1001

MCSE

TIPS

By Shane Stigler, MCSE, MCT
and Mark A. Linsenbardt, MCSE, MCT

JP

JAMSA
P·R·E·S·S
...a computer user's best friend

Published by
Jamsa Press
A Division of Gulf Publishing Company
3301 Allen Parkway
Houston, TX 77019 U.S.A.
http://www.jamsa.com

For information about the translation or distribution of any Jamsa Press book, please write to Jamsa Press at the address listed above.

1001 MCSE Tips

Printed in the United States of America.
98765432

ISBN 1-884133-62-2

Performance Manager	*Technical Advisor*	*Proofer*
Kong Cheung	Phil Schmauder	Jeanne K. Smith
		Rosemary Pasco
Copy Editors	*Cover Photograph*	*Technical Editor*
Rosemary Pasco	O'Gara/Bissell	Lars Klander
Ann Edwards		
Dorothy Oppenheimer		
Renee Wesberry		
Composition	*Illustrators*	*Cover Design*
New Vision Media	James Rehrauer	James Rehrauer
	Phil Schmauder	Debbie Jamsa

Indexer
   Kong Cheung

Gulf Publishing Company
Book Division
P.O. Box 2608
Houston, TX 77252-2608
U.S.A.

http://www.gulfpub.com

Acknowledgements

I would like to thank my family, Sue, Max, and Mollie for their patience and support during the writing of this book. I would also like to thank the following members of the extended family: Don Stigler, Sharon Stigler, Bob and Ann Samuelson, Robin and Terry Dunlap, Scott Dunlap, Tom and Connie Morrison, Christi Stigler, and the list goes on. I would like to acknowledge Michada Computers for providing equipment, Dave Carter for helping provide important research, and last, but not least, Lars Klander, without whom this book would never have been completed.

Shane

Invariably, the pages of a book contain some words of thanks to those people whose efforts would otherwise be unknown. So that the efforts of those shining few do not pass without note, I gratefully acknowledge Lars Klander for his work, advice, and support, Harold Ross of Michada Computers for providing me with equipment, and Shane Stigler who made this project possible for me. Mostly, I would like to thank my wife Denisa for putting up with me while I sat home writing and firmly dedicate all my own efforts to my parents, Leroy and Gladys Linsenbardt, without whose love and guidance I would be nothing.

Mark

1   UNDERSTANDING THE MICROSOFT CERTIFIED PROFESSIONALS (MCP) PROGRAM

Q: *A recent salary survey conducted by MCP Magazine found that MCSEs between the ages of 25-34, on average, earned how much more per year than comparably experienced professionals who had passed only one certification exam?*

Choose the best answer:

    A.   *$2,400*

    B.   *$3,600*

    C.   *$4,800*

    D.   *$5,000*

In the last 20 years, the Information Services department has become one of the most important determinations of a business' success. The centerpiece of many Information Services (IS) departments is the organization's computer network. In recent years, as Microsoft products have become more central in the network, determining how proficient computer professionals are at managing Microsoft products has become a real concern for IS decision makers.

In its role as one of the dominant forces in computing today, and as a means of helping to drive their expansion into the network marketplace, Microsoft is striving to set professional standards that clearly distinguish between the computer user and the computer professional. With its Microsoft Certified Professionals (MCP) program, Microsoft provides a standard means of evaluating the knowledge and proficiency that computer professionals have with Microsoft products. If you have purchased this book, you probably intend to become some level of Microsoft Certified Professional. You will find that becoming an MCP will not only bring you respect in the marketplace and provide you with evidence of your computing achievements, but its likely to translate to improvements in your bottom-line as well.

Answer C *is the correct answer. The MCP Magazine Third Annual Salary Survey found that MCSEs between the ages of 25-34 earned an average of $61,300, while comparably experienced MCPs passing only a single certification exam earned an average of $56,500.*

2   UNDERSTANDING THE DIFFERENT LEVELS AND TYPES OF MICROSOFT CERTIFICATIONS

Q.   *Which of the following are valid levels of Microsoft certification?*

Choose all correct answers:

    A.   *MCSE (Microsoft Certified Systems Engineer)*

    B.   *MCSD (Microsoft Certified Solutions Developer)*

    C.   *MCP (Microsoft Certified Professional)*

    D.   *MCWM (Microsoft Certified Web Master)*

Because there are so many different protocols, programs, operating systems, file systems, and other common components for networking, the continual presence of acronyms wherever there are computer professionals is not particularly surprising. People in and around the computer industry love to use initials instead of the actual words the initials refer to, which saves time, but can often lead to confusion. For example, over the years, one of the most common protocols in networking, the Transmission Control Protocol (TCP), has also been known as the Transport Control Protocol. Similarly, while Microsoft is commonly referred to as MS (as in MS-DOS, for Microsoft Disk Operating System), in the series of certification tests to become a *MCSE*, or *Microsoft Certified Systems Engineer*, which this book discusses, Microsoft omits the "S" in Microsoft.

Becoming fluent in the acronyms that come hand-in-hand with knowledge of the Microsoft networking products (and, for that matter, networking in general) is a crucial task that you must accomplish as you work toward certification. Finding a meaning for each new acronym is a by-product of the more important goal of learning the material that Microsoft tests, and that you will use every day. This book deals with the knowledge you will need to pass the series of MCSE exams, Microsoft's top-level certification. Other certification levels are available too, and along the way to your MCSE, you may find it valuable to add these certifications to your "pedigree."

Answers A, B, and C are all correct. Answer D is incorrect because Microsoft does not offer a MCWM (Microsoft Certified Web Master) certification. Microsoft does, however, offer the MCP+I title, which is a Microsoft Certified Professional + Internet, which requires passing of the Windows NT Server 4.0 exam, the TCP/IP for Windows NT 4.0 exam, and the Internet Information Server 4.0 exam.

3   CHOOSING THE MCP TRACK

Q: Which of the following exams must you pass to receive the Microsoft Certified Professional certification?

Choose the best answer:

     A.   The Microsoft Windows NT Server 4.0 exam

     B.   The Microsoft Windows NT Workstation 4.0 exam

     C.   The Microsoft Windows 95 exam

     D.   Any one of the operating system exams

As you have learned, Microsoft offers several different levels and types of certifications. The simplest level of certification to achieve is the *Microsoft Certified Professional* certification (MCP). Microsoft uses MCP to refer to anyone who has achieved any of the four qualification levels of certification, although one of those levels is itself called MCP. To achieve the MCP certification level, you must pass only one of the operating system exams to show you have proficiency in a current Microsoft Windows client or server operating system. The following list shows the exam numbers and their titles, passing any one of which will qualify you as an MCP. Note that some of the tests are about to be discontinued (marked with an asterisk and, in some cases, a date), as they refer to operating systems that are gradually becoming obsolete:

- *Exam 70-042: Implementing and Supporting Microsoft Windows NT Workstation 3.51* (Microsoft will retire this test when they release Windows NT 5.0 Workstation)*

- *Exam 70-043: Implementing and Supporting Microsoft Windows NT Server 3.51* (Microsoft will retire this test when they release Windows NT 5.0 Server)*

- *Exam 70-064: Implementing and Supporting Microsoft Windows 95*

- *Exam 70-067: Implementing and Supporting Microsoft Windows NT Server 4.0*

- *Exam 70-073: Implementing and Supporting Microsoft Windows NT Workstation 4.02*

- *Exam 70-160: Microsoft Windows Architecture I * (June 30, 1999)*

- *Exam 70-061: Microsoft Windows Architecture II * (June 30, 1999)*

Passing any one of the exams will qualify you to claim the Microsoft Certified Professional title. However, as you will learn in later Tips, you must pass several different exams, including at least two from the list in this Tip, to qualify as a Microsoft Certified Systems Engineer (MCSE).

*Note: Microsoft occasionally changes the number designations on its exams. The company generally posts these changes on its World Wide Web site at **http://www.microsoft.com/mcp**.*

Answer D is the correct answer because you must pass any one of the operating system exams to receive the MCP certification. Answers A, B, and C are all incorrect because, even though passing any of the exams in those answers will result in an MCP certification, none of those exams specifically is required for MCP certification.

4   CHOOSING THE *MCSD* TRACK

Q: *If you intend to create custom applications to run on Windows operating system platforms, which of the following certifications is likely the best certification for you?*

Choose the best answer:

     A.   *Microsoft Certified Systems Engineer (MCSE)*

     B.   *Microsoft Certified Professional (MCP)*

     C.   *Microsoft Certified Professional + Internet (MCP+I)*

     D.   *Microsoft Certified Solutions Developer (MCSD)*

As you have learned, there are several different types of MCP certifications. For professional developers and applications programmers, the most helpful track is the MCSD certification track. *MCSD* stands for *Microsoft Certified Solutions Developer*. To achieve this level of certification, you must pass two core technology exams and two elective exams. Microsoft refers to its various operating systems as the "core technologies." Electives refer to less essential, but helpful, support subject groups. The MCSD certification level requires a thorough knowledge of the Microsoft Windows 32-bit architecture, programming code, Object Linking and Embedding (OLE), and User Interface (UI) design. The required exams for the MCSD certification include:

- *Exam 70-160: Microsoft Windows Architecture I*

- *Exam 70-161: Microsoft Windows Architecture II*

The elective exams, for which you must pass two, include:

- *Exam 70-015: Designing and Implementing Distributed Applications with Microsoft Visual C++ 6.0*

- *Exam 70-016: Designing and Implementing Desktop Applications with Microsoft Visual C++ 6.0*

- *Exam 70-027: Implementing a Database Design on Microsoft SQL Server 6.5 (you must take either this exam or 70-279, you cannot get exam credit for both)*

- *Exam 70-029: Implementing a Database Design on Microsoft SQL Server 7.0 (you must take either this exam or 70-277, you cannot get exam credit for both)*

- *Exam 70-024: Developing Applications with C++ Using the Microsoft Foundation Class*

- *Exam 70-025: Implementing OLE in Microsoft in Microsoft Foundation Class Applications*

- *Exam 70-165: Developing Applications with Microsoft Visual Basic 5.0 (you must take either this exam, 70-175, or 70-176, you cannot get exam credit for more than one exam)*

- *Exam 70-069: Microsoft Access for Windows 95 and the Microsoft Access Developer's Toolkit*

- *Exam 70-052: Developing Applications with Microsoft Excel 5.0 Using Visual Basic for Applications*

- *Exam 70-055: Designing and Implementing Web Sites with Microsoft FrontPage 98*

- *Exam 70-057: Designing and Implementing Commerce Solutions with Microsoft Site Server 3.0 Commerce Edition*

- *Exam 70-091: Designing and Implementing Solutions with Microsoft Office and Visual Basic for Applications*

- *Exam 70-152: Designing and Implementing Web Solutions with Microsoft Visual InterDev 6.0*

Note: *In the fourth quarter of 1998, Microsoft introduced the new MCSD track. The new track focuses on application development types (stand-alone, distributed, and OLE-based applications), rather than the Windows architecture. In accordance with the new track, Microsoft will retire the Windows Architecture I and II classes on June 30, 1999. If you are considering an MCSD certification, you should check the Microsoft Web site at* **http://www.microsoft.com/mcp.**

Answer D *is the correct answer. If you intend to create applications to run on Windows-based platforms, you should acquire the Microsoft Certified Solutions Developer (MCSD) credential.* **Answers A, B,** *and* **C** *are all incorrect because those certifications do not indicate developer-specific knowledge.*

5	CHOOSING THE **MCT** TRACK

Q: *To become a Microsoft Certified Trainer, you must first be a fully-certified MCSE or MCSD, depending on which courses you will be teaching.*

True or False?

MCT stands for a *Microsoft Certified Trainer*. Microsoft Certified Trainers teach the Microsoft courses that most professionals take in preparation for the Microsoft Certified Professional exams—generally in conjunction with one or more books and other study tools.

Although you might assume Microsoft would require the highest certification qualification to become one of its Certified Trainers, in reality, the company requires its trainer candidates to pass only the exam they expect to teach, and to prove their training skills. To become an MCT, you must first submit an MCT application approval form, available from Microsoft. Upon approval, you have 90 days to get your first course certification. You must also prove that you have professional training skills. Such skills can include previous training in one of the other software products, such as Novell or Lotus.

Note: *If you do not have training skills, Microsoft recommends you get the requisite skills by becoming a* **Certified Technical Trainer (CTT)**. *(The Chauncey group conducts CTT testing. Information about its training is available from its World Wide Web site at* **http://www.chauncey.com/.**)

Microsoft makes other stipulations in the process of becoming an MCT, such as submitting additional forms by mail for Microsoft's approval and reviewing supplementary material in preparation for teaching the course. You also might have to take additional exam requirements that pertain to the course you will teach. After you achieve MCT status, Microsoft will grant you access to a special Web site with materials for MCT's, and you will receive your official MCT certificate. Microsoft will guide you through the process of becoming a MCT and will supply full information, as well as documents that you may need to submit, on its World Wide Web site at *http://www.microsoft.com/mcp/certstep/mct.htm.*

*The answer is **False**. You need only pass the exams that you will teach, as well as completing a Microsoft-certified "train-the-trainer" course, and apply for approval from Microsoft to be an MCT.*

6   GETTING ON TRACK TO MCSE CERTIFICATION

Q: *For network administrators, the most valuable Microsoft Certification level is which of the following?*

Choose the best answer:

      A.   *Microsoft Certified Systems Engineer (MCSE)*

      B.   *Microsoft Certified Professional (MCP)*

      C.   *Microsoft Certified Professional + Internet (MCP+I)*

      D.   *Microsoft Certified Solutions Developer (MCSD)*

MCSE stands for *Microsoft Certified Systems Engineer*. It is the highest certification level Microsoft offers in its family of MCP's. You must pass four operating system exams and two electives to achieve the MCSE certification. The exams will test your proficiency in client, server, and networking elements.

Some of the exams will also test your expertise with Microsoft *BackOffice* products. Microsoft is currently offering a complete set of requirements for the NT 3.51 track, but this book deals only with the requirements for the NT 4.0 track, as the 3.51 track is close to retirement. You will also find that some courses in the 4.0 track are close to retirement. The following list explains the core requirements for fulfilling your MCSE requirements:

- *Exam 70-067: Implementing and Supporting Windows NT Server 4.0*

- *Exam 70-068: Implementing and Supporting Windows NT Server 4.0 in the Enterprise*

- *Exam 70-064: Implementing and Supporting Microsoft Windows 95 (you must take either this exam, 70-073, or 70-098, you cannot get exam credit for more than one exam)*

- *Exam 70-073: Microsoft Windows NT Workstation 4.0 (you must take either this exam, 70-064, or 70-098, you cannot get exam credit for more than one exam)*

- *Exam 70-098: Implementing and Supporting Microsoft Windows 98 (you must take either this exam, 70-064, or 70-073, you cannot get exam credit for more than one exam)*

- *Exam 70-058: Networking Essentials*

The following list contains the electives available to you in the MCSE exam structure. You can pick only one exam from each grouping of exams, and must pass a total of two elective exams:

- *Exam 70-013 Implementing and Supporting Microsoft SNA Server 3.0 (you must take either this exam or 70-085, you cannot get exam credit for more than one exam)*

- *Exam 70-085 Implementing and Supporting Microsoft SNA Server 4.0 (you must take either this exam or 70-013, you cannot get exam credit for more than one exam)*

- *Exam 70-018 Implementing and Supporting Microsoft Systems Management Server 1.2 (you must take either this exam or 70-086, you cannot get exam credit for more than one exam*

- *Exam 70-086 Implementing and Supporting Microsoft SNA Server 2.0 (you must take either this exam or 70-018, you cannot get exam credit for more than one exam)*

- *Exam 70-027 Implementing a Database Design on Microsoft SQL Server 6.5 (you must take either this exam or 70-029, you cannot get exam credit for more than one exam)*

- *Exam 70-029 Implementing a Database Design on Microsoft SQL Server 6.5 (you must take either this exam or 70-027, you cannot get exam credit for more than one exam)*

- *Exam 70-026 System Administration for Microsoft SQL Server 6.5 (you must take either this exam or 70-028, you cannot get exam credit for more than one exam)*

- *Exam 70-028 System Administration for Microsoft SQL Server 7.0 (you must take either this exam or 70-026, you cannot get exam credit for more than one exam)*

- *Exam 70-053 Internetworking Microsoft TCP/IP on Windows NT (3.5-3.51) (you must take either this exam or 70-059, you cannot get exam credit for more than one exam)*

- *Exam 70-059 Internetworking Microsoft TCP/IP on Windows NT 4.0 (you must take either this exam or 70-053, you cannot get exam credit for more than one exam)*

- *Exam 70-056 Implementing and Supporting Web Sites Using Microsoft Site Server 3.0*

- *Exam 70-076 Implementing and Supporting Microsoft Exchange Server 5.0 (you must take either this exam or 70-081, you cannot get exam credit for more than one exam)*

- *Exam 70-081 Implementing and Supporting Microsoft Exchange Server 5.5 (you must take either this exam or 70-076, you cannot get exam credit for more than one exam)*

- *Exam 70-077 Implementing and Supporting Microsoft Internet Information Server 3.0 and Microsoft Index Server 1.1 (you must take either this exam or 70-087, you cannot get exam credit for more than one exam)*

- *Exam 70-087 Implementing and Supporting Microsoft Internet Information Server 4.0 (you must take either this exam or 70-087, you cannot get exam credit for more than one exam)*

- *Exam 70-078 Implementing and Supporting Microsoft Proxy Server 1.0 (you must take either this exam or 70-088, you cannot get exam credit for more than one exam)*

- *Exam 70-088 Implementing and Supporting Microsoft Proxy Server 2.0 (you must take either this exam or 70-078, you cannot get exam credit for more than one exam)*

- *Exam 70-079 Implementing and Supporting Microsoft Internet Explorer 4.0 Using the Internet Explorer Administration Kit*

In late 1997, Microsoft began offering two new certification levels, which focus specifically on Internet development. The first new certification level is called the *MCSE+Internet Certification*. To achieve this certification level, you must take the four core technology courses for the standard MCSE certification level, plus three others Microsoft includes in the "core" for the MCSE+Internet certification.

The extra three core courses are Exam 70-059: Internetworking with Microsoft TCP/IP on Microsoft Windows NT 4.0, Exam 70-087: Implementing and Supporting Microsoft Internet Information Server 4.0, and Exam 70-079: Implementing and Supporting Microsoft *Internet Explorer 4.0* By Using the Internet Explorer Administration Kit. After you pass these seven exams (the four standard core and the three additional core exams), you must also choose any two of the electives (that you have not yet taken) from the course list. The other new certification level Microsoft now offers is the *MCP+Internet Certification*. To become a Microsoft Certified Professional with a specialty in the Internet, you must pass the following three exams:

- Exam 70-059: Internetworking with Microsoft TCP/IP on Microsoft Windows NT 4.0

- Exam 70-067: Implementing and Supporting Microsoft Windows NT Server 4.0

- Exam 70-087: Implementing and Supporting Microsoft Internet Information Server 4.0

Answer A is the correct answer. Network administrators should achieve the Microsoft Certified Systems Engineer (MCSE). Answers B, C, and D all detail useful certifications, but not the best one for the network administrator.

7   PICKING THE MCSE COURSE COMBINATION THAT IS RIGHT FOR YOU

Q: *All MCSE candidates will take the same set of exams to achieve certification.*

    True or False?

As you learned in Tip 6, the MCSE certification requires two separate and distinct achievements: completion of the four core exams, three of which everyone will take, and completion of two elective exams, which you can select from over a dozen different tests. Clearly, there are several different specialties that you focus on when pursuing your MCSE certification.

While the core technologies will give you operating system and networking basics, the electives you choose will determine how you apply your core knowledge. Microsoft is taking notice of the recent popularity in Internet electives, and is offering the new MCSE+Internet certification discussed in Tip 6. However, people who want to develop their mainframe connectivity skills might want to instead choose the Systems Management Server (SNA) course. The Systems Management Server elective will help you learn how to audit and do such things as push installations in large-scale networks. Furthermore, electives such as the SQL Server, Database Design on SQL, and Database Administration cover the many different components of successful corporate database administration.

The continued need for mail and groupware services makes the Exchange Server elective inviting to many MCSE candidates. As a recent addition to the family of Microsoft *BackOffice* products, Exchange Server is proving its value as a first-class messaging utility in such programs as Microsoft *Office* and *Outlook*.

Proxy Server is also a fairly late addition to Microsoft's suite of *BackOffice* products. Microsoft considers this elective mandatory for those candidates hoping to master Internet Security and firewall issues.

To decide the course combination that is right for you, you should both consider the direction you want your professional career to take, as well as the current skill set you may possess. For instance, if you have a great deal of experience with SQL Server, you are probably better served to receive your MCSE certification with the SQL Server electives. You can always take the Exchange Server tests, for example, later in your career, after you have become an MCSE. In addition, talk with a Microsoft Certified Trainer, or anyone involved in an Information Management department, to gather advice on your best career move.

*The answer is **False**. Despite the fact that all MCSE candidates will take three exams that are the same, there is great diversity among the electives, which will help you specialize in the areas most important to you.*

Q: Which course should you take to prepare yourself for the Networking Essentials exam?

Choose the best answer:

> A.   *Course 578: Networking Essentials Self-Paced Training*
>
> B.   *Course 689: Supporting Microsoft Windows NT Server 4.0–Enterprise Technologies*
>
> C.   *Course 865: Enterprise Series: Implementing Directory Services Using Microsoft Windows NT Server 4.0*
>
> D.   *Course 922: Supporting Microsoft Windows NT 4.0 Core Technologies*

As you have learned, the MCSE certification requires that you pass four core exams and two elective exams. Microsoft offers a series of courses to help prepare you for the exams before you take them. A Microsoft Certified Trainer (MCT) teaches all Microsoft-approved curriculum courses. The core courses in the curriculum will teach you the fundamentals of the current operating systems around which Microsoft designs its networks. The heart of the core courses is the combination of Course 803: Administering Microsoft Windows NT 4.0, and Course 922: Supporting Microsoft Windows NT 4.0 Core Technologies.

Because Windows NT 4.0 is Microsoft's networking product of choice, you should familiarize yourself with all aspects of Windows NT 4.0 to best prepare yourself for network management if you intend to specialize in the Microsoft products. Therefore, you will likely benefit more from taking Course 689: Supporting Microsoft Windows NT Server 4.0–Enterprise Technologies, than you will from taking the Windows 95 courses. Moreover, Course 689 is a good supplement to help you understand the implementation of Microsoft NT Workstation 4.0 and Windows NT Server 4 in wide area networks (WANs).

Finally, the Networking Essentials exam is a self-paced course that Microsoft recommends you complete before proceeding with any other courses (although Microsoft does not make strong mention of this prerequisite in its course materials). Students on the MCSE track must purchase the Networking Essentials book and CD, which Microsoft Press publishes. The course contains information you will have to memorize by rote to pass the exam. Topics such as basic network design, types of cabling, WAN's, and network security comprise the tested subjects on this mostly hardware-oriented examination. The following list shows the core courses that Microsoft recommends that you complete before you take the core MCSE examinations, and their corresponding course numbers:

- *Course 564: Supporting Microsoft Windows 95 Self-Paced Training*

- *Course 578: Networking Essentials Self-Paced Training*

- *Course 798: Supporting Microsoft Windows 95*

- *Course 689: Supporting Microsoft Windows NT Server 4.0–Enterprise Technologies*

- *Course 803: Administering Microsoft Windows NT 4.0*

- *Course 865: Enterprise Series: Implementing Directory Services Using Microsoft Windows NT Server 4.0*

- *Course 922: Supporting Microsoft Windows NT 4.0 Core Technologies*

In general, you will find that most of the courses will apply to a variety of different exams. In general, you should closely evaluate the content of courses before you take them, and consult closely with the instructor, to ensure the course targets the information you want to learn.

Answer A is the correct answer because Course 578 prepares you for the Networking Essentials exam. Answer B is incorrect because Course 689 prepares you for the Windows NT Server 4.0 in the Enterprise exam. Answer C is incorrect because Course 865 prepares you for the Windows NT Server 4.0 in the Enterprise exam. Answer D is incorrect because Course 922 prepares you for the Windows NT Server and Workstation exams.

9   EXAMINING THE ELECTIVE COURSES

Q: *Which courses should you take to best prepare yourself for Exam 70-029: Implementing a Database Design on Microsoft SQL Server 7.0?*

Choose all correct answers:

    A.   *Course 243: Implementing a Database Design on Microsoft SQL Server for Windows NT*

    B.   *Course 750: Implementing a Database Design on Microsoft SQL Server 6.5*

    C.   *Course 833: Implementing a Database Design in Microsoft SQL Server 7.0*

    D.   *Course 933: Accelerated Training for Microsoft SQL Server 6.5*

As you have seen, Microsoft designed the core courses and their corresponding MCSE examinations to closely integrate with the core courses, preparing you fully for the MCSE examinations. Similarly, Microsoft designed the pool of elective courses to directly support the elective technology examinations. However, you should generally complete the core courses (or examinations) before you take the elective examinations.

You can enhance your true understanding of the Systems Network Architecture (SNA) server, for example, by fully-understanding the Microsoft vision of Windows NT in the Enterprise. The term "Enterprise" is widely accepted as a general description of large geographic network, but Microsoft also uses the term to include acceptance of the integration of different networking products within those geographic networks. Successfully completing the Enterprise-based courses and passing the Windows NT Server 4.0 in the Enterprise examination are crucial steps you should complete before you pursue the elective examinations.

After you complete the core criteria, and before you take the elective examinations, you should generally take the elective course that corresponds to the examination before you try to take the examination. The following list shows some of the elective courses and their corresponding course numbers:

- *Course 213: Systems Administration for Microsoft SQL Server for Windows NT*

- *Course 243: Implementing a Database Design on Microsoft SQL Server for Windows NT*

- *Course 286: New Features of Microsoft SQL Server for Windows NT for System Administrators*

- *Course 633: Microsoft SQL Server Training*

- *Course 667: Implementing Microsoft Mail 3.5*

- *Course 684: Supporting Microsoft SNA Server 3.0*

- *Course 688: Internetworking Microsoft TCP/IP on Microsoft Windows NT 4.0*

- *Course 709: Microsoft Exchange Server 5.0 Multisite and Internet Environments*

- *Course 732: Supporting Microsoft Systems Management Server 1.2*

- *Course 735: Microsoft Internet Information Server 2.0 Training*

- *Course 750: Implementing a Database Design on Microsoft SQL Server 6.5*

- *Course 771: Core Technologies of Microsoft Exchange Server 5.0*

- *Course 826: Creating and Configuring a Web Server Using Microsoft Tools*

- *Course 833: Implementing a Database Design in Microsoft SQL Server 7.0*

- *Course 836: Secure Web Access using Microsoft Proxy Server 2.0*

- *Course 867: System Administration for Microsoft SQL Server 6.5*

- *Course 868: Microsoft Exchange Server 5.0 Enterprise Series*

- *Course 869: MS Exchange Server 5.0 Performance and Troubleshooting*

- *Course 933: Accelerated Training for Microsoft SQL Server 6.5*

- *Course 936B: Creating and Configuring a Web Server Using Microsoft Internet Information Server 4.0*

- *Course 956: Implementing Microsoft Internet Explorer 4.0*

- *Course 973: Supporting Microsoft Exchange Server 5.5*

- *Course 981: Supporting Microsoft SNA Server 4.0*

- *Course 1026: Administering Microsoft Exchange Server 5.5*

You should note that most of the courses are product version specific—that is, if you are planning to take the SQL Server 7.0 exam, you should take Course 833 rather than Course 750 (which covers SQL Server 6.5). Microsoft adds new courses to the curriculum every month—you should check the Microsoft MCP Web site at *http://www.microsoft.com/ mcp/* regularly to see what new courses Microsoft is offering.

Answer C is the only correct answer. Answer A is incorrect because Course 243 discusses SQL Server implementation on SQL Server 4.2, rather than 7.0. Answers B and C are incorrect because the Courses are SQL Server 6.5 specific.

---

10   IDENTIFYING THE TEST NUMBERS

Q: *The two examinations that you would take to have a specialization in database administration and development would be which of the following?*

Choose all correct answers:

    A.   *Exam 70-027: Implementing a Database Design on Microsoft SQL Server 6.5 or Exam 70-029: Implementing a Database Design on Microsoft SQL Server 7.0*

    B.   *Exam 70-026: System Administration for Microsoft SQL Server 6.5 or Exam 70-028: System Administration for Microsoft SQL Server 7.0*

    C.   *Exam 70-068: Implementing and Supporting Microsoft Windows NT Server 4.0 in the Enterprise*

    D.   *Exam 70-073: Implementing and Supporting Microsoft Windows NT Workstation 4.0*

As you work your way through the possible MCSE tracks that you might pursue, you will find that there are a dizzying array of examination numbers, some of which seem to follow a pattern, and others of which do not. Do not be confused by Microsoft's exam numbering system. As you have seen, the numbering system does not necessarily follow any logical pattern. Moreover, as Microsoft retires certain exams and brings new products online, the examination numbers will change.

Moreover, as Microsoft retires certain operating systems (such as Windows 3.x), Microsoft will retire the courses and the related exam numbers that correspond to those operating systems. Microsoft will also add new courses and exams as new technologies come to market (the Exam 70-098: Implementing and Supporting Microsoft Windows 98, for example, is relatively new).

Finally, Microsoft may change the numbers for exams as they redesign the product, the course, or the exam. For example, Microsoft retired the core technologies examination it offered under MCSE for Windows 95, 70-063, to make room for 70-064 because of the differences between Windows 95 OSR1 and OSR2. As a result of changes to the Windows 95 operating system, Microsoft will also update the course and the corresponding exam for the operating system.

At present, a good core course combination is the exam numbers 70-067, 70-073, 70-068, and 70-058, which correspond respectively to the NT4.0 Server, the NT 4.0 Workstation, the NT 4.0 in the Enterprise, and the Networking Essentials exam numbers.

Answers A and B are correct, as you would take either Exam 70-027: Implementing a Database Design on Microsoft SQL Server 6.5 and Exam 70-026: System Administration for Microsoft SQL Server 6.5 or Exam 70-029:Implementing a Database Design on Microsoft SQL Server 7.0 and Exam 70-028: System Administration for Microsoft SQL Server 7.0, depending on whether you intended to specialize in SQL Server 6.5 or 7.0. Answers C and D are incorrect because both Exam 70-068: Implementing and Supporting Microsoft Windows NT Server 4.0 in the Enterprise and Exam 70-073: Microsoft Windows NT Workstation 4.0 are core exams.

11 COMPARING COURSE CONTENT WITH TEST CONTENT

Q: *If you plan to take Exam 70-073: Implementing and Support Windows NT Workstation 4.0, which of the following courses should you take?*

Choose all correct answers:

A. *Course 753: Microsoft Windows NT 4.0 Network Administration Training*

B. *Course 770: Installing and Configuring Microsoft Windows NT Workstation 4.0*

C. *Course 803: Administering Microsoft Windows NT 4.0*

D. *Course 922: Supporting Microsoft Windows NT 4.0 Core Technologies.*

While the MCSE examinations test a consistent body of knowledge, which you will learn about later in this book for the core exams, the courses that provide that knowledge may not always directly correspond in a one-to-one relationship to the examination. In fact, the content of MCSE courses will almost always not have a direct correspondence to the content of a matching exam. Therefore, you should not expect to enroll in any one of the core or elective courses and then take a single exam over that exact material. Generally, Microsoft will spread the information in one exam across two, three, or even more courses.

In other words, you can not always count on the courses to give you the prerequisite knowledge in order to pass the requisite exams. For example, very little of the content of Course 689: Supporting Microsoft Windows NT Server 4.0–Enterprise Technologies appears on the test with almost an identical name, Exam 70-068: Implementing and Supporting Microsoft Windows NT Server 4.0 in the Enterprise. More frequently, you will find that the courses cover a series of concepts in-depth (such as Course 770), but the examination will test you with only a few questions on those concepts.

Note: Microsoft has a suggested order of taking the courses and exams, as Tip 34 will discuss.

Answers A, B, C, and D are all correct. Microsoft recommends that you take Course 753, Course 770, Course 803, and Course 922 all in preparation for Exam 70-073. In fact, Microsoft recommends that you take a total of as many as 10 courses in preparation for Exam 70-073.

12   UNDERSTANDING MICROSOFT'S **MCSE** VISION

Q: *The MCSE examinations do not test real knowledge of networking; instead, they test rote memorization of facts about Microsoft software, and result in Microsoft's "rubber-stamp" of approval of your knowledge.*

True or False?

Part of Microsoft's strategy is to establish excellence in education for its products. If Microsoft can "out do" its competition in turning out qualified technicians who have high proficiency in their networking products, the product will do better in the marketplace. So the Microsoft's education branch is a high-budget department. with professional educators who "know their business." Their research in this area is highly developed, and test design is very closely controlled. The MCSE exams are hard—Microsoft means them to be.

The course material that the exams cover is substantial and people who pass the series of tests qualifying them as Microsoft Certified Systems Engineers have truly reached a mastery of range of Microsoft networking products. However, before you think that Microsoft provides these fine services simply for the benefit of the MCSE candidates, it is important to recognize a single goal behind Microsoft's training programs. Simply put, the family of Windows NT products will win in the marketplace only if there are as many qualified technicians as possible to implement, maintain, and service the product.

Understanding the impact that this will have on many network administrators is important. It is not entirely unlikely that, in the near future, your ability to be hired as a network administrator may depend as much on your MCSE exam scores as it does on your college degree. In fact, the MCSE exams are becoming an important standard for determining a computer professional's knowledge and experience.

*The correct answer is **False**. The Microsoft Certified Professional exams do focus on Microsoft technologies, but receiving certification requires an in-depth knowledge not only of how the technologies work, but of how to use them in the field.*

13   UNDERSTANDING HOW MICROSOFT CREATES ITS TESTS

Q.   *Microsoft Certified Professional examinations contain how many questions?*

Choose the best answer:

A.   *Less than 40*

B.   *Exactly 40*

C.   *Exactly 50*

D.   *More than 45*

When you take your MCSE examinations, each exam will test you with a set of roughly 50 questions. Microsoft takes the questions that comprise your test at random from a pool of hundreds of potential test questions, and sends them to the testing center the morning of the test. If you do not pass a test the first time and try to take the test again, your second test will, again, be about 50 questions (though it may have more or fewer questions than the first examination), and the questions will be *different* from the first 50 you encountered.

Additionally, while questions per section breakdowns remain relatively consistent, there will likely be slight changes in the distribution from examination to examination. For example, there may be more questions in your second test on user accounts than there were on the first test. However, the second examination might, in turn, contain fewer questions on installation. On balance, the difference is statistically minor, and you should not focus on it as a testing benefit or detriment, simply recognize that the differences exist.

You may also find that a question you have seen before is slightly altered from the first time you saw. The alteration may not change the correct answer at all, or it may make the correct answer the exact opposite of what it was the first time you saw the question. Therefore, you should read every question on each test carefully. (Tip 29 discusses more about how to read test questions.)

Finally, you should recognize that it is not out of the ordinary to have to take a test more than twice before you pass it. Each time you take a test, Microsoft will present you with new questions in a familiar format that cover the same content.

Answer D is the correct answer because the examinations will contain at least 45 questions, and may contain more. Answers A, B, and C are incorrect because the examinations will always contain at least 45 questions, and may contain exactly 50 questions, but may contain more or less than 50 questions.

14   USING THIS BOOK TO HELP YOU TAKE YOUR TESTS

Q: *Which examination should you take first?*

Choose the best answer:

    A.   *Exam 70-068: Implementing and Supporting Microsoft Windows NT Server 4.0 in the Enterprise*

    B.   *Exam 70-073: Implementing and Supporting Microsoft Windows NT Workstation 4.0*

    C.   *Exam 70-067: Implementing and Supporting Microsoft Windows NT Server 4.0*

    D.   *Exam 70-058: Networking Essentials*

This book will give you the full content you need to prepare for the core MCSE examinations. Additionally, the book will provide you with sample questions in the MCSE examination style, reiterating information in different ways to help make sure that you retain the information that the Tips teach you. You should not read this book from front to back; rather, you should work through the Tip series that corresponds to a given examination before you take the examination. You will find all the information in this book that you will need to pass the MCSE core exams.

The 1001 Tips are arranged by topic, according to the five most common exams that network administrators must choose from to receive the MCSE certification. The sections cover Exam 70-067 (Windows NT Server), then Exam 70-073 (Windows NT Workstation), then Exam 70-068 (Windows NT Server in the Enterprise), then Exam 70-058 (Networking Essentials), and finally Exam 70-064 (Windows 95).

While the Windows NT Server section begins at Tip 36, the authors designed the first thirty-five Tips in the book to help you better prepare for the test. The first 14 Tips helped you to understand what Microsoft expects from you for certification. The next 20 Tips will help you to study and prepare yourself for the MCSE exams.

The authors designed the questions this book includes within each Tip (with the exception of the questions in the first 35 Tips) to be as similar to the Microsoft exam format as possible. Taken as a whole, the questions in this book also reflect a similar distribution of the different types of questions you will see in an authentic MCSE test. About 40% of the questions in this book will be in multiple choice style and 40% in multiple choice/multiple answer format, while the remaining 20% are true or false questions.

Answer C is the correct answer. While there is great variation and general disagreement in the order in which people should take the examinations, Microsoft and most professional trainers agree that you should successfully pass Exam 70-067 before you try to complete the remaining tests within the MCSE track. Answers A, B, and D are all incorrect. Note that most professionals also agree that you should take Exam 70-058 last.

15   SEARCHING THE INTERNET FOR HELP WITH THE EXAMS

Q: *Because the Microsoft Certified Professional exams are proprietary, there are no non-Microsoft-approved resources available to help you study for the exams.*

True or False?

If you enter the initials MCSE into an Internet search engine, the engine will return numerous references to MCSE resources. Individuals post many of the sites (detailing their own performance, and providing Tips about their experiences), while companies that specialize in MCSE examination study and preparation will post other sites. Some people are helpful in giving you personal testimony about how they made it through the MCSE courses and exams.

You will find MCSE Web pages in foreign languages, suggestions on which books to read, and lists of locations where you can take courses and exams. As with any information you find on the Web, you should confirm the information's validity through some other medium—be especially careful of supposed "questions directly from the test" that people post on the Internet. In general, you should recognize that the Web can be a useful additional resource, you should build your primary study for the examinations around the Microsoft-approved curriculum and test question study, including working through all the Tips in each section in this book.

In addition to the complete MCSE test summary this book provides, you can also find information on the MCSE exams at the following Web sites:

- Microsoft at *http://www.microsoft.com/mcp/*
- Transcender Corporation at *http://www.transcender.com*
- MCP Online at *http://www.saluki.com/mcp/*
- Microsoft's MCP Magazine as *http://www.mcpmag.com/*
- Public site at *http://www.hardcoremcse.com*
- Sylvan Prometric at *http://www.microsoft.com/Train_cert/mcp/certstep/sylvan.htm*

In addition to information that you can locate on the World Wide Web, there are thousands of newsgroups serving numerous personal and professional interests throughout the Internet. Several newsgroup sites specifically discuss MCSE courses and exams. To find useful MCSE information newsgroup sites, you can start with the *DejaNews* search engine at *http://www.dejanews.com*. In addition, three of the top newsgroups with discussions about MCSE and Windows NT networking are *comp.os.ms-windows.nt*, *comp.networks*, and *comp.os.ms-windows.networking.misc*. Remember, you should always try to validate the information you obtain from newsgroups, but most do contain valuable information that may help you achieve certification.

*The correct answer is **False**, because there are a broad variety of resources available on the Internet to help you prepare for the examinations.*

16   SEEKING OUT SANCTIONED MICROSOFT COURSE INSTRUCTION

Q: *How and where can you obtain Microsoft-approved course instruction to help prepare you for the MCSE examinations?*

Choose the best answer:

     A.   *The Microsoft-approved curriculum is taught only at the Microsoft campus and in Microsoft-owned educational facilities.*

     B.   *All state universities and community colleges offer the Microsoft-approved curriculum.*

     C.   *Microsoft-approved instruction is available only from Authorized Technical Education Centers.*

     D.   *Microsoft courses are taught entirely by individuals and companies who may or may not have received Microsoft approval.*

Microsoft-approved education facilities are spread across the world. In the U.S., one is probably located within driving distance of you. Various independent locally owned and nationally franchised companies (such as Productivity Point International, Executrain, and New Horizons) offer the courses and aggressively advertise their classes in trade publications and local daily newspapers. Microsoft calls these places ATEC's, or Authorized Technical Education Centers. Microsoft also offers Microsoft On Line Institute (MOLI). MOLI is a Web-based medium that provides students with on-line instruction, course materials, and feedback.

Finally, for highly self-directed individuals, there are a wide variety of books and other study materials available for preparation for the MCSE examinations. These self-study courses require discipline on your part to complete the work in reasonable time on your own. However, many people prefer receiving instruction in classroom-like settings. Course material Microsoft provides can cost in the thousands of dollars for the entire set, but many people choose this method for getting MCSE information. Most of these classes give students the opportunity to work at a computer station with the NT software loaded and running on a network. Prospective students should inquire about the credentials of the instructor of the class they intend to take.

When selecting a teacher, you should look for one with real-world experience in addition to certification. Microsoft Certified Trainers follow a rigid, pre-determined lesson plan in conducting the class. The trainers encourage their students to ask questions. The price of the tuition includes all course materials Microsoft provides, including evaluation software in CD-ROM format. Upon completion, the student receives a certificate for having satisfied the course requirements.

*Answer **C** is the correct answer because Microsoft-approved instruction is available only from Authorized Technical Education Centers. Answer **A** is incorrect because other companies offer the Microsoft-approved curriculum. Answer **B** is incorrect because most state universities and community colleges do not offer the Microsoft-approved curriculum. Answer **D** is incorrect because you should generally enroll only in Microsoft courses taught by Microsoft Certified Trainers.*

FINDING QUALITY THIRD-PARTY HELP

17

Q: *Aside from the Microsoft-approved curriculum, which of the following companies offer third-party support to help you prepare for your Microsoft Certified Professional exams?*

Choose all correct answers:

    A.   *Transcender Corporation*

    B.   *QuickCert Corporation*

    C.   *Prep Technologies*

    D.   *Productivity Point International*

You can find help with MCSE courses and exams outside of the standard Authorized Technical Education Centers (ATEC) and Microsoft-related sources. Some people may have work acquaintances or friends in the industry they can rely on, but any quality third-party help typically comes through books such as this, or through on-line sources. Many popular book stores carry a wide selection of books relating to the NT 4.0 operating system and supplemental course material.

In addition, the Transcender Corporation (at *http://www.transcender.com*) makes a business of MCSE test preparation. Transcender's sample tests are quite similar to the real thing, and it offers a money-back guarantee if you do not pass the exam. You can also try the Prep Technologies software from the Prep Technologies Web site at *http://www.mcpprep.com* or the QuickCert Corporation software from the QuickCert Web site at *http://www.quick-cert.com*.

Answers A, B, and C are all correct, as each company designs and markets test preparation software. Answer D is incorrect, as Productivity Point International is an Authorized Technical Education Center.

FINDING NT EVALUATION COPIES TO PRACTICE ON

18

Q: *If you do not already own Windows NT server and workstation, you will be unable to work with the operating systems at home unless you purchase the operating systems.*

    True or False?

People taking the Microsoft MCSE courses at an Authorized Technical Education Center get valuable course materials with their instruction. Part of the course material is a set of CD-ROMs that include evaluation copies of the NT operating system students study in the course. The license on the software usually lasts for 120 days, and is full-featured until it expires.

Microsoft also offers many of its latest *BackOffice* products (including NT 4.0) for download at the Web site *http://backoffice.microsoft.com/downtrial/default.asp*. Some of the items for download on this page are upgrades and service packs, while others are fully featured 120-day evaluation products.

*The correct answer is **False**, as Microsoft and the Authorized Technical Education Centers offer trial software that lets you work with the operating systems for up to 120 days without purchasing the entire software package.*

19 — SIGNING UP TO TAKE YOUR TEST

Q: Which of the following companies might administer your MCSE examinations?

Choose all correct answers:

    A.   Transcender Corporation

    B.   Microsoft Corporation

    C.   Sylvan Prometric

    D.   Virtual University Enterprises

Microsoft has an exclusive worldwide contract with the Sylvan Prometric Corporation and Virtual University Enterprises, Inc., to administer the Microsoft Certified Professional examinations. Sylvan Prometric's toll-free number is 1-800-755-EXAM (3926), while Virtual University Enterprises' toll-free number is 1-888-837-8616. You can find both Sylvan Prometric and Virtual University Enterprises on the Web at Microsoft's certification home page at *http://www.microsoft.com/mcp*. The Web page explains both companies' three-step process for registering to take an exam, and you can actually register online at this site. The typical approach, however, is to call the toll-free number and find the location of the nearest testing centers. Not all testing centers are the same, so if there are multiple centers in your area, you should take the time to find the one that is most comfortable for you. The testing location should be a quiet room with only one exam desk (some have two), as few distractions as possible, preferably no windows, and a cooperative staff. You may want to actually visit the test center in advance of the scheduled exam to become as familiar as possible with its environment.

Both Sylvan Prometric and Virtual University Enterprises can arrange for you to take the exam the day you call with only a few minutes notice if the schedule is open at the exam site you have chosen. Sylvan Prometric says you can actually call from the testing center, make payment arrangements, and take your test within minutes. However, both Sylvan Prometric and Virtual University Enterprises recommend calling at least 24 hours in advance to avoid any problems. Sylvan Prometric also now offers scheduling and payment options on the Internet at *http://www.slspro.com* or at *http://www.prometric.com*, while Virtual University Enterprises offers scheduling and payment at *http://www.vuew.com/ms/*. You must have 2 forms of ID (one of which must be a picture ID) when you present yourself to take the exam. Both Sylvan Prometric and Virtual University Enterprises will make available electronically, at the exam site, an exam with your name on it the day of the scheduled exam.

Answers C and D are the correct answers. Answers A and B are incorrect, as neither of the companies listed offer MCSE examination testing.

20 — PAYING FOR YOUR EXAM

Q: The Microsoft Certified Professional exams are prohibitively expensive to take.

True or False?

You pay for your exam when you schedule it. Sylvan Prometric accepts only major credit cards as payment when you schedule your exam. The cost of each exam is $100.00. You will get a receipt for your exam purchase in the mail within two weeks. The receipt may arrive after you take the exam, but you do not need the receipt at the time you appear for your exam. Microsoft has traditionally offered fully enrolled college students a significant student discount on its operating system software products. People who are in the full-time students category should inquire at their college bookstore for details on Microsoft's program, or inquire at Microsoft's home page at *http://www.microsoft.com*. It is important to note that, while the exams themselves are relatively inexpensive, the Microsoft-approved course curriculum is not. Courses may run $1,500, $2,000, or even more.

*The correct answer is **False**; the exams themselves are not expensive, it the training necessary for the exams that is expensive.*

21   ## PREPARING YOURSELF FOR YOUR EXAMS BEFORE YOU WALK INTO THE TEST CENTER

Q: *How long before the exam should you arrive at the center?*

Choose the best answer:

    A.   *At least fifteen minutes*

    B.   *Half an hour*

    C.   *One hour or more*

    D.   *At the exact time the exam starts*

Successful exam graduates generally agree that it helps to arrive at the exam site as far in advance of the actual test time as you need to look over last minute notes and compose yourself. You can sit in your car or a private area of the test center and do a last-minute review of difficult areas. You should try to commit to short-term memory any items you feel sure the test will include. That time may be as little as fifteen minutes and as much as an hour or more. You can jot down these thoughts immediately upon entering the test room while they are still fresh in your mind. Fear of test-taking can be a powerful deterrent to success, especially if it has been several years since you have taken an exam. Remember, however, all the work you have done thus far to be able to take the exam. Luckily, most test-takers will count it as an advantage that the test is taken alone with no one else in the room, unless you have chosen one of the test centers that has two desks, and another person has scheduled the same time. Finally, well-known suggestions for test preparation include getting good sleep the night before, entering the exam with no hunger pangs, and reviewing key points rather than staying up late with stressful "cramming."

Answer A is the correct answer. You should always arrive at the testing center at least fifteen minutes in advance of the test, to ensure that your paperwork is processed and you are ready to begin. Answers B and C are incorrect because, while they are also appropriate times to arrive, they will depend on your personal preference. Answer D is incorrect because arriving at the exam's exact start time may cause you to miss the exam.

22   ## USING EXAM MATERIALS THE TEST CENTER PROVIDES TO YOU

Q: *You will be unable to use which of the following materials when you take the tests?*

Choose all correct answers:

> A.   Center-provided markers and pencils
>
> B.   Your own notes
>
> C.   Center-provided paper or laminated paper
>
> D.   Your own pencil and paper

When you go to the testing center, the proctors at the center will not let you bring into the exam room any books, notes, or other papers of your own. In general, you should either leave such materials in your car, at home, or look for a safe storage space in the testing center when you make your "get acquainted" visit, as Tip 20 discusses. In addition, you do not need to bring your own materials, such as pen, pencil, eraser, or paper into the test—because the test is administered entirely on computer. However, depending on the test location, staff at the exam site may make available at the exam desk either paper and pencil that you can use to write notes, or laminated paper with a dry-erase marker that you can use. As soon as you sit down to take the exam, you can use these supplies to jot down any helpful concepts you committed to memory before the test. You can also make notes to yourself about test questions, if you think it will be helpful later in the test. Keep in mind, however, that the test administrator or the staff at the site will collect these materials before you leave the room.

Answers A and C are correct; you can use any center-provided materials while you take the tests. Answers B and D are incorrect because you cannot use any of your own materials while you take the tests.

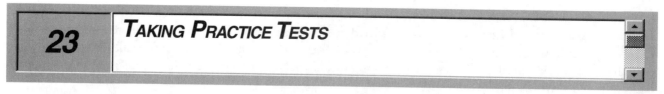

23   **TAKING PRACTICE TESTS**

Q: *Where can you acquire practice exams to prepare for the test?*

Choose all correct answers:

> A.   You can purchase software from the Transcender Corporation.
>
> B.   You can find sample questions with many study books.
>
> C.   Training centers will provide sample questions to you during your course preparation.
>
> D.   You can acquire sample questions from the Microsoft Certified Professional Web site.

When preparing for the Microsoft exams, taking practice exams and working with Microsoft-style practice questions are both crucial parts of your study process. As with many standardized exams, understanding how to take the test itself is very important—although not as important as having the knowledge itself; understanding the exams' structure runs a very close second. A large number of practice exams are available in books, on CD-ROM, and online. Many simulate the actual test-taking experience with a clock timer on the screen and the same on-screen percentage test score you will see on your real exam afterward. This book contains sample test questions with most Tips, and also includes a companion CD-ROM with sample exams.

The Transcender Corporation, one of the best-known sellers of test preparation software for the MCSE, sells study programs for each of the Microsoft Certified Professional tests. Additionally, the Transcender Corporation posts new sample questions each day on its Web site, at *http://www.transcender.com,* with discussions of the correct answers. Finally, Transcender also makes available shortened versions of sample tests on its Web site. Microsoft's Certified Professional Web site at *http://www.microsoft.com/mcp* provides detailed information about the contents and sections of each test. In addition, the Web site will let you download Personal Exam Preparation (PEP) tests by Self Test Software,

Inc., to practice with. Additionally, Microsoft's online Certified Professional Magazine is also a good reference for sample exams and online MCSE resource material at *http://www.mcpmag.com/*.

Practicing with many different sample exams is invaluable in preparation for the actual exam. Programs that simulate the exam experience are especially helpful because they include the built-in time factor, forcing you to complete the test in the amount of time you will have during the test's actual administration.

Answers A, B, C, and D are all correct. You can obtain sample tests from the Transcender Corporation, from many study books, from training centers, and from the Microsoft Certified Professional Web site.

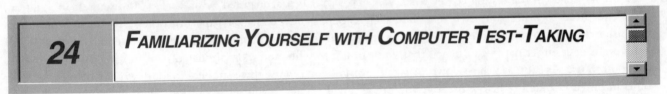

24   FAMILIARIZING YOURSELF WITH COMPUTER TEST-TAKING

Q: *When taking the examinations, you will have the choice of taking the test on paper or online at the testing center.*

    True or False?

One of the biggest problems that many people run into when they start to study for the Microsoft Certified Professional exams is the difference in format from most of the tests that they have taken previously. Because most people have taken standardized tests, whether the Scholastic Aptitude Test (SAT), California Aptitude Test (CAT), or some other educational test, most people are familiar with the ScanTron™ format of such exams. The Microsoft Certified Professional exams, on the other hand, are administered in a slightly different fashion. The entire test for any Microsoft Certified Professional exam is administered on computer. You will have the ability to answer all the questions using only the mouse. Additionally, the exam program will provide you with navigation buttons that you can use to move backwards and forwards through the test.

As you can see, the interface lets you answer most questions with the radio buttons to the left of the answer selections. You can use the navigation buttons at the interface's bottom to move backward and forward through the questions, and to end the exam when you finish. The entire question is displayed within the question area, and no other question or information is displayed until you leave the current question. Even though you may not have ever taken an exam by computer, your comfort level with the computer should work to your advantage. In fact, most people find that, after study and actually taking the exam, they much prefer the computerized exam to the old-fashioned pencil and paper-style exam.

*The correct answer is **False**. The testing centers offer the Microsoft Certified Professional exams only online. There is no paper exam for you to take.*

25   MAXIMIZING EVERY SECOND OF YOUR EXAM TIME

Q: *How long are the exams, and how many questions does each exam contain?*

Choose the best answer:

    A.   *The exams are each one hour long and contain 36 questions.*

    B.   *The exams are each one and one-half hours long, and contain 55 questions.*

C.   *The exams are each one and one-half hours long, and will contain a variable number of questions.*

D.   *The exams are each two hours long, and will contain a variable number of questions.*

In a standardized testing environment, understanding how long you have to answer each question (or all the questions) is often as or more important than knowing how many questions there are in total. For the Microsoft Certified Professional exams, you will have no more than one hour and thirty minutes to complete the exam. If you should run out of time, the examination will automatically stop and will generate your score based on your progress when the examination stopped. Use every second of the hour and one-half that the exam provides you, even if you are sure after one hour that you have answered every question correctly. The wording of many questions is often tricky, so rereading the elements of each question after your initial haste is gone can sometimes reveal that your answer is the exact opposite of what the correct answer is. Many experienced MCSE test-takers argue that you should *read through the entire exam first*, marking each question as you go so you can revisit them all, even though it may be tempting to stop and immediately answer questions that seem "easy." However, many test-takers also argue that doing so is a waste of time—because you will end up reading each question twice before you enter your answers. Your testing method will depend on you—when you practice, you should try to take the test both ways, and see how you perform. In the event that you do read through all the questions before you begin answering any of the questions, do not take too long to do so. Half an hour should be the most you will need and, in any event, should be the most you allot, as doing so will leave you about one minute per question to actually answer the questions. This method often tends to help you relax, and may help you to avoid frustration in the event that the early questions on the exam are exceptionally difficult.

Answer C is correct because the exams are each one and one-half hours long, and will contain a variable number of questions. Answer A is incorrect because both the duration and the number of questions is incorrect. Answer B is incorrect because, while the exams are each one and one-half hours long, and some exams may contain 55 questions, other exams may contain more or fewer questions. Answer D is incorrect because the exams are each one and one-half hours long.

26   **EXPLORING TEST QUESTION FORMATS**

Q: *Each MCSE exam has two essay questions worth 50% of your score.*

    True or False?

The MCSE exam questions will almost invariably take the form of multiple choice, multiple choice/multiple answer, or True/False. Microsoft test designers tend to put more information in the questions than you actually need to give the correct answer. Read carefully through each question's entire text, gleaning only the information you need to answer the question correctly. Some question information may have no bearing on the correct answer. MCSE exam questions tend more toward the "situational," which means the exam writers present problematic scenarios within a typical corporate networking environment. You are often in troublesome scenarios as a network administrator, so the exam questions will explain not only your hypothetical challenge, but also what the limits are on the equipment or resources available to you in a given environment. As the administrator involved in the scenario, your answers will resolve the question within its limiting factors.

*The answer is **False**. The MCSE exams do not have essay questions.*

27   **UNDERSTANDING THE MULTIPLE-CHOICE QUESTION FORMAT**

Q: *Microsoft Certification exams contain which of the following approximate percentages of question types?*

Choose the correct answer:

    A.   *50% multiple choice, 25% multiple-choice with multiple correct answers, and 25% true or false*

    B.   *40% multiple choice, 40% multiple-choice with multiple correct answers, and 20% true or false*

    C.   *25% multiple choice, 50% multiple-choice with multiple correct answers, and 25% true or false*

    D.   *25% multiple choice, 50% multiple-choice with multiple correct answers, and 15% true or false, and a single essay question worth 10%*

Many of the questions in the MCSE exams will be in a multiple choice with only a single correct answer format. Questions that the test present in such a format means that only one of the provided answers will be correct. Generally, the test will preface questions of this type with a phrase such as "Choose the best answer," and will provide your selection choices to you as a series of radio buttons.

Answer B is the correct answer, as the Microsoft exams are generally composed of approximately 40% multiple choice questions, 40% multiple-choice questions with multiple correct answers, and 20% true or false questions.

28   UNDERSTANDING THE TRUE OR FALSE QUESTION FORMAT

Q: *Microsoft Certification exams will contain simple True or False questions.*

    True or False?

Some of the questions in the MCSE exams will be in a true or false question format. Unfortunately, most questions that have a true or false answer are not simple. Instead, it is more likely that you will see a question in the following format:

Q: *You have several hundred users in your company. You will soon hire fifty temporary workers. The temporary workers will be at your company for time periods ranging from one to three months. Your boss asks you to submit a plan administering the temporary user accounts. You must allow for account expirations and account restrictions, and optionally you should be able to audit the temporary users' server activity.*

When you submit your plan, you recommend the following:

    You will create each user account from a template that you have created specifically for temporary users. You will use User Manager for Domains and configure each user account to have an appropriate expiration. You will use the Account Policies option in User Manager for Domains to configure the temporary users to forcibly disconnect when the users' log-on hours expire. In addition, you will use the Event Viewer weekly to examine temporary user activity.

Your plan responds to all the requirements, including the optional requirements.

    True or False?

Generally, the test will preface questions with a True or False response with a statement. You must then determine whether the statement is accurate. Because the questions may have very complex constructions, true or false questions may actually be the most difficult questions on the test in some situations.

The correct answer is False, as certification exams will generally include more difficult true or false questions.

29   UNDERSTANDING MULTIPLE CHOICE QUESTIONS WITH MORE THAN ONE ANSWER

Q.   *Microsoft Certification exams contain two types of questions: multiple-choice and true or false.*

True or False?

Many of the questions in the MCSE exams will be in a multiple choice with multiple correct answer format. Questions that the test presents in such a format means that all, some, or only one of the provided answers may be correct. Generally, the test will preface questions of this type with a phrase such as "Choose all correct answers," and will provide your selection choices to you as checkboxes, instead of radio buttons as the test does with multiple choice and single answer questions. This format is particularly difficult for some test-takers, in part because they often consider one or more of the answers simultaneously.

Instead, the best approach for you to take may be to deal with multiple choice with multiple correct answer questions as a series of true and false questions. In other words, you can ask yourself whether the first answer is true or false in the context of the question. If it is false, it will always be false—do not mark it. If it is true, it will always be true, immaterial of the other selections, so mark the answer. After you decide for each answer, move on to the next answer.

Do not compare the value of each answer to the next; doing so can be even more confusing. If one statement is true given the question and information provided, it stands on its own without regard to the truth or falsehood of the other possible answers.

*The correct answer is **False** because Microsoft exams include multiple choice, true and false, and multiple choice with multiple answer questions.*

30   UNDERSTANDING SOLUTION-BASED QUESTIONS

Q: *Which of the following types of questions are likely to appear on an MCP exam?*

Choose all correct answers:

    A.   Simple, fact-based questions

    B.   Questions that ask you how to perform a certain task

    C.   Questions that propose a situation, and a solution, and ask you to evaluate the solution

    D.   Questions about specific key sequences to perform an action from a given start point

The most common types of questions on the MCP examinations are questions that either ask you to verify facts (such as the name of a computer on a network), or that ask you how to perform a certain task (such as adding a new user to the network domain). However, there are also more complex questions which deal with solutions to particular problems or situations. In general, such questions will include the question "Which results does the proposed solution produce?" You should use the question as your cue that the question is of the solution-based type. Consider, for example, the sample test question from a Transcender sample exam shown in Figure 30.

As you can see, the question describes a specific situation. Next, the question describes the minimal solution you must achieve, and then describes optional results that you may also desire. Finally, the question proposes a solution to the problem. You must then evaluate the solution and determine whether it achieves only the desired result, the desired result and some of the optional results, the desired result and all the optional results, or achieves none of the results. These questions are generally very time consuming, simply because you must evaluate the solution in detail to ensure what requirements it meets. As a test-taking strategy, you may want to mark questions of the solution type and return to them after you complete the other questions on the exam.

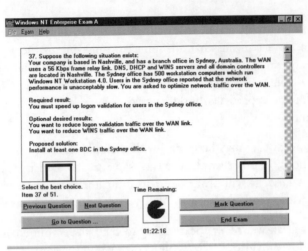

Figure 30 A solution-based question within a Transcender sample examination.

*Answers A, B, and C are all correct. **Answer D** is incorrect because the examinations do not test knowledge of specific key sequences to perform an action from a given start point.*

31 UNDERSTANDING "RECOMMENDED APPROACH" QUESTIONS

Q.   When responding to "Recommended Approach" questions, which of the following answers should you provide?

Choose the best answer:

> *A.   The method that the Microsoft Curriculum specifies for addressing the problem*
>
> *B.   The method that your trainer taught you was a "shortcut," requiring fewer steps than the Microsoft Curriculum's method*
>
> *C.   A method that you have used "in the field," but which Microsoft's Curriculum makes no mention of.*
>
> *D.   An undocumented method that the Microsoft Curriculum mentions*

As you learned in Tip 30, MCP exams will often include questions of the solution-based type, which describe a specific situation and a set of actions taken to resolve the situation, and will then ask you whether the actions fully or partially resolve the situation. Similarly, the MCP exams will often include questions that ask you to respond with the "Recommended Approach" for solving a problem. Figure 31 shows a sample question in the "Recommended Approach" format.

"Recommended Approach" questions expect you to respond with the Microsoft-recommended approach to solving a problem. In fact, such questions may include other answer choices which will solve the problem the question describes, but which do not use Microsoft's recommended approach to do so. You must be careful with such questions to ensure that the answer you provide matches the information the Microsoft-approved curriculum provides to solve the problem.

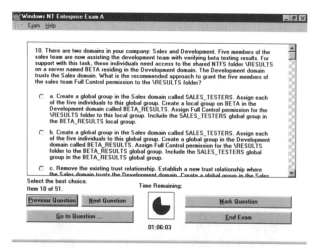

Figure 31 *A "Recommended Approach" question within a Transcender sample examination.*

Note: *The solutions this book describes adhere to the Microsoft-approved curriculum. In such cases where the book may make a suggestion for use in the field that does not adhere to the curriculum, the text in the Tip will clearly indicate that such is the case.*

Answer A *is the correct answer because you should respond with the method that the Microsoft Curriculum specifies for addressing the problem.* **Answers B, C,** *and* **D** *are incorrect because, while all the answers may provide an effective solution to the problem, they are not the Microsoft-recommended method for responding to the problem.*

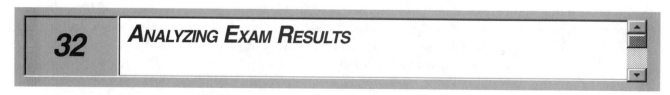

32	ANALYZING EXAM RESULTS

Q: How long will you have to wait to view the results of your test?

Choose the best answer:

A.   *You will receive the results almost immediately.*

B.   *You will receive the results within about ten minutes.*

C.   *You will receive the results within one business day.*

D.   *You will receive the results within one week.*

After you finish the exam, the exam PC will post your individual results almost immediately. The results will not show how you did on each question (that is, which specific questions you got right or wrong). Rather, the program will display a bar graph that shows the percentage of questions you answered correctly in the Microsoft-specified sections of the exam. For example, the program may show you that correctly answered 74% of "planning" questions, but only 43% of "installation" questions. In such a case (assuming you failed the entire exam), you would study to maintain your planning percentage, but focus your efforts on installation questions to better your score in that section. The program will also display, in percentage form, Microsoft's pre-determined threshold of correct answers for passing the test. For example, the Windows NT Server exam (70-067) requires an 85% passing grade. Compare this value to your overall percentage of correct answers to reveal whether you passed or not. You should examine your results particularly carefully if you did not pass (although even a passing score will likely require closer study). Subject headings with low percentage scores will indicate to you the areas where you must most diligently re-apply yourself in your studies.

*Answer A is the correct answer because your testing computer will display the test results almost immediately. **Answers B, C, and D** are all incorrect because receiving the results does not take as long as any of them indicate.*

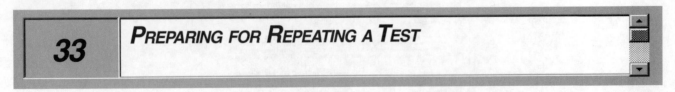

33 **PREPARING FOR REPEATING A TEST**

Q: *Once you fail a test for the MCSE certification, the odds are high that you will never pass the test.*

True or False?

After all the preparation that you might perform for the test, after all the study that you will do within this book, and any other resources that you may take advantage of, it is still possible that you may not pass the exam. In fact, Microsoft plans for about 60% of all test-takers to fail the exams their first time.

If you did not pass, before you leave the test center, immediately make detailed notes of whatever you can remember from the questions on the exam, especially those that were hard for you. Doing this, in addition to having the bar-graph results that the center will provide to you that ranks your performance, should indicate which subject areas you must study again.

The next test you take will have the same relative subject portions. In other words, gear your study toward gathering the additional material that you did not know on your first exam, but also be sure to maintain the knowledge that you applied successfully on the first exam.

Usually, facing a test over the same subject material comes with a little less fear and a little more confidence—because you know that you know most of the material, and you likely need just a little "extra" study to put you "over the hump." Preparation for repeating the same exam will be much the same as your original approach, except you will be operating from a position of strength because of your experience.

*The correct answer is **False**. In fact, many very successful MCSEs failed one or more exams on their way to certification.*

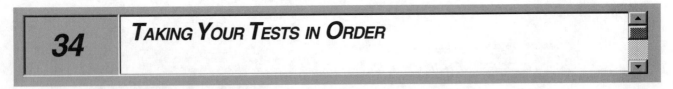

34 **TAKING YOUR TESTS IN ORDER**

Q: *There is a specific order that you must follow when taking the MCSE exams.*

True or False?

As you have learned, you will have to take a minimum of six exams, four required exams and two electives, to receive your Microsoft Certified Systems Engineer certification. While professional trainers generally recommend that you follow a pre-planned sequence of tests, you are free to choose whatever sequence of courses and exams you want. Microsoft recommends the self-paced Networking Essentials course to start. It covers a broad spectrum of basic network concepts and is a good refresher for those already proficient with networking principles. Beginners will find that it is loaded with facts they must memorize. Almost all MCSE graduates say the Networking Essentials *exam*, however, should be the last one you take because of the sheer number of facts you must commit to memory. (Keep in mind that Microsoft suggests taking the self-paced training course on Networking Essentials *first*.)

Next, you should attend courses 922 and 803 to prepare for the 70-067 Exam, Implementing and Supporting Microsoft Windows NT Server 4.0. You should then be able to also take the 70-073 Exam, Implementing and Supporting

Microsoft Windows NT Workstation 4.0 Enterprise. Next, most trainers suggest that you take the 689 course, Supporting Microsoft Windows NT Server 4.0–Enterprise Technologies. Even though very little material from the course is on the Exam 70-068 (Implementing and Supporting Microsoft Windows NT Server 4.0 in the Enterprise), you will find the content valuable when you take electives.

After you take the two Windows NT Server exams, but before you take the Networking Essentials exam, most trainers recommend that you take the Windows NT Workstation or Windows 95 exam, depending on the track you want to pursue. In general, you should take the elective exams after you pass the four core exams.

*The answer is **False**. While there is an order that most training professionals, and Microsoft professionals themselves, recommend that you should follow, you can take the exams in any order you want.*

35   FAMILIARIZING YOURSELF WITH THE WINDOWS FAMILY

Q: *The currently-tested Windows family of operating systems includes which of the following operating systems?*

Choose all correct answers:

      A.   *Microsoft Windows NT Server 4.0*

      B.   *Microsoft Windows NT Workstation 4.0*

      C.   *Microsoft Windows 95*

      D.   *Microsoft Windows for Workgroups 3.11*

The Microsoft Windows family of operating systems have grown and evolved significantly in the last decade. The early releases of the Microsoft Windows platform were not always very stable, but after MS Windows became popular, it continued to grow and improve. MS Windows has gone through several versions. The first to really succeed was MS Windows 3.x. Windows 3.x was fairly stable and let PC users have a graphical interface on an otherwise boring screen. The next highly successful platform was Windows for Workgroups. Windows for Workgroups gave users the same features as the previous versions of Windows, but with network support.

About the same time that Windows for Workgroups was becoming a household name, Windows NT Advanced Server was becoming an industry name. Users speculated that Microsoft had really intended to impact the "rock solid" Unix market, but instead of becoming the next Unix, Windows NT has become an industry-standard file and print server system. The first version to catch on in the corporate world was NT 3.5 (with a slightly altered 3.51 soon thereafter). Today, most users use version 4.0 of Windows NT. Microsoft intends to release Windows NT version 5.0 in the near future.

Finally, Windows 95 was the first 32-bit operating system from Microsoft intended for home use. Microsoft made it available to the general public shortly after the first commercial versions of NT came to the corporate world. Windows 95 brought such innovations as Plug and Play and a more intuitive user interface, along with limited networking capabilities. Today, with an expanding Internet market driving the development of software, Microsoft is "converging" its Internet browser applications with its operating system software and its networking designs in the next generation. While Windows 98 fulfills much of that promise of convergence, Microsoft does not recommend Windows 98 as a business operating system, and instead recommends that companies should upgrade their Windows 95 workstations to Windows NT 4.0 Workstation.

***Answers A, B, and C** are all correct. **Answer D** is incorrect because Microsoft has retired the Microsoft Windows for Workgroups 3.11 exam.*

36   COMPARING WINDOWS *NT* SERVER AND *NT* WORKSTATION

Q: *You have just recently installed Windows NT as your company platform. Your boss calls you and wants to know why you installed Windows NT Workstation instead of Windows NT Server on his machine. Why did you install NT Workstation on his machine and what could you tell him to eliminate his fears of not having the most powerful operating system?*

Choose the best answer:

     A.   *Windows NT networks permit only one machine on the network to use the Windows NT Server version of the operating system.*

     B.   *Windows NT Workstation will perform faster than Windows NT Server for the type of tasks he will perform.*

     C.   *If he were to run Windows NT Server, other computers on the network would constantly access his machine, impacting the security of his documents and slowing his machine's performance.*

     D.   *Windows NT Workstation will provide him with the performance that he wants without giving him the opportunity to damage important setup information on the network.*

Windows NT Server is a powerful 32-bit network operating system Microsoft designed to handle numerous simultaneous network connections. Windows NT Workstation, on the other hand, is a powerful Workstation operating system Microsoft optimized to run applications locally. Although both operating systems have a lot in common, they are not the same.

To test this for yourself, you can run an application (such as Microsoft *Word*) on a Windows NT Server, but you will experience sluggish performance. If you initiate the same application on a Windows NT Workstation, you will see that it executes much more quickly. Likewise, if you try to use your Windows NT Workstation as a file and print server (that is, a computer that lets other computers access files or print to printers on that computer), you will immediately become aware of its limitations as a server. To achieve the best results, you should use the correct "tools" for the job. In general, Windows NT Server computers should be computers that provide services to other computers on the network, while Windows NT Workstation computers should be computers that request services from other computers on the network.

Answer B is correct because Windows NT Workstation will perform faster than Windows NT Server for the type of tasks he will perform. Answer A is incorrect because a Windows NT network can support as many different Windows NT Server computers as your network may require. Answer C is incorrect because the Windows NT network security setup would control access to his machine. Answer D is incorrect because, even with Windows NT Server on his desktop, he could not damage the network without the appropriate rights.

37   COMPARING WINDOWS *NT* WORKSTATION AND WINDOWS 95

Q: *An employee who has Windows 95 at home comes to you, the administrator of the network in the company you both work for, to ask why he cannot use Windows 95 in the office too, rather than having to learn a new operating system (NT 4.0 Workstation).*

Choose all correct answers:

A.   *Windows 95 will not work correctly with a Windows NT network.*

B.   *Windows NT is a more stable operating system than Windows 95.*

C.   *Some applications that the network must run will only run on Windows NT, so he must use the Windows NT Workstation client.*

D.   *Windows 95 does not provide the security of Windows NT workstation.*

In many networking environments, users will be familiar with Windows 95 from the home computers. Many corporate environments will use Windows 95 as their network clients, as well. However, in some organizations, you may have a need for the security and other corporate-specific features of Windows NT Workstation as the client. In general, you should try to determine what operating system is the best fit for your client computers, and install that operating system throughout your organization. To understand the difference between Windows 95 and Windows NT Workstation, study Table 37, which lists some features of both operating systems, and the differences in their implementations.

Windows 95	Windows NT Workstation
32-bit operating system	32-bit operating system
Multitasking	Multitasking (Windows 95 does not support multiple processors for true multitasking)
Multithreading	Multithreading
Hardware profiles	Hardware profiles
Plug and Play support	No Plug-and-Play Support
Windows Messaging	Windows Messaging
No built-in Web services	Peer Web services
Compatibility with existing (16-bit) software	Compatibility with some existing (16-bit) software
No Security	Security
Compatibility with existing hardware	Compatibility with some existing hardware
Less Stable	More Stable

Table 37 Windows 95 and Windows NT Workstation features.

Although you can find many of the Windows 95 features in Windows NT Workstation, there are many differences between the two operating systems. Windows 95, for example, supports Plug-and-Play devices, making it easier for users to add new hardware to their operating system, while Windows NT does not. On the other hand, Windows NT Workstation supports true multi-tasking, Peer Web services, and security. Additionally, Windows NT Workstation provides greater operating system stability than Windows 95.

One of the most important considerations, however, is Windows 95's higher level of compatibility with most 16-bit applications. Microsoft built the Windows 95 operating system with the specific goal of ensuring that the majority of Windows 3.x applications could still run on the new operating system, and that most hardware originally designed for Windows 3.x would still work correctly in Windows 95. Windows NT Workstation's support is not as strong, and you should carefully evaluate any legacy applications or hardware in your organization before upgrading to Windows NT Workstation 4.0. Such applications and hardware may not work correctly after the upgrade.

Answers B *and* ***D*** *are both correct. Although more users recognize Windows 95, which has Plug and Play along with networking capabilities, it does not provide the security most work settings need, and is a less stable operating system.* ***Answer A*** *is incorrect because Windows 95 will work correctly with a Windows NT network.* ***Answer C*** *is incorrect because most commercial applications will run correctly on either Windows NT Workstation or Windows 95.*

38	### CHOOSING BETWEEN WINDOWS 95 AND WINDOWS NT WORKSTATION

Q: *Your boss has asked you to recommend a new operating system for all client computers in your company. Each machine has the hardware to support Windows NT or Windows 95. Each client will run accounting software and an office suite. Users must be able to secure files and folders on their local machines as well as access secured files and folders on the server. In such an environment, you should recommend Windows NT Workstation as the client operating system.*

True or false?

As Tip 37 discusses in detail, there are significant differences in the implementation of Windows NT Workstation and Windows 95. Microsoft calls Windows NT Workstation "a robust 32-bit operating system designed to support mission critical applications," which means that Microsoft expects industries, not home users, to use Windows NT Workstation. On the other hand, Microsoft designed Windows 95 to be backward compatible with older software and hardware. For light office use or the home, a user should choose the Windows 95 operating system. If the user's needs involve heavy office, industrial, or security issues, then the user should choose the Windows NT Workstation operating system. As you learned in Tip 37, the most significant reason to select Windows 95 as a client operating system in most organizations is probably backward compatibility with older applications and hardware.

However, if your workstations must provide file and data security at both the local computer and on the network, you have no choice but to upgrade to Windows NT Workstation for your client operating system. In the event that you have both important legacy applications that may not work correctly on Windows NT and specific security needs for your local computers, you will have to determine which is more important and install the appropriate operating system.

The correct answer is **True***, you should use Windows NT Workstation because the operating system will provide you with tight local security, while Windows 95 has no local security.*

39	### MICROSOFT WINDOWS NT EXAM 70-067: IMPLEMENTING AND SUPPORTING MICROSOFT WINDOWS NT SERVER 4.0

Q: *To get the Microsoft Certified Systems Engineer (MCSE) certification, you must pass four core exams and two electives. Of the four core exams, three test your knowledge on a specific operating system, while one exam tests your general knowledge of networks. Which of the following exams test your general knowledge of Windows NT Server 4.0?*

Choose all correct answers:

> *A.* *Exam 70-073: Implementing and Supporting Microsoft Windows NT Workstation 4.02*
>
> *B.* *Exam 70-067: Implementing and Supporting Microsoft Windows NT Server 4.0.*
>
> *C.* *Exam 70-068: Implementing and Supporting Microsoft Windows NT Server 4.0 in the Enterprise*
>
> *D.* *Exam 70-069: Implementing and Supporting Microsoft Windows NT Server 4.0 In Networks*

As you have learned, there is a series of exams that you must pass to receive your MCSE certification. You have also learned that Microsoft provides a series of courses that you may take before you take the exams. In fact, Microsoft recommends attending its Official Curriculum Courses before taking your exams. Although the official courses are generally a good idea, one course does not always completely prepare you for an exam.

For example, in the case of Exam 70-067: Implementing and Supporting Microsoft Windows NT Server 4.0, you would have to take two courses to fully prepare yourself for this one exam. You must first take Course 803: Administering Microsoft Windows NT 4.0, which is a three-day course that contains 11 sections, or modules. Table 39 shows the eleven modules in Course 803: Administering Microsoft Windows NT 4.0.

Course 803: Administering Microsoft Windows NT 4.0 is a good course for you if must know how to perform general system administration. However, this course will only give you about half the information you need to pass Exam 70-067: Implementing and Supporting Microsoft Windows NT Server 4.0.

The other information you will need is in Course 922: Supporting Microsoft Windows NT 4.0 Core Technologies. Course 922 discusses key Windows NT technologies that are common to both Windows NT Server and Windows NT Workstation. In taking Course 922, you will help prepare yourself for both the Windows NT Server exam and the Windows NT Workstation exam.

Modules in Course 803: Administering Microsoft Windows NT 4.0
Introduction to Administering Windows NT
Setting Up User Accounts
Setting Up Group Accounts
Administering User and Group Accounts
Securing Network Resources with Shared Folder Permissions
Securing Network Resources with NTFS Permissions
Setting Up a Network Printer
Administering Network Printers
Auditing Resources and Events
Monitoring Network Resources
Backing Up and Restoring Data

Table 39 Modules in Course 803: Administering Microsoft Windows NT 4.0.

Answer B is the correct answer, you should take Exam 70-067: Implementing and Supporting Microsoft Windows NT Server 4.0 to test your basic Windows NT Server 4.0 knowledge. Answer A is incorrect because Exam 70-073: Implementing and Supporting Microsoft Windows NT Workstation 4.02 tests your knowledge of Windows NT Workstation. Answer C is incorrect because Exam 70-068: Implementing and Supporting Microsoft Windows NT Server 4.0 in the Enterprise tests you on specific networking issues with Windows NT. Answer D is incorrect because there is no Exam 70-069: Implementing and Supporting Microsoft Windows NT Server 4.0 In Networks.

40	## WHAT EXAM 70-067: IMPLEMENTING AND SUPPORTING MICROSOFT WINDOWS NT SERVER 4.0 COVERS

Q: *Exam 70-067: Implementing and Supporting Windows NT Server 4.0 will contain questions on, among other things, creating user accounts.*

   True or False?

Knowing what is going to be on an exam can help you to prepare for that exam. Exam 70-067 measures your ability to implement, administer, and troubleshoot information systems that incorporate Windows NT Server version 4.0 in a simple computing environment. A simple computing environment is typically a Windows NT-only local-area network. The network might include one or more servers, a single domain, and a single location; and it might have file-sharing and print-sharing capabilities. Before taking the exam, you should be proficient in six main categories of job skills. The exam is in six sections that correspond with those job skills.

The Planning section tests you on your ability to plan and layout the configuration of a Windows NT Server to meet various network requirements. Specific areas tested include the following:

- Choosing a file system

- Choosing a fault-tolerance method

- Selecting the appropriate network protocol for your networking, with your choices including TCP/IP, NWLink IPX/SPX Compatible Transport, and NetBEUI

The Installation and Configuration section tests you on your ability to install Windows NT Server on Intel-based platforms. Specific areas the exam tests include:

- Installing Windows NT Server to perform various server roles, including primary domain controller, backup domain controller, and member server

- Using all the different possible methods to install Windows NT Server, including installation from CD-ROM, installation over the network, Network Client Administrator, and express versus custom installation

- Configuring the possible protocols and protocol bindings for your Windows NT Server, including the TCP/IP protocol, the NWLink IPX/SPX Compatible Transport protocol, and the NetBEUI protocol

- Configuring network adapters for the server, including changing IRQ, IObase, and memory addresses, and configuring multiple adapters

- Configuring Windows NT Server core services, including the Directory Replicator, the License Manager, and other core services

- Configuring peripherals and devices, including communication devices, SCSI devices, tape device drivers, UPS devices and the UPS service, and mouse drivers, display drivers, and keyboard drivers

- Configuring hard disks to meet various server requirements, including allocating disk space capacity, providing redundancy, improving performance, providing security, and formatting

- Configuring printers, including adding and configuring a printer, implementing a printer pool, and setting print priorities

- Configuring a Windows NT Server computer for different types of client computers, including Windows NT Workstation, Microsoft Windows 95, and Microsoft MS-DOS-based clients

The Managing Resources section tests you on your knowledge and ability to manage users, groups, and resources on the Windows NT network. Specific areas tested include the following:

- Managing user and group accounts, including managing Windows NT groups, managing Windows NT user rights, administering account policies, and auditing changes to the user account database

- Creating and managing policies and profiles for efficient network administration, including local user profiles, roaming user profiles, and system policies.

- Administrating remote servers from client computers, including both Windows 95 and Windows NT Workstation client computers

- Managing disk resources, including copying and moving files between file systems, creating and sharing resources, implementing permissions and security, and establishing file auditing

The Connectivity section tests you on your ability to perform interoperation and remote access tasks with Windows NT server. Specific areas tested include the following:

- Configuring Windows NT Server for interoperability with NetWare servers using Gateway Service for NetWare and the Migration Tool for NetWare

- Installing and configuring Remote Access Service (RAS), including configuring RAS communications, configuring RAS protocols, configuring RAS security, and configuring Dial-Up Networking clients

The Monitoring and Optimization section tests you on your ability to monitor the performance of your Windows NT Server, and to optimize the server for maximum performance. Specific areas tested include the following:

- Monitoring performance of various functions by using Performance Monitor, including Processor, Memory, Disk, and Network functions

- Identifying performance bottlenecks

The Troubleshooting section tests your ability to solve problems with Windows NT Server installations or implementations. Specific areas tested include the following:

- Choosing the appropriate course of action to take to resolve installation failures

- Choosing the appropriate course of action to take to resolve boot failures

- Choosing the appropriate course of action to take to resolve configuration errors

- Choosing the appropriate course of action to take to resolve printer problems

- Choosing the appropriate course of action to take to resolve RAS problems

- Choosing the appropriate course of action to take to resolve connectivity problems

- Choosing the appropriate course of action to take to resolve resource access problems and permission problems

- Choosing the appropriate course of action to resolve fault-tolerance failures, including tape backup failures, mirroring failures, stripe set with parity failures, and disk duplexing failures

The correct answer is **True**. *The Managing Resources section of the exam will test you on your ability to create and manage user accounts.*

41 | **INTRODUCTION TO THE WINDOWS NT 4.0 INTERFACE**

Q: *You will perform most administration tasks within Windows NT in system-provided tool and utility programs. Where are most of these programs located on the Windows NT Desktop?*

Choose the best answer:

A.   *The Start menu Programs option Accessories group*

B.   *The Start menu Programs option Administrative Tools group*

C.   *The Start menu Settings option Control Panel group*

D.   *The Start menu Settings option Services group*

When Microsoft designed Windows NT 4.0, they updated the interface significantly from Windows NT 3.51, making the interface very similar to the Windows 95 interface most computer users are familiar with. An *interface* is simply what the user sees and interacts with on the computer's display. Many people refer to the Windows NT 4.0 interface as the Windows 95 interface. In reality, Microsoft released the Windows NT 4.0 interface early in Windows 95. The purpose of the interface change was to better accommodate new Windows platform users. The new Windows NT 4.0 interface is easier to use than previous Windows interfaces, such as Windows for Workgroups. Microsoft included features such as single-click icons to help users who had difficulty with double-clicking their mouse. To find anything in Windows NT 4.0 that is not already an icon on the Desktop, you should click your mouse on the Start button. Windows NT, in turn, will display the Start menu. In general, you will work with one of two submenus under the Start menu—the Programs menu or the Settings menu. The Programs menu will contain icons that correspond to most applications and utilities present on a computer, while the Settings menu lets you configure certain operating system features, including printers and the Taskbar's appearance. Figure 41 shows an example of a standard Windows NT interface that contains icons, the Taskbar, and the Start menu.

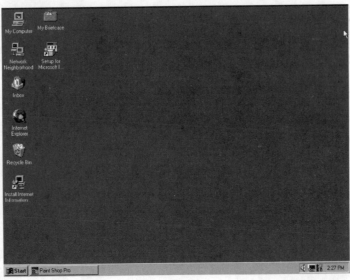

Figure 41 The standard Windows NT Interface.

Answer B *is the correct answer. Most Windows NT administration tools are within the Administrative Tools group.* **Answer A** *is incorrect because the Accessories group contains helper programs, such as the Windows* **Calculator**. **Answer C** *is incorrect because the Control Panel group contains icons that let you access Windows NT configuration options, such as the Desktop's appearance.* **Answer D** *is incorrect because there is no Services group.*

42   USING THE WINDOWS NT 4.0 TASKBAR

Q: *What is the quickest way to set the correct time on a Windows NT computer?*

Choose the correct answer:

A.   *Select the Start menu Settings option Control Panel group. Within the Control Panel window, double-click the mouse on the Date/Time icon.*

B.   *Select the Start menu Programs option Accessories group. Within the Accessories group, select the Date/Time program option.*

C.   *Double-click your mouse on the Taskbar clock.*

D.   *Select the Start menu Programs option Command Prompt option. At the command prompt, enter the* **Time** *command.*

One of the first features that most users will notice the Windows NT 4.0 Desktop is the Windows NT Taskbar. The Taskbar lets a user easily access applications that are already running in the background by simply clicking the mouse on the title of the application displayed on the Taskbar (which is usually at the bottom of the Desktop). If you click your mouse on any application you see on the Taskbar, that application will come to the foreground of the screen. Using the Taskbar, you can type information into a word processor and then quickly switch to a spreadsheet program. In addition to toggling between programs, you can use the Taskbar to view the time, change the volume control of your computer's speakers (making them louder or quieter), and arrange open windows.

One of the features of the Taskbar is its flexibility. For example, you can move the Taskbar to any outside edge of the screen—for example, to the left side of the screen, if your applications need more vertical space and less horizontal space. To do so, point your mouse to a blank area of the Taskbar, click and hold down your left mouse button, and drag the Taskbar to the side of the screen where you want the Taskbar to reside. You can also resize the Taskbar, making it larger or smaller. To do so, move your mouse pointer to the edge of the Taskbar until the pointer becomes a double-sided arrow, hold down your left mouse button, and drag the mouse until the Taskbar is the size you want. Figure 42 shows a possible Windows NT Taskbar view.

Figure 42 *A possible Taskbar view.*

Answer C *is the correct answer because you should double-click your mouse on the Taskbar clock.* **Answer A** *is incorrect because, while you can set the current Date and Time in the manner detailed, it is not as efficient as double-clicking on the Taskbar clock.* **Answer B** *is incorrect because there is no Date/Time program option within the Accessories group.* **Answer D** *is incorrect because the steps it details will only let you set the time, not the date, and because it is not as efficient as double-clicking on the Taskbar clock.*

43   INTRODUCTION TO THE WINDOWS NT RECYCLE BIN

Q: *You have deleted several files on your Windows NT Workstation 4.0. Can you get the deleted files back?*

Choose the best answer:

A.   *Yes, provided you have not emptied the Recycle Bin.*

B.   *Yes, provided the files were on a hard drive and you have not emptied the Recycle Bin.*

C.   *Yes, provided the files were not on a floppy drive and you have not emptied the Recycle Bin.*

D.   *No, you cannot retrieve the files.*

In many older file systems, a common problem was the user's accidental deletion of files on the computer. Windows NT creates a Recycle Bin for recovery of files that you have deleted, provided those files are on a hard drive. Older MS-

DOS utilities people used to recover deleted files are not compatible with Windows NT, so Microsoft created the Recycle Bin to let users undelete files. The system does not actually remove any file you delete from a hard drive. Instead, the system sends the files to a holding area where you can retrieve them later. To retrieve lost files, perform the following steps:

1. From the Windows NT Desktop, double-click your mouse on the Recycle Bin icon on the Desktop. Windows NT will display the Recycle Bin window.

2. Within the Recycle Bin window, use the mouse to select the file or files you want to restore. After you select the files, select the File menu Restore option. Windows NT will restore the files to their original location.

Answer B is correct because the files must be on a hard drive and you must not have emptied the Recycle Bin. Answer A is incorrect because you can delete files on removable media and thereafter be unable to recover them. Answer C is incorrect because there are other types of removable media than floppy disks, including Zip® disks and optical disks. Answer D is incorrect because you can retrieve the files, provided they meet certain criteria.

44   INTRODUCTION TO ACCOUNTS IN WINDOWS NT

Q: *What constitutes an account in Windows NT?*

Choose all correct answers:

     A.   Users

     B.   Groups

     C.   Windows NT computers

     D.   Shared resources

To work with Windows NT, you must understand accounts. A Windows NT *account* represents some user or users of the resources the network maintains. An account is a crucial, yet somewhat slippery, concept. It is perhaps best to define an account by its permissions. Account *permissions* tell the operating system what resources a particular account can access. For example, just as you need an account number to access funds in your bank, Windows NT requires account authorization to access network resources. In Windows NT, users, groups, and Windows NT computers all have accounts. Each user in a Windows NT network will have an account on the network. Similarly, each group (a logical construct that maintains permissions information) and Windows NT computer on the network will have its own account.

As you will learn in detail in Tip 46, Windows NT has a practical limitation of 40,000 accounts per domain. In large network environments, administrators must consider account limitation when they set up user accounts. If you structure your domain properly and watch the number of accounts you create, you can accommodate far more users than you would be able to otherwise. Knowing when to create an account is important.

Each user in your network constitutes a single account. You must have an account for each user who will access resources, so you cannot cut down on the number of users to conserve on account numbers. Each group you use to "containerize" your users is also an account. Each computer running Windows NT will have an account in the domain. Windows 95 computers do not need accounts, so if you select the proper operating system for each type of user in your network, you may be able to reduce the number of computer accounts in your domain.

Answers A, B, and C are all correct because Users, Groups, and Windows NT computers all comprise accounts in Windows NT. Answer D is incorrect because Windows NT does not create accounts for shared resources.

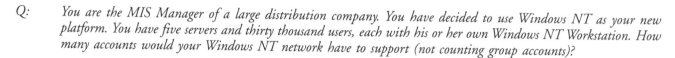

45 — UNDERSTANDING THE NUMBER OF ACCOUNTS A SINGLE DOMAIN MODEL CAN SUPPORT

Q: *You are the MIS Manager of a large distribution company. You have decided to use Windows NT as your new platform. You have five servers and thirty thousand users, each with his or her own Windows NT Workstation. How many accounts would your Windows NT network have to support (not counting group accounts)?*

Choose the best answer:

> A.   *Thirty thousand five (30,005)*
>
> B.   *Thirty-five thousand (35,000)*
>
> C.   *Sixty thousand five (60,005)*
>
> D.   *Two hundred ten thousand (210,000)*

As Tip 44 explains, Windows NT creates a single account for each user, group, and Windows NT computer on the network. Tip 44 also indicated that Windows NT 4.0 has a practical limitation of forty thousand accounts in a single domain. Microsoft bases this limitation on its testing policies in optimum situations—however, depending on your hardware and the time your Windows NT Server requires to boot, your effective limit may be much lower. Windows NT stores information about all accounts, including all users, groups, and all Windows NT computers, within the Directory Database. The *Directory Database* maintains all of the account information while the server runs. Windows NT uses the information within the Directory Database to validate user logons, approve resource access, and more. When you shut down the server, it will write the Directory Database to disk or discard it, depending on the server's network role.

The operating system loads the entire Directory Database into RAM when the Windows NT Server Domain Controller boots. Therefore, a large Directory Database can cause significant performance loss when the operating system boots. Moreover, a large Directory Database can slow down network performance significantly, because of the amount of network traffic that the network's servers may generate when they copy the Directory Database from the primary domain controller to the backup domain controllers.

Note: Microsoft says that although it has tested Directory Databases above forty thousand, it does not recommend exceeding this limit because doing so tends to cause a significant decline in network performance.

Answer C is correct, because the users alone generate thirty thousand accounts. The users' Windows NT Workstations generate another thirty thousand accounts. Finally, the Windows NT Servers generate five more accounts. You would then have a total of sixty thousand five accounts. Answers A, B, and D are all incorrect.

46 — INTRODUCTION TO SECURITY IDENTIFICATION NUMBERS

Q: *You are the network administrator for a company. You have just been informed that Bob Jones has quit, so you delete the user account Bobj. Then your boss tells you that he talked Bob into staying with the company. You create a new user account called Bobj with the same properties as the previous Bobj account. This solution will provide Bob Jones with full access to all the network resources he had access to with his old account.*

True or False?

As you have learned, Windows NT maintains an account for each user, group, and Windows NT computer on a Windows NT network. In addition to the human-readable information that Windows NT maintains about an account, Windows NT maintains a Security Identification Number (SID) for each account in a domain. The *Security Identification Number (SID)* is a unique, 32-bit number (meaning that its value falls somewhere between 0 and 2^{32}). The SID for each account is (in theory) unique throughout a domain, and the operating system will never (again, theoretically) regenerate a new SID that matches an SID that the domain is currently using or has used in the past. SIDs are only theoretically unique because it is conceivable (if extremely unlikely) that a single domain could use up 2^{32} accounts (a total of 4,294,967,296, or just under 4 billion 3 million accounts), over time.

When a user or computer tries to gain access to an object on the network, the operating system compares permissions set on the object to the SID of the account requesting access to the object. If the account has sufficient permissions to access the object, the operating system will grant access; otherwise, the system will deny the user access to the object. After the operating system generates a SID, the operating system will never regenerate it (again, subject to the 2^{32} SIDs limitation discussed earlier). For example, suppose that you created an account and gave that account permissions to an object, and then deleted that account. Suppose further that you later created an account of the same name. The new account would not have the same access to the object as did the original account—because the SID for the new account is different than the SID for the original account.

Note: In the event that you do run out of SIDs, you will have to reinstall your Windows NT Server software—the operating system will not let you use repeat SIDs, even if it runs out of new SIDs.

*The correct answer is **False**. The original account's Security Identification Number (SID) is different from the SID the operating system assigns to the new account. The new Bobj account will not have the same access to objects that the original account did because the new account does not have the original SID.*

| 47 | **USING ADMINISTRATIVE WIZARDS TO CREATE ACCOUNTS** |

Q: *What component has Microsoft added to Windows NT 4.0 Server to simplify account management?*

Choose the correct answer:

  A.   The User Manager for Domains utility

  B.   The Server Manager utility

  C.   The NewUser Wizard

  D.   The Administrative Wizards

There are different utilities that the Windows NT Server 4.0 installation includes with the operating system. You will work extensively with many of these utilities—particularly the User Manager for Domains and the Server Manager utilities. However, Windows NT 4.0 also includes a new feature to simplify network administration—the Windows NT Administrative Wizards. The Administrative Wizards let system administrators with little experience manage accounts in a Windows NT network using a simple, step-by-step process. The Administrative Wizards use the Windows Wizard interface (a series of dialog boxes, which you navigate through with Next and Back buttons) to take system administrators "by the hand" and lead them through the process of account creation and management. To invoke the Administrative Wizards from within Windows NT, perform the following steps:

  1.   Select the Start menu Programs option Administrative Tools group. Within the Administrative Tools group, select the Administrative Wizards program. Windows NT will display the Administrative Wizards dialog box will appear on your screen.

2. From the Administrative Wizards dialog box, select the type of function that you want to perform. For example, if you wanted to create a new user account, you would select the Add User Account Wizard option.

There are several different Administrative Wizards that you can access from the Wizard's main screen, each of which simplifies a specific administration task. Table 47 details the Administrative Wizards and how you would use them.

Administrative Wizard	Use
Add User Accounts	Creates new user accounts
Group Management	Creates new groups and manage existing groups
Managing File and Folder Access	Assigns shared and access permissions to files and folders
Add Printer	Adds support for a new printer to the server
Add and Remove Programs	Adds and remove programs from the Windows NT Server
Install New Modem	Adds support for a new modem to the server
Network Client Administrator	Installs or updates network client workstations
License Compliance	Checks licensing for installed applications and the operating system

Table 47 The Windows NT Administrative Wizards.

Figure 47 shows the Windows NT 4.0 Server Administrative Wizard's opening screen, with the icons for the eight different Administrative Wizards.

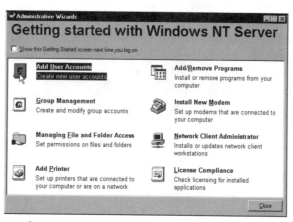

Figure 47 The Windows NT 4.0 Server Administrative Wizards.

Answer D is the correct answer because the Administrative Wizards are new to Windows NT 4.0. Answers A and B are incorrect because Windows NT 3.51 included both the User Manager for Domains utility and the Server Manager utility. Answer C is incorrect because there is no such wizard.

48 | **USING THE SERVER MANAGER UTILITY TO CREATE A COMPUTER ACCOUNT**

Q: *You have decided to have your Windows NT Workstation join a domain. You can log in normally from a Windows 95 computer. However, when you try to join the domain from your Workstation, the operating system denies you access. What could be causing this denial of access?*

Choose the best answer:

> A.   The system administrator did not create a computer account for the workstation.
>
> B.   Your user account does not have access to the domain.
>
> C.   The domain does not support Windows NT Workstation client computers.
>
> D.   Your network cable is not correctly connected to both the client and the server.

One of the most important tasks that you will perform as a Windows NT administrator is the management of accounts on the network. Each Windows NT Computer in a domain must have a computer account. For a Windows NT Workstation to join a domain, the system administrator must create a computer account for the workstation. System administrators can create Windows NT computer accounts using the Server Manager. You can use the Server Manager to perform a variety of system management tasks. Such tasks include configuring directory replication, viewing shared resources, disconnecting users from resources, stopping and starting services on servers, sharing remote resources, and creating computer accounts. (Later Tips will examine the Server Manager's other features.)

To create a computer account, perform the following steps:

1. Select the Start menu Programs option Administrative Tools group. Within the Administrative Tools group, select the Server Manager program. Windows NT will run the Server Manager.

2. Within the Server Manager, select the Computer menu Add to Domain option. Windows NT will display the Add Computer to Domain dialog box, as shown in Figure 48.

3. Within the Add Computer to Domain dialog box, select the type of computer account you want to create, either Windows NT Workstation or Server, or Windows NT Backup Domain Controller. Then, enter the computer account name for the new account. Click your mouse on OK when you finish to return to the Server Manager window.

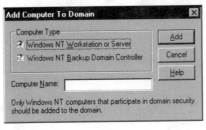

Figure 48 *The Add Computer to Domain dialog box.*

Answer A is the correct answer because the system administrator most likely did not create a computer account for the workstation. Answer B is incorrect because, if your user account does not have access to the domain, you would not have been able to log in from the Windows 95 computer. Answer C is incorrect because Windows NT domains always support Windows NT Workstation client computers. Answer D is incorrect because, if your network cable was not correctly connected to both the client and the server, you would not receive a network login prompt.

---

49   INTRODUCTION TO USER MANAGER FOR DOMAINS

Q: *Where in Windows NT 4.0 Server would you configure Trust Relationships?*

Choose the correct answer:

    A.   *In User Manager for Domains from the User menu*

    B.   *In User Manager for Domains from the Policies menu*

    C.   *In Server Manager from the Computers menu*

    D.   *In User Manager for Domains from the Trusts menu*

As you have learned, there are several important administrative tools that Windows NT will provide to you when you install the operating system. One of the tools that administrators use most is the User Manager for Domains utility program. You can use the User Manager for Domains to create user accounts, establish Trust Relationships, configure a system policy, change user rights, and administer other domains.

You must be very familiar with User Manager for Domains to pass Exam 70-067: Implementing and Supporting Microsoft Windows NT Server 4.0. Rather than trying to cram all the information that the test will expect you to know into a single Tip, upcoming Tips will discuss specific features of User Manager for Domains in detail—the program is, needless to say, very powerful.

To learn more about User Manager for Domains, you should spend some time examining User Manager for Domains' various menus and dialog boxes. You should also notice that the application will present you with many more options when you select an account before choosing a menu. Figure 49 shows the User Manager for Domains main window.

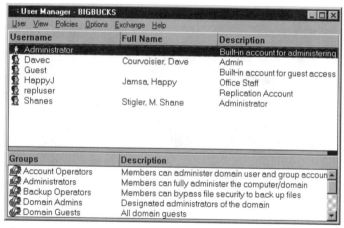

Figure 49 *The User Manager for Domains window.*

Answer B *is correct because you would configure trust relationships from User Manager for Domains from the Policies menu.* **Answer A** *is incorrect because the User menu is not the right menu for the task.* **Answer C** *is incorrect because you do not use the Server Manager to maintain trust relationships.* **Answer D** *is incorrect because there is no Trusts menu.*

---

50   USING USER MANAGER FOR DOMAINS TO CREATE A USER ACCOUNT

Q: *You have decided to create several user accounts for the sales department. The Administrative Wizards would be the best utility for the job.*

    True or False?

If you intend to administer a Windows NT domain, you should be very familiar with the User Manager for Domains program. While there are many different tasks that you will perform from within the User Manager for Domains, administrators most commonly use User Manager for Domains to create new user accounts or modify existing user accounts.

You will have to create a user account for every person in your organization who will access network resources. You should create a single user account for every person in your organization—no user, with the notable exception of the system administrator (who actually should have two accounts, as you will learn in later Tips) should have more than one account. To create a new user account, perform the following steps:

1. Select the Start menu Programs option Administrative Tools group. Within the Administrative Tools group, select the User Manager for Domains program.

2. Within the User Manager for Domains, select the User menu and New User option. Windows NT will display the New User dialog box.

3. When you create new accounts, you must specify to which groups a user belongs, the user's profile and log-on hours, computers the user can log on from, the type of account you are creating, and password restrictions. Within the New User dialog box, you will add basic information about the user's account, as well as using the button's along the box's bottom to specify additional information about the user.

Upcoming Tips discuss in detail many of these options. Figure 50 shows the New User Accounts dialog box.

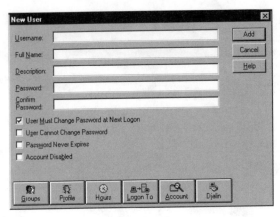

Figure 50 *The New User Accounts dialog box.*

*The correct answer is **False**. While the Administrative Wizards can perform this function, you will not have complete access to all the features if you use the Administrative Wizards that you will have with the User Manager for Domains.*

51	REFRESHING THE USER ACCOUNTS LIST

Q: *You are the administrator of a medium-size network. You have offices in Los Angeles and New York. The Primary Domain Controller is in the New York office. You are in Los Angeles with the Backup Domain Controller. You know that the New York administrator has just added users to the domain, but in Los Angeles you cannot see the new users on the Backup Domain Controller in User manager for Domains. What is your first action to locate these new users on the Backup Domain Controller in Los Angeles?*

Choose all correct answers:

A. *Close and then re-open the User Manager for Domains.*

B. *Shut down the server and restart it. After you restart the server, enter User Manager for Domains.*

C. *Have the New York administrator shut down the server there. When it restarts, User Manager for Domains will contain the updated list.*

D. *Select the View menu Refresh option to update the display within the User Manager for Domains.*

The User Manager for Domains user list does not automatically refresh itself, which means that while you have the user list open you will not see new accounts administrators in other sites have created. To show new entries within the user list, you must refresh the list, which will query the Directory Database for any new users and groups. To refresh the user list, perform the following steps:

1. Select the Start menu Programs option Administrative Tools group. Within the Administrative Tools group, select the User Manager for Domains program.

2   Within User Manager for Domains, select the View menu Refresh option. User Manager for Domains will update the list of users and groups.

Figure 51 shows the User Manager for Domains Refresh selection.

Answers A and D are the correct answers because User Manager for Domains will not display the new accounts until you close and re-open User Manager for Domains or until you refresh the user list. Answers B and C are incorrect because, while they would work, you would bring down either the entire network or your local node to update the list.

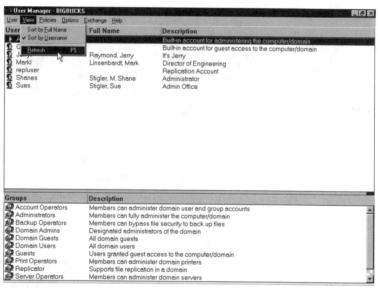

Figure 51 Refreshing user accounts in User Manager for Domains.

52   SORTING THE USER ACCOUNTS LIST

Q: *You administer a large domain. You are having difficulty finding particular user accounts when you make changes to user properties. How do you simplify the process of finding user accounts in a large user accounts list?*

Choose the correct answer:

A.   *You can filter the user accounts by criteria you specify.*

B.   *You should break your network up into smaller domains to reduce the number of users you must administer within a given domain.*

C.   *Use the Edit menu Search option to search the list by name.*

D.   *You can sort the user accounts by full name instead of user name to facilitate your search.*

By default, the User Manager for Domains window will list user accounts by user name. While listing by user name is often convenient, the sheer size of the user list can make account administration in a large network environment quite difficult.

To make matters worse, in many networks, the user name is a user's first name and last initial, or even a user name which does not reflect the user's real name at all—such as *KP08563*. There are two ways to resolve the problem. The first is to sort the accounts by user name, rather than simply displaying them in a list.

To change the sorting order of User Manager for Domains, select the View menu and then select the option which corresponds to the sorting order you prefer. Figure 52.1 shows the User Manager for Domains window with a list of accounts after sorting by user name.

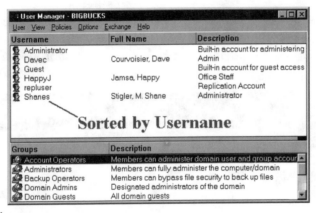

Figure 52.1 Sorting user accounts by user name.

In larger domains, or domains where the user name is not reflective of the actual user, you may wish to sort user accounts by the user's full name. Doing so will let you quickly and easily find users without regard for their user account names. Figure 52.2 shows the User Manager for Domains window with a list of accounts after sorting by the users' full names.

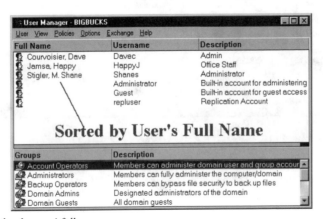

Figure 52.2 Sorting user accounts by the users' full names.

Answer D is correct because you can sort the list of user accounts to help in your search. Answer A is incorrect because you cannot filter the user accounts. Answer B is incorrect because you should not change your domain model simply because you have difficulty locating users within User Manager for Domains. Answer C is incorrect because there is no Edit menu Search option in User Manager for Domains.

53 INTRODUCTION TO THE EVENT VIEWER PROGRAM

Q: *A power outage occurred overnight in the same area where your company's network server resides. However, the system is up and running when you get to work the next morning. The server may have automatically rebooted, but power outages can cause damage in the system. How can you tell if the system indeed shut down while you were away?*

Choose the correct answer:

A. *Run Scandisk and check to see if any files on the drive were corrupted overnight.*

B. *Assume that the shutdown corrupted the network server and restore from a backup.*

C. *Use the Event Viewer to determine if the system shut down.*

D. *Open all files within their respective programs to determine if any of the files were corrupted.*

Windows NT furnishes the Event Viewer utility, which you can use to view three distinct types of system events. The Event Viewer displays the activity for the log files of application, system, and security functions. Log files contain all events within Windows NT that the operating system automatically (or by instruction) maintains records about. The *application log file* will contain application-specific information. In general, applications and non-system services that you run within Windows NT will log messages to the application log file. The *system log file* will contain operating-system-specific information. Any system services (such as Winlogon, the Server service, and so on) will write information to the system log file. For example, if the Server service fails to start correctly, it will write an error message to the system log file with a code or textual explanation of the error. The *security log file* will contain information about log-ins, security access, failed resource access attempts, and so on. For example, if a user tries to access a folder that the user does not have rights for, Windows NT will note in the security log file both the user's access attempt and the failure that resulted. Windows NT will automatically monitor some events (such as a system shutdown or startup). However, you must, in general, configure other events that you wish Windows NT to monitor. Such events will vary from installation to installation, and later Tips will discuss them in detail. For now, simply recognize that the Event Viewer lets you view information about occurrences on your network or server. Figure 53 shows the Event Viewer window.

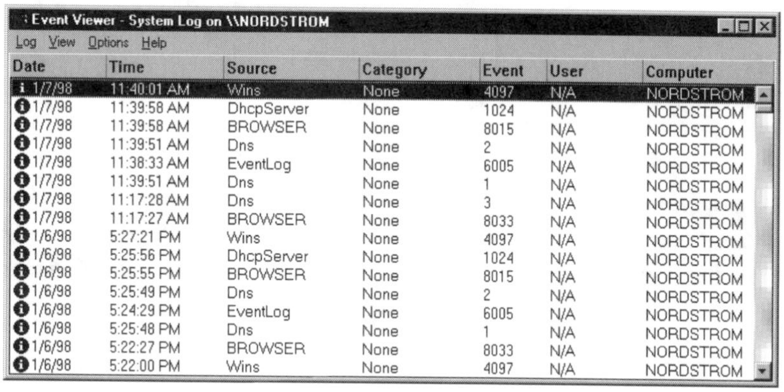

Date	Time	Source	Category	Event	User	Computer
1/7/98	11:40:01 AM	Wins	None	4097	N/A	NORDSTROM
1/7/98	11:39:58 AM	DhcpServer	None	1024	N/A	NORDSTROM
1/7/98	11:39:58 AM	BROWSER	None	8015	N/A	NORDSTROM
1/7/98	11:39:51 AM	Dns	None	2	N/A	NORDSTROM
1/7/98	11:38:33 AM	EventLog	None	6005	N/A	NORDSTROM
1/7/98	11:39:51 AM	Dns	None	1	N/A	NORDSTROM
1/7/98	11:17:28 AM	Dns	None	3	N/A	NORDSTROM
1/7/98	11:17:27 AM	BROWSER	None	8033	N/A	NORDSTROM
1/6/98	5:27:21 PM	Wins	None	4097	N/A	NORDSTROM
1/6/98	5:25:56 PM	DhcpServer	None	1024	N/A	NORDSTROM
1/6/98	5:25:55 PM	BROWSER	None	8015	N/A	NORDSTROM
1/6/98	5:25:49 PM	Dns	None	2	N/A	NORDSTROM
1/6/98	5:24:29 PM	EventLog	None	6005	N/A	NORDSTROM
1/6/98	5:25:48 PM	Dns	None	1	N/A	NORDSTROM
1/6/98	5:22:27 PM	BROWSER	None	8033	N/A	NORDSTROM
1/6/98	5:22:00 PM	Wins	None	4097	N/A	NORDSTROM

***Figure 53** The Event Viewer program window.*

*Answer C is the correct answer because you can use the Event Viewer to determine if the system shut down. The system log under Event Viewer keeps track of all system activities, including a shut down (and the subsequent reboot). **Answer A** is incorrect because Scandisk may not report errors even if a shutdown has corrupted files. **Answer B** is incorrect because it will take some time to restore from a backup, and you may not actually need to do so. **Answer D** is incorrect because, while opening all the files would work, it is not the most effective way to determine whether any files were corrupted.*

54 **FILTERING EVENTS IN THE EVENT VIEWER**

Q: *Your server recently experienced problems running a certain application. You want to see all events pertaining to the troublesome program. How can you do this in Event Viewer?*

Choose the correct answer:

     A.   *Sort the Event Viewer listings by source.*

     B.   *View only the Application Event Log and then identify each entry individually.*

     C.   *Turn on Event Viewer's Event Filtering option.*

     D.   *You cannot filter events in Event Viewer.*

Event Viewer lets you filter events to reveal only the ones you want to monitor. To turn on event filtering, click your mouse on the View menu and select Filter Events. From the Filter dialog box, configure the events you want to see. You can even choose to filter events for a certain computer or user account. You can also select specific types of events or sources of event code. Figure 54 shows the Event Viewer's Filter dialog box.

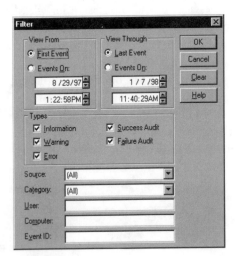

Figure 54 Filtering events in the Event Viewer program.

*Answer C is the correct answer because you should user Event Viewer's Event Filtering option. **Answer A** is incorrect because you cannot sort the Event Viewer listings by source, only by date and time. **Answer B** is incorrect because, while you could use this method, it is not the most efficient way to accomplish your task. **Answer D** is incorrect because you can filter events in Event Viewer.*

55 GRANTING USER RIGHTS FOR LOCAL LOGON

Q: *You ask a high-level user to assist you in system administration. When the user tries to log on at the Windows NT Server, the computer denies the person access with an error message that states: "The local policy of this machine does not permit you to interactively log on." What could be causing this message?*

Choose the best answer:

    A.   The user's password has expired.

    B.   The user does not have a valid user name.

    C.   The system administrator has not granted this user the right to log on locally in the User Manager for Domains.

    D.   The user is trying to log on from a trusted domain.

By default, Windows NT 4.0 Server only gives administrators, account operators, server operators, and print operators the right to log on locally. Windows NT applies the security constraint to prevent non-administrative users from gaining direct access to the server. To maintain administrative security, you must make log-on access to the server selective. However, you may grant to a user or group the right to log on locally if the need arises. To give a user the right to log on locally, perform the following steps:

1.   Select the Start menu Programs option Administrative Tools group. Within the Administrative Tools group, select the User Manager for Domains program.

2.   In the User Manager for Domains program, select the user account to which you want to assign log-on time limitations. Select the Policies menu User Rights option. User Manager for Domains will display the User Rights dialog box.

3.   Within the User Rights dialog box, click your mouse on the drop-down list of Rights, and select Log on locally. Below the Rights list will be the list of users and groups that have that particular right.

4.   Click your mouse on Add and then select the user or group you want to add. After you do so, click your mouse on the Ok button. Windows NT will grant the user the local log-on right and return to the User Manager for Domains window.

Figure 55 shows the User Rights dialog box, within which an administrator grants users the right to log on locally.

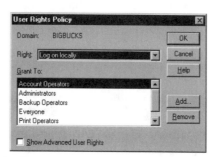

Figure 55 Configuring a user's right to log on locally.

Answer C is the correct answer because Windows NT will only display this message if the system administrator has not granted this user the right to log on locally in the User Manager for Domains. Answer A is incorrect because, if the user's password has expired, Windows NT will display a different error message. Answer B is incorrect because Windows NT will display a different error message if the user does not have a valid user name. Answer D is incorrect because the user can log on from a trusted domain without receiving an error message.

| 56 | **USING THE WINDOWS NT DIAGNOSTICS UTILITY TO VIEW SYSTEM CONFIGURATION** |

Q: *Your boss asks you to provide an inventory of your company's computers, including the operating system, processor, amount of memory, and disks in each machine. How can you accomplish this without opening each computer?*

Choose the best answer:

A.   *Maintain an installation and setup list for each computer you create.*

B.   *Send a message to each user on the network asking them to send you information about their computer.*

C.   *Reboot each computer, and during the power-on self-test (POST), enter the system BIOS management tool.*

D.   *Use the Windows NT Diagnostics utility to gather information about the computer.*

The Windows NT Diagnostics utility lets you view and print a report on your system configuration. Windows NT Diagnostics offers several different tabs for you to choose from for information display and reporting. The tabs include Version, System, Display, Drives, Memory, Services, Resources, Environment, and Network. Each tab corresponds to a general setup category within the computer. For example, if you want to see information pertaining to your computer memory, you would select the Memory tab. Similarly, if you want to see information about your system, you should select the System tab. In turn, the System tab will display system BIOS information and processor information. If your system has multiple processors, the System tab will display each processor individually. To open Windows NT Diagnostics and print a report, perform the following steps:

1.   From the Windows NT Desktop, click your mouse on the Start button and select the Programs menu Administrative Tools group. In the Administrative Tools menu, select the Windows NT Diagnostics program option. The Windows NT Diagnostics window will open.

2.   After the Windows NT Diagnostics window opens, you can select a tab to view information pertaining to a general category.

3.   After you select a tab, select the File menu Print Report option to print information about that tab.

After you print a report, you may use that report to keep track of standard configuration for your servers, as a template for configuration for other servers in your organization, or in any manner that you need to use it. Figure 56 shows the Windows NT Diagnostics window.

Answer D is the correct answer because you should use the Windows NT Diagnostics utility to gather information about the computer. Answer A is incorrect because, while maintaining an installation and setup list is a good policy, you cannot implement it after the fact. Answer B is incorrect because you cannot be sure that the users will respond, or that they will send the correct information when they do respond. Answer C is incorrect because, while you could obtain the necessary information from the BIOS manager, rebooting all of the computers on the network is not the most efficient solution.

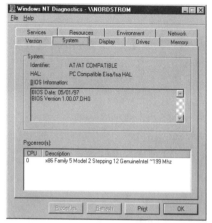

Figure 56 *The Windows NT Diagnostics window that you use to print information about system configuration.*

57   INVOKING THE WINDOWS NT SECURITY DIALOG BOX

Q: *You must leave your Windows NT Workstation for several minutes. You are working on sensitive information you do not want others to see. How do you secure your workstation while you are away?*

Choose the best answer:

       A.   *Invoke the Security dialog box and select Lock Workstation*

       B.   *Logoff your computer*

       C.   *Shut down Windows NT*

       D.   *Both B and C*

A significant security concern for many administrators is workstation security, particularly if the workstation is currently logged-into the network. As a user, it is relatively easy for you to secure your computer from casual intrusions. While there are several methods to make Windows NT unavailable if you leave your desk, the quickest and most efficient way is to lock your workstation. You will lock your workstation from the Security dialog box.

You will invoke the Security dialog box by pressing and holding down the CTRL and ALT keys simultaneously, while pushing the DELETE key once (you will often see this combination referred to in text as CTRL+ALT+DEL). When you first open the Security dialog box, the Lock Workstation option is selected (and is therefore the default selection). If you then press the ENTER key, the workstation will lock. If you choose to lock your workstation through the Security dialog box, only you or an administrator can unlock the workstation, with a password.

In addition, the Windows NT Security dialog box offers functions other than locking your Windows NT computer. The Windows NT Security dialog box also lets you change your network password, shut down your computer, and access the Task Manager.

Answer A is the correct answer because the most efficient way to secure your workstation is to invoke the Security dialog box and select Lock Workstation. **Answer B** *is incorrect because, while logging-off your computer would work, it is not the most efficient means to secure your workstation.* **Answer C** *is incorrect because, while shutting down Windows NT would work, it is not the most efficient means to secure your workstation.* **Answer D** *is incorrect because both Answers B and C are incorrect.*

58   UNDERSTANDING THE LOG-ON VALIDATION PROCESS

Q: *What analogy best describes the Windows NT log-on process?*

Choose the best answer:

> A.   *The sequence of events you use to access a bank ATM machine most closely resembles the Windows NT log-on process.*
>
> B.   *The sequence of events you use to start the engine of your car most closely resembles the Windows NT log-on process.*
>
> C.   *The sequence of events you use when you make a credit-card purchase most closely resembles the Windows NT log-on process.*
>
> D.   *The sequence of events you use when you make a phone call most closely resembles the Windows NT log-on process.*

One of the most important components of the Windows NT security model is the Windows NT log-on process. The Windows NT log-on process follows a simple progression of events, much like withdrawing cash at a bank ATM machine. For example, suppose you bank at Bank X and you want to use an ATM machine Bank Y owns. Bank X maintains your account information, and Bank Y has no knowledge of your account information.

When you use Bank Y's ATM machine, you must supply your ATM card and personal identification number (PIN). The ATM card provides your name and the information about where Bank X stores your accounts. Your transaction ID would include your name, bank, and PIN (for example, Bob Smith, Bank X, 1234). In order for you to use Bank Y's ATM machine, Bank Y must have a trust relationship with Bank X (that is, Bank Y must trust that Bank X will pay them back for the money you are removing from their ATM). Moreover, you must validate your identity—by inserting your ATM card and entering your secret PIN.

The same basic elements you find in a bank ATM transaction are also present during a Windows NT logon. You must supply a user name, password (PIN), and domain (bank) to which you belong.

The file that executes when you enter your account information during a Windows NT logon is *Winlogon.exe*. You supply your account information and the *Winlogon* process sends the log-on request to the *Local Security Authority* (LSA) on the computer you are using, called the *local machine* (Bank X).

The Local Security Authority is part of the Security Subsystem (a complex set of interconnected pieces that manage security on your local Windows NT machine) that Tip 274 discusses. The *Security Subsystem* passes the log-on request to the local machine's *Net Logon* service. The local Net Logon service queries the local *Security Accounts Manager* (SAM) for your user account information. (In other words, the Security Accounts Manager is Bank Y, which has a trust relationship with the Local Security Authority in the local machine, or Bank X.)

The local Net Logon service might send a query for a domain logon instead of a local logon. If the request is for a domain logon, the operating system sends the request to a domain controller's Net Logon service, where the remote domain controller's Net Logon service will query the domain's Security Accounts Manager. Whether or not the account is validated, the remote domain controller sends the results back to the requesting machine. If either the local machine or the domain controller validates the user's account, then the local machine's Local Security Authority issues an Access Token with the granted rights and starts a new process. Figure 58 shows the flow of a Windows NT log-on process.

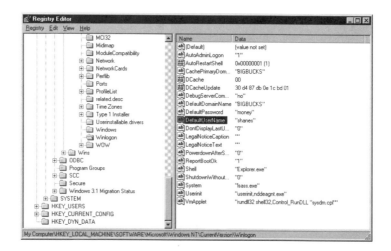

Figure 58 *The Windows NT log-on process.*

Answer A is correct because, when you log onto Windows NT, you enter a username (analogous to an ATM card), then a password (analogous to a PIN number), and then the domain server validates your identity (as does the remote bank computer). All three steps must be correct before the server grants access. Answer B is incorrect because inserting the key and turning on the key is only a two-step process, without the validation. Answer C is incorrect because swiping a credit card and signing the card (and, at best, local verification by a store clerk of your signature) does not correspond to the three-step Windows NT logon process. Answer D is incorrect because, when you make a phone call, you simply dial the phone and place your money into the phone—there is no validation of your identity.

59	**UNDERSTANDING ACCESS TOKENS**

Q: *A user complains to you, a system administrator, that he does not have access to a previously accessible resource. You examine the user's account properties and discover the user is not a member of the group with access to the resource. After adding the user to the appropriate group, the user still complains of denied access. What can the user do to gain the proper access?*

Choose the best answer:

A. *The user can manually navigate to the shared resource.*

B. *The user will not gain access to the new group until the user logs off and then logs on again.*

C. *The user can join the Administrators group.*

D. *The user cannot gain access to the resource through membership in the group.*

Access Tokens contain the security identifier (SID) of logged-on users and any group to which the users belong, as well as the users' rights. As Tip 58 discusses, the Local Security Authority (LSA) generates an Access Token for the user when the user successfully logs on. The Local Security Authority compares the Access Tokens of a user who requests access to the permission set on an object. If the Access Tokens are within the permission set on an object, the Local Security Authority will grant the user access to the resource. If the Access Tokens are not within the permission set on an object, the Local Security Authority will not grant the user access to the resource. Because the Local Security Authority creates Access Tokens only when a user first logs on, a user must log off and then log back on in order for the system to issue a new Access Token that reflects changes (additions, deletions, or modifications) to the set of groups to which the user belongs.

Note: Refer to Tip 46 for more information on SIDs.

*Answer B is the correct answer because the user will not gain access to the new group until the user logs off and then logs on again. **Answer A** is incorrect because the user will be unable to navigate to the shared resource by any means until the user logs off and then back on. **Answer C** is incorrect because it will still not grant the user immediate access. **Answer D** is incorrect because the user can gain access to the resource through membership in the group.*

60   INTRODUCTION TO WINDOWS *NT* DIRECTORY SERVICES

Q: What component of Windows NT lets a user have access to all network resources through a single user account?

Choose the best answer:

> A.   Windows NT's Directory Services gives a user access to all network resources through a single-user account.
>
> B.   Windows NT's Workstation service gives a user access to all network resources through a single-user account.
>
> C.   Windows NT's Server service gives a user access to all network resources through a single-user account.
>
> D.   Windows NT's Net Logon service gives a user access to all network resources through a single-user account.

Directory Services is the name for Windows NT's Domain and Security models. In its *Official Curriculum*, Microsoft most often defines Windows NT Directory Services as "universal access to resources." Understanding the Microsoft definition is very important not only for exam preparation but because universal access to resources is a key Directory Services requirement.

Universal access to resources means that a user can gain access to network resources anywhere in the organization using only a single network log-on—one account, one password, complete access (within the security model). To maintain a proper Directory Services structure, the administrator must maintain only a single-user account for each user—and, in fact, users should never need more than that single account. Moreover, the same Directory Services that let a user have one log-on password within an organization also let an administrator manage a large enterprise network—because you only work with a single user account for access to the operating system and the applications that the user runs, making administration significantly simpler.

Directory Services are a complex topic, and are tested in detail on Exam 70-068: Windows NT Server Enterprise Technologies. For now, you must simply understand that Directory Services are what makes users able to access all their files, printers, and other resources, as well as many applications, using only the user account and password that they log onto Windows NT with. This book's "Windows NT Server in the Enterprise" section takes a closer look at all the components that make up Windows NT's Directory Services.

*Answer A is the correct answer because Windows NT's Directory Services gives a user access to all network resources through a single-user account. **Answer B** is incorrect because Windows NT's Workstation service does not play a role in granting access to resources. **Answer C** is incorrect because Windows NT's Server service does not play a role in granting access to resources. **Answer D** is incorrect because, while the Windows NT Net Logon service does transmit logon information across the network, its role ends after it gives validation (or refusal) to the Local Security Authority (LSA).*

61 UNDERSTANDING HOW WINDOWS NT CONSTRUCTS THE USER ACCOUNTS DATABASE

Q: *Why is centralized administration so important?*

Choose all correct answers:

A   *Without centralized administration, your network would have multiple user account databases.*

B.   *Without centralized administration, you would have to create duplicate accounts for each user in each domain.*

C.   *Without centralized administration, you would be unable to manage access to resources efficiently.*

D.   *Without centralized administration, you would be unable to build trust models and multiple domain relationships.*

Microsoft uses the term "centralized administration" to describe Windows NT's structure. *Centralized administration* implies a single location, usually a Windows NT Domain, where a system administrator can create and maintain all computer, user, and group accounts. In contrast, Windows NT Workstations in a workgroup do not provide a single point of administration. Windows NT Workstations you configure as a workgroup use multiple user accounts databases. A user hoping to gain access to a network resource in a Windows NT Workgroup must have an account on the computer where he or she is sitting, as well as an account at the Windows NT Workstation that has the resource the user wants. Maintaining multiple user accounts databases is a problem even in small networks. Windows NT domains eliminate many of the problems associated with multiple user accounts databases.

Answers A, B, C, and D are all correct, because they are all features of centralized administration.

62 USING THE CTRL+ALT+DEL KEYPRESS COMBINATION IN WINDOWS NT

Q: *Why did Microsoft choose CTRL+ALT+DEL as the keypress combination for logon in Windows NT?*

Choose the best answer:

A.   *It is not a combination that user's would be likely to invoke accidentally.*

B.   *IBM-compatible computer users traditionally invoke CTRL+ALT+DEL to reboot the computer. Therefore, NT software designers chose the same combination for log on to keep users from accidentally rebooting their machine.*

C.   *To force users to only reboot the system from the Start menu Shutdown option.*

D.   *Because it was the combination used in Windows NT 3.51, so Microsoft maintained it for backwards compatibility.*

Windows NT users and administrators have long debated why Microsoft chose the CTRL+ALT+DEL keypress combination for logon. Many reasons have been suggested—some in support of Microsoft, some suggesting that Microsoft had some self-serving goal in mind. For example, some users believe the combination keeps screen password-capturing software from working in NT. Regardless, Microsoft maintains that it chose these keys simply to keep a user or even the administrator from accidentally restarting the computer.

If you are not currently logged in to Windows NT, the CTRL+ALT+DEL keypress combination will invoke the *Winlogon.exe* file and display the logon dialog box. After you have logged on, you can use the CTRL+ALT+DEL keypress combination to invoke the Security dialog box, from which you can manage tasks, lock out the workstation, and so on.

Answer B is correct because IBM-compatible computer users traditionally invoke CTRL+ALT+DEL to reboot the computer. Therefore, NT software designers chose the same combination for log on to keep users from accidentally rebooting their machine. Answer A is incorrect, because while it makes sense, it is not the primary reason for the decision. Answer C is incorrect because users can still reboot the system with a forced power-off. Answer D is incorrect because Microsoft used the combination in Windows NT 3.51 for the reason Answer B details.

63 CONFIGURING A WINDOWS NT COMPUTER TO AUTO LOGON

Q: *Your boss asks you to configure a computer that sits in the lobby of your company so customers can access your corporate intranet. You have already installed Windows NT Workstation and all other required software. How can you configure this machine so that each morning this computer works by someone simply turning it on?*

Choose the best answer:

A.   *Disconnect the Windows NT workstation from the corporate domain and force all users to login as guests.*

B.   *Write a batch file that sends a series of logon commands to the system.*

C.   *Enable auto logon.*

D.   *You cannot enable a Windows NT workstation to start the Windows NT Desktop automatically.*

As you have learned, the Windows NT security model will not let users gain access to a Windows NT machine without logging on. However, you can automate the log-on process. To enable auto logon, you must edit the Registry database. You can edit the Registry to enable auto logon in one of three ways: editing the Registry directly; using utilities provided with the Windows NT Resource Kit; or using the System Policy Editor. You can manually edit the Registry using the *Regedit.exe* program that Windows NT provides. To manually edit the Registry, perform the following steps:

1.   Select Start button Run option. Windows NT will display the Run dialog box.

2.   Type the **REGEDIT** command in the dialog box and press ENTER. Windows NT will run the Windows NT Registry Editor.

3.   The Windows NT Registry Editor window will display a split, Windows Explorer-style window. In the left column, double-click your mouse on *HKEY_LOCAL_MACHINE*. You will see a list of subdirectories under *HKEY_LOCAL_MACHINE*.

4.   In the *HKEY_LOCAL_MACHINE* list, double-click your mouse on the word *SOFTWARE*. Another subdirectory structure will open beneath the word *SOFTWARE*.

5.   Within the subdirectory structure, double-click your mouse on the word *Microsoft*, then *Windows NT*, then *CurrentVersion*, and finally *Winlogon*. In the screen's right column, you will see a name list. In the name list locate *DefaultUserName*.

6.   Double-click your mouse on *DefaultUserName* and type in the user account that you want this machine to use for auto logon.

You must now add several values to the Registry to enable auto logon. To do so, perform the following steps:

1.   Within the Registry Editor, click your mouse on the Edit menu at the top of your screen and highlight the word New.

2. Select String Value. A String Value dialog box will open on your screen.

3. In the String Value dialog box, type **AutoAdminLogon** and press ENTER.

4. Double-click your mouse on the new string value you have created to change its data. Type the number 1, which tells Windows NT to perform auto login

5. Repeat Steps 1, 2, and 3 to create a new string value called DefaultPassword.

6. Change the string value's data to the password of the auto-logon user account.

After you perform these steps, the computer will automatically log on the next time it boots. Figure 63 shows the Registry Editor window within Windows NT.

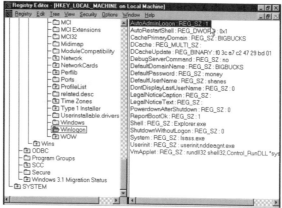

***Figure 63** Configuring auto logon through the Windows NT Registry.*

***Answer C** is the correct answer because you should enable auto-logon from within the Windows NT Registry. **Answer A** is incorrect because users will be unable to access the intranet if they are outside the domain. **Answer B** is incorrect because you cannot write a batch file that sends a series of logon commands to the system. **Answer D** is incorrect because you can enable a Windows NT workstation to start the Windows NT Desktop automatically.*

64 CHANGING A PASSWORD IN WINDOWS NT

Q: How can you change your user account password in a Windows NT domain?

Choose the best answer:

> *A   To change your password in a Windows NT domain, press the CTRL+ALT+DEL keyboard combination. Windows NT will display the Security dialog box. Within the dialog box, select Change Password.*

> *B.   To change your password in a Windows NT domain, press the CTRL+ALT+DEL keyboard combination. Windows NT will reboot the system. When the logon prompt appears, enter your new password within the password field.*

> *C.   To change your password in a Windows NT domain, run the User Manager for Domains program. Within User Manager for Domains, select your user account. Next, select the User menu Password option. Windows NT will display the Password dialog box. Within the dialog box, change your password.*

> *D.   To change your password in a Windows NT domain, run the Server Manager program. Within Server Manager, select your user account. Next, select the User menu Password option. Windows NT will display the Password dialog box. Within the dialog box, change your password.*

As an administrator, you will generally configure Windows NT to force users to change their passwords frequently (once a month is common). However, users may, from time to time, want to change their passwords without waiting for the system to prompt them to do so. As a user, you can change your password from the Windows NT Security dialog box. To change your user account password, perform the following steps:

1. From within Windows NT (that is, at any time after login), use the CTRL+ALT+DEL key combination that you use to log off and shut down the system. Windows NT will display the Security dialog box.

2. Within the Security dialog box, click your mouse on the Change Password button. Windows NT will open the Change Password dialog box.

3. Within the Change Password dialog box, enter your old password and new password, and confirm your new password within the three fields that the dialog box provides for such purpose. Click your mouse on the OK button. Windows NT will verify that your old password entry is correct, and also that your new password and the confirming password match.

You now have a new password. The next time you log on, you must use the new password you have created, or Windows NT will not validate your logon. Remember to observe common password security. Do not tell anyone your new password or write it down where someone might find it.

Answer A is the correct answer because you can change your password from within the Security dialog box. Answer B is incorrect because you must be logged in to Windows NT to change your password. Answer C is incorrect because, while the administrator can change user passwords from within User Manager for Domains, the administrator will do so from the Account Properties dialog box. Answer D is incorrect because Server Manager has nothing to do with password changes.

65 — LOGGING ON USING DIAL-UP NETWORKING

Q: How can you configure a Windows NT Server in a remote location to be a domain controller without using a wide area network (WAN) link?

Choose the best answer:

A. *Do not connect the server in the remote location to the main network.*

B. *Configure the server as a Backup Domain Controller.*

C. *You can configure the Server in a remote location to be a domain controller by configuring the server to act as a Dial-Up Networking client.*

D. *You cannot configure a Server in a remote location to be a domain controller.*

One common occurrence in many businesses today is the placement of Windows NT computers in a wide variety of locations—for example, in both the company's home office and the company's warehouse. Wherever the computers reside, you will still want to validate logons from all locations against your domain controller (which maintains the central copy of the Directory Database). However, WAN connections can be very expensive, running to thousands of dollars a month or more. For smaller organizations that do not send large amounts of traffic back and forth between the remote location and the central network, a better alternative is to let the remote server login to the network over a regular telephone line. You can configure your Windows NT servers to support this type of remote login with the Dial-Up Networking protocol.

The Dial-Up Networking protocol lets you use a regular modem to dial-in to a remote network and access the network as if you had a direct physical connection to the network. A Windows NT computer you configure to be a Dial-Up Networking client will display a log-on dialog box slightly different than a normal log-on dialog box, in that you have the option to use Dial-Up Networking to connect to a domain controller for log-on validation. To connect to a domain controller through Dial-Up Networking, check the Use Dial-Up Networking checkbox on the log-on dialog box displayed at system startup. Windows NT will prompt you for the Dial-Up connection to use. Then, using a regular modem and telephone line, you will be able to log on to your network as if you were connected through a normal network interface card.

Note: This Tip explains only how to use Dial-Up Networking at logon. Later Tips will show you how to create a Dial-Up Networking client and specific implementation issues that you must address when you do so.

Answer C is the correct answer because you can configure the server in a remote location to be a domain controller by configuring the server to act as a Dial-Up Networking client. Answer A is incorrect because the server will not let users access the network if you do so. Answer B is incorrect because you still need to connect the server to the network. Answer D is incorrect because you can configure a server in a remote location to be a domain controller.

66   COPYING A USER ACCOUNT

Q: *You want to create a user account very similar to an existing user account. What is the most efficient way to create the new user account?*

Choose the best answer:

    A.   *From within User Manager for Domains, create a new user account by copying the existing similar user account and renaming the user.*

    B.   *From within User Manager for Domains, use the User menu Replicate option to create the new user account.*

    C.   *From within User Manager for Domains, select the similar user account. Next, select the View menu Properties option. From within the Properties dialog box, click your mouse on the Set As Default checkbox.*

    D.   *You must create the new user from scratch; there is no more efficient way to create the user account.*

Network system administrators will frequently have opportunities to create an account almost identical to an existing account. For example, most users within a given department will share the same rights for most resources, particularly if the users all share the same job description. User Manager for Domains lets you easily create a copy of any account in the user account list. Most of the properties of the copied account carry over to the new account. The user properties that do not carry over are the user name, password, full name, and the account disabled property. To copy a user account for the creation of a new account, perform the following steps:

1. Select the Start menu Programs option Administrative Tools group. Within the Administrative Tools group, select the User Manager for Domains program.

2. In User Manager for Domains, select the user account which you want to use as a template for the new account. Next, press the F8 function key, or select the User menu Copy option.

3. Enter the properties that do not carry over from the original account and click your mouse on OK when you finish. Windows NT will create the new user account.

Answer A is the correct answer because you should copy the existing user account and rename for the target user. Answer B is incorrect because there is no User menu Replicate option. Answer C is incorrect because there is no Set As Default checkbox in the Properties dialog box. Answer D is incorrect because you can use the copy function.

---

67 CREATING A USER ACCOUNT TEMPLATE TO SIMPLIFY MULTIPLE ACCOUNT CREATION

Q: You must create user accounts for your company's sales staff. All the sales staff want access to the same resources and want the same user properties. How do you simplify this administrative task?

Choose the best answer:

A. *From within User Manager for Domains, create a new user account by copying an existing user account from the Sales department and renaming the user. Repeat the process for each new account you want to create.*

B. *Create similar user accounts by making a user account template for the Sales department. Copy the template to create the new Sales user accounts.*

C. *Create a batch file that uses the CreateUser command-line utility to create all the new users.*

D. *From within User Manager for Domains, select the User menu Template option. Windows NT will display the User Template wizard. Enter the default properties for the template within the appropriate Wizard dialog boxes.*

As you learned in Tip 66, if you need to create a single user account that is similar to an existing user account, you can simply copy the existing user account. However, you will often need to create many user accounts that share similar features. The most efficient way to do so is to create a user account template. You should create a user account template if you must create several similar accounts with the same properties, especially if you anticipate the same need in the future. A *user account template* is an account that has all the general user account properties set, but which you have disabled—that is, no user can login to the network with the template account. When you copy this account, all the group associations the template defines will remain in the new account, as well as any log-on restrictions, account type information, profile information, and dial-in settings. Figure 67 shows a user account template.

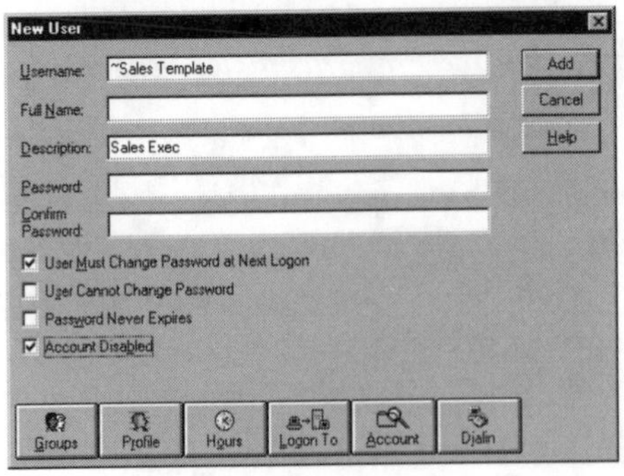

Figure 67 A user account template.

Note: *Microsoft recommends that you use a special character as the first character of the user account name. As the software alphabetizes the list, the character causes the account to move to the top of the user accounts list, making it easier for you to find. As you can see in Figure 67, one of the most commonly used special characters is the tilde (~) character.*

Answer B is the correct answer because you should use a user account template. Answer A is incorrect because, while you could copy existing accounts, doing so is not the most efficient process. Answer C is incorrect because there is no CreateUser command-line utility. Answer D is incorrect because there is no User Template wizard.

68   DELETING AND RENAMING USER ACCOUNTS

Q: *Your boss calls you to inform you that a particular user just quit the company. You hang up and delete the user's account from the Directory Database. Your boss calls back and says the user has been rehired and needs the old account restored. You create a new account with the same user name as before and configure all the properties to match the original account. A few minutes later you receive a call from the user, who complains that he cannot gain access to the home directory. What could be causing this problem?*

Choose the best answer:

> A.   *When you deleted the original account, you also deleted the user's home directory. You will have to create a new home directory for the user.*

> B.   *Windows NT has not yet updated the Directory Database. Tell the user to logoff and then log back on. The new access token will contain the correct security information.*

> C.   *When you created the new user account, Windows NT automatically created a new home directory for the user. You will have to move the files from the user's old home directory to the new home directory.*

> D.   *User accounts have unique security identification numbers (SID'). When you deleted the original account, Windows NT removed the user's SID from the Directory Database. When you created the new account, the account names matched but the SIDs were different, so the user could not gain access to the home directory.*

As an administrator, you will frequently have to enable and disable user accounts as employees start and leave your organization. When deciding whether to delete an account, consider disabling the account instead and keeping the account for future use. Windows NT will permanently remove a security identification number (SID) from the Directory Database whenever you delete a user account. Even if you create another account with the same user name and properties, the new account will have a different SID.

The new user account of the same name will not have access to any resources you granted the old account. You will have to re-grant all of those permissions to the new user account. When you have to choose whether to delete a user account, you should consider the possibility of needing an account of the same type in the near future. For example, if an employee left your company and you anticipate a new employee coming to fill that position, consider disabling the user account for the employee who is leaving. When you hire the new employee to fill the open position, just rename and enable the old account.

To rename a user account from User Manager for Domains, perform the following steps:

1. Select the Start menu Programs option Administrative Tools group. Within the Administrative Tools group, select the User Manager for Domains program.

2. In User Manager for Domains, select the user account you want to rename. Select the User menu Rename option. User Manager for Domains will display the Rename dialog box, as shown in Figure 68.

3. Within the Rename dialog box, type the new account name and click your mouse on OK.

On the other hand, if you must delete a user account in User Manager for Domains, select the user account you want to delete and press the DELETE key, or select the User menu Delete option. Windows NT will remove the user account from the Directory Database.

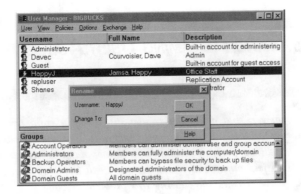

Figure 68 *Renaming a user account.*

*Answer D is the correct answer because, when you deleted the original account, Windows NT removed the user's SID from the Directory Database. When you created the new account, the account names matched but the SIDs were different, so the user could not gain access to the home directory. **Answer A** is incorrect because you must manually delete the home directory—Windows NT will not do so automatically. **Answer B** is incorrect because, if Windows NT had not yet updated the Directory Database, the user would be unable to logon. **Answer C** is incorrect because Windows NT will not automatically create home directories.*

69	UNDERSTANDING THE IMPORTANCE OF PROTECTING THE DEFAULT ADMINISTRATOR ACCOUNT

Q: *A person who should not have been able to get into the system accessed your company's Remote Access Server. When you examine the Event Viewer Security log, you find that someone made five log-on attempts last night to the default administrator account. You have configured your Windows NT Remote Access Server so that it disables user accounts after three bad log-on attempts. How would the unauthorized individual be able to circumvent your security precautions?*

Choose the best answer:

A.   *The Remote Access Server cannot lock out user accounts if the user tries to login from a Dial-Up Networking connection.*

B.   *Windows NT does not hold the default Administrator account within the constraints of bad log-on attempt policies.*

C.   *The Remote Access Server granted the user Guest access, which let him enter the server and view all available resources.*

D.   *The user can avoid the lock out provisions if the user closes the Dial-Up Networking connection and then dials back in to the server.*

In most networking environments, administrators commonly configure some sort of protection against unauthorized access to the system. In many cases, configuring accounts involves setting restrictions on how many log-on attempts a user can perform with incorrect account information, such as passwords or user names. You will learn more about lock out provisions in later Tips. However, for now it is sufficient to understand that Windows NT lets you configure lock out security.

However, Windows NT does not hold the default Administrator account within the constraints of the lock-out policy. Therefore, if you have left the default Administrator account name, a person can try to logon as long as he or she wants without fear of locking the account, which would give a person ample time to guess the administrative password, simply by trying to log in as Administrator.

Microsoft allows this potential hole in security to ensure administrative capabilities. If the administrative account could be locked, someone could accidentally lock the only account that has permissions to unlock accounts. If you understand the potential for security breaches, you can help stop unauthorized access before it occurs. While stopping login attempts through the default Administrator account is only part of a unified security policy, it is a very important part. In the next Tip, you will learn how to rename the account to make it less susceptible to unauthorized access.

Answer B is the correct answer because Windows NT does not hold the default Administrator account within the constraints of bad log-on attempt policies. Answer A is incorrect because the Remote Access Server can lock-out user accounts if the user tries to login from a Dial-Up Networking connection. Answer C is incorrect because Guest access will not let the user view resources. Answer D is incorrect because Windows NT will apply the lock-out rule based on attempts, not the connection's persistence.

70 | **RENAMING THE ADMINISTRATOR ACCOUNT TO ZACK**

Q: *Some documentation on Windows NT states that no one can disable the default Administrator account. Understanding the potential security risks of this, what can you do to secure your system against unauthorized access?*

Choose the best answer:

    A.   *Create a new administrator account and then delete the default Administrator account.*

    B.   *Delete the default Administrator account.*

    C.   *Rename the default administrator account.*

    D.   *Turn the network off at the end of the day.*

As Tip 69 explains in detail, the default administrator account is a potential security risk. Although you cannot disable this account, you can rename it. Renaming the default administrator account does not eliminate the security risk, but does reduce the chance of a common hacker getting into the network. Try using an uncommon name, such as Zack, Zeta, or Zenon for your new default administrative account name. Using a name with a Z as the first character will place the administrator account at the bottom of the user accounts list so that you can easily find it. However, you can use any name you want. Be careful to ensure that you use a name you are unlikely to choose for a user account in the future. After you rename the default Administrator account, give it a difficult-to-guess password. Use upper- and lowercase characters or numbers in your password, such as *MyPaSsWorD, Numb3r,* or *UPPERlower.*

Answer C is the correct answer because you should rename the Administrator account. Answers A and B are incorrect because you should never delete the default Administrator account. Answer D is incorrect because doing so will not secure the network against attacks during the business day.

71 | **UNDERSTANDING THE DEFAULT GUEST ACCOUNT**

Q: *You painstakingly secured your network, only to discover that an unauthorized user gained access through a Windows 95 computer without even logging on to the network. How could a user gain access to the Windows NT Server's resources without NT validating the user?*

Choose the best answer:

> A.   *A user could gain access to the Windows NT server's resources through the default Guest account.*

> B.   *Because Windows 95 is an unsecure operating system, you can access the Windows NT server's resources without validation.*

> C.   *The user logged onto a trusted domain and then accessed the resources on the server.*

> D.   *Any user can access resources on the server, but you can keep the user from editing or deleting those resources.*

As you have learned, Windows NT Server 4.0 creates two default accounts when you install the operating system: the default Administrator account and the default Guest account. Windows NT Server 4.0 disables the Guest account by default. If you then enable the default Guest account, you will certainly create a security risk. The Guest account, like all other domain accounts, is part of the *Everyone* group (you will learn more about the Everyone group in later Tips).

When the Windows NT server installation creates the *Everyone* group, it automatically grants the group full control over all shared and local New Technology File System (NTFS) resources. If a user tries to access any resource to which he or she does not have any explicit permissions Windows NT Server will let the user gain access through the default Guest account.

To avoid creating such a hole, you should either not enable the Guest account, or remove the *Everyone* group from the Guest account's permission set. If you have a specific need for a Guest account, either remove the *Everyone* group or rename the default Guest account and create a new Guest account, much as you did for the default Administrator account.

Answer A is correct because a user could gain access to the Windows NT server's resources through the default Guest account. Answer B is incorrect because Windows NT will validate users for server access without concern for the client's operating system. Answer C is incorrect because the user would still have logged-on to the network to enter the trusted domain. Answer D is incorrect because you can secure all resources on the server.

---

72   WHERE WINDOWS NT CREATES ACCOUNTS

Q: You create a new user account for someone in a remote location who has a backup domain controller. After you created the new account, the user cannot log on. What could be the cause of the user's log-on difficulties?

Choose the best answer:

> A.   *The user's backup domain controller is not functioning correctly.*

> B.   *You created the user account within the wrong domain.*

> C.   *The Directory Database is not yet synchronized.*

> D.   *You did not assign sufficient access permissions to the new account for the user to logon.*

Several previous Tips used the term *Centralized Administration* to describe Windows NT Server's single point of administration. The *single point of administration* refers to a single Directory Database that maintains all accounts in a domain model.

An administrator can replicate the Directory Database to other domains to validate users through a domain controller geographically close to the user. No matter where the Administrator is when creating new accounts, the accounts appear on the primary domain controller (PDC). The *primary domain controller* is the single point of administration in a domain model.

The only time you do not create accounts on the primary domain controller is when you configure Windows NT Servers as Member Servers (which typically maintain applications, file and print services, or other specific user services).

Although Member Servers can set permissions to resources using domain accounts, the Member Servers have their own Directory Databases that contain completely different accounts—typically, the accounts for the applications that execute on the Member Server, such as Microsoft's SQL Server.

Answer C is the correct answer because the most likely cause is that Windows NT has not yet synchronized the Directory Databases on the two machines. Answer A is incorrect because the system would automatically pass the request on to another backup domain controller or the primary domain controller in the event that the user's Backup Domain Controller was not functioning correctly. Answer B is incorrect because it is very unlikely that you created the user account within the wrong domain. Answer D is incorrect because, as long as an account is enabled, it will have sufficient access permissions for the user to logon.

73 SETTING PASSWORD RESTRICTIONS

Q: *You want your users to change their passwords every thirty days. How can you force this policy upon your users?*

Choose the best answer:

    A.   *Every month, set the User must change password at next login flag from within User Manager for Domains.*

    B.   *Implement an Account Policy in User Manager for Domains.*

    C.   *Set the account's properties to force a password change every thirty days in the Account Properties dialog box.*

    D.   *Windows NT will automatically force the user to change the password every thirty days.*

As you have learned, password security is an important part of maintaining the integrity of your Windows NT network. The Windows NT User Manager for Domains utility lets you set Account Policies to restrict password age, uniqueness, and length, as well as many other parameters.

Before setting any kind of password restrictions, you may want to consider your company's security needs and the administrative overhead associated with maintaining tight password security.

Many companies experience difficulties in managing user-password expirations. People can become frustrated with stringent password policies. Changing passwords on a regular basis can become tiresome and users will often forget their passwords, thereby adding to the network administrative duties.

After you decide on a password policy, you will implement the policy through User Manager for Domains. In User Manager for Domains, select the Policies menu Account option. The Account Policy dialog box has many options, some of which are specific to password security management. Table 73 contains a list of password options with descriptions of their use that you may set from within the Account Policy dialog box:

Password Option	Description
Maximum Password Age	Controls the length of time a user can keep the same password before being required to change it.
Minimum Password Age	Makes users keep a password for a preset length of time after they have changed it.
Minimum Password Length	Dictates the minimum number of characters in a user's password.
Password Uniqueness	Forces users to always use a new password. You can specify the number of passwords the user must use before the user can repeat a password from within the Account Policy dialog box.

Table 73 *Password options that you can set from within the Account Policy dialog box.*

Figure 73 shows a sample Account Policy dialog box with password restriction options.

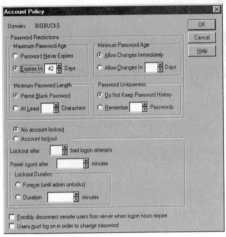

Figure 73 *A sample Account Policy dialog box showing password restrictions.*

Answer B is the correct answer, because you can force password changes by implementing an Account Policy in User Manager for Domains. Answer A is incorrect because, while you could set the User must change password at next login flag from within User Manager for Domains every month, it would be very time consuming and inefficient. Answer C is incorrect because you cannot force a password change from the Account Properties dialog box, you must use an Account Policy. Answer D is incorrect because Windows NT does not automatically force the user to change the password every thirty days.

74 | **CONFIGURING LOGON LOCATIONS FOR USERS**

Q: You want to restrict certain users from being able to wander around in your company and randomly log on to any computer. How can you restrict these users?

Choose the best answer:

A.   *From within the Account Policy dialog box, set the Only logon from home computer option to True.*

B.   *From within the Account Policy dialog box, disable the Roaming Logins option.*

C.   *Configure the Only logon from home computer option in the Account Properties dialog box.*

D.   *Configure the Logon To Computers option in the Account Properties dialog box.*

Depending on your company's security needs, you may want to configure user accounts so all or just certain users can only logon to a specified machine. You might do this, for example, to constrain the administrator's login to only the computer on his desk, which would help prevent other users from trying to log in as the administrator from other machines on the network. You can configure between one and eight computers where users can have permission to log on to the domain. To configure specific computers where users can log on, perform the following steps:

1. Select the Start menu Programs option Administrative Tools group. Within the Administrative Tools group, select the User Manager for Domains program.

2. In User Manager for Domains, select the user account you want to configure for log-on computers' access. From the User menu select the Properties option. Windows NT will display the Account Properties dialog box.

3. Within the Account Properties dialog box, click your mouse on the Logon To button at the bottom of the dialog box. Windows NT will display the Logon Workstations dialog box.

4. Within the Logon Workstations dialog box, enter the name of the computer or computers where you want users to have logon rights. After you finish, click your mouse on OK to return to the Account Properties dialog box.

Figure 74 shows the Logon Workstations dialog box, within which you can set constraints on the workstations that a user can log in from.

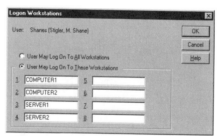

Figure 74 *The Logon Workstations dialog box lets you limit the computers that a user can log in from.*

Answer D *is the correct answer because you should configure Logon To Computers in from the Account Properties dialog box in User Manager for Domains to prevent random logons anywhere in your network.* **Answers A, B,** *and* **C** *are all incorrect because those options do not exist.*

75	CREATING HOME FOLDERS

Q: Each user in your network must have a location to save private information. The administrator must regularly back up users' personal directories. How could you give each user a personal data storage location and simplify the backup process?

Choose the best answer:

A. Create user home directories to simplify the backup process during network administration.

B. Configure the backup program to backup from each user's local drive.

C. Use the Replicator service to copy the files from the user's local drive to the server.

D. Create a User Documents folder on the server and instruct all users to save their private information within that directory.

User home directories are an industry-standard way to provide users with a secure private location where they can save private information. By creating all user home directories on a server, a single backup operation can back up the users' directories.

Creating user directories is a relatively simple process. First, to properly structure your user home directories, create a central location for storage. You will generally create a *Users* directory as this central location. Under the *Users* directory, create a directory for each user who wants to have a home directory. For example, if the user's account were JohnS, you would create a *Users\JohnS* directory.

Next, you should share each individual user's home directory as the user name with a $ sign appended as the last character, meaning that you would share the *Users\JohnS* directory as *JohnS$*. The $ sign will hide the shared directory from network browsing, meaning that other users will be unable to see the *JohnS* directory.

After you create the directories and share them, use the User Manager for Domains utility to configure each individual user account's properties to point to the respective user home directory. To point a user's account to a home directory location, perform the following steps:

1. Select the Start menu Programs option Administrative Tools group. Within the Administrative Tools group, select the User Manager for Domains program.

2. In User Manager for Domains, select the user account to which you want to assign a home directory. Select the User menu Properties option. User Manager for Domains will display the User Properties dialog box.

3. Within the User Properties dialog box, click your mouse on the Profile button. Windows NT will display the User Environment Profile dialog box.

4. In User Environment Profile dialog box, select the drive letter for the home folder within the Connect drop-down list. Next, in the To field, type the location of the server and directory that the user account should use as the home directory. Each time the user logs on, the user's account will connect to the home directory as the drive letter that you indicate. Figure 75 shows the User Environment Profile dialog box after entering a user's home folder.

The properties set in Figure 75 will automatically connect the *Shanes* user to the *\\server\shanes$* shared folder. The connection will be available to *Shanes* as his *H:* drive.

*Answer A is the correct answer because you should create user home directories to simplify the backup process during network administration. **Answer B** is incorrect because configuring the backup program to backup from each user's local drive will be, at best, difficult and, at worst, impossible. **Answer C** is incorrect because you will only use the Replicator service with scripts and other system information. **Answer D** is incorrect because the User Documents folder will let everyone access the share, rather than keeping private information private.*

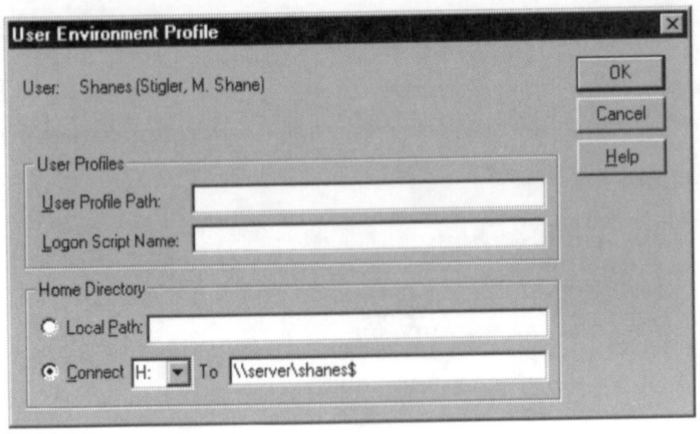

Figure 75 Creating a home directory for one user.

76 SETTING LOG-ON HOURS FOR USERS

Q: *Your boss tells you that she is concerned about temporary workers in the company logging on when no one is supervising them. As the administrator, what would you do to solve this problem?*

Choose only the correct answer:

A.   *Click your mouse on the Restrict Logon Hours option in Server Manager.*

B.   *Set the Hours option in the users' account properties.*

C.   *Install the Microsoft Zero Administration Kit.*

D.   *You cannot restrict hours in Windows NT.*

Some companies' security needs dictate specific log-on times for users. For example, management may decide that users can only log on during the standard 8:00 a.m. to 5:00 p.m. work day. In situations where you want to restrict the log-on times for one or many users, you must use the Hours option. To set the Hours option, perform the following steps:

1. Select the Start menu Programs option Administrative Tools group. Within the Administrative Tools group, select the User Manager for Domains program.

2. In User Manager for Domains, select the user account to which you want to assign log-on time limitations. Select the User menu Properties option. User Manager for Domains will display the User Properties dialog box.

3. Click your mouse on the Hours button and then select the times you will let the user account log on. To set the specific time for user logon, hold down your left mouse button and drag your mouse over the cells that include the times you want to select.

4. Within the Logon Hours window, click your mouse on either the Allow or the Disallow button. Figure 76 shows the Logon Hours window in the Properties dialog box.

Answer B is correct because you will set the Hours option in the users' account properties. Answer A is incorrect because there is no Restrict Logon Hours option in Server Manager. Answer C is incorrect because the Microsoft Zero Administration Kit's purpose is to help you limit user administration in generalized ways, and will not help you to restrict a user's logon hours. Answer D is incorrect because you can restrict hours in Windows NT.

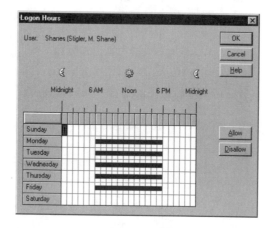

Figure 76 Setting logon hours.

77   CREATING ACCOUNTS FOR TEMPORARY EMPLOYEES

Q: *You have several hundred users in your company. You will soon hire fifty temporary workers. The temporary workers will be at your company for time periods ranging from one to three months. Your boss asks you to submit a plan for administering the temporary user accounts. You must allow for account expirations and account restrictions, and optionally you should be able to audit the temporary users server activity.*

When you submit your plan, you recommend the following:

You will create each user account from a template that you have created specifically for temporary users. You will use User Manager for Domains and configure each user account to have an appropriate expiration. You will use the Account Policies option in User Manager for Domains to configure the temporary users to forcibly disconnect when the users' log-on hours expire. In addition, you will use the Event Viewer weekly to examine temporary user activity.

Choose only the correct answer:

A.   *Your recommendation meets all requirements and the optional criterion.*

B.   *Your recommendation meets all requirements but does not meet the optional criterion.*

C.   *Your recommendation meets one requirement and the optional criterion.*

D.   *Your recommendation does not meet any of the requirements or the optional criterion.*

Administrators for larger networking environments may have difficulty tracking temporary users. Some temporary users may be at your company for months at a time while others may only stay a few days. A high temporary employee turnover rate justifies your creating a single *Temp* account for all short-term employees to use. When you have temporary employees who require an individual logon, a good security policy will generally recommend that you set account expirations for those users. Setting an account expiration eliminates concern about users coming back to your company and logging on to your network after they no longer work for your company. You will probably want to use other security measures besides account expirations. You may also want to configure an audit policy, as Tip 171 discusses, or configure accounts to forcibly log off users when the users' log-on hours expire, as Tip 80 discusses. To set an account expiration, perform the following steps:

1.   Select the Start menu Programs option Administrative Tools group. Within the Administrative Tools group, select the User Manager for Domains program.

2.   In User Manager for Domains, select the user account to which you want to assign an account expiration date. Select the User menu Properties option. User Manager for Domains will display the User Properties dialog box.

3.   Within the User Properties dialog box, click your mouse on the Account button. Windows NT will display the Account Information dialog box, as shown in Figure 77.

4.   In the Account Expires section of the dialog box, enter a date in the *End Of* field.

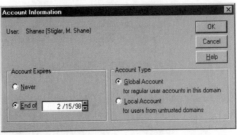

Figure 77 Configuring a user account with an expiration date.

Answer B is correct because your recommendation will ensure that temporary users cannot log-on outside the hours you specify, but will not provide audit support for user activity. Answer A is incorrect because your recommendation does not satisfy the optional criterion. Answers C and D are incorrect because your recommendation meets all the requirements.

78 RESETTING USER ACCOUNT PASSWORDS

Q: *You just received a call from a user telling you that he forgot his password. How will you handle this problem?*

Choose the correct answer:

A.   Reset the user's password to a generic password and select the User Must Change Password at Next Logon option in User Manager for Domains.

B.   Delete the user's account and then create a new account of the same name.

C.   Click your mouse on the Reset Password option in User Manager for Domains.

D.   Restore the user's account properties from the Windows NT Emergency Repair Disk.

Network administrators will eventually run into the problem of users forgetting their passwords. In Windows NT, an administrator cannot see a user's password because of the security risk that exposing any user's password would create. Therefore, if you have a user who cannot log on because of an incorrect password, you will have to create a new password for that user. The best way to help a user who cannot log on because of a forgotten password is to simply select a new password at random and set the user's account to the new password. After you tell the user his or her new password, instruct the user that the new password will work only on the next logon, after which time the user must create his or her own new password. To reset a user password, perform the following steps:

1.   Select the Start menu Programs option Administrative Tools group. Within the Administrative Tools group, select the User Manager for Domains program.

2.   In User Manager for Domains, select the user account to which you want to assign the new password. Select the User menu Properties option. User Manager for Domains will display the User Properties dialog box.

3.   Highlight the password within the User Properties dialog box, as shown in Figure 78. The password will not appear as letters, but as fourteen asterisks.

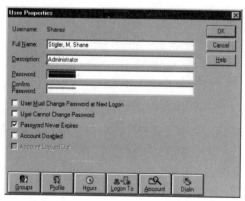

Figure 78 Resetting a user's account password.

4.   Within the dialog box, delete the user password (the asterisks) and enter the new password. Next, press the TAB key. Doing so will highlight the *Confirm Password* field.

5. Delete the *Confirm Password* field's contents and enter the confirmation for your new password.

6. Select the User Must Change Password at Next Logon checkbox in the user account properties. Click your mouse on OK to exit the User Properties dialog box.

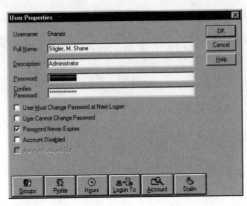

Figure 78 Resetting a user's account password.

Note: *Never reset a user's password unless you are sure (either because you recognize the user's voice or the user shows you identification) that you are talking to the user. One way hackers break into systems is by requesting administrators to change the password for a specific user account.*

Answer A is the correct answer because you should both reset the password and force the user to enter a new password at the user's next logon. Answer B is incorrect because deleting the user's account will change the security identifier for the user and create other issues that you must solve. Answer C is incorrect because there is no Reset Password option in the User Manager for Domains utility. Answer D is incorrect because using the Windows NT Emergency Repair Disk would restore everyone's accounts to their previous status, not just that user's.

79 | **MODIFYING MULTIPLE USER ACCOUNTS**

Q: *You want to set log-on hours for several users to match your company's hours of business. What is the easiest way to accomplish this task?*

Choose the correct answer:

A. *You cannot simultaneously change multiple account properties.*

B. *Use the ALT key to select all the accounts you want to change, and then select the User menu Properties option. Set the users' log-on hours to the company's business hours.*

C. *You must use the Administrative Wizards to accomplish multiple-account administration.*

D. *Use the CTRL key to select all the accounts you want to change and then select the User menu Properties option. Set the users' log-on hours to the company's business hours.*

Network administrators may find it necessary to change group memberships, log-on hours, or other account properties that affect multiple-user accounts. You can accomplish all these tasks with User Manager for Domains. If you make simultaneous changes to multiple user accounts, User Manager for Domains will update all the accounts you select with the new account information. If some accounts have unique account properties, you will want to make individual changes to such accounts.

To select multiple accounts and change their properties, perform the following steps:

1. Select the Start menu Programs option Administrative Tools group. Within the Administrative Tools group, select the User Manager for Domains program.

2. In User Manager for Domains, select the first account you want to change. To select the first account, click your mouse once on the account name. To select additional accounts, press and hold down the CTRL key while you click your mouse on each account you want to add to the group of selected accounts.

3. After you select all the accounts you want to modify, select the User menu Properties option. Windows NT will display the User Properties dialog box.

4. Make your changes—such as setting log-on time limitations—and click your mouse on the OK button. Windows NT will close the User Properties dialog box and set the properties for all the accounts you selected.

Figure 79 shows a selection of multiple accounts in User Manager for Domains.

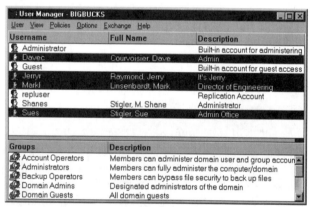

***Figure 79** Using multiple-account selection in User Manager for Domains.*

*Answer D is the correct answer because you will use the CTRL key to select all the accounts you want to change and then select the User menu Properties option to display the dialog box within which you will set the users' log-on hours to the company's business hours. **Answer A** is incorrect because you can simultaneously change multiple account properties. **Answer B** is incorrect because you will use the CTRL key, not the ALT key, to select all the accounts you want to change. **Answer C** is incorrect because you can administer multiple accounts from within User Manager for Domains.*

80 AUTOMATICALLY LOGGING OFF USERS WHO HAVE RESTRICTED HOURS

Q: *You configured your Windows NT domain so that all users have restricted log-on hours. You notice that several users can continue working after their log-on hours have passed. Why is this occurring and what can you do to fix the problem?*

Choose the correct answer:

A. *The Hours option in the Users Account Properties dialog box only sets the hours the operating system will validate the user's account. The Hours option does not force the user to log off when the user's hours expire. You can configure the Account Policy to force log off when the log-on hours expire.*

B. *You cannot configure Windows NT to forcibly log off a user's account.*

C.   *You must configure the account to forcibly log off the user when the user's log-on hours expire. You can configure forcible log offs within the Windows NT Registry by changing the value in the HKEY_LOCAL_MACHINE\SOFTWARE\Microsoft\WindowsNT\CurrentVersion\Winlogon key.*

D.   *The users are logging on with administrative accounts. Find out how the users have obtained administrative accounts, and issue new accounts.*

Many new administrators are confused when users with restricted log-on hours can still access resources even though the users' log-on hours have expired. The Hours option in User Manager for Domains sets only the hours that a domain controller will validate a user's log-on request, not the hours that the user can remain logged-on to the domain. In other words, if a user signs in at 4:59 PM, and the user's log-on hours expire at 5:00 PM, the user can nevertheless work all night after that successful login, unless you perform additional configuration. If you want to restrict the hours a user can access resources, you can do so from within the User Manager for Domains utility. To restrict the hours a user can access resources, perform the following steps:

1. Select the Start menu Programs option Administrative Tools group. Within the Administrative Tools group, select the User Manager for Domains program.

2. In User Manager for Domains, select the user account for which you want to control resource access. Select the Policies menu Account option. Windows NT will display the Account dialog box.

3. In the Account dialog box, select *Forcibly disconnect remote users from server when logon hours expire* check box. Next, click your mouse on OK. Windows NT will return the display to the User Manager for Domains.

Answer A is the correct answer because the Hours option in the Users Account Properties dialog box only sets the hours the operating system will validate the user's account. You must configure the Account Policy to force log off when the log-on hours expire. Answer B is incorrect because you can configure Windows NT to forcibly log off a user's account. Answer C is incorrect because you do not need to change the value in the HKEY_LOCAL_MACHINE\SOFTWARE\Microsoft\WindowsNT\CurrentVersion\Winlogon key, you can do it from within the User Manager for Domains. Answer D is incorrect because, while it is possible that the users are logging on with administrative accounts, it is not the likely solution.

---

81   REQUIRING USERS TO CHANGE THEIR PASSWORDS AT NEXT LOGON

Q: *How would you configure Windows NT Server so that no one except the users will know their passwords?*

Choose the correct answer:

A.   *Have each user meet you at the Windows NT Server and let each user configure his or her own password.*

B.   *Set generic initial passwords and tell users to change their password within the first 24 hours.*

C.   *Configure each account so that the user must change his or her password at the next logon.*

D.   *Have Windows NT randomly generate passwords. Use the Messenger Service to electronically notify the users of their new passwords.*

Log-on security is always an issue for a network administrator—because poor log-on security can compromise any other security in place on the network. Even in small companies, lack of proper security can cause concern for both administrators and managers. As an administrator, you must consider that a large majority of your corporate information will exist on the network. A single security breach can cause a company significant losses, even force the company out of business. If a user gives their password to an employee who subsequently leaves the company, that employee will still be able to access the network with the other user's password—perhaps even stealing corporate information and selling it to a competitor. Administrators will often find that users give their passwords to other users, and eventually the password is no longer a secret. Remind your users that they should not give their password to anyone, just as they should never give their bank ATM personal identification number (PIN) to anyone.

One of the many features Windows NT Server supports is several different methods that administrators can use to force a user to change his or her password at the next logon. Most system administrators find forced password changes to be a useful tool to maintain system security. To force a user to change his or her password at the next logon, perform the following steps:

1. Select the Start menu Programs option Administrative Tools group. Within the Administrative Tools group, select the User Manager for Domains program.

2. In User Manager for Domains, select the user account for which you want to force a password change at next logon. Next, select the User menu Properties option. Windows NT will display the User Properties dialog box.

3. Within the User Properties dialog box, click your mouse on the User Must Change Password at Next Logon checkbox. Click your mouse on OK to close the User Properties dialog box. Windows NT will force the user to change his or her account password at the next logon.

Figure 81 shows the User Properties dialog box showing the User Must Change Password at Next Logon checkbox.

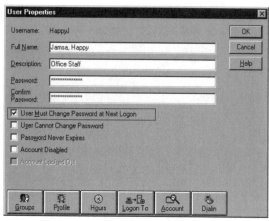

Figure 81 *The User Properties dialog box.*

Answer C is the correct answer because you must configure each account so that the user must change his or her password at the next logon. Answer A is incorrect because the user can change the password from the workstation, and does not require access to the server. Answer B is incorrect because you must force users to change the passwords, not simply inform them. Answer D is incorrect because Windows NT cannot randomly generate passwords.

82 SETTING ACCOUNT POLICIES

Q: *Your boss just finished reading a book about network security and is now concerned that users can guess other users' passwords. Your boss asks you to implement a plan to lock out users if they attempt to log on with an incorrect password. Your plan should let users try three logons before the account locks them out. How can you implement your plan?*

Choose the best answer:

    A.   *Set each account with an account policy that locks out the user after three bad log-on attempts.*

    B.   *Use the Account Policies dialog box and configure the Account Lockout section. The values you set in the Account Lockout section will apply to all users.*

    C.   *Use the Rights dialog box and turn on the Bad Logon right. The right will default to three bad logon attempts and apply to all users.*

    D.   *Set the value of the HKEY_LOCAL_MACHINE\SOFTWARE\Microsoft\WindowsNT\CurrentVersion \Winlogon key's BadLogonLockout sub-key's value to 3.*

In Tip 73, you learned about the Account Policy dialog box for password restrictions. You can also use the Account Policy dialog box to configure Windows NT so that the system locks out users' accounts after an arbitrary number of bad log-on attempts. Configuring lockouts is an important security step because, even in small networks, you will not want unauthorized users to gain access to your system. When you configure Windows NT to lock out users after several bad log-on attempts, you take steps toward a more secure networking environment. To configure Windows NT to lock out users after several bad log-on attempts, perform the following steps:

1.   Select the Start menu Programs option Administrative Tools group. Within the Administrative Tools group, select the User Manager for Domains program.

2.   Within User Manager for Domains, select the Policies menu Account option. The Account Policy dialog box will open.

3.   Within the Account Policy dialog box, click your mouse on the Account Lockout radio button. Windows NT will enable the account lockout fields within the Account Policy dialog box. To set the number of attempts to 3 before lock-out, enter the value 3 within the *Lockout after* field. Click your mouse on OK to close the Account Policy dialog box.

You can configure a number of different lock-out options within the Account Policy dialog box, such as whether to lock out after a specific number of log-on attempts or after a certain time period. You must also decide when to reset the account and what the lock-out duration (that is, how long the user will be forbidden from trying to log-in to that account) will be. The *Lockout after* field lets you specify a variable number of times that a user can attempt to log on with incorrect account information before Windows NT locks the account.

The *Reset count after* field lets you configure the number of minutes that must pass before Windows NT resets the bad log-on attempt counter. For example, if the administrator did not select a time value for the counter reset, and a user tried to log on Monday and accidentally entered the wrong account password, Windows NT would consider that one bad log-on attempt. If on Tuesday the user tried to log on again with the incorrect account password, Windows NT would consider that two bad log-on attempts. If the user continued to use incorrect passwords in his or her log-on attempts, the system could lock out the user by Wednesday or Thursday. The reset counter would have reset the bad log-on attempt count back to zero by Monday afternoon. If, on the other hand, the reset counter is set to one hour, the user must have three bad log-on attempts within a single hour for the operating system to lock out the user.

Configuring the lock-out duration lets a system administrator configure a predetermined time period the system will have to wait before it unlocks a locked-out user's account. The user will be unable to gain access to the system again until the system unlocks the account. Many administrators use the Forever (until admin unlocks) option, which helps the system administrator know which users are having password difficulties or if hackers are violating the system (because the administrator must manually unlock the account).

Figure 82 shows the Account Policy dialog box, where you configure Windows NT to lock out users after several bad log-on attempts.

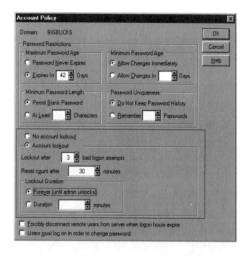

***Figure 82** The Account Policy dialog box.*

Answer B *is correct because you will configure lock outs within the Account Policies dialog box and the values you set in the Account Lockout section will apply to all users.* **Answer A** *is incorrect because you do not need to manually set lock outs for every user.* **Answer C** *is incorrect because there is no Bad Logon right.* **Answer D** *is incorrect because there is no HKEY_LOCAL_ MACHINE\SOFTWARE\Microsoft\WindowsNT\CurrentVersion\Winlogon\BadLogonLockout sub-key.*

83 CONFIGURING A USER'S PASSWORD TO NEVER EXPIRE

Q: What is the best reason to configure a specific user's account to have a password that never expires?

Choose the best answer:

> A.   *The user is an administrator.*
>
> B.   *The Windows NT operating system, a service, or a program uses the user account.*
>
> C.   *The user is a temporary worker who will not be at the company for very long.*
>
> D.   *The user is in upper management at your company and you do not want the user to have to remember new passwords.*
>
> E.   *You cannot configure a user's account password to never expire.*

One frequently misunderstood Windows NT feature is the ability for a system administrator to configure a user's account password to never expire. The non-expiring password feature means that, even though you may have configured Windows NT so users must change their passwords every 30 days, Windows NT does not "hold" certain users to the policy's constraints. While you may initially think this is a good feature to use for administrator accounts or upper management users, that is not the user Microsoft intended. Furthermore, doing so creates a significant security hole within your network. Instead, Windows NT supports the feature for your use with specific system features, services, and programs.

An administrator must be able to disable password expiration for system accounts that no person uses, but that applications crucial to the system do use. Certain programs, such as Microsoft's *Internet Information Server* (IIS), need a user account to access resources. As an example of account expiration, when you install Microsoft's Internet Information Server, the program creates a user account called *IUSR_servername*. The Internet Information Server will use the

IUSR_servername account to access published Web sites that reside on the Windows NT server. An Internet user will then enter a Web site address that resides on the server. In turn, Windows NT will use the *IUSR_servername* account as if it were an actual user who requested the network resource.

If you do not configure the *IUSR_servername* account's properties so that the password never expires, every time the password changes (for example, every 30 days), you will have to remember to manually change the *IUSR_servername* account's password. Frequently changing account passwords (particularly system-required accounts) creates a lot of unnecessary work for you, as well as being work that is easy for you to forget. In the case of the *IUSR_servername* account, if you forget to change the password, remote users will be unable to access Web pages on the server. For most programs that require a user account for resource access, the administrator must manually configure the account and the password properties. To configure an account so that the password never expires, perform the following steps:

1. Select the Start menu Programs option Administrative Tools group. Within the Administrative Tools group, select the User Manager for Domains program.

2. In User Manager for Domains, select the user account to which you want to assign a never-expiring password. Select the User menu Properties option. User Manager for Domains will display the User Properties dialog box.

3. In the User Properties dialog box, click your mouse on the Password Never Expires checkbox, as Figure 83 shows.

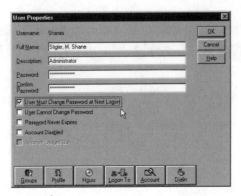

Figure 83 *Configuring a user's password to never expire.*

Answer B is the correct answer because the only time you should set a never-expiring password is if the account is a Windows NT system, service, or program user account. Answer A is incorrect because even the administrator should have to change the password regularly. Answer C is incorrect because a temporary worker should have close constraints, not a non-expiring password. Answer D is incorrect because upper management probably has access to important information, and the managers should be forced to change their access passwords just as everyone else does. Answer E is incorrect because you can configure a user's account password to never expire from within User Manager for Domains..

84 DISABLING A USER ACCOUNT

Q: *When is it appropriate to disable a user's account?*

Choose the best answer:

A.   *When you want to perform routine server maintenance.*

B.   *Nightly at system shut-down.*

C.   When you make changes to a user's account.

D.   When a user has quit or been fired and you anticipate that the company will hire someone to fill the position.

As you learned in Tip 46, each time you create a new user account, Windows NT creates a unique 32-bit number (called a Security Identifier, or SID) that identifies the account. After Windows NT generates a SID, the system will never duplicate that exact number. If the system administrator deletes a user's account, the SID that identifies that account will never identify any other account.

Because the SID truly represents the account and not the account user name, all group memberships, rights, and log-on hours are SID-specific. If a user leaves your network and a new user performs the same job, do not create a new account for the new user. Disable the account for the user who is leaving, then rename and enable the account when the new user replaces the one who left. To disable a user account, perform the following steps:

1. Select the Start menu Programs option Administrative Tools group. Within the Administrative Tools group, select the User Manager for Domains program.

2. In User Manager for Domains, select the user account to which you want to give dial-in permission. Select the User menu Properties option. User Manager for Domains will display the User Properties dialog box.

3. In the User Properties dialog box, click your mouse on the Account Disabled checkbox. Next, click your mouse on OK to exit the User Properties dialog box. Windows NT will disable the account.

Figure 84 shows the User Properties dialog box after you disable an account.

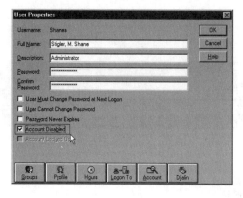

Figure 84 *Disabling a user account.*

Answer D is the correct answer because you should disable a user's account when a user has quit or been fired and you anticipate that the company will hire someone to fill the position. Answer A is incorrect because you do not need to disable a user's account when you want to perform routine server maintenance. Answer B is incorrect because you will generally not shut-down the Windows NT server. Answer D is incorrect because you do not need to disable a user's account when you make changes to a user's account.

85   UNLOCKING A USER'S ACCOUNT AFTER A BAD LOG-ON ATTEMPT

Q: *How do you unlock a user account after a bad log-on attempt locked the user's account?*

Choose the best answer:

A.   *Delete the user account and then create another account of the same name.*

B.   *Uncheck the Account Locked Out checkbox in the User Properties dialog box for the user with the locked account.*

C.   *In Server Manager, use the Unlock Accounts tab.*

D.   *In User Manager for Domains, use the Account Policies dialog box and click your mouse on the Unlock account button.*

As you learned in Tip 82, you can configure Windows NT to lock out users who attempt to log on to the system using incorrect account information. You also learned that, once the system locks out a user, the user cannot log back in to the system until either the operating system or the administrator unlocks the user's account. While you can configure the system to unlock the user's account after a specific amount of time, you will often need to manually unlock a user account after a bad log-on attempt lock out. Unlocking a user account after a bad log-on attempt is a relatively easy administrative task, and is almost always necessary at one time or another in most networking environments. You can unlock several accounts at the same time if the system has locked out more than one user. However, unlocking user accounts is generally a one-at-a-time task—because it is unlikely that multiple users will forget their passwords simultaneously. To unlock user accounts, perform the following steps:

1. Select the Start menu Programs option Administrative Tools group. Within the Administrative Tools group, select the User Manager for Domains program.

2. In User Manager for Domains, select the user account that you must unlock. Select the User menu Properties option. User Manager for Domains will display the User Properties dialog box.

3. Within the User Properties dialog box, uncheck the Account Locked Out checkbox. Click your mouse on OK to close the User Properties dialog box. Windows NT will unlock the user's account.

Figure 85 shows the User Properties dialog box before you unlock the locked account.

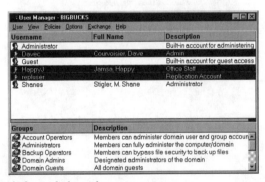

Figure 85 *The User Properties dialog box before unlocking the user account.*

Answer B *is the correct answer because you should uncheck the Account Locked Out checkbox in the User Properties dialog box for the user with the locked account to unlock the account. **Answer A** is incorrect because deleting the user account and then creating another account of the same name will create significant administrative work for you. **Answer C** is incorrect because there is no Unlock Accounts tab in Server Manager. **Answer D** is incorrect because there is no Unlock account button in the Account Policies dialog box.*

Q: *You are the system administrator of a large network you configured as a Windows NT Multiple Master Domain model. You have three master domains and thirty resource domains. You established trust relationships between the resource domains and the master domains. Therefore, each resource domain trusts each master domain and, in turn, each master domain trusts other master domains.*

Your boss has asked you to initiate a backup strategy that will let a small team of administrators back up all domains. The backup team members are Ron, Mark, Jerry, and Don. You have created and placed each backup team member's user account into a global group called Backupteam.

What else must you do in order for the backup team members to perform back ups on all domains?

Choose the best answer:

A.   *Place the Backupteam global group into the default Backup Operators global group in each domain.*

B.   *Place the Backupteam global group into the default Server Operators global group in each domain.*

C.   *Place the Backupteam global group into the default Backup Operators local group in each domain.*

D.   *Place the Backupteam global group into the default Server Operators local group in each domain.*

The answer to this Tip's question extends into the next three Tips. To understand the answer, you must understand the concept of Windows NT groups, which this Tip introduces, as well as user and group permissions, user and group rights, and the differences between the two, as the next three Tips explain. *Groups* let an administrator pool users with similar job responsibilities so the administrator can assign them resource permissions as one administrative unit. In contrast, if a system does not use groups, an administrator would have to identify individual users from the domain users' list to assign resource permissions to a specific resource, such as a printer.

A network administrator's job encompasses many time-consuming responsibilities. For example, to configure resources so appropriate users have access and others do not can take an administrator a long time (particularly if your network has hundreds of users). You can assign user permissions to a specific resource on a per user basis, but it is a much better approach to assign permissions to a group of users with common resource access. Some groups an administrator will need in Windows NT are built in to the system. The administrator can create any other groups he or she many need.

To learn more about groups, consider an example in which you are the system administrator for a small company that has five sales people, two bookkeeping staff, and a manufacturing staff of twenty people. If everyone in the company must use a single printer, then all users must have specific permissions to that resource. As an administrator, you could give specific permissions by setting printer permissions for the default *Everyone* group. However, creating individual accounts might create problems in the future. As your company grows, so too will the number of employees in your company. In particular, when your sales department has fifteen people, accounting has eight people, and manufacturing has fifty people, you may find that the original printer cannot handle the number of users trying to print to it. You may need to add another printer to your network. If you decide that all sales and accounting staff will use a new printer and all manufacturing staff will use the old printer, you will have to assign permissions accordingly.

To divide resource permissions between staff members, you must identify and pool each set of users—sales, accounting, and manufacturing—into its own group. You must then assign permissions to each group for the printer to which each group should print. You should begin pooling accounts and assigning groups to your company's employees even when the company is small, because you will only add to your workload by waiting until you have a large number of users to group.

When you pool user accounts with similar responsibilities, you will place those accounts within one or more groups. Windows NT lets an administrator create and use two types of groups: global and local. Administrators can use *global groups* to pool users. Global groups cannot contain users from other domains or any other global groups. Global groups also cannot contain local groups. Administrators can use global groups in the domain in which the administrators created the groups, as well as in any trusting domain.

Administrators use *local* groups to assign resource access. The administrators will pool users into global groups and place the global groups into local groups. The administrator grants the local groups permissions to the actual resources. Local groups cannot contain other local groups. Local groups can contain global groups from other trusted domains.

Answer C is the correct answer because you should place the Backupteam global group into the default Backup Operators local group in each domain. Answer A is incorrect because you cannot place the Backupteam global group into the default Backup Operators global group. Answer B is incorrect because you cannot place the place the Backupteam global group into the default Server Operators global group. Answer D is incorrect because placing the Backupteam global group into the default Server Operators local group in each domain grants the users in the Backupteam group more access than necessary.

87 — UNDERSTANDING USER AND GROUP PERMISSIONS

Q: *Windows NT lets administrators place users into groups whose members require access to similar resources.*

True or False?

An administrator can assign Windows NT permissions to individual user accounts or to groups to which the user belongs. Only an authorized user account can access a Windows NT resource, such as a printer, folder, or application. (For more information about the resource access process, see Tip 128.)

Windows NT attaches an object called an Access Control List (ACL) to each resource when you create the resource, and updates the list whenever you make a change to the access permissions for the resource. The Access Control List contains a list of users and groups that have access to a resource as well as what level of access each user or group has to that specific resource.

As you have learned, each user in a system has an account number called a security identifier (SID). Access Control Lists and Access Tokens contain only the security identifiers that represent the users and groups within the system. However, to illustrate Windows NT's security model, Microsoft tests (as well as most other texts on the topic) will always show actual user or group names instead of the security identifiers that represent the names.

Windows NT checks the Access Control List's contents against a user's Access Token to see if the Access Control List contains the user or any of the groups to which the user belongs. Windows NT then decides what level of access, if any, the user has to the resource.

The answer is **True.**

88 — UNDERSTANDING USER AND GROUP RIGHTS

Q: *Within Windows NT, a user's rights or his or her group's rights controls the operations the user can perform.*

True or False?

Windows NT rights let users or groups have different levels of access to the operating system, as well as any resources on the network. Windows NT pre-configures many groups with system rights. Windows NT predominantly assigns rights to groups.

However, you can assign rights to individual user accounts, although you should do so only as a rare exception. Sometimes Windows NT will assign an individual user a specific right while you are configuring a service, such as when you configure Windows NT directory replication (a system service that you will learn more about in later Tips). Windows NT will automatically assign the user account you specify as the directory replicator account the right to log on as a service.

For a complete description of the common Windows NT rights and their functions, refer to the Microsoft Windows NT 4.0 Resource Kit (which you can buy at most computer stores). The following list contains some common Windows NT rights:

- *Access this computer from the network*
- *Add workstations to a domain*
- *Backup files and directories*
- *Change the system time*
- *Force shutdown from a remote system*
- *Load and unload device drivers*
- *Log on locally*
- *Manage auditing and security log*
- *Restore files and directories*
- *Shut down the system*
- *Take ownership of files or other objects*

To give a user or group a specific right, perform the following steps:

1. Select the Start menu Programs option Administrative Tools group. Within the Administrative Tools group, select the User Manager for Domains program.
2. In User Manager for Domains, select the user account to which you want to give dial-in permission. Select the Policies menu User Rights option. The User Rights Policy dialog box will open.
3. Within the User Rights Policy dialog box, click your mouse on the Right drop-down list and select a right. After you select a right, the *Grant To* field will display the users and groups to which Windows NT has already granted your right.
4. Within the User Rights Policy dialog box, click your mouse on the Add button and then select a user or group to which you will assign the right. Windows NT will display the Add user or Groups dialog box.
5. Within the Add User or Groups dialog box, click your mouse on the Add button and then on the OK button. Windows NT, in turn, will display the User Rights Policy dialog box, within

which you select the right you want.

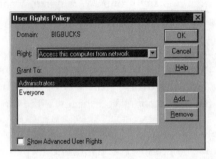

Figure 88 *Selecting a right in the User Rights Policy dialog box.*

The answer is **True***. A user or his or her group's rights, controls the operations the user can perform.*

89 CLARIFYING PERMISSIONS VERSUS RIGHTS

As you learned in Tip 87, Windows NT controls resource access by assigning users or groups permissions to each resource. User permissions are different then user rights. Permissions let users or groups access specific network resources, such as printers, folders, and applications, On the other hand, rights let users or groups access Windows NT operating system functions or objects. Operating system functions or objects include a user's right to bypass Windows NT's security in order to back up the system, to let a user log on locally to the server, and to shut down the server.

If you want to let a user or group back up the system, even though the individual user may not have permissions to all server resources, you would add the user or a group to which the user belongs to the Backup Operators local group. The Backup Operators local group is a built-in Windows NT group that exists on all Windows NT machines and that has the Windows NT *Backup files and directories* and *Restore files and directories* system rights. These rights let a user bypass the usual Windows NT security to back up or restore files to the Windows NT machine.

90 SETTING GROUP MEMBERSHIPS

Q: *Your boss informs you that while you were away yesterday he tried to create an account for a new user in User Manger for Domains, and he was unable to perform this task. He wants to know why he cannot create new user accounts. Your boss is a member of the Domain Users and Management groups. What would you tell your boss?*

Choose the best answer:

   A.   *He used the wrong system utility.*

   B.   *He must be a member of the Server Operators group to create user accounts.*

   C.   *He must be a member of the Account Admin group to create user accounts.*

   D.   *He must be a member of the Account Operators group or an administrator to create user accounts.*

Group memberships (that is, what groups a given user is a member of) are very important to system administrators in Windows NT, because they will be your primary tool for administering users on your network. As a system administrator, you must know when to create groups and when to use a system's built-in groups.

Built-in groups have predefined permissions to perform system tasks, while custom groups will let you set specific permissions for resources on the network. For example, to create new user accounts on a Windows NT Server, you would have to be a member of the Account Operators built-in group or an administrator. The Account Operators group is a predefined Windows NT Server local group with rights to create and manage user accounts.

A system administrator will find it relatively easy to set group memberships (which you will do for almost every user account, and, in many cases, multiple times for the same account). To set a group membership, perform the following steps:

1. Select the Start menu Programs option Administrative Tools group. Within the Administrative Tools group, select the User Manager for Domains program.
2. In User Manager for Domains, select the user account which you want to place within a group. Select the User menu Properties option. User Manager for Domains will display the User Properties dialog box.
3. In the User Properties dialog box, click your mouse on the Groups button. Windows NT will display the Group Memberships dialog box.
4. Within the Group Memberships dialog box, click your mouse on the *Not member of* field and then select the group where you want to put the new account.
5. Click your mouse on the Add button to add the new group membership. When you finish adding group memberships, click OK to close the Group Memberships dialog box. Windows NT will close the dialog box and return you to the User Properties dialog box.

Answer D is the correct answer because he must be a member of the Account Operators group or an administrator to create user accounts. Answer A is incorrect because User Manager for Domains is the correct system utility. Answers B and C are the incorrect answer because he must be a member of the Account Operators group or an administrator to create user accounts.

---

91 UNDERSTANDING GLOBAL ACCOUNTS

Q: *You are a member of the Manager of Information Services (MIS) department at your company. There are several other departments in your organization. Each department has a separate Windows NT domain. You are the administrator of your company's master domain, where all user accounts reside. You must create new user accounts to which you will assign resource permissions in all department domains. What type of user accounts would you create?*

Choose the best answer:

    A.   *Universal User Account*

    B.   *Local User Account*

    C.   *Global User Account*

    D.   *Trust User Account*

Windows NT will automatically create new user accounts as global user accounts. A system administrator can assign global user account permissions to any resource in the user's home domain as well as to any trusted domain. Most accounts that you create as an administrator are global accounts: Windows NT's two default global accounts are

Administrator and Guest. When you assign permissions on a resource to any group from your domain, you will only include global accounts in the group.

*Answer C is correct because all users are automatically Global User Accounts. **Answer A** is incorrect because there is no Universal User Account. **Answer B** is incorrect because users are not automatically added as Local User Accounts. **Answer D** is incorrect because there is no Trust User Account.*

92 UNDERSTANDING LOCAL ACCOUNTS

Q: *You are the administrator of a single Windows NT domain. Your company leases space in a building with two other companies in it. All three companies share a single T1 line to the Internet. Because you share a T1 line to the Internet, all three companies are on the same subnet and can see each other's servers on the network. You are friends with one of the other company's employees in your building. You would like to let your friend at the other company have access to some of the resources on your domain. How would you give your friend access to network resources without establishing a trust relationship with the other domain?*

Choose the best answer:

    A.   *Create a global account for your friend with the same user name and password as the user's home domain account.*

    B.   *Create a local account for your friend with any user name and password, and give your friend the account information.*

    C.   *Enable the Windows NT Server's Guest account.*

    D.   *You cannot give your friend access without establishing a trust relationship.*

Windows NT Server can create accounts for any user who will access your domain's servers from untrusted domains. In situations where you do not want to establish trust relationships between domains, but you still want to provide users in other domains access to resources in your domain, you will want to create local accounts. A user who uses a local account from an untrusted domain (that is, a domain without a trust relationship with your domain) to access resources in your domain will be able to do so only if his or her log-on computer is from an untrusted domain. If the user for whom you created the local account tries to log on using a computer in your domain, the system will not validate the user's account. Although creating local accounts can let users in untrusted domains access resources in your domain, if the number of out-of-domain users is large (relative to your network size), you may want to establish a trust relationship between the two domains.

To create a local user account for users in untrusted domains, perform the following steps:

1. Select the Start menu Programs option Administrative Tools group. Within the Administrative Tools group, select the User Manager for Domains program.

2. In User Manager for Domains, select the user account to which you want to give dial-in permission. Select the User menu Properties option. User Manager for Domains will display the User Properties dialog box.

3. In the User Properties dialog box click your mouse on the Account button. Windows NT will display the Account Information dialog box, shown in Figure 92.

4. Within the Account Information dialog box, click your mouse in the *Account Type* field. Then click your mouse on the Local Account radio button. Click your mouse on OK to exit the Account Information dialog box. Windows NT will make the account a local account.

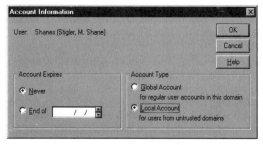

Figure 92 *Creating Local user accounts in the Account Information dialog box.*

Answer B is the correct answer because you should create a local account for your friend. **Answer A** is incorrect because you cannot create a global account from an untrusted domain. **Answer C** is incorrect because the Guest account will not let the user log in from an untrusted domain. **Answer D** is incorrect because you can use a local account.

93	**DEFINING THE EVERYONE GROUP**

Q: You are a Windows NT domain administrator. You have established trust relationships with another domain but have not yet assigned any user permissions to resources from the other domain. When you examine your security log, you discover that users from the trusted domain are already accessing resources in your domain. You examine the permissions you set on your server's resources and discover that all default permissions are in place. Why would users from the trusted domain be able to access your resources without you explicitly granting any permissions yet?

Choose the best answer:

A.   You established trust relationships in the wrong direction.

B.   The users are logging on as accounts from your domain.

C.   The Windows NT Security Accounts Manager service has stalled.

D.   The Everyone group is the permission set on your server's resources. The Everyone group includes users from trusted domains.

The Everyone group, which has the full control permission, is the default group that Windows NT sets on all resources in a system. The Everyone group includes all users, except users in untrusted domains. If you have established trust relationships with other domains, the Everyone group includes the trusted domain's users, which means that even though you may think you have not given any permissions to users in the trusted domain, in fact you have.

To avoid the problem of users from other domains gaining access to resources to which you have not explicitly granted permissions, you should remove the default permission (that is, the Everyone group) that Windows NT sets on all resources. After you remove the default permission, you should configure the resources so that the Domain Users group, instead of the Everyone group, has the full control permission.

Answer D is the correct answer because the Everyone group includes users from trusted domains. **Answer A** is incorrect because a trust relationship in the wrong direction would not let the users access resources at all. **Answer B** is incorrect because the security log indicates that the users are logging on from the trusted domain. **Answer C** is incorrect because, if the Windows NT Security Accounts Manager service stalled, the operating system would not execute.

94   **DEFINING THE NETWORK GROUP**

Q: *The Network group contains accounts of network users accessing resources from trusted domains.*

     True or False?

There are groups in Windows NT, such as the Network group, whose membership an administrator cannot control. The Network group includes all users who access resources on the local computer, regardless of where the users access the resource from. If you, as the system administrator, want to configure a resource so that users who access the resource from the network will have different permissions than users who locally access the resource, use the Network group to set permissions. You could, for example, configure a single file so that when a user accesses it from the network, the user cannot even open the file to view its contents. However, if the user were to access the resources from the physical Windows NT computer with the resources on it, the user can access the resources with full control.

*The answer is **True**, because the Network group contains all users who access resources remotely from anywhere.*

Note: *See Tip 127 to learn how to set permissions on resources so that the Network group can access the resources with a specific permission.*

95   **DEFINING THE INTERACTIVE GROUP**

Q: *The user who is locally logged on to a Windows NT computer is not a member of the Interactive group.*

     True or False?

You must become familiar with the term interactive because Microsoft uses it often in its exams. The term *interactive* refers to any user who is logged on at a local computer. If you are sitting at, and using, a Windows NT computer, you are the *interactive user* with that computer. The Interactive group contains only the one user account that corresponds to the user who is currently logged on to the local machine. An administrator cannot control the Interactive group's membership. When users log on, the Windows NT operating system automatically makes them members of the Interactive group. An administrator can use the Interactive group to grant different permissions to users who locally access resources, as opposed to remotely accessing resources from the network.

*The correct answer is **False** because the Interactive group contains only the currently logged-on user's account.*

96   **DEFINING THE ADMINISTRATORS GROUP**

Q: *You are the administrator of your company's enterprise network. You must create an account for a new employee who will be your assistant and who must have administrative permissions on the network. When you open User Manager for Domains, you notice that there are two groups that appear to be administrative groups—Administrators and Domain Admins. Which group should you make your assistant a member of?*

Choose the correct answer:

    A.   *Administrators*

    B.   *Domain Admins*

    C.   *Both of these*

    D.   *Neither of these*

A common cause of confusion for new Windows NT domain administrators is which group to make a user a member of for administrative permissions. Both the Administrators and Domain Admins groups provide a user with administrative permissions; however, the Administrators group is more restrictive because it is a local group. Administrators can assign local groups permissions only to resources on the local machine, which means that an administrator cannot assign local groups a Windows NT Workstation that defines permissions anywhere else in the domain. However, domain controllers provide the one exception to the rule of administrators assigning resource permissions on the local machine. Windows NT domain controllers share the same Directory Database, so local the groups one domain controller defines, are available to all other domain controllers.

The Domain Admins is a global group. Administrators can assign permissions to resources to global groups everywhere in the local domain as well as in any other trusted domain. As you learned in Tip 86, global groups contain user accounts, while local groups generally contain global groups but can contain user accounts. The local Administrators group automatically contains the global Domain Admins group. So, if you want a user to have domain-wide administrative permission as well as trusted domains permission, you should make the user a member of the global Domain Admins group. If you want to make a user an administrator only in the local domain and only on the domain controllers, you should make the user a member of the local Administrators group.

Answer B is the correct answer because, although either group would let this user perform administrative duties in your domain, the Domain Admins group would be the best choice because this would give the user administrative permissions on all computers—not just the domain controllers—in your domain. Answer A is incorrect because the Administrators group will only give the user administrative rights on the local machine (or on all domain controllers, depending on the local machine's network role). Answers C and D are incorrect because Answer B is the only correct answer to the question.

97   DEFINING THE SERVER OPERATORS GROUP

Q: *You receive a call from a user who has been entrusted to help you administer your Windows NT domain. The user tells you that he was denied access when he tried to extend a volume set on a Windows NT Server that is a domain controller in your domain. You examine the user's group memberships in User Manager for Domains and discover that he is a member of the Account Operators, Print Operators, and Backup Operators groups. Why is the system denying this user access when he extends a volume set?*

Choose the best answer:

    A.   *The user must be a member of the Server Operators group or an administrator to create or extend a volume set.*

    B.   *You cannot extend volume sets in Windows NT.*

    C.   *Only the default Administrator account can extend volume sets.*

    D.   *The user cannot be a member of the Print Operators, Account Operators, and Backup Operators groups. Remove membership of one of the groups and the user will be able to extend a volume set.*

You may need to enlist help in administering your domain, even in small environments. After you select a user to help you perform administrative duties, you do not have to make the user's account a member of the Domain Admins or Administrator groups. Instead, you can use one of Windows NT's local groups that contain a subset of administrative rights.

The local groups to which you can assign your assistant are the Account Operators, Backup Operators, Print Operators, and Server Operators. Each of these groups has a part of the total administrative rights. Tips 100 through 102 will examine the Account Operators, Backup Operators, and Print Operators groups. The Server Operators group gives its members the rights to back up files and directories, change the system time, force shutdown from a remote system, restore files and directories, and shut down the system, among other things. One of the possible tasks that a Server Operator can perform is to extend a volume set, provided the volume set bridges only NTFS drives. You will learn more about volume sets in later Tips.

Answer A is correct because the user must be a member of the Server Operators group or an administrator to create or extend a volume set. Answer B is incorrect because you can extend volume sets in Windows NT, provided the volume set is across NTFS drives. Answer C is incorrect because members of the Server Operators group or an administrator can create or extend a volume set. Answer D is incorrect because those groups have nothing to do with volume set extensions.

98   THE GUESTS GROUP DEFINED

Q: *You would make temporary employees members of the Guests group to let the users access system resources.*

True or False?

The Guests group is a local group administrators use for low-level access to system resources. You would not typically assign membership to this group. Windows NT will, by default, make the global Domain Guest group a member of the local Guests group. Because the system Guest account is a member of the Domain Guests group, the system can validate any user who does not have a valid user account to log on as the system's guest and gain access to resources domain wide. If a user without a domain account tries to access a system resource, the system will deny the user's request. The system will then automatically use the system Guest account to try to log on the user. By virtue of the Guest account's membership in the Domain Guests group, and because the Domain Guests group is a member of the Guests local group, users can access (without a valid domain account) any resource that has the default Everyone permission.

*The correct answer is **False** because the system will only log users in with the system Guest account if a user without a domain account tries to access a system resource.*

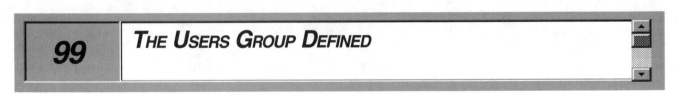

99   THE USERS GROUP DEFINED

Q: *You administer a large network consisting of several Windows NT domains. You configured your domains in a master domain model. You have one master domain and six resource domains. What steps must you perform to ensure that users from the master domain can access resources in each of the resource domains?*

Choose the best answer:

> A. *Establish trust relationships between the domains so that the master domain trusts all resource domains, and make the Domain Users global group from each resource domain a member of the Users local group in the master domain.*
>
> B. *Establish trust relationships between the domains so that each resource domain trusts the master domain, and then make the Domain Users global group from each resource domain a member of the Users local group in the master domain.*
>
> C. *Establish trust relationships between the domains so that the master domain trusts all resource domains, and make the Domain Users global group from the master domain a member of the Users local group in each of the resource domains.*
>
> D. *Establish trust relationships between the domains so that each resource domain trusts the master domain, and then make the Domain Users global group from the master domain a member of the Users local group in each resource domain*

By default, the Domain Users global group from the local domain is a member of the Users local group. As earlier Tips have discussed in detail, the default permission for Windows NT resources is the Everyone group with the full control permission. Microsoft recommends that you remove the default permission from all resources and replace it with the Users local group that has full control. Microsoft recommends that you do so specifically because the Everyone group contains users from untrusted domains. If you assign the Users local group permissions to a resource, you will grant only users from your domain and any trusted domains access, provided that you have taken the Domain Users groups from any trusted domains and made them members of the Users local group. You will learn more about the concept of multiple domains and their relationships in the "Windows NT Server in the Enterprise" section of this book.

Answer D is the correct answer because you should establish trust relationships between the domains so that each resource domain trusts the master domain, and then make the Domain Users global group from the master domain a member of the Users local group in each resource domain. **Answer A** is incorrect because the trust relationship is backwards and because you should make the Domain Users global group from the master domain a member of the Users local group in the resource domains. **Answer B** is incorrect because you should make the Domain Users global group from the master domain a member of the Users local group in the resource domains. **Answer C** is incorrect because the trust relationship is backward.

---

100 — THE PRINT OPERATORS GROUP DEFINED

Q: Any user who must print must be a member of the Print Operators group.

True or False?

As you learned in Tip 97, there are built-in groups in Windows NT Server that will let you, as the administrator, break up your administrative duties. You can assign membership of these administrative assistant groups to users who you will entrust with a subset of administrative responsibilities. The Print Operators group lets you give a user all the rights he or she must have to create and manage print devices. The actual rights you give to the Print Operators group from within the User Manager for Domains in the Rights dialog box are *Log on locally* and *Shut down the system*. Users who are members of the Print Operators group can create printers, assign forms to paper trays, schedule times that the printer will be available, set permission for other users, create printer pools, and perform many other tasks.

The correct answer is **False** because a user requires only access to a print resource to print to that resource. Membership in the Print Operators group would grant the user control of the resource.

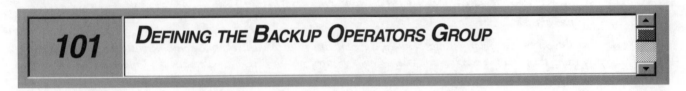

101   DEFINING THE BACKUP OPERATORS GROUP

Q: Backup Operators is a global group.

Q: True or False?

As you learned in previous Tips, administrators generally use local groups to assign permissions to resources, as opposed to using global groups that contain user accounts and do not have permission to any resources. There are some circumstances where the administrator may choose to include user accounts in a local group. For example, an administrator might place individual user accounts into Windows NT Server's built-in local groups that have subsets of administrative rights (administrators call such groups *sub-administrative groups*). An administrator might want to include a single user account in one of the sub-administrative groups because to create a global group, "containerize" one user account in the new global group, and then place the global group in the local sub-administrative group would be more work than to place the single user account into the local sub-administrative group. The Backup Operators group is a default local group that all Windows NT computers have.

The Backup Operators group provides a system administrator with a built-in local group that has all the rights it needs to perform system backup operations. Windows NT domain administrators who want to grant backup privileges to users can make individual user accounts members of the Backup Operators group. Administrators can also make global groups that contain user accounts members of the Backup Operators group. After a user is in the Backup Operators global group, the system administrator can assign that user membership in the Backup Operators local groups in any domain where the user may need to perform backup operations. Windows NT Server does not automatically include user accounts in the Backup Operators group. An administrator must assign membership to the Backup Operators group to any user account that the administrator wants to grant backup rights in the domain or on the local computer. To review how administrators can set group memberships, review Tip 90.

The correct answer is **False** because Backup Operators is a local group that provides group members the rights to perform system backups, while there is no Backup Operators global group.

102   THE ACCOUNT OPERATORS GROUP DEFINED

Q: You are seeking help with administering your Windows NT domain. You want help in the area of account creation and management. What group or groups would you make your administrative assistant a member of?

Choose the best answer:

A.   Account Operators

B.   Account Operators and Server Operators

C.   Server Operators

D.   Domain Admins and Server Operators

Microsoft Windows NT Server provides several built-in sub-administrative groups that divide administrative tasks into categories. As you examine the sub-administrative groups, you should consider the following categories which Microsoft defines as sub-administrative group responsibilities: backups, server operations, print management, and account management. Each sub-administrative group is part of the total administration replication tasks category. For example, a common sub-administrative group is the Account Operators group. Account Operators is a local group available on any Windows NT Server domain controller. The Account Operators group provides administrators with a built-in local group that will let any member of the group create and manage user accounts in the domain. Windows NT grants to members of the Account Operators group the specific rights to log on locally and shut down the system. In addition to the system rights Windows NT grants to members of the Account Operators group, members in this group can also create new user accounts, change group memberships, set log-on hours, and perform many other administrative tasks that deal with account management.

Administrators can use the Account Operators group in the local domain or in complex multiple domain models to break up system administration. Windows NT will not automatically assign users membership to the Account Operators group. The Windows NT system administrator must assign Account Operators group membership to any user account that will assist in account creation and in management of other user accounts. Tip 90 explained in detail how administrators or Account Operators group members can assign group memberships.

Answer A is correct because Account Operators is the only group membership Windows NT requires for a user to create and manage other user accounts. Answer B is incorrect because the answer includes the Server Operators group, which gives members permissions to make changes on the system setting and hardware. Answer C is incorrect because the Server Operators group will not give the user the proper rights or permissions. Answer D is incorrect because, although Domain Admins group membership would give a user rights and permission to create and manage user accounts, the answer also included the Server Operators group, which would provide the user with redundant permission.

103   DEFINING THE REPLICATOR GROUP

Q: *What purpose does the Replicator group serve in Windows NT?*

Choose the best answer:

    A.   *Windows NT uses the Replicator group as a system group to manage Directory Database synchronization.*

    B.   *Members of the Replicator group can manage directory replication in Windows NT.*

    C.   *Windows NT uses the Replicator group to establish trust relationships.*

    D.   *Windows NT copies all user accounts to the Replicator group to back up a domain's user account information.*

Microsoft uses the terms *replication* and *synchronization* to describe two very similar functions of the Windows NT operating system. Because replication and synchronization perform similar functions, administrators can sometimes confuse the terms. Microsoft uses the term synchronization to describe the process Windows NT uses to copy the Directory Database from one domain controller to another and ensure that all domain controllers maintain consistent copies of the Directory Database (that is, the databases are *synchronized*).

Microsoft uses the term replication to describe the process of a Windows NT Server copying (or replicating) its *system_root\system32\Repl\Export* directory to the *system_root\system32\Repl\Import* directory on another Windows NT Server or a Windows NT Workstation. Administrators use replication to copy key files, such as logon scripts or policy files from one system (the export system) to another (the import system).

Although the terms, in general, describe completely different operations in Windows NT, the two terms can also describe components of the process of the other operation. Sometimes, you will find that Microsoft will use the terms replication and synchronization to describe part of another process, which process might, in its entirety, be known by another name. To understand this better, consider the following examples:

- Windows NT Server uses Directory Replication to synchronize the export server's *system_root\system32\Repl\Export* directory with that of the import computer *system_root\system32\Import* directory. Note that, in this case, synchronization is a crucial step before replication.

- A Windows NT Server Primary Domain Controller will replicate its Directory Database to other Windows NT Server domain controllers. Microsoft calls this replication process *directory synchronization*. Note that, in this case, replication is a crucial step before synchronization.

Throughout this book's Tips, you will learn more about the different types of synchronization and replication, and how they relate to specific operating system processes. For now, it is enough that you understand that, in the current context, replication describes the process of a Windows NT Server copying (or replicating) its *system_root\system32 \Repl\Export* directory to the *system_root\system32\Repl\Import* directory on another Windows NT Server or a Windows NT Workstation. The process of replicating *Export* to *Import* is known as *directory replication*.

The Replicator group is a local group that all Windows NT machines contain. The Replicator group does not have any special system rights in User Manager for Domains; however, Replicator group members can configure and manage the Windows NT directory replication process. As discussed, Windows NT uses directory replication to copy system policies, log-on scripts, and small read-only files to other Windows NT computers. The system administrator must create the system policies, log-on scripts, and read-only files that Windows NT will replicate. The administrator must also configure Windows NT's directory replication on all machines that will export or import data.

Note: *To learn more about how to configure Windows NT's directory replication, see Tips 432 through 437.*

Answer B is correct because members of the Replicator group can configure and manage directory replication. Answer A is incorrect because the Replicator group has nothing to do with Windows NT's Directory Database synchronization process. Answer C is incorrect because administrators do not have to use the Replicator group to establish trust relationships. Answer D is incorrect because administrators do not use the Replicator group as any sort of user accounts backup.

104 — DEFINING THE DOMAIN GUESTS GROUP

Q: For what reason would you assign users membership to the Domain Guests group?

Choose the best answer:

A. *To ensure some level of access to all system resources in your local domain.*

B. *So you can group temporary workers' accounts together, but separate from your company's full-time employees.*

C. *This group would be most useful in multi-domain environments where you want to let users from trusted domains access resources in trusting domains as guests.*

D. *You cannot assign memberships to the Domain Guests group. Windows NT manages this group.*

Any built-in group in Windows NT Server that begins with the word domain is a global group. Administrators use global groups to "containerize" user accounts. Administrators then place global groups into local groups, which the administrator then grants access to network resources. Some local groups are built-in Windows NT groups that all domain users are members of (such as the Everyone group), while other groups require an administrator to assign membership to the group. In Windows NT Server, the Guests local group contains, by default, the Domain Guests global group. In turn, the Domain Guests global group contains the user account Guest as a system default. The administrator can assign other users membership to the Domain Guests group.

In networks that consist of multiple Windows NT domains, the administrator can place the master domain's Domain Guests group into each resource domain's Guests local group, which is an easy way to grant users guest privileges in multiple domains. A system administrator must design and implement each group association this Tip discusses. Later Tips, in the "Windows NT Server in the Enterprise" section of this book, discuss master and resource domains.

Answer C is correct because the best use of this group would be in multi-domain environments where the system administrator wants to grant low-level access to resources in one domain that users of another domain access. Answer A is incorrect because Windows NT automatically assigns users membership to the Domain Users group, which will grant to all domain users low-level access to resources. Answer B is incorrect because you would not assign membership in the Domain Guests group for use in your local domain. Answer D is incorrect because Windows NT does not manage the Domain Guests group; an administrator manages the Domain Guests group.

105 THE DOMAIN USERS GROUP DEFINED

Q: *The Domain Users group is a global group you can use to grant users from one domain access to resources in another domain.*

       True or False?

You can use the Domain Users group in the same manner you use the Domain Guests group, which Tip 104 discussed. In situations where trust relationships link multiple Windows NT domains, the system administrator can use the Domain Users global group to let users from one domain access resources in another domain.

It is quite common for system administrators of a Windows NT multi-domain network to take the Domain Users group from a master domain and place it into the Users local group in a resource domain. Doing so lets users from the master domain access the remote domain's resources as if their accounts were from the remote domain.

The Domain Users group also has practical applications in the local domain. Microsoft recommends that you remove the default Windows NT Everyone group's Full Control permission from all resources and instead assign the Domain Users group Full Control permission to the resources.

As you will learn in later Tips, doing so is a relatively simple process. When you give permissions to the Domain Users group, all user accounts from the local domain will have access to resources, but users from other domains (even trusted domains) will not have access to any resources.

*The correct answer is **True**, because Windows NT automatically assigns Domain Users group membership to all user accounts in the domain. Administrators can use the Domain Users global group in the local domain or across trust relationships in multi-domain environments.*

106   DEFINING THE DOMAIN ADMINS

Q: *You are the administrator of a small organization. You have configured your network as a Microsoft Windows NT single domain model. You have three Windows NT Servers and all client machines are Windows NT Workstations. Your boss has asked you to make her an administrator so that during times when you are not in the building, there will still be a system administrator who can perform any task you would typically perform. Your boss must be able to create users, back up any Windows NT computer on the network, and assign permissions to resources located not only on your Windows NT Servers, but also on some Windows NT Workstations in your domain. What group should you make your boss a member of?*

Choose the best answer:

    A.   *Administrators*

    B.   *Server Operators*

    C.   *Domain Admins*

    D.   *Account Operators*

Many system administrators face the dilemma of deciding which group to use to give a user full administrative rights and permissions in the domain. You might initially think that making a user a member of the Administrators group would make the user a full administrator. However, while membership to the Administrators group does give its members administrative rights and permissions, the Administrators group is a local group and therefore only gives the member user administrative rights and permissions on the local machine.

All Windows NT machines have a local Administrators group. If an administrator installs Windows NT Server as a Member Server or installs Windows NT Workstation and joins a domain, the local machine will place the Domain Admins group from the domain in the Administrators local group, giving Domain Admins members administrative rights and permissions on the local machine. In cases where there are no Windows NT Workstations or Windows NT Member Servers in the domain, membership in the Administrators group on the Primary Domain Controller will grant the user administrative rights and permissions to the whole domain. Windows NT Server domain controllers share the same Directory Database of accounts.

The Administrators local group the Primary Domain Controller defines is the same on all domain controllers from the same domain. Windows 95 and Windows for Workgroups machines do not have Directory Databases, so they cannot be members of a Windows NT domain. Windows 95 or Windows for Workgroups machines can act only as clients to Windows NT domain controllers; they cannot participate in domain security. Because only Windows NT machines can be domain members, if you do not have Windows NT machines other than the domain controllers, membership to the Administrators local group will provide its members with full domain administration rights and permissions.

In large organizations that encompass multiple domains, the network administrator may place the Domain Admins group from the domain that has the administrator's user account into the Administrators local group, which will exist independently within each of the domains for which the administrator is responsible. If the administrator places the Domain Admins global group into the Administrators local group in each of the domains, one user account can centrally administer the entire domain. In multiple-domain models, Windows NT will not automatically assign the Domain Admins group to any other domain's Administrators group—the domain administrator must assign memberships.

Answer C is correct because Domain Admins group membership will give its members administrative rights and permission on every machine in a domain. An administrator can use the Domain Admins group to assign administrative rights and permissions in trusting domains. Answer A is incorrect because the Administrators group is a local group that an adminis-

*trator can use only on the local machine. **Answer B** is incorrect because Server Operators have only a subset of administrative rights and permissions. **Answer D** is incorrect because Account Operators have only a subset of administrative rights and permissions.*

107   GRANTING DIAL-IN PERMISSIONS

Q: *What steps must the system administrator perform in order to let network users access the Windows NT domain remotely?*

Choose all answers that apply:

A.   *Make any user who requires remote network access a member of the Remote Users group.*

B.   *In User Manager for Domains, open the account properties for any user who requires remote access and click your mouse on the Dialin button. In the Dialin information dialog box, check the Grant dialin permission to user checkbox.*

C.   *Install the Remote Access Server service on the Windows NT machine that will act as the dial-in server.*

D.   *Install a network router connected to the Internet.*

E.   *Install the Dial-up Networking software on Windows 95 or Windows NT Workstation clients.*

Whether your network is large or small, you may require remote access for your users. Remote access lets users dial in from home or any other location and interact with the Windows NT domain as if the remote computer were connected to the local area network (LAN). You will learn more about the specifics of local area networks in later Tips. After a remote user connects to the network, the connection is no different from any other computer directly connected to the LAN. The type of connection Windows NT lets remote computers make is known as *remote noding*. In remote noding, the Windows NT network treats the remote computer as if it were simply another computer connected directly to the network, rather than treating it differently because it connects across a phone line.

Windows NT will not automatically grant dial-in permission to all users. The system administrator must grant dial-in permission to users who need remote access. To grant dial-in permission, perform the following steps:

1. Select the Start menu Programs option Administrative Tools group. Within the Administrative Tools group, select the User Manager for Domains program.

2. In User Manager for Domains, select the user account to which you want to give dial-in permission. Select the User menu Properties option. User Manager for Domains will display the User Properties dialog box.

3. In the User Properties dialog box, click your mouse on the Dialin button. User Manger for Domains will display the Dialin Information dialog box, as shown in Figure 107.

4. In the Dialin Information dialog box, click your mouse on the Grant dialin permission to user checkbox. Click your mouse on the OK button. User Manager for Domains will close the Dialin Information dialog box.

5. In the User Properties dialog box, click your mouse on the OK button. User Manager for Domains will close the User Properties dialog box.

6. In User Manager for Domains, select the User menu Exit option. Windows NT will close User Manager for Domains.

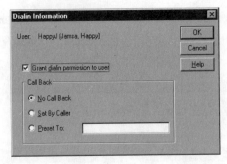

Figure 107 The Dialin Information dialog box.

Answers B, C, and E are correct because all three steps are required. A Windows NT domain administrator who wants to let users remotely access network resources must grant the Dialin permission to each user who requires remote access. In addition, the administrator must install the Remote Access Service (RAS) on the Windows NT machine that will be the dial-in server. The administrator must also configure each client computer by installing the Dial-up Networking client software on any Windows NT or Windows 95 machine. Answer A is incorrect because there is no default Remote Users group. Answer D is incorrect because you do not have to use a network routing device with a modem to remotely access a Windows NT network.

108   U**NDERSTANDING** U**SER** P**ROFILES**

Q: *A user calls you and complains that when he logs on to machines other than the one at his own desk, he does not get the same screen colors and Desktop settings. What could you tell this user to explain why his settings are different on other machines?*

Choose the best answer:

A.   *The user is logging on using different user accounts.*

B.   *User settings will be different on each Windows NT machine. The administrator must manually configure the settings to look the same.*

C.   *User profiles contain all user-defined settings and, by default, reside on the local machine. To have the user's settings centrally stored so that they are the same everywhere in the network, the administrator must create a server-based profile for the user.*

D.   *If the user's machine is in one domain and the other computers the user logs on to are in different domains, the user profile will not follow the user.*

In older networks, users encountered a problem in which if more than one user used a single Windows for Workgroups or Windows 3.x machine, all the machine's users would have to share the machine's Desktop settings. If one user liked a neon-pink Desktop, all the other users would have to suffer. In Windows 95 and in Windows NT, each machine locally stores the user Desktop settings. Each user has a unique user profile that defines the user screen colors, background image, screen saver, network drives, mapped printing devices, and icon placement on the screen. In Tip 110, you will learn how to make a user's profile available anywhere in the network.

Windows NT creates a user profile for each user that logs on to the local machine. The *system_root\profiles* directory stores each profile locally in individual sub-directories. If an administrator plans on using only locally stored profiles, he or she can maintain the profiles without using administrative intervention. Each Windows NT machine will manage its own locally stored user profiles. An administrator can view a list of locally stored user profiles, as Figure 108 shows.

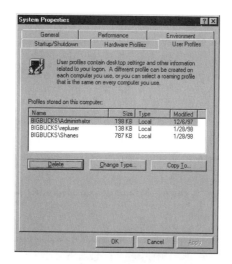

Figure 108 *Locally stored user profiles.*

To see a list of user profiles locally stored on any Windows NT machine, perform the following steps:

1. From the Windows NT Desktop, click your right mouse button on the My Computer icon. Windows NT will display a pop-up menu.

2. Within the pop-up menu, select the Properties option. Windows NT will display the System Properties dialog box.

3. In the System Properties dialog box, click your mouse on the User Profiles tab. In the User Profiles tab of the System Properties dialog box, review the *Profiles stored on this computer* list. Note that you can copy, change, or delete profiles within the list.

4. Click your mouse on the OK button and Windows NT will close the System Properties dialog box.

Answer C is correct because, by default, Windows NT stores user profiles on the local machine. Each new computer you log on to will create a new locally stored user profile that contains all user-definable settings. Answer A is incorrect because, although different user accounts will have separate user profiles, this answer is not the likely cause of the problem—most users will not (and should not) have access to multiple user accounts. Answer B is incorrect because an administrator can centrally store user profiles so that a user would not have to reset Desktop settings on each machine the user logs on to. Answer D is incorrect because an administrator can configure user profiles to cross trust relationships between domains.

| 109 | CREATING AND USING LOG-ON SCRIPTS FOR WINDOWS USERS |

Q: *Administrators can configure Windows NT profiles to work for Windows 3.x and MS-DOS clients.*

True or False?

For years network administrators have used log-on script files to map local-drive letters to volumes on servers. For example, you might use a local-drive letter to point to a server disk that contains your home directory. The administrator creates home directories for each user, and then maps a local drive to them using a log-on script file. Normally, the user will have a local drive letter (generally H:) that points to the individual user's home directory.

When a user wants to save personal data he or she can save the data to the H: drive. Each user would have an H: drive, but each user's H: drive would point to a different directory on the network server. Having all users' home directories in one location lets administrators protect the network users' personal data. Moreover, the network administrator can back up one volume on the server, thereby protecting all users' home directories with a single backup operation. Network administrators also use log-on scripts to map users to public directories and to point users to network printers.

A Windows NT system administrator can create and use log-on scripts, but not all Microsoft clients can take advantage of the commands the administrator might use in the scripts. Microsoft recommends not using log-on scripts for any Windows NT or Windows 95 clients. Instead, Windows NT and Windows 95 clients can take advantage of Microsoft's *roaming user profiles*, which Tip 110 details. Roaming profiles can do everything a log-on script can do and a lot more. Microsoft recommends system administrators use log-on scripts if there are any Windows 3.x or MS-DOS clients in the network.

To write a log-on script, you must learn the basic construction of a log-on script for Microsoft clients. The commands a Windows NT system administrator can use in log-on scripts are *Microsoft LAN Manager* commands. *LAN Manager* was an early Microsoft network operating system (integrated with early versions of Windows NT, it provided close support for Windows 3.x and MS-DOS client machines). For a list of *LAN Manager* commands and their use, see Tips 452 through 473.

Log-on scripts are batch files (short text files that contain operating system commands), which you must name with the *.bat* suffix. In Windows NT, you must place log-on scripts within the *system_root\system32\ Repl\Import\Scripts* subdirectory on a domain controller. You can use *Notepad* or any other text editor to create your log-on scripts.

Note: *You must place your log-on scripts within the* **system_root\system32\Repl\Import\Scripts** *subdirectory so that Windows NT can automatically copy them to new workstations that sign on to the network.*

A system administrator can use variables to create log-on scripts. *Variables* let you specify information that the log-in script will require without constraining it to a specific value. For example, a log-on script might need to look at the user's operating system. You could write different log-on scripts for client computers running Windows 95,

Windows NT, MS-DOS, and so on, or you could (more efficiently) place a variable within the script that tells the server what the user's operating system is. Table 109 shows variables that the system administrator can use in log-on scripts.

Variable	Description
%HOMEDRIVE%	The drive letter that connects to the user's home directory.
%HOMEPATH%	The actual path to the user's home directory.
%HOMESHARE%	The share point of the user's home directory.
%OS%	The operating system on the user's machine.
%PROCESSOR%	The processor on the user's machine.
%USERDOMAIN%	The domain where the user's account is from.
%USERNAME%	The name of the user's account.

Table 109 Variables in log-on scripts.

The following is an example of a basic log-on script:

```
NET TIME \\Server /SET
NET USE H: /HOME
NET USE P: \\Server\Public
NET USE LPT1: \\Server\Printer
```

In this example, the first line sets the client computer's time to match the time of a target computer (usually a domain controller). In the second line, the *NET USE* command maps the drive letter *H:* to the user's home directory. In the third line, the *NET USE* command maps the drive letter *P:* to a computer called *Server* to a share point called *Public*. In the last line, the *NET USE* command maps the local *LPT1:* port to a network printer called *Printer*, which in this particular example, resides on a computer called *Server*.

*The correct answer is **False**, because Windows 3.x and MS-DOS clients are not compatible with Windows NT profiles.*

110   CREATING A ROAMING USER PROFILE

Q: *You are the administrator of a Windows NT domain. You want everyone in the company's Sales Department to have the same Desktop settings (screen colors, backgrounds, screen savers, and mapped drives). All the people working on Windows NT Workstations are in the sales department. What is the best way to accomplish your objective?*

Choose the best answer:

A.   *Physically configure each user's machine so that all machines have the same settings.*

B.   *Make everyone from the Sales Department part of a global group called Sales. Create a user account and log on to any Windows NT computer as the new account. Change all Desktop settings, including screen colors, screen savers, background, and mapped network drives and printers. Copy the profile of the user account you logged on as to a Profiles directory on a domain controller. Grant the right to use the profile to the Sales group you created earlier. Assign the Sales group the profile you created earlier.*

C.   *Make everyone from the Sales Department part of a global group called Sales. Create a user and log on to a Windows NT computer as the new account. Change all Desktop settings, including screen colors, screen savers, background, and map network drives and printers. Copy the profile of the user account you logged on as to a Profiles directory on a domain controller. Grant the right to use the profile to the Sales group you created earlier. Assign each user who requires a common profile to the profile you created earlier.*

D.   *Make everyone from the Sales Department part of a global group called Sales. Create a user account and log on to a Windows 95 computer as the new account. Change all Desktop settings, including screen colors, screen savers, background, and map network drives and printers. Copy the profile of the user account you logged on as to a Profiles directory on a domain controller. Grant the right to use the profile to the Sales group you created earlier. Assign each user who requires a common profile to the profile you created earlier.*

In Tip 108, you learned what a Windows NT profile is. Although Windows 95 uses profiles, its profiles are not compatible with Windows NT (because of differences in Microsoft's design of the two profile types). If you want to administer a network where Windows 95 and Windows NT machines will co-exist, you must create and use separate Windows NT and Windows 95 profiles for each user who will operate both platforms. If you do not, and you try to use a Windows 95 profile on a Windows NT workstation, or vice versa, the computer may operate incorrectly, may not even load the Desktop at all, or may simply ignore the profile entirely.

As you also learned in Tip 108, profiles store all user-defined Desktop information (screen colors, background image, screen saver, mapped network drives, and mapped network printers). Windows NT automatically creates and stores profiles for each user who logs on to the local machine. If a user logs on to one Windows NT machine and makes changes to his or her Desktop settings, Windows NT will save the changes to the user's local profile. When the user logs back on to a machine that he or she has used before, Windows NT will use the user's individual profile to restore all Desktop settings. By default, if a user logs on to a machine he or she has not logged on to before, Windows NT will create a new user profile. Because of the way Windows NT creates and manages profiles, unless you make modifications to the way your network creates profiles, the user will have a separate profile at each machine that the user logs on to.

As an administrator, you can choose to implement roaming user profiles for your Windows NT users. There are advantages and disadvantages to creating roaming user profiles. One advantage to creating roaming user profiles is that you can assign one profile to many users, and even configure the profile so that users cannot change the Desktop settings or mapped network connections. One disadvantage of creating roaming user profiles is that it uses a lot of an administrator's time. If you must create and manage a profile for each user in your network, consider the time you will require for profile administration (which will vary by user, by network, and by configuration). If your network consists of several hundred or thousand users, profile administration could be a big job—and might become so time consuming as to make you unable to perform other administrative difficulties. You should also closely evaluate whether the majority of your users move between computers. If they do most of their work on a single computer, the benefit of roaming user profiles will likely be minimal.

Because Windows NT creates profiles only when a user logs on to a Windows NT machine, you, as an administrator, must log on to a machine as a valid user account in order to create the profile you will make into a roaming user profile. After you logon, to create a roaming user profile, perform the following steps:

1. Select the Start menu Programs option Administrative Tools group. Within the Administrative Tools group, select the User Manager for Domains option. Windows NT will open the User Manager for Domains program.

2. Within User Manager for Domains, select the User menu New User option. User Manager for Domains will display the New User dialog box.

3. Within the New User dialog box, type the name of the new user account in the *Username* field (Microsoft recommends typing Profile User). Click your mouse on the OK button. User manager for Domains will close the New User dialog box.

4. Within User Manager for Domains, select the User menu Exit option. Windows NT will close User manager for Domains.

5. Log off the Windows NT machine and log back on as the *Profile User* account.

6. After you log on as the Profile User account, use Windows *Explorer* to map network connections and change any Desktop setting you want. Log off the local machine. Windows NT will save the user profile of the *Profile User* account.

7. Next, log on as an administrative account. On the Windows NT Desktop, click your right mouse button on the My Computer icon. Windows NT will display a pop-up menu.

8. Within the pop-up menu, select the Properties option. Windows NT will display the System Properties dialog box.

9. Within the System Properties dialog box, select the User Profiles tab and select the profile of the *Profile User* account. Click your mouse on the Copy To button. Windows NT will display the Copy To dialog box.

10. Within the Copy To dialog box, browse to or type the pathname where you want the profiles copied (probably a shared resource on a server that all accounts have access to).

11. From the Copy To dialog box in the Permitted to use section, click your mouse on the Change button. Windows NT will display the Choose User dialog box.

12. Within the Choose User dialog box, select the user or group you will let use the profile you copied. Click your left mouse on the Add button. Windows NT will add the selected user to the *Add name* field. Then, click your mouse on the OK button. Windows NT will close the Choose User dialog box.

13. Within the Copy To dialog box, click your mouse on the OK button. Windows NT will close the Copy To dialog box.

14. Within the System Properties dialog box, click your mouse on the OK button. Windows NT will close the System Properties dialog box.

After you have created and copied the *Profile User's* profile, you must configure each user's account to point to the *Profile User's* profile. After you associate the user's account with the *Profile User's* profile, the user will use the profile that you created, from any machine on the network. To configure a user account, perform the following steps:

1. Select the Start menu Programs option Administrative Tools group. Within the Administrative Tools group, select the on User Manager for Domains option. Windows NT will open the User Manager for Domains program.

2. Within User Manager for Domains, select the user or users to whom you want to assign the *Profile User* profile. Open the properties of the selected accounts.

3. In the User Properties dialog box, click your mouse on the Profile button. User Manager for Domains will display the User Environment Profile dialog box.

4. Within the User Environment Profile dialog box, type the pathname where you previously saved the *Profile User* profile in the *User Profile Path* field in the User Profile section. Click your mouse on the OK button. User Manager for Domains will close the User Environment Profile dialog box.

5. Within the User Properties dialog box, click your mouse on the OK button. User Manager for Domains will close the User Properties dialog box.

6. Close User Manager for Domains.

Answer C is correct because it describes the process of creating the user profile and assigning permissions, as the steps outline. Answer A is incorrect because configuring each user's computer so that the Desktops appear the same will only deceive the user. If the user makes any changes to his or her Desktop, the administrator must manually update all other machines. Answer B is incorrect because an administrator cannot assign profiles to groups; the administrator must assign profiles to users. Answer D is incorrect because, although a user logging on to a Windows 95 client will create a profile, the Windows 95 profile will not be compatible with Windows NT machines.

111   CREATING A MANDATORY USER PROFILE

Q: *You are a Windows NT domain administrator. You have configured all user accounts from your company's Sales Department with mandatory profiles. If the mandatory profile is not available when a user from the sales department logs on, what will occur?*

Choose the best answer:

    A.   *Windows NT will log on the user with cached profile information. Windows NT will not save any changes the user makes to the Desktop.*

    B.   *Windows NT will log on the user with the default system profile. Windows NT will not save any changes the user makes to the Desktop.*

    C.   *Windows NT will log on the user with cached profile information. Windows NT will save any changes the user makes to the Desktop in the cached profile. When the user's mandatory profile becomes available, the cached profile will update the user's mandatory profile.*

    D.   *The user will not be able to log on.*

In Tip 110, you learned that roaming user profiles will let a user have the same Desktop appearance and network connections on every machine the user logs on to in the domain. Although letting individual users have the same Desktop everywhere the user logs on makes the user happy, it does not ease the administrative workload. One way administrators can take advantage of roaming profiles to reduce administrative work is to configure multiple user accounts to use the same roaming user profile. The only problem with having users share the same profile is that the system saves changes one user makes to the Desktop, so the next user who shares the profile will see the changes.

To solve the problem of shared profiles, the system administrator can make the user profile mandatory. A *mandatory profile* means the user cannot save any changes to the profile. Suppose a user with a mandatory profile logs on to your domain. If the user changes the Desktop colors, the system will place the changes within the cached copy of the profile on the local machine, but will not save the changes to the mandatory profile when the user logs off. In addition, if a user attempts to log on and the user's mandatory profile is unavailable (because the network is down, the administrator removed the profile, or for any other reason), the user cannot log on to the domain.

Making a user profile mandatory is a two-step process. First, before you perform the steps to make a user profile mandatory, you must be sure you have first made the profile a roaming user profile. After you have performed all the steps in Tip 110, and created as many roaming user profiles as you need, you can then make the profiles mandatory. To make a user profile mandatory, perform the following steps:

1. Within the directory that you saved the profile into in Tip 110, locate the profile you want to make mandatory. Double-click your mouse on the Profile folder. Windows NT will open the Profile folder.

2. Within the Profile folder, locate the *User.dat* file. Click your right mouse button on the *User.dat* file. Windows NT will display a pop-up menu.

3. Within the pop-up menu, select the Rename option. Windows NT will highlight the file name. In the highlighted file name area, change the *.dat* extension to *.man* and press ENTER.

When a user logs on with a profile that has a *User.man* file, Windows NT saves the mandatory profile status. In Tip 112, you will learn how to assign the mandatory profile to the user accounts. For now, Figure 111 shows the contents of a profile folder and the *User.man* file.

Figure 111 *Profile folder contents after you set the profile to mandatory use.*

Answer D is correct because a user with a mandatory profile must have access to the profile or he or she cannot log on to the domain. Answer A is incorrect for mandatory profiles, but would be correct if a user logging on has a regular profile that is not available. Answer B is incorrect because the user account properties will state the profile of the user logging on. If a user does not have a profile set in the user properties from the User Manager for Domains utility, the user can log on using the default profile. Answer C is incorrect because Windows NT will not update cached profiles with user profiles.

112 | **ASSIGNING A PROFILE TO A USER ACCOUNT**

Q: Which utility would you use to assign a profile to a user account in Windows NT?

Choose the best answer:

    A.   Server Manager

    B.   System Profile Editor

    C.   User Manager for Domains

    D.   Network Client Administrator

In previous Tips, you learned about user profiles, how to make roaming user profiles, and how to make mandatory user profiles. After you make a user profile a roaming profile, you must specify the profile path in the user properties for the user within the User Manager for Domains utility. If you want to assign a single profile to multiple users, select all accounts that will share the single profile and open the user accounts' properties. To assign a roaming profile to one or more user accounts, perform the following steps:

1. Select the Start menu Programs option Administrative Tools group. Within the Administrative Tools group, select the on User Manager for Domains option. Windows NT will open the User Manager for Domains program.

2. Within User Manager for Domains, open the user account properties of the account to which you want to assign a profile. The User Properties dialog box will open.

3. Within the User Properties dialog box, click your mouse on the Profile button. User manager for Domains will display the User Environment Profile dialog box.

4. Within the User Environment Profile dialog box (in the User Profile section *Profile Path* field), type the pathname for the roaming profile. Click your mouse on the OK button. User Manager for Domains will close the User Environment Profile dialog box.

5. Close User Manager for Domains.

Figure 112 shows a sample pathname for the roaming profile in the *Profile Path* field.

Figure 112 Assigning a roaming profile in the User Environment Profile dialog box.

Answer C *is the correct answer because the administrator will use User Manager for Domains to point user accounts to roaming profiles.* **Answer A** *is incorrect because an administrator would use Server manager for computer account management, not for user account management.* **Answer B** *is incorrect because no such utility exists.* **Answer D** *is incorrect because the system administrator will use Network Client Administrator to install client software or to create the client software diskettes.*

113 USING VARIABLES WHEN YOU CREATE ACCOUNTS

Q: *You are the administrator of a your company's domain. You never created user home directories when you originally set up your domain. You now want to configure user home directories for each user. What is the easiest way for you to create home directories for all domain users?*

Choose the best answer:

A.   *Use the %USERNAME% variable.*

B.   *Use the %USERDOMAIN% variable.*

C.   *Manually create directories for each user and assign each user to his or her respective directory.*

D.   *Use the Windows NT Administrative Wizards to automate home directory creation.*

In Tip 109, you learned about variables that administrators can use to create log-on scripts. A system administrator can use the same variables as you learned about in Tip 109 to create user accounts. For example, suppose you plan to create several hundred user accounts. You know it would take a considerable amount of time (probably upward of 8 hours or more) to create user home directories for each user and configure permissions so that each user is the only account with permission to the home directory. To save you administrative time, you can use system variables. Instead of manually creating each user home directory and configuring permissions, you can use variables to let Windows NT create and configure for you.

In User Manager for Domains, type the *%USERNAME%* variable in the user properties of each user who needs a home directory. Windows NT will create the home directory and configure permissions so that only the individual user will have access to his or her home directory.

You can also use the *%USERNAME%* variable to create roaming profiles for users. To do so, place the text line *\\computer_name\share\%USERNAME%* in the *User Profile Path* field in the User Environment Profile dialog box. When the user logs on, Windows NT will create a profile for the user and place the newly created profile in a folder with the same name as the user account name. An administrator can use the *%USERNAME%* variable when creating support directories and other information for an account, as Figure 113 shows.

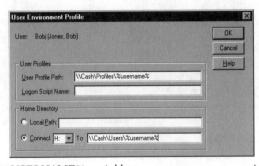

Figure 113 An administrator using the %USERNAME% variable to automate account creation tasks.

In Figure 113, notice that in the *User Profile Path* field, the path points to a computer with the name *Cash* and to a shared folder with the name *Profiles*. In the Home Directory section in the *To* field, the path points to a computer with the name *Cash* and to a shared folder with the name *Users*. The *%USERNAME%* variable will create a subfolder within the *Users* share with the same name as the user name.

Answer A is the correct answer because the %USERNAME% variable would let Windows NT create a home directory for existing user accounts or you can use it to create a new account. Answer B is incorrect because the %USERDOMAIN% variable would create a home directory with the domain's name. All users for whom you created the %USERDOMAIN% variable would have the same home folder location. Answer C is incorrect because manually creating the user home directories would take the most time. Answer D is incorrect because the Administrative Wizard would not create home directories for users.

114	CREATING RANDOM INITIAL PASSWORDS

Q: *You are a Windows NT domain administrator. Your boss is concerned about password security. You have implemented password restrictions so that all users must use passwords at least five characters in length and must change their passwords often. You use upper- and lowercase characters to create the password FirstPass, and you require new users to change their password at first log on. What else can you do to better secure your domain?*

Choose the best answer:

A.   *From User Manager for Domains in the Account Policy dialog box, put a check in the User Must Logon in Order to Change Password checkbox.*

B.   *Use random initial passwords. Only tell each individual user the random password the user will use for his or her account.*

C.   *Configure the Minimum Password Age option in the Account Policy dialog box.*

D.   *Do nothing: your domain is already as secure as you can make it.*

Windows NT will force each of your users to logon to the network with a unique user name and password. If you are worried about security in your organization, you might want to consider implementing a password policy that incorporates several additional password-securing features, including the following:

- *password age*, which specifies how long a user can keep the same password

- *password uniqueness*, which specifies how many passwords Windows NT will remember so that the user cannot use a previously used password

- *minimum password length*, which specifies how many characters a user password must have

- *random initial passwords*, which generates random initial passwords that the system administrator gives the user for the user's first logon

Many network administrators accept the Windows NT default that requires all users to change their passwords at first logon. However, if the administrator has also configured the Windows NT Server so that the system requires a minimum password length, the administrator must create an initial password for the user to log on with. Many administrators will use a common password (such as *PASSWORD*) for the initial password. Doing so, however, will increase the likelihood that someone may make an unauthorized logon. Microsoft recommends that you use random initial passwords instead of a single common password. As the system administrator, you can create random initial passwords for new users (such as a series of letters and numbers) and then let only the individual users know the initial password. Remember to leave the User Must Change Password at Next Logon checkbox checked.

Answer B is the correct answer because you could use random initial passwords for new users to better secure the system. Answer A is incorrect because using the User Must Logon in Order to Change Password option will not let the administrator use the User Must Change Password at next Logon option. Answer C is incorrect because configuring a minimum password age makes the user keep a password for a variable length of time before the user can change the password. Answer D is incorrect because there are further steps that you can take to make your system more secure.

115	UNDERSTANDING BUILT-IN GROUPS

Q: You are the administrator of a large Windows NT master-domain model. You want to have a group of administrative staff members be responsible for performing system backups in all domains. All staff members who will perform the backups are from a single domain. What steps must you take to let your backup administration staff perform system backups on all domains?

Choose the best answer:

A.   Create a Backup global group to "containerize" the administrative backup staff.

B.   Create a Backup Operators local group on each machine that requires backups.

C.   Assign the Backup Operators groups rights to perform backups on all machines.

D.   Place the Backup global group that contains all backup administrative staff in the Backup Operators local group on each machine that requires backups.

There may be times when you might have to grant individuals or groups of users rights to perform system operations. You can better grant such rights if you understand Windows NT's built-in groups and their rights. To let a group of users perform system backups on several machines spanning domains, you might create a global group to containerize the group of user accounts that require back-up rights. You must create a global group to do so because there is no predefined Windows NT group that would suit your needs. After you create the global group, you would place all users you will entrust with back-up rights into the global group. Next, you would place the backup global group into the Backup Operators local group on each machine that requires backups. Backup Operators is a Windows NT built-in group with rights to back up and restore data. Table 115 lists Windows NT's built-in groups and the operating system in which you will find each group.

Group	Windows NT Server Domain Controllers	Windows NT Member Servers	Windows NT Workstations
Users	X	X	X
Administrators	X	X	X
Guests	X	X	X
Backup Operators	X	X	X
Replicator	X	X	X
Power Users		X	X
Account Operators	X		
Server Operators	X		
Print Operators	X		
Domain Users	X		
Domain Admins	X		
Domain Guests	X		
Everyone	X	X	X
Creator Owner	X	X	X
Interactive	X	X	X
Network	X	X	X

Table 115 Windows NT's built-in groups.

*Answers A and D are the correct answers because you must create the global group in which to place all backup administrative staff. You must place the Backup global group in the Backup Operators local group on each machine you must back up. **Answer B** is incorrect because the Backup Operators group is a built-in local group on all Windows NT machines. **Answer C** is incorrect because the Backup Operators group has predefined rights to perform system backups.*

116	UNDERSTANDING GROUP STRATEGIES

Q: *You should place users into local groups. You should place local groups into global groups. You should grant global groups permissions to resources.*

True or False?

You have learned in several previous Tips how administrators place users into global groups and global groups into local groups and assign local groups permissions to resources. You should remember that although it is possible for a system administrator to assign resource permissions to a global group, Microsoft does not recommend or discuss it in its documentation. The Windows NT exams will test you extensively on group administration issues. You will answer many of the group administration questions using the Microsoft relationship principals of *user into global,* and *global into local.* Group strategies—that is, techniques for effectively managing resources using groups—are actually quite simple to understand. It is much easier, more efficient, and generally more secure, for a system administrator to assign access permissions for a specific resource to a group of users rather than to each individual user account that needs access. As you have learned, Windows NT uses two types of groups: global groups and local groups. Local groups can contain users and global groups that a local domain or any trusted domain defines. Administrators can assign resource access permissions to a local group and users can thereafter gain access to the resource because of their group memberships.

On the other hand, global groups can contain only users from the domain within which the administrator defines the global group. Global groups cannot contain other global groups, local groups, or user accounts from other domains. The major difference between local and global groups is that an administrator can assign permissions to local groups only on the local machine, while an administrator can place global groups into local groups anywhere in the network.

As a general rule, you, as an administrator should assign users to global groups that define the users' functions. For example, suppose you have a Sales Department. All sales people will probably access the same network resources (for example, client databases and company product information). You should, therefore, group all the sales people together in a global group named Sales. You can then assign the Sales global group membership to any local group that has access to resources the sales staff wants—such as the client databases, proposal printers, and so on. Table 116 shows the differences between global and local groups.

Function	Local Groups	Global Groups
Administrator can use to group users	X	X
Can contain local groups		
Can contain global groups	X	
Can contain users from other domains	X	
Will grant permissions to resources	X	
Administrator can use domain wide		X
Administrator can use across trusts		X

Table 116 Understanding the differences between global and local groups.

*The correct answer is **False** because you should place users into global groups, global groups into local groups, and you should assign local groups permissions to resources.*

Q: *You are training an administrator from your company's New York office. The New York administrator tells you that he has noticed something interesting in User Manager for Domains. In the Groups dialog box within User Properties, there is a Set Primary Group button. The New York administrator wants to know what the Set Primary Group button does. What would you tell the New York administrator?*

Choose the best answer:

A.   *The Primary Group establishes an order in which Windows NT will look for permissions to resources.*

B.   *Although Windows NT requires each user account to have a Primary Group, only Macintosh computer users will use the Primary Group setting.*

C.   *An administrator can set a Primary Group to make it easier to group users with similar job functions.*

D.   *You have to use the Primary Groups only when you operate in mixed environments where there are Novell NetWare clients.*

A big part of Windows NT's appeal is Windows NT's ability to fuse mixed networking environments into one network, which lets many administrators upgrade to Windows NT without eliminating legacy systems in their organization. Microsoft refers to the practice of using dissimilar network operating systems as *heterogeneous networking*. Many network administrators will have heterogeneous networking environments that consist of Novell, Unix, or even Macintosh computers in the same network with Windows NT machines. Microsoft has provided many tools—such as specific clients for Windows NT servers that run on Macintosh computers, utilities to access Novell File and Print Services, and more—to facilitate Windows NT operating in heterogeneous networking environments. You will learn about many of the Microsoft Windows NT utilities for heterogeneous networking in upcoming Tips.

Microsoft has built into Windows NT many of the features that let Windows NT connect dissimilar networks. One example of a built-in heterogeneous networking feature is the Primary Group. An administrator can find the Primary Group in every user's account properties. Windows NT requires every user to have a Primary Group (a special type of global group), although Windows NT will use the Primary Group only when Macintosh clients connect to Windows NT Servers.

As you will learn in later Tips, to make a Windows NT server computer available to Macintosh client computers, you must create Macintosh Accessible Volumes on the Windows NT server, which the Macintosh clients will access as shared folders. Macintosh Accessible Volumes on a Windows NT Server have permissions similar to regular shared folders. Windows NT configures Macintosh resource permissions in a way that Macintosh client machines expect to see them—which is not the way that Windows NT normally grants permissions.

To "sidestep" the permissions issue, part of Windows NT's Macintosh compatibility is Windows NT's use of Primary Groups. An administrator will configure permissions on Macintosh resources so that three groups, Everyone, Owner, and Primary Group, will have access to the resource. Everyone is all users in the network, Owner is the user who created the object, and Primary Group is the Primary Group set for each user. You will learn more about Macintosh clients in Windows NT networks in Tips 420 through 422.

To set a Primary Group that your Macintosh computers will use, perform the following steps:

1. Select the Start menu Programs option Administrative Tools group. Within the Administrative Tools group, select the User Manager for Domains program.

2. Within User Manager for Domains, open the Properties of the user or users for whom you want to set a Primary Group. In the Properties dialog box, click your mouse on the Groups button. User Manager for Domains will open the Group Memberships dialog box, as shown in Figure 117.

3. Within the Group Memberships dialog box, select the group you want to make the Primary Group. Click your mouse on the Set button. User Manager for Domains will set the Primary Group.

4. Close the Group Memberships dialog box.

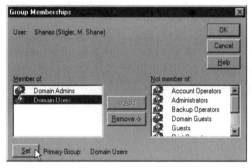

Figure 117 The Group Memberships dialog box.

Answer B is the correct answer because Windows NT requires a Primary Group for each user account, although Windows NT will use the Primary Group only for Macintosh clients that need access to Macintosh resources on Windows NT Servers. Answer A is incorrect because Windows NT does not use group orders when it determines resource access permissions. Answer C is incorrect because an administrator would use global groups to "containerize" users with similar job duties. Answer D is incorrect because Novell NetWare clients will not use the Primary Group setting.

118   UNDERSTANDING THE IMPLICATIONS OF DELETING A GROUP

Q: *You have deleted the Sales global group from your Windows NT Primary Domain Controller (PDC). The Sales group contained 20 users, and was assigned permissions to several resources. If you create another group with the same name, which of the following answers would be true?*

Select two answers:

     A.   *You must recreate all user accounts that were part of the original group.*

     B.   *You must assign membership to the new Sales group, all user accounts that were part of the original group.*

     C.   *You must reassign permissions to all resources the original Sales group had, so the new Sales group has access to them.*

     D.   *You could not create another group of the same name until you removed the original group from the Recycle Bin.*

     E.   *No administrative intervention is required. Creating the new group of the same name will fix all the problems.*

In Tip 46, you learned about security identification numbers (SIDs). A security identification number represents each object in Windows NT. If an administrator creates a new user or group, Windows NT generates a security identification number for that object. If the administrator creates a user or group using the name of a previously deleted user or group, the new user or group will have a different SID than did the original.

Before it allows access to a resource, Windows NT compares the security identification numbers that represent a user and all groups a user belongs to with the permissions on a resource. If an administrator deletes a user account, the system irrevocably discards the security identification number that represents the account. If the administrator creates a new account for the deleted user, the security identification number that represents the new account will not match the original. You will then have to reassign resources to which the user had access before you deleted the original account so the user has access to them again.

Before you delete a group, you should consider whether you might want the group for future use. If you delete a group, you will lose only the security identification number of the group itself. All members of a group are separate objects represented with their own representative security identification numbers. You might have to assign memberships to new or existing global groups when you delete a group that contains users so the users can still have resource access.

Answers B and C are correct because you would have to assign membership to the new Sales group to all users that were members of the original Sales group. You would have to reassign permissions to all resources the original Sales group had access to so that the new Sales group has permissions to the resources. Answer A is incorrect because when you delete groups, you do not also delete the group members. Answer D is incorrect because the system will not send deleted users and groups to the Recycle Bin. Answer E is incorrect because administrative intervention is required—creating a new group with the same name will not solve the problem.

119 INTRODUCTION TO DOMAIN CONTROLLERS

Q: *Any Windows NT Server can validate a user log-on request.*

True or False?

In several previous Tips, you have seen the term domain controller. A *domain controller*, loosely, is a Windows NT server that maintains information about users, and independently validates a user's access to any resource on the network from the server. It is a crucial part of the Windows NT security model. In fact, the very heart of a Windows NT network is the domain concept. In this Tip, you will learn just the basic domain concept and the function of a domain controller. In upcoming Tips, you will learn more about the components that comprise a domain and how they work.

In Tip 58, you learned that the way users log on to Windows NT is similar to a bank's ATM machine. The ATM machine itself does not validate the user's request to remove money. Rather, it sends the information to a central computer, which verifies the user's account and available funds. Similarly, in most networks, the local computer does not validate the user's request to logon. Instead, the local computer passes on the log-on request to another computer that can validate the request. In Windows NT, the computer that can validate a user's log-on request is called a domain controller.

There are two types of domain controllers in Windows NT. The first type of domain controller is the *primary domain controller* (PDC). Only a Windows NT Server can be a primary domain controller. The first Windows NT Server the administrator installs on a new network is generally the primary domain controller. There can be only one primary domain controller in each Windows NT domain. The primary domain controller has the active *Directory Database*. Any new user, group, or computer accounts the administrator creates will result in new entries within the primary domain controller's Directory Database. A primary domain controller by itself actually constitutes a domain, although a domain controller without clients would serve no purpose.

The other type of domain controller is the *backup domain controller* (BDC). You can have up to 2,000 backup domain controllers in a single Windows NT domain (which is probably more than you will ever need). Although you do not have to have a backup domain controller to have a domain, Microsoft recommends always having at least one backup domain controller. Only a Windows NT Server can be a backup domain controller. Backup domain controllers store a copy of the Directory Database which the backup domain controller receives from the primary domain controller. You will learn in Tip 124 how the Directory Databases of the primary domain controller and the backup domain controller are synchronized.

Administrators place backup domain controllers in geographical locations where there are a significant number of network users. When a user logs on to the domain, any domain controller (primary or backup) can validate the log-on request. If you have a domain controller close to the users, log-on requests will not have to pass through wide area network (WAN) links, which can be quite slow, or create additional network traffic by needing to all access the same machine.

When you place backup domain controllers, you should take into consideration that although you will decrease WAN network traffic for user logon validation, you may increase network traffic to handle the backup domain controllers updating their Directory Databases with the primary domain controllers. Much of the Windows NT Server in the Enterprise section of this book will examine the Directory Database synchronization process and synchronization issues—for now, it is enough to understand that the backup domain controllers will receive regular updates of the Directory Database from the primary domain controller.

*The correct answer is **False** because only a Windows NT Server domain controller can validate a user's log-on request.*

120   **INTRODUCTION TO MEMBER SERVERS**

Q: *You are a Windows NT domain administrator. You have just received a new server machine that will act as the company's new Microsoft SQL Server. How should you install Windows NT?*

Choose the best answer:

    A.   *As a Windows NT Primary Domain Controller.*

    B.   *As a Windows NT Backup Domain Controller.*

    C.   *As a Windows NT Member Server.*

    D.   *Windows NT installation is not required; SQL Server is its own operating system.*

To make a Windows NT Server a domain controller, you must specify the domain controller option at system installation. In turn, Windows NT Member Servers are the same way. You cannot change a domain controller to a Member Server after system installation. The major difference between a Windows NT domain controller and a Windows NT Member Server is that Member Servers will not validate domain user's log-on requests. Because it does not have to validate user's log-on requests, the server is free to perform client–server application processes. If you plan to implement a Microsoft SQL Server, Microsoft Internet Information Server, or Microsoft Exchange Server, you might want to consider making the server a Member Server, because the server will not lose cycles responding to log-on requests, but will instead focus its processing on performing activities specific to its purpose. Windows NT domain controllers make adequate file and print servers, but for anything more extensive you should consider using a Member Server.

One thing to watch for when you take your Microsoft Windows NT exams is that Microsoft will use three terms to describe a Member Server. The first term, *Member Server,* is obvious. Another term Microsoft will use to describe Member Servers is *Application Server.* Typically, you will see *Application Server* when Microsoft is tying the question to another server installation, such as *SQL Server*. You will also see Microsoft describe a Member Server as a *Server Only*. Be careful when you take your tests, because Member Server, Application Server, and Server Only all mean the same thing on Microsoft exams.

*The correct answer is **Answer C** because you should install Windows NT as a Member Server. **Answers A, B**, and **D** are all incorrect because the question clearly states that a domain already exists. Because you can validate the user by the existing domain controllers, you could better use the new server as a Member Server than as a domain controller.*

121   PROMOTING A BACKUP DOMAIN CONTROLLER

Q: *Your Windows NT primary domain controller is going into the repair shop for upgrades. The primary domain controller is also a file and print server. What should you do, if anything, before sending the server into the shop?*

Choose the best answers:

A.   *Promote a Windows NT backup domain controller to the role of a primary domain controller.*

B.   *Notify users that the primary domain controller will be down and they may not be able to access some network resources.*

C.   *Pause the Netlogon service on each backup domain controller so that the operating system will not send the users' log-on request to the primary domain controller.*

D.   *Reroute print jobs from Print Manager to another print server.*

There may be times when you must take a server off line. If the server that you are taking off line is the Windows NT primary domain controller, you might want to consider the dangers in doing so. The primary domain controller is the only machine with an active copy of the Directory Database. If you want to create new users, groups, or computers while the server is out of commission, you will not be able to. To lessen these dangers, Microsoft built into the Server Manager program the ability to *promote* a backup domain controller to the role of a primary domain controller. When you promote a backup domain controller, it becomes the primary domain controller, and its copy of the Directory Database becomes the active copy.

If you promote a backup domain controller to a primary domain controller, the primary domain controller will demote itself to the role of a backup domain controller. You can then make changes to the Directory Database while the original primary domain controller is off line. When the original primary domain controller comes back online, you can promote the original primary domain controller (which is now a backup domain controller) to the role of a primary domain controller and your domain controllers will be back in their original roles. To promote a backup domain controller to the role of a primary domain controller, perform the following steps:

1. Select the Start menu Programs option Administrative Tools group. Within the Administrative Tools group, select the Server Manager program. Windows NT will open Server Manager.

2. Within Server Manager, select the backup domain controller you want to make a primary domain controller. Select the Computer menu Promote to Primary Domain Controller option. Server Manager will display a warning message.

3. Within the warning message dialog box, click your mouse on the Yes button. Server Manager will start the promotion process.

4. After the promotion completes, close Server Manager.

Figure 121 shows the Server Manager program's Computer menu.

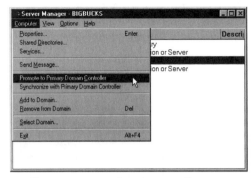

Figure 121 *Promoting a backup domain controller to a primary domain controller.*

*The correct answers are **Answers A and B**. If a Windows NT primary domain controller were going off line for an extended time period, you would promote a backup domain controller to the role of a primary domain controller. Additionally, you would notify users the original primary domain controller was down. **Answer C** is incorrect because if you pause the Netlogon service, you would render the backup domain controller useless. Users could not log on at all. **Answer D** is incorrect because if the original primary domain controller were the print server, all users would point to the missing server for printer re-routing.*

122 DEMOTING A PRIMARY DOMAIN CONTROLLER TO A BACKUP DOMAIN CONTROLLER

Q: *Your boss learns that to install Windows NT as a backup domain controller, he must be connected to the primary domain controller or the installation will fail. Your boss comes up with a plan to do an off-site installation of a Windows NT Server and then import the server into an existing Windows NT domain. Your boss' plan is to install Windows NT Server as a primary domain controller, name the domain the same as the existing domain, and then transport the primary domain controller to the existing network. Your boss wants to then connect the server to the network and demote the new primary domain controller to the role of a backup domain controller. Will your boss' plan work and why (or why not)?*

Choose the best answers:

A. *Yes, the plan will work. After the new Windows NT Server installed as a primary domain controller is connected to the network, it will receive an error message that states there are two primary domain controllers on the network. You can then demote the second primary domain controller to a backup domain controller and the backup domain controller will synchronize with the real primary domain controller.*

B. *No, the plan will not work. When the new primary domain controller connects to the existing network, you will receive an error message stating that there are two primary domain controllers for the same domain. However, the two domain controllers will not have the same security identification number representing the domain, even though they share the same domain name. You will have to reinstall Windows NT.*

C. *Yes, the plan will work. However, Windows NT will automatically demote the second primary domain controller to the role of a backup domain controller and then synchronize the domain controllers.*

D. *No, the plan will not work. As soon as the system detects the second primary domain controller, the two primary domain controllers will negotiate for dominance. The system will pause and shut down both domain controllers' networking service.*

In Tip 121, you learned how you can promote Windows NT Server backup domain controllers within their domains. In some circumstances, you will want to demote a primary domain controller to the role of a backup domain controller—such as, for example, when the previous primary domain controller returns from the shop. You can demote a primary domain controller in Server Manager. However, the Demote to Backup Domain Controller option only appears in rare situations.

For example, suppose you have a Windows NT Server primary domain controller that unexpectedly goes off line. You send the primary domain controller in for repairs. During the period of time when the primary domain controller is gone, you have promoted a backup domain controller to the role of a primary domain controller. When the original primary domain controller comes back online, you will have two primary domain controllers. Because the primary domain controllers share the same domain security identification numbers, Windows NT understands these two machines are part of the same domain, and will display the Demote to Backup Domain Controller option in Server Manager when you select the most recently booted primary domain controller in the computer list.

An administrator cannot install a primary domain controller with the same domain name as an existing domain and then connect the primary domain controller to the existing domain and demote it. The two domains will have different security identification numbers that represent the domains.

When a primary domain controller comes on-line in a domain where a backup domain controller has been promoted, the most recently booted primary domain controller will have its *Netlogon* service paused so it cannot validate users' log-on requests.

*The correct answer is **Answer B** because the domain will have different security identification numbers. **Answer A** is incorrect because you cannot migrate a domain controller from another domain without reinstalling Windows NT Server. **Answer C** is incorrect because Windows NT will not automatically promote domain controllers. **Answer D** is incorrect because even if the primary domain controller were originally from the same domain, the first primary domain controller up will remain up and unaffected by the second primary domain controller being booted.*

123   PROMOTING A MEMBER SERVER TO A DOMAIN CONTROLLER

Q: What is the easiest way to promote a Member Server to a domain controller?

Choose the best answer:

    A.   Within Server Manager, select the Member Server and from the Computer menu, click your mouse on the Promote to Backup Domain Controller option.

    B.   Use the Windows NT Emergency Repair Disk and select the Promote to Domain Controller option.

    C.   From the Command prompt, type Convert D: /fs:NTFS.

    D.   You cannot promote a Member Server to a domain controller.

When you install Windows NT Server, the system prompts you for an installation server type of either domain controller or Member Server. After installation you cannot migrate from one type to the other. In other words, a Windows NT Server domain controller cannot become a Windows NT Member Server if you do not reinstall Windows NT. Likewise, a Window NT Member Server cannot become a Windows NT Server domain controller without reinstallation. On your MCSE exams, you will encounter questions about promoting Member Servers to domain controllers, so be sure to remember that Windows NT Server domain controllers cannot become Member Servers, and Member Servers cannot become domain controllers.

*The correct answer is **Answer D** because a Member Server cannot become a Windows NT domain controller. **Answers A, B,** and C are all wrong because each describes a non-existent technique for promoting a Member Server to a domain controller.*

124	SYNCHRONIZING DOMAIN CONTROLLERS

Q: *You are a Windows NT domain administrator. You have offices in Los Angeles, Las Vegas, and New York. Your company's primary domain controller is in Los Angeles. You have backup domain controllers in Las Vegas and New York. You create a user account for a new user who will work in the New York office. After you create the new account and tell the new user to log on, the computer gives the user an error message stating that the user's account cannot be validated and the user name or password is incorrect. You check the user name and password and find that you gave the correct information to the user. The user tries again and receives the same message. What is the most probable cause of the log-on error?*

Choose the correct answer:

> A.   *A corrupt Directory Database on the primary domain controller.*
>
> B.   *A corrupt Directory Database on the backup domain controller.*
>
> C.   *The user account is disabled.*
>
> D.   *The backup domain controller in New York has not yet synchronized with the primary domain controller in Los Angeles.*

In a Windows NT domain there is only one active Directory Database. When an administrator creates a new account, the system actually creates the account in the primary domain controller's Directory Database. After Windows NT places the new account in the primary domain controller's Directory Database, the primary domain controller will notify all backup domain controllers that a change has occurred in the master Directory Database. All backup domain controllers will then contact the primary domain controller and request the changes. The process of updating the backup domain controllers' Directory Databases is *Directory Synchronization.* Simply put, directory synchronization is the copying of the Directory Database from the primary domain controller to each backup domain controller on the network.

In general, all Windows NT Server backup domain controllers will manage their own synchronization with the primary domain controller. However, there may be times when you want to force a synchronization event. In this Tip's question, the problem is that the backup domain controller located where the user is, in New York, has not synchronized with the primary domain controller in Los Angeles. In a case where a user is waiting for a synchronization event to occur prior to being able to log on, you would probably force the synchronization event. To force a synchronization event, perform the following steps:

> 1.   Click your mouse on Start menu Programs option Administrative Tools group. Within the Administrative Tools group, select the Server Manager option. Windows NT will open Server Manager.
>
> 2.   Within Server Manager, select the backup domain controller that you want to synchronize with the primary domain controller. Select the Computer menu Synchronize with Primary Domain Controller option. (If you select the primary domain controller before you open the Computer menu, you will see the Synchronize Entire Domain option, which is otherwise not enabled). Server Manager will display the message box "Synchronizing the domain could take several minutes."
>
> 3.   Within the Synchronizing the domain could take several minutes message box, click your mouse on the Yes button. Server Manager will perform domain controller synchronization.

Figure 124 shows the Server Manager Computer menu with the Synchronize Entire Domain option selected.

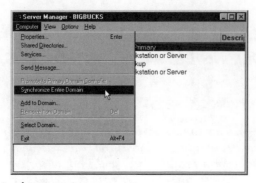

Figure 124 *Selecting the Synchronize entire domain option.*

*The correct answer is **Answer D** because the Directory Database on the backup domain controller has not synchronized with the primary domain controller. **Answers A** and **B** are incorrect because, although a corrupt Directory Database could cause this problem, it is an unlikely source of the problem. **Answer C** is incorrect because a disabled user account will generate a different message.*

125   INTRODUCTION TO NETWORK SHARED RESOURCES

Q: *You want to access a folder named Data. You know the Data folder is on a Windows NT Server named Server1. When you browse Server1 using Network Neighborhood, you do not see the Data folder. Why is the Data folder not showing up in Server1's list of resources?*

Choose the correct answer:

     A.   *The Data folder is read-only.*

     B.   *You must refresh the list of Server1's resources.*

     C.   *No user has shared the Data folder.*

     D.   *Another user is using the Data folder.*

In some networking environments, the system administrator must make network volumes that network clients can see. In Microsoft networking, any Windows for Workgroups or later Microsoft operating system can function as a file and print server. If an administrator wants to have network users access resources on any Windows for Workgroups or later operating system, he or she has only to share the resource, such as a printer, folder, or application. Not every user can share resources on Windows NT machines. Table 125 shows which users can share folders on a Windows NT machine.

Group	Operating System
Administrators	Can share folders on any computer with Windows NT installed.
Server Operators	Can share folders only on Windows NT Server domain controllers.
Power Users	Can share folders on Windows NT Member Servers and Windows NT Workstations.

Table 125 *How different groups can share folders within Windows NT.*

Users who access shared network resources can see each server's resources within the resource list that each Microsoft machine running the Server service generates. Figure 125 shows a resource list of a computer named *Cash*.

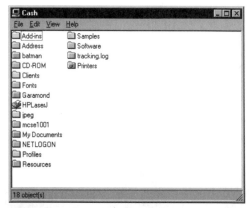

Figure 125 *List of network-shared resources on* ***Cash***.

To share a folder, perform the following steps:

1. From the Windows NT Desktop, double-click your mouse on the My Computer icon. Windows NT will open the My Computer window.
2. Within the My Computer window, double-click your mouse on the drive letter that has the folder you want to share. Windows NT will open a window that contains the folders on the drive letter you selected.
3. Within the window representing the drive you selected, identify the folder you want to share. Click your right mouse button on the folder. Windows NT will display a pop-up menu.
4. Within the pop-up menu, select the Sharing option. Windows NT will display the Sharing dialog box.
5. Within the Sharing dialog box, click your mouse on the Shared As radio button. Windows NT will highlight the Share Name field.
6. Within the *Share Name* field, type the name you want the network user to see the share as (such as *MyShare1*) in the server resource list.
7. Click your mouse on the OK button and close all open windows.

Note: *Tip 150 will discuss how to share a printer.*

*The correct answer to the question is **Answer C** because the administrator (or some other user with sufficient rights) must share a resource before network users can see the resource. **Answer A** is incorrect because a read-only folder can still be shared. Read-only is just a file or folder attribute and has nothing to do with sharing a resource. **Answer B** is incorrect because the list of resources will be refreshed every time a user opens the Network Neighborhood. **Answer D** is incorrect because a folder that has reached a maximum number of connections will display a message that states that the system has reached the maximum number of connections and you must try again later.*

126 | INTRODUCTION TO NAMING CONVENTIONS IN LAN ENVIRONMENTS

Q: *What does the universal naming convention (UNC) style pathname \\Apex\Data\Public describe?*

Choose the best answer:

  A.   *Apex is a subdirectory of the Data directory located on a computer named Public.*

  B.   *Apex is a computer name. Data is a share point and Public is a folder within the Data share.*

  C.   *Apex is a maproot, Data is a directory, and Public is a data file.*

  D.   *The universal naming convention is invalid.*

In order for users to access network resources, the resources must have names with which users can specify the resource they want. Different network operating systems use various naming conventions to make network resources accessible to clients. For example, the NetWare naming convention appears as *Servername\Volume_name:Directory\Subdirectory*. Novell NetWare uses a naming convention that specifies the file-server name, the volume the user wants to access, and the directory and subdirectory the user wants. In contrast, Microsoft uses a completely different naming convention—the universal naming convention (UNC) style. The universal naming convention style represents a logical path to a shared network resource, such as *\\ComputerName\ShareName*. The universal naming convention style uses a double backslash (\\) to denote the name of the computer you want to access. Universal naming convention-style pathnames always begin with a double backslash (\\).

After the double backslash, the user will specify a single backslash (\), which separates the computer name from the *share name*—the names an administrator gives to network resources. After the user specifies the share name, the user can use multiple single backslashes to specify subdirectory names (for subdirectories that reside beneath the share name). For example, if the user wants to access a computer named *BIGBEN*, and the share the user wants to access is named *Data*, and the subdirectory of the share is *Personal*, the universal naming convention pathname would be *\\BIGBEN\Data\Personal*.

For a network client to access a network resource, the administrator must first share the resource. When an administrator shares a network resource in a Microsoft network, the administrator must specify a share name with which users can access the resource. Users can share only folders, volumes, and printers. When a network user wants to access a specific network resource, the user must know the name of the computer on which the resource resides, as well as the share's name. In Windows NT, some applications let users browse the network in a graphical user interface (GUI) so the users can see all the names of the computers in the network and then select one computer name to see all the share names on that computer. Other Windows NT applications require the user to know the name of the computer and the share the user is accessing. Most applications that require the user to know the computer and share require the user to specify the universal naming convention-style pathname to the resource. For example, one Windows NT component that requires users to specify universal naming convention pathnames is the Map Network Drive dialog box, which Figure 126 shows.

Figure 126 The Map Network Drive dialog box.

Answer B is correct because the universal naming convention-style path always starts with the computer name, followed by the share point and any subdirectories. Answer A is incorrect because the answer does not follow the universal naming convention style. Answer C is incorrect because Microsoft networking does not use maproots. Answer D is incorrect because the universal naming convention-style path in the question is valid.

127   SETTING SHARED FOLDER PERMISSIONS

Q: *You are the administrator of a small Windows NT domain. You have one Windows NT Server domain controller. You have configured the permissions on all your Windows NT Server shares so that the Everyone group has the Read permission. One of the users in your network uses the Windows NT Server as a workstation. The user who uses the server as a workstation has opened and made changes to several files. How can this user be making changes to files to which the user has the Read permission?*

Choose the best answer:

     A.   *Administrators apply shared permissions only when users access the shares from a remote computer.*

     B.   *The user is a member of the Administrators group.*

     C.   *Local New Technology File System (NTFS) permissions may be giving users a higher access level.*

     D.   *The files the user is changing have a different permissions level.*

In Tip 126, you learned that administrators must share folders so that network users can access the folders. When an administrator shares a folder or a printer, the administrator can accept the operating system's default permissions or configure his or her own share permissions. The default share permissions for any resource in Windows NT is that all users in the Everyone group have access, and all those users have Full Control permissions. Any user who accesses the shared resources from across the network will be subject to that resource's permissions structure. Windows NT will not apply the shared permissions security structure to users who access resources locally. In Tip 134, you will learn how administrators should effectively combine shared and NTFS permissions to determine users' permissions to a resource.

Before you can set shared permissions to a resource, you must first share the resource. For example, to share a folder, perform the following steps:

     1.   From within the My Computer window or the Windows *Explorer*, double-click your mouse on the folder you want to share. Windows NT will display a pop-up menu.

     2.   Within the pop-up menu, select the Sharing option. Windows NT will display the Properties dialog box for the folder with the Sharing tab selected.

     3.   On the Sharing tab in the folder's Properties dialog box, click your mouse on the Shared As radio button. Windows NT will highlight the *Share Name* field.

     4.   Within the *Share Name* field, type a unique share name (the share name will be specific to your network. For example, if you have a share with the name *TomsShare*, and you want to create a new one in addition to the first share, you might name it *TomsShare2*). Click your mouse on OK to close the Properties dialog box and share the resource, or click your mouse on the Permission button to set user permissions.

After you share a resource, you can set shared permissions on the resource. There are only four levels of shared permissions: *No Access, Read, Change,* and *Full Control.* Table 127 shows each permission and what type of access users will have with each.

Permission	Description
No Access	Users can establish a connection to a shared resource, but the system will deny access to the resource and the users will not see any of the files or folders in the share.
Read	Users can access the share and view files and folders under the share. Users cannot add new files or folders.
Change	Users will access the resource with the same access level as Read, but they can also create files and folders, add data to existing files, change file attributes, and delete files and folders.
Full Control	Users get all the permissions of Read and Change, as well as the ability to change file permissions and take ownership of files and folders on NTFS volumes.

Table 127 *The four shared permissions levels.*

To set permissions on a shared resource, perform the following steps:

1. Within the Properties dialog box for the folder, select the Sharing tab and click your mouse on the Permissions button. Windows NT, in turn, will display the Access Through Share Permissions dialog box, as shown in Figure 127.

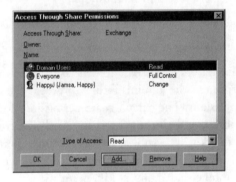

Figure 127 *The Access Through Share Permissions dialog box.*

2. Within the Access Through Share Permissions dialog box, click your mouse on the Add button. Windows NT will display the Add Users and Groups dialog box.

3. Within the Add Users and Groups dialog box, select the user or group to which you want to give permissions. Within the Type of Access drop-down menu, select the type of access you want to give the user or group. Click your mouse on the Add button. Windows NT will add the user or group name to the *Add Names* field.

4. Click your mouse on OK. Windows NT will close the Add Users and Groups dialog box.

Answer A *is correct because shared permissions will affect a user only when the user accesses a resource from a remote computer.* ***Answer B*** *is incorrect because it is unlikely the user would be a member of the Administrators group. Even if the user is an administrator, if the permissions on the share were set so the Everyone group has Read access, the system would still hold the administrator within the constraints of the permissions.* ***Answer C*** *is incorrect because when the operating system applies NTFS and shared permissions to a single folder, the most restrictive of the two will become the effective level of permissions to the resource.* ***Answer D*** *is incorrect because administrators can set share permissions only at the folder level. Files cannot have different share permissions than the folder the files are in.*

| **128** | **APPLYING USER AND GROUP FOLDER PERMISSIONS WHEN YOU ACCESS A RESOURCE** |

Q: You are the administrator of a small network with a single Windows NT Server primary domain controller. You have configured a shared network folder named Data so the shared permissions match Table 128. User SamR is a member of the Sales, Managers, and Research groups. What will the effective permissions of SamR be to the Data folder?

Group	Shared Permissions
Everyone	Read
Sales	Read
Research	Change
Managers	Full Control

Table 128 *The shared network folder Data with its groups and shared permissions.*

Choose the best answer:

A.   SamR will have the Read permission.

B.   SamR will have the Change permission

C.   SamR will have the Full Control permission

D.   SamR will have no access to the resource

Of all the Windows NT issues that will require administrative troubleshooting abilities, Windows NT permission problems are among the easiest to fix. Administrators can set permissions only at one of two levels—the share level or the file system (NTFS) level. To determine if a user has the correct permissions, the administrator must perform only two steps. First, the administrator must determine to which groups a user belongs. Second, the administrator should check the permissions previously set on the resource. To do so, the administrator will first check the share-level permissions for the resource and then check the NTFS permissions for the resource. If the user is a member of the right groups and the permissions are set correctly on the shared and NTFS levels, the user can access the server resource successfully.

You must understand how an administrator combines user and group permissions to give the user access to a resource not only to pass the exams, but also to effectively administer a Windows NT domain. When Windows NT examines the Access Token of a user requesting access to a resource, Windows NT compares the groups the user belongs to against the Windows NT security manager's list of shared permissions. Windows NT adds up the permissions to find the "most permissive" permission (that is, the one that grants the user the most control of the resource) of all the individual and group permissions. The most permissive permission becomes the resource's effective permission.

The only exception to the most permissive permission being the effective permission is when an administrator uses the No Access permission. If an administrator grants the No Access permission to an individual user or to any group to which the user belongs, No Access will be the effective permission to the resource, regardless of any other explicit permission the administrator granted.

Answer C is correct because, on the share level, the most permissive permission will be a user's effective permission. The exception to the "most permissive" rule is in the case of the No Access permission, which overrides all other permissions. Answers A, B, and D are incorrect because Read and change are not the most permissive permissions.

129   USING INTUITIVE SHARE NAMES

Q: *You are the administrator of a small Windows NT network. You want to install Windows NT Workstation on an Intel-based client machine. You know that you have shared a folder containing the Windows NT Workstation installation files on the server, but you cannot remember what share name you gave to it. You notice a share named i386 and because i386 is the folder from the Windows NT Workstation CD-ROM for Intel-based installations, you assume that i386 must be the correct share point. You connect to the i386 share and find the WINNT.EXE file and execute it. When the Windows NT installation begins, you realize that the installation is for Windows NT Server, not Workstation. Why did the share contain an unexpected installation file and what could you have done differently?*

Choose the best answer:

A.   *WINNT.EXE defaults to a server installation. You should have used WINNT.EXE with the /w option to denote a Windows NT Workstation installation.*

B.   *Although i386 is the folder from the Windows NT Workstation CD_ROM for Intel-based installations, most Microsoft BackOffice products use the same folder name. Using a more intuitive share name, such as NT4WKS, would have reduced your confusion about share names.*

C.   *When you created the folder on the server containing the i386 files, you accidentally used the Windows NT Server CD-ROM instead of the Windows NT Workstation CD-ROM. Make sure to carefully create all software installation folders.*

D.   *You were using the wrong share name—i386 is for Windows NT Server installations. You must perform Windows NT Workstation installations from the i386w folder.*

When any user with the correct permissions shares a folder, the default share name will be the same as the local machine's shared folder name. The user who shares the resource can enter a unique share name instead of accepting the default folder name. Users must make share names unique to the computers where users created the names. Users perform Windows NT Server and Windows NT Workstation installations from the i386 folder in the users' respective CD-ROMs. For example, if you were to share the installation files for NT Workstation and NT Server on the same server, and you accepted the defaults when sharing the folders, you could name the first share you created i386. However, you could not name the second share you created i386—because of Windows NT's constraints on share name duplication. You would, instead, have to assign a different name to the second share.

Using intuitive share names—that is, share names that clearly reflect the contents of the share—will make it easier for you and other users who access the resources from the network to know which specific resources are on the server. Microsoft recommends keeping your share name to a short length, no more than eight characters. If you keep your share names short, you will ensure that all Microsoft network clients, even older MS-DOS clients, can access the share. Figure 129 shows a user assigning an intuitive share name to a resource—in the Fgure's case, *WinNTWks*, which is a share that would likely contain Windows NT workstation-specific programs—such as the installation.

Answer B is correct because you install Windows NT Server and Windows NT Workstation from the i386 directory on the servers' respective CD-ROMs. You could have reduced confusion by using a more intuitive share name. Answer A is incorrect because the /w option does not exist in Windows NT installations. Answer C is incorrect because it is not the most likely cause of the problem the question described, even though you could have used the wrong CD-ROM to install the Windows NT Workstation installation files. Answer D is incorrect because i386 is the correct folder name for a Windows NT Workstation installation.

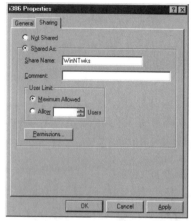

Figure 129 *Assigning an intuitive share name to a resource.*

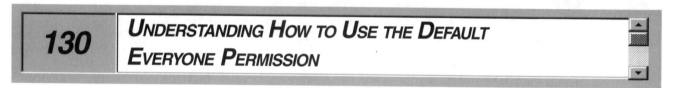

130   **UNDERSTANDING HOW TO USE THE DEFAULT EVERYONE PERMISSION**

Q: *You are the administrator of a Windows NT multiple domain model. You have configured several shared resources on a Windows NT server in the resource domain Sales, and you accepted the default permissions on all resources. You know that when an administrator establishes trust relationships, the administrator must assign users in the trusted domains permissions to resources in the trusting domain before any remote user can access the resources. After you examine the Event Viewer, you discover that users from the trusted domain have been accessing resources in the Sales domain. Why are users from the trusted domain able to access the Sales domain's resources when you have not given any trusted domain user permission to the resources?*

Choose the best answer:

    A.   *Trust relationships grant all users in the trusted domain access to all resources in the trusting domain, regardless of permissions.*

    B.   *Users in the trusted domain are logging on using accounts from the Sales domain.*

    C.   *The system logs on users from the trusted domain as guest accounts in the trusting domain.*

    D.   *The default permission in Windows NT is Everyone Full Control. The Everyone group includes users from untrusted domains.*

Many network administrators are concerned about network security. Although administrators can configure Windows NT to be very secure (and most do), the default settings for shared or NTFS permissions apply little or no security to the shared or file system resource. When an administrator shares or assigns NTFS permissions to any resource in Windows NT, the system sets the default permission as the Everyone group with Full Control permissions. The Everyone group is a built-in Windows NT group that includes all users from the local domain as well as any users from trusted domains. Because of the broad definition of the Everyone group, unless you take specific action to secure a share, every user on the local domain and any trusted domains will have complete access to the share.

Microsoft recommends removing the default Everyone group with Full Control permissions from every resource and instead assigning the Full Control permissions to the Domain Users group, which includes only users from the local domain. To prevent users from trusted domains accessing resources from other domains, you should have removed the Everyone group with Full Control permissions and instead placed the Domain Users group from the trusted domain in a local group to which you would then have assigned resource permissions.

To effectively control resource access, you will almost always want to remove the Everyone group with Full Control permissions from the resource. However, to audit resource access (that is, if you want to see who has tried to access a resource), you will want to audit the Everyone group because the Everyone group will include users from other domains. You will learn more about auditing in later Tips.

Answer D is correct because the Everyone group with Full Control permissions is the default permission in Windows NT. Answer A is incorrect because trust relationships alone do not grant any permissions. Answer B is incorrect because trusted domain users cannot log on using trusting accounts. Answer C is incorrect because Windows NT will, by default, disable the Guest account.

131 USING ADMINISTRATIVE SHARES

Q: *You are the administrator of your company's Windows NT domain. You are at a remote location and must access network diagnostic utilities that are on your server back at your office. You have a wide area network link to the location where your server is, but the folder that contains the utility is unshared. As an administrator, how can you access this utility?*

Choose the best answer:

A. *Use User Manager for Domains to share the directory that contains the network diagnostic utility. Access the network diagnostic utility share.*

B. *Use Server Manager to map a network drive to the path of the network diagnostic utility.*

C. *Use the administrative shares to map a network drive. Access the network diagnostics utility's folder through the administrative shares.*

D. *You cannot access the resource. If a resource is unshared, you cannot access it from anywhere in the network.*

There may be times when network administrators must access unshared folders. Administrators can access unshared folders because Microsoft created *administrative shares* to let administrators access resources network-wide, regardless of whether the resource is unshared or shared. Every Windows NT machine will share each volume on the local machine every time the machine boots, which ensures an administrator access to any folder on any Windows NT machine in the domain.

Users cannot see each administrative share, which administrators can access only by knowing the path to the administrative share. In addition, only users who have administrative permissions in the domain or on the local machine can access administrative shares. By default, the operating system will share each volume by naming each volume and putting the dollar ($) symbol after the name.

The dollar ($) symbol indicates that the share is hidden (that is, the *hidden* attribute is set) and therefore users cannot see the share no matter what network resources they browse with. In addition to the volume shares, Windows NT will create the *Admin$* share. The *Admin$* share is the Windows NT *%SystemRoot%* folder, usually *WINNT.*

You can use the System Policy Editor utility to stop the system from creating the administrative shares at system startup, in the event that you do not want the shares to exist at all (which you may want to do for security reasons). You will learn more about the System Policy Editor in Tip 293. Figure 131 shows the administrative shares in the Server Manager shared resources list.

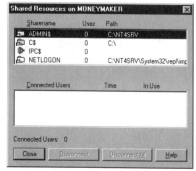

Figure 131 Shared administrative resources in the Server Manager.

Answer C *is correct because you could use the administrative share to access the network diagnostics utility.* **Answer A** *is incorrect because you cannot share folders with User Manager for Domains.* **Answer B** *is incorrect, although Server Manager will let you create shares on remote machines. However, this is not the best answer for the question.* **Answer D** *is incorrect because administrators can access unshared resources.*

132 SHARING A SERVER RESOURCE FROM A WINDOWS 95 CLIENT

Q: *How would you share a CD-ROM from a Windows 95 client on a Windows NT Server?*

Choose the best answer:

  A.   *Install the Client Administration Tools on the Windows 95 client and then use Server Manager to create the share.*

  B.   *Install the Client Administration Tools on the Windows 95 client and then use Windows Explorer to create the share.*

  C.   *Make sure the user account with which you are logging onto the domain is a member of the Administrators group. Use Windows Explorer to create the share.*

  D.   *You cannot create a share on a Windows NT Server from a Windows 95 client, regardless of what additional tools the administrator has installed.*

Most network operating systems do not let an administrator directly access the server. Administrators perform all network administration at client computers running administrative software. Windows NT Server is unique among operating systems in that it does let administrators use the server not only for network administration but also as a workstation that can locally run application software. However, Microsoft does not recommend using your Windows NT Server as a workstation, both because of the potential security risks that arise from direct access to the server and because of the performance slowdown that may arise from working on the server directly. In some large environments, you may not even want to perform network administration on your Windows NT Server because of the possible large number of network requests and the system overhead required to use your server for administration.

Microsoft includes on the Windows NT Server 4.0 CD-ROM the Administration Tools utilities, which they designed specifically for use from a client machine on the network. The Client Administration Tools let you perform the vast majority of server administration tasks from a client machine, rather than requiring direct access to the server. Microsoft includes administration tools for Windows NT Workstations and for Windows 95. If you install the Windows 95 Client Administration Tools utility, you can perform most of the administrative tasks you can perform from the actual server. To learn how to install the Windows 95 Client Administration Tools utility and to see what tools it includes, see Tip 182.

After you install the Windows 95 Client Administration Tools utility, you can, for example, share a resource located on a Windows NT machine from the Windows 95 client computer. To share a resource from the Windows 95 client computer with the Administration Tools utility installed, perform the following steps:

1. Within Windows 95, click your mouse on the Start menu Programs option. Select the Windows NT Server Tools group. Within the Windows NT Server Tools group, click your mouse on the Server Manager option. Windows 95 will open Server Manager.

2. Within Server Manager, select the Windows NT machine on which you want to share a resource. Select the Computer menu Shared Directories option. Server Manager will open the Shared Directories dialog box.

3. Click your mouse on the New Share button. Server Manager will open the New Share dialog box.

4. Within the New Share dialog box, enter in the *Share Name* field a name for the new share you want to create. Enter the path to the resource as if you were on the remote machine. (For example, if you wanted to share a Window NT Server machine's CD-ROM drive and the machine's CD-ROM drive letter was E:, you would enter the letter E in the path field.) In addition to creating shares from the client, you can also assign access permissions to the share from the client, just as you learned to do from the server in earlier Tips. Click your mouse on the OK button. Windows 95 will close the New Share dialog box.

Figure 132 shows the New Share dialog box from a Windows 95 machine with the Client Administration Tools utility installed.

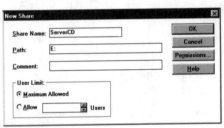

Figure 132 Sharing a resource within the New Share dialog box

Answer A is correct because you would install the Client Administration Tools utilities for the Windows 95 client and then use Server Manager to create the share. Answer B is incorrect because you cannot share remote resources from Windows 95 Explorer. Answer C is incorrect because you do not want regular users to be members of the administrators group and Windows 95 Explorer will not let you share remote resources. Answer D is incorrect because the Server Manager utility within the Administration Tools client will let you create remote shares.

133   UNDERSTANDING ACCESS CONTROL LISTS

Q: *Your boss asked you to remove a user's permissions to a database. The database is on a computer named Server1 on a share named Accounting. You configure the new permissions on the database so that the user's account is no longer listed in the permissions list. A few minutes after you set the new permissions, a manager calls you to complain that the restricted user made changes to the database after you set the new permissions. How could the user make changes to the database?*

Select all answers that apply:

A.   *The user logged on using someone else's account, which had access to the resource.*

B.   *The user had the database open when the administrator configured the new permissions.*

C.   *The user logged on to the computer where the database is and made changes locally.*

D.   *The user is a member of another group that had permissions to the resource.*

E.   *The user changed his or her password.*

In Tip 46, you learned how unique security identification numbers represent each object in Windows NT. In Tip 58, you learned how Windows NT uses Access Tokens to compare a user's personal security identification number and the security identification number for each group the user is a member of against a resource's permissions. In this Tip, you will learn that Windows NT stores resource permissions in objects called *access control lists (ACL)*. An access control list will contain all groups and individual user accounts that have permissions to a resource. Each resource has its own access control list with specific permissions to a resource. When a user logs on to a Windows NT domain, Windows NT issues the user an Access Token. The Access Token contains the security identification number that represents the user, as well as the security identification number for each group the user is a member of. Windows NT will use the Access Token by comparing the contents of the Access Token against the access control list for each object the user requests access to. Each object's access control list will contain the individual permissions an administrator has set for the specific resource. The comparison process ensures that only authorized users can access a resource.

After Windows NT checks a user's Access Token against a resource's access control list, the user can open the resource. While the user has an open file handle to a resource, the system does not have to again validate the user for access to the resource. Therefore, if an administrator changes a resource's permissions, Windows NT will not hold users who have the resource open at the time of the change within the new permissions' constraints until the user releases the object and establishes another connection to the resource. For this reason, if you make changes to resources during the business day, you may want to disconnect your users from the resource to which you will make permissions changes and then let the users reconnect to the resources.

Answer A is correct because if the user logged on to the system using an account different from his or her own, the user might have a higher access level than he or she should. Answer B is correct because if the user had the database open at the time you changed the permissions, the user would have no change in access until the user disconnected from and then reconnected to the resource. Answer C is incorrect because you can set permissions on an individual file, such as a database, only at the NTFS level and NTFS permissions are restrictive, even at the local machine. Answer D is correct because when you made the permission changes, you might not have realized the user was a member of another group that has access to the resource. Answer E is incorrect because changes in a user's password would have no effect on permissions you set on a resource.

134	**COMBINING SHARED AND NTFS PERMISSIONS**

Q: *You configured a user's permissions as shown in Table 134. The user's name is Happyj, who is a member of the Sales, Marketing, and Research groups. What will be Happyj's effective permissions to a resource?*

Groups	Shared Permissions	NTFS Permissions
Happyj	No permissions set	No permissions set
Sales	Read	Read
Marketing	Read	Change
Research	No permissions set	Change

Choose the best answer:

A. The user's permissions will be Read.

B. The user's permissions will be Change.

C. The user's permissions will be the "Read and Change" special permission.

D. The user will not have access to the resource.

Microsoft's Windows NT exams will test heavily on the subject of permissions; however, the exams are not the only reason you should understand NTFS and shared permissions. If you plan to become or are currently a systems administrator, you must have a strong understanding of Windows NT security to properly administer your network. In Tip 127, you learned how to set and apply share permissions. You learned that the most permissive permission will become the user's effective permission to the resource and that the exception is the No Access permission. The system will cut off any user or group with the No Access permission from any level of access to the resource. NTFS permissions work the same way that shared permissions do. Windows NT compares a user's Access Token to the access control list of the resource a user requests. Whatever permission is the most permissive will become the user's effective permission to the resource, unless the permission is No Access: the No Access permission will override any other permissions.

When a single shared folder has both NTFS permissions and shared permissions, things change somewhat. Windows NT uses the same process as before to determine the user's effective permissions. The system adds up the shared permissions and grants the accessing user the most permissive permission. Next, Windows NT examines the NTFS permissions and, again, grants the accessing user the most permissive permission. Finally, Windows NT examines the NTFS most permissive permission and the shared most permissive permission, and between the two selects the most *restrictive* permission. The most restrictive permission among the NTFS and shared permissive permissions will become the user's effective permissions to a resource.

Answer A is correct because the user's effective permission will be Read. The user belongs to all the groups in the access control list. If you compare the shared permissions, you will see that the most permissive permission is Read. Compare the NTFS permissions and you will see that the most permissive permission is Change. Between Read and Change, the most restrictive permission is Read. Read will become the user's effective permission to the resource. Answer B is incorrect because Change is a less restrictive permission than Read is. Answer C is incorrect because there is no "Read and Change" special permission in Windows NT. Answer D is incorrect because the user will have access to the resource.

---

135 TAKING OWNERSHIP OF NTFS OBJECTS

Q: *A user has just quit your company. After the user has left, your boss realizes that several important documents are in the user's home folder. Your boss has called the user and asked for the password to the user's account. The user refused to give your boss the account password. No other copies of these documents exist. You try to access the user's home folder and receive an Access Denied message. What can you do to access the important documents?*

Select all answers that apply:

A. Copy the folder to a File Access Table volume and then access the documents.

B. Within User Manager for Domains, change the user's account password and log on and copy the documents to a folder where your boss can access them.

C. Take ownership of the user's home folder and reset permissions so your boss can access the documents.

D. You cannot access the user's home folder without the original password. Recreate the documents.

In some network environments, the network administrator will not have access to all network resources. There may be times when users leave the organization or are otherwise unavailable when an administrator needs resources the user owns. When an administrator must access resources he or she does not control, the administrator can *take ownership* of the resources. After the administrator takes ownership of a resource, the administrator cannot give the ownership back to the original owner without giving the original owner special permissions to take ownership.

All objects in Windows NT will have owners. An object's owner can set permissions or even give another user permission to take ownership. Regardless of how an administrator has configured any resource, an administrator can always take ownership of objects, such as printers, files, and folders. To take ownership of an object, perform the following steps:

1. Log on to the domain as an administrator. Using Explorer or My Computer, click your mouse on the file or folder you want to take ownership of. Windows NT will display the Quick Menu for the file or folder. From the Quick Menu select the Properties option. Windows NT will display the object's Properties dialog box.

2. Within the Properties dialog box, select the Security tab. Within the Security tab, click your mouse on the Ownership button. Windows NT will display the Ownership dialog box, as shown in Figure 135.

3. Within the Ownership dialog box, click your mouse on the Take Ownership button. Windows NT will display a dialog box asking you to confirm the change in Ownership.

4. Click your mouse on the OK button. Windows NT will change ownership to your user account.

Figure 135 *The Ownership dialog box.*

Answer B is correct because changing the user's password and logging on to the domain with the user account will let you assign new permissions to the resources the user owns. Answer C is correct because, as the administrator, you could take ownership of a user's resources. Answer A is incorrect because you cannot copy a file to which you do not have at least the Read permission. Answer D is incorrect because there are ways to access resources that users have denied administrators access to.

---

136 UNDERSTANDING NTFS PERMISSIONS

Q: NTFS permissions are only effective when a user accesses a resource from across the network.

True or False?

As you have learned in previous Tips, the New Technology File System (NTFS) is a file system, like the File Access Table (FAT) file system or IBM's OS/2 High Performance File System (HPFS). *File systems*, in general, provide a unified way to access the contents of drives and disks. No computer which supports storage media—in short, no personal computer, and very few workstation computers—is without a file system. Microsoft designed Windows NT to support both FAT and HPFS.

Microsoft originally designed FAT as a file system for floppy disks. Although FAT works well on small volumes (under 2Gb), it does have limitations that make it a poor choice for a network server. FAT supports only the Read Only,

Archive, System, and Hidden file attributes, which do not provide the file-level security most network environments require. A network administrator must be able to restrict access to specific resources on a file-by-file basis, but because FAT is unable to do so, it falls short of the standards for network operating system use. However, you will use a small FAT partition when you install Windows NT on a Reduced-Instruction Set Chip (RISC) architecture machine. To run Windows NT on a RISC-architecture machine, you will require the small FAT partition because the firmware (that is, the RISC-equivalent of PC-BIOS) that comes with most RISC computers does not support NTFS. Other than installing Windows NT on RISC computers, the only other reason you should format your volumes with FAT is for dual-boot Windows NT machines.

Note: *Neither MS-DOS nor Windows 95 can interpret NTFS volumes, so if you intend to boot either operating system, you must maintain a FAT partition for the operating system.*

Unlike FAT, NTFS lets you apply a high level of access control to specific system resources. NTFS permissions let system administrators configure which users in the network can access specific resources and to which users the system will deny access. Administrators rarely give users individual NTFS permissions—that is, the administrator will rarely assign access permissions to individuals on the network, one user at a time. Instead, administrators will create groups of individual permissions that they most often use (or use the groups Windows NT creates). In turn, administrators assign the group permissions to users and groups—letting you control a user's access with fewer steps and less repetition. Table 136.1 shows the access levels that the NTFS individual permissions for folders grant to users or groups who receive the permissions.

NTFS Permissions	Effect on Folders
Read	Group or user can display folder names, attributes, owners, and permissions.
Write	Group or user can add files and folders, change a folder's attributes, and display owner and permissions.
Execute	Group or user can display folder attributes, make changes to folders within a folder, and display owner and permissions.
Delete	Group or user can delete a folder.
Change Permissions	Group or user can change a folder's permissions.
Take Ownership	Group or user can take ownership of a folder.

Table 136.1 The effects of the NTFS individual permissions on folders.

Table 136.2 shows the access rights that the NTFS individual permissions for files grant to groups or users.

NTFS Individual Permissions	Effect on Files
Read	Group or user can display file data, attributes, owner, and permissions.
Write	Group or user can display owner and permissions, change file attributes, create data in and append data to a file.
Execute	Group or user can display file attributes, owner, and permissions and can run a file if it is an executable.
Delete	Group or user can delete a file.
Change Permissions	Group or user can change a file's permissions.
Take Ownership	Group or user can take ownership of a file.

Table 136.2 The effects of the NTFS individual permissions on files.

Although you should understand the NTFS individual permissions, you will not generally use them. Instead, you will generally use Windows NT's *standard permissions* to assign grouped permissions. Standard permissions are sets of the individual permissions administrators most often use, which Windows NT groups together to make them more easy to assign. Table 136.3 shows the NTFS standard permissions and the level of access each will provide.

NTFS Standard Permissions	Folder Permissions	File Permissions
No Access	None	None
Read	Read, Execute (RX)	Read, Execute (RX)
Change	Read, Write, Execute, Delete (RWXD)	Read, Write, Execute, Delete (RWXD)
Add	Write, Execute (WX)	N/A
Add and Read	Read, Write, Execute (RWX)	N/A
List	Read, Execute (RX)	N/A
Full Control	All	All

Table 136.3 The standard NTFS permissions.

In Table 136.3, the individual permissions are shown for the folder first and the files next. For example, in the table the Change permission shows (RWXD) as the first part of the permissions. The abbreviation (RWXD) corresponds to the individual permissions Read, Write, Execute, and Delete, and is what Windows NT will display when you select the permissions. To set NTFS standard permissions, perform the following steps:

1. Within My Computer or in Windows Explorer, select the icon for the file or folder on which you want to configure NTFS standard permissions. Click your right mouse button on file or folder. Windows NT will display a pop-up menu.

2. Within the pop-up menu select the Properties option. Windows NT will display the Properties dialog box.

3. Within the Properties dialog box, select the Security tab. Within the Security tab, click your mouse on the Permissions button. Windows NT will display the Object Permissions dialog box, as shown in Figure 136.

4. Within the Object Permissions dialog box, click your mouse on the Add button. Windows NT will display the Add Users and Groups dialog box.

5. Within the Add User and Groups dialog box, select the user or group to which you want to assign permissions. Click your mouse on the Add button. Windows NT will add the user or group to the *Add Names* field.

6. Within the Add Users and Groups dialog box, in the *Type of Access* field, select the type of access to give the user or group and then click your mouse on the OK button. Windows NT will close the Add Users and Groups dialog box.

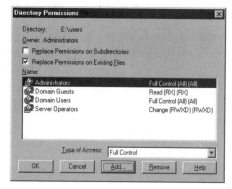

Figure 136 The NTFS Permissions dialog box.

*The answer is **False** because NTFS permissions are effective whether a user or group accesses the resource locally or from a remote computer.*

137   BETTER UNDERSTANDING THE DELETE PERMISSION

Q: *A user cannot delete a file using only the Delete permission; the user must also use the Execute permission.*

True or False?

An administrator can assign the individual NTFS permissions, or *special permissions*, to users. The individual NTFS permissions can be dangerous if an administrator misuses the permissions. For example, users can use Delete, which is an individual permission, by itself to delete files and folders. This is dangerous because, normally, users must have the Read permission to the parent folder to see any of the files and folders and to delete them from within Windows NT's graphical interface. However, if a user has the Delete permission, they can go directly to the command prompt and delete the file and folders if they know the names of the files and folders. Therefore, an administrator must be careful when assigning the standard NTFS permissions because some include the Delete permission.

*The answer is **False** because users can use the Delete permission by itself to delete files and folders.*

138   BETTER UNDERSTANDING THE NO ACCESS PERMISSION

Q: *If an administrator assigns the No Access permission to a specific resource to a group to which a user belongs, the user cannot access that resource even if the administrator explicitly granted the Full Control permission to the individual user's account.*

True or False?

As you learned in Tip 128, the No Access permission is the one exception to the rule that states that a user's effective permission to a resource will be the most permissive of the possible permissions that may apply to the user. In several Tips, you have seen how a system evaluates permissions to give the user the most permissive permission and you know that the No Access permission overrides all other permissions. If an administrator has assigned the No Access permission to any resource for a group a user belongs to, the user cannot gain any level of access to the resource.

For example, suppose you are the administrator of a Windows NT domain. You do not want any sales people at your company to access your research database. However, if you assign the Sales group the No Access permission, you might restrict users who should have access to other resources. If you restrict all Sales group members, including the sales manager, who should have access to the research database, the sales manager would not be able to gain access to the research database, regardless of any other groups the sales manager belongs to.

Note: Never assign the Everyone group the No Access permission to any resource. You will deny everyone (including yourself) access to the resource.

The answer is **True** *because if an administrator grants any user in a group the No Access permission, the user will have no access to that resource, regardless of other permissions the user does have.*

139   **BETTER UNDERSTANDING THE LIST PERMISSION**

Q: *Windows NT will let a user who has the List permission perform what functions?*

Choose the best answer:

     A.   *Add files and folders and open and read existing files.*

     B.   *Add files and folders.*

     C.   *View folders only in the folder where the user has the list permission.*

     D.   *View files and folders in the folder where the user has the list permission.*

The List permission will let users view the contents of the folder to which they have List permission. An administrator will find the List permission useful in situations where an individual user or a group can verify the existence of files or folders but cannot add to the folders, make changes to existing files or folders, or even read the contents of the existing files or folders. The List permission includes the individual permissions Read and Execute for the folder, and no file permissions. The individual permissions let users read the files to view the main folder contents, but do not grant other access to the files. Therefore, users will not have any access to the files or folders within the main folder.

Answer D *is correct because users can view the names of the files and folders, but cannot make any changes to or even read the contents of the files or folders.* **Answer A** *is incorrect because permission to add files and folders and open and read existing files are not part of the List permissions.* **Answer B** *is incorrect because the List permission does not grant the right to add files and folders.* **Answer C** *is incorrect because the List permission lets users view both files and folders.*

140   **BETTER UNDERSTANDING THE READ, ADD, AND ADD AND READ PERMISSIONS**

Q: *You want to grant a user a permission to a folder that will let the user copy files into the folder but not view the contents, including the files the user copies into the folder. Which NTFS permission should you assign the user?*

Choose the best answer:

     A.   *Add*

     B.   *Add and Read*

     C.   *Read*

     D.   *List*

As you learned in Tip 139, you should use the List permission if you want to assign a permission that will let users view the names of, but not change the contents of, files and folders in a folder. You might, however, want to grant users permissions that will let the users view the names of and copy or create the files and folders in a folder. To do so, you can use several standard NTFS permissions Windows NT provides that will let users have the type of access they require.

The NTFS standard permission Read lets users access files or folders, but only to view the contents. If a user with the Read permission opens a folder, the user can see the names of all files and folders the folder contains for which the user has the Read permission. In addition, the user can open any file or folder and view the file or folder's contents. The user cannot, however, add files or folders or make changes to any files or folders under the folder for which the user has the Read permission.

The NTFS standard permission Add let users add files or folders in the folder to which the users have the Add permission. Administrators can apply the Add permission only to folders. A user with the Add permission cannot view, make changes to, or copy any files or folders, even files and folders the user has created. An administrator might use the Add permission in situations where certain users must be able to add confidential documents to a primary storage folder that contains other confidential documents.

The NTFS standard permission Add and Read lets users perform all the same tasks as the Read permission, but with the added permissions of the Add permission. Like the Add permission, administrators can apply the Add and Read permission only to folders. A user with the Add and Read permission can view the contents of all files and folders and can add files and folders to the folder for which the user has the Add and Read permission. Windows NT will not let a user with the Add and Read permission make any changes to existing files or folders. An administrator would use the Add and Read permission much like the Add permission; that is, to let users add to folders but to restrict users' ability to change the information in folders. An administrator can use the Add and Read permission when a user must add files and folders to a folder but should not make changes to any of the files or folders.

Answer A is correct because the Add permission will let the user copy or create files or folders in the folder for which the user has the Add permission. Answer B is incorrect because the Add and Read permission would let the user view the folder's contents. Answer C is incorrect because the Read permission would let the user view the folder's contents but would not let the user create or copy any files or folders into the folder for which the user has the Read permission. Answer D is incorrect because the List permission would let the user view only the names of the contents of the folder for which the user has the List permission.

141 BETTER UNDERSTANDING THE CHANGE AND FULL CONTROL PERMISSIONS

Q: *If an administrator gives the Full Control permission to a user, the user can take ownership of a file or folder and assign permissions to other users.*

True or False?

As you learned in previous Tips, the default permission in Windows NT is the Everyone group with Full Control permissions. Administrators should not give every user or group the Full Control permission—because doing so will entirely defeat your security model. Full Control is the highest level of access to a resource in Windows NT that users can have. Users with the Full Control permission can read, write, execute, delete, and change permissions or even take ownership of files or folders. As an administrator, you should be careful when you assign users the Full Control permission. In fact, when you want to give a user or group Full Control, you should consider giving the user the Change permission.

Like the Full Control permission, the Change permission is quite permissive. Using the Change permission, a user can read, write, execute, and delete file or folders. However, the user cannot change permissions or take ownership of an object for which the user has the Change permission. An administrator might use the Change permission for folders such as the public folder, where users will read and possibly make changes to files or folders, but where they should not change permissions.

*The answer is **True** because any user who has the Full Control permission can take ownership and even change the permissions on a file or folder.*

142   UNDERSTANDING SPECIAL ACCESS PERMISSIONS

Q: *You are the owner of a database at your company and you are the only one who administers the database. You will soon transfer to another company location, so you must transfer ownership of the database to another user. How do you transfer the ownership of a database if you are only one who has any permissions to it?*

Choose the best answer:

   A.   *Assign the Full Control permission to the user to whom you want to transfer ownership and instruct the user to take ownership of the database.*

   B.   *Assign the user the Take Ownership (O) special permission. Do not assign the user any other permissions. Instruct the user to take ownership.*

   C.   *Assign the user the Change permission and instruct the user to take ownership.*

   D.   *You cannot transfer ownership. You must have the user create a database and then give your permissions to the new database. You will then transfer all the data in the old database to the new database.*

You learned in Tip 136 that although an administrator typically assigns the NTFS standard permissions, an administrator can also assign NTFS individual (special) access permissions. As an administrator, you might want to give a user permission to take ownership of a file or folder without assigning any other permissions. If you assign the Take Ownership special permission to a user, the user can take ownership. Without any other permissions granted, the user would then have to take ownership of a file or folder, and then reset the permissions for the new user's access to even view the file or folder.

Administrators can assign special permissions at the file or folder level. When you examine a user's NTFS permissions, you will see two areas of information, each with parentheses around it. The parentheses contain the NTFS special permissions. The first information area contains the permissions to the folder. The second information area contains the permissions for the files the folder contains. For example, the information areas (RWX)(RX) mean, respectively, that the folder permissions are Read, Write, and Execute and the file permissions are Read and Execute. The folder-level permissions will let the user add files or folders and open and view the existing files and folders. The file-level permissions will let the user read the contents of the files in the folder. To assign special permissions to a resource, perform the following steps:

   1.   Within Windows Explorer or the My Computer window, click your right mouse button the file or folder for which you want to assign NTFS permissions. Windows NT will display a pop-up menu.

   2.   Within the pop-up menu, select the Properties option. Windows NT will display the Properties dialog box.

   3.   Within the Properties dialog box, select the Security tab. In the Security tab click your mouse on the Permissions button. Windows NT will display the File or Folder Permissions dialog box.

   4.   Within the File or Folder Permissions dialog box, add the user or group or select the existing user or group to which you want to assign the special permissions. In the Type of Access drop-down list, select Special Directory Access or Special File Access. Windows NT will display either the Special Directory Access or Special File Access dialog box (depending on which one you selected). Figure 142 shows the Special Directory Access dialog box.

5. Within the Special Access dialog box, select the special access permissions you want to grant to the user or group. Click your mouse on the OK button. Windows NT will close the Special Permissions dialog box.

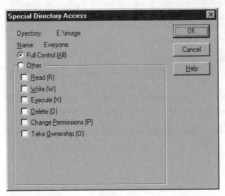

Figure 142 Selecting the individual permissions you will grant to a user or group.

Answer B is correct because by giving the user the Take Ownership (O) special permission, the user cannot do anything with the resource until the user takes ownership and reassigns permissions, thereby giving the user permissions to the resource. **Answer A** is incorrect because if you give the user the Full Control permission, the user would not have to take ownership of the resource to view or change its contents. **Answer C** is incorrect because the user cannot take ownership with the Change permission. **Answer D** is incorrect because you can transfer ownership using the Take Ownership special permission.

143 COPYING AND MOVING NTFS FILES AND FOLDERS

Q: *You have a database on an NTFS volume in the C:\Data folder, with the permissions configured so that the Sales global group has the Full Control permissions. You want to copy the database to the C:\Sales folder, where the Sales group currently has the Read permissions. After you copy the database to the C:\Sales folder, what will be the Sales group's effective permissions to the database?*

Choose the best answer:

A. *Full Control, Windows NT will retain the permissions from the previous NTFS folder.*

B. *The Sales group will inherit the Read permission from the new parent folder.*

C. *Windows NT will reset the permissions to the default Everyone, Full Control NTFS permission.*

D. *Windows NT will reset the permissions to the Guest, Read permission.*

As you have learned, proper security in your Windows NT environment is very important. Therefore, if you do not fully understand how NTFS permissions work, you will probably experience administrative difficulties. As you have learned in previous Tips, the default NTFS permission is Everyone, Full Control. The Everyone, Full Control permission is the default only when an administrator first creates a NTFS volume. After an administrator creates a NTFS volume, the administrator could change the default permission at the volume root.

For example, if you, as an administrator, created a new NTFS volume with the drive letter *E*, drive *E* would have the default Windows NT NTFS permission of Everyone, Full Control. However, if, before you create any new folders, you change the drive *E* permissions to Domain Users, Full Control, the new default permission for all new folders would be Domain Users, Full Control.

Whenever you create a file or folder, the file or folder will automatically inherit the parent folder's (that is, the folder within which you create the file or folder) permissions. However, if you copy or move the files or folder from another folder to the NTFS folder, the NTFS permissions might not be the same as the parent folder, as you can see in Table 143.

Location	Copy	Move
Another volume	Inherits parent's permissions	Inherits parent's permissions
Same volume	Inherits parent's permissions	Retains previous folder's NTFS permissions

Table 143 Moving and copying NTFS files and folders.

Answer B is correct because the file will inherit the new parent folder's permissions. Answer A is incorrect because when you copy a file, it will inherit the permissions of the parent folder where you copy the file. Answer C is incorrect because the default NTFS permission Everyone, Full Control is only the default for new NTFS volumes. Answer D is incorrect because the Guest, Read permission would be the default permission for the folder only if that was the permission you set expressly for the folder.

144	DELETING FILES THAT HAVE THE NO ACCESS PERMISSION

Q: *You are the administrator of a Windows NT network. You have assigned the Everyone group Full Control permission to the C:\Data folder. You have configured NTFS permissions on the folders and files in C:\Data so that a user named Happyj has the No Access permission to them. When you examine the event logs, you discover that Happyj has been deleting files in the C:\Data folder. How can Happyj delete files for which Happyj has the No Access permission?*

Choose the best answer:

A.   *Administrators can give the No Access permission only to groups, not individual users.*

B.   *Windows NT lets any user with the Full Control permission to a folder delete any file in the folder, even if the user's file permissions include No Access.*

C.   *The No Access permission means that the user cannot read or write to the file, but the user can delete the file.*

D.   *The Full Control permission overrides the No Access permission.*

Microsoft appeals to a wide market audience with Windows NT because it designed Windows NT to meet the requirements of large organizations, such as the U.S. Government. For example, Windows NT meets C2-level security restrictions (the commercial-level security classification described by the U.S. government), and is also *POSIX 1.x*-compliant. *POSIX* is a standard for UNIX-type applications that the U.S. government (as well as other large, historically UNIX-based organizations) frequently uses. One aspect of the *POSIX* standard is that in certain, very specific situations, users must be able to delete files to which they usually do not have access. Visualizing this *POSIX* security policy is easier if you consider a "hard copy" example. In high-security environments, at certain times, personnel may be asked to shred documents that they are not to read, and would normally not have access to, but they are nevertheless responsible for shredding the documents.

In Windows NT, administrators or other network policy-setters may also ask users to delete documents that the user has no access permissions to. By default, the No Access permission lets users delete files, in keeping with the *POSIX* security model.

If you want to secure a folder so that users cannot delete files to which they have the No Access permission, give all the users special permissions instead of the Full Control permission. If you do so, users cannot delete any files to which they have the No Access permission.

Answer B is correct because one aspect of the POSIX standard requires that users with the Full Control permission can delete files in folders for which the users have the No Access permission. Answer A is incorrect because administrators can assign the No Access permission to users or groups. Answer C is incorrect because the No Access permission does not let the user delete the file. The user can delete the file because of the combination of the Full Control permission on the folder and the No Access permission on the file. Answer D is incorrect because the Full Control permission does not override the No Access permission.

145 UNDERSTANDING WHY CHANGED PERMISSIONS MAY NOT TAKE IMMEDIATE EFFECT

Q: *A user calls you and complains that he cannot gain access to the company client database. You ask the user's boss about the user's data requirements and learn that the user should have permissions to the database. You make the user a member of the Sales group. You previously assigned the Sales group permissions to the company client database. After you notify the user that he can now gain access to the company client database, the user calls you and complains that he still cannot gain access to the database. What could be causing the problem?*

Choose the best answer:

A.   *You must assign permissions for the Sales database directly to the user's account.*

B.   *The user must log off and then log back on to gain access to the Sales database.*

C.   *The user must wait five minutes for the server to update the permissions to the resource.*

D.   *The user is logging on using the wrong account.*

As a Windows NT administrator, you will spend a lot of your time securing the network. Therefore, you must have a thorough understanding of the log-on process and how Windows NT uses Access Tokens. If your Windows NT security knowledge is weak, a simple task such as giving a user access to a database can become a real problem.

In Tip 59, you learned about Access Tokens and how Windows NT uses them. Windows NT will generate an Access Token only when a user logs on. After the user has logged on, the system will check the Access Token against the ACL for a requested object to see if the user has any permissions. As the system administrator, you will occasionally give users permissions while the users are logged onto the Windows NT domain.

If you change permissions on a resource so that a group of which the user is a member has access to the resource, the user will then have immediate access to the resource. However, if you change a user's group memberships so the user can gain access to a resource, the user must log off and then log back on in order for Windows NT to generate a new Access Token.

Answer B is correct because the user must log off the domain and then log back on in order for Windows NT to issue the user a new Access Token. Answer A is incorrect because you should always assign permissions to groups when possible. Answer C is incorrect because resource permissions take effect immediately. Answer D is incorrect because there should only be one user account for each user in your organization.

146 — *UNDERSTANDING MICROSOFT PRINT TERMINOLOGY*

Q: *In Microsoft print terminology, the term "Printer" refers to the physical printing device.*

True or False?

Microsoft has changed some of the standard industry terminology that describes network printing processes and components. If you are coming from a NetWare background, you might have to familiarize yourself with Microsoft's new use of old terms.

In most network operating system environments, the term *Print Queue* refers to the software interface an administrator uses to perform network printer administration. In Microsoft terminology, the term Print Queue refers to the line of print jobs waiting to be printed. In most network operating system environments, the term *Printer* refers to the physical printing device. In Microsoft terminology, the term Printer describes the software interface the Windows NT administrator will use to administer the network print device. Instead of Printer (which refers to the software interface), Microsoft uses the term *Physical Print Device* to describe the piece of hardware (the printer) that handles print jobs.

The answer is **False** *because, in Microsoft terminology, the term Printer refers to the software interface, not the physical device.*

147 — *UNDERSTANDING THE NT PRINT PERMISSIONS*

Q: *You want a user to be an administrative assistant to help manage your network printers. You want the user to be able to schedule print jobs, cancel print jobs, and set priorities between users' print jobs. What NT print permission could you give the user?*

Choose the best answer:

    A.   *Print*

    B.   *Full Control*

    C.   *Manage Documents*

    D.   *Supervisor*

Network printer administration accounts for a great deal of the total administrative overhead associated with network administration. You may be an administrator for a small network where you will perform all the network administration by yourself, or you may be in a large environment where you will delegate the network administration to several people. Whether you are in a small or large Windows NT environment, you will want to have a solid understanding of Windows NT printer administration.

In several previous Tips, you have examined Windows NT's shared and NTFS permissions. In Windows NT, print permissions work in much the same way that the NTFS or shared permissions do. You even access the Permissions dialog box for printers the same way that you do for NTFS or shared permissions. In Windows NT there are four print permissions, as Table 147 shows.

Capabilities	No Access	Print	Manage Documents	Full Control
Print Documents		X	X	X
Pause, resume, restart, and cancelthe user's own print jobs		X	X	X
Connect to a printer		X	X	X
Control job settings for all documents			X	X
Pause, restart, and delete all documents.			X	X
Share a printer				X
Change printer properties				X
Delete printers				X
Change printer permissions				X

Table 147 The four Windows NT print permissions.

***Answer C** is correct because the Manage Documents permission will let the user perform all the required tasks. **Answer A** is incorrect because the Print permission will not let the user manage any other user's print jobs. **Answer B** is incorrect because the Full Control permission is too permissive. Full Control would let the user take ownership of the printer and reassign permissions. **Answer D** is incorrect because the Supervisor permission is not a Windows NT permission.*

148   SETTING PRINTER PERMISSIONS

Q: To set printer permissions, you should configure printer permissions from User Manager for Domains.

True or False?

In Tip 147, you learned about Windows NT print permissions. As an administrator, you will have to create and administer network printers. After you create printer permissions, you may choose to delegate the responsibilities for your network printer to other users. As you learned in Tip 147, the four Windows NT print permissions are No Access, Print, Manage Documents, and Full Control. You will assign the configuration of Windows NT print permissions the same way that you assign NTFS or shared permissions. To configure print permissions, perform the following steps:

1. Select the Start menu Settings groups Printers option. Windows NT will display the Printers window.

2. Within the Printers window, select the printer you want to set permissions on and click your right mouse button on the selected printer. Windows NT will display a pop-up menu. Within the pop-up menu, select the Properties option. Windows NT will display the Printer Properties dialog box.

3. Within the Printer Properties dialog box, click your mouse on the Security tab. In the Security tab, click your mouse on the Permissions button. Windows NT will display the Print Permissions dialog box, as shown in Figure 148.

4. Within the Print Permissions dialog box, click your mouse on the Add button. Windows NT will display the Add Users and Groups dialog box.

5. Within the Add User and Groups dialog box, add the user or group to which you want to give permission to use the printer and select the type of access you want to grant the user or group.

6. Click your mouse on OK. Windows NT will close the Add Users and Groups dialog box.

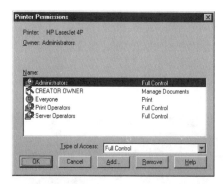

Figure 148 *The Print Permissions dialog box.*

The answer is **False** *because administrators assign Windows NT print permissions from the Printer Properties dialog box.*

149   CREATING A NEW PRINTER

Q: *Only members of the Administrators group can create and share printers.*

True or False?

As a network administrator, you will create and share printers to make them accessible to network users. Windows NT does not require any special software to create a print server: simply sharing a printer makes the computer that manages the printer a print server. (In Tip 150, you will learn how to share an existing printer.)

Creating a printer in Windows NT is actually quite easy. Windows NT uses an installation Wizard that will lead you through the process of creating the printer. Any user who is a member of the Administrators, Print Operators, Server Operators, or Power Users (on a Windows NT Workstation) groups can create and share a printer. To create a printer, perform the following steps:

1. Select the Start menu Settings group Printers option. Windows NT will open the Printers window.

2. Within the Printers window, double-click your mouse on the Add Printer icon. Windows NT will open the Add Printer Wizard dialog box.

3. Within the Add Printer dialog box, click your mouse on the Next button. The Add Printer Wizard dialog box will advance to the next dialog box in the Wizard.

4. Within the Add Printer Wizard dialog box, click your mouse on the port your printing device is on. Next, click your mouse on the Next button. The Add Printer Wizard dialog box will advance to the next dialog box in the Wizard.

5. Within the Add Printer Wizard dialog box, select the manufacturer and model of your printing device. Click your mouse on the Next button. The Add Printer Wizard dialog box will advance to the next dialog box in the Wizard.

6. Enter a name you will use to manage your printer. Choose whether or not you want this printer to be the default printer. Click your mouse on the Next button. The Add Printer Wizard dialog box will advance to the next dialog box in the Wizard.

7. Click your mouse on the radio button to indicate whether or not you want to share the printer. Click your mouse on the Next button. The Add Printer Wizard dialog box will advance to the next dialog box in the Wizard.

8. Click your mouse on the Finish button. Windows NT will now complete the printer installation.

Figure 149 shows the Add Printer Wizard main screen.

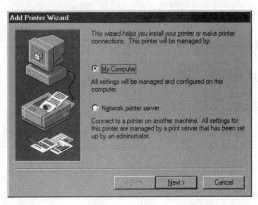

Figure 149 The Add Printer Wizard main screen.

*The answer is **False** because any user who is a member of the Administrators, Server Operators, or Print Operators groups can create and share a printer. In addition, on Windows NT Workstations, any user that is a member of the Power Users group can create and share a printer.*

150 SHARING AN EXISTING PRINTER

Q: Users can share printers only when the users first create the printer.

True or False?

In several previous Tips, you learned about Windows NT printer administration. You might at times want to share a printer and make the computer the printer manages into a print server. You can easily share a printer that you have already created. To do so, you can follow the same process you use to configure permissions and then simply click your mouse on a checkbox to share an existing printer.

When you share a printer, you should remember to keep the share name intuitive and short. An intuitive share name will let users very easily distinguish network printers. For example, if you were sharing a printer in the Sales office, you might want to name the printer Sales. You should keep your printer share names short (8 characters or fewer) so that if an MS-DOS client ever needs to access to the shared printer, that client will be able to see the printer on the network. MS-DOS clients cannot see more than 8-character names.

To share an existing printer, perform the following steps:

1. Select the Start menu Settings group Printers option. Windows NT will open the Printers window.

2. Within the Printers window, click your right mouse button on the printer you want to share. Windows NT will display a pop-up menu. Within the pop-up menu, select the Sharing option. Windows NT will display the Sharing sheet in the Printer Properties dialog box, as shown in Figure 150.

3. Within the Printer Properties dialog box, click your mouse on the Shared radio button. In the *Share Name* field, enter a unique printer name that users will see on the network. Click your mouse on the OK button. Windows NT will close the dialog box and share the printer.

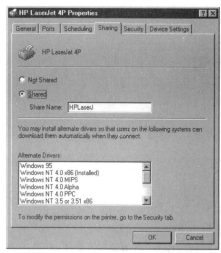

Figure 150 *The Printer Properties dialog box.*

*The answer is **False** because at any time any member of the Server Operators, Print Operators, or Administrators groups can share printers. On Windows NT Workstations, members of the Power Users group can also create and share printers.*

151 ASSIGNING FORMS TO PAPER TRAYS

Q: *You have created and shared a printer on your Windows NT Server. The printer is a HP LaserJet 4Si. The Accounting Department is complaining of having to share the printer with the rest of the network because users from other departments are accidentally printing on company checks. What could you do to eliminate the problem?*

Choose the best answer:

A.   *Have the company purchase another HP LaserJet 4Si and have everyone other than accounting staff print to the new printer.*

B.   *Configure the printer so that between certain hours only the Accounting Department has access to the printer. Instruct the accounting department to print between the configured hours.*

C.   *Assign a paper type to a specific printer tray. Put the company checks in a separate paper tray and instruct the accounting staff to print to the checks' paper tray.*

D.   *Issue a company memo instructing all network users to notify the Accounting Department before printing any documents.*

To be a Windows NT network administrator can mean performing many dissimilar tasks. For example, you might create user accounts in the morning and manage printers in the afternoon. Although there are many tasks that make up an administrator's day, a major part of network administration is managing printers. One aspect of managing printers is to make sure users are able to use the print devices without any problems. However, one consistent problem network administrators face is that users often print on preprinted documents that other users intended to use. As an example, someone from the Accounting Department at your company could place company checks in a printing device, and another user from a different department could accidentally print on the checks before the person intending to use the checks even got back to his or her desk.

There are many ways to solve such a problem. You could issue a company memo stating that all users should notify the Accounting Department when a given department is planning to print. However, companies that have tried the memo approach have had little success because users forget to notify the appropriate department when they start printing and the same problem occurs again. You could create multiple printers (the software interface) that point to one print device. You would then schedule the different printers so that between certain hours only the Accounting Department would have access to the printing device. However, the drawback to the multiple printer approach is that users who are not members of the accounting department must wait to print their documents. Finally, you could have your company purchase multiple print devices and assign the Accounting Department one of the printers. However, you might find it unnecessary (and a pointless expense) to purchase another printing device because you can simply assign different paper trays to specific departments.

Different print devices have different paper tray options. You must learn how to manage your network print device by examining the documentation that comes with your specific print device. If the printing device you manage is designed for heavy network use, the print device should have multiple paper trays you can use to assign different paper sizes or types to the different paper trays. You might have one letter-size tray and one legal-size tray, or one tray that contains plain paper and one that contains letterhead. Some print devices may not come with the additional paper trays, but you can purchase the paper trays from the print device manufacturer. Check with your network print device's manufacturer to see if it makes paper trays for your model.

Because every print device model has different paper tray configuration options, this Tip will explain how to use only one print device model. The steps you must perform to assign forms to paper trays are similar in various models. To assign forms to paper trays for a Hewlett Packard LaserJet 4P (one of the most commonly used models), perform the following steps:

1. Click your mouse on the Start menu and select the Settings submenu Printers option. Windows NT will display the Printer window.

2. Within the Printers window, click your right mouse button on the icon for the printer to which you want to assign forms. Windows NT will display the pop-up menu. Within the pop-up menu, select the Properties option. Windows NT will display the Printer Properties dialog box,.

3. Within the Printer Properties dialog box, select the Device Settings tab. Within the Device Settings tab, select the *Assign Forms to Tray* field and select the tray name to which you want to assign a paper type. Within the *Change Tray Setting* field, select the paper type. Click your mouse on the OK button. Windows NT will assign the paper to the tray and close the Printer Properties dialog box.

Answer C is correct because if you assign specific paper to printer trays, you will not have to purchase any additional parts. Answer A is incorrect because purchasing another print device would be expensive. Answer B is incorrect because configuring the print device so that only the Accounting Department would have access to it during certain hours would mean users who were not members of the Accounting Department would not be able to print at times. Answer D is incorrect because issuing a company memo, while being the most cost-effective method of solving the printer problem, would probably be ineffective in stopping users from printing on Accounting Department forms.

152 | UNDERSTANDING HOW CLIENT COMPUTERS PRINT

Q: If a Window NT Workstation prints to a shared printer on a Windows NT Server, the print job will go to a captured print port on the client side.

True or False?

Any Microsoft operating system with a shared printer constitutes a print server in a Microsoft network. In many other network operating system environments, a network administrator must install and configure special software that lets the computer that will act as the print server accept network print requests from client computers. Although any Microsoft Windows for Workgroups or later operating system can be a print server, you should only use Windows NT machines because they can handle the network print request workload much better than a Windows for Workgroups computer can.

Now that you are familiar with the Microsoft print terminology and some of the basic printing concepts, you will learn the process a network client goes through when it prints to a network printer. If you want to print a document to a network printer, you can, in almost any application, click your mouse on a Print icon in your application or use the File menu Print option. If that were all there is to network printing, a network administrator's job would be much easier. However, what goes on "behind the scenes" is a bit more complicated. To understand the complicated printing process, consider the following scenario, which assumes for simplicity that the client computer is a Windows NT Workstation and the print server is a Windows NT Server.

First, when you click your mouse on the Print icon, your computer contacts the print server, sending a message that contains a printer driver version. The print server checks your computer's printer driver version against the locally stored printer driver. If the printer driver on the server is newer than the printer driver on the client, the print server will send the newer printer driver to the client computer to update the client's local printer driver. After Windows NT establishes the proper printer driver, the client machine takes the data from the application and sends the data to the print server. The print server then formats the data for the type of print device the server manages and writes the data onto the server's hard drive. The server then waits for the print device to be ready to accept the print job. When the print device is ready to accept the print job, the server sends the data to the print device. If any step in this process fails, the print job will not print.

The process described in the previous paragraph is a bit over-simplified, however it illustrates that managing a network print server is not as simple as knowing to click your mouse on a Print icon.

Various client platforms print to Windows NT print servers in slightly different ways. For example, the following paragraph describes the ways that Microsoft platforms print to Windows NT print servers.

Windows for Workgroups and MS-DOS clients print to Windows NT print servers in the same way they would print to a locally connected print device. If you were to print to a print device attached to your local machine, the local machine would *render* (format a document for the specific print device) the print job and then send the job to your local printer port (usually *LPT1*). *Rendering* is the process of translating print commands from the application into commands the printing device can use. When managing printing for Windows 3.x and MS-DOS clients, an administrator would capture the local print port of the Windows or MS-DOS client and route the local port to the network print server. *Capturing* a printer port is the process of intercepting data sent to the port and forwarding it across the network to a remote printer. The local computer would perform all rendering and then the local operating system would send the print job to the print server. Administrators can use log-on scripts to automate the capturing of a client's printer ports. (Tip 109 describes the process of creating and using log-on scripts.)

Windows 95 and Windows NT machines do not use network print servers the same way that Windows 3.x and MS-DOS clients do. You must never capture a printer port for Windows NT or Windows 95 clients (unless you intend to print from an MS-DOS application). A captured printer port on a Windows NT or Windows 95 client will cause the print job to stall in the printer.

To print from Windows 95 and Windows NT client machines, the computer must first connect to a network print server. When the client connects to a Windows NT print server, the print server will send the correct printer driver for the platform of the client requesting the connection. (Remote retrieval of the printer driver works only for Windows 95 and Windows NT clients.) Windows NT machines will then check the version of the local printer driver against the printer driver on the print server every time the Windows NT machine prints. If the printer driver on the print server is newer than the one on the NT client, the system will copy the newer version to the client, thereby updating the printer driver. You can always update your printer drivers for Windows NT clients from a centralized location. The process of centrally updating printer drivers will work only on Windows NT machines because Windows 95 clients will not check for newer printer driver versions. In Tip 168, you will learn how to install printer drivers for multiple platforms for automatic updates.

The answer is **False** *because you must never print to a captured printer port on a Windows NT client. If you do so, the print job will stall and never print.*

153   **ACCESSING A NETWORK PRINTER**

Q: *You are administering a Windows NT Workstation. You want to connect to a network printer. How would you connect to the printer?*

Choose the best answer:

    A.   *From the command prompt, type NET USE LPT1: \\Server\Printer.*

    B.   *Create a new printer and then at the prompt for the printer port, select Network Port and enter the path to the network printer.*

    C.   *From Server Manager, select the machine with the shared printer from the server list. In the Properties dialog box for the server, select the printer and click your mouse on the Attach button.*

    D.   *Add a printer. When the Add Printer Wizard prompts you, select Network Printer Server instead of Create Printer.*

In some network environments, the system administrator will let users connect to the network print server on their own. In most environments, however, the system administrator will either perform the network printer connections or select someone else to perform the network printer connections on the administrator's behalf. Whether you, as the administrator, decide to connect network printers yourself or have someone do it for you, the process is the same. First, the person connecting to the printer must have at least the Print permission to the network printer, or the print server will deny the connection. You will connect to a network printer in much the same way you created a printer in Tip 149. To connect to a network printer, perform the following steps:

    1. Click your mouse on the Start menu and select the Settings submenu Printers option. Windows NT will display the Printers Window.

    2. Within the Printers Window, double click your mouse on the Add Printer icon. Windows NT will display the Add Printer Wizard.

3. Within the Add Printer Wizard, click your mouse on the Network Printer Server radio button. Then click your mouse on the Next button. Windows NT will advance to the next dialog box.

4. Within the next Wizard dialog box, select the network printer server and printer to connect to. Click your mouse on the OK button. Windows NT will ask you if you want this to be the default printer. Click your mouse on the Next button. Windows NT will prompt you to click on the Finish button.

5. Click your mouse on the Finish button. Windows NT will connect to the network printer and download the printer driver.

Answer D is correct because you will connect to a network printer from within the Add Printer Wizard, and you will use the select Network Printer Server option. Answer A is incorrect because using the NET USE command would capture the printer port and cause Windows NT print jobs to print incorrectly. Answer B is incorrect because creating a printer and then selecting a network printer port would also capture the printer port. Answer C is incorrect because you cannot use Server Manager to connect to or to manage printers.

154   **MANAGING A PRINTER REMOTELY**

Q: *You have created and shared a printer on a Windows NT Server domain controller. Who can administer the printer?*

Select all answers that apply:

     A.   *Server Operators*

     B.   *Print Operators*

     C.   *Administrators*

     D.   *Account Operators*

Microsoft has included several sub-administrative groups with the Windows NT operating system for you to use to break up the administration of your network. In Tips 97 and 100 through 102, you examined the Windows NT sub-administrative groups. Managing printers is one administrative task you might want to delegate to someone else in your department, because it is a relatively low-security issue. Table 154.1 lists the groups that can administer printers and on what computers the group members will be able to administer the printers.

Group Member	Administrative Permissions
Administrators	Any computer in the domain running Windows NT Workstation or Windows NT Server
Print Operators	Any domain controller
Server Operators	Any domain controller
Power Users	Any computer in the domain in which the Power Users group exists (Windows NT Workstation or Windows NT Server-Member Server)

Table 154.1 Group members that can administer printers.

If you decide to break up your Windows NT domain administration by selecting someone to be a print administrator, you will first have to assign membership to one of the groups in Table 154.1 to the user whom you want to make a print administrator. After you establish the group memberships, you might have to instruct the print administrator on how to remotely administer network printers.

An administrator or someone who is a member of one of the groups listed in Table 154.1 can administer the network printer from any Windows NT or Windows 95 computer that is connected to the network printer. The administration computer must have the client version of the Windows NT Administration Tools installed. As you learned in Tip 153, creating and connecting to a printer are very different actions. When you create a printer, you configure the printer so your local machine will manage it. After you create a printer, you can share the printer, but the local machine still manages the print job you sent to the printer.

When you connect to a printer, however, you simply establish a connection to a remote computer that has a shared printer. Your local machine is only a client front-end to the network print process when you are connected to a network printer. You can always look in the Printer window to see which printers are local to your machine and which printer are network printers another machine manages. Network printers always have a different icon than local printers (the icon will have either a network cable or a hand superimposed). To remotely administer a network printer, perform the following steps:

1. Click your mouse on the Start menu. Select the Settings submenu Printers option. Windows NT will open the Printers Window.
2. Within the Printers Window, select the Printer you want to administer. Double-click your mouse on the Printer icon. Windows NT will open the Print Manager window for the selected printer.

After the Print Manager window is open for the selected network printer, you can administer the documents in the printer. To administer documents, perform the following steps:

1. Select the document you want to administer. Right-click your mouse on the document. The Print Manager will display the pop-up menu for the selected document.
2. Select an administration option from the pop-up menu, using the options in Table 154.2

Option	Use
Pause	To pause the print job. Other print jobs will continue to print.
Resume	To resume printing of a paused document.
Restart	To restart the print job from the beginning.
Cancel	To delete the print job from the printer.
Properties	To view various document configuration options.

Table 154.2 *Document administration options.*

Answers A, B, and C are correct because the Server Operators, Print Operators, and Administrators groups can all administer network printers on a domain controller. Answer D is incorrect because the Account Operators group cannot create or manage printers.

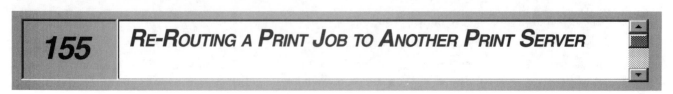

155   *RE-ROUTING A PRINT JOB TO ANOTHER PRINT SERVER*

Q: *You must take a printing device off line for repairs. How would you re-route print jobs to another printer on the network?*

Select all answers that apply:

A. *Create or edit a log-on script for the domain users. In the log-on script, use the NET USE LPT1: command and specify the universal naming convention-style pathname (\\server_name\printer) to the network printer that will accept print jobs. Configure each user's account to use the log-on script.*

B. *At each machine, change the port location for the network printer to point to the network printer that will accept print jobs while you repair the other printer.*

C. *Within the Properties dialog box for the printer that is going offline, specify the port location as the universal naming convention (UNC) style pathname to the replacement network printer.*

D. *You cannot re-route print jobs in Windows NT. Each client must remove the network printer and connect to the new printer that will take the original printer's place.*

Your hardware will, inevitably, require repairs or upgrades that necessitate having the hardware offline. For example, your server might require a new hard drive or a printer might require adjustments that you can perform only while the hardware is offline. If your printer requires repairs or upgrades, you can re-route print jobs to another printer in the network quite easily. When you re-route print jobs, the print server that manages the printer that will go offline will still receive print jobs. However, instead of managing the print job locally, the print server will send the print request to another print server, which will print the document. After you re-route the print job, all you must do is notify users about where they should pick up their printed documents. To re-route a printer, perform the following steps:

1. Click your mouse on the Start menu and choose the Setting submenu Printers option. Windows NT will open the Printers window.

2. Within the Printers window, select the printer you want to re-route. Right-click your mouse on the icon that represents the printer. Windows NT will display a pop-up menu for the printer.

3. Within the pop-up menu, select the Properties option. Windows NT will display the printer's properties in the Properties dialog box.

4. Within the Properties dialog box, click your mouse on the Ports tab. In the Ports tab, click your mouse on the Add Port button. The Print Manager will display the Printer Ports dialog box.

5. Within the Printer Ports dialog box, select Local Port and click your mouse on the New Port button. The Print Manager will display the Port Name dialog box.

6. Within the Port Name dialog box, enter the universal naming convention-style pathname (\\server_name\printer_name) in the Enter a Port Name field. Windows NT will search the network for the server you have specified in the pathname and check to see if the printer specified in the pathname is present on the remote computer. Windows NT will then add the port for the local printer.

Answer C *is correct because you should specify the universal naming convention-style pathname to the new printer as a printer port for the local machine.* **Answer A** *is incorrect because log-on scripts would capture the clients' printer ports, causing the printer problems you learned about in Tip 152.* **Answer B** *is incorrect because it would require a lot of administrative work.* **Answer D** *is incorrect because you can re-route printers in Windows NT.*

156 INTRODUCTION TO PRINTER POOLS

Q: *You are the administrator for a large company. Your company's Accounting Department is printing to a HP LaserJet 4Si. The accounting staff is complaining that they have to wait too long for print jobs to print because of their volume of print jobs. Your company's Sales Department is in the office next to the Accounting Department. The Sales Department also has a HP LaserJet 4Si, which it seldom uses. What could you do as the system administrator to solve the Accounting Department's problem?*

Choose the best answer:

> A.   Move the sales printer to the Accounting Office and implement a printer pool.

> B.   Give the accounting staff permissions to print to the sales printer. Instruct the accounting staff to use the sales printer when the Accounting Department's print job volume is high.

> C.   Create a spreadsheet detailing a schedule of the times each accounting staff member can use the printer.

> D.   Instruct accounting staff members to schedule large print jobs to print at night.

Windows NT administrators have many tools at their disposal to help them solve printing problems. One of the weapons in the "administrative arsenal" is the *printer pool*. A printer pool is one printer (the software interface) connected to multiple printing devices. Windows NT lets administrators use multiple printer ports to connect one printer to multiple printing devices. In turn, the printer pool software manages the printing devices as one printer. Therefore, when a user sends a print job to the printer, the printer pool software will actually send the print job to whichever printing device is available to accept the print job. Printer pools are useful when users send a large volume of print jobs to one printer. However, because the printer pool software manages all the print devices in a printer pool as one printer, users will not know which print device is actually going to print their documents. Therefore, you, as an administrator, should place printers in a printer pool so the printers are geographically close to each other.

Answer A is correct because implementing a printer pool would solve the print job volume problem. Answer B is incorrect because accounting staff members who print more frequently than Sales Department staff members would have to pick up print jobs in the sales office. Answers C and D are incorrect because accounting staff members might need to use the printer outside of their scheduled hours.

157   CREATING A PRINTER POOL

Q: You are the network administrator of your company's Windows NT domain. You have decided to implement a printer pool. Your company will not authorize the purchase of another print device. The Accounting Department has an HP LaserJet 4Si and the Sales Department has an HP LaserJet 4P. You do not have any other print devices to use in the printer pool. How will you implement the printer pool?

Choose the best answer:

> A.   Move the sales printer to the accounting office. In the Properties dialog box for the printer managing the accounting office's print device, specify additional ports to print to and add the port for the new printer.

> B.   Create another printer on the print server managing the accounting office's printer. In the Printer Properties dialog box, specify that the new printer is a slave to the current accounting printer.

> C.   Install the Printer Pool Administrator utility from the Microsoft Windows NT Server CD-ROM. Move the print device from the sales office to the accounting office and then use the Printer Pool Administrator utility to specify that the printer should manage the two print devices as one print device.

> D.   You cannot implement a printer pool with your current hardware.

As you learned in Tip 156, you can use a printer pool to help you manage large volumes of print jobs you are sending to one printer. Printer pools can also be very useful in large Windows NT networks. However, before you set up a printer pool, you should understand some basic rules or printer pool use.

First, because Windows NT manages all printing devices as one device, Windows NT uses the same printer driver for all printers in a printer pool. Therefore, you must ensure that all your printing devices are of the same make and model in order for them to work in a printer pool. Second, you should place printers in a printer pool geographically close together so users will have an easy time locating their printed documents. In Tip 158, you will learn more about how to geographically place printing devices in a printer pool. After you have made sure that your printing devices can share the same printer driver and are close together, you can create your printer pool. To create a printer pool, perform the following steps:

1. Click your mouse on the Start menu and select the Setting submenu Printer option. Windows NT will open the Printers window.

2. Within the Printers window, select the printer you want to make the printer pool manager. Right-click your mouse on the icon representing the printer. Windows NT will display a pop-up menu.

3. Within the pop-up menu, select the Properties option. Windows NT will open the Printer Properties dialog box.

4. Within the Printer Properties dialog box, click your mouse on the Ports tab. In the Ports tab, click your mouse on the Enable Printer Pooling checkbox. Select the additional ports to which you want to print and then click your mouse on the OK button. Windows NT will close the Printer Properties dialog box and enable the printer pool.

Figure 157 shows the Printer Properties dialog box Ports tab. Notice the Enable Printer Pooling checkbox in the lower left corner of the dialog box.

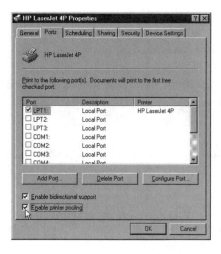

Figure 157 Enabling a printer pool.

Answer D is correct because printing devices in a printer pool must be able to use the same printer driver. Answer A is incorrect because although the steps to creating a printer pool are accurate, the two printing devices specified will not work together in a printer pool. Answers B and C are incorrect because no such options or utilities exist for Windows NT.

---

158 GEOGRAPHICALLY PLACING PRINTERS IN A PRINTER POOL

Q: *You are the administrator of a small company. You recently implemented a printer pool. You are now receiving calls from angry users who complain that when they print to the printer pool they never know where their print jobs are going to print. Sometimes the users' print jobs come out in the sales office, and other time the users' print jobs come out in the accounting office. What is causing this problem?*

    A.   *The printing devices are not properly configured as a printer pool.*

    B.   *The users are printing to the wrong printer.*

    C.   *The printer pool is corrupt.*

    D.   *The printer pool administrator did not place the printing devices in the printer pool together.*

As you learned in Tip 157, you should always place printing devices in a printer pool close to each other. The reason you want to place your printing devices in a printer pool geographically close together is because Windows NT considers the numerous printing devices as one printing device. When Windows NT sends a print job to the printer pool, Windows NT does not know to which printing device in the pool the print job will go. Therefore, if you do not place the printing devices in the printer pool together, the users will have a much harder time knowing where to pick up their print jobs than if you had placed the printing devices together.

As an administrator, you will find that it is sometime better to consolidate your printing devices into a printer pool instead of letting each department or office have its own printing device. For example, in many companies there are entire offices or departments that will print much more than others. As the administrator, it is your job to make the network as streamlined as possible. You can do so by taking the printing device from an office or department that does not print frequently and placing the printing device in a printer pool in another office or department that produces a large volume of print jobs. By consolidating printing devices in a central printer pool, you can increase overall user productivity.

Answer D is correct because the printing devices in the printer pool were not geographically close together. Answer A is incorrect because, in a printer pool, the users' print jobs should go to different printers. Answer B is incorrect because if the users were printing to the wrong printer, the same print device would print all the print jobs. Answer C is incorrect because a corrupt printer pool would not accept any print jobs.

---

159   SETTING ACCESS PRIORITIES FOR PRINTERS

Q: *You are the administrator of a small company that has only one printing device. You are having problems because the Accounting Department is complaining of having to wait for users from the Sales Department to print their documents before the Accounting Department can print important documents, such as company checks. Your company will not authorize another printing device purchase. How can you solve this problem?*

Choose the best answer:

    A.   *Create multiple printers pointing to the same printing device. Set priorities between the printers so the Accounting Department has a higher priority.*

    B.   *Give all users in the Accounting Department the Manage Documents permission to the printer, and instruct accounting department staff to set priorities on their documents higher than the documents the other network users print.*

    C.   *Configure the printer to process print jobs from the accounting staff with a higher priority.*

    D.   *You cannot solve this problem without purchasing another printing device.*

In previous Tips, you learned how to create printer pools by making one printer (software interface) point to multiple printing devices. In turn, you can also create multiple printers (software interfaces) that point to one printing device. While you will learn the implementation specifics of doing so in Tip 161, for now simply recognize that multiple printer objects from the user's Desktop can all refer to the same printer device.

When you create multiple printers for one printing device, you can set priorities between the printers. Administrators may choose to set priorities between printers so that users printing to the printer with the higher priority will get to print first. For example, if you wanted your company's Accounting and Sales Departments to share a printing device, you could create multiple printers—one called accounting and one called sales—for the one printing device. You would then set the priority on the accounting printer higher than the priority on the sales printer. You could even schedule times when users can print to the printers. To set priorities on printers, perform the following steps:

1. Click your mouse on the Start menu and select the Setting submenu Printers option. Windows NT will display the Printers window.

2. Within the Printers window, select the printer you want to set the priority for. Click your mouse on the icon representing the printer. Windows NT will display a pop-up menu.

3. Within the pop-up menu, select the Properties option. Windows NT will display the Printer Properties dialog box, as shown in Figure 159.

4. Within the Printer Properties dialog box, click your mouse on the Scheduling tab. Within the Scheduling tab, click on and hold down your mouse on the Priority slide bar and drag your mouse to the right side of the dialog box. Doing so will increase the priority of the printer.

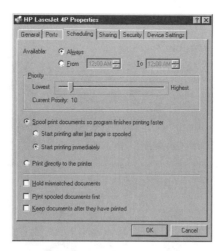

Figure 159 *Setting priorities on printers.*

Answer A is correct because the best solution is to create multiple printers and set priorities between them. This solution would require the least administrative overhead. Answer B is incorrect because giving the accounting staff members permissions to manage the Sales Departments documents could cause animosity between the sales and accounting staff members. Answer C is incorrect because you cannot set an automatic printer priority for specific user's print jobs. Answer D is incorrect because you can solve the problem described in the question.

160   SCHEDULING LARGE PRINT JOBS

Q: *You want to print a large print job that might last more than one hour. You do not want to tie up the network printer during the regular business day for the print job but you will need the document for a meeting the next morning. What can you do to print the document without causing anyone else to wait for your print job?*

Choose the best answer:

A.   *Instruct someone from the evening shift to print the document for you.*

B.   *Stay late until everyone else has left and then print your document.*

C.   *Come in to work in the morning at least an hour early and print your document before the meeting.*

D.   *Schedule your document to print late at night when the network will be idle. Come in early and pick up your document.*

Any users who have the Print permission to a printer can manage their own documents. One document management ability that each user has is the right to schedule his or her own documents to print at specific times. In addition, users who are members of the Print Operators or Administrators groups can schedule other people's documents. Small documents will probably spool and start to print before you can schedule the documents for printing—but, in such cases, the benefits of scheduling are minimal anyway. With larger print jobs, however, you will generally have more than sufficient time to set scheduling properties for the print job. You will configure notifications, priorities, and print times all from the same dialog box.

To set a specific time for an individual document, you must first print the document from within your application, which tells the operating system to send it to a printer object. Then, to set a specific time for the document to print from the printer object to the actual print device, perform the following steps:

1.   Click your mouse on the Start menu and select the Setting submenu Printer option. Windows NT will display the Printers window.

2.   Within the Printers window, select the printer to which you sent your print job. Double-click your mouse on the Printer icon. Windows NT will display the Print Manager window for the selected printer.

3.   Within the Print Manager window, select the print job you want to schedule. Right-click your mouse on the print job. Print Manager will display a pop-up menu.

4.   Within the pop-up menu, select the Properties option. Print Manager will display the Properties dialog box for the document you selected, as shown in Figure 160.

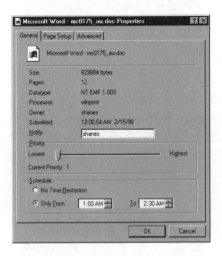

Figure 160 Scheduling a document to print.

5.   Within the document's Document Properties dialog box, select the Schedule section at the bottom of the dialog box and click your mouse on the Only From radio button. Enter the times you would like your print job to print. Click your mouse on the OK button. Windows NT will close the Document Properties dialog box and schedule the document to print during the hours you specified.

Answer D is correct because it is easiest for you to schedule the document to print during off hours. Answers A, B, and C are incorrect because they are labor intensive and do not use much computer technology, and therefore are not the best solutions.

161 CREATING MULTIPLE PRINTERS FOR THE SAME PRINT DEVICE

Q: You are the administrator of your company's Windows NT domain. Your company's Accounting Department and sales department share the same HP LaserJet 4Si printing device. Accounting staff members have asked you if there is any way that the Accounting Department could have exclusive access to the printing device between the hours of 2:00 and 3:00 p.m. How can you give the Accounting Department exclusive access to the printing device between 2:00 and 3:00 p.m.?

Choose the best answer:

A.   Within the Printer Properties dialog box, choose the Scheduling tab and click your mouse on the Advanced button. In the Advanced dialog box, set the exclusive access hours for the accounting staff.

B.   Within the Printer Properties dialog box, choose the Scheduling tab and set the schedules for the Accounting Department to All and the sales department to 3:00 p.m. to 2:00 p.m.

C.   Create multiple printers that point to the same printing device. Name the printers sales and accounting. In the sales printer Properties dialog box, choose the Scheduling tab and configure the available hours as 3:00 p.m. to 2:00 p.m.

D.   You cannot give the Accounting Department exclusive access to a printer without purchasing another printing device.

In most companies, there are times when, for various reasons, multiple departments must share a single printing device. If one of the departments sharing a printing device is the department responsible for cutting company checks or using any other special printing forms, you, as the administrator, might encounter some problems. For example, sometimes users from one department will accidentally print on company checks because the users were not aware that the Accounting Department (or whatever department is responsible for printing company checks) had placed the checks in the printing device the two departments share. Luckily, there are several way to solve the problem of users printing on the wrong forms. One way to solve such a problem is to create multiple printers and point them to one printing device. Creating multiple printers will let the administrator set priorities and schedules between the two printers. In the case of users accidentally printing over company checks, an administrator could make the Accounting Department's documents print before the Sales Department's documents. To do so, the administrator could give exclusive access to the printing device to one printer by scheduling the other printer to be available only during certain hours.

To create multiple printers, follow the steps outlined in Tip 149 for creating a new printer. When you create the second printer and the system prompts you for the port of the printing device, select the same port as the first printer you created. When you do so, you will have two printers using the same printing device. After you create the multiple printers, you can tailor each printer to the specific requirements of the groups to which you will assign the printers. For example, to schedule a printer's availability, perform the following steps:

1.   Click your mouse on the Start menu and select the Settings submenu Printers option. Windows NT will open the Printers window.

2.   Within the Printers window, select the printer on which you want to set the schedule. Right-click your mouse on the icon representing the printer. Windows NT will display a pop-up menu.

3.   Within the pop-up menu, select the Properties option. Windows NT will display the Printer Properties dialog box for the selected printer.

4. Within the Printer Properties dialog box, click your mouse on the Schedule tab. Within the Schedule tab, click your mouse on the Available radio button and specify the From and To times you want the printer to be available. Click your mouse on the OK button. The Print Manager will close the Printer Properties dialog box and set the schedule on the printer.

Answer C is correct because you should create multiple printers for the same printing device and configure schedules for the printers. Answer A is incorrect because there are no Advanced buttons on the Schedule tab of the Printer Properties dialog box. Answer B is incorrect because you can set a schedule only for the printer, not for different groups for the same printer. Answer D is incorrect because answer C solves the problem.

162   SETTING A SEPARATOR PAGE

Q: *You have a printer to which users are sending a large number of print jobs. Users are complaining they are having difficulty separating the print jobs as they come off the printing device, and some jobs are getting mixed up with other jobs. As the administrator, what can you do to help the users?*

Choose the best answer:

A.   *Have your company purchase another printing device. Create a new printer and assign half the users to the one printer and the other half to the existing printer.*

B.   *Hire a new employee to separate users' print jobs.*

C.   *Create multiple printers and schedule the printers to have access to the printing device at different times.*

D.   *Go to the Printer Properties dialog box for the printer, and set a separator page on the General tab.*

The number of jobs users send to a printer varies from company to company. If, in your company, a particular printing device processes a large volume of print jobs, you may find that users' print jobs will become mixed with other users' print jobs. If you are having problems with mixed-up print jobs, you may want to set a separator page.

When an administrator configures a printer to use a separator page, the printer will send an extra page with each print job to the printing device. The extra page will have information printed on it detailing who printed the job, when it was printed, and how may pages the print job has. Separator pages separate print jobs and can therefore greatly reduce mixed-up print job issues. To set a separator page, perform the following steps:

1. Click your mouse on the Start menu and select the Settings sub menu Printers option. Windows NT will display the Printers window.

2. Within the Printers window, right-click your mouse on the printer for which you want to configure a separator page. Windows NT will display a pop-up menu.

3. Within the pop-up menu, select the Properties option. Windows NT will display the Printer Properties dialog box.

4. Within the Printer Properties dialog box's General tab, click your mouse on the Separator Page button. The Print Manager will display the Separator Page dialog box.

5. Within the Separator Page dialog box, enter the name of the separator page you want to use. Table 162 lists the separator pages you can use.

6. Click your mouse on the OK button. The Print Manager will set the separator page for the printer.

Table 162 shows the separator page files and their uses.

File Name	Use
Pcl.sep	Switching the printing mode to *PCL* for HP series printing devices, and printing a page before each print job.
Pscript.sep	Switching the printing mode to *PostScript* for HP series printing devices, but not printing a page before each print job.
Sysprint.sep	Printing a page before each document on *PostScript* printing devices.

Table 162 The Windows NT separator pages.

Answer D *is correct because you should set a separator page in the printer's Printer Properties dialog box.* **Answer A** *is incorrect because it would not solve the problem and would be expensive.* **Answer B** *is incorrect because although hiring a new employee might solve the problem, it might be an expensive solution.* **Answer C** *is incorrect because users might continue to lose pages of their documents in other users' print jobs.*

163   **INTRODUCTION TO THE PRINT PROCESS**

Q: *You have just printed a document. Your hard drive light shows access consistent with sending a print job, but the print job never reaches the print server. What could be causing the problem?*

Choose the best answer:

     A.   *Your network connection is down.*

     B.   *You are out of hard disk space.*

     C.   *The print job is too large for the printer you are using.*

     D.   *You are using the wrong printer driver or your printer driver is corrupt.*

If you plan to administer a Windows NT network in which users will be printing, you should understand the Windows NT printing process. The following steps describe the basic Windows NT print process. First, when a user invokes the print command, the client queries the server for the printer driver version. If the printer driver version on the server is newer than the printer driver on the client, the client will download the newer printer driver and load it into memory.

Second, the application produces the print job and passes it to the spooler. The *print spooler* is an interface between the application that is printing and the print monitor and is responsible for routing (that is, transmitting) print jobs to the correct printer. The spooler is responsible for the following tasks: it tracks print jobs, routes print jobs to the correct ports, tracks which ports are connected to printers, and assigns priorities to print jobs. The spooler then passes the print job to the print processor. Third, the print processor renders (translates) the print commands from an application into commands the printing device can understand. As you learned in Tip 152, *rendering* is the process of translating print commands (for example, formatting and drawing instructions) from the application into commands the printing device can use. After the print processor completes the rendering, it returns the job to the spooler.

Next, the client-side spooler contacts the server-side spooler and sends the document to the server-side spooler. The server-side spooler then passes the document to the server-side print processor. If you use a separator page in the print job, the separator page processor creates the page and attaches it to the beginning of the print job. The spooler then passes the print job to the print monitor. The print monitor performs the following functions:

- Controls the data stream to one or more printer ports.

- Gains access to the correct printer port.

- Writes the print job to an output destination.

- Releases access to the port.

- Searches for unsolicited error messages, such as "out of toner."

- Handles true end-of-job notification. The print monitor waits until the printer has printed the last page of the print job and then tells the spooler that the job is finished and the spooler can delete the job.

- Monitors the printer status to detect printing errors. In case of an error, it notifies the spooler to restart the print job from the beginning.

Finally, the print monitor waits for the printer port to be available and then sends the job to the printing device. The printing device receives the print job and prints the document.

Note: When Windows NT spools a document (whether the document's destination is a printer on the server or a printer attached to the client), the operating system first writes the data to the local hard drive. If a hard drive performs constant access and a print job does not reach the printing device, the problem is a lack of disk space to spool the document.

Answer B is correct because the client does not have sufficient disk space to spool the print job. Answer A is incorrect because you would receive a message telling you the network device is not found. Answer C is incorrect because a print job can be too big for the amount of memory on a printing device to handle, but a print job cannot be too big for the printer to handle. Answer D is incorrect because a corrupt or incorrect printer driver would not cause the hard drive to thrash.

164	DELETING A DOCUMENT

Q: You have decided to add some additional information to a large document you just printed. The document has not reached the printing device yet. How can you stop the document from printing so you can add the additional information?

Choose the best answer:

    A.   Ask the system administrator to cancel the print job.

    B.   Add the additional information and reprint the document. If the original document has not reached the printing device, the new document will override the previous document.

    C.   Double-click the mouse on the Printer on your local machine. In the Print Manager's list of jobs waiting to print, right-click your mouse on your print job. From the pop-up menu, select Cancel.

    D.   You cannot stop a print job without clearing the entire printer and losing all other print jobs.

Occasionally, you or users in your network will want to stop a print job from printing. Any users who have the Print permission can stop their own print jobs from printing. In addition, any users who have the Manage Documents or

Full Control permissions can stop any other user's print job. In any event, users can only stop a print job as long as the job has not left the print monitor. To stop a print job from printing, perform the following steps:

1. Click your mouse on the Start menu and select the Setting submenu Printers option. Windows NT will display the Printers window.

2. Within the Printers window, double-click your mouse on the icon representing the printer to which you sent your print job. Windows NT will display the Print Manager for the printer you selected.

3. Within the Print Manager for the printer, select the print job you want to stop from printing. Right-click your mouse on the print job you want to cancel. Windows NT will display the pop-up menu for the document.

4. Within the pop-up menu, select the Cancel option. The Print Manager will delete the print job, as Figure 164 shows.

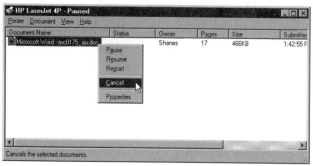

Figure 164 Canceling a print job within the print monitor.

Note: *If you prefer to use your keyboard, you can skip Steps 3 and 4 and press the* DELETE *key instead.*

Answer C is correct because you would cancel the print job from the pop-up menu. ***Answer A*** *is incorrect because although the administrator can cancel your print job, each user has the permission to cancel his or her own print job.* ***Answer B*** *is incorrect because reprinting the document will send another print job to the printer and the first document will print unchanged.* ***Answer D*** *is incorrect because any user with the proper permissions can cancel a print job.*

165   SETTING A NOTIFICATION, PRIORITY, AND PRINT TIME

Q: *You are leaving for an important meeting. Your assistant will remain behind at the office until an important document you will need at your meeting prints. Your assistant will join you as soon as the document prints. How can you have your assistant join you with the least amount of down time?*

Choose the best answer:

A. *Have your assistant stand at the printing device so as soon as the document prints he can leave to join you at the meeting.*

B. *Have your assistant work at your desk logged on as you. When the document prints, it will notify the machine your assistant is using.*

C. *Open your document's properties and configure the Notification option to notify your assistant. Have your assistant keep working at his desk. Windows NT will notify him when the print job is done printing.*

D. *Configure the printer to notify your assistant when any print job completes printing.*

As you have learned, users with the Print permission can manage their own print jobs. You also learned that to set any management options on a print job, you must open a print job's Properties dialog box. When you open a print job's Properties dialog box, you can do any of the following procedures:

- Set a notification to send to any user you specify

- Set a priority on your document relative to other documents you have printed

- Schedule a time for your document to print.

To manage a document, perform the following steps:

1. Click your mouse on the Start menu and select the Setting submenu Printers option. Windows NT will display the Printers window.

2. Within the Printers window, double-click your mouse on the icon representing the printer to which you sent your print job. Windows NT will open the Print Manager for the selected printer.

3. Within the Print Manager window, right-click your mouse on the document you want to manage. The Print Manager will display a pop-up menu.

4. Within the pop-up menu, select the Properties option. The Print Manager will display the Document Properties dialog box.

5. Within the Document Properties dialog box, enter which user to notify when the print job is complete, set a priority for the print job, or schedule a time for the document to print.

You will set a notification to tell the printer to notify a specific user when the print job has completed printing. The default notification is the user that printed the job. You will set a priority to tell the printer in what order your print jobs should print. Users with the Full Control and Manage Documents permissions can configure not only the order of the printing for their own print jobs but also all other users' documents. You will schedule a print time to tell the printer when to start the print job. If the print time you specify falls outside the hours the printer is available, the print job will never print.

Answer C is correct because you should set a notification for the document to notify your assistant. Answer A is incorrect because having your assistant wait at the printing device would be inefficient. Answer B is incorrect because you should never let anyone use your logon ID and password. Answer D is incorrect because you can configure a notification only on a document, not on a printer.

166 PAUSING, PURGING, AND RESUMING A PRINTER

Q: When would you pause a printer?

Choose all answers that apply:

A. When you change a toner cartridge.

B. Before you re-route the printer to another printer.

C. When a print job is stuck at the head of the queue.

D. When you set permissions on the printer.

Printer administration includes taking a printer offline so you can perform a variety of administration tasks on the printer, clearing all print jobs from the printer, and starting the printer after you have taken it offline. Any user who is a member of the Administrators, Server Operators, or Print Operators groups can manage a printer.

As part of normal printer administration, you might want to pause a printer any time you want the printer to accept but not process print jobs (for example, if you need to perform some work on the printer, but want users to still be able to queue jobs).

When a printer is paused, the print jobs the printer receives queue in the printer. When the printer resumes, the print jobs will start to process as if the printer were never paused. Examples of times when you may want to consider pausing a printer are when you take the printer offline for quick minor repairs, when you change the printer toner cartridge, and when you re-route print jobs.

An administrator may want to purge the document queue (that is, cancel all pending jobs) for a printer when there is a problem with the printer or the printing device. For example, imagine there are a large number of print jobs in the printer when you realize that each print job is coming out of the printing device garbled. You would then want to purge the printer to clear all print jobs while you change the printer driver or send the printer in for repair. You might also purge a printer if a large number of corrupt print jobs are in the printer queue.

However, before you purge a printer, consider re-routing the print jobs to another printer or pausing the printer until you fix the problem. When you purge a printer, you will lose all current print jobs. To pause, purge, or resume printing, perform the following steps:

1. Click your mouse on the Start menu and select the Setting submenu Printers option. Windows NT will display the Printers window.

2. Within the Printers window, right-click your mouse on the icon representing the printer you want to pause, purge, or resume. Windows NT will display a pop-up menu.

3. Within the pop-up menu, select the option you want to perform—either Pause Printing or Purge Print Documents. To resume printing (which you can only do after printing has previously been paused), click your mouse on the Pause option when the checkmark is present, as Figure 166 shows.

Figure 166 You will pause, purge, and resume a printer from the pop-up menu.

*Answers A and B are correct because you might want to pause a printer when you change the printer's toner cartridge or before you re-route print jobs through the printer. **Answer C** is incorrect because you would not have to pause a printer when a print job is stuck in the queue. No jobs will print until you clear the stuck job. **Answer D** is incorrect because you can set permissions on the printer without pausing it.*

---

167 STOPPING AND RESTARTING THE SPOOLER SERVICE

Q: *You receive a call from a user complaining that the user cannot print. You examine the printer and discover a print job at the head of the queue is stuck. The stuck print job has a byte size of 0. You try to delete the print job but cannot. How can you clear the one stuck print job without losing the other print jobs in the printer?*

Choose the best answer:

    A.   *Remove the printer. Create a new printer and give it the same name as the previous printer.*

    B.   *Pause and the resume the printer.*

    C.   *Stop and restart the spooler service from the Services utility in the Control Panel.*

    D.   *Purge the printer.*

As you learned in Tip 163, the Windows NT print spooler tracks print jobs, routes print jobs to the ports, tracks ports that are connected to printers, and assigns priorities to print jobs. When the print spooler is stalled, you will not receive any administrative messages or alerts. Instead, no documents will come out of the printing device. One symptom of a stalled spooler is when the print job at the head of the queue is stuck and has a byte size of 0. In turn, if you cannot remove the print job, you have a stalled spooler service. You can fix a stalled spooler by stopping and then restarting the spooler service. To stop and then restart the spooler service, perform the following steps:

1.   Click your mouse on the Start menu and select the Settings submenu Control Panel option. Windows NT will open the Control Panel window.

2.   Within the Control Panel window, locate the Service icon (which looks like two gears meshing). Double-click your mouse on the Service icon. Windows NT will open the Services program.

3.   Within the Services program, find and select the Spooler service. On the right side of the Service program dialog box, click your mouse on the Stop button. Windows NT will stop the Spooler service. Figure 167 shows the Services program with the Spooler service selected.

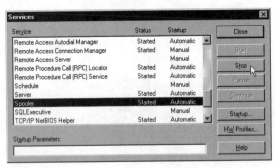

Figure 167 Stopping and restarting the Spooler service.

4.   Click your mouse on the Start button. Windows NT will start the Spooler service.

5.   Close the Services program. Open the printer and you should see that the job at the head of the queue is gone and subsequent jobs are now printing.

Answer C is correct because you should stop and restart the Spooler service. Answer A is incorrect because removing the printer would lose all print jobs currently in the printer. Answer B is incorrect because pausing and resuming the printer would have no effect when the Spooler service is stalled. Answer D is incorrect because purging the printer would remove all print jobs except the one that is stuck.

168   UPDATING A PRINTER DRIVER IN WINDOWS *NT*

Q: *You have configured a Windows NT Server to be a print server. You recently installed a new printer driver for the print device you are using. When Windows NT Workstations connect to the printer, the Windows NT Workstations update their local printer driver to the new printer driver you have installed. When Windows 95 clients print to the print server, they do not receive the new printer driver. Why are Windows NT machines receiving the new printer driver and Windows 95 machines are not?*

Choose the best answer:

A.   *The printer driver is for a Windows NT machine. Install the printer driver for a Windows 95 client and all Windows 95 machines will automatically receive printer driver updates when they next print to the print server.*

B.   *Windows 95 clients will access the printer driver on the server only when the Windows 95 clients first connect to the printer. Windows 95 clients will not receive printer driver updates. Print driver updates will require manual administrative intervention.*

C.   *The Windows 95 clients are configured in a workgroup instead of a domain. Configure the Windows 95 clients to log on to the domain and the clients will receive automatic printer driver updates.*

D.   *The portion of the printer driver for Windows 95 clients is corrupt. Replace the printer driver and Windows 95 clients will receive printer driver updates.*

One unique aspect of the Windows NT printing process is that Windows NT clients will check the print server's printer driver version to see if it is newer than the local machine's printer driver. If the printer driver version is newer, the local machine will update its own printer driver to the newer version. You can update all Windows NT printer drivers from one location. If you update the printer driver on the server, all Windows NT machines of the same platform will receive new printer drivers when the clients next print. If you have dissimilar platforms, such as Alpha and MIPS, along with Intel machines, you will have to load to additional Windows NT printer drivers for each platform. To install printer drivers for platforms other than the local machine's platform, perform the following steps:

1. Click your mouse on the Start menu and select the Settings submenu Printers option. Windows NT will display the Printers window.

2. Within the Printers window, right-click your mouse on the icon representing the Printer for which you want to install additional drivers. Windows NT will display the pop-up menu.

3. Within the pop-up menu, select the Properties option. Windows NT will open the Printer Properties for the selected printer.

4. Within the Printer Properties dialog box, select the Sharing tab. In the *Alternate Drivers* field, click your mouse on the additional drivers you want to install. Click your mouse on the OK button. Windows NT will prompt you for the source file location of the driver you have chosen to install. Windows NT will then close the Printer Properties dialog box.

Unlike Windows NT clients, Windows 95 clients will not check the print server's printer driver version when the clients print. The only time a Windows 95 client will use the printer driver on the server is when an administrator first connects to the print server from the client. When the Windows 95 client first connects to a printer, Windows NT will copy to the client from the server the printer driver for the client.

Answer B is correct because Windows 95 clients will receive printer drivers from a Windows NT machine only when the Windows 95 machine first connects to the Windows NT print server. Answer A is incorrect because Windows 95 clients will not update their local printer drivers without removing the printer and reconnecting. Answer C is incorrect because Windows 95 clients will not function any differently in a workgroup than in a domain. Answer D is incorrect because Windows NT and Windows 95 use different printer drivers.

---

169   INTRODUCTION TO AUDITING EVENTS IN WINDOWS NT

Q: *You want to examine recent user activity on your server. What utilities would you use to accomplish your task?*

Choose all answers that apply:

    A.   *Server Manager*

    B.   *User Manager for Domains*

    C.   *Event Viewer*

    D.   *Administrative Wizards*

As you have learned, the Event Viewer program lets Administrators, Server Operators, and, on Windows NT Workstations, Power Users groups view system, application, and security events. One example of an *event* which users from these three groups could view would be a user logging on to a domain. Windows NT will automatically audit many system and application events. For example, Windows NT will keep within the audit log a record of all services that start (and those that fail to start) when the operating system starts execution.

However, you, as the administrator, must manually configure security events in order for Windows NT to record them. To enable security event auditing, you must perform two steps: first, you must enable auditing from User Manager for Domains and, second, you must turn on the auditing of the specific resource you want to audit. In Tip 171, you will learn how to turn on auditing in User Manager for Domains and for specific resources.

While you will most often use the Event Viewer to view events that you specifically choose to audit, you can always use the Event Viewer to review the audit log for system and application events. However, you must open the Event Viewer program to view the actual events. Event Viewer will let you filter the events to more easily locate specific events. To filter events in Event Viewer, perform the following steps:

1. Click your mouse on the Start menu and select the Programs submenu Administrative Tools group Event Viewer program. Windows NT will open the Event Viewer program.

2. Within Event Viewer, use the Log menu to select the log file—Security, System, or Application—in which you want to view events. After you have selected a log file, Windows NT will display the log file. For example, to display System log information, select the Log menu System option.

3. Select the View menu Filter Events option. Event Viewer will display the Filter Events dialog box, as shown in Figure 169.

4. Within the Filter Events dialog box, select the dates, times, types, sources, and categories of events you want to filter.

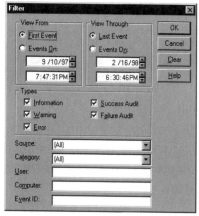

Figure 169 The Filter Events dialog box in Event Viewer.

Answer C is correct because you would use Event Viewer to view events, including user activity on the server. Answer A is incorrect because Server Manager will let you examine services and active connections on the Windows NT machine, but will not record any Windows NT system events. Answer B is incorrect because User Manager for Domains does not record any system event information. Answer D is incorrect because there are no Administrative Wizards for configuring or viewing events.

170   **PLANNING AND IMPLEMENTING AN AUDIT POLICY**

Q: *It is generally a good idea to audit all system events on each of your Windows NT servers.*

True or False?

Now that you have learned that Windows NT supports auditing, not only of System and Application events, but also of user activities (Security events), you might want to implement an auditing policy that will audit all users accessing all system resources. However, you must carefully plan your audit policy so it is not too comprehensive. That is, if you turn on auditing on all system resources, you will most likely create a log file so large that by the time you examine it, the system will have overwritten some of the recorded events. To create audit policies that are not too cumbersome for an administrator to use, you should review your events and audit only the important ones. For example, you might want to audit the Public folder on your Windows NT Server, but you might not want to audit users who have read-only access to the Public folder. You probably do not want to view events related to normal network activity. On the other hand, you will probably want to audit users who delete files or folders in a given folder. You may even, depending on the security level of items within a given folder, audit all users who access that folder.

Planning your audit policy will help you implement a long-term strategy for archiving and viewing system events. To get started, determine which events to record and plan a schedule for viewing your logs. Unfortunately, many network administrators implement audit policies but never find the time to view the audit logs. Windows NT will not notify you when it records events. Instead, you will have to find time to open Event Viewer and view your event logs. The Event Viewer log files display different kinds of events. The system and application logs will display one of three icons—a blue *i*, a yellow exclamation point, or a red stop sign—each of which represents a type of event. Each icon represents the severity of an event (from simply informational to a critical system error). The blue *i* represents a normal system event, which you should not be concerned about. The yellow exclamation point represents a system error that Windows NT deemed a non-critical, though noteworthy, event. You should generally closely watch such events, however, as they may degrade to critical system errors if you do not correct the problem that caused the non-critical event. The red stop sign represents a critical system error. You should examine closely any event the red stop sign represents.

*The answer is **False** because you should audit only events critical to your network administration.*

171 TURNING ON AUDITING FOR FILES, FOLDERS, AND PRINTERS

Q: *You suspect users of accessing unauthorized files and folders. What can you do as the administrator to check users' access to restricted documents?*

Choose the best answer:

A.   *In Server Manager, select the machine you want to audit events on. From the Computer menu, select Auditing. Windows NT will audit all disk resources. Use Event Viewer to view the users' access.*

B.   *In User Manager for Domains, turn on Auditing. Within the Properties dialog box, select the Security tab and select the resources you want to audit. Click your mouse on the Auditing button. Within the Auditing dialog box, add the users or groups you want to audit. Use Event Viewer to view the users' access.*

C.   *In the Properties dialog box for the resource you want to audit, select the General tab and add the users or groups you want to audit. Use Event Viewer to view the users' access.*

D.   *You cannot view users' access to resources.*

Configuring the system to record security events requires two steps. You must first turn on auditing in User Manager for Domains, and then turn on auditing at each resource you want to audit. You can also select what type of auditing you want to perform—auditing of successful actions, auditing of unsuccessful actions, and auditing of both successful and unsuccessful actions. When you audit successful actions, you keep a record of each user who performed the action successfully—for example, each user who actually opened a file in that folder. You may also want to keep a record of users whose actions failed—that is, each user who tried to open a file in that folder and failed because of their security permissions. Both types of events will provide you with different (but useful) information. To turn on system auditing, perform the following steps:

1. Click your mouse on the Start menu and select the Programs submenu Administrative Tools group User Manager for Domains option. Windows NT will open User Manager for Domains.

2. Within User Manager for Domains, select the Policies menu Audit option. User Manager for Domains will open the Audit Policy dialog box, as shown in Figure 171.1.

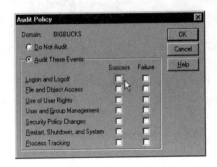

Figure 171.1 The Audit Policy dialog box.

3. Within the Audit Policy dialog box, select the checkboxes of the event you want Windows NT to audit. Click your mouse on the OK button. Windows NT will close the Audit dialog box.

After you have turned on the auditing from within Windows NT's User Manager for Domains, you can then set auditing on individual resources. To set auditing on individual resources, perform the following steps:

1. Open My Computer or *Windows Explorer.* Select the file or folder on which you want to configure auditing. Right-click your mouse on the selected file or folder. Windows NT will display the pop-up menu.

2. Within the pop-up menu, select the Properties option. Windows NT will open the Properties dialog box for the file or folder.

3. Within the Properties dialog box, select the Security tab. In the Security tab, click your mouse on the Auditing button. Windows NT will open the Auditing dialog box, as shown in Figure 171.2.

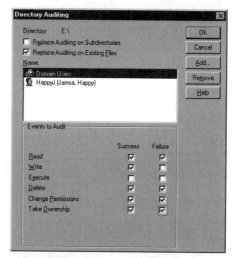

Figure 171.2 Using the Auditing dialog box to audit a resource.

4. Within the Auditing dialog box (which will say Directory Auditing if you are accessing a folder, and File Auditing if you are accessing a specific file), click your mouse on the Add button to add the users or groups you want to audit. Windows NT will display the Add Users or Groups dialog box.

5. Within the Add Users or Groups dialog box, select the user or group to audit. Click your mouse on the OK button. Windows NT will close the Add User or Groups dialog box. Repeat Step 5 until you have added to the audit list all the groups and users you want.

6. Within the Auditing dialog box, select the user or group you want to configure the specific audit policy for. In the Success or Failure checkboxes, click your mouse on each event you want to audit either the success or failure of. Click your mouse on the OK button. Windows NT will close the Audit dialog box and set the auditing policy.

Answer B is correct because you should turn on auditing in User Manager for Domains and then turn on auditing for the specific resource you want to audit. Answer A is incorrect because you cannot set an audit policy from Server Manager. Answer C is incorrect because you cannot turn on auditing from the General tab in the resource's Properties dialog box. Answer D is incorrect because you can audit resource events.

172 — USING EVENT VIEWER TO EXAMINE AUDITED EVENTS

Q: You can use Event Viewer to check for a specific user's unauthorized access to a specific resource.

True or False?

In the last several Tips, you learned how to plan an audit policy and enable auditing on your system's resources. You have also learned that system administrators use Event Viewer to view events Windows NT generates. An administrator can view any automatic or administrator-enabled event a system has audited. In addition,

Event Viewer will let administrators sort, filter, or even find specific events. Administrators can also archive the logs to enable long-term trend tracking. (In Tip 173, you will learn how to use Event Viewer to generate audit log files you can save to disk, which will then let you maintain archives of server activity.) To view events on your Windows NT machine, perform the following steps:

1. Click your mouse on the Start menu and select the Programs submenu Administrative Tools group Event Viewer program. Windows NT will open the Event Viewer program.

2. Within the Event Viewer, click your mouse on the Logs menu and select the Security, Application, or System log. Event Viewer will display the log you select.

3. After Event Viewer displays the log, double-click your mouse on the event you want to view. Event Viewer will open the Event Details dialog box, as shown in Figure 172.

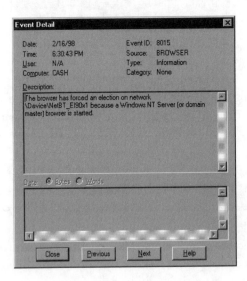

Figure 172 The Event Details dialog box.

4. Within the Event Details dialog box, you can view the actual event information.

*The answer is **True** because an administrator can use Event Viewer to view any audited system event.*

173 ARCHIVING THE SECURITY LOG

Q: *You are the administrator of a Windows NT Domain. As part of your regular duties, you must make permanent records of the security log. What steps would you take to make permanent security log records?*

Choose the best answer:

A.   *Use Event Viewer to save the security log as a file to a secure location.*

B.   *Use Server Manager to configure replication of the logs to another server.*

C.   *Use Event viewer to configure the auto-save feature for logging.*

D.   *Use Event Viewer to enable archiving on all logs.*

A Windows NT domain administrator has many responsibilities. For example, there may be times the administrator must maintain a history of security issues—in the event that the administrator wants to later review the logs, or pass them on to a third-party, such as a departmental manager. Fortunately, Windows NT automatically keeps track of security-related events with Event Viewer. Event Viewer keeps a running log of events concerning system operation, applications, and security. These logs have a finite amount of space that they may use. An administrator can configure the maximum amount of space that the logs may use. Event Viewer will record over older events after a certain amount of time has passed since the events occurred in order to comply with the space limitations the administrator sets. The administrator is responsible for archiving—ensuring that there is a record of—domain events. Company policy usually dictates how long a record is and how long to keep the record. Each administrator should ask the company management how long to keep event records and which events are most important to the management. In addition, administrators might decide to keep a history of events for their own use. Event history can be of tremendous assistance in determining server performance or troubleshooting problems that arise. To archive the security log, perform the following steps:

1.   Click your mouse on the Start menu and select the Programs submenu Administrative Tools group Event Viewer program. Windows NT will open the Event Viewer program.

2.   Within the Event Viewer, select the Log menu Security option. Event Viewer will display the current security log.

3.   Click your mouse on the Log menu Save as option. Event Viewer will open a Save As dialog box.

4.   Within the Save As dialog box, enter in the *File Name* field a file name for the log. Event Viewer will display the file name as you type it. Change the drive and directory if necessary. Event Viewer will save the file to whatever drive and directory you have selected. Ensure that you have set the value within the File Type drop-down list to Event Log Files (which it should be by default). If you have not set the File Type to Event Log Files, do so by clicking your mouse on the Save as Type button and selecting Event Log Files from the list that appears.

5.   Click your mouse on the Save button. Event Viewer will save the file.

Answer A is correct because Event Viewer can save its logs as files. An administrator can save these files as Event Log Files, as Plain Text, or as Comma Delimited Files. Answer B is incorrect because Windows NT cannot replicate unsaved log files. Answer C is incorrect because Event Viewer has no auto-saving feature. Answer D is incorrect because Event Viewer has no archiving feature.

174	USING SERVER MANAGER TO VIEW IN-USE RESOURCES

Q: *You are the administrator of a Windows NT Domain. As part of your duties, you must monitor the servers in the domain to see which users are accessing which shares on which servers in the domain. What program or function within Windows NT lets the administrator view connected users, open shares, and resources?*

Choose the best answer:

A.   Network Client Administrator

B.   Event Viewer

C.   The Properties screen for Network Neighborhood

D.   Server Manager

As a Windows NT domain administrator, occasionally you must monitor the access to your servers, what shares are in use at any given time, what shares are available to users on a given server, the status or configuration of server replication, and the status or configuration of the *Alerts* function. Windows NT lets the administrator use Server Manager to perform all these activities in a single location.

Server Manager is the program within Windows NT that can monitor and change any configuration for shares and functions. Server Manager can manage shares and functions on any server within your domain or any server within any domain that you have sufficient rights to access and manage.

To access Server Manager, click your mouse on the Start menu and select the Programs menu Administrative Tools group Server Manager option. Windows NT will open the Server Manager program. When Server Manager opens, it will list all the computers active in the domain within the program's client area. Each computer in the list will have a type, and some of them may also have a description. Server Manager will use a heading at the top of each column in its display to indicate what information it is displaying.

In order to manage any single server, there are two ways to open the Server Properties dialog box for that server. First, you can select the server you want to manage by clicking your mouse once on the name of the server, then select the Computer menu Properties option. Server Manager will open the Server Properties dialog box for the server you selected. Alternatively, you can open the Server Properties dialog box by double-clicking your mouse on the server you want to manage. Server Manager will open the Server Properties dialog box for the server you selected.

The Server Properties dialog box contains a usage summary, a description line, and five buttons that let administrators make various management choices. The button choices are Users, Shares, In-use, Replication, and Alerts, and each lets you perform management tasks related to the button's caption. For example, the Users button lets you perform management activities on Users currently accessing the server in question. Upcoming Tips will describe each button choice.

You can view resources that users are currently accessing by clicking your mouse on the In-Use button. When you do so, Server Manager will open the In-Use dialog box. The In-Use dialog box will list the following information about resources on the server:

- All resources that are currently in use
- Which user opened the resource

- How long the resource has been open

- Any access locks that are in place on the resource as a result of current use by a user

- The path to the resource.

Answer D is correct because Server Manager is the program Windows NT provides that lets an administrator manage users, shares, resources, replication, and alerts. Answers A, B, and C are incorrect because none of these programs will let you view in-use resources.

175   DISCONNECTING A USER FROM THE SERVER

Q: You are the administrator of a Windows NT domain. Your boss has asked you to disconnect a user from the network. Besides disabling the user's account, what would you do to disconnect a user from the Windows NT Server?

Choose all answers that apply:

A.   Within Server Manager, select the appropriate server and open the Properties dialog box. Click your mouse on the Users button. The Server Manager, in turn, will display the Connected Users list.

B.   From the Server Manager Connected Users list, select the user you want to disconnect and click your mouse on the Disconnect button.

C.   Within the Connected Users list, select the user you want to disconnect and click your mouse on the Connection Options button.

D.   Within the Connection Options menu, choose Disconnect User.

There may be times when a Windows NT Server administrator must manually disconnect users from a Windows NT Server or Workstation. As an administrator, you might disconnect users from the network for a variety of reasons. For example, your company might fire an employee or you might perform routine system maintenance. Any member of the Server Operators, Administrators, or Account Operators groups (or the Power Users group on a Windows NT Workstation) can disconnect a user from a Windows NT Server or Workstation.

Windows NT lets the administrator manually disconnect users from the server at any time. To disconnect users from a Windows NT server, perform the following steps:

1. Click your mouse on the Start menu and select the Programs option Administrative Tools group Server Manager program. Windows NT will open the Server Manager dialog box.

2. Within Server Manager, select the appropriate server in the computer list. Any commands the menus issued will now affect the selected server. Click your mouse on the Computer menu Properties option. Windows NT will open the Server Properties dialog box. (The server name will appear in the title bar, followed by the word Properties.)

3. Click your mouse on the Users icon in the bottom left corner of the dialog box. Windows NT will display a list of users currently connected to the server (the same dialog box will also contain a list of open connections), as shown in Figure 175.

4. Select the user you want to disconnect. Windows NT will enable the Disconnect button at the bottom of the dialog box.

5. Click your mouse on the Disconnect button. Windows NT will terminate the user's connection.

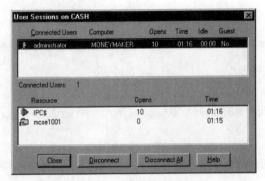

Figure 175 Disconnecting a user in the User Sessions dialog box.

Note: *This process will disconnect a user from the server. However, if the user retains a valid account and has the appropriate log-on rights, the user will be able to reconnect to the server.*

Answers A and B are correct because a Windows NT Server administrator would use Server manager to disconnect a user from the server. The Properties dialog box for any server contains the command buttons to disconnect users. Answers C and D are incorrect because Server Manager does not have a Connection options buttons or a Connection options menu.

176   SETTING ADMINISTRATIVE ALERTS

Q: *By default, Windows NT will send administrative messages to the default Administrator account any time a critical system event occurs. You want Windows NT to send the administrative alerts both to your user account and to your assistant's user account. How can you make Windows NT send administrative alerts to you and to your assistant's user accounts?*

Choose the best answer:

A.   *In User Manager for Domains, select the Policies menu Account option. In the Account Policies dialog box, click your mouse on the Send Administrative Alerts to All Domain Admins checkbox.*

B.   *In Server Manager, select the computer you want to receive alerts from. Open the server properties and click your mouse on the Alerts button. In the Alerts on Computer dialog box, add the users you want to receive administrative alerts.*

C.   *Edit the Windows NT Registry HKEY_LOCAL_MACHINE\SOFTWARE\Microsoft\Windows NT\CurrentVersion\Winlogon key. Add the value, administrative alerts, and specify users who should receive administrative alerts.*

D.   *You cannot alter the Windows NT default administrative alert settings.*

Windows NT will send *administrative alerts* any time a system event occurs that Windows NT views as a potential problem. The administrative alerts are intended only for system administrators and are not of any significance to general network users. An example of a system event that could cause Windows NT to generate an administrative alert would be when a server is low on hard disk space. When Windows NT sees that the system is close to running out of disk space, it will issue an administrative alert, which it then sends to the default Windows NT Administrator account.

As you learned in Tip 70, you should not use your default Administrator account, but instead rename your default administrator account to protect it, and create your own user account that is a member of the Domain Admins group. If you are logged on to the system as any account other than the default Administrator account, however, you will not receive any administrative alerts. You can use Server Manager to configure the Windows NT system to send administrative alerts to any user or computer you specify. Each server in your network will require you to manually configure the administrative alerts for that machine. To configure administrative alerts on a Windows NT machine, perform the following steps:

1. Click your mouse on the Start menu and select the Programs submenu Administrative Tools group Server Manager program. Windows NT will open the Server Manager program.

2. Within Server Manager, double-click your mouse on the server you want to configure alerts for. Server Manager will open the Computer Properties dialog box.

3. Within the Computer Properties dialog box, click your mouse on the Alerts button. Server Manager will display the Alerts dialog box, as shown in Figure 176.

4. Within the Alerts dialog box, enter the user name or computer name to send alerts to in the *New Computer* or *Username* field. Click your mouse on the Add button. Server Manager will add the user or computer to the list of administrative alert recipients.

5. Click your mouse on the OK button. Windows NT will return you to the Computer Properties dialog box.

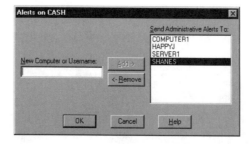

Figure 176 *The Alerts dialog box.*

Answer B is correct because setting the administrative Alerts option in Server Manager will notify the users you have selected when critical system events occur. Answer A is incorrect because Account Policies in User Manager for Domains will not let you view or configure administrative alerts. Answer C is incorrect because the registry location in the answer does not contain administrative alert information. Answer D is incorrect because you can configure administrative alerts from Server Manager.

177 — SENDING ADMINISTRATIVE MESSAGES TO USERS

Q: You are planning to shut down your Windows NT Server for system repairs. What is the easiest way to notify users who are connected to the server of the impending system shutdown?

Choose the best answer:

A. Send users connected to the server an e-mail detailing when and for how long the server will be down.

B. Configure the administrative Alerts in Server Manager to notify all users. Windows NT will automatically notify users after the administrator initiates system shutdown.

C. Issue a company memo explaining that the system will be down and when users can expect the system to be up again.

D. In Server Manager, select the computer from which you want to send an administrative message. Next, select the Computer menu Send Message option. Enter a message explaining that you will shut down the system and when the system will be back on-line.

There are many instances when an administrator might want to send a message to users who are logged on to a Windows NT Server. You might, for instance, want to shut down the server for system repair or upgrade. To do so, you would send users an *administrative message*. In Tip 176, you learned how administrators can configure the Windows NT Server to send administrative alerts when the system encounters problems. Sending administrative messages is not the same as sending administrative alerts. The Windows NT system generates administrative alerts to warn the administrator of system events, but the administrator generates administrative messages to send users specific information. When you send an administrative message, all users who are connected to the machine from which you send the message from will receive the message. Any member of the Server Operators or Administrators groups can send administrative messages to users. To send administrative messages to users, perform the following steps:

1. Click your mouse on the Start menu and select the Programs submenu Administrative Tools group Server Manger program. Windows NT will open the Server Manager program.

2. Within Server Manager, select the server from which you want to send an administrative message. Next, select the Computer menu Send Message option. Server Manager will display the Send Message dialog box, as shown in Figure 177.

3. Within the Send Message dialog box, type the message you want users to receive. Click your mouse on the OK button. Server Manager will send the message to all computers connected to the server from which you sent the message.

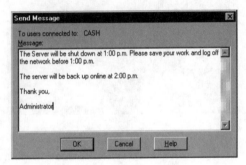

Figure 177 Sending an administrative message.

Answer D is correct because sending an administrative message from Server Manager would notify all users who are connected to the server. Answer A is incorrect because sending an e-mail to all company users could be time consuming and you might be sending messages to users who are not connected to the server. Answer B is incorrect because configuring the server to send administrative alerts to all users would send only system events; it would not send the message to notify users that you are shutting down the server. Answer C is incorrect because a company memo would be time consuming and would waste paper.

178 · REMOTELY SHUTTING DOWN A WINDOWS NT COMPUTER

Q: *You are the administrator of a Windows NT domain. While monitoring network resources, you discover that a user has accessed a restricted area and has opened confidential company files. According to your access list, this user should not have had rights to open these files, and you must take administrative action. You first disable the user's account and you then disconnect the user from the server. However, the user could have by now copied the information in the opened files to the user's local system. In order to prevent further access to files that might now exist on the user's Windows NT computer, you decide to shut down the remote computer. What steps must you take to shut down the remote computer?*

Choose the best answer:

A. *Use the AT command to issue a time to shut down the system*

B. *Use the Shutdown Manager in the Windows NT Resource Kit to shut down the remote computer..*

C. *Use Server manager to shut down the remote computer.*

D. *Use the AT command to issue an immediate shutdown sequence.*

A Windows NT domain administrator might have many reasons to remotely shut down a workstation or server. For example, an administrator might shut down a Windows NT Machine to quickly shut down a system that is for some reason interfering with the network, or to shut down a server that the administrator remotely upgraded with new software components and must restart. Windows NT Server does not come with a built-in means for remotely shutting down machines. To remotely shut down a Windows NT machine, an administrator must first install the Windows NT Server Resource Kit. The Windows NT Server Resource Kit is a technical reference aid that contains both written information and software components designed to assist the Windows NT Server administrator with the tasks that he or she might need to perform. To remotely shut down a Windows NT machine, perform the following steps:

1. Ensure that you have installed the Windows NT Resource Kit.

2. Click your mouse on the Start menu and select the Programs submenu Resource Kit group Management subgroup Shutdown Manager program. Windows NT will open the Shutdown Manager program.

3. Within the Shutdown Manager, click your mouse on the Ellipses icon. Windows NT will open the Select Computer dialog box.

4. Within the Select Computer dialog box, click your mouse on the Kill applications without saving data option, or the Reboot after shutdown option if you want the operating system to perform these tasks. Shutdown Manager will send the options you check, along with the shutdown command to the operating system when you activate it.

5. Type in any warning message you want to send and enter the amount of time the remote machine should wait before it performs the shutdown. Shutdown Manager is now ready to send your instructions.

6. Click your mouse on the OK button. Shutdown Manager will send the shutdown sequence to the remote computer. The remote computer will accept or reject the sequence, based on your rights.

Answer B is correct because Shutdown Manager is the correct program to use to remotely shut down a Windows NT machine. Answer A is incorrect because you cannot use the AT command to shut down a remote system. Answer C is incorrect because Server Manager has no remote shutdown capabilities. Answer D is incorrect because you cannot use the AT command to shut down a remote system.

179 USING THE WINDOWS NT SYSTEM PROPERTIES DIALOG BOX

Q: *You are the administrator of your company's Windows NT domain. Users are calling you and complaining that their Windows NT Workstations are displaying Out of Virtual Memory messages. Where can you set the virtual memory configuration on a Windows NT Workstation?*

Choose the best answer:

A. *From Server Manager in the Server Properties dialog box.*

B. *In User Manager for Domains.*

C.   *From the Control Panel Memory dialog box.*

D.   *From the Control Panel System Properties dialog box Performance tab.*

As part of an administrator's duties, the administrator might have to configure users' Windows NT Workstations in addition to the network's Windows NT Servers. Administrators may configure Windows NT workstation options, such as the system's virtual memory settings, hardware profiles, and user profiles. *Virtual memory* is Windows NT's ability to use the system's hard disk space to emulate Random Access Memory (RAM). In Tip 277, you will learn more about Windows NT's virtual memory.

Windows NT uses *hardware profiles* to set Windows NT machines' configuration, depending on what hardware—such as a network interface card—the machines have attached. In Tip 232, you will learn about hardware profiles. As you learned in Tip 107, *user profiles* let network users save different Desktop environments on the same machine. Administrators will configure many Windows NT system parameters from the System Properties dialog box.

The System Properties dialog box has six tabs with system information or administrator-configurable options. The six tabs in the System Properties dialog box are: General, Performance, Environment, Startup/Shutdown, Hardware Profiles, and User Profiles. Each tab in the System Properties dialog box has its own function.

- The General tab contains system information such as the operating system version, the registered software owner, and the amount of RAM in the machine. There are no configurable options on the General tab.

- The Performance tab has only two administrator-configurable options. The first option is the Application Performance Boost slide bar, which lets an administrator configure the foreground application responsiveness. (In Tip 271, you will learn more about how to change the foreground application responsiveness and why you would want to do so.) The Performance tab also contains the Virtual Memory settings. Administrators can click the mouse on the Change button and Windows NT will display the Virtual Memory settings dialog box. Administrators can then change the Virtual Memory settings, which you will learn how to do in Tip 197.

- The Environment tab contains *system environment variables*, which the system sets, and which contain information that the operating system will use during execution. Windows NT automatically sets some environment variables, such as the operating system path and the number of system processors. Other environment variables are user-specific environment variables that will point to the folder location some programs use to save temporary files.

- The Startup/Shutdown tab contains two sections—System Startup and System Recovery— that serve distinctly different administrative configuration requirements. The System Startup section contains the default operating system and the *Show List For* field. The computer will boot the default operating system if the person who boots the Windows NT machine does not make another operating system choice. The *Show List For* field defines for how long the system will display the choice of operating systems at system startup before initializing the default operating system. The other section of the Startup/Shutdown tab is the System Recovery section, which you will learn more about in later Tips.

- The Hardware Profiles tab contains hardware-specific configuration information. Windows NT will let you create hardware profiles so that when you have certain hardware attached to your computer, Windows NT will load device drivers for the hardware, and when you remove certain pieces of hardware, Windows NT will not load the hardware device drivers. Because the device drivers do not load for hardware not currently attached to your computer, you save on system resources.

- The User Profiles tab contains the individual user profile for any user who has logged on to the local machine. As you learned in Tip 108, user profiles store specific users' desktop configuration information, such as the background patterns and colors and the mapped network drives and printers. The administrator can use the User Profiles tab to create roaming profiles, which, as you learned in Tip 110, you can use to assign a user one profile which the system automatically loads, regardless of what computer he or she is currently using.

Answer D is correct because the System Properties dialog box Performance tab is where the system stores its virtual memory settings. Answers A and B are incorrect because neither the Server Manager nor the User Manager for Domains programs lets you configure virtual memory. Answer C is incorrect because Windows NT does not have a Memory program in the Control Panel.

180 INTRODUCTION TO WINDOWS NT DIAGNOSTICS

Q: *You are having trouble configuring a peripheral device. You want to see a list of the local machine's Interrupt Request (IRQ) settings. Where could you locate the local machine's IRQ settings?*

Choose the best answer:

A.   *In Server Manager*

B.   *In Windows NT Diagnostics*

C.   *In the Windows NT Device log*

D.   *You must view each resource separately from within the Resources dialog boxes*

There will be many times when you, as an administrator, must know the resource allocations on a particular machine, such as when you install a new network interface card. If you do not know what IRQ and I/O bases are available, you will not know which IRQ and I/O base you can assign to the new network interface card. Fortunately, Windows NT offers the Windows NT Diagnostics program, which is designed to let system administrators view system configuration information to help make hardware configuration choices. However, an administrator cannot use Windows NT Diagnostics to alter any system configurations. Instead, Windows NT Diagnostics can only show system configuration information. The Windows NT Diagnostics dialog box has nine tabs—Version, System, Display, Drives, Memory, Services, Resources, Environment, and Network—that contain system configuration information. The tabs have intuitive names, which means that you can easily identify the tab with the configuration information you want. To use the Window NT Diagnostics program, perform the following steps:

1. Click your mouse on the Start menu and select the Programs submenu Administrative Tolls group Windows NT Diagnostics program. Windows NT will open the Windows NT Diagnostics program.

2. Within Windows NT Diagnostics, click your mouse on the tab representing the system configuration information you want. Figure 180 shows the Windows NT Diagnostics program.

Answer B is correct because Windows NT Diagnostic will let you view system configuration information. Answer A is incorrect because Server Manager does not have the capability to show system configuration information. Answer C is incorrect because Windows NT uses Device logs for tracking remote access problems. Answer D is incorrect because although you could open each resource's configuration dialog box and view the IRQ and I/O bases the resources are using, to do so would be very time consuming.

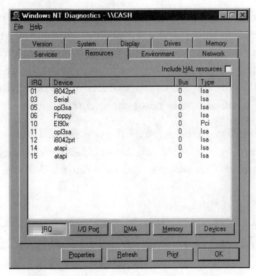

Figure 180 *The Windows NT Diagnostics program.*

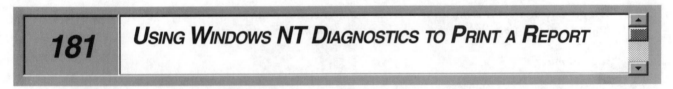

181   USING WINDOWS NT DIAGNOSTICS TO PRINT A REPORT

Q: *You are the administrator of a multi-server Windows NT domain. As part of documenting your network, you want to include a complete printout of the servers in your domain. What steps would you take to create a complete report of any given server?*

Choose the best answer:

     A.   *Copy the system properties to a word processor and print the results.*

     B.   *Use the System Reporting tool in the Windows NT Server Resource Kit to create and print a detailed report.*

     C.   *Use the Print function in Windows NT Diagnostics to create and print a detailed report.*

     D.   *Use Disk Administrator to print a detailed report of the system contents.*

A Windows NT domain administrator may be called upon at any time to answer questions or provide others with details about the network. For example, you as an administrator might have to give reports to management at regular intervals or provide specific information to an application specialist who is tuning a custom application for your company. Windows NT Diagnostics provides more detailed information about your system than any other program or sub-procedure available in Windows NT. Therefore, it is often easier for you to view and understand the information in printed form than on the screen. In addition, in order to configure applications properly, application specialists from outside the company might need system information that they can find only in Windows NT Diagnostics. Because a good administrator keeps physical access to the network servers at a low level, the administrator can print a report the application specialists (or anyone else) can read without actually having physical access to the servers. To print a detailed report of your Windows NT Diagnostics information, perform the following steps:

1.   Click your mouse on the Start menu and select the Programs submenu Administrative Tools group Windows NT Diagnostics program. Windows NT will open the Windows NT Diagnostics program.

2.   Within Windows NT Diagnostics, click your mouse on the Print button at the bottom of the program window. Windows NT Diagnostics will open the Create Report dialog box.

3. Within the Create Report dialog box, use your mouse and the fields the dialog box provides to choose the appropriate scope, detail level, and destination for the report you want to create. Windows NT Diagnostics will create the report based on the choices you selected.

4. Click your mouse on the OK button. Windows NT Diagnostics will create the report.

Answer C is correct because Windows NT Diagnostics can create detailed reports without a need for an exterior reporting tool. Answer A is incorrect because Profiles is the only option in System Properties you can copy, and the Profiles option does not contain the detailed system information you need. Answer B is incorrect because no such tool exists in the Windows NT Server Resource Kit. Answer D is incorrect because Disk Administrator does not have printing abilities and does not track system information other than hard disk information.

182 INSTALLING WINDOWS NT ADMINISTRATIVE TOOLS ON A WINDOWS 95 CLIENT

Q: *You are a Windows NT domain administrator. You have chosen to work from a standard Windows 95 client machine when you perform day-to-day duties. You decide to install the Administrative tools for Windows NT on your Windows 95 workstation so that you can perform simple management operations on the Server. What steps would you take to install the Windows NT administrative tools to a Windows 95 workstation?*

Choose the best answer:

A.   *Use the Setup program on the Windows NT Server CD-ROM to install the administration tools to any computer you want.*

B.   *Use the Add/Remove Programs option in the Windows 95 Control Panel to install the tools one at a time from the Windows NT server CD-ROM.*

C.   *Use the Add/Remove Programs option in the Windows 95 Control Panel to install all the tools simultaneously from the Windows NT Server CD-ROM.*

D.   *Use the installation utility on the Windows NT Server Resource Kit CD-ROM to install all the tools simultaneously to any computer you want.*

One of the primary responsibilities of a Windows NT server or domain administrator is to minimize the chance that a server will crash, becoming unavailable to users on the network. To do so, most administrators agree that administrators should not perform, from the server itself, any normal, day-to-day work that has nothing to do with the actual manipulation of the server or network. Instead, administrators should perform most of their computer-related work on a single, remote computer whose sole purpose is network management.

Alternatively, administrators may choose to perform remote administration or monitoring from their client machines. Windows NT domain administrators will, if given the choice, often select Windows NT Workstation as the operating system for their primary workstations. In smaller companies or those that have existing installations, administrators will often not have a choice or, in some cases, will choose Windows 95 (for consistency with the other workstations, for example) for their client machines. When the administrator computer is a Windows 95 machine, you, as the administrator, must install the Client Administration Tools for a Windows NT network. To install the Client Administration Tools for Windows NT on your Windows 95 client machine, perform the following steps:

1. Place the Windows NT Server CD-ROM in a CD-ROM drive that is accessible from the Windows 95 workstation (either a local drive or a shared network CD-ROM resource).

2. Click your mouse on the Start menu and select the Settings submenu Control Panel option. Windows 95 will open the Control Panel.

3. Within the Control Panel, double-click your mouse on the Add/Remove Programs option. Windows 95 will open the Add/Remove Programs dialog box.

4. Within the Add/Remove Programs dialog box, click your mouse on the Windows Setup tab. The Control Panel will switch to the Windows Setup installation screen. Click your mouse on the Have Disk button. Windows 95 will open the Install From Disk dialog box.

5. Within the From Disk dialog box, click your mouse on the Browse Button. Windows 95 will open the Browse dialog box.

6. Within the Browse dialog box, change the drive and directory to the Windows NT Server CD-ROM *Clients* directory *svrtools* subdirectory *Win95* subdirectory. The Browse dialog box will now act on files found in this location.

7. Within the Browse dialog box, select the *Svrtools* entry and click your mouse on the Open button. Windows 95 will insert the path to *Svrtools* into the *Copy Manufacturers Files From* field.

8. Within the Browse dialog box, click your mouse in the checkbox to the left of the words *Svrtools*. Windows 95 will target this file as the installation instructions it requires. Click your mouse on the Install button. Windows 95 will install the Server Tools.

Answer C is correct because you use the Add/Remove Programs option in the Windows 95 Control Panel to install the Windows NT Server administrative tools. Answer A is incorrect because you do not use the set-up programs on the Windows NT Server CD-ROM to install administrative tools. Answer B is incorrect because it is impossible to select only a single program in the Install Programs dialog box. Answer D is incorrect because the Windows NT Server Resource Kit does not contain the Windows 95 installable administrative tools.

---

183 INTRODUCTION TO THE WINDOWS NT BACKUP UTILITY

Q: *You are the administrator of a new Windows NT domain. You have just completed installing your new server and configuring and installing the applications. You now want to ensure that you can restore the system to its current state if any problems occur. What should you do to ensure that a system failure will not result in your having to repeat your efforts?*

Choose the best answer:

    A.   Create an emergency repair disk.

    B.   Use the Registry Editor to back up the registry to a secure location.

    C.   Use Disk Administrator to mirror the system partition.

    D.   Use the Windows NT Backup utility to create a complete system backup.

One of a Windows NT domain administrator's most important responsibilities is to ensure that the chance of a system failure is at a minimum. Another very important administrator responsibility is to ensure that, should a system failure occur, a reliable backup is ready to restore the system to a state of readiness with a minimum loss of data. Windows NT provides the Backup utility to assist with the system backup task. The Windows NT Backup utility ensures that a new system is ready to perform backups as soon as the administrator installs it, without the need to purchase additional software tools.

There are many software companies that sell a wide variety of Windows NT-compatible backup utilities. Many administrators choose to use these third-party products, but you should note that Windows NT has its own backup utility that provides all the features you need to conduct an effective backup routine. In addition, the Windows NT Backup utility is the backup solution that many MCSE exams will test you on. You should also note that, unlike the Windows 95 Backup utility, which will let the administrator backup to a floppy disk, a network location, or a hard drive, the Windows NT Backup utility requires you to install a tape drive. The tape drive requirement is a natural one, because network drives tend to be larger, and a backup that does not exist separately from the network is arguably not truly a backup. The Windows NT Backup utility will not back up to a floppy disk, a directory on your hard drives, or a network drive. You can use the Windows NT Backup utility to back up a remote computer, but you cannot back up data to anything other than tape devices.

A Windows NT domain administrator must develop a back-up strategy to ensure that the systems and data on the network are safe. Different networks may require different back-up strategies—some may require full-system backups every night, while others may require only incremental backups once a week. Therefore, an administrator must have a proper understanding of backup types and concepts. Figure 183 shows the Windows NT Backup utility.

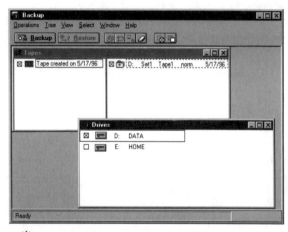

Figure 183 The Windows NT Backup utility.

Answer D is correct because you use the Windows NT Backup utility to create backups that you can later use to restore information to the machine. Answer A is incorrect because the emergency repair disk does not contain actual files the system needs in order to operate. Answer B is incorrect because merely backing up the registry would not include necessary system files or data files the system needs to operate correctly. Answer C is incorrect because, although a mirror would, in fact, provide a complete duplicate of the server, the system would then mirror a software failure or configuration problem and so would provide no real security.

184   **UNDERSTANDING NORMAL BACKUPS IN WINDOWS NT**

Q.   *What type of backup should you perform before any other type of backup?*

Choose the best answer:

      A.   *System Backup*

      B.   *Normal Backup*

      C.   *Differential Backup*

      D.   *Incremental Backup*

Administrators must be concerned with how to provide the greatest level of protection to servers and data while at the same time minimizing the amount of time the servers and administrators spend when they perform backups. In addition, administrators must consider the amount of server downtime users will experience when administrators perform backups, as well as the company's costs to perform backups. Administrators will deal with these concerns based on the amount of data they back up, the number of servers in the domain, the number of users connected to the files to be backed up, the times these users are connected, and the budget companies provide to accomplish these backup goals. Various backup types require different amounts of tape space and varying amounts of time to perform (depending on type and size of network drives). There are three general backup types administrators use: Normal, Differential, and Incremental. Of the three backup types, the Normal Backup takes up the greatest amount of tape space and performance time—because it backs up every single selected file on the server. Because of the sheer volume of data, a Windows NT administrator might think initially that a Normal backup would not be a good choice for backups because of its space and time requirements.

Differential and Incremental backups, however, use a file-level reference (technically, they check a file's archive property) to determine if an administrator has previously backed up a file. Differential and Incremental Backups do not stand alone; rather, they augment the Normal backup in a typical backup strategy—meaning that you must always have at least one Normal backup of the system for the other backup types to use as a baseline. The Normal backup is the foundation, and therefore, the most important type of backup. Some backup strategies might require the administrator to perform the Normal backup infrequently (such as once a month) or perhaps even only once. Most good strategies, however, include a regularly scheduled Normal backup to provide a constantly changing base from which to perform the other backups. To execute a Normal backup, perform the following steps:

1. Click your mouse on the Start menu and select the Programs submenu Administrative Tools group Backup program. Windows NT will open the Backup program.

2. Within the Backup program, double-click the Drives window title bar. Windows NT will maximize the Drives window, making it easier to view.

3. Within the Backup program, click your mouse in the checkbox to the left of the drive letter to select files and folders. Windows NT Backup will place a check mark in the checkbox to indicate your selection.

4. To select individual files or folders on any single drive, double-click your mouse on the letter that corresponds to the drive. Windows NT Backup will open a window that displays the details of that drive. Click your mouse on any file or folder you want to back up. Windows NT Backup will indicate your selection by placing a check mark in the checkbox. Click your mouse on the Close button in the top-right corner of the window. Windows NT Backup will close the window and return you to the Drives window. Windows NT Backup will place a shaded checkbox in the Drives window to indicate your selection.

5. Click your mouse on the Backup button. Windows NT will open the Backup Information dialog box.

6. Within the Backup Information dialog box, type a name for the tape in the *Tape Name* field. (Note that if you have selected the Append option, the *Tape Name* field will be disabled.)

7. Select your choices for the backup from the available options. (Tip 192 contains a complete list of the options.) To perform a Normal backup, choose Normal in the *Backup Type* field.

8. Click your mouse on the OK button. Windows NT Backup will proceed with the backup.

Answer B is correct because you must perform a Normal backup before any other type of backup will function. Answer A is incorrect because System backup is not a real backup type. Answer C is not correct because you cannot use a Differential backup without first performing a Normal backup. Answer D is incorrect because an Incremental backup relies on the record the Normal backup made in the file attributes.

185	**UNDERSTANDING INCREMENTAL BACKUPS IN WINDOWS NT**

Q.   You are a Windows NT domain administrator. You want to back up only those files that contain changes since the last Normal or Incremental backup. What type of backup would you perform?

Choose the best answer:

A.   *Normal Backup*

B.   *Incremental Backup*

C.   *Copy Backup*

D.   *Daily Copy Backup*

As you learned in Tip 184, you must perform a Normal backup first if you want to perform a restore from any other type of backup. You will use the Incremental backup to back up all files that have changed since the most recent Normal backup. The Incremental Backup marks the files as it performs the backup so that it creates a record within each file's attributes. In turn, future Incremental backups can use this record (which will revert back to its unsaved state when a user changes the file) to identify new files that it should back up.

As an example of when to use an Incremental backup, imagine that an administrator creates a Normal backup once a week—on Sunday—for a company with a seven-day work week. The administrator has chosen Sunday because it is the day with the fewest users connected to files on the network, and, as a result, users' down time will be minimal. Remember, in order to create the Normal backup, the administrator must disconnect all users from the server that the administrator will back up. One reason the administrator would disconnect users is because some files the backup would record are locked and the Windows NT Backup utility cannot back up locked files. Therefore, the administrator must disconnect the users to ensure that the Normal backup will contain all the necessary files.

After the administrator performs the Normal backup on Sunday, the administrator performs an Incremental backup on Monday. The Incremental backup will back up all files that have changed since the last Normal backup (on Sunday) and will ignore all other files. As the Incremental backup executes, it marks the files it has backed up in a file called the *catalog*, which it stores on the last tape in the backup set (if multiple tapes are necessary for the backup). After the administrator backs up the system files on Sunday and Monday, the administrator performs another Incremental backup on Tuesday. As with the Monday Incremental backup, the Tuesday Incremental backup will back up only the files that have changed since the last Incremental backup and will ignore all other files. The administrator will follow this back up strategy so that if the server suffers a catastrophic event on Wednesday of the work week, the administrator can use the Normal backup tape from Sunday and each Incremental backup tape for Monday and Tuesday to restore the system. The administrator must use these tapes in sequential order from first to last to accomplish a complete restore, because the Normal tape set will return the server to its state on Sunday. The administrator must then restore the server to its state on Monday, and finally to its state on Tuesday (before the crash occurred).

As you will learn, you can use several strategies to back up the Windows NT domain. The Incremental backup strategy's primary advantage is that of all the backup methods, it uses the least amount of backup time and tape space for routine backup. As a result, users experience very little down time, compared to other backup strategies. The Incremental backup strategy's disadvantage is that if an administrator must restore server data after a catastrophic event, the administrator must have the most recent Normal backup tape, as well as all the Incremental backups since the Normal backup. Therefore, the restore process will require more backup time (and usually tapes) than other backup strategies.

To perform an Incremental backup, perform the following steps:

1. Click your mouse on the Start menu and select the Programs submenu Administrative Tools group Backup program. Windows NT will open the Backup program.

2. Within the Backup program, double-click the Drives window title bar. Windows NT will maximize the Drives window, making it easier to view.

3. Within the Backup program, click your mouse in the checkbox to the left of the drive letter to select files and folders. Windows NT Backup will place a check mark in the checkbox to indicate your selection.

4. To select individual files or folders on any single drive, double-click your mouse on the letter that corresponds to the drive. Windows NT Backup will open a window that displays the details of that drive. Click your mouse on any file or folder you want to back up. Windows NT Backup will indicate your selection by placing a check mark in the checkbox. Click your mouse on the Close button in the top-right corner of the window. Windows NT Backup will close the window and return you to the Drives window. Windows NT Backup will place a shaded checkbox in the Drives window to indicate your selection.

5. Click your mouse on the Backup button. Windows NT will open the Backup Information dialog box.

6. Within the Backup Information dialog box, type a name for the tape in the *Tape Name* field. (Note that if you have selected the Append option, the *Tape Name* field will be disabled.)

7. Select your choices for the backup from the options available. (Tip 192 contains a complete list of the options.) To perform an Incremental backup, choose Incremental in the *Backup Type* field.

8. Click your mouse on the OK button. Windows NT Backup will proceed with the backup.

Answer B is correct because an Incremental backup backs up all the files that have changed since the last Normal or Incremental backup. Answer A is incorrect because a Normal backup backs up all files you select and pays no attention to when you last backed them up. Answer C is incorrect because Copy backup backs up all files you selected and pays no attention to when you last backed them up. Answer D is incorrect because a Daily Copy backup backs up only files that changed during a given day.

---

186   UNDERSTANDING COPY BACKUPS IN WINDOWS NT

Q: *You are a Windows NT domain administrator. As part of your regular backup procedure, you must create a midweek backup of an outside accounting firm's financial data, without affecting your Normal backup strategy. To do so, what type of backup would you perform?*

Choose the best answer:

     A.   *Incremental Backup*

     B.   *Differential Backup*

     C.   *Normal Backup*

     D.   *Copy Backup*

Windows NT's Copy backup is one of the more interesting backup types, in part because of its usefulness and in part because many other backup programs do not include it. The Copy Backup is a relatively new concept that resolves a problem that occurs in many backup strategies. The problem with many backup strategies is that if administrators must make a backup for any reason that falls outside their regular backup strategy, the new backup would alter the reference in the file attributes and, as a result, would alter the entire backup plan for that cycle.

For example, imagine that a national company with many locations makes a midweek request for the administrator to send a complete backup of the local server to the national office for archiving or review. To comply with such a request, the administrator could send the existing tapes, but doing so would mean the administrator could not restore files if the server failed. The administrator could create a new Normal backup to send, but that would mark all the files as backed up and would throw off Incremental or Differential backups. (You will learn about Differential backups in Tip 187.) In a well-planned backup strategy that involves many tapes, making new Normal backups could create administrative confusion. Instead, the administrator could perform a Copy backup, which backs up all selected files and folders but does so without marking the files the same way a Normal backup does. Therefore, administrators can perform Copy backups at any time, without affecting the records of Differential or Incremental backup files and tapes—because all the files will maintain their currently indicated backup status. To perform a Copy backup, perform the following steps:

1. Click your mouse on the Start menu and select the Programs submenu Administrative Tools group Backup program. Windows NT will open the Backup program.

2. Within the Backup program, double-click the Drives window title bar. Windows NT will maximize the Drives window, making it easier to view.

3. Within the Backup program, click your mouse in the checkbox to the left of the drive letter to select files and folders. Windows NT Backup will place a check mark in the checkbox to indicate your selection.

4. To select individual files or folders on any single drive, double-click your mouse on the letter that corresponds to the drive. Windows NT Backup will open a window that displays the details of that drive. Click your mouse on any file or folder you want to back up. Windows NT Backup will indicate your selection by placing a check mark in the checkbox. Click your mouse on the Close button in the top-right corner of the window. Windows NT Backup will close the window and return you to the Drives window. Windows NT Backup will place a shaded checkbox in the Drives window to indicate your selection.

5. Click your mouse on the Backup button. Windows NT will open the Backup Information dialog box.

6. Within the Backup Information dialog box, type a name for the tape in the *Tape Name* field. (Note that if you have selected the Append option, the *Tape Name* field will be disabled.)

7. Select your choices for the backup from the options available. (Tip 192 contains a complete list of the options.) To perform a Copy backup, select Copy in the *Backup Type* field.

8. Click your mouse on the OK button. Windows NT Backup will proceed with the backup.

Answer D is correct because a Copy backup backs up all selected files and folders but does not change the files' backup indicators in any way. Answer A is incorrect because an Incremental backup backs up only those files that have changed since the last Normal or Incremental backup and also marks the files it backs up as backed up. Answer B is incorrect because a Differential backup backs up only the files that have changed since the last Normal or Incremental backup. Answer C is incorrect because a Normal backup would mark the files as having been backed up and would therefore alter the backup strategy.

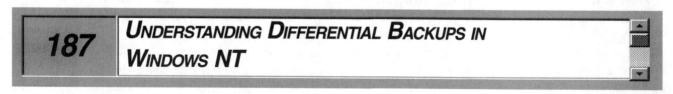

187 **UNDERSTANDING DIFFERENTIAL BACKUPS IN WINDOWS NT**

Q.   *What type of backup will back up only files and folders that have changed since the last Normal or Incremental backup without marking the file archive attributes?*

> A.   Copy Backup
>
> B.   Incremental Backup
>
> C.   Normal Backup
>
> D.   Differential Backup

The Differential backup is similar to the Incremental Backup in that it backs up all files and folders that have changed since the last Incremental or Differential backup. However, unlike the Incremental Backup, it does not change the file flag that marks the files as backed up.

An example of a strategy that uses the Differential backup would be if an administrator created a Normal backup on Monday and Differential backups on Tuesday through Friday, and then on Saturday the server failed. To restore the files, the administrator would need only the Normal backup tape from Monday and the Differential backup from Friday, before the server failed. The advantage to a strategy that uses the Differential backup is that you will need less time and fewer tapes to restore the files if a problem occurs.

The disadvantage to using a Differential backup strategy is that, as the number of days between the Differential backup and the Normal backup increases, it takes more time to back up files than the Incremental backup does (because it is copying more files). To execute a Differential backup, perform the following steps:

1. Click your mouse on the Start menu and select the Programs submenu Administrative Tools group Backup program. Windows NT will open the Backup program.

2. Within the Backup program, double-click the Drives window title bar. Windows NT will maximize the Drives window, making it easier to view.

3. Within the Backup program, click your mouse in the checkbox to the left of the drive letter to select files and folders. Windows NT Backup will place a check mark in the checkbox to indicate your selection.

4. To select individual files or folders on any single drive, double-click your mouse on the letter that corresponds to the drive. Windows NT Backup will open a window that displays the details of that drive. Click your mouse on any file or folder you want to back up. Windows NT Backup will indicate your selection by placing a check mark in the checkbox. Click your mouse on the Close button in the top-right corner of the window. Windows NT Backup will close the window and return you to the Drives window. Windows NT Backup will place a shaded checkbox in the Drives window to indicate your selection.

5. Click your mouse on the Backup button. Windows NT will open the Backup Information dialog box.

6. Within the Backup Information dialog box, type a name for the tape in the *Tape Name* field. (Note that if you have selected the Append option, the *Tape Name* field will be disabled.)

7. Select your choices for the backup from the options available. (Tip 192 contains a complete list of the options.) To create a Differential backup, choose Differential in the *Backup Type* field.

8. Click your mouse on the OK button. Windows NT Backup will proceed with the backup.

Answer D is correct because a Differential backup backs up all files and folders that have changed since the last Normal or Incremental backup and does not change the file attributes of files it backs up. Answer A is incorrect because a Copy backup backs up all files and folders and pays no attention to when you last backed them up. Answer B is incorrect because an Incremental backup backs up all files and folders that have changed since the last Normal or Incremental backup and marks the files as backed up. Answer C is incorrect because a Normal backup backs up all files and folders and pays no attention to when you last backed them up. The Normal backup also marks the files as backed up while it executes.

188 — UNDERSTANDING DAILY BACKUPS IN WINDOWS NT

Q.   *You are a Windows NT domain administrator. You want to create a backup of all files that have changed during a given day. What type of backup would you perform?*

Choose the best answer:

A.   *Incremental Backup*

B.   *Differential Backup*

C.   *Daily Copy Backup*

D.   *Copy Backup*

Windows NT domain administrators must often create backups for reasons outside of the regular backup strategy. For example, if an administrator wants to create a backup of all work users performed on a server in a given day, but does not want to affect the regular backup cycle, the administrator would use the Daily Copy backup. The Daily Copy backup backs up all files and folders that have changed during one given day.

The Daily Copy backup does not mark the files as it backs up and therefore will not interfere with an administrator's regular backup strategy. The Daily Copy is useful in certain situations, but is generally not helpful as part of a regular backup strategy, because a Thursday restoration would require Sunday's Normal backup, and Monday, Tuesday, and Wednesday's Daily Copy backup. Therefore, Daily Copy backups are generally not a cornerstone of a backup policy, but are instead used to respond to specific situations. To execute a Daily Copy backup, perform the following steps:

1. Click your mouse on the Start menu and select the Programs submenu Administrative Tools group Backup program. Windows NT will open the Backup program.

2. Within the Backup program, double-click the Drives window title bar. Windows NT will maximize the Drives window, making it easier to view.

3. Within the Backup program, click your mouse in the checkbox to the left of the drive letter to select files and folders. Windows NT Backup will place a check mark in the checkbox to indicate your selection.

4. To select individual files or folders on any single drive, double-click your mouse on the letter that corresponds to the drive. Windows NT Backup will open a window that displays the details of that drive. Click your mouse on any file or folder you want to back up. Windows NT Backup will indicate your selection by placing a check mark in the checkbox. Click your mouse on the Close button in the top-right corner of the window. Windows NT Backup will close the window and return you to the Drives window. Windows NT Backup will place a shaded checkbox in the Drives window to indicate your selection.

5. Click your mouse on the Backup button. Windows NT will open the Backup Information dialog box.

6. Within the Backup Information dialog box, type a name for the tape in the *Tape Name* field. (Note that if you have selected the Append option, the *Tape Name* field will be disabled.)

7. Select your choices for the backup from the options available. (Tip 192 contains a complete list of the options.) To create a Daily Copy backup, choose Daily Copy in the *Backup Type* field.

8. Click your mouse on the OK button. Windows NT Backup will proceed with the backup.

Answer C is correct because the Daily Copy backup backs up only files that have changed during a given day. Answer A is incorrect because an Incremental backup backs up files and folders that have changed since the last Normal or Incremental backup. Answer B is incorrect because a Differential backup backs up all files and folders that have changed since the last Normal or Incremental backup. Answer D is incorrect because a Copy Backup backs up all selected files and folders regardless of their current "backed up" status.

189   BACKING UP THE REGISTRY IN WINDOWS NT

Q.   *You are the administrator of a Windows NT domain that consists of one primary domain controller, one backup domain controller, two standalone servers, and a variety of client machines. You have installed tape backup units in each of the servers. You want to back up the backup and primary domain controllers' Registries. What steps would you take to perform the backups?*

Choose the best answer:

     A.   *Create drive mappings to each server and back up the Registries from the primary domain controller.*

     B.   *Create drive mappings to each server and perform the backups from the backup domain controller.*

     C.   *Perform the backup for each machine locally.*

     D.   *Create drive mappings to each server and perform the backups from one of the standalone servers.*

One of the most important aspects of the backup strategy is to back up the Registry which contains vital configuration information that a Windows NT machine must have to function. An administrator who does not back up the Registry and then later tries to restore the system files after a server failure may well find that the machine will not function as it did at the time of the backup because the administrator cannot restore the Registry. An administrator who restores the system files without the Registry will only fix a problem with the files themselves but will not resolve a problem that exists in the Registry. Worse, the current Registry might have information that no longer functions with the system files from the backup, resulting in a server that does not function at all. Therefore, as an administrator, you must back up the Registry on a regular basis.

Before you back up the Windows NT Registry, however, there are a few things you must know. First, you can only back up the Windows NT Registry *locally*, which means that the event or process you perform can only occur at the machine the event or process will affect. In other words, you cannot backup the Windows NT registry on a server to a tape drive on a remote machine on the network, and you cannot backup the Windows NT Registry from a remote machine to the server's tape drive, either. Second, you can back up the Windows NT Registry only if you back up an additional file from the same partition as the Registry at the same time. For example, imagine that you have a Windows NT Server with a single hard drive installed. You divided the hard drive into two partitions and the logical drives for these partitions are C: and D:. In turn, you have installed the Windows NT system files on the D: drive (where the Registry resides). In order to back up the Registry for this machine, you must also select at least one file from the D: drive to back up. To back up the Windows NT Registry, perform the following steps:

1.   Click your mouse on the Start menu and select the Programs submenu Administrative Tools group Backup program. Windows NT will open the Backup program.

2.   Within the Backup program, double-click the Drives window title bar. Windows NT will maximize the Drives window, making it easier to view.

3.   Within the Backup program, click your mouse in the checkbox to the left of the drive letter to select files and folders. Windows NT Backup will place a check mark in the checkbox to indi-

cate your selection.

4. To select individual files or folders on any single drive, double-click your mouse on the letter that corresponds to the drive. Windows NT Backup will open a window that displays the details of that drive. Click your mouse on any file or folder you want to back up. Windows NT Backup will indicate your selection by placing a check mark in the checkbox. Click your mouse on the Close button in the top-right corner of the window. Windows NT Backup will close the window and return you to the Drives window. Windows NT Backup will place a shaded checkbox in the Drives window to indicate your selection.

5. Click your mouse on the Backup button. Windows NT will open the Backup Information dialog box.

6. Within the Backup Information dialog box, type a name for the tape in the *Tape Name* field. (Note that if you have selected the Append option, the *Tape Name* field will be disabled.)

7. Select your choices for the backup from the options available. (Tip 192 contains a complete list of the options.) To back up the Windows NT Registry, click your mouse on the Backup Registry checkbox. Windows NT will insert a check mark into the Backup Registry checkbox.

8. Click your mouse on the OK button. Windows NT Backup will proceed with the backup.

*Answer **C** is correct because you can only back up the Windows NT Registry locally. **Answers A, B**, and **D** are incorrect because you cannot back up the Windows NT Registry from a remote machine.*

190   **ROTATING BACKUP TAPE SETS**

Q.   *Which of the following definitions best describes the term Tape Rotation?*

Choose the best answer:

     A.   *Part of your backup strategy in which you reuse tapes, remove tapes from the backup cycle for archiving, and introduce new tapes to the backup cycle.*

     B.   *The act of turning over a tape so you can use the other side.*

     C.   *The act of using a different tape for each backup you perform.*

     D.   *The speed at which a tape device rotates to advance the tape.*

Tape backup systems and parallel backup drives (additional hard drives used solely for backups) use *magnetic media*. Magnetic media, which consists of a magnetic coating over a base of plastic, metal, or glass, is the storage method floppy disks and hard drives use. The magnetic coating in magnetic media can deteriorate over time and repeated use will increase this deterioration.

Because the magnetic media administrators use to perform backups can deteriorate, administrators must include in their backup strategies a way to remove aging tapes from the backup cycle, introduce new tapes into the backup cycle, and create an archive of the backup tapes. To do so, administrators will use *tape rotation*.

Tape rotation is the process of removing existing tapes from, and introducing new tapes into, the backup cycle. You should consider tape rotation an important aspect of your backup strategy. The number of tapes you will need depends on the amount of data that you must back up, what kind of tape rotation schedule you implement, and the life cycle of the tapes themselves. Tape life is based on the quality of the tapes you buy and the manner in which you store them. If you choose inexpensive tapes, they might deteriorate faster than more expensive tapes. You should store all tapes in a secure location that is both cool and dry. Some companies even choose to store their tapes at facilities that specialize in tape storage.

As an example of tape rotation, imagine that you are the administrator for a small company with a single Windows NT Server. Because you back up a small amount of data and users' down time is minimal, you perform a Normal backup every day. After you perform the Normal backup on Friday of a given week, you remove the tape from the cycle and place it into the archive. Then, on Monday you perform the Normal backup on a new tape. On Tuesday, you use Monday's tape for Tuesday's backup and continue to use the same tape in the same manner throughout the week. Finally, on Friday you perform your Normal backup again and send the week's full tape to the archive. If you continue this practice and always introduce a new tape on Monday, you will eventually cycle all your tapes into the archive.

Answer A is correct because when you use tape rotation in your backup strategy, you reuse the same tapes, remove tapes from the backup cycle for archiving, and introduce new tapes to the backup cycle.

191 UNDERSTANDING BACKUP RECORDS AND STORAGE ROTATION

Q.   *When you make backup sets, you should always keep the sets as physically close to the server as possible.*

True or False?

Your Windows NT backup strategy must provide the most data security possible. Tape security is just as important as the backup itself. If you, as a Windows NT administrator, keep all your backup tapes in the same location, a single catastrophic event, such as a fire, could destroy both the server and all your backups, in which case you would lose all your data permanently.

Storage rotation is one aspect of your backup strategy that you can use to avoid unintentional tape destruction. Storage rotation is the act of storing one complete backup tape set at a site separate from the server and other backup tape sets. To have effective storage rotation, you must ensure that the tape set you keep at the remote location is a complete backup of the system and its data. For example, to store a complete backup at a remote location, you would include a Normal backup and any Incremental or Differential backup tape sets. You would not store a Normal backup remotely without the Incremental or Differential backup tape sets because, in order to restore data, you must have the information on both the Normal backup and on any other backup tape sets.

Storage rotation is generally an administrative part of the backup process because you do not need technical skills to store tapes. Another administrative task that is an important part of storage rotation is to keep *backup records*. Backup records are, simply, printed or electronic lists of what files and folders you backed up and when you did so. You will usually make backup records by printing the backup log and storing it in a physical folder you can easily access. When you keep backup records, you make it much easier to locate storage locations if someone requests a list of files you have backed up. Another reason you would keep printed backup records is for reference in case you need old files you no longer use, as in the case of audits or litigation.

*The answer is **False** because you should keep at least one complete system backup at a remote location to prevent a single catastrophic event from destroying all data.*

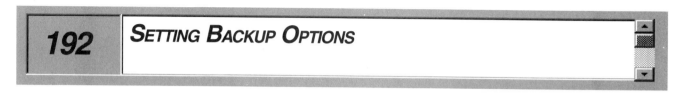

192 | **SETTING BACKUP OPTIONS**

Q. *The Windows NT Registry automatically backs up when you back up the Windows NT system folder.*

True or False?

As you have learned, a Windows NT domain administrator will perform many different kinds of backups. Before you, as an administrator, perform a backup, however, you must configure your backup options from within the Backup Information dialog box. To open the Backup Information dialog box, perform the following steps:

1. Click your mouse on the Start menu and select the Programs submenu Administrative Tools group Backup program. Windows NT will open the Backup program.

2. Within the Backup program, double-click your mouse on the Drives window title bar. Windows NT will maximize the Drives window, making it easier to view.

3. Within the Drives window, click your mouse on the Backup button. Windows NT will open the Backup Information dialog box, as shown in Figure 192.

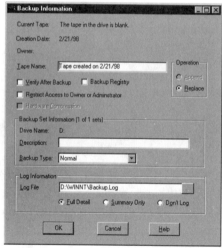

Figure 192 Using the Backup Information dialog box.

Within the Backup Information dialog box, you can choose from the following options, which will control how the Backup program performs your backups:

- *Operation:* Lets you either append or replace data. If you select the Append option, Windows NT Backup will add a new backup set after the last backup set on the tape. If you select the Replace option, Windows NT Backup will overwrite all the data on the tape with the new backup set.

- *Verify After Backup:* Confirms that you backed up all files accurately.

- *Backup Registry:* Adds a copy of the Registry to the backup.

Note: *The Backup Registry option is available only if you select a minimum of one other file from the volume containing the Registry file.*

- *Restrict Access to Owner or Administrator:* Limits access to administrators, backup operators, or the users who performed the backup.

- *Hardware Compression:* Enables hardware compression if you are using a compression-supporting tape drive.

- *Description:* Contains a field that lets you enter a name for the backup set.

- *Backup Type:* Lets you choose what type of backup to perform.

- *Log File:* Contains a field that lets you specify a file name for backup logging and three checkboxes. The checkboxes—which determine the amount of detail, if any, you will keep in the log file— are Full Detail, Summary Only, and Don't Log.

*The answer is **False** because the Windows NT registry will back up only if you have configured it to do so in the Backup Information dialog box.*

193	USING WINDOWS NT BACKUP TO RESTORE DATA

Q.   *You are a Windows NT domain administrator. The Primary Domain Controller has suffered a hard drive failure. After you replace the hard drive, what steps would you take to restore the primary domain controller to service?*

Choose the best answer:

A.   *Install Windows NT server from the original installation files and reconstruct the data from client machines.*

B.   *Install Windows NT server from the original installation files and reconstruct the data from a backup domain controller.*

C.   *Install Windows NT server from the original installation files and use the Windows NT Backup utility to restore all files and folders from the backup tapes.*

D.   *Install Windows NT server and restore the data files from backups on floppy disk.*

One of a Windows NT administrator's biggest potential problems is a server failure. Factors such as the wear and tear computer parts receive, environmental issues (such as extreme heat or flooding), and unexplained software failure contribute to the likelihood that sooner or later a Windows NT administrator will experience a server failure. Server failure is precisely the reason that administrators perform system backups. A properly backed up server is at minimal risk should a server failure occur. When a complete server failure does occur, the administrator must repair or replace the failed component, perhaps reinstall the Windows NT operating system, and even, in some cases, replace the installation with a backup of the original server. To restore data from a backup tape to the system, perform the following steps:

1. Click your mouse on the Start menu and select the Programs submenu Administrative Tools group Backup program. Windows NT will open the Backup program.

2. Double-click your mouse on the Tapes window title bar, which will maximize the Tapes window, making it easier to view. Windows NT will scan the tape drive, list the backup sets on that tape, and attempt to load a catalog file, which lists the files and folders the backup set contains.

3. Within the Backup program, click your mouse in the checkbox to the left of the drive letter to select files and folders. Windows NT Backup will place a check mark in the checkbox to indicate your selection.

4. To select individual files or folders on any single drive, double-click your mouse on the letter that corresponds to the drive. Windows NT Backup will open a window that displays the details of that drive. Click your mouse on any file or folder you want to back up. Windows NT Backup will indicate your selection by placing a check mark in the checkbox. Click your mouse on the Close button in the top-right corner of the window. Windows NT Backup will close the window and return you to the Tapes window. Windows NT Backup will place a shaded checkbox in the Tapes window to indicate your selection.

5. Click your mouse on the Restore button. Windows NT will open the Restore Information dialog box. Click your mouse on OK. Windows NT Backup will proceed with the restore.

In Tip 192, you learned about the various options you can choose to back up your system. To restore your system, you can choose from the following options:

- *Restore to Drive:* Lets you choose the drive to which you want to restore the data.

- *Alternate Path*: Lets you specify a path for the restore other than the path that existed when you made the backup.

- *Restore Local Registry*: Restores a backed up registry to the local system.

- *Restore File Permissions*: Adds the original file permissions to the files as you restore them. You cannot restore file permissions to a FAT partition.

- *Verify After Restore*: Compares the restored files to the files on the tape to ensure integrity.

- *Log Information*: Contains a field that lets you specify a file name for backup logging and three checkboxes. The checkboxes—which determine the amount of detail, if any, you will keep in the log file—are Full Detail, Summary Only, and Don't Log.

Answer C is correct because you use the Windows NT Backup utility within the Windows NT operating system to restore files and folders from tape to a system. Answer A is incorrect because client machines would not have any of the system data the primary domain controller needs to function. Answer B is incorrect because the backup domain controller would not have the local registry or data files the primary domain controller needs to function. Answer D is incorrect because the standalone servers would not have the local registry or any of the data files the primary domain controller needs to function.

194 — CREATING A BACKUP SCRIPT FOR A SCHEDULED BACKUP

Q: *You are a Windows NT domain administrator. You must perform system backups on all network servers. How can you use the Windows NT Backup program so that the backups will execute automatically at night?*

Choose the best answer:

A. *Within the Windows NT Backup program, use the Schedule option from the Backup menu and specify the backup times.*

B. *From the Windows NT Backup program on the Backup Properties dialog box, click your mouse on the Schedule button.*

C. *Create a batch file that contains the command-line scripts which will instruct Windows NT to perform the backup you want. Use the AT command to schedule the batch file to execute.*

D. *From the Windows NT Command prompt, type the command NTBackup.exe Backup /Shed.*

As you learned in Tip 183, you can use the Windows NT Backup utility to establish an effective system backup routine. Windows NT Server and Windows NT Workstation both include the Windows NT Backup program on the installation CD-ROM. The Windows NT Backup program includes most of the features that third-party backup utilities have, with one exception: The Windows NT Backup utility does not include built-in support to let you schedule automatic backups. To schedule a backup means that no one has to be present to start the backup procedure—the system will start the backup at the time the administrator previously scheduled. The Windows NT Backup program, however, requires the person who will perform the backup to start the backup procedure manually (which is not so wonderful at 1 A.M., or some other time of low network use). In turn, imagine how cumbersome backups would be if every backup required a person to click the mouse on the Backup button for each system backup procedure.

Although the Windows NT Backup program does not include built-in support to let you schedule an automatic backup, you can use other Windows NT features to make a backup occur at a scheduled time. To create a Windows NT scheduled backup, you must perform two steps. First, create a backup batch file that contains a command script to control the backup procedure. Second, use the Windows NT AT command to schedule the backup batch file to execute. (You will learn how to perform the second step in Tip 195.) To create a backup batch file, you must open the *Notepad* program. To open *Notepad*, click your mouse on the Start menu and select the Programs submenu Accessories group *Notepad* program. Windows NT will open the *Notepad* program. In the *Notepad* program, enter the following syntax (square brackets indicate that Windows NT does not require a parameter):

```
NTBACKUP operation path [/A] [/B] [/D "text"] [/E] [/HC:[ON|OFF]] [/L "filename"] [/R]
    [/T option] [/Tape :n] [/V]
```

The *NTBACKUP* invocation runs the Windows NT backup utility. Table 194 lists the parameters and options for invoking *NTBACKUP* from the command-line.

Parameters	Options
Operation	An administrator will specify the Backup or the Restore option.
Path	Specifies the path to the folders or volumes Windows NT will back up.
/A	Include /A to have *NTBACKUP* append the backup job to the tape. Omit /A to let *NTBACKUP* overwrite the tape.
/B	Include /B to back up the Windows NT Registry.
/D "text"	Use /D to specify a description of the backup on the tape. Place the description within the quotation marks.
/E	Use /E to have the backup log include exceptions only. Without the /E, *NTBACKUP* will create a full backup log.
/HC:[ON|OFF]	Use /HC to force the tape device to turn hardware compression on or off.
/L "filename"	Use /L to specify the name of the backup log file. Include the name and path within the quotation marks.
/R	Use /R to restrict tape access to the owner or administrator. Only the user who performed the backup or an administrator can restore a tape backed up with /R.
/T option	Use /T to specify the backup type. Replace *option* with the word Normal, Copy, Incremental, Differential, or Daily.
/Tape:n	Use /Tape to specify the desired tape device for the backup routine only when the machine has more than one tape device.
/V	Use /V to verify the backup after the backup completes.

Table 194 The NTBACKUP program's parameters and options.

Answer C is correct because you must create a backup batch file and schedule the batch file to execute when you want the backups to occur. Answers A, B, and D are incorrect because Windows NT Backup (NTBACKUP.exe) does not have a scheduling service.

---

195   USING THE AT COMMAND TO SCHEDULE A BACKUP

Q: *You have created a backup batch file. You now want to schedule the backup batch file to execute at midnight, while the network is idle. What command can you use to schedule Windows NT to execute a backup batch file named* **backup.bat** *at 12 a.m.?*

Choose the best answer:

     A.   *At the Windows NT command prompt, type Schedule backup.bat 12:00a. Windows NT will automatically start the backup.bat file every night at 12 a.m.*

     B.   *At the Windows NT command prompt, type AT \\servername 00:00 /every:m,t,w,th,f "C:\backup.bat".*

     C.   *Install the Windows NT Workstation Resource Kit. From the command prompt, type Set backup.bat 12:00 a.m. /every: 1,2,3,4,5.*

     D.   *You cannot schedule the Windows NT backup program.*

Although the Windows NT Backup program does not have built-in scheduling ability, you can use the Windows NT *AT* command to schedule a backup time. An administrator can use the *AT* command to schedule any batch file or program to execute at a set time and date. An administrator can also configure the command to execute just one time or on a regular schedule.

The following lists the *AT* command syntax, which you will only use from the command-line within a console window:

```
AT \\computername time /EVERY:date "command"
```

An example of an actual *AT* command is *AT \\Cash 00:00 /every:m,t,w,th,f "C:\backupdir\backup.bat"*. This example would schedule the *backup.bat* file to execute on a computer named Cash every Monday, Tuesday, Wednesday, Thursday, and Friday at midnight (12:00 a.m.). For a complete list of Windows NT *AT* command syntax and options, perform the following steps:

1. Click your mouse on the Start menu and select the Programs submenu Command Prompt program. Windows NT will open the Command Prompt window.

2. Within the Command Prompt window, type *AT /?*. Windows NT will display the *AT* syntax and command options.

Administrators can use the command-line switches in Table 195 with the *AT* command to modify how the command executes.

Answer B is correct because you must use the AT command from the Windows NT command prompt. Answer A is incorrect because Windows NT does not have a Schedule command. Answer C is incorrect because although the Windows NT Server Resource Kit contains the **Winat** *program interface, the Kit relies on the AT command to schedule commands. Windows NT does not support the syntax in Answer C. Answer D is incorrect because you can use the AT command to schedule commands.*

AT Switch	Uses
computername	Specifies a remote computer to schedule an event on. If an administrator omits this parameter, Windows NT schedules commands on the local machine.
id	Identifies the scheduled command by number. (The first scheduled command will have *id 1*, the second command will have *id 2*, and so on.)
/delete	Cancels a scheduled command. If an administrator omits *id*, Windows NT deletes all scheduled commands.
/yes	An administrator will use /yes with the /delete option to cancel all scheduled commands without requiring that Windows NT prompt the user to press the Y key.
Time	Specifies the time the command is to execute.
/interactive	Lets the command interact with the Desktop of the user who is currently logged on when the command executes.
/every:date	Executes the command on the specified day or days. If the administrator omits the date, Windows NT assumes the current date of the month.
/next:date	Executes the command on the next occurrence of the day (for example, next Friday would be /next:Friday).
"command"	The batch file or program Windows NT executes.

Table 195 The AT command options.

196 USING THE NT BACKUP UTILITY WITH PARALLEL DEVICES

Q: *You have just purchased a new tape backup device. The backup device is an external tape device that uses the parallel port. You cannot get the backup device to work in Windows NT. Why does the tape backup device not work in Windows NT?*

Choose the best answer:

A. *You must use the Control Panel Tape Device dialog box to specify the type of device you are using.*

B. *You must have the backup device connected when you boot the machine. Windows NT will automatically detect the device.*

C. *You must install special device drivers for the specific tape device you are using.*

D. *You cannot use backup parallel devices with the Windows NT Backup utility. You can purchase special drivers from the hardware vendor that will let Windows NT see the tape device, but you will also need proprietary tape backup software for your tape device to work.*

Windows NT is guaranteed to work only on hardware on the Microsoft Windows NT Hardware Compatibility List (HCL). The Hardware Compatibility List is a list of machines and model numbers that Microsoft considers as compatible with Windows NT. The Hardware Compatibility List also lists peripheral devices (such as SCSI controllers, scanners, modem, network cards, and tape devices). You will learn more about the Hardware Compatibility List in Tip 221, "Introduction to the HCL." Windows NT does not support parallel tape devices (that is, tape drives that connect to the computer through the parallel port), so Microsoft does not include parallel tape devices on the Hardware Compatibility List. In turn, the Windows NT Backup program will work only with supported tape devices from the

Hardware Compatibility List. Some vendors will produce special drivers for their tape devices to work with Windows NT, but you will then have to load special software to work with the tape devices.

Answer D is correct because you cannot use the Windows NT Backup utility with a parallel tape device. Answer A is incorrect because, although you would use the Tape Devices dialog box to specify the type of tape device connected to your Windows NT machine, you can specify supported tape devices only. Windows NT does not support the parallel tape device. Answer B is incorrect because Windows NT will detect supported tape devices only when you use the Detect button in the Tape Devices dialog box. Answer C is incorrect because, although you could install special device drivers for your tape device, the device will still be incompatible with the Windows NT Backup program.

197 INTRODUCTION TO WINDOWS NT'S VIRTUAL MEMORY MODEL

Q: *Which of the following describes Windows NT's Virtual Memory?*

Choose the best answer:

     A.   *Windows NT uses cache memory from the system board as RAM.*

     B.   *Windows NT sets aside a small amount of RAM for system processes.*

     C.   *Windows NT uses a file on the hard drive named pagefile.sys to emulate RAM.*

     D.   *Windows NT will write the physical memory contents to the hard drive during a system crash.*

Virtual memory occurs when an operating system uses hard drive space to convince applications and the portions of the operating system that there is more physical memory than actually exists. Windows NT uses a local hard drive to create the virtual memory. When the physical memory fills up, Windows NT uses the hard drive as an extension to the regular physical memory. The process the operating system performs when it moves information from physical memory (RAM) onto the hard drive (virtual memory) is known as *paging*. Windows NT uses a *virtual memory manager* to handle all paging requests.

The virtual memory manager constantly chooses sections of RAM that you have not used recently and moves those sections to the pagefile (which has the name *pagefile.sys*) on the hard drive that emulates RAM. When an application requires information from RAM, the virtual memory manager finds the requested information, either in RAM or in the pagefile. If the information is in the pagefile, the virtual memory manager will move information in RAM that you have not used recently to the pagefile and then move the information the application requested to the newly available RAM. The process of the operating system's moving information to and from RAM back and forth to the pagefile is called *demand paging*. Although virtual memory's major benefit is in the computer's ability to execute more programs with a limited amount of RAM, virtual memory's major drawback is that it is much slower than RAM because hard drives are mechanical devices and RAM is electronic.

Windows NT uses a *flat, linear address space*, which runs from 0 to 4Gb, which means that Windows NT does not use any conventional or extended memory. Older operating systems, such as MS-DOS, use conventional and extended memory, which let them bypass the limitation of the Intel microchip to only 640Kb of system RAM. In other words, on a computer with 128Mb of memory, 640Kb would be conventional memory and the remainder would be extended memory. Windows NT, however, uses its entire amount of physical memory as one memory area—there are no divisions in the memory. Windows NT can access up to four gigabytes of physical memory. Windows NT uses two gigabytes of the total memory for user applications and reserves two gigabytes for the operating system. Most computers will not have four gigabytes of physical memory, so Windows NT uses the virtual memory manager to emulate the missing physical memory. Therefore, because of the virtual memory manager, each application that runs in Windows NT acts as if it has access to a full 4Gb of RAM.

*Answer C is correct because Windows NT uses the **pagefile.sys** file to emulate physical memory. **Answer A** is incorrect because Windows NT uses cache memory to store recently requested information, not to emulate physical memory. **Answer B** is incorrect because Windows NT does not set aside RAM for paging purposes. **Answer D** is incorrect because the process of writing physical memory to the hard drive in the event of a system crash is called a memory dump, and does not involve virtual memory.*

198 CREATING MULTIPLE PAGEFILES

Q: *You want to improve your Windows NT Server's performance. Which of the following would be the best way to implement pagefiles to improve performance?*

Choose the best answer:

    A.   *One pagefile on the system partition on the first physical hard drive.*

    B.   *One pagefile on the system partition of the first physical hard drive, and one pagefile on an extended partition of the first physical hard drive.*

    C.   *One pagefile on the system partition of the first physical hard drive, and one pagefile on a primary partition on the second physical hard drive.*

    D.   *One pagefile on a partition other than the system partition on the first physical hard drive, and one pagefile on a primary or extended partition of the second physical hard drive.*

An administrator can configure the amount of virtual memory Windows NT will use. To do so, an administrator can place multiple pagefiles on one or more hard drives on the local machine. The virtual-memory manager will manage the pagefile as one area of virtual memory. If you have multiple pagefiles, you can improve system performance; however, having multiple pagefiles increases system performance only if the pagefiles are on different physical drives. To improve system performance, Microsoft also recommends moving your pagefile off of the partition that stores your Windows NT system files. Remember that whenever you suggest a pagefile solution to enhance your system's performance, you must consider the location of the pagefiles. Make sure that each pagefile is on its own physical drive. If pagefiles are not on different physical drives, the drive where multiple pagefiles exist will use the same read and write heads to access the pagefile, thus creating no performance enhancement. To create multiple pagefiles or manage existing pagefiles, perform the following steps:

1.   Right-click your mouse on the My Computer icon on the desktop. Windows NT will display the Quick menu.

2.   Within the Quick menu, select the Properties option. Windows NT will display the System Properties dialog box.

3.   Within the System Properties dialog box, select the Performance tab. Within the Performance tab in the Virtual Memory section, click your mouse on the Change button. Windows NT will display the Virtual Memory dialog box, as shown in Figure 198.

4.   Within the Virtual Memory dialog box, either select the drive on which you want to configure a pagefile or select the default pagefile. In the *Initial Size* field, enter the minimum size for the new pagefile (this value should never be lower then the physical memory on your machine). In the *Maximum Size* field, enter the maximum size your pagefile will grow to.

5. Click your mouse on the Set button. Windows NT will create the pagefile.

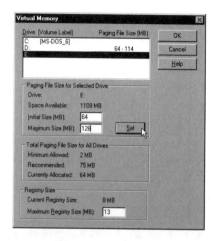

Figure 198 The Virtual Memory dialog box.

Answer D is correct because you would want to create multiple pagefiles on different physical hard drives and move the pagefile off of the system partition. Answer A is incorrect because a single pagefile on the system partition would provide the least amount of system performance. Answer B is incorrect because creating a pagefile on the extended partition of the first physical disk where the pagefile is on the system partition would be redundant and would not improve performance. Answer C is incorrect because one of the pagefiles is on the system partition, which will result in system performance degradation.

199 UNDERSTANDING THE WINDOWS NT WORKGROUP MODEL

Q: You have configured your Windows NT Workstations in a workgroup. Which of the following statements are true?

Choose all answers that apply:

> *A.   You will have only one user account in the workgroup for each user.*
>
> *B.   You will not have universal access to resources.*
>
> *C.   You can use your local user account to administer any resources in the workgroup from your local machine.*
>
> *D.   You must create multiple user accounts for each machine users will access.*
>
> *E.   An administrator on one Window NT Workstation will be an administrator on all Windows NT Workstations.*

You can set up Windows NT Workstations in a *workgroup configuration*. A workgroup configuration is a low-security network implementation that lets small organizations set up LANs and share resources. For example, imagine an insurance office with six employees where everyone must be able to access a customer list file and print. For users to use files and printers without a network, each computer would have to have duplicate customer lists and its own printer. If the insurance office used a workgroup, however, the office would need only one copy of the client list and one printer. One of the workstations would simply share the resource and the other users would access the object through the network. A user must log on to a Windows NT Workstation in order to use the Windows NT Workstation's resources. In a workgroup configuration, the local workstation would perform the user's account validation, which means that in order to reach remote resources, the user's logon name and password must exist on each workstation that shares resources. The resulting user account and password duplication can create significant administrative overhead, because an administrator must maintain user accounts on each Windows NT Workstation. If a user wants to change his or her password, the administrator would then have to change the password on each Windows NT Workstation in the workgroup. Because of the work an administrator must perform to maintain a Windows NT workgroup, any more then ten workstations would be quite cumbersome to the administrator, and Microsoft (and most network administrators) do not recommend doing so.

In a workgroup configuration, in order to reach a remote resource, a user must have a duplicate account on the computer where the resource is. Suppose a user named "Bob" wants to access a printer on a remote workstation. When Bob accesses the printer, the following events occur. Bob logs onto his local machine (Computer 1) as "Bob" with a password of "Password." When Bob tries to print to Computer 2, the Windows NT software running on Computer 2 checks its local Directory Database to see if the requesting user has an account. When Windows NT locates the account and password and validates the account, Windows NT issues the user an Access Token for Computer 2. Windows NT matches the local (Computer 2) Access Token against the Access Control List for the printing device and gives the user the appropriate access level.

Answer D is correct because you will have one user account for each user in the workgroup at each Windows NT Workstation in the workgroup. Answer A is incorrect because you will have multiple user accounts in a workgroup configuration. Answer B is incorrect because universal access to resources implies that one user account can access all network resources. Answer C and E are incorrect because, as you have learned, there will be multiple user accounts for each user in the workgroup. In order to be an administrator, you would have to have an administrative account on each Windows NT machine in the workgroup.

200 | **INTRODUCTION TO WINDOWS NT DOMAINS**

Q: Which of the following best describes a Windows NT domain model?

Choose the best answer:

A.   Windows NT domains require an administrator to create a user account for each user in the domain on all Windows NT Servers.

B.   Windows NT domains are administrative units where only one user account for each user exists and which you can centrally administer from any Windows 95 or Windows NT machine.

C.   A Windows NT domain must have at least two, and not more then ten, Windows NT Servers.

D.   Windows NT domains are only for administering user accounts.

Windows NT domains are centrally administered administrative units that let system administrators create and manage users and resources. *Centralized administration* means that one user account (username and password) exists for each user in the network and that the administrators can create and manage the user accounts within the domain from any location. To create a Windows NT domain, you need only one machine—a Windows NT Server that an administrator has installed as a Windows NT Server *Primary Domain Controller (PDC)*. The Windows NT Primary Domain Controller will log on users to the domain.

When the Windows NT Server Primary Domain Controller logs on a user to the domain, the user will have access to all resources in the domain to which the administrator has granted the user permissions. The Windows NT Server Primary Domain Controller maintains the entire domain's user accounts database (the directory database). The directory database contains the accounts for all users, groups, and Windows NT machines in the domain. When a user tries to access a resource located on a Windows NT machine, the Windows NT machine will check the user's Access Token to see if the user has the permissions required to access the resource the user requested.

Although in a Windows NT domain, you require only one Primary Domain Controller, you can install several machines to assist the Primary Domain Controller in granting users' log-on requests. The machines that assist the primary domain controller are called *Backup Domain Controllers (BDCs)*. Backup domain controllers maintain read-only copies of the Directory Database the Primary Domain Controller stores. Backup Domain Controllers can log on users, but cannot make changes to the Directory Database that local machines store. The operating system will directly update only the Directory Database on the Primary Domain Controller. After an administrator updates the Primary Domain Controller's Directory Database, the network operating system will replicate the changes to the Backup Domain Controllers. After the network operating system replicates the changes to the Backup Domain Controllers, the Primary Domain Controller or the Backup Domain Controllers can validate any user who requests a log-on validation—whichever machine receives the request first will respond. You will learn more about domains in the "Windows NT Server in the Enterprise Technologies" section of this book.

Answer B is correct because domains are administrative units that let system administrators create and manage user accounts and system resources from anywhere in the domain. Answer A is incorrect because user accounts should reside only on the Primary Domain Controller. Answer C is incorrect because a Windows NT domain requires only one computer, the Primary Domain Controller. Answer D is incorrect because Windows NT domains let administrators create and manage users as well as resources.

201 | **INTRODUCTION TO TRUST RELATIONSHIPS**

Q.   *You are the administrator of a medium-sized network that has three Windows NT domains. You have placed all user accounts within Domain A. What steps must you take to ensure that users can access resources in Domain B and Domain C?*

Choose all answers that apply:

A.   *Create a two-way trust relationship between all domains.*

B.   *Create a one-way trust relationship so that Domain A trusts Domain B and Domain B trusts Domain C.*

C.   *Create a one-way trust relationship so that Domain B trusts Domain A and Domain C trusts Domain A.*

D.   *Create a one-way trust relationship so that Domain A trusts Domain B and Domain A trusts Domain C.*

Windows NT administrators often must implement security across multiple domains. Windows NT directory services provide inter-domain security through *trust relationships*. Trust relationships enable the inherent Windows NT security in one domain to affect one or more additional domains or create a single administrative unit that is able to authenticate user log-on requests from all domains. Within multiple domain models, the administrator must decide where the authentication process will take place or if all affected domains will have an equal ability (and authority) to authenticate users. After you make such a decision, you will use trust relationships to implement your chosen model. There are two kinds of trust relationships: one-way trusts and two-way trusts.

In a *one-way trust relationship*, one domain passes the right to authenticate users to a different domain. For example, if an administrator created a one-way trust relationship from Domain B to Domain A, the domain controllers in Domain A could then grant access rights to users from both domains to resources on Domain B. In turn, Domain B would still be able to grant its own users access to its own resources, but would have no authentication rights on Domain A.

In a *two-way trust relationship*, the domains pass authentication rights to each other. For example, if the administrator created a two-way trust relationship between Domain A and Domain B, the domain controllers from both domains could grant access rights to all users to all resources in both domains. A two-way trust relationship is actually two one-way trusts established between domains (a one-way trust running from one domain to the other, and a second one-way trust from that domain back to the first). This trust pair is described as a two-way trust to imply its purpose (of sharing information in both directions between domains).

Most documentation illustrates trust relationships in the form of arrows. The arrows represent the relationship between the trusting domain and the trusted domain, with the arrow pointing toward the domain that will receive authentication rights. Microsoft uses the terms *trusting* and *trusted* extensively to describe the relationship that trusts establish. The trusting domain is the domain that passes the authentication rights to another domain, and the trusted domain is the domain that receives the authentication rights.

To establish even a one-way trust, an administrator must perform configuration changes on both domains. First, the administrator must configure the trusted domain to receive a specific trust relationship. Then, the administrator can configure the trusting domain to pass authentication rights to the trusted domain. An administrator establishes trust relationships from the Trust Relationship dialog box, as Figure 201.1 shows.

Figure 201.1 The Windows NT Trust Relationships dialog box.

To establish a trust relationship in the trusted domain, perform the following steps:

1. Click your mouse on the Start menu and select the Programs submenu Administrative tools group User Manager for Domains program. Windows NT will open the User Manager for Domains program.

2. Within User Manager for Domains, click your mouse on the Policies menu Trust Relationships option. User Manager for Domains will open the Trust Relationships window.

3. Within the Trust Relationships window, click your mouse on the Add button to the right of the *Trusting Domains* field. User Manager for Domains will open the Add Trusting Domain window.

4. Within the Add Trusting Domain window, type in the *Trusting Domain* field the name of the domain you want to allow trusts from and press the TAB key. User Manager for Domains will insert the name you type and move the cursor to the *Initial Password* field.

5. Type a password in the *Initial Password* field if you want to attach an initial password to the trust, and then press the TAB key. User Manger for Domains will insert the password you type into the *Initial Password* field and move the cursor to the *Confirm Password* field.

6. If you entered a password in Step 5, retype the same password in the *Confirm Password* field. Windows NT will insert the password you type in the *Confirm Password* field.

7. Click your mouse on the OK button. User Manager for Domains will insert the name of the domain into the *Trusting Domains* field. If the information the *Initial Password* and *Confirm Password* fields contain does not match, User Manager for Domains will prompt you to retype the passwords.

To establish a trust relationship in the trusting domain, perform the following steps:

1. Click your mouse on the Start menu select the Programs submenu Administrative tools group User Manager for Domains option. Windows NT will open the User Manager for Domains.

2. Within the User Manager for Domains, select the Policies menu Trust Relationships option. User Manager for Domains will open the Trust Relationships window.

3. Within the Trust Relationships windows, click your mouse on the Add button to the right of the *Trusted Domains* field. User Manager for Domains will open the Add Trusted Domain window.

4. Type in the *Domain* field the name of the domain you want to trust and press the TAB key. User Manager for Domains will insert in the *Domain* field the name you typed and move the cursor to the *Password* field.

5. Type a password (which, again, is optional) in the *Password* field. User Manager for Domains will insert in the *Password* field the password you typed.

6. Click your mouse on OK. User Manager for Domains will establish the trust relationship.

Answer C is correct because in order for users in Domain A to access resources on Domain B and Domain C, Domains B and C must trust Domain A. Answer A is correct because a two-way trust relationship between all domains would let the operating system authenticate all users to all domains. Answer B and C are incorrect because in order for users in Domain A to access resources in Domain B and Domain C, Domains B and C would have to trust Domain A.

202 INTRODUCTION TO THE SINGLE DOMAIN MODEL

Q.   *You are the administrator of a small network that consists of seven Windows NT Workstations, five Windows 95 clients, and one Windows NT server. You have installed the Windows NT server as a Primary Domain Controller, and all computers receive log-on authentication to the network from the Primary Domain Controller. What domain model best describes this network?*

Choose all answers that apply:

    A.   *Master Domain*

    B.   *Multiple Master Domain*

    C.   *Single Domain*

    D.   *Complete Trust*

The network administrator must often design new networks or redesign existing networks to support growth. Fortunately, you can use the Windows NT domain structure in networks of different sizes and needs. An administrator can use the Windows NT domain model, along with carefully planned trust relationships, to get the scaleability (that is, the ability to expand the network) to address the different needs of small, medium, and large networks, while making network administration as simple or complex as the administrator wants. *Domain structure* refers to the relationship between all the domains on a network.

Domain structure includes all the conceptual designs administrators commonly refer to as *domain models*, which provide administrators with guidelines to assist in network design. The domain models are *Single Domain, Master Domain, Multiple Master Domain, Complete Trust,* and *Hybrid.* (You will learn more about individual domain models in the following Tips.) To determine which domain model to implement, administrators will consider the quantity of machines in the entire network, the location of machines and offices, the burden or load on each server, and other issues. However, the primary factors in accurately defining domain models are the nature of the Primary Domain Controllers and trust relationships between them. For example, the Single Domain model is the simplest of all the models because it has only one set of domain controllers. Therefore, no matter how many machines you find in the network, if you have only one Primary Domain Controller, you have a Single Domain model. A network that has one Primary Domain Controller and ten Backup Domain Controllers would still be a Single Domain mode.

Answer C is correct because the network has only one Primary Domain Controller and therefore is a single domain model. Answers A,B, and C are incorrect because each of the listed domain models has more than one Primary Domain Controller.

203   INTRODUCTION TO THE MASTER DOMAIN MODEL

Q.   *You are the administrator of a medium-sized network that consists of five domains—Engineering, Accounting, Human Resources, Sales, and Administration. The Administration domain holds all user accounts. A one-way trust relationship has been established with Engineering, Accounting, Human Resources, and Sales as the trusting domains and Administration as the trusted domain. All users log on to the network through the Administration domain. Which of the following domain models best describes this network?*

Choose the best answer:

     A.   Master

     B.   Multiple Master

     C.   Hybrid

     D.   Complete Trust

An administrator might find that as the network grows he or she must break the network into multiple domains, especially if there are Windows NT Workstations on the network. As you learned in Tip 45, there is a limited number of accounts each domain can support. For example, if your network had 30,000 users and they were all using Windows NT Workstation, their use would exceed the logical limitation of 40,000 accounts (1 for each user and 1 for each computer = 60,000 accounts).

In such a case, you could solve the account limitation problem by breaking up the network into multiple domains. After you break the network into multiple domains, you use trust relationships to establish a relationship in which the newly formed domains trust the original domain for authentication, thereby creating a Master domain model.

The Master domain model is an excellent model to use to reduce administration time in a medium-sized network that has more than one domain. The Master domain model consists of two or more domains with a one-way trust relationship established so that one domain will act as the authentication domain (the Master), while all other domains trust the Master domain for authentication and become *Resource domains*. The Resource domains, in turn, pass all authentication requests to the Master domain for users to access resources. The Master domain contains all the user accounts for the network, thereby creating a single administration point.

Answer A is correct because a network with multiple Resource domains that all trust one Master domain describes the Master Domain model. Answer B is incorrect because Multiple Master domains contain more than one Master domain. Answer C is incorrect because Hybrid domains contain blends of two or more established domain models. Answer D is incorrect because in Complete Trust domains, all domains are equal.

204 INTRODUCTION TO THE MULTIPLE MASTER DOMAIN MODEL

Q. *You are the administrator of a large network that has 25 Windows NT domains. All user accounts reside in one of five domains. The domains where the user accounts reside are Domain1, Domain2, Domain3, Domain4, and Domain5. You have established a two-way trust relationship between each of the five domains that contain the user accounts. In each of the domains that do not contain user accounts (Domain6 through Domain25), you have established one-way trust relationships so that Domain6 through Domain25 trusts the domains that contain the user accounts (Domain1 through Domain5). What domain model best describes the network?*

Choose the best answer:

    A.   *Master*

    B.   *Multiple Master*

    C.   *Complete Trust*

    D.   *Single*

Large organizations, such as large corporations, with individual divisions that maintain their own information in their own locations on the network will often still require a single network. For example, there might be users who must access resources in a different division or users who must submit data updates to a central location. However, sheer numbers of computer and user accounts in very large organizations may prevent you from implementing a Master domain model. Moreover, administrative issues and internal politics may also provide reasons to break up the Master domain model. When the overall design of the network seems to dictate a Master domain model, but for various reasons you cannot use this model, you can use the Multiple Master domain model instead. A Multiple Master domain model is simply two or more Master domains in which each Master domain trusts all other Master domains.

Answer B is correct because the example accurately describes the Multiple Master domain model. Answer A is incorrect because a Master domain model would have only one domain in which user accounts would reside. Answer C is incorrect because a Complete Trust domain model would require that each domain trust all other domains. Answer D is incorrect because a Single domain model would have only one domain.

205 INTRODUCTION TO THE COMPLETE TRUST MODEL

Q. *In a Complete Trust domain model, all domains completely trust all other domains.*

True or False?

You can find the Complete Trust domain model in networks of all sizes, ranging from those that support only two domains to very large networks that support 20 or more domains. A Complete Trust domain model is one in which each domain trusts all others and all domains are equal on the network. However, there are very few good reasons for implementing the Complete Trust domain model. In general, the Complete Trust domain model is security-weak and potential-problem strong.

You might implement a Complete Trust domain model to merge two independent, self-sustaining organizations that previously maintained their own Windows NT domains. You will find, however, that when the organizations merge, Windows NT does not provide a service to migrate the user accounts from one domain to the other. To fix this problem, you could implement the Complete Trust model, which would let you manage users and resources from either domain.

The answer is **True** *because a complete trust domain model is a network in which all domains trust all other domains.*

206 — **INTRODUCTION TO THE HYBRID DOMAIN MODEL**

Q.   *You are the network administrator for a school district. You have established a domain model in which each school is its own single domain. All student accounts and school resources are in the School domains. You also have a District Office domain. Each School domain trusts the District Office domain. The School domains do not trust each other. The District Office domain does not trust any domains. All user accounts for administrative staff and teachers are in the District Office domain. What type of domain model best describes this domain?*

Choose the best answer:

   A.   *Master*

   B.   *Multiple Master*

   C.   *Hybrid*

   D.   *Complete Trust*

The Hybrid domain model is not an official model that Microsoft describes in its official Windows NT documentation. The Hybrid domain model is, however, a concept Windows NT administrators must understand because they will find it in actual Windows NT domain implementations and they might have to implement a Hybrid domain model in their own organizations.

The Hybrid domain model is a network that combines two or more of the other domain models to solve some specific authentication or administrative issue. As this Tip's example question illustrates, each of the resource domains (School domains) have established trust relationships that pass the authentication rights for the resource domains to the Administration domain (District Office domains). The trust relationships make the Administration domain the Master domain, which creates a Master domain model. The School domains, however, maintain their own user accounts for the students, which means that the School domains are Single domains. Because the network contains what would be both a Master and a Single domain model. You would administer it as a single unit, but, it is actually a Hybrid domain model.

Answer C is correct because the question describes the Hybrid domain model. Answer A is incorrect because although the question describes a Master domain, it also describes Single domains in the same administrative unit. Answer B is incorrect because a Multiple Master domain would have more than one domain with user accounts and each resource domain would trust it. Answer D is incorrect because a Complete Trust domain model would require trust relationships between each domain.

207 — **UNDERSTANDING BOOT AND SYSTEM PARTITIONS**

Q.   *The partition that contains the files required to boot the Windows NT operating system is always the system partition.*

True or False?

As you have learned, the prospective Microsoft certified systems engineer must learn many new and confusing terms. However, you must know and understand Microsoft terminology to pass the required Microsoft exams so you can become a Microsoft certified systems engineer. As you learn Microsoft's terminology, you will find that one set of terms that is difficult to understand is *system partition* and *boot partition*. Microsoft uses the terms system and boot to describe what a partition contains and how the terms apply to a Windows NT computer's initialization.

When an administrator installs Windows NT, the administrator can choose to install the system to any available partition formatted with a supported file system. If the administrator installs Windows NT to the active partition (on the boot drive), which is, in most cases, the C: drive, the system and boot partitions are the same partition. If however, the administrator installs the operating system on a partition other than the active partition, the system and boot partitions are different partitions.

To understand a common Windows NT install and its different partitions, consider the following example. If you install Windows NT onto a personal computer that has a single hard drive you divided into two partitions, the logical drive assignment will be C: and D:, with the C: drive as the active partition. When you install Windows NT, the setup program gives you the option to manage partitions. Assume you choose to install Windows NT to the D: drive. Therefore, Windows NT Setup will copy all the files it needs to boot the operating system to the D: drive, but because the C: drive is the active partition, Windows NT Setup must still copy its system files to the C: drive. As you can see in this example, the active partition receives the system files. The active partition is, therefore, the system partition. In turn, the partition that contains the files an operating system requires to boot is the boot partition.

The answer is **False** *because the system partition does not always contain the files the system requires to boot the Windows NT operating system.*

Q.   *You are the network administrator of a small network with five Windows 95 clients and four Macintosh clients. You are installing a new Windows NT server to provide centralized data storage and administration. What file system would you choose in order to provide data storage to all client computers?*

Choose the best answer:

A.   FAT

B.   NTFS

C.   CDFS

D.   HPFS

Windows NT supports a variety of file systems and can, in fact, support multiple file systems on a single computer. The administrator chooses what file systems to implement based on operating systems and security requirements. Each file system has its own unique properties, and Windows NT supports it to provide compatibility with other operating systems and applications, as Table 208 shows.

File System	Characteristics
FAT	Stands for File Allocation Table. It is an enhanced version of the same file system MSDOS, Windows 3x, Windows 95, and computers with RISC-based architecture use. Note that Windows NT 4.0 does not support FAT32, a derivative of FAT.
HPFS	Stands for High Performance File System. IBM designed and OS2 uses this file system.
CDFS	Stands for Compact Disk File System. The file system you use to access compact disk storage methods.
NTFS	Stands for NT File System. The file system Microsoft designed for Windows NT.

Table 208 *Windows NT's supported file systems.*

Windows NT supports all the file systems Table 208 lists. However, you, as an administrator, will use NTFS and FAT more often on a day-to-day basis than HPFS and CDFS, which Windows NT supports for compatibility reasons and, therefore, an administrator uses less often. In this Tip, you will learn about NTFS, and in Tip 210 you will learn about the FAT file system.

NTFS is the file system Microsoft designed specifically for use with the Windows NT operating system. NTFS grants the administrator a greater level of functionality and security than other file systems. In part, the features the following paragraphs discuss implement that security and functionality. Other features that you will learn about throughout this book also contribute to Windows NT's robustness and usefulness.

NTFS supports long file naming conventions. Long file names make it easier for a user to identify documents. Older file systems had cryptic methods for naming files. (In Tip 210, you will learn more about the file naming convention the original implementation of the FAT file system used.) NTFS file names can be up to 255 characters in length and can contain any characters except the following: *space* / \ : | * ? " < >. In addition, NTFS file names are not generally case sensitive but preserve case, which means that although most applications do not differentiate between upper- and lowercase, the NTFS file system will understand the difference in case and preserve it. For example, consider the difference between MyDocument and mydocument. NTFS provides case preservation to accommodate rare applications, such as those you write to the Portable Operating System Interface (POSIX) standard, which lets two or more file names have the same name so long as they differ in case.

The NTFS file system provides file system security such as transaction-based recoverability, cluster re-mapping, and local security (which the next few paragraphs discuss) to address the Windows NT administrator's security concerns. *File system security* is a general term that deals with a variety of issues, such as reliability of file storage, protection from unauthorized access, and recoverability.

NTFS uses a concept called *transaction logging* to store information about all changes to files and folders. Windows NT can use information the transaction log contains in the event of a system failure to reconstruct a file if a change (such as a move or a copy) operation failure occurs. For example, if you were moving a file from one computer to another and halfway through the moving operation your building had a power failure, the file would revert back to its original location. *Transaction-based recoverability* is the term that describes the feature in the NTFS file system that lets Windows NT reconstruct data after a system failure.

In Tip 190, "Rotating Backup Tape Sets," you learned that magnetic media can deteriorate. The deterioration of magnetic media and weaknesses in the base material in the media can sometimes result in a bad cluster on the disk. A *cluster* is an area on the disk that you can use for storage. When a cluster *fails*, it can no longer store data and can cause disk I/O problems. The NTFS file system uses cluster re-mapping to deal with cluster failure. *Cluster re-mapping* means that if NTFS detects an error a bad cluster caused, NTFS will simply store the information in a new cluster and store the bad cluster's address so that it does not use it again. The file system performs cluster re-mapping entirely behind the scenes, and applications cannot detect the re-mapping. NTFS writes files to disk in a contiguous manner to reduce fragmentation—doing so can lead to a longer disk life and help slow down cluster deterioration.

Note: Windows NT will perform cluster re-mapping only on NTFS volumes on SCSI hard drives.

NTFS inherently supports a high level of local file-level security. *Local file-level security* means that a user can apply security to files and folders that would prevent any other user who uses that computer from accessing the files or folders. Local file-level security operates independently of network security. An administrator can restrict files and folders at the file level so that no user can access them at the local computer, and simultaneously share those same files and folders across the network to users for access. Although NTFS and HPFS can both support local file-level security (making them different from FAT and CDFS), an administrator cannot format a drive with HPFS (IBM's High Performance File System). Windows NT will, however, let an administrator retain an HPFS volume if one exists on a computer.

Another interesting feature of the NTFS file system is that NTFS can compress individual files or folders while leaving the rest of the partition uncompressed. File compression grants the administrator the ability to compress old or infrequently used files in order to save space, while at the same time leaving frequently accessed files uncompressed so that file access speed is unaffected.

Windows NT is a POSIX 1.x-compliant system and can run many different POSIX applications. NTFS is the POSIX 1.x-compliant file system within Windows NT and supports, in addition to case-sensitive naming, a time stamping feature that marks the time and date a user last accessed the file, and hard link support. *Hard links* occur when two or more file names, possibly in different folders, point to the same data. Some POSIX applications can run under Windows NT with any file system. Many POSIX applications, however, utilize file-system resources as part of their internal workings and, as a result, require the NTFS file system to function.

NTFS supports the largest partition size of any file system currently available in the commercial market. Windows NT with the NTFS file system can support up to 16 *exabytes* of storage capacity on each partition, with maximum file sizes ranging from 4 gigabytes to 64 gigabytes, depending on system hardware limitations. (In theory, a file's size could be as large as 16 exabytes, but, because of current hardware limitations, a 16-exabyte file is not possible.)

All the features available in the NTFS file system result in a large amount of system overhead (the resources NTFS requires) to implement the NTFS file system. Because of the overhead you require to implement NTFS, Microsoft recommends a minimum partition of 50Mb (smaller partitions will likely degrade operating system performance).

Answer B is correct because you must have the NTFS file system in order to use Windows NT Server as a file server for Macintosh clients. Answers A, C, and D are incorrect because other file systems do not support Macintosh file storage.

209 | **UNDERSTANDING MULTIPLE RECYCLE BINS ON NTFS PARTITIONS**

Q.   *You are the administrator of a Windows NT domain. While browsing through an NTFS partition on the primary domain controller, you notice that there are 12 Recycle Bins. What steps must you take to restore the Windows NT Recycle Bin to normal operation?*

Choose the best answer:

    A.   Delete the Recycle Bin on the desktop and restart the server.

    B.   Use Disk Administrator to regenerate the Recycle Bin.

    C.   Do nothing, Windows NT supports multiple Recycle Bins.

    D.   Click the Consolidate Recycle Bins option in the Server Properties dialog box.

One concern for both users and administrators has always been the issue of files and folders they accidentally deleted. In turn, over the years different operating systems have implemented many solutions to inadvertently deleted files. Older operating systems often employed an undelete utility that could provide several levels of file deletion protection, depending on the operating system's configuration. Windows NT provides protection against mistakenly deleted files with the *Recycle Bin*. The Recycle Bin is a utility that stores deleted files so that a user who deletes a file, whether on purpose or by mistake, has the option of getting it back. Windows NT supports independent Recycle Bins for each user, as long as the location of the user's home directory is on an NTFS partition. If all the user home directories are on a partition formatted with a file system other than NTFS, there will be only one Recycle Bin (which the administrator can configure) for all users.

The Recycle Bin is fully configurable and uses an area of disk space to store deleted files, unless the administrator or individual user has configured the Recycle Bin not to store files. If the user configures the Recycle Bin not to store files, the system immediately removes all deleted files from the disk so the user cannot recover the files. Users who configure the Recycle Bin to store deleted files can retrieve the files, if necessary, as long as they have not exceeded the size limitation the administrator has set for their Recycle Bin.

Answer C is correct because Windows NT supports multiple Recycle Bins on NTFS partitions. Answers A, B, and D are incorrect because the Recycle Bin is already functioning normally.

210   CONSIDERING *FAT* CHARACTERISTICS IN *NT*

Q.   *Windows NT supports long file names on FAT file systems.*

True or False?

Operating systems such as MS-DOS and Windows 95 have used the File Allocation Table (FAT) file system for years. In addition, the Windows NT implementation of the FAT file system has several enhancements to increase its functionality. The following paragraphs discuss the enhanced properties of the FAT file system under Windows NT.

- Using the FAT file system, you can make file names up to 255 characters in length. FAT file names may contain multiple spaces or periods and any characters except / \ : | * = ? " [ ] , ^ and will preserve case, but are not case-sensitive.

- A FAT partition size can be up to 4Gb.

There are several important considerations that the administrator must pay attention to when implementing the FAT file system, as detailed in the following paragraphs:

- Windows NT must support the FAT file system because other operating systems or computer architectures require access to FAT. For example, a Windows NT computer you have installed as a dual-boot so that it would also run the Windows 95 operating system would require the FAT file system because Windows 95 does not support the NTFS file system. Another reason to use the FAT file system is that Advanced RISC Computing (ARC)-compliant computers that use Reduced Instruction Set Computing (RISC) chips require that the system partition is formatted with the FAT file system—they cannot correctly process NTFS volumes.

- An administrator cannot undelete a file on a FAT volume while Windows NT is operating. If the file is on a FAT partition, however, the administrator can reboot the computer into MS-

DOS and then use common undelete tools that might be able to retrieve the file, as long as other data did not overwrite it.

- As the number of files on a FAT partition grows, overall performance will degrade because of the way in which a FAT file system's linked-list directory structure functions (a table holds pointers to the files themselves). In turn, file access speeds will decline as fragmentation grows with the increase in files.

- FAT file systems do not support local security.

*The answer is **True** because Windows NT does support long file names on FAT partitions.*

211 — **MIGRATING NT COMPUTERS TO OTHER DOMAINS**

Q.   *You can use the Backup Domain Controller only in the domain in which the administrator originally installed the controller.*

True or False?

The administrator of a medium- to large-sized network might frequently want to move client computers and servers from one domain to another. Moving a Windows NT computer between domains is simply a matter of changing the domain to which the computer authenticates—except when the computer is a domain controller.

You, as an administrator, cannot move Domain controllers from one domain to another because the security identifiers in the registry are specific to the domain, and the operating system creates the security identifiers for the domain when you install the Primary Domain Controller for the first time. Backup Domain Controllers copy the security identifiers from the Primary Domain Controller when you install the Backup Domain Controllers. After you have installed a domain controller, it is forever a participating member of domain authentication and you cannot use it to authenticate in a different domain—with one exception. If you move a domain controller from another network model to an independent network and that controller is the only domain controller for the domain, it will function normally.

Because you cannot move domain controllers between domains, your network planning must include the number of domain controllers you need for each domain. If you face a scenario in which you must move a domain controller from one domain to another, you must "wipe clean" from the domain controller all traces of the installation and then re-install the domain controller. Unlike domain controllers, you can move Windows NT standalone servers and workstations between domains without requiring re-formatting of the hard drive.

*The answer is **True** because you can use Windows NT domain controllers only in the domain in which you originally installed the controllers.*

212 — **UNDERSTANDING NT LICENSING**

Q: *You are the administrator of a Windows NT domain with 30 client computers and one Windows NT Server. You have purchased 10 copies of Windows NT Workstation to install on existing computers. In addition, you have 20 copies of Windows 95 that you have installed on 10 client computers. Each copy of Windows NT Workstation and*

Windows 95 came with its own software license. Your Windows NT Server software came with 10 client access licenses. How many additional licenses must you have?

Choose the best answer:

A.   20

B.   10

C.   5

D.   None

Many administrators are concerned not only with their network administration, but also with network license issues. Software manufacturers require consumers to purchase software licenses to use the software manufacturers' programs. Frequently, it is your responsibility as an administrator to secure software licenses. There are two types of licenses: software installation and network client access. First, *software installation licenses* permit consumers to install software legally. Many people are under the misconception that if they have a program's installation disks, they have the right to install and use the software. However, in most cases they must also have the software installation license to use a program legally.

Second, a *Client Access License (CAL)* is the license to connect to a network operating system server legally. Microsoft requires consumers to purchase client access licenses for each client who will connect to a Windows NT computer. In addition to the client access licenses that you must have for each computer in the network, you must also have a software installation license for each Windows for Workgroups, Windows 95, Windows NT Workstation, and Windows NT Server in the network. Microsoft licenses are paper documents that legally permit administrators to install or connect to Microsoft software. As you learn about Microsoft software installation and client licenses, you will find that understanding Microsoft's client license requirements is more difficult than understanding Microsoft's software licenses. Windows NT Server has two client licensing modes: *Per Server* and *Per Seat*. In order to configure your Microsoft network so that it is legal and cost efficient, you must understand Microsoft's Windows NT Server license modes. Table 212 shows the two Windows NT client license modes.

Client License Mode	Description
Per Server	The Per Server mode is the default client license mode when you install Windows NT Server. In the Per Server mode, you specify how many client licenses you have purchased. The number of client licenses you specify is the total number of users in your network that will be connecting to the server on which you have specified the Per Server mode. If more than one server is present in your network, you must purchase additional client access licenses for each user in your network.
Per Seat	You should choose the Per Seat mode when installing Windows NT Server in a multi-server environment. After you select the Per Seat mode, you must specify how many client access licenses to install. The number of client access licenses should be directly proportionate to the number of users in the network. Regardless of how many Windows NT computers (acting as servers) are present in the network, you will need to install only the exact number of client access licenses for the number of users in the network.

Table 212 The two Windows NT Server licensing modes.

As Table 212 shows, if you are using the Per Server mode, you must have client access licenses for the number of users in your network multiplied by the number of servers in your network (client access licenses = users * servers). As you can see, in a Per Server mode you might have more client access licenses then users in your network. On the other hand, the Per Seat mode lets you buy only the number of client access licenses you will need for the number of users in the network. You will learn more about Microsoft licensing and administration in Tips 407 through 410 and in Tip 883.

Answer A is correct because you will have to purchase an additional 20 client access licenses to have the total 30 client access licenses you need. Although each Windows operating system comes with its own software license, you still need client access licenses to operate legally. Because your Windows NT Server came with 10 client access licenses, you need an additional 20. Answers B, C, and D are incorrect because you will require client access licenses for each computer that will connect to your Windows NT Server.

213   **INTRODUCTION TO WINDOWS NT INSTALLATION TYPES**

Q: *You are installing Windows NT Server on a new computer. You want to install all the standard Windows NT system files as well as some additional components. Which Windows NT installation type would you choose?*

Choose the best answer:

     A.   *Typical*

     B.   *Portable*

     C.   *Custom*

     D.   *Compact*

     E.   *You cannot choose a Windows NT Server installation mode*

Microsoft has learned that people who perform software installation tend to fall into groups that install similar components—for example, Microsoft generally creates a Typical installation (which installs the most common options), a Minimum installation (which installs only the files necessary to execute the program), and a Custom installation. Therefore, when you install most Microsoft products, you will see installation types that reflect most consumers' installation requirements. These installation types are usually *Compact, Typical, Portable*, or *Custom*. You can choose an installation type only when you are installing a Windows NT Workstation. Windows NT Server does not give the person performing an installation any choices about installation type; rather, all Windows NT Server installations are the *Custom* type.

Understanding what the different installation types will place onto the target computer is important, both for the MCSE exams and for effective installation administration. The following paragraphs discuss the different installation types and the features of each.

Typical: As its name denotes, the Typical installation will install the most typical components that system administrators install. Typical installations will install the following components of the operating system:

     •   Accessibility Options (options for users with special physical needs)

     •   All the Windows NT accessories, except Desktop Wallpaper, and mouse pointers

     •   All Communications programs

     •   All the Multimedia components, except the Sound Schemes

Portable: As the system administrator, you might perform installations on company notebook computers. You should use the Portable installation type on notebook computers. Portable installations will install the following components of the operating system:

- Accessibility options (options for the physically challenged)

- All the Windows NT accessories, except Desktop Wallpaper and mouse pointers

- All Communications programs

- All Multimedia components your hardware supports

- Dial-Up Networking

Compact: This installation type is intended for computers with limited disk space. The Compact installation will install only the components Windows NT requires to run. Compact installations will not install any optional components.

Custom: When you want to perform an installation that falls outside the other installation types, you should use the Custom installation type. Custom installations let you choose any optional components. You will learn more about Windows NT installation issues in Tips 281 through 290.

Answer E is correct because you cannot choose a Windows NT Server installation type. Answers A, B, C, and D are incorrect because all four answers are installation types you can choose only for Windows NT Workstation installations.

214 CREATING A BACKUP COPY OF THE THREE SETUP DISKS

Q: *You must perform a Windows NT Server installation on a computer without a current operating system. You cannot find the three setup disks that came with your Windows NT Server software. How can you obtain a new copy of the three setup disks?*

Choose the best answer:

A. *Download the three setup disks from the Microsoft Web site.*

B. *Download the three setup disks from the Microsoft Download Library.*

C. *Buy another copy of Windows NT Server.*

D. *From the Windows NT Server CD-ROM, execute Winnt.exe with the /OX option.*

You can install Windows NT from the three installation disks Microsoft provides with the Windows NT CD-ROM. You will use the three setup disks if you are installing Windows NT on a computer without an operating system already installed on it. You will place the first disk in the floppy drive of the computer on which you are installing Windows NT and reboot the computer. The computer will start a Windows NT installation when it accesses the floppy disk on the drive. The installation program will prompt you for each disk until you reach the third disk. After the installation program reaches the third disk, the installation program will automatically search for a supported CD-ROM drive. Check the Microsoft Hardware Compatibility List (HCL), about which you will learn more in Tip 221, for supported CD-ROM drives. You can create a copy of your three setup disks in case you lose or misplace them. To create a copy of your Windows NT setup disks, perform the following steps:

1. Insert the Windows NT CD-ROM into your computer's CD-ROM drive. Click your mouse on the Start menu and select the Programs submenu Command Prompt program. Windows NT will open the Command Prompt window.

2. Within the Command Prompt window, navigate to the drive letter that corresponds to the drive on which contains the Windows NT CD-ROM disk in it. On the NT CD-ROM, navigate to the *i386* directory.

3. Within the *i386* directory, type *Winnt /OX*. Windows NT will prompt you to insert the first diskette in your floppy disk drive. Follow the onscreen prompts to insert each disk.

4. When the utility finishes, you will have a new set of three setup disks.

The setup disks are not computer-specific so you can use them to install Windows NT on any Intel processor-based computer.

Answer D is correct because you will use Winnt /OX on the Windows NT Server CD-ROM to create the three setup disks. Answers A and B are incorrect because you cannot download the three Windows NT setup disks from either the Microsoft Download Library or the Microsoft Web site. Answer C is incorrect because although you could obtain the three setup disks by purchasing the Windows NT Server product again, it would not be cost effective and would be unnecessary because you can create the three disks from the Windows NT Server CD-ROM.

215 **UNDERSTANDING RISC ARCHITECTURE INSTALLATION**

Q: *You are going to perform a Windows NT Server installation on a RISC chip architecture computer. Which of the following are supported installation methods?*

Select all correct answers:

A. *CD-ROM*

B. *Over the network*

C. *The three Windows NT Server Setup disks*

D. *You cannot perform a Windows NT Server installation on a RISC chip architecture computer*

Windows NT is a cross-platform network operating system. You can install Windows NT on Intel, Alpha, MIPS, and PowerPC platforms. Alpha, MIPS, and PowerPC platforms are Reduced Instruction Set Computing (RISC) architecture processors. RISC architecture is faster than other processors, but RISC chips are not compatible with the majority of the software sold currently. Instead, application manufacturers would have to write an application to specifically work with a particular RISC architecture in order to run on a Windows NT computer. Nevertheless, many companies will choose to use Windows NT Server on RISC architecture computers because of their processing power. However, because RISC chips are so different from Intel chips, there are some installation considerations you should be aware of before you begin.

When you install Windows NT on a RISC architecture computer, you must have (or create) a small FAT partition. RISC hardware requires a supported file system to which it can boot. Of the file systems you can use in Windows NT, FAT is the only RISC-supported file system. RISC hardware specification requires no fewer than a 2Mb FAT partition to which it can boot. You can perform RISC architecture installations only from the Windows NT CD-ROM, and then only from a SCSI CD-ROM drive that Windows NT supports. You cannot install Windows NT on a RISC architecture computer using the three Windows NT Setup disks you learned about in Tip 214, nor can you use an over-the-network installation to install Windows NT on a RISC computer.

Answer A is correct because you can install Windows NT on RISC architecture computers only if you use the Windows NT CD-ROM. Answers B and C are incorrect because Windows NT only supports installing from the setup disks or from a network server when you perform a Windows NT installation on an Intel architecture computer. Answer D is incorrect because you can install Windows NT on a RISC architecture computer.

216 ***RUNNING WINDOWS NT ON POWERPC SYSTEMS***

Q: *Your company's purchasing agent just bought a Macintosh PowerPC for you to use a Windows NT Server. Windows NT will let you use the PowerPC computer as your server.*

True or False?

The *PowerPC* architecture is an IBM product which is based on the RISC architecture chip. As you learned in Tip 215, Microsoft Windows NT supports PowerPC installations. However, you can install Windows NT on the PowerPC only if the PowerPC's *firmware* (hardware configuration) supports a Windows NT installation. For the past few years, Macintosh has used PowerPC chips in some of its computers. Macintosh PowerPC computers do not support a Windows NT installation—you must upgrade your firmware in order to install Windows NT.

*The answer is **False** because you cannot install Windows NT on a Macintosh PowerPC computer without a firmware upgrade (which Macintosh does not provide). Therefore, you cannot use the Macintosh PowerPC computers for Windows NT installations.*

217 ***PERFORMING A SERVER-BASED INSTALLATION***

Q: *Of the following options, which is the fastest Windows NT installation method?*

Choose the best answer:

> A.   *By CD-ROM*
>
> B.   *Over the network*
>
> C.   *By floppy disks*

You can install Windows NT using one of the following three methods: with floppy disks, with CD-ROMs, or over the network. You cannot use floppy disks to install Windows NT if you want an English language installation because Microsoft does not manufacture floppy disks for English language installations. Instead, Microsoft says in its official curriculum courses that the CD-ROM installation method is Microsoft's preferred installation method. Although the latest CD-ROM drives may provide a faster installation than the over-the-network installation method, Microsoft lists the over-the-network installation as the fastest Windows NT installation method. If you are the system administrator and you want to perform over-the-network Windows NT installations because of your network configuration or security considerations, you must first create a distribution server.

A *distribution server* is a computer that can receive network connections and that stores the Windows NT source file. After you create the distribution server, you can install Windows NT on computers from the distribution server. To create a distribution server on a Windows NT computer, perform the following steps:

> 1.   Double-click your mouse on the My Computer icon on your Desktop. Windows NT will open the My Computer window.

2. Within the My Computer window, select a target drive on which to place the Windows NT source files. (A *target drive* is the location where you will place your Windows NT source files.) Double-click your mouse on the target drive. Windows NT will open a window that displays the contents of the target drive.

3. Place the Windows NT CD-ROM disk in your computer's CD-ROM drive. Within My Computer, double-click your mouse on the CD-ROM drive. Windows NT will open the Windows NT CD-ROM Setup window.

4. Within the Windows NT CD-ROM Setup window, click your mouse on the Browse this CD button. Windows NT will display the contents of the Windows NT CD-ROM.

5. Arrange the windows on your Desktop so you can see the contents of the Windows NT CD-ROM and the target drive window. Click and hold down your mouse on the *i386* folder and then drag the *i386* folder to the target drive. Windows NT will copy the *i386* folder to your target drive.

6. Within the target drive window, select the *i386* folder. Right-click your mouse on the *i386* folder. Windows NT will display a pop-up menu.

7. Within the pop-up menu, select the Sharing option. Windows NT will display the folder Properties dialog box Sharing sheet.

8. Within the Sharing sheet, click your mouse on the Share As radio button. Then click your mouse on the OK button. Next, click your mouse on the Permissions button. Windows NT will display the Access Through Share Permissions dialog box.

9. Within the Access Through Share Permissions dialog box, click your mouse on the Type of Access drop-down list. Windows NT will display the list of permissions.

10. Click your mouse on the Read permission. The Access Through Share Permissions dialog box will accept the Read permission.

11. Click your mouse on the OK button. Windows NT will return you to the Sharing tab in the Folder Properties dialog box. Click your mouse on the OK button in the folder Properties dialog box. Windows NT will share the *i386* folder.

*Answer B is correct because although a fast CD-ROM may actually yield faster installation times, Microsoft lists the over-the-network installation as the fastest installation method. **Answers A and C** are incorrect because Microsoft states that a network installation is faster than any other method.*

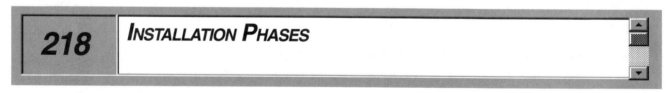

218   **INSTALLATION PHASES**

Q: *How many phases does a Windows NT installation go through?*

Choose the best answer:

   A.   One

   B.   Two

   C.   Four

   D.   Six

When you perform a Windows NT Workstation or Server installation, the installation will go through four phases. Each phase performs a specific series of tasks in the installation, and each phase prepares the computer for the next phase. The four installation phases are: *Initializing Installation, Gathering Information, Installing Windows NT Networking*, and *Finishing Setup*, which the following paragraphs detail.

First, during the Initializing Installation phase, the Windows NT Setup program copies a limited version of Windows NT (just enough to boot into NT) to the hard drive. The Windows NT Setup program will then prompt you for the following information:

- To determine if there is a Windows NT version already on your computer and decide whether to upgrade that Windows NT version to Windows NT 4.0 or to install a new Windows NT version.

- To confirm the presence of the hardware that the Windows NT setup program has already detected.

- To locate the disk partition on which to install Windows NT.

- To choose a file system for Windows NT to use—either FAT or NTFS.

- To find the location to install the Windows NT files.

Second, during the Gathering Information phase, the Windows NT Setup program will switch to a graphical mode and initialize the Setup Wizard. The Setup Wizard will prompt you for the following information:

- If you are performing a Windows NT Workstation installation, you will be prompted for an installation type, such as Typical or Custom.

- The Setup Wizard will prompt you for your name and organization.

- If you are performing a Windows NT Server installation, the program will prompt you to select a licensing mode (either Per Server or Per Seat).

- The Windows NT Setup Wizard will prompt you for a name for your computer. You can make the name between one and fifteen characters in length. The name must be unique in your network.

- If you are installing Windows NT Server, the Windows NT Setup Wizard will prompt you for a server type (either Domain Controller or Member Server).

Third, during the Installing Windows NT Networking portion of the setup program, the Windows NT Setup Wizard will prompt you:

- To choose whether or not to install networking.

- To install Internet Information Server.

- For the configuration information for the network adapter card in your computer.

- For the network protocols you want to install. (You will learn about the network protocols in Tips 727 through 739.)

- For any additional network services you want to install.

- For the domain or workgroup name your computer will be a member of.

Finally, during the Finishing Setup phase, the Windows NT Setup program will prompt you:

- For the time zone, current date, and current time.

- To configure the Exchange Inbox, if you selected it earlier in the installation.

- For the video graphics card drive and configuration information.

Answer C is correct because Windows NT has four installation phases. Answers A, B, and D are incorrect because Windows NT will go through four installation phases.

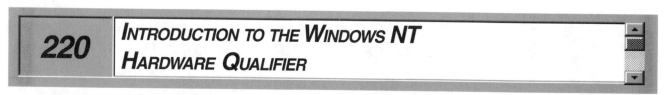

219 | **WINDOWS NT INSTALLATION HARDWARE REQUIREMENTS**

Q: *Of the following computers, choose which ones you will be able to install Windows NT Workstation 4.0 on.*

Choose all the correct answers:

> A. *486 DX 33MHz computer with 16Mb of RAM, a 500Mb hard disk, and an EGA video graphics adapter.*
>
> B. *386 DX 33MHz computer with 16Mb of RAM, a 1Gb hard disk, and a VGA video graphics adapter.*
>
> C. *486 DX/2 66MHz computer with 32Mb of RAM, a 2Gb hard disk, and a VGA video graphic adapter.*
>
> D. *Pentium 100MHz computer with 32Mb of RAM, a 2Gb hard disk, and a VGA video graphics adapter.*
>
> E. *486 DX/2 66MHz computer with 12 Mb of RAM, a 2Gb hard disk, and a VGA video graphics adapter.*

All operating systems have minimum hardware requirements (such as hard drive space, processor speed, and so on), which differ substantially between the various versions on the market. If you are in a position to recommend an operating system, check the hardware you currently have and make sure all the hardware meets the minimum hardware requirements for a Windows NT installation before you recommend Windows NT as the best operating system. You must also ensure the hardware meets the Microsoft Windows NT Server or Workstation minimum hardware requirements. In addition, you should check the Microsoft Hardware Compatibility List (HCL) to see if the hardware you have is compatible with Windows NT. The Hardware Compatibility List is a complete list of all hardware Microsoft knows to be compatible with Windows NT. You will learn about the Microsoft Windows NT Hardware Compatibility List in Tip 221.

Answers C, D, and E are correct because each of the computers answers C, D, and E describe meet the minimum hardware requirements Figure 219 lists. Answer A is incorrect because the display adapter is only an Enhanced Graphic Adapter (EGA) card. EGA is an old architecture graphic card that Windows NT does not support. Answer B is incorrect because an Intel 386 computer does not meet the minimum hardware requirements.

220 | **INTRODUCTION TO THE WINDOWS NT HARDWARE QUALIFIER**

Q: *You have a computer at your office that you cannot find on the Windows NT Server Hardware Compatibility List. You must try to use the computer as a Backup Domain Controller. How can you check to see if this computer will work with Windows NT Server?*

Choose the best answer:

A.   *Install Windows NT and then use the Windows NT Diagnostics to check computer compatibility.*

B.   *Install Windows 95. If Windows 95 will install without problems, this computer will work with Windows NT Server.*

C.   *Use the NT Hardware Qualifier (NTHQ) disk. Boot the computer from the NTHQ disk. NTHQ will check the computer's hardware and identify all components. You can then use the information to determine if your hardware will work with Windows NT.*

D.   *If the computer is not on the Windows NT Hardware Compatibility List, it will not work with Windows NT.*

The *Windows NT Hardware Qualifier* (NTHQ) is a utility that will check and identify a computer's hardware. You can use the NT Hardware Qualifier to determine if your hardware will work with Windows NT. The NT Hardware Qualifier comes with the CD-ROM you use to install Windows NT. The NT Hardware Qualifier works only on Intel computers. You install the NT Hardware Qualifier on an MS-DOS formatted floppy disk, which you will then use to boot the computer (because the hardware qualified needs to control the boot and run outside Windows NT).

To create the NT Hardware Qualifier disk, you must have one MS-DOS *boot disk*, which is a disk the MS-DOS system files require to boot a computer in MS-DOS mode. To create the NT Hardware Qualifier disk from the MS-DOS boot disk, perform the following steps:

1. Place your MS-DOS boot disk in your computer's 3½" floppy disk drive. Insert the Windows NT Server or Workstation CD-ROM into your computer's CD-ROM drive. Double-click your mouse on the My Computer icon on your Desktop. Windows NT will open the My Computer window.

2. Within the My Computer window, double-click your mouse on the CD-ROM drive icon. Windows NT will open the CD-ROM window.

3. Within the CD-ROM window, double-click your mouse on the Support folder icon. Windows NT will open the Support folder window.

4. Within the Support folder window, double-click your mouse on the HQTool folder icon. Windows NT will open the HQTool folder window.

5. Within the HQTool folder window, double-click your mouse on the *Makedisk.bat* file's icon. *Makedisk.bat* will prompt you for the MS-DOS boot disk.

6. Press ENTER on your keyboard. The *Makedisk.bat* file will place the NT Hardware Qualifier files on your MS-DOS boot disk.

Answer C is correct because you would use the NT Hardware Qualifier to identify your computer's hardware and then use the list of identified hardware to determine if your computer will work with Windows NT. Answer A is incorrect because you are installing Windows NT on a computer that you are not sure will work with Windows NT. Answer B is incorrect because Windows 95 does not have the same hardware requirements that a Windows NT computer does. Answer D is incorrect because the NT Hardware Qualifier can help you determine whether your hardware will work with Windows NT.

221   INTRODUCTION TO THE HARDWARE COMPATIBILITY LIST

Q: *You are going buy several new computers on which you will install Windows NT Workstation. You are concerned about the computers working with Windows NT. What would you do first to ensure that the new computers will be Windows NT-compatible?*

Choose the best answer:

A.   Ask the computer vendor to boot the computers from the NT Hardware Qualifier disk.

B.   Ask the computer vendor if the computers will work with Windows NT.

C.   Check the Microsoft Windows NT Hardware Compatibility List (HCL).

D.   Buy one of the computers. If Windows NT does not work, return the computer and try another computer brand.

In older operating systems, it was not very important what type of hardware you installed the operating system on, as long as your hardware met the minimum hardware requirements. However, as hardware manufacturers made advances in computer design and software manufacturers improved their operating systems, you will often find that the operating systems now not only have minimum hardware requirements, but also require certain hardware brands in order to function properly. For example, if a hardware vendor designed a disk drive to work only with Macintosh computers, the drive will not work correctly with Windows NT. Microsoft started using the Microsoft Hardware Compatibility Lists with earlier Windows NT releases. Now Windows NT Workstation and Server, as well as Windows 95, have Hardware Compatibility Lists (one list for each operating system).

The Hardware Compatibility List for each operating system is brand name and model number specific. The Hardware Compatibility List contains information about computer brand names and model numbers as well as peripheral devices (modems, network adapters, and Scanners). All computer manufacturers that want to sell computers to organizations that need Windows NT Server computers should select their computers from those listed on the Microsoft Windows NT Server Hardware Compatibility List. The following paragraph describes the process a computer manufacturer would go through to have a computer on the Hardware Compatibility List.

If you are a computer manufacturer and want to put your newest computer on the Windows NT Server Hardware Compatibility List, you must send one of your computers to Microsoft, which will test it and determine if it is compatible with Windows NT Server. If your computer is Windows NT Server-compatible, Microsoft will issue your company a document that states your computer (by brand name and model number) is Windows NT-server compatible. Microsoft will then place your computer on the Microsoft Windows NT Server Hardware Compatibility List. If later you decide to change any components in your computer, such as the motherboard or processor, you must send the computer back to Microsoft for it to test the new configuration.

Windows NT Workstation and Server both come with a Hardware Compatibility List book. However, the most up-to-date Hardware Compatibility List is on Microsoft's Web site at *http://www.microsoft.com* for each operating system. To find information, search with the keyword *HCL*. Microsoft's Web site will return the Hardware Compatibility Lists for all the Microsoft products that have Hardware Compatibility Lists.

Answer C is correct because the Microsoft Windows NT Server Hardware Compatibility List will list computers that Microsoft has determined are compatible with Windows NT. Answer A is incorrect because the Hardware Compatibility List would be a faster way to determine whether the computer you want to buy is compatible with Windows NT. Answer B is incorrect because asking the computer vendor if its computers are compatible with Windows NT would rely on the salesperson's opinion about how compatible the computers are. Answer D is incorrect because buying a computer simply to test its compatibility would be unnecessary. Instead, the Windows NT Hardware Compatibility List would list all the computers Microsoft knows to be NT-compatible.

222   SETTING THE TIME ZONE

Q: You want to change your Windows NT Server's time zone registry entry. Where would you go in Windows NT Server to change the time zone?

Choose the best answer:

     A.   *Within the Control Panel, select the Time Zone utility.*

     B.   *Within Server Manager, select the computer on which you want to change the Time Zone and then, in the Computer menu, select Time Zone.*

     C.   *Within the Control Panel, select the Date/Time utility.*

     D.   *You must change the Time Zone from the computer's configuration program.*

When you install Windows NT Workstation or Server, you will specify the *time zone* that your computer is in. If you later move the computer (such as from Las Vegas to Houston), you might have to reconfigure the computer's time zone. The time zone lets Windows NT interact with other computers in different time zones while maintaining a time perspective between the computers. Windows NT lets you choose between 50 different time zones.

Windows NT provides the *Date/Time* utility to configure a computer's date, time, and time zone. You can find the Date/Time utility in the Control Panel. When you open the Date/Time utility, you can click your mouse on a drop-down list of time zones and select the time zone that your computer is in, as Figure 222 shows.

Figure 222 *The Windows NT Date/Time utility.*

To configure a Windows NT computer's time zone, perform the following steps:

1. Click your mouse on the Start menu Settings submenu Control Panel option. Windows NT will display the Control Panel window.

2. Within the Control Panel window, find the Date/Time icon. Double-click your mouse on the Date/Time icon. Windows NT will display the Date/Time dialog box.

3. Within the Date/Time dialog box, select the Time Zone tab. The Date/Time Properties dialog box will switch to the Time Zone tab.

4. On the Time Zone tab, click your mouse on the drop-down Time Zones list. Select the Time Zone you are in. Click your mouse on the OK button. Windows NT will set the Time Zone and close the Date/Time Properties dialog box.

Answer C *is correct because you would use the Date/Time utility in the Control Panel to configure the computer's time zone.* **Answer A** *is incorrect because there is no Time Zone utility in the Control Panel.* **Answer B** *is incorrect because you cannot configure the computer's time zone in Server Manager.* **Answer D** *is incorrect because a computer setup program will not let you configure a time zone.*

223 INTRODUCTION TO THE WINDOWS NT REGISTRY

Q: *Which of the following best describes the Windows NT Registry?*

Choose the best answer:

>   A.   *It is the central repository of the system's configuration information.*
>
>   B.   *It is the program you use to register your copy of Windows NT.*
>
>   C.   *It is a Microsoft list of MCSEs.*
>
>   D.   *It is the component in Windows NT that schedules processes and threads.*

Since the first personal computers became available, users could configure computer operating systems to meet the individual requirements of the users using the systems. On computers with the MS-DOS operating system, the files that let you configure your system are *config.sys* and *autoexec.bat*. Both the *autoexec.bat* and *config.sys* files are scripting files that let users specify such configuration options as the mouse driver to use or memory settings. Windows NT itself does not use an *autoexec.bat* or *config.sys* file. Instead, Windows NT uses a special system component called the *Registry*. The Registry is a database that acts as a central repository for configuration information about a given Windows NT computer. The Windows NT Registry is very stable. For example, if the system crashes while Windows NT is writing changes to the Registry, Windows NT will put the Registry back into the uncorrupted state before the crash occurred.

The Windows NT Registry stores a considerable amount of information. Most data the Registry stores is of little concern to the user; rather, the data is for system use only. A great deal of information in the Registry is in a binary format that users could not easily interpret or edit. In the vast majority of cases, users will edit the Registry with a utility (either *regedit* or *regedt32*). Only users with considerable experience—that is, users who have advance knowledge of what they intend to accomplish and how to do so—should directly edit the Registry. Before you examine the Windows NT Registry, you should be familiar with some basic Windows NT Registry terms. Table 223.1 describes the terms Microsoft uses to describe the Windows NT Registry components.

Registry Terms	Description
Subtree	The root of a body of hives containing keys that have system configuration information. The Windows NT Registry has five subtrees, which Table 223.2 describes.
Hive	A discrete body of keys, subkeys, and values.
Key and subkeys	Keys and subkeys reside in hives. Keys and subkeys are just like folders and subfolders. You can have a folder within another folder, which would be called a subfolder.
Values	Just as keys and subkeys are like folders and subfolders, values are like files. You can find many values in keys and subkeys.
Value Data Type	Each value must have a data type, which specifies what type of data a value can contain. The data types are: *REG_DWORD* The key can store only one value and it must be a string of one to eight hexadecimal digits.

Table 223.1 Common Windows NT Registry terms. (continued on the next page)

Registry Terms	Description
REG_SZ	The key can store only one value and Windows NT interprets it as the string to be stored.
REG_EXPAND_SZ	This data type is similar to *REG_SZ*, except you can place variables in the string.
REG_BINARY	The key can store only one value, which must be a string of hexadecimal digits, each pair of which Windows NT will interpret as a byte value.
REG_MULTI_SZ	The key can store multiple values. A *NULL* character separates entries.

Table 223.1 Common Windows NT Registry terms. (continued from the previous page)

The Windows NT Registry stores data in one of the five subtrees which comprise the entire registry. Table 223.2 describes the five subtrees.

Registry subtree	Description
HKEY_LOCAL_MACHINE	Contains the configuration information for the local computer. The Windows NT operating system, device drivers, and applications use the information in the *HKEY_LOCAL_MACHINE* subtree. Windows NT uses some of the information in this key when booting. Windows NT determines which device drivers and services to load from this subtree.
HKEY_USERS	Contains two subkeys: Default, which is the system's default configuration, and the currently logged-on user's security identifier (SID).
HKEY_CURRENT_USER	Contains information about the currently logged-on user. Windows NT will save a copy of the *HKEY_CURRENT_USER* subtree for each user who logs on to the local computer.
HKEY_CLASSES_ROOT	Points to the *HKEY_LOCAL_MACHINE\SOFTWARE\Classes* subkey, and contains application configuration information.
HKEY_CURRENT_CONFIG	Contains information about the active hardware profile.

Table 223.2 The Windows NT Registry's five subtrees.

Note: In Tip 224, you will examine the Registry's contents.

Answer A is correct because the Registry is a central repository of system configuration information. Answer B is incorrect because there is no program to register your copy of Windows NT. Answer C is incorrect because at the time of this book's release, Microsoft does not issue a list of Microsoft Certified System Engineers. Answer D is incorrect because the component in Windows NT that schedules processes and threads is the microkernel.

224 EXAMINING THE HKEY_LOCAL_MACHINE SUBTREE

Q: *In which Registry subtree does Windows NT store the system hardware descriptions?*

Choose the best answer:

A.   *HKEY_CURRENT_CONFIG*

B.   *HKEY_USERS*

C.   *HKEY_CURRENT_USER*

D.   *HKEY_LOCAL_MACHINE*

As you learned in Tip 223, the Windows NT Registry is a central repository for configuration information. In this Tip, you will learn more about the *HKEY_LOCAL_MACHINE* subtree in the Windows NT Registry. You will make almost every Windows NT Registry configuration change in the *HKEY_LOCAL_MACHINE* subtree. The *HKEY_LOCAL_MACHINE* subtree has five subkeys: *HARDWARE, SAM, SECURITY, SOFTWARE,* and *SYSTEM.* Each subkey has a specific purpose in Windows NT, as Table 224 shows.

Subkey	Description
HARDWARE	Windows NT creates this subkey from information Windows NT gathers each time the computer boots. You can find hardware descriptions in the *HARDWARE* subkey. The system does not save the information in the *HARD-WARE* subkey to disk because Windows NT builds it each time the computer starts.
SAM	The *Security Accounts Manager (SAM)* is a hive (a discrete body of keys, subkeys, and values). The *SAM* contains the directory database of all users, Windows NT computers, and groups in the domain. Even as an administrator, you cannot view the *SAM's* contents. Only the Windows NT system can access the *SAM* directly.
SECURITY	*SECURITY* is a hive that contains all the security information for the local computer. Administrators cannot view the *SECURITY* hive's contents. Applications that need security information can call to the security APIs.
SOFTWARE	*SOFTWARE* is a database hive that contains information about the devices and services on the system. When you install new device drivers or Windows NT services, they will add or modify information in the *SOFTWARE* hive.
SYSTEM	The *SYSTEM* hive contains indirect pointers to the other four hives detailed previously.

Table 224 The five **HKEY_LOCAL_MACHINE** *subkeys.*

Answer D is correct because the **HKEY_LOCAL_MACHINE** *subtree stores all hardware descriptions. Answer A is incorrect because the* **HKEY_CURRENT_CONFIG** *subtree contains information about the current hardware profile. Answer B is correct because the* **HKEY_USERS** *subtree contains information about the currently logged-on user. Answer C is incorrect because the* **HKEY_CURRENT_USER** *subtree also contains information about the currently logged-on user.*

225 E**XAMINING THE** **HARDWARE** K**EY**

Q: *If you wanted to know what type of system processor was on your computer, in which Registry subkey would you look?*

Choose the best answer:

A.   *HKEY_LOCAL_MACHINE\HARDWARE*

B.   *HKEY_LOCAL_MACHINE\SYSTEM*

C.   *HKEY_LOCAL_MACHINE\SOFTWARE*

D.   *HKEY_CURRENT_USER*

Some applications require hardware descriptions or configuration information (for example, to work directly with a graphics card). The *HARDWARE* subkey contains information about a computer's hardware descriptions and configuration. The Description subkey under *HKEY_LOCAL_MACHINE\HARDWARE* displays information from the hardware database the computer's firmware, together with the *NTDETECT* utility and the Executive (a modular component within Windows NT that contains various managers that handle system calls), built when you booted the computer. *NTDETECT* is a Windows NT system file that detects hardware when a Windows NT system is booting. The Windows NT *Executive* is a modular component within Windows NT that contains various managers that handle system calls. If your computer is RISC-based, the *HARDWARE* subkey will be a copy of the ARC configuration database taken from the computer's firmware. If your computer is Intel-based, the *HARDWARE* subkey will contain the data the *Hardware Recognizer* found. The *Hardware Recognizer* is a program that runs as part of the Windows NT startup sequence. The *Hardware Recognizer* on Intel-based computers is *NTDETECT.COM*. If your computer is not PC-compatible, the computer manufacturer must provide its own version of *NTDETECT.COM* as the *Hardware Recognizer*. The *Hardware Recognizer* for *x86*-based computers detects the following:

- Bus/adapter type
- Communication ports
- Floating point coprocessor
- Floppy drives
- Keyboard
- Machine ID
- Mouse
- Parallel ports
- SCSI adapters
- Video adapter

The *HARDWARE* subkey also contains the subkeys *Device Map*, *Owner Map*, and *Resource Map*. The *Device Map* subkey contains information about each device on the computer. There are several subkeys in the *Device Map* subkey that contain one or more values to specify the location in the Registry for specific driver information about the device the driver manages. The *Resource Map* points device drivers to the devices that use them. Windows NT uses the *Owner Map* subkey for computers that have PCI card slots.

Answer A is correct because the HKEY_LOCAL_MACHINE\HARDWARE subkey stores hardware descriptions, such as what type of processor your computer has. Answer B is incorrect because the HKEY_LOCAL_MACHINE\SYSTEM subkey points to software configurations. Answer C is incorrect because the HKEY_LOCAL_MACHINE\SOFTWARE subkey also points to software configurations. Answer D is incorrect because Windows NT uses the HKEY_CURRENT_USER subtree to configure the system for the currently logged-on user and has no hardware configuration information.

226   EXAMINING THE **SAM** AND **SECURITY** SUBKEYS

Q   *Administrators occasionally must edit the Security Accounts Manager (SAM) and the SECURITY subkeys in the Windows NT Registry in order to create user accounts.*

True or False?

As you learned in Tip 223, there are sections in the Windows NT Registry to which you will not make changes. Two of the sections that you will never directly access and change are the Security Accounts Manager (SAM) and the *SECURITY* subkeys. The *SAM* subkey contains the Security Identification numbers (SID) for every object in your Windows NT domain. (Remember, a domain is an administrative unit of computers, users, groups, and resources.) Windows NT does not provide any permissions or rights you can give a user that will let the user directly access the *SAM* or *SECURITY* subkeys—because the subkeys are such a critical part of the NT security system, exposing them directly to a user would undermine the entire security model.

The *HKEY_LOCAL_MACHINE\SECURITY* subtree contains security information about the local computer, including user rights, password policy, and the membership of local groups you have configured in User Manager for Domains. Windows NT maps (points) the *HKEY_LOCAL_MACHINE\SECURITY\SAM* subkey to the *HKEY_LOCAL_MACHINE\SAM* subkey, so changes the operating system makes in one subkey automatically appear in the other. Because you cannot access the subkeys directly, you must use a Windows NT-provided security utility to change security-related items. If you want to change global group membership or other security-related items, such as creating a user account, you must use User Manager (on a Windows NT Workstation) or User Manager for Domains (on a Windows NT Server).

The *HKEY_LOCAL_MACHINE\SAM* key contains the user and group account information in the Directory Database (which Microsoft called the Security Account Manager in Windows NT 3.x, and maintained the key with the same initials for backwards compatibility) for the local computer. For a computer running Windows NT Server, this key also contains security information about the domain. The information from the *SAM* subkey appears in User Manager for Domains. Also, on computers with NTFS partitions, you can view and edit security information for a file using Windows NT *Explorer* or My Computer.

System administrators must use User Manager (Windows NT Workstation) or User Manager for Domains (Windows NT Server) to add or remove users, change information about accounts, or change security information for the local computer or for the domain.

The answer is **False** *because you cannot edit the SAM or the SECURITY subkeys. Windows NT uses these subkeys to configure security information. (However, you can edit the SAM and SECURITY subkeys only indirectly, by using User Manager for Domains or by setting security information on files or folders.)*

227 EXAMINING THE SOFTWARE SUBKEY

Q: *What purpose does the* **HKEY_LOCAL_MACHINE\Software** *subkey serve?*

Choose all answers that apply:

A.   *To provide a description of the software on the local computer.*

B.   *To let administrators configure log-on options on the local computer.*

C.   *To record which program groups users are using on the local computer.*

D.   *To provide a central repository of software configuration information on the local computer.*

The *HKEY_LOCAL_MACHINE\Software* subkey contains specific configuration information about software (such as file locations, startup directories, and so on) installed on your computer. The entries under the *HKEY_LOCAL_MACHINE\Software* subkey apply to any computer user and show what software a computer has. This subkey also contains several subkeys. Table 227 describes the subkeys under the *HKEY_LOCAL_MACHINE\Software* subkey.

HKEY_LOCAL_MACHINE\Software	Description
Classes	Filename-extension subkeys that associate applications with file types by their filename extension. These subkeys contain information you add by using the File Types tab in Windows NT *Explorer*, information that Windows-based applications add during their installation, and information about applications Windows NT installs.
Description	Contains the names and version numbers of the software installed on the local computer. (Windows NT stores information about the configuration of the installed applications on a per-user basis under the *HKEY_CURRENT_USER* subkey.)
ODBC	Stores Windows NT system data sources. *ODBC* stands for the Open Database Connectivity standard, a Microsoft-based standard that lets Windows applications access a variety of database formats.
Microsoft	Contains settings for installed Microsoft software.
Program Groups	Records—as a *Yes (0x1)* or *No (0x0)* value—whether Windows NT has converted all former program groups to the new Windows NT 4.0 directory structure. Microsoft redefined the *Program Groups* subkey in Windows NT 4.0. In previous Windows NT versions, it contained a list of the program groups that all the local computer's users used. In Windows NT 4.0, the Windows NT *Explorer* directory structure has replaced the *Program Groups* subkey and no longer maintains a program groups list.
Secure	Provides a convenient place for applications to store configuration information that only an administrator should change.
Windows 3.1 Migration Status	Contains data if you have updated the computer from Windows 3.x to Windows NT 4.0. The values in this subkey indicate whether *.ini* and *Reg.dat* files have migrated (that is, Windows NT 4.0 has converted them) successfully to the Windows NT 4.0 format. If you delete this subkey, Windows NT will again attempt to migrate the files when you restart the system.

Table 227 The HKEY_LOCAL_MACHINE\Software subkeys.

Answers A, B, and D are correct because the HKEY_LOCAL_MACHINE\Software subkey does describe and configure software installed on your local computer. In addition, this subkey will let administrators configure log-on parameters. Answer C is incorrect because Windows NT maintained a list of the program groups all the local computer's users used in previous Windows NT versions.

228   EXAMINING THE *SYSTEM* SUBKEY

Q: *The SYSTEM subkey contains information about the last configuration the local computer was booted under.*

True or False?

The Windows NT Registry's *HKEY_LOCAL_MACHINE\System* subkey contains information about system startup, device drivers, and services to load. The system can save in the *System* subkey all startup-related data it must store (rather than computing the data during system startup). The *System* subkey contains several subkeys of its own. Table 228 describes the sections you will typically find in the *System* subkey.

System Subkey	Description
Clone	Contains information about the last configuration you booted the local computer under. Windows NT uses the *Clone* subkey to build the *CurrentControlSet* subkey when you boot the system. Tip 449 discusses how the *Clone* subkey builds the *CurrentControlSet* subkey and updates the *ControlSet00x* subkey.
ControlSet001	Is the *Current* and the *Default* control set. *ControlSet001* is the subkey the system will modify if you use the options in the Control Panel to make any changes. The system will use *ControlSet001* for the *Default* control set the next time you start the computer.
ControlSet00x	Contains the *LastKnownGood* configuration. The *x* is a variable which can be any number between 1 and 4. Tip 449 discusses the *LastKnownGood* configuration (which contains information about the last successful boot) in detail.
CurrentControlSet	Changes *ControlSet001* when you change information in this subkey. When you use Control Panel options or the Registry Editor to change the Registry, you are changing information in the *CurrentControlSet* subkey.
Select	Points to the *ControlSet* that is the *LastKnownGood* configuration.
Setup	Points to the Windows NT system files' location.

Table 228 The HKEY_LOCAL_MACHINE\System subkeys.

The answer is **True** because the *SYSTEM* subkey does contain information about the last configuration you booted the computer under.

229   EXAMINING THE *HKEY_LOCAL_MACHINE\CURRENTCONTROLSET\SERVICES*

Q: *You have configured your Windows NT Workstation to use Dial-up networking to connect to a Windows NT Server. When you try to connect to the Windows NT Server, your connection fails. Where in the Registry can you configure a log file to help you troubleshoot this problem?*

Choose the best answer:

A.   *HKEY_LOCAL_MACHINE\Software\RAS\Logging*

B.   *HKEY_LOCAL_MACHINE\SYSTEM\CurrentControlSet\Services\RASMAN\ppp\logging*

C.   *HKEY_LOCAL_MACHINE\Hardware\Modems\RAS\logging*

D.   *You cannot configure a log file of modem activity*

Although this Tip's question deals with a specific problem that you could use the *HKEY_LOCAL_MACHINE \SYSTEM\CurrentControlSet\Services* subkey to solve, this Tip will simply introduce you to the subkey. The *HKEY_LOCAL_MACHINE\System\CurrentControlSet\Services* subkey contains the configuration information of all the services on your Windows NT computer.

A *service* is a Windows NT component that serves users or the Windows NT operating system in some way. Services run in the background, performing actions on behalf of the operating system or specific applications. Windows NT services include the Server, Workstation, and Messenger services. These services are integral components of the overall Windows NT operating system. For example, without the Workstation service, you could not connect to other computers through the network. The number of subkeys you will see in the *HKEY_LOCAL_MACHINE\System\CurrentControlSet \Services* subkey will vary, depending on how many Windows NT services you have installed.

Answer B *is correct because, as you will learn in Tip 398, "Troubleshooting RAS," you can enable a Remote Access Service (RAS) log file from the Service\PPP\RASMAN\logging subkey.* **Answers A and C** *are incorrect because these Registry subkeys do not exist.* **Answer D** *is incorrect because you can enable a log file of modem activity.*

---

230   INTRODUCTION TO REGEDIT

Q: *You want to remotely edit the Registry of a Windows 95 computer. Which utility would you use to do so?*

Choose the best answer:

A.   Server Manager

B.   User Manager for Domains

C.   Regedit

D.   Regedt32

Windows NT Server and Workstation both come with two Registry editing utilities, *Regedit* and *Regedt32*. Although both utilities will let you view and change your local or remote computer's Registry, Microsoft intended for you to use Regedit only on Windows 95 computers, so that you can remotely administer them in your network. The Windows 95 and the Windows NT Registries are not compatible, and require you to use different Registry editing tools when you make changes to the Registries. If you use the Regedit utility on a Windows NT Registry, you might corrupt it.

Regedit is a fairly simple utility to use on Windows 95 computers. It displays the registry structure in a format that resembles a file directory structure (tree), with the folder metaphor applying to keys and subkeys and the file metaphor applying to key values. You can drill down through the different subkeys and make changes to the values. Double-click your mouse on any directory tree branch and Regedit will expand that branch. If you want to change values in a subkey, double-click your mouse on the value you want to change and Regedit will display the data in the value on which you clicked. To use the Regedit utility, you must manually open the file because no icon or program group contains the Regedit (or Regedt32) utility. To open the Regedit utility, click your mouse on the Start menu Run option. Windows NT will display the Run dialog box. Within the Run dialog box, enter *Regedit* in the Open field and then click your mouse on the OK button. Windows NT will open the Regedit utility in the Registry Editor window, as Figure 230 shows.

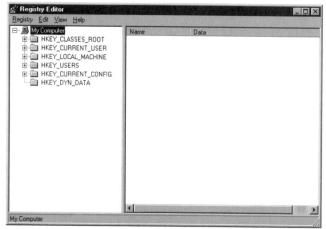

Figure 230 *The Registry Editor window after you start the Regedit utility.*

Note: *Never edit your Registry unless you know specifically what value you are changing and what the consequences to what your change might be. You may accidentally make changes that render Windows NT unable even to boot—for example, to the configuration keys within the* ***CurrentControlSet*** *subkey.*

Answer C *is correct because* ***Regedit*** *is the appropriate utility to use to edit the Windows 95 Registry.* ***Answers A*** *and* ***B*** *are incorrect because you cannot use these utilities to edit the Registry.* ***Answer D*** *is incorrect because you would only use the* ***Regedtr32*** *utility to edit a Windows NT computer's Registry.*

231   **INTRODUCTION TO REGEDT32**

Q: *You want to edit your Windows NT Server's Registry. Which utility would you use to do so?*

Choose the best answer:

    A.   *Regedit*

    B.   *Regedt32*

    C.   *User Manager for Domains*

    D.   *Notepad*

As you learned in Tip 230, an administrator can use the Regedit Registry Editor utility to edit the Registry on a Windows 95 computer. You also learned that, while you can use Regedit to view the Windows NT Registry, you should not use Regedit to make changes to the Windows NT Registry, as it may corrupt values within the Registry. On the other hand, an administrator can use the Regedt32 utility to edit a Windows NT computer's Registry.

The Windows NT Registry is quite a bit different from the Windows 95 Registry in the way that the operating system constructs the Registry. Because of the differences between the Windows NT and the Windows 95 Registries, Microsoft included both the Registry Editor for Windows NT (Regedt32) and the Registry Editor for Windows 95 (Regedit) in the Windows NT operating system.

Although you can view, and even edit, the Windows NT Registry using Regedit, you might cause Registry corruption (because the Registry Editor for Windows 95 may incorrectly write Registry values), resulting in a Windows NT computer that will not function properly.

The Regedit and Regedt32 utilities are almost identical in appearance, so you must pay close attention to which one you use. To open the Regedt32 utility, click your mouse on the Start menu, Run option. Windows NT will display the Run dialog box. Within the Run dialog box, type *Regedt32* and click your mouse on the OK button. Windows NT will open the Regedt32 utility, as Figure 231 shows.

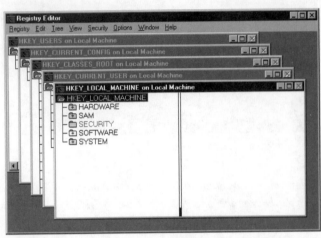

Figure 231 The Registry Editor for Windows NT window displaying the Regedt32 utility.

Note: *Because of the similarities in appearance between the two Registry Editors, if you are unsure which version you have opened, you should check the Help menu About Registry Editor option. Furthermore, you cannot open the Registry Editor for Windows NT from within Windows 9x.*

*Answer B is correct because you would use the **Regedt32** utility to edit a Windows NT computer's Registry. **Answer A** is incorrect because you would only use the **Regedit** utility to edit a Windows 95 computer's Registry. **Answers C and D** are incorrect because you could not use the User Manager for Domains or the Notepad utilities to edit any computer's Registry.*

232 CONFIGURING HARDWARE PROFILES

Q: *You have a notebook computer with Windows NT Workstation installed on it. The notebook computer has a docking station where you installed the network adapter card. You want to configure the notebook computer so that when it is docked, it will load the network adapter drivers, and when the notebook is not docked it will not install the network adapter drivers. How can you configure your Windows NT Workstation to sometimes load the network device drivers and other times not?*

Choose the best answer:

A.   *Configure hardware profiles for the docked and undocked states the notebook computer could be in.*

B.   *Install Windows NT Workstation twice. Once with the network adapter drivers, and once without the network adapter drivers.*

C.   *Configure multiple user profiles and configure one with the network adapter drivers and one without the network adapter drivers.*

D.   *You cannot configure your Windows NT Workstation to have different configurations based on its docked or undocked state.*

There may be times when you must configure a notebook computer to load different device drivers based on a hardware state the computer is in. For example, if you have a notebook computer that has its network adapter card in the docking station, you would not want to load the device drivers for the network adapter card when the notebook computer is not docked (because no network adapter card would be present).

To handle such a situation, Windows NT lets administrators create hardware profiles for computers. A *hardware profile* contains configuration information about the computer's hardware. You can configure one profile to load certain device drivers and another profile to not load the same device drivers. To configure hardware profiles in Windows NT, perform the following steps:

1. Right-click your mouse on the My Computer icon. Windows NT will display the Quick menu.

2. Within the Quick menu, click your mouse on the Properties option. Windows NT will display the System Properties dialog box.

3. Within the System Properties dialog box, click your mouse on the Hardware Profiles tab. System Properties will change to the Hardware Profiles tab, as shown in Figure 232.

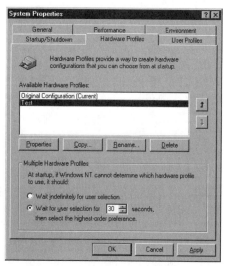

Figure 232 The Windows NT Hardware Profiles tab in the System Properties dialog box.

4. Within the Hardware Profiles tab, in the *Available hardware Profiles* field, select the profile Original Configuration (Current). Click your mouse on the Copy button. Windows NT will open the Copy Profile dialog box and prompt you to name the new profile.

5. Within the Copy Profile dialog box, type the name you want to give the new profile and click your mouse on the OK button. Windows NT will create the new profile.

6. Double-click your mouse on the profile you just created. Windows NT will open the new profile's Profile Properties dialog box.

7. Within the Profile Properties dialog box, you may now click on the radio buttons to turn on docking station support and network adapter drivers.

Answer A is correct because you would create hardware profiles for the docked and undocked states. Answer B is incorrect because, although installing Windows NT twice would let you create two configurations, it would be a waste of disk space. Answer C is incorrect because you cannot control hardware configurations from a user profile. Answer D is incorrect because you can configure hardware profiles.

233 | CONFIGURING COMMUNICATIONS PORTS

Q: *You are installing a new modem on your Windows NT computer. You want to use COM4 on your computer for the new modem, but COM4 is not present. How can you add COM4?*

Choose the best answer:

A.   *Use Server Manager*

B.   *Use Windows NT Diagnostics*

C.   *Use the Ports utility in the Control Panel*

D.   *Windows NT automatically detects COM ports, you cannot manually add COM ports*

Your computer uses COM (communication) ports for serial communication devices, such as modems. Typically, Windows NT will detect COM ports when you install the system. However, you might occasionally have to add or configure COM ports—for example, if you add a modem to a Windows NT computer after the operating system's installation. If you need to add or configure a COM port, you can use the Ports utility in the Control Panel. (Remember, the Windows NT Control Panel stores your computer's hardware configuration information.)

When you open the Ports utility, you will see a list of the ports currently installed on your computer. If a device is attached to the serial port or another device is using the same memory interrupt (an internal hardware issue) as the COM port, the COM port will not show up in the Ports dialog box. For example, if you have a mouse connected to the COM1 serial port, you will not see COM1 show up in the Ports list. To add a COM port, perform the following steps:

1. Click your mouse on the Start menu and select the Settings submenu Control Panel option. Windows NT will display the Control Panel window.

2. Within the Control Panel, double-click your mouse on the Ports icon. Windows NT will open the Ports utility, as shown in Figure 233.

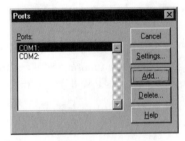

Figure 233 The Ports utility in the Control Panel.

3. Within the Ports utility, click your mouse on the Add button. Windows NT will display the Advanced Settings for New Port dialog box.

4. Within the Advanced Settings for New Port dialog box, click your mouse on the drop-down lists for the following settings: COM Port Number, Base Input Output Address, and Interrupt Request Line (IRQ). Click your mouse on the OK button. Windows NT will add the COM port and close the Advanced Settings for New Port dialog box.

Answer C is correct because to add or configure COM ports, you would use the Ports utility in the Windows NT Control Panel. Answers A and B are incorrect because neither the Server Manager nor Windows NT Diagnostics will let you configure or add COM ports. Answer D is incorrect because, although Windows NT will attempt to detect COM ports when you first install the system, you might have to add or configure new COM ports.

234   CONFIGURING DISPLAY SETTINGS

Q: *You have just changed your monitor on your Windows NT Server to a 21 inch monitor. You now want to change your monitor's resolution to 1024 pixels x 768 pixels. Where in Windows NT would you change your monitor's resolution?*

Choose the best answer:

     A.   *Server Manager*

     B.   *User Manager for Domains*

     C.   *Control Panel Monitor*

     D.   *Control Panel Display*

People call the device you use to view the information your computer displays many different names, such as display, screen, CRT, and monitor. All these names mean the same thing, however. In this book, the term *monitor* will describe the location where you will view a computer's output. In turn, your monitor's *resolution* refers to the number of dots (pixels) on the actual screen that make up the total picture. A monitor's resolution is expressed as the number of pixels across the screen (horizontal resolution) by the number of pixels running down the screen (vertical resolution). An example of a monitor's resolution is 640x480. The number 640 refers to the number of horizontal pixels that make up your monitor's display area. The number 480 refers to the number of vertical pixels that make up your monitor's display area. To configure a monitor's resolution in Windows NT, perform the following steps:

1. Click your mouse on the Start menu and select the Settings submenu Control Panel option. Windows NT will display the Control Panel window.

2. Within the Control Panel window, double-click your mouse on the Display icon. Windows NT will open the Display Properties dialog box.

3. Within the Display Properties dialog box, click your mouse on the Settings tab. The Display Properties dialog box will change its display to show the Settings tab.

4. Within the Settings tab, locate the Desktop Area section. Click and hold down your mouse on the Less-More slide bar and drag to the desired monitor resolution. Click your mouse on the Test button. Windows NT will test the new display settings.

5. When Windows NT is done testing the new display settings, if the setting change was successful, click your mouse on the OK button. Windows NT will close the Display dialog box and set the new Display options, as Figure 234 shows.

Answer D is correct because you would configure display settings from the Display Properties dialog box. Answers A and B are incorrect because you cannot change Windows NT display settings, such as monitor resolution, from either the Server Manager or the User Manager for Domains programs. Answer C is incorrect because the Monitor option does not exist in Windows NT.

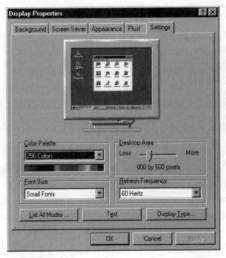

Figure 234 *The Windows NT Display Properties dialog box.*

235   **ADDING SCSI ADAPTERS**

Q: *You have added a new Small Computer System Interface (SCSI) controller and a SCSI hard drive. You want to configure the SCSI devices to work with Windows NT. What must you do before you can manage the SCSI devices in Windows NT?*

Choose the best answer:

   A.   Use the Add New Hardware utility to add the SCSI devices in the Control Panel.

   B.   Add the SCSI controller in the Control Panel from the SCSI Adapters utility. Restart your computer. Windows NT will automatically detect the SCSI hard drive.

   C.   Add the SCSI devices in Server Manager.

   D.   Do nothing—Windows NT will automatically detect and configure the new SCSI devices.

The *Small Computer System Interface (SCSI)* standard defines a protocol set for communications among devices, and supports many different types of devices—from scanners to hard drives. Most network administrators consider SCSI hard drives to be the most reliable of all disk types, because of their performance, maintainability, support for mirroring, and other data protection techniques. The SCSI standard, however, does define a set of communications rules— meaning that almost any device, not just hard drives, can adhere to the SCSI standard. Other SCSI devices include scanners, tape backup devices, and external storage devices, among others.

To use a SCSI device, you must first have a SCSI controller card in your computer. The SCSI controller card converts the information that comes from the SCSI-compatible device into information that your Windows NT computer can understand. After you have installed a SCSI controller card, your Windows NT computer can manage any device you connect to the controller card. To add a SCSI controller card to your Windows NT computer, perform the following steps:

   1.   After you install the SCSI controller card in your computer, click your mouse on the Start menu and select the Settings submenu Control Panel option. Windows NT will open the Control Panel.

2. Within the Control Panel, double-click your mouse on the SCSI Adapters icon. Windows NT will open the SCSI Adapters dialog box, as shown in Figure 235.

3. Within the SCSI Adapters dialog box, click your mouse on the Drivers tab. The SCSI Adapters dialog box will change its display to the Drivers tab.

4. Within the Drivers tab, click your mouse on the Add button. Windows NT will display the Install Driver dialog box.

5. Within the Install Driver dialog box, select the brand and model of SCSI controller you have installed. Click your mouse on the OK button. Windows NT will add the SCSI drivers for your SCSI controller and close the Install Driver dialog box.

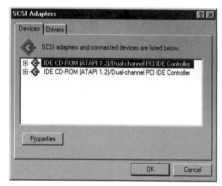

Figure 235 The Windows NT SCSI Adapters dialog box, which lists available SCSI controllers.

Answer B is correct because you must use the Control Panel SCSI Adapters utility to add the SCSI controller. After you add the SCSI controller, you will not have to do anything else: Windows NT will automatically detect the SCSI hard drive. Answer A is incorrect because Windows NT does not have an Add New Hardware utility. Answer C is incorrect because you cannot use Server Manager to add SCSI devices or controllers. Answer D is incorrect because you must use the SCSI Adapters dialog box in the Control Panel to add the SCSI controller.

236 CONFIGURING DEVICES THAT RESPOND IN THE EVENT OF A POWER FAILURE

Q.   *Which of the following best describes the term UPS?*

Select the best answer:

    A.   *Universal Parallel Support*

    B.   *Uninterruptible Power Supply*

    C.   *Uninterruptible Power Source*

    D.   *Unprotected Power Source*

Power failure is an event that can cause various kinds of damage to any operating system or its data, including loss of data, damage to computer hardware add-ons, and damage to the computer itself. As a Windows NT administrator, you should take as many precautions as you can to guard against damage or loss a power failure can cause.

Network administrators commonly use an *Uninterruptable Power Supply (UPS)* to protect their servers against power failure. An Uninterruptable Power Supply is basically a self-charging battery that maintains a charge of electricity that attached equipment will use if the power fails. An Uninterruptable Power Supply typically has the ability to notify a computer that power is lost and that the computer is now running on battery.

Windows NT supports many Uninterruptable Power Supply models and has a built-in set of software components that let Windows NT perform actions based on signals the Uninterruptable Power Supply sends it. The Windows NT Uninterruptable Power Supply software components consist of the Uninterruptable Power Supply service and its configuration dialog box, which you can find in the Windows NT Control Panel.

Because the software components in Windows NT must work with more than one kind of Uninterruptable Power Supply, there are configuration options within the Uninterruptable Power Supply dialog box that let you tell the software how and where to listen for notifications from the Uninterruptable Power Supply model you chose. Understanding the unique method your Uninterruptable Power Supply will use to communicate is vital to properly configuring the Uninterruptable Power Supply software Windows NT includes. The Windows NT UPS configuration dialog box contains the following options:

- The *Uninterruptible Power Supply is installed on* is an option that lets you tell Windows NT what COM port to use for the Uninterruptable Power Supply.

- The *UPS Configuration* lets you tell Windows NT which of (or all) three actions to perform, and choose which *interface voltages* will trigger the actions. Interface voltages indicate active communication from the Uninterruptable Power Supply. If you choose *Negative*, it means that the Uninterruptable Power Supply normally sends a positive signal that changes to negative when power fails. If you choose *Positive*, the opposite is true; The options that require an interface voltage setting are *Power failure signal, Low battery at least 2 min before shutdown,* and *Remote UPS shutdown*. You can enable each of these options only if your Uninterruptable Power Supply supports the option. Tip 237 teaches you more about the interface voltage signals.

- The *Execute Command File* option lets you specify a *command file,* which is a file with an extension of .EXE, .COM, .BAT, or .CMD, to execute when a power failure occurs. The command file option has the limitation that it must complete execution within 30 seconds or Windows NT will terminate it.

- The *UPS Characteristics* option contains two numeric settings that let you tell Windows NT the amount of time your Uninterruptable Power Supply is expected to provide power and how long it will take to recharge the battery.

- *Expected Battery Life* and *Battery recharge time per minute of run time* are the names of the options set within the Uninterruptable Power Supply characteristics area.

- *UPS Service* provides you with the ability to decide the *Time between power failure and initial warning message,* and *Delay between warning* messages, which are options Windows NT executes and have nothing to do with the model Uninterruptable Power Supply you have.

To configure an Uninterruptable Power Supply to work with the Windows Uninterruptable Power Supply service, perform the following steps:

1. Click your mouse on the Start menu and select the Settings submenu Control Panel option. Windows NT will open the Control Panel Window.

2. Double-click your mouse on the UPS icon. Windows NT will open the UPS dialog box, as shown in Figure 236.

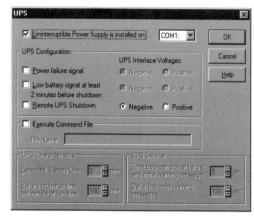

Figure 236 *The UPS dialog box displays several options to let you configure a UPS.*

3. Within the UPS dialog box, choose your configuration options and click your mouse on the OK button. Windows NT will store your configuration options and apply them to the Uninterruptable Power Supply communications.

Answer B *is correct because UPS stands for Uninterruptable Power Supply.* **Answers A, C, and D** *are incorrect because they do not represent the meaning of UPS.*

| 237 | USING SPECIAL SERIAL CABLES WITH AN UNINTERRUPTABLE POWER SUPPLY |

Q.   *You are a Windows NT domain administrator. You are installing a new Uninterruptable Power Supply to the server and want to configure the Windows NT Uninterruptable Power Supply service to react if power fails. What kind of cable do you need to connect the Uninterruptable Power Supply to the server?*

Choose the best answer:

A.   *Parallel*

B.   *Serial*

C.   *SCSI*

D   *Serial with special pinout*

After you install and configure an Uninterruptable Power Supply (UPS), Windows NT must communicate with the UPS in order to perform the actions you have configured. Therefore, you first must establish a means of communication. Windows NT uses a communication (COM) port to receive information from the Uninterruptable Power Supply and may require a special serial cable (with hardwired pins to control configuration differences) to accurately read the signals some models of UPS will send. You must establish communication because Windows NT uses certain *connector pins* (pins that connect to wires in the cable that connect to other pins at the UPS) to read interface voltage signals (which Table 23.17 lists) which may not be the same as your Uninterruptable Power Supply's *pin assignments*.

If your Uninterruptable Power Supply's pin assignments do not match those Windows NT uses, you might have to purchase or manufacture a special serial cable which will cross the wires to ensure that the pins match. Table 237.1 shows the UPS and RS-232 signals.

Serial 9 Pin Connector	Serial 25 Pin	UPS signal	RS-232 Signal
4	20	UPS Remote Shutdown	DTR
1	8	Low Battery	DCD
8	5	Power Failure	CTS

Table 237.1 Interface voltage pin assignments.

Each of the signals that the Uninterruptable Power Supply can send will create a resulting action on the Windows NT computer. If the pins on the computer do not match the pins on the UPS, you can have serious problems because the computer may interpret a message from the UPS incorrectly or not read the message at all. Table 237.2 describes in detail each signal the Windows NT computer might receive from a UPS and the result it produces.

Shutdown Signal	Result
Remote UPS	The Windows NT computer sends to the Uninterruptable Power Supply when a system shutdown has completed its operation. This signal tells the Uninterruptable Power Supply that it may turn off the battery power.
Low Battery	The Uninterruptable Power Supply sends when battery power is close to failing. You must check the Low Battery signal checkbox if your Uninterruptable Power Supply supports this feature.
Power Failure	Produces one of two effects on the Windows NT computer, based on the ability of the Uninterruptable Power Supply to send a low battery signal.

Table 237.2 Uninterruptable Power Supply signals and their results.

If the Uninterruptable Power Supply can send a low battery signal, the Windows NT computer will wait the amount of time you specified in the *Time between power failure and initial warning message* field and then send a message to all connected users that a power failure has occurred.

Users will be unable to connect after Windows NT sends the power failure message. If the Uninterruptable Power Supply signals that power has been restored, the Windows NT computer will resume normal operation and accept user connections once more. If the Uninterruptable Power Supply sends a low battery signal, the Windows NT computer will execute the file you specified in the *Execute Command File* field and initiate a system shutdown. When it completes shutdown operations, Windows NT will signal the Uninterruptable Power Supply that it can turn off battery power (and, probably, start to recharge).

If the Uninterruptable Power Supply cannot send a low battery signal, the Windows NT computer will compute the expected battery life by dividing the amount of time Windows NT has been running by the information in the *Battery recharge time per minute of run time* field. If the remaining battery life is more than two minutes, Windows NT will wait the amount of time the *Time between power failure and initial warning message* field specifies and then send a message to all connected users indicating a power failure, while at the same time preventing new connections. If the Uninterruptable Power Supply sends a signal that power has been restored before the calculated battery life reaches two minutes, Windows NT will resume normal operation and users can once again connect.

If or when the calculated battery life reaches two minutes, Windows NT will execute the file you specified in the *Execute Command File* field and initiate a system shutdown. When it completes shutdown operations, Windows NT will signal the Uninterruptable Power Supply that the UPS can turn off battery power.

Answer D is correct because you use a serial cable to connect an Uninterruptable Power Supply to Windows NT, which serial cable may require special pin configurations to work correctly. Answers A, B, and C are incorrect because you use a serial cable to connect an Uninterruptable Power Supply to Windows NT.

238 ADDING AND REMOVING WINDOWS NT COMPONENTS

Q.   *You are a Windows NT domain administrator. You want to remove the Windows NT games from all Windows NT computers. What program would you use to remove the games?*

Choose the best answer:

    A.   *Add/Remove Programs*

    B.   *Services*

    C.   *Program Manager*

    D.   *Add-in Manager*

The Windows NT operating system has many optional features that you can remove or add to your computer, as you want. For example, you might want to add or remove the program set you must use to implement workgroup-level *Microsoft Mail* functionality. Not all networks use this component, and you would have to add it in order to use workgroup-level *Microsoft Mail*. The interface Windows NT provides that lets you select components to add or remove from a computer is the Add/Remove Programs option in the Windows NT Control Panel. To view the Add/Remove Programs dialog box, perform the following steps:

1. Click your mouse on the Start menu Settings submenu Control Panel option. Windows NT will open the Control Panel window.

2. Double-click your mouse on the Add/Remove Programs option. Windows NT will open the Add/Remove Programs dialog box.

The Add/Remove Programs dialog box contains two tabs at the top, Install/Uninstall and Windows NT Setup, which let you choose, respectively, between installing or uninstalling applications and selecting the Windows NT setup components. The Install/Uninstall tab provides you with an Install button, which lets you install applications, a list of installed applications, and an Add/Remove button, which lets you uninstall applications you have selected from the list or install new applications. Figure 238.1 shows the Install/Uninstall tab.

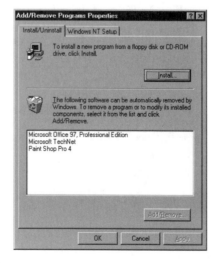

Figure 238.1 Using the Install/Uninstall tab.

The Windows NT Setup tab lets you choose which of the optional components in Windows NT to install or remove. The components are divided into groups that contain one or more components to choose from. Each group has a checkbox to the left of it that shows you if you selected a group or part of a group for installation. If the checkbox has a check mark in it against a white background, the options in that group are already installed or will be installed when you click your mouse on OK. If the checkbox has a checkmark in it against a colored background, some of the options in that group are already installed or will be installed when you click your mouse on OK. If the checkbox does not have a checkmark in it, you have either not selected any of the options in that group for install or all options in that group will be removed when you click your mouse on OK.

In addition, you must double-click your mouse on a group name or select the group name and click your mouse on the Details button to view a group's options. Finally, the Windows NT Setup tab also has a Have Disk button, which lets you install components from a source other than the Windows NT Setup source files. Figure 238.2 shows the Windows NT Setup tab.

Figure 238.2 *Using the Windows NT Setup tab.*

Answer A is correct because you use the Add/Remove Programs option in the Control Panel to add or remove optional Windows NT components. *Answer B is incorrect because the Services dialog box does not let you add or remove anything and does not apply to optional components.* *Answer C is incorrect because there is no Program Manager in Windows NT 4.0. Answer D is incorrect because there is no Add-in Manager in Windows NT 4.0.*

239	UNDERSTANDING SYSTEM POLICIES

Q.   You are the administrator of a Windows NT domain that consists of one Windows NT Server and 38 Windows NT Workstations. You want to restrict certain users from making changes to computers. What steps would you follow to ensure that only approved users can make changes to computers while preventing other users from making changes?

Choose the best answer:

   A.   *Create a system policy that contains the appropriate restrictions.*

   B.   *Create log-on scripts with appropriate rights for each user.*

C.   *Modify the Registry on each machine to reflect appropriate rights.*

D.   *Modify the log-on server's Registry to restrict the users.*

As the administrator of a Windows NT domain, you might have to impose certain restrictions on computers or users at the local computer level. If the operating systems on the users' computers are Windows NT or Windows 95, you can use system policies to implement local restrictions. You implement system policies by creating a policy file and saving it in the authenticating server's log-on directory. You will use the System Policy Editor to create the policy file. The policy file's name depends on the remote computer's operating system. If the operating system is Windows NT, the file name will be *NTCONFIG.POL*. If the operating system is Windows 95, the file name will be *CONFIG.POL*.

Each client computer sends its operating system version to the domain controller. The domain controller will search the *Netlogon* share looking for the appropriate policy file. If the domain controller finds the appropriate policy file, it will search through the file for information that corresponds to the client computer name, user name, or group that the user belongs to. If the domain controller finds the information, it will download the policy file and update the remote computer's registry so that it will comply with the restrictions that the policy file establishes.

You can use policy files to effectively implement local restrictions on your network. Policy files let you implement changes on computers throughout your network without you having to visit each computer. They also let you apply restrictions to users who might log on to different computers, while ensuring that those restrictions apply only to the users you specify.

Answer A is correct because you use policy files to implement restrictions at the local computer. Answer B is incorrect because log-on scripts cannot enforce restrictions at the local computer. Answer C is incorrect because modifying each Registry would take too much time and would not let you apply restrictions to roving users. Answer D is incorrect because changes you make to the log-on server's Registry would not apply to the local machine.

240   CONVERTING A **FAT** PARTITION TO **NTFS**

Q.   *You are the administrator of a Windows NT domain. You want to compress certain files on your Primary Domain Controller, but cannot because the files reside on a FAT partition. What is the best method to change the partition to NTFS?*

Choose the best answer:

A.   *Back up the files to tape, delete, and recreate the partition.*

B.   *Back up the files to tape and use Disk Administrator to format the partition NTFS.*

C.   *Use Disk Administrator to convert the partition to NTFS.*

D.   *Use the Convert.exe utility to convert the partition to NTFS.*

As a Windows NT administrator, you must often convert an existing FAT partition to NTFS, because of the need to apply security constraints to files on the partition, for effectiveness, or for any one of a number of other reasons. The *Convert.exe* utility lets you change a FAT partition to NTFS without damaging files on the partition, which means you do not have to first back up and restore information in order to accomplish the conversion. The *Convert.exe* utility is a command-line executable program, which means that there is no window for it and you must execute it from the *console*. The console is a Windows NT term for the command prompt, which people also call the MS-DOS window.

At the console prompt, you will type the following syntax to invoke the *Convert.exe* utility (type within the brackets the letter that corresponds to the drive you want to convert):

```
C:\> CONVERT [drive letter]: /fs:ntfs  <ENTER>
```

If any process is currently accessing the drive when you execute the *Convert.exe* utility, Windows NT will display an error message and give you the option of scheduling the conversion for the next system restart. To convert a FAT partition to NTFS, perform the following steps:

1. Click your mouse on the Start menu and select the Programs submenu Command Prompt option. Windows NT will open the Console window.

2. Within the Console window, type CONVERT [DRIVE LETTER]: /FS:NTFS and press the ENTER key. Windows NT will try to convert the drive you specified and, if it cannot, it will display an error message and give you the rescheduling option.

Answer D is correct because you use the Convert.EXE utility to convert FAT partitions to NTFS. Answer A is incorrect because the option is unnecessary and time-consuming. Answer B is incorrect because Disk Administrator cannot perform conversions. Answer C is incorrect because Disk Administrator cannot perform conversions.

241 COMPRESSING A FILE

Q. *You are a Windows NT domain administrator and you want to compress several infrequently accessed files on an NTFS partition. What is the best method for compressing the files?*

Choose the best answer:

A. *You cannot compress files on an NTFS partition.*

B. *Use Disk Manager.*

C. *Use Wincompress from the Windows NT Resource Kit.*

D. *Use Windows NT Explorer to check the compress attribute for the file or folder.*

As you learned in Tip 208, Windows NT supports file-level compression on independent files and folders on an NTFS partition. Files and folders on NTFS partitions have an additional attribute, *Compress*, which lets you compress them individually. The operating system will automatically compress any file that has the Compress attribute enabled. The operating system will automatically compress any files that you create within a folder with the *Compress* attribute enabled. Figure 241 shows a file's Properties dialog box and clearly displays the *Compress* attribute.

You can configure Windows NT to display compressed files and folders in blue, simply by checking the Display compressed files and folders with an alternate color checkbox in the Windows NT *Explorer* View menu. Windows NT can use only the color blue to indicate compression, so you should not use a blue background within the *Explorer*. However, a folder containing compressed files is not always blue—Windows NT *Explorer* might not display the blue color if the folder itself is not compressed. You will see this lack of blue coloring most often when you move compressed files into uncompressed folders. In addition to the Compress attribute in Windows *Explorer*, Windows NT provides another method, the *Compact.exe* utility, to compress files and folders. In Tip 242, you will learn how to use the *Compact.exe* utility to compress a file.

Note: Windows NT *Explorer* and the *Compact.exe* utility cannot compress an open file.

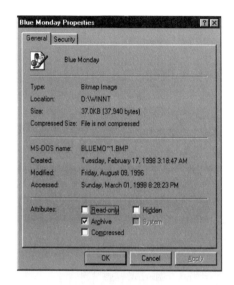

Figure 241 *The File Properties dialog box.*

To compress a file or folder in Windows NT *Explorer*, perform the following steps:

1. Click your mouse on the Start menu and select the Programs submenu Windows Explorer option. Windows NT will open the Windows NT *Explorer*.

2. Click your mouse on a file or folder. Windows NT *Explorer* will indicate your selection by highlighting the file or folder.

3. Click your mouse on the File menu Properties option. Windows NT *Explorer* will open the Properties dialog box for the file or folder.

4. Click your mouse on the Attributes option Compressed checkbox. Windows NT will indicate your selection by placing a check mark in the checkbox.

5. Click your mouse on the OK button. Windows NT *Explorer* will compress the file or folder.

Answer D *is correct because a file or folder's Properties window in Windows NT Explorer can compress files or folders.* ***Answer A*** *is incorrect because you can compress files or folders on an NTFS partition.* ***Answer B*** *is incorrect because Disk Manager cannot compress files and folders.* ***Answer C*** *is incorrect because the Windows NT Resource Kit does not contain a utility called Wincompress.*

242 — **COMPRESSING A FILE FROM THE CONSOLE**

Q.   *You are a Windows NT domain administrator. While compressing files on an NTFS partition, you lost power to your computer before the compression completed. How can you force compress operations to complete even on files that you have already marked as compressed?*

Choose the best answer:

A.   *Do nothing: the compress attribute will reapply compression when the system restarts.*

B.   *Use Compact.exe /f to force compression on all designated files.*

C.   *Use Chkdsk to repair and recompress all files.*

D.   *Use Compress.exe /f to force compression on all designated files.*

You learned in Tip 241 how to compress individual files and folders on NTFS partitions using Windows NT *Explorer*. Windows NT provides an additional tool, the *Compact.exe* utility, to let you compress files and folders on NTFS partitions. The *Compact.exe* utility is a command-line utility that lets you perform compression operations on files and folders with variables that are not available in Windows NT *Explorer*. The *Compact.exe* utility can compress and uncompress files and folders normally on NTFS partitions and can also perform, using command-line switches, additional compression operations, as Table 242 shows.

Switch	Operation
A	Displays a list of files with Hidden or System attributes.
C	Compresses files and folders you specified and marks the *Compressed* attribute.
F	Forces the program to complete compression operations even if you have set the *Compressed* attribute.
I	Program performs compression operations even if errors occur.
Q	Displays summary information.
S	Performs compression on files in the current or specified folder and all subfolders.
U	Uncompresses files and folders you specified and removes the Compressed attribute.
None	Displays compression status on all files in the current folder.

*Table 242 The command-line switches you can use with **Compact.exe** to perform compression operations.*

The *Compact.exe* utility is a very useful tool and, in some cases, the only tool you will have to accomplish a compression goal. If, for example, you wanted to compress an entire drive or a folder with many subfolders in it, as well as all the files inside them, you could compress each folder in turn, one at a time. However, doing so would take much more time than using *Compact.exe* with the /s switch to compress the drive, folder, subfolders, and files.

Answer B is correct because you can use the Compact.exe utility to force compression operations on files or folders already marked as compressed. Answer A is incorrect because Windows NT does not reapply compression to marked files unless you use the Compact.exe utility. Answer C is incorrect because the CHKDSK utility does not perform compression operations. Answer D is incorrect because Compress.EXE does not exist.

243 — COPYING AND MOVING COMPRESSED FILES

Q.   You are a Windows NT domain administrator. While performing routine maintenance on your Windows NT server, you move a file from a compressed folder to an uncompressed folder. What will be the copied file's compression status?

Choose the best answer:

A.   The file will retain its original compression status from the original folder.

B.   The file will inherit the target folder's compression status.

C.   The file will not copy until you have compressed the target folder.

D.   The file will not copy until you have uncompressed the original folder.

The compression attribute of files you copy or move on NTFS partitions can change. A file's compression status depends on the copy or move operation you perform. If you copy a file from one folder to another, the file will inherit the target folder's compression attribute status. Therefore, if you copy a compressed file to an uncompressed folder, the new file will be uncompressed. The original file will be unaffected.

If you copy an uncompressed file to a compressed folder, the system first copies and then compresses the file. Therefore, there must be enough room on the partition containing the compressed folder to fit the file in its uncompressed state. If you move a file from one folder to another, the file will retain its original compression attribute status. Therefore, if you move a compressed file to an uncompressed folder, the file will still be compressed in its new location.

Answer B is correct because a copied file will inherit the target folder's compression attribute status. Answer A is incorrect because a copied file will inherit the target folder's compression attribute status. Answers C and D are incorrect because you can copy files between folders without changing the folders' compression attribute.

244 | INTRODUCTION TO THE DISK ADMINISTRATOR UTILITY

Q.   *You are a Windows NT domain administrator. You have just installed an additional hard drive in your Windows NT server. What utility should you use to partition and format the drive?*

Choose the best answer:

   A.   *User Manager*

   B.   *Disk Administrator*

   C.   *Backup*

   D.   *Event Viewer*

Disk management is a task you will undoubtedly have to perform as a Microsoft Certified System Engineer. Disk management involves creating, deleting, and modifying disk partitions. You will use the Windows NT Disk Administrator utility to perform necessary disk management operations. The Disk Administrator produces a graphical representation of your fixed disk drives so that you can view the partition status of all drives and make configuration changes without having to learn complex command-line sequences. To open the Disk Administrator program, click your mouse on the Start menu and select the Programs submenu Administrative Tools group Disk Administrator option. Windows NT will open the Disk Administrator program window. Figure 244 shows the Disk Administrator window.

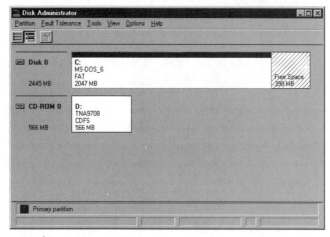

Figure 244 The Disk Administrator window.

Answer B is correct because the Disk Administrator is the correct tool for managing disk partitions. **Answer A** is incorrect because User Manager has no disk administration abilities. **Answer C** is incorrect because the Backup utility cannot make changes to hard drives. **Answer D** is incorrect because you cannot use the Event Viewer to manage fixed disks.

245 — UNDERSTANDING PRIMARY PARTITIONS

Q.   Windows NT can support up to six primary partitions.

True or False?

Primary partitions are partitions the computer can mark as active and use to execute a system start. Therefore, only an active partition can have the boot sector, which the computer will read to find the operating system boot files. You cannot divide primary partitions into logical partitions, and the primary partitions will remain the size they were when you created them until you destroy them.

Fixed disks can have up to four active partitions, although some operating systems and partitioning tools will support only one. The four primary partition limit is based on a hardware constraint that prevents more than four partitions of any kind on a single disk.

The answer is **False** because a single fixed disk can have only up to four primary partitions.

246 — UNDERSTANDING EXTENDED PARTITIONS

Q.   Windows NT can support up to three extended partitions.

True or False?

As you learned in Tip 245, a single fixed disk can support up to four total partitions, all of which can function as primary partitions unless an *extended partition* is present. An extended partition is not a data partition, but rather a structure that holds logical drives within itself.

A single hard drive can have only one extended partition, but you can divide the partition into multiple logical drives. You must create at least one logical drive to use an extended partition because you cannot format or assign a drive letter to the extended partition itself. Instead, you must format and assign a drive letter to the logical drive.

Using an extended partition lets you go beyond the four-partition limitation on a single drive. You can, for example, create three primary partitions and one extended partition and then divide the extended partition into four or more logical drives; doing so would provide you with more than seven independent drive letters to use. Windows NT can use extended partitions to store data or even the operating system's boot files and root folder, but the system files for Windows NT must reside on a primary partition.

The answer is **False** because a single fixed disk can support only one extended partition.

247 — UNDERSTANDING PARTITION NUMBERING

Q.   *Windows NT assigns partition numbers first to all primary partitions on drive 0, then to all extended partitions on drive 0, then to primary partitions on drive 1, and then to extended partitions on drive 1, continuing this path until all partitions are numbered.*

True or False?

Windows NT assigns numbers to partitions based on partition value. Windows NT assigns partition value first according to the partition type, with primary partitions having the highest value and logical drives having the lowest value, and then according to partition location. Partitions can receive different values, based on where they are on the hard drives and what hard drives they are on. For example, if you have two drives with an extended partition on each of them, the extended partition on drive 0 will have a higher value than the extended partition on drive 1.

The following example illustrates how partition values determine the partition number. Imagine you have a Windows NT computer with three hard drives: drive 0, drive 1, and drive 2. There are two primary partitions and one extended partition on drive 0. Drive 1 has one primary partition and one extended partition. Drive 2 has one primary partition and no extended partitions.

*The answer is **False** because Windows NT numbers primary partitions first, regardless of what disk they are on, because they have a greater value than extended partitions.*

248 — COMMITTING CURRENT CHANGES FROM THE DISK ADMINISTRATOR

Q.   *You are a Windows NT domain administrator. You have just created a new partition in Disk Administrator. What must you do before you can format the new partition?*

Choose the best answer:

    A.   *Mark the partition active*

    B.   *Reboot the computer*

    C.   *Commit changes so that the operating system saves the new partition*

    D.   *Run CHKDSK on the new partition*

As you learned in Tip 244, the Disk Administrator utility provides you with a graphical representation of your disk and partition status. The Disk Administrator reads the disk and partition information and creates the graphic representations of the information when it starts. The Windows NT does not actually save changes you make in the Disk Administrator until you tell the Disk Administrator to do so.

There are two ways that you can make changes in the Disk Administrator. First, if you have made changes to the partition structure and then you try to close the Disk Administrator, the utility will display a message box that prompts you to save changes. If you choose to continue, the Disk Administrator will save all changes you made to the partition structure to the *partition table*, where the changes will take effect. If you choose not to continue, the Disk Administrator abandons your changes and the partition table will remain unaffected.

The second way to save changes you made to the partition structure is to use the Commit Changes Now option in the Disk Administrator's Partition menu. The Commit Changes Now option will save changes to the partition structure so that the structure matches the graphical representation you see in the Disk Administrator. This method is useful if you must update the partition structure before you can continue. For example, if you are creating a new partition, you must save the changes to the partition table before you can format the partition for use. Figure 248 shows the Commit Changes Now option.

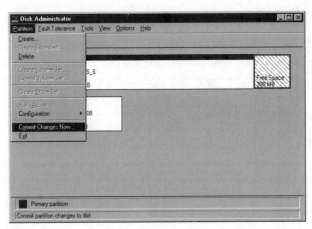

Figure 248 The Commit Changes Now option in the Disk Administrator dialog box.

Answer C is correct because you must commit changes before you format a new partition. Answer A is incorrect because you do not have to make a partition active to format it. Answer B is incorrect because rebooting the computer is not required and would not reflect the new partition information unless you saved the changes. Answer D is incorrect because you cannot execute the CHKDSK utility on an unformatted partition.

249 UNDERSTANDING STRIPE SETS

Q.   Which of the following can improve disk I/O performance?

Choose the best answer:

A.   *Disk Mirroring*

B.   *Disk Duplexing*

C.   *Stripe sets*

D.   *Volume sets*

Windows NT supports a wide variety of disk configurations to help you enhance data security, disk performance, and effective use of space. One way to effectively increase disk drive performance is to create a *stripe set*. A stripe set is a disk configuration in which you use two or more physical disks to act as a single logical drive. All disks in a stripe set function as if they were a single disk, which means that the operating system can perform disk input output (I/O) commands on all disks simultaneously, thereby increasing disk performance. A stripe set is much like a volume set because it uses free space from multiple disks. A volume set, however, provides no increase in disk I/O performance. You will learn more about volume sets in Tip 259.

Stripe sets must use an equal portion of disk space on each disk but can combine free space from different types of fixed disks, such as Small Computer System Interface (SCSI) and Integrated Device Electronics (IDE). Because of the equal space limitation, you may have free space left unused after you create a stripe set. A stripe set writes the data evenly in strips of equal space across all disks in the set, as Figure 249 shows.

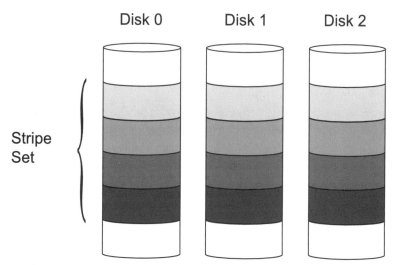

Figure 249 *The stripe set writes data in strips across all disks it contains.*

Because the disks function as if they were a single disk, the loss of a single disk in a stripe set would result in the complete loss of data from the entire set.

Note: *A stripe set cannot contain Windows NT system and boot partitions.*

Answer C is correct because stripe sets can improve disk I/O performance. Answer A is incorrect because disk mirroring can actually reduce disk I/O performance. Answer B is incorrect because disk duplexing provides no additional speed to a mirror set and can also reduce disk I/O performance. Answer D is incorrect because a volume set does not increase disk I/O performance.

250 CREATING A STRIPE SET

Q.   *You are a Windows NT domain administrator. You want to create a stripe set on your Windows NT Server to store a large database file. What program would you use to create the stripe set?*

Choose the best answer:

  A. *Disk Administrator*

  B. *User Manager*

  C. *Disk Manager*

  D. *Event Viewer*

As you learned in Tip 249, you can use Windows NT-created stripe sets to increase disk performance. However, other operating systems can produce stripe sets, and hardware components exist that make the stripe set transparent to the operating system. You must be sensitive to configurations that result from outside Windows NT in a real-world environment. However, Windows NT inherently supports stripe sets, and Microsoft will test you on how to implement the Windows NT-controlled stripe sets in your quest to be a Microsoft Certified System Engineer. The Disk Administrator utility program creates and manages stripe sets Windows NT controls. To create a stripe set in Windows NT, perform the following steps:

1. Click your mouse on the Start menu and select the Programs submenu Administrative Tools group Disk Administrator program. Windows NT will open the Disk Administrator program.

2. Within the Disk Administrator, hold down your CTRL key and click your mouse on the free space indicator of at least two disks. The Disk Administrator will outline the disk representations to indicate your selection.

3. Select the Partition menu Create Stripe Set option. The Disk Administrator will open the Stripe Set Size dialog box that lets you determine stripe set size.

4. Within the Stripe Set Size dialog box, enter the size you want into the *Create stripe set of total size* field. The Disk Administrator will insert the number into the *Create stripe set of total size* field.

5. Click your mouse on the OK button. The Disk Administrator will create the stripe set.

Figure 250 shows the Disk Administrator with three disks.

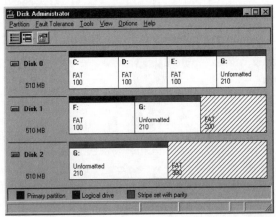

Figure 250 The Disk Administrator utility with three disks displayed. The G: drive is a stripe set with parity, about which you will learn more in Tip 251.

Answer A is correct because you use the Disk Administrator utility to create stripe sets in Windows NT. **Answer B** is incorrect because User Manager cannot create a stripe set. **Answer C** is incorrect because there is no Disk Manager program in Windows NT. **Answer D** is incorrect because Event Viewer cannot create a stripe set.

251   ## UNDERSTANDING STRIPE SETS WITH PARITY

Q.   *Which of the following disk configurations provide a RAID level-five data protection standard?*

Choose the best answer:

A.   *Volume sets*

B.   *Mirror sets*

C.   *Stripe sets*

D.   *Stripe sets with parity*

As you learned in Tip 249, stripe sets can enhance disk I/O performance. A stripe set, however, does not provide you with data protection of any kind. If even one disk that is a member of a stripe set fails, you will lose all data in the set. You can implement a *stripe set with parity* to obtain increased disk I/O performance and a high level of data protection at the same time. A stripe set with parity, then, writes the data across disks similar to the way a normal stripe set does, but it uses at least one additional disk to provide parity information that the operating system can reference if one of the striped disks fails to rebuild lost data.

Parity is a mathematical method of data verification that writes additional information that Windows NT can reference to reconstruct information lost because of disk failure. Disk I/O performance in a stripe set with parity is lower than that in a normal stripe set, but the stripe set with parity does outperform other methods of providing data protection, such as a mirror set.

Because of the additional data the stripe set with parity requires and the method which Windows NT uses to write the data, to implement a stripe set with parity, you must have at least one more disk than a normal stripe set requires. The additional disk means that Windows NT requires a minimum of three disks to implement a stripe set with parity. The maximum number of disks that Windows NT can support in a stripe set is 32. For each disk in the stripe set, Windows NT will produce one stripe that writes data across the disks in *strips*. A strip is the portion of a stripe that a single disk contains. Each stripe will contain one parity strip and multiple data strips. The following paragraph explains how Windows NT would write parity information across a four-disk stripe set with parity.

Because four disks comprise the set, Windows NT creates four stripes. Disk 1 contains parity information for stripe 1, and Windows NT writes the first strip so that only strips on disks 2, 3, and 4 will contain data. Disk 2 contains parity information for stripe 2, and is the second strip that Windows NT writes so that only strips on disks 1, 3, and 4 contain data. This method of never writing data from a particular stripe to the same disk that contains the parity information for that stripe continues until all stripes have been accounted for, as shown in Figure 251. The method, in turn, protects the data in the stripe set from corruption or loss in the event a disk is damaged, because the parity data is on another disk entirely.

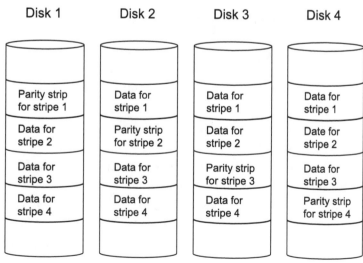

Figure 251 A stripe set with parity uses multiple disks and multiple strips to protect data.

If disk 1 fails, you will not lose any data because no data from stripe 1 was written to disk 1, and the parity strips for the remaining stripes are unaffected—because they are duplicated across multiple drives. To return the system to normal operation, you must replace the failed disk and restart the computer. Windows NT will create a new parity strip for stripe 1 from the data strips on disks 2, 3, and 4 and reconstruct the data you lost in stripes 2, 3, and 4 using the available parity strips on the remaining disks.

Note: *As with a normal stripe set, Windows NT boot and system partitions cannot be part of a stripe set with parity—because boot and system partitions must always be on a single drive, the boot drive.*

The type of data protection this Tip discusses is industry-classified as a *Redundant Array of Independent Disks (RAID)* level five. RAID is an industry-standard rating system that describes the data protection level a specific disk configuration provides. You will learn more about RAID in Tip 263.

*Answer D is correct because only a stripe set with parity provides the classification RAID level five. **Answer A** is incorrect because volume sets do not provide any level of data protection and have no RAID classification. **Answer B** is incorrect because mirror sets provide only a RAID level one classification. **Answer C** is incorrect because stripe sets do not provide any level of data protection and have a RAID level zero classification.*

252   CREATING A STRIPE SET WITH PARITY

Q.   *You must have a minimum of four physical disks to create a stripe set with parity.*

True or False?

As you have learned in previous Tips, you will use the Disk Administrator program to perform most disk management operations. You have also learned that stripe sets with parity provide a high degree of data protection with a minimal impact on disk I/O performance. Because a stripe set with parity is a disk management operation, you will use the Disk Administrator to create one.

Creating a stripe set with parity is a simple process. Because the Disk Administrator produces a graphical representation of installed disks and their associated partitions, to create a stripe set, you must only select free space on the appropriate fixed disk drives and tell the Disk Administrator to create the set. To create a stripe set with parity, perform the following steps:

1. Click your mouse on the Start Menu and select the Programs submenu Administrative Tools group Disk Administrator program. Windows NT will open the Disk Administrator program.

2. Within the Disk Administrator, hold down the CTRL key and click your mouse on sections of free space from at least three fixed disks. The Disk Administrator will outline the disks with a dark line to indicate your selection.

3. Select the Fault Tolerance menu Create Stripe Set with Parity option. The Disk Administrator will open the Create Stripe Set with Parity dialog box.

4. Enter the desired size for the entire stripe set in the *Create Stripe Set of Total Size* field. The Disk Administrator will insert the number in the *Create Stripe Set of Total Size* field.

5. Click your mouse on OK. The Disk Administrator will create the stripe set with parity.

Creating a stripe set with parity is a quick process that you can complete in just a few seconds. However, when you create your first stripe set with parity, you should give the operating system extra time for formatting because the stripe set is likely to have more space than you are accustomed to formatting. Because the stripe set with parity crosses over multiple disks, it may use many times as much space as you would normally encounter on a single disk.

*The answer is **False** because you must have a minimum of three disks to create a stripe set with parity in Windows NT.*

253   **MARKING A PARTITION AS ACTIVE**

Q.   *The Windows NT system partition must be an active partition.*

     True or False?

As you learned in Tip 207, a computer must have an active partition to start the operating system. In turn, the active partition is always a primary partition and contains necessary startup information in the *Master Boot Record (MBR)* area. When you turn on a computer, it performs a *Power On Self Test (POST)*, which performs various other tests (such as checking the keyboard connection, testing the computer's RAM, and so on) on the computer hardware. After the computer checks the hardware components, it will find the active partition and look in the master boot record for the location of the operating system's startup files.

If you are currently running Windows NT and want to run a different operating system that is on a different partition, you must mark the other partition as active and restart the system. As you have learned, the utility for disk and partition management in Windows NT is the Disk Administrator. When you mark a partition as active, Windows NT will remove the active status of any other partition.

Therefore, if you mark a partition other than the one that contains the Windows NT startup files as active, subsequent restarts of the computer will not start Windows NT until you once again make the Windows NT system partition active. Because the partition and its active status are implemented at a hardware level, any disk management utility (such as *fdisk* or other MS-DOS-based utilities) can restore the Windows NT system partition to active status.

An alternative method of resetting the active partition to the Windows NT system partition would be to use a Windows NT boot diskette and the Disk Administrator to mark the Windows NT system partition as active. You will learn more about creating a Windows NT boot diskette in Tip 269. To mark a partition as active in Windows NT, perform the following steps:

1. Click your mouse on the Start menu Programs submenu Administrative Tools group Disk Administrator program. Windows NT, in turn, will open the Disk Administrator program.

2. Within the Disk Administrator, click your mouse on the partition you want to make active. The Disk Administrator will outline the partition with a dark line to indicate your selection.

3. Click your mouse on the Partition menu Mark Active option. The Disk Administrator will mark the partition as active.

4. Restart the computer. The computer will perform a Power On Self Test and search the master boot record on the new active partition.

*The answer is **True** because the Windows NT system partition must be the active partition or Windows NT will not start.*

254   INTRODUCTION TO THE *BOOT.INI* FILE

Q.   *Which of the following Windows NT system files contains information about the location of the Windows NT boot partition?*

Choose the best answer:

    A.   *NTLDR*

    B.   *NTDETECT.COM*

    C.   *BOOT.INI*

    D.   *BOOTSECT.DOS*

As you learned in previous Tips, the Windows NT boot partition can be separate from the system partition. Therefore, although the startup files for Windows NT must be on the active partition, the boot partition can be any partition on the computer. If the Windows NT boot partition can reside on any partition in the computer, the system partition must have a means to identify the boot partition. The file that contains the information the computer uses to determine the boot partition is the *BOOT.INI* file. The *BOOT.INI* file is a text file that has two sections: the *Boot loader* section and the *Operating systems* section.

The Boot loader section contains the *Timeout* and *Default* variables. The *Timeout* variable determines the amount of time the computer will wait before it starts the operating system the *Default* variable designates. The *Default* variable indicates which operating system to start if the user takes no action during the wait time the *Timeout* variable provides.

The Operating system section contains an entry for each operating system you can load from the active partition. For example, you can install Windows NT Workstation, Windows NT Server, and Windows 95 so that you can start any one of the operating systems from a single active partition. The startup menu would then display the operating system entries as choices when the machine starts. Each entry in the Operating system section contains a description of the operating system (usually its name) and an Advanced RISC Computing (ARC) pathname that identifies the boot partition's location. You will learn more about ARC paths in Tip 255.

Answer C is correct because the BOOT.INI file contains information about the boot partition's location. Answer A is incorrect because the NTLDR file loads the operating system and does not contain boot partition information. Answer B is incorrect because NTDETECT.COM examines the available hardware in the computer and does not contain any boot partition information. Answer D is incorrect because BOOTSECT.DOS is a file the NTLDR executable loads if the user selects an operating system other than Windows NT from the boot menu at the time of system startup, and it does not contain any boot partition information.

255   UNDERSTANDING ADVANCED RISC COMPUTING (ARC) PATHS

Q.   *The following is a typical example of an ARC path: C:\Winnt\system32.*

True or False?

As you learned in Tip 254, the *BOOT.INI* file uses Advanced RISC Computing (ARC) pathnames to identify the boot partition's location. As a Microsoft certified system engineer, you must frequently edit the *BOOT.INI* file to restore functionality to a Windows NT computer. You must understand ARC paths in detail if you are to successfully edit a *BOOT.INI* file.

ARC pathnames are four units of information written together so that they form a single line of data. The syntax an ARC pathname uses is *multi(x)disk(x)rdisk(x)partition(x)*. By interpreting the information in each unit (which consists of a word and an ordinal number, such as *(multi(0))*, and then combining the completed whole, a computer can determine the boot partition's exact location. Table 255 describes each unit.

Unit	Function
multi or *scsi*	Identifies whether the type of disk controller is *Small Computer System Inter-face (SCSI)*, or *multi*, which is any other type of controller, such as Integrated Device Electronics (IDE) or SCSI devices that use the SCSI BIOS.
x	Identifies the disk controller's ordinal number. The first adapter to load determines the ordinal number of the disk controllers. Ordinal numbering begins with 0 for the first adapter, and progresses in order to the second and third adapters, and so on.
disk(x)	Identifies the SCSI disk number. This entry will be *disk(0)* for ARC entries that use *multi* rather than *scsi*.
rdisk(x)	Identifies the disk's ordinal number. The computer will ignore this entry for ARC entries that use *scsi* as the disk controller type.
partition(x)	Identifies the partition's ordinal number.

Table 255 The Advanced RISC Computing (ARC) pathname information units.

Consider an ARC pathname that is *multi(0)disk(0)rdisk(1)partition(1)*. If you break apart the information in the ARC pathname and compare it to the information in Table 255, you will find that the boot partition is located on the second partition, *partition(1)*, of the second physical disk, *rdisk(1)*. The first or only disk controller in the computer, either a SCSI controller using the SCSI BIOS or a different type of controller, *multi(0)*, controls the boot partition. Remember that in an ARC pathname that uses *multi*, the computer will ignore the *disk* variable.

*The answer is **False** because the example is a demonstration of a standard computer pathname on a single partition. An example of an ARC pathname would be **multi(0)disk(0)rdisk(1)partition(0)**.*

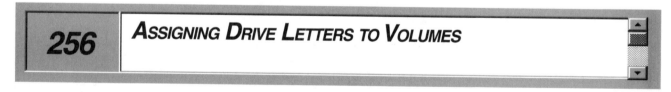

256   ASSIGNING DRIVE LETTERS TO VOLUMES

Q.   *You are a Windows NT domain administrator. You have an application which has been preprogrammed to search for data on drive C:. Because of disk space limitations, you had to install the application on a second partition to which Windows NT has assigned the drive letter D:. The application does not support internal changes to the data path and will not function on logical drive D:. What can you do to enable the application's functionality?*

Choose the best answer:

    A.   *Share the application folder as C.*

    B.   *Nothing; you must reinstall the computer.*

    C.   *Install REMAP.EXE from the Windows NT Resource Kit.*

    D.   *Use the Disk Administrator to change the partition drive letter assignment.*

As a Windows NT domain administrator, you will often find reasons to change a partition's or a CD-ROM's logical drive letter. As a Microsoft certified system engineer, you might also have to change drive letter assignment. You can make drive letter changes to any partition that doesn't contain the Windows NT system files without restarting the computer. If you must change the boot partition's drive letter, the computer will require a system restart to function properly. In addition, you must be careful if you change the drive letter assignment of a partition that has applications installed on it. Changing the drive letter might make the application unable to start, or other problems may develop.

You can change drive letter assignments in Windows NT with the Disk Administrator. With the Disk Administrator, you can change a partition or CD-ROM to any unassigned drive letter. To change a drive letter assignment, perform the following steps:

1. Click your mouse on the Start menu and select the Programs submenu Administrative Tools group Disk Administrator program. Windows NT will open the Disk Administrator program.

2. Click your mouse on the drive you want to change. The Disk Administrator will indicate your selection by outlining the drive with a dark line.

3. Select the Tools menu Assign drive letter option. The Disk Administrator will open the Assign drive letter dialog box.

4. Within the Assign drive letter dialog box, choose the letter you want from the drop-down list. The Disk Administrator will insert the letter you have chosen into the drop-down list box.

5. Click your mouse on the OK button. The Disk Administrator will change the drive letter. If the drive you changed was the Windows NT boot partition, Windows NT will prompt you to restart the computer.

Answer D is correct because the Disk Administrator lets you change drive letter assignments. Answer A is incorrect because sharing the drive will have no effect on its drive letter assignment. Answer B is incorrect because you are not required to reinstall a computer to reassign the drive letter in Windows NT. Answer C is incorrect because the Windows NT Resource Kit does not contain a REMAP.EXE program.

257 CREATING, FORMATTING, AND DELETING PARTITIONS

Q. You are a Windows NT domain administrator. You want to create and format two new partitions on your Windows NT server. What program or programs must you use to accomplish this task?

Choose the best answer:

A. Disk Administrator

B. FDISK.EXE

C. Disk Manager

D. Disk Administrator and FDISK.EXE

As you have learned, you must define and format partitions on computer disks before any computer program or operating system can use them and before they can store data. The creation, deletion, and formatting of partitions on a fixed disk drive are disk management operations: therefore, the Disk Administrator program in Windows NT performs such operations. Previous Tips have shown you that the Disk Administrator program is easy to use because it produces a graphical representation of the fixed disks and their associated partitions. For you to create, delete, or format a partition is merely a matter of knowing where to click your mouse. The following list explains each operation for partition management. For each set of instructions, assume you have already started and are within the Disk Administrator. To create a partition, perform the following steps:

1. Click your mouse in an area of free space on the disk on which you want to create the partition. The Disk Administrator will indicate your selection by outlining the free space with a dark line.

2. Click your mouse on the Partition menu Create or Create extended option, depending on what type of partition you want to create. The Disk Administrator in turn will open the Create Primary or Create Extended dialog box. (If you choose Create Primary, a warning will appear indicating you are about to create a partition not compatible with MS-DOS and ask you if you want to continue. You must choose Yes to create a primary partition.)

3. Enter the size you want in the *Create partition of size* field. The Disk Administrator will insert your entry in the *Create partition of size* field.

4. Click the OK button. The Disk Administrator will create the partition.

To delete an existing partition, perform the following steps:

1. Click your mouse on the partition you want to delete. The Disk Administrator will indicate your selection by outlining the partition with a dark line.

2. Select the Partition menu Delete option. The Disk Administrator will display a warning dialog box that asks if you are sure you want to delete the partition.

3. Click the Yes button. The Disk Administrator will delete the partition.

After you have created a partition, you must format it for use. When you choose the Format Drive option in the Disk Administrator, Windows NT will display the Format drive dialog box that lets you make decisions about your new partition. Table 257 describes each of the fields in the Format drive dialog box.

Field	Description
Capacity	A drop-down list box that determines the amount of space the partition will have with the file system you choose.
File System	A drop-down list box that lets you choose the file system to format with: your choices will be FAT or NTFS.
Allocation Unit Size	A drop-down list box that will display default allocation sizes only if you choose the FAT file system. It will let you choose from a list of variable allocation unit sizes if you choose the NTFS file system.
Volume Label	Lets you enter a name for the logical drive.
Quick Format	A checkbox that lets you perform a quick format of an existing partition.
Enable Compression	Sets an NTFS partition to compress files automatically.

Table 257 The Format drive dialog box fields.

To format a partition, perform the following steps:

1. Click your mouse on the partition you want to format. The Disk Administrator will indicate your selection by outlining the partition with a dark line.

2. Click your mouse on the Tools menu Format option. The Disk Administrator will open the Format dialog box.

3. Choose the capacity, file system, allocation unit size, volume label, and compression or quick format options, if applicable. The Disk Administrator will read the variable information you have chosen and apply it to the format.

4. Click the Start button in the Format drive dialog box. The Disk Administrator will format the partition.

Answer A is correct because the Disk Administrator can create, delete, and format partitions. Answer B is incorrect because FDISK.EXE cannot format partitions. Answer C is incorrect because there is no such program as Disk Manager in Windows NT. Answer D is incorrect because the Disk Administrator is the only program you must have to create, delete or format partitions.

258 REMOVING WINDOWS NT FROM A COMPUTER

Q.   You want to remove Windows NT Workstation from your computer and install Windows 95. Windows NT has been installed on an extended partition. How can you remove Windows NT and grant Windows 95 full access to the entire hard drive?

Choose the best answer:

A.   From a Windows 95 boot disk, use fdisk.exe to remove and recreate all partitions and then use format.com to format the partitions as FAT.

B.   Use the Disk Administrator to remove all partitions and then use a Windows 95 boot disk to create and format new partitions.

C.   Use the three Windows NT setup diskettes to remove all partitions and then use a Windows 95 boot disk to create and format new partitions.

D.   Install Windows 95 normally. Windows 95 can use or delete the NTFS partition, as required.

You may, at some point, find it necessary to remove a Windows NT installation—for example, if you install a new server and convert an old server to a client machine. How difficult it will be to remove Windows NT will depend on how you installed it. If, for example, you have installed the Windows NT computer on a single fixed disk with a single partition you have formatted with the FAT file system, you can format or *sys* the logical drive with the new operating system. To sys a drive is to install system files to a drive so that the operating system will start. The term sys comes from the *sys.com* utility that came with many MS-DOS versions.

On the other hand, if you have installed Windows NT to an extended partition that you formatted with the NTFS file system, a unique situation arises. Because only Windows NT can read the NTFS file system and, because in order to remove an extended partition you must first remove the logical drives, most disk management utilities will be unable to remove the extended partition.

Only the three Windows NT setup disks or some third-party utilities specially crafted for the purpose (such as *System Commander*™) can remove the Windows NT installation. After you have removed the NTFS partition, normal disk-management utilities, such as those found on a Windows 95 or MS-DOS boot disk, can create and format new partitions.

Answer C is correct because only the three Windows NT setup diskettes can remove logical drives from an extended partition you formatted with NTFS. Answer A is incorrect because the Windows 95 implementation of FDISK.EXE is unable to remove logical drives from an NTFS partition. Answer B is incorrect because the Disk Administrator cannot remove the boot partition. Answer D is incorrect because Windows 95 cannot read NTFS partitions.

259 UNDERSTANDING VOLUME SETS

Q.   *You are a Windows NT Server administrator. Your server has three hard drives with the following amounts of free space: disk 1 has 150 megabytes of free space; disk 2 has 100 megabytes of free space; and disk 3 has 50 megabytes of free space. What is the largest volume set you can create?*

Choose the best answer:

     A.   *200 megabytes*

     B.   *250 megabytes*

     C.   *150 megabytes*

     D.   *300 megabytes*

Imagine you are a Windows NT Server administrator. Your server has multiple physical disks, upon which you have created several partitions and a stripe set. Each physical disk has a small amount of free space left on it, but no single disk has enough space to create a partition of any useful size. You must decide what to do with the fragments of free space spread across the disks. Windows NT will help you solve this problem with Windows NT *volume sets*. A volume set is simply a combination of free space from one or more physical disks merged so they act as a single partition. Each area of disk space from a separate drive that Windows NT uses when it creates the volume set is known as a *member*. Together, the members make up a volume set that applications treat as a single logical drive. Windows NT can create a volume set that can store files or folders too large to store on any single disk's remaining free space by combining the free space from different disks. In addition, you can create volume sets from different types of fixed disks. For example, you could create a volume set using space from both a SCSI and an IDE disk. Moreover, you could take the free space for a volume set from unpartitioned disk space or from unallocated space on an extended partition.

Volume sets save data one member at a time, which means that the first member (which is based on the disk's ordinal position) in a set will fill up completely before the volume set saves to the next member. If you have formatted the volume set with the NTFS file system, you can add members to the set at any time. The process of adding a member to a volume set is called *extending the volume*. You cannot, however, extend a volume set you formatted with the FAT file system or reclaim space from a volume set after you have added it without destroying the entire set. Because most operating systems do not support volume sets, MS-DOS or Windows 95 installations also running on the computer (dual-boot) will not have access to the data on the volume set. Finally, another disadvantage to volume sets is that they do not provide you with any kind of data protection. If any member of the volume set fails, you will lose all data from the entire set.

Answer D is correct because the largest volume set possible for the example is 300 megabytes. **Answers A, B, and C are** incorrect because the largest possible volume set is 300 megabytes.

260 CREATING A VOLUME SET

Q.   *What is the minimum number of physical disks you require to create a volume set?*

Choose the best answer:

A.   Two

B.   Three

C.   One

D.   Four

Creating a volume set is a similar operation to the one you learned in Tip 250, "Creating a Stripe Set." As you have learned, the Disk Administrator performs Windows NT disk management operations. You also know that you can create a volume set from free space on one or more disks. For example, in theory, you could create a volume set with members from both unallocated space on an extended partition and unpartitioned space on the same disk. As long as the Disk Administrator can select the areas separately, you can combine them into a volume set. To create a volume set, perform the following steps:

1. Click your mouse on the Start menu and select the Programs submenu Administrative Tools group Disk Administrator program. Windows NT will open the Disk Administrator program.

2. Within the Disk Administrator, hold down the CTRL key and click your mouse on the areas of free space you want to include in the volume set. The Disk Administrator will indicate your selection by outlining the areas with a dark line.

3. Select the Partition menu Create Volume Set option. The Disk Administrator will open the Create Volume Set dialog box.

4. Within the *Create volume set of total size* field, enter your desired size for the volume set. The Disk Administrator will insert the size into the *Create volume set of total size* field.

5. Click your mouse on the OK button. The Disk Administrator will create the volume set and prompt you to restart the system.

Note: *The new volume set will be unformatted.*

Answer C *is correct because you can create a volume set from free space on one or more disks.* **Answers A, B, and D** *are are incorrect because you require partitions from only one disk to create a volume set.*

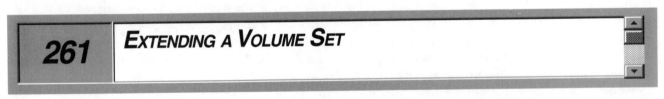

261   EXTENDING A VOLUME SET

Q.   *You can use the Disk Administrator to extend a volume set you formatted with the FAT file system.*

True or False?

As you have learned, you can extend a volume set if you have some free space to add and you have formatted the volume set with the NTFS file system. If you have formatted the volume set with the FAT file system, you can convert the file system to NTFS and then proceed with the extension. (In Tip 240, you learned how to convert a FAT partition to NTFS.) Whenever you extend a volume set, you must restart the computer. During startup after the forced restart, the operating system will format the new member of the volume set. To extend a volume set, perform the following steps:

1. Click your mouse on the Start menu Programs submenu Administrative Tools group Disk Administrator program. Windows NT will open the Disk Administrator program.

2. Within the Disk Administrator, hold down the CTRL key and click your mouse on the volume set and the free space you want to add. The Disk Administrator will indicate your selection by outlining the areas with a dark line.

3. Select the Partition menu Extend volume set option. The Disk Administrator will open the Extend Volume Set dialog box.

4. Within the *Create volume set of total size* field, enter the size you want the new volume set to be. The Disk Administrator will insert your entry into the *Create volume set of total size* field.

5. Click your mouse on the OK button. The Disk Administrator will extend the volume set and prompt you to restart the system.

6. Click your mouse on the Yes button to restart Windows NT. Windows NT will restart and format the new member of the volume set during startup.

The answer is **False** *because you can extend a volume set only if you have formatted it with the NTFS file system.*

262   **INTRODUCTION TO FAULT TOLERANCE**

Q: *You are the administrator of your company's Windows NT Server. You are concerned about hardware failures resulting in lost data. You perform frequent backups. What else can you do to improve your Windows NT Server's data fault tolerance?*

Choose the best answer:

     A.   Create a disk stripe set

     B.   Create a volume set

     C.   Extend a volume set

     D.   Create a stripe set with parity

A big concern for most network administrators is losing company data due to a hardware failure. In fact, disks and controllers will eventually fail. However, you, as an administrator, can safeguard yourself against a disaster in several ways. One way to protect your data is to perform frequent system backups to tapes and then keep the tapes in a safe location. Another way to protect your data is to implement *disk fault tolerance*, which is a term that describes a system's ability to recover from a hard disk or disk controller card failure. There are several types of disk fault tolerance.

Windows NT Server comes with the ability to provide two types of disk fault tolerance: *stripe sets with parity* and *disk mirroring*, also called *disk duplexing* (when two disk controllers are present). In a disk fault tolerant environment, your computer can completely lose one hard disk, but not lose any data that was on the fault tolerant disk. In turn, you can recover data from a lost disk because in either implementation of Windows NT Server's disk fault tolerance, the system writes data on the fault-tolerant disk to multiple disks. When one disk fails, Windows NT will use the information on the other disk(s) to regenerate the lost disk's data. Tips 263 through 266 will discuss Windows NT Server's disk fault tolerance and how you will create the fault-tolerant drives.

Answer D is correct because a stripe set with parity is the only answer that would provide any fault tolerance. Answer A is incorrect because although a stripe set will write data across multiple disks, it will not provide disk fault tolerance. Answers B and C are incorrect because volume sets fill one drive before starting to write data on the next drive and provide no fault tolerance.

263	### INTRODUCTION TO **RAID** LEVELS

Q: *Which of the following Redundant Array of Independent Disks (RAID) levels provides fault tolerance?*

Choose all answers that apply:

     A.   *Volume set*

     B.   *Stripe set with parity (RAID 5)*

     C.   *Stripe set (RAID 0)*

     D.   *Mirror set (RAID 1)*

     E.   *Duplex set (RAID 1)*

The Computer Science Department at the University of California (UC) at Berkeley first developed the *Redundant Array of Independent Disks (RAID)* standard in the 1980s. The standard defines a set of processes that administrators can use to protect data stored on fixed disks from loss in the event of the catastrophic failure of a single disk.

The developers originally used the word inexpensive instead of independent to represent the I in RAID, but they later thought that independent was a better description of the disks than was inexpensive. Since UC Berkeley's original RAID design, there have been many advances in RAID technology.

Although there are several significant levels of RAID, in this Tip you will only learn about the six core levels. In a RAID array, a computer uses two or more disks when it writes data to the *disk subsystem*, a term that refers to your computer's disk drives and controllers.

In some RAID levels, the data you write to the disk subsystem will write to two disks: one disk has the data you wrote to the disk subsystem and the other disk receives a copy of the data for data redundancy. If one disk fails, you can use the other disk to recover the lost data.

Other RAID levels use *parity* (a mathematical equation for ensuring data integrity) information written across several disks to provide data redundancy. RAID is a standard that makes the data on disks more accessible and less susceptible to inadvertent loss.

RAID is not, however, a data backup and a network administrator should never use RAID in place of a system backup; rather, an administrator should use RAID in addition to system backups. If you accidentally save over an important file, a RAID array will not be of use—because it does not maintain a static "image" of the drive's contents.

Each RAID level provides something a little bit different than its preceding level, as Table 263, which details the six core RAID levels.

Answers B, D, and *E are correct because each of these RAID levels provide data redundancy. **Answer A** is incorrect because a volume set is not a RAID level and would not provide any data redundancy. **Answer C** is incorrect because although a stripe set is a RAID level, it does not provide any data redundancy.*

RAID Level	Description
Level 0	RAID level 0 stripes data across multiple disks without data redundancy or parity. You will best use this RAID level for maximized data transfer rates. RAID level 0 does not provide data protection.
Level 1	RAID level 1 mirrors data across multiple disks. The operating system will duplicate data saved onto a disk to a second disk or disk set. If one disk fails, an administrator can use the other disk to recover the lost data. This RAID level has one of the highest costs for each megabyte of disk space—because the operating system creates two complete copies of all data.
Level 2	In general, people do not use the RAID level 2. This level bit interleaves data across multiple disks with parity information the operating system creates using a *Hamming code*, which detects errors that occur. This RAID level specifies that you use a total of 39 disks with 7 disks of error-recovery coding—making it relatively useless in most enterprise environments.
Level 3	RAID level 3 stripes data across multiple disks, just as RAID level 0 does. However, this RAID level will write the data at the byte level and will also write parity information to a dedicated disk in the set. In RAID level 3, the operating system calculates parity information at write time, which will tend to cause significant system performance downgrades.
Level 4	RAID level 4 is identical in implementation to level 3, except that RAID level 4 writes data at the block level (as opposed to the byte level). Like level 3, RAID level 4 requires a dedicated parity disk for data redundancy.
Level 5	A RAID level 5 disk array will write data across multiple disks, using striping like levels 1, 3, and 4. However, it will use the next available disk for parity information, rather then a dedicated parity disk, as levels 3 and 4 do. Writing parity information in such a manner protects against a loss of parity information in the event the dedicated parity disk fails.

Table 263 The six core RAID levels you may implement.

264   **UNDERSTANDING MIRROR SETS**

Q: *You are the administrator of your company's Windows NT Server. You want to implement a level of disk fault tolerance that will protect your system's boot partition. Which of the following RAID levels will let you implement fault tolerance on your computer's boot partition?*

Choose the best answer:

A.   *Stripe set with parity*

B.   *Stripe set*

C.   *Mirror set*

D.   *Volume set*

As you have learned, RAID level 1uses the *disk mirroring* technique to provide data protection. Although there are hardware implementations of RAID level 1 that can use more than two hard disks to create the mirror set, Windows NT Server's software mirror set implementation can use only two physical disks. In addition, you cannot mirror the system or boot partitions (Tip 207 discusses both partitions) in a Windows NT Server disk mirror set implementation. In a Windows NT Server mirror set implementation, when the operating system writes data to the drive that is the mirror set, the system will write the data to both disks in the mirror set drive.

Answer C is correct because a mirror set is the only level that provides fault tolerance and that you can implement on boot or system partitions. Answer A is incorrect because, although a stripe set with parity will provide fault tolerance, you cannot use a stripe set with parity on a system or boot partition. Answers B and D are incorrect because not only does neither level provide fault tolerance, but you cannot implement either level on a system or boot partition.

265   **UNDERSTANDING DISK DUPLEXING**

Q: *You are a Windows NT Server administrator. You are concerned about disk fault tolerance and you want to protect the system partition that is also the boot partition. Which of the following techniques would let you protect the system boot partition, as well as protect you against a hard disk controller failure?*

Choose the best answer:

     A.   *Mirror set*

     B.   *Stripe set with parity*

     C.   *Duplex set*

     D.   *Volume set*

In Tip 264, you learned about Windows NT Server's mirror sets. Remember, a mirror set provides data redundancy by taking anything the operating system writes to one disk and duplicating the data to another disk, called the *mirror*. In turn, a *disk duplex set* is identical to a mirror set in every way except one: in a disk duplex set, you will use two controller cards to manage the disk's I/O (Input/Output), compared to the mirror set's one controller card. Having two disk controllers provides a higher level of disk fault tolerance because it would take more than a disk controller failure to bring your server down; it would take a disk failure and a disk controller failure for your server to be inoperable.

Answer C is correct because a disk duplex set would provide not only fault tolerance but would also let you recover from a disk controller failure, and you can put the system or boot partitions on a disk duplex set. Answer A is incorrect because although a mirror set will provide fault tolerance and you can use a mirror set on the system or boot partitions, a disk mirror uses only one disk controller. Answer B is incorrect because although a stripe set with parity will let you use multiple disk controllers and provides fault tolerance, you cannot use a stripe set with parity on the system or boot partitions. Answer D is incorrect because you cannot place the system or boot partitions on a volume set, and volume sets provide no fault tolerance at all.

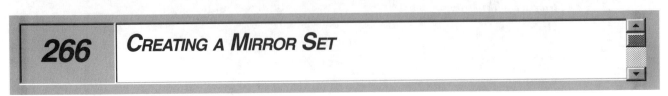

266   **CREATING A MIRROR SET**

Q: *What utility would you use to create a mirror set?*

Choose the best answer:

> A.   *User Manager for Domains*
>
> B.   *Server Manager*
>
> C.   *Windows NT Diagnostics*
>
> D.   *Disk Administrator*

In Tips 264 and 265, you learned how an administrator can use either a mirror set or a duplex set to provide disk fault tolerance. As you learned, the only difference between a mirror and a duplex set is that a duplex set uses two disk controllers instead of one. In turn, the steps you perform to create a mirror or a duplex set are identical. To create a mirror or duplex set, you must have a disk with an equal or greater amount of disk space than the disk you want to mirror. You must use unformatted and unpartitioned free disk space to create the mirror set. To create a mirror or duplex set, perform the following steps:

1. Click your mouse on the Start menu and select the Programs submenu Administrative Tools group Disk Administrator program. Windows NT will open the Disk Administrator program.

2. Within the Disk Administrator program, click your mouse on the disk you want to mirror. Hold down the CTRL key on your keyboard and click your mouse on the free space of the disk you want to use to create the mirror image. (Both the disk you want to mirror from and the disk that will contain the mirror image should now have black lines around the perimeters of the boxes representing the drives.)

3. Within the Disk Administrator program, select the Fault Tolerance menu Establish Mirror option. Windows NT will establish the mirror set (which will be a duplex set if the drives are on different controllers).

Answer D is correct because you can create mirror sets using only the Disk Administrator program. Answers A, B, and C are incorrect because you cannot use any of these programs to create or manage disk fault tolerance.

---

267   RECOVERING A MIRROR SET AFTER DRIVE FAILURE

Q: *The hard drive on your server has crashed. The drive that crashed was the boot disk section of a mirror set. How would you recover the lost data and restore the server to its previous state?*

Choose the best answer:

> A.   *Install a new hard disk and then use the Windows NT Emergency Repair Disk (ERD) to create a new mirror.*
>
> B.   *Install a new hard disk and then start the computer with an emergency boot disk. Use the Disk Administrator to create a new mirror.*
>
> C.   *Install a new hard disk. Boot Windows NT normally and then use the Disk Administrator to create a new mirror.*
>
> D.   *You cannot recover from a disk failure if the boot disk was the failure.*

After you have learned all about mirrors and duplex sets and how to create them, you must know how to recover from a hard drive failure should one occur. If the drive that fails is the mirror disk (the one that Windows NT uses for data redundancy), you will only have to remove the drive that failed and install a new one. After you have installed the new hard drive, you will start Windows NT and use the Disk Administrator to *break* (that is, stop mirroring) the mirror. Next, you must re-establish your mirror. To break a mirror, perform the following steps:

1. Shut down Windows NT, turn off the power, and install the new hard drive. When you finish, reboot Windows NT.

2. Click your mouse on the Start menu and select the Programs submenu Administrative Tools group Disk Administrator program. Windows NT will open the Disk Administrator program.

3. Within the Disk Administrator program, Select the Fault Tolerance menu Break Mirror option. Windows NT will break the mirror and assign a new drive letter to the drive that was the mirror.

4. Then establish a mirror with the new drive you installed. (You learned in Tip 266 how to create a mirror set).

The steps you perform to recover from a disk failure will be different if the disk that fails is the disk that your system boots to. In such a case, you cannot boot your server normally. You will need an *emergency boot disk*, which is a Windows NT-formatted diskette that has the files Windows NT requires to boot your server. You will learn in Tip 269 how to create an emergency boot disk. To recover from a disk failure where the disk that failed is the disk that your system boots to, perform the following steps:

1. Shut down your server and replace the failed hard disk. Then, insert your emergency boot disk into the floppy disk drive in your server and start the computer.

2. After you boot the computer, click your mouse on the Start menu and select the Programs submenu Administrative Tools group Disk Administrator program. Windows NT will open the Disk Administrator program.

3. Within the Disk Administrator program, select the Fault Tolerance menu Break Mirror option. Windows NT will break the mirror.

4. After Windows NT breaks the mirror, select the drive you want to mirror and the new drive you installed and click your mouse on the Fault Tolerance menu Establish Mirror option. Windows NT will create the new mirror set.

Answer B is correct because in the question the boot disk was the disk that failed. Therefore, you would have to boot to an emergency boot disk, break the mirror, and then establish a new mirror. Answer A is incorrect because an administrator would use an emergency repair disk to restore a corrupt Registry or startup files, not for a failed hard disk. Answer C is incorrect because the answer would work only if the failed hard disk was not the boot hard disk. Answer D is incorrect because you can recover from a boot disk failure.

---

268   RECOVERING A STRIPE SET WITH PARITY AFTER FAILURE

Q: *One of the hard drives on your Windows NT Server has failed. The drive that failed was part of a stripe set with parity. How can you recover the lost data and restore the system to working order?*

Choose the best answer:

    A.   *Use an emergency boot disk to boot the server. From the Disk Administrator program, re-establish the stripe set with parity.*

B.   *Remove the failed hard disk and then install a new hard disk. Boot the server normally and then do nothing; Windows NT will automatically regenerate the stripe set using the new disk.*

C.   *Remove the failed hard disk and then install a new hard disk. Boot the server normally and then use the Disk Administrator program to regenerate the stripe set with parity.*

D.   *Remove the disk that failed. Install a new disk. Delete the stripe set with parity. Create a new stripe set with parity and then restore the lost data from a tape backup.*

The purpose of disk fault tolerance is to provide a way of either keeping the system up and running or getting your system back up in a the shortest time possible. If you have implemented a disk stripe set with parity, you can lose any one disk in the stripe set with parity and quickly be back "up and running" again. If you lose more than one disk, however, you will not be able to recover.

As you learned in Tip 251, a stripe set with parity writes data across multiple physical disks in stripes. One piece of each disk has parity (a mathematical equation that will let the system recover from disk failures) on it. If any one disk fails, Windows NT will use the parity information from the other disks to rebuild the lost disk's data.

Although Windows NT will generate the data from a failed disk in the Windows NT Server's system memory, doing so takes a considerable amount of the system resources and will cause the system to run very slowly. Therefore, you should replace a failed disk in a stripe set with parity as soon as possible. To recover from a failed hard disk in a stripe set with parity, perform the following steps:

1.   Shut down your server and remove the failed hard drive. Install a new hard drive and restart your server.

2.   After your computer boots to Windows NT Server, click your mouse on the Start menu and select the Programs submenu Administrative Tools group Disk Administrator program. Windows NT will open the Disk Administrator program.

3.   Within the Disk Administrator program, click your mouse on the stripe set with parity. Then, hold down the CTRL key on your keyboard and click your mouse on the new hard disk you installed.

4.   Within the Disk Administrator program, select the Fault Tolerance menu Regenerate option. Windows NT will regenerate the data from the lost hard disk.

Answer C is correct because you will only have to replace the failed hard disk and then use the Disk Administrator program to regenerate the data from the lost disk. Answer A is incorrect because stripe sets with parity cannot be on the system or boot partitions, so you will not have to boot from an emergency boot disk. Answer B is incorrect because Windows NT will automatically generate the data from the lost disk in system memory with severe system performance loss. To completely restore the system to its working state, you would have to use the Disk Administrator program to regenerate the lost disk's data. Answer D is incorrect because, although this solution will get you back to the state the server was in before the hard disk failure, it is an unnecessary procedure.

| 269 | **CREATING A FAULT-TOLERANT BOOT DISK** |

Q: *You have created a mirror set on your server's boot partition. How would you create a fault-tolerant boot disk to use in case of emergency?*

Choose the best answer:

A.   Format a floppy diskette using the command format /s.

B.   Use any DOS-formatted diskette and copy the Windows NT system file to the DOS diskette.

C.   Format a floppy diskette on any Windows NT computer. Copy the Windows NT system files to the diskette. Edit the boot.ini file on the floppy diskette to reflect the boot partition to use in case of a hard disk failure.

D.   Format a floppy diskette in Windows NT and check the System checkbox.

If you are mirroring or duplexing the system or boot partition, you must have a fault-tolerant boot disk. The fault-tolerant boot disk (also called an *emergency boot disk*) lets you boot your Windows NT Server in the event that your boot hard drive crashes. A fault-tolerant boot disk is nothing more than a regular floppy diskette formatted in Windows NT that has the system files that Windows NT requires to boot. To create a fault-tolerant boot disk, perform the following steps:

1. Insert a diskette in your Windows NT Server's floppy diskette drive. Double-click your mouse on the My Computer icon on your desktop. Windows NT will open the My Computer window.

2. Within the My Computer window, right-click your mouse on the letter that corresponds to your floppy diskette drive. Windows NT will display the floppy diskette drive's pop-up menu.

3. Within the pop-up menu, select the Format option. Windows NT will display the Format dialog box, as shown in Figure 269.

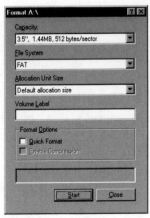

Figure 269 *The Format dialog box for the floppy diskette drive.*

4. Within the Format dialog box, click your mouse on the Start button. Windows NT will format the floppy diskette.

5. After Windows NT formats the diskette, close the Format dialog box. Windows NT will return you to the My Computer window.

6. Within the My Computer window, double-click your mouse on the C: drive icon. Windows NT will open the C: drive window.

7. Within the C: drive window, select the View menu Options option. Windows NT will open the Options dialog box.

8. Within the Options dialog box, select the View tab and click your mouse on the Show all files radio button. Click your mouse on the OK button. Windows NT will close the Options dialog box and display all files.

9. Locate the files *NTLDR, NTDETECT.COM,* and *BOOT.INI* (and *NTBOODD.SYS* if you have a SCSI disabled hard disk controller). Click your mouse on one of these files and then, holding down the CTRL key on your keyboard, click each additional file. When you finish, the files will all appear in reverse video, indicating their selection. Hold down your mouse and drag the files to your floppy diskette drive.

Table 269 show the Windows NT boot files and brief descriptions of each. (In Tip 439 you will learn about the entirety of the Windows NT boot process.)

File	Description
NTLDR	Loads Windows NT through the multi-boot loader program.
NTDETECT.COM	Detects the computer's hardware.
BOOT.INI	Describes the boot partitions' location, which the Advanced RISC Computing (ARC) naming conventions specify.
BOOTSECT.DOS	Points to the location of a previous operating system.
NTBOOTDD.SYS	Required only if you are using the *SCSI* syntax in place of *multi* syntax in *BOOT.INI*.

Table 269 *The Windows NT boot files.*

Answer C *is correct because you must first format a floppy diskette in Windows NT and then copy the Windows NT boot files to the floppy diskette. In addition, you must edit the boot.ini file on the floppy disk to point to the Windows NT boot partition.* **Answer A** *is incorrect because Windows NT does not have a format /s command.* **Answer B** *is incorrect because a DOS-formatted diskette will not work.* **Answer D** *is incorrect because there are no system format options in the Format dialog box in Windows NT.*

270 USING THE START COMMAND

Q: *You want to cause an application to start with a higher priority than other applications. How can you start an application with a higher than normal priority?*

Choose the best answer:

A. *Within the System Properties dialog box on the Performance tab, use the Application Performance slidebar.*

B. *Use the Start /high command.*

C. *Use the Priority /high command.*

D. *You cannot start programs with different priorities.*

Windows NT prioritizes applications and distributes the system processing time among them. You can change an application's priority to enhance or inhibit that application's performance. The priorities range from 0 to 31, with 0 having the lowest priority and 31 having the highest priority.

Windows NT breaks up the priority levels into two general categories: dynamic application priorities and real-time application priorities. Applications that run with priority levels from 0 to 15 are *dynamic applications*. Most applications start with the system-defined "normal" priority of 8. Windows NT can write dynamic applications to the *pagefile* (virtual memory). Applications that run with priority levels from 16 to 31 are *real-time applications*. Windows NT cannot write these applications to the *pagefile*.

You can use the command-line *start* command to force an application to start with a priority other than the normal priority of 8. Table 270 shows the *start* command options.

Options	Description
start /realtime	Sets the base priority at 24
start /high	Sets the base priority at 13
start /normal	Sets the base priority at 8
start /low	Sets the base priority at 4

*Table 270 Windows NT's **Start** command options.*

*Answer B is correct because you can set an application's priority by using the Start command. **Answer A** is incorrect because the answer describes how to configure the foreground and background application responsiveness, not configure an application's priority. **Answer C** is incorrect because the Priority /high command does not exist in Windows NT. **Answer D** is incorrect because you can configure an application's priority.*

271 SETTING FOREGROUND AND BACKGROUND APPLICATION RESPONSIVENESS

Q: You want to be able to download information from the Internet in the background while working on a word processor. You want the download to receive as much processor time as the word processor. How can you configure your Windows NT computer to give equal processor time to the application you are working on and to the background application?

Choose the best answer:

A. Use the Start /high command.

B. Within the System Properties dialog box on the Performance tab, use the Application Performance Boost slidebar.

C. Edit the Windows NT Registry HKEY_LOCAL_MACHINE subkey.

D. You cannot change the foreground and background application responsiveness.

Anyone familiar with the Microsoft Windows family of operating systems has seen how an application you minimize or place in the background so that you can work on another application will experience a significant performance slowdown. For example, imagine you are downloading data from an on-line service, such as the Internet, while working on a word processor. Your download will occur very slowly until you bring the Internet application to the foreground, and then the download speed will increase substantially.

In Windows NT, you can control how responsive background applications are. The utility you will use to configure background and foreground application responsiveness, the Performance utility, is located on the System Properties dialog box, as Figure 271 shows.

To configure foreground and background application responsiveness, perform the following steps:

1. On your Desktop, right-click your mouse on the My Computer icon. Windows NT will display a Quick menu.

2. Within the Quick menu, click your mouse on the Properties option. Windows NT will open the System Properties dialog box.

3. Within the System Properties dialog box, click your mouse on the Performance tab.

4. On the Performance tab, click and hold down your mouse on the Application Performance Boost slidebar and drag the Boost slide-bar to your performance preference.

5. Click your mouse on the OK button. Windows NT will close the System Properties dialog box and set your preferences.

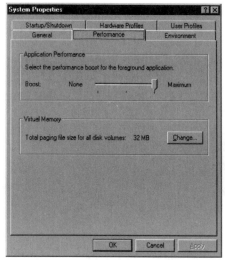

Figure 271 *Setting foreground and background application responsiveness.*

Note: *The operating system does not specifically lower the priority of applications executing in the background; instead, it adds additional priority to the application executing in the foreground. Reducing the amount of performance boost to the foreground application will result in greater similarity in the execution speeds between foreground and background applications.*

Answer B is correct because you would change foreground and background application responsiveness from the Application Performance Boost slide-bar in the System Properties dialog box. **Answer A** is incorrect because you would use the **Start /high** command to set the application's processor priority, not the application's foreground or background responsiveness. **Answer C** is incorrect because you do not have to edit the Registry in order to set the foreground and background application responsiveness. **Answer D** is incorrect because you can set the foreground and background application responsiveness.

272   IMPLEMENTING AND SUPPORTING MICROSOFT WINDOWS NT WORKSTATION 4.0 EXAM (70-073)

Q: Which Microsoft exam would you take to test your knowledge of Microsoft Windows NT Workstation 4.0?

Choose the best answer:

    A.   70-067

    B.   70-058

    C.   70-068

    D.   70-073

As you learned in the beginning of this book, Microsoft requires you to take and pass six exams to be a Microsoft Certified System Engineer. As part of this requirement, you must take and pass four core exams and two elective exams. Although you have a choice about which Microsoft exams you want to take (particularly the elective exams), for three of the four core exams you will have no choice. You must pass the following exams: Implementing and Supporting Microsoft Windows NT Server 4.0 (70-067), Implementing and Supporting Microsoft Windows NT Server 4.0 in the Enterprise (70-068), and Networking Essentials (70-058). The Implementing and Supporting Microsoft Windows NT Workstation 4.0 (70-073) exam is not a requirement for you to become a Microsoft Certified System Engineer. You are given a choice on the last exam of your four core exams: you can take the Implementing and Supporting Microsoft Windows NT Workstation 4.0 (70-073) exam or the Implementing and Supporting Microsoft Windows 95 (70-063) exam.

If you choose to take the Implementing and Supporting Microsoft Windows NT Workstation (70-073) exam, you will prepare yourself not only for supporting Windows NT Workstation, but also for supporting Windows NT Server. A lot of information the 70-073 exam tests you on is common core technology for both Windows NT Workstation and Server. The 70-073 exam will test your knowledge of topics such as Remote Access Service, Windows NT's architecture, and networking Windows NT in heterogeneous networking environments. Conversely, the 70-063 exam will test you specifically on Windows 95-only issues.

Answer D is correct; 70-073 is the Implementing and Supporting Microsoft Windows NT Workstation 4.0 exam. Answer A is incorrect because 70-067 is the Implementing and Supporting Microsoft Windows NT Server 4.0 exam. Answer B is incorrect because 70-058 is the Networking Essentials exam. Answer C is incorrect because 70-068 is the Implementing and Supporting Microsoft Windows NT Server 4.0 in the Enterprise exam.

| 273 | **UNDERSTANDING THE SEVEN SECTIONS OF THE 70-073 EXAM** |

Q: *The Implementing and Supporting Microsoft Windows NT Workstation 4.0 (70-073) exam will test you on your knowledge of how applications run in Windows NT.*

True or False?

Each Microsoft certification exam has various sections that categorize the test items. In turn, each exam has a different number of sections. The Implementing and Supporting Microsoft Windows NT Workstation 4.0 (70-073) exam has seven sections it will test you on. The following list shows the seven sections:

- Planning
- Installation and Configuration
- Managing Resources
- Connectivity
- Running Applications
- Monitoring and Optimization
- Troubleshooting

Planning: In the planning section, you will test on topics such as unattended installations, strategies for sharing and securing resources, and choosing the appropriate file system to use in a given situation.

Installation and Configuration: In the Installation and Configuration section, you will test on the following topics:

- Installing Windows NT on Intel platforms.
- Installing Windows NT on RISC platforms.

- Configuring a Windows NT computer for dual-boot situations.

- Removing Windows NT from a computer.

- Installing, configuring, and removing network adapter cards, SCSI device drivers, tape device drivers, Uninterruptable Power Supplies (UPS), multimedia devices, display adapters, keyboard drivers, and mouse drivers.

- Using the Control Panel applications to configure Windows NT.

- Upgrading to Windows NT Workstation 4.0.

- Using server-based Windows NT installations in a given situation.

Managing Resources: In the Managing Resources section, you will test on the following topics:

- Creating and managing local user accounts.

- Setting up and changing user profiles.

- Setting up shared folders and permissions.

- Configuring NT File System (NTFS) permissions.

- Installing and configuring printers.

Connectivity: In the Connectivity section, you will test on the following topics:

- Adding and configuring networking components of Windows NT.

- Accessing network resources.

- Implementing a Windows NT Workstation as a client in a NetWare network.

- Installing Windows NT Workstation as a Transmission Control Protocol/Internet Protocol (TCP/IP) client.

- Installing and configuring Dial-Up networking in given situations.

- Using Microsoft Peer Web Services.

Running Applications: In the Running Applications section, you will test on the following topics:

- Running Applications on Intel and RISC platforms.

- Starting applications at various priorities.

Monitoring and Optimization: In the Monitoring and Optimization section, you will test on the following topics:

- Monitoring system performance using various tools.

- Identifying and resolving a given performance problem.

- Optimizing system performance in a given situation.

Troubleshooting: In the Troubleshooting section, you will test on the following topics:

- Choosing the appropriate course of action to take when the boot process fails.

- Choosing the appropriate course of action to take when a print job fails.

- Choosing the appropriate course of action to take when the installation process fails.

- Choosing the appropriate course of action to take when an application fails.

- Choosing the appropriate course of action to take when a user cannot access a resource.

- Modifying the registry using the appropriate tool in a given situation.

- Implementing advanced techniques to resolve various problems.

*The answer is **True** because Microsoft will test you on how applications run on various platforms.*

274 — **PREPARING FOR YOUR 70-073 EXAM**

Q: *The Implementing and Supporting Microsoft Windows NT Workstation 4.0 exam will test you only on topics from the Microsoft Official Curriculum courses.*

True or False?

In preparation for any of your Microsoft exams, you should be familiar with the printed documentation as well as have a strong practical knowledge of the product that you are testing on. In addition, Microsoft suggests that you should not take any Microsoft exam without practical experience with the product. For the Implementing and Supporting Microsoft Windows NT Workstation 4.0 (70-073) exam, you should spend a considerable amount of time installing and configuring Windows NT Workstation 4.0 in various situations, such as over the network and locally. Be sure to perform an unattended installation (that is, one that is pushed entirely from the network server, without your direct interaction), as well. Another good idea is to open and become familiar with every dialog box and application Windows NT Workstation 4.0 includes.

Not everyone has the opportunity to install and configure Windows NT on multiple computers, but if you can, you should install Windows NT Workstation 4.0 on one computer and install Windows NT Server 4.0 on another computer. Configure the server to be a Primary Domain Controller (PDC) and configure the Windows NT Workstation to be a client to the Windows NT Server. Then, try out various Tips from this book on your test computers.

Note: *Although this book provides you with the tools you need to take the Microsoft MCSE core exams, it is up to you to gain "hands-on" experience with various systems.*

*The answer is **False** because Microsoft will test you on the topics from its Official Curriculum as well as actual "hands-on" experience.*

275 — **UNDERSTANDING WORKSTATIONS AND CLIENTS**

Q: *Which of the following best describes a workstation?*

Choose the best answer:

    A.   *A computer that is connected to a network server.*

    B.   *A powerful computer that runs mission-critical applications and may connect to a network server.*

    C.   *A computer that other computers connect to for file and print services.*

    D.   *Any computer in the network.*

In Tip 38, you learned that Windows 95 is a client operating system, but Windows NT Workstation is a workstation operating system. A *workstation* (the term is originally from the UNIX environment) is a computer with a powerful operating system capable of running mission-critical applications in its own right, with or without server interaction. A *mission critical application* is an application that you cannot afford to crash during execution, such as an accounting package or a Computer Aided Design (CAD) program.

A *client* refers to a computer that connects to a network server. Typically, the term client describes a computer that performs no server function at all and only connects to a server, which means that no computers, workstation or client, can connect to client computers. However, Windows 95, although considered a client operating system, does have a server service, which simply means that a Windows 95 computer can share its folders and printers. Although this appears to be contradictory information, because Windows 95 is not capable of running mission-critical applications, it does not qualify as a workstation. Therefore, Windows 95 more closely resembles a client than a workstation.

In short, any computer that connects to another computer can be a client, but only computers capable of running mission-critical applications can be workstations.

Answer B is correct because a computer that runs mission-critical applications is a workstation. Answer A is incorrect because the answer describes a client. Answer C is incorrect because the answer describes a server. Answer D is incorrect because a workstation is a computer that runs mission-critical applications.

276   UNDERSTANDING WHY YOU SHOULD TAKE THE 70-073 EXAM

Q: *You are the administrator of a network that consists of one Windows NT Server and several Windows 95 computers. Which of the following would be the best reason to take the Implementing and Supporting Microsoft Windows NT Workstation (70-073) exam instead of the Implementing and Supporting Microsoft Windows 95 (70-063) exam?*

Choose the best answer:

    A.   *Because the Implementing and Supporting Microsoft Windows NT Workstation 4.0 (70-073) exam is easier than the Implementing and Supporting Microsoft Windows 95 (70-063) exam.*

    B.   *Because the Implementing and Supporting Microsoft Windows NT Workstation 4.0 (70-073) exam is harder than the Implementing and Supporting Microsoft Windows 95 (70-063) exam and will teach you more.*

    C.   *Because the Implementing and Supporting Microsoft Windows NT Workstation 4.0 (70-073) exam tests not only your Windows NT Workstation knowledge, but also your Windows NT Server knowledge.*

    D.   *You have to take the Implementing and Supporting Microsoft Windows NT Workstation in order to be a Microsoft Certified Systems Engineer.*

To become a Microsoft certified systems engineer, you must take the Implementing and Supporting Microsoft Windows NT Server, the Implementing and Supporting Windows NT Server in the Enterprise, and the Networking Essentials exams. For the remaining core exam, you have a choice of either the Implementing and Supporting Microsoft Windows NT Workstation or the Implementing and Supporting Microsoft Windows 95 exams.

Although there is nothing wrong with taking the Windows 95 exam, the Windows NT Workstation exam tests your knowledge of not only Windows NT Workstation, but also of technical support information that is standard to Windows NT Workstation and Windows NT Server. Even if you are not planning to have any Windows NT Workstations in your network, you should take the Implementing and Supporting Microsoft Windows NT Workstation 4.0 (70-073) exam to expand on your general Windows NT knowledge.

Answer C is correct because the Implementing and Supporting Microsoft Windows NT Workstation 4.0 (70-073) exam tests your knowledge of Windows NT Server and Workstation common features. Answers A and B are incorrect because the Implementing and Supporting Microsoft Windows NT Workstation 4.0 (70-073) exam is not any easier or harder than any other exam. Answer D is incorrect because you can choose which exam you want to take—either the Implementing and Supporting Microsoft Windows NT Workstation 4.0 (70-073) or the Implementing and Supporting Microsoft Windows 95 (70-063) exams.

277   **UNDERSTANDING WINDOWS NT ARCHITECTURE**

Q: *You can describe Windows NT's architecture as having four modes.*

True or False?

Windows NT architecture is *modular* by design, because Microsoft created Windows NT with an eye toward making upgrades easy for the user and administrator. Having a modular design means that, if someone creates a new component for Windows NT, you can plug the new component into Windows NT without major system upgrades. In this Tip, you will learn the basic concept of Windows NT's architecture, and in future Tips you will learn more details.

Windows NT's architecture (although having multiple components) consists of two major executable sections: *User mode* and *Kernel mode* (in other words, at any given time, a program is running in either user mode or kernel mode). In general, you can think of User mode as where application programs run. An application running in User mode does not have direct access to hardware. To perform hardware specific operations (such an input or output operation), applications running in the user mode must make calls to Kernel-mode routines (such as device managers). Only managers (operating-system software) running in the Kernel mode can directly access hardware attached to the system. In Tip 278, you will learn more about the User and Kernel mode components.

Windows NT Workstation and Server 4.0 both have four environment subsystems, all of which run in User mode. The *environment subsystem* acts as a miniature operating system. The four Windows NT environment subsystems are: Win32, OS/2, Portable Operating System Interface for Computing Environments (POSIX), and the Security subsystem.

Each environment subsystem has specific duties: The Win32 subsystem handles screen I/O (Input Output) and any Windows or MS-DOS applications. The OS/2 subsystem handles OS/2 2.x non-graphical applications. The Security subsystem handles user logons. (When the Security subsystem is active, no other subsystem can run. In this way Windows NT protects the log-on process from password-capturing programs and makes Windows NT more secure.)

*The answer is **False** because Windows NT has only two modes: User and Kernel.*

278   **BETTER UNDERSTANDING USER MODE AND KERNEL MODE**

Q: The user log-on process runs completely in User mode on a Windows NT computer.

True or False?

As you have learned, Windows NT uses a two-mode architecture (also called a *ring architecture*). You also learned that Windows NT uses the two modes—User and Kernel—to keep applications from having direct access to hardware. Applications and the subsystems that support them run in User mode. In turn, User-mode processes have the following limitations:

- User-mode processes have no direct access to hardware.

- The operating system limits User-mode processes to a Windows NT-assigned memory address space.

- User mode processes run with a lower priority than Kernel mode processes.

Any process running in User mode must submit calls for system resources to a Kernel-mode component that can process the request. An example of a Kernel mode component is the *I/O Manager*. If you save a file, for example, your application sends a request for disk I/O access to the I/O Manager. The I/O Manager, in turn, then uses the appropriate device driver to access the hard disk.

Another example of how User and Kernel mode processes work together is the Windows NT log-on process. When you enter your username and password and click your mouse on the OK button, you are using the *Winlogon* process that runs in User mode. *Winlogon* sends the information you entered at the logon (username, password, and domain) to Windows NT to validate the user log-on request. The operating system, in turn, sends the information to the Security Manager (SAM), which runs in Kernel mode. The Security Manager passes the log-on information to the Local Security Authority (LSA, also in Kernel mode), which then processes the log request.

The answer is **False** *because the log-on process runs in both User and Kernel modes.*

279 | INTRODUCTION TO THE WINDOWS NT EXECUTIVE

Q: Which of the following best describe the Microsoft Windows NT Executive?

Choose the best answer:

>   *A.   A two-ring architecture that separates application and system processes.*

>   *B.   A virtual memory manager that works on a demand-paged basis (that is, it allocates pages as the system demands them).*

>   *C.   Runs in Kernel mode and provides underlying services for applications and the environment subsystems.*

>   *D.   Lets Windows NT recover from system crashes by writing information to a debugging file.*

As you have learned, Windows NT's architecture is modular in design. Part of the modular design includes the *Windows NT Executive*, which maintains the lower half of the Windows NT architecture. The Windows NT Executive provides support for the applications and the environment subsystems.

The Windows NT Executive has many components. Each component falls into one of three categories: *Executive Services,* the *Microkernel,* and the *Hardware Abstraction Layer (HAL)*. Table 279 shows and describes each of the three Windows NT Executive component categories.

Component Category	Description
Executive Services	Consists of the hardware device drivers and various managers that manage system I/O, security, screen I/O, virtual memory, and other system managers.
Microkernel	Schedules threads and handles interrupt requests (IRQs).
HAL	Is a dynamic link library (DLL) that isolates the actual hardware on your system from the operating system, making Windows NT more portable.

Table 279 The Windows NT Executive component categories.

Answer C is correct because the Windows NT Executive provides underlying services for applications and the environment subsystems. Answer A is incorrect because the answer describes Windows NT's architecture, not the Windows NT Executive. Answer B is incorrect because the answer describes Windows NT's Virtual Memory Manger, not the Windows NT Executive. Answer D is incorrect because the answer describes Windows NT's Crash debugging, not the Windows NT Executive.

280 UNDERSTANDING THE BENEFITS OF WINDOWS NT'S MEMORY MODEL

Q: *Of the following, which are advantages of the Windows NT memory model?*

Choose all answers that apply:

    A.   *The addressing scheme lets Windows NT run on other platforms, such as Alpha, and MIPS R4000 computers.*

    B.   *Applications will not share memory.*

    C.   *The Windows NT memory model lets a user run more applications than the physical memory would otherwise allow.*

    D.   *One application that crashes will not bring down another application.*

In Tip 197, you learned about the Windows NT virtual-memory model and that Windows NT's virtual memory manger works on a flat, linear address space that gives processes access to up to 4Gb of virtual memory. You also learned that Windows NT creates the large virtual-memory space by performing a *paging* operation, in which Windows NT writes information to the hard disk and uses a paging table to treat the information written to the disk as if it were random-access memory (RAM).

Windows NT's memory model has some distinct advantages over other memory models. Of those advantages, two are most significant. First, the linear addressing scheme Windows NT uses is compatible with RISC chip architectures, such as MIPS R4000 and Alpha, which makes Windows NT more portable. Second, users can run more applications than the physical memory would otherwise permit.

Answers A and C are correct because Windows NT's memory model is compatible with RISC chip architecture processors and users will be able to run more applications simultaneously than the physical memory would otherwise permit. Answer B is incorrect because most applications will use shared memory. Answer D is incorrect because, although one application crashing will not cause another application to crash, this is not because of the Windows NT memory model, but rather because Windows NT is a preemptively multitasked operating system.

281   UNDERSTANDING THE ADVANTAGES OF CENTRALIZED ADMINISTRATION

Q: *Which of the following best describes the centralized administration of a Windows NT domain model?*

Choose the best answer:

     A.   *An administrator will create user accounts for each user in the domain at each server.*

     B.   *An administrator must create system policies at each server.*

     C.   *An administrator must create only one user account for each user in the network.*

     D.   *The administrator can create and manage user accounts only from the Windows NT Server Primary Domain Controller (PDC).*

As a network grows, administration becomes increasingly more time consuming. You can imagine how much work would be involved in adding a new user to a 25-computer network if you had to visit each computer to add the new user and apply the user's rights. Consider the hours you would require to perform the same operation on a 50- or 100-computer network.

You can see why administrators often choose to implement a domain model. As you have learned, you create a domain by installing at least one domain controller through which all users log on. The domain controller provides *centralized administration*, which means that you can perform most administrative tasks from one location.

Centralized administration does not mean that you must perform administrative tasks from the physical domain controller, but that the domain controller, instead of each computer, maintains authentication data.

In a domain model, the administrator creates one user account for each user on the network. Each participating computer in the network will check with the domain controller at logon to see if the user is valid and what rights the user has.

The domain model is much more efficient than the workgroup model you learned about in Tip 199, in which each computer maintains its own list of users and rights. Centralized administration, then, occurs when you store user information (particularly information about resource rights) at a central location that all participating computers on the network can access.

Centralized administration lets you set rights and privileges one time and access and use them from any location on the network. Several of the Tips that follow will examine benefits of centralized administration.

Answer C is correct because you can best describe centralized administration in a domain model as the creation of a single user account for each user on the network. Answer A is incorrect because it describes multiple user accounts for each user, which is not centralized administration. Answer B is incorrect because centralized administration does not require system policies. Answer D is incorrect because the administrator can create and manage user accounts from many places in the domain. The Primary Domain Controller centrally stores the accounts and their associated rights, but is not the only place you can create and manage accounts and rights.

282   LOGGING ON TO A WINDOWS NT DOMAIN

Q.   *In a Windows NT domain, domain controllers validate log-on requests by comparing the log-on data with data the Directory Database stores.*

True or False?

As you learned in Tip 58, when you log on to a Windows NT computer, the Local Security Authority (LSA) queries the Security Accounts Manager (SAM) to see if your log-on information is authorized. The Security Accounts Manager will check your username and password against information the Directory Database contains and return the results to the Local Security Authority, which will approve or reject the log-on request and issue an access token, if approved.

When you log on to a Windows NT computer that is participating in a domain, Windows NT must perform additional steps in the log-on process. Because the computer is participating in a domain structure, a domain controller must validate the log-on request. In general, after you enter a username and password in the fields on a client computer's log-on screen (which the *WinLogon* process displays), *Winlogon* passes the information to the Local Security Authority as it normally would for a standalone computer. For a standalone computer, the Local Security Authority would then evaluate the logon and grant or deny access.

However, if you are logging on to a domain, the Local Security Authority then passes the information to the client computer's Net Logon service, which then passes the request to the domain controller's Net Logon service. In turn, the domain controller's Net Logon service passes the request to the domain controller's Security Accounts Manager (SAM). The domain controller's Security Accounts Manager then checks the information in the request against stored information in the Directory Database on the domain controller and passes the results to the domain controller's Net Logon service. Then, the domain controller's Net Logon service passes the results to the client computer's Net Logon service which, in turn, passes the results to the client computer's Local Security Authority. If the Security Accounts Manager approves access, the client computer's Local Security Authority issues an access token with the user's rights and passes the token to the *WinLogon* process. The *WinLogon* process calls a new process (usually *Explorer*) and passes the Access Token to the new process.

The answer is **True,** *because in a domain, the Security Accounts Manager (SAM) references the Directory Database stored on domain controllers against log-on requests.*

283   MIGRATING FROM WINDOWS 95 TO WINDOWS NT

Q.   *You can install Windows NT as an upgrade to Windows 95 and it will retain application and user settings.*

True or False?

When you first examine both the Windows 95 and the Windows NT operating systems, you might get the impression that the two operating systems are very similar in design. Windows NT does, in fact, have an almost identical interface to Windows 95 and this similarity can be confusing. However, the similarities between NT and Windows 95 stop with the interface. Because of the system structure differences, you cannot install either operating system as an upgrade to the other.

If you have a Windows 95 computer and you want to install Windows NT in its place, you will not have the option to perform an upgrade. Instead, your choices are to install Windows NT as a dual-boot operating system with Windows 95 or to replace the Windows 95 installation with Windows NT.

If you have a Windows NT computer and want to install Windows NT, you will also be unable to upgrade. Instead, you must install Windows 95 as an original install. Because the Windows 95 install will copy system files and modify the primary partition's master boot record, you cannot create a dual-boot operating system installation unless Windows 95 was the first operating system you installed.

*The answer is **False** because you cannot install Windows NT as an upgrade to Windows 95.*

284 | **CHOOSING A SERVER ROLE**

Q.   Which of the following are available choices for the server's role when you install Windows NT Server?

Choose all answers that apply:

> *A.   Primary Domain Controller*
>
> *B.   Member Server*
>
> *C.   Backup Domain Controller*
>
> *D.   Standalone Server*

Part of planning your domain is to decide how many Windows NT servers you require and what role they will play in the network. You can install Windows NT Server in one of three roles that affect both the installation and the function the servers will perform after you have installed them.

During the setup process, the Windows NT installation will provide you with three choices for the server's role: Primary Domain Controller, Backup Domain Controller, and Standalone Server. Each of these choices will significantly affect both the setup process and the server's operation after you have installed it.

Note: Accurately determining the server's role before you install the operating system is very important because you cannot change the server's role in some installations without completely reinstalling the operating system.

If you choose to install your server as a Primary Domain Controller (PDC), your computer will act as the central repository of user accounts, group accounts, and the associated rights to resources that apply to the accounts. The Directory Services Database contains all the information that you store within the repository.

All other computers participating in the domain will depend for verification on information the Primary Domain Controller stores. The operating system and the network will authenticate standalone Server and user machines to the Primary Domain Controller or to one of its Backup Domain Controllers (BDC), which are basically helper servers that assist the Primary Domain Controller with user authentication.

Backup Domain Controllers will verify their Directory Services Database copies against the original on the Primary Domain Controller. You cannot change Primary Domain Controllers to standalone Servers without a complete reinstall of Windows NT.

Backup Domain Controllers copy the Directory Services Database from the Primary Domain Controller. The operating system regularly verifies the copy at the Backup Domain Controller against the original database that the Primary Domain Controller stores.

Backup Domain Controllers can validate user accounts and therefore help decrease the Primary Domain Controller's workload. If you choose to install your server as a Backup Domain Controller, the server must be network-connected and able to contact the Primary Domain Controller to copy the Directory Services Database, or the setup will fail.

As you will learn in greater detail in later Tips, if the Primary Domain Controller fails, you can promote a Backup Domain Controller to take its place. You cannot, however, change Backup Domain Controllers to stand-alone Servers without performing a complete reinstall of Windows NT.

Standalone servers act as data storage machines. They are optimized for background data transfer and do not participate in domain security, which means that a standalone server cannot validate a user account and contains no copy of the Directory Services Database. Standalone servers are also called Member servers.

Answers A, C, and D are correct because they are valid choices for the server role. Answer B is incorrect because although Member server is another name for Standalone server, it is not a valid choice during setup.

285   **UNDERSTANDING THE USE OF INSTALLATION SWITCHES**

Q.   *How can you create a new set of the three Windows NT setup diskettes?*

Choose the best answer:

    A.   *Use WINNT /x*

    B.   *Use WINNT /f*

    C.   *Use WINNT /OX*

    D.   *Use the Disk Administrator*

As you have learned, installing a Windows NT server is an operation in which you must make many choices and perform complex planning. Actually, installing Windows NT is less difficult than the planning and research you do to make good decisions about domain structure.

The Windows NT installation process begins with the *WINNT.EXE* file. *WINNT.EXE* is a command-line executable file that, in addition to initializing the portion of setup that takes place outside of a Windows environment, can create the Windows NT setup diskettes and specify variables for custom installations.

Table 285 provides a complete list of command-line switches for *WINNT.EXE*.

Answer C is correct because the /OX switch will create a new set of the Windows NT setup diskettes. Answer A is incorrect because the /X switch instructs Windows NT not to create the setup diskettes. Answers B and D are incorrect because these options do not create the Windows NT setup diskettes.

Switch	Effect
B	Instructs Windows NT to install without the use of the setup diskettes (you must use the /*b* switch together with the *s* switch, although either /*sb* or /*bs* is acceptable).
C	Instructs Windows NT to not check for free space on setup diskettes.
E	Specifies the file which Windows NT should execute at the end of setup.
F	Instructs Windows NT to not verify files as it copies them to setup diskettes.
I	Specifies a setup information file filename (the default name that *WINNT.EXE* will search for is *DOSNET.INF*).
OX	Creates the three NT setup diskettes but does not install Windows NT.
R	Specifies the optional directory into which Windows NT should install.
RX	Specifies the optional directory which Windows NT should copy.
S	Specifies an alternate location for Windows NT source files. You must follow /*s* with a valid pathname (such as *c:\files*) or a Universal Naming Convention pathname (that is, *computername\sharename\files*).
T	Specifies a drive for temporary setup files. (If you do not use this switch, Windows will try to find a drive automatically.)
U	Instructs Windows NT to perform unattended installation with an optional script file (you must use the /*u* switch together with the *s* switch, although either /*su* or /*us* is acceptable).
X	Instructs Windows NT to not create the three Windows NT setup diskettes during setup.

Table 285 The WINNT.EXE command-line switches.

286 **JOINING A DOMAIN**

Q. *You must install Windows NT Workstation as part of a domain or workgroup during setup, and you cannot change it after you have installed it.*

True or False?

Windows NT Workstations are basically client computers that can operate independently or as part of a domain. You can choose independent operation or domain participation by properly configuring the network properties. To join a domain, you must either be logged on as a user with the rights to add computers to the domain or know the account information of a user with those rights. Then, you will enter the name of the domain you want to join and choose whether to create a computer account in the domain within the Network Properties dialog box, as shown in Figure 286.

To join a domain, perform the following steps:

1. Right-click your mouse on the Network Neighborhood icon and choose the Properties option from the menu that appears. Windows NT will open the Network Properties dialog box.

2. Click your mouse on the Change button. Windows NT will open the Identification Changes dialog box.

3. Click your mouse in the checkbox to the left of the word Domain. Windows NT will indicate your selection by inserting a dot in the checkbox.

4. Type the name of the domain you want to join in the *Domain* field.

5. After you enter the domain name, click your mouse on the checkbox to the left of the Create a Computer Account in the Domain option. (Doing so is optional.) Windows NT will place a checkmark in the check box and enable the *User Name* and *Password* fields.

6. Type both the username of a user who has the right to add computer accounts in the domain and the appropriate user's password.

7. After entering the user name and password, click your mouse on the OK button. Windows NT will attempt to join the domain and, if you choose to do so, will create a computer account in the domain. If you successfully join the domain, Windows NT will prompt you with the message *Welcome to the* [domain name] *domain.*

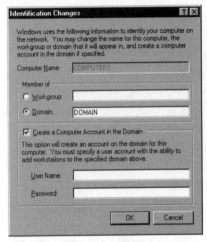

Figure 286 *The Identification Changes tab in the Network Properties dialog box.*

The answer is **False** because you can change a Windows NT Workstation configuration to make it a member of a domain or a workgroup.

287   TROUBLESHOOTING INSTALLATION PROBLEMS

Q.   You are the administrator of a 25-station network. You are trying to install a Windows NT Server, but a SCSI adapter that Windows NT does not support controls the computer's CD-ROM drive. How can you install Windows NT?

Choose the best answer:

A.   Load an operating system that does support the SCSI adapter, change to the CD-ROM drive, and install Windows NT from the I386 folder.

B.   Install a new SCSI adapter that Windows NT supports.

C.   Perform the installation across the network from a shared CD-ROM.

D.   All of the above.

As you have learned, the Windows NT installation process can be simple or complicated, depending on what you want your installation to do. Even simple installations from time to time can have problems that will require you to perform some troubleshooting. Table 287 details some installation problems and possible solutions.

Problem	Solution
Non-supported SCSI adapter	Start the computer with an operating system that does support the adapter and install Windows NT from the i386 folder, install from a remote location across the network, or simply change the adapter to one that Windows NT supports. *Note: If the non-supported adapter controls all physical disks, you must change the adapter or Windows NT will not start.*
Cannot start the network	Return to the Network Settings dialog box and make sure your settings match the network card's. If you do not know the card settings, you can install the *MS LOOPBACK* adapter, which is a network card driver that requires no physical card. Doing so will let you complete the install and configure the network card later. *Note: The MS LOOPBACK adapter will not let you install a Backup Domain Controller.*
Cannot connect to the domain controller	Make sure that the Primary Domain Controller is on-line. Check your network card settings. Check your network cable. Make sure you have the correct protocols installed. Add the computer account to the domain again.
Not enough disk space	Remove and re-create the partitions. Compress an NTFS partition. Delete unnecessary files and folders.
Error copying files	Try using a different compact disk or install from a remote location over the network.

Table 287 Common installation errors and solutions you can use to troubleshoot the errors.

Answer D is correct because all the answers are valid solutions to the problem. Answers A, B, and C are also correct but the question limits you to a single answer and all answers are correct.

288 UNDERSTANDING UNATTENDED INSTALLATIONS

Q: *You want to perform a series of Windows NT Workstation 4.0 installations. All the computers on which you will perform the installations have the same hardware. What is the easiest way to perform your installations?*

Choose the best answer:

A. *Copy the Windows NT Workstation source files to a server. Share the Windows NT Workstation 4.0 source files. At each computer on which you want to install Windows NT Workstation, connect to the share where the Windows NT Workstation source files are and use WINNT.EXE to start your installation.*

B. *Copy the Windows NT Workstation source files to a server. Share the Windows NT Workstation 4.0 source files. At each computer on which you want to install Windows NT Workstation, start a Windows NT Workstation installation using the WINNT.EXE /u:answerfile.txt /UDF:ID,database.*

    C.   *At each computer on which you want to install Windows NT Workstation, insert the Windows NT Workstation 4.0 CD-ROM into the computer's CD-ROM drive. Use the WINNT.EXE command to perform your Windows NT Workstation installation.*

    D.   *At each computer on which you want to install Windows NT Workstation, insert the Windows NT Workstation 4.0 CD-ROM into the computer's CD-ROM drive. Use the WINNT32.EXE command to perform your Windows NT Workstation installation.*

There may be times when you, as the administrator, must install Windows NT on several computers in a short time. Through creating a *distribution server* (a computer where the Windows NT source files are shared) and performing your Windows NT installations from the distribution server, you can speed your server-based installations using a technique known as an *unattended installation.*

An unattended installation occurs when you start an installation with options that will provide all the specific information that Windows NT requires during an installation. There are two files you can use to perform unattended Windows NT installations: the first file, an *answer file*, is required. An answer file is a text file that will answer some or potentially all the prompts that the user would otherwise have to answer during a Windows NT installation. The second file, a *Uniqueness Database File (UDF)*, is optional. A Uniqueness Database File is a database file you create that has individual records for each computer on which you will install Windows NT.

Note: The Windows NT 4.0 Resource Kit contains sample answer files and Uniqueness Database Files. (The Resource Kit is a set of books and utilities that you can buy from most bookstores, which you will learn more about in later Tips.)

Answer B is correct because if you perform Windows NT Workstation installations on several computers, you should use both an answer file and a Uniqueness Database File. Answer A is incorrect because although it would not be a bad solution, it is not the best answer. Answer C is incorrect because it would be the slowest installation method. Answer D is incorrect because you cannot use WINNT32.EXE unless you are performing your installation on a computer that already has Windows NT on it.

289   USING AN UNATTENDED INSTALLATION ANSWER FILE

Q: *What specific information would you find in an unattended installation answer file?*

Choose all answers that apply:

    A.   *Computer name*

    B.   *Video display settings*

    C.   *User accounts to create*

    D.   *Domain to join (only if Windows NT Workstation or Server)*

Answer files provide the information that a user typically must specify during a Microsoft Windows NT installation. To use an answer file, you must specify the switch */U* (which you learned about in Tip 285) when you start your Windows NT installation.

Most administrators could benefit from unattended Windows NT installations because this installation type often reduces administrative time and costs. For example, if you are an administrator of a small company, performing Windows NT installations on new computers your company purchases could be quite time consuming. Microsoft created the installation option */U* to reduce the time necessary to perform new Windows NT installations.

As you learned in the previous Tip, when performing an unattended installation, you must use an answer file. Although you must customize an answer file to fit your specific needs, Microsoft includes a sample answer file, *unattend.txt*, in the Microsoft Windows NT 4.0 Resource Kit, and on the Windows NT Workstation 4.0 CD-ROM. You might want to use one of these answer files as a template to create your own answer files. The installation answer file will include information such as the display settings, computer name, the Windows NT domain to join, and network adapter card parameters and settings. Table 289 shows some of the common sections within an answer file.

Section	Description
[Unattended]	This section defines the Setup program's behavior during text mode setup. You can specify this section only in the answer file, not in the Uniqueness Database File.
[OEMBootFiles]	To install onto x86 computers, you must list in this section a reference to the *OEM\OEMFILES\TXTSETUP.OEM* file and all files it lists (HALs and drivers). You can specify this section only in the answer file, not in the Uniqueness Database File. You can also use this section to include user application software installations.
[MassStorageDrivers]	You use this section to specify SCSI drivers and you can specify this section only in the answer file, not in the Uniqueness Database File.

Table 289 *Common settings within a Setup answer file.*

Answer A, B, *and* **D** *are correct because the installation answer file specifies each answer.* **Answer C** *is incorrect because the answer file does not specify any information about the creation of user accounts.*

| 290 | **UNDERSTANDING THE INITIAL PARAMETER FILES** |

Q: *You are a Windows NT network administrator. A user has tried a Windows NT Workstation installation that has failed. How can you determine what type installation the user tried to perform?*

Choose the best answer:

A.   *Open and view the contents of the bootlog.txt file.*

B.   *Open and view the $winnt$.inf file on your computer's hard drive.*

C.   *Ask the user what type of installation they tried to perform.*

D.   *You cannot determine, with certainty, what type of installation the user tried to perform.*

In previous Tips, you have learned how to install Windows NT Workstation and Server. You have also learned that you can use an answer file and, optionally, a Uniqueness Database File to install Windows NT without being present. In addition, you will learn about the *initial parameter files* that Windows NT creates when it first starts an installation. The initial parameter files are useful because if an installation fails, you, as an administrator, can examine the initial parameter files to see what type of installation someone performed and what options that person specified for the installation.

Windows NT creates the initial parameter files automatically when you start your Microsoft Windows NT installation. Either the information the unattended installation answer file supplies or the command-line switches you used during installation specify the information that Windows NT uses to create the files.

There are two initial parameter files that specify how Windows NT will install onto the computer and how it will configure options during an installation. First, the *Winnt.sif* text mode setup file specifies whether the installation was 32-bit or 16-bit. It also specifies whether the user used floppy diskettes. In addition, *Winnt.sif* specifies (if multiple installations of Windows NT exist on the computer) which installation the install will upgrade.

The second initial parameter file is *$winnt$.inf*, which is the graphical mode initial parameter file. The *$winnt$.inf* file specifies information such as whether an installation is an upgrade or not, if the installation is an unattended installation, and whether the user started the installation from an operating system other than a previous installation of Windows NT.

Answer B is correct because you could open and view the $winnt$.inf file's contents to see what options the user specified during installation. Answer A is incorrect because bootlog.txt is a file you use to troubleshoot other Windows operating systems that are having trouble booting. Answer C is incorrect because the user might not remember what type of installation he or she performed, or you might get inaccurate information from the user. Answer D is incorrect because you can determine quite a bit about the failed installation from the initial parameter files.

291 USING THE OEM\OEMFILES FOLDER TO SCRIPT SOFTWARE INSTALLATIONS

Q: *You are installing Windows NT Workstation 4.0 on several computers in your network. You want to install an application at the same time that Windows NT is installing. The application you want to install does support scripted installations. How can you install this application while installing Windows NT?*

Choose the best answer:

    A.   *Use the Compare.exe program.*

    B.   *Use the Setupadd.exe program.*

    C.   *Use the Oem\Oemfiles folder to script the installation.*

    D.   *Place the program you want to install in the same folder as the Windows NT Workstation source files. Windows NT will automatically install the additional application.*

Windows NT 4.0 can install additional components and applications when you are installing Windows NT. However, doing so is not necessarily very easy because there are no dialog boxes or Microsoft Wizards to help you. You can use the *Oem\Oemfiles* folder only when you perform server-based installations. You will create the *Oem\Oemfiles* folder in the network share that stores the Windows NT source files. Within the *Oem\$Oemfiles* folder, you must create subfolders for each component you want to install. In turn, the subfolders you create depend on what components you want to install. Files you must install during the text mode portion of the Windows NT installation, such as hardware device drivers, must be in the *Oem\Oemfiles\Textmode* folder. You must create one folder for each device driver you want to install. You can use the *Oem\Oemfiles* folder to install System files (files that will supplement or replace Windows NT system files during installation), Network components, and Application files. Because using the *Oem\Oemfiles* folder to script installations (that is, to perform special installation actions without interacting directly with Windows NT) is very complex, for complete information on how to install components or applications using *Oem\Oemfiles*, refer to the Microsoft Windows NT Resource Kit.

Answer C is correct because it is the only answer that will let you script installations of Windows NT components or applications. Answers A and B are incorrect because neither of the answers are programs that exist in Windows NT. Answer D is incorrect because Windows NT will not automatically install additional components or applications.

292 — USING SYSDIFF.EXE TO PERFORM UNATTENDED SOFTWARE INSTALLATIONS

Q: *You are the administrator of your company's network, which consists of two Windows NT Servers and several computers on which you want to install Windows NT Workstation. While you install Windows NT Workstation, you want to install some applications that do not support scripted installations. How can you install applications that do not support scripted installations at the same time you install Windows NT Workstation?*

Choose the best answer:

    A.   *Use Oem\Oemfiles\.*

    B.   *Use Sysdiff.exe.*

    C.   *Place the application you want to install into the same folder from which you are installing Windows NT Workstation.*

    D.   *You cannot perform unattended installations of applications that do not support scripted installations.*

If you are planning to install Windows NT on several computers, you may want to perform unattended installations, which are installations you manually start but in which an answer file will respond to some or all the prompts you typically would have to respond to. In many situations, when you install Windows NT you might also want to install applications that users will require later (for example, office suites that all users have).

You can script application installations or Windows NT component installations (components are optional or required pieces of Windows NT) by using the *Oem\Oemfiles* folder where your Windows NT source files are stored. You cannot use the *Oem\Oemfiles* folder to install applications that do not support scripted installations. For applications that do not support scripted installations, Microsoft created the *Sysdiff* utility.

You can use *Sysdiff* to create a snapshot (image) of the information on a computer's hard disk. After you create a snapshot, you can install applications on the computer and then use *Sysdiff* to create a *difference file*, which will contain all the differences between the computer at the initial snapshot and the computer when you created the difference file. You can then use the difference file on other computers to match installations on several computers. The following paragraph is an example of how you could use *Sysdiff* to install applications on several computers:

Suppose you have many computers on which you want to install Windows NT Workstation 4.0 and several applications. The easiest way for you to install Windows NT Workstation is to perform unattended installations. If the applications you want to install do not support scripted installation, the only other way to automate the installation of these applications is to use *Sysdiff*. To do so, you would first install Windows NT on a single computer and then run *Sysdiff.exe* to create a snapshot file.

Next, install all the applications whose installation you want to automate and run *Sysdiff.exe* to create a difference file. Then, place the difference file in a folder you must create and call *Oem\$$*. The *Oem\$$* folder must be on the same share from which you are installing Windows NT Workstation. Finally, you must also add the following command to the *OEM\Cmdlines.txt* file (which you may have to create if it does not already exist):

```
sysdiff /apply /m [/log:log_file ] difference_file
```

*Note: For more detailed instructions on how to use the **Sysdiff** utility, refer to the Microsoft Windows NT Resource Kit.*

*Answer B is correct because you can use the Sydiff utility to automate the installation of an application that does not support scripted installations. **Answer A** is incorrect because you can only use the oem\Oemfiles folder to perform automated installations of applications that support scripted installations. **Answer C** is incorrect because placing the application you want to install into the same folder as the Windows NT source files would not work. **Answer D** is incorrect because you can use the Sysdiff utility to install applications that do not support scripted installations.*

---

293   PERFORMING A WINDOWS NT UPGRADE WITH WINNT32.EXE

Q: *You want to upgrade a Windows NT Workstation 3.51 computer to Windows NT Workstation 4.0. Which of the following would be the fastest way to install Windows NT Workstation 4.0, upgrading your previously installed version?*

Choose the best answer:

    A.   *Use Winnt.exe /u at the command prompt from within Windows NT Workstation 3.51.*

    B.   *Use Winnt.exe at the command prompt from within Windows NT Workstation 3.51.*

    C.   *Use Winnt32.exe at the command prompt or from the graphical user interface from within Windows NT Workstation 3.51.*

    D.   *Boot to a DOS boot disk and use Winnt.exe to start your Windows NT Workstation 4.0 installation from the command prompt.*

There may be times when you want to *upgrade* older Windows NT Workstation versions to the latest Windows NT Workstation version. Upgrading is not hard to do, but you should make sure to properly plan your upgrades to ensure a smooth transition. To upgrade means to move up to a newer version of existing files or components. As you have learned, you cannot upgrade a Windows NT Workstation to a Windows NT Server.

To upgrade an existing version of Windows NT, all you must do is run *Winnt32.exe* from the Windows NT 4.0 source files. Although you can run *Winnt.exe* to upgrade a previous version of Windows NT, it is not the preferred installation method for upgrades because it will be considerably slower than *Winnt32.exe*. The *Winnt32.exe* program is a 32-bit Windows NT installation you use to upgrade previous Windows NT versions to the latest version. You will follow the on-screen prompts just like any other installation, but this installation will run a lot faster than a normal installation.

*Answer C is correct because to use the fastest method, you would use Winnt32.exe to upgrade an existing Windows NT installation. **Answer A** is incorrect because you use Wint.exe /u to perform unattended installations, not upgrades. **Answer B** is incorrect because, although you can upgrade Windows NT using Winnt.exe, it is not the fastest method of upgrade. **Answer D** is incorrect because booting under DOS and performing an installation would be the slowest installation method.*

---

294   USING BOOKS ONLINE

Q.   *You are a Windows NT domain administrator. You have a question about an advanced domain structure but you do not have any Windows NT manuals to answer the question. Where can you find detailed information about the domain structure in Windows NT?*

Choose the best answer:

> A.   *DOMAIN.TXT*
>
> B.   *DOMAIN.DOC*
>
> C.   *Books Online*
>
> D.   *Windows NT Help*

If you had been a network administrator ten years ago, you would have unwrapped the operating systems you purchased and found in the package a wide assortment of owner manuals and user guides. In fact, you could find some support information only in the books that originally shipped with the operating systems. As computers became more popular, however, reference manuals about an operating system became easier to find and software companies began to ship their product with less documentation. Finally, in recent years, most information you previously could find only in reference manuals has become available in electronic form.

The Windows NT CD-ROM contains support information in the form of *Books Online*, a utility that Microsoft implemented as a Windows NT help file that you can easily search or index to find specific information. To open the Books Online utility, perform the following steps:

1. Click your mouse on the Start menu and select the Programs submenu Books Online option. Windows NT will open the Windows NT *Help* program and load Books Online.

2. Within the Help window, double-click your mouse on the Microsoft Windows NT Server Books Online icon. Books Online will expand the view to display the book choices. You can navigate the book choices to answer common and not-so-common questions.

Note: *The first time you open Books Online you will be prompted to enter the path to the books.*

Microsoft divides Books Online into three separate texts: Concepts and Planning, Network Supplement, and Copyright Information. Each book contains a group of expandable categories you can browse through to easily find specific information. The three books cover topics ranging from basic domain management to advanced network protocol configuration. Figure 294 shows the Books Online utility within the Help window.

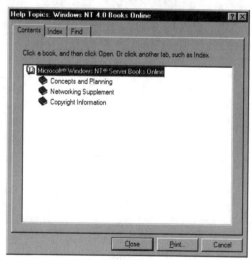

Figure 294 The Windows NT Books Online utility within the Help window.

Answer C *is correct because Books Online contains domain management information.* **Answer A** *is incorrect because there is no such file as DOMAIN.TXT in Windows NT.* **Answer B** *is incorrect because there is no such file as DOMAIN.DOC in Windows NT.* **Answer D** *is incorrect because Windows NT Help does not contain advanced domain configuration information.*

295 INTRODUCTION TO THE SYSTEM POLICY EDITOR

Q. *What program can you use to create a system policy?*

Choose the best answer:

A. *Disk Administrator*

B. *System Policy Editor*

C. *Policy Maker*

D. *User Manager*

As you learned in Tip 239, system policies are a method you can use to enforce restrictions to users, groups, and computers on your network. The Windows NT and Windows 95 operating systems automatically search the authenticating server's log-on folder for the presence of system policy files. If the operating system finds an appropriate system policy file, it will search through the file for restrictions that it should apply to the current computer, user, or groups that the current user is part of.

You create system policy files with the System Policy Editor (*POLEDIT.EXE*), which the Windows NT setup automatically copies to the Windows NT root folder when you install Windows NT. You can access the System Policy Editor from the Start menu Programs option Administrative Tools group. Creating a system policy that works for your organization, creates no problems, and does not apply restrictions when it should not, means you must understand the log-on process and how Windows NT uses system policies. You will learn more about how Windows NT uses system policies in Tip 297. Figure 295 shows the System Policy Editor.

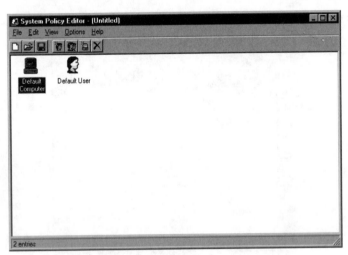

Figure 295 The Windows NT System Policy Editor.

Answer B is correct because the System Policy Editor creates system policies. Answer A is incorrect because the Disk Administrator cannot create system policies. Answer C is incorrect because there is no such program as Policy Maker in Windows NT. Answer D is incorrect because although User Manager can create and manage account Policies, it cannot create or manage system policies.

296   UNDERSTANDING SYSTEM POLICY EDITOR MODES

Q.   *The System Policy Editor can make changes to policy files and to the Windows NT Registry directly.*

True or False?

The System Policy Editor operates in one of two modes, Registry or Policy, depending on what you are using it for. In Policy mode, you can use the System Policy Editor to create and manage policy files. In Registry mode, you can use the System Policy Editor to make direct changes to the Windows NT Registry.

Registry mode means that you have opened the Registry and the computer will incorporate any changes you make in the Registry almost immediately. The System Policy Editor can open the local machine's or the remote computer's Registry. Changes you make in a Registry, however, affect only the computer that owns that Registry.

Policy mode means that you have opened a policy file and the computer or computers subject to that policy will incorporate any changes at the time of the next logon. Policy files can affect many computers when they log on.

The System Policy Editor window will remain empty until you either open or create a new policy file or open a Registry. To create a new system policy file, perform the following steps:

1. Click your mouse on the Start menu and select the Programs submenu Administrative Tools group System Policy Editor program. Windows NT will open the System Policy Editor.

2. Within the System Policy Editor, click your mouse on the File menu New Policy File option. *POLEDIT.EXE* will create a new, unsaved policy file in the System Policy Editor window.

When you look at a new policy file, you will see the Default User and Default Computer icons. As you will learn more about in Tip 297, the Default settings help keep policy files efficient (because you can set default policies for all computers, and then only apply specific policies, as necessary). To edit the local Registry, perform the following steps:

1. Click your mouse on the Start menu and select the Programs submenu Administrative Tools group System Policy Editor program. Windows NT will open the System Policy Editor.

2. Within the System Policy Editor, click your mouse on the File menu Open Registry option. *POLEDIT.EXE* will open the local registry in the System Policy Editor window.

The answer is **True** *because the System Policy Editor can manage policy files and make changes directly to the Windows NT registry.*

297   UNDERSTANDING THE SYSTEM POLICY PROCESS

Q.   *System policies consist of restrictions the operating system applies to a computer, a user, or a group. In what order does the system read and apply the components of a policy?*

Choose the best answer:

A.   *User, Computer, Group*

B.   *Computer, User, Group*

C.   *User, Computer, Group*

D.   *User, Group, Computer*

During the logon process, a variety of things take place, depending on what the user is logging in to. For example, Tip 282 taught you what happens when logging on to a Windows NT domain. As you learned, after approving the login, Windows NT will load the user's profile.

After the user profile loads, Windows NT will search the *Netlogon* share (located at *systemroot\SYSTEM32\REPL \IMPORTS\SCRIPTS*) for a system policy file (*NTCONFIG.POL*). If Windows NT finds *NTCOFIG.POL*, Windows NT will search the file for a policy that applies to the user. If a policy for the user exists, Windows NT will download and apply it. If a user policy does not exist, Windows NT will search the file for a group policy that the user is a member of. If there is a valid group policy that includes the user, Windows will download and apply it. If there is not a valid group policy that includes the user, Windows NT will download and apply the default user policy. After applying a policy for the user, Windows NT will search for a policy that applies to the computer the user is logging on to. If a policy exists for the computer, Windows NT will download and apply it. If there is no policy for the computer, Windows NT will apply the default user policy.

Note: Because a user may belong to more than one group, administrators must assign groups priorities when they create them. Windows will load as the policy the group with the highest priority that also includes the user.

Answer D is correct because Windows NT searches for policy restrictions in the order of User, Group, Computer. Answers A, B, and C are incorrect because they do not accurately describe the correct search order.

298   I**MPLEMENTING** S**YSTEM** P**OLICIES ON A** D**OMAIN** C**ONTROLLER**

Q: *In what folder on the Primary Domain Controller does Windows NT keep system policy files?*

Choose the best answer:

A.   *SYSTEMROOT\SYSTEM32\REPL\IMPORT\SCRIPTS*

B.   *SYSTEMROOT\SYSTEM32\REPL\EXPORT\SCRIPTS*

C.   *SYSTEMROOT\SYSTEM32\REPL\IMPORT\NETLOGON*

D.   *SYSTEMROOT\SYSTEM32\REPL\EXPORT\NETLOGON*

Windows NT computers automatically check for the system policy file on the Primary Domain Controller (PDC) in the *Netlogon* share. The *Netlogon* share is a folder that Windows NT creates during installation and automatically shares as *Netlogon*. The actual folder name is *systemroot\system32\repl\import\scripts*.

If your domain has Backup Domain Controllers (BDCs), you must enable *replication* so that the policy files copy to the *Netlogon* share on the Backup Domain Controllers. (You will learn more about the Windows NT replication feature in Tip 435.) To implement system policies on a Primary Domain Controller, simply create the policy file and save it to the primary domain controller's *Netlogon* folder.

Answer A is correct because the Netlogon share's physical location is systemroot\system32\repl\import\scripts. Answer B is incorrect because the path contains the export folder rather than the import folder. Answers C and D are incorrect because Netlogon is a share name, not a folder.

299 | **IMPLEMENTING A SYSTEM POLICY ON A NON-DOMAIN CONTROLLER**

Q: Which of the following accurately describes the location of system policy files you have implemented on a non-domain controller?

Choose the best answer:

A.   SYSTEMROOT\SYSTEM32\REPL\IMPORT\SCRIPTS

B.   *In any folder you choose*

C.   SYSTEMROOT\SYSTEM32\REPL\EXPORT\SCRIPTS

D.   SYSTEMROOT

As you learned in Tip 298, Windows NT computers automatically check for the system policy file on the Primary Domain Controller in the *Netlogon* share. It is possible, however, to change the automatic search path to a folder and computer that you specify. One reason to specify an alternative search path for system policies would be if you wanted to implement more than one set of system policies in the same domain. Because the system policy file's filename cannot change, the only way to implement multiple system policies is to save the files to different locations. Therefore, you would also have to alter the search path that Windows NT computers automatically use. You can change a Windows NT computer's default search path by creating a local system policy for each computer. To change a Windows NT computer's automatic search path, perform the following steps:

1. Click your mouse on the Start menu and select the Programs submenu Administrative Tools group System Policy Editor program. Windows NT will open the System Policy Editor.

2. Within the System Policy Editor, click your mouse on the File menu New policy option. *POLEDIT* will open a new policy file in the System Policy Editor window.

3. Within the System Policy Editor window, double-click your mouse on the Default Computer icon. *POLEDIT* will open the Default Computer Properties dialog box.

4. Within the Default Computer Properties dialog box, click your mouse on the plus symbol to the left of the Network option. *POLEDIT* will expand the Network option.

5. Within the Default Computer Properties dialog box, click your mouse on the plus symbol to the left of the System Policies Update option. *POLEDIT* will expand the System Policies update option.

6. Within the Default Computer Properties dialog box, click your mouse on the checkbox to the left of the Remote update option. *POLEDIT* will enable the Settings for Remote update area at the bottom of the dialog box and insert a check mark in the Remote update checkbox.

7. Within the Default Computer Properties dialog box, choose Manual from the Update mode drop-down list box. *POLEDIT* will insert your choice in the *update mode* field.

8. Type the pathname for the manual update into the *Path for manual update* field. Make sure to include the filename. *POLEDIT* will insert the path you type into the *Path for Manual update* field. (The path must match the root folder of the drive containing the remote computer's Windows NT *systemroot* folder.)

9. Click your mouse on the Display error messages checkbox (optional). *POLEDIT* will insert a check mark in the Display error messages checkbox.

10. Click your mouse on the Load balancing checkbox (optional). *POLEDIT* will insert a check mark in the Load balancing checkbox.

11. Click your mouse on the OK button. *POLEDIT* will close the Default Computer Properties dialog box.

12. Click your mouse on the File Menu Save option. *POLEDIT* will open the Save As dialog box.

13. Choose Network Neighborhood from the Save In drop-down list box and double-click your mouse on the name of the remote computer you want to change. *POLEDIT* will identify the remote computer as the location to save in.

14. Type a name for the policy file into the *File Name* field (the filename should match the one you typed into the path in step 8.).

15. Click your mouse on the Save Button. *POLEDIT* will save the file to the remote computer and close the Save As dialog box.

Answer C *is correct because you can specify any location you want for the local policy file.* **Answers A, C, and D** *are incorrect because they specify folders.*

300	USING SYSTEM POLICY EDITOR CHECK BOX SELECTION LEVELS

Q: A gray checkbox in the System Policy Editor indicates what?

Choose the best answer:

  A.   *Some options are selected*

  B.   *All options are selected*

  C.   *Options are untouched*

  D.   *Options are unavailable*

Using the System Policy Editor is easy. To create restrictions (that is, limitations that apply to users, groups, and computers), you simply check the restriction you want to apply and fill in the appropriate variables for the restriction. Each policy inside a policy file has an expandable list of restrictions with their associated checkboxes. Each check box indicates the restriction or option status (that is, enabled or disabled). Table 300 describes the checkbox status variables.

Check box	Meaning
Clear	Option is not implemented
Grayed	Option is unmodified
Checked	Option is implemented

Table 300 Checkbox implementation status.

Answer C *is correct because a gray checkbox in the System Policy Editor means that the options are unmodified.* **Answers A, B, and C** *are incorrect because a gray checkbox indicates that an option is unchanged.*

301 REMOVING THE LAST USER LOGGED ON FROM THE LOGON DIALOG BOX

Q: *Windows NT always displays the name of the last user who logged on to the system locally. You cannot change this feature.*

True or False?

Microsoft designed Windows NT with high security. One of the features Windows NT provides is to insert the username of the last user who logged onto the system locally into the *username* field in the Windows NT logon dialog box—a convenience feature that might be a security risk, depending on your security policy. You might, for security reasons, decide to remove this feature on some networks. Although it is possible to remove the last username logon feature by directly editing the Windows NT Registry, using the System Policy Editor to edit the Registry or actually removing the feature with a system policy file is much easier and prevents you from duplicating your efforts. To remove the last username logon feature, click your mouse on the check box in the Default Computer policy, as Figure 301 shows.

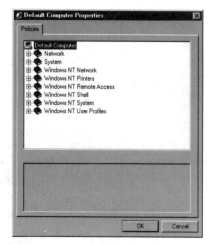

Figure 301 *Disabling the last username logon feature.*

The answer is **False** *because you can disable the last username logon feature using a system policy or the Windows NT Registry.*

302 CONFIGURING A LOGON BANNER

Q: *What do you call the dialog box that appears prior to the Windows NT logon screen?*

Choose the best answer:

A.   *Pre-logon screen*

B.   *Logon Banner*

C.   *Logon text*

D.   *Logon warning*

The Windows NT logon banner is a feature that lets you place warnings the user must read before logging on. Your reasons for implementing logon banner warnings range from a gentle warning to the user to log off when finished to legal warnings informing potential hackers not to log on without authorization. To implement logon banners, you should always use system policies rather than change the local Registry. You can then perform changes to the logon banner one time and then implement the changes on every Windows NT computer in the network. If you were to place the logon banners directly into each machine's Registry, you would have to make the same change individually on every machine, which would take a lot of administrative time. To implement a logon banner, place a checkmark in the check box to the left of the logon banner option in the Default Computer policy and type the text you want into the *Caption* and *Text* fields, as Figure 302 shows.

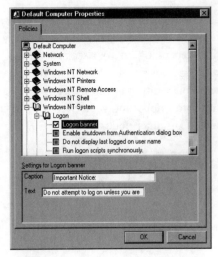

Figure 302 *Using the system policy logon banner option.*

Answer B is correct because a dialog box that appears prior to the Windows NT logon screen is a logon banner. Answers A, C, and D are incorrect because they are not the names of a dialog box that appears prior to the Windows NT logon screen.

303 VIEWING THE PROGRAMS WINDOWS NT IS CURRENTLY RUNNING

Q: To view a list of the programs Windows NT is currently running, press the Ctrl-Esc keyboard combination.

True or False?

Within in Windows NT, you can view the programs your system is currently running (the applications as well as the system processes) using the *Task Manager*. Within the *Task Manager*, you can view a list of active applications within the Applications sheet and specifics about systems processes within the Processes sheet. By clicking your mouse on an application within the Applications sheet, you can switch quickly to the application's window. To display the Windows NT Task Manager, perform these steps:

1. Right click your mouse on an unused region of the Taskbar. Windows NT, in turn, will display a small pop-up menu.

2. Within the pop-up menu, select the Task Manager option.

*The answer is **False**, because the Ctrl-Esc keyboard combination directs Windows NT to display the Start menu.*

304 INTRODUCTION TO THE MICROSOFT ZERO ADMINISTRATION KIT (ZAK)

Q: You can best describe the Microsoft Zero Administration Kit as a series of tools and guidelines to help administrators reduce the Total Cost of Ownership for personal computers.

True or False?

Many individuals within the computer industry use the term *Total Cost of Ownership (TCO)* to explain the actual costs of implementing any new product—whether software or hardware. When the product is a software application or operating system, costs may include items such as training for the users, a consultant for installation and configuration, and optional components or specialized hardware. Microsoft's Zero Administration initiative provides administrators with a way to reduce the Total Cost of Ownership for Microsoft products by reducing the administration costs. The Microsoft *Zero Administration Kit* (ZAK) is a series of tools and guidelines that Microsoft has created, as part of the Zero Administration initiative, that use Microsoft product features to reduce administrator workloads. Specifically, the ZAK includes samples of system policies and utilities that use and supplement the system policies and user profiles in Windows NT.

Many problems administrators find in the average network are due to users who change software configurations or install unsupported applications. If you implement restrictions and effectively manage operating systems and applications at a server level, you can reduce administrative hours because you will not have to spend as much time fixing network problems.

*The answer is **True** because the Microsoft Zero Administration Kit is a series of tools and guidelines designed to reduce the Total Cost of Ownership for personal computers.*

305 SYSTEM POLICY TROUBLESHOOTING

Q: You are a Windows NT domain administrator. You have implemented a system policy that includes a specific wallpaper. Not all the computers in the network are displaying the wallpaper. What is the most likely reason some of the computers are not displaying the wallpaper?

Choose the best answer:

    A.   The policy file is corrupt.

    B.   The server contains another policy file with the same name.

    C.   The remote computers' video adapters do not support the wallpaper.

    D.   You have not copied the wallpaper to the remote computers.

You can attribute many problems you discover as you work with system policies to an oversight during policy creation. If you experience unexpected results from your system policies, frequently you can review the policy file to find solutions. Table 305 lists some system policy problems and possible solutions.

Problem	Solution
Computers take too long to log on	If you have a large policy file with many individual policies defined in it, or many users are logging on at the same time, downloading a policy can take a long time. To decrease log-on time, you can specify other locations for some computers to obtain the system policy file, or you can enable load balancing on Windows 95 computers.
Windows 95 users are receiving NT policies	Remember to create a user policy in both *NTCONFIG.POL* and *CONFIG.POL* to let a user log on to either operating system.
Wallpaper does not display on all computers	Policy files implement restrictions. Settings for files that policy files require must include a complete network or local path and, in some cases, such as with wallpaper, you must store the files on the remote computer.
A computer does not enforce restrictions	Check the Registry to ensure that you pointed the computer to the correct location for the system policy file.

Table 305 Identifying some system policy problems and solutions.

Answer D *is correct because you must store the wallpaper on the local computer in order for the system policy to load it.* **Answer A** *is incorrect because all computers would have problems if the policy file was corrupt.* **Answer B** *is incorrect because you cannot store two policy files with the same name in the same folder.* **Answer C** *is incorrect because the video adapter has no bearing on loading wallpaper.*

306   UNDERSTANDING LONG FILENAMES

Q: *Windows NT supports filenames that can be up to how many characters in length?*

Choose the best answer:

     A.   8

     B.   255

     C.   256

     D   125

As you have learned, Windows NT supports long filenames on both the New Technologies File System (NTFS) and the File Allocation Table (FAT) file systems. Long filenames let users name their files more completely (as opposed to the old MS-DOS 8.3 naming convention, for example), which makes the files easier for users to identify. Filenames on Windows NT partitions can be up to 255 characters in length and can include any characters, except for ? " / \ > < * | :. Windows NT will automatically generate filenames compliant with the MS-DOS (8.3) standard, whether on an NTFS partition or a FAT partition. However, you should name files carefully if you want to use the files with MS-DOS-based applications because the applications may not be able to use the long filename and may, in fact, destroy the filename, renaming the file with a fully MS-DOS-style filename. You will learn more about the automatic generation of MS-DOS filenames in the following Tip. When you use long filenames from the console, you must place the filenames in quotations. For example, if you are executing a command called *OPEN.EXE* on a file named *HELLO_MCSE.TXT*, which the C: drive's *FILES* subfolder contains, your command is *OPEN "C:\FILES\HELLO_MCSE.TXT"*.

Answer B *is correct because Windows NT filenames can be up to 255 characters.* **Answers A, C,** *and* **D** *are incorrect because they do not list the correct number of filename characters.*

| 307 | AUTOMATICALLY GENERATING MS-DOS FILENAMES |

Q: *You have just created and saved a file as NewFile.txt. How will Windows NT convert this filename when you save it to a FAT partition?*

Choose the best answer:

     A.   *No conversion will take place*

     B.   *newfile.txt*

     C.   *NEWFILE.TXT*

     D.   *NEWFIL~1.txt*

MS-DOS-based applications and some 16-bit Windows applications cannot read long filenames. To ensure a file is compatible with as many applications as possible, Windows NT will automatically convert long filenames to the 8.3 naming convention (the MS-DOS file naming method that has 8 characters, a period, and 3 characters) that older applications require. From within a normal Windows NT window or application, you will see only the long filename. Windows NT will also convert a filename with uppercase and lowercase characters in it if you save or copy the file to a FAT partition. For example, a valid filename on an NTFS partition would be *NewFile.doc*. If you save or copy the file to a FAT partition, however, Windows NT will convert the filename to *NEWFILE.DOC* because the FAT file system does not preserve case. Windows NT generates 8.3 filenames on an as-needed basis on any file system you use. Windows NT will not, however, generate 8.3 filenames for files a POSIX application creates. If you create a filename inside a POSIX application that does not comply with the 8.3 naming convention, MS-DOS and 16-bit Windows applications will not be able to access it.

Additionally, as you learned in the previous Tips, some 16-bit applications will save their files in a way that removes the automatically generated 8.3 filenames (and long filenames) and NTFS permissions, and saves the file purely as a 16-bit file with an MS-DOS based name.

How Windows NT converts a filename depends on how many filenames within the same directory have similar names to each other. Standard filename conversion takes the first six characters from the long filename, removes the spaces, and uses a tilde (~) followed by a number. Windows NT moves the file extension to the file's end and reduces it to three characters, if necessary. For example, Windows NT would change a file named *Our financial data first quarter.text* to an 8.3 filename of *OURFIN~1.TEX*. If you then saved a file named *Our financial data second quarter.text*, the generated 8.3 filename would be *OURFIN~2.TEX*. Windows NT will use this reduction method for the first four files with similar names. After the first four filenames, Windows NT will take only the first two characters and generate the remaining characters randomly for any other similar filenames. Table 307 illustrates how Windows NT converts similar long filenames.

Long Filename	8.3 Filename
Our financial data first quarter.TXT	*OURFIN~1.TXT*
Our financial data second quarter.TXT	*OURFIN~2.TXT*
Our financial data third quarter.TXT	*OURFIN~3.TXT*
Our financial data fifth quarter.TXT	*OUPQ52~1.TXT*
Our financial data sixth quarter.TXT	*OU8741~1.TXT*

Table 307 Understanding how Windows NT converts long filenames.

Answer C is correct because the FAT file system does not preserve case and Windows NT will convert the filename to uppercase. Answer A is incorrect because a conversion does take place. Answer B is incorrect because Windows NT will convert filenames to uppercase on a FAT partition. Answer D is incorrect because the file already complies with the 8.3 naming convention, therefore Windows NT will not generate a new filename.

308   LONG FILENAMES ON *FAT* PARTITIONS

Q: *Where does Windows NT keep long filenames on a FAT partition?*

Choose the best answer:

     A.   *In the master boot record*

     B.   *In the file attributes*

     C.   *In secondary directory entries*

     D.   *In a hidden database of filenames called LFN.REF*

How Windows NT stores long filenames is an interesting set of workarounds because Microsoft did not design the file system to support long filenames. When you create and name a file, Windows NT reads the filename to see if it is a long filename—that is, if the name is longer than 12 characters (the 8.3 filenames are 12 characters). If Windows NT finds that the filename is a long filename and that its destination is a FAT partition, Windows NT will generate an 8.3 filename for it. Windows NT will then save the file with its new 8.3 filename and save the long filename as a series of secondary directory entries in the table. Windows NT creates one directory entry for the 8.3 filename and one secondary directory entry for every 13 characters in the long filename (including spaces and punctuation marks).

Note: *Because the FAT root directory has a limit of 512 directory entries, too many long filenames in the root folder can quickly take up the available entries, resulting in Windows NT being unable to create files and folders.*

If you have stored long filenames on a FAT partition, you should be careful about running third-party disk-management applications or booting the computer into MS-DOS because the applications or MS-DOS may not understand the long filename storage method and might therefore destroy the long filename entry. Unfortunately, the applications that may destroy the long filename entry are many, and it is difficult or impossible to know the effect that an application will have on a long filename entry until you use the application to change one.

Windows NT protects against the possibility of long filename corruption by adding the *Volume, Read only, System,* and *Hidden* attributes to the long filename directory entry. Adding all four attributes is unique because no other MS-DOS filename entry has these attributes all at one time—in fact, only the operating system can attach all four attributes to a file. The file attribute protection for the long filename, however, is not foolproof, and so you must be careful to avoid destroying the long filename.

Programs such as *SCANDISK, DEFRAG,* and *CHKDSK,* which Microsoft provides with MS-DOS version 6.0 and higher and all Windows 95 versions, have all been verified by both Microsoft and independent third-parties as programs that do not corrupt long filenames.

Answer C is correct because, on a FAT partition, Windows NT stores long filenames in secondary directory entries. Answers A, B, and D are incorrect because they do not accurately describe where Windows NT stores long filenames.

309 UNDERSTANDING *FAT* PARTITION AND FILE SIZE LIMITATIONS

Q: What is a FAT partition's maximum possible size?

Choose the best answer:

> A.   *1Gb*
>
> B.   *2Gb*
>
> C.   *3Gb*
>
> D.   *4Gb*

The Windows NT implementation of the File Allocation Table (FAT) file system provides many enhancements to the original implementation of FAT. Windows NT's enhancements grant the administrator a higher level of functionality when he or she uses the FAT than the administrator would have with, for example, an MS-DOS 5.0 implementation of the file system. However, the FAT file system does have limitations and boundaries, including size limitations, number of files within each directory, and other limitations, within which operating systems and applications must operate. For example, the FAT file system maximum partition size is 4Gb, which means that no single partition, whether it is primary or extended, can be larger that 4Gb. The FAT file system also limits file sizes to 4Gb.

FAT partitions are subject to high levels of fragmentation as file size increases, which can also cause performance degradation. *Fragmentation* describes files whose data the operating system is storing in non-consecutive locations on the disk. You will learn more about fragmentation in Tip 313.

Answer D is correct because the maximum partition size under the FAT file system is 4Gb. Answers A, B, and C are incorrect because they do not accurately describe the FAT file system's partition size limit.

310 RISC ARCHITECTURE-BASED COMPUTERS REQUIRE A SMALL *FAT* PARTITION

Q: RISC architecture-based computers require a FAT partition. What Windows NT files must the administrator store on a RISC architecture-based computer FAT partition?

Choose the best answer:

> A.   *All Windows NT files*
>
> B.   *The Windows NT boot files*
>
> C.   *The Windows NT system files*
>
> D.   *None. RISC architecture-based computers require the partition for specific processor-related files that they use.*

As you learned in Tip 215, Reduced Instruction Set Computing (RISC) installations have special considerations that are not a concern when you install Windows NT to other architectures. One consideration is that RISC-based installations require you to store the Windows NT system files on a FAT partition. In Tip 207, you learned that the

Windows NT system partition is a primary partition and contains the system files a computer requires to locate and start an operating system. RISC-based installations will start only from a FAT partition, which means you must store the Windows NT system files on a FAT partition in order for a RISC-based computer running Windows NT to start.

Because you cannot apply Windows NT local security to FAT file systems (because FAT does not support security), the system partition on a RISC-based computer is vulnerable to unauthorized file access. The Disk Administrator provides some protection through the Secure System Partition feature. If you apply the Secure System Partition command, only Administrators group members will have access to the system partition.

Note: You must restart the computer after applying the **Secure System Partition** *command to implement it.*

Answer C is correct because you must store the Windows NT system files on a FAT partition in RISC-based installations. Answer A is incorrect because only the Windows NT system files must be on the FAT partition. Remaining files can be on a partition formatted with any file system. Answer B is incorrect because you can store the Windows NT boot files on a partition formatted with any file system. Answer D is incorrect because you do have to store the Windows NT system files on a FAT partition.

311 UNDERSTANDING NTFS PARTITION AND FILE SIZE LIMITATIONS

Q: What is an NTFS partition's maximum size?

Choose the best answer:

    A.   *16 gigabytes*

    B.   *16 exabytes*

    C.   *16 terabytes*

    D.   *16 megabytes*

As you learned in Tip 208, an NTFS partition or file's maximum theoretical size is 16 exabytes. However, because of hardware limitations, the maximum size of a single partition you can actually create is two terabytes and a file's actual maximum size is between four and 64Gb.

When you implement an NTFS partition, the only disk configuration currently able to exceed the two terabyte hardware limitation is a volume set, which uses multiple physical partitions to make up a logical drive (therefore the hardware limitation only applies to the members of the set). Tips 259 through 261 discuss volume sets in more detail.

Answer B is correct because an NTFS partition's maximum size is 16 exabytes. *Answers A, C, and D are incorrect because they are smaller than the actual limitation.*

Note: As you have learned, to become a Microsoft Certified Systems Engineer you must pass a series of exams. Remember, as you prepare for your exams, to read the questions carefully. Questions on many of the exams will ask you about an NTFS partition's maximum size in the same manner as this Tip's question does. The answer is 16 exabytes because the question is asking about the NTFS limitation, not the hardware.

312   NTFS POSIX.1 COMPLIANCE

Q: *Which of the following POSIX.1 compliant features are available in an NTFS file system?*

Choose all answers that apply:

     A.   *Case sensitive naming*

     B.   *Additional Time Stamping*

     C.   *Linked-list directory structure*

     D.   *Hard links*

The New Technologies File System (NTFS), as you learned in Tip 208, is the Portable Operating System Interface (POSIX) compliant file system that Windows NT supports. To provide POSIX.1 compliance, Windows NT includes the features Table 312 describes in an NTFS file system.

Feature	Description
Case Sensitive Naming	POSIX supports filenames that vary only in case. For example, POSIX considers NEWFILE.TXT, *NewFile.txt*, and *newfile.txt* different files.
Additional Time Stamp	The stamp that adds the time a user last accessed the file.
Hard Links	The process wherein two or more files stored in different folders point to the same data (a file with more than one name that you may access from different folders).

Table 312 The NTFS file system's POSIX.1 compliant features.

Answers A, B, and **C** are correct because case sensitive naming, additional time stamping, and hard links are all POSIX.1 compliant features available in the NTFS file system. **Answer D** is incorrect because only FAT uses the linked-list directory structure.

313   DEFRAGMENTING AN NTFS PARTITION

Q: *Which of the following tools performs defragmentation in Windows NT?*

Choose the best answer:

     A.   *The Disk Administrator*

     B.   *DEFRAG.EXE*

     C.   *Windows NT does not provide a defragmentation tool*

     D.   *Disk Manager*

As you have learned, file systems store files and folders on partitions. As a file grows, Windows NT may store data from the same file at different locations on the partition. *Fragmentation* describes files whose contents the operating system is storing in non-consecutive locations on the disk. Many operating systems provide a utility that can defragment hard drives by restoring a file's contents in consecutive disk locations. The *defrag.exe* program, for example, is an MS-DOS utility that provides defragmentation.

Windows NT does not have a built-in defragmentation utility, so you must manually defragment partitions. The level of fragmentation you will find depends on which file system you choose. FAT partitions are much more susceptible to fragmentation than NTFS, because of structural differences in the way the operating systems save files. Therefore, you probably will have to defragment FAT partitions more often than NTFS partitions. To defragment a partition, you will have to manually copy the files you want to defragment to a different location (such as a different disk drive or a tape drive), delete the original files, and then copy the files back again. When you copy the files back to their original locations, Windows NT will try to store the file's contents in consecutive locations (provided the disk has consecutive locations large enough to hold a file).

Instead of copying all the files on the hard drive to reduce fragmentation, another (generally more attractive) choice is to implement a third-party defragmentation utility. You must be careful when you implement third-party disk utilities in Windows NT because they might create problems, such as interfering with the security model. Tip 315 discusses some problems with third-party disk utilities in detail.

Answer C is correct because Windows NT does not provide a defragmentation tool. Answer A is incorrect because the Disk Administrator does not perform defragmentation. Answer B is incorrect because Microsoft does not provide DEFRAG.EXE with Windows NT. Answer D is incorrect because Windows NT does not contain a program named Disk Manager.

314 REMOVABLE MEDIA AND WINDOWS NT

Q: *Windows NT does not support removable media.*

True or False?

Removable media is a standard industry term that refers to disks which a user can remove from the computer without tools and frequently can remove without restarting the system. Floppy disks are examples of removable media. In addition to floppy disks, Windows NT also supports SCSI-based and magneto-optical-based removable disk drives (a type of drive that uses a special, high-density storage disk). Removable media has limitations other forms of storage do not. For example, you cannot format floppy disks with the NTFS file system, which means that you cannot store files you compress under NTFS or that have NTFS permissions and security limitations onto a floppy disk without losing the compression or permissions. The following bulleted list describes some other removable media limitations:

- Windows NT limits removable media support to a single primary partition, which means that Windows NT is unable to read multiple partitions on removable disks.

- Removable disks cannot be part of a stripe or volume set.

- Removable media does not support Write-Once/Read-Many (WORM) and other types of media that you can write to only one time.

The file system also affects removable media's functionality. Windows NT supports removable drives formatted with the FAT file system differently from removable drives formatted with NTFS. You can remove removable drives formatted with the FAT file system while Windows NT is running, unless the pagefile (the system's virtual memory storage) is on the drive. You must unmount removable drives formatted with the NTFS file system before you can remove them. In most cases, unmounting a removable drive means you must shut down the Windows NT computer.

One indicator that quickly tells you if you can remove a disk is Drive icon. If you right-click your mouse on the Drive icon and the resulting pop-up menu has the Eject option, you may safely eject and remove the disk. If the Eject option is not in the Drive icon's menu, you may not safely remove the disk.

*The answer is **False** because Windows NT does support many types of removable media.*

315   **UNDERSTANDING PROBLEMS WITH RUNNING THIRD-PARTY DISK UTILITIES**

Q: *You should never use disk utilities not designed for Windows NT.*

True or False?

Disk management and virus protection utilities designed for other operating systems do not understand or comply with Windows NT architecture and cannot read NTFS partitions or understand long filenames. As a result, if you use these utilities, you may experience damage to files, data loss, or other problems with Windows NT.

For example, virus protection programs not designed for Windows NT might interpret NTFS partitions or long filenames on FAT partitions as viruses and try to remove them. In addition, disk management utilities not designed for Windows NT may destroy long filenames on FAT and try to destroy NTFS partitions. As a basic rule, never implement a utility which does not explicitly list compliance with Windows NT on a computer that uses Windows NT as an operating system.

*The answer is **True** because disk utilities not designed for Windows NT can cause problems in Windows NT and, therefore, you should not use them.*

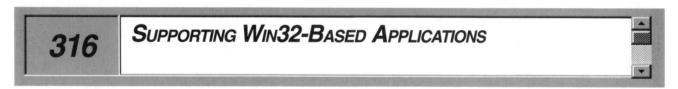

316   **SUPPORTING WIN32-BASED APPLICATIONS**

Q: *Which of the following best describes the term multithreading?*

Choose the best answer:

     A.   *An operating system's ability to run multiple applications at the same time.*

     B.   *An operating system's ability to have multiple applications access the same data source.*

     C.   *An application's ability to support multiple execution units.*

     D.   *A server's ability to manage multiple client computers simultaneously.*

In order to provide the highest possible level of functionality, Microsoft designed Windows NT to support applications designed to run on other operating systems, such as MS-DOS, Windows *3.x*, Windows 95, OS/2, and POSIX. Windows NT can support different kinds of applications because it uses *application translation programs* (called subsystems) to understand application instructions whether or not software companies designed the applications specifically for Windows NT.

Applications specifically designed to take advantage of Windows NT's multithreading features are *Win32-based applications*. *Multithreading* is an application's ability to support multiple execution units (code units the processor can execute) simultaneously. A multithreaded application might, for example, use one thread to print a document in the background while a second thread spell checks the current paragraph.

Win32-based applications each have an independent 2Gb range of virtual-memory addresses within which to run. Independent memory addressing prevents Win32-based applications that fail or hang up from affecting the memory addresses of other Win32-based applications. (A failed Win32-based application will also not hang up other applications because Windows NT preemptively multitasks the still-operating applications.)

Multitasking is an operating system's ability to run multiple applications simultaneously. Win32-based applications use *preemptive multitasking*. In preemptive multitasking, a special program called a *Scheduler* decides which application gets to use the processor and for how long. The *Scheduler* also controls the processor and can interrupt an application if a higher-priority thread comes along. Because the applications do not have control of the processor and the *Scheduler* can interrupt (preempt) them, this form of multitasking is known as preemptive multitasking.

Answer C is correct because multithreading is an application's ability to support multiple execution units. **Answer A is** incorrect because an operating system's ability to simultaneously operate multiple applications describes multitasking, not multithreading. **Answers B and D are** incorrect because they do not describe multithreading.

317	## UNDERSTANDING WINDOWS NT'S SUPPORT OF ADDITIONAL TECHNOLOGIES

Q: *Which of the following technologies lets you embed controls in Web pages on the Internet?*

Choose the best answer:

    A.   *OLE*

    B   *Active X*

    C.   *Open GL*

    D.   *All of the above*

As you have learned, Windows NT supports a variety of applications that software companies did not specifically design for the Windows NT operating system. To support other applications, Windows NT understands a variety of Application Programming Interfaces (APIs), such as the Open Graphics Language (GL) API and technologies such as ActiveX. The Open Graphics Language (GL) API provides services programs can use to produce two- and three-dimensional graphics. The Windows NT implementation of Open GL supports the 16-color mode Video Graphics Adapter (VGA), which differs from other Open GL API implementations that usually require a minimum of 256 colors. Windows NT includes some examples of Open GL programs as screen savers. Tip 318 describes Windows NT Open GL screen savers in more detail.

Object Linking and Embedding (OLE) has been available since Microsoft implemented Windows *3.x*. OLE lets applications interact with one another. Without OLE, creating documents that contain embedded data from a different application would be very difficult. Microsoft based OLE on the Component Object Model (COM), which provides a "behind-the-scenes" engine that enables separate program components to communicate with each other.

Windows NT supports both 16-bit and 32-bit OLE, which means that 16-bit and 32-bit applications can communicate with each other as easily as two 16-bit applications could in Windows *3.x*. The ActiveX technologies support a series of relatively new APIs that give controls and objects embedded in Web pages with the communication functionality that the OLE API provides to applications, as well as other extended functionality.

Answer B is correct because ActiveX is the technology that lets you embed controls in Web pages. Answers A and C are incorrect because these APIs do not give Web pages any functionality. Answer D is incorrect because only ActiveX lets you embed controls in Web pages.

---

318 — KNOWING WHEN NOT TO USE OPEN GL SCREEN SAVERS

Q: *The Windows NT operating system includes several Open GL screen savers. Which of the following are valid reasons why an administrator should not use an Open GL screen saver?*

Choose all answers that apply:

A. *Microsoft does not test Open GL screen savers with Windows NT and therefore the screen savers could cause computers to hang up.*

B. *Open GL screen savers can damage monitors.*

C. *Open GL screen savers are processor intensive and may cause performance loss to background operations.*

D. *Open GL screen savers are memory intensive and administrators should not implement them on computers with less than 64Mb of RAM.*

Windows NT provides several examples of screen savers that use the Open Graphics Language (GL) API, which include the following:

- 3D Flower Box
- 3D Flying Objects
- 3D Maze
- 3D Pipes
- 3D Text

Open GL screen savers are very processor intensive, meaning, an Open GL screen saver will take up many of the processor's execution cycles and other running applications may suffer a performance loss. Because Open GL screen savers can take up so much processor time, a Windows NT administrator should never use them on a File, Print, or Application server. Much of what the File, Print, and Application servers do is background execution because they primarily perform services for other machines and seldom perform foreground operations, such as word processing or data entry. The performance degradation on background operations when you use a processor-intensive Open GL screen saver could produce a drastic reduction in network speed and impact all users.

Answer C is correct because a valid reason not to implement an Open GL screen saver is they are processor intensive and could cause a loss of performance in background operations. Answer A is incorrect because Windows NT supports the Open GL API and the screen savers will not cause a system hang up. Answer B is incorrect because Open GL screen savers do not damage monitors any more than any other type of screen saver. Answer D is incorrect because Open GL screen savers are not memory intensive and administrators can run them safely on systems with less than 64Mb of RAM.

319 UNDERSTANDING THE DIRECTX APIS

Q: Which of the following DirectX APIs does Microsoft include in Windows NT?

Choose all answers that apply:

    A.   DirectDraw

    B.   DirectPlay

    C.   DirectSound

    D.   DirectExecution

DirectX is a term that describes a set of low-level Application Programming Interfaces (APIs) specifically designed to provide a real-time response to user actions for high-performance applications, such as games, 3-D virtual reality, and so on. Each DirectX API that Windows NT supports provides a level of functionality between the application and the hardware. A DirectX API function communicates directly with an internal component of Windows NT architecture. Hardware specifically designed to support DirectX APIs can communicate directly with the application through the API. Windows NT supports three DirectX APIs, which Table 319 describes.

API	Function
DirectDraw	Provides accelerated drawing speed to increase realism in video motion
DirectSound	Provides sound control features, such as real-time mixing of audio streams, extended sound card support, and so on
DirectPlay	Provides simplified communications between computers over a modem or network

Table 319 The DirectX APIs that Windows NT supports.

Answers A, B, and *C are correct because they name DirectX APIs that Windows NT supports.* **Answer D** *is incorrect because there is no such DirectX API.*

320 SUPPORTING WIN16-BASED AND MS-DOS-BASED APPLICATIONS

Q: *Microsoft designed Win16-based applications for use in Windows 3.x operating systems.*

True or False?

Win16-based applications are applications that Microsoft designed for use with Windows 3.x operating systems. Win16-based applications share processor time is *cooperative multitasking,* as opposed to the Win32 preemptive multitasking method.

In cooperative multitasking, each application will use and then release the processor so that another application can use it. Programmers call cooperative multitasking "cooperative" because the application controls the processor and must release control of the processor before a different application can use it. Because the application has control of the processor, a Win16-based application that hangs may also hang all other Win16-based applications currently running.

Within Windows NT, all Win16 applications will cooperatively share a given thread that Windows NT will preemptively multitask with other Win32 threads. Implementing the Win16 execution in this manner keeps 16-bit applications from hanging up the entire operating system in the event of a program failure.

Even before Win16-based applications, PCs supported MS-DOS-based applications, which remain the most limited applications that Windows NT supports. Microsoft did not design the MS-DOS operating system for multitasking, which means that MS-DOS-based applications can run only one application at a time, and they use the MS-DOS system files *IO.SYS* and *MSDOS.SYS*—which Windows NT must take into account when it executes MS-DOS programs from within the Windows NT operating system. Because certain MS-DOS-based applications continue to be popular, Windows NT includes a set of components that let most MS-DOS-based applications run under Windows NT. Tip 321 describes the Windows NT components that support MS-DOS in detail.

*The answer is **True** because Microsoft did design Win16-based applications for the Windows **3.x** operating system.*

321   INTRODUCTION TO THE NEW TECHNOLOGIES VIRTUAL DOS MACHINE (NTVDM)

Q: How does Windows NT run applications designed for MS-DOS?

Choose the best answer:

> *A.   Windows NT cannot run applications designed for MS-DOS.*
>
> *B.   Windows NT will shutdown and temporarily load MS-DOS for the application to run.*
>
> *C.   Windows NT runs MS-DOS-based applications in an NTVDM.*
>
> *D.   Windows NT converts MS-DOS-based applications into Windows applications.*

Windows NT runs MS-DOS-based applications using a special Win32-based program called a *New Technologies Virtual DOS Machine (NTVDM)*. The NTVDM program impersonates (programmers call this process *emulating*) a computer with an MS-DOS operating system, with which the MS-DOS-based application then communicates. Windows NT creates a separate NTVDM instance for each MS-DOS-based application. Each NTVDM has its own memory address space and a single processor thread, which means you can run multiple MS-DOS-based applications simultaneously and the Scheduler program will preemptively multitask them with other Win32-based applications.

MS-DOS-based applications frequently make requests directly to hardware, such as a printer, mouse, or keyboard. However, Windows NT does not let applications communicate directly with hardware, so NTVDMs have special software components called *virtual device drivers (VDDs)*. Virtual device drivers intercept signals from the MS-DOS-based application, interpret the signals, and then pass them to the Windows NT device drivers. Windows NT device drivers are the components in Windows NT that can communicate with hardware.

As you learned in Tip 320, MS-DOS-based applications use the MS-DOS system files *IO.SYS* and *MSDOS.SYS*. For an MS-DOS-based application to run under Windows NT, NTVDMs must have components that impersonate the MS-DOS system files. The NTVDM components that provide system file functionality are *NTIO.SYS* and *NTDOS.SYS*. Figure 321 illustrates an NTVDM's functionality.

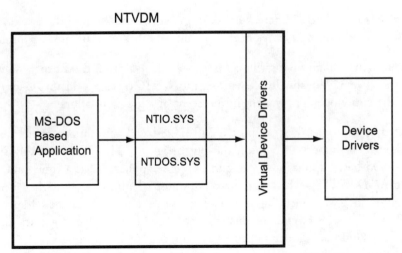

Figure 321 *The New Technologies Virtual DOS Machine (NTVDM) interacts with the MS-DOS application and Windows NT.*

Note: *NTVDMs on Reduced Instruction Set Computing-based (RISC-based) computers have the Instruction Execution Unit (IEU) component, which Microsoft provides to let RISC-based computers emulate an Intel 80486 processor.*

Answer C is correct because Windows NT runs MS-DOS-based applications in an NTVDM. Answer A is incorrect because Windows NT can run MS-DOS-based applications. Answer B is incorrect because Windows NT does not shutdown to run MS-DOS-based applications. Answer D is incorrect because Windows NT does not convert MS-DOS-based applications into Windows applications.

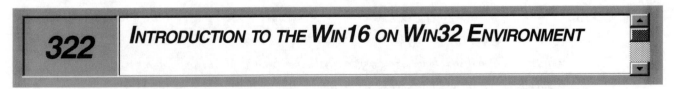

322 INTRODUCTION TO THE WIN16 ON WIN32 ENVIRONMENT

Q: *Which of the following terms describes the process of translating 16-bit code to 32-bit code?*

Choose the best answer:

    A.   *Conversion*

    B.   *Transference*

    C.   *Thunking*

    D.   *Transmigration*

You learned in Tip 321 that Windows NT runs MS-DOS-based applications inside New Technologies Virtual DOS Machines (NTVDMs). Because the Windows *3.x* operating system is actually an MS-DOS-based application, Windows NT also runs Win16-based applications from within an NTVDM.

To run a Win16-based application, Windows NT produces an NTVDM with additional components that emulate the Windows *3.x* environment. Programmers refer to the special NTVDM as a Win16 on Win32 (WOW) environment because Windows NT must translate commands from a Win16 environment (Windows *3.x*) to a Win32 environment (Windows NT). Table 322 describes the NTVDM's additional WOW components.

The WOW software intercepts program requests the Win16-based application makes and translates them into Win32-compatible requests before passing the requests to the Win32 (Windows NT) components responsible for the requested action. In the same way, WOW software intercepts Win32 (Windows NT) responses and translates them into

Win16-compatible signals before passing the signals to the Win16-based application. The process of translating program requests between 16-bit and 32-bit components is *thunking*. Figure 322 illustrates how Windows NT runs Win16-based applications in an NTVDM WOW.

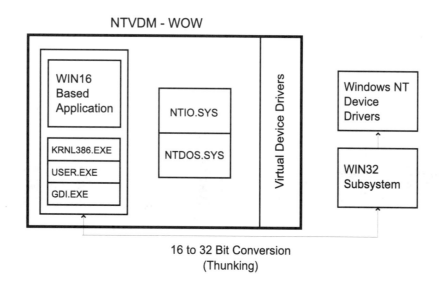

Figure 322 Windows NT running a Win16-based application in an NTVDM WOW.

Component	Description
WOWEXEC.EXE	Provides the Windows *3.x* emulation structure
WOW32.DLL	Emulates the Windows *3.x* Dynamic-Link Library (DLL) functionality
KRNL386.EXE	A modified version of the Windows *3.x* system file that Windows NT uses to simulate execution
USER.EXE	A modified version of the Windows *3.x* system file that Windows NT uses to simulate execution
GDI.EXE	A modified version of the Windows *3.x* system file that Windows NT uses to simulate execution

Table 322 The NTVDM's additional WOW components.

Win16-based applications operate cooperatively with other Win-16-based applications in the Windows *3.x* environment. Windows NT automatically starts all Win16-based applications in the same NTVDM. After the NTVDM that provides the enhanced Win16 support starts, it remains open even if you close all Win16-based applications. You can choose to run a Win16-based application in its own NTVDM. However, without your input the applications will all run in a single NTVDM. You will learn how to configure a Win16-based application in its own NTVDM in Tip 323.

Answer C is correct because the term that describes the translation of 16-bit to 32-bit code is thunking. Answers A, B, and D are incorrect because they do not describe the translation of 16-bit to 32-bit code.

323 RUNNING MULTIPLE NEW TECHNOLOGIES VIRTUAL DOS MACHINES (NTVDMs)

Q: *Windows NT can run Win16-based applications in separate NTVDMs.*

True or False?

As you learned in Tip 321, Windows NT uses multiple NTVDMs (and, therefore, preemptive multitasking) to run multiple MS-DOS-based applications. In contrast, Windows NT, by default, runs all Win16-based applications in a single NTVDM and the applications cooperatively multitask themselves within that NTVDM. However, you can configure Windows NT to run a single Win16-based application in its own NTVDM, which effectively separates it from all other applications and causes the Scheduler to preemptively multitask it the same way as a Win32-based or MS-DOS-based application. Table 323 describes some advantages of running a Win16-based application in its own NTVDM.

You must specify to the operating system that the Win16-based application must run in its own NTVDM before the application starts. You will specify how Windows NT should run the Win16-based application differently, depending on the method with which you choose to start the application. If you want to start the Win16-based application from the Run option in the Start menu, you must simply place a check mark in the Run dialog box's Run in Separate Memory Space checkbox. To start a Win16-based application in its own NTVDM from the Start menu, perform the following steps:

1.   Click your mouse on the Start menu and select the Run option. Windows NT will open the Run dialog box.

2.   Within the Run dialog box, type the complete pathname, *drive letter:\folder\application name*, of the application you want to run.

3.   Next, within the Run dialog box, click your mouse on the Run in Separate Memory Space check box. Windows NT will insert a check mark in the box to indicate your selection. Figure 323.1 shows the Run dialog box after you select the Run in Separate Memory Space check box.

Figure 323.1 The Run dialog box's Run in Separate Memory Space checkbox after you select it.

4.   Click your mouse on the OK button. Windows NT will start the application you specified in a separate NTVDM.

If you have created a shortcut to the Win16-based application and you want to run the application in a separate NTVDM, you must configure the shortcut properties to indicate a separate NTVDM to Windows NT. As with starting the application from the Start menu, you can indicate a separate NTVDM by placing a check mark in the Shortcut Properties dialog box's Run in Separate Memory Space check box. Figure 323.2 shows the Shortcut Properties dialog box before you select the Run in Separate Memory Space check box.

If you are already running an NTVDM (Command Prompt) and want to start a Win16-based application from inside it, simply enter the following instruction at the command prompt (make sure to use the */separate* switch):

```
C:\> Start /separate "drive letter:\folder\application name"   <ENTER>
```

Note: *Win16-based applications that rely on shared memory, instead of OLE and DDE specifications to communicate with other Win16-based applications, cannot interoperate with other Win16-based applications that you run in separate memory spaces on a Windows NT computer.*

Figure 323.2 The Shortcut Properties dialog box's Run in Separate Memory Space check box before you select it.

Advantage	Description
Enhanced reliability	A Win16-based application running in a separate NTVDM cannot hang up other Win16-based applications if it fails.
Preemptive Multitasking	Under normal operating conditions, a Win16-based application that is busy brings all other Win16-based applications to a halt until it releases the processor. When you run a Win16-based application in its own NTVDM, you force it to share time with other NTVDMs and Win32-based applications.
Multiprocessing	Because all Win16-based applications usually run under a single NTVDM, even on computers with multiple processors, all Win16-based applications share time with a single processor. Running Win16-based applications in separate NTVDMs lets Windows NT assign a processor to each application.

Table 323 The advantages of running Win16-based applications in separate NTVDMS.

The answer is **True** because Windows NT can run Win16-based applications in separate NTVDMs.

324 RUNNING AN APPLICATION IN THE OS/2 SUBSYSTEM

Q: *Windows NT installations on RISC-based architecture can run which of the following OS/2 applications?*

Choose the best answer:

> *A.   All OS/2 applications*
>
> *B.   Only those applications designed to use the Presentation Manager*
>
> *C.   Only Bound applications*
>
> *D.   None. Windows NT installations on RISC-based architectures cannot support OS/2 applications.*

In Tip 316, you learned that Windows NT can support OS/2 applications. Windows NT limits support of OS/2 applications to Bound applications and OS/2 *1.x* character-based applications. *Bound applications* are applications software companies specifically design to run on either OS/2 or MS-DOS. *Character-based applications* are applications that do not use the OS/2 graphical user interface (GUI), the Presentation Manager. OS/2 applications designed to use the Presentation Manager require a third-party add on, which Microsoft does not include with Windows NT. You will learn more about supporting OS/2 applications designed to use the Presentation Manager in Tip 326.

To support OS/2 applications, Windows NT provides a subsystem dedicated to OS/2 (that is, the subsystem runs only OS/2 applications). OS/2 applications communicate directly with the OS/2 subsystem which, in turn, communicates with Windows NT. OS/2 bound applications run in a New Technologies Virtual DOS Machine (NTVDM) and communicate with Windows NT the same way as any MS-DOS-based application. Windows NT installations on Reduced Instruction Set Computing-based (RISC-based) architectures do not include an OS/2 subsystem. Because there is no OS/2 subsystem support within RISC-based architectures, if you have installed Windows NT onto a RISC-based computer, it will support only Bound applications.

Answer C is correct because Windows NT supports only Bound applications, which run in an NTVDM, in installations on RISC-based architectures. Answer A is incorrect because Windows NT does not support all OS/2 applications. Answer B is incorrect because Windows NT does not natively support applications designed to use Presentation Manager. Also, applications that use Presentation Manager require a third-party add on. Answer D is incorrect because Windows NT installations on RISC-based architectures can run Bound applications.

325 OS/2's CONFIG.SYS FILE

Q: How do native OS/2 applications running on Windows NT get configuration information for the OS/2 session?

Choose the best answer:

    A.   OS/2 applications read OS/2 session information from the CONFIG.SYS file in the system partition's root folder.

    B   OS/2 applications read OS/2 session information from the Windows NT Registry.

    C.   OS/2 applications contain their own OS/2 session information.

    D.   Windows NT is unable to run OS/2 applications.

As you have learned, when you run OS/2 applications in the Windows NT operating system environment, those applications will either use the NTVDM or the OS/2 subsystem to execute. OS/2 applications get configuration information about their operating environment from different locations, depending on the type of application. For example, bound applications read the information from the CONFIG.SYS file located in the system partition's root folder. Software companies also design native OS/2 applications (those that use the Presentation Manager) to read information from the CONFIG.SYS file. The OS/2's CONFIG.SYS file, however, does not actually exist on Windows NT installations. Instead, Windows NT stores the information normally found in the OS/2's CONFIG.SYS file in the System Registry. When a native OS/2 application calls the CONFIG.SYS file, or requests information from the CONFIG.SYS file, Windows NT intercepts the call and returns the information from the Registry.

If you try to use an OS/2 text-based editor to change CONFIG.SYS entries, Windows NT will store the information in a temporary file for display. When you save the file, Windows NT saves the information to the Registry without making changes to the actual CONFIG.SYS file stored in the system partition's root folder—because the CONFIG.SYS file in the system partition's root folder is a Windows NT file, rather than an OS/2 file.

Note: If you use a text-based editor that is not a native OS/2 application, Windows NT will use the actual CONFIG.SYS file (the Windows NT configuration) stored in the system partition's root folder.

Answer B is correct because Windows NT keeps OS/2 session information in the Windows NT system registry, so OS/2 applications will read the session information from there. Answer A is incorrect because native OS/2 applications cannot use information from the CONFIG.SYS file in the system partition's root folder. Answer C is incorrect because OS/2 applications do not contain OS/2 session information. Answer D is incorrect because Windows NT does support OS/2 applications.

326 | **RUNNING PRESENTATION MANAGER APPLICATIONS**

Q: *Windows NT can natively support which of the following OS/2 applications?*

Choose all answers that apply:

    A.   *OS/2 1.x character-based applications*

    B.   *OS/2 1.x Presentation Manager applications*

    C.   *OS/2 1.x Bound applications*

    D.   *OS/2 2.x applications*

As you learned in Tip 324, Windows NT requires a third-party add-on to support OS/2 Presentation Manager applications. The add-on replaces the OS/2 subsystem, which Windows NT includes. Microsoft does not ship this add-on with any Windows NT version. In addition, it is compatible only with *x*86 based installations and you must purchase it separately. No Presentation Manager add-on exists for RISC-based architectures.

The Presentation Manager is a graphical interface for applications in OS/2. As you have learned, Windows NT natively supports (that is, without additional drivers) only OS/2 1.*x* character-based applications and bound applications, which means that without the add-on replacement subsystem for Windows NT, Presentation Manager applications cannot operate.

The first time a Presentation Manager application starts (after you install the replacement subsystem), Windows NT creates a new Desktop for Presentation Manager applications. The Windows NT Desktop and the Presentation Manager Desktop are not compatible and are not integrated.

Answers A and C are correct because Windows NT natively supports only OS/2 1.x character-based and Bound applications. Answer B is incorrect because Presentation Manager requires a third-party add on for support. Answer D is incorrect because Windows NT does not support OS/2 2.x applications.

327 | **UNDERSTANDING HOW WINDOWS NT SUPPORTS POSIX-BASED APPLICATIONS**

Q: *Windows NT can support a maximum of how many POSIX applications running at the same time?*

Choose the best answer:

A.   32

B.   256

C.   255

D.   1

The *Portable Operating System Interface* (POSIX) is a standard set of rules for UNIX-based programs and similar applications. Applications that programmers write to conform with the POSIX standard meet the U.S. Federal Information Processing Standard. Windows NT includes a dedicated subsystem that provides functionality for POSIX-compliant applications. You can divide the POSIX subsystem into three basic files that each provide a service to POSIX applications. Table 327 describes each POSIX subsystem component.

Component	Function
PSXSS.EXE	Provides a compatible environment for POSIX applications.
POSIX.EXE	Provides communication translations between the POSIX subsystem and Windows NT. Windows NT requires one copy of *POSIX.EXE* for each POSIX application that is currently executing.
PSXDLL.DLL	Manages the address space available to all POSIX applications and governs communication between POSIX applications and *PSXSS.EXE*.

Table 327 The Windows NT POSIX subsystem's components.

The Windows NT POSIX subsystem can support 32 POSIX applications running at the same time. POSIX requires a compliant file system to let POSIX applications save any data to the hard drive. The New Technology File System (NTFS) is a POSIX.1-compliant file system for Windows NT. POSIX.1 compliance means that the NTFS file system supports an application's ability to communicate directly with the file system.

Not all POSIX applications require access to the file system. If an application does not require access to the file system, you can run it on any Windows NT-supported file system. However, you can implement an application that does require file system access only on an NTFS partition.

Answer A is correct because Windows NT can support only 32 POSIX applications running at the same time. Answers B, C, and D are incorrect because they list either too many or too few maximum applications.

328   SUPPORTING APPLICATIONS ACROSS PLATFORMS

Q: *Which of the following is an industry standard term that describes an application that can run on any Windows NT installation, regardless of platform, without recompiling the application?*

Choose the best answer:

A.   *Source-compatible*

B.   *Binary-compatible*

C.   *Processor-independent*

D.   *Platform-independent*

As you have learned, Windows NT is an operating system that you can install on many different platforms (architectures). Depending on what platform you have, you will have different application choices. Application types are divided into two categories: *binary-compatible* and *source-compatible*. Binary-compatible applications can operate on any platform and do not require you to recompile the application code. Source-compatible applications are applications whose program code is written and then compiled to run specifically on a certain platform, and you must recompile them for use on a different platform.

Windows 3.*x* (Win16) and MS-DOS-based applications are excellent examples of binary compatibility because Win16 and MS-DOS-based applications can run on platforms such as *x*86 and RISC and do not require you to recompile the application code. Win32 based applications are examples of source compatibility because their designers must write and compile them specifically for the *x*86-based platform, and therefore the applications cannot run on other platforms unless you recompile the code.

Table 328 lists application types that Windows NT supports and their Binary or Source compatibility designation.

Application Type	Compatibility designation
Win32	Source
Win16	Binary
MS-DOS	Binary
POSIX	Source
OS/2 1.*x*	Binary (bound applications only)

Table 328 The five basic application types and their compatibility designations.

Answer B *is correct because the industry standard term Binary-compatible refers to applications that can run on multiple platforms and do not require you to recompile the code.* **Answer A** *is incorrect because it describes applications that require you to recompile the code for use on different platforms.* **Answers C and D** *are incorrect because processor-independent and platform-independent are not industry standard terms.*

329 INTRODUCTION TO THE DISTRIBUTED COMPONENT OBJECT MODEL

Q: *Which of the following industry-standard terms is interchangeable with the term Distributed Processing?*

Choose the best answer:

    A.   *Network Topology*

    B.   *Domain*

    C.   *Client-Server*

    D.   *Symmetric Multiprocessing*

Distributed processing is an industry standard term that describes the distribution of a single application's duties across multiple computers. The term *client–server* is sometimes interchangeable with distributed processing.

In client–server applications, the client (sometimes called the *front-end*) application usually performs user-level operations such as data entry and screen display. The server (sometimes called the *back-end*) application performs server operations such as mass data storage, searching, and manipulation. The client–server application divides the operational workload between computers to achieve a greater level of responsiveness, particularly when the application's implementation model has many client applications accessing a single server application. Although there is actually more than one application at work in the client–server model, most administrators treat all the components as a single application because neither application can function without the other.

Microsoft's Distributed Component Object Model (DCOM) enhances the functionality of existing client–server applications, and provides the ability to distribute processing to applications that were not specifically designed as client–server. Existing applications that use the Object Linking and Embedding (OLE) standard can also use DCOM. In other words, with minor adjustments to an application's configuration, you can enhance an application so that it may take advantage of distributed processing. Those modifications, however, take place in the Registry, and are beyond the scope of this Tip's discussion.

For distributed processing models to function, there must be communication between programs (sometimes called Processes)—the programs must be able to share information with each other, because they are executing on entirely different computers. Programmers call direct communication between two or more processes *inter-process communication (IPC)*. Windows NT provides the following nine inter-process communication mechanisms:

- Server Message Blocks (SMBs)
- Network Dynamic Data Exchange (NetDDE)
- Mailslots
- NetBIOS
- Windows Sockets
- Named Pipes
- Local Procedure Calls (LPCs)
- Remote Procedure Calls (RPCs)
- Distributed Component Object Model (DCOM)

Inter-process communication mechanisms sometimes use each other to perform certain functions—for example, a named pipe uses NetBIOS to locate the pipe's opposite end. DCOM is an excellent example of IPCs working together to achieve functionality. DCOM uses Remote Procedure Calls (RPCs) to establish communication between applications. RPCs, in turn, can use Named Pipes, NetBIOS, or Windows Sockets to send and receive signals over a network.

Table 329 describes the RPC mechanism's components.

Component	Functionality
Server Stub	Packages remote procedure calls that the RPC Run Time Library will send.
RPC Run Time Library	Sends and receives Remote Procedure Calls.
Application Stub	Unpackages Remote Procedure Calls.
Remote Procedure Call	The actual program request the RPC Run Time Library sends.

Table 329 RPC components and their functionality.

Figure 329 illustrates how DCOM implements the four RPC components to achieve client–server communications.

Answer C is correct because the term client–server is interchangeable with the term distributed processing. Answers A, B, and D are incorrect because these terms do not describe the distribution of application workload across multiple computers.

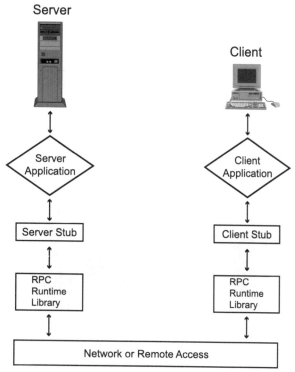

Figure 329 Using client and server stubs to implement RPC communication

330   CONFIGURING DCOM

Q: *How can you configure the default variables for Windows NT's DCOM implementation?*

Choose the best answer:

>   *A.   Use the Dconfig utility in Administrative Tools*
>
>   *B.   Use Disk Administrator*
>
>   *C.   You cannot configure DCOM*
>
>   *D.   Use DCOMCNFG.EXE*

You can configure DCOM to perform differently for each application based on choices you make in the DCOM configuration utility. The DCOM Configuration Properties dialog box lets you choose between default configuration and specifying a custom configuration for each application. To configure DCOM, perform the following steps:

1.   From the Windows NT Desktop, click your mouse on the Start menu and select the Run option. Windows NT will open the Run dialog box

2.   Within the Run dialog box, type *DCOMCNFG* in the *Open* field.

3.   Click your mouse on the OK button. Windows NT will open the DCOM Configuration Properties dialog box.

The DCOM Configuration Properties dialog box has three tabs, Applications, Default Properties, and Default Security, as shown in Figure 330.

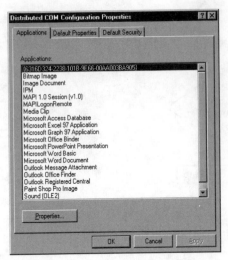

Figure 330 *The DCOM Configuration Properties dialog box.*

The Applications tab lets you specify custom configurations for each application. To specify an option, select the application you want to configure and click your mouse on the Properties button. Table 330 describes configuration options.

Option	Function
Location	Lets you specify where you want to run the application.
Security	Lets you specify user permissions for access, execution, and application-specific configurations.
Identity	Lets you specify which users can run the application.

Table 330 *Custom DCOM configuration options.*

The Default Properties tab lets you enable or disable DCOM (if you disable DCOM, applications will not be able to remotely access other components). Additionally, it lets you configure packet-level security and the application's ability to identify who is making requests and whether the application can perform operations based on that identification. These properties apply to all DCOM applications. The Default Security tab lets you configure user permissions for access, launch, and application configuration for all applications.

Answer D is correct because DCOMCNFG.EXE is the correct application you use to configure DCOM functionality. Answer A is incorrect because there is no such utility as Dconfig. Answer B is incorrect because Disk Administrator cannot configure DCOM. Answer C is incorrect because you can configure DCOM.

331   SETTING PRIORITIES ON APPLICATIONS

Q: *Which of the following is the maximum base priority at which you can start an application?*

Choose the best answer:

A.   30

B.   24

C.   13

D.   8

As you learned in Tip 316, application requests to the processor (threads) each have a priority. A thread's base priority is the priority the application issues the thread and is based on the application that issues it. The thread's priority will determine how frequently the computer's processor checks the thread and performs the thread's requested operations. Windows NT assigns priorities to all applications and uses these priorities, together with the thread-specific priorities, to determine how much time the processor gives to threads from a specific application. To give users a high-level application control, Windows NT lets you change an application's base priority to enhance or inhibit its performance. You can also change the base priority of a given thread within the application.

Applications have 32 priority levels. Priorities 0 through 15 are typically user applications and non-critical system components. The operating system reserve priorities 16 through 31 for real-time applications that cannot be paged (that is, they must stay in real memory, and the operating system cannot pass them to virtual memory) and critical system components, such as the operating system kernel.

You can use command line switches to manually set application base priority to four levels. To manually designate a specific base priority at startup, you must start the application from the command prompt. You start an application from the command prompt with the Start command and use the following syntax:

```
C:\> start /variablename executable   <ENTER>
```

For example, to start Word for Windows with the highest possible base priority, you would enter the following line at the command prompt:

```
C:\> start /realtime winword.exe   <ENTER>
```

After an application has started, you can change its base priority within the Windows NT Task Manager. You will learn more about the Windows NT Task Manager in the following Tip.

Table 331 describes an application's command line switches and the resulting base priority.

Command line switch	Base priority
realtime	24
high	13
normal	8
low	4

*Table 331 The **start** command line switches that affect base priority.*

Note: Only users with administrator privileges can use the realtime switch.

Answer B is correct because 24 is the highest base priority a user can specify. Answers A, C, and D are incorrect because the answers are either higher or lower than the maximum base priority possible.

332 INTRODUCING THE WINDOWS NT TASK MANAGER

Q: What Windows NT program displays information about running applications, memory, and CPU usage?

Choose all answers that apply:

> A.   *Disk Administrator*
>
> B.   *User Manager*
>
> C.   *Task Manager*
>
> D.   *Event Viewer*

The Windows NT administrator can use the Task Manager to view information about the computer and applications that are currently running. To help categorize the information (which can be quite sizeable on a busy server), the Task Manager dialog box has three tabs: Applications, Processes, and Performance, as shown in Figure 332.

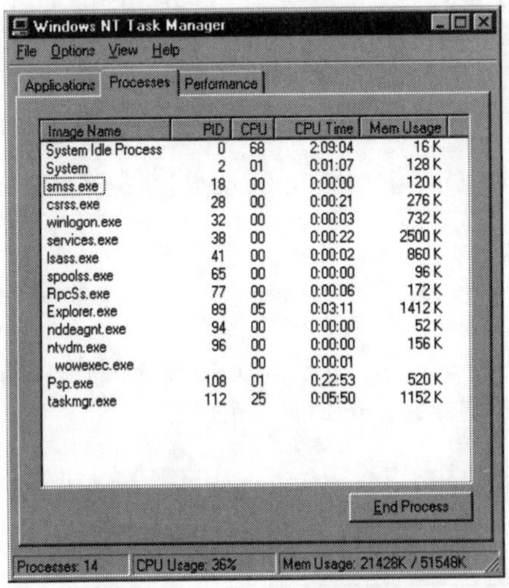

Figure 332 *The Windows NT Task Manager displays three tabs which categorize system tasks.*

Each Windows NT Task Manager tab lets you view current system information and configuration options differently. To display the Task Manager, right-click your mouse on an unused part of the Taskbar. Windows NT, in turn, will display a small pop-up menu. Within the menu, click your mouse on the Task Manager option. Table 332 describes each tab and its function.

Tab	Function
Application	Displays each application's name and describes the application's status.
Processes	Displays currently running processes and statistics about the processes.
Performance	Graphically displays CPU and memory usage. Also provides numeric values for a variety of system components.

Table 332 *Windows NT Task Manager tabs and their functions.*

You can also change applications' or processes' configurations and start or halt processes within the Task Manager. To change an application's or process's configuration, right click your mouse on its name in the appropriate list. To start or halt an application or process, use the corresponding buttons at the bottom of Task Manager.

Answer C is correct because Task Manager can display information about running applications, memory, and CPU usage. Answer A, B, and D are incorrect because these programs cannot configure or view information about an application or process.

333   **INTRODUCING THE MICROSOFT WINDOWS NT NETWORK ARCHITECTURE**

Q: *What are the Windows NT network architecture's three layers?*

Choose all answers that apply:

> A.   *Foundation*
>
> B.   *File system drivers*
>
> C.   *Protocols*
>
> D.   *Network adapter card drivers*

Network architecture defines the layers or components that make up the network hardware and software. The Windows NT network architecture consists of different components that have three basic layers: file system drivers, protocols, and network adapter card drivers. The Windows NT network also has two special layers, *boundary layers*, which provide standardized communication between the other layers. Boundary layers consist of the Transport Driver Interface (TDI) and Network Device Interface Specification (NDIS) 4.0.

To establish network communication, any operating system must perform four basic steps. First, it must identify the information that the network hardware must transport. Next, the operating system breaks down the information into pieces that it can transport (often called packets or frames).

After creating the packets, the operating system applies rules for transportation (which rules will depend on *network protocols*) of those packets. Finally, the operating system and the computer's internal hardware convert the information into a form that the network hardware can understand—generally, electrical pulses.

When Windows NT has information that a computer must send over the network, the operating system passes the information through the layers, which break it into smaller pieces, apply transportation rules to the pieces, and translate the information into a form the network card can understand.

When a network card on a Windows NT computer receives information, it passes that information to the operating system, which then passes the information back up through the layers. The layers, in turn, strip away the transportation rules, translate the information from packets back into its original form, and reassemble the pieces to form the original information. Figure 333 illustrates the Windows NT network architecture.

Answers B, C, and D are correct because they name Windows NT network architecture's layers. Answer A is incorrect because there is no Foundation network layer.

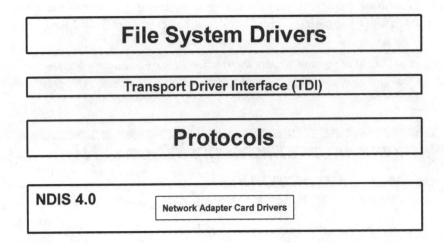

Figure 333 *The Windows NT network Architecture.*

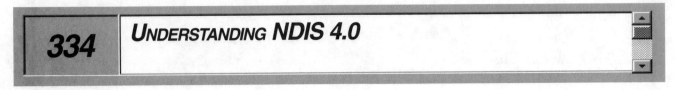

Q: Which of the following best describes NDIS 4.0?

Choose the best answer:

    A.   *A standard method of network communication*

    B.   *A set of standard regulations for applications*

    C.   *A standard for communication between protocols and network interface card drivers*

    D.   *A standard for network interface cards that understand all protocols*

The Network Device Interface Specification (NDIS) 4.0 is a set of rules that define a method for protocols to communicate with network interface card (NIC) drivers. Providing a standard for communication between protocols and network card drivers lets developers produce a protocol without including code for specific hardware. Because Windows NT supports the NDIS 4.0 standard, any NDIS 4.0-compliant network interface card will be NT compatible. The following list describes features that NDIS 4.0 provides in Windows NT:

- Unlimited number of network interface cards

- Unlimited number of protocols that the operating system can bind to a single network interface card

- Communication between the network interface card and its associated Windows NT driver

- Independence between network interface cards and protocols

The file in Windows NT that provides the NDIS 4.0 functionality is *NDIS.SYS*, which programmers sometimes refer to as the NDIS wrapper because it is a code library that produces a layer around device drivers to separate the drivers from the network interface card and the protocol. Figure 334 illustrates the NDIS layer that surrounds the network interface card device drivers.

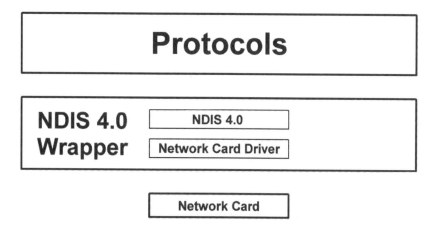

Figure 334 The NDIS 4.0 wrapper separates the device drivers from the network interface card and the network protocol..

Answer C *is correct because NDIS 4.0 correctly describes a standard for communication between protocols and network interface card drivers.* **Answers A, B,** *and* **D** *are incorrect because they do not accurately describe NDIS 4.0.*

335   **INTRODUCING NETWORK PROTOCOLS IN WINDOWS NT**

Q: *Which of the following best describes an agreed upon set of communication standards that governs data transport over a network?*

Choose the best answer:

> A.   *Application Programming Interface*
>
> B.   *Protocol*
>
> C.   *Dynamic Link Library*
>
> D.   *Executable*

Throughout this book, you have and will continue to repeatedly encounter the term network protocol (sometimes transport protocol). As you have learned, the word "network" describes both the physical and virtual connection that establishes communication between computers. The word "protocol" describes an agreed upon set of standards that govern a specific task or event. For example, military protocol sets standards, such as the salute two officers exchange when they meet.

The lesser-ranked officer must salute first, but the higher-ranking officer can wait for the initial salute. However, after the lesser-ranked officer gives the salute, the higher-ranking officer must return the salute. Because of the rules the protocol establishes, officers exchange salutes the same way every time and think little about what to do. A network protocol is therefore a set of communication standards that govern information transportation across a network—standards that operate automatically, without direct instruction from the operating system. Network protocols provide a set of rules for network communications that reduce the amount of processing the operating system must perform to achieve data transport.

Windows NT includes the following transport protocols:

- TCP/IP
- NWLINK
- NetBEUI
- AppleTalk

Windows NT also includes the DLC protocol. However, programmers do not consider DLC a transport protocol, because they primarily use DLC to establish communication between printers and computers physically connected to the network, or to access Systems Network Architecture (SNA) computers.

Programmers must implement and configure the same transport protocol the same way, with the same configuration specifics, on each computer in the network to establish communication.

Answer B is correct because the term protocol best describes an agreed upon set of communication standards that governs data transport over a network. Answer A is incorrect because the term Application Programming Interface (API) describes a set of standards for application design. Answer C is incorrect because a Dynamic-Link Library is a file that stores code that multiple programs can access. Answer D is incorrect because the term executable describes a file that initiates a program.

| 336 | INTRODUCING THE MULTIPLE UNC PROVIDER (MUP) | |

Q: Which Windows NT component maintains a list of active UNC names and determines the most appropriate redirector for UNC-compliant applications?

Choose the best answer:

A.   *Multiple Provider Router (MPR)*

B.   *Multiple UNC Provider (MUP)*

C.   *NT Virtual DOS Machine (NTVDM)*

D.   *Distributed Component Object Model (DCOM)*

As you have learned about other Windows NT components, Microsoft designed the Windows NT network architecture in a modular fashion so that third-party programmers can write components that they can then seamlessly add to Windows NT. A component that networking systems manufacturers may want to include in Windows NT is a *redirector*.

The redirector is responsible for pointing application requests to specific computers on the network. Each network structure may require its own redirector to pass application requests to the network.

Many applications include internal support for the Universal Naming Convention (UNC), and can use the UNC to point to a remote computer.

The Windows NT Multiple UNC Provider (MUP) maintains a list of active UNCs on the network, which it then provides to UNC-compliant applications. This prevents applications from having to maintain their own UNC lists and reduces network traffic.

The Windows NT Workstation service requires the Multiple UNC Provider, which it considers as part of the File and Print sharing components. The Windows NT Server service does not require the Multiple UNC Provider, but you will almost always install it anyway, because most network protocols will require it.

Answer B is correct because the term that best describes the Windows NT component that maintains a list of active UNC names and determines the most appropriate redirector for UNC-compliant applications is the Multiple UNC Provider. Answer A is incorrect because the Multiple Provider Router determines the most appropriate redirector for non-UNC-compliant applications. Answer C is incorrect because an NT Virtual DOS Machine provides a shell in which MS-DOS and Win16-based applications can run. Answer D is incorrect because the Distributed Component Object Model provides applications enhanced Client–Server functionality.

337 INTRODUCING THE MULTIPLE PROVIDER ROUTER (MPR)

Q: *Which of the following Windows NT components determines the most appropriate redirector for non-UNC-compliant applications?*

Choose the best answer:

      A.   *Multiple UNC Provider (MUP)*

      B.   *Multiple Provider Router (MPR)*

      C.   *Primary Domain Controller (PDC)*

      D.   *NT Virtual DOS Machine (NTVDM)*

As you learned in the previous Tip, Windows NT can support multiple redirectors and must determine the most appropriate redirector for an application to use. UNC-compliant applications receive this determination from the Multiple UNC Provider (MUP).

However, non-UNC-compliant applications may still require a redirector. Windows NT, therefore, provides the Multiple Provider Router (MPR), a component that determines the most appropriate redirector for non-UNC-compliant applications.

The MPR is similar to the MUP in that it determines the most appropriate redirector for an application to use. Each redirector has its own dynamic-link library (DLL) file, which establishes communication between the redirector and the MPR. The MPR intercepts application requests for a network resource.

The MPR then queries the redirectors for the one with the highest priority that indicates it can establish a path to the remote computer. The MPR functions slightly differently from the MUP. Figure 337 illustrates the MPR's functionality as compared to the MUP's functionality.

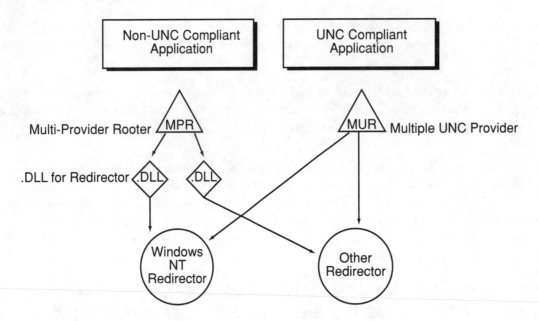

Figure 337 *The MPR uses network redirectors without UNC conformance.*

Answer B *is correct because the component that determines the most appropriate redirector for non-UNC-compliant applications is the Multiple Provider Router (MPR).* **Answer A** *is incorrect because the Multiple UNC provider determines the most appropriate redirector for UNC-compliant applications.* **Answer C** *is incorrect because a Primary Domain Controller designates a Windows NT server's role on the network.* **Answer D** *is incorrect because an NT Virtual DOS Machine provides a shell in which MS-DOS and Win16-based applications can run.*

338 — **UNDERSTANDING THE TRANSPORT DRIVER INTERFACE (TDI)**

Q: *Which of the following Windows NT architectural components separates the protocol drivers from the file system drivers?*

Choose the best answer:

    A. *Transport Driver Interface (TDI)*

    B. *Network Device Interface Specification (NDIS)*

    C. *Multiple Provider Router (MPR)*

    D. *Multiple UNC Provider (MUP)*

In Tip 333, you learned that the Windows NT network architecture has three standard layers that two boundary layers separate. The Transport Driver Interface Driver (TDI) is the boundary layer that separates the file system drivers from the protocol layer.

Separating the file system drivers from the protocol layer lets developers produce protocols without including code for every possible redirector. This separation also lets developers produce redirectors for networking systems without including code for every possible protocol. Because the protocol layer is separate from the file system, developers can add or remove protocols without reconfiguring the entire networking architecture.

Answer A is correct because the Transport Driver Interface (TDI) separates the protocol drivers from the file system drivers. Answer B is incorrect because Network Device Interface Specification (NDIS) describes a standard for network interface card drivers. Answer C is incorrect because the Multiple Provider Router (MPR) provides redirector decisions for non-UNC-compliant applications. Answer D is incorrect because the Multiple UNC Provider (MUP) provides redirector decisions for UNC-compliant applications.

339   **UNDERSTANDING FILE SYSTEM DRIVERS**

Q: Which of the following standard layers of the Windows NT network architecture contains the Workstation service and redirectors?

Choose the best answer:

     A.   File system drivers

     B.   Protocols

     C.   Network Adapter Card Drivers

     D.   Transport Driver Interface

As you have learned, the Windows NT network architecture has three standard layers and two boundary layers that separate the standard layers from each other. The uppermost standard network architecture layer contains the *file system drivers*. The file system drivers layer contains the Server service, which is responsible for file and printer sharing to the network. This layer also contains the Workstation service, which is responsible for connecting to remote computers, and the redirectors, which are responsible for diverting information to remote locations on the network. File system drivers communicate with the protocol layer (the next standard layer in the architecture) through the Transport Driver Interface (TDI) boundary layer.

Answer A is correct because the standard layer in the Windows NT network architecture that contains the Workstation service and redirectors is the file system drivers layer. Answer B is incorrect because the protocols layer contains only protocol drivers. Answer C is incorrect because the network adapter card layer contains network interface card drivers. Answer D is incorrect because the Transport Driver Interface (TDI) is a boundary layer that separates the file system driver and protocol layers.

340   **UNDERSTANDING A DISTRIBUTED PROCESS**

Q: Which of the following best describes the term distributed process?

Choose the best answer:

     A.   An application that distributes information to remote computers.

     B.   A Windows NT networking component that distributes packets to the network.

     C.   An application divided into two or more parts with components that run on more than one computer.

     D.   A popular method of selling computers.

As you learned in Tip 329, the computer industry uses the terms client–server and distributed processing to describe an application that has two or more components that run on separate connected computers. An excellent example of a distributed process is a network electronic mail (e-mail) system. In an e-mail system, users run a client-based application to create and read e-mails, while a server-based application acts as a post office, which distributes and sometimes stores e-mails. Because neither the client nor the server application will work without the other, an e-mail system is functionally a single application that has separate components. A client–server application is a distributed process because either application can cause its remote counterpart to perform operations on its host computer.

Answer C is correct because the term distributed process is an application that has two or more parts with components that run on more than one computer. Answers A, B, and D are incorrect because the answers do not describe the term distributed process.

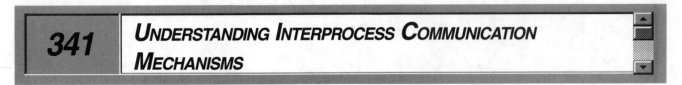

341   UNDERSTANDING INTERPROCESS COMMUNICATION MECHANISMS

Q: *Which of the following are Interprocess Communication (IPC) Mechanisms that Windows NT supports?*

Choose all answers that apply:

    A.   *TCP/IP*

    B.   *NetBIOS*

    C.   *Named Pipes*

    D.   *MailSlots*

To communicate effectively, a distributed process must be able to establish direct communication between the client and server applications. The system objects that establish this connection between the two inter-communication components are known as *Interprocess Communication Mechanisms (IPCs)*. Windows NT includes the following IPCs:

- Server Message Blocks (SMBs)
- Network Dynamic Data Exchange (NetDDE)
- Mailslots
- NetBIOS
- Windows Sockets
- Named Pipes
- Local Procedure Calls (LPCs)
- Remote Procedure Calls (RPCs)
- Distributed Component Object Model (DCOM)

The operating system implements each IPC differently and each has its strengths and weaknesses. Because Windows NT includes many IPCs, it can support several different client–server application structures.

Answers B, C, and D are correct because they are Interprocess Communication Mechanisms that Windows NT supports. Answer A is incorrect because TCP/IP is a transport protocol suite, not an IPC.

342 ACCESSING FILE AND PRINT RESOURCES

Q: Which Windows NT component determines whether a requested resource is on the local computer or at a remote location on the network?

Choose the best answer:

    A.   Server service

    B.   Multiple Provider Router (MPR)

    C.   Multiple UNC Provider (MUP)

    D.   Workstation service

The main reason computer scientists created computer networks was so that client computers could access remote printers and store files in a central location. The Windows NT file and print sharing components consist of the Multiple Provider Router (MPR), the Multiple UNC Provider (MUP), the Server service, and the Workstation service.

The Workstation service is responsible for locating the correct component that can provide an application with resources it requests. This means that the Workstation service is the Windows NT component that determines whether an application request is for the local computer or for a network resource. As you learned in Tips 337 and 338, the Workstation service requires the MUP and MPR components.

The Server service is a direct counterpart to the Workstation service and is responsible for advertising available resources to the network (by sending resource lists to the appropriate network protocols). It is also responsible for passing network requests to the I/O manager. The I/O manager governs all communications to file systems and network resources. Figure 342 illustrates the relationship between the server and workstation services.

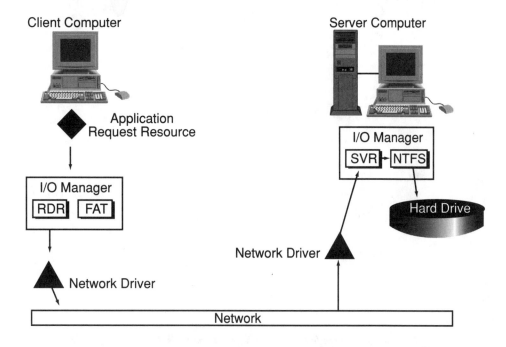

Figure 342 A client computer accessing a network resource.

*Answer D is correct because the workstation service determines whether a requested resource is on the local computer or at a remote location on the network. **Answer A** is incorrect because the server service is responsible for receiving network requests and passing them to the I/O manager. **Answer B** is incorrect because the MPR determines the most appropriate redirector for non-UNC-compliant applications. **Answer C** is incorrect because the MUP determines the most appropriate redirector for UNC-compliant applications.*

---

343   INTRODUCING THE DISTRIBUTED FILE SYSTEM

Q: *How can you install the Distributed File System utility?*

Choose the best answer:

     A.   *From the support folder on the Windows NT compact disk*

     B.   *From the Add/Remove Programs option in the Windows NT Control Panel*

     C.   *You must get the Distributed File System (DFS) utility from Microsoft and install it as a service*

     D.   *There is no such thing as a Distributed File System Utility*

The *Distributed File System (DFS)* is a network share management utility that lets you build a single tree of resources from shares on multiple computers. Because Windows NT and Windows 95 support the Distributed File System, you can take network shares from all computers with these operating systems and combine the shares into a single tree that the user may browse through to locate a resource. Figure 343 illustrates the DFS concept.

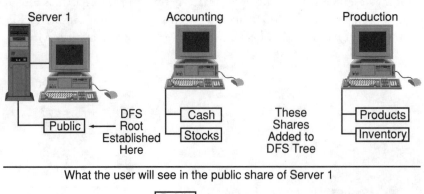

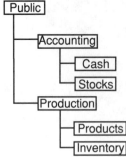

Figure 343 The Distributed File System (DFS) lets you combine and view network shares within a single tree.

Note: Computers must have DFS support installed so that a user can view a DFS tree.

You can get the DFS support for Windows NT and Windows 95 from Microsoft. If you have an Internet connection, you can download the system and tools free from Microsoft's Web site at *http://www.microsoft.com*. If you do not have an Internet connection, contact Microsoft for instructions on how to get DFS. You install DFS as a Windows NT service and manage it through the DFS Administrator program, which you can find in the Administrative Tools group after you have installed DFS.

Answer C is correct because the DFS tool must be obtained from Microsoft and is installed as a service. Answers A and B are incorrect because the DFS tool is not included in Windows NT. Answer D is incorrect because there is a Distributed File System(DFS) tool.

| 344 | INTRODUCING THE NETWORK PROGRAM IN THE CONTROL PANEL |

Q: You are a Windows NT domain administrator. You have just installed a new Network Interface Card (NIC) on a Windows NT standalone server and want to install and configure the card's device drivers. What option in the Windows NT Control Panel lets you install and configure Network Adapter Cards?

Choose the best answer:

   A.   Devices

   B.   Network

   C.   System

   D.   Services

As you have learned, developers designed Windows NT for networking; therefore, it supports a wide range of networking products. The Windows NT computer administrator must be able to make configuration changes to networking components. Such components may include the computer's name on the network, the domain's name, what protocols the computer will use to access the network and how to configure them, and what kind of Network Interface Cards (NICs) are installed in the computer and their configurations. You perform network configuration from the Network dialog box. The Network option in the Windows NT Control Panel lets you configure network-specific components. You can also access the Network dialog box as the Properties screen for the Network Neighborhood (by right-clicking your mouse on the Network Neighborhood icon and then selecting Properties from the pop-up menu). The Network dialog box has five tabs, Identification, Services, Protocols, Adapters, and Bindings, that categorize the configuration options, as shown in Figure 344. Each tab within the Network dialog box gives you different configuration options. Table 344 describes each tab and its configuration options.

Tab	Configuration options
Identification	Lets you change the computer's name, or change the computer's workgroup-domain configuration.
Services	Lets you add or remove services and configure their properties.
Protocols	Lets you add or remove protocols and configure their properties (if the protocol is configurable).
Adapters	Lets you add, remove, or configure Network Interface Cards (NICs).
Bindings	Lets you view and change the properties and order of the relationship between services, protocols, and adapters.

Table 344 The Network dialog box tabs and their configuration options.

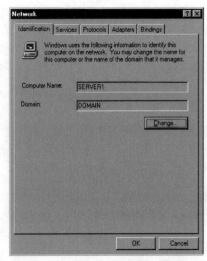

Figure 344 *The Network dialog box that you will use to configure Network access options.*

Answer B is correct because the Network option in Windows NT Control Panel lets you install and configure Network Adapter Cards. Answers A, C, and D are incorrect because these options will not let you install, configure, or remove Network Interface Cards.

345 INSTALLING NETWORK PROTOCOLS

Q: *You are a Windows NT domain administrator. You have just installed a new protocol to your Windows NT server. You must restart the computer before this new protocol will function.*

True or False?

As you have learned, a network protocol is a set or rules that define how two programs will communicate across the a network. Installing a network protocol in Windows NT is really quite easy. Although different protocols will have a greater or lesser number of configurable options—which may make getting the protocol to work correctly difficult— the protocol's actual installation is very simple. For example, the TCP/IP protocol has many options that you can configure. When you install TCP/IP, Windows NT will prompt you to supply your network's configuration information. On the other hand, you can install the NetBEUI protocol in a single step because it has no configuration options. You install both protocols from the Network dialog box. To install a network protocol, perform the following steps:

1. Within Windows NT, click your mouse on the Start menu Settings submenu Control Panel option. Windows NT will open the Control Panel window.

2. Within the Control Panel window, double click your mouse on the Network option. Windows NT will open the Network dialog box.

3. Within the Network dialog box, click your mouse on the Protocols tab. Windows NT will change your view to the Protocols tab.

4. Within the Protocols tab, click your mouse on the Add button. Windows NT will build and open the Select Network Protocol dialog box.

5. Within the Select Network Protocol dialog box, click your mouse on the protocol name you want to install in the Network Protocol list. Windows NT will highlight the protocol name to indicate your selection.

6. Click your mouse on the OK button. Windows NT will install the protocol and prompt you for any additional input the protocol may require—such as computer names and addresses, DHCP configuration, and so on. (Each protocol will require different inputs, except NetBIOS which, of course, requires no inputs.)

7. Click your mouse on the OK button. Windows NT will close the Network dialog box and display a message box that prompts you to restart your computer.

8. Within the message box, click your mouse on the Yes button. Windows NT will restart your computer.

Windows NT includes six protocols you can choose from, as shown in Figure 345.

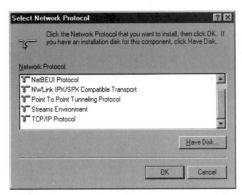

Figure 345 Protocol Choices Windows NT includes.

*The answer is **True** because you must restart the computer before a newly added protocol will function.*

346   **INTRODUCTION TO MICROSOFT *TCP/IP***

Q: *What does the acronym TCP/IP stand for?*

Choose the best answer:

     A.   *Transport Carrier Protocol / Internet Protocol*

     B.   *Transport Contention Protocol / Internal Protocol*

     C.   *Transmission Control Protocol / Internet Protocol*

     D.   *Transmission Control Protocol / Internal Protocol*

In Tip 335, you learned that a protocol is an agreed on set of standards. For example, in most countries, people expect you to offer your hand and say hello when you meet someone. However, in other countries, you may offend someone by offering to shake their hand, and they may not understand your greeting.

In computer networking, a protocol is a method a computer uses to communicate information to another computer. Just as a human protocol dictates behavior, a networking protocol dictates how a computer packages and transmits data along a network cable. If one computer does not understand or share the other protocol, the computers will be unable to communicate. Several networking protocols exist, but this Tip introduces you to only one, the Transmission Control Protocol / Internet Protocol (TCP/IP) protocol suite.

The TCP/IP protocol is actually many protocols working together. Over the last 28 years, several different individuals and organizations have collaborated to create TCP/IP, and those applications continue to work on the various components of the protocol to this day. Networking professionals often refer to TCP/IP as a *protocol suite* because it encompasses many different protocols. TCP/IP is a big subject that an entire book could cover—in fact, entire books have been written about the Internet Protocol, which is only a portion of the TCP/IP suite. In fact, Microsoft has an official curriculum five-day course (taught at Authorized Technical Education Centers (ATEC)) on TCP/IP, which is one of the MCSE elective exams.

As you have learned, TCP/IP is a suite of protocols. The two major protocols that make up TCP/IP are Transmission Control Protocol (TCP), and Internet Protocol (IP). TCP packages the data and ensures proper delivery of the data to the remote computer. IP is responsible for addressing the package that TCP creates to ensure that the right computer receives the data. Although none of the core exams require in-depth TCP/IP knowledge, several questions throughout the core exams require you to have a basic TCP/IP understanding. The TCP/IP knowledge that the core exams might test you on includes: configuring TCP/IP, testing TCP/IP, and troubleshooting TCP/IP. To become familiar with the TCP/IP protocol, you must know the TCP/IP core protocols. Table 346 lists the TCP/IP core protocols.

Protocol	Description
NetBIOS	Network Basic Input Output System (NetBIOS) provides a standard interface for TCP/IP.
WinSockets	Windows Sockets (WinSocks) is an Application Programming Interface (API) that provides a way for applications to use TCP/IP.
TCP	Transmission Control Protocol (TCP) provides connection-oriented, reliable communication sessions between two computers. TCP is a transport protocol, which means that TCP packages the data and delivers information across the network cable.
UDP	User Datagram Protocol (UDP) provides connectionless communications. UDP does not establish sessions between computers, and does not provide reliable data transmission. The application is responsible for reliable data delivery.
IP	Internet Protocol (IP) addresses and routes data packages (frames). IP does not guarantee that the frames will reach the intended computer. Higher-level protocols ensure that the intended computer receives the data properly.
IGMP	Internet Group Management Protocol (IGMP) reports host group memberships to local multicast routers.
ICMP	Internet Control Message Protocol (ICMP) reports errors and sends messages at the time of a frame's delivery.
ARP	Address Resolution Protocol (ARP) gets the destination computer's hardware address. Programmers refer to a hardware address as a Media Access Control (MAC) address.

Table 346 The TCP/IP core protocols.

TCP/IP uses an addressing scheme in which each computer that is using TCP/IP will have a unique address the administrator normally assigns (unless you are using a DHCP server). A TCP/IP address is actually a 32-bit number, which you can express as a binary, hexadecimal, or dotted decimal notation. Binary numbers are 1s or 0s; to have a 32-bit number you would have a combination of 32 ones and zeros that make up each computer's TCP/IP address. Because TCP/IP addresses are like your home address (no two locations can have the exact same address), using a binary notation to address your computers would be inconvenient. Hexadecimal notation is a series of numbers and letters that make up your total address, and would also be hard to administer. Because binary numbers and hexadecimal notation are so complex, the most common (and generally, easiest to understand) way to express your computers' TCP/IP addresses is to use dotted decimal notation (such as 111.212.211.112).

You express dotted decimal notation in sections called *octets*. An octet is one quarter of the total 32-bit number, so each TCP/IP address has four octets. Each octet can have a number between zero and 255, which means that one octet has a possible 256 combinations. Because each address has four octets, each with a possible 256 combinations, an entire TCP/IP address has a total of 4,294,967,296 combinations. Although over four billion possible TCP/IP addresses exist, it is still likely that the Internet will run out, because of the way the addresses are constructed.

A computer's TCP/IP address includes two sections: the *network identification* and the *host identification*. The network identification tells your computer which addresses are on your local network, and which addresses are in remote networks. This distinction is important for routing information between computers in different networks. The other TCP/IP address section is the host identification, which identifies the local computer. The network and host identifications are similar to your postal code and home address—one identifies your general area, and the other identifies the exact location within the general area.

You must configure the TCP/IP address you are assigning to the computer and the *subnet mask* so that TCP/IP will function properly. You express a subnet mask the same as a computer's TCP/IP address; in dotted decimal notation. TCP/IP uses a subnet mask to determine whether the destination address you computer is trying to reach is in the local network, or on a remote network. Subnet masks are very complex, and you probably will not have to determine your own subnet mask in your own network. You will most likely get your TCP/IP address range from your local service provider, who will also give you your network's proper subnet mask. In Tips 347 and 348, you will examine the dialog box that you will use to configure TCP/IP, and how to configure TCP/IP automatically.

Answer C is correct; TCP/IP stands for Transmission Control Protocol / Internet Protocol. ***Answer A, B, and D are incorrect*** *because none of these are correct acronyms for TCP/IP.*

347   CONFIGURING *TCP/IP* MANUALLY

Q: *What two pieces of information must you specify in order to use the TCP/IP protocol on a computer?*

Choose all correct answers:

     A.   *IP address*

     B.   *Default Gateway*

     C.   *Subnet Mask*

     D.   *DNS IP Address*

In Tip 346, you learned that Transmission Control Protocol / Internet Protocol (TCP/IP) requires every computer in your network to have a unique address. Network administrators refer to a computer's unique TCP/IP address as the IP address. In addition to the IP address that you must specify for each computer in your network, you must specify a subnet mask.

Remember, the subnet mask helps TCP/IP determine if the destination computer is on the local network, or a remote network. An administrator must assign an IP address and a subnet mask, either manually or by using a Dynamic Host Configuration Protocol (DHCP) server. A DHCP server automatically assigns TCP/IP addresses to computers that the administrator configures to use DHCP. You will learn more about DHCP in Tip 348.

You will configure TCP/IP properties from the Network dialog box in the Control Panel. In the Network dialog box, you can also specify additional information such as the *Domain Name System (DNS)* server. A DNS server is a computer that resolves computer names (such as *www.jamsa.com*) to IP address (such as 111.212.112.112). Programs use the DNS to access Web sites and to access computers in remote networks by computer name, therefore, DNS is an essential TCP/IP component. To manually configure a TCP/IP Windows NT computer, perform the following steps:

1. Within Windows NT, click your mouse on the Start menu Settings submenu Control Panel option. Windows NT will open the Control Panel window.

2. Within the Control Panel window, double-click your mouse on the Network icon. Windows NT will open the Network dialog box.

3. Within the Network dialog box, click your mouse on the Protocols tab. The Network dialog box will switch to the Protocols tab.

4. Within the Protocols tab, double-click your mouse on the TCP/IP protocol in the *Network Protocols* field. Windows NT will open the Microsoft TCP/IP Properties dialog box.

5. Within the Microsoft TCP/IP Properties dialog box, specify the IP address and subnet mask, as shown in Figure 347.

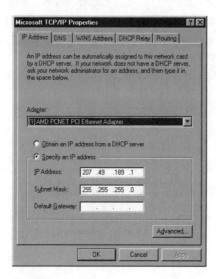

Figure 347 Configuring TCP/IP manually.

6. Within the Properites dialog box, click your mouse on the OK button. Windows NT will close the Microsoft TCP/IP Properties dialog box.

7. Within the Network dialog box, click your mouse on the OK button. Windows NT will close the Network dialog box and prompt you to restart Windows NT.

Answers A and C are correct because you must have an IP address and a subnet mask to use the TCP/IP protocol. Answers B and D are incorrect because you would only configure the Default Gateway if you were connecting to remote networks, and you would only use a Domain Name System (DNS) server address for computer name resolution of computers in remote networks.

348   CONFIGURING *TCP/IP* AUTOMATICALLY

Q: *What must you do to have a Windows NT Workstation get a TCP/IP address from a DHCP server?*

Choose all correct answers:

A.   *Install the TCP/IP protocol.*

B.   *Manually specify a DNS server.*

C.   *Select an IP address from a DHCP server option in the TCP/IP Properties dialog box.*

D.   *Do nothing. Your computer will automatically find a DHCP server and configure itself.*

As you have learned, TCP/IP requires each computer in your network to have a unique address, and that the addresses are 32-bit numbers expressed in dotted decimal notation. Because it is a difficult task to set up several computers that each have a different IP address, Microsoft included the *Microsoft Dynamic Host Configuration Protocol (DHCP)* server software with the Windows NT Server CD-ROM.

DHCP is a service you can install on a Windows NT server computer. In general, a DHCP server will provide IP addresses to DHCP client computers. Not all computers can get their IP addresses from a DHCP server; only computers that have a DHCP client running will be able to automatically obtain IP addresses from DHCP servers. To configure a DHCP client to get an IP address from a DHCP server, perform the following steps:

1. Within Windows NT, click your mouse on the Start menu Settings submenu Control Panel option. Windows NT will open the Control Panel window.

2. Within the Control Panel window, double-click your mouse on the Network icon. Windows NT will open the Network dialog box.

3. Within the Network dialog box, click your mouse on the Protocols tab. The Network dialog box will switch to the Protocols tab.

4. Within the Protocols tab, double-click your mouse on the TCP/IP protocol in the *Network Protocols* field. Windows NT will open the Microsoft TCP/IP Properties dialog box.

5. Within the Microsoft TCP/IP Properties dialog box, click your mouse on the Obtain an IP address from a DHCP server radio button. Click your mouse on the OK button. Windows NT will close the Microsoft TCP/IP Properties dialog box.

6. Within the Network dialog box, click your mouse on the OK button. Windows NT will close the Network dialog box.

Figure 348 shows how to configure a DHCP client Windows NT computer.

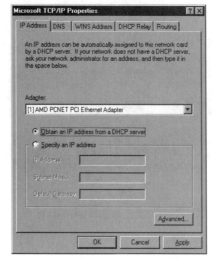

Figure 348 Configuring a DHCP client in a Windows NT computer's TCP/IP Properties dialog box.

*Answers A and C are correct because you must install the TCP/IP protocol and check the Obtain IP address from a DHCP server radio button. **Answer B** is incorrect because it is not necessary to specify a DNS server. DNS servers provide computer name resolution to IP addresses, and TCP/IP does not require them. **Answer D** is incorrect because Windows NT computers will require you to specify that you are using a DHCP server.*

349	USING **PING** TO TEST **TCP/IP** CONNECTIVITY

Q: *You are a Microsoft network administrator. You have just installed TCP/IP on all your client computers. You now want to test your TCP/IP configuration. What is the best way to test TCP/IP to see if you can connect to another computer?*

Choose the best answer:

> A.   *Use a cable tester.*
>
> B.   *Use a multimeter.*
>
> C.   *Use PING.*
>
> D.   *Use Network Neighborhood.*

In Tips 346, 347, and 348, you have learned what TCP/IP is, and where to make configurations on a computer to use TCP/IP. After you have installed TCP/IP, you must test your configuration to see if it works. The Packet Internet Groper (PING) utility lets you send a test message to a computer and receive a reply. PING lets you know if your TCP/IP protocol is working properly. When you use PING, you will specify a target computer that you want to reach. PING will send a series of four packets to the target computer. After the target computer receives the packets, it will return a series of four timed responses. When your computer receives the responses, it will display the times for each packet the target computer sent, as Figure 349.1 shows.

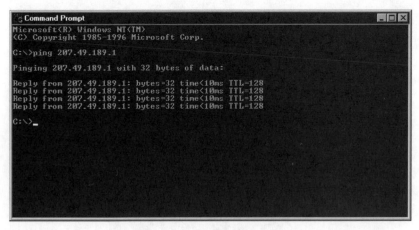

Figure 349.1 A PING response.

The syntax you will use for PING is PING *IP_address*. For example, you might invoke PING, as shown here:

```
C:\> PING 127.0.0.0   <ENTER>
```

If the target computer does not respond, PING will display the four messages as negative responses, such as Destination Host Unreachable, as Figure 349.2 shows.

Figure 349.2 *A PING negative response.*

Answer C *is correct because you can use PING to test the TCP/IP protocol.* **Answer A** *is incorrect because a cable tester cannot test the TCP/IP protocol.* **Answer B** *is incorrect because you would not use a multimeter to test TCP/IP.* **Answer D** *is incorrect because using the Network Neighborhood would not specifically test TCP/IP.*

350	USING **IPCONFIG** TO VERIFY **TCP/IP** CONFIGURATION

Q: You have just installed TCP/IP. You used PING to test your TCP/IP configuration. PING did not work—you received negative responses from the test packets. What would you do next to troubleshoot your TCP/IP configuration?

Choose the best answer:

        A.   *Remove TCP/IP and install it again.*

        B.   *Use IPCONFIG.*

        C.   *Shut down your computer, and then restart it.*

        D.   *Call Microsoft's tech support.*

After you have used PING to test TCP/IP, the next step is to use *IPCONFIG* to verify your TCP/IP configuration. *IPCONFIG* is a utility that lets you see all TCP/IP configuration information. If you type *IPCONFIG* at the command prompt, *IPCONFIG* will display the local computer's IP address and subnet mask.

You can use *IPCONFIG* to check for errors in IP address assignment, or other TCP/IP configuration parameters. *IPCONFIG* has several switches that will either expand the information that *IPCONFIG* will display, or let you change settings, as Figure 350.1 shows.

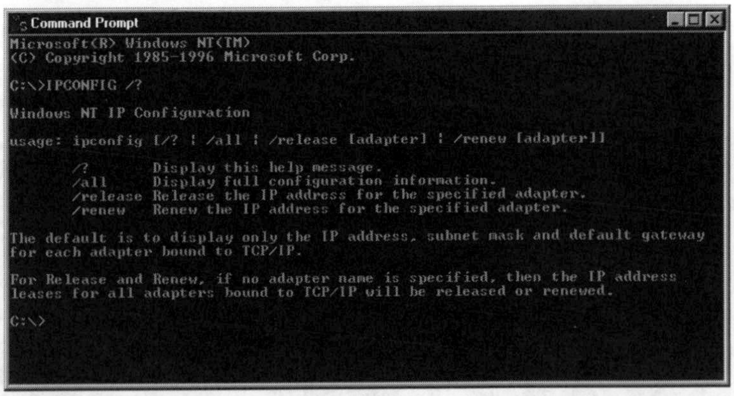

Figure 350.1 *IPCONFIG switches.*

IPCONFIG will not show you any configuration information that you cannot see in the Network dialog box. However, IPCONFIG will display all the TCP/IP configuration information on one screen, as Figure 350.2 shows, as opposed to the several tabs you must navigate in the Network dialog box.

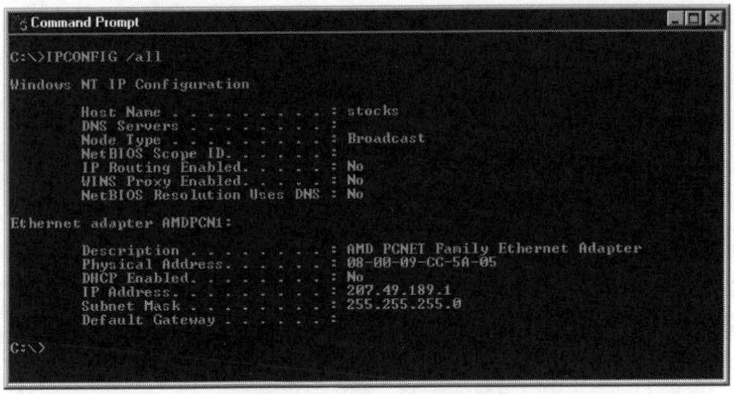

Figure 350.2 *IPCONFIG showing all configuration information.*

Answer B is correct because after you have used PING to test the TCP/IP protocol, you must use IPCONFIG to verify your computer's TCP/IP configuration. Answer A is incorrect because you may only have a minor TCP/IP configuration error that you can use IPCONFIG to find. Answer C is incorrect because shutting down your computer and then restarting it would not accomplish anything. Answer D is incorrect because calling Microsoft tech support may be unnecessary if you use IPCONFIG to solve the problem yourself.

351 INTRODUCTION TO **NWLINK**

Q: Which of the following network protocols is most commonly used for communicating with NetWare?

Choose the best answer:

     A.   *TCP/IP*

     B.   *NetBEUI*

     C.   *NWLINK*

     D.   *AppleTalk*

As you have learned, Windows NT uses various network protocols to establish communication with remote computers. One of the many useful network protocols Windows NT includes is *NWLINK*. NWLINK is the Microsoft implementation of the Novell NetWare proprietary IPX/SPX protocol (think of NWLINK as meaning NetWare Link). NWLINK is a NDIS 4.0-compliant 32-bit network protocol (sometimes called a transport protocol). NWLINK is a *routable* protocol, which means that it lets intermediate networks pass along data packets as the packets travel from the source computer to their destination.

For example, suppose that you have a computer that has two network interface cards and is physically connected to two separate networks, network 1 and network 2. In such a case, a signal from a remote computer on network 1 that is destined for a computer on network 2 can pass through the computer with the two network interface cards to the computer on network 2. In this example, the computer with two network interface cards is a router because its primary job is to pass packets from network 1 to network 2. To pass packets between networks in this way, the software must use a routable protocol.

Windows NT computers that require access to Novell NetWare servers commonly use the NWLINK protocol. Novell NetWare client computers that require access to applications or data on a Windows NT server will also use the NWLINK protocol. Small networks consisting of only Windows NT and Microsoft clients may also use NWLINK as the primary or only network protocol. NWLINK supports a variety of transport mechanisms:

- Novell NetBIOS

- Windows Sockets (WinSock)

- Remote Procedure Calls (RPC)

- Named Pipes

Answer C is correct because Windows-based systems commonly use the NWLINK protocol to communicate with Novell NetWare installations. Answers A, B, and D are incorrect because they list protocols Windows-based systems do not commonly use to communicate with Novell NetWare installations.

352   **CONFIGURING *NWLINK***

Q: *What is the Windows NT default Frame Type for NWLINK?*

Choose the best answer:

     A.   *802.2*

     B.   *802.3*

     C.   *802.5*

     D.   *Auto-detected*

NWLINK is a complex protocol with internal variables that must be the same for all computers in order for those computers to communicate correctly. For example, the sending PC and receiving PC must use the same frame size. To configure NWLINK, you will use the Windows NT Network dialog box. Specifically, to configure NWLINK, perform the following steps:

1. On the Windows NT Desktop, right-click your mouse on the Network Neighborhood icon and choose the Properties option from the pop-up menu that appears. Windows NT will open the Network dialog box.

2. Within the Network dialog box, click your mouse on the Protocols tab. Windows NT will display the Protocols sheet.

3. Within the Protocols sheet, double-click your mouse on the NWLINK IPX/SPX protocol. Windows NT will open the NWLINK IPX/SPX Properties dialog box. Within the NWLINK IPX/SPX Properties dialog box, you will perform network-specific configuration steps for NWLINK.

NWLINK has two major configuration options: the *Internal Network Number* and the *Frame Type*. For each network interface card you install on a computer, Windows NT lets you configure a different Network Number and Frame Type. The Windows NT default setting for NWLINK is a Network Number of 00000000 and the *auto-detected* Frame Type (which means that Windows NT will check the network for the Frame Type in use and set the NWLINK Frame Type to match). If Windows NT detects more than one in-use Frame Type on the Network, it will set the NWLINK Frame Type to 802.2. You will learn more about the 802.2 standard in the Networking Essentials section of this book.

The NWLINK IPX/SPX Properties dialog box has two tabs: *General* and *Routing*. The General tab, shown in Figure 352, lets you set the Network Number for all network interface cards and determine whether the Frame Type for each network interface card is auto-detected or manually set.

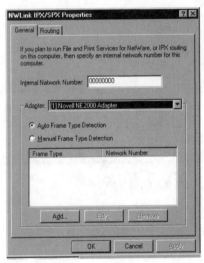

Figure 352 *The NWLINK Properties dialog box General tab.*

The Routing tab is available only if you have installed the *Routing Information Protocol (RIP)* for NWLINK that enables a single computer to act as a router for NWLINK. If you have installed the Routing Information Protocol, you can use the Routing tab to enable or disable routing for NWLINK.

Answer D is correct because Windows NT will auto-detect the Frame Type for NWLINK by default. Answers A, B, and C are incorrect because although they list valid Frame Types, each Frame Type would be set only if Windows NT detected it or if the administrator manually changed it.

353   INTRODUCTION TO NETBEUI

Q: *Where can you make configuration changes to the NetBEUI protocol?*

Choose the best answer:

     A.   *From the Network dialog box*

     B.   *From the Command Prompt*

     C.   *You cannot configure NetBEUI*

     D.   *From the Windows NT Control Panel*

The *Network Basic Input Output System Extended User Interface (NetBEUI) protocol* is perhaps the simplest network protocol to setup for use on Windows NT. As it turns out, NetBEUI is completely *self-configuring* and *self-tuning*, which means that you have no configuration options for the NetBEUI protocol.

NetBEUI is designed for small networks and is not routable, which means that you can use the NetBEUI protocol only in a single network (including bridge-connected networks, which administrators consider to be a single network). The NetBEUI protocol uses a very small amount of memory and processor time and is ideal for computers with slow processors or low amounts of physical memory. Because they cannot configure NetBEUI, new administrators with limited networking experience often choose this protocol.

One disadvantage to the NetBEUI protocol is that it is *broadcast-based,* which means that the protocol uses message broadcasting to locate network resources and to register remote computer names. Broadcast-based protocols often create excessive network traffic which can reduce network speed.

Answer C *is correct because the NetBEUI protocol is self-configuring and you cannot change it.* **Answers A, B, and D** *are incorrect because there is no location for NetBEUI configuration.*

354   UNDERSTANDING NETWORK BINDINGS

Q: *Which of the following best describes the term network bindings?*

Choose the best answer:

     A.   *Restrictions to network users that prevent unauthorized access.*

     B.   *Forcing a user to log onto a single computer.*

     C.   *The communication between different levels of networking components.*

     D.   *Forcing a single computer to authenticate all log-on requests.*

Network bindings is a term that refers to the communication between networking components that exist in different levels of the Windows NT network architecture. As you will learn, Windows NT lets you control this communication.

The Windows NT network architecture consists of five layers. Each layer consists of components that either directly contribute to network communication or serve as layer separators. For example, file system drivers, protocols, and network-adapter card drivers are all standard network layers that contain components necessary for network communication. The transport driver interface (TDI) and network device interface specification (NDIS) are boundary layers that separate the other layers to provide component independence.

Network bindings are the communication ties between components in standard layers. For example, the workstation service that the file-system-drivers layer contains must be bound to at least one component in the protocols layer, such as NetBEUI. In the same way, NetBEUI must be bound to at least one network-adapter card driver. The communication path from the workstation service to NetBEUI and from NetBEUI to the network-adapter card driver, then, corresponds to the network bindings for that particular set of components.

Windows NT automatically binds all components to each other when you install them. Windows NT will, however, let you enable or disable any binding you choose and change the order in which Windows NT binds the components. You will learn more about how to configure bindings in the next Tip.

Answer C *is correct because you can best describe the term network bindings as the communication between different levels of networking components.* **Answers A, B** *and* **D** *are incorrect because the descriptions do not describe network bindings.*

| 355 | CONFIGURING NETWORK BINDINGS |

Q: Which of the following are valid configuration options for Windows NT network bindings?

Choose all answers that apply:

    A.   *Enable*

    B.   *Disable*

    C.   *Primary*

    D.   *Secondary*

As you learned in Tip 354, Windows NT lets you control and configure all vital aspects of network bindings. Within NT, you perform binding configurations within the Network dialog box Bindings sheet. The configuration options you can set include: Enable, Disable, Move up, and Move down. You can use the configuration options to determine which bindings are enabled or disabled and the order in which Windows NT binds a protocol to an adapter or service.

There are a variety of reasons why you might choose to alter the Windows NT default bindings. For example, if you have a network that operates only on the NWLINK protocol, but you installed the NetBEUI protocol to a Windows NT server strictly to support dial-in access for the Remote Access Service (RAS), you might choose to disable the bindings between NetBEUI and the network interface card.

Similarly, you can base your reason for altering the binding order on multiple protocols and multiple network-interface cards. For example, assume you have a Windows NT Workstation with TCP/IP, NWLINK, and NetBEUI protocols installed, but which connects most frequently to servers you installed only with NWLINK. If you configure the bindings for the Workstation Service so that Windows NT binds the NWLINK protocol first, you will improve performance by ensuring that the Workstation will check to see if it can establish the connection using NWLINK first and then the other protocols subsequently.

You can best understand bindings by considering how they relate to services, protocols, or adapters. Figure 355 shows the Bindings sheet within the Network dialog box, which indicates the order that the computer will use when trying to bind.

Answers A *and* **B** *are correct because they are valid configuration options for network bindings.* **Answers C** *and* **D** *are incorrect because they are not valid configuration options for network bindings.*

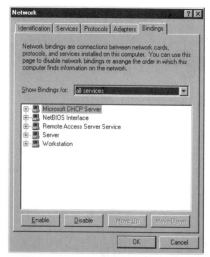

Figure 355 *The Network dialog box Bindings sheet.*

356   INTRODUCTION TO WINDOWS NT NETWORK SERVICES

Q: *Where can you install or modify configuration settings for network services?*

Choose the best answer:

> *A.*   *From the Services option in Windows NT Control Panel.*
>
> *B.*   *From the System Properties dialog box.*
>
> *C.*   *From the Network dialog box.*
>
> *D.*   *You cannot. Windows NT installs all network services automatically and you cannot configure them.*

Think of a *service* as a packaged set of installable components that, together, provide Windows NT with an ability it would otherwise not have. For example, to provide network client computers with the ability to dynamically obtain a TCP/IP address from a Windows NT Server, you must install the Dynamic Host Configuration Protocol (DHCP) server service.

However, conceptualizing a service can be difficult because each service provides a unique level of functionality to Windows NT. Some services may be crucial for Windows NT to function correctly, while other services may only be necessary to perform a specific task or series of tasks. You can add or remove some services from Windows NT, although others you must install at the time of setup and they must remain installed for Windows NT to function properly.

Windows NT includes a variety of installable services that you may or may not install during setup, depending on your Windows NT computer's specific requirements, but which you can install separately at any time. You can add or remove a network service from the Services sheet within the Network dialog box, as shown in Figure 356.

Answer C is correct because you install or remove Windows NT services from the Services tab in the Network dialog box. *Answer A is incorrect because you cannot add or remove a service from the Services dialog box.* *Answer B is incorrect because the System Properties dialog box does not contain any information about services.* *Answer D is incorrect because not all Windows NT services are automatically installed and you can configure some services.*

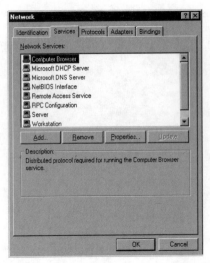

Figure 356 *The Network dialog box Services sheet.*

357 INTRODUCTION TO THE DYNAMIC HOST CONFIGURATION PROTOCOL (DHCP)

Q: You are the administrator of a Windows NT domain consisting of one Windows NT Server and 53 Client computers. Your organization has decided on TCP/IP as the primary protocol for network communication. What would be the least time-consuming method of distributing valid TCP/IP addresses to the client computers?

Choose the best answer:

A. Manually assign TCP/IP addresses to the client computers.

B. Implement the Dynamic Host Configuration Protocol (DHCP).

C. Use the Internet Control Message Protocol (ICMP).

D. All of the above.

The Dynamic Host Configuration Protocol (DHCP) provides automatic assignment of Transmission Control Protocol/Internet Protocol (TCP/IP) addresses (which users refer to as IP addresses) to client computers in your network. Because your network may consist of many PCs, each of which requires a unique TCP/IP address, manual configuration of TCP/IP addresses could become quite time consuming. The DHCP lets you configure a range of IP addresses that you can manage from a single location. Client computers within your network will (dynamically) receive (from the DHCP server) an IP address from this range of addresses. By you configuring a range of IP addresses from a single location, you eliminate many problems you might encounter if you manually assign TCP/IP addresses. For example, when you manually configure IP addresses, you might incorrectly enter the IP address or duplicate the address on more than one client computer (remember, TCP/IP requires each computer to have a unique address). Because the TCP/IP protocol suite has changed over the years to include many functions, the DHCP also lets you manage various TCP/IP enhancements. You will learn more about the TCP/IP enhancements in the following Tips.

*Answer B is correct because using the Dynamic Host Configuration Protocol (DHCP) is the least time-consuming method of address distribution. **Answer A** is incorrect because manually configuring TCP/IP addresses would be the most time-consuming method of address distribution. **Answer C** is incorrect because the Internet Control Message Protocol (ICMP) reports status and errors of the TCP/IP protocol and does not assign TCP/IP addresses. **Answer D** is incorrect because Answers A and B are different methods of address distribution.*

358 UNDERSTANDING *DHCP* REQUIREMENTS

Q: *You are the administrator of a Windows NT domain. You want to configure a Windows NT Workstation as a DHCP server. Where can you install the DHCP server service on a Windows NT Workstation?*

Choose the best answer:

    A. *From the Services option in the Windows NT Control Panel.*

    B. *From the Services tab on the Network dialog box.*

    C. *From the DHCP Setup program on the Windows NT setup CD-ROM.*

    D. *You cannot configure a Windows NT Workstation as a DHCP server.*

There are two sides to the Dynamic Host Configuration Protocol (DHCP) process: the DHCP client (which requests an IP address) and the DHCP server (which provides the address from the range of IP addresses the network administrator specifies). Windows NT includes the DHCP client components in its TCP/IP protocol implementation. Windows NT will automatically use DHCP unless you manually change the TCP/IP configuration.

To provide DHCP server support on a Windows NT Server, you must install the DHCP server service. To install the DHCP server service on a Windows NT Server, perform the following steps:

1. Right-click your mouse on the Network Neighborhood icon and choose Properties from the menu that appears. Windows NT will open the Network dialog box.

2. Within the Network dialog box, click your mouse on the Services tab. Windows NT will display the Services sheet.

3. Within the Services sheet, click your mouse on the ADD button. Windows NT will open a list of installable services Windows NT Server includes.

4. Within the list, click your mouse on the DHCP Server service. Windows NT will indicate your selection by highlighting the DHCP Server service in the list.

5. Click your mouse on the OK button. Window NT will prompt you to enter the pathname to the Windows NT setup files (usually the *I386* folder on the Windows NT Server CD-ROM).

6. Type the pathname to the Windows NT setup files and click your mouse on the Continue button. Windows NT will install the DHCP Server service and prompt you to restart your computer.

7. Click your mouse on the Yes button to restart Windows NT. Windows NT will restart, putting your changes into effect.

After you have installed the DHCP server service, you can create and manage the TCP/IP address ranges. You will learn more about creating and managing DHCP range of TCP/IP addresses in Tip 361.

Note: *Not all operating system can support DHCP.*

Answer D *is correct because you cannot use a Windows NT Workstation as a DHCP server. Only Windows NT Servers can be DHCP servers.* **Answers A, B,** *and* **C** *are incorrect because you cannot use a Windows NT Workstation as a DHCP server.*

359   **UNDERSTANDING THE DHCP PROCESS**

Q: *DHCP clients will obtain their DHCP configuration information from a DHCP client that an administrator has configured with a range of TCP/IP addresses.*

True or False?

As you have learned, there are two sides to the Dynamic Host Configuration Protocol (DHCP) process: the client and the server. In order for a DHCP client to get its TCP/IP configuration information, the DHCP client must contact a DHCP server, which must then respond to the client requesting configuration information. There are four phases in the process of a DHCP client getting its TCP/IP configuration information from a DHCP server.

The first phase in the DHCP process is the *Discovery* phase, during which the DHCP client sends a broadcast network message looking for any DHCP server. The DHCP client sends the broadcast message to the IP address 255.255.255.255. Each of your network-connected computers with the TCP/IP protocol suite installed will receive the broadcast message, but only DHCP servers will respond.

The second phase in the DHCP process is the *Offer* phase, in which the DHCP servers that received the Discovery message the DHCP client sent out in the Discovery phase will respond to the message. All DHCP servers will send back to the DHCP client an *Offer message*. The Offer message will have the TCP/IP address and all other configuration information for the DHCP client to use. The DHCP client must then select one of the DHCP server responses.

The third phase in the DHCP process is the *Selection* phase, within which the DHCP client will send a *Selection message* to the DHCP server. The Selection message contains a request for the TCP/IP configuration information that the DHCP server offered in the Offer phase.

The last phase in the DHCP process is the *Acknowledgement* phase, within which the DHCP server sends a message back to the DHCP client, informing the DHCP client that it can use the TCP/IP address and the other configuration information the DHCP server offered in the Offer phase. Then, the DHCP client will *bind* (associate) the TCP/IP protocol with the network-adapter card in the DHCP client computer. In addition, in the Acknowledgement phase, all DHCP servers, other than the one the DHCP client got its configuration information from, will withdraw their TCP/IP offers from the DHCP client.

*The answer is **False** because DHCP clients must obtain their TCP/IP configuration information from a DHCP server. A DHCP client cannot be a DHCP server.*

360   **CREATION AND CONFIGURATION OF DHCP SCOPES**

Q: *You are a Windows NT domain administrator. You have decided to use DHCP to configure all your client computers. You have installed the DHCP server service on your Windows NT Server, but when client computers boot they do not receive any TCP/IP configuration information from the DHCP server. You have checked the client computers to ensure that you have TCP/IP installed, and you have configured the clients to use DHCP. What could be causing the DHCP clients not to receive their TCP/IP configuration information from the DHCP server?*

Choose the best answer:

A.   *There is a problem with the DHCP client computers' TCP/IP protocol.*

B.   *You installed the DHCP server service incorrectly.*

C.   *You have not created a DHCP scope.*

D.   *Your DHCP server is also a DHCP client.*

As you know, TCP/IP addresses uniquely identify devices in your network. Typically, you would assign TCP/IP addresses to computers, but you could also assign TCP/IP addresses to other devices, such as routers. As an example of how you could use a TCP/IP address, assume that some East Coast university students made some modifications to a vending machine and then assigned a TCP/IP address to it.

The university students created special software for the vending machine so they could see how many of each kind of soft drink was available in the vending machine. Then, the students attached the vending machine to the network—making the information accessible from anywhere on the network. Although this is an unusual use of a TCP/IP address, it illustrates that you can assign TCP/IP addresses to various devices.

However, you will probably not be making any radical modifications to devices to which you will assign TCP/IP addresses. In fact, most devices that will use TCP/IP will already be able to use the TCP/IP protocol without any major administrative intervention.

As you have learned, assigning TCP/IP addresses to a large number of computers would be tedious and time consuming. Assigning TCP/IP addresses manually would be a lot like entering a range of telephone numbers—with area codes—on every computer in your network. If each computer must have a different telephone number, you might make a mistake in address assignment by entering a number incorrectly.

In such a case, a DHCP server could simplify your TCP/IP addresses management. As you learned in Tip 358, after you have decided to use a DHCP server, you must install the DHCP server service on your Windows NT Server. Then, you must create a range of TCP/IP addresses to manage. A range of TCP/IP addresses and other TCP/IP configuration options is a *scope*. When you install the DHCP server service, it will not automatically create a scope. Instead, an administrator must personally create the scope.

One Windows NT Server with the DHCP server service on it can manage one or many scopes. A DHCP scope includes the start and end addresses in a TCP/IP address range, such as 207.49.189.1 through 207.49.189.223. To define a DHCP scope, perform the following steps:

1.   Click your mouse on the Start menu and select the Programs submenu Administrative Tools group DHCP Manager program. Windows NT will open the DHCP Manager program.

2.   Within the DHCP Manager program, click your mouse on the Scope menu Create option. The DHCP Manager will open the Create Scope dialog box, as shown in Figure 360.

3.   Within the Create Scope dialog box, click your mouse in the *Start Address* field. Enter the start TCP/IP address for the scope you want to create. Click your mouse in the *End Address* field. Enter the last address in the range of TCP/IP addresses you are using. Click your mouse in the *Subnet Mask* field. Enter the subnet mask for your network.

4.   Click your mouse on the OK button. DHCP Manager will prompt you to set the scope as active. Click your mouse on the OK button. The DHCP Manager will close the Create Scope dialog box and create the scope.

After you create the scope, you might want to configure optional DHCP settings. Tip 361 discusses DHCP options.

Answer C is correct because you must create a DHCP scope after you install the DHCP server service. Answers A and B are incorrect because it is unlikely that you have a problem with the TCP/IP protocol or that you installed the DHCP server service incorrectly. Answer D is incorrect because a DHCP server cannot be a DHCP client.

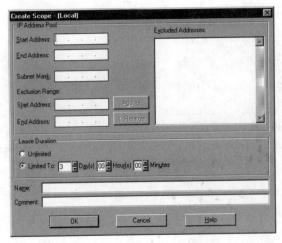

Figure 360 The Create Scope dialog box.

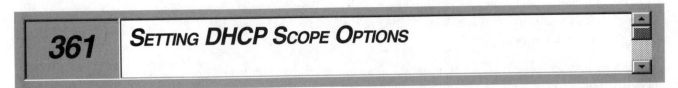

361   SETTING DHCP SCOPE OPTIONS

Q: *You are the administrator of a Windows NT domain with one Windows NT Server and several Windows NT Workstations. You have installed the DHCP server service on your Windows NT Server. You have created a scope. DHCP client computers can get their TCP/IP addresses from the DHCP server, but when you examine the DHCP client computers, you find that they are not receiving any WINS configuration information. Why are your DHCP clients not getting the WINS configuration information?*

Choose the best answer:

    A.   *A DHCP server cannot configure WINS.*

    B.   *To have a DHCP server give WINS configuration information to the DHCP clients, the administrator must configure the DHCP server to provide WINS configuration information manually.*

    C.   *You must manually configure the DHCP clients to get WINS configuration information from the DHCP server.*

    D.   *You can use WINS only on Windows NT Servers, not on Windows NT Workstations.*

As you learned in Tip 360, after you install the DHCP server service on your Windows NT Server, you must create a scope. After you create a scope, you can choose to configure optional settings that your DHCP server will send to DHCP clients when the clients request configuration information. Scope options let administrators push (send) optional configuration information to clients. Without "pushing" that information, the administrator (or some other professional) would have to access each client computer to configure the DHCP options. Although there are over 50 DHCP scope options you can configure, there are only five you can use on Microsoft clients. The other options are for non-Microsoft clients, such as Macintosh computers. Table 361 lists the five scope options you can assign to Microsoft clients. To configure a DHCP scope's options, perform the following steps:

1. Click your mouse on the Start menu and select the Programs submenu Administrative Tools group DHCP Manager program. Windows NT will open the DHCP Manager program.

2. Within the DHCP manager program, click your mouse on the scope you want to set options for. The DHCP Manager will highlight the scope.

3. Within the DHCP Manager program, click your mouse on the DHCP Options menu Scope option. Windows NT will open the DHCP Options: Scope dialog box, shown in Figure 361.

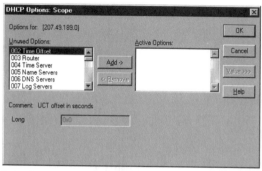

Figure 361 The DHCP Options: Scope dialog box.

4. Within the DHCP Options: Scope dialog box, select the options you want to add from the *Unused Options* field and then click your mouse on the Add button. The DHCP Manager will add the options you selected into the *Active Options* field. After you have added the options you want to configure, click your mouse on the Value button. The DHCP Options: Scope dialog box will expand to display the Edit Array button.

5. Within the DHCP Options: Scope dialog box, click your mouse on the Edit Array button. The DHCP Manager will display the IP Address Array Editor dialog box. Enter the TCP/IP address for the specific option you are configuring. Click your mouse on the OK button. DHCP Manager will close the IP Address Array Editor dialog box.

6. Within the DHCP Options: Scope dialog box, click you mouse on the OK button. The DHCP Manager will close the DHCP Options: Scope dialog box and set the options.

Scope Option	Description
003 Router	You can use this option to specify the TCP/IP address of the router the DHCP client will use to route network packets to foreign networks. The router's TCP/IP address is also called the *Default Gateway*.
006 DNS servers	You can use this option to specify the TCP/IP address of the Domain Name System (DNS) servers, your DHCP clients will use. DNS servers resolve a computers host name to an IP address (that is, they convert it from human-readable text to computer-readable numbers). For example, if you enter the address *www.microsoft.com* on your computer's Web browser, the DNS server must resolve the address *www.microsoft.com* to an IP address (such as 111.22.121.12). You will learn more about DNS servers in Tip 365.
044 WINS/NBNS servers	Where DNS servers resolve host names to IP addresses, WINS servers resolve NetBIOS names to IP addresses. You can use option *044 Windows Internet Name Service (WINS)/NetBIOS Name Servers (NBNS)* to configure the IP address of the WINS server that will resolve the computer's NetBIOS names to IP addresses.
046 WINS/NBT node type	You can use this option to configure a computer's WINS/NetBIOS over TCP/IP node type. The configuration options are: *1=B-node (broadcast), 2=P-node (peer), 4=M-node (mixed), and 8=H-node (hybrid)*. Tip 362 details WINS and the different node types.
047 NetBIOS Scope ID	You can configure your Microsoft computers to use a NetBIOS *Scope ID*, which will separate your computers into different groups that will not be able to communicate with each other. Only computers with the same NetBIOS Scope ID can establish connections with each other.

Table 361 The five Microsoft DHCP scope options.

*Answer B is correct because you must manually configure the DHCP server's WINS settings. **Answer A** is incorrect because you can use a DHCP server to push WINS configuration information to DHCP clients. **Answer C** is incorrect because you cannot configure which options a DHCP client will receive from a DHCP server. **Answer D** is incorrect because Windows NT Workstations and Servers can be DHCP clients, as long as the DHCP server is not also a DHCP client.*

362	INTRODUCTION TO WINDOWS INTERNET NAME SERVICE (WINS)

Q: *You are the administrator of a medium-sized Windows NT domain. You have two Windows NT servers and all other client computers are Windows NT Workstations. You want to reduce broadcast network traffic. What is the easiest way to reduce network broadcast traffic?*

Choose the best answer:

> A.   *Implement a DHCP server.*
>
> B.   *Implement a WINS server.*
>
> C.   *Implement WINS clients.*
>
> D.   *Both B and C.*

In Microsoft networking, a computer can have two names that users can use to establish a connection: the NetBIOS name and the host name. Microsoft uses the *Network Basic Input Output System (NetBIOS) name* to identify each computer whenever you use an application that supports *browse lists*, which are graphical interfaces that show all the computers in your network by their NetBIOS name. Within a browse list, you can click your mouse on a computer's NetBIOS name to establish a connection to that computer. TCP/IP uses a different naming scheme, *host names*. If you are using TCP/IP on a Microsoft operating system, you will use both a NetBIOS name and a host name for the computer. The computer's NetBIOS name and host name do not have to match, although they can.

For one computer to communicate with another computer using TCP/IP, each computer must have the other's TCP/IP address. Because Microsoft networking uses browse lists that let users see the names of computers in the network, the operating system (depending on the programs that are running) may have to resolve the human-readable NetBIOS names of the computers into TCP/IP addresses. Typically, the requesting computer will resolve NetBIOS names to TCP/IP addresses by sending a NetBIOS *name resolution broadcast message*, as Figure 362 shows.

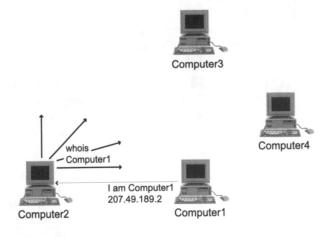

Figure 362 NetBIOS name resolution broadcast network traffic.

When a computer must resolve a NetBIOS name, the computer sends a NetBIOS name resolution broadcast message. When the computer with the NetBIOS name to be resolved receives the broadcast message, that computer sends a directed message back to the requesting computer that includes the computer's name and the computer's TCP/IP address. The problem with broadcasting for a computer's NetBIOS name is that each computer in the network must process the broadcast message until it determines that the broadcast message was not intended for it. Such broadcast activity can generate a lot of useless network traffic.

In small networks the broadcast traffic is not a concern, but in large networks too much broadcast traffic can hurt the overall network performance because it can saturate the network's *bandwidth* (total amount of data that can transmit at one time).

To reduce the amount of broadcast network traffic, you can implement a *Windows Internet Name Service (WINS)* server, which runs as a service on a Windows NT Server computer. WINS can greatly reduce the amount of broadcast network traffic on your network by resolving NetBIOS names to TCP/IP addresses without broadcasting for a computer's name resolution. When you implement the Windows Internet Name Service, you must configure computers on the network to be WINS clients. When the WINS client boots, it will register its NetBIOS name with the WINS server, which will then keep the WINS clients' NetBIOS name and IP addresses in the WINS database for name resolution.

When a WINS client wants to resolve a NetBIOS name of another computer on the network, it queries the WINS server for the name. The WINS server, in turn, will respond with the requested computer's TCP/IP address, provided the requested NetBIOS name is a WINS client. If the destination computer is not a WINS client, the operating system must use some other name resolution method—such as a NetBIOS broadcast message.

How the client computer will resolve the address if it is not a WINS client will depend on the computer's NetBIOS setup. There are four different NetBIOS node types: *B, P, M,* and *H.* A *node* is another word for a client computer. Each NetBIOS node type describes how the client will resolve NetBIOS computer names. Table 362 details the node types and how they will resolve addresses.

Node Type	Resolution Method
B-node	The default node type, which will broadcast for NetBIOS computer name resolution.
P-node	The P-node type will not broadcast for NetBIOS name resolution. If the P-node node cannot resolve a computer's name with the WINS server, the node will not be able to connect to the other computer.
M-node	The M-node type will broadcast first and, if the node does not resolve the NetBIOS name through the broadcast, it will try to use the WINS server.
H-node	The H-node type will use the WINS server first. If the H-node cannot resolve the NetBIOS name with the WINS server, it will then broadcast for name resolution.

Table 362 The four NetBIOS node types and their resolution processes.

Answer D is correct because you would implement a WINS server and then configure all your client computers to be WINS clients. Answers B and C are incorrect because neither step alone is sufficient to reduce network traffic. Answer A is incorrect because a DHCP server would not provide any NetBIOS name resolution.

363 UNDERSTANDING *WINS* REQUIREMENTS

Q: *You are the administrator of your company's Windows NT domain. You have one Windows NT Server and several Windows NT Workstations. You want to use one of your Windows NT Workstations for a WINS server. Can you use a Windows NT Workstation as a WINS server?*

Choose the best answer:

A. *Yes, you can use any Windows NT computer as a WINS server.*

B. *Yes, but you will have to install the Microsoft Windows NT Workstation Resource Kit.*

C. *No, only Windows NT Servers can be WINS servers.*

D. *No, you can only use Windows NT Workstations as WINS servers when there are no Windows NT Servers in your network.*

The WINS server service is designed to run only on Windows NT Servers. You cannot, for example, use a Windows NT Workstation as a WINS server. If you try to install the WINS server service on a Windows NT Workstation, the system will return a message stating that you must have a Windows NT Server to install the WINS service. In addition to having a Windows NT Server, you must also have a static TCP/IP address and subnet mask on the Windows NT Server on which you will install the WINS server service. In order for a client computer to use (query) a WINS server, the client must be one of the following:

- Windows NT Server *3.x* or *4.x*

- Windows NT Workstation *3.x* or *4.x*

- Windows 95 or Windows 98

- Windows for Workgroups *3.x* running the Microsoft TCP/IP-32

- Microsoft Network Client *3.0* for MS-DOS

- LAN Manager *2.2c* for MS-DOS

Answer C *is correct because you can install the WINS server service only on a Windows NT Server.* **Answers A, B and D** *are incorrect because you cannot install the Microsoft WINS server service on a Windows NT Workstation.*

364 **UNDERSTANDING *WINS* CONFIGURATION**

Q: *You have just installed the WINS server service on your Windows NT Server. You have configured all your network clients to use the WINS server. What additional configuration must you perform in order to use WINS?*

Choose the best answer:

A. *You must open the WINS Manager and manually configure the client settings.*

B. *You must open the WINS Manager and manually configure the server settings.*

C. *You must open the WINS Manger and enable the WINS service.*

D. *Do nothing: WINS is configured automatically.*

You do not have to perform any administrative configuration to the Microsoft WINS server service for it to resolve client Network Basic Input Output System (NetBIOS) computer names to Internet Protocol (IP) addresses. After you install the WINS server service and configure your client computers to use WINS, all WINS clients will automatically register their NetBIOS computer names with the WINS server and use the server when they must resolve NetBIOS computer names to TCP/IP addresses. (There are some configuration settings to which an administrator can make changes on the WINS server to enhance WINS performance and reliability, but the MCSE core exams do not test you on these settings.)

Answer D is correct because you do not have to configure WINS in order to get it to work. Answers A, B, and C are incorrect because you do not have to manually configure any settings in WINS in order to get it to work.

| 365 | **INTRODUCTION TO THE DOMAIN NAME SYSTEM (DNS) SERVERS** |

Q: *DNS resolves computers' NetBIOS names into TCP/IP addresses.*

True or False?

What computer users now call the *Internet* was originally called the *ARPANet*, which stands for the United States government's Advanced Research Projects Agency Network. ARPANet developed in the late 1960s from a collaboration between leading U.S. educational institutions' research and the U.S. government's funding. By the early 1980s, there were only a few hundred computers connected to the ARPANet.

However, because people could not remember every computer's Internet Protocol (IP) address (no one had developed TCP yet), they recognized the need for a naming scheme. Therefore, the ARPANet designers created the *host naming convention*, a means of converting human-readable host names into computer-readable IP addresses. The designers mapped every computer's IP address that was connected to the ARPANet to the computer's host name in one central file called *hosts.txt*. In turn, California's Stanford University stored the *hosts.txt* file in the Stanford Research Institute Network Information Center (SRI-NIC).

Initially, the one *hosts.txt* file worked well because of the ARPANet's small size, but as the ARPANet grew, its designers realized they needed a more scaleable name resolution method. In fact, the problems the designers began to have from using only one *hosts.txt* file were the following:

- The *hosts.txt* file grew too large, because of the increasing number of addresses it needed to resolve.

- Because there was only one *hosts.txt* file, network traffic trough SRI-NIC became a problem.

- Because there was only one file maintaining the names of all computers on the network, computer host names had to be unique across the whole network.

- As the network grew, administrators had to edit the *hosts.txt* file more than once a day.

Because of the problems associated with the *hosts.txt* file, the ARPANet designers created the *Domain Name System (DNS)*. The DNS is a distributed database containing the host names and IP addresses of computers on the ARPANet. (The Internet did not start using the Transport Control Protocol until 1982. Only since then have network administrators referred to a computer's address as the TCP/IP address.)

Microsoft includes a DNS server service with the Windows NT Server CD-ROM. By installing a DNS server within your network, your system can resolve local host names (host names known only within your network—as opposed to global names, such as *microsoft.com*) to local IP addresses. To install the DNS server service, perform the following steps:

1. Right-click your mouse on the Network Neighborhood icon. Windows NT will display a Quick menu.

2. Within the Quick menu, select the Properties option. Windows NT will open the Network dialog box.

3. Within the Network dialog box, click your mouse on the Services tab. Windows NT will display the Services sheet.

4. Within the Services sheet, click your mouse on the Add button. Windows NT will open the Select Network Service dialog box.

5. Within the Select Network Service dialog box, click your mouse on the Microsoft DNS Server option. Windows NT will highlight the Microsoft DNS Server option.

6. Within the Select Network Service dialog box, click your mouse on the OK button. Windows NT will install the Microsoft DNS server service.

DNS is similar in many ways to WINS. Where WINS resolves a computer's NetBIOS name (to an IP address), DNS resolves a computer's host name. In contrast, however, whereas WINS is dynamic because WINS clients register their names at the time the system boots, an administrator must create IP *address-to-host name records* in DNS. You will learn more about DNS host records in Tip 367. The process a DNS client goes through to resolve a host name to an IP address is similar to the WINS process. When you enter an Internet Universal Resource Locator (URL) address (for example, *www.jamsa.com*) your computer must query a DNS server for the IP address of the Internet site you want. This process is a simple query and response, as Figure 365 shows.

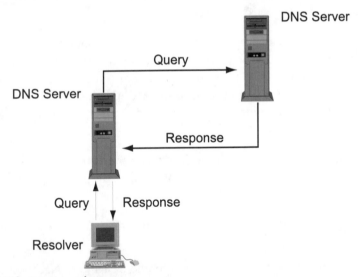

Figure 365 The Microsoft DNS host name resolution process.

*The answer is **False** because DNS resolves host names to IP addresses, not NetBIOS names to IP addresses.*

366 UNDERSTANDING DOMAIN NAME SYSTEM (DNS) ZONES

Q: *You want to resolve host names to IP addresses in the companyxyz.com domain. You have installed the Microsoft DNS server service and configured all of your network client computers to use the DNS server you created. What further configuration must you perform prior to clients being able to use the DNS server?*

Choose the best answer:

A.   *You must create a zone and then create host records for each computer in your network that you must have host name resolution for.*

B.   *You must create a DNS server, a zone, and a host record for each computer in your network that will require host name resolution.*

C.   *You must stop and then restart the DNS server service to enable it.*

D.   *Do nothing: the Microsoft DNS server service is self-configuring.*

One confusing fact for most newcomers to networking with TCP/IP is that Microsoft uses the term *domain* to refer to its Windows NT Server's administrative unit, but on the Internet and in UNIX environments the term domain refers to a hierarchical naming scheme. Although there is no definitive way to discern between the Microsoft domain and the other type of domain, most of the time you can just look at the word domain's context. For example, if a sentence's context refers to the Internet, you can assume that the meaning is the UNIX-type domain. If the context refers to a Windows NT Server, it is a Microsoft domain.

To understand fully how the Domain Name System (DNS) works, you must have a basic understanding of the *Domain Name Space*, which is a naming convention for Internet resources. The Domain Name Space consists of three sections: the *top-level domain*, the *sub-domain*, and the *host name*. You can best describe the Domain Name Space with the term hierarchical, which describes how the Domain Name Space names are structured—from a general group to a specific computer. An example of a Domain Name Space name is *www.jamsa.com*. The final part of the name, *com*, means that the top-level domain is *com*, which stands for commercial. Currently, on the Internet there are only eight top-level domains, as Table 366 shows.

Top-level domain	Use
arpa	Administrators can use this domain name to create reverse DNS lookup zones.
com	Represents all commercial organizations.
edu	Represents all educational institutions.
gov	Represents government organizations.
mil	Represents the military.
net	Represents the networks that make up the Internet.
num	Represents phone numbers.

Table 366 Top-level domains on the Internet.

If you examine the Domain Name Space name *www.jamsa.com* from right to left, you can quickly determine what the name refers to. The *com* suffix indicates that this is a commercial site. The name *jamsa* indicates that this is the sub-domain name of the company that registered the name. The last part of the name at the far left, *www*, indicates that there is a host computer with the host name *www* in the domain *jamsa*, in the top-level domain *com*. In general, *www* indicates that the server is an HTTP-based server, though sub-domain servers can have many names. For example, if the *jamsa.com* domain also included a secure book purchasing server, that server might have the Domain Space Name *buybooks.jamsa.com*.

After you learn how the Domain Name Space works, you will learn how DNS uses the Domain Name Space names and how to create a zone to administer. A *zone* is simply an administration point. For example, in the domain name *www.jamsa.com*, the administration zone is *jamsa.com*, indicating that Jamsa Press is responsible for administration of the server, and other servers in the zone (such as *buybooks.jamsa.com*). In turn, a DNS server must have a zone in order to create host records that will resolve host names to IP addresses. You can create a zone quite easily, but before you can create a zone, you must first create a DNS server. You will create a DNS server after you install the Microsoft DNS server service. To create a DNS server, perform the following steps:

1. Click your mouse on the Start menu and select the Programs submenu Administrative Tools group DNS Manager program. Windows NT will open the DNS Manager program.
2. Within the DNS Manager program, click your mouse on the DNS menu New Server option. DNS Manager will display the Add DNS Server dialog box.
3. Within the Add DNS Server dialog box, type the local computer's name or IP address and click your mouse on the OK button. DNS Manager will close the Add DNS Server dialog box and create the DNS server.

After you create the new DNS server, you must then create the zone. To create a new zone in the new DNS server, perform the following steps:

1. Within the DNS Manager program, right-click your mouse on the new server you created. DNS Manager will display a Quick menu.
2. Within the Quick menu, click your mouse on the New Zone option. DNS Manager will display the Creating new zone for Wizard's opening dialog box.
3. Within the Creating new zone for Wizard dialog box, click your mouse on the Primary radio button and then click your mouse on the Next button. The Creating new zone for Wizard will advance to the next step, displaying a different dialog box with the same caption.
4. Within the Creating new zone for Wizard dialog box, enter a zone name, such as *jamsa.com*, in the *Zone Name* field and then press the TAB key on your keyboard. The Creating new zone for Wizard will create the field entry in the *Zone File* field. Click your mouse on the Next button. The Creating new zone for Wizard will create the zone file for your zone and advance to the next step.
5. Click your mouse on the Finnish button. The Creating new zone for Wizard will close and create your new zone.

After you create the new zone, you can create host records in that zone. You will learn how to create host records in Tip 367.

Answer B is correct because you must create a new DNS server, a zone, and host records for each computer in your network. Answer A is incorrect because you must create a new DNS server. Remember, even though you installed the Microsoft DNS server service, you still must create a new DNS server within the DNS server service. Answer C is incorrect because stopping and then restarting the DNS server service would not accomplish anything. Answer D is incorrect because you must configure Microsoft DNS: it is not self-configuring.

367	**CREATING DOMAIN NAME SYSTEM (DNS) HOST RECORDS**

Q: *Whenever users try to connect to a computer with the host name computer1, users connect to a computer with the host name computer2. Of the following, which is the most likely reason users are connecting to the wrong computer?*

Choose the best answer:

A. *There are no DNS servers for the client computers.*

B. *There are no WINS servers for the client computers.*

C.   *There is no host record for computer1 on the DNS server.*

D.   *The host record for computer1 on the DNS server points to the wrong IP address.*

You have learned in previous Tips how Domain Name System (DNS) servers work and the operations the DNS servers perform. As you learned, TCP/IP clients that use another computer's host name to establish a connection must resolve the destination computer's host name into an IP address. The client computer will then use the destination computer's IP address to make a network connection.

To resolve a host name to an IP address, the client computer queries a DNS server. The DNS server then checks its DNS database for the client's host name. After the DNS server finds the record for the requested host name, it will respond to the requesting computer with a network packet that contains the destination computer's host name and IP address.

Unfortunately, if the record in the DNS database points to an incorrect IP address, the DNS server will direct the client computer requesting DNS host name resolution to the wrong computer. Remember, DNS database entries are *static* (that is, the network administrator enters them). To create a DNS record for a host computer, perform the following steps:

1. Click your mouse on the Start menu and select the Programs submenu Administrative Tools group DNS Manager program. Windows NT will open the DNS Manager program.

2. Within the DNS Manager program, right-click your mouse on the zone in which you want to create a host record. Windows NT will display a Quick menu.

3. Within the Quick menu, click your mouse on the New Host option. The DNS Manager will display the New Host dialog box.

4. Within the New Host dialog box, type a name for the host in the *Host Name* field. Click your mouse in the *Host IP Address* field and type the IP address of the host.

5. Click your mouse on the Add Host button. The DNS Manager will add the host record to the DNS database. Close the DNS manager when you finish adding host records.

Answer D is correct because the client computer is connecting to the wrong IP address. Answer A is incorrect because if there were no DNS server, the client computer would not connect to any computer using a host name. Answer B is incorrect because WINS does not resolve host names to IP addresses, so a WINS server is unnecessary. Answer C is incorrect because if there were no host record for computer1, the client that requested the DNS host name resolution would have received a "destination host unreachable" message.

368	CONFIGURING A DNS SERVER TO FORWARD CLIENT REQUESTS

Q: *You want to implement a DNS server solution that will let you create host records for internal company use and that will let your network users browse the Internet. You have installed the Microsoft DNS server service on your Windows NT Server. You have created host records for the computers in your network. What additional steps must you take to meet your objective?*

Choose the best answer:

A.   *Install a WINS server and configure it to allow Internet access.*

B.   *Configure your DNS server to forward client host name resolution requests to other DNS servers.*

C.   *Configure each client computer with the IP address of a second DNS server that the computer will use to resolve Internet host names.*

D.   *You cannot implement your own DNS server and meet your objective.*

In the DNS process, the client that requests a host name resolution is the *resolver*. To obtain a computer's IP address, the resolver will send a request for a host-name resolution to a DNS server. If the DNS server does not have the host name resolution that the resolver requested, the DNS server will do one of two things: it will either return a "destination host unreachable" message or forward the resolver's request to another DNS server.

If you have not configured your DNS server to forward resolver host-name queries, your network clients will receive "destination host unreachable" messages for any host that is not in your DNS database. Even if you configure multiple DNS servers on the client computer in your network, your local computers will not be able to access any host not in your DNS database. Note that a Microsoft DNS client will use a secondary DNS server only if the primary DNS server does not respond to a host name query. If the primary DNS server responds with a "destination host unreachable" message, the client will not use the secondary DNS.

If you want your DNS server to resolve addresses for systems for which you have not created host records, you must configure your DNS server to forward host-name resolution requests to another DNS server. To configure a Microsoft DNS server to forward host name resolution requests, perform the following steps:

1. Click your mouse on the Start menu and select the Programs submenu Administrative Tools group DNS Manager program. Windows NT will open the DNS manager.

2. Within the DNS Manager program, right-click your mouse on your DNS server in the Server List section. Windows NT will display a pop-up menu.

3. Within the pop-up menu, select the Properties option. DNS Manager will display the Server Properties dialog box.

4. Within the Server Properties dialog box, click your mouse on the Forwarders tab. Windows NT, in turn, will display the Forwarders sheet. Within the Forwarders sheet, click your mouse on the Use Forwarders checkbox. Then, type the IP address of the DNS server to which you want to forward the host-name-resolution request.

5. Click your mouse on the Add button. DNS Manager will add the DNS server to the Forwarders list, as shown in Figure 368.

Figure 368 *The DNS Manager Forwarders tab in the Server Properties dialog box.*

6. Click your mouse on the OK button. DNS Manager will close the Server Properties dialog box.

Answer B is correct because you must configure your DNS server to forward host name resolution requests to other DNS servers in order to have your network clients access both your local network and the Internet using host names. Answer A is incorrect because WINS will not let you use host names to access the Internet. Answer C is incorrect because you can use a secondary DNS server only if the first DNS server does not respond at all. Answer D is incorrect because you can meet your objective by configuring your DNS server to forward host name resolution requests.

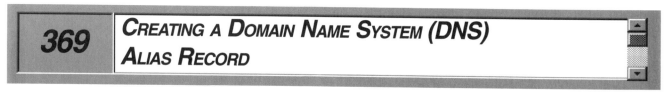

369 CREATING A DOMAIN NAME SYSTEM (DNS) ALIAS RECORD

Q: *Your Windows NT Server's host name is server1. You have just created a Web site on server1. You want Internet users to access your Web site using www.companyx.com as the address. The best way to configure the DNS server to accomplish this is to create two host records for your Windows NT Server: one for server1 and a second record for www.*

True or False?

Administrators for networks that have Web sites will often use an *alias* host name for servers that have Web sites on them. Administrators use alias host names so they can have one host name that local clients will use to access the server and one name that Internet clients will use to access the Web site on the server.

In Microsoft DNS, the record that creates an alias for a host record is a *canonical name record (CNAME)* record, which the administrator must create. A canonical name record in the Microsoft DNS implementation points to a given computer's host record. For example, you might create a canonical name record *www* that points to the host record for a computer named *server1.companyx.com*. To create an canonical name record for a host, perform the following steps:

1.   Click your mouse on the Start menu and select the Programs submenu Administrative Tools group DNS Manager program. Windows NT will open the DNS Manager program.

2.   Within the DNS Manager program, right-click your mouse on the zone in which you want to create an alias record. Windows NT will display a Quick menu.

3.   Within the Quick menu, select the New Record option. The DNS Manager will display the New Resource Record dialog box.

4.   Within the New Resource Record dialog box, click your mouse on the CNAME Record option in the *Record Type* field. In the *Alias name* field, type the alias name. In the *For Host DNS Name* field, type the host name of the record you are creating the alias for (for example, *www.companyx.com*).

5.   Click your mouse on the OK button. The DNS Manager will close the New Resource Record dialog box and create the alias record.

The answer is **False** because the best way to create an alias for a host record is to create a canonical name (CNAME) record that is an alias for the host record.

370 CONFIGURING A DOMAIN NAME SYSTEM (DNS) SERVER TO INTEGRATE WINDOWS INTERNET NAME SERVICE (WINS)

Q: *You want to use a DNS server to let network clients resolve host names to IP addresses. You are using a DHCP server to provide IP addresses to your client computers. You are concerned about IP address assignments changing on your local computers and affecting the DNS server's ability to resolve names. How can you have a reliable network design that lets client computers lease IP addresses through DHCP and lets your client computers use DNS to resolve host names, without you worrying about the static entries in the DNS server's database being incorrect?*

Choose the best answer:

> A.   *Configure your DNS server to use a WINS server.*
>
> B.   *Configure your DNS server so that it runs in Dynamic mode.*
>
> C.   *Configure your client computers to use both WINS and DNS.*
>
> D.   *You cannot use DNS and DHCP in the same network.*

In this Tip, you will learn how you can use DNS, DHCP, and WINS together in your network to create a design that requires the least amount of administrative intervention. As you know, DNS uses only static entries (which means you must manually enter all information). Unfortunately, if a client computer's IP address changes (which will occur each time the client starts in a DHCP environment), you must change the DNS database entry. Therefore, in a large network, changing host names could be a tedious process.

Although DNS uses static entries, Windows Internet Name Service (WINS) uses *dynamic client name registration*, which means that it acquires addresses during execution. Both DNS and WINS resolve computer names into IP addresses. However, DNS resolves computer host names and WINS resolves computer NetBIOS names.

As you have learned, the Dynamic Host Configuration Protocol (DHCP) *leases* (assigns) IP addresses to DHCP client computers (which almost any Microsoft client can be). Because a DHCP server leases IP addresses *dynamically* (automatically), the IP address it assigns to a particular client might change if the client computer is turned off or otherwise disconnected from the network beyond a period of time the DHCP server's configuration specifies. (The DHCP server can reclaim an IP address it leased to a client computer when the client computer has not used the IP address for a given period of time, which can vary from as little as 10 minutes on an online service's server to weeks on a local network.)

As you can see, DNS, DHCP, and WINS all serve different purposes within your network and all can be useful to you. Your administrative challenge, however, is to integrate DNS, DHCP, and WINS together in your network. If you must use DNS, you should integrate WINS with it. To do so, first install your DNS server service on your Windows NT Server. Then, create your organization's zone and the host records for any computer that you know will never have a different IP address. Do not create any host records for the rest of your computers. Next, configure the DNS server to forward host name queries to your WINS server. Finally, configure all your network clients as WINS clients.

After you integrate DNS and WINS, if one of your client computers must resolve a computer's name, the client requesting the host-name resolution will first send the host-name query to the DNS server. The DNS server will check its database to see if the requested zone is in the DNS database. If the zone is present in the DNS database, the DNS server will look for the host record. If the host record is not present in the DNS database, the DNS server will send a query to the WINS server for the host's IP address and the WINS server will look in its database for the host name. If the WINS server finds the host name that the DNS server is looking for as a NetBIOS name a client has registered, the WINS server will return the IP address of the computer with the NetBIOS name that the WINS server found. The DNS server will then add both the NetBIOS name the WINS server found and the IP address from the WINS server to a query reply. Finally, the computer that originally requested the host name resolution will receive the reply as if the DNS server had the host record to begin with. Because you integrated WINS and DNS, computers that must resolve host names of other computers that have at some point received different IP addresses because their original leases expired can still contact the destination computers.

To configure your DNS server to forward name resolution queries to a WINS server, perform the following steps:

1. Click your mouse on the Start menu and select the Programs submenu Administrative Tools group DNS Manager program. Windows NT will open the DNS Manager program.

2. Within the DNS Manager program, right-click your mouse on your organization's zone. Windows NT will display a Quick menu.

3. Within the Quick menu, click your mouse on the Properties option. The DNS manager will open the Zone Properties dialog box.

4. Within the Zone Properties dialog box, click your mouse on the WINS Lookup tab. Windows NT will display the WINS Lookup sheet.

5. On the WINS Lookup sheet, click your mouse on the Use WINS Resolution checkbox and then type your WINS server's IP address in the *WINS Servers* field.

6. Click your mouse on the OK button. The DNS Manager will close the Zone Properties dialog box.

*Answer A is correct because to have DHCP lease IP addresses to your client computers without the possibility of incorrect DNS database entries, you must configure your DNS server to use WINS. **Answer B** is incorrect because DNS is static and you cannot configure it to be dynamic. **Answer C** is incorrect because if you configure your client computers to use DNS and WINS, you will not be able to access your company's Web site unless you create a static entry for it in the DNS server database. WINS would provide no additional connectivity. **Answer D** is incorrect because you can use DNS and DHCP in the same Microsoft network.*

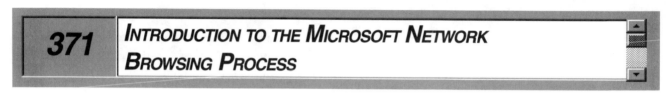

371   INTRODUCTION TO THE MICROSOFT NETWORK BROWSING PROCESS

Q: *You have received several calls from angry users complaining that they sometimes can see computers in browse lists, but when the users try to connect they get messages that state the computer name "cannot be found." Other users are complaining that they sometimes cannot see computers that the users know are up and on the network. What is causing some computers to be visible, but not accessible, while other computers are not visible, but they are accessible?*

Choose the best answer.

    A.   *You are having a physical network problem, such as network cabling.*

    B.   *You have a corrupt browser service on the Windows NT Server that is the domain master browser.*

    C.   *Your Windows NT Server has a faulty network adapter card.*

    D.   *There is nothing wrong with your network. What your users are describing is a normal Microsoft browsing issue.*

Some aspects of networks, the Internet, Microsoft products, or nearly any other computer program or protocol, can appear "broken" even when they're not, if the users are unfamiliar with the product or its process. The Microsoft browsing process is one such case in which users may become confused. In Microsoft networks, you can see all the computers on the network in *browse lists*, which is a term Microsoft uses to describe the list of computers in the network. You can access a browse list from one of many locations. One example of a browse list is the Network Neighborhood window. When you double-click your mouse on the Network Neighborhood icon on your Desktop, you will see a list of all the workgroups and domains that are connected to your computer. However, the Microsoft browsing process will sometimes let computers that are no longer available show up in a browse list, and it may sometimes not show computers that are available. Therefore, you can see why users might get confused and think there is something wrong with the network.

To understand the browsing process, consider the following series of events: When a Microsoft computer comes on-line, it will broadcast its presence to the network, where there are computers listening for these broadcasts. The computers that listen for broadcast of network availability are called *Master Browsers*. There can be only one Master Browser for each Microsoft domain in each *Local Area Network (LAN)*—the Domain Master Browser. You can link multiple LANs together, each having its own Master Browser. When you connect multiple LANs, you create a *Wide Area Network (WAN)*. If you are operating in a WAN environment, you will have one Master Browser for each Microsoft domain in each LAN. You will also have one *Domain Master Browser* for each Microsoft Windows NT domain. The Master Browsers elect other computers to be *Backup Browsers*. When a computer announces its presence to the network, the Master Browser takes the computer's announcement and puts it into a list of *network resources*. Periodically, the Master Browser sends the network-resources list to the Backup Browsers.

When a client computer needs the list of network resources, it must go through a specific process to retrieve the network-resource list. First, the client computer contacts the Master Browser in the LAN. The client computer then requests a list of all the Backup Browsers in the LAN. After the client receives the list of Backup Browsers, it will choose the first Backup Browser in the list and send that Backup Browser a request for the network-resources list. Finally, the Backup Browser will send the network-resources list to the client that requested it. (You will learn more about Microsoft Browser roles in Tip 372.)

Periodically, the Master Browser in each LAN will contact the Domain Master Browser and the two will exchange their network-resources lists. In this way, all network clients will see all computers in the network, regardless of the client's location within the domain.

However, the computers on the network do not always correctly update the browse lists as to the computer's status. For example, when you properly shut down a Windows computer, it will announce it is going offline. The Master Browser will then remove the computer from the list of network resources. However, if the computer shuts down unexpectedly, it could be up to 45 minutes before the Master Browser will remove the computer from the list of network resources. In such a case, the computer will show up in browse lists, but will not be available.

Similarly, when a computer starts up it will announce it is on-line. During the time it takes the Master Browser to send the startup information to the Backup Browsers, the computer will not show up in browse list, but will be available on the network.

Answer D is correct because the question is describing normal Microsoft browser operation. Answer A is incorrect because although a physical problem with the network cabling could cause problems with establishing connections to other computers, it is unlikely. Answer B is incorrect because a corrupt browser service would typically cause the computer not to browse at all, rather than generate an intermittent problem. Answer C is incorrect because a faulty network adapter card would typically cause the server to not browse at all.

---

372 UNDERSTANDING COMPUTER BROWSER ROLES

Q: *What is the function of a Backup Browser in a Microsoft network?*

Choose the best answer:

>   *A.*   *To receive computer service announcements.*
>
>   *B.*   *To function as the Master Browser in case the Master Browser fails.*
>
>   *C.*   *To service client requests for available computers in the network.*
>
>   *D.*   *To maintain all browse lists from all Master Browsers in other LANs.*

You have learned how the Microsoft browse process requires computers to announce their presence in the network, and how Master Browsers take these announcements and build a list of network resources called a browse list. You have also learned that when a client computer needs the browse list, it will contact the Master Browser and request a list of all the Backup Browsers in the LAN. In this Tip, you will learn about the browser roles that Microsoft computers play. Table 372 describes the browsers and their roles.

Browser	Role Description
Non-Browser	A computer configured to be a non-browser will not participate in the Microsoft browser process. It can still request the network browse list, but it will never become any other type of browser.
Backup Browser	Maintains a backup copy of the network browse list from the Master Browser. A Backup Browser will reply to client requests for the network browse list. Backup Browsers will not register client announcements.
Master Browsers	Receives client service announcements. When a computer with a Microsoft operating system that has a server service, such as Windows 95, initializes, it will announce its presence on the network. The Master Browser registers this announcement.
Domain Master Browser	Only one Domain Master Browser can reside in each Microsoft Windows NT domain. The Domain Master Browser is responsible for building all Master Browsers' network browse lists into one enterprise network browse list within which all computers (regardless of location) are contained.

Table 372 The Microsoft browser roles.

*Answer C is correct because a Backup Browser will service client requests for network resources by providing a list of the computers in the network. **Answer A** is incorrect because Master Browsers, not Backup Browsers, receive client computer service announcements. **Answer B** is incorrect because the purpose of a Backup Browser is not to take over for a Master Browser in case of the Master Browser's failure. **Answer D** is incorrect because the Domain Master Browser, not the Backup Browser, maintains the browse lists from all Master Browsers in the network.*

373 UNDERSTANDING BROWSER ELECTIONS

Q: What will happen if your Domain Master Browser fails?

Choose the best answer.

A.   One of the computers in the network will call for an election and a new Domain Master Browser will be elected.

B.   You will not be able to see any new computers that come on-line until your Domain Master Browser is back on-line.

C.   The first Backup Browser that tries to contact the Domain Master Browser and fails will just take over as the new Domain Master Browser.

D.   You will have to create a new Domain Master Browser.

The entire Microsoft browser process is completely automatic. When a browser fails, an *election process* will replace it. When any browser misses three announcement periods, a computer in the network will send an *election criteria packet*. The election criteria packet contains the information from the computer that sent the election criteria packet (operating system, version number, and NetBIOS name). The election criteria packet broadcasts to every computer in the network. Any computer that you have configured to not participate in the browser process will not respond to the election criteria packet. Any computer that can participate in the browser process will examine the election criteria packet. When a potential browser receives the election criteria packet, it will examine the packet to see if it has more recent information than what the election packet contains, or if it has a higher-priority operating system. For example, if one computer is running the Windows 95 operating system and another is running the Windows NT operating system, the one with the Windows NT operating system will win the election. This process continues until every computer has had a chance to examine the election criteria packet. At the end of this process, the computer with the highest election criteria packet wins the election and calls for every computer in the network to announce its presence. This computer is not the Domain Master Browser, but is rather simply a replacement browser for the one that failed. In turn, the same process of election determines the Master Browsers for each LAN.

*Answer A is correct because whenever a browser fails, a computer will call for an election. **Answer B** is incorrect because Microsoft allows for a computer failure by providing the election process. **Answer C** is incorrect because the first Backup Browser that contacts the Master Browser unsuccessfully will not automatically become the Master Browser. **Answer D** is incorrect because you cannot create browsers.*

374 CONFIGURING A COMPUTER NOT TO PARTICIPATE IN THE BROWSER PROCESS

Q: *You have a Windows NT Member Server in a LAN that you do not want to participate in the browsing process. How can you configure the Windows NT Member Server to not participate?*

Choose the best answer.

   A.   *Stop the Netlogon service on the Windows NT Member Server.*

   B.   *Stop the Browser service on the Windows NT Member Server.*

   C.   *Edit the Registry on the Windows NT Member Server and set the MaintainServerList value to No.*

   D.   *You cannot stop a Windows NT Server from becoming a browser if it is elected to do so.*

You can configure any Windows NT computer to be a preferred browser or not to be a browser at all. If there is a computer you would like to be the Master Browser in a LAN, you can configure that computer to win the elections. You can do so only in a network that the Primary Domain Controller is not in. If the Primary Domain Controller is in the LAN where an election is held, the Primary Domain Controller will win the election regardless of how you have configured the computers.

You can also configure a Windows NT computer to not participate in the browser process. If a Windows NT computer you have configured to not participate in the browser process is in a network where an election is held, the Windows NT computer will not respond to the election criteria packet. To configure a Windows NT computer to not participate in the browser process, perform the following steps:

   1.   Click your mouse on the Start menu and select the Run option. Type *Regedt32.exe* into the Open field. Windows NT will open the Registry Editor program for Windows NT.

   2.   Within the Registry Editor program, click your mouse on the *System* hive in the *HKEY_LOCAL_MACHINE*. The Registry Editor will expand the *System* hive.

   3.   Within the System hive, click your mouse on the *CurrentControlSet* key. The Registry Editor will expand the *CurrentControlSet* key.

4. Within the *CurrentControlSet* key, click your mouse on the *Services* subkey. The Registry Editor will expand the *Services* subkey.

5. Within the *Services* subkey, click your mouse on the *Browser* subkey. The Registry Editor will expand the *Browser* subkey.

6. Within the *Browser* subkey, click your mouse on the *Parameters* subkey. The Registry editor will expand the *Parameters* subkey.

7. Within the *Parameters* subkey, double-click your mouse on the *MaintainServerList* value. The Registry editor will open the Edit String dialog box.

8. Within the Edit String dialog box, type *No* in the *Value Data* field. Click your mouse on the OK button. The Registry editor will close the Edit String dialog box.

9. Close the Registry editor. Restart your Windows NT computer. It will now not participate in the browser process.

*Answer C is correct because you must edit the Registry to stop a Windows NT computer from participating in the browser process. **Answer A** is incorrect because stopping the Netlogon service would cause the Windows NT computer not to show up on browse lists. **Answer B** is incorrect because stopping the browser service would mean that the Windows NT computer would not see any computers on the network. **Answer D** is incorrect because you can stop a Windows NT computer from participating in the browser process by editing the Registry.*

375   **UNDERSTANDING NETWORK DATAGRAMS**

Which of the following are valid datagrams that systems exchange within a browsing environment?

Choose all answers that apply:

     A.   *Force election datagram*

     B.   *Query browsers server datagram*

     C.   *Server announcement datagram*

     D.   *Request announcement datagram*

To maintain browsing within a Microsoft network, clients and servers exchange a variety of messages that they package within datagrams. For example, when a client cannot access any of three backup browsers and then cannot access the master browser, the client can send a *force election datagram* to initiate the master browser election process.

When a client first enters the network, the client sends a *server announcement datagram* that identifies the client to the Master browser, which then adds the client to the browse list. Later, the client can sends a *query browers server datagram* to the Master browser to get a list of backup browsers the client can use.

In a similar way, when a Master browser joins a network, it may broadcast a *request announcement datagram* that requests all clients to identify themselves to the browser (using *server announcement datagrams*).

Answers A, B, C, and D are all correct answers.

376   INTRODUCTION TO WINDOWS NT'S REMOTE ACCESS SERVICE (RAS)

Q: *You are the administrator of a Windows NT domain that consists of one Windows NT Server, 32 Windows NT Workstations, and 15 Windows 95 laptop computers. The Windows 95 users travel frequently and cannot always connect to the network locally. How can you give the Windows 95 users the ability to connect to the network when a local connection is not available?*

Choose the best answer:

A.   *Install modems on the Windows NT Server and all the Windows 95 computers and install RAS on the Windows NT Server.*

B.   *Install Modems on all the Windows 95 computers and on 15 of the Windows NT Workstations and configure Dial-Up Networking on the Windows NT Workstations to accept calls.*

C.   *You cannot. Windows NT requires computers to be locally connected to the network in order to authenticate users.*

D.   *Install modems on the Windows NT Server and all Windows 95 computers and configure Dial-Up Networking on the Windows NT Server to accept calls.*

In today's distributed business environment, many networks include both permanently connected desktop computers and remotely connected laptop computers. Within Windows NT, the *Remote Access Service (RAS)* is the component that lets the network server accept remote logins from remote computers across normal phone lines. For example, if you required a user in your organization to travel frequently and, while traveling, the user needed to connect to the network with a laptop and modem, you would have to configure your server with a modem and the RAS software. The user would then use a RAS client, such as the Dial-Up networking components that Windows NT 4.0 or Windows 95 include, to dial into the Windows NT computer over a standard phone line. After the user connects, the user could access all network resources as if the user's computer were connected to the network locally.

Answer A is correct because you must have modems to use normal phone lines for connection and the Remote Access Service (RAS) for Windows NT to answer calls. **Answer B** is incorrect because you cannot configure Windows NT Dial-Up Networking to answer calls. **Answer C** is incorrect because you can configure RAS to answer calls and connect remote computers over normal phone lines. **Answer D** is incorrect because you cannot configure Windows NT Dial-Up Networking to answer calls.

377   COMPARING REMOTE ACCESS SERVICE (RAS) AND REMOTE CONTROL SOFTWARE (RCS)

Q: *Which of the following Windows NT components lets you take control of a Windows NT computer from a remote client and perform operations as if you were sitting at the local computer?*

Choose the best answer:

A.   *Remote Access Service (RAS)*

B.   *Remote Control Service (RCS)*

C.   *Remote Console Utility (RCU)*

D.   *None. Windows NT does not include a component that lets you take control of a computer from a remote client*

As you learned in Tip 376, the Remote Access Service (RAS) lets remote computers connect to a Windows NT network over standard phone lines. You should be careful to not confuse the remote access service with the remote control software, that lets the user take control of the local computer (sometimes called a *host computer*) and perform operations as if the user were actually performing the operations at the local computer.

You would use remote control software if you want to let a remote user perform operations, such as disk management or hardware configuration, from a remote location. You would use the remote access service if you want to perform normal network operations as a client computer.

Answer D is correct because Windows NT does not include a component that lets you take control of a local computer from a remote client. Answer A is incorrect because, although the Remote Access Service (RAS) lets you connect to a Windows NT computer from a remote client, the client performs as if it were a client computer on the same network and does not let you take control of local operations. Answer B is incorrect because Windows NT does not contain a component called Remote Console Service. Answer C is incorrect because Windows NT does not contain a component called Remote Console Utility.

378   **USING THE REMOTE ACCESS SERVICE (RAS) AND DIAL-UP NETWORKING**

Q: *Which of the following Windows NT components lets you dial into a host and connect as if you were a client computer on the local network?*

Choose the best answer:

     A.   *Remote Access Service (RAS)*

     B.   *Dial-Up Networking*

     C.   *The Modems option in the Windows NT Control Panel*

     D.   *The Phone Dialer in the Accessories group*

As you have learned, the Remote Access Service (RAS) is the component in Windows NT that can use a modem to answer calls and to provide a connection to a remote computer over normal phone lines. To actually create a connection between two computers, you must have software that can dial-out from the remote computer as well. The client software you use to dial-out from a remote computer in Windows NT is known as *Dial-Up Networking*.

Dial-Up Networking works together with the Remote Access Service to extend a network beyond a single location. For example, if you want to connect a Windows NT Workstation in your home to a Windows NT Server in your office, you would install RAS on the Windows NT Server and then use Dial-Up Networking on the Windows NT Workstation to dial into the Windows NT Server's modem. After you establish the connection, the link will operate in the background and you can perform operations on the Server as if you were a client computer on a local network with a direct connection to the Server. In this example, the Windows NT server takes the role of a host computer while the Windows NT Workstation acts as a remote client.

Answer B is correct because Dial-Up Networking is the component in Windows NT that lets you dial out to a remote host and connect as if you were on the local network. Answer A is incorrect because RAS is the component that lets Windows NT act as a remote host. Answer C is incorrect because the Modems option in Windows NT Control Panel lets you manage modems but provides no connection abilities. Answer D is incorrect because the Phone Dialer in the Accessories group lets you dial a phone number for voice communication but does not establish network-like connections and will not pass data.

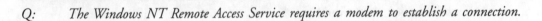

379   INTRODUCTION TO THE POINT-TO-POINT TUNNELING PROTOCOL

Q: *The Windows NT Remote Access Service requires a modem to establish a connection.*

True or False?

As you have learned, the Windows NT 4.0 Remote Access Service (RAS) lets remote users connect to the network over a modem and normal phone line. The Windows NT 4.0 RAS can also establish secure connections across the Internet through the implementation of the operating system's *Point-to-Point Tunneling Protocol (PPTP)*. PPTP is a new technology that supports the creation of virtual networks over TCP/IP, which means that users can establish a connection to the Internet and then establish a secure link to the remote network through the Internet.

Because the Point-to-Point Tunneling Protocol's protocol stack manages the connections internally, you can make the host computer's connection to the Internet from an external source and connect through the local network. Therefore, a Windows NT computer can establish a remote connection without a modem if another connection to the Internet is present. Establishing a connection through PPTP provides the same functionality as having a direct connection via a modem, with the added benefits Table 379 lists.

Benefit	Description
Lower connection costs	Remote users can establish a local connection to the Internet wherever they are, so the connection cost is reduced because users will not have to pay for the cost of long distance or 800 number calls.
Lower hardware costs	The connections are established through the Internet, so the host computer requires only one connection to the Internet and you will not have to purchase multiple modems or expensive modem cards for multiple users.
Easy to manage	RAS manages the PPTP directly. You perform configuration only on dial-in permissions for users and actual user accounts.

Table 379 PPTP features.

*The answer is **False** because Windows NT RAS can establish a connection through the Internet. In turn, you can establish Internet connections externally and connect through the local area network (LAN), which eliminates the need for a modem.*

380   INTRODUCTION TO THE MULTI-LINK PROTOCOL

Q: *Which of the following best describes the multi-link protocol?*

Choose the best answer:

     A.   *A protocol that supports simultaneous connection to more than one location through the same modem.*

     B.   *A protocol that can interpret signals from other protocols.*

C.   *A protocol that can combine more than one connection into a single logical channel of communication that is transparent to applications.*

D.   *A protocol that functions on any operating system.*

As you have learned, you can use the Remote Access Service (RAS), together with Dial-Up Networking, to support remote user connections over a normal phone line. You can also use a modem within a server to communicate with other remote computers, such as an Internet Service Provider (ISP) for remote

Web site hosting. One limitation of using modems, however, is that a modem's speed is generally confined to no more than 56 kilobits per second (56Kbs). You can avoid a modem's speed limitations, however, using the *multi-link protocol*. The multi-link protocol provides Windows NT with the means to increase the data transmission rate by binding multiple connections together to form a single communication channel. For example, imagine you have a

Windows NT computer installed with two modems, each of which can send and receive data at 28.8 kilobytes per second. In this case, you could connect both modems at the same time and use the multi-link protocol to create a single communication channel that can send and receive data at 57.6 kilobytes per second.

The multi-link protocol's combination of multiple channels is completely transparent to applications and operating system utilities, such as Windows NT *Explorer*. Windows NT makes the connection available to applications and will separate or reassemble data for each physical link in the background. Figure 380 illustrates the concept of the multi-link protocol.

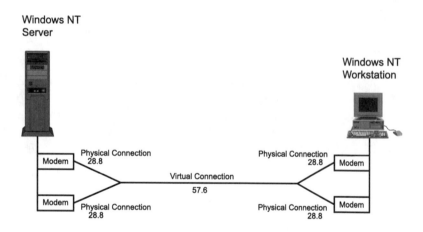

Figure 380 *Using the multi-link protocol with complex hardware to gain remote access.*

Using the multi-link protocol can reduce connection costs by increasing the data transfer rate which, in turn, reduces the amount of connection time required to complete a process. The cost of hardware, however, increases because the multi-link protocol requires more than one physical connection.

In addition to combining two similar modems, Windows NT can use the multi-link protocol to combine different connection types. For example, you could use the multi-link protocol to combine an Integrated Services Digital Network (ISDN) line and a standard modem.

Answer C is correct because the multi-link protocol can combine multiple physical links into a single logical communication channel that is transparent to applications. Answer A is incorrect because the multi-link protocol cannot connect a single modem to multiple locations simultaneously. Answer B is incorrect because the multi-link protocol cannot interpret other protocols. Answer D is incorrect because the multi-link protocol will not function on all operating systems.

381 | UNDERSTANDING REMOTE ACCESS SERVICE (RAS) PROTOCOLS

Q: *Which of the following are protocols for Remote Access Service?*

Choose all answers that apply:

A.   *Point-to-Point Protocol (PPP)*

B.   *Transport Control Protocol/Internet Protocol (TCP/IP)*

C.   *Serial Line Internet Protocol (SLIP)*

D.   *Network Basic Input Output System Extended User Interface (NetBEUI)*

As you learned in Tip 335, network protocols (sometimes called transport protocols) play a very important role in the Windows NT network architecture. As you have also learned, Windows NT supports numerous protocols dedicated to establishing remote communication. A *protocol* is a set of rules that govern a specific process or event. Remote Access Service (RAS) protocols are those protocols Microsoft and other vendors specifically designed to govern the communication between computers, and which are connected remotely instead of through a local-area network (LAN).

Windows NT includes two RAS protocols in addition to the basic protocols that you have learned in previous Tips: *Serial Line Internet Protocol (SLIP)* and *Point-to-Point Protocol (PPP)*. SLIP is an industry standard protocol that governs Transport Control Protocol/Internet Protocol (TCP/IP) connections over serial lines. Windows NT Dial-Up Networking supports SLIP and can connect to SLIP servers.

SLIP supports only TCP/IP as a transport protocol, and the host computer must have a static IP assignment (that is, a registered IP address) to function. In other words, SLIP connections cannot use the Dynamic Host Configuration Protocol (DHCP) or the Windows Internet Naming Service (WINS). The PPP is an enhancement to the original SLIP standard and is now itself an industry standard protocol for establishing remote connections. The PPP supports the following transport protocols:

- AppleTalk
- DECnet
- Open Systems Interconnection (OSI)
- TCP/IP
- IPX

Note: *The Windows NT PPP implementation supports only TCP/IP, IPX, and NetBEUI.*

Windows NT uses RAS protocols to establish a communication link through a modem or other remote connection device and then uses network protocols to transfer data for applications through the RAS protocols.

Answers A and C are correct because SLIP and PPP are remote access service protocols. Answers B and D are incorrect because TCP/IP and NetBEUI are transport protocols.

382 **UNDERSTANDING THE REMOTE ACCESS SERVICE (RAS) NETBIOS GATEWAY**

Q: *You are a Windows NT domain administrator. You want to establish a RAS session between a remote client computer running Windows NT Workstation and a local computer running Windows NT Server. You must install the same network protocols for both the Windows NT Workstation and the Server for the Workstation to access shared folders and printers.*

True or False?

As you have learned, the Windows NT Remote Access Service (RAS) consists of multiple protocols that let you connect remote computers to a network in several different ways, including direct dial-in access and access across the Internet. Another feature of the Windows NT Remote Access Service is the Network Basic Input Output (NetBIOS) gateway function, which lets RAS clients running only the NetBIOS Extended User Interface (NetBEUI) protocol access RAS servers, regardless of what protocol is running on the RAS server. The RAS software will automatically translate NetBEUI communications into TCP/IP or IPX formats that the network servers using these protocols can understand. Similarly, RAS will automatically translate communications from TCP/IP or IPX to the NetBEUI protocol and pass the information from the server to the NetBEUI client, as Figure 382 shows.

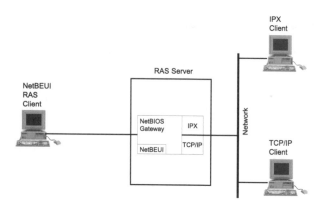

Figure 382 RAS protocols use the Windows NT RAS NetBIOS gateway to convert data between network protocol types.

*The answer is **False** because the Remote Access Service's NetBIOS gateway feature can translate NetBEUI communication from the client computer into IPX or TCP/IP communication for the local network.*

383 **UNDERSTANDING NETBEUI AND REMOTE ACCESS SERVICE (RAS)**

Q: *Which of the following network protocols operates the fastest over a RAS connection?*

Choose the best answer:

A.   TCP/IP

B.   NetBEUI

C.   IPX

D.   DLC

As you have learned, NetBEUI is a transport protocol that requires no configuration because it is completely self-configuring and self-tuning—that is, the Windows NT operating system handles the configurations for you. NetBEUI is the Microsoft-recommended protocol for the Remote Access Service (RAS) because it has the fastest data transfer speed of any transport protocol that Windows NT RAS supports.

In addition, to enable browsing over a connection, the RAS requires the NetBEUI protocol. Although Windows NT RAS supports clients that use TCP/IP, IPX, or NetBEUI, only NetBEUI clients can browse over a RAS connection. You must install NetBEUI on both the client computer and the host server in order to enable browsing.

Answer B is correct because NetBEUI is the fastest performing transport protocol over RAS. Answers A and C are incorrect because although Windows NT RAS supports TCP/IP and IPX, neither of them are the fastest performing over a RAS connection. Answer D is incorrect because RAS does not support DLC.

384   UNDERSTANDING THE **TCP/IP** AND **NWLINK** ROUTERS

Q: *Which of the following transport protocols can Windows NT Remote Access Service (RAS) route?*

Choose the best answers:

A.   NetBEUI

B.   NWLINK

C.   TCP/IP

D.   SLIP

As you have learned, the Windows NT Remote Access Service (RAS) lets computers communicate using different protocols, and will even translate automatically from some protocols (such as TCP/IP) to other protocols (such as NetBEUI). The Windows NT Remote Access Service can also route TCP/IP and NWLINK protocol messages so that two or more different networks can pass information among themselves. Usually, if two networks use different protocols, a single network's protocols cannot communicate with another network's protocols, even if both networks are connected to the same cable. Because TCP/IP networks use a numbering sequence to determine a computer's physical location, and IPX networks use a network number to determine a computer's physical location, translating messages between networks is not normally possible.

However, *routers* let units of communication pass from one network into another and out again. For example, imagine that your organization has two offices that one cabling system connects but that each have an independent TCP/IP network numbering sequence. In order for a computer on one network to communicate with a computer on the other network, you must have a machine or computer that can route the units of communication between the numbering sequences. The TCP/IP and NWLINK routers in Windows NT RAS perform routing functions for RAS clients so that client computers on other networks can access information on the RAS server's network.

*Answers B and C are correct because Windows NT RAS can route the TCP/IP and NWLINK transport protocols. **Answer** A is incorrect because NetBEUI is not routable. **Answer D** is incorrect because SLIP is not a transport protocol.*

385 INTRODUCTION TO REMOTE ACCESS SERVICE (RAS) SECURITY

Q: Which of the following are security features of the Remote Access Service (RAS)?

Choose the best answer:

A. Callback security

B. Encrypted authentication

C. PPTP filtering

D. All of the above

As you have learned, Windows NT includes the Remote Access Service (RAS), which will let users access the network from a remote location. In turn, because the risk of unauthorized parties accessing your computer network (*hacking your network*) is higher for servers that are connected to the outside world with a modem or over the Internet, the Windows NT Remote Access Service (RAS) implements several security measures. RAS-implemented security measures are specifically targeted at preventing unauthorized access to the network from the remote location. Table 385 describes the Windows NT RAS security features.

Feature	Description
Integrated Domain Security	Windows NT authenticates all domain users through a single account whether they are connected to the Local Area Network (LAN) or through RAS. Doing so ensures that the user will have all appropriate rights on the network when dialing in as the user does when connected to the LAN locally.
Encrypted Authentication	Windows NT automatically encrypts authentication and logon information when it is transmitted over RAS. This option is completely under your control and you can configure RAS to pass logon and authentication data as clear text, or to transmit all data in encrypted format.
Callback Security	You can configure RAS to disconnect and call a user back before access is granted to the computer or network. Callback options include the ability to call back a specific number, the number the user dialed in from, or not to call back at all.
Auditing	You can configure Windows NT to audit events that take place on the computer, including authentication, logons, and actions performed.
Third-party Security Hosts	You have the option to purchase and install a third-party host, which adds a level of security to RAS connections.
PTP Filters	The Windows NT TCP/IP implementation has an advanced option for the Point-to-Point Tunneling Protocol—*PPTP filtering*. When PPTP filtering is turned on, all protocols other than PPTP are disabled for the chosen network interface card (NIC). This can prevent access to network resources operating on the specified NIC.

Table 385 Windows NT RAS security features.

Answer D is correct because answers A, B, and C are all security features of the Remote Access Service. Answers A, B, and C are incorrect because although they are all valid security features in the Remote Access Service, Answer D includes these features and is the correct answer.

386   **INTRODUCTION TO CALLBACK VERIFICATION**

Q: *Which of the following are valid configuration options for Callback Verification?*

Choose all answers that apply:

    A.   *No Call Back*

    B.   *Set By Caller*

    C.   *Preset To*

    D.   *There are no configuration options for Callback Verification*

As you learned in Tip 385, one security feature which the Windows NT Remote Access Service (RAS) supports is known as *Callback Verification* or *Callback Security*. This feature lets Windows NT disconnect an incoming call (before Windows NT grants the user access to the computer or network) and call a user back either at a pre-specified number or at a connection-time number the user specifies each time he or she connects.

Callback verification can be very effective because, at its most restrictive setting, for an unauthorized user to gain access to the network the user would have to know the number to dial, know a valid user name and password, and dial from the user's preset number. Then, when the computer called back, the unauthorized user's computer would be able to answer the phone.

In addition to providing a high level of security, the callback verification feature can save an organization money by using phone lines that receive a cheaper rate from phone companies than would be available to a single user trying to dial in. You can configure callback verification from the User Manager or from the Remote Access Permissions dialog box, as Figure 386 shows.

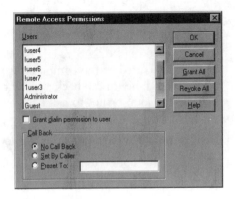

Figure 386 Using the Remote Access Permissions dialog box to configure callback verification.

Answers A, B, and C are correct because they are all valid configuration options for callback verification. Answer D is incorrect because you can configure callback verification.

387   INTRODUCTION TO THIRD-PARTY SECURITY HOSTS

Q: *A third-party security host is a person your organization employs to monitor remote access events.*

True or False?

As you have learned, enabling your network for remote access introduces new security issues to the network that you must consider. While Windows NT's Remote Access Service (RAS) includes several built-in security safeguards that you can easily implement to provide security to your system, you may find that your system requires more extensive security protections. *Third-party security host* is a term that describes a large number of devices designed for administrators to implement between the phone line and the Remote Access Service (RAS) server. These devices provide an additional security level by introducing a manufacturer-specific security system that must themselves independently authenticate the caller before the RAS server receives the call—in other words, the systems intercept the call before it ever connects to the host computer.

An example of a third-party security host is a *key-card verification device*. Key-card RAS systems consist of two components you implement at each end of a RAS connection. For example, you would install the host component at the RAS server's location between the phone lines and the server, and install the client component on the remote user's computer. Then, when the user tries to access the RAS server, the host component intercepts the call and issues a challenge to the client computer requesting the client component.

The client component and the host component identify each other and begin a cycle wherein the host component uses a preset *algorithm* (a mathematical function) to produce a pass-code value and, in turn, requests confirmation from the client component. The client component then produces the pass-code value using the same preset algorithm and sends the code to the host component. If the pass-code values match, the host component will pass the call to the RAS server. The RAS server, in turn, will perform normal Windows NT authentication on the remote user's access request. Throughout the call's length, the host component will issue a new challenge at regular intervals to the client component, which must then respond accurately or the host will terminate the call. Other examples of third-party security hosts include fingerprint recognition or other advanced identification methods prior to a Windows NT authentication.

*The answer is **False** because a third-party security host is a device you implement between the phone lines and a RAS server to enhance RAS security.*

388   UNDERSTANDING REMOTE ACCESS SERVICE (RAS) INSTALLATION

Q: *Windows NT Workstation supports 256 inbound RAS connections but only one outbound connection.*

True or False?

As you have learned, you can use the Remote Access Service (RAS) to provide remote access to your Windows NT network. You have also learned that RAS supports multiple protocols you can implement to let users access the network in different ways. Before you can use RAS, however, you must install it onto the Windows NT Server that will support remote access. You can install RAS during Windows NT setup by choosing the support Remote Access to the Network option during installation. Selecting this option will install both RAS and Dial-Up Networking (both of which you can also install individually any time after setup).

Choosing the correct operating system for Remote Access Services can be important because of differences in the RAS functionality on Windows NT Server and Workstation. Windows NT Server can support up to 256 concurrent inbound RAS connections (that is, concurrent users dialing into the server), while Windows NT Workstation can support only one. You will install the Dial-Up Networking or RAS features the same way on either operating system. To install Dial-Up Networking on a Windows NT Workstation after system setup, perform the following steps:

1. Click your mouse on the Start menu and select the Programs submenu Accessories Group Dial-Up Networking option. Windows NT will open a dialog box that tells you Dial-Up Networking is currently uninstalled and to press the Install button to install it.
2. Click your mouse on the Install button. Windows NT will install Dial-Up Networking. (If you are prompted for the location of install files, type in the appropriate pathname and click your mouse on the OK button.)

To install RAS on a Windows NT Server after system setup, perform the following steps:

1. Right-click your mouse on the Network Neighborhood icon. Windows NT will open the Network dialog box.
2. Within the Network dialog box, click your mouse on the ADD button. Windows NT will open a list of installable services.
3. Within the list of installable services, click your mouse on the Remote Access Service option. Windows NT will indicate your selection by highlighting the Remote Access Service option.
4. Click your mouse on the OK button. Windows NT will open the Remote Access Setup dialog box.
5. Within the Remote Access Setup dialog box, click your mouse on the modem you want to use for RAS and then click the Continue button. Windows NT will accept your modem choice and open the Network Configuration dialog box.
6. Within the Network Configuration dialog box, click your mouse on the OK button to continue. Windows NT will install RAS.

*The answer is **False** because Windows NT Workstation can support only one inbound RAS connection.*

389   CONFIGURING A REMOTE ACCESS SERVICE (RAS) SERVER

Q: *The Windows NT Remote Access Service functions only with modems.*

True or False?

As you learned in Tip 388, you can install the Remote Access Service (RAS) to your Windows NT server either during the system's initial installation or at any time. After you install RAS, you must then configure RAS to support the remote services you want for the network. When you configure a RAS server, it will have many options for you to choose from. The first and most important decision you will have to make is what modem or other communication device (including PPTP) the Remote Access Service will use. If you have only one device, the decision is easy, but you still must designate the device for use.

You can perform configuration for RAS modems in the Remote Access Setup dialog box. The Remote Access Setup dialog box includes the options Table 389.1 lists.

Option	Description
Add	Lets you add devices from a list of installed RAS-compatible devices.
Remove	Lets you remove an existing RAS device.
Configure	Lets you specify what the port will be used for: options include Dial-out Only, Receive calls only, and Dial-out and Receive calls.
Clone	Lets you duplicate an entry from an existing device for multiple access (some devices can support multiple connections for each device).
Network	Lets you access the Network Configuration dialog box.

Table 389.1 The RAS device options.

You must also accept or make changes to the network configuration for RAS. You will make such changes in the Network Configuration dialog box. The Network Configuration dialog box includes the options Table 389.2 details.

Option	Description
Dial-out Protocols	Lets you specify which protocols are available for outgoing calls. You can enable or disable NetBEUI, TCP/IP, or IPX.
Server Settings	Lets you specify which protocols are available for incoming calls. You can enable, disable, or configure NetBEUI, TCP/IP, or IPX.
Encryption Settings	Lets you specify the encryption level for the RAS session. Options include Allow any authentication including clear text, Require encrypted authentication, Require Microsoft encrypted authentication, and Require Data encryption.
Enable Multilink	Lets you enable the multi-link protocol abilities for this modem.

Table 389.2 The Network Configuration options for Windows NT RAS.

*The answer is **False** because the Windows NT Remote Access Service supports a variety of communication devices, including the virtual device PPTP.*

390 CONFIGURING *TCP/IP* FOR REMOTE ACCESS SERVICE (RAS)

Q: *You are a Windows NT domain administrator. You are configuring the Remote Access Service to provide Internet access. Where in Windows NT RAS can you specify TCP/IP settings for RAS clients?*

Choose the best answer:

A. *From the Protocols tab in the Network dialog box.*

B. *From the Network Configuration dialog box.*

C. *You cannot configure TCP/IP for RAS clients.*

D. *From the Dial-Up Networking Properties dialog box.*

As you have learned, the Windows NT Remote Access Service (RAS) lets you configure each compatible network protocol through the Network Configuration dialog box, shown in Figure 390.1.

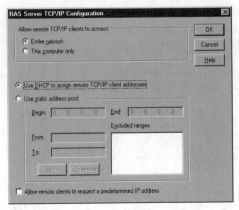

Figure 390.1 The Network Configuration dialog box.

Table 390 describes the configuration options for TCP/IP over RAS.

Option	Description
Allow remote TCP/IP clients to access	Lets you enable or disable TCP/IP client access and specify access to only the RAS server or to the entire network.
Use DHCP to assign remote TCP/IP client addresses	Lets you use a DHCP server to allocate an IP address to remote clients.
Use static address pool	Lets you specify a range of IP addresses available to RAS clients and exclusions.
Allow clients to request A predetermined IP address	Lets remote clients request a specific IP address.

Table 390 The TCP/IP configuration options for Remote Access Service.

Figure 390.2 shows the RAS Server TCP/IP Configuration dialog box.

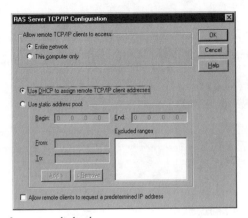

Figure390.2 The RAS Server TCP/IP Configuration dialog box.

Answer B is correct because you perform TCP/IP configuration for RAS clients in the Network Configuration dialog box. Answer A is incorrect because the Network dialog box lets you perform TCP/IP configuration for the local computer, not for RAS clients. Answer C is incorrect because you can configure TCP/IP for RAS clients. Answer D is incorrect because you cannot configure TCP/IP for RAS clients anywhere in Dial-Up networking.

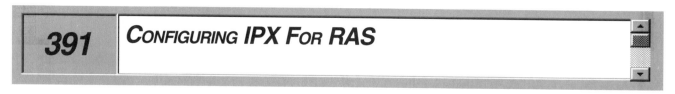

391 **CONFIGURING IPX FOR RAS**

Q: *You are a Windows NT domain administrator. You are configuring your RAS server to provide functionality to IPX-based RAS clients. Which of the following are valid configuration options for IPX clients?*

Choose all answers that apply:

   A.   *Allocate network numbers automatically.*

   B.   *Assign same network number to all IPX clients.*

   C.   *Allow remote clients to request IPX node number.*

   D.   *Route IPX.*

In previous Tips, you learned that you can independently configure network protocols for clients connecting through the Remote Access Service (RAS). One of the common protocols that you will use with RAS is the NetWare IPX/SPX protocol stack. The options Table 391 describes can affect client computers connecting with the IPX protocol.

Option	Description
Allow Remote IPX clients to access	Lets you specify the access level for IPX clients. Choices include This computer and Entire network.
Allocate network numbers automatically	Lets Windows NT automatically assign network numbers to IPX clients.
Allocate network numbers	Lets you specify a range of network numbers that RAS can assign to IPX clients.
Assign same network number to all IPX clients	Forces all network clients to receive the same network number.
Allow remote clients to request IPX node number	Lets potential IPX clients request a specific network number from the available numbers the Allocate network numbers option specifies.

Table 391 The RAS client IPX configuration options.

Figure 391 shows the RAS Server IPX Configuration dialog box.

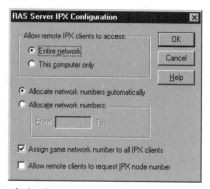

Figure 391 The RAS Server IPX Configuration dialog box.

Answers A, B, and C are correct because they are valid configuration options in the RAS Server IPX Configuration dialog box. Answer D is incorrect because there is no option to enable or disable IPX routing for RAS clients.

| 392 | CONFIGURING NETBEUI FOR REMOTE ACCESS SERVICE |

Q: *The NetBEUI protocol has no configuration options as a protocol for the Local Area Network (LAN) or for RAS clients.*

True or False?

As you have learned, the NetBEUI protocol is completely self-configuring and has no configuration options as a network protocol. However, because Remote Access Service (RAS) servers have unique requirements you must apply to the network protocols that RAS clients use, there is a configuration dialog box for the NetBEUI protocol. The RAS Server NetBEUI Configuration dialog box lets you choose the access level for NetBEUI-based RAS clients. Options include This computer only and Entire network. Figure 392 shows the NetBEUI Configuration dialog box.

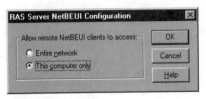

Figure 392 *The RAS Server NetBEUI Configuration dialog box.*

The answer is **False** *because, although the NetBEUI protocol has no configuration options as a network protocol, you can specify access level for NetBEUI clients in the RAS Server NetBEUI Configuration dialog box.*

| 393 | INTRODUCTION TO THE TELEPHONY APPLICATION PROGRAMMING INTERFACE (TAPI) |

Q: *Which of the following Application Programming Interfaces governs communication with telephone networks?*

Choose the best answer:

    A.   *Win16*

    B.   *Win32*

    C.   *TAPI*

    D.   *OpenGL*

The *Telephony Application Programming Interface (TAPI)* lets Windows NT interact with telephone networks by providing functions such as answering or terminating calls. TAPI lets you configure a computer's dialing properties and provides that information to TAPI-compliant applications. You can also use TAPI to govern advanced functions present in some phone systems (such as a PBX system)—which functions may include features such as Hold, Conference call, Call Transfer, and Call Park.

Answer C is correct because the Telephony Application Programming Interface (TAPI) governs communication with telephone networks. Answer A is incorrect because the Win16 API governs the structure of applications written for the Windows 3.x operating systems. Answer B is incorrect because the Win32 API governs the structure of applications written for Windows NT or Windows 95. Answer D is incorrect because the OpenGL API governs applications written to produce two- and three-dimensional graphics.

394 — UNDERSTANDING TELEPHONY **API (TAPI)** SETTINGS

Q: Which of the following settings are necessary for TAPI to function properly?

Choose all answers that apply:

    A.   Location
    B.   Calling cards
    C.   Tone-Pulse
    D.   Drivers

As you learned in Tip 393, the Telephony Application Programming Interface (TAPI) lets Windows NT interact with telephone networks by providing functions such as answering or terminating calls. The TAPI has three controllable settings, which include *Location*, *Calling cards*, and *Drivers*. TAPI uses information the Location setting contains to determine the correct sequence of numbers to dial when the user requests that the computer place a phone call. For example, if your computer is a laptop computer, you might dial to remote hosts from both your office and your home. To reach an outside line at your office, you must first dial 9, but you can reach an outside line from your home without special dialing procedures. In this example, you might choose to create two locations that include the different dialing procedures the computer must follow for each location.

TAPI uses the information the Calling card setting contains to create the sequence of numbers required to activate a calling card's special billing features (because you may not always use a calling card, this setting is optional). You must configure TAPI with device drivers that are appropriate for the communication hardware the computer uses. TAPI uses information the Drivers setting contains to identify additional drivers that special communication devices require—such as high-speed modem settings. Windows NT installs the normal TAPI driver (a file named *unimodem.tsp*) during system setup.

Answers A, B, and D are correct because the settings for TAPI are Location, Calling cards, and Drivers. Answer C is incorrect because there is no setting called Tone-Pulse in TAPI.

395 — CONFIGURING A TELEPHONY **API (TAPI)** LOCATION

Q: You are a Windows NT domain administrator. You are configuring a Windows NT Workstation to dial-out to remote hosts. Where can you specify TAPI configuration settings?

Choose the best answer:

     A.   *From the RAS Properties dialog box.*

     B.   *From the Modems option in Windows NT Control Panel.*

     C.   *From the Telephony option in Windows NT Control Panel.*

     D.   *From the Telephony Manager program.*

As you learned in Tip 394, the Telephony Application Programming Interface (TAPI) has three basic settings that you must configure for TAPI to function properly. You will perform TAPI configuration in the Dialing Properties dialog box. To open the Dialing Properties dialog box, perform the following steps:

1. Click your mouse on the Start Menu and select the Settings submenu Control Panel option. Windows NT will open the Windows NT Control Panel.
2. Within the Control Panel, double-click your mouse on the Telephony icon. Windows NT will open the Dialing Properties dialog box.

The Dialing Properties dialog box has two tabs: My Locations and Telephony Drivers. The My Locations tab lets you create and manage locations, special dialing procedures, and calling cards. Figure 395.1 shows the My Locations tab within the Dialing Properties dialog box.

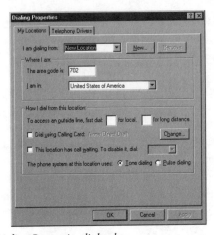

Figure 395.1 The My Locations tab in the Dialing Properties dialog box.

The Telephony Drivers tab lets you add, remove, or configure TAPI drivers. Figure 395.2 shows the Telephony Drivers tab within the Dialing Properties dialog box.

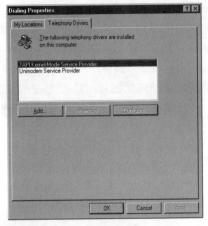

Figure 395.2 The Telephony Drivers tab in the Dialing Properties dialog box.

Answer C is correct because you can manage TAPI settings from the Telephony option in Windows NT Control Panel. Answer A is incorrect because there are no TAPI configuration options in the RAS Properties dialog box. Answer B is incorrect because you cannot manage TAPI configurations from the Modems option in Windows NT Control Panel. Answer D is incorrect because there is no program call Telephony Manager in Windows NT.

396 LOGGING ON THROUGH DIAL-UP NETWORKING

Q: *You are a Windows NT domain administrator. You want to configure a remote Windows NT Workstation to log on to the domain and to authenticate its access through the Remote Access Service at the network's domain controller. You perform this configuration on the Windows NT Workstation and it is part of the Dial-Up Networking configuration.*

True or False?

You can configure a Windows NT Server or Workstation to log on to a domain remotely through Dial-Up Networking. This feature lets you connect to the network from a remote location with the same functionality you would have if you were connected to the Local Area Network (LAN) locally.

To configure Dial-Up Networking to log on to a domain, you must specify, while you install Dial-Up Networking, that you will log on and Windows NT will authenticate you remotely. After you have specified remote logon through Dial-Up Networking, you will have the option of connecting remotely from the log-on screen, which the operating system will display when you press the CTRL+ALT+DELETE keystroke. You can configure the dialing options for login in the Logon Preferences dialog box. Figure 396 shows the Logon Preferences dialog box.

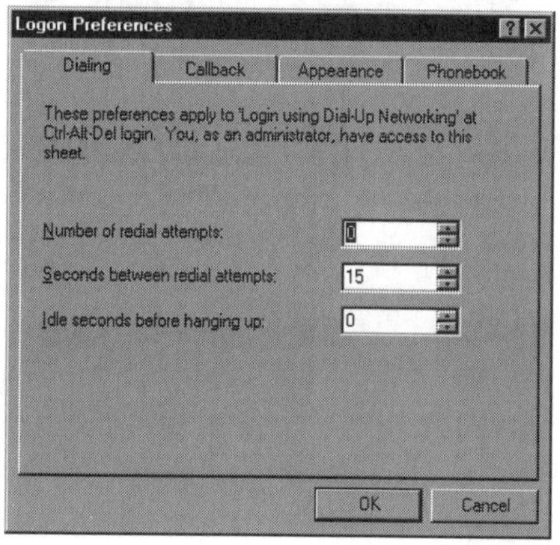

Figure 396 *The Logon Preferences dialog box.*

Within the Logon Preferences dialog box, each option performs a specific function. First, the "Number of redial attempts" option lets you specify how many times Windows NT will attempt to connect to the remote host before giving up. Second, the "Seconds between redial attempts" option lets you specify how long Windows NT will wait between connection attempts. Finally, the "Idle seconds before hanging up" option lets you specify how long Windows NT will keep the line open to receive a response from the remote host before hanging up and trying again.

*The answer is **True** because you can specify Dial-Up Networking to dial a remote host for log-on validation.*

397 — CONFIGURING THE AUTODIAL MANAGER

Q: *You can configure Windows NT applications that require a remote connection to automatically dial a number when they start.*

True or False?

As you have learned, you can configure a Windows NT Server or Workstation to log onto a domain remotely through Dial-Up Networking. In addition, you can configure Dial-Up Networking to automatically dial a number in response to a specific event (such as when you start a program). In turn, you must install the *Remote Access AutoDial Manager* for the automatic dialing to function correctly. In other words, you must run the AutoDial Manager service or Windows NT will disable the automatic dialing feature. You can enable the AutoDial Manager service within the Windows NT Services dialog box. To do so, choose Automatic for the Startup Type of the AutoDial Manager service.

You can configure each entry individually in the Dial-Up Networking phone book to automatically redial the number if the connection somehow breaks. In other words, if you lose your Remote Access Service (RAS) connection, you can configure Dial-Up Networking to try and re-connect you automatically—without direct interaction from you.

Note: *The AutoDial Manager does not support IPX client connections.*

*The answer is **True** because Windows NT can use the Dial-Up Networking AutoDial features.*

398 — TROUBLESHOOTING REMOTE ACCESS SERVICE (RAS)

Q: *You are a Windows NT domain administrator. Several users are complaining that they have problems when trying to connect to the network through the Remote Access Service. What program in Windows NT lets you review errors and see details about each error?*

Choose the best answer:

    A.   *User Manager*

    B.   *Disk Administrator*

    C.   *Error Viewer*

    D.   *Event Viewer*

As with any computer service, from time to time the Windows NT Remote Access Service (RAS) may not function as you planned. When you troubleshoot (locate and eliminate) problems in RAS, you should understand where the problem takes place. For example, users who complain that they are unable to connect through RAS might actually have a problem in the Dial-Up Networking settings for their computers. In such a case, you would be unable to find a problem with the RAS server and would have to troubleshoot the remote client to solve the problem.

One of the first items to check when troubleshooting a RAS problem is the Windows NT Event Viewer, which keeps a record of events that might include problems in the RAS. Table 398 details additional troubleshooting steps you can perform to help solve RAS problems.

Problem Type	Troubleshooting Description
Point-to-Point Protocol connections	You can create a *ppp.log* file to provide debugging information for problems over Point-to-Point Protocol connections. To enable the log file feature, change the *\HKEY_LOCAL_ MACHINE\SYSTEM\CurrentControlSet\Services\Rasman \PPP\Logging* Registry key's value to 1.
Authentication	Try changing the authentication setting for the client. Start at the lowest authentication and, if successful, move the authentication level up one at a time until you reach the highest level that still can connect.
Dial-Up Networking monitor	Windows NT includes a Dial-Up Networking monitor in the Control Panel that lets you monitor a connection status, including data-transfer speeds and multi-link connections.
AutoDial during logon	Mapped drives or other persistent connections will initiate an automatic dialing sequence as soon as *Windows Explorer* starts. To prevent this, disable AutoDial on connections.

Table 398 RAS troubleshooting tips.

Answer D is correct because the Event Viewer displays information about events and errors that have taken place on a Windows NT computer. Answer A is incorrect because User Manager does not display errors. Answer B is incorrect because the Disk Administrator does not display errors. Answer C is incorrect because there is no program called Error Viewer in Windows NT.

399 INTRODUCTION TO MICROSOFT'S INTERNET INFORMATION SERVER (IIS)

Q: *You want to build and publish a corporate Internet site. Which of the following services will you need to publish your Internet site?*

Choose the best answer:

    A.   WINS

    B.   DHCP

    C.   IIS

    D.   DNS

The high demand for corporate Internet and intranet Web sites has encouraged Microsoft to design the *Internet Information Server (IIS)*, which lets you publish Hypertext Transfer Protocol (HTTP), File Transfer Protocol (FTP), and Gopher sites. When you make HTTP, FTP, and Gopher sites available on the Internet for computers from outside your own network to access, it is known as *publishing* those sites.

Servers that support HTTP-type communications are also known as *Web sites*, which users can view from Web browser applications, such as *Internet Explorer*. Web sites are graphical information stores that provide users with interactive data manipulation features.

FTP-type sites let users browse file directories located on FTP servers, which users will access through the Internet to download files. Although Web sites are graphical, FTP sites are character-based and do not provide interactive content. Gopher-type sites, like FTP sites, are character-based and let users download files.

Microsoft's Internet Information Server lets you publish all three protocol types—HTTP, FTP, and Gopher. However, you can install IIS only on a Windows NT Server (Windows NT 4.0 Server setup will, by default, install IIS).

Answer C is correct because the Internet Information Server is the program you use to publish Web sites. Answer A is incorrect because WINS will not let you publish Web sites. WINS provides name resolution. Answer B is incorrect because DHCP will not let you publish Web sites. DHCP provides automatic IP addressing to IP client computers. Answer D is incorrect because DNS will not let you publish Web sites. DNS provides hostname resolution.

400 INSTALLING THE INTERNET INFORMATION SERVER (IIS)

Q: *Windows NT Server 4.0 will automatically install the Internet Information Server.*

True or False?

As you have learned, to support various Internet protocols from your Windows NT Server, you must also install the Internet Information Server (IIS) with the operating system. The Windows NT Server 4.0 installation CD-ROM will automatically install IIS unless you specifically instruct the setup program not to install it.

After your system setup completes, you can still install from within the Windows NT Desktop. To install IIS from the Install IIS icon on the Desktop, perform the following steps:

1.   Double-click your mouse on the Install IIS icon. Windows NT will open the IIS Setup program.

2.   Within the IIS Setup program, click your mouse on the OK button to begin setup. Windows NT will open the IIS options dialog box.

3.   Within the IIS options dialog box, select the services you want to install (such as FTP or WWW). Windows NT will indicate your selection by inserting an X in the checkbox to the right of each option.

4.   Within the IIS options dialog box, click your mouse on the OK button to continue. Windows NT will prompt you to verify the appropriate folder for service installation.

5.   Verify that the installation folders are where you want to install and click your mouse on the OK button. Windows NT will install IIS.

The answer is **True** *because Windows NT Server will install IIS automatically unless you specify otherwise.*

401   UNDERSTANDING INTERNET AND INTRANET SITES

Q: *Which of the following best describes the difference between an Internet site and an intranet site?*

Choose the best answer:

> *A.*   *An Internet site is on the network known as the Internet. An intranet is on a government information server.*
>
> *B.*   *An Internet site is interactive. An intranet site contains read-only information.*
>
> *C.*   *An Internet site is available to any user worldwide that has access to the Internet. An intranet site is internal to a company or organization.*
>
> *D.*   *There is no difference between Internet and intranet sites. These are just two terms that people use to describe the same thing.*

Most people have heard of the Internet, but cannot explain what it is. Even some computer veterans find it difficult to explain what the Internet is because the Internet is not something that you can touch or see. The Internet is a vast number of computer networks that physical lines connect, much like telephone lines.

The United States government originally conceived the Internet. In the late 1960s, the U.S. government's Department of Defense Advanced Research Projects Agency (DARPA) wanted to link Defense Department contractors with e-mail. Later, DARPA became the Advanced Research Projects Agency (ARPA) and formed the ARPAnet. ARPA eventually changed ARPAnet's name to the Internet.

The Internet originally linked only government sites and universities; later the government opened it up for public use. However, the government did not make the Internet accessible for commercial use until the 1990s. Now companies all around the world buy, sell, and exchange information, products, and ideas.

Companies, organizations, and even individuals use Internet sites for everything from distributing information about new products, to showing off family vacation pictures. Anything you can imagine, you can probably find somewhere on the Internet.

In contrast, a company or organization uses an intranet site only for internal purposes, such as information about products that are still in developmental stages. For example, an intranet site is the perfect way to distribute information if you want sales people to see how a new product is coming along, but you do not want that information available to your competitors.

Companies and organizations publish Internet sites so the site's content is available worldwide, while an intranet site is available only for limited use internal to an organization. Other than where a company or organization publishes a site, Internet and intranet sites have no major distinction in the nature of their construction.

Answer C is correct because companies and organizations publish Internet sites for worldwide public use and intranet sites are for internal company or organization use. Answer A is incorrect because an intranet site does not have to be on a government server. Answer B is incorrect because both Internet and intranet sites can be interactive. Answer D is incorrect because, although there are no differences in how an Internet and an intranet site are constructed, companies and organizations use the two types of sites for different reasons. You can use an Internet site from anywhere in the world where you can get access to the Internet. You can use an intranet site only if you are using a computer in the same network as the intranet site.

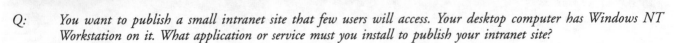

402 | INTRODUCTION TO PEER WEB SERVICES ON A WINDOWS NT WORKSTATION

Q: *You want to publish a small intranet site that few users will access. Your desktop computer has Windows NT Workstation on it. What application or service must you install to publish your intranet site?*

Choose the best answer:

A. *WINS*

B. *DHCP*

C. *IIS*

D. *PWS*

In previous Tips, you have learned about Microsoft's Internet Information Server (IIS), and how you can use IIS to publish Internet or intranet sites. A limitation of IIS is that you can install IIS only on a Windows NT Server computer. If you have a Windows NT Workstation computer, you will have to install the Peer Web Services (PWS) program in order to publish an Internet or intranet site.

PWS is similar to IIS in that they both can publish Hypertext Transfer Protocol (HTTP), File Transfer Protocol (FTP), and Gopher sites. Any of these sites can be either an Internet or an intranet site, depending on whether the publisher connected the site to the Internet. In a Windows NT Server, the Windows NT Server setup will automatically install IIS. You would have to stop the setup program from installing IIS if you did not want it to install. However, on a Windows NT Workstation, the Windows NT *Workstation Setup* program will not automatically install PWS. If you want to use PWS, you will have to install the Microsoft Peer Web Services (PWS) service from the Network dialog box. To install PWS on your Windows NT Workstation, perform the following steps:

1. Click your mouse on the Start menu and select the Setting submenu Control Panel option. Windows NT will open the Control Panel window.

2. Within the Control Panel window, double-click your mouse on the Network icon. Windows NT will open the Network dialog box.

3. Within the Network dialog box, click your mouse on the Services tab. Windows NT will display the Services sheet. Within the Services sheet, click your mouse on the Add button. Windows NT will open the Select Network Service dialog box.

4. Within the Select Network Service dialog box, click your mouse on the Microsoft Peer Web Services option. Then, click your mouse on the OK button. Windows NT will open the Microsoft *Peer Web Services Setup* program.

5. Within the Microsoft *Peer Web Services Setup* program, click your mouse on the OK button. The Microsoft *Peer Web Services Setup* program will display the Options dialog box.

6. Within the Microsoft Peer Web Services Setup Options dialog box, select the Peer Web Services components that you want to install. For example, Gopher Service or World Wide Web Service. Click your mouse on the OK button. Microsoft *Peer Web Services Setup* will display the Publishing Directories dialog box.

7. Within the Publishing Directories dialog box, verify the directories that the Microsoft *Peer Web Services Setup* program will create. Click your mouse on the OK button. The Microsoft *Peer Web Services Setup* program will create the directories, copy the files it requires to operate to your hard drive, and prompt you to restart your Windows NT Workstation.

*Answer D is correct because you must install PWS to publish an intranet site from a Windows NT Workstation. **Answer A** is incorrect because you cannot use the Windows Internet Name Service (WINS) to publish an Internet or an intranet site. **Answer B** is incorrect because the Dynamic Host Configuration Protocol (DHCP) assigns IP addresses to DHCP clients, but has nothing to do with Internet or intranet publication. **Answer C** is incorrect because the Internet Information Server (IIS) will work only with a Windows NT Server.*

403	CONFIGURING INTERNET INFORMATION SERVER AND PEER WEB SERVICES

Q: IIS and PWS share the same user interface for site administration.

True or False?

An Internet or intranet site's actual configuration is much more complex than a single Tip could possibly explain, and Internet site configuration is not on any of the core exams. However, this Tip's purpose is simply to make you aware of how to publish a basic Internet or intranet site, which will help you with your MCSE core exams by providing a foundation for Internet-related questions.

Internet Information Server (IIS) and Peer Web Services (PWS) are almost identical programs. The main difference between IIS and PWS is IIS can handle a large number of users accessing the IIS server's content at the same time. Microsoft designed PWS to handle a much lighter load. A PWS server can comfortably handle up to ten simultaneous users connecting and accessing the PWS server's content. To publish your Internet or intranet sites, you will use the Microsoft *Internet Service Manager* program, whether you use IIS or PWS for the underlying service.

Whether you publish your Internet or intranet sites from IIS or PWS, you will have to use Windows NT security to protect your site because IIS and PWS do not have any built-in security features. To secure a site that IIS or PWS publishes, you will have to set Windows NT security at the file level. You will learn more about how to secure your sites in Tip 404. IIS and PWS can publish either HTTP, FTP, or Gopher sites. Most Internet and intranet sites today are HTTP (Web) sites. Therefore, this Tip will outline how to publish an HTTP site only. To publish an HTTP site, perform the following steps:

1. Click your mouse on the Start menu and select the Programs submenu Microsoft *Internet Information Server* (Microsoft Peer Web Service on a Windows NT Workstation) group *Internet Service Manager* program option. Windows NT will open the Microsoft *Internet Service Manager* program.

2. Within the Microsoft *Internet Service Manager* program, click your mouse on the Computer icon that has the WWW caption to the right of it. Windows NT will highlight the icon. Next, click your mouse on the Properties menu Service Properties option. The Microsoft *Internet Service Manager* program will open the "WWW Service Properties For" dialog box.

3. Within the WWW Service Properties For dialog box, click your mouse on the Directories tab. Within the Directories tab, click your mouse on the Add button. The Microsoft *Internet Service Manager* will open the Directory Properties dialog box.

4. Within the Directory Properties dialog box, type the pathname to the directory on your computer that has the Internet or intranet site. Then, click your mouse on the OK button. The Microsoft *Internet Service Manager* will publish the pathname you specify—that is, it will make all the files in that and any subdirectories beneath that path available for access from the Internet or intranet.

5. Within the WWW Service Properties For dialog box, click your mouse on the OK button to close the dialog box and return to the Microsoft *Internet Service Manager* program.

6. Within the Microsoft *Internet Service Manager* program, click your mouse on the Properties menu and select the Exit option. Windows NT will close the Microsoft *Internet Service Manager* program.

*The answer is **True** because IIS and PWS both share the same user interface—the Internet Service Manager.*

404 USING WINDOWS NT SECURITY TO SECURE INTERNET AND INTRANET SITES

Q: *You would configure all security information for your Internet site from the Microsoft Internet Service Manager program.*

   True or False?

As you have learned, you will use either Internet Information Server (IIS) or Peer Web Services (PWS) to publish Internet and intranet sites. However, neither program supports built-in security. Instead, both programs use the integrated Windows NT security model. Microsoft often boasts about Back Office integration with Windows NT—the way Microsoft applications use the Windows NT security model rather than implementing their own, proprietary model. The way that IIS and PWS rely on Windows NT's security model is an excellent example of what Microsoft is so proud of.

Windows NT's major market strength is its secure network architecture. When Microsoft designed IIS, they did not want to create a security structure for it if Windows NT could provide all the security that most companies would require. Microsoft decided to have IIS use Windows NT's existing security model for all IIS security needs. IIS will run only on a Windows NT Server, so using Windows NT's security model made sense.

A company or organization constructs a Web site out of files that contain a scripted language called Hypertext Markup Language (HTML). In HTML, one file might point to another file and so on, creating an intricate document structure through which a user can browse. To secure a Web site published with IIS or PWS, you must use Windows NT's built-in file and directory security model to secure access to HTML files that you do not want open access. To secure any file with NTFS security (and specifically an HTML file), perform the following steps:

1. In My Computer or Windows *Explorer*, select the file or folder on which you want to configure NTFS permissions. Right-click your mouse on the file or folder. Windows NT will display the pop-up menu.

2. Within the pop-up menu, select the Properties option. Windows NT will display the file's or folder's Properties dialog box.

3. Within the Properties dialog box, select the Security tab. On the Security tab, click your mouse on the Permissions button. Windows NT will display the Object Permissions dialog box.

4. Within the Object Permissions dialog box, click your mouse on the Everyone group. Next, click your mouse on the Remove button. Windows NT will remove the Everyone group from the Permissions list.

5. Within the Object Permissions dialog box, click your mouse on the Add button. Windows NT will display the Add Users and Groups dialog box.

6. In the Add Users and Groups dialog box, select the user or group to which you want to assign permissions. Next, click your mouse on the Add button. Windows NT will add the user or group to the *Add Names* field.

7. In the Add Users and Groups dialog box in the *Type of Access* field, select the type of access to give the user or group and click your mouse on the OK button. Windows NT will close the Add Users and Groups dialog box.

After you have assigned NTFS security permissions to the HTML file that you want to restrict, when an Internet user tries to access the file, Windows NT will deny access. Windows NT will then send the Internet user a challenge, requesting the user's username and password. When the user enters his or her username and password, Windows NT will check the user's account information against the Directory Database. If the user's account information is valid, Windows NT will check the permissions for the HTML file to which the user requested access. If the user's account, or if any group account the user belongs to is on the Permissions list, Windows NT will let the user gain the level of access you granted to the user's account on the Permissions list.

The answer is **False** *because you would use Windows NT's NTFS security with IIS to secure a Web site.*

405   PUBLISHING MULTIPLE VIRTUAL WEB SERVERS

Q: *If you want to publish the following Web sites: www.companyx.com, www.corporate.com, and www.experimental.com, how many Windows NT Servers running Internet Information Server will you need?*

Choose the best answer:

A.   One

B.   Two

C.   Three

D.   Four

In previous Tips, you have learned the basics of publishing Web sites. However, there may be times when you will want to publish more than one Web site. For example, if you were opening your own Internet Service Provider (ISP) company, you may have to publish Web sites for your customers. If you had to purchase a Windows NT Server for each Web site that your company publishes, you could spend a lot of money on servers, and you may not have enough space to store all the servers you purchase. Microsoft recognized companies would need to publish multiple Web sites and made Windows NT able to publish as many Web sites as you have Internet Protocol (IP) addresses on your Windows NT Server.

Until version 4.0, Windows NT had a limitation of five IP addresses for each network-adapter card in a computer. For Internet Service Providers, five IP addresses per network-adapter card was not adequate room to publish their customers' Web sites. Now, in Windows NT 4.0, you can have a virtually unlimited number of IP addresses on your network-adapter card, which is important because you will need one IP address for each virtual Web server (that is, published pathname that users will access through an independent domain name) you host.

This Tip's question asks how many Windows NT Servers you will need to create virtual Web servers for *www.companyx.com*, *www.corporate.com*, and *www.experimental.com*. The answer is one. You need only one Windows NT Server, but that one server will require multiple IP addresses, one for each site. To bind multiple IP addresses to one network adapter card, perform the following steps:

1. Right-click your mouse on the Network Neighborhood icon on your desktop. Windows NT will display a pop-up menu.

2. On the pop-up menu, select the Properties option. Windows NT will open the Network dialog box.

3. Within the Network dialog box, click your mouse on the Protocols tab. Windows NT will display the Protocols sheet. Within the Protocols sheet, double-click your mouse on the TCP/IP Protocol option. Windows NT will display the Microsoft TCP/IP Properties dialog box.

4. Within the Microsoft TCP/IP Properties dialog box, click your mouse on the Advanced button. Windows NT will display the Advanced TCP/IP Addressing dialog box.

5. Within the Advanced TCP/IP Addressing dialog box in the IP Addresses section, click your mouse on the Add button. Windows NT will display the TCP/IP Address dialog box.

6. Within the TCP/IP Address dialog box, enter the IP address and subnet mask for the new IP address you want to use. Next, click your mouse on the OK button. Windows NT will close the TCP/IP Address dialog box, and return you to the Advanced TCP/IP Addressing dialog box.

7. Within the Advanced TCP/IP Addressing dialog box, click your mouse on the OK button. Windows NT will close the Advanced TCP/IP Addressing dialog box, and return you to the Microsoft TCP/IP Properties dialog box.

8. Within the Microsoft TCP/IP Properties dialog box, click your mouse on the OK button. Windows NT will close the Microsoft TCP/IP Properties dialog box.

After you have configured multiple IP addresses on your Windows NT Server, you must configure the IIS *Internet Service Manager* to point the IP addresses to the contents of the virtual server sites you want to create. To create virtual Web servers, perform the following steps:

1. Click your mouse on the Start menu and select the Programs submenu Internet Information Server group Internet Service Manager program. Windows NT will open the *Internet Service Manager* program.

2. Within the *Internet Service Manager* program, double-click your mouse on your server's name with the WWW caption to the right. The *Internet Service Manager* will open the WWW Service Properties For dialog box.

3. Within the WWW Service Properties For dialog box, click your mouse on the Directories tab. Windows NT will display the Directories sheet. Within the Directories sheet, click your mouse on the Add button. The *Internet Service Manager* will open the Directory Properties dialog box.

4. Within the Directory Properties dialog box, in the *Directory* field type the pathname to the virtual Web server site. For example, *C:\inetpub\experiment*. Click your mouse on the Home Directory radio button.

5. Within the Directory Properties dialog box, click your mouse on the Virtual Server checkbox, placing a check mark within the box. Then, type the IP address of the virtual server site that you want to create in the *Virtual Server IP Address* field. Next, click your mouse on the OK button. The *Internet Service Manager* will close the Directory Properties dialog box, and return you to the WWW Service Properties For dialog box.

6. Within the WWW Service Properties For dialog box, click your mouse on the OK button. The *Internet Service Manager* will close the WWW Service Properties For dialog box, and return you to the *Internet Service Manager* program window.

7. Within the *Internet Service Manager* program window, select the Properties menu Exit option. Windows NT will close the *Internet Service Manager* program.

Answer A is correct because you will not need more than one Windows NT Server with multiple IP addresses to publish the multiple Web sites. Answers B, C, and D are incorrect because a single Windows NT Server with multiple IP addresses can handle a virtually unlimited number of Web sites.

406 LOCKING A WINDOWS NT WORKSTATION

Q: *You are an administrator for a medium-sized network'. All the client computers are Windows NT Workstations. Several users explain they have to leave their desks frequently, and they are concerned about someone seeing sensitive information on their screens. Of the following options, which ones would you recommend to your users?*

Choose the best answers:

A.   *The users could log off the Windows NT Workstation.*

B.   *The users could set screen savers with the password option to come on after a short time of no use.*

C.   *The users could disconnect their keyboards and take the keyboards with them.*

D.   *The users could lock the Windows NT Workstations using the Lock Workstation option in the Windows NT Security dialog box.*

Depending on the type of work a user performs, he or she might need to secure a workstation. Microsoft recognized this and built into Windows NT several security features that let users secure their workstations. One quick way to secure your Windows NT computer is to use the CTRL+ALT+DEL keystroke combination, then click your mouse on the Lock Workstation button in the Windows NT Security dialog box. Using the CTRL+ALT+DEL keystroke combination will lock your workstation. Only an administrator or the person who locked a Windows NT computer can unlock the computer. After you lock Windows NT, you can use the CTRL+ALT+DEL keypress combination to invoke the Windows NT Unlock Workstation dialog box. Within the Windows NT Unlock Workstation dialog box, you can enter your username and password. Then, click your mouse on the OK button and Windows NT will unlock the workstation.

Another way to secure a Windows NT computer is to configure a Windows NT screen saver and set a password for it. In Windows NT, only a user who has a valid Windows NT account can unlock a screen saver with a password. To configure a screen saver with a password, perform the following steps:

1.   Click your mouse on the Start menu and select the Settings submenu Control Panel option. Windows NT will open the Control Panel window.

2.   Within the Control Panel window, double-click your mouse on the Display icon. Windows NT will open the Display Properties dialog box.

3.   Within the Display Properties dialog box, click your mouse on the Screen Savers tab. Windows NT will display the Screen Savers sheet. Within the Screen Savers tab, click your mouse on the Screen Savers drop-down list. Click your mouse on any screen saver in the list. Next, click your mouse on the Password Protected checkbox.

4.   Click your mouse on the OK button. Windows NT will close the Display Properties dialog box and configure the screen saver you selected.

Finally, a third option for securing your Windows NT computer is simply to log off the computer. Unlike locking the workstation, when you log off, users can still use your workstation, but they will not gain access to any files or folders on which you have set security.

*Answers A, B, and D are correct because you can secure your Windows NT computer by logging off the computer, configuring a screen saver with a password, or using the Lock Workstation option in the Windows NT Security dialog box. **Answer C** is incorrect because you should never remove a keyboard from a computer when the computer is on. Removing the keyboard could result in hardware damage.*

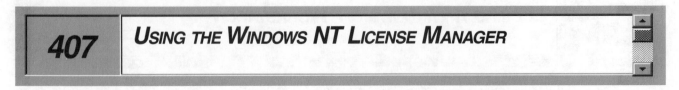

407   **USING THE WINDOWS NT LICENSE MANAGER**

Q: *You will need separate Microsoft licenses for your Microsoft Back Office products.*

True or False?

Most network operating systems require some type of licensing structure and information to ensure that businesses install the correct number of software packages for the number of users the network contains. Microsoft licensing works a little differently than most network operating systems. For example, NetWare requires you to purchase additional licenses in the form of software and you must physically install the licenses to use them (as opposed to just indicating that you have a license). In contrast, on a Microsoft Windows NT Server, you can add licenses by using the *License Manager* program. The *License Manager* program lets you add licenses for Windows NT Server Client Access Licenses (CALs), or for your Microsoft Back Office products. The *License Manager* keeps track of when you purchase licenses and how many licenses are in use.

The *License Manager* will also let you replicate licenses from one Windows NT Server to other Windows NT Servers. You will want to replicate licenses to other Windows NT Servers when you have configured your Windows NT Servers to operate in the Per Seat licensing mode. In Tip 408, you will learn more about Microsoft Windows NT Server license replication.

Windows NT Server has two licensing modes, Per Server and Per Seat. In the Per Server mode, Windows NT requires you to have duplicate licenses if you have more than one server. In the Per Seat mode, Windows NT will let the number of users for which you have licenses connect to your Windows NT Server. In Tip 212, you learned about the Per Server and Per Seat license modes in detail.

*The answer is **True** because you must purchase and then add licenses for your network clients that will access your Windows NT Server, as well as licenses for your Back Office products.*

408   **CONFIGURING LICENSE REPLICATION**

Q: *You have switched your Windows NT Server Primary Domain Controller from the Per Server license mode to the Per Seat license mode. You do not want to have to go to each Windows NT Server in your network to manage the licenses. How can you manage your Client Access Licenses (CALs) from one location?*

Choose the best answer:

    A.   *Configure your Windows NT Server Primary Domain Controller to replicate its license information to the other Windows NT Servers in your network, using the License Manager program.*

    B.   *Configure your Windows NT Server Primary Domain Controller to replicate its license information to the other Windows NT Servers in your network, using the Windows NT Replication service.*

C.   *Configure all your Windows NT Servers to replicate the license information from the Windows NT Server Primary Domain Controller, using the License Manager program.*

D.   *Configure all your Windows NT Servers to replicate the license information from the Windows NT Server Primary Domain Controller, using the Windows NT Replication service.*

As you have learned, Windows NT supports two licensing modes, Per Seat and Per Server. If you place your Windows NT Server Primary Domain Controller into the Per Seat mode, you will want to configure the other Windows NT Servers in your network to replicate the license information from your Windows NT Server Primary Domain Controller. The only exceptions are the Windows NT Servers that are domain controllers. If you configure licensing on any domain controller in your domain, the information that you configure on that domain controller will automatically be the same on every other domain controller in the domain, so you will only have to manually configure license replication on the non-domain controllers. You cannot use the Windows NT Replication service to replicate a server's licensing information. You can use the Windows NT Replication service for files only, not for licenses. To replicate the licensing information from a server to other Windows NT Servers, you must use the *License Manager* program's Replication option. To configure license replication, perform the following steps:

1.   Click your mouse on the Start menu and select the Programs option Administrative Tools group License Manager program icon. Windows NT will open the *License Manager* program.

2.   Within the *License Manager* program, click your mouse on the Server Browser tab. Within the Server Browser tab, under the domain name, click your mouse on the name of your Windows NT Server to highlight it. Next, click your mouse on the License menu Properties option. The *License Manager* will display the Properties dialog box.

3.   Within the Properties dialog box, click your mouse on the Replication tab. Within the Replication tab, click your mouse on the Enterprise Server radio button and type the name of the server from which you want to get your license information. Next, click your mouse on the OK button. The *License Manager* will configure the replication, so that it will occur at the set times, and close the Properties dialog box.

4.   Within the *License Manager* program window, click your mouse on the License menu Exit option. Windows NT will close the *License Manager* program.

Answer C is correct because you will use the License Manager program to configure all your Windows NT Servers to replicate the license information from the domain controllers. Answers A and B are incorrect because you cannot configure your Windows NT Server Primary Domain Controller to replicate its license information to other Windows NT Servers. Answer D is incorrect because you cannot use the Windows NT Replication service to replicate licensing information.

409   ADDING AND REMOVING CLIENT ACCESS LICENSES (CALs)

Q: *You have just purchased 20 new Client Access Licenses (CALs) and you must add the licenses to your Windows NT Server. What program would you use to add your CALs?*

Choose the best answer:

A.   *Server Manager*

B.   *License Manager*

C.   *User Manager for Domains*

D.   *System Policy Editor*

As you have learned in previous Tips, you can add or remove Client Access Licenses (CALs) with the *License Manager* program. The *License Manager* program shows you a purchase history for the Client Access Licenses that you previously purchased. The program will also show you what products you have purchased licenses for, and how many users are currently using licenses. You can use the *License Manager* program to administer licenses on other servers or in other domains. To add licenses to your Windows NT Server, perform the following steps:

1. Click your mouse on the Start menu and select the Programs submenu Administrative Tools group License Manager program option. Windows NT will open the *License Manager* program.

2. Within the *License Manager* program, click your mouse on the License menu New License option. The *License Manager* will open the New Client Access License dialog box.

3. Within the New Client Access License dialog box, click your mouse on the Product drop-down list and select the product for which you want to add licenses. In the *Quantity* field, type the number of licenses you purchased. Next, click your mouse on the OK button. The *License Manager* will close the New Client Access License dialog box and add the new licenses to the operating system.

4. Within the *License Manager* program window, click your mouse on the License menu Exit option. Windows NT will close the *License Manager* program.

Answer B is correct because the License Manager program lets you add new Client Access Licenses. Answer A is incorrect because you cannot use Server Manager to administer Client Access Licenses. Answer C is incorrect because you would use User Manager for Domains to administer user account properties, not Windows NT Server Client Access Licenses. Answer D is incorrect because you cannot use the System Policy Editor to administer Client Access Licenses.

410 CREATING LICENSE GROUPS

Q: *You are your company's Windows NT domain administrator. You want to assign the cost of Client Access Licenses to each department in your company, so the license costs do not come out of the Computer Department's budget. How can you tell how many users each department has logging on to the Windows NT Server?*

Choose the best answer:

A. *Install multiple network adapter cards in your Windows NT Server. Configure your network so you connect each network adapter card to a specific department. From Server Manager, you can see how many clients log on from each network adapter card.*

B. *In the License Manager program, create one license group for each department in your organization. Add the users from each department to their respective license groups. Use License Manager to view how many licenses each department is using.*

C. *Server Manager will list each user who has logged onto the Windows NT Server. Use the company's employee roster to determine to which department each user belongs, then print the results and distribute them to the various departments.*

D. *You cannot determine to which department a user belongs.*

As you have learned, you must purchase a license for each user or seat in your network. However, one concern for many companies is the annual budget—and distributing the cost for all those licenses among the departments is an important consideration. If you are the person responsible for your department's budget, you do not want any expenses that result from supporting other departments coming out of your budget. In many companies, the Client Access License (CAL) costs come out of the Computer Department's budget. Although the Computer Department absorbing CAL costs may work well for some companies, other companies may not like how large the department's budget grows. Therefore, you may want to charge to each department its respective CAL costs.

In order to charge to each department its CAL costs, you must determine the number of users in each department. You can determine the number of users by creating license groups. A *license group* is an administrative unit you can use to contain users from different departments for license management. To create a license group, perform the following steps:

1. Click your mouse on the Start menu and select the Program submenu Administrative Tools group License Manager program option. Windows NT will open the *License Manager* program.

2. Within the *License Manager* program, click your mouse on the Options menu and select the Advances submenu New License Group option. The *License Manager* will open the New License Group dialog box.

3. Within the New License Group dialog box, type the name for the group in the *Group Name* field. Click your mouse on the *Licenses* field and type the number of licenses you want to assign to this group. Next, click your mouse on the Add button. The *License Manager* will open the Add Users dialog box.

4. Within the Add Users dialog box, click your mouse on the List User From drop-down list and select the domain from which you want to group users. Hold down the CTRL key on your keyboard and, in the *Users* field, click your mouse on each user you want to group (Windows NT will highlight each user after you click on them). Next, click your mouse on the Add button. The *License Manager* will add the users to the *Add Users* field.

5. Within the Add Users dialog box, click your mouse on the OK button. The *License Manager* will close the Add Users dialog box, and return you to the New License Group dialog box.

6. Within the New License Group dialog box, click you mouse on the OK button. The *License Manager* will close the New License Group dialog box, and return you to the License Manager program window.

7. Within the License Manager program window, click your mouse on the License menu Exit option. Windows NT will close the *License Manager* program.

Answer B is correct because, to assign the cost of CALs to each department, you will create license groups in the License Manager program. Answer A is incorrect because each network adapter card must use the Windows NT Server's system resources and installing multiple network adapter cards in your server would create unnecessary system resource overhead. Answer C is incorrect because using Server Manager to determine how many users from each department are logging on to your Windows NT Server would require too much administrative effort, when you can create license groups instead. Answer D is incorrect because you use license groups to manage each user's CAL from the various departments in your company.

411 | **INTRODUCTION TO THE NETWORK CLIENT ADMINISTRATOR PROGRAM**

Q: *You want to perform a Windows 95 installation. The client computer you want to install Windows 95 on does not have a CD-ROM drive. You do have the Windows 95 source files on your Windows NT Server. Of the following, which would be the fastest method of installing Windows 95 on your client computer?*

Choose the best answer:

A.   *Install a CD-ROM drive on the client computer. Use the Windows 95 CD-ROM to install the operating system.*

B.   *Use the Network Client Administrator program to create an Installation Startup disk for Windows 95. Boot the client computer using the Windows 95 Installation Startup disk to connect to the Windows NT Server. Perform an over-the-network installation of Windows 95.*

C.   *Copy the Windows 95 source files onto a removable media disk. Connect the removable media disk to the computer you want to install Windows 95 on, and perform the Windows 95 installation from the removable media disk.*

D.   *Purchase the diskette version of Windows 95, and install it from the diskettes.*

Microsoft Windows NT Server comes with many tools to help you administer your Windows NT network. One tool is the *Network Client Administrator* program. The *Network Client Administrator* program lets you create network Installation Startup disks and Installation Disk Sets, and configure the setup of Microsoft Client Administration tools.

A *Network Installation Startup disk* is a 1.44Mb floppy diskette that contains the files a computer requires to boot and to access the network. When a computer boots with a Network Installation Startup disk, it will boot and then access the network and start installing the operating system you specify, such as Windows 95. If you are performing several operating system installations, you may find the network Installation Startup disk to be a useful resource.

An *Installation Disk Set* is one or more 1.44Mb floppy diskettes with the installation software for a given application, such as the MS-DOS Network Client 3.0. Table 411 lists the software for which you can use the *Network Client Administrator* program to create Installation Disk Sets.

Software	Description
MS-DOS Client 3.0	You can use the Network Client 3.0 for MS-DOS and Windows to connect older DOS or Windows *3.x* operating systems to any Microsoft operating system that has a server service, such as a Windows NT Server. You will find the Network Client 3.0 useful when you want to perform over-the-network installations of operating system software.
RAS 1.1 for MS-DOS	You can use the Remote Access client version 1.1 for MS-DOS to remotely connect to Windows NT Servers from MS-DOS clients.
TCP/IP 32 for WFW 3.11	TCP/IP 32 for Windows for Workgroups is an enhancement to the TCP/IP protocol stack that comes with Windows for Workgroups 3.11.
LAN Manager 2.2c for MS-DOS	The LAN Manager 2.2c for MS-DOS is an older version of the MS-DOS Client 3.0. You can use the LAN Manager 2.2c client if your have an older computer that does not have the minimum hardware to run another operating system.
LAN Manager 2.2c for OS/2	LAN Manager 2.2c for OS/2 is the Microsoft OS/2 client for connecting to Microsoft Windows NT Servers.

Table 411 The Windows NT Server's network client software.

The *Network Client Administrator* will also let you copy the client-based Network Administration Tools from your Windows NT Server CD-ROM to your Windows NT Server, so you can install them on your client computers. The Network Administration Tools are the utilities that let administrators manage their Microsoft Windows NT networks from Windows 95 or Windows NT Workstation computers, as you will learn in Tip 414. Figure 411 shows the *Network Client Administrator* program with the Make Installation Disk Set radio button selected.

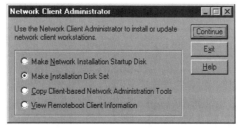

Figure 411 The Network Client Administrator program with a radio button selected.

Answer B *is correct because the quickest way to install the Windows 95 operating system on the client computer is to create a Windows 95 Installation Startup disk and boot the client computer from the disk. The Windows 95 Installation Startup disk will connect to the Windows NT Server where it has the Windows 95 source files, and then perform the installation from across the network.* **Answer A** *is incorrect because to install a CD-ROM drive and perform the installation from the Windows 95 CD-ROM would be more difficult and take longer than using a Windows 95 Installation Startup disk over the network.* **Answer C** *is incorrect because it would take longer to copy the Windows 95 source files to a removable media disk, connect the removable media disk to the client computer, and perform a Windows 95 installation, than the over-the-network installation.* **Answer D** *is incorrect because installing Windows 95 from diskettes is the slowest software installation method.*

412   **CREATING A NETWORK CLIENT INSTALLATION STARTUP DISK**

Q: *You have created a Network Installation Startup disk for a Windows 95 installation. You have put the disk into the client computer on which you want to install Windows 95 and restarted the computer. The disk boots the system, but cannot access the network. What is the most likely cause of this problem?*

Choose the best answer:

   A.   *The Network Installation Startup disk is corrupt.*

   B.   *The client computer does not have a network adapter card.*

   C.   *The network adapter card you specified when you created the disk is incorrect for the computer on which you are using it.*

   D.   *The diskette drive on the client computer is having intermittent problems.*

Using the *Network Client Administrator* program, you can create a boot diskette to use to boot a computer. After the computer boots from the diskette, the computer will initialize the network card on the computer, connect to a Windows NT Server, and start an over-the-network installation of the operating system that you specified when you created the disk. If you decide to use the *Network Client Administrator* program to create a Network Installation Startup disk, have a formatted floppy disk ready. Insert the diskette in your floppy disk drive on your Windows NT Server, and perform the following steps:

   1.   Click your mouse on the Start menu and select the Programs submenu Administrative Tools group Network Client Administrator program option. Windows NT will open the *Network Client Administrator* program.

   2.   Within the *Network Client Administrator* program, click your mouse on the Make Installation Startup disk radio button. Next, click your mouse on the Continue button. The *Network Client Administrator* program will open the Share Network Client Installation Files dialog box.

3. Within the Share Network Client Installation Files dialog box, click your mouse on the OK button. The *Network Client Administrator* will open the Target Workstation Configuration dialog box.

4. Within the Target Workstation Configuration dialog box, select the client operating system you want to install in the *Network Client* field. In the *Network Adapter* field, click your mouse on the drop-down list and select the type of network adapter card on your client computer. Next, click your mouse on the OK button. The *Network Client Administrator* will open the Network Startup Disk Configuration dialog box.

5. Within the Network Startup Disk Configuration dialog box, type the NetBIOS name you want to give to the client computer in the *Computer Name* field. In the *Network Protocol* field, click your mouse on the drop-down list and select the network protocol you want to use. Next, click your mouse on the OK button. The *Network Client Administrator* will display a message box that prompts you to insert a blank, formatted diskette into your floppy disk drive.

6. After you insert a diskette in the floppy disk drive, click your mouse on the OK button. The Network Client Administrator will create your Network Installation Startup disk.

Note: *When you are creating the Network Installation Startup disk, make sure you select the correct network adapter card. If you do not select the correct card, the diskette will not let you boot up the computer and access the network.*

Answer C is correct because if you select the wrong network adapter card type when you create the Network Installation Startup disk, the disk will not work. Answer A is incorrect because the Network Installation Startup disk is not usually corrupt. Answer B is incorrect because if the client computer did not have a network adapter card, you would see an error stating that the operating system could not bind the network protocol to the network adapter card. Answer D is incorrect because a faulty diskette drive is rare.

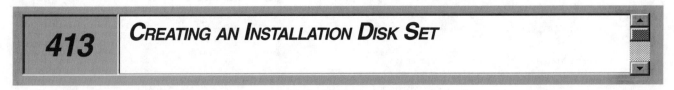

| 413 | CREATING AN INSTALLATION DISK SET |

Q: You are the administrator of a Windows NT domain that contains some Windows for Workgroups computers. You want to update the TCP/IP protocol on the Windows for Workgroups computers. How can you accomplish this?

Choose the best answer:

A. *Purchase the TCP/IP upgrade for Windows for Workgroups 3.x from Microsoft, and install the upgrade.*

B. *Remove the TCP/IP protocol from the Windows for Workgroups computer. Reinstall the TCP/IP protocol using the Windows NT CD-ROM.*

C. *Use the Network Client Administrator program to create an Installation Disk Set for TCP/IP 32 for Windows for Workgroups.*

D. *Download and use the TCP/IP patch file (TCPIP32.exe) from the Microsoft Web site to upgrade the TCP/IP protocol on the Windows for Workgroups computers.*

As you have learned, you can use the *Network Client Administrator* program to create Installation Disk Sets. You can use the Installation Disk Sets to install clients or service software for clients. The software you can make Installation Disk Sets for are the MS-DOS Client, RAS for MS-DOS, TCP/IP 32 for WFW, and the LAN Manager 2.2c clients for DOS and OS/2, which Table 411 describes in detail.

Creating an Installation Disk Set is similar to creating a Network Installation Startup disk. You will need at least one blank, formatted 1.44Mb floppy diskette. Then, you will follow the on-screen prompts that the *Network Client Administrator* program generates. To create an Installation Disk Set, perform the following steps:

1. Click your mouse on the Start menu and select the Programs submenu Administrative Tools group Network Client Administrator program option. Windows NT will open the *Network Client Administrator* program.

2. Within the *Network Client Administrator* program, click your mouse on the Make Installation Disk Set radio button. Next, click your mouse on the Continue button. The *Network Client Administrator* program will open the Share Network Client Installation Files dialog box.

3. Within the Share Network Client Installation Files dialog box, click your mouse on the OK button. The *Network Client Administrator* program will open the Make Installation Disk Set dialog box.

4. Within the Make Installation Disk Set dialog box, click you mouse on the network client or service for which you want to make a disk set. Next, click your mouse on the OK button. The *Network Client Administrator* will prompt you to insert a diskette into your floppy disk drive.

5. After you insert a diskette in the floppy disk drive, click your mouse on the OK button. The Network Client Administrator will create your Make Installation Disk Set dialog box.

6. Within the *Network Client Administrator,* click your mouse on the Exit button. Windows NT will close the *Network Client Administrator* program.

Answer C is correct because you can create the TCP/IP 32 for Windows for Workgroups Installation Disk Set in the Network Client Administrator program. ***Answer A*** *is incorrect because the TCP/IP 32 for Windows for Workgroups upgrade is free on the Windows NT Server CD-ROM.* ***Answer B*** *is incorrect because you cannot use the TCP/IP protocol stack from the Windows NT Server product on Windows for Workgroups, because the protocol is not compatible with Windows for Workgroup.* ***Answer D*** *is incorrect because the TCPIP32.exe file does not exist.*

---

414   CLIENT-BASED NETWORK ADMINISTRATION TOOLS

Q: *You are the administrator of a small Windows NT domain. You have decided to perform all network administration from the Windows NT Workstation on your desk. You have noticed that not all the same programs and utilities exist on your Windows NT Workstation that you use on the Windows NT Server, some of which you require for network administration. How will you administer your Windows NT domain from your Windows NT Workstation computer?*

Choose the best answer:

     A.   *Copy the Network Administration Tools from your Windows NT Server to your Windows NT Workstation.*

     B.   *Use the Network Client Administrator program to copy the client-based Network Administration Tools to your Windows NT Server, and then install the client tools to your Windows NT Workstation.*

     C.   *Purchase and install the Microsoft Windows NT Workstation Network Administration Kit.*

     D.   *You cannot use a Windows NT Workstation to administer a Windows NT domain.*

Most network administrators agree that performing network administration on your network server is unwise. You might accidentally do something that could leave your server in an inoperable state. Generally, using a client computer to perform network administration makes damaging the server significantly less likely. If you examine Windows NT Workstation or Windows 95, you may notice that critical Network Administration Tools are missing, such as User Manager for Domains and Server Manager. However, you can add these tools and other valuable utilities to either Windows NT Workstation or Windows 95.

The Windows NT Server Tools for 32-bit, Windows-based clients let a Windows NT Workstation computer administer a Windows NT Server domain. The tools for 32-bit, Windows-based clients include the following utilities: Dynamic Host Control Protocol (DHCP) Manager, Remote Access Administrator, Remoteboot Manager, Server Manager, User Manager for Domains, User Profile Editor, and Windows Internet Services (WINS) Manager.

After you install them onto the target computer, the Windows NT Server Tools will function exactly as they do on a Windows NT Server computer. You will learn about the Network Administration Tools for Windows NT Workstation and Windows 95 in the next several Tips. You can use the *Network Client Administrator* program to copy the client-based Network Administration Tools to your Windows NT Server, and then install the tools on the client computer that you will use for network administration.

Answer B is correct because you would use the Network Client Administrator program to copy the client-based Network Administration Tools to your Windows NT Server, and then install the administration tools from your Windows NT Server. Answer A is incorrect because you would use the Network Client Administrator program to copy the proper tools for a Windows NT Workstation to a location from which you could install them. Answer C is incorrect because the Microsoft Windows NT Workstation Network Administration Kit does not exist. Answer D is incorrect because you can install the client-based Network Administration Tools and use a Windows NT Workstation to administer your Windows NT domain.

415 NETWORK ADMINISTRATION TOOLS FOR WINDOWS NT WORKSTATION

Q: *You are performing network administration from your Windows NT Workstation. When you create user accounts, the accounts are not showing up in the domain. What is the most likely cause of the user accounts not showing up in the domain?*

Choose the best answer:

A. *You are administering a different domain.*

B. *Your domain's Directory Database is corrupt.*

C. *The accounts are not showing up because of Microsoft browsing. The accounts will show up if you give them enough time.*

D. *You have not installed the client-based Network Administration Tools for Windows NT Workstation on your Windows NT Workstation. The accounts that you are creating are on the Windows NT Workstation, not the domain.*

As you learned in Tip 414, you can perform almost all the Microsoft Windows NT domain administration you will ever need from a Windows NT Workstation. You will have to do very little at the Windows NT Server Domain Controller. Although you can perform most network administration from a Windows NT Workstation, it does not come with many of the tools that you will need to administer your Windows NT domain. The extra tools that you will need are on the Windows NT Server CD-ROM. However, you do not install the Windows NT Workstation client-based Network Administration Tools from the Windows NT Server CD-ROM. Instead, you will use the *Network*

Client Administrator program to copy the client-based Network Administration Tools to your Windows NT Server, and then share the files. From your Windows NT Workstation, you will connect to the client-based Network Administration Tools share on your Windows NT Server, and then install them to your Windows NT Workstation.

On a Windows NT Workstation, the operating system will automatically install the following utilities: the Dynamic Host Control Protocol (DHCP) Manager, the Remote Access Administrator, the Remoteboot Manager, the Server Manager, the User Manager for Domains, the User Profile Editor, and the WINS Manager. In Tip 416, you will learn how to install the Network Administration Tools.

Answer D is correct because you can create accounts on a Windows NT Workstation but, if you do not have the client-based Network Administration Tools, the accounts that you create will only be on the local Windows NT Workstation's Directory Database, not in the domain's Directory Database. Answer A is incorrect because administering a different domain is most likely not the problem's cause. Answer B is incorrect because your domain's Directory Database being corrupt is unlikely. Answer C is incorrect because Microsoft browsing has nothing to do with user accounts.

416 SYSTEM REQUIREMENTS FOR INSTALLING ADMINIS- TRATION TOOLS ON AN NT WORKSTATION

Q: You want to install the client-based Network Administration Tools on your Windows NT Workstation. You have a 486 computer with a 1Gb hard disk drive and 32Mb of RAM. You have only 1.5Mbs of hard disk space available. Will you be able to install the client-based Network Administration Tools?

Yes or No?

As you learned in Tip 415, to use Windows NT Workstation to manage your networks, you must install the client-based Network Administration Tools. Before you can install the client-based Network Administration Tools on a Windows NT Workstation, you must understand the installation system requirements Table 416 lists.

Category	Minimum Requirement
Processor	80486, Pentium, Alpha, MIPS, or PowerPC
Memory	8Mb of extended memory
Hard disk space	2.1 to 3.2Mb, depending on which hardware platform you use
Network card	One NDIS 4.0 compliant network card, installed

Table 416 The minimum hardware requirements you need to install the client-based Network Administration Tools on a Windows NT Workstation computer.

Remember, you must copy the client-based Network Administration Tools to a Windows NT server on the network before you can place them on the workstation. To copy the client-based Network Administration Tools to your Windows NT Server, perform the following steps:

1. Click your mouse on the Start menu and select the Programs submenu Administrative Tools group Network Client Administrator program option. Windows NT will open the *Network Client Administrator* program.

2. Within the *Network Client Administrator* program, click your mouse on the Copy Client-based Network Administration Tools radio button. Next, click your mouse on the Continue button. The *Network Client Administrator* will open the Share Client-based Administration Tools dialog box.

3. Within the Share Client-based Administration Tools dialog box, click your mouse on the OK button. The *Network Client Administrator* will copy the client-based Network Administration Tools to your Windows NT Server and place them into a client-accessible share. The *Network Client Administrator* will then close the Share Client-based Administration Tools dialog box.

After you have copied the client-based Network Administration Tools to your Windows NT Server, you can install the tools on your Windows NT Workstation. To install the client-based Network Administration Tools to your Windows NT Workstation, perform the following steps:

1. On your Windows NT Workstation, click your mouse on the Start menu and select the Run command. Windows NT will display the Run dialog box.

2. Within the Run dialog box, type the UNC pathname *server**SetupAdm* (where *server* corresponds to the name of your Windows NT Server with the shared client-based Network Administration Tools). Next, click your mouse on the OK button. Windows NT will connect to the SetupAdm share on the Windows NT Server and display the SetupAdm window.

3. Within the SetupAdm window, double-click your mouse on the *Winnt* folder. Windows NT will open the *Winnt* folder.

4. Within the *Winnt* folder, double-click your mouse on the *setup.bat* file. Windows NT will run the *setup.bat* file. The *setup.bat* file will install the Windows NT Workstation client-based Network Administration Tools to your Windows NT Workstation.

*The answer is **No** because you do not have sufficient hard disk space available to install the client-based Network Administration Tools.*

417 NETWORK ADMINISTRATION TOOLS FOR WINDOWS 95

Q: *If you install the client-based Network Administration Tools on a Windows 95 computer, you will get all the same tools that you get when you install them on a Windows NT Workstation.*

True or False?

As you have learned, you can perform most Windows NT domain administration tasks from a client computer. Just as you can perform most administration tasks with a Windows NT Workstation computer, you can also perform them with a Windows 95 client computer. If you are planning to use a Windows 95 client computer as an administrative workstation, you will have to install the client-based Network Administration Tools to the Windows 95 computer just as you would with a Windows NT Workstation, although the actual steps are slightly different. Although you can install the client-based Network Administration Tools on a Windows 95 client computer, you do not get all the same tools that you get on a Windows NT Workstation, because of operating system implementation differences between Windows 95 and Windows NT. You will still get the Event Viewer, Server Manager, and User Manager for Domains, and have the ability to administer printers and NTFS permissions. You will not get the DHCP Manager, Policy Editor, and WINS Manager tools, or the RAS Admin utility. You do not install the client-based Network Administration Tools for Windows 95 the same way that you install them for Windows NT Workstation, because of differences in the operating systems' implementations. To install the client-based Network Administration Tools for Windows 95, perform the following steps:

1. On your Windows 95 Client computer, click your mouse on the Start menu and select the Settings submenu Control Panel option. Windows 95 will open the Control Panel window.

2. Within the Control Panel window, click your mouse on the Add/Remove Programs option. Windows 95 will open the Add/Remove Programs dialog box.

3. Within the Add/Remove Programs dialog box, click your mouse on the Windows Setup tab. Within the Windows Setup tab, click your mouse on the Have Disk button. Windows 95 will display the Install From Disk dialog box.

4. Within the Install From Disk dialog box, click your mouse on the Browse button. Windows 95 will display the Open dialog box.

5. Within the Open dialog box, click your mouse on the Network button. Windows 95 will display the Map Network Drive dialog box.

6. Within the Map Network Drive dialog box, type the pathname to the Windows NT Server where you shared the client-based Network Administration Tools. For example, *\\server\SetupAdm*. Next, click your mouse on the OK button. Windows 95 will close the Map Network Drive dialog box, map the network drive, and return you to the Open dialog box.

7. Within the Open dialog box, click your mouse on the Drives drop-down list and select the drive that you created in the Map Network Drive dialog box. Next, click your mouse on the OK button. Windows 95 will close the Open dialog box and return you to the Install From Disk dialog box.

8. Within the Install From Disk dialog box, click your mouse on the OK button. Windows 95 will close the Install From Disk dialog box and display the Have Disk dialog box.

9. Within the Have Disk dialog box, click your mouse on the Windows NT Server Tools checkbox. Windows 95 will display a check mark in the box. Next, click your mouse on the Install button. Windows 95 will install the client-based Network Administration Tools onto your Windows 95 Client computer.

*The answer is **False** because you will only get a subset of the client-based Network Administration Tools.*

418 SYSTEM REQUIREMENTS FOR INSTALLING ADMINISTRATION TOOLS ON WINDOWS 95

Q: *You want to install the client-based Network Administration Tools on Windows 95 on a computer in your network. The computer is a 486 with 16Mb of RAM and a 500Mb hard disk drive. There are 2.5Mb of hard disk space free. Will you be able to install the client-based Network Administration Tools on this computer?*

Yes or No?

Although the client-based Network Administration Tools for Windows 95 have minimum hardware requirements, the minimum requirements are not extensive. In fact, you can install the client-based Network Administration Tools for Windows 95 on almost any Windows 95 client computer in your network. Table 418 shows the minimum hardware requirements you need to install the client-based Network Administration Tools for Windows 95.

Category	Minimum requirement
Microprocessor	386SX, 486SX, 386, 486, or Pentium
Memory	8Mb of extended memory
Hard disk space	2.2Mb
Network card	One supported network card, installed

Table 418 The minimum hardware to install the client-based Network Administration Tools on a Windows 95 computer.

*The answer is **Yes** because the computer the question describes does meet the minimum hardware requirements for installing the client-based Network Administration Tools.*

419	INTRODUCTION TO THE CLIENT SOFTWARE MICROSOFT INCLUDES WITH WINDOWS NT SERVER 4.0

Q: Of the following software, which does Microsoft include with the Windows NT Server 4.0 CD-ROM?

Choose all correct answers:

    A.   Gateway Services for NetWare (GSNW)

    B.   Services for Macintosh

    C.   Windows 95

    D.   Windows for Workgroups

Because Windows NT Server 4.0 is the cornerstone of Microsoft's networking environment, Windows NT Server 4.0 comes with a lot of add-on software at no additional charge. Some software that comes with Windows NT Server is for network administration and some is for connecting dissimilar networks together. For example, you may have Macintosh computers you want to connect to your Windows NT Server. Table 419 lists the client software Microsoft includes with Windows NT 4.0.

Client	Description
GSNW	Gateway Services for NetWare lets you create a gateway to a NetWare server. Microsoft clients (regardless of the protocols clients are using) can establish a connection to a NetWare server through the Windows NT Server running the GSNW service. Tip 424 explains GSNW in more detail.
Services for Macintosh	You can use the Services for Macintosh to let Macintosh computer clients connect to your Windows NT Server for file and print services.
Windows 95	Windows 95 is on the Windows NT Server 4.0 CD-ROM. Windows 95 is an operating system with a client for Microsoft networks.

Table 419 The client software Microsoft includes with Windows NT Server 4.0.

You will often see Windows 95 referred to as a client. However, Windows 95 is not just a client, it is also an operating system—meaning that it can run the computer on its own, without a network connection to a Windows NT Server, unlike the other clients. You will learn more about each client Table 419 lists in the next several Tips. For more information on Windows 95, see this book's Windows 95 Exam section, in Tips 806 through 1001.

Answers A, B, and C *are correct because Microsoft includes the GSNW, Services for Macintosh, and Windows 95 clients with the Windows NT Server 4.0 CD-ROM.* ***Answer D*** *is incorrect because Microsoft does not include Windows for Workgroups with Windows NT Server 4.0.*

420	INTRODUCTION TO THE CLIENT SERVICES FOR MACINTOSH

Q: *You are a Windows NT domain administrator. You have several Macintosh computers that you want to have access to your Windows NT Server Primary Domain Controller (PDC). What will you need on your Windows NT server to give the Macintosh clients access to the Windows NT Server?*

Choose all correct answers:

    A.   *AppleTalk protocol*

    B   *Macintosh MacServer*

    C.   *The Microsoft Windows NT Services for Macintosh*

    D.   *An Apple router*

As Tip 419 indicates, Microsoft designed Windows NT Server with the idea that companies do not always have standard equipment throughout their organizations. A company that has network operating systems other than Microsoft's is likely. However, Windows NT makes connecting dissimilar networks together easy, including connecting Macintosh computers to a Windows NT Server. The ability to connect Macintosh computers to a Windows NT Server is important because Apple (the maker of Macintosh computers) has established a strong market base. Computer users who use Macintosh computers tend to be loyal to Macintosh and not willing to change computers. Also, many companies that perform graphic-intensive operations require Macintosh computers.

Because of both user loyalty and corporate business requirements, you might therefore have to connect Apple Macintosh computers together with your Windows NT Servers. Microsoft includes the Services for Macintosh on the Windows NT Server CD-ROM for this purpose. The Services for Macintosh service lets you create Macintosh-Accessible Volumes. A *Macintosh-Accessible Volume* is a folder on your Windows NT Server that both Macintosh and Microsoft clients can access. You can also have Macintosh clients print to your Windows NT Server. To install the Services for Macintosh, perform the following steps:

1. Right-click your mouse on the Network Neighborhood icon on the desktop. Windows NT will display a pop-up menu.

2. On the pop-up menu, click your mouse on the Properties option. Windows NT will open the Network dialog box.

3. Within the Network dialog box, click your mouse on the Services tab. Within the Services tab, click your mouse on the Add button. Windows NT will display the Select Network Service dialog box.

4. Within the Select Network Service dialog box, click your mouse on the Services for Macintosh option. Then, click your mouse on the OK button. Windows NT will close the Select Network Service dialog box and display the Network dialog box.

5. Within the Network dialog box, click your mouse on the OK button. Windows NT will close the Network dialog box, install the Services for Macintosh, and prompt you to restart your computer.

When you install the Services for Macintosh, Windows NT will install the AppleTalk protocol for communicating with Macintosh computers. You can install the Services for Macintosh only on a Windows NT Server (you cannot install it onto a Workstation or a Windows 95 computer, because neither supports the AppleTalk protocol). You will learn more about the Services for Macintosh in Tip 421.

Answers A and C are correct because you will need the AppleTalk protocol and the Services for Macintosh installed on your Windows NT Server to provide Macintosh clients with access to the Windows NT Server. Answer B is incorrect because you will not need a Macintosh MacServer in your Windows NT domain. Answer D is incorrect because you will not need any routing devices for simple connectivity.

421   CREATING A MACINTOSH-ACCESSIBLE VOLUME

Q: *Of the following, on which file systems can you create a Macintosh-Accessible Volume?*

Choose all correct answers:

     A.   FAT

     B.   CDFS

     C.   NTFS

     D.   HPFS

In Tip 420, you learned that in order to have Macintosh clients access your Windows NT Server, you must install the Services for Macintosh service, and then you must create the Macintosh-Accessible Volume. Understanding what limitations Windows NT imposes on your ability to create Macintosh-Accessible Volumes is important. Although the Windows NT Server supports the Compact Disk File System (CDFS), High Performance File System (HPFS), File Allocation Table (FAT), and NT File System (NTFS), you can create Macintosh-Accessible Volumes only on NTFS partitions on your Windows NT Server computer. You must use the NTFS file system because Macintosh computers use a completely different file system than any of the Windows NT supported file systems, and the NTFS file system is the most compatible.

When you create a Macintosh-Accessible Volume, you cannot create another Macintosh-Accessible Volume below the first one in the directory tree. For example, you can create a Macintosh-Accessible Volume of *C:\Public*. However, you cannot then create a *C:\Public\Sales* Macintosh-Accessible Volume. Creating a share, and then creating another share under the first one is *nesting*. While you can nest standard Windows NT shares, you cannot nest Macintosh-Accessible Volumes (which are Macintosh-based shares). If you plan to create Macintosh-Accessible Volumes, you will want to carefully plan on which NTFS partition you want to create your Macintosh-Accessible Volumes, as well as how you want to structure them. After you decide on which NTFS partition you want to create a Macintosh-Accessible Choose the best answer:olume, you must use the Windows NT *Server Manager* program to create the Macintosh-Accessible Volumes. To create a Macintosh-Accessible Volume, perform the following steps:

1. Click your mouse on the Start menu and select the Programs submenu Administrative Tools group Server Manager program option. Windows NT will open the *Server Manager* program.

2. Within the *Server Manager* program, click your mouse on the MacFile menu Volumes option. *Server Manager* will display the Macintosh-Accessible Volumes dialog box.

3. Within the Macintosh-Accessible Volumes dialog box, click your mouse on the Create Volumes button. *Server Manager* will display the Create Macintosh-Accessible Volume dialog box.

4. Within the Create Macintosh-Accessible Volume dialog box, type the name for the volume (such as *MacVolume1*) in the *Volume Name* field. Click your mouse on the *Path* field and type the pathname to the folder that you want to make a Macintosh-Accessible Volume (for example, "c:\public\GraphArt." Next, click your mouse on the OK button. The *Server Manager* will close the dialog box and create the Macintosh-Accessible Volume.

Answer C is correct because you can create a Macintosh-Accessible Volume only on an NTFS partition. Answers A, B, and D are incorrect because you cannot create a Macintosh-Accessible Volume on the FAT, CDFS, or HPFS file systems.

422 | **SERVICES FOR MACINTOSH REQUIREMENTS**

Q: *You want to install the Services for Macintosh on your Windows NT Workstation 4.0. Your computer is a Pentium processor with 64Mb of RAM and a four gigabyte hard disk drive with 2Gb free. You will be able to install the Services for Macintosh on your computer.*

True or False?

As you have learned, you can create Macintosh-Accessible Volumes only on an NTFS partition. Additionally, both the Windows NT Server and the Macintosh computers will have to meet minimum hardware requirements for you to successfully implement the Services for Macintosh service. You can install the Services for Macintosh only on a computer with a Windows NT Server installation. If you try to install the Services for Macintosh on a Windows NT Workstation, you will receive a message from the operating system stating that you need a Windows NT Server to install the Services for Macintosh service.

The computer that you want to install the Services for Macintosh on must be a Windows NT Server operating system with at least one NTFS partition that has at least 2Mb of free disk space. The Macintosh computers must have the Macintosh operating system (MacOS) version 6.0.7, or later, and the *AppleShare* service.

The answer is **False** *because you cannot install the Services for Macintosh on a Windows NT Workstation.*

423 | **INTRODUCTION TO CLIENT SERVICES FOR NETWARE**

Q: *You are in a network where there are Windows NT Servers and Novell NetWare servers. You use a Windows NT Workstation computer. You want to connect to both the Windows NT Servers and the Novell NetWare servers for file and print services. Using just the tools that Microsoft supplies with Windows NT Workstation, how will you accomplish this goal?*

Choose the best answer:

A.   *Install just the IPX/SPX transport protocol.*

B.   *Install the Client Services for NetWare. The Client Services for NetWare will install the IPX/SPX transport protocol.*

C.   *Install just the TCP/IP transport protocol.*

D.   *Configure a WINS server for your Windows NT Workstation.*

Novell NetWare has been the leading client–server-based network operating system for many years. Today, thousands of companies are still using the NetWare operating system. However, as companies purchase new computer equipment, many are choosing to use Windows NT Server as their server network operating system. However, companies usually will not just throw away the old NetWare servers and replace them with new Windows NT Servers. Rather, changes of operating systems generally occur over an extended time period. While a company is phasing out one network operating system and bringing in a new one, it needs the two operating systems to be compatible. Microsoft includes many features in Windows NT Server and Workstation to help operating system migrations occur smoothly. One service you can use to help integrate your Windows NT computers with Novell NetWare servers is the *Client Services for NetWare (CSNW)*. CSNW will install only on a Windows NT Workstation. (Windows NT Server has a separate service called Gateway Services for NetWare (GSNW) that you will learn about in the next Tip.) CSNW will let you establish connections to Novell NetWare servers for file and print services. After you connect to a Novell NetWare server, you can print to the NetWare server's print queues, and open, save, and copy data to and from the NetWare server.

You cannot use CSNW unless you have the *Internet Packet Exchange/Sequenced Packet Exchange (IPX/SPX)* transport protocol installed on your Windows NT Workstation. The IPX/SPX protocol is the NetWare compatible protocol. To install CSNW, perform the following steps:

1. Right-click your mouse on the Network Neighborhood icon on the desktop. Windows NT will display a pop-up menu.

2. On the pop-up menu, click your mouse on the Properties option. Windows NT will open the Network dialog box.

3. Within the Network dialog box, click your mouse on the Services tab. Windows NT will display the Services sheet. Within the Services sheet, click your mouse on the Add button. Windows NT will display the Select Network Service dialog box.

4. Within the Select Network Service dialog box, click your mouse on the Client Services for NetWare option. Then, click your mouse on the OK button. Windows NT will install the IPX/SPX protocol, close the Select Network Service dialog box, and display the Network dialog box.

5. Within the Network dialog box, click your mouse on the OK button. Windows NT will close the Network dialog box and display a message box prompting you to restart your computer.

After you install CSNW, not only will you be able to use the NetWare servers for file and print services, but you will also be able to use NetWare utilities, such as Syscon and Pconsole.

Answer B is correct because you must install only the Client Services for NetWare to connect to Novell NetWare servers for file and print services. Answer A is incorrect because the IPX/SPX transport protocol alone will let you connect to Novell NetWare servers only for client–server applications. Answer C is incorrect because you will not be able to connect to the Novell NetWare servers using the TCP/IP protocol. Answer D is incorrect because a WINS server will not help you connect to a Novell NetWare server.

424 — INTRODUCTION TO THE GATEWAY SERVICES FOR NETWARE

Q: *You want to let your Microsoft client computers access a NetWare server. Your client computers need access to the NetWare server only one time each day. You want all your Microsoft client computers to access the NetWare server through your Windows NT Server. Which of the following Microsoft services lets you accomplish this task?*

Choose the best answer:

A   GSNW

B.   DHCP

C.   WINS

D.   CSNW

In Tip 423, you learned how the Microsoft Client Services for NetWare (CSNW) will let you connect to a NetWare server from a Windows NT Workstation, for file and print services. If you have Microsoft computers that occasionally need file and print service connections, but you do not want to install a NetWare client service, you can install the *Gateway Services for NetWare (GSNW)*. GSNW lets you create a gateway to the NetWare server so your Microsoft client computers can access the NetWare server by going through your Windows NT Server computer.

The Microsoft GSNW translates Microsoft Server Message Blocks (SMB) into NetWare Core Protocol (NCP) transmissions. The NetWare Core Protocols are the underlying communication mechanisms for client-to-server communications in their respective environments. For example, when a Microsoft Windows 95 client computer connects to a Windows NT Server, the Windows NT Server and the Windows 95 client computer must communicate using the same Server Message Block dialect. After the client and the server establish the Server Message Block dialect, the client computer can then request a tree connect. A *tree connect* is a request to connect to a specific folder on the server. To the user, the process of translating Server Message Blocks to NetWare Core Protocol transmissions is invisible—they never know that it occurs. When a Microsoft client computer uses GSNW, the client will connect to the Windows NT Server where the GSNW service is running. The Windows NT Server will connect to the NetWare server for the client that is requesting service. To install the GSNW, perform the following steps:

1. Right-click your mouse on the Network Neighborhood icon on the desktop. Windows NT will display a pop-up menu.

2. On the pop-up menu, click your mouse on the Properties option. Windows NT will open the Network dialog box.

3. Within the Network dialog box, click your mouse on the Services tab. Windows NT will display the Services sheet. Within the Services sheet, click your mouse on the Add button. Windows NT will display the Select Network Service dialog box.

4. Within the Select Network Service dialog box, click your mouse on Gateway Services (and Client) for NetWare option. Then, click your mouse on the OK button. Windows NT will install the IPX/SPX protocol, close the Select Network Service dialog box, and display the Network dialog box.

5. Within the Network dialog box, click your mouse on the OK button. Windows NT will close the Network dialog box and display a message box prompting you to restart your computer.

Answer A is correct because in order to let your Microsoft client computers access the NetWare server through your Windows NT Server, you must use the Gateway Services for NetWare (GSNW). Answer B is incorrect because the Dynamic Host Configuration Protocol (DHCP) assigns IP addresses to DHCP clients and has nothing to do with NetWare connectivity. Answer C is incorrect because the Windows Internet Name Service (WINS) has nothing to do with NetWare connectivity. Answer D is incorrect because the Client Service for NetWare (CSNW) will only let Microsoft Windows NT Workstations connect to NetWare servers.

425	WHEN TO USE GATEWAY SERVICES FOR NETWARE (GSNW)

Q: *You have several Microsoft client computers that need constant access to a NetWare server for file and print services. Of the following, which is the best way to connect your Microsoft clients to the NetWare server?*

Choose the best answer:

    A.   *Install a NetWare client service on each Microsoft client computer.*

    B.   *Install just the IPX/SPX protocol on each Microsoft client computer.*

    C.   *Install the Gateway Services for NetWare (GSNW) on your Windows NT Server, and then configure a gateway to the NetWare server on your Windows NT Server.*

    D.   *Configure a small group of NetWare client computers and let your users share the computers.*

In Tip 424, you learned that you can install the Gateway Services for NetWare (GSNW) on servers to let Windows clients connect to NetWare servers. However, the Microsoft GSNW service is not right for every situation where you must connect Microsoft client computers to NetWare servers. To correctly administer NetWare server connections, you must know when to use the GSNW.

Microsoft designed the GSNW for Microsoft client computers that require occasional access to NetWare servers. If you have client computers that require more than just occasional (light) NetWare server use, you will want to install NetWare client software on those clients. You do not want to use GSNW for client computers that require heavy use of the NetWare server because the Windows NT Server that has the GSNW service running will act as a proxy to the NetWare server. Whenever a client requests file or print service through the gateway, the Windows NT Server must process the request and send it to the NetWare server. As you can see, such a proxy structure will create a network bottleneck (slow point). To avoid a bottleneck problem, you should install a NetWare client service on any computer that will require more than occasional access to the NetWare server.

Answer A is correct because, if a client computer needs constant access to a NetWare server, you will want to install a NetWare client service on each Microsoft client computer. Answer B is incorrect because the IPX/SPX protocol will only let a Microsoft client computer access a NetWare server for client–server applications. Answer C is incorrect because the Gateway Service for NetWare (GSNW) would not let all the Microsoft client computers have sufficient access. Answer D is incorrect because configuring a small group of NetWare client computers is unnecessary. Instead, you can have all your Microsoft client computers use a NetWare client service, such as Client Service for NetWare (CSNW), to access the NetWare servers.

---

426   INTRODUCING FILE AND PRINT SERVICES FOR NETWARE

Q: *You have a mixed network with both Windows NT Servers and Novell NetWare servers. Many client computers in your network are Microsoft clients; the rest are NetWare clients. The NetWare clients must be able to access the Microsoft Windows NT Servers. What would be the easiest way to have the NetWare clients connect to the Windows NT Servers for file and print services?*

Choose the best answer:

    A.   *Install and configure the Microsoft file and print services for NetWare (FPNW) on your Windows NT Servers that you want the NetWare clients to access.*

    B.   *Install the IPX/SPX protocol on each of the Windows NT Servers that you want the NetWare clients to access.*

    C.   *Install and configure the Microsoft NetWare Connectivity Kit on each of the Windows NT Servers that you want the NetWare clients to access.*

    D.   *You cannot have Novell NetWare clients access your Microsoft Windows NT Servers.*

As you have learned in previous Tips, Client Service for NetWare (CSNW) and Gateway Services for NetWare (GSNW) let computers running Windows NT connect to NetWare servers for file and print services. If you want to integrate

NetWare clients into a Windows NT environment, you must have File and Print Services for NetWare (FPNW). If you install the File and Print Services for NetWare, your NetWare clients will see the Windows NT Server as if it were actually a NetWare *3.x* server. In other words, to the client, there is no difference between the NetWare servers and the Windows NT Servers. The NetWare client will not require that you make any changes to the client software to operate correctly.

File and print services for NetWare (FPNW) does not come with Windows NT; instead, you must purchase File and Print Services for NetWare from Microsoft or an authorized reseller. You can use the File and Print services for NetWare to integrate a Windows NT Server into a NetWare environment as an application server. Because of the intermediate layer that FPNW provides, you will not be required to add any software to the NetWare clients to understand Server Message Blocks (SMB) protocol (the underlying Microsoft protocol the Windows NT Server will use).

Answer A is correct because the Microsoft file and print services for NetWare (FPNW) will let you connect Novell NetWare clients to Microsoft Windows NT Servers. Answer B is incorrect because the IPX/SPX protocol alone will only let you connect NetWare clients to Windows NT Servers for client-server applications. Answer C is incorrect because the Microsoft NetWare Connectivity Kit does not exist. Answer D is incorrect because you can install FPNW on a Windows NT Server to have NetWare clients connect to your Microsoft Windows NT Server.

427   INTRODUCTION TO THE NETWARE MIGRATION UTILITY

Q: *You are a Novell NetWare network administrator. Your company has decided to change all the NetWare servers to Microsoft Windows NT Servers and you must make this transition as smooth as possible. How would you move the user accounts and other data to the new Microsoft Windows NT Server?*

Choose the best answer:

A.   *Copy the data from the NetWare server to the Microsoft Windows NT Servers, then copy the user accounts from the NetWare servers to the Windows NT Servers.*

B.   *Copy the data from the NetWare server to the Microsoft Windows NT Servers, then create the user accounts that are on the NetWare servers on the Windows NT Servers.*

C.   *Use the NetWare Migration utility to copy all user accounts and data in one operation.*

D.   *Perform a tape backup operation of all data on the NetWare servers that you want to move to the Windows NT Servers. Use the NetWare Migration utility to copy all user accounts to the Windows NT Servers, then restore the tape backup of the data from the NetWare servers on the Windows NT Servers.*

As you have learned, many companies are migrating their existing NetWare networks to Windows NT networks. If you are a Novell NetWare network administrator, your company may ask you to migrate the NetWare servers to Windows NT. To do so, you must be familiar with the Windows NT NetWare Migration utility. The NetWare Migration utility lets you migrate user accounts, group accounts, and data from a NetWare server to a Windows NT Server.

When you are migrating from one network operating system to another, you must consider important issues, such as what to do about duplicate user names, what to do about duplicate group names, and what data you should copy from the old operating system. The NetWare Migration utility will help you to manage these issues. You can use the NetWare Migration utility's graphical user interface (GUI) to select checkboxes that will handle most migration issues.

To use the NetWare Migration utility, you must have the IPX/SPX protocol installed on your Windows NT Server. Windows NT automatically installs the NetWare Migration utility when you install Windows NT. To perform a trial migration, perform the following steps:

1. Within Windows NT, click your mouse on the Start menu and select the Programs submenu Administrative Tools group Migration Tool for NetWare option. Windows NT will display the Select Server for Migration dialog box.

2. Within the Select Server for Migration dialog box, type the name of the NetWare server you want to migrate from in the *From NetWare Server* field. In the *To Windows NT Server* field, type the name of the Windows NT Server you want to migrate to. Click your mouse on the OK button. The NetWare Migration utility will display the Migration Tool for NetWare dialog box.

3. Within the Migration Tool for NetWare dialog box, click your mouse on the Trial Migration button. The NetWare Migration utility will start the trial migration.

Answer C is correct because the NetWare Migration utility will let you copy all user accounts and data in one operation. Answers A, B, and D are incorrect because the NetWare Migration utility is the most efficient and accurate way to copy all user accounts and data to your Microsoft Windows NT Servers.

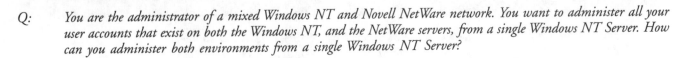

428   INTRODUCING THE DIRECTORY SERVICE MANAGER FOR NETWARE (DSMN)

Q: You are the administrator of a mixed Windows NT and Novell NetWare network. You want to administer all your user accounts that exist on both the Windows NT, and the NetWare servers, from a single Windows NT Server. How can you administer both environments from a single Windows NT Server?

Choose the best answer:

A.   Install the GSNW service and use the NetWare Client Administration utility to administer your user accounts.

B.   In User Manager for Domains, configure each user account's individual properties to be NetWare compatible. The network operating system will automatically push back all user accounts from the Windows NT Server to the NetWare servers in your network.

C.   Install the DSMN service on your Windows NT Server. Use User Manager for Domains to administer all user accounts.

D.   You cannot administer NetWare user accounts from a Windows NT Server.

As you have learned in previous Tips, Windows NT provides services that let you connect different operating systems to your Windows NT network. Microsoft Directory Service Manager for NetWare (DSMN) is a Microsoft Windows NT Server utility that enables synchronization of user accounts between Windows NT Server domains and Novell NetWare servers versions 2.x and 3.x as well as 4.x (provided the 4.x machine is running in the bindery emulation mode). DSMN extends the Windows NT Server directory database service features for user and group account management to NetWare servers. You can manage NetWare servers as part of a Windows NT domain and you can use User Manager for Domains to create and manage users and groups across the network. DSMN does not come with a Windows NT Server; instead, you must purchase DSMN from Microsoft as part of the Services for NetWare package. For more information on the Services for NetWare package, visit Microsoft's Web site at *http://www.microsoft.com*.

Answer C is correct because the Directory Service Manager for NetWare will let you administer NetWare user accounts from a Windows NT Server. Answer A is incorrect because the Gateway Services for NetWare (GSNW) will let you connect Microsoft clients to a NetWare server, not administer user accounts. Answer B is incorrect because you can only use User Manager for Domains to administer NetWare user accounts if you have installed the DSMN service. Answer D is incorrect because you can install the DSMN and then use User Manager for Domains to administer your NetWare user accounts.

429 CONFIGURING THE GATEWAY SERVICES FOR NETWARE (GSNW)

Q: *You want to configure the Gateway Services for NetWare (GSNW). Which of the following will the operating system require for you to implement the gateway?*

Choose all correct answers:

    A.   *You must be a member of the Administrators local group in the domain where you want to implement the gateway.*

    B.   *You must install and configure the IPX/SPX protocol.*

    C.   *You must create a user account at the NetWare server. You must also create a NTGATEWAY group and assign it Supervisor rights. You must make the user account that you created a member of the NTGATEWAY group.*

    D.   *You must install and configure the TCP/IP protocol.*

    E.   *You must install and configure the GSNW service.*

As you learned in Tip 424, the Gateway Services for NetWare (GSNW) lets you connect Microsoft clients to Novell NetWare servers. After you install GSNW, you must configure it correctly for your installation. Windows NT will then create a new icon in the Control Panel, GSNW. The GSNW icon will open the Gateway Services for NetWare program. You can use the GSNW program to create and manage a *gateway*, which is a central point at which Microsoft client computers can access the Novell NetWare server. Before you can use GSNW to establish the gateway, you must perform some steps on the NetWare server. First, you must create a user account. Second, you must create a *NTGATEWAY* group. Third, you must make the user account you created a member of the *NTGATEWAY* group. Finally, you must assign the NTGATEWAY group Supervisor rights. After you have performed these steps, you can use GSNW to create the gateway. To use GSNW to create the gateway, perform the following steps:

1. Within Windows NT, click your mouse on the Start menu and select the Setting submenu Control Panel option. Windows NT will open the Control Panel window.

2. Within the Control Panel window, double-click your mouse on the GSNW icon. Windows NT will open the GSNW program.

3. Within the GSNW program, click your mouse on the Gateway button. GSNW will display the Configure Gateway dialog box.

4. Within the Configure Gateway dialog box, click your mouse on the Enable Gateway check box. GSNW will highlight the *Gateway Account, Password,* and *Confirm Password* fields.

5. Within the Configure Gateway dialog box, type the user account that is a member of the NTGATEWAY group on the NetWare server in the *Gateway Account* field. Then, type the user account's password in the *Password* field, and in the *Confirm Password* field. Click your mouse on the Add button. GSNW will display the New Share dialog box.

6. Within the New Share dialog box, type the gateway name you want Microsoft clients to see in the *Share Name* field. Next, type the pathname to the NetWare server in the *Network Path* field. For example, if the NetWare server for which you are creating the gateway is Server1, the volume on the NetWare server to which you want the gateway to point is the Sys volume, and the directory on the Sys volume to which you want the gateway to point is Public, the pathname will be \\Server\Sys\Public. Click your mouse on the OK button. GSNW will create the gateway and return you to the Configure Gateway dialog box.

7. Within the Configure Gateway dialog box, click your mouse on the OK button. GSNW will close the Configure Gateway dialog box and return you to the GSNW main window.

8. Within the GSNW main window, click your mouse on the OK button. Windows NT will close GSNW.

Answers A, B, C, and E are correct. You must be a member of the Administrators local group on the Windows NT Server on which you want to implement the gateway. You must also create a user account on the NetWare server and an NTGATEWAY group. In addition, you must make the user account a member of the NTGATEWAY group. Finally, you must install and configure the IPX/SPX protocol. Answer D is incorrect because the TCP/IP protocol is not necessary to implement GSNW.

430   CONFIGURING THE CLIENT SERVICE FOR NETWARE (CSNW)

Q: *You want to configure the Client Service for NetWare (CSNW). Which of the following must you do to implement CSNW?*

Choose all correct answers:

     A.   *Install and configure GSNW.*

     B.   *Install and configure the IPX/SPX protocol.*

     C.   *Install and configure DNS.*

     D.   *Install and configure CSNW.*

As you learned in Tip 423, you can use the Client Service for NetWare (CSNW) service on a Windows NT Workstation to connect to a Novell NetWare server for file and print services. After you install CSNW, you must configure the CSNW service to specify a NetWare server that will validate your username and password. CSNW will ask you for the preferred NetWare server to validate your user account.

If you choose not to select a preferred NetWare server when you log onto your Windows NT Workstation, you can select a preferred server later in the Windows NT Workstation's Control Panel. You might not select a preferred server if, for example, you are at the top of the user tree, and actually validate to several different servers when you log in, depending on what you are trying to accomplish during a session. To configure the CSNW preferred server from the Windows NT Workstation's Control Panel, perform the following steps:

1. Within Windows NT, click your mouse on the Start menu and select the Settings submenu Control Panel option. Windows NT will display the Control Panel window.

2. Within the Control Panel window, double-click your mouse on the CSNW icon. Windows NT will open the Client Service for NetWare dialog box.

3. Within the Client Service for NetWare dialog box, click your mouse on the Select Preferred Server drop-down list. CSNW will display the list of NetWare servers in your network.

4. Within the Select Preferred Server list, click your mouse on the NetWare server that you want to validate your user account. Click your mouse on the OK button. Windows NT Workstation will close the Client Services for NetWare and set your preferred NetWare server.

Answers B and D are correct because you must install and configure both the IPX/SPX protocol and the Client Service for NetWare. Answer A is incorrect because the Gateway Services for NetWare let you connect to a NetWare server through a Windows NT Server, but not as an actual client to the NetWare server. Answer C is incorrect because the Domain Name System (DNS) service resolves host names to IP addresses in a TCP/IP environment, and has nothing to do with a NetWare network.

431 CONFIGURING FILE AND PRINT SERVICES FOR NETWARE (FPNW)

Q: *You are your company's network administrator. You have a mixed Windows NT and Novell NetWare environment. You want your NetWare clients to be able to use the Windows NT Servers with no special software or configuration on the NetWare clients. What steps must you take to set up your Windows NT Servers so that the NetWare clients can use the servers for file and print services?*

Choose all correct answers:

A. *Install and configure the IPX/SPX protocol.*

B. *Install the Gateway Services for NetWare (GSNW).*

C. *Install and configure file and print services for NetWare (FPNW).*

D. *Do nothing. NetWare clients can use Windows NT Server automatically.*

If you administer a mixed Windows NT and Novell NetWare environment that has both Microsoft and NetWare clients, you may want to implement file and print services for NetWare (FPNW). FPNW will let you connect NetWare client computers to a Windows NT Server.

To the NetWare clients, the Windows NT Server is a NetWare *3.x* server. As you learned in Tip 426, "Introducing File and Print Services for NetWare," you must purchase FPNW from Microsoft. To install and configure FPNW, perform the following steps:

1. On your Windows NT Workstation's Desktop, right-click your mouse on the Network Neighborhood icon. Windows NT will display a pop-up menu.

2. Within the pop-up menu, select the Properties option. Windows NT will display the Network dialog box.

3. Within the Network dialog box, click your mouse on the Add button. Windows NT will display the Select Network Service dialog box.

4. Within the Select Network Service dialog box, click your mouse on the Have Disk button. Windows NT will display the Insert Disk dialog box.

5. Insert the floppy disk that contains FPNW into a drive. Within the highlighted field, type the drive letter that corresponds to the drive where you inserted the Services for NetWare disk, and click your mouse on the OK button. Windows NT will display the Select OEM Option dialog box.

6. Within the Select OEM Option dialog box, click your mouse on the File and Print Services for NetWare option. Click your mouse on the OK button. Windows NT will display the Install File and Print Services for NetWare dialog box.

7. Within the Install File and Print Services for NetWare dialog box, type the location for the *SYSVOL* directory that is equivalent to the NetWare SYS: volume in the *Directory for SYS Volume* field.

8. Within the Install File and Print Services for NetWare dialog box's *Server Name* field, type the computer name that the NetWare client computers will use to access the server. Type a password for the Supervisor's account in the *Supervisor Account* field, and then type the same password in the *Password* and *Confirm Password* fields. Click your mouse on the OK button. Windows NT will configure the option you set and exit the Install File and Print Services for NetWare dialog box.

9. Restart your Windows NT Server so that the changes will take effect.

Answers A and C are correct because you must install and configure both the IPX/SPX protocol and FPNW. Answer B is incorrect because the Gateway Services for NetWare (GSNW) lets you connect Microsoft clients to Novell NetWare servers through a single Windows NT Server, and has nothing to do with connecting NetWare clients to Windows NT Servers. Answer D is incorrect because you must install and configure both the IPX/SPX protocol and FPNW on your Windows NT Server.

---

432 | INTRODUCING WINDOWS NT DIRECTORY REPLICATION

Q: Which of the following are examples of data that you should use Windows NT's Directory Replication utility to copy to other Windows NT computers?

Choose all correct answers:

    A.   A list of all the office phone numbers for staff at your company.

    B.   Windows NT System Policy files.

    C.   A database that contains your company's inventory.

    D.   Logon script files.

Windows NT comes with the ability to replicate data from one Windows NT Server to any Windows NT Server or Workstation. Although it might appear at first glance that such ability is a great way to create backups of data on other servers, Windows NT's Directory Replication is not suitable for such purposes. Windows NT's Directory Replication would take too much of your network's bandwidth (capacity) to replicate large amounts of data. Microsoft designed Windows NT's Directory Replication to replicate only three things: system policy files, logon scripts, and small read-only files. You must manually configure Windows NT's Directory Replication on the Windows NT computer that will send the data (the *Export server*), and on the Windows NT computer that will receive the data (the *Import server*). You will learn how to configure Windows NT's Directory Replication in Tips 434 and 435.

Answers A, B, and D are correct because you should use Windows NT's Directory Replication only for small read-only files, logon scripts, and Windows NT System Policy files. Answer C is incorrect because a database file for your company's inventory would be a constantly changing file.

---

433 | UNDERSTANDING THE DIRECTORY REPLICATION PROCESS

Q: *In the Windows NT Directory Replication process, the Export server checks its export directory for changes every five minutes. If the Export server finds any changes in the export directory, it will send a network message to each Import server, notifying the Import servers that someone has made changes to the export directory. The Import servers will then contact the Export server and request the changes.*

This statement accurately describes the Windows NT Directory Replication process.

True or False

As you learned in Tip 432, you must use an Export server and an Import server when you use the Windows NT Directory Replication process. In fact, you can configure a Windows NT computer to be only one of two types of replication servers—either an Import server (Windows NT will replicate data to an Import server), or an Export server (Windows NT will replicate data from an Export server). Either a Windows NT Server or a Windows NT Workstation can be an Import server, but only a Windows NT Server can be an Export server. Windows NT relies on the Directory Replicator service to manage directory replication. If the Directory Replicator service fails to start, directory replication will not occur.

The Windows NT Server (Export server) checks its export directory every five minutes to see if the administrator has changed any data. If Windows NT determines that a change in the export directory's data has occurred, the Windows NT Export server will contact all Windows NT Import servers, and notify them of the change. The Import servers will then send a message to the Export server requesting the changes. You will learn more about Windows NT's Directory Replication in Tips 434-437.

The answer is **True** *because the question accurately describes the Windows NT Directory Replication process.*

Q: *Which of the following can be Windows NT Directory Replication Export servers?*

Choose the best answer:

> *A.* *Windows NT Server Primary Domain Controller (PDC)*
>
> *B.* *Windows NT Server Backup Domain Controller (BDC)*
>
> *C.* *Windows NT Workstation*
>
> *D.* *Windows NT Server Member Server*

In Tip 433, you learned how the directory replication process occurs and what you can use it for. You have also learned that the directory replication process has two sides: the Export server, which sends data, and the Import server, which receives the data the Export server sends. You must configure each side of the directory replication process individually. In this Tip, you will learn how to configure the Export server. Before you can perform the steps to configure directory replication, you must configure the Directory Replicator service. To configure the Directory Replicator service, perform the following steps:

> 1. Within Windows NT, click your mouse on the Start menu and select the Setting submenu Control Panel option. Windows NT will display the Control Panel window.

2. Within the Control Panel window, double-click your mouse on the Services icon. Windows NT will open the Services dialog box.

3. Within the Services dialog box, double-click your mouse on the Directory Replicator service icon. Windows NT will open the Service dialog box.

4. Within the Service dialog box in the Startup Type section, click your mouse on the *Automatic* radio button. In the Log On As section of the Service dialog box, click your mouse on the *This Account* radio button. Type the name of a user account for the Windows NT directory replication to use. Finally, within the *Password* and *Confirm Password* fields, enter and re-enter the password of the user account that you are using for directory replication. Click your mouse on the OK button. Windows NT will configure the Service dialog box, and return you to the Services dialog box.

5. Within the Services dialog box, click your mouse on the Close button. Windows NT will close the Services dialog box.

After you configure the Directory Replicator service, you must configure the computer as an Export server. To configure a Windows NT Server as an Export server for directory replication, perform the following steps:

1. Within Windows NT, click your mouse on the Start menu and select the Programs submenu Administrative Tools group *Server Manager* program. Windows NT will open the *Server Manager* program.

2. Within the *Server Manager* program, double-click your mouse on the Windows NT Server that you want to configure as the Export server. *Server Manager* will open the Properties for Server dialog box.

3. Within the Properties for Server dialog box, click your mouse on the Replication button. Windows NT will display the Directory Replication on Server dialog box.

4. Within the Directory Replication on Server dialog box, click your mouse on the *Export Directories* radio button, then click your mouse on the Add button. Server Manager will display the Select Domain dialog box.

5. Within the Select Domain dialog box, click your mouse on the Windows NT computer to which you want to replicate data. Click your mouse on the OK button. *Server Manager* will add the Windows NT computer you selected to the *To List* field. Click your mouse on the OK button. *Server Manager* will close the Directory Replication on Server dialog box, and return you to *Server Manager*.

Answers A, B, and D are correct because any Windows NT computer, except a Windows NT Workstation, can be a Directory Replication Export server. Answer C is incorrect because Windows NT Workstations can be only Directory Replication Import servers.

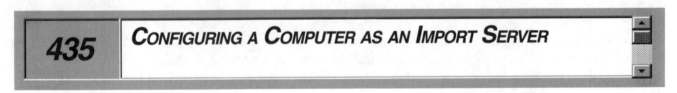

435 CONFIGURING A COMPUTER AS AN IMPORT SERVER

Q: *When you are setting up a Windows NT Directory Replication Import server, you must be an administrator on the Import server.*

True or False?

In Tip 434, you learned how to configure a Windows NT Server to be an Export server for directory replication. In this Tip, you will learn how to configure a Windows NT Server or Workstation computer to be an Import server. A Windows NT computer must be an Import server for directory replication because other Windows NT computers that validate user log-on requests will look in their *Winnt\System32\Repl\Import\Scripts* directory for log-on scripts, and system policy files. If no log-on scripts or system policy files are in the *Winnt\System32\Repl\Import\Scripts* directory, Windows NT will log the user on without setting policies that an administrator may have set for the user. You will configure directory replication so that log-on scripts and system policies will be on the Windows NT computers that log on users.

Note: *Before you can configure your Windows NT computer to be a directory replication Import server, you must configure the Directory Replicator service just as you did for the Export server in Tip 434.*

After you configure the Directory Replicator service, you must configure the computer as an Import server. To configure a Windows NT computer as an Import server for directory replication, perform the following steps:

1. Within Windows NT, click your mouse on the Start menu and select the Programs submenu Administrative Tools group *Server Manager* program. Windows NT will open the *Server Manager* program.

2. Within the *Server Manager* program, double-click your mouse on the Windows NT Server that you want to configure as the Import server. *Server Manager* will open the Properties for Server dialog box.

3. Within the Properties for Server dialog box, click your mouse on the Replication button. Windows NT will display the Directory Replication on Server dialog box.

4. Within the Directory Replication on *Server* dialog box, click your mouse on the *Import Directories* radio button, then click your mouse on the Add button. *Server Manager* will display the Select Domain dialog box.

5. Within the Select Domain dialog box, click your mouse on the Windows NT computer from which you want to replicate data. Click your mouse on the OK button. *Server Manager* will add the Windows NT computer you selected to the *From List* field. Click your mouse on the OK button. *Server Manager* will close the Directory Replication on Server dialog box, and return you to *Server Manager*.

The answer is **True** *because you must be an administrator of the Windows NT computer that you are configuring as a Directory Replication Import server.*

Q: *You can replicate only the Winnt\system32\Repl\Export directory.*

     True or False?

As you learned in previous Tips, if you accept the default setting (that is, unless you specify otherwise) when you configure directory replication, you will replicate the *Winnt\System32\Repl\Export* directory tree (which may include the \Scripts directory, as well as other directories) to the Import server's *Winnt\System32\Repl\Import* directory. To replicate other directories, you must use the Windows NT directory replication Manage button. You must also use the

Windows NT directory replication Manage button to lock certain files in directory replication so that the Windows NT replication process will not corrupt those files while you are editing them. The Directory Replication on Server dialog box has two sections: the Export section and the Import section, which both have a Manage button. When you click your mouse on the Manage button, *Server Manager* will open the Manage Imported Directories dialog box, or the Manage Exported Directories dialog box (depending on which section the button is in).

Within the Manage Exported Directories dialog box, you can lock a directory so that Windows NT will not replicate data to the Import server while you are editing the files in the directory. You can also add new directories to export to the Import servers. In addition to adding locks to directories so that you can edit the data in the import directory without corruption, you can also find out the last time Windows NT replicated the data within the Manage Imported Directories dialog box.

*The answer is **False** because you can replicate any directory on your Windows NT Server.*

437   *TROUBLESHOOTING THE REPLICATION PROCESS*

Q: *You are a Windows NT domain administrator. You are configuring Windows NT to replicate throughout the domain. You choose a user account with which the Directory Replicator service will operate. What Windows NT user rights must the user account for the Directory Replicator have?*

Choose the best answer:

     A.   *The Log on as part of the operating system right.*

     B.   *Sufficient rights to read the files on the Export server.*

     C.   *The Log on locally right.*

     D.   *The user account does not require any rights.*

Although directory replication has many advantages, it is also a process that can produce unique problems. If the Directory Replicator service encounters an error, it will write an event to the Windows NT Event log. You can use Event Viewer to view the error. Most often, you must only read the error message to identify and solve the problem. One important thing you must check is whether the account the Directory Replicator is using has sufficient rights to read the files on the Export server. Insufficient rights can result in an Access Denied error. If the password for the user account that the Directory Replicator service is using expires, Directory Replication will cease until you change the password. In such cases, the Directory Replicator service will not initialize or execute correctly.

*Answer **B** is correct because the user account that the Directory Replicator uses must have sufficient rights to read the files on the Export server. **Answer A** is incorrect because the Directory Replicator service user account does not require the act as part of the operating system right. **Answer C** is incorrect because the Directory Replicator account does not require the Log on locally right. **Answer D** is incorrect because the user account that the Directory Replicator uses must have sufficient rights to read files on the Export server.*

438   *UNDERSTANDING WINDOWS NT VGA MODE*

Q: *You are a Windows NT domain administrator. You have just installed a new video graphics card into a Windows NT Workstation and now the computer display is blank. How can you get Windows NT to produce a display so that you can configure the video card drivers?*

Choose the best answer:

A. *Restart the computer with a different operating system and copy each new driver to the boot partition.*

B. *Hold the SHIFT key during startup to force VGA mode.*

C. *Choose VGA mode from the boot menu.*

D. *You cannot force a display and must re-install Windows NT.*

One of the most common changes that users and administrators will make to a computer is to change its display properties. Because changes to video settings can sometimes result in display problems at restart, Windows NT provides an additional item, *VGA (Video Graphics Adapter) mode,* in the boot menu that system start produces. VGA mode is a set of additional commands at the end of *boot.ini's* command sequence that forces Windows NT to use the standard (VGA) driver, rather than extended or custom Super VGA (SVGA) drivers—which may limit the resolution of displays on the computer, but will generally ensure that the video driver boots correctly. Table 438 describes the difference between *boot.ini's* command lines.

Menu Choice	Runs Command Sequence
Normal mode	SCSI(0)disk(0)rdisk(0)partition(1)\WINNT="Windows NT Workstation Version 4.00"
VGA mode	SCSI(0)disk(0)rdisk(0)partition(1)\WINNT="Windows NT Workstation Version 4.00 [VGA mode]" /basevideo

*Table 438 The **boot.ini** command sequence for normal mode and VGA mode.*

Answer C *is correct because you can choose VGA mode from the boot menu to force Windows NT to use the standard VGA driver.* **Answer A** *is incorrect because copying files will not change Windows NT's internal configuration to use the new drivers.* **Answer B** *is incorrect because holding the SHIFT key during startup will not force Windows NT into VGA mode.* **Answer D** *is incorrect because you can force Windows NT to use the standard VGA driver to produce a display.*

439 UNDERSTANDING THE WINDOWS NT BOOT PROCESS ON INTEL x86-BASED COMPUTERS

Q: *Which of the following Windows NT boot files do systems booting only from SCSI drives require?*

Choose the best answer:

A. *ntdetect.com*

B. *boot.ini*

C. *ntbootdd.sys*

D. *ntoskrnl.exe*

As an MCSE, it is likely that at some point you will be asked to troubleshoot a Windows NT computer which will not start. Therefore, you must understand the sequence of events that Windows NT performs as it starts. When you install

Windows NT on an x86-based computer, the boot sequence performs the following steps:

1. The computer's hardware will perform a Power On Self Test (POST).

2. The Built-In Operating System (BIOS) locates the Master boot record and runs the program the Master boot record contains (generally the operating system bootstrap files).

3. The bootstrap files load the boot sector from the active partition into memory and identify the location of system files.

4. The bootstrap files load the *NTLDR* program into memory.

5. *NTLDR* instructs the microprocessor to use the flat memory model, which reads all physical memory as a single range of available addresses.

6. *NTLDR* loads the appropriate mini-file system drivers (mini-file system drivers read file systems like FAT and NTFS).

7. *NTLDR* reads the *boot.ini* file and creates and displays the boot menu.

8. *NTLDR* loads the correct operating system. If the user selects an operating system other than Windows NT, *NTLDR* loads the *bootsect.dos* file and passes control to the other operating system. If the user selects Windows NT, the Windows NT boot process continues.

9. *NTLDR* runs *ntdetect.com*. The *ntdetect.com* system file scans the computer's hardware and provides *NTLDR* a list of hardware it detects.

10. *NTLDR* loads *ntoskrnl.exe*, *hal.dll*, and the Windows NT Registry's system hive. *NTLDR* scans the keys within the system hive and loads the appropriate device drivers.

11. *NTLDR* passes control to *ntoskrnl.exe*.

After NTLDR passes control to *ntoskrnl.exe*, the Windows NT boot sequence is finished. Windows NT then begins the load phases during which Windows NT loads advanced functions and services. You will learn more about the Windows NT load phase in Tip 441. Each file that Windows NT uses to perform a system boot serves a specific purpose. Table 439 describes the Windows NT boot files for x86-based installations.

File	Function
NTLDR	Loads the operating system and controls the boot sequence.
boot.ini	Contains information for building the boot menu and locates the system partition for each choice in the menu.
bootsect.dos	Contains the boot sector information that was present before you installed Windows NT, provided you kept a FAT partition on the drive.
ntdetect.com	Scans the computer's hardware and provides NTLDR details on hardware it detects.
ntbootdd.sys	Present only on systems that boot from a SCSI hard drive with the SCSI BIOS for the adapter disabled. The *ntbootdd.sys* file identifies devices attached to the adapter during the Windows NT boot sequence.
ntoskrnl.exe	The Windows NT kernel file.
hal.dll	The Windows NT Hardware Abstraction Layer that separates Windows NT from physical hardware and enables Windows NT to run on multiple platforms.
system	The file that contains a collection of system configuration settings. The *system* file determines the device drivers Windows NT will load.
Device drivers	The control files for such device drivers as *ftdisk* and *scsidisk*.

Table 439 The Windows NT system boot files for x86-based installations.

*Answer C is correct because Windows NT installations require ntbootdd.sys only when it boots from a SCSI hard drive (which a SCSI adapter with its SCSI BIOS disabled controls). **Answer A** is incorrect because all Windows NT installations require ntdetect.com. The ntdetect.com file scans the computer for its hardware configuration and provides NTLDR details about hardware it detects. **Answer B** is incorrect because all Windows NT installations require boot.ini. The boot.ini file contains information Windows NT requires to build the boot menu and provides each menu choice's boot partition location. **Answer D** is incorrect because ntoskrnl.exe is the Windows NT kernel file that all Windows NT installations require.*

440 UNDERSTANDING THE WINDOWS NT BOOT PROCESS ON RISC ARCHITECTURES

Q: Which of the following Windows NT boot files do installations on RISC architectures not require?

Choose the best answer:

> A.   *ntoskrnl.exe*
>
> B.   *ntdetect.com*
>
> C.   *hal.dll*
>
> D.   *system*

The Windows NT boot process on a Reduced Instruction Set Computing-chip (RISC) based computer differs from the boot process on an Intel x86-based computer in that RISC architectures have a different boot sequence and different boot files. The Windows NT boot sequence for a RISC-based computer performs the following steps:

1. ROM firmware chooses a device from which to boot, and then determines if the device has a bootable partition.

2. The ROM firmware verifies that the boot partition contains a RISC-supported file system.

3. Finally, ROM firmware locates and loads *osloader.exe* and passes to it control of the boot process.

4. The *osloader.exe* file loads *ntoskrnl.exe*, *hal.dll*, **.pal* files (Alpha only), and the Windows NT Registry's system hive.

5. The *osloader.exe* file scans the system hive and loads the appropriate device drivers.

6. The operating system passes control to *oskrnl.exe*.

After the operating system passes control to *oskrnl.exe*, the Windows NT boot sequence is finished. Windows NT then begins the load phases during which Windows NT loads advanced functions and services. You will learn more about the Windows NT load phase in Tip 441. Each file that Windows NT uses to perform a system boot serves a specific purpose. Table 440 describes the Windows NT boot files for RISC-based installations.

File	Function
osloader.exe	Loads the operating system and controls the boot sequence.
ntoskrnl.exe	The Windows NT *kernel* file.
hal.dll	The Windows NT Hardware Abstraction Layer.
*.pal Files	Files that contain the PAL code that let an operating system access the processor directly. Only Alpha-based installations require PAL files.
system	The file that contains a collection of system configuration settings.
Device drivers	The control files for such device drivers as *ftdisk* and *scsidisk*.

Table 440 The Windows NT system boot files for RISC-based installations.

Note: *RISC installs do not need Ntdetect.com because the ROM firmware identifies all hardware.*

*Answer B is correct because RISC-based installations have ROM firmware that identifies all hardware so they do not require ntdetect.com. **Answer A** is incorrect because ntoskrnl.exe is the Windows NT kernel file that all Windows NT installations require. **Answer C** is incorrect because all Windows NT installations require hal.dll. The hal.dll file separates Windows NT from the hardware and enables Windows NT to run on different platforms. **Answer D** is incorrect because all Windows NT installations require the system file. The system file contains system configuration settings and determines the device drivers Windows NT will load.*

441 UNDERSTANDING THE WINDOWS NT LOAD PHASES

Q: *The Windows NT startup sequence is finished when the Win32 subsystem loads.*

True or False?

As you learned in Tips 439 and 440, both the RISC-based and x86-based architectures' boot sequences are finished when the loading program passes operating-system control to *ntoskrnl.exe*. After *ntoskrnl.exe* receives control, Windows NT begins the load phases, which are the same for the RISC-based architecture and the x86-based architectures. The following list describes the five load phases in Windows NT's startup sequence:

1. The *Kernel Load:* phase begins when Windows NT loads *ntoskrnl*. You can tell when this portion of system start takes place because the screen clears after *ntdetect.com* has run. Progress periods (....) appear across the top of the screen. The following events then take place:

    a. Windows NT loads the Hardware Abstraction Layer (HAL). The HAL separates Windows NT from the actual hardware that lets Windows NT operate on different platforms.
    b. Windows NT loads the system hive and scans it for information. Windows NT then divides devices and services into groups and loads them into memory, but they do not start.

Note: *To view the files that Windows NT is loading during the **Kernel Load** phase, add /sos to the end of the [Kernel Load] command line in BOOT.INI.*

2. During the *Kernel Initialization:* phase, the screen turns blue and Windows NT starts the drivers that it loaded into memory during Kernel Load. At Kernel Initialization, Windows NT saves the Registry's *CurrentControlSet* and creates the *CloneControlSet*, but does not initialize it. (Refer to Tip 229 for more information on the *CurrentControlSet* key in the Windows NT Registry.)

3. During the *Services Load* phase, the *Session Manager* (*sms.exe*) loads and carries out instructions the *BootExecute, Memory Management, DOS Devices,* and *Subsystems* registry keys contain. Table 441 describes the four registry keys.

4. During the *Win32 Subsystem start* phase, the Win32 subsystem begins executing and immediately invokes *winlogon.exe*, which starts the Local Security Authority and displays the CTRL+ALT+DELETE log-on dialog box. The *Service Controller* (*screg.exe*) simultaneously reads the registry and loads services the registry indicates it should automatically load at startup,

such as the Server and Workstation Service.

5. The *User Logs On* phase is the final load phase. A startup sequence is not complete until a user successfully logs on. After the user successfully logs on, the operating system copies the *CloneConrolSet* to the *LastKnownGood* control set and saves the *LastKnownGood* control set.

Key	Purpose
BootExecute	Although you can add additional programs or utilities that you want to execute during the boot phase, before Windows NT starts, this registry key usually contains only directions to run *autocheck.exe,* the startup version of *chkdsk*. The *autocheck.exe* checks and displays the *chkdsk* information you see on the blue screen during system start.
Memory Management	Information this key stores tells Windows NT how and where to set up page files.
DOS Devices	Information this key stores defines information Windows NT will use to support DOS-based applications.
Subsystems	This key contains instructions to start necessary subsystems for Windows NT. The default entry starts the Win32 subsystem. For example, you might add an additional entry to start the POSIX subsystem.

Table 441 The Session Manager's registry keys.

The answer is **False** *because the Windows NT startup sequence is not finished until a user successfully logs on.*

442	**INTRODUCING THE SERVICE ERROR LEVELS IN THE LOAD PHASES**

Q: *Which of the following ErrorControl Values will produce an error message and permanently halt the Windows NT startup sequence?*

Choose the best answer:

A.   *0x3 Critical*

B.   *0x0 Ignore*

C.   *0x1 Normal*

D.   *0x2 Severe*

As Tip 441 details, Windows NT has five load phases. The first load phase loads the Windows NT kernel, and the second load phase initializes the kernel.

If an error occurs while Windows NT is initializing drivers during the Kernel Initialization phase, Windows NT will use a preset range of values, called *ErrorControl values,* to determine the appropriate course of action. Table 442 describes the *ErrorControl* values.

ErrorControl Value	Description
0x0 (Ignore)	The boot sequence will ignore the error and proceed without displaying any error message.
0x1 (Normal)	The boot sequence will display an error message, ignore the error, and proceed.
0x2 (Severe)	The boot sequence will halt and use the values the *LastKnownGood* control set stores to restart. If the boot sequence is using the *LastKnownGood* control set when the error occurs, the boot sequence will ignore the error and proceed.
0x3 (Critical)	The boot sequence will halt and use the values the *LastKnownGood* control set stores to restart. If the boot sequence is using the *LastKnownGood* control set when the error occurs, the boot sequence will halt and display an error message.

*Table 442 The **ErrorContol** values.*

*Answer A is correct because an ErrorControl value of 0x3 (Critical) will halt the Windows NT startup sequence even if Windows NT is currently using the LastKnownGood control set. **Answer B** is incorrect because an ErrorControl value of 0x0 (ignore) will not halt the Windows NT startup sequence. **Answer C** is incorrect because an ErrorControl value of 0x1 (normal) will not halt the Windows NT startup sequence. **Answer D** is incorrect because although an ErrorControl value of 0x2 (severe) will halt the Windows NT startup sequence, it will restart and use the LastKnownGood control set to complete startup. If an ErrorControl value of 0x2 occurs while Windows NT is using the LastKnownGood control set, the boot system will ignore the error and system startup will proceed.*

443 EDITING THE BOOT.INI FILE

Q: *You are a Windows NT domain administrator. Your Windows NT Server will not start. You suspect the problem is in the boot.ini file's path variables. What must you do before you can edit the boot.ini file?*

Choose the best answer:

    A.   *Remove the System, Hidden, and Read-Only file attributes.*

    B.   *Remove the Hidden and Read-Only file attributes.*

    C.   *Remove the System, Hidden, Read-Only, and Archive file attributes.*

    D.   *Nothing. You can edit boot.ini without performing additional steps.*

Despite Windows NT's robustness, there may be situations when Windows NT will not start correctly or at all. If Windows NT will not start, the problem is most likely an error in the *boot.ini* file. As you learned in Tip 254, Windows NT uses information the *boot.ini* file contains to build the boot menu and locate the boot partition for the user's chosen operating system. Windows NT marks the *boot.ini* file with the *System, Hidden*, and *Read-Only* file attributes. The *Read-Only* and *Hidden* attributes prevent you from editing the *boot.ini* file unless you change them before you try to edit the file. Because you may not be able to start Windows NT in the event of errors in the *boot.ini* file, you must know how to change the *Read-Only* and *Hidden* file attributes from the command prompt.

When you boot the computer with an MS-DOS or a Windows 95 Boot disk, you will be able to manage and edit files on FAT partitions. At the command prompt, you can type the following command in the system partition's root folder to remove the restrictions on the *boot.ini* file:

```
C:\> ATTRIB -R -H -S BOOT.INI   <Enter>
C:\>
```

Answer B *is correct because you must remove the Hidden attribute to see the boot.ini file, and the Read-Only attribute to save changes.* **Answer A** *is incorrect because the System attribute has no affect on editing the file.* **Answer C** *is incorrect because neither the System or Archive attributes affect your ability to edit a file.* **Answer D** *is incorrect because you must remove the Hidden and Read-Only attributes to edit the* **boot.ini** *file.*

444 UNDERSTANDING COMMON BOOT ERRORS

Q: *You are a Windows NT domain administrator. You are experiencing a problem on a computer that you have installed to dual-boot Windows NT and Windows 95. The problem is that the computer displays no boot menu and automatically starts Windows 95. Which of the following solutions consumes the least amount of time and will both enable the boot menu and ensure that Windows NT is the operating system that starts automatically?*

Choose the best answer:

    A. *Format the hard drive, reinstall Windows 95, then reinstall Windows NT.*

    B. *Restore the entire computer from a backup which was made before the problem began.*

    C. *Edit the boot.ini file and change the Timeout and Default sections appropriately.*

    D. *Reinstall Windows NT over the existing installation.*

Some of the most common errors you will experience with Windows NT occur during the startup sequence. These problems can range from files that are missing due to user error, to problems with the computer hardware, such as a bad hard drive. As you have learned, the *boot.ini* file is often the cause of most errors. Table 444 describes some common boot errors.

Problem	Solution
Will not boot	Check to see if a floppy disk or compact disk is currently in the computer. Many computers now support bootable CD-ROMs and will try to boot from a compact disk or a floppy disk that is not system-enabled.
Automatically starts wrong operating system	Edit your *boot.ini* file and ensure Windows NT is the operating system set in the Default section.
No boot menu is displayed	Edit the *boot.ini* file and increase the value in the Timeout section.

Table 444 Common boot problems and solutions.

You can edit or replace a file to solve many problems you will experience during the Windows NT startup sequence. Although reinstalling the operating system onto the computer will frequently solve a problem, a less time-consuming method is often available. Thoroughly understanding how Windows NT starts is vital to properly diagnosing a problem and restoring the computer to a state of readiness in the shortest possible time. For example, although you can reinstall the operating systems on the computer to solve problems with the *boot.ini* file, simply editing the *boot.ini* file is a much faster way to restore the computer to a state of readiness.

*Answer C is correct because settings in the boot.ini file determine both a boot menu's production and the operating system that will start automatically. Therefore, editing this file is the least time-consuming solution. **Answer A** is incorrect because, although formatting and completely reinstalling both operating systems would solve the problem, it is not the least time-consuming solution. **Answer B** is incorrect because, although restoring the computer from a backup would solve the problem, it is not the least time-consuming solution. **Answer D** is incorrect because, although reinstalling Windows NT as an upgrade over the existing installation would solve the problem, it is not the least time-consuming solution.*

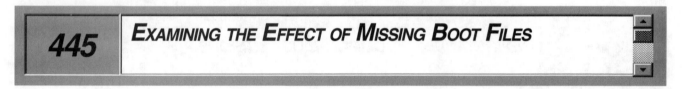

445	EXAMINING THE EFFECT OF MISSING BOOT FILES

Q: *You are a Windows NT domain administrator. When you boot your Windows NT Server, you get the following message:*

```
Error accessing boot sector file multi (0)disk (0)rdisk (0)partition (1):\bootss
```

Which of the following Windows NT boot files will produce this message if the file is missing?

Choose the best answer:

A.   *ntdetect.com*

B.   *ntoskrnl.exe*

C.   *bootsect.dos*

D.   *NTLDR*

As you know, the Windows NT system start process consists of five steps. You can use the error message the currently executing operating-system loader displays to diagnose some problems you may encounter during the Windows NT startup sequence. For example, you can identify a missing boot file by the message the operating-system loader displays during the boot process. Table 445 lists the messages Windows NT will display when a specific boot file is missing.

Missing File	Windows NT message
NTLDR	*BOOT: Couldn't find NTLDR Please insert another disk.*
ntdetect.com	*NTDETECT V4.0 Checking Hardware... NTDETECT failed.*
ntoskrnl.exe	*Windows NT could not start because the following file is missing or corrupt: <winnt root> \system32\ntoskrnl.exe. Please reinstall a copy of the above file.*
bootsect.dos	*I/O Error accessing boot sector file multi (0)disk (0)rdisk (0)partition (1):\bootss.*
boot.ini	Windows NT will boot if you have installed it to the WINNT folder on the first physical hard drive's first partition. All other installations will result in the following message: *Windows NT could not start because the following file is missing or corrupt: <winnt root> \system32\ntoskrnl.exe. Please reinstall a copy of the above file.*

Table 445 Error messages for missing boot files.

*Answer C is correct because the operating system loader will display the error message Error accessing boot sector file multi (0)disk (0)rdisk (0)partition (1):\bootss when the bootsect.dos file is missing or corrupt. **Answers A, B, and D** are incorrect because the operating system does not produce this error message if the bootsect.dos files are missing.*

446 USING EXPAND.EXE TO REPLACE MISSING OR DAMAGED FILES

Q: *You are a Windows NT Server administrator. You are experiencing an error during system boot and have determined that the problem is a missing boot file. What program does the Windows NT Server CD-ROM provide that will let you decompress and copy a single file to the location you choose?*

Choose the best answer

A.   *Extract.exe*

B.   *Expand.exe*

C.   *Uncompress.exe*

D.   *There is no such utility on the Windows NT CD-ROM*

In Tip 445, you learned how to recognize common Windows NT boot problems that missing or damaged boot files cause. After you have identified the problematic file, you must know how to replace it with a new copy that will return your computer to a state of readiness. Planning ahead for such problems is an excellent way to ensure that you can repair the system quickly, no matter what file has been destroyed or corrupted. Planning ahead, in the case of addressing boot problems, means that you should make a copy of all boot files for your computer.

In Tips 339 and 340, you learned what files the operating system requires to boot a Windows NT computer. If you copy the boot files to a floppy disk that you have formatted from within Windows NT, you will have copies for replacement, and a floppy disk that can start Windows NT from the floppy drive.

If you must replace missing or damaged boot files and no copy of the files exist, you can use the *expand.exe* command to decompress and copy a single file from the Windows NT compact disk. Installation files on the Windows NT compact disk are compressed. You must decompress and copy the file or files to the proper location so that you can use the files. Each installation folder on the Windows NT compact disk stores the *expand.exe* utility. You can use the *expand.exe* utility to decompress and to copy individual files to any location the computer is capable of writing to. For example, if you wanted to expand the *ntdetect.com* file for an x86-based computer that has Windows NT installed on the C drive, you would simply access the command prompt, change to the CD-ROM drive's i386 directory, and type the following command:

```
C:\i386> EXPAND NTDETECT.CO_  C:\NTDETECT.COM   <ENTER>
```

Because the files are compressed, the *compress.exe* program (which performed the compression) replaces each file name's last letter with the underscore character (_). You must supply the last letter in the new name you specify at the command line's end, as shown here:

```
C:\> expand testfile.ex_  testfile.exe   <ENTER>
```

You can also use an Emergency Repair Disk (ERD) to replace missing boot files. You will learn more about the ERD in Tip 447.

Answer B is correct because the expand.exe command line utility can both decompress files and copy files to a location you specify. Answers A and C are incorrect because the Windows NT compact disk does not contain any such utilities. Answer D is incorrect because you can expand individual files from the Windows NT compact disk.

447   CREATING AN EMERGENCY REPAIR DISK (ERD)

Q: *You are a Windows NT Workstation administrator. You want to create an Emergency Repair Disk (ERD). What Windows NT utility will let you create an ERD?*

Choose the best answer:

    A.   *Disk Administrator*

    B.   *User Manager*

    C.   *RDISK*

    D.   *FDISK*

You can use an Emergency Repair Disk (ERD) to repair bad or missing boot files and to replace the Windows NT Registry. The Emergency Repair Disk is an important part of system maintenance, because of its necessity for boot file replacements. You should create a new Emergency Repair Disk each time you make an important change to the Windows NT configuration, such as the addition or removal of hard drives or user accounts, which will ensure that all that information will restore from the boot disk as well. You start the utility that creates an Emergency Repair Disk from the command prompt, but it runs in a window. To start the RDISK utility, simply access the command prompt and type "RDISK."

The RDISK utility has two options: Update Repair Info and Create Repair Disk. Update Repair Info overwrites the files in the system root folder that the Repair folder contains and then prompts you to create a Repair Disk. The Repair folder contains the following files:

- *SYSTEM._*
- *SOFTWARE._*
- *DEFAULT._*
- *SECURITY._*
- *SAM._*
- *NTUSER DA_*
- *AUTOEXEC.NT*
- *CONFIG.NT*

These files represent the majority of Windows NT configuration options that the user controls and include a copy of the security accounts database and the system registry. Neither the Emergency Repair Disk nor the repair directory store hardware configurations such as port assignment and video driver configurations. Instead, the Create Repair Disk utility prepares the Repair disk (a floppy disk) that Windows NT setup requires to execute a repair process. The Repair disk contains the same files as the Repair folder. You can get boot and system files the repair process may require from the Windows NT setup diskettes or compact disk.

Answer C is correct because the RDISK utility can create Emergency Repair Disks (ERDs). Answer A is incorrect because Disk Administrator can manipulate disks and partitions but cannot create an ERD. Answer B is incorrect because User Manager can manipulate users and groups but cannot create an ERD. Answer D is incorrect because FDISK is an MS-DOS disk management utility and cannot create an ERD.

448   **USING THE EMERGENCY REPAIR DISK (ERD)**

Q: *You are a Windows NT domain administrator. You are experiencing a boot problem with a Windows NT Workstation and have determined that the problem is corrupted boot files. To repair the problem, you can use the Emergency Repair Disk and execute the repair command to boot the computer.*

True or False?

You must have the Windows NT setup diskettes to use the Emergency Repair Disk to repair a Windows NT installation, because the repair process takes place in the character-based portion of Windows NT setup that executes from the diskettes. To repair a Windows NT installation, perform the following steps:

1. Insert disk 1 of the three Windows NT setup diskettes in a bootable floppy drive and restart the computer. The bootable diskette will begin the Windows NT setup process.

2. At the character-based setup screen that asks if you want to install Windows NT or repair files, choose R to repair files. Windows NT setup will prompt you to insert an Emergency Repair Disk (ERD). If you do not have an ERD, Windows NT setup will search the boot partition for repair folders and present you with a list of choices.

3. Follow the instructions on the screen, inserting whichever individual disks from the setup process the repair process asks for. The Windows NT setup will perform the repair and prompt you to restart the computer.

4. Remove the ERD and restart the computer. If the repair process solved the problem, Windows NT will start normally. If it did not, you will need to pursue other solutions.

Note: *If you replace the Security Account Manager database during repair, you must know the administrator password, which was stored on the Emergency Repair Disk when it was made (either by you or another administrator).*

The answer is **False**. The Emergency Repair Disk is not bootable. You must use it with the three Windows NT setup diskettes to repair corrupted files.

449   **INTRODUCING THE LASTKNOWNGOOD CONFIGURATION**

Q: *You are a Windows NT domain administrator. You have just finished making changes to the video driver configuration on a Windows NT Workstation, which prompted you to restart your computer. When the computer restarts, everything appears to be normal until the blue screen disappears and the screen goes black. No other signs of malfunction are present. What steps should you take to restore the computer's functionality?*

Choose the best answer:

     A.   *Replace the monitor.*

     B.   *Do not try to log on. Restart the computer, and press the spacebar when the computer prompts you to use the LastKnownGood configuration.*

C.   *Restore the system from a backup.*

D.   *Use the Emergency Repair Disk to replace the video configuration.*

As you learned in Tip 441, the Windows NT startup process is not complete until a user successfully logs on to the system. If you experience problems that relate specifically to changes you made in the last session, or make a configuration change that results in an unstable system, you can restore the computer to its previous state prior to logon.

The operating system saves the Windows NT configuration as the Default control set when you shut down Windows NT. Windows NT will automatically try to use the Default control set configuration the next time it restarts. Additionally, Windows NT will save the configuration that existed when you last successfully logged on to your computer. This configuration is the *LastKnownGood* control set.

You can use the *LastKnownGood* configuration to solve problems that result from changes you make to hardware configuration, such as port assignment or video drivers. If a problem occurs that you believe you can use the *LastKnownGood* configuration to solve, do not try to log on, restart your computer, and press the spacebar for *LastKnownGood* when the computer prompts you during the Windows NT startup's character-based portion.

Answer B is correct because you can use the LastKnownGood configuration to restore the video driver configuration, provided you have not logged on. Answer A is incorrect because the problem is not likely to be the monitor because the monitor appears to function normally until the blue screen portion of the Windows NT startup is done. Answer C is incorrect because, although restoring the computer from backup would solve the problem, it is not the best answer because it is more time-consuming to perform a restore than it is to use the LastKnownGood configuration. Answer D is incorrect because the Emergency Repair Disk does not contain hardware configurations.

| **450** | **UNDERSTANDING HOW WINDOWS NT CREATES THE LASTKNOWNGOOD CONFIGURATION** | |

Q: When does Windows NT create the LastKnownGood Configuration?

Choose the best answer:

A.   *When you shut the computer down.*

B.   *When you log off from Windows NT.*

C.   *When you Log on to Windows NT.*

D.   *During the Kernel Initialization phase of the Windows NT startup process.*

As you learned in the previous Tip, part of the Windows NT startup process lets you specify that Windows NT should load the *LastKnownGood* control set. The key to understanding when to use the *LastKnownGood* configuration is that the operating system creates the *LastKnownGood* configuration when you successfully log on to the computer. If you have been unable to complete an entire boot sequence and log onto the operating system, *LastKnownGood* will contain the last configuration that you successfully logged on with.

During the Windows NT startup Kernel Initialization phase, Windows NT reads information from the Default control set to create both the current control set and the clone control set. When a user successfully logs on, the operating system copies the clone control set to the *LastKnownGood* control set. The operating system does not change the *LastKnownGood* control set again until the next time a user successfully logs on.

Answer C is correct because the operating system saves the LastKnownGood control set when you log onto Windows NT. Answer A is incorrect because the operating system creates the Default control set when you shut down a Windows NT computer. Answer B is incorrect because the operating system does not create or save a control set when you log off from Windows NT. Answer D is incorrect because the operating system creates Current and Clone control sets during the Windows NT startup process's Kernel Initialization phase.

---

451 UNDERSTANDING REMOTE PROCEDURE CALLS IN WINDOWS NT

Q: Which of the following best describes the use of Remote Procedure Calls?

Choose the best answer:

    A.   A message-passing facility that lets applications distributed across the network communicate with each other.

    B.   An internal Windows NT component that maintains a list of remote resources.

    C.   An application Windows NT includes that lets administrators use a remote to control Workstations.

    D.   An internal Windows NT component that sends warning messages across the network.

As you have learned in previous Tips, Windows NT supports distributed processing, which is the basis for client–server computing. Distributed processing lets applications request information from other applications and resources from other computers in the network. When applications distribute the workload across the network, they can work more quickly and efficiently.

Microsoft's *SQL Server,* a large multi-user database program, is an excellent example of client–server computing. Client computers on the network that use *SQL Server* can run a client application that performs user-level tasks, such as data entry and information display. Simultaneously, the server computer runs a server-level application that searches databases and indexes the data within the database. A user can create a request for database entries that meets specific criteria, and then send that request to the server. The server then acts on the client's request and returns the results to the client computer which, in turn, displays the search results.

To perform such processing, the client and server computers must communicate. Client and server applications in Windows NT networks use the Remote Procedure Call (RPC) protocol to send and receive messages. The RPC protocol acts as a direct interface between the client application and the server application.

Answer A is correct because a Remote Procedure Call is best described as a message passing facility which lets applications distributed across the network communicate with each other. Answers B, C, and D are incorrect because they do not accurately describe the term Remote Procedure Call (RPC).

---

452 USING THE NET ACCOUNTS COMMAND

Q: Which of the following commands can you use to modify password and log-on requirements for all accounts?

Choose the best answer:

    A.   *Net Use*

    B.   *Net Accounts*

    C.   *Net Stop*

    D.   *Net File*

As you have learned, Windows NT primarily uses a Graphical User Interface (GUI) for systems administration. There are, however, reasons to include character-based command (as opposed to mouse-command based, like the GUI) sets for configuring information in Windows NT. Some common reasons for you to use character-based command sets include creating scripts or batch files which make configuration changes automatically run, or creating scripts to perform large-scale changes to accounts which would take more time to accomplish with the Windows NT GUI.

Many character-based commands are *Net* commands, which you may find difficult to differentiate between because they all start with Net. Although you may find NET commands intimidating now, with practice, you will soon learn that each NET command has its own unique function, which will help you understand how each one works. Because the Net commands are important tools for your use in administering Windows NT, and because the MCSE exams may test you on each individual command, Tips 453 through 473 discuss each Net command separately.

Answer B is correct because the Net Accounts command modifies password and log-on requirements for all accounts. Answer A is incorrect because the Net Use command connects and disconnects a computer to and from a resource the network shares. Answer C is incorrect because the Net Stop command stops a Windows NT service. Answer D is incorrect because the Net File command displays all the filenames the network shares and how many locks each file has. Net File can also remove file locks and close shared files.

453   USING THE NET COMPUTER COMMAND

Q: *Which of the following commands can add and remove computers from a domain database?*

Choose the best answer:

    A.   *Net Computer*

    B.   *Net Accounts*

    C.   *Net File*

    D.   *Net Share*

As you learned in Tip 452, you can perform many administrative tasks within Windows NT's Graphical User Interface (GUI) that you can also use simple text commands to perform. Most text commands you will use begin with the *Net* command. For example, there may be times when you must add or remove a computer from the Windows NT Domain database and you are not sitting at a Windows NT domain controller. To add or remove computers from the Domain database, you can use the *Net Computer* command sequence from any Windows NT computer on the network, as shown in the following code example:

```
C:\> NET COMPUTER \\computername /ADD   <ENTER>
C:\> NET COMPUTER \\computername /DEL   <ENTER>
```

Computername corresponds to the name of the computer that you wish to add or remove from the database, while the */ADD* and */DEL* switches either add or remove the computer from the Domain database, as the name indicates.

Answer A is correct because the Net Computer command can add and remove a computer to and from a Domain database. Answer B is incorrect because the Net Accounts command modifies password and log-on requirements for all accounts. Answer C is incorrect because the Net File command displays all the filenames the network shares and how many locks each file has. Net File can also remove file locks and close shared files. Answer D is incorrect because the Net Share command creates, deletes, or displays resources the network shares.

454 | **USING THE NET CONFIG SERVER OR WORKSTATION COMMAND**

Q: *Which of the following commands will display the Workstation service's current configuration?*

Choose the best answer:

    A.   *Net Config Server*

    B.   *Net Config Workstation*

    C.   *Net Statistics*

    D.   *Net Share*

In Tip 453, you learned how to use the *Net Computer* command to add and remove a computer from a network's domain database. Similarly, you can use the *Net Config Server* command to display configuration information about the Server, and the *Net Config Workstation* command to control the Workstation services' configuration. The information each command displays will help you quickly determine if the administrator has properly configured the services for your network. In addition to displaying the current configuration, you can also configure the services from the command prompt. Some configuration options for services can only be changed using the *Net Config Server* and *Net Config Workstation* commands. To display the configuration list, simply enter the entire command at the command-line, as shown here for the server:

```
C:\> net config workstation   <ENTER>
```

Answer B is correct because the Net Config Workstation command will display the Workstation service's current configuration. Answer A is incorrect because the Net Config Server command will display current configuration of the Server service. Answer C is incorrect because the Net Statistics command will display statistics about a service you specify; it will not display configuration information. Answer D is incorrect because the Net Share command will create, delete, and display network resources.

455 | **USING THE NET CONTINUE COMMAND**

Q: *Which of the following commands will reactivate a service that a user has paused?*

Choose the best answer:

    A.   *Net Continue*

    B.   *Net Start*

C.   *Net Use*

D.   *Net Help*

As you have learned in previous Tips, there may be times when you will pause a service before you stop it so that users can finish what they are doing before the service stops. When you pause a service, users who are already connected to that service can finish their work with the service, but new users cannot log on and connect to the network. As you have learned, you can use text commands to pause a service from both the Windows GUI and the console. Although you cannot pause all Windows NT services, the *Net Pause* command lets you specify which Windows NT service you want to pause. The following list contains some Windows NT services you can pause with the *Net Pause* command:

- File Server for Macintosh

- FTP Publishing service

- LPDSVC

- Netlogon

- Network Dynamic Data Exchange

- Network DDE DSDM

- NT LanManager Security Support Provider

- Remoteboot

- Remote Access Server

- Schedule

- Server

- Simple TCP/IP services (such as SMTP)

- Workstation

After you pause a service, you can use the *Net Continue* command to reactivate the service. You can only use *Net Continue* on a service if you have not already stopped it. If the service has been stopped, you will actually need to re-start the service. The following code example shows the *Net Continue* command-line syntax:

```
C:\> NET CONTINUE service   <ENTER>
```

In the command, *service* corresponds to the registered name of the service. For example, to continue the *Workstation* service, you would enter the following command at the command line:

```
C:\> NET CONTINUE workstation   <ENTER>
```

Answer A is correct because the Net Continue command will reactivate a service that you have used the Net Pause command to pause. Answer B is incorrect because the Net Start command will start a service you specify or display a list of services you have already started. Answer C is incorrect because the Net Use command connects or disconnects a computer to and from a shared resource. Answer D is incorrect because the Net Help command displays help information about Net commands.

---

456   USING THE NET FILE COMMAND

Q: *Which of the following commands can remove file locks from a shared file?*

Choose the best answer:

    A.   Net File

    B.   Net Share

    C.   Net Stop

    D.   Net Continue

As the previous Tips have detailed, you can often perform a network administration activity (such as continuing a paused service) from the console with textual commands. You have also learned that it is sometimes more convenient to use the console than it is to use the Windows NT Graphical User Interface (GUI) when performing network administration. Another console command you can use to administer files and permissions on your Windows NT network is the *Net File* command. When a user on a remote computer opens a file from a shared folder, the operating system considers the file a shared file. Sometimes, however, files which users try to access may only be able to support only one user. When more than one user tries to access a file, but cannot because another user already has it open, a file lock occurs.

You can use the *Net File* command to view shared files and their associated file locks. The *Net File* command will also let you remove file locks and close a file another user accidentally left open or if a software error did not unlock the file after the user closed the file. You will use the *Net File* command from the console, as shown in the following code (the items within the brackets are optional):

```
C:\> NET FILE [id [/CLOSE]] <ENTER>
```

If you invoke the *NET FILE* command without parameters, the operating system will display a list of files. You can then use the *NET FILE* command with a ID returned by the original *NET FILE* invocation.

Answer A is correct because the Net File command can display shared files and their file locks, as well as remove file locks and close shared files. Answer B is incorrect because the Net Share command creates, deletes, and displays shared resources such as folders or printers, but cannot remove file locks. Answer C is incorrect because the Net Stop command stops a Windows NT service you specify. Answer D is incorrect because the Net Continue command reactivates services you paused with the Net Pause command.

---

457   USING THE NET GROUP COMMAND

Q: *Which of the following commands can add a new global group on a Windows NT domain?*

Choose the best answer:

A.   *Net Share*

B.   *Net Start*

C.   *Net Group*

D.   *Net Accounts*

Suppose you are a network administrator whom a major company has asked to configure a series of ten Windows NT servers. The servers are at different locations and are not connected to the other servers. The configuration contains multiple global groups which are the same for each location. Because you know that it would be time-consuming to create a global group at each server, you decide to instead create a *batch file,* which will automatically create the groups on all the servers. The batch file is a special text file that contains command sequences you can execute from the command line. The Windows NT operating system processes each command in order, as though you had entered them from the keyboard one at a time.

You can use standard commands, which work individually at the Windows NT Command Prompt, to create the batch file in any text editor program. To do so, you must use a separate line for each command to create the file and then save the file with the *.bat* extension, which indicates to the operating system that the file is a batch file. To create a simple batch file that will, in turn, create multiple global groups, you must include invocations to the *Net Group* command. You will implement the *Net Goup* command in accordance with the following command format (the items within the brackets are optional):

```
NET  GROUP [groupname [/COMMENT:"text"]  [/DOMAIN]
        groupname </ADD [/COMMENT:"text"]  |  /DELETE> [/DOMAIN]
        username [...] </ADD  |  /DELETE> [/DOMAIN]
```

The *Net Group* command is the command that you must use, either from the command line or within a batch file, to create global groups on a Windows NT computer. The *Net Group* command lets you add, modify, and display global group information (including names and comments).

Answer C is correct because the Net Group command lets you add, display, and modify global groups on a Windows NT domain. ***Answer A*** *is incorrect because the Net Share command lets you create, delete, and display network resources, such as shared folders and printers, but cannot create or modify global groups.* ***Answer B*** *is incorrect because the Net Start command lets you start a Windows NT service you specify, and will display a list of services you have started.* ***Answer D*** *is incorrect because the Net Accounts command lets you display and modify password and log-on requirements for all accounts.*

458   **USING THE NET HELP COMMAND**

Q: *Which of the following commands will display help information about a Net command you specify?*

Choose the best answer:

A.   *Net Statistics*

B.   *Net Help*

C.   *Net Config*

D.   *None; you must access Windows NT's on-line Help for help information on Net commands*

As Tips 452 through 457 indicate, you will use several different *Net* commands to manage a Windows NT network from the command-line prompt. However, there may be times when you will not remember each *Net* command's function. If you require help with *Net* commands, you can use the *Net Help* command to list each *Net* command and display help information about a command you specify. To get help for an individual *Net* command, type the command name and the support string */help;* or type *Net Help,* then the command name itself.

Answer B is correct because the Net Help command displays help information about a Net command you specify. **Answer A** is incorrect because the Net Statistics command displays statistical information about a service you specify, such as Server or Workstation. **Answer C** is incorrect because the Net Config command displays and modifies the settings for a service you specify, such as Server or Workstation. **Answer D** is incorrect because the Net Help command displays help information about a Net command you specify.

459   **USING THE NET HELPMSG COMMAND**

Q: *Which of the following commands provide information about Windows NT error messages?*

Choose the best answer:

     A.   *Net Help*

     B.   *Net Helpmsg*

     C.   *Net Statistics*

     D.   *None; you must look up error messages in the Windows NT Resource Kit*

Although typing in Net commands at the console might seem more convenient because they automate otherwise time-consuming processes, you also have a larger margin for error when you type a command, rather than click the mouse on your selection. Sometimes if you type a Net command incorrectly, Windows NT will display an error message that ends with a numeric code. You can use the *Net Helpmsg* command with this numeric code to find the error. When you invoke the *Net Helpmsg* command with the numeric error code from the incorrect entry, Windows NT will display information that describes the error in the original command that displayed the error. You will implement the *Net Helpmsg* command, as shown in the following code:

```
C:\> NET HELPMSG message#   <ENTER>
```

The *message#* parameter corresponds to the error message that the operating system previously returned to you.

Answer B is correct because the Net Helpmsg command displays information about a Windows NT error message you specify. **Answer A** is incorrect because the Net Help command displays help information about Net commands. **Answer C** is incorrect because the Net Statistics command displays statistical information about a service you specify, such as Server or Workstation. **Answer D** is incorrect because the Net Helpmsg command displays information about a Windows NT error message you specify.

460   **USING THE NET LOCALGROUP COMMAND**

Q: *Which of the following commands let you add a new Local group to a Windows NT Server?*

Choose the best answer:

   A.   Net Group

   B.   Net Localgroup

   C.   Net Start

   D.   Net Share

As you learned in Tip 457, you can use the *Net Group* command to add, modify, and display information about Global groups. Similarly, you can use the *Net Localgroup* command to manage Local groups. If you type the *Net Localgroup* command, Windows NT will list Local groups. You can use command-line variables to add and remove users to and from the Local group. Command-line variables can also add new groups and comments to the Local group, which makes it more descriptive. You will implement the *Net Localgroup* command, as shown in the following command format (the items within brackets are optional):

```
NET LOCALGROUP [groupname [/COMMENT:"text"] [/DOMAIN]
               groupname </ADD [/COMMENT:"text"] | /DELETE> [/DOMAIN]
               username [...] </ADD | /DELETE> [/DOMAIN]
```

As you can see, the *groupname* and *username* variables, like with the *Net Group* command, let you specify users and groups to add and delete.

Answer B is correct because the Net Localgroup command adds, displays and modifies Local groups. **Answer A** is incorrect because the Net Group command adds, displays, and modifies Global groups. **Answer C** is incorrect because the Net Start command starts a Windows NT service you specify. **Answer D** is incorrect because the Net Share command creates, deletes, and displays network shares.

461 USING THE NET NAME COMMAND

Q: *Which of the following commands let you create an alias to send and receive messages on the network?*

Choose the best answer:

   A.   Net User

   B.   Net View

   C.   Net Name

   D.   Net Group

As you have learned, Windows NT computers can send messages to each other across the network. In order for a Windows NT computer to send a message to another computer, it must know the computer's name to which it is sending the message. The operating system obtains a computer's list of names from three different places: a *computername*, which you specify in the Network dialog box, a *username*, which Windows NT adds to the list when you log on, and a *messagename*, which you use the *Net Name* command to add. The *messagename*, or *alias*, is an additional name in the computer's list of names. The alias directs messages to a computer that already has a name in the sending computer's list. You can use the *Net Name* command to view your current names or add a *messagename*. You will implement the *Net Name* command, as shown in the following command format (the items within brackets are optional):

```
C:\> NET NAME [name [/ADD | /DELETE]] <ENTER>
```

The *name* parameter corresponds to the computer name to add or delete.

*Answer C is correct because the Net Name command adds, deletes, and displays messaging names. **Answer A** is incorrect because the Net User command adds, deletes, and displays user account information. **Answer B** is incorrect because the Net View command displays a list that contains domains, computers and resources a computer shares. **Answer D** is incorrect because the Net Group command adds, modifies, and displays information about Global groups.*

462	USING THE NET PAUSE COMMAND

Q: *Which of the following commands can you use to pause many Windows NT services?*

Choose the best answer:

    A.   *Net Stop*

    B.   *Net Pause*

    C.   *Net Session*

    D.   *Net Continue*

As you learned in Tip 455, you may decide to pause a Windows NT service so that users can finish what they are doing before you stop the service. When you pause a service, users who are already connected to the network can finish their work, but new users cannot log on and connect to the network. Although you cannot pause all Windows NT services, you can use the Net Pause command to specify which service you want to pause. The following list contains some Windows NT services you can pause with the Net pause command:

- File Server for Macintosh
- FTP Publishing service
- LPDSVC
- Netlogon
- Network Dynamic Data Exchange
- Network DDE DSDM
- NT Lan Manager Security Support Provider
- Remoteboot
- Remote Access Server
- Schedule
- Server
- Simple TCP/IP services (such as SMTP)
- Workstation

Note: *Although you can use **Net Pause** on almost any Windows NT service, each network will have its own restrictions that specify the services you can pause and those you cannot.*

You will implement the *Net Pause* command, as shown in the following example:

```
C:\> NET PAUSE service   <ENTER>
```

The *service* value corresponds to the name of the service that you want the operating system to pause.

Answer B is correct because the Net Pause command pauses currently running Windows NT services. Answer A is incorrect because the Net Stop command stops the Windows NT services you specify. Answer C is incorrect because the Net Session command displays a computer and its remote clients, and disconnects a computer from its remote clients. Answer D is incorrect because the Net Continue command reactivates a service you have paused with the Net pause command.

463 USING THE NET PRINT COMMAND

Q: *Which of the following commands can cancel and delete a print job on a network printer?*

Choose the best answer:

A.   *Net Stop*

B.   *Net Print*

C.   *Net Computer*

D.   *Net Accounts*

As you have learned, you can type Net commands at the command prompt, or click your mouse on the commands in the Windows NT Graphical User Interface (GUI). You can use the *Net Print* command to manage print jobs and print queues from the command prompt. The *Net Print* command lets you view current print jobs in a remote share, hold a print job (pause it), release a print job (unpause it), and cancel a print job (delete it from the queue). To use the *Net Print* command to manage a printer, you must have sufficient network rights. You will implement the *Net Print* command, as shown in the following command format (the items within brackets are optional):

```
NET PRINT \\computername\sharename
          [\\computername\ job# [/HOLD | /RELEASE | /DELETE]
```

In the prototype, the *computername* is the name of the computer on which the share resides, while the *sharename* corresponds to the share itself.

Answer B is correct because the Net Print command controls and displays information about print jobs and print queues. Answer A is incorrect because the Net Stop command stops a Windows NT service you specify. Answer C is incorrect because the Net Computer command adds and deletes computers to and from a Windows NT domain database. Answer D is incorrect because the Net Accounts command displays and modifies password and log-on information for all Windows NT accounts.

464 USING THE NET SEND COMMAND

Q: *Which of the following commands can send a message to a remote computer on the network?*

Choose the best answer:

     A.   *Net Session*

     B.   *Net Computer*

     C.   *Net User*

     D.   *Net Send*

As you have learned, the Windows NT operating system uses messages to communicate between computers. You can use the *Net Send* command to send a message to a specific computer or user. The *Net Send* command lets you send a text message to a *computername*, *username*, or *messagename* that you specify when you create the message. You will implement the *Net Send* command, as shown in the following command format (the items within brackets are optional):

```
NET SEND <name | * | /DOMAIN[:name] | /USERS> message
```

The *name* variable corresponds to the *computername*, *username*, or *messagename* of the target computer. The *message* variable contains the string that you want to display on the remote computer.

Answer D *is correct because the* **Net Send** *command sends messages to other computers in the network.* **Answer A** *is incorrect because the Net Session command displays information about remote computers on the network, as well as disconnects remote computers from the network.* **Answer B** *is incorrect because the Net Computer command adds and deletes computers from a Windows NT domain database.* **Answer C** *is incorrect because the Net User command adds to and modifies user account information.*

465   **USING THE NET SESSION COMMAND**

Q: *Which of the following commands can disconnect a connection from a remote computer on the network?*

Choose the best answer:

     A.   *Net Stop*

     B.   *Net Accounts*

     C.   *Net Session*

     D.   *Net Use*

As you have learned, the fastest way to execute Net commands is to type them at the command prompt. To view the computers that are on your network, or to disconnect a specific computer from yours, you can use the *Net Session* command. The *Net Session* command lets you list current connections, and disconnect specific computers from your shared resources.

When you type only the *Net Session* command, Windows NT will display all the current network computers to which your computer is connected. Typing *Net Session*, and then a Universal Naming Convention (UNC) string that specifies a *computername*, will display all the connections that referenced computer holds. Typing *Net Session*, and then a UNC that specifies a *computername* with the additional */delete* option, will disconnect the computer from all shared resources.

You will implement the *Net Session* command, as shown in the following command format (the items within brackets are optional):

```
C:\> NET SESSION [\\computername] [\DELETE] <ENTER>
```

*Answer C is correct because the Net Session command displays information about and disconnects connections from remote computers on the network. **Answer A** is incorrect because the Net Stop command stops a Windows NT service you specify. Although stopping the Server service will disconnect all connections, this is not the best answer because Windows NT developers did not specifically design the Net Stop command to remove connections. **Answer B** is incorrect because the Net Accounts command displays and controls password and log-on information for all Windows NT accounts. **Answer D** is incorrect because the Net Use command adds, deletes, and displays information about connections to remote resources, but not from remote computers.*

466   USING THE NET SHARE COMMAND

Q: *Which of the following commands can give network access to a local folder?*

Choose the best answer:

     A.   *Net Use*

     B.   *Net Share*

     C.   *Net View*

     D.   *Net Start*

As you have learned in previous Tips, one of the administrator's most important responsibilities is to manage shared resources. The *Net Share* command displays all your computer's current shared resources, and lets you add and delete shares. If you type the *Net Share* at the command prompt, Windows NT will display a list of shares (including hidden shares, which will not normally display within the Windows GUI).

Using the command line variables lets you specify new shares, limit the number of users who can access each share, add remarks to each share, or delete existing shares. You will implement the *Net Share* command as shown, in the following command formats (the items within brackets are optional):

```
NET SHARE sharename
        sharename=drive:path [/USERS:number | /UNLIMITED]
                          [/REMARK:"text"]
        sharename [/USERS:number | /UNLIMITED]
              [/REMARK:"text"]
        <sharename | devicename | drive:path> /DELETE
```

*Answer B is correct because the Net Share command creates, deletes, and displays information about locally shared resources. **Answer A** is incorrect because the Net Use command connects, disconnects, and displays information about connections to remote resources. **Answer C** is incorrect because the Net View command lists Windows NT domains, computers, and shared resources on a computer. **Answer D** is incorrect because the Net Start command starts a Windows NT service you specify.*

467 USING THE NET START COMMAND

Q: *Which of the following commands can start a Windows NT service you specify?*

Choose the best answer:

    A.   *Net Start*

    B.   *Net Computer*

    C.   *Net Config*

    D.   *Net Accounts*

As previous Tips have detailed, you can pause and then continue services that are already running with the *Net Pause* and *Net Continue* commands. Additionally, you can use the *Net Start* command to get a list of currently running services on a Windows NT computer and to start new services. The *Net Start* command lets you display services that you have started, and start services you specify from the command line.

When you type only the *Net Start* command, Windows NT will display all the services you have already started. To start a specific service with the *Net Start* command, you will implement the *Net Start* command, as shown in the following command format:

```
C:\> NET START service   <ENTER>
```

Answer A is correct because the Net Start command starts a Windows NT service you specify. Answer B is incorrect because the Net Computer command adds, deletes and displays a list of computers in a Windows NT Domain database. Answer C is incorrect because the Net Config command displays and modifies configuration information about a Windows NT service you specify such as Server or Workstation. Answer D is incorrect because the Net Accounts command displays and modifies password and log-on information for all Windows NT accounts.

468 USING THE NET STATISTICS COMMAND

Q: *Which of the following commands displays statistical information about a Windows NT service you specify?*

Choose the best answer:

    A.   *Net View*

    B.   *Net Help*

    C.   *Net Statistics*

    D.   *Net Config*

As you have learned, the fastest way to get information about the network is to type a Net command at the command prompt. You can use the *Net Statistics* command to get information about certain services running on the machine.

When you type only the *Net Statistics* command, it will display a list of services for *Workstation* or *Server*, and give statistical information about the services. Similarly, if you specify a service's name after the *Net Statistics* command, Windows NT will list statistical data about that service. For example, if you type "*Net Statistics* Workstation," Windows NT will display a range of statistical data the *Net Statistics* command gathered from the *Workstation* service. You will implement the *Net Statistics* command as shown in the following command format:

```
C:\> NET STATISTICS service   <ENTER>
```

Answer C is correct because the Net Statistics command displays statistical information about a Windows NT service you specify, such as Server or Workstation. Answer A is incorrect because the Net View command displays a list of Windows NT domains, computers, or shared resources on a computer. Answer B is incorrect because the Net Help command displays help information about a Net command you specify. Answer D is incorrect because the Net Config command controls and displays configuration information about a Windows NT service you specify, such as Server or Workstation.

469 USING THE NET STOP COMMAND

Q: Which of the following commands can stop a Windows NT service you specify?

Choose the best answer:

    A.   Net Pause

    B.   Net Stop

    C.   Net Config

    D.   None. You must stop Windows NT services from within the Windows NT Control Panel

As you have learned in previous Tips, you can start Windows NT services from the command line with the *Net Start* command. Similarly, you can use the *Net Stop* command to stop Windows NT services from the command line. Many installation programs use the *Net Stop* and *Net Start* commands because you must stop and then restart some Windows NT services during installation so that new applications can use them. You will implement the *Net Stop* command, as shown in the following command format:

```
C:\> NET STOP service   <ENTER>
```

Answer B is correct because the Net Stop command stops a Windows NT service you specify. Answer A is incorrect because the Net Pause command pauses a Windows NT service you specify, but does not stop it. Answer C is incorrect because the Net Config command controls and displays configuration information about a Windows NT service you specify, such as Server or Workstation. Answer D is incorrect because you can use the Net Stop command to stop a specific Windows NT service.

470 USING THE NET TIME COMMAND

Q: Which of the following commands can set a computer's time to match a network time server's time?

Choose the best answer:

A.   *Net Time*

B.   *Net Config*

C.   *Net Session*

D.   *Net Continue*

Many applications, such as large databases and accounting applications, require all client computers to operate with the same *time value*. Client computers that operate with different time values can produce undesirable results in some applications. To prevent undesirable results, you can use the *Net Time* command to synchronize the clock on all network computers to the current date and time on a single computer. You can synchronize the network's time value to any computer or domain you specify. You will implement the *Net Time* command, as shown in the following command format:

```
C:\> NET TIME [\\computername | DOMAIN[:domainname]] [/SET] <ENTER>
```

If you use the /SET switch, the command will set the time based on the clock in the current computer. Otherwise, the NET TIME command will seek out the *computername* computer, which can even be in a remote domain, in which case you must specify the *DOMAIN* switch and the *domainname* parameter.

Answer A is correct because you can use the Net Time command to synchronize the time between a local computer and a network server. Answer B is incorrect because the Net Config command controls and displays configuration information about a Windows NT service you specify, such as Server or Workstation. Answer C is incorrect because the Net Session command displays information about remote computers, and disconnects connections from remote computers on the network. Answer D is incorrect because the Net Continue command reactivates Windows NT services you have paused with the Net Pause command.

471   USING THE NET USE COMMAND

Q: *Which of the following commands can you use to create a connection from a local computer to a remote network resource?*

Choose the best answer:

A.   *Net Use*

B.   *Net User*

C.   *Net Share*

D.   *Net Name*

As you have learned, you can perform many network administration tasks in Windows NT either from the Windows GUI or from the command-line interface. You can frequently implement the *Net Use* command in log-on scripts to create drive mappings (a drive letter you assign to a network share) for specific users. The *Net Use* command lets you add, delete, and display information about connections to remote network resources. You will implement the *Net Use* command, as shown in the following command formats (the items within brackets are optional):

```
NET USE
NET USE [devicename | *] [\\computername\sharename[\volume] [password | *]]
        [/USER:[domainname\]username]
        [[/DELETE] | [/PERSISTENT:<YES | NO>]]
NET USE [devicename | *] [password | *]] [/HOME]
NET USE [/PERSISTENT:<YES | NO>]
```

Answer A is correct because the Net Use command adds, deletes, and displays information about connections to remote network resources. Answer B is incorrect because the Net User command adds, modifies, and displays user account information. Answer C is incorrect because the Net Share command creates, deletes, and displays information about local shares. Answer D is incorrect because the Net Name command creates and deletes messaging names, or aliases.

472 USING THE NET USER COMMAND

Q: Which of the following commands can display user information you specify?

Choose the best answer:

    A.   Net Statistics

    B.   Net User

    C.   Net Name

    D.   Net Accounts

As you have learned, the *Net Accounts* command lets you obtain information about all accounts on the network. Similarly, the *Net User* command is a valuable tool you can use to get information about user accounts. The *Net User* command lets you set all user account variables. Additionally, the *Net User* command can give you statistical information about user accounts, such as when the password was last set or what groups the user account belongs to. You will implement the *Net User* command, as shown in the following command formats (items within brackets are optional):

```
NET USER [username [password | *] [options]] [/DOMAIN]
        username <password | *> [options] [/DOMAIN]
        username [/DELETE] [/DOMAIN]
```

*Answer B is correct because the Net User command adds, modifies, and displays information about user accounts. Answer A is incorrect because the Net Statistics command displays statistical information about a Windows NT service you specify, such as Server or Workstation. Answer C is incorrect because the Net Name command adds, deletes, and displays information about messaging names, or aliases. Answer D is incorrect because the **Net Accounts** command controls and displays password and log-on information for all Windows NT accounts.*

473 USING THE NET VIEW COMMAND

Q: Which of the following commands can display a list of Windows NT Domains?

Choose the best answer:

    A.   *Net Use*

    B.   *Net View*

    C.   *Net Statistics*

    D.   *Net Share*

As you have learned, one of the most important features of networks is their ability to share resources. If you are unsure about what resources have been shared from a specific computer, you can view the computer's non-hidden shares using the *Net View* command. In addition, the *Net View* command can list the Windows NT domains on the network, and list the computers in each domain. You will implement the *Net View* command, as shown in the following command formats (the items within brackets are optional):

```
NET VIEW [\\computername  |  /DOMAIN[:domainname]]
NET VIEW /NEWORK:NW [\\computername]
```

Answer B is correct because the Net View command displays a list of Windows NT domains, computers, and shared resources. Answer A is incorrect because the Net Use command adds, deletes, and displays information about connections to remote resources. Answer C is incorrect because the Net Statistics command displays statistical information about a Windows NT service you specify, such as Server or **Workstation**. *Answer D is incorrect because the Net Share command adds, deletes, and displays information about local resources the network shares.*

474   **IMPLEMENTING AND SUPPORTING MICROSOFT WINDOWS NT SERVER 4.0 IN THE ENTERPRISE, EXAM (70-68)**

Q: *Which of the following counts as an MCSE core exam?*

Choose all answers that apply:

    A.   *Implementing and Supporting Windows NT Server (70-67)*

    B.   *Implementing and Supporting Windows NT Server in the Enterprise (70-68)*

    C.   *Implementing and Supporting Windows NT Workstation (70-73)*

    D.   *Networking Essentials (70-58)*

Microsoft designed Exam (70-68), Introduction to Implementing and Supporting Microsoft Windows NT Server 4.0 in the Enterprise exam, to measure how well you administer the Windows NT Server 4.0. As you know, the Windows NT Server 4.0's environment can include multiple servers, multiple domains, and connectivity that extends beyond the Local Area Network (LAN) to Wide Area Networks (WAN) and other distributed network configurations. As organizations grow, your ability to manage computer systems in a Wide Area Network (WAN) configuration will become an increasingly important skill—because more and more organizations will use WANs instead of simple LANs. Microsoft designed its testing methods so that each exam stands alone and ensures that people who pass the exam can support the product in the environment tested. As a result of this testing method, you will notice that many subjects are tested repeatedly on different exams and that some of the testable information for this exam you have already learned in previous Tips.

Answers A, B, C, and D are all correct. Each exam in the answer lists counts as an MCSE core exam.

| 475 | UNDERSTANDING THE SIX SECTIONS OF THE *70-68* EXAM | |

Q: Each Microsoft Exam tests different subject matter each time you take the same exam.

True or False?

The 70-68 Exam contains the following six sections:

- Planning
- Installation and Configuration
- Managing Resources
- Connectivity
- Monitoring and Optimization
- Troubleshooting

The following bulleted lists give the testable information for each section as Microsoft describes it:

Planning

In the Planning section of the exam, the test will measure your ability to plan various parts of the Enterprise model's implementation. For example, to plan a directory services architecture implementation, you must consider the following:

- Selecting the appropriate domain model
- Supporting a single logon account
- Allowing users to access resources in different domains

You will also be tested on your ability to plan the disk drive configuration for various requirements, which include choosing a fault-tolerance method. Additionally, you must choose an appropriate network protocol for various installation situations, such as mixed networks, intranets, and so on. Tested protocols on the exam include the following:

- TCP/IP
- TCP/IP with DHCP and WINS
- NWLink IPX/SPX Compatible Transport Protocol
- Data Link Control (DLC)
- AppleTalk

Installation and Configuration

In the Installation and Configuration section, the exam tests your ability to both determine the possible roles for the server computer within a network, as well as what steps you must perform to install the Windows NT server correctly for that role. As you have learned, there are three server roles that a Windows NT server generally falls into, as detailed in the following list:

- Primary domain controller

- Backup domain controller

- Member server

In addition to simply building the server, you must be able to determine how to make the server communicate with the other computers on your network. Specifically, you must be able to configure network protocols and protocol bindings. Protocols the exam tests will include the following:

- TCP/IP

- TCP/IP with DHCP and WINS

- NWLink IPX/SPX Compatible Transport Protocol

- DLC

- AppleTalk

You must also know how to configure other important aspects of the Windows NT Server configuration. Other tested configurations include the NT Server core services, hard drives, printers, and appropriate configuration of the Windows NT Server computer to handle connections from different types of client computers.

Managing Resources

To succeed on the test you must show competency in the management of user and group accounts. Tested resource management categories will include the following:

- Managing Windows NT user accounts

- Managing Windows NT user rights

- Managing Windows NT groups

- Administering account policies

- Auditing changes to the user account database

Additionally, the Managing Resources section will test you on your ability to manage policies and profiles, administer remote servers from client computers, and manage disk resources

Connectivity

In the Connectivity section of the exam, you will be tested on your ability to configure Windows NT Server for interoperability with NetWare servers by using various tools, including:

- Gateway Service for NetWare

- Migration Tool for NetWare

You will also need to be able to install and configure multi-protocol routing, install and configure Internet Information Server, install and configure Internet services, and install and configure Remote Access

Monitoring and Optimization

In the Monitoring and Optimization section, you will need to show competency in establishing a baseline for measuring system performance. Tasks you must perform will include creating a database of measurement data and monitor performance of various functions with Performance Monitor.

You will also need to monitor network traffic by using Network Monitor. Finally, you will need to be able to identify performance bottlenecks and optimize performance to achieve specific results, such as controlling server load.

Troubleshooting

Finally, in the Troubleshooting section, you will need to be able to display competency in choosing the appropriate course of action to take to resolve installation failures, the appropriate course of action to take to resolve boot failures, and the appropriate course of action to take to resolve configuration errors.

Additionally, you must show how to resolve printer problems, resolve RAS problems, resolve connectivity problems, resolve resource access and permission problems, and resolve fault-tolerance failures. Finally, you must be able to perform advanced problem resolution, including the performance of the following tasks:

- Diagnosing and interpreting a blue screen
- Configuring a memory dump
- Using the Event Log service

*The answer is **False**. Although the questions may be different, Microsoft Exams test the same material on an exam every time.*

476   ***REVIEWING MICROSOFT WINDOWS NT DOMAINS***

Q: Which of the following answers best describe a Microsoft Windows NT domain?

Choose the best answer:

> A.   *Any Windows NT Server computer.*
>
> B.   *An abstract concept for grouping computers.*
>
> C.   *An administrative unit for managing computers, resources, and user accounts.*
>
> D.   *None of the above.*

As you learned in Tip 200, "Introduction to Domains," a Microsoft Windows NT domain is an administrative unit you can use to manage users, groups, resources, and computers. To create a domain, you must have one Windows NT Server that you have installed as a Primary Domain Controller. Then, you can also create multiple Windows NT Servers that you have installed as Backup Domain Controllers. You have also learned that the Primary Domain Controller's Directory Database stores all user, group, and computer accounts. Whether you administer these accounts from a Backup Domain Controller or from another client computer, you will actually make all changes on the Primary Domain Controller.

*Answer **C** is correct because a Microsoft Windows NT domain is an administrative unit for managing computers, resources, and user accounts. **Answer A** is incorrect because although a single Windows NT Server can be a domain, not all Windows NT Servers can be domains. Only a Windows NT Server that you have installed as a domain controller can be a domain. **Answer B** is incorrect because a Windows NT domain is more then just a group of computers. **Answer D** is incorrect because a Windows NT domain is an administrative unit, as **Answer C** states.*

477   ***REVIEWING WINDOWS NT DOMAIN TRUST RELATIONSHIPS***

Q: Which of the following answers best describe a Windows NT domain trust relationship?

Choose the best answer:

      A.   A logical link between two Windows NT domains for administrative purposes.

      B.   Two Windows NT domains sharing the same network cabling.

      C.   When a single Windows NT Server domain controller lets users access resources.

      D.   When the Windows NT Primary Domain Controller copies its Directory Database to Windows NT Server Backup Domain Controllers.

As you have learned, Windows NT domains are administrative units that you can use to manage networks, users, and groups. Some companies grow too large for a single Microsoft Windows NT domain (making the single-domain model inefficient and difficult to administer), while others choose to use multiple domains (without outgrowing a single domain) to simplify administration. Whether your company fits into the first category or the second, if you administer a multiple domain environment, you must administer Microsoft Windows NT domain trust relationships.

As you have learned in earlier Tips, a Microsoft Windows NT domain trust relationship is a logical link between two or more Microsoft Windows NT domains. Only an administrator can create a trust, and the administrator must configure the trust on all domains that will participate in the trust relationship. After you, as the administrator, configure the trust relationship, you can administer multiple Microsoft Windows NT domains from a single administration point (such as a client computer or a Backup Domain Controller).

Answer A is correct because a Windows NT domain trust relationship is a logical link between two Windows NT domains for administrative purposes. Answer B is incorrect because you can have two Windows NT domains on the same network cable segment and not have a trust relationship between them. Answer C is incorrect because a single Windows NT Server sharing resources does not describe a trust relationship. Answer D is incorrect because when a Windows NT Server Primary Domain Controller copies its Directory Database to Windows NT Server Backup Domain Controllers, it is called Directory Database Synchronization, and has nothing to do with a trust relationship.

478 REVIEWING WINDOWS NT DIRECTORY SERVICES

Q: You can install Windows NT Directory Services from the Control Panel in the Network dialog box.

True or False?

Well after Microsoft Windows NT Server 3.51 had become popular, Microsoft introduced a new service for Windows NT called *directory services* to users. As you have learned, Windows NT directory services is a term that Microsoft uses to describe the overall Windows NT Server operating system and file services when you use it as a domain controller. Microsoft updated and improved the Windows NT directory services model for Windows NT 4.0.

Microsoft uses some key words and phrases to describe directory services, such as *centralized administration, single-user logon,* and *universal access to resources.* First, centralized administration means that you can create and manage user, group, and computer accounts from any Microsoft client computer in the network on a single database located on the Primary Domain Controller. Second, single user logon means that each user will have one, and only one, user account in the network, regardless of how many domains encompass your organization. Finally, universal access to resources means that no matter where in the network a user logs on from, the user can gain access to resources at any other location where you have granted the user access. Directory services is, simply, a concept for total network administration, regardless of how large your network has grown or will grow in the future. Grossly simplified, directory services let users work with directories and files on any server in the domain within a simple tree model under the domain, just as they work with directories and files on a single hard drive on their local computer. The three concepts this Tip explains all work together to provide the user with the coherent interface to the files and directories throughout the network.

*The answer is **False** because you cannot install Windows NT directory services, which is a conceptual way for you to administer your Windows NT domain.*

479 | **BUILDING AN EFFECTIVE WINDOWS NT DIRECTORY SERVICES STRUCTURE**

Q: *Building an effective Windows NT directory services structure includes which of the following?*

Choose all answers that apply:

    A. *Administering resources.*

    B. *Configuring directory replication.*

    C. *Installing new computer software.*

    D. *Planning your Windows NT domain model.*

As you have learned, installing Microsoft Windows NT Server is, in practice, not very difficult—in fact, the simplest installations are not much more difficult than installing Windows 95 or another client operating system. The challenge in administering a Microsoft Windows NT domain is not installing the Servers; rather, the challenge is in building an effective directory services structure (including a domain model, the network shares, and so on) that will work for you now and well into the future.

Before you learn how to build an effective directory services structure, you should know what your objectives are. An effective directory services structure is one that takes into account the number of objects in the network (an object is any user, group, or Windows NT computer), as well as how many administrative units make sense for your organization. An administrative unit can be anything you would like to use, such as a department or even a geographical location. For example, you might create separate domains for the Sales, Accounting, and Research departments in your company and then have one "umbrella" company domain for all user accounts. In this way, you can break up resources and user administration. You could administer all user accounts in the company domain, and you could assign administrative responsibility to different users for each of the multiple department domains. Because Microsoft recommends not going beyond 40,000 accounts in a single domain, sometimes multiple domains are not an administrative option, but a necessity.

After you take into account the number of accounts and how many administrative units you will use, you must consider the Wide Area Network (WAN) links between locations and how many accounts you will synchronize across the WAN links. Every Windows NT Server Primary Domain Controller must copy its entire Directory Database to all Backup Domain Controllers in the domain. You will generally place these Backup Domain Controllers where your user accounts are—probably across WAN links—so you should understand that it might take a long time for all the account information to cross the links to the Backup Domain Controllers. To calculate how long it will take to *synchronize* a Directory Database (that is, make sure the directory database is consistent throughout a domain) across a particular WAN link, you will need the calculations that Tip 485 explains in detail. To calculate the amount of time (each month) it will take to synchronize account information from the Primary Domain Controller to a particular Backup Domain Controller, perform the following steps:

1. Divide by 30 the number of calendar days in which your users' passwords will expire, and then multiply your answer by the number of users in your domain. Call the result Answer A.

2. Add up the number of new users, computers, and groups you expect to create each month, and then add that figure plus 5% of Answer A together. (The 5% of Answer A is for additional, unforeseen changes.) Call this total Answer B.

3. Add Answers A and B together and then multiply by 1,000. The result is the total amount of data (in bytes) that you expect to synchronize each month. You will call this result Answer C.

4. Calculate your line speed (that is, how quickly information transits your network) in bits per second (BPS). To determine your line speed in BPS, take your line speed in kilobits per second (Kbs) and multiply by 1,024. Call the result Answer D.

5. Divide Answer D by 8, and then divide that result by 60 (seconds) and then again by 60 (minutes). Call the result Answer E.

6. Divide Answer C by Answer E. The result is the total amount of time (in hours) your Directory Database will consume when you synchronize it over your WAN link.

Answers A, B, and D are correct because each describes a part of what you will have to do in order to build an effective Windows NT directory services structure. Answer C is incorrect because you installing software has nothing to do with Windows NT directory services structure.

480 **DETERMINING THE NUMBER OF DOMAIN CONTROLLERS TO USE**

Q: *A single Windows NT Server domain controller can support 40,000 users effectively.*

True or False?

The optimum number of domain controllers you should have depends on key factors, such as the domain controllers' size and speed, the number of master domains, the number of resource domains, and the number of users in your organization. Each of these factors help establish the total number of domain controllers you should have.

As you know, Microsoft recommends not exceeding 40,000 accounts in a single Windows NT domain. Remember that an account is any user, group, or computer in your domain, so if you have 15,000 users and each has his or her own Microsoft Windows NT Workstation, you will have 30,000 accounts, not including groups. However, companies do not always break up their Microsoft Windows NT domains because of the number of users; sometimes, a company will break up Microsoft Windows NT domains for administrative purposes.

As you have learned, every domain in your organization will have its own Microsoft Windows NT Primary Domain Controller. Each domain may also have additional domain controllers to validate user log-on requests. These domain controllers will be Microsoft Windows NT Server Backup Domain Controllers. You will place Microsoft Windows NT Server Backup Domain Controllers in any location where you have a significant number of users or where there is a user who must always be able to log on to the network. In addition, Microsoft recommends having one Backup Domain Controller for every 2,000 users. To determine the total number of domain controllers your network will require, take the total number of domains you will have and add the number of Backup Domain Controllers you will need (based on the number of users and the locations at which you will place Backup Domain Controllers).

Note: *In Tip 484, you will learn how to calculate the number of Backup Domain Controllers you will need for a single domain.*

*The answer is **False** because in a network with 40,000 users, you will want to break up the network into multiple domains. Each domain will require a domain controller and, in addition, you might require multiple domain controllers for each domain.*

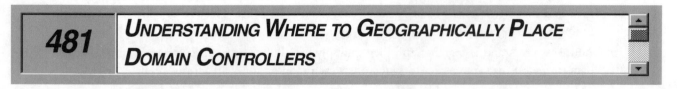

481 | **UNDERSTANDING WHERE TO GEOGRAPHICALLY PLACE DOMAIN CONTROLLERS**

Q: *For better performance, you should place your Windows NT Server domain controllers in segmented networks away from where your users are.*

True or False?

You can configure your Microsoft Windows NT domain in a variety of ways. If you are administering a multiple domain environment, you will place your Backup Domain Controllers anywhere you have a significant number of users. You might not, for example, want to place a Backup Domain Controller in a location where you have 10 users if there are 10,000 users in your domain. Because Windows NT will have to copy all user accounts from the Primary Domain Controller to all Backup Domain Controllers, your Windows NT Server Backup Domain Controller in the location with 10 users will have 10,000 user accounts on it. Therefore, it would likely be more efficient if you let the users log on to the network across the WAN link rather than have 10,000 accounts replicate across the same link.

On the other hand, if the WAN link goes down, users in that location will not be able to log on to the network. If the 10 users must always be able to log onto the network, you might want to place a Backup Domain Controller in that site, even though it will take longer to synchronize the Directory Database than it will if users log on to the domain remotely.

*The answer is **False** because you should place your Windows NT Server domain controllers as close to your users as possible.*

482 | **UNDERSTANDING DOMAIN CONTROLLER SIZE AND SPEED**

Q: *Of the following, which is a true statement about domain controllers?*

Choose the best answer:

A.   *The most powerful computer in your network should be the Primary Domain Controller. Backup Domain Controllers should be the next most powerful computers, and application servers should have the least powerful computers.*

B.   *The most powerful computers in your network should be the application servers. The next most powerful computer should be the Primary Domain Controller, and then the Backup Domain Controllers.*

C.   *The most powerful computers in your network should be the application servers. The next most powerful computers should be the Backup Domain Controllers, and then the Primary Domain Controller.*

D.   *All Windows NT computers will have to have exactly the same hardware.*

Many administrators, particularly new administrators, often mistakenly think that the most powerful computer in the network should be the Microsoft Windows NT Server Primary Domain Controller. In fact, the most powerful computers in your network should be any *application servers*, which are computers with a lot of memory and fast processors that respond to user requests for application processes.

The next most powerful computer should be the Microsoft Windows NT Server Backup Domain Controllers. A Backup Domain Controller must log on users to the domain and, in many cases, run additional processes, such as Windows Internet Name Service (WINS) or Domain Name System (DNS). To optimize your Microsoft Windows NT domain environment, you should make the least powerful computer the Primary Domain Controller.

The Primary Domain Controller's overall function is to update Directory Database information to the Backup Domain Controllers. Therefore, the Primary Domain Controller does not have to be very powerful. For example, a 486 computer with 32 megabytes of memory can make a fine Primary Domain Controller in some domains.

Table 482 shows the Microsoft recommended minimum requirements for a Primary Domain Controller. You will use the requirements in Figure 482 to configure your domain model based on your hardware's limitations.

Database Size	Number of Accounts	Minimum CPU	Recommended Memory
10Mb	7500	486DX/66	32Mb
15Mb	10,000	Pentium or RISC-based	48Mb
20Mb	15,000	Pentium or RISC-based	64Mb
30Mb	20,000 to 30,000	Pentium or RISC-based	96Mb
40Mb	30,000 to 40,000	Pentium or RISC-based	128Mb

Table 482 The minimum Microsoft-recommended Primary Domain Controller requirments.

Answer C is correct because application servers will require the most processing power to run the application the users must use. If you configure your Windows NT directory services structure properly, you will make the Backup Domain Controllers more powerful then the Primary Domain Controller. Answer A is incorrect because the Primary Domain Controller will not require as much processing power as an application server or the Backup Domain Controllers. Answer B is incorrect because if you configure your Windows NT Server Primary Domain Controller to only synchronize user account information, it will not require a very powerful computer. Answer D is incorrect because there will be no need for all computers to be equally powerful; domain controllers do not require as much processing power as application servers do.

483 CALCULATING THE NUMBER OF MASTER DOMAINS YOU NEED

Q: *You are the administrator of a large organization with 30,000 users. All users have their own Windows NT Workstations. What is the minimum number of master domains you will require?*

Choose the best answer:

    A.   *One*

    B.   *Two*

    C.   *Three*

    D.   *None*

You can determine the number of master domains to create based on one of two factors: the total number of accounts your network organization will have or the number of administrative units you want to break administration into. As you have learned, the master domain model lets you configure a single domain with access rights, user and groups IDs, and other access parameters, and then make every domain of which that domain is the master use the master domain's Directory Database. If you configure your master domains based on the number of accounts in your organization, you can easily calculate the number of master domains you will require. However, if you base the number of master domains on administrative units, a subjective determination (or one based on a non-system specific formula), you will find it more difficult to determine the proper number of master domains to create.

To calculate the number of master domains to create, you must divide the Directory Database size (the users, groups, and computers in your network) by the largest Directory Database size your hardware will support. (Use Figure 482 to see how big a Directory Database your hardware will support.)

Answer A is correct because you will need at least one Windows NT master domain. A single Windows NT domain can support up to 40,000 accounts. Each Windows NT computer in your network will require an account. If you have 30,000 users and they all have their own Windows NT Workstations, you will have a minimum of 60,000 accounts. Answers B and C are incorrect because, although you can use two or even three master domains, the question asks what is the minimum number of master domains you will need. Answer D is incorrect because you will need at least one master domain.

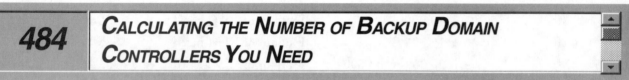

484 **CALCULATING THE NUMBER OF BACKUP DOMAIN CONTROLLERS YOU NEED**

Q: *You are the administrator of a medium-sized network. You will soon be implementing a Windows NT domain model. You have 5,000 users. How many Windows NT Server Backup Domain Controllers will you need to meet Microsoft's recommended standards?*

Choose the best answer:

A.   *One*

B.   *Two*

C.   *Three*

D.   *Four*

As your network continues to grow, it is likely that you will have many Microsoft Windows NT Server Backup Domain Controllers in your network. You have learned in earlier Tips that most Microsoft Windows NT domains will have many more than Microsoft's recommended minimum number of domain controllers. In fact, it is always a good idea to have at least one Backup Domain Controller in the same location as your Primary Domain Controller. Doing so will ensure that if the Primary Domain Controller fails, there will still be another domain controller your network can promote to take the Primary Domain Controller's place.

Microsoft recommends having at least one Backup Domain Controller for every 2,000 users in your domain. Use Table 484 as a quick guide to determine the number of Backup Domain Controllers you will need.

Users	Backup Domain Controllers
Up to 2,000	1
5,000 users	3
10,000 users	5
20,000 users	10
40,000 users	20

Table 484 Determining the number of Backup Domain Controllers you will need.

*Answer C is correct because you should have one Backup Domain Controller for every 2,000 users in your network. For 5,000 users you should have two Backup Domain Controllers for the first 4,000 users and one more for the extra 1,000 users, to provide room for growth. **Answer A** is incorrect because one Backup Domain Controller would be inadequate for the number of users your network has. **Answer B** is incorrect because Microsoft recommends having one Backup Domain Controller for every 2,000 users in your network. **Answer D** is incorrect because, although there would not be anything wrong with having the extra Backup Domain Controller, the question asks how many Windows NT Server Backup Domain Controllers you will need to meet **Microsoft's** recommended standards.*

485 CALCULATING THE SPACE USERS AND GROUPS NEED

Q: How much space in the Directory Database does a user account take?

Choose the best answer:

    A.   1 byte

    B.   1Kb

    C.   512 bytes

    D.   512Kb

In previous Tips, you have learned that the size of the Directory Database is important when determining how long it will take your network to backup the Primary Domain Controller to the Backup Domain Controller. As the administrator of a Microsoft Windows NT domain, you must know how big your Directory Database is. You can find the Directory Database size by calculating how much space user and group accounts take up. Then, add the space computer accounts take up, and the result is the total Directory Database size. To calculate the total Directory Database size for your domain, you can use the amount of space in kilobytes (Kb) objects will take up in the Directory Database, as Table 485 shows.

Object	Space
User	1Kb
Computer account	0.5Kb
Global group	0.5Kb, plus 12 bytes for each user that is a member of the group
Local group	0.5Kb, plus 36 bytes for each user that is a member of the group

Table 485 Calculating the Directory Database size.

*Answer B is correct because a single user account will take 1Kb of space in the Directory Database. **Answers A, C, and D** are incorrect because none of the answers accurately state the size of a user account.*

486 UNDERSTANDING THE ENTERPRISE CHALLENGE

Q: Which of the following answers best describe the Windows NT Enterprise Challenge?

    Choose the best answer:

A.   *The Windows NT Enterprise Challenge is to have only one user account for each person who will access network resources. It is also to provide universal access to the network resources to the correct users and, finally, to have the ability to administer the entire network from a single location.*

B.   *The Windows NT Enterprise Challenge is to design a network so users will be able to log on to the network at specific times and gain access to only the resources to which the administrator assigns the users access.*

C.   *The Windows NT Enterprise Challenge is to design and implement a network that will withstand the load placed on it by your organization and to provide a quick method of recovery if the network should fail.*

D.   *The Windows NT Enterprise Challenge is to work with other network administrators in your company's divisions to create a smooth network operation.*

The Microsoft Windows NT Enterprise Challenge—a Microsoft term to refer to *why* you will use enterprise-style networks in your organization—is to administer a large network environment where you might have hundreds of sites and thousands of users. The Enterprise Challenge includes creating and managing a single user account for each user, a centralized user account and resource administration, universal resource access, and password policies.

A *single user account* for each person in your organization is essential because if you have multiple accounts for users, it is hard for you, as the administrator, to manage the accounts. That is, you could easily assign resource permissions to the wrong account. Therefore, one user account for each user ensures that if you assign permissions to an account, you assign the permissions to the correct account.

Another aspect of the Enterprise Challenge is *universal resource access*, which means that users can access the network resources they should have access to, from any location within your organization. Universal resource access ties together with *centralized administration*, which lets you, as the administrator, log on from anywhere in the network and assign permissions to resources at any location within your network. In addition, you can create and manage user accounts, password policies, and groups.

Answer A is correct because the Windows NT Enterprise Challenge is to manage your network so each user has only one user account and can access network resources from anywhere in your company and you have the ability to administer the network from a single location in your organization. Answers B and C are incorrect because the answers describe network management in general, but not specifically the Enterprise Challenge. Answer D is incorrect because the Enterprise Challenge specifically deals with central administration, not multiple points of administration.

487 UNDERSTANDING THE ONE USER, ONE ACCOUNT PRINCIPLE

Q: *Microsoft recommends having only one user account for each user in your network, with one exception. Which of the following is the exception to the one user, one account principle?*

Choose the best answer:

A.   *When you have a user who will require access to resources in multiple domains.*

B.   *When you have multiple Windows NT Server computers and you must assign access to resources located on the various servers.*

C.   *When network administrators must have a regular user account to access network resources for reasons other than network administration.*

D.   *There is no exception to Microsoft's one user, one account principle.*

As you learned in Tip 486, you should have only one user account for each user in your network. In other (non-Microsoft) network operating systems, such as Novell NetWare *3.x*, each server in your organization must have a user account for everyone who will access network resources. If you work in a non-Microsoft operating system, imagine having one user account for each user in your organization on every server in your network. Then, imagine the work you would do to create a simple password change for one user. That is, if User Bob has a password of *password1* and he wants to change his password to *password2*, he will have to change his password on each server in the network individually. Then, if user Bob forgets to change his password on any one of the servers in the network, he will have created different passwords for the same user account in your network. Over time, user Bob could create several passwords on the various servers in your network.

To understand how frustrating having several different user passwords for your one network account would be, consider what would happen if you had a different personal identification number (PIN) for every ATM machine you use to access your bank accounts. You might find it difficult to remember all the PINs. Then, imagine that you are far away from all but one ATM machine and you desperately need money, but you have forgotten the PIN and so you cannot access your bank accounts. Networks are no different from this example: if you have more than one password in your network (more than one PIN), you will probably forget one of them at some point and find yourself frustrated and inefficient.

The only exception to the one user, one account principle is for the administrators. Microsoft recommends that all administrators have a second account. The reason for the second account is so you, as an administrator, will have one account you use to perform network administration and a second account for when you must access network resources as a user. If you use your regular user account when you access network resources, you cannot accidentally do something on the network (such as grant permissions) because you have too high an access level.

Answer C is correct because administrators should have two user accounts: one for administrative duties and one for accessing network resources as a user. Answer A is incorrect because you will still only have one account for each user in multiple domain environments. Answer B is incorrect because you will still only have one account for each user when you have multiple servers in your network. Answer D is incorrect because administrators should have one administrator account and a regular user account for accessing the network.

488   WINDOWS NT DIRECTORY DATABASE PARTITIONING

Q: How would you partition your Windows NT Directory Database?

Choose the best answer:

> A. *From Server Manager, open the Primary Domain Controller properties and then select Database Partitions from the Computer menu. Then, configure your database partition and restart your Windows NT Server.*
>
> B. *Within User Manager for Domains, open the Policies menu and select the Database option. In the Database dialog box, configure your Windows NT domain Directory Database partition scheme.*
>
> C. *Directory Database partitioning is not something you do within a single domain and there is no utility to configure Directory Database partitioning. To partition a Directory Database means to create multiple Windows NT domains and separate your network user accounts into the various domains.*
>
> D. *To partition a Windows NT Directory Database, you will need the Microsoft Windows NT Resource Kit. Install the Resource Kit and then use the Directory Services Manager program to configure the Windows NT Directory Database partition scheme.*

As your Directory Databases grow larger, you will likely want to segment or partition your Directory Database into a more usable size (because doing so makes the Directory Database and, by extension, the operating system, faster). You cannot actually break up, or divide, a single Microsoft Windows NT Directory Database. Rather, Microsoft uses the term *Directory Database partitioning* to describe using multiple Microsoft Windows NT domains to separate your accounts. As you have learned, a single Microsoft Windows NT domain can accommodate up to 40,000 accounts. If you are the network administrator for an organization that has more than 40,000 users, a single Microsoft Windows NT domain will not be sufficient for your needs. Remember, 40,000 accounts includes all the users, groups, and Windows NT computers in a domain.

Many organizations will divide and organize their users into multiple Microsoft Windows NT domains long before reaching the 40,000 account limitation. When organizations separate their users, they *partition the Directory Database*. You, as an organization's administrator, would partition the Directory Database for administrative purposes. For example, imagine you are the administrator for a company that has 10,000 users and each user has a Windows NT Workstation computer. Your company has large Sales, Accounting, and Manufacturing departments. Therefore, you might want to create one Windows NT domain for your company and one Windows NT domain for each department. You would then create all user accounts in the company domain and all resources (including computer accounts) in the department domains. By doing so, you can break up your network administration so that each department is responsible for administering its own resources.

Answer C is correct because you cannot actually partition a Windows NT Directory Database. The term Directory Database partitioning is a term Microsoft uses to describe separating your network users into various Windows NT domains. Answers A, B, and D are incorrect because you cannot actually separate a single Windows NT Directory Database into partitioned pieces.

489	**UNDERSTANDING THE DIRECTORY DATABASE SYNCHRONIZATION PROCESS**

Q: *A Windows NT Server Primary Domain Controller will check its Directory Database every ___ minutes, by default, to look for changes. If any changes have occurred, the Primary Domain Controller will contact all Windows NT Server Backup Domain Controllers to notify them of the changes.*

Choose the best answer:

A.   One

B.   Five

C.   Twelve

D.   Fifteen

As you have learned, a Microsoft Windows NT Server Primary Domain Controller will periodically send notifications to the Windows NT Server Backup Domain Controllers in the domain to inform the Backup Domain Controllers of changes in the Directory Database. In turn, the Backup Domain Controllers will request the changes. This process is *Directory Database synchronization*.

During the Directory Database synchronization process, the Primary Domain Controller will check its Directory Database every five minutes for any changes. Administrators, server operators, and account operators can make changes to the Directory Database. *Changes* include any addition of user, group, or computer accounts, and any modification of existing user, group, or computer accounts, including access permissions, passwords, and so on.

When the Primary Domain Controller checks the Directory Database for changes, it performs a *Pulse*. If the Primary Domain Controller finds any changes to the Directory Database (during a Pulse), the Primary Domain Controller will send a notification to the group of Backup Domain Controllers. The number of Backup Domain Controllers to which a Primary Domain Controller can send notification at one time is the *Pulse Concurrency*.

When the Backup Domain Controllers receive the notifications, each Backup Domain Controller will request the changes at random intervals. In turn, the Primary Domain Controller will not send all the changes at once. Instead, each Backup Domain Controller will tell the Primary Domain Controller how much data to send and then when to send more, which prevents Directory Database synchronization traffic from saturating the network. If a Backup Domain Controller finds that it is not keeping up with the number of changes in the Directory Database, the Backup Domain Controller will call for a *full synchronization event*, which instructs the Primary Domain Controller to synchronize the entire Directory Database across the network in a single action.

The entire Directory Database synchronization process occurs automatically. However, you can configure some aspects of Directory Database synchronization. You will learn more about Directory Database synchronization in Tips 491 through 495.

Answer B is correct because a Windows NT Server Primary Domain Controller will check its Directory Database every five minutes to see if any changes have occurred. Answers A, C, and D are incorrect because none of the answers correctly state the frequency of minutes for a Primary Domain Controller to check the Directory Database.

490   **CHANGING YOUR DOMAIN NAME**

Q: *What utility or program would you use to change the name of your Windows NT domain?*

Choose the best answer:

      A.   *User Manager for Domains*

      B.   *The Network dialog box Identification sheet*

      C.   *Server Manager*

      D.   *You cannot change your Windows NT domain name*

You, as an administrator, can change your Windows NT domain's name at any time. However, you may want to consider the consequences before you change a domain's name. That is, if you change your Windows NT domain name, you can encounter problems such as trust relationships not working or Microsoft Windows NT Server Member Servers no longer participating in domain security. When you change a Windows NT domain name, you should consider the risks before you continue. Additionally, be sure to back up the network information where possible, and have a definitive troubleshooting plan on how to solve problems if and when you encounter them after the name change. To change a Windows NT domain name, perform the following steps:

1.   Right-click your mouse on the Network Neighborhood icon on your Desktop. Windows NT will display the pop-up menu.

2.   Within in the pop-up menu, select the Properties option. Windows NT will open the Network dialog box.

3. Within the Network dialog box click your mouse on the Identification tab. Windows NT will display the Identification sheet. Within the Identification sheet, click your mouse on the Change button. Windows NT will display the Identification Change dialog box.

4. Within the Identification Change dialog box, type the new domain name in the *Domain Name* field. Click your mouse on the OK button. Windows NT will change the domain name and return you to the Network dialog box.

5. Within the Network dialog box, click your mouse on the OK button. Windows NT will prompt you to restart your computer. Click your mouse on the OK button to confirm the restart. Windows NT will restart with the new domain name.

Answer B is correct because you will use the Network dialog box Identification sheet to change your Windows NT domain's name. Answer A is incorrect because you cannot change your Windows NT domain name from User Manager for Domains. Answer C is incorrect because you cannot use Server Manager to change your Windows NT domain name. Answer D is incorrect because you can change your Windows NT domain name on the Identification tab in the Network dialog box.

491 — CONFIGURING THE REPLICATIONGOVERNOR PARAMETER

Q: The *ReplicationGoverner* parameter will let you configure _____.

Choose the best answer:

A.   The frequency of calls to the Primary Domain Controller from the Backup Domain Controller for Directory Database changes, and how much data to send at a time.

B.   The frequency of calls to the Backup Domain Controller from the Primary Domain Controller for Directory Database changes, and how much data to send at a time.

C.   How often the Primary Domain Controller checks the Directory Database to see if any changes have occurred.

D.   How often the Backup Domain Controller checks the Directory Database to see if any changes have occurred.

As you learned in Tip 489, every five minutes the Primary Domain Controller checks its Directory Database for changes and then notifies all Backup Domain Controllers if any changes have occurred. The next step in the Directory Database synchronization process is when the Backup Domain Controller contacts the Primary Domain Controller and requests the changes. You also learned that when the Backup Domain Controller contacts the Primary Domain Controller to request the changes, the Backup Domain Controller informs the Primary Domain Controller how much data to send and when to send it.

Windows NT will automatically manage the Directory Database synchronization process. However, in some circumstances, you might want to adjust both the amount of data the Primary Domain Controller sends to the Backup Domain Controller during Directory Database synchronization, and how much time will elapse before the Primary Domain Controller will send more. To do so, you will use the *ReplicationGovernor parameter*.

A Microsoft Windows NT Server Backup Domain Controller uses the *ReplicationGovernor* parameter in the Registry to increase Directory Database synchronization performance over slow Wide Area Network (WAN) links. When you adjust the *ReplicationGovernor* parameter, you control both the size of the data transferred on each call (the *replication call*) to the Primary Domain Controller and the frequency of those calls. For example, setting *ReplicationGovernor* to

50 percent will use a 64Kb buffer (that is, transfer size limit) rather than a 128Kb buffer and will have a replication call processing on the network only a maximum of 50 percent of the time. The *ReplicationGovernor* parameter is not in the Windows NT Server Backup Domain Controller Registry by default—you must add this parameter and configure it. To add and configure the *ReplicationGovernor* parameter, perform the following steps:

1. Click your mouse on the Start menu and select the Run option. Windows NT will open the Run dialog box.

2. Within the Run dialog box, type *Regedt32* and click your mouse on the OK button. Windows NT will open the *Registry Editor* program.

3. Within the *Registry Editor* program, double-click your mouse on the *HKEY_LOCAL_MACHINE\SYSTEM* hive. The *Registry Editor* program will expand the *SYSTEM* hive.

4. Within the *SYSTEM* hive, double-click your mouse on the *CurrentControlSet* subkey. The *Registry Editor* will expand the *CurrentControlSet* subkey.

5. Within the *CurrentControlSet* subkey, double-click your mouse on the *Service* subkey. The *Registry Editor* will expand the *Service* subkey.

6. Within the *Service* subkey, double-click your mouse on the *Netlogon* subkey. The *Registry Editor* will expand the *Netlogon* subkey.

7. Within the *Netlogon* subkey, double-click your mouse on the *Parameters* subkey. The *Registry Editor* will expand the *Parameters* subkey.

8. Within the *Parameters* subkey, click your mouse on the Edit menu Add Value option. The *Registry Editor* will display the Add Value dialog box.

9. Within the Add Value dialog box, type *ReplicationGovernor* in the *Value Name* field. Click your mouse on the Data Type drop-down list and select REG_DWORD. Click your mouse on the OK button. The *Registry Editor* will display the DWORD Editor dialog box.

10. Within the DWORD Editor dialog box, type a value between 0 and 100. Click your mouse on the OK button. The *Registry Editor* will close the DWORD Editor and Add Value dialog boxes.

11. Shut down and restart your Windows NT Server Backup Domain Controller. Windows NT will set the *ReplicationGovernor* parameter.

Answer B is correct because the ReplicationGovernor parameter will let you configure both the Backup Domain Controller's requests for Directory Database changes and how much data the Primary Domain Controller will send at a time. Answer A is incorrect because a Primary Domain Controller will not request any Directory Database changes from the Backup Domain Controllers. Answers C and D are incorrect because only a Primary Domain Controller will check the Directory Database for changes, and that process is called the Pulse.

492 **CONFIGURING THE PULSE PARAMETER FOR REPLICATION**

Q: *As a Windows NT network administrator, you may have to configure the Pulse parameter on your Windows NT Server Primary Domain Controller to change the frequency with which the Windows NT Server will check the Directory Database for changes. Where in Windows NT will you configure this?*

Choose the best answer:

A. *In Server Manager, within the Primary Domain Controller Server Properties dialog box*

B. *In User Manager for Domains from the Policies menu*

C. *In the Windows NT Registry in the following location: HKEY_LOCAL_MACHINE\SYSTEM \CurrentControlSet\Services\Netlogon\Parameters*

D. *In the Windows NT Server's Control Panel*

As you have learned, a Microsoft Windows NT Server Primary Domain Controller will automatically check its Directory Database every five minutes looking for changes. You can control this process so that your Primary Domain Controller will check its Directory Database every 10 minutes, or whatever time interval you prefer. To change the amount of time between Directory Database checks, you must add and configure the *Pulse* parameter in the Registry.

The *Pulse* parameter defines the frequency (in seconds) of the Primary Domain Controller's Directory Database checks (Pulses). The Primary Domain Controller collects all Directory Database changes made since the last Pulse. After the *Pulse* time lapses, the Primary Domain Controller sends a pulse to each Backup Domain Controller that needs the changes (each of which, in turn, sends a series of replication calls back to the Primary Domain Controller). However, the Primary Domain Controller does not send a pulse to a Backup Domain Controller that has an up-to-date Directory Database. You can set a value for the Pulse parameter of anywhere from 60 (seconds) to 172,800 (seconds), although the default setting is 300 (five minutes). When the Registry does not specify a *Pulse* parameter value, the *NetLogon* service determines the optimal values for your Primary Domain Controller, depending on the Primary Domain Controller's load. To add and configure the *Pulse* parameter, perform the following steps:

1. Click your mouse on the Start menu and select the Run option. Windows NT will open the Run dialog box.

2. Within the Run dialog box, type *Regedt32* and click your mouse on the OK button. Windows NT will open the *Registry Editor* program.

3. Within the *Registry Editor* program, double-click your mouse on the *HKEY_LOCAL_ MACHINE\SYSTEM* hive. The *Registry Editor* program will expand the *SYSTEM* hive.

4. Within the *SYSTEM* hive, double-click your mouse on the *CurrentControlSet* subkey. The *Registry Editor* will expand the *CurrentControlSet* subkey.

5. Within the *CurrentControlSet* subkey, double-click your mouse on the *Service* subkey. The *Registry Editor* will expand the *Service* subkey.

6. Within the *Service* subkey, double-click your mouse on the *Netlogon* subkey. The *Registry Editor* will expand the *Netlogon* subkey.

7. Within the *Netlogon* subkey, double-click your mouse on the *Parameters* subkey. The *Registry Editor* will expand the *Parameters* subkey.

8. Within the *Parameters* subkey, click your mouse on the Edit menu Add Value option. The *Registry Editor* will display the Add Value dialog box.

9. Within the Add Value dialog box, type *Pulse* in the *Value Name* field. Click your mouse on the Data Type drop-down list and select REG_DWORD. Click your mouse on the OK button. The *Registry Editor* will display the DWORD Editor dialog box.

10. Within the DWORD Editor dialog box, type a value between 60 and 172,800. Click your mouse on the OK button. The *Registry Editor* will close the DWORD Editor and Add Value dialog boxes.

11. Shut down and restart your Windows NT Server Backup Domain Controller. Windows NT will set the *Pulse* parameter.

Answer C is correct because you must configure the Pulse parameter from the Windows NT Server Primary Domain Controller's Registry. Answers A and B are incorrect because you cannot configure any aspect of Directory Database synchronization from either Server Manager or User Manager for Domains. Answer D is incorrect because there are no utilities in the Windows NT Server's Control Panel that will let you configure the Pulse parameter for Directory Database synchronization.

493   CONFIGURING THE PULSEMAXIMUM PARAMETER FOR REPLICATION

Q: *The PulseMaximum parameter in the Registry determines the maximum interval at which the Primary Domain Controller will pulse all Backup Domain Controllers.*

True or False?

As you have learned, when a Microsoft Windows NT Server Primary Domain Controller checks its Directory Database and finds changes, it will then notify only the Backup Domain Controllers that need the change information. Whether or not a Backup Domain Controller needs Directory Database information, every Backup Domain Controller will receive a pulse (notification) at the time the *PulseMaximum* parameter specifies. You can configure the amount of time you want between these mandatory calls.

The *PulseMaximum parameter* defines the maximum pulse frequency (in seconds). The Primary Domain Controller will send every Backup Domain Controller at least one pulse at the *PulseMaximum* parameter frequency, regardless of whether the Backup Domain Controller's database is up-to-date. The default value for *PulseMaximum* is 7,200 seconds (2 hours)—which means that the mandatory pulse will occur every 2 hours at a minimum. To configure the *PulseMaximum* parameter, perform the following steps:

1. Click your mouse on the Start menu and select the Run option. Windows NT will open the Run dialog box.

2. Within the Run dialog box, type *Regedt32* and click your mouse on the OK button. Windows NT will open the Registry Editor program.

3. Within the Registry Editor program, double-click your mouse on the *HKEY_LOCAL_MACHINE\SYSTEM* hive. The Registry Editor program will expand the *SYSTEM* hive.

4. Within the *SYSTEM* hive, double-click your mouse on the *CurrentControlSet* subkey. The Registry Editor will expand the *CurrentControlSet* subkey.

5. Within the *CurrentControlSet* subkey, double-click your mouse on the *Service* subkey. The Registry Editor will expand the *Service* subkey.

6. Within the *Service* subkey, double-click your mouse on the *Netlogon* subkey. The Registry Editor will expand the *Netlogon* subkey.C C

7. Within the *Netlogon* subkey, double-click your mouse on the *Parameters* subkey. The Registry Editor will expand the *Parameters* subkey.

8. Within the *Parameters* subkey, click your mouse on the Edit menu Add Value option. The Registry Editor will display the Add Value dialog box.

9. Within the Add Value dialog box, type *PulseMaximum* in the *Value Name* field. Click your mouse on the Data Type drop-down list and select REG_DWORD. Click your mouse on the OK button. The Registry Editor will display the DWORD Editor dialog box.

10. Within the DWORD Editor dialog box, type a value between 60 and 86,400. Click your mouse on the OK button. The Registry Editor will close the DWORD Editor and Add Value dialog boxes.

11. Shut down and restart your Windows NT Server Backup Domain Controller. Windows NT will set the *PulseMaximum* parameter.

*The answer is **True** because the PulseMaximum parameter in the Registry will control the maximum amount of time before the Primary Domain Controller will force a pulse to each Backup Domain Controller, whether or not its Directory Database is up-to-date.*

494 CONFIGURING THE CHANGELOGSIZE PARAMETER FOR REPLICATION

Q: *The default setting for the change log will allow for 2,000 changes.*

True or False?

As you have learned, from time to time, a Backup Domain Controller will request a full synchronization event. Windows NT uses information within the *change log* to determine whether a full or partial synchronization event occurs. Each change—remember a change is an addition of or modification to the set of users, groups, and computers in the domain—to the Directory Database is typically 32 bytes in size. The default change log is 64 kilobytes in size, so the default change log will hold approximately 2,000 changes (divide 64,000 by 32). Each change in the change log has a version number that Windows NT assigns. When the Primary Domain Controller records enough changes, Windows NT overwrites the change log entry with the lowest version number. When a Windows NT Server Backup Domain Controller accesses the change log and determines that the Primary Domain Controller has overwritten the change version the Backup Domain Controller is requesting, the Backup Domain Controller will call for a full synchronization event.

If you notice a Backup Domain Controller performing an excessive number of full synchronizations (by tracking of network traffic and entries in the Event Viewer), you should probably increase the *ChangeLogSize* parameter in the Primary Domain Controller's Registry. As with the change log, the default value for the *ChangeLogSize* parameter is 64 kilobytes and it will hold approximately 2,000 changes. The maximum size for a change log is four megabytes (which would hold over 100,000 changes). To add and configure the *ChangeLogSize* parameter, perform the following steps:

1. Click your mouse on the Start menu and select the Run option. Windows NT will open the Run dialog box.

2. Within the Run dialog box, type *Regedt32* and click your mouse on the OK button. Windows NT will open the Registry Editor program.

3. Within the Registry Editor program, click your mouse on the *HKEY_LOCAL_ MACHINE\SYSTEM* hive. The Registry Editor program will expand the *SYSTEM* hive.

4. Within the *SYSTEM* hive, double-click your mouse on the *CurrentControlSet* subkey. The Registry Editor will expand the *CurrentControlSet* subkey.

5. Within the *CurrentControlSet* subkey, double-click your mouse on the *Service* subkey. The Registry Editor will expand the *Service* subkey.

6. Within the *Service* subkey, double-click your mouse on the *Netlogon* subkey. The Registry Editor will expand the *Netlogon* subkey.

7. Within the *Netlogon* subkey, double-click your mouse on the *Parameters* subkey. The Registry Editor will expand the *Parameters* subkey.

8. Within the *Parameters* subkey, click your mouse on the Edit menu Add Value option. The Registry Editor will display the Add Value dialog box.

9. Within the Add Value dialog box, type *ChangeLogSize* in the *Value Name* field. Click your mouse on the Data Type drop-down list and select REG_DWORD. Click your mouse on the OK button. The Registry Editor will display the DWORD Editor dialog box.

10. Within the DWORD Editor dialog box, type a value between 65,536 and 4,194,304. Click your mouse on the OK button. The Registry Editor will close the DWORD Editor and Add Value dialog boxes.

11. Shut down and restart your Windows NT Server Backup Domain Controller. Windows NT will set the *ChangeLogSize* parameter.

The answer is **True** *because the change log for Directory Database synchronization default will hold 2,000 changes.*

| 495 | CONFIGURING THE PULSECONCURRENCY PARAMETER FOR REPLICATION |

Q: *The PulseConcurrency parameter in the Registry will control the number of Backup Domain Controllers to which the Primary Domain Controller will send synchronization information at one time.*

True or False?

When a Windows NT Server Primary Domain Controller sends a Pulse to the Backup Domain Controllers in the domain, the Primary Domain Controller will send pulses only to a limited number of Backup Domain Controllers at one time. A Windows NT Server Primary Domain Controller will, by default, send pulses to only 20 Backup Domain Controllers before sending any more pulses. Limiting the number of Backup Domain Controllers receiving pulses at any one time ensures that the pulses and the resulting Directory Database synchronization will not saturate the network bandwidth. To control the number of Pulses that a Primary Domain Controller will send at one time, set the *PulseConcurrency* parameter in the Registry. To set the *PulseConcurrency* parameter in the Registry, perform the following steps:

1. Click your mouse on the Start menu and select the Run option. Windows NT will open the Run dialog box.

2. Within the Run dialog box, type *Regedt32* and click your mouse on the OK button. Windows NT will open the Registry Editor program.

3. Within the Registry Editor program, double-click your mouse on the *HKEY_LOCAL_ MACHINE\SYSTEM* hive. The Registry Editor program will expand the *SYSTEM* hive.

4. Within the *SYSTEM* hive, double-click your mouse on the *CurrentControlSet* subkey. The Registry Editor will expand the *CurrentControlSet* subkey.

5. Within the *CurrentControlSet* subkey, double-click your mouse on the *Service* subkey. The Registry Editor will expand the *Service* subkey.

6. Within the *Service* subkey, double-click your mouse on the *Netlogon* subkey. The Registry Editor will expand the *Netlogon* subkey.

7. Within the *Netlogon* subkey, double-click your mouse on the *Parameters* subkey. The Registry Editor will expand the *Parameters* subkey.

8. Within the *Parameters* subkey, click your mouse on the Edit menu Add Value option. The Registry Editor will display the Add Value dialog box.

9. Within the Add Value dialog box, type *PulseConcurrency* in the *Value Name* field. Click your mouse on the Data Type drop-down list and select REG_DWORD. Click your mouse on the OK button. The Registry Editor will display the DWORD Editor dialog box.

10. Within the DWORD Editor dialog box, type a value between 1 and 500. Click your mouse on the OK button. The Registry Editor will close the DWORD Editor and Add Value dialog boxes.

11. Shut down and restart your Windows NT Server Backup Domain Controller. Windows NT will set the *PulseConcurrency* parameter.

The answer is **True** *because the PulseConcurrency parameter lets you specify how many Backup Domain Controllers will receive Directory Database update information at one time.*

496   **USING SERVER MANAGER TO FORCE A SYNCHRONIZATION EVENT**

Q: When you use Server Manager to force a synchronization event, what type of synchronization will occur?

Choose the best answer:

     A.   *A full synchronization*

     B.   *A partial synchronization*

     C.   *A full synchronization, but only to the Backup Domain Controllers you have selected*

     D.   *A full synchronization, but only to Backup Domain Controllers that require Directory Database updates*

There may be times when you want the Primary Domain Controller to send updated Directory Database information to the Backup Domain Controllers immediately. Just as you can always change your domain's name, as a Windows NT domain administrator you can also cause a synchronization event to occur at any time. To do so, the *Server Manager* program will let you select either the Primary Domain Controller or any Backup Domain Controller and then synchronize the domain controllers. If you select the Primary Domain Controller and cause a synchronization event, you will synchronize the entire domain. If you choose a Backup Domain Controller and cause a synchronization event, you will synchronize only that one Backup Domain Controller with the Primary Domain Controller. When you use *Server Manager* to cause a synchronization event, you only cause the Primary Domain Controller to send a Pulse to the Backup Domain Controllers. You do not call for a full synchronization, so this process is a different type of *partial synchronization*. To cause a synchronization event using *Server Manager*, perform the following steps:

1. Click your mouse on the Start menu and select the Programs submenu Administrative Tools group *Server Manager* program. Windows NT will display the *Server Manager* program.

2. Within the *Server Manager* program, select the Backup Domain Controller to which you want to send a Pulse. Click your mouse on the Computer menu Synchronize with Primary Domain Controller option. *Server Manager* will display a confirmation dialog box.

3. Click your mouse on the Yes button. *Server Manager* will make the Primary Domain Controller send a pulse to the Backup Domain Controller you selected.

Answer B *is correct because when you use* **Server Manager** *to force a synchronization event, you will cause only a partial synchronization to occur.* **Answers A, C,** *and* **D** *are incorrect because you cannot force a full synchronization event to occur from Server Manager.*

497 **CALLING FOR A FULL SYNCHRONIZATION EVENT**

Q: How can you force a full synchronization event to occur?

Choose the best answer:

> A.   *In Server Manager, select the Backup Domain Controller that you want to synchronize. From the Computer menu, select the Synchronize with Primary Domain Controller option.*
>
> B.   *Install the Windows NT Server Resource Kit. Open the Synchronization utility and select the Synchronize Now option from the Synchronize menu.*
>
> C.   *From the Windows NT Command Prompt, type the command Net Accounts /Sync.*
>
> D.   *From the Windows NT Command Prompt, type the command Synchronize /Yes.*

As you learned in Tip 496, you can use the *Server Manager* program to force a Windows NT Server Primary Domain Controller to send a pulse to one or all Windows NT Server Backup Domain Controllers. However, when you use *Server Manager* to force a synchronization event, you only cause the Primary Domain Controller to send a pulse, which will cause only a partial Directory Database synchronization. As you know, you cannot use *Server Manager* to force a full synchronization. Instead, to force a full Directory Database synchronization, you must use the *net accounts /sync* command from the Windows NT Command Prompt, as Figure 497 shows.

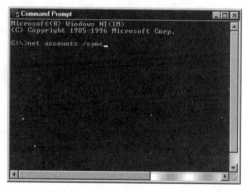

Figure 497 *Using the Command Prompt to force a full Directory Database synchronization event.*

Answer C *is correct because the only way for you to force a full synchronization event is to use the Net Accounts /sync command.* **Answer A** *is incorrect because you cannot use Server Manager to force a full synchronization event.* **Answer B** *is incorrect because there is no Synchronization utility in the Windows NT Server Resource Kit.* **Answer D** *is incorrect because there is no Synchronize command.*

498 **SCHEDULING DIFFERENT REPLICATION RATES**

Q: You are the administrator of a Windows NT domain that encompasses multiple sites throughout the United States. You are having problems with Directory Database synchronization in some of your sites because of slow WAN links between the sites. Some locations do not have up-to-date Directory Databases. What can you do, as the administrator, to solve this problem?

Choose the best answer:

A. Upgrade the slow WAN links to faster lines.

B. Remove the Backup Domain Controllers from the sites where the slow links are.

C. Create multiple Windows NT domains and make each site its own domain.

D. Schedule different synchronization rates for day and night. Configure the nighttime synchronization to use the full network bandwidth.

If you are the administrator of a Microsoft Windows NT domain that spans multiple locations using WAN links, you may want to configure one or more of your Windows NT Server Backup Domain Controllers to have nighttime *replication rates* different from the daytime replication rates you set. Doing so will let you reduce network traffic from replication during the day time, and perform the majority of replication at night. The term replication refers to the Directory Database synchronization process—so the replication rate is the frequency of the Directory Database synchronization process.

You can implement different replication rates by adjusting the *ReplicationGovernor* parameter in the Registry and then stopping and restarting the *NetLogon* service from within a batch file that you will schedule using the AT command. You can use the *regini.exe* command from the Windows NT Resource Kit to make the changes in the Registry, as shown in the following command format (the items within the brackets are optional):

```
C:\> regini [scriptfile name]   <ENTER>
```

The *scriptfile* would contain the full pathname in the Registry to the *ReplicationGovernor* parameter and the new value you want to apply to it. For detailed information on what a *scriptfile* will contain to control replication rates, see the Microsoft Windows NT Resource Kit.

Answer D is correct because you can schedule different synchronization times for different synchronization rates. Answer A is incorrect because although replacing slow links with faster ones may solve your problem, it is expensive and therefore not the best answer. Answer B is incorrect because removing the Backup Domain Controllers from sites where you have slow links will eliminate the synchronization problem, it will also create a problem with users having to log on across the WAN links. Answer C is incorrect because creating multiple domains would not necessarily create trust relationships problems, so it is not the best answer.

499   UNDERSTANDING UNIVERSAL RESOURCE ACCESS

Q: Users should be able to access resources only in their own domains.

True or False?

Whether your network is small, medium, or large, all users must have access to network resources. As you have learned in previous Tips, efficient control of access to resources is one of Windows NT's strongest features. For example, if you are a traveling sales person, you must have access to documents and databases no matter where you are—so the network should be smart enough to recognize your log-in, even if you are across the country, and grant access to your directories and files. *Universal resource access*—the ability to access files and folders from any computer on the network—is essential in any Windows NT network.

In a multiple-domain environment, the administrator must assign resource access permissions across domains. In general, the administrators will use the Master domain model, trust relationships, and other Windows NT features that you have learned about to perpetuate access permissions across domains on the network. The ultimate goal of passing resource access permissions across domains is that, regardless of what domain validates a user's account, the user should still have access to the appropriate resources, as their home domain specifies, and as Figure 499 shows.

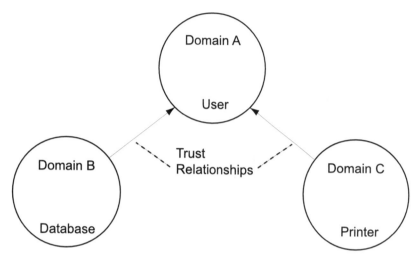

Figure 499 Users obtain universal resource access in remote domains through different domain models and trust relationships..

*The answer is **False** because users should be able to access resources in any domain to which the administrator has granted them permissions.*

500 UNDERSTANDING ADVANCED TRUST RELATIONSHIPS

Q: You can configure a Windows NT trust relationship between which of the following?

Choose the best answer:

> *A.   Any Windows NT Server and any Windows NT Workstation*
>
> *B.   Any Windows NT Server and any other Windows NT Server*
>
> *C.   A Windows NT Server Primary Domain Controller and any other Windows NT Server Primary Domain Controller*
>
> *D.   Any Windows NT Server Primary Domain Controller and any other Windows NT Server*

As you learned in Tip 477, in a Windows NT domain model, a trust relationship is a logical administrative link between two or more Windows NT domains. A trust relationship lets an administrator manage users and resources in multiple domains from any location in the network. Only an administrator can configure Windows NT domain trust relationships, and the administrator must have a minimum of two Microsoft Windows NT domains to establish the trusts. You, as an administrator, can establish a trust relationship only between Windows NT Server Primary Domain Controllers. Anytime you configure more than two trust relationships, you will deal with advanced trust relationship issues. Trust relationships require only initial configuration. After you configure your trust relationships, you will not have to perform any other administrative duties on the trusts. However, this does not mean that you should not plan trust relationships carefully. In fact, when you plan your advanced trust relationships, you should consider the network traffic, Directory Database synchronization, and resource access you expect in your network. As an example of how you might use advanced trust relationships, imagine that you are the network administrator of a school district. The district has asked you to examine the network and make recommendations about how to improve the network design. When you examine the network, you find that the school district has one district office and 10 grade schools. Each of the 11 locations is configured as its own Microsoft Windows NT domain and, because there are no trust relationships, each domain requires its own administrator. User accounts for the district office are in the district office domain, and all teacher and student accounts are in their respective school domains, as Figure 500.1 shows. After you question several school district employees, you learn that each year more than 100 teachers change schools within the district. Because you cannot migrate a user account from one Windows NT domain to another Windows NT domain, you must delete the account for a teacher leaving a given school and create a new account for the new, replacement teacher. If you do this, you must perform 200 administrative tasks just to accommodate the teachers moving from one school to another each year, and this work does not include the students with user accounts who move from school to school.

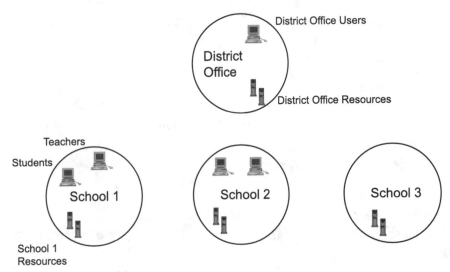

Figure 500.1 The school district domain model.

After careful consideration, you recommend changing the network's configuration so that all user accounts are in the district office domain. By doing so, you can centralize all user account administration. In addition, you will not have to create or delete accounts for users who move from one school to another, as Figure 500.2 shows.

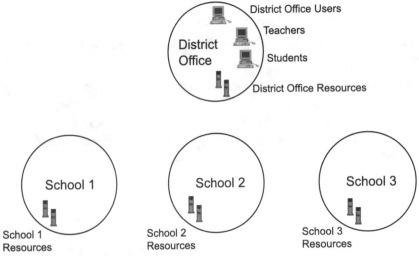

Figure 500.2 Creating your recommended domain model.

Answer C is correct because you can configure a trust relationship only between two Windows NT domains, and you must configure the trust relationship through the Primary Domain Controllers. Answers A, B, and D are incorrect because you can configure a trust relationship only between two Windows NT Server Primary Domain Controllers.

501	DETERMINING THE NUMBER OF TRUST RELATIONSHIPS FOR MULTIPLE MASTER DOMAIN MODELS

Q: *You are the administrator of your company's Microsoft Windows NT network. You will be implementing a Multiple Master Domain model soon, in which you will have two master domains and four resource domains. How many trust relationships will you need?*

Choose the best answer:

> A. *Four*
>
> B. *Six*
>
> C. *Ten*
>
> D. *None*

As you have learned in previous Tips, trust relationships between servers are one of the most important determinations that you will make as an administrator. If you are the administrator for a company that is migrating to Microsoft Windows NT, and you will be implementing a Multiple Master Domain model, you must know how many trust relationships to configure.

Multiple Master Domain models always have a two-way trust relationship between all master domains. Additionally, you will have to implement one-way trust relationships from each resource domain to each master domain. To determine the number of trust relationships you will need to implement the Multiple Master Domain model, you must multiply the number of master domains, *M*, by the number of master domains minus 1, *(M-1)*. The formula *(M*(M-1))* yields the number of two-way trust relationships you must use.

You must also multiply the number of resource domains, *R*, by the number of master domains, *(R*M)*, which yields the number of one-way trust relationships to use. Then, you add *(M* (M-1))* to *(R*M)* and your final formula is *(M*(M-1) + (R*M))*. For example, if you have three master domains and six resource domains, your formula would be 3*(3-1) + (3*4) = 18. Therefore, you would need 18 trust relationships to implement the Multiple Master Domain model.

Answer C is correct because you will need ten trust relationships for a Microsoft Windows NT Multiple Master Domain model that has two master domains and four resource domains (2*(2-1) + (4*2) = 10). Answers A, B, and D are incorrect because for you to configure a Microsoft Windows NT Multiple Master Domain model, you must create a two-way trust relationship between each master domain, and then one one-way trust relationship between each resource domain and each master domain—meaning none of these answers includes enough trust relationships for the model.

502	DETERMINING THE NUMBER OF TRUST RELATIONSHIPS FOR COMPLETE TRUST DOMAIN MODELS

Q: *You have four Microsoft Windows NT domains. You want to configure the Microsoft Windows NT domains into a Complete Trust Domain model. How many trust relationships will you need to establish a Complete Trust Domain model?*

Choose the best answer:

    A.   Four

    B.   Eight

    C.   Ten

    D.   Twelve

As you have learned, in a Microsoft Windows NT Complete Trust Domain model, each domain will have two-way trust relationships with every other domain on the network. If you are implementing a Complete Trust Domain model, you will have to know how to calculate the total number of trust relationships to configure. To calculate the number of trust relationships, simply multiply the number of domains, N, by the number of domains minus one $(N-1)$. For example, in a Complete Trust Domain model that has five domains, you would calculate $5 * (5-1) = 20$.

Answer D is correct because you will need 12 trust relationships for a Microsoft Windows NT Complete Trust Domain model that has four Microsoft Windows NT domains. **Answers A, B,** and **C** are incorrect because you must have 12 trust relationships for a four domain, Complete Trust Domain model.

503   TROUBLESHOOTING ADVANCED TRUST RELATIONSHIPS

Q: *You have implemented a Microsoft Windows NT Multiple Master Domain model. You have configured all the trust relationships and verified they are correct. When you try to administer domains other than the one your account is in, you cannot perform any administrative activities. What could be causing this problem?*

Choose the best answer:

    A.   You have not placed the Domain Admins group from your domain into the Administrators group of the other domains.

    B.   You have not placed the Administrators group from your domain into the Domain Admins group in the other domains.

    C.   You have not established the trust relationships properly.

    D.   You must synchronize the entire network in order for the trust relationships to work properly.

In domain models where you have several domains, you may have complex trust relationship issues, such as how many trusts to configure or how to implement groups across the trusts. You will want to plan every procedure before you actually implement anything—because a single missed step can make the entire model useless.

The biggest issue regarding trust relationships is the initial configuration of the trust relationships. Planning your domain model's trusts includes drawing initial sketches of your domain model and the trust relationships between domains on paper, choosing the domain model, and deciding where you will configure the trust relationships between the domains in the domain model.

When you are drawing the sketches for your domain model, you should always make sure that the arrows that you use within your sketches to represent trust relationships point toward the trusted domain. If Domain One trusts Domain Two, the arrow will point from Domain One to Domain Two. Users from Domain Two will be able to access Domain One's resources.

After you plan your model, you should implement it carefully, in accordance with how you designed your sketch. However, even after you establish your trust relationships, users will not automatically get access to resources in the trusting domain. For example, if have a friend you trust, you may or may not let that friend use your car. The friendship implies a trust, but you will have to explicitly grant permission to use any of your possessions. When a Microsoft Windows NT domain trusts another Microsoft Windows NT domain, the administrator will have to assign users from the trusted domain access to resources in the trusting domain.

When you configure a Multiple Master Domain model, you must also configure the necessary rights to let administrators perform administration from within the various domains in the model. You will have to place the Domain Admins global group from each trusted domain into the Administrators local group on each trusting domain. Moving the Domain Admins group lets you copy an administrative account from the trusted domain into an administrative account in the trusting domain.

If you are troubleshooting problems in a Microsoft Windows NT Multiple Master Domain model, you should check the group associations first. Make sure that you have placed the global groups from the trusted domain into the proper local groups in the trusting domains.

*Answer A is correct because you must place the Domain Admins global group from your domain into the Administrators local group in all other domains. **Answer B** is incorrect because you cannot place the Administrators local group into the Domain Admins global group. **Answer C** is incorrect because the question states that you have verified the trust relationships. **Answer D** is incorrect because Windows NT will validate your account from your domain, which Windows NT will have already synchronized after you established the trust relationships.*

504   **UNDERSTANDING BACKOFFICE INTEGRATION**

Q: *What does the term BackOffice integration mean?*

Choose the best answer:

A.   *Installing and configuring Microsoft BackOffice on a Microsoft Windows NT server.*

B.   *BackOffice applications will use Microsoft Windows NT user and group accounts so you can configure security.*

C.   *Mixing Microsoft Windows NT server Primary Domain Controllers and Microsoft Windows NT member servers in the same network.*

D.   *Planning strategies for using BackOffice applications.*

As you have learned, Windows NT is a network environment which Microsoft has specifically targeted at what they refer to as the Enterprise—businesses in need of cost-effective, high-powered solutions. Most analysts agree that Windows NT delivers admirably on that goal. However, Microsoft has taken the network solution one step further than other network operating system providers by integrating a large number of server-based applications within the operating system itself. Microsoft BackOffice is a suite of server products that Microsoft designed for high-end business solutions. The Microsoft BackOffice suite includes the following servers:

- Microsoft Windows NT server

- Microsoft Structured Query Language (SQL) server

- Microsoft Exchange server

- Microsoft Systems Network Architecture (SNA) server

- Microsoft Internet Information server

- Microsoft Systems Management server (SMS)

Microsoft designed all the BackOffice products to integrate with a Microsoft Windows NT server. In addition to the Windows NT server itself, all BackOffice products run on top of a Windows NT server as Windows NT services. Because the BackOffice products run as a service for Windows NT, each one weaves itself into the Windows NT architecture—for example, most BackOffice products use the Users and Groups that the Windows NT server itself implements as the basis for their security model.

For example, you do not have to create new user or group accounts in an *SQL Server* installation; instead, you can use the existing Windows NT domain accounts. Similarly, you do not have to create separate accounts for users of the *Exchange* server; you can have the *Exchange* server create the Windows NT accounts when it creates mailboxes for users. In fact, like *SQL Server* and *Exchange* server, each BackOffice product works with the Windows NT server to provide smooth, consistent operation.

Answer B is correct because Microsoft BackOffice products will use the preexisting Microsoft Windows NT server domain accounts to let you configure BackOffice security. Answers A, C, and D are incorrect because they do not give the proper definition for BackOffice integration.

505   **UNDERSTANDING THE NETLOGON SERVICE**

Q: *Which of the following are functions of the NetLogon service?*

Choose all correct answers:

     A.   *Managing Directory Database synchronization*

     B.   *Logging on domain users*

     C.   *Performing directory replication*

     D.   *Performing pass-through authentication*

The Microsoft Windows NT NetLogon service is vital to network operations, because it is the access point that all users will go through to get to the network itself. In other words, if the NetLogon service on your Windows NT server fails, your domain users will not be able to log on to the network. The NetLogon service is responsible for the following functions in Windows NT:

- Pass-through authentication

- Directory Database synchronization

- Log-on validation

Pass-through authentication (for user and group rights) occurs when your Windows NT computer passes a log-on request to a domain controller, or when a domain controller from one domain passes a log-on request to another Windows NT domain controller in another domain. The NetLogon service is responsible for all pass-through authentication. You will learn more about pass-through authentication in Tip 511. The NetLogon service is also responsible for managing Directory Database synchronization. If the NetLogon service fails to start, your domain controllers will not synchronize their Directory Databases—which, as you have learned, will cause significant problems for backup domain controllers across your network. Furthermore, depending on your domain model, users may be unable to access domains other than their home domain in NetLogon fails. In addition to Directory Database synchronization and pass-through authentication, the Windows NT NetLogon service is also responsible for user log-on validation. If a user tries to log on to the network and have a domain controller validate the log-on where the NetLogon service is not running, NetLogon will not authenticate the user's log-on request.

Answers A, B, and D are all correct because the NetLogon service is responsible for Directory Database synchronization, user log-on validation, and pass-through authentication. Answer C is incorrect because the NetLogon service is not responsible for directory replication.

506   ## ACCOUNT PLACEMENT IN MULTIPLE-DOMAIN ENVIRONMENTS

Q: *In a Microsoft Windows NT Multiple Master Domain environment, you will create all user accounts in the master domains.*

True or False?

In a Microsoft Windows NT multiple-domain model, you may have more than one domain in which user accounts reside. You would separate your accounts for a variety of reasons, ranging from wanting to break up the administration of the user accounts, to having too many users to fit into a single domain. Regardless of your reasons for using a Microsoft Windows NT multiple-domain model, you should understand where to place your user accounts.

In a Microsoft Windows NT multiple-domain model, the domains where user accounts reside are *master domains* and the domains where you administer your network resources are *resource domains*. If you have placed user accounts into more than one domain, you have a Multiple Master Domain model. You will have to place the Domain Users global group from the master domains into the Users local groups on the resource domains. Moving the Domain Users global group lets you copy the users from the master domains, making them also users in the resource domains. To administer your entire network, you will have to place the Domain Admins global groups from each master domain into the Administrators local groups in each other domain. When you move the Domain Admins groups, you copy the administrators from the master domains, making them administrators in all domains into which you copy the groups.

*The answer is **True** because you will always create all user accounts in Multiple Master Domain models in the master domains.*

507   ## INTRODUCTION TO CENTRALIZED ADMINISTRATION

Q: *Which of the following best describes the term centralized administration?*

Choose the best answer:

    A.   *The administrator has the ability to create users, groups, and computer accounts from anywhere in the network.*

    B.   *The administrator must manage the entire Microsoft Windows NT domain from one computer only.*

C.   *Multiple network administrators sharing the administrative load.*

D.   *The distributed database design of Microsoft Windows NT domains.*

When you take your MCSE exams, Microsoft will repeatedly refer to the term *centralized administration* because it is the "heart" of the Microsoft Windows NT server domain structure. Centralized administration means one active database contains all user, group, and computer accounts. The Directory Database is the central database of accounts.

Windows NT copies the Directory Database to Windows NT server Backup Domain Controllers (BDC) and the Backup Domain Controllers will act as log-on validation servers. When a user logs on to the network, either a Windows NT server Backup Domain Controller or the Primary Domain Controller containing the Directory Database will respond by authenticating the user's log-on request.

While the Directory Database resides only on the Primary Domain Controller and Backup Domain Controllers, you can administer the Directory Database from any computer in the network. Regardless of what computer you use to access the Directory Database, you will be accessing the Directory Database on the Primary Domain Controller. You cannot view the Directory Database copy on the Backup Domain Controller—a restraint that Windows NT forces to ensure that you do not inadvertently change the wrong copy of the Directory Database.

Microsoft Windows NT server's centralized administration is important because it lets you administer the network from any computer in the network. However, if the Primary Domain Controller goes off-line unexpectedly, the drawback is you cannot perform any domain administration. You would have to promote the Backup Domain Controller to the Primary Domain Controller's role to perform any domain administration. You learned how to promote Backup Domain Controllers to Primary Domain Controllers in Tip 121.

Answer A is correct because centralized administration is the administrator's ability to manage the network from any computer. Answers B, C, and D are incorrect because none of the answers properly describe centralized administration.

508   CONFIGURING ONE-WAY AND TWO-WAY TRUSTS

Q: *A two-way trust relationship is actually two one-way trusts.*

True or False?

As the network administrator for a Microsoft Windows NT domain, you will have to configure Microsoft Windows NT domain trust relationships. After you configure domain trust relationships, you are mostly done with them administratively because Microsoft Windows NT domain trusts do not need any maintenance—unless, for some reason, you decide to change trust relationships within your network (which can result in serious configuration issues, as you learned previously). As Tip 201 explains in detail, a two-way trust relationship is actually two one-way trusts. If you must configure a two-way trust, you can simply configure a one-way trust from each domain. To configure a trust relationship, from your Windows NT server Primary Domain Controller in the domain that will be the trusted domain, perform the following steps:

1. Click your mouse on the Start menu and select the Programs submenu Administrative Tools group User Manager for Domains program. Windows NT will open the *User Manager for Domains* program.

2. Within *User Manager for Domains,* click your mouse on the Policies menu and select the Trust Relationships option. *User Manager for Domains* will display the Trust Relationships dialog box.

3. Within the Trust Relationships dialog box, click your mouse on the Add button in the Trusting Domains section. *User Manager for Domains* will display the Add Trusting Domain dialog box.

4. Within the Add Trusting Domain dialog box, type the name of the domain that you want to be the trusting domain. Optionally, you can use a password for configuring this trust (that is, you can place a password within the Password field that the administrator must enter before modifying or deleting the trust). Then, click your mouse on the OK button. *User Manager for Domains* will close the Add Trusting Domain dialog box and display the Trust Relationships dialog box.

5. Within the Trust Relationships dialog box, click your mouse on the OK button. *User Manager for Domains* will create the new trust relationship and close the Trust Relationships dialog box.

To configure the trusting domain side of the trust relationship, on the Microsoft Windows NT server Primary Domain Controller in the trusting domain, perform the following steps:

1. Click your mouse on the Start menu and select the Programs submenu Administrative Tools group User Manager for Domains option. Windows NT will open the *User Manager for Domains* program.

2. Within *User Manager for Domains,* click your mouse on the Policies menu and select the Trust Relationships option. *User Manager for Domains* will display the Trust Relationships dialog box.

3. Within the Trust Relationships dialog box, click your mouse on the Add button in the Trusted Domains section. *User Manager for Domains* will display the Add Trusted Domain dialog box.

4. Within the Add Trusted Domain dialog box, type the name of the domain that you want to be the trusted domain. Then, click your mouse on the OK button. *User Manager for Domains* will close the Add Trusted Domain dialog box and display the Trust Relationships dialog box.

5. Within the Trust Relationships dialog box, click your mouse on the OK button. *User Manager for Domains* will create the Primary Domain Controller's side of the two-way trust relationship and close the Trust Relationships dialog box.

The answer is **True** *because a two-way trust relationship is actually two one-way trusts.*

509 UNDERSTANDING THE DIFFERENCE BETWEEN TRUSTING AND TRUSTED DOMAINS

Q: In Microsoft diagrams, the arrows point toward the Trusting domain.

True or False?

The two types of domains in a Microsoft Windows NT trust relationship are the trusting and the trusted domains. The *trusting domain* is the domain in which the administrator will grant permission to use resources. The *trusted domain* is the domain in which the user accounts reside. In a Microsoft Windows NT domain, the domain that trusts the other domain is stating that users in the trusted domain may use its resources.

When you draw your domain model, you should use arrows to denote the flow of trust relationships (which is the same way that Microsoft draws the trust relationship diagrams). The arrows in your model should always point from the trusting domain toward the trusted domain.

The answer is **False,** *because in Microsoft diagrams, the arrows point toward the Trusted domain.*

510 USING BUILT-IN GROUPS TO MANAGE TRUSTS

Q: Which of the following are built-in groups on a Microsoft Windows NT server computer?

Choose all correct answers:

    A.   Administrators

    B.   Sales

    C.   Backup Operators

    D.   Printer Managers

As you have learned, establishing trust relationships is one of the most important tasks for the administrator. After the administrator establishes trust relationships, the administrator must then perform account administration activities to let users access resources in the newly-accessible domains. Additionally, the administrator must duplicate certain information within both domains on either side of the trust in order to grant themselves sufficient rights to perform their administrative duties.

Generally, when you build a trust relationship, you will use the Directory Database from the trusted domain to verify user access and permissions. However, although you may create groups to contain users in a multiple-domain environment, you will nevertheless use some built-in groups to administer the network and to grant users access to resources. You must ensure that you duplicate these groups within the trusting domain.

Windows NT stores all user accounts in a Windows NT domain in the Domain Users global group. You can copy the Domain Users group from any trusted domain into the Users local group in any trusting domain—thereby copying the information Windows NT needs about user accounts into the trusting domain. Moving the Domain Users group gives you the ability to grant access to resources in the trusting domain to users from the trusted domain. You also must place the Domain Admins global group from the trusted domain into the Administrators local group in the trusting domains. Moving the Domain Admins group lets you make any member of the Domain Admins global group an administrator in the trusting domain. Table 510 lists the built-in Microsoft Windows NT groups.

Microsoft Windows NT Groups

Account Operators	Administrators	Backup Operators	Creator Owner
Domain Admin	Domain Guests	Domain Users	Everyone
Guests	Interactive	Network	Power Users
Print Operators	Replicator	Server Operators	Users

Table 510 The built-in groups that Windows NT includes.

Answers A and C are correct because both Administrators and Backup Operators are built-in groups on Microsoft Windows NT server computers. **Answer B and D** *are incorrect because neither groups exist by default on Microsoft Windows NT server computers.*

511 UNDERSTANDING PASS-THROUGH AUTHENTICATION

Q: Which service in Microsoft Windows NT manages pass-through authentication?

Choose the best answer:

    A.   Server service

    B.   Workstation service

    C.   NetLogon service

    D.   Replicator service

In earlier Tips, you learned about the Windows NT log-on process. If you are logging on to the domain, your Windows NT computer will have to send the log-on request to a domain controller. The service that sends the request is the NetLogon service. The process of the Windows NT computer sending the request is *pass-through authentication*, because no authentication happens at the computer where you make the log-on request—instead, the computer passes all the information through to a domain controller which, in turn, performs the actual authentication of your request.

Pass-through authentication occurs in only three circumstances. First, pass-through authentication can happen when a Windows NT computer sends a log-on request to the domain. Second, when a Windows NT computer that you are using to access the network is part of a domain other than the domain where your user account resides, the network will use pass-through authentication to authenticate you within your home domain. Third, pass-through authentication occurs when a user tries to access a resource in a domain that does not contain the user's account.

Pass-through authentication will most frequently occur when you are in a Master Domain or Multiple Master Domain model. For example, if you are logging on from a computer in a resource domain, and your user account is in the master domain, your Windows NT computer will send the log-on request to its domain controller. The domain controller from the resource domain will then pass the request to the domain where your user account resides (the Master Domain). The Master Domain then passes the authentication information back to the local computer (through its domain controller). The entire process—from initial authentication entry to the networks grant of access—uses pass-through authentication.

Answer C is correct because the NetLogon service manages pass-through authentication. Answers A, B, and D are incorrect because the neither the Server, Workstation, nor the Replicator services manage pass-through authentication.

512   GRANTING USERS PERMISSIONS TO RESOURCES ACROSS TRUSTS

Q: What makes it possible for you to grant users permissions to resources across trusts?

Choose the best answer:

    A.   The Server service

    B.   The Workstation service

    C.   Administrative shares

    D.   Pass-through authentication

As the administrator of a Windows NT network, you are responsible for making sure that users can access resources in the network. In a multiple-domain environment, you will have to grant access to resources in more than one domain, which means that you will have to grant access to the resources across trust relationships. After you have established trust relationships between your domains, you can add users and groups from trusted domains to local groups that have access to the resources in the resource domains. To assign permissions to users and groups from trusted domains to a resource on an NTFS volume, perform the following steps:

1. Double-click your mouse on the My Computer icon on your desktop. Windows NT will open the My Computer window.

2. Within the My Computer window, double-click your mouse on the NTFS volume that contains the resource (for example, a folder) to which you want to grant access. Windows NT will open the Volume window of the resource you select.

3. Within the Volume window, right-click your mouse on the folder to which you want to assign permissions. Windows NT will display a pop-up menu.

4. Within the pop-up menu, click your mouse on the Properties option. Windows NT will open the Properties dialog box.

5. Within the Properties dialog box, select the Security tab. On the Security tab, click your mouse on the Permissions button. Windows NT will display the Directory Permissions dialog box.

6. Within the Directory Permissions dialog box, click your mouse on the Add button. Windows NT will display the Add User and Groups dialog box.

7. Within the Add User and Groups dialog box, click your mouse on the List Names From drop-down list and select the trusted domain name that contains the Directory Database. Windows NT will get the list of user accounts from the trusted domain.

8. Within the Add User and Groups dialog box, select the user or groups to which you want to assign permissions. Click your mouse on the Type of Access drop-down list and select the type of access you want to assign to these users. Then, click your mouse on the OK button. Windows NT will close the Add User and Groups dialog box.

Answer D is correct because pass-through authentication makes it possible for an administrator to grant permissions to resources across trusts. Answers A and B are incorrect because the Server and Workstation services have nothing to do with accessing resources across trusts. Answer C is incorrect because only an administrator can use administrative shares.

513   MANAGING BROKEN TRUST RELATIONSHIPS

Q: *If an administrator breaks a trust on one side, you must reestablish the trust only on the side where the administrator broke the trust in order to fix it.*

True or False?

As you have learned, after you establish a trust relationship, it does not require that you perform any regular maintenance in the normal course of operations. However, if a trust relationship becomes corrupt, or if an administrator accidentally removes the trust, you may have problems trying to fix it. The two sides to a Microsoft Windows NT server domain trust relationship are the trusting and the trusted domains. If either side of the trust ends the trust relationship, you cannot reestablish the trust on the broken side—Windows NT will not let you. Instead, you must break the trust on both sides, and then reestablish the trust from both sides. Therefore, if you ever have difficulty establishing a trust relationship, you should break the trust from both sides, and then create the trust again.

*The answer is **False** because if a Trust Relationship is broken on one side, the administrator must break the trust on the other side and reestablish the trusts from both sides.*

514   UNDERSTANDING NON-TRANSITIVE TRUST ISSUES

Q: Domain A trusts Domain B, and Domain B trusts Domain C. Therefore, Domain A also trusts Domain C.

True or False?

One limitation of using trust relationships is trusts are *non-transitive*. In other words, when you establish a trust relationship with a single domain, you do not establish trust relationships with any other domains automatically—even domains already having trust relationships with the trusted domain. Simply put, when you establish a trust relationship with a domain, you do not inherit that domain's trust relationships, nor does it inherit your trust relationships. Each domain that uses another domain's resources must configure a trust relationship with that domain, as Figure 514 shows.

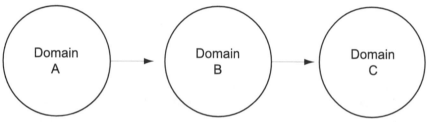

Figure 514 *Understanding how domain trust relationships are non-transitive.*

In Figure 514, Domain A trusts Domain B and Domain B trusts Domain C. A user in Domain A can access resources in Domain A only. A user in Domain B can access resources in Domains A and B. A user in Domain C can access resources only in Domains C and B.

The answer is **False** *because trusts are non-transitive. When a domain trusts another domain, the first domain does not inherit the trust relationships of the second domain.*

515   INTRODUCTION TO SERVER ANALYSIS AND OPTIMIZATION

Q: Which of the following are part of Windows NT server analysis and optimization?

Choose the best answers:

> *A.   Creating a server measurement baseline to define the server's current activity.*
>
> *B.   Tracking resource trends.*
>
> *C.   Monitoring client access licenses.*
>
> *D.   Analyzing Performance Monitor data to find and resolve system problems.*

Server analysis and optimization is the term used for monitoring your server's activity to improve the server's overall performance. You must take several steps to perform server analysis and optimization. First, you must determine the resources to monitor, and then you must establish a measurement baseline. A *measurement baseline* is a sample of server activity while the server is under a normal workload. You should take measurements at several times over the course of several workdays to determine the most accurate measurement baseline. Later, you can compare your measurement baseline to subsequent measurements to determine if the server's performance is suffering. You will learn more about measurement baselines in Tip 524.

After you establish your measurement baseline, you will have to record resource use trends to see if your server is experiencing a heavier workload over time. You will use the *Performance Monitor* program to record and view performance data related to your server. Analyzing the data you record from the *Performance Monitor* program is essential to server analysis and optimization. Tip 516 explains the *Performance Monitor* program in detail.

*Answers A, B, and C are correct. Server analysis and optimization includes creating a measurement baseline so you will know where to look for system resource problems. You must also track resource trends so you can determine your system's normal workload. In addition, you must analyze the Performance Monitor program's data to determine if the server is having any system resource problems. **Answer C** is incorrect because server analysis and optimization does not include monitoring client access licenses.*

516	INTRODUCTION TO THE PERFORMANCE MONITOR PROGRAM

Q: *You can use the Performance Monitor program to perform which of the following functions?*

Choose all correct answers:

    A.   *To track resource usage over a period of time.*

    B.   *To view real-time data about system performance.*

    C.   *To receive alerts when a particular object reaches a threshold.*

    D.   *To start and stop Microsoft Windows NT server services.*

As the network administrator, ensuring that the network is performing adequately is an ongoing task. To help you measure network performance, you should have a regular schedule for running *Performance Monitor*, a utility program that provides Windows NT administrators with a graphical interface for recording and viewing server performance data. The *Performance Monitor* program will let you view data from one or more Windows NT servers and workstations at the same time.

You can use *Performance Monitor* to record resource usage over time or to view real-time performance data. You can even configure *Performance Monitor* to alert you when a computer or the network reaches meets a specific resource usage threshold. You will view most of the server's performance data in the *Performance Monitor* Chart view, as Figure 516 shows.

*Answers A, B, and C are correct because you can use the Performance Monitor program to track resource use trends, view real-time data, and receive alerts when a particular object reaches a threshold you have set. **Answer D** is incorrect because you cannot use Performance Monitor to start or stop Windows NT server services.*

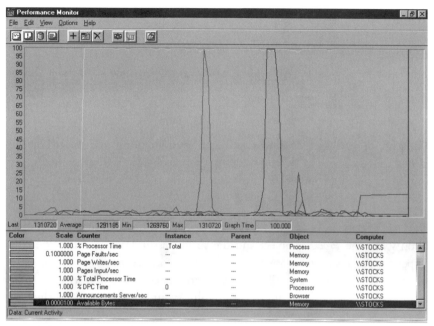

*Figure 516 The **Performance Monitor** program showing the Chart view.*

517 UNDERSTANDING OBJECTS IN PERFORMANCE MONITOR

Q: An object in the Performance Monitor program is a general category of server performance.

True or False?

To use the *Performance Monitor,* you must select which specific item's performance you want to view. *Performance Monitor* lets you track the performance of almost everything in the system. Whenever you want to monitor something occurring on the network, you must first select a general category of system performance called an *object*. For example, *Performance Monitor* objects include *Process, Processor, Memory,* and *PhysicalDisk.*

Although objects cover general areas of system performance, you cannot use *Performance Monitor* to track an object, such as memory. Instead, you must use a specific resource within the object called a *counter.* Counters provide specific information about various properties of the object—such as how much memory the system is currently using, how much is still available, and so on. You will learn about counters in Tip 518.

*The answer is **True** because an object is a general category of server performance, such as PhysicalDisk or Processor.*

518 UNDERSTANDING COUNTERS IN PERFORMANCE MONITOR

Q: Which of the following answers best describe a counter in the Performance Monitor program?

Choose the best answer:

    A.   *An object that counts statistics for a specific service.*

    B.   *A specific category of server performance within an object, such as Memory: Available Bytes.*

    C.   *A service that provides support for other services.*

    D.   *None of the above.*

As you learned in Tip 517, objects are general categories of system performance within the *Performance Monitor* program. You also learned that *Performance Monitor* does not track objects, but rather tracks a specific system resource or function within an object, called a counter. For example, after you select the *Memory* object, you could then select the Available Bytes counter.

Within the counter, you can specify an instance (a single occurrence of the counter) to get even more specific information. For example, if you select the *Processor* object and the % Processor Time counter, you could also select a specific instance, such as the specific processor you want to track. When you use *Performance Monitor,* you will always work with objects and counters, and you may optionally work with instances of counters as well. In later Tips, you will learn about specific objects and counters that you can use to establish your measurement baseline.

Answer B is correct because a counter is a specific category of server performance within an object in Performance Monitor. Answers A, C, and D are incorrect because none of the answers describe a counter.

519   THE PERFORMANCE MONITOR CHART VIEW

Q: *The Performance Monitor Chart view provides you with a graphical view of system data.*

True or False?

In the last several Tips, you learned how you can use the *Performance Monitor* program and its objects, counters, and instances to record and view your server's performance data. In addition, *Performance Monitor* has four separate views you can choose from to view the data: *Chart view, Alert view, Log view,* and *Report view.* However, only the Chart view is useful for a quick analysis of system performance data. (The following three Tips discuss the Alert, Log, and Report views in detail.) You can use the Chart view to see a graphical real-time chart of system activity or to examine previously saved data in a graphical view. However, you will use the chart view most often to view real-time system activity. To examine a real-time view of system activity, perform the following steps:

1.   Click your mouse on the Start menu and select the Programs submenu Administrative Tools group Performance Monitor program option. Windows NT will open the *Performance Monitor* program.

2.   Within the *Performance Monitor* program, click your mouse on the Edit menu and select the Add to Chart option. *Performance Monitor* will open the Add to Chart dialog box.

3.   Within the Add to Chart dialog box, click your mouse on the Object drop-down list and select the object you want to chart, such as *Processor*.

4.   Within the Add to Chart dialog box, click your mouse on the Counter drop-down list and select the counter you want to chart, such as % Processor Time. You can also, optionally, select an Instance (if the server has multiple processors).

5. After you have selected the object, counter, and instance, click your mouse on the Add button within the Add to Chart dialog box. *Performance Monitor* will add the items you select to the Chart view.

Figure 519 shows the Add to Chart dialog box with the Processor object, % Processor Time counter, and the 0 instance selected.

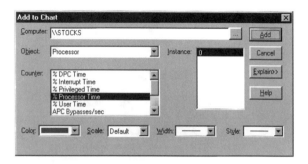

Figure 519 The *Performance Monitor's* Add to Chart *dialog box with an object, counter, and instance selected.*

The answer is **True** *because the Chart view will provide you with a graphical view of system data.*

520 | **USING THE PERFORMANCE MONITOR ALERT VIEW**

Q: The Performance Monitor Alert view will let you view system errors.

True or False?

As the network administrator, you should be concerned about your server's resources. One way to check your server's resources and how heavily the network is utilizing the resources is to use the *Performance Monitor* Alert view. You can use the Alert view to configure the *Performance Monitor* program so when your server meets a specific resource threshold, *Performance Monitor* will alert you that the specific resource has reached your threshold setting. To use the Alert view, perform the following steps:

1. Click your mouse on the Start menu and select the Programs submenu Administrative Tools group Performance Monitor program option. Windows NT will open the *Performance Monitor* program.

2. Within the *Performance Monitor* program, click your mouse on the View menu and select the Alert option. *Performance Monitor* will display the Alert view window.

3. Within the Alert view window, click your mouse on the Edit menu and select the Add to Alert option. *Performance Monitor* will display the Add to Alert dialog box.

4. Within the Add to Alert dialog box, click your mouse on the Object drop-down list and select the object on which you want to receive alerts, such as *Processor*.

5. Within the Add to Alert dialog box, click your mouse on the Counter drop-down list and select the counter you want to chart, such as % Processor Time. You can also, optionally, select an Instance (if the server has multiple processors).

6. Within the Alert If section, click your mouse on either the *Over* or *Under* radio button. *Performance Monitor* will display a dot on the button you select.

7. Within the Alert If section, type the value at which you want to receive an alert, as Figure 520 shows. Next, click your mouse on the Add button. *Performance Monitor* will close the Add to Alert dialog box and start waiting for the counter to reach its alert level.

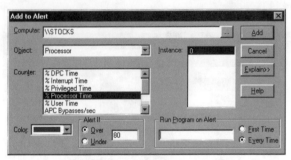

Figure 520 The Add to Alert dialog box before you click your mouse on the Add button.

The answer is **False** *because the Alert view will not let you view errors. The Alert view lets you configure Performance Monitor so it will alert you when a specific counter reaches a threshold you have set.*

521	USING THE PERFORMANCE MONITOR LOG VIEW

Q: Why would you use the Performance Monitor Log view?

Choose the best answer:

A.   *To chart activity from the Microsoft Windows NT Event Viewer.*

B.   *To save system performance data to a file for you to view later.*

C.   *To see errors Performance Monitor has generated during system activity.*

D.   *To see a log file that shows the last time an administrator ran the Performance Monitor.*

When you administer a network, it is likely that some problems on the network will occur only intermittently. It is difficult to track such problems in real-time (that is, when you cannot watch the system activity on *Performance Monitor*). Instead, you may want to use the Performance Monitor Log view to save *Performance Monitor* data to a file. You can then use the Chart view to view the data file's contents. To create a *Performance Monitor* Log view file, perform the following steps:

1. Click your mouse on the Start menu and select the Programs submenu Administrative Tools group Performance Monitor program option. Windows NT will open the *Performance Monitor* program.

2. Within the *Performance Monitor* program, click your mouse on the View menu and select the Log option. *Performance Monitor* will display the Log view window.

3. Within the Log view window, click your mouse on the Edit menu and select the Add to Log option. *Performance Monitor* will display the Add to Log dialog box.

4. Within the Add to Log dialog box, click your mouse on the objects you want to log while holding down the CTRL key on your keyboard. *Performance Monitor* will highlight the objects you select.

5. After you finish selecting objects, click your mouse on the Add button, and then click your mouse on the Done button. *Performance Monitor* will close the Add to Log dialog box and return you to the Log view.

6. Within the Log view, select the Options menu Log option. *Performance Monitor* will display the Log Options dialog box.

7. Within the Log Options dialog box, click your mouse in the *File Name* field and type a name for your log file. Then, click your mouse on the Start Log button. *Performance Monitor* will start the log file.

Answer B is correct because you would use the Performance Monitor Log view to save data to a file that you can view later. Answer A is incorrect because you cannot chart activity from the Windows NT Event Viewer. Answer C is incorrect because any errors the Performance Monitor generates would go to the Event Viewer, not to the Performance Monitor program. Answer D is incorrect because Performance Monitor will not keep a log showing when you have run the Performance Monitor program.

522 THE PERFORMANCE MONITOR REPORT VIEW

Q: *The Performance Monitor Report view will show you Performance Monitor data in an easy-to-read text format.*

True or False?

As you have learned, you can configure *Performance Monitor* to use four views, the Chart, Alert, Log, and Report views, and each view has a specific function. For example, you can capture your system performance data using the Log view, and then you can use either the Chart or Report view to examine the performance data. To use the Report view to examine performance data, perform the following steps:

1. Click your mouse on the Start menu and select the Programs submenu Administrative Tools group Performance Monitor program option. Windows NT will open the *Performance Monitor* program.

2. Within the *Performance Monitor* program, select the View menu Report option. *Performance Monitor* will display the Report view window.

3. Within the Report view window, click your mouse on the Edit menu and select the Add to Report option. *Performance Monitor* will display the Add to Report dialog box.

4. Within the Add to Report dialog box, select the objects and counters on which you want a report. Click your mouse on the Add button, and then the Done button. *Performance Monitor* will close the Add to Report dialog box and return you to the Report view window.

5. Within the Report view window, the *Performance Monitor* program will update the performance output every five seconds, as Figure 522 shows.

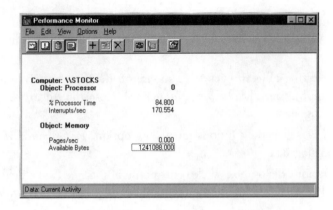

Figure 522 *The **Performance Monitor** Report view showing a performance update.*

*The answer is **True** because the **Performance Monitor** Report view will show you Performance Monitor data in an easy-to-read text format.*

523   **USING THE PERFORMANCE MONITOR TIME WINDOW**

Q: Why would you use the Performance Monitor Time window?

Choose the best answer:

     A.   To view all Performance Monitor data from several Performance Monitor sessions.

     B.   To view a portion of time from a Performance Monitor session.

     C.   To configure Performance Monitor to track specific objects for a specific period of time.

     D.   None of the above.

As you have learned, you can track data from the *Performance Monitor* within a log file and then view it later within the Chart view. When you are using the *Performance Monitor* Chart view to examine data from a log file, you can use the Time window option. A Time window lets you take a portion of a Chart view and examine it more closely—a useful technique when you try to analyze eight hours worth of log files because the *Performance Monitor* program displays the data results in the log file within a single window, no matter how long you log data. If you are charting several counters over a long period of time, you will likely find reading the captured data results difficult because the individual counters show up as a complicated graphical image in the Chart view. Using the Time window will simplify your review. The Time window lets you take a segment of time and examine exactly what occurred during that period, as Figure 523 shows.

To use the Time window, you must open a log file's contents in a Chart view, and then perform the following steps:

    1.   Within the *Performance Monitor* program, select the View menu Report option. *Performance Monitor* will display the Report view window.

    2.   Next, select the Edit menu Time Window option. *Performance Monitor* will display the Input Log File Time Frame dialog box.

3. Within the Input Log File Time Frame dialog box, to select the system data on which you want to use the Time window, click and hold down your mouse on the beginning of the data. Next, drag your mouse to the end of data you want. *Performance Monitor* will highlight the data you select.

4. Next, click your mouse on the OK button. *Performance Monitor* will display the time frame you select in the Chart view.

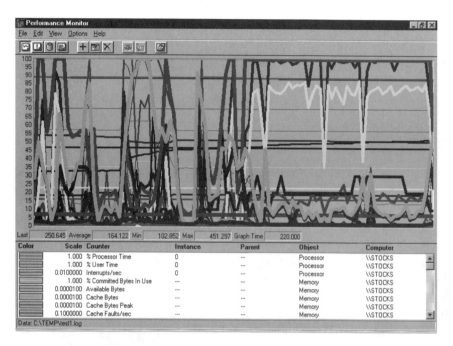

*Figure 523 The **Performance Monitor** program showing a segment of time in the Time window.*

Answer B is correct because you would use the Performance Monitor Time window to view a portion of time from a Performance Monitor session. Answer A is incorrect because you cannot use the Time window to view data from multiple Performance Monitor sessions. Answer C is incorrect because you would not use the Performance Monitor Time window to configure a Performance Monitor session. Answer D is incorrect because you can use the Performance Monitor Time window to view a portion of time from a Performance Monitor session.

524 CREATING A PERFORMANCE MEASUREMENT BASELINE

Q: A performance measurement baseline is a measurement of current system activity under a normal load.

True or False?

As you have learned, tracking your server's workload—both in total and for individual resources on the server—is an important part of network administration. To determine if your server is experiencing an abnormal workload, you must know what the normal workload is for your server. A performance measurement baseline will let you determine if the workload on your server is increasing. If you are experiencing network growth, you might need to add system resources to your server, such as memory or hard drive space.

A performance measurement baseline is simply a log of server activity under normal conditions. You will want to take samples of server activity over the course of a normal workday. Microsoft recommends the following objects for to you log to establish your performance measurement baseline:

- Cache

- Logical disk

- Memory

- Network adapter

- Network segment activity on at least one server in the segment

- Physical disk (if you use RAID)

- Processor

- Server

- System

*The answer is **True** because a performance baseline is a measurement of current server activity under a normal load.*

525   INTRODUCTION TO THE NETWORK SUBSYSTEM

Q: *The network subsystem is a Microsoft Windows NT environment subsystem that can process application requests.*

True or False?

When you are an administrator of a Microsoft Windows NT network, one important task is to keep your network running smoothly. One of the most important considerations for smooth-running networks is making sure that your server performs at a sufficient level for your network. Your server's overall performance breaks down into four basic groups of system resources, the disk subsystem, memory subsystem, processor subsystem, and network subsystem. Unlike the Windows NT network subsystems (a group of computers on a network segment), Microsoft simply uses the term *subsystem* to refer to a category of server performance, many of which loosely correspond to *Performance Monitor* objects.

The network subsystem includes your network interface card, protocols, and any other Windows NT component that deals with your server's network performance. When you run *Performance Monitor* to chart system activity, the network subsystem is one of the key areas to examine. Slow network cards, for example, can slow your server's effective performance on the network.

*The answer is **False** because Microsoft uses the term network subsystem to describe the overall operation of the network components within your Windows NT server.*

526   INTRODUCTION TO THE DISK SUBSYSTEM

Q: The disk subsystem includes RAID controllers?

True or False?

As you have learned in previous Tips, you will often analyze the performance of servers on your network. When you analyze server performance, you will generally do so by looking at the server's subsystems. One of the most common performance concerns for servers is the *disk subsystem*. If you were to characterize all the components of disk performance on your server, you would consider more than just your hard disks—you would also note your disk controller cards, because the computer communicates with the hard disks through the cards themselves. Microsoft uses the term *disk subsystem* to describe both the hard disks and the disk controller cards.

When you examine your disk subsystem's performance, you should examine the type and speed of your hard disks. Certainly, a faster hard disk can produce faster access times for your server. Disk types can also make a significant performance difference, particularly for larger disks. In addition, you should also examine the type, number, and speed of your hard disk controllers. Hard disk controllers can range from simple, Integrated Device Electronics (IDE) hard disk controllers to complex, RAID-5 compliant disk controller arrays. When you have multiple hard disks in a server, you will benefit from having multiple hard disk controllers to break up the disks so that various controllers manage different hard disks, thereby improving performance.

*The answer is **True** because RAID controllers are part of the disk subsystem.*

527 UNDERSTANDING DISK CONTROLLER TYPES AND SPEEDS

Q: Of the following, which type of hard disk and controller would best suit a Microsoft Windows NT server computer that you use as an application server?

Choose the best answer:

> A.   SCSI
>
> B.   MFM
>
> C.   IDE
>
> D.   ESDI

Not all hard disks are the same; in fact, some hard disks (and their corresponding controllers) are better suited for servers than others. When you choose the type of hard disk and controller for your server, remember that each type of hard disk requires its own special controller card to operate. Although there are several types of controllers, at present there are only two that people frequently use: *Integrated Device Electronics (IDE)* and *Small Computer System Interface (SCSI)*. The Older Modified Frequency Modulation (MFM), Run Length Limited (RLL), and Enhanced Small Devices Interface (ESDI) controllers are no longer in use, and are even becoming hard to find.

Because of their popularity, you will probably use either IDE or SCSI disks and controllers in your Windows NT 4.0 computers. IDE disks and controllers are widely used in desktop computers. IDE disks and controllers are inexpensive and fairly reliable, so they are a good choice for non-critical computers. On the other hand, if you are deciding what type of disk to place in your production server, you may want to choose a SCSI disk (which is the industry standard for server-class computers). SCSI disks have advanced features such as *sector sparing*, which occurs when the disk determines if there are any bad areas of the disk. The SCSI disk will then move data off the bad areas to good areas, and mark the bad area so the operating system will not write any more data to that section of the disk. In addition, SCSI disks normally perform much faster than current IDE disks.

*Answer A is correct because Microsoft recommends that you use SCSI hard disks and controllers for your server. **Answers B** and **D** are incorrect because MFM and ESDI are older hard disk types that do not have the capacity newer drives have and, therefore, would not be sufficient in size for a server's needs. **Answer C** is incorrect because, although you can use an IDE drive, which comes in large sizes, IDE drives do not have all the same capabilities as SCSI drives.*

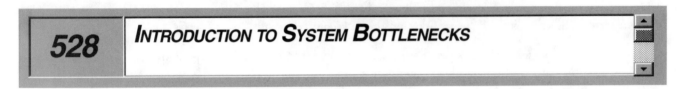

528   **INTRODUCTION TO SYSTEM BOTTLENECKS**

Q: *Which of the following answers best describe a system bottleneck?*

Choose all answers that apply:

     A.   *Lack of sufficient system memory*

     B.   *The systems processor running at a constant 100% usage*

     C.   *Applications not running properly*

     D.   *A network adapter card that cannot keep up with the system's request for network service*

Within the computer industry, you will frequently hear the term *bottleneck* to describe the slowest part of a system. You will hear about how awful system bottlenecks are and how administrators should eliminate them. However, it's important to recognize that you will always have slow sections in your systems. The trick to eliminating bottleneck problems is to make sure that the bottlenecks you address first are the ones that currently restrict the flow of data within your system. An example of a system bottleneck could be your processor. If you have an older processor, or too many applications running on one computer, your processor could become a bottleneck simply because it can't keep up. Likewise, when you work with networks, especially distributed resources on networks, you must watch your resources closely to see if they are causing bottlenecks. To determine where your system's bottlenecks are and if they are restricting data flow, you will use the *Performance Monitor* program.

*Answers A, B, and D are correct because any system resource that is restricting data flow is a system bottleneck. **Answer C** is incorrect because a system bottleneck is a system resource restricting data flow, not a misbehaving application.*

529   **USING PERFORMANCE MONITOR TO FIND MEMORY BOTTLENECKS**

Q: *Which utility in Windows NT would you use to locate memory bottlenecks?*

Choose the best answer:

     A.   *Server Manager*

     B.   *Performance Monitor*

     C.   *User Manager for Domains*

     D.   *Windows NT Diagnostics*

As you learned in Tip 528, you will use the *Performance Monitor* program to detect system bottlenecks. When you use the *Performance Monitor* to find bottlenecks, you will often discover that the cause of a system's bottleneck is memory—either insufficient memory or slow memory. System memory is a resource that you can never have too much of, and which you almost always need more of when your system begins to slow down.

To find memory bottlenecks, use *Performance Monitor* and capture data (use the Report View to log the data) from a period of the day when your server experiences the most traffic. Use the following counters from the *Memory* object to find your memory bottlenecks: Available Bytes, Committed Bytes, Pages/sec, and Pool Non-paged Bytes.

The *Available Bytes* counter is the total amount of physical memory available on the system. You should have as high a value as possible in this counter. Microsoft recommends having no less than 4Mb of available memory (an absolute minimum). If you find that your server does not have at least 4Mb of memory available, you should look for a process that may be using your server's memory and not releasing it. However, in almost every situation where your available memory falls below 4Mb, you will almost always find that you should add more memory to your system.

The *Committed Bytes* counter is the total amount of virtual memory the system has set aside for application and system use. If the amount of committed bytes is larger than the total amount of physical memory in your computer, you may want to add memory to the system.

The *Pages/sec* counter is the number of application or system requests for data that the Virtual Memory Manager could not immediately retrieve from physical memory (and, instead, went to the paging file to retrieve that data, as you have learned about in previous Tips). Therefore, the data had to be read from the disk (a slow process) or other data had to be written to the disk to make room for the requested data in physical memory. Microsoft recommends adding more memory if you find values above 5 in the *Pages/sec* counter in the *Performance Monitor*.

The *Pool Non-paged Bytes* counter is somewhat more complex than the other counters. To understand the Pool Non-paged Bytes counter, you must first understand *pool non-paged memory*. As you have learned, Windows NT uses two types of memory: physical memory (actual physical memory) and virtual memory (memory space the operating system creates and manages by combining your system's RAM and disk space). To improve performance and for operational purposes, the operating-system should not swap some objects from RAM to disk (if the operating system swapped out its program code that controls virtual memory, for example, your system would fail to function). To provide such key objects with memory locations that it will not swap (page) to disk, the operating system defines a pool of non-paged memory locations. The Pool Non-paged Bytes counter tracks the amount of memory the operating system has allocated for non-paged objects. Because non-paged objects consume memory locations on a permanent basis, they reduce the amount of memory available for other resources.

Answer B is correct because you will use Performance Monitor to look for memory bottlenecks. Answers A, C, and D are incorrect because you cannot use Server Manager, User Manager for Domains, or Windows NT Diagnostics to look for system resource bottlenecks.

---

530 USING PERFORMANCE MONITOR TO FIND PROCESSOR BOTTLENECKS

Q: *You have used the Performance Monitor to look for system bottlenecks. You have found that the system's processor is running constantly at 90%. A system running with a processor at a sustained rate of 80% or above is always a processor bottleneck.*

True or False?

As you learned in Tip 528, a bottleneck is a slow part of your system. In this Tip, you will learn which counters to use to look for a *processor* bottleneck, which occurs when your system's processor cannot keep up the requests it receives. To determine if you have a processor bottleneck, use the following counters:

- The *Processor: % Privileged Time* counter is the total amount of time the processor spends on system processes that run in privileged processor mode (that is, processes that automatically take priority over any other currently-executing process). You want a value below 75%.

- The *Processor: % Processor Time* counter is the total amount of processor that all system components use. Microsoft recommends not having a sustained rate over 75%. If you find a sustained rate of over 75%, you might want to move applications to other servers to distribute the processor load or add more and faster processors.

- The *Processor: % User Time* counter is the total amount of time the processor spends on user mode requests. Applications and environment subsystems run in user mode. You want a value below 75%.

- The *Server Work Queues: Queue Length* counter is the total number of requests waiting for a specific processor. If this value is above 2, Microsoft recommends upgrading your processor.

*The answer is **False** because a high sustained rate of processor usage may not always be a processor bottleneck; it could be a lack of memory or some other bottleneck causing the processor to work harder.*

531	USING PERFORMANCE MONITOR TO FIND DISK SUBSYSTEM BOTTLENECKS

Q: *A slow disk controller can cause a virtual memory bottleneck.*

True or False?

As you have learned, one of the primary causes of system slowdown is a performance bottleneck. In addition to the memory and processor bottlenecks that you have learned about in previous Tips, you will often experience bottlenecks in your disk subsystem's performance. When you are looking for disk subsystem bottlenecks, you should consider the type and speed of controller card in your server before running the *Performance Monitor* program. A slow controller will impede performance no matter how fast your hard disk is. To use *Performance Monitor* to look for disk subsystem bottlenecks, use the following counters:

- The *Physical Disk: Avg. Disk Bytes/Transfer* counter is the average number of bytes the disk is transferring to and from the system. If two disks have the same transfer rates, the disk with the higher value (that is, the more bytes per transfer to and from the disk) will have the better performance.

- The *Physical Disk: Avg. Disk Queue Length* counter is the number of Input Output (I/O) requests waiting for this disk. Microsoft recommends not having more than a value of 2 for this counter. If your value is over 2, you may want to consider upgrading your disk.

- The *Physical Disk: Disk Bytes/sec* counter is the transfer rate of your disk during read or write operations. You want a high value (indicating that the disk is reading more bytes per second) for this counter.

- The *Physical Disk: % Disk Time* counter is the total amount of time the system uses the disk. You want a low value for this counter. Microsoft recommends upgrading your disk if this value remains above 50% for an extended period of time (that is, if it is above 50% during normal workload on your server).

*The answer is **True** because a slow disk controller can cause the system's virtual memory to be less responsive than the system requires.*

532 USING PERFORMANCE MONITOR TO FIND NETWORK SUBSYSTEM BOTTLENECKS

Q: *Of the following, which are objects and counters you will use to help determine if you have a network subsystem bottleneck?*

Choose all answers that apply:

A. *Server: Bytes Total/sec*

B. *Server: Logon/sec*

C. *Server: Logon/max*

D. *Server: Logon Total*

Locating disk and memory subsystem bottlenecks is generally a relatively simple process, although it is often tedious. However, finding network subsystem bottlenecks can be difficult because there are so many components that make up the network subsystem, such as the network card, the protocol, and the client software. Although difficult, it is not impossible to find network bottlenecks. To find network subsystem bottlenecks, use the *Server* object and the following of its component counters:

- The *Server: Bytes Total/sec* counter is the total amount of data your *Server* service is managing. The value will give you an indication of the server's workload. You should track this number relative to the server's performance. If the server seems slow and the number is high, the server's load may be greater than the server can handle.

- The *Server Logon/sec* counter is the total number of user log-on requests your server is processing each second. You want a high value for this counter—although a low value may indicate that you do not have many log-on requests to process, not necessarily that the server is slow, depending on your network's size.

- The *Server: Logons Total* counter is the total number of log-on requests since the last time the administrator booted the server. The counter's value may give you an indication of the server's demands.

Note: *There are many other counters you can use to determine whether your server has a network subsystem bottleneck; however, these are the most common indicators that you will use when tracking network bottlenecks. For a complete list of network counters and their values, refer to the **Windows NT Resource Kit** from Microsoft Press.*

*Answers A, B, and D are correct because you will use each of the counters listed to determine the network subsystem's performance. **Answer C** is incorrect because there is no Server: Logon/max counter in Performance Monitor.*

533   ANALYZING FILE AND PRINT SERVER PERFORMANCE

Q: *Of the following, which are objects and counters you will use to analyze file and print server computers?*

Choose all answers that apply:

> A.   *Server: Server Sessions*
>
> B.   *PhysicalDisk: Application Request/sec*
>
> C.   *PhysicalDisk: % Disk Time*
>
> D.   *Network Segment: % Network Utilization*

When you consider system resources, it is important to understand the type of server that you are analyzing. The system resources you will rely on for an application server to perform adequately (such as disk-access times) are not necessarily the same as the resource requirements for a domain controller's performance (such as log-on processing speed). So, it is not surprising that the system resources you will examine on a file and print server are different from either of the other server types. To analyze a file and print server, use the following counters:

- The *Physical Disk: Avg. Disk Bytes/Transfer* counter is the average amount of data users are transferring to and from the server's disk. If this number is very high, your disk may be the server's bottleneck.

- The *Physical Disk: % Disk Time* counter is the total amount of time that users and the system are using the disk. You can use this counter to examine how often the disk is in use.

- The *Physical Disk: % Disk Read Time* counter is the total amount of time the disk spends performing read operations.

- The *Physical Disk: % Disk Write Time* counter is the total amount of time the disk spends on write operations.

- The *Server: Server Sessions* counter will let you know how many user sessions your server is handling. You may want to watch this value over time, to identify trends.

- The *Server: Files Open* counter is the total number of files that users currently have open on the server. Again, you may want to watch this value over time, to identify trends.

*Answers A, C, and D are correct because you will use each of the listed objects and counters to analyze file and print server computers. **Answer B** is incorrect because Performance Monitor does not have a PhysicalDisk: Application Request/sec counter.*

534   ANALYZING APPLICATION SERVER PERFORMANCE

Q: *Of the following, which are objects and counters you will use to analyze application server performance?*

Choose all answers that apply:

A.   *WinNT: Environment Subsystems*

B.   *Processor: % Processor Time*

C.   *Memory: Available Bytes*

D.   *Memory: Pages/sec*

In most network environments, administrators will include servers that have applications on them for users to access through the network. These server computers are *application servers*, which can be mail servers, database servers, or any other client/server applications. Depending on what programs an application server runs (for example, your customer-service database), the server's performance can be very important to your company—in some cases, even critical. To keep the server "up and running" to its full capacity, you should monitor the server regularly using *Performance Monitor* on it. To analyze an application server in *Performance Monitor*, use the following counters:

- The *Cache: Copy Read Hits %* counter identifies your server's cache effectiveness—the percentage of read operations for which the server found the requested data in its cache which, in turn, eliminated a slow disk read operation.

- The *Memory: Available Bytes* counter is the total amount of physical memory available on the system. You want as much available memory as possible (generally, with most application servers, you will have 128Mb of available memory or more).

- The *Memory: Pages/sec* counter is the total number of page faults the server is experiencing per second. As your server's use increases, so too will this value. If the value becomes high, you will want to add more memory.

- The *Physical Disk: Avg. Disk Bytes/Transfer* counter is the average amount of data the system is transferring to and from the disk with each transfer operation.

- The *Physical Disk: % Disk Time* counter is the total amount of time the system is using the disk. As this value increases, your disk may become a server bottleneck.

- The *Server: Server Sessions* is a counter you can use to examine the number of user sessions this server is handling. You may want to watch this value over time, to identify trends.

Answers B, C, and D are correct because you will use each of the objects and counters listed to help you analyze an application server. Answer A is incorrect because Performance Monitor does not have a WinNT object (meaning it does not have an environment subsystems counter, either).

535	ANALYZING DOMAIN CONTROLLER PERFORMANCE

Q: Of the following, which are objects and counters you will use to analyze a domain controller?

Choose all answers that apply:

A.   *Server: Logon/sec*

B.   *Server: Error Logon*

C.   *Network Segment: % Network Utilization*

D.   *WINS Server: Queries/sec*

As you learned in the previous two Tips, you can use the *Performance Monitor* program to analyze both application servers and file and print servers. However, you will generally use a different group of counters to analyze a *domain controller,* a Windows NT server that logs users onto the network. A domain controller does not have to be a powerful computer; the workload placed on a domain controller is relatively low. Nevertheless, you should ensure the domain controller is running at its potential. To analyze a domain controller, use the following counters:

- The *Memory: Available Bytes* counter is the total amount of physical memory available on the server.

- The *Server: Error Logon* counter is the total number of invalid Microsoft client log-on requests. You might monitor this value to identify system break-in attempts.

- The *Server: Logon/sec* counter is the total number of user log-on requests the server is processing each second. You may want to watch this value over time, to identify trends.

- The *Server: Logon Total* counter is the total number of logons since the administrator last booted the domain controller. You may want to watch this value over time, to identify trends.

Answers A, B, C, and D are all correct because each is a counter you will use in Performance Monitor to analyze a domain controller.

536   **UNDERSTANDING WORKLOAD CHARACTERIZATION**

Q: *A workload characterization is a process by which you can determine the entire workload your server is under.*

True or False?

As the administrator of your network, you must have realistic expectations of your network's performance. To a large degree, your network's performance will depend on such things as the network's speed, the speed of the servers that deliver information to the clients, and the speed of the client computers themselves. However, before you can determine what your network capacity is, you must also determine how much and what type of work the network will support. Microsoft calls this process *workload characterization.* In turn, Microsoft calls the individual objects that make up the workload total *workload units.* An example of a workload unit is the amount of time it takes the server to respond to one user making a typical file access request. To determine your server's total workload, you must use *Performance Monitor* to measure a single user making normal (expected) transactions. After measuring the typical user's workload units, you can then multiply the single user's measurements by the total number of users in your network to get a good idea of how many users your server can support and the total resulting workload. If, when you multiply your workload units by the number of users in your network and you find that your server cannot support the number of requests the users are making, you can then add servers to your network.

*The answer is **True** because a workload characterization is a process by which you can determine your server's total workload.*

537   **UNDERSTANDING FILE AND PRINT SERVER RESOURCES**

Q: *There are four main categories of system resources: the system's memory subsystem, processor subsystem, disk subsystem, and network subsystem. In order of importance to a file and print server, which resource subsystems are most and least important?*

Choose the best answer:

A.   *Memory subsystem, processor subsystem, network subsystem, and disk subsystem*

B.   *Memory subsystem, processor subsystem, and then the network and disk subsystems, equally*

C.   *Processor subsystem, memory subsystem, disk subsystem, and network subsystem*

D.   *All four resources are equally important*

As you have learned in previous Tips, each type of server—application, domain controller, and file and print—has its own specific resource needs and bottleneck concerns. An application server, for example, must have a fast processor, while a domain controller does not need a fast processor but, instead, lots of memory within which to store and access the Directory Database. In turn, understanding what types of resources a specific type of server will require is one aspect of being a good network administrator.

As you have learned, the resources that a server relies on are in four categories: disk subsystem, network subsystem, memory, and processor. Each of these categories is important for server performance. However, depending on the type of server you have, some resources are more important than others, which results in a ranked order of resource importance. For example, the ranked order of resource importance for a file and print server is, from most important to least important: memory, processor, and then, of equal importance, both the disk and network subsystems.

Answer B *is correct because a file and print server will use memory to cache files that users open. The processor must process every network request, so having a strong processor helps improve performance. Finally, the disk subsystem and the network subsystem are of equal importance.* **Answers A, C, and D** *are incorrect because they do not list the proper order of importance.*

---

538   CALCULATING THE NUMBER OF USERS A FILE AND PRINT SERVER CAN SUPPORT

Q: *The number of users a file and print server can support depends on which of the following resources?*

Choose all answers that apply:

A.   *Processor*

B.   *Memory*

C.   *Disk subsystem*

D.   *Network subsystem*

As a network administrator, you should be familiar with your servers and know how many users each server can support. As you learned in Tip 536, the best way to determine how many users a server can support is to test a single user making a normal transaction, and then multiply the performance results by how many users you have in your network. If you have the means to do so, Microsoft recommends using a segmented network (that is, one not connected to your main network) with only the test server and one client computer in it. By creating a network with only the two computers in it, you can accurately determine how much time it takes to perform a single transaction. When you test, remember to allow for users having multiple connections—that is, if a user can connect from multiple computers simultaneously (meaning there are more computers than users on your network), that you add those additional computers and their workload requirements into the total.

The number of users a file and print server can support depends on all four resource categories—memory, processor, disk subsystem, and network subsystem. Even though all system resources determine how many users your file and print server will support, you should watch the most important file and print server resources, which you have previously learned are the memory and processor resources. When system slowdowns occur at the file or print server, the memory or processor is most often responsible.

Answers A, B, C, and D are all correct because the number of users a file and print server can support depends on all system resources.

539   UNDERSTANDING APPLICATION SERVER RESOURCES

Q: *There are four main categories of system resources: the system's memory, processor, disk subsystem, and network subsystem. In order of importance to an application server, which resources are most and least important?*

Choose the best answer:

     A.   *Memory, processor, network subsystem, and disk subsystem*

     B.   *Processor, memory, and then the disk and network subsystems, equally*

     C.   *Processor, memory, disk subsystem, and network subsystem*

     D.   *Network subsystem, disk subsystem, processor, and memory*

As you have learned, different types of servers will require various resource strengths. Of the four resource categories—memory, processor, disk subsystem, and network subsystem—an application server's most important resource is its processor. Application servers frequently respond to user requests for service, such as a request for a database query. In such a case, the client sends a query request to the server, which will then process the query and return the results of the query operation across the network to the client. All the processing power for handling the query resides on the server, so the application server must have a lot of memory to support the system. For the application server, after processor and memory resources, the next most needed resource is the disk subsystem (because the server will often have to access file resources to respond to the user's application request). Users will make requests for system resources and the server must then retrieve the resources from the disk. The least important resource on an application server is the network subsystem, which, of the four resource categories, plays the least important role, because all the processing occurs on the server, and the server simply transmits the response across the network.

Answer C is correct because the order of importance for an application server is the system's processor, memory, disk subsystem, and network subsystem. Answers A, B, and D are incorrect because they do not list the proper order of importance.

540   CALCULATING THE NUMBER OF USERS AN APPLICATION SERVER CAN SUPPORT

Q: To calculate the number of users an application server can serve, you would use specific counters in Performance Monitor to capture data from a single user making a transaction and then multiply the results by the number of users who will be making similar requests.

True or False?

In Tip 536, you learned that you can analyze a single user's transaction and then multiply the transaction's results by the number of users in your network to determine the total number of user transactions your server can effectively support. In addition, you can use the same technique to determine the number of users an application server can support.

When you monitor the single user transaction on the application server, you will examine different system resources than you did on the file and print server. Remember that an application server's most important resource is its processor. Therefore, you should examine the system's processor activity when you make the test user transaction requests (and then multiply that activity by the number of users on the network to determine maximum workload). In addition, you should pay attention to the system's memory, watching the *Performance Monitor* counters for memory usage. If your application server does not have sufficient memory, your applications will run slowly. Using the *Performance Monitor's* Report View to log information on access will help you compute your server's maximum workload, and whether the server is capable of handling that workload.

The answer is **True** *because to determine the number of users an application server can support, you will log data within the Performance Monitor from a single user performing the type of transaction you expect your users to make, and then multiply the results by the number of users in your network.*

541   UNDERSTANDING DOMAIN CONTROLLER RESOURCES

Q: There are four main categories of system resources: the system's memory, processor, disk subsystem, and network subsystem. In order of importance to a domain controller, which resources are most and least important?

Choose the best answer:

    A.   Memory and the network subsystem equally, then the processor, and disk subsystem

    B.   Memory and the network subsystem equally, then the disk subsystem, and processor

    C.   Memory, network subsystem, processor, and disk subsystem

    D.   Network subsystem, memory, processor, and disk subsystem

As you learned in Tip 535, a domain controller is a server that will log users onto the network. Unlike application and file and print servers, a domain controller does not have to be a very powerful computer. You can use a computer with a slower processor and not see any performance degradation. When you make a decision about which computers in your organization to use as domain controllers, you must consider only two resource categories: memory and the network subsystem. Memory is important because the entire Directory Database is in memory. The Windows NT server domain controller will access the Directory Database to find users' account information. In addition, your network subsystem is important because users will log on from across the network.

The final two resource categories are the system's processor and the disk subsystem, in that order of importance. You must use the processor to process user log-on requests. You will use the disk subsystem resource the least because a domain controller will access the disk only for virtual memory.

Answer A is correct because the order of importance for system resources on a domain controller is: memory and network subsystem equally, processor, and disk subsystem. Answers B, C, and D are incorrect because they do not list the proper order of importance for resources on a domain controller.

---

542   CALCULATING THE NUMBER OF USERS A DOMAIN CONTROLLER CAN SUPPORT

Q: *Which of the following factors is most important in supporting users on a domain controller computer?*

Choose the best answer:

     A.   *The system's memory*

     B.   *The computer's operating system configuration*

     C.   *The system's network subsystem*

     D.   *The computer's total hardware*

As you have learned, domain controllers (Microsoft Windows NT server computers that log on users to the network) do not have to be powerful computers. In fact, a 486 computer with 16Mb of memory can make a fine domain controller for networks with thousands of users. The only time a domain controller's performance will become an issue is when it executes duties other than logging on users, such as name resolution using a Windows Internet Naming Service (WINS) or Domain-Name Service (DNS) server.

If your domain controllers will not be performing additional duties, you probably will not have any performance concerns. To check for performance issues on your domain controllers, just capture the data from a single user logging on to the network, and then multiply by the number of users in your network. You will get a good idea of the potential log-on traffic each morning.

Answer D is correct because it is the computer's total hardware that determines the number of users a domain controller can support. Answers A and C are incorrect because, although the system's memory and the network subsystem are part of the hardware, it is the system's collective hardware you will use to determine the total number of users the system can support. Answer B is incorrect because the operating system's configuration has little to do with the number of users a domain controller can support.

---

543   USING PERFORMANCE MONITOR TO MONITOR NETBEUI AND NWLINK

Q: *The Performance Monitor counters for NetBEUI and for NWLINK are the same.*

     True or False?

When you are working with the Performance Monitor to track information about the network subsystem, you will generally start by looking at the performance of network-related hardware within the computer. In addition to using *Performance Monitor* to track information about the network hardware card, you can also use it to monitor the Network Basic Input and Output (NetBIOS) communications and the Extended User Interface (NetBEUI) and NetWare Link (NWLINK) protocols.

The NetBEUI and NWLINK protocols' counters are the same within their respective objects. In addition to monitoring the *Network Segment* object to examine overall network activity, you should monitor the individual protocols you have installed on your Windows NT computer so you can determine whether your protocols are functioning properly. To monitor either the NetBEUI or NWLINK protocol, Microsoft recommends using the following counters within the *Network Segment* object:

- The *Network Segment: Bytes Total/sec* counter will let you examine the total number of bytes sent in frames and datagrams (broadcasts and acknowledgements).

- The *Network Segment: Datagrams/sec* counter will let you examine the total number of datagrams your computer sent and received.

- The *Network Segment: Frames/sec* counter will let you examine the total number of frames (packages of data) your computer sent or received.

*The answer is **True** because the Performance Monitor counters for monitoring the NetBEUI and NWLINK protocols are the same.*

544   USING PERFORMANCE MONITOR TO MONITOR *TCP/IP*

Q: *Of the following, which are not Performance Monitor counters for monitoring TCP/IP?*

Choose all answers that apply:

    A.   *TCP Segments/sec*

    B.   *Work Queues*

    C.   *UDP Datagrams/sec*

    D.   *Pages/sec*

In Tip 543, you learned that NetBEUI and NWLINK have very similar counters in the *Performance Monitor* program. The Transmission Control Protocol/Internet Protocol (TCP/IP) *Performance Monitor* counters within the *Network Segment* object serve a similar purpose (that is, they help you track the performance of the TCP/IP protocol), but are quite different in nature—because TCP/IP uses different communications methods than either NetBEUI or NWLINK.

Windows NT will add the TCP/IP counters only when you install the Simple Network Management Protocol (SNMP) service in the Network dialog box. When you are using *Performance Monitor* to capture TCP/IP data, you should use the following counters:

- The *Network Interface: Output Queue Length* counter will let you examine the length of the output packet queue (packets waiting to be sent). More than two packets in the queue indicates a potential bottleneck.

- The *TCP Segments/sec* counter is useful because it will let you know the number of TCP frames (segments) that your computer has sent or received.

- The *TCP Segments Re-translated* counter will let you examine the total number of frames that your computer has re-translated on the network.

- The *UDP Datagrams/sec* counter displays the number of User Datagram Protocol (UDP) datagrams your computer sent or received.

Answers B and D are correct because you would not use Work Queues or Pages/sec to analyze TCP performance. Answers A and C are incorrect because TCP Segments/sec and UDP Datagrams/sec are both actual counters for analyzing TCP/IP performance.

545   ESTABLISHING A PLAN FOR LONG-TERM RECORD KEEPING

Q: *Which of the following can you use for long-term record keeping?*

Choose all answers that apply:

    A.   *Windows NT Diagnostics*

    B.   *Microsoft Excel*

    C.   *Performance Monitor*

    D.   *Server Manager*

As a network administrator, your job is to ensure that the network remains in good running order. Part of maintaining a network is to establish and maintain a record of *Performance Monitor*-captured data. In addition, you should archive *Performance Monitor* data because you can use the recorded data to determine whether your server is experiencing a heavier workload than before. Then, if a server is not experiencing a heavier workload, but *Performance Monitor* data shows that a system resource is stressed, you may have a hardware problem.

As the administrator, it is your choice to determine what type of record-keeping plan is right for your network. For example, some network administrators prefer to save the *Performance Monitor* data in log files, while others prefer to import the data into Microsoft *Excel* or a database program such as Microsoft *Access*.

Answers A, B, and C are correct because you can use either Windows NT Diagnostics, Microsoft Excel, or Performance Monitor for long-term record keeping. Answer D is incorrect because Server Manager does not provide any long-term record keeping abilities.

546   MONITORING MULTIPLE SERVERS WITH PERFORMANCE MONITOR

Q: *How many Windows NT computers can you monitor using Performance Monitor?*

Choose the best answer:

    A.   5

    B.   10

    C.   25

    D.   50

When you use the *Performance Monitor* program on a Windows NT computer, you cause the computer to work harder than it would otherwise, and then you record the results of the extra stress in *Performance Monitor*. To eliminate the extra stress associated with running *Performance Monitor* locally (which may skew your testing results), you can monitor one Windows NT computer from another Windows NT computer.

You might even want to monitor the performance of several Windows NT computers at one time. You can monitor up to 25 Windows NT workstation or server computers at one time from a single Windows NT computer running *Performance Monitor*. On the other hand, you could start *Performance Monitor* on more than one Windows NT computer and monitor different Windows NT computers from each *Performance Monitor* session. Then, you could take the data from each *Performance Monitor* session and import it into a database.

Answer C is correct you can monitor up to 25 Windows NT computers at a time using **Performance Monitor**. *Answers A, B, and C are incorrect because they do not state the correct number of concurrent Windows NT computers you can monitor with* **Performance Monitor**.

547   **SETTING PERFORMANCE MONITOR ALERTS**

Q: *You can use a Performance Monitor alert so that* **Performance Monitor** *will alert you when the counter you are tracking meets or exceeds a threshold.*

True or False?

As the administrator of a Microsoft Windows NT network, you should set aside time for using the *Performance Monitor* program. In fact, you may spend entire days capturing and reviewing *Performance Monitor* data. You can use the Alert view to notify you when a resource becomes over-consumed, and then take immediate action to determine the cause. To set an alert within *Performance Monitor*, perform the following steps:

1. Click your mouse on the Start menu and select the Programs submenu Administrative Tools group Performance Monitor program. Windows NT will open the *Performance Monitor* program.

2. Within the *Performance Monitor* program, click your mouse on the View menu Alert option. *Performance Monitor* will display the Alert view window.

3. Within the Alert view window, click your mouse on the Edit menu Add to Alert option. *Performance Monitor* will display the Add to Alert dialog box, as Figure 547 shows.

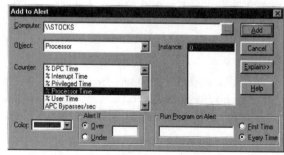

Figure 547 *The Add to Alert dialog box.*

4. Within the Add to Alert dialog box, click your mouse on the Object drop-down list and select the object for which you want to receive alerts. Then, select the specific counter within the

object. In the Alert If section, click your mouse on either the *Over* or *Under* radio button and then type the value for which you want to receive an alert. Click your mouse on the Add button. *Performance Monitor* will close the Add to Alert dialog box and start the capture.

The answer is **True** *because you can use the* **Performance Monitor** *Alert view to have Performance Monitor alert you when a counter you are tracking meets or exceeds a threshold value.*

548   CREATING A PERFORMANCE MONITOR LOG

Q: *You can create a log file in which of the following Performance Monitor views?*

Choose all answers that apply:

     A.   Alert view

     B.   Chart view

     C.   Log view

     D.   Report view

Network administrators find that the most useful tool in *Performance Monitor* is its ability to save captured data to a log file you can review at your leisure. Creating a log is not very difficult, but reviewing a log file's contents can be confusing. You can create a log file only in the Log view. You can, however, read a log file's contents in either the Report or Chart view. In this Tip, you will review how to create a log file, and then you will learn how to open a log file to read its contents. To create a log file, perform the following steps:

1.   Click your mouse on the Start menu and select the Programs submenu Administrative Tools group Performance Monitor program. Windows NT will open the *Performance Monitor* program.

2.   Within the *Performance Monitor* program, select the View menu Log option. *Performance Monitor* will switch to the Log view.

3.   Within the Log view, select the Edit menu Add to Log option. *Performance Monitor* will display the Add to Log dialog box.

4.   Within the Add to Log dialog box, hold down the CTRL key on your keyboard and click your mouse on the objects you want to log. Click your mouse on the Add button and then the Done button. *Performance Monitor* will close the Add to Log dialog box and return you to the Log view in *Performance Monitor*.

5.   Within the Log view, click your mouse on the Options menu Log option. *Performance Monitor* will display the Log Options dialog box.

6.   Within the Log Options dialog box, click your mouse in the *File Name* field. Type a name for your log file. Click your mouse on the Start Log button. *Performance Monitor* will start the log.

7.   Minimize the *Performance Monitor* and continue to work normally. *Performance Monitor* will continue to log activity.

After you start a log file, you must at some point stop *Performance Monitor* from collecting any more data. To stop a *Performance Monitor* log, perform the following steps:

1.   Re-open *Performance Monitor*. Within the *Performance Monitor* program, click your mouse on the Options menu Log option. *Performance Monitor* will open the Log Options dialog box.

2. Within the Log Options dialog box, click your mouse on the Stop button. *Performance Monitor* will stop data collection for the log.

3. Within the Log Options dialog box, click your mouse on the Cancel button. *Performance Monitor* will close the Log Options dialog box.

After you have stopped your log from gathering any more data, you should view the log file's contents. To view a log file's contents, perform the following steps:

1. Within *Performance Monitor*, click your mouse on the View menu Chart option. *Performance Monitor* will switch to the Chart view.

2. Within the Chart view, click your mouse on the Options menu Data From option. *Performance Monitor* will open the Data From dialog box.

3. Within the Data From dialog box, click your mouse on the Log File radio button and then type the path- and filename for the log file. Click your mouse on the OK button. *Performance Monitor* will open the log file. (An open log file does not automatically display any data.)

4. Click your mouse on the Edit menu Add To Chart option. *Performance Monitor* will display the Add To Chart dialog box.

5. Within the Add To Chart dialog box, click your mouse on the Object drop-down list and select the object on which you want to view information. Click your mouse on the counter you want to view. Click your mouse on the Add button. *Performance Monitor* will add the counter to the chart.

6. Continue adding objects and counters until you have added all the data you want to view, and then click your mouse on the Close button. *Performance Monitor* will close the Add To Chart dialog box.

Answer C is correct because you can use the Log view to capture performance data. Answers A, B, and D are incorrect because you cannot use the Alert, Report, or Chart views to capture performance data.

549   **PRINTING A PERFORMANCE MONITOR REPORT**

Q: *You would print a Performance Monitor report to use for long-term record keeping.*

True or False?

You can create a *Performance Monitor* report from real-time data (that is, as the activity occurs) or from data you collected in a *Performance Monitor* log file. Whether you use real-time or collected data, creating the report is very easy. To create a report from data collected in a log file, perform the following steps:

1. Click your mouse on the Start menu and select the Programs submenu Administrative Tools group Performance Monitor program. Windows NT will open the *Performance Monitor* program.

2. Within the *Performance Monitor* program, click your mouse on the View menu Report option. *Performance Monitor* will switch to the Report view.

3. Within the Report view, click your mouse on the Options menu Data From option. *Performance Monitor* will open the Data From dialog box.

4. Within the Data From dialog box, click your mouse on the Log File radio button and then type the path- and filename for the log file. Click your mouse on the OK button. *Performance Monitor* will close the Data From dialog box.

5. Within the Report view, click your mouse on the Edit menu Add to Report option. *Performance Monitor* will display the Add to Report dialog box.

6. Within the Add to Report dialog box, select the objects and counters you want a report on. Click your mouse on the Add button and then the Done button. *Performance Monitor* will close the Add to Report dialog box and return you to the Report view.

After you have created your report, you should print it, either for archive purposes or to show someone else the server performance report. To print a *Performance Monitor* report, perform the following steps:

1. Within the *Performance Monitor* program, click your mouse on the File Menu Print option. *Performance Monitor* will display the Print dialog box.

2. Within the Print dialog box, click your mouse on the Print button. *Performance Monitor* will print your report.

*The answer is **True** because you would print a Performance Monitor report to use for long-term record keeping.*

550   **UNDERSTANDING TREND ANALYSIS**

Q: *Why would you analyze system performance trends?*

Choose the best answer:

A.   *To better understand fluctuations in server performance.*

B.   *To practice using Performance Monitor.*

C.   *To make sure that your server resources will meet your utilization expectations.*

D.   *To determine which users are using which resources.*

As you have learned, you should use the Performance Monitor program to regularly check your system's performance. Unfortunately, many network administrators overlook the importance of regularly using the *Performance Monitor* program. If you do not run frequent *Performance Monitor* sessions, you will not know what type of system performance is abnormal. The process of running frequent *Performance Monitor* sessions to determine normal performance levels is called *trend analysis*.

The easiest way, by far, to perform trend analysis is to chart data in a graph. You can use *Performance Monitor's* Chart view to examine real-time data, but most network administrators agree that captured data is easier to work with. Whether you are using real-time or captured data, you should keep a record of performance levels so you can compare those levels against previous *Performance Monitor* sessions.

For this reason, creating a log file makes the most sense—otherwise, you will have to memorize information from previous real-time sessions. In general, you will create log files at various workload times, on a regular basis, and over an extended period of time (weeks or longer), you will be able to determine important trends on your network.

Answer C is correct because you analyze system performance trends to ensure that your server will meet future resource needs. ***Answer A*** *is incorrect because you will have to understand server performance fluctuations.* ***Answer B*** *is incorrect because you will not analyze performance trends to practice using Performance Monitor.* ***Answer D*** *is incorrect because you cannot analyze performance trends to determine which users are using which resources.*

551   **MONITORING DESKTOP COMPUTERS**

Q: *You can use Performance Monitor to analyze all the desktop computers in your network.*

    True or False?

As a network administrator, you must have a good idea of how the computers in your network are performing. If you do not know what type of performance to expect from the different computers in your network, you will not know if a computer is running abnormally slow. You have learned that you can use Microsoft Windows NT's *Performance Monitor* program to capture performance data from computers in your network, store the data in a log file, and then view the captured data to determine what a computer's normal operation performance level is. However, you can use *Performance Monitor* only on Windows NT computers—it will not function on Windows 95 systems.

To view performance data on non-Windows NT computers, you must purchase Microsoft's Systems Management Server (SMS), which is part of Microsoft's *BackOffice* suite. The Systems Management Server will let you inventory the computers in your network, as well as check the performance of a desktop computer in your network.

Note: *The Systems Management Server exam is an MCSE elective exam. For more information on Microsoft Systems Management Server, see the Microsoft Web site at* ***www.microsoft.com.***

The answer is ***False*** *because you must use Microsoft's Systems Management Server to monitor your desktop computers.*

552   **INTRODUCTION TO RESPONSE PROBE**

Q: *You are the administrator of a Microsoft Windows NT domain. You want to test your server's response to a simulated load. What utility will you use to simulate a load?*

Choose the best answer:

      A.   *Windows NT Diagnostics*

      B.   *Server Manager*

      C.   *Response Probe*

      D.   *Testcpu*

As you have learned, when you track performance of your servers on the network, you will analyze the workload on the server in various areas, such as memory availability, processor usage, and so on. The *Response Probe* is a utility that lets you design a simulated workload—that is, it lets you specify how heavy the workload on the server should be. It then uses the simulated workload that you created to test the performance of your hardware and software configurations.

When you use the *Response Probe*, the response of your server's configuration becomes the only independent variable in the workload test (as opposed to during a normal workload test, when even the slightest access by another user of process can skew results). You can make changes to your configuration, and you can be more confident that any changes in performance will result from the new configuration you created. The Microsoft *Response Probe* utility comes with the Microsoft *Windows NT Resource Kit*, to which you can refer for more information.

Answer C is correct because you would use the Microsoft Response Probe to test a computer response to a simulated workload. Answers A and B are incorrect because you cannot use either Windows NT Diagnostics or Server Manager to test a computer using a simulated workload. Answer D is incorrect because there is no such utility.

553 **AUTOMATING PERFORMANCE MONITOR DATA COLLECTION**

Q: *You want to capture server performance data at night. Unfortunately, you must start data collection at the server.*

True or False?

In previous Tips, you have learned that the *Performance Monitor* is a powerful tool for analyzing performance and performance problems on your Windows NT network computers. A Windows NT administrator should use the *Performance Monitor* program any time the administrator suspects a loss in server performance. For example, imagine you are the administrator and you suspect a significant slowdown in server performance occurs at night. You can make *Performance Monitor* start collecting data at a specific time, but to do so you must also use the command-line *AT* scheduler utility and the Microsoft *Windows NT Resource Kit*.

First, you must install the Microsoft *Windows NT Resource Kit*, which includes the *Performance Monitor* service (a version of the performance monitor that the operating system can control directly). You can use the *Performance Monitor* service to force the *Performance Monitor* program to start, and use predefined counters to collect data. The *Performance Monitor* service does not have a graphical interface; instead, you will control the service using the *monitor.exe* utility.

After you have installed the *Performance Monitor* service, you must create a *workspace file*, which contains the objects and counters for a specific *Performance Monitor* session. To design a workspace file, use *Performance Monitor* and add any objects and counters for any resources you want to capture. After you have added all your objects and counters, within the Performance Monitor, use the File menu Save Workspace option to save the workspace file.

After you have installed the Microsoft *Windows NT Resource Kit* and created your workspace file, you must configure the *Performance Monitor* service to use the workspace file. To configure the *Performance Monitor* service to use the workspace file you created, perform the following steps:

1. Click your mouse on the Start menu and select the Programs submenu *Command Prompt* program. Windows NT will open the Command Prompt window.

2. Within the Command Prompt window at the command line, type *Monitor \\computername workspace_file_name*. Doing so will configure the *Performance Monitor* service to use the workspace file you created. After the service configures, the Command Prompt window will display the command line. Then close the Command Prompt.

After you have configured the *Performance Monitor* service to use the workspace file you created earlier, you must schedule the *Performance Monitor* service to start at a specific time. Because you have already installed the Microsoft *Windows NT Resource Kit*, you can use the graphical interface for the *Command Scheduler* program. To schedule the *Performance Monitor* service to start at a specific time, perform the following steps:

1. Click your mouse on the Start menu and select the Programs submenu Resource Kit 4.0 group Configuration subgroup Command Scheduler program. Windows NT will open the *Command Scheduler* program.

2. Within the *Command Scheduler* program, click your mouse on the Edit menu Add option. The *Command Scheduler* program will display the Add Command dialog box.

3. Within the Add Command dialog box, type *Monitor Start* in the *Command* field. In the *Time On Client* field, type the time you want the *Performance Monitor* service to start. Click your mouse on the OK button. The *Command Scheduler* will close the Add Command dialog box and schedule the *Performance Monitor* service to start at the time you specified.

4. Within the *Command Scheduler*, click your mouse on the File menu Exit option. Windows NT will close the *Command Scheduler* program.

*The answer is **False** because you can use the command line and the Monitor service to automate Performance Monitor data collection.*

554 **APPLICATIONS THAT WILL IMPORT PERFORMANCE MONITOR DATA**

Q: *You can import Performance Monitor data into Microsoft Excel.*

True or False?

After you use the *Performance Monitor* program to capture and analyze performance data, you must find a way to archive your captured data. How you archive your data will generally depend on how often you capture performance data, how long you intend to maintain the data, and how large your network is. Fortunately, you can use a variety of applications to archive your *Performance Monitor* data. After you import your captured performance data into an application other than *Performance Monitor*, you can use the new application's features to enhance your viewing of the captured data. For example, you might create extended graphs to show performance trends over a year or more. The following is a list of applications you can use to store and view performance data:

- Microsoft *Access*
- Microsoft *Excel*
- Microsoft *FoxPro*
- Microsoft *SQL Server*

Each of these applications will let you manipulate the *Performance Monitor* data using any of the individual application's built-in features—although most are databases, so you will generally use the queries and other database tools to organize the data.

*The answer is **True** because you can import Performance Monitor data into Microsoft Excel.*

555   USING MICROSOFT EXCEL TO TRACK SYSTEM PERFORMANCE

Q: *How would importing Performance Monitor data into Microsoft Excel be useful to you?*

Choose the best answer:

     A.   *Microsoft Excel can automatically determine system bottlenecks.*

     B.   *You can chart Performance Monitor data in Microsoft Excel.*

     C.   *You can use Microsoft Excel to import several captured performance monitoring sessions into one record.*

     D.   *You must use Microsoft Excel to read Performance Monitor data.*

As Tip 554 details, you can import data from *Performance Monitor* into several other programs which may help you more efficiently manage the data. Of the several applications that you can use to manipulate *Performance Monitor* data, administrators most frequently use the Microsoft *Excel* application. Microsoft *Excel* lets you use the captured *Performance Monitor* data to create elaborate charts and spreadsheets.

To use Microsoft *Excel* to view *Performance Monitor* data, you must first create a performance log file. After you have captured all the data you want to import into Microsoft *Excel*, you must open the performance data in a Chart view. Add all counters that you want to export within the Chart view, and then use the *Performance Monitor's* File menu Export option to save the chart as a *.csv* file.

After you have saved your performance data in a *.csv* file, you can open Microsoft *Excel* and then open the *.csv* file. Microsoft *Excel* will automatically detect the data type and import the performance information. Then you can chart or otherwise manipulate the captured performance data. If you are familiar with the Microsoft *Excel* macro language or Visual Basic, you can even create automated bottleneck-locating processes.

Answer C is correct because you will use Microsoft Excel to import data from multiple data-capturing sessions into one record for long-term record keeping. Answer A is incorrect because Microsoft Excel cannot automatically determine system bottlenecks. Answer B is incorrect because, although you can chart performance data in Microsoft Excel, you can also do it in Performance Monitor. Answer D is incorrect because you can view Performance Monitor data in the Performance Monitor program.

556   SETTING YOUR EXPECTATIONS OF SYSTEM USAGE AND AVAILABILITY

Q: *Achieving realistic expectations of system usage and availability involves analyzing your company's business plan.*

     True or False?

As you have learned in previous Tips, a domain controller does not require a very powerful computer. However, application and file and print servers must have computers with powerful processors and lots of physical memory. As an administrator, you must choose the right computers as the various types of servers in your network. You must also know what performance to expect from each server.

Knowing what your servers' capacities are is essential to predicting your future resource needs. One of the best ways to analyze your company's server needs is to examine your organization's business plan. Your company will have a detailed plan of how it will reach its business objectives, and when you examine that plan you will learn what your company's primary objectives are. For example, if you know that the most important thing to your business is customer billing, you may want to make sure that the most powerful servers in your organization are the servers in the customer billing areas.

After you decide where to place your servers, you should use the *Performance Monitor* program to establish how much you can reasonably expect each server to perform. Then, periodically run *Performance Monitor* again using the same counters to determine if you must upgrade system resources.

*The answer is **True** because you must analyze your company's overall business plan to reach realistic expectations about system performance.*

557 | **INTRODUCTION TO THE NETWORK MONITOR PROGRAM**

Q: You want to capture network packets and examine their contents. Which Microsoft utility will you use?

Choose the best answer:

      A.   Server Manager

      B.   Network Monitor

      C.   Microsoft Protocol Analyzer

      D.   Performance Monitor

One of the most crucial tasks a network administrator must perform is to maintain and troubleshoot the network. There are many variables in network troubleshooting: You could have problems with a network card in a computer, with physical cabling, hubs, or routers, and so on. A good network administrator will not discount any aspect of the network as the cause of a problem. To aid you in network troubleshooting and maintenance, Microsoft includes the *Network Monitor* program with Windows NT 4.x. However, there are two versions of *Network Monitor*. The simple version is included with Microsoft Windows NT Server. The full version of *Network Monitor* is sold only with Microsoft System Management Server (SMS).

Network Monitor is a Microsoft utility an administrator can use to capture network traffic and examine the contents of the network packages that contain data sent across the network. The simple version of *Network Monitor* is fine for capturing network frames (packets) that are destined to or sent from your local computer. Only the full version of *Network Monitor* has the ability to capture network data from anywhere on the network.

***Answer B** is correct because you will use Network Monitor to capture and examine network packets. **Answers A and D** are incorrect because you cannot capture network packets with either Server Manager or Performance Monitor. **Answer C** is incorrect because there is no such product as Microsoft Protocol Analyzer.*

558 | **UNDERSTANDING THE NETWORK MONITOR INTERFACE**

Q: You can use Network Monitor to perform which of the following?

Choose all answers that apply:

> A.   *Capture network packets*
>
> B.   *Find computer NetBIOS names*
>
> C.   *Find router names*
>
> D.   *Re-send network packets*

Microsoft's *Network Monitor* full version will let you both capture network packets from anywhere on the network and also find the NetBIOS names of routers and computers. You can even capture packets and then alter and re-send the packets. Navigating through the *Network Monitor* interface is quite simple. The interface is in four major sections: the *Graph pane, Total Statistics pane, Station Statistics pane,* and *Session Statistics pane.* Each pane provides an administrator with information about network utilization, as Figure 558 shows.

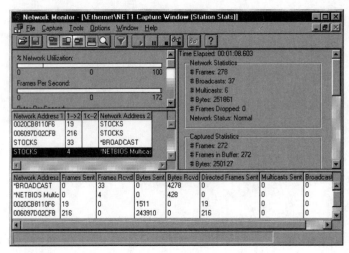

Figure 558 The Network Monitor interface.

Answers A, B, C, and D are all correct because you can use the Network Monitor program to capture network packets, find NetBIOS and router names, and re-send network packets.

| 559 | USING NETWORK MONITOR TO CAPTURE NETWORK TRAFFIC |

Q: You can capture all network traffic with the full version of Network Monitor.

True or False?

As you have learned, *Performance Monitor* lets you analyze the performance of a specific computer, while the *Network Monitor* lets you analyze the information passing between computers over the network. Before you can open the *Network Monitor* program, you must install it. Each version of *Network Monitor* installs differently, so see your Windows NT Online documentation or the Microsoft SMS documentation for details on how to install the *Network Monitor* version you have. To capture network frames (packages of data moving across the network), perform the following steps:

1. Within *Network Monitor*, select the Start menu Capture option. *Network Monitor* will begin to capture network frames.
2. When you want to stop capturing network frames, select the Capture menu Stop option. *Network Monitor* will stop capturing network frames.

*The answer is **True** because you can capture all network traffic with the full version of Network Monitor.*

560   **UNDERSTANDING NETWORK FRAMES**

Q: *Which of the following answers best describe a network frame?*

Choose the best answer:

     A.   *A window in Network Monitor*

     B.   *A package of data*

     C.   *One protocol acting as another*

     D.   *None of the above*

When one computer sends information to another computer, the sending computer breaks up the information into small, manageable pieces called *network frames* (sometimes called *packets*). A *network frame* contains more than just a piece of data; it also contains addressing and protocol information. As a receiving computer processes an incoming network frame, network software running on the computer will examine a piece of the network frame (which, generally, contains information about what computer sent the network frame, values to help the computer check the frame's validity, and so on) in much the same way that you would open a package mailed to your family during the holidays. When you receive the package at your house, it will be addressed to your family; so, too, must the frame be addressed to your computer for your computer to receive it. You will then open the package and retrieve the gifts from within the package (as the computer will do with the data in the network frame). In the same way that you would open a package addressed to you, a computer receiving a network frame will look for addressing information within the frame. If a network frame has the correct address on it, the receiving computer will strip the address off, process the frame, and strip away protocol information until it finds the actual data within the frame. If a network frame does not have your computer's address on it, the computer will ignore the frame or send it down the network, depending on your network's architecture.

Note: *You will learn more about network frames and packets in Tips 624-800, which detail information for the Networking Essentials exam and define frames in detail.*

Answer B *is correct because a network frame is a package of data.* **Answers A** *and* **C** *are incorrect because neither answer describes a network frame.* **Answer D** *is incorrect because B contains the correct answer.*

561   **UNDERSTANDING FRAME TYPES**

Q: *Which of the following are frame types?*

Choose all answers that apply:

>   A.   *Broadcast*
>
>   B.   *Single*
>
>   C.   *Multicast*
>
>   D.   *Directed*

As you have learned, network frames are small, manageable pieces of data that computers send over the network. While you can think of network frames as simply data within a wrapper, there are three specific major network frame types that you will use the *Network Monitor* program to capture. The three major network frame types are *broadcast, multicast,* and *directed.* Each network frame type has a specific function in the network.

Broadcast frames travel to every computer in a network. When one computer sends a broadcast message, every computer connected to the same cabling segment must process the frame. Broadcast frames are similar to postal junk mail. When you receive junk mail at your house, you may or may not be interested in the contents of the message, so you might open the package to view what is inside. If the junk mail contents are something you can use, you might keep reading; otherwise, you would discard the rest of the information. Computers handle broadcast frames the same way. After the receiving computer examines a broadcast frame's addressing information it will view the frame's next section. Each section of the network frame contains information to help network software process the frame. In general, you can think of the receiving computer's network software as stripping away frame sections, one by one, until it reaches the section that actually contains the data it requires. Because every computer in a network must process a broadcast frame, most administrators will try to reduce the number of broadcasts their networks send.

Multicast frames are similar to broadcast frames, in that they travel to more than one destination. However, a multicast frame is addressed to a group of computers (just as you might send a letter to a client and three carbon copies to managers in your organization), instead of to every computer in the network. After each computer in the target group receives the network frame, it will process the network frame and pass the information the network frame contains to the application receiving it.

Directed frames are addressed to only one computer. Every computer in the network will see the frame, but only the computer to which the frame is addressed will open it. Using directed frames reduces your network computers' workload because only the one destination computer must process the frame. In general, most applications that you will run on the network will use directed frames—for example, when you send a print job, your computer directs those network frames solely at the print server.

Answers A, C, and D are correct because Microsoft Windows NT supports broadcast, multicast, and directed frame types. Answer B is incorrect because single is not a frame type.

562 MAKING A SIMPLE COMPARISON OF NETWORK PROTOCOLS

Q: *Which one of the Microsoft Windows NT-supported protocols is the fastest?*

Choose the best answer:

> *A.* *NetBEUI*
>
> *B.* *TCP/IP*
>
> *C.* *NWLINK*
>
> *D.* *AppleTalk*

As you have learned, a network frame contains small pieces of information. When the transmitting computer sends information, it will generally break the information into a number of network frames whose contents make up a complete piece of information. When the receiving computer gets all the network frames, it will reassemble the pieces and work with the complete piece of information. The number of pieces the sending computer will break up data into depends on the protocol you are using in your network. Microsoft Windows NT supports several network protocols, such as TCP/IP, NWLINK, NetBEUI, and AppleTalk. Each protocol uses its own method of breaking up data and then reassembling it on the receiving side.

Each protocol has a specific use. For example, if you are integrating Novell NetWare into your Microsoft Windows NT environment, you would use the NWLINK protocol. If you want to access the Internet, you would require TCP/IP. In turn, NetBEUI makes a fine protocol for a small network because it requires no tuning or configuration. Of the protocols that Windows NT supports, Microsoft lists NWLINK as the fastest. However, you could not determine this without using a protocol analyzer, such as *Network Monitor*.

Answer C is correct because NWLINK is the fastest of all the Microsoft Windows NT-supported protocols. Answers A, B, and D are incorrect because in tests Microsoft performed, the NWLINK protocol is the fastest network protocol of these four.

563 INTRODUCTION TO HOST NAMES

Q: *A computer's host name and NetBIOS name are always the same.*

True or False?

In a computer network, users might find it difficult to remember the physical address of each computer to which they want to connect—especially considering that network addresses are generally a twelve-digit stream of numbers. Instead, you, as the administrator, will name each computer with a textual (or *human readable*) name. Then, when users want to connect to a computer in your network, they must know only the computer's name. You can think of network computer names the same way you might think of the speed-dial function on your telephone. When you use speed dial, you do not have to remember the phone number of the people you want to contact; you must remember only the programmed button numbers that correspond to specific phone numbers. Computer networks work the same way: you must know only the name (not the address) of the computer to which you want to connect. The network will resolve (that is, convert from name to address) the computer's name into an address that the client computer can use to connect to the other computer.

Microsoft generally uses Network Basic Input Output (NetBIOS) names for network addressing. Typically, computers will resolve NetBIOS computer names to network addresses using a broadcast method. When you try to connect to another computer in the network, your computer will send a broadcast frame querying (asking) for the address of the computer name to which you want to connect. Every computer in the network will receive the broadcast, but only the computer with the correct name will respond to the query.

In contrast, other network types use different name resolution processes. TCP/IP networks have traditionally used a *host name* resolution method. Although Microsoft networks can use broadcasts to resolve computer names (using TCP/IP), Microsoft networks also use a host naming resolution method on TCP/IP computers. Whether a computer will broadcast for the name of another computer in a TCP/IP environment depends on what type of name the client computer is using to connect to the other computer. Microsoft Windows NT computers can have two names: a *host name* and a *NetBIOS name*. A computer cannot broadcast to resolve a host name, only a NetBIOS name. The host name is associated with the TCP/IP protocol itself. The NetBIOS name is the Microsoft client computer's name. The two names can be the same, or the administrator can assign different NetBIOS and host names.

*The answer is **False** because a computer's NetBIOS name may be the same as the host name, but it does not have to be.*

564 **INTRODUCTION TO THE DOMAIN NAME SYSTEM (DNS) SERVER**

Q: *Microsoft DNS is compatible with existing DNS servers, and you can use it for Internet name resolution.*

True or False?

As you have learned, a computer will broadcast for another computer's NetBIOS network name, and only the computer with the correct name will respond. On the other hand, you must resolve a computer's host name using a different method. To resolve a computer's host name, you use a database of host names and the IP addresses to which these host names belong. You can keep this database on a file on each computer in the network, or you can use a centralized database. The most widely used centralized database system for resolving host names to IP addresses is the *Domain Name System (DNS) server*.

If you are using a DNS server, resolving host names and IP addresses is a three-step process. First, the computer in your network trying to connect to another computer using its host name will send a directed frame to the DNS server. The directed frame will query the server for the host name resolution (that is, the IP address) of the desired connection. The DNS server will send back a query reply with the destination host computer's IP address. The sending computer will then use the IP address in the query reply to directly connect to the destination host computer.

If, when the DNS server receives the query, it does not have a name resolution for the requested host, it can (if the administrator has configured it to do so) send the query on to another DNS server, and that DNS server can do the same thing. The idea is that somewhere along the line, one of the DNS servers will have the host name resolution. The process of the first computer sending the request and the DNS server querying on the original computer's behalf is called *recursion*. Only the first query from the client to the DNS server is actually a recursive query—all other queries from the first DNS server to other DNS servers are *iterative* queries. However, Microsoft refers to the entire process as recursion.

Note: *An administrator must install and configure the Microsoft DNS server on a Windows NT Server computer.*

*The answer is **True** because Microsoft's DNS server is completely compatible with existing Internet DNS servers, and you can use Microsoft's DNS server for Internet name resolution.*

565 **MINIMIZING DOMAIN NAME SYSTEM (DNS) SERVER RECURSION**

Q: *To minimize DNS recursion is to reduce the number of resolution requests your DNS server sends to other DNS servers.*

True or False?

As you learned in Tip 564, recursion is the process of a computer sending a DNS query to a DNS server, and the DNS server then querying another DNS server on behalf of the original computer. As the administrator of your company's DNS server, you should reduce recursion because the recursion process creates network traffic.

There are only three ways to reduce DNS recursion: you can configure your DNS server to not forward DNS queries; you can configure your DNS server to resolve more hosts names so it will not have to forward DNS queries; or you can configure each host computer to provide its own host name resolution. If you configure your DNS server to not forward DNS queries, clients' computers will not be able to connect to any host for which you have not configured a DNS record on your DNS server. If you configure each host computer to provide its own host name resolution, you will have to maintain each computer's host name resolution file.

*The answer is **True** because to minimize DNS recursion does mean to reduce the number of DNS-forwarded requests.*

566   **CONFIGURING THE DOMAIN NAME SYSTEM (DNS) MINIMUM DEFAULT TIME TO LIVE (TTL) PARAMETER**

Q: *The default DNS cached entry minimum Time To Live (TTL) is 60 minutes.*

True or False?

To administer a Microsoft DNS server, you must be the administrator of the Windows NT server on which the DNS server is running. One of the configuration parameters you can set on a DNS server is the default *Time To Live (TTL)* that specifies how long a DNS server, after it receives a response (from another DNS server), can cache the result.

When a host computer sends a host name query to the DNS server, the DNS server will attempt to resolve the name locally. If the DNS server cannot resolve the name locally, it will send an iterative query to another DNS server. When the original DNS server receives the query results, it will return the query results to the host computer that originally sent the request. The DNS server will then cache (store locally in a temporary file) the DNS results, so that if another host computer sends a DNS query for the same host name resolution, the DNS server will not have to send an iterative query. The amount of time the DNS server will cache the DNS query is the TTL.

Note: *For information on how to change the default DNS TTL, refer to the Microsoft **Windows NT Resource Kit**.*

*The answer is **True** because the default Microsoft DNS cached TTL is 60 minutes.*

567   **IMPLEMENTING A HOSTS FILE**

Q: *A Hosts file is a file of users who have recently accessed your server.*

True or False?

In Tip 563, you learned that computers that use the TCP/IP protocol have computer names (host names) different from the Microsoft NetBIOS name. When you connect to a computer using its host name, your computer must resolve the destination computer's host name into an IP address. Your computer can resolve the name using a DNS server, or it can use its own local *Hosts* file.

In the early days of the Internet, all computers had to resolve their own host names. For example, if you wanted to connect to a computer in another network using the computer name *Server1*, you would have had to create a *Hosts* file entry on your computer that would resolve the name *Server1* into the remote host's IP address. Today, you would use recursive DNS lookup to resolve the name, as you learned about previously. However, you can still use a *Hosts* file if you want to.

The problem with a *Hosts* file is that if any computers change their IP addresses, you must change the *Hosts* file on every computer in your network. However, you might still have reasons why you choose to implement a local *Hosts* file on Windows NT computers in your network (generally, you would do so to speed host name resolution). If you choose to use the local *Hosts* file, you can use the sample *Hosts* file that comes with Microsoft Windows NT as a starting point in your *Hosts* file's design. The sample *Hosts* file, which you can edit with any text editor, is located in the *Winnt\system32\drivers\ect* directory.

*The answer is **False** because a Hosts file is a file you can implement on your local computer that resolves host names to IP addresses.*

568	### INTRODUCTION TO THE DYNAMIC HOST CONFIGURATION PROTOCOL (DHCP) SERVICE

Q: DHCP will perform which of the following functions?

Choose all answers that apply:

> A.   Assign IP addresses to client computers
>
> B.   Assign subnet masks to DHCP clients
>
> C.   Assign host names to DHCP clients
>
> D.   Share the root of every volume on each DHCP client

Transmission Control Protocol/Internet Protocol (TCP/IP) requires each computer to have its own unique 32-bit address. In Windows NT 4.0, you will specify the IP addresses using dotted-decimal notation (a series of four byte values separated by periods). For example, a computer might have the IP address 204.31.13.1. Each number in the IP address has a specific meaning to the IP protocol. In the 204.31.13.1 IP address, the numbers 204.31.13 represent the actual network that computer is on, while the number 1 indicates the address of the computer itself. As you can see, to assign IP addresses to many computers could be a very tedious job—because you would have to create a computer address for each computer on the network.

To simplify the process of assigning IP addresses to host computers, Microsoft has included the *Dynamic Host Configuration Protocol (DHCP) service* with Windows NT Server. DHCP lets you create a pool (range) of IP addresses that host computers can use. When a computer you have configured to be a DHCP client starts, it will announce its presence to the network and broadcast for a DHCP server (a server running the DHCP service). When the DHCP server receives the DHCP client request, it will send back to the client an IP address, as well as other configuration information, such as the subnet mask, default gateway, WINS server, and DNS server information. Because a single, central location assigns all the addresses on the network, using DHCP helps eliminate configuration errors.

Answers A and B are correct because a DHCP server will assign both an IP address and a subnet mask to each DHCP client computer. Answers C and D are incorrect because a DHCP server will not assign a host name to a DHCP client, nor will it share the root of every volume on the DHCP client computer.

569   INTRODUCTION TO THE WORKSTATION SERVICE

Q: *Another name for the Workstation service is the _____?*

Choose the best answer:

    A.   *The Server service*

    B.   *The Redirector service*

    C.   *The Proxy service*

    D.   *The Slave service*

Microsoft sometime gives more than one name to the same components of their products. For example, a Windows NT Server can be a Server Only, Member Server Standalone Server, or an Application Server. Each of these are the same thing—a Microsoft Windows NT Server that is not a domain controller. One of the key services in Windows NT has three names: the *Workstation* service, the *Redirector* service, and the *Client* service. All three names, however, refer to the same service. Depending on where you are in Windows NT, you will see each of these different names. For example, in the Network dialog box you will see the *Workstation* service.

Whether you are talking about the *Workstation* service, *Redirector* service, or the *Client* service, you should understand the service's function and purpose. The *Workstation* service provides a Windows NT computer with the ability to connect to another Microsoft computer. When you change to a drive, for example the F: drive, the *Workstation* service helps the computer determine whether the F: drive is local to your computer, or somewhere on the network. When your computer determines that the destination computer is on the network, the *Redirector* (*Workstation* service) will redirect your request to the network, instead of handling the request locally.

Answer B is correct because another name for the Workstation service is the Redirector. Answers A, C, and D are incorrect because they do not correctly state another Microsoft-accepted name for the Workstation service.

570   INTRODUCTION TO THE DIRECTORY REPLICATOR SERVICE

Q: *The Directory Replicator service is responsible for synchronizing the Directory Database, which contains all user, group, and computer accounts in the domain.*

    True or False?

You have been introduced to the concept of Directory Database synchronization (the replication of the Directory Database from Primary Domain Controllers to Backup Domain Controllers). A similar process can copy data from one Windows NT server to any other Windows NT computer.

In large, complex Windows NT domain, you must have system policies and log-on scripts on all domain controllers. When your Windows NT servers are in several different locations, ensuring that the policies and scripts are consistent throughout the network can become an administrative concern. Therefore, it is essential that you make sure all domain controllers have up-to-date log-on scripts and system policies.

Microsoft has given Windows NT the ability to automatically copy a directory's contents from one Windows NT server to any other Windows NT computer. Microsoft calls this process *Directory Replication*. In turn, the *Directory Replicator* service manages the Directory Replication process. Generally, you will only use *Directory Replication* to replicate log-on scripts, system policies, and occasionally small read-only files essential to your administration of domains on the network.

*The answer is **False** because as an administrator, you will use the Directory Replicator service to replicate log-on scripts, system policies, and small read-only files to other Windows NT computers.*

571   **REVIEWING THE COMPUTER BROWSER SERVICE**

Q: *Why would computers that are up on the network and able to see all network resources not show up in browse lists?*

Choose the best answer:

> A.   *The computer's NetLogon service is not running.*
>
> B.   *The computer's Workstation service is not running.*
>
> C.   *The computer has not been up long enough for the Master Browser to build it into the browse list.*
>
> D.   *The Computer's network card is not functioning properly.*

When a Microsoft client computer starts, it will announce its presence on the network with a *host announcement*. Other computers called *Master Browsers* listen for these host announcements. When a Master Browser hears a host announcement, it will take the information from the host announcement and build it into the *master browse list*, a list of every computer, workgroup, and domain in the network. Much as Primary Domain Controllers send the Directory Database to Backup Domain Controllers, the Master Browser sends the complete master browse list to computers called *backup browsers*, computers that keep a copy of the master browse list.

When a client computer wants to see the master browse list, it will send a request to the Master Browser asking for a list of all backup browsers. After the client computer receives the list of backup browsers, it will contact one of the backup browsers and request the master browse list.

A client computer will go through the process of retrieving the master browse list any time the computer's user opens a dialog box or program that displays a list of network resources. For example, when you open Network Neighborhood, the computer retrieves the master browse list and displays the browsing information within the Network Neighborhood window.

Answer C *is correct because, if a computer has just come on-line, it will be several minutes before it shows up in the browse list.* **Answer A** *is incorrect because the NetLogon service not running would not stop you from showing up as a network resource, it would just keep you from logging on to the domain.* **Answer B** *is incorrect because the computer's Workstation service not running would keep you from connecting to other network resources.* **Answer D** *is incorrect because, if the computer's network card was not functioning properly, you would not be able to connect to the network.*

572 LOCATING A LOG-ON SERVER

Q: *Every time a user logs onto the network, the local computer must contact a domain controller to validate the log-on request. Which of the following are ways the local computer can find a domain controller?*

Choose all answers that apply:

  A. *By looking in the local controller.txt file*

  B. *By broadcasting a request to NetLogon*

  C. *By querying a WINS server*

  D. *By contacting a DHCP server*

When a user logs onto the network from a Windows NT computer, the computer sends a broadcast frame to the *NetLogon* mailslot (a *mailslot* is a communication mechanism). The Windows NT computer sends the broadcast to the physical Ethernet broadcast address of the *NetLogon* mail slot, and additionally sends a subnet broadcast at the IP level to UDP port 138. The sending computer's destination for the broadcast is the domain's NetBIOS name, with the sixteenth character appended by Windows NT as *<00>*. If the domain's NetBIOS name has fewer than fifteen characters, Windows NT will append zeros at the end of the domain name. For example, if the domain name is *domain*, Windows NT will send the *NetLogon* broadcast to *domain0000000<00>*.

The only other way a client computer can locate a log-on server is if the client computer is a WINS client. When a user with a WINS client computer logs onto the network, the WINS client will send a directed frame to the WINS server and request a list of domain controllers' names. The client computer will then send a directed message to each domain controller, requesting log-on validation. The domain controller that responds first will be the domain controller that validates the client's log-on request.

Answers B and **C** are correct because to locate a log-on server, the local computer must either send a broadcast to NetLogon or directly query a WINS server. **Answer A** is incorrect because the Controller.TXT file does not exist. **Answer D** is incorrect because a DHCP server will not have domain controller information.

573 UNDERSTANDING SETTINGS FOR THE SERVER SERVICE

Q: *You are the administrator of a Microsoft Windows NT network. You have several Windows NT servers, one of which is going to be an application server. You want to maximize the performance of the application server. Which of the following Server service settings would be best for an application server?*

Choose the best answer:

  A. *Minimize Memory Used*

  B. *Balance*

  C. *Maximize Throughput for File Sharing*

  D. *Maximize Throughput for Network Applications*

Windows NT servers automatically configure their *Server* service for the optimal number of user connections. However, an administrator can choose to manually configure the *Server* service of a Windows NT server. An administrator may do so when he or she thinks that the *Server* service is not configured optimally for the specific use the administrator intends for the Windows NT server. You can adjust the *Server* service from the *Network* program in the Control Panel. The *Server* service has four settings, as shown in Table 573.

Setting	Description
Minimize Memory Used	Optimizes the Windows NT server's memory use for 10 remote users, allowing more memory for local processes.
Balance	Optimizes the system for up to 64 remote users.
Maximize Throughput for File Sharing	The default *Server* service setting. This setting optimizes the server for more than 64 remote users.
Maximize Throughput for Network Applications	Will optimize the server to run as an application server with more than 64 remote users.

Table 573 The Server service settings for a Windows NT server.

Answer D is correct because the Maximize Throughput for Network Applications option is optimal for an application server. Answers A, B, and C are incorrect because they would configure the system's memory for optimal use as an application server.

574 **ANALYZING CLIENT INITIALIZATION TRAFFIC**

Q: *Which of the following are examples of Microsoft client initialization traffic?*

Choose all answers that apply:

    A.   *DHCP*

    B.   *WINS*

    C.   *File copying*

    D.   *Log-on validation*

As the administrator of your Microsoft network, you must know what type of network traffic to expect during the various peak times of the workday. One of the busiest times will most likely be in the morning when users first arrive at work and they all start their computers and log onto the network.

When a Microsoft Windows NT computer first starts, it will generate some client initialization traffic, such as locating a Dynamic Host Configuration Protocol (DHCP) server, Windows Internet Name Service (WINS) server, and making host announcements. Each of these tasks will generate a small amount of network traffic; in fact, a single client computer's initialization traffic is fairly insignificant. It is only when you combine the total network traffic of all your network users that the client initialization traffic can become an issue. Therefore, you should use the *Network Monitor* program to analyze the total network traffic in the morning to determine if you are saturating your network bandwidth (that is, if logons are slow because there is too much consecutive traffic on the network).

Answers A, B, and D are correct because DHCP, WINS, and log-on validation are all part of client initialization traffic. Answer C is incorrect because copying a file is not part of the network traffic associated with client initialization traffic.

575   **ANALYZING CLIENT LOG-ON VALIDATION TRAFFIC**

Q: *Client log-on validation causes a large amount of network traffic.*

True or False?

Any time a user logs onto the network, there will be client logon network traffic. In turn, the network protocol you are using in your network will determine the amount of traffic your network will experience. However, in any case, the relative impact on the network will actually be light because client log-on validation does not generate much traffic. Microsoft states in its official curriculum courses that the minimum network traffic generated during a client's logon is 3,105 bytes sent in 24 frames. However, if you are using log-on scripts, system policies, or system profiles, you will experience a much higher level of network traffic—but even so, your logon traffic will generally only be a few Kb of data.

Although local network traffic for log-on validation is low, if you have slow Wide Area Network (WAN) links to remote sites, downloading system polices and system profiles can cause network bandwidth saturation—causing extremely slow logons. Therefore, you should use the *Network Monitor* program to analyze WAN links if you find that users are having a difficult time logging on over a remote connection.

*The answer is **False** because client log-on validation causes only a minimal amount of network traffic.*

576   **ANALYZING DYNAMIC HOST CONFIGURATION PROTOCOL (DHCP) CLIENT TRAFFIC**

Q: *How many frames of network traffic are generated during a DHCP client lease acquisition?*

Choose the correct answer:

     A.   *Two*

     B.   *Four*

     C.   *Six*

     D.   *Eight*

In Tip 568, you learned how an administrator can use a Dynamic Host Configuration Protocol (DHCP) server to automatically lease IP addresses to DHCP client computers. In Tip 575, you learned that whenever a user logs onto the network, the operating system generates a certain minimum amount of network traffic. When you use DHCP on your network, user logons generate more network traffic than they would if you were not using DHCP.

When a DHCP client computer initializes, it will send one network frame, called a *discovery frame,* as a broadcast frame. The discovery frame contains the sending computer's physical address (also known as the MAC address, which you will learn more about in Tip 586) and the sending computer's NetBIOS name. When it sends the discovery frame, the DHCP client does not yet have an IP address, so the client uses the IP address 0.0.0.0 as its source address. The DHCP client then broadcasts the discovery frame to all network computers.

Every computer in the network will receive the broadcast discovery frame from the DHCP client, but only a DHCP server will respond. After a DHCP server receives a request for a DHCP IP address lease, the DHCP server will send an *offer frame* back to the requesting client computer. The offer frame contains the IP address, subnet mask, and any other configuration information (such as proxy server addresses and so on) from the DHCP sever. After the DHCP server sends the offer frame and the client computer receives the offer frame, the DHCP client computer will then send a DHCP *request frame*. The request frame is a simple reply to the DHCP server's offer that states that the client computer will accept the IP address assignment the DHCP server offered. In response, the DHCP server will send an acknowledgment back to the DHCP client (the *acknowledgement frame*), which gives the client the lease duration, and any other TCP/IP configuration parameters.

Answer B is correct because DHCP client lease acquisition generates only four frames of network traffic. Answers A, C, and D are incorrect because none of the answers correctly state how many frames a DHCP client lease acquisition generates.

577   **INTRODUCING NETBIOS NAMES**

Q: *How many characters can a computer's NetBIOS name have?*

Choose the best answer:

     A.   Fourteen

     B.   Fifteen

     C.   Sixteen

     D.   Eighteen

In a Microsoft network, each computer must have a unique identification name, or a *NetBIOS name*. Network Basic Input Output System (NetBIOS) names are human-readable, fifteen-character names. You can use any characters except the following standard special characters: \ / | [{] } ( ) * % $ # @ . ,. NetBIOS names are actually sixteen characters long, but the operating system hides the sixteenth character, which is a variable that the operating system sets that determines the type of name that is registered on the network. For example, a sixteenth character of hexadecimal value <20> represents the Server service. To see a list of your local NetBIOS names, use the *NBTStat* command. (Tip 580 explains *NBTStat* in detail.) Table 577 shows some possible NetBIOS names a computer can register on the network if you are logged onto a computer whose name is Server1 with the username *Shanes*, in a domain whose name is Domain1.

Name	16TH	Type	Description
Server1	<00>	UNIQUE	Workstation Service name
Server1	<20>	UNIQUE	Server Service name
Domain1	<00>	GROUP	Domain name
Domain1	<1C>	GROUP	Domain Controller name
Domain1	<1B>	UNIQUE	Master Browser name
Shanes	<03>	UNIQUE	Messenger name
Server1.	<BF>	UNIQUE	Network Monitor name

Table 577 A NetBIOS name table.

*Answer B is correct because a computer's NetBIOS name can have only fifteen characters. **Answers A** and **D** are incorrect because neither answer correctly states the number of characters you can use in a NetBIOS name. **Answer C** is incorrect because although a NetBIOS name technically has sixteen characters, the sixteenth character is a hidden variable that the operating system sets.*

578   **UNDERSTANDING HOST ANNOUNCEMENTS**

Q: *When a Microsoft client starts, the client will make a host announcement every minute for the first five minutes, then it will make additional host announcements every twelve minutes thereafter.*

True or False?

As you have learned, in a network that uses the DHCP service to assign IP addresses to client computers, the client computer must announce its presence to the DHCP server to request an address. However, even if computers on the network already have fixed IP address, in a Microsoft network, every computer must announce its presence so that it will appear in the list of network resources. Each computer follows a process to announce its presence, starting with the initial announcement to the network.

When a Microsoft client computer (host) first connects to the network, it sends a network broadcast frame that announces its availability on the network. The broadcast contains information about services the host can provide. The host will make this announcement every minute for the first five minutes that the host is up. After the first five minutes, each host will broadcast another host announcement every twelve minutes.

*The answer is **True**. Microsoft clients will make host announcements every minute for the first five minutes after the client connects to the network, and every twelve minutes thereafter.*

579   **UNDERSTANDING NETBIOS NAME RESOLUTION**

Q: *You can use broadcasts or a NetBIOS name server to resolve NetBIOS names to a computer's address.*

True or False?

As you have learned, Microsoft client computers send host announcements, which make the computer available on the network. Because the two processes occur almost simultaneously, it is important to understand how the announcement process works together with the resolution of the names during a client log-on. As you have also learned, when Microsoft client computers (hosts) announce their presence to the network, a *master browser* gathers information about the new client computer. The master browser then takes the information, and distributes it to *backup browsers*. The backup browsers will make the list of computers in the network available to all clients.

A Microsoft client computer may show up in a browse list, but you may not be able to connect to the client computer (for example, if the client signed off the network after the last browse list update). After you select a computer to connect to in a browse list, the computer's name to which you want to connect must be resolved to an address your computer can use to establish the connection. By default, Microsoft networks will resolve computer NetBIOS names by broadcasting. To look for the computer NetBIOS name you want to connect to, a Microsoft client will send a broadcast to the network. Only the remote computer with the matching NetBIOS name will respond to your broadcast, and send the remote computer's address information.

As you know, you may experience network congestion problems in large networks where there is a lot of network broadcast traffic. To avoid the traffic, you may want to use another form of NetBIOS name resolution, a Windows Internet Name Service (WINS) server, instead of the default broadcast method.

Another way to configure your Microsoft network to perform NetBIOS name resolution is to use a WINS server. A WINS server will eliminate broadcast name resolution traffic. When a Microsoft client computer must resolve another computer's name to an IP address, the client computer sends a directed frame to the WINS server (rather than a broadcast frame).

The directed frame is a simple query for the resolution of a computer's NetBIOS name to an IP address. The WINS server sends back the name resolution, and then the client can directly connect to the remote host without using broadcast traffic to get the remote host's name first—which will result in a reduction of network traffic.

The answer is **True** *because the default method a Microsoft computer uses to resolve another computer's NetBIOS name is to broadcast for the computer's address. However, you can configure a WINS server, which is a NetBIOS name server, to greatly reduce broadcast network traffic.*

580 | ## USING THE NBTSTAT UTILITY

Q: *Which NBTStat switch will let you view your local NetBIOS name cache?*

Choose the best answer:

     A.   -a

     B.   -n

     C.   -c

     D.   -x

As you learned in Tip 577, you can use the *NBTStat* command-line utility to see a list of your local NetBIOS names. Microsoft's Transmission Control Protocol/Internet Protocol (TCP/IP) implementation comes with utilities, such as *NBTStat*, to help you diagnose TCP/IP-related problems, as well as better understand your TCP/IP configurations.

NBTStat is a command line utility that will show you statistical information about your TCP/IP protocol, such as your local computer's NetBIOS name cache. Like most command-line applications, *NBTStat* lets you use switches (options) to view specific statistical information. A switch in *NBTStat* is a "-" (dash) with a letter that designates the option you want. Figure 580 shows the *NBTStat* command help screen.

Answer C *is correct because when you use the -c switch with the NBTStat command, you can view the local* **NetBIOS** *name cache.* **Answer A** *is incorrect because when you use the -a switch with the NBTStat command, you can view a remote computer's name table.* **Answer B** *is incorrect because when you use the -n switch with the NBTStat command, you can view your local NetBIOS names.* **Answer D** *is incorrect because you cannot use a -x switch with the NBTStat command.*

Figure 580 *The NBTStat command help screen.*

581 CONFIGURING YOUR NETBIOS NAME CACHE

Q: *The default Time To Live (TTL) for your Windows NT computer's NetBIOS name cache is ten minutes.*

True or False?

To reduce network traffic for name-resolution broadcast messages (and to improve your system performance when your software must resolve an name to an address), Microsoft client computers will automatically store the NetBIOS computer names that it has recently resolved within the local NetBIOS name cache.

When your network software must resolve a computer's name to an address, the software will first look in the NetBIOS name cache to see if it has already resolved the name. If your computer does not have a name resolution for the computer you want to connect to, your computer will initiate the name resolution process (using the slow broadcast-message technique or a WINS server request) which you have learned about previously.

Although you can configure the time length that your computer will store a recently resolved NetBIOS name, the default value is ten minutes. Microsoft calls the time amount that your computer will store recently resolved NetBIOS names the *NetBIOS Name Cache Time To Live (TTL)* interval. To change the NetBIOS name cache's Time To Live (TTL), perform the following steps to edit the Windows NT Registry:

1. Click your mouse on the Start menu and select the Run option. Windows NT will display the Run dialog box.

2. Within the Run dialog box, type *Regedt32.exe* in the *Open* field. Click your mouse on the OK button. Windows NT will open the *Registry Editor* program.

3. Within the *Registry Editor* program, click your mouse on the *HKEY_LOCAL_MACHINE* subtree. Within the *HKEY_LOCAL_MACHINE* subtree, expand the following pathname: *SYSTEM\CurrentControlSet\Services\NetBT\Parameters*. The *Registry Editor* program will display the *Parameters* subkey.

4. Within the *SYSTEM\CurrentControlSet\Services\NetBT\Parameters* subkey (in the right pane of the *Registry Editor*), double-click your mouse on the *CacheTimeout* value. The *Registry Editor* will display the DWORD Editor dialog box.

5. Within the DWORD Editor dialog box, type a value for the time length you want your NetBIOS name cache to store computer names it has recently resolved. (The *Registry Editor* shows the values in hexadecimal). Click your mouse on the OK button. The *Registry Editor* will close the DWORD Editor dialog box and set the NetBIOS name cache value.

The answer is **True**, *because a Windows NT computer's NetBIOS name cache default TTL is ten minutes.*

582 — **IMPLEMENTING AN LMHOSTS FILE**

Q: LMHOSTS file will resolve which of the following?

Choose the best answer:

A.   Host names to IP addresses

B.   NetBIOS names to IP addresses

C.   IP addresses to physical addresses

D.   IP addresses to Host names

As you have learned, a Microsoft computer will broadcast for NetBIOS name resolution, or use a Windows Internet Name Service (WINS) server to resolve the NetBIOS name of other computers on the network to IP addresses. However, you can also implement a *LMHOSTS* file to resolve computer NetBIOS names to IP addresses. A LMHOSTS file is a LAN Manager HOSTS file your local computer stores, which you can edit and which the operating system will then use to create mappings that resolve computer NetBIOS names to IP addresses. LAN Manager is an old Microsoft network operating system, some of whose features, including the LMHOSTS file, Microsoft carried over into Windows NT.

Windows NT includes a sample LMHOSTS file that you can view. Go to your Windows NT system root (usually *Winnt*), and open *System32\Drivers\ECT* to view the file. In an LMHOSTS file, you will specify the IP address first, then the name you want to resolve to that IP address. For example, the following entry resolves *Server2* to an IP address:

```
206.49.190.10    Server2
```

Answer B is correct because a Windows NT computer will use a LMHOSTS file to resolve NetBIOS names to IP addresses. Answers A, C, and D are incorrect because a LMHOSTS file will not resolve Host names to IP addresses, IP addresses to physical addresses, or IP addresses to Host names. A LMHOSTS file can only resolve NetBIOS names to IP addresses.

583 — **ANALYZING WINS CLIENT TRAFFIC**

Q: Which of the following can you use to optimize your WINS client traffic?

Choose all answers that apply:

A.   Disable unnecessary Windows NT services.

B.   Use the Windows NT Resource Kit's WINS optimizer.

    C.   *Implement a LMHOSTS file.*

    D   *Increase the NetBIOS name cache.*

As you have learned, as soon as a Microsoft client computer starts, it will first initialize its IP address and will then register its NetBIOS names. To register its NetBIOS names, the client may use a broadcast frame, or a directed frame to a Windows Internet Name Service (WINS) server. If you have configured the client computer to use WINS, the client will send a registration frame every time the client computer starts. The WINS server will respond with a name registration acknowledgment frame.

After the first name registration, the client computer will renew its name registration periodically. The frequency with which a WINS client renews its name registration with a WINS server depends on how you have configured the WINS server. After the WINS client registers its names with a WINS server, the WINS server will send the client the name registration acknowledgment, which includes a name registration Time To Live (TTL) value. A WINS server's default configuration will set the name registration TTL at six days. WINS clients must renew their names at one half the TTL; therefore, WINS clients will, by default, renew their names every three days.

The only other network traffic that WINS generates (aside from name registration acknowledgements) is name resolution traffic. When a WINS client wants to connect to another computer, the WINS client must get a name resolution of the remote computer's NetBIOS name. The WINS client will send a directed frame to the WINS server that requests the name resolution. The entire process generates only two frames of traffic: the name resolution request and the server's response.

Answers A, C, and D *are correct because you can disable unnecessary Windows NT services, implement a LMHOSTS file, and increase the NetBIOS name cache CacheTimeout value to optimize a WINS client.* **Answer B** *is incorrect because the Windows NT Resource Kit does not have a WINS optimizer.*

| 584 | CONFIGURING THE **DHCP** SERVICE TO OPTIMIZE NETWORK TRAFFIC |

Q: *Which of the following methods can you use to optimize your DHCP server service?*

Choose all answers that apply:

    A.   *Extend the lease duration.*

    B.   *Adjust the ReplicationGovernor parameters in the Registry.*

    C.   *Extend the DHCP threshold on your routers.*

    D.   *Configure your DHCP servers to replicate IP address information to each other.*

As the administrator of your Windows NT network, you will want to optimize every aspect of your network's performance. Although you can do very little to optimize your DHCP server, there are a couple of things you can do to enhance its performance. For example, all DHCP clients receive lease duration information from their DHCP servers. You can change the lease duration settings to enhance network performance. A DHCP server's default configuration will lease IP addresses to DHCP clients for three days. All DHCP clients will renew their IP address lease assignments at one-half the lease duration. You can change the lease duration from within *DHCP Manager*. To change a DHCP service's lease duration, perform the following steps:

    1.   Click your mouse on the Start menu and select the Programs submenu Administrative Tools group *DHCP Manager* program. Windows NT will open the *DHCP Manager*.

2. Within the *DHCP Manager,* click your mouse on the scope for which you want to set lease duration. The *DHCP Manager* will highlight that scope.

3. Within the *DHCP Manager,* select the Scope menu Properties option. The *DHCP Manger* will open the Scope Properties dialog box.

4. Within the Scope Properties dialog box, click your mouse in the *Limited To* field, type the lease duration you want to set, and click your mouse on the OK button. The *DHCP Manager* will set the new lease duration

Other than the lease duration, the only configuration change you can make to a DHCP server to enhance its performance are to the DHCP threshold on your routers. Most newer routers will forward DHCP client broadcasts to other subnets on the network. You can configure how much time the router will wait before forwarding the broadcast. This gives the DHCP client enough time to get its address from a local DHCP server before the router forwards the request onward to a remote DHCP server. You must read your router's documentation to configure it.

*Answers A and C are correct because you can extend the IP address lease duration, or extend the DHCP threshold on your routers to optimize your DHCP server service, or do both. **Answer B** is incorrect because you use the ReplicationGovernor parameter to configure Directory Database synchronization; it has nothing to do with DHCP. **Answer D** is incorrect because you cannot configure DHCP servers to replicate their IP address information to each other.*

| 585 | ANALYZING *TCP/IP* FILE SESSION TRAFFIC |

Q: Within TCP/IP file session establishment, there will not be a NetBIOS session establishment.

True or False?

In computer networking, you will often hear about connection, and *connectionless-oriented networking.* A *connection-oriented protocol* requires a session establishment and connection between two computers before the sending computer can transmit any data. Additionally, in connection-oriented networking, if a computer sends any part of the transmission incorrectly, the sending side of the connection will request that the sending computer re-send any part received which was not correct. In connectionless-oriented networking, the protocol does not ensure the data's safe delivery.

Each of the three major protocols Windows NT includes provide both connection and connectionless-oriented networking communication. Because TCP/IP is a suite of protocols, there are connection and connectionless protocols within it. TCP is a connect-oriented protocol that is built into TCP/IP, while User Datagram Protocol (UDP, which is also part of TCP/IP) is a connectionless-oriented protocol.

When you use the TCP/IP protocol suite to establish a connection to a remote computer, you will use the TCP protocol to send and receive files and folders. TCP establishes a session between the two computers before you can transmit any file or folder.

If you use TCP/IP to connect to a remote computer, the first step in the process is for your computer to resolve the remote computer's NetBIOS name to an IP address. After your computer gets the remote computer's IP address, your computer must then resolve the IP address to the physical address of the network adapter card in the remote computer. Your computer will use the Address Resolution Protocol (ARP) to get the remote computer's network card's physical address. After your computer gets the remote computer's physical address, the next step is for your computer to establish a TCP session. The TCP session establishment is sometimes called a *TCP three-way handshake.* The TCP session establishment generates three frames of traffic, and a total of 180 bytes.

After you establish your TCP session, you must also establish a NetBIOS session with the remote computer. As you have learned, Microsoft networking requires that you create a NetBIOS session before any further communication can take place between the two computers. Every transport protocol in Windows NT will establish NetBIOS sessions before data transfer takes place.

The Answer is False because you will always have a NetBIOS session when you use any protocol in Windows NT.

---

586 — UNDERSTANDING MAC ADDRESS RESOLUTION

Q: A MAC address is also known as a _____ address.

Choose the best answer:

    A.   Host address

    B.   IP address

    C.   Physical address

    D.   Memory address

In Tip 585, you learned that client computers must resolve a remote computer's physical address before a connection can take place. Whether you are using TCP/IP or any other protocol in Windows NT, the client computer must resolve the remote computer's network address to the physical address of the network card on the remote computer. For the MCSE exams, you must only know about TCP/IP physical address resolution.

When a computer using TCP/IP wants to connect to a remote computer, the entire process consists of two general steps. First, the client computer must resolve the remote computer's NetBIOS name to an IP address. Second, the client computer must resolve the IP address to a physical address for the remote computer's network interface card.

TCP/IP uses the Address Resolution Protocol (ARP) to determine the physical addresses for network adapter cards from a computer's IP address. ARP is more than just a protocol within Windows NT, it is also a utility. At the command prompt, you can type *ARP address*, where *address* represents the IP address of the remote computer, to find the physical network card address for a remote computer. Physical network adapter card addresses are also known as Media Access Control (MAC) addresses.

Answer C is correct because the terms physical address and MAC address are interchangeable. Answers A, B, and D are incorrect because none of the answers correctly state another name for the MAC address.

---

587 — UNDERSTANDING TREE-CONNECT REQUESTS

Q: Which of the following does the client send to a server during a tree-connect request?

Choose all correct answers:

A.   *The name of the user sending the request.*

B.   *The password of the user sending the request.*

C.   *The domain the user is from.*

D.   *The share name the user wants to connect to.*

Over the past several Tips, you have learned that when a client computer wants to connect to a host computer, the client computer must first establish a series of sessions and address resolutions. The last thing a client computer must do before it transfers files or folders is send a *tree-connect request* to the server.

After the client computer finishes all name resolution, address resolution, and session establishment, it must then send a *Server Message Block (SMB) session setup* and a tree-connect request to the server. The SMB session setup and tree-connect request-frame contains the user's name, password, and the share name of the share to which the user is requesting a connection. The server, after it receives the SMB session setup and tree-connect request, will respond to the client with an acknowledgment frame.

Answers A, B, and D are correct because a tree connect request includes the user name, password, and the share name the connection request is for. Answer C is incorrect because the tree-connect request does not include the requesting user's domain name.

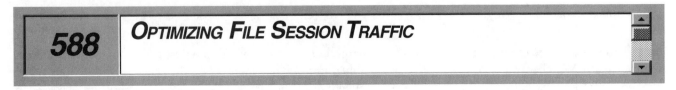

588   OPTIMIZING FILE SESSION TRAFFIC

Q: *You can remove protocols you are not using in your network to optimize your file session traffic.*

     True or False?

A network administrator should constantly strive to enhance the network's performance. One area a network administrator can optimize is the *file session traffic*, which occurs when users transfer files and directories across the network. Most file session traffic occurs after the computer establishes the protocol session. Microsoft makes recommendations on two performance areas, the number of protocols to install, and the distance between clients and servers. The more transport protocols you have installed, the more connection requests each computer will send each time it tries to make a connection across the network. In Microsoft networking, each protocol you have installed will send connection requests simultaneously with the other protocols, which will create unnecessary network traffic. Therefore, you should remove from the network any protocols you are not using because only one transport protocol (or, at most, two) is generally necessary in most networks. The other way you can enhance network performance is to situate clients and servers close together. This does not mean within the same LAN—that is, geographically close together. "Close together" means only that you should try not to place servers on the other side of WAN links. Try to keep servers in the same LAN as the clients that access them most frequently.

*The answer is **True** because you can remove unnecessary protocols to optimize file session traffic.*

589   UNDERSTANDING THE TRAFFIC GENERATED BY CLIENT BROWSERS

Q: Which of the following are examples of client browser traffic?

Choose all correct answers:

> *A.   Host announcements*
>
> *B.   Get browse list*
>
> *C.   Get backup list*
>
> *D.   Get share list*

In Tip 372, you learned how Microsoft networks rely on the browsing process to see computers within the network. In other Tips, you have learned about host announcement, browser elections, and the different browser types. When you consider network performance, it is also important that you understand the network traffic these browser components generate.

Every Microsoft computer will send a host announcement every minute for the first five minutes the computer is up, and then one time every twelve minutes thereafter. Each host announcement will generate one 243-byte frame of network traffic. After a Microsoft computer is up and has made its host announcements, the client computer must retrieve a browse list of the computers that have shared resources, so the client can connect to any available network resources. The client will send one 215-byte frame only once to the master browser to request a list of backup browsers. Your computer must repeat this connection process only if you have shut it down. After the server receives the request for a list of backup browsers, it will respond with a *get backup list* response frame. The *get backup list* response frame's length varies because each backup browser will add 27 bytes to the frame's size. The more backup browsers you have, the larger the response frame's length will be.

After the client computer receives the get backup list response frame, it will select a backup browser from the list and send the backup browser a *get browse list* frame. The backup browser's response can generate either very little or a great deal of network traffic, depending on the number of entries in the list. When a client computer receives a browse list, it can use entries in the list to select a computer in the network to connect to. The last thing the client computer will do before it connects to a remote computer is send a *get share list* frame to the remote computer. The *get share list* frame is a request for the shared resources on the remote computer.

Answers A, B, C, and D are all correct because each describes a client browser function that generates network traffic.

Q: Which of the following are examples of optimization methods you can use to enhance client browser traffic?

Choose correct answer:

> *A.   Disable unnecessary protocols.*
>
> *B.   Pause the NetLogon service on your domain controllers.*
>
> *C.   Reduce the number of potential browsers.*
>
> *D.   Eliminate unnecessary services.*

To optimize your client browser traffic, you must examine your servers to see if they have any unnecessary services or protocols. In previous Tips, you have learned how Microsoft computers announce their presence in the network and register their NetBIOS names. Each service a Microsoft computer can provide will register another NetBIOS name (in addition to the computer's NetBIOS name). On just one computer, the additional NetBIOS names will not generate much network browser traffic, but if you have several servers that have unnecessary services, the additional names may become an issue.

In addition to eliminating unnecessary services or protocols, you can optimize your Windows NT networks by reducing the number of transport protocols you have installed. Each network transport protocol will send simultaneously with all the other transport protocols, which will create unnecessary network traffic. To avoid such traffic, remove any unused protocols.

The last client browser traffic area you can optimize is to reduce how many potential browsers can be on the network. Every Microsoft computer, by default, is a potential browser, which means each one has the potential to become a backup or a master browser. You can configure your Microsoft computers to not be potential browsers; the method you use to do so is different on each Windows operating system. See the applicable Microsoft Resource Kit for details on how to prevent your Microsoft client computers from becoming potential browsers.

Answers A, C, and D are correct because you can disable unnecessary network protocols, disable unnecessary services, and reduce how many potential browsers optimize browser traffic. Answer B is incorrect because if you pause the NetLogon service on your domain controllers, it will stop your domain controller from logging any users onto the network.

591	## UNDERSTANDING A NETWORK'S APPROXIMATE CLIENT TRAFFIC PERCENTAGES

Q: In an average Microsoft Windows NT network, you should expect client browsing to take up approximately what network traffic percentage?

Choose the best answer:

A.   10 percent

B.   20 percent

C.   30 percent

D.   40 percent

When you analyze network traffic, it is important to recognize that the client initiates the vast majority of network traffic. Understanding the composition of that traffic is important for determining the network's capacity and workload. Microsoft's official curriculum courses state the following figures:

- Approximately 48 percent of your client-to-server network traffic will be Internet browsing traffic

- Approximately 30 percent of your client-to-server network traffic will be LAN browser traffic

- Approximately 12 percent of your client-to-server network traffic will be file sessions

- Approximately 6 percent of your client-to-server network traffic will be log-on validation traffic

- The remaining 6 percent of your client-to-server network traffic will be equally divided between DHCP, WINS, and DNS

If you know where most of your client traffic comes from, you can better optimize the services that will support your network users. You must run your own tests to determine your actual breakdown of network usage on your network.

Answer C is correct because you should expect client browsing to take up approximately 30 percent of your total client network traffic. Answers A, B, and D are incorrect because none of the answers correctly state the average percentage of browsing network traffic.

592   ESTABLISHING SESSIONS AND SECURE CHANNELS

Q: *Windows NT Server Primary Domain Controllers and Windows NT Server Backup Domain Controllers must establish a session, and then a secure channel to verify the Directory Database.*

True or False?

As you have learned, although Windows NT domains can contain only one Primary Domain Controller (PDC), they can contain numerous Backup Domain Controllers (BDCs). The Windows NT Server Primary Domain Controller manages the entire Directory Database, which contains every user, group, and computer account in the domain. Periodically, the Primary Domain Controller will give each Backup Domain Controllers in the domain an updated copy of the Directory Database so that users can log on from anywhere in the network. How frequently the Primary Domain Controller updates the Backup Domain Controllers will vary from network to network, but is generally every ten minutes or less.

When a Backup Domain Controller comes on-line, it must verify the Directory Database with the Primary Domain Controller—that is, it must make sure that its Directory Database matches the Primary Domain Controller's database. To verify the Directory Database, the Backup Domain Controller must establish a session, and then a secure channel it will use to communicate with the Primary Domain Controller.

The Backup Domain Controller generates approximately nine frames (containing about 1,200 bytes of traffic) to establish a session. After the Backup Domain Controller establishes the session, it must set up a secure channel, which will generate approximately eight frames (containing about 1,550 bytes of traffic). After the Windows NT Server Domain Controller verifies the Directory Database, the Backup Domain Controller can synchronize with the Primary Domain Controller.

*The answer is **True** because Windows NT Server Domain Controllers must establish a session, and then a secure channel to verify the Directory Database.*

593   UNDERSTANDING IMPORTING TRUSTED ACCOUNTS

Q: *Every time you assign permissions to a group account or a user account from a trusted domain, you must import the accounts list from the trusted domain.*

True or False?

If you are the administrator of a large Windows NT network, you will likely have multiple domains on the network. A Microsoft multi-domain environment will always have Trust Relationships between the domains that make up the network. As you have learned, a Trust Relationship is a logical link between two Windows NT domains. You will establish a Trust Relationship for administrative purposes—such as duplicating Directory Database information be-tween domains. Trust Relationships in a Microsoft multi-domain environment enable an administrator to manage the entire network with one administrative user account.

In most Microsoft multi-domain environments, you will separate the users from the resources. You will have domains that contain only user accounts, and you will have domains that have resources, but no user accounts. Domains that contain user accounts in a Microsoft multi-domain environment are *master domains*. Domains that contain only resources are *resource domains*.

When an administrator wants to grant permissions to a resource in a resource domain, or to a user from a master domain, the Windows NT Server in the resource domain must import the user accounts from the Trusted domain. Importing the user accounts between domains generates a varying amount of network traffic (depending on the num-ber of users and groups, the number of different permissions, and so on). Every time an administrator grants permis-sions to a user or to a group from a Trusted domain, the Windows NT Server in the Trusting domain must import the accounts from the Trusted domain.

The answer is **True** *because every time you assign users or groups permission to resources in your domain, from a Trusted domain, you must import the list of accounts from the Trusted domain.*

594   **CONFIGURING THE REGISTRY MASTERPERIODICITY KEY**

Q: *The MasterPeriodicity subkey in the Registry specifies how often a backup browser will contact the master browser.*

True or False?

As you have learned, one of the most traffic-generating procedures that the network must perform during normal operation is the browsing process. Although Windows NT will automatically manage most network traffic that com-puters produce through browsing, you must do some things to enhance the Microsoft browsing service's performance, such as removing unnecessary network transport protocols. When you remove such protocols, network traffic related to browser announcements will decrease throughout the network. You can also disable the browser entries service. Each Microsoft computer that runs a server service, such as Windows NT Workstation, Windows NT Server, Windows 95, and Windows for Workgroups, will announce its presence on the network. You only need the server service to run on that computer if you want users to be able to connect to that computer. If you have client computers that will not be acting as servers, you should turn off the server service on those client computers. Because each operating system is different, if you want to disable the server service on your Microsoft clients, refer to the applicable Microsoft Resource Kit for details on how you will disable your server service.

To enhance your browser traffic's performance, you can also change the *MasterPeriodicity*, or the *BackupPeriodicity* subkeys within the Registry. You can edit the Registry and add a *MasterPeriodicity* value to optimize Windows NT computers that are master browsers. The *MasterPeriodicity* value controls how often the master browser will contact the domain master browser. The default setting is twelve minutes. If you change the default setting's value, you can control the network traffic that Microsoft browsing generates when it sends updated browse lists to the domain master browser. Remember, the longer you make the time between calls to update the network browse list, the less network traffic. However, if you make the amount of time between browse list updates too long, users will not see up-to-date browse lists (meaning that the browse lists that they see may be inaccurate). To add the *MasterPeriodicity* value to the Registry of the Windows NT computer that maintains the master browser, perform the following steps:

1. Click your mouse on the Start menu and select the Run option. Windows NT will open the Run dialog box.

2. Within the Run dialog box, type *Regedt32* and click your mouse on the OK button. Windows NT will open the *Registry Editor* program.

3. Within the Registry Editor, double-click your mouse on the *HKEY_LOCAL_MACHINE \SYSTEM* hive. *Registry Editor* will expand the *SYSTEM* hive.

4. Within the *SYSTEM* hive, double-click your mouse on the *CurrentControlSet* subkey. The *Registry Editor* will expand the *CurrentControlSet* subkey.

5. Within the *CurrentControlSet* subkey, double-click your mouse on the *Service* subkey. The *Registry Editor* will expand the *Service* subkey.

6. Within the *Service* subkey, double-click your mouse on the *Browser* subkey. The *Registry Editor* will expand the *Browser* subkey.

7. Within the *Browser* subkey, double-click your mouse on the *Parameters* subkey. The *Registry Editor* will expand the *Parameters* subkey.

8. Within the *Parameters* subkey, click your mouse on the Edit menu and select the Add Value option. The *Registry Editor* will display the Add Value dialog box.

9. Within the Add Value dialog box, type *MasterPeriodicity* in the *Value Name* field. Click your mouse on the Data Type drop-down list and select REG_DWORD. Click your mouse on the OK button. The *Registry Editor* will display the DWORD Editor dialog box.

10. Within the DWORD Editor dialog box, type a value between 300 and 4,294,967 (these values range from five minutes to forty-nine days and eight hours). Click your mouse on the OK button. The *Registry Editor* will close the DWORD Editor and the Add Value dialog boxes.

The answer is **False** *because the MasterPeriodicity subkey in the Registry will let you configure the frequency with which the master browser will contact the domain master browser.*

595   CONFIGURING THE REGISTRY BACKUPPERIODICITY KEY

Q: *The BackupPeriodicity setting in the Registry will let you configure the frequency with which a backup browser will contact the Master Browser.*

True or False?

In Tip 594, you learned how to add the *MasterPeriodicity* value to your Master Browser's Registry and to change the frequency with which a Master Browser will contact the domain Master Browser to enhance your master browser's performance. You can also enhance the performance of your backup browsers' calls to the Master Browser in the subnet. Each backup browser will, by default, contact the master browser every twelve minutes to request an up-to-date browse list. As the administrator, you can add the *BackupPeriodicity* value to the Registry of the computers that contain your backup browser list to change the frequency with which a backup browser will contact the master browser. To add the *BackupPeriodicity* value to the Registry, perform the following steps:

1. Click your mouse on the Start menu and select the Run option. Windows NT will open the Run dialog box.

2. Within the Run dialog box, type *Regedt32*, and click your mouse on the OK button. Windows NT will open the *Registry Editor*.

3. Within the *Registry Editor*, double-click your mouse on the *HKEY_LOCAL_MACHINE \SYSTEM*. The *Registry Editor* program will expand the *SYSTEM* hive.

4. Within the *SYSTEM* hive, double-click your mouse on the *CurrentControlSet* subkey. The *Registry Editor* will expand the *CurrentControlSet* subkey.

5. Within the *CurrentControlSet* subkey, double-click your mouse on the *Service* subkey. The *Registry Editor* will expand the *Service* subkey.

6. Within the *Service* subkey, double-click your mouse on the *Browser* subkey. The *Registry Editor* will expand the *Browser* subkey.

7. Within the *Browser* subkey, double-click your mouse on the *Parameters* subkey. The *Registry Editor* will expand the *Parameters* subkey.

8. Within the *Parameters* subkey, click your mouse on the Edit menu and select the Add Value option. The *Registry Editor* will display the Add Value dialog box.

9. Within the Add Value dialog box, type *BackupPeriodicity* in the *Value Name* field. Click your mouse on the Data Type drop-down list and select REG_DWORD. Click your mouse on the OK button. The *Registry Editor* will display the DWORD Editor dialog box.

10. Within the DWORD Editor dialog box, type a value between 300 to 4,294,967 (these values range from five minutes to forty-nine days and eight hours) and click your mouse on the OK button. The *Registry Editor* will close the DWORD Editor and the Add Value dialog boxes.

11. Shut down and restart your Windows NT computer for these registry changes to take effect.

The answer is **True** *because the BackupPeriodicity subkey in the Registry will let you configure the frequency with which a backup browser will contact a master browser.*

596   **INTRODUCING ADVANCED BROWSING ISSUES**

Q: *You are the administrator of a large Windows NT network that has multiple sites. You are having problems with users being able to see computers in browse lists. Specifically, when a user tries to connect to the computer, the user receives a messages that states, "the computer cannot be found." After you examine the problem, you discover that this only happens when users connect to computers in other subnets than their own. What is the most probable cause of this problem?*

Choose the best answer:

A. *The master browser in the other subnet is down.*

B. *The remote subnet is not connected to the internetwork.*

C. *The user can see the computer in the browse window because of the way that Microsoft network browsing works, but when the user tries to connect to the computer, the user's computer can not get NetBIOS name resolution.*

D. *The NetLogon service is not running on the remote subnet's master browser.*

In complex Windows NT multi-domain environments, browsing can be a problem because it is possible for a Microsoft client computer to be visible in a browse list, but unavailable on the network. Generally, seeing computers in the browse window but being unable to access them is because most routers will not forward NetBIOS broadcasts. Because the routers in the network will not forward the NetBIOS broadcasts that every Microsoft client uses to resolve a computer's NetBIOS name into an IP address, the server never receives the request for name resolution and the client never connects. The best way to eliminate the user's problem of being unable to access computers the user sees in the browse window is to implement a Windows Internet Name Service (WINS) server.

A single WINS server will work for multiple subnets. You will configure each WINS client computer with the WINS server's IP address in the network. When you do so, all WINS-related network traffic will be directed to the WINS server's IP address, and will not require any name resolution.

Answer C is correct because Microsoft browsing will let you see computers in remote subnets, but you may not be able to resolve the remote computer's NetBIOS name to an IP address. Answer A is incorrect because if the master browser in the other subnet is down, Windows NT will automatically elect another Master Browser. Answer B is incorrect because if the remote subnet were not connected to the internetwork, you would not see the remote computer in a browse list. Answer D is incorrect because the NetLogon service does not have to be running on the remote master browser to connect to remote resources.

597   INTRODUCING *WINS* REPLICATION

Q: *WINS replication is the process of copying the WINS database from one WINS server to another, for local-name resolution of remote computers.*

True or False?

As you learned in Tip 363, Microsoft's Windows Internet Name Service (WINS) resolves NetBIOS computer names to IP addresses dynamically. In a large Microsoft Windows NT network, it is likely that a single WINS server will not be sufficient to handle every client's name resolution needs. A single WINS server can comfortably accommodate up to 10,000 WINS clients. However, Microsoft always recommends having at least one backup WINS server—just as you have Backup Domain Controllers. Whether you are implementing multiple WINS servers for backup or you have more than 10,000 users, you will want to configure your WINS servers to replicate to each other.

WINS replication is the process of one WINS server copying its WINS database to another WINS server. You should replicate your WINS databases so that every WINS client will be able to resolve all computers' NetBIOS names to IP address, network wide. You will learn more about WINS replication in Tips 598 and 599.

The answer is True because WINS replication is the process you use to copy the WINS database from one WINS server to another. You would copy the WINS database so that a local WINS server could handle a remote computer's name resolution.

598   CONFIGURING A *WINS* PUSH PARTNER

Q: *You should configure a WINS Push Partner if you have fast WAN links between your WINS server.*

True or False?

In Tip 597, you learned about Microsoft's WINS server replication. An important part of WINS server replication is configuring a WINS server to be *a push partner*. A WINS push partner is a WINS server that notifies its partners when the WINS server reaches an administrator-defined number of database entries. The default number of changes that a WINS server that you have configured as a push partner will reach before it sends an announcement is 20. You should implement a WINS push partner when you have fast WAN links between sites because a WINS push partner will replicate only when it reaches the administrator-defined number of changes, as shown in Figure 598.

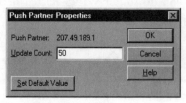

Figure 598 The WINS Server Push Partner Properties dialog box.

To configure your WINS server as a push partner, perform the following steps:

1. Click your mouse on the Start menu and select the Programs submenu Administrative Tools group *WINS Manager* program. Windows NT will start the *WINS Manager*.

2. Within the *WINS Manager*, select the Server menu Replication Partners option. The *WINS Manager* will display the Replication Partners dialog box.

3. Within the Replication Partners dialog box, click your mouse on the Add button. The *WINS Manager* will display the Add WINS Server dialog box.

4. Within the Add WINS Server dialog box, click your mouse on the *WINS Server* field, and type the name, or WINS server IP address you want to add as a push partner. Click your mouse on the OK button. *WINS Manager* will close the Add WINS Server dialog box, and return you to the Replication Partners dialog box.

5. Within the Replication Partners dialog box, click your mouse on the *Push Partner* checkbox in the Replication Options section of the dialog box. Click your mouse on the Configure button. The *WINS Manager* will display the Push Partner Properties dialog box.

6. Within the Push Partner Properties dialog box, click your mouse on the *Update Count* field, and type the number of database entries you want to trigger a replication event. Click your mouse on the OK button. The *WINS Manager* will configure the WINS replication, and return you to the Replication Partners dialog box.

7. Within the Replication Partners dialog box, click your mouse on the OK button. Windows NT will close the *WINS Manager*.

The answer is **True** *because Microsoft recommends that you configure a WINS push partner when you have fast links between your WINS server. A WINS server that you have configured as a push partner will replicate its database only when it reaches a pre-configured number of updates.*

599   CONFIGURING A *WINS* PULL PARTNER

Q: *In which of the following circumstances would you configure your WINS server to be a pull partner?*

Choose all correct answers:

A.   *If you have fast WAN links between your WINS server.*

B.   *If you have slow WAN links between your WINS servers.*

C.   *When you need NetBIOS name resolution for remote computers at the WINS server that will be the Pull Partner.*

D.   *When you need NetBIOS name resolution at the WINS server to which your pull partner is connected.*

As you have learned, in any Windows NT network that includes routers between its subnets, you will generally configure a WINS server to perform name resolution. As the administrator of a Windows NT network, you must make decisions on how to configure your WINS server. One thing you must decide is whether to make a WINS server a push partner or a *pull partner*. A pull partner is a WINS server that will request any new WINS database entries from its partners. A pull partner requests database updates by requesting only the entries that have version numbers greater than the last version number the WINS pull partner received on the last replication.

As you learned in Tip 598, you should make your WINS servers push partners when you have fast WAN links between sites. You should configure a WINS server to be a pull partner when you have slow WAN links between sites. This is because an administrator can configure a WINS pull partner to replicate at specific times, such as when the network is quiet (for example, overnight). To configure your WINS server as a pull partner, perform the following steps:

1. Click your mouse on the Start menu and select the Programs submenu Administrative Tools group *WINS Manager* program. Windows NT will start the *WINS Manager* program.

2. Within the *WINS Manager,* select the Server menu Replication Partners option. The *WINS Manager* will display the Replication Partners dialog box.

3. Within the Replication Partners dialog box, click your mouse on the Add button. The *WINS Manager* will display the Add WINS Server dialog box.

4. Within the Add WINS Server dialog box, click your mouse on the *WINS Server* field, and type the name, or the WINS server's IP address, you want to add as a pull partner. Click your mouse on the OK button. The *WINS Manager* will close the Add WINS Server dialog box, and return you to the Replication Partners dialog box.

5. Within the Replication Partners dialog box, click your mouse on the Pull Partner checkbox in the dialog box's Replication Options section. Click your mouse on the Configure button. The *WINS Manager* will display the Pull Partner Properties dialog box, as Figure 599 shows.

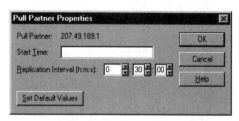

Figure 599 *The WINS server Pull Partner Properties dialog box.*

6. Within the Pull Partner Properties dialog box, click your mouse on the *Start Time* field and type the start time that you want to trigger a replication event. Click your mouse on the *Replication Interval* field and set the time amount you want between replication events. Click your mouse on the OK button. The *WINS Manager* will configure the WINS replication and return you to the Replication Partners dialog box.

7. Within the Replication Partners dialog box, click your mouse on the OK button. Windows NT will close the *WINS Manager*.

Answers B and C are correct because you will configure a WINS server as a pull partner to resolve NetBIOS names to IP addresses on your pull partner, and because you have slow WNA links between your WINS servers. Answers A and D are incorrect because neither answer correctly states why you would configure a WINS server to be a pull partner.

600   ANALYZING DOMAIN NAME SYSTEM (DNS) NETWORK TRAFFIC

Q: *Which of the following are examples of DNS network traffic?*

Choose all correct answers:

> A.   DNS Query
>
> B.   DNS Query Response
>
> C.   DNS NetBIOS Name Resolution
>
> D.   DNS Replication

A *Microsoft Domain Name System (DNS)* server is a service running on top of a Windows NT Server operating system. The Microsoft DNS service is completely compatible with existing Internet DNS architecture. As the administrator of your Microsoft Windows NT network, you may choose to install a DNS server. Remember, DNS servers resolve computers' host names into IP addresses. In order to access a site on the Internet, you must have a DNS server resolve the Internet site name into the IP addresses that your computer will use to access the site. DNS does not generate a lot of network traffic but, as the administrator, you should know what all of your network traffic is.

A host computer requiring DNS name resolution will send one small network frame to the DNS server which requests the server, provide the host with the name resolution. The DNS server will respond with a one frame response, if it has the name resolution in its local database. If the DNS server does not have the host name resolution in the local database, the DNS server must perform an iterative DNS lookup. This means the DNS server will contact other DNS server's on the host's behalf. An iterative lookup will likely generate several frames of network traffic, but all frames will be small. The only other network traffic you will see from DNS is when an administrator has configured DNS servers to replicate their database information to each other. When the administrator configures the DNS servers to replicate to each other, there will be several network frames, and depending on the size of the DNS database the servers are replicating, a varying amount of network traffic.

Answers A, B, and D are correct because hosts will send DNS queries to DNS servers, the DNS servers will respond with DNS query responses, and DNS server can replicate their databases to each other. Answer C is incorrect because DNS does not have anything to do with NetBIOS name; DNS resolves host names.

601   UNDERSTANDING DOMAIN NAME SYSTEM (DNS) REPLICATION

Q: *You would configure DNS database replication to reduce DNS lookups across WAN links.*

True or False?

Microsoft Domain Name System (DNS) servers resolve computers' host names into Internet Protocol (IP) addresses that clients can use to connect to the remote hosts. Resolving host names into IP addresses is an essential step before clients can communicate with the host server over the Internet or through any other connection that uses Transport Control Protocol/Internet Protocol (TCP/IP) as its underlying communications protocol. Administrators manually create and maintain all records in a DNS server. In other words, an administrator must create each resource record on the DNS server, as opposed to WINS, which resolves NetBIOS names and is dynamic.

To improve system performance within a large organization, you may need more than one DNS server. When you require multiple DNS servers, you will create a primary DNS server, and then make each additional server a secondary name server. Each secondary name server will receive database updates from DNS servers you have configured as master name servers (usually, your primary name server). (Receiving database updates means you will have the same DNS database on multiple computers, which will provide redundancy of the DNS database.)

Clients requiring DNS hostname resolution can get it faster if the local-area network (LAN) has a DNS server because the LAN will not have to route the client's DNS name resolution request to another subnet on the WAN.

*The answer is **True** because you would configure DNS servers to replicate their databases to each other to reduce the amount of DNS traffic that crosses wide area network (WAN) links in your network.*

602   ANALYZING DOMAIN NAME SYSTEM (DNS) REPLICATION TRAFFIC

Q: *What do you call the process when a DNS server updates its database from another DNS server?*

Choose the best answer:

    A.   *DNS database replication*

    B.   *DNS synchronization*

    C.   *A zone transfer*

    D.   *DNS update transfer*

As you have learned, in Microsoft Windows NT networks that have multiple Domain Name System (DNS) servers, the secondary name servers will receive DNS database updates from a master DNS server. When a DNS master name server replicates its DNS database to a secondary name server, the process is known as a *zone transfer*.

The first step in the zone transfer process is for the secondary name server to query the primary name server to verify that it is active as the primary name server. After verifying the primary name server, the zone transfer process generates one query frame and one response frame. The next step in the process is for the secondary name server to establish a Transmission Control Protocol (TCP) session, which is a standard three-frame conversation.

After the secondary name server establishes the TCP session with the primary name server, the secondary name server requests the zone transfer. The actual zone transfer will generate a varying amount of network traffic—depending on the size of the DNS database.

*Answer **C** is correct because a DNS server's replication process is a zone transfer. Answer **A** is incorrect because DNS database replication describes the process, but is not the correct name for the process. Answers **B** and **D** are incorrect because neither answer is a proper description or name for a DNS zone transfer.*

603 CONFIGURING THE DOMAIN NAME SYSTEM (DNS) REFRESH INTERVAL

Q: *By default, a Microsoft DNS server that you have configured as a secondary name server will contact the primary name server every 60 minutes to request a zone transfer.*

True or False?

As an administrator, you must know what network traffic exists on your Windows NT network, including both normal workflow traffic and specialized traffic, such as DNS replication traffic. You can optimize your DNS replication traffic in three areas: *Refresh Interval*, *Retry Interval*, and *Expire Time*. You will learn how to configure the Retry Interval and the Expire Time settings in Tips 604 and 605.

The Refresh Interval lets you configure the amount of time a secondary name server will wait before it queries the DNS primary name server to see if the primary name server's database has changed. If the primary name server's database has changed, the secondary name server will request a zone transfer. The default value for the Refresh Interval is 60 minutes. You can use Windows NT's *DNS Manager* program to configure the Refresh Interval. To configure the Refresh Interval, perform the following steps:

1. Click your mouse on the Start menu and select the Programs submenu. Within the Programs submenu, select the Administrative Tools group *DNS Manager* program. Windows NT will open the *DNS Manager* program.
2. Within the *DNS Manager* program, right-click your mouse on the zone for which you want to configure DNS replication. *DNS Manager* will display a pop-up menu.
3. Within the pop-up menu, click your mouse on the Properties option. *DNS Manager* will display the Zone Properties dialog box.
4. Within the Zone Properties dialog box, click your mouse on the *Refresh Interval* field and type the value you want to set for the Refresh Interval (between 1 minute and 999,999 years). Next, click your mouse on the OK button. *DNS Manager* will close the Zone Properties dialog box and return you to the *DNS Manager* window.
5. Within the *DNS Manager*, select the DNS menu and Exit option. Windows NT will close the *DNS Manager*.

The answer is **True** *because a secondary name server will (by default) contact its primary name server every 60 minutes to request a zone transfer if the primary name server has changed its database.*

604 CONFIGURING THE DOMAIN NAME SYSTEM (DNS) RETRY INTERVAL

Q: *The Retry Interval is the amount of time a secondary name server will wait before it tries to initiate a zone transfer after a failed zone transfer.*

True or False?

In Tip 603, you learned how an administrator can configure the Domain Name System (DNS) Refresh Interval to optimize replication performance. You can also change the Retry Interval to help you optimize your DNS replication traffic. You configure the Retry Interval to set the amount of time a secondary name server will wait before initiating a zone transfer after a failure. For example, when a DNS secondary name server tries to contact a master name server and fails, it looks at the Retry Interval to determine how long to wait before trying again. Typically, a zone transfer will fail because of network traffic, because of some communication error between the two systems, or some other similar situation which is independent of the zone transfer itself. You will, as with the Refresh Interval, use the *DNS Manager* program to configure the Retry Interval. To configure the Retry Interval, perform the following steps:

1. Click your mouse on the Start menu and select the Programs submenu. Within the Programs submenu, select the Administrative Tools group *DNS Manager* program. Windows NT will open the *DNS Manager* program.

2. Within the *DNS Manager* program, right-click your mouse on the zone for which you want to configure DNS replication. *DNS Manager* will display a pop-up menu.

3. Within the pop-up menu, click your mouse on the Properties option. *DNS Manager* will display the Zone Properties dialog box.

4. Within the Zone Properties dialog box, click your mouse on the *Retry Interval* field and type the value you want to set for the Retry Interval (between 1 minute and 999,999 years). Next, click your mouse on the OK button. *DNS Manager* will close the Zone Properties dialog box and return you to the *DNS Manager* window.

5. Within the *DNS Manager,* select the DNS menu Exit option. Windows NT will close the *DNS Manager.*

*The answer is **True** because the Retry Interval is the amount of time a secondary name server will wait before trying a zone transfer after one has failed.*

605   **CONFIGURING THE DOMAIN NAME SYSTEM (DNS) EXPIRE TIME**

Q: *The Expire Time is the maximum amount of time a secondary name server will wait before initiating a full replication of the primary name server's DNS database.*

True or False?

In Tips 603 and 604, you have learned how you can configure the Refresh Interval and the Retry Interval using the Zone Properties dialog box. You will use the same dialog box to configure the Expire Time setting. As you have learned, a secondary name server will contact the master name server at the Refresh Interval. If the secondary name server cannot find the master name server, the secondary name server will wait for the amount of time the Retry Interval specifies before trying to perform the zone transfer again. However, if the secondary name server cannot find the master name server after a period of time you specify (or if the zone transfers continue to fail beyond a given length of time), the secondary name server will no longer respond to name queries. The period of time you specify beyond which the secondary name server should no longer respond to name queries is the *Expire Time*. You can configure the Expire Time from the Zone Properties dialog box in the *DNS Manager* program. To set the Expire Time, perform the following steps:

1. Click your mouse on the Start menu and select the Programs submenu. Within the Programs submenu, select the Administrative Tools group *DNS Manager* program. Windows NT will open the *DNS Manager* program.

2. Within the *DNS Manager* program, right-click your mouse on the zone for which you want to configure DNS replication. *DNS Manager* will display a pop-up menu.

3. Within the pop-up menu, click your mouse on the Properties option. *DNS Manager* will display the Zone Properties dialog box.

4. Within the Zone Properties dialog box, click your mouse on the *Expire Time* field and type the value you want to set for the expire time (between 1 minute and 999,999 years). Next, click your mouse on the OK button. *DNS Manager* will return you to the *DNS Manager* window.

5. Within the *DNS Manager*, select the DNS menu Exit option. Windows NT will close the *DNS Manager*.

The answer is **False** *because the Expire Time is the maximum amount of time the secondary name server will continue to respond to name queries even though it cannot contact the primary name server.*

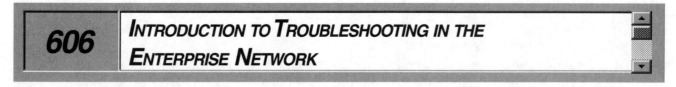

606 | **INTRODUCTION TO TROUBLESHOOTING IN THE ENTERPRISE NETWORK**

Q: Which of the following are examples of administrative troubleshooting responsibilities a Windows NT network administrator would perform?

Choose all answers that apply:

A.   Diagnose problems using your Windows NT architectural knowledge.

B.   Creating new user accounts.

C.   Troubleshooting the Windows NT boot process.

D.   Researching documentation on Microsoft Windows NT.

When you take the Microsoft Certified Systems Engineer (MCSE) track, you will take exams that test your knowledge of Microsoft products and how to implement them in networks as large as 80,000 users. Most people will never work on networks of such a substantial size. However, Microsoft still expects you to know how its products work in diverse environments. When considering networks of such large size, or other networks of unknown composition, Microsoft will generally refer to such networks as enterprise networks. Microsoft defines an *enterprise network* as a network that encompasses multiple sites and, potentially, dissimilar network operating systems, such as Novell NetWare and Unix systems combined with your Windows NT systems. Microsoft will not test your knowledge of how other vendors' products work, but it will require you to know how Microsoft products interact with other network operating systems. To troubleshoot your Microsoft Windows NT enterprise network, you will have to diagnose problems using your knowledge of the Microsoft Windows NT architecture. Much like a surgeon will operate using knowledge of human anatomy, you will strategically diagnose and repair your Windows NT systems. You also must know how a Windows NT system boots. You must know what files Windows NT requires and what happens when one file is missing or corrupt. Additionally, you must know what Windows NT documentation to use to help you administer your Windows NT systems. When you are troubleshooting problems within an enterprise network, a crucial tool that you must have is the *Microsoft Windows NT Resource Kit*, which provides great assistance in resolving network management issues. Troubleshooting in the enterprise network is not that different from how you would troubleshoot a single Windows NT system—except in the sheer number of possible difficulties that can arise, and in the occasional issue that results from integrating multiple operating systems. In fact, in many cases you will use your troubleshooting skills to fix a single system within your network, while other times you may have to use the *Windows NT Resource Kit* to help you decide the best way to fix a major domain problem. Whatever your network problem, your knowledge of basic Microsoft Windows NT troubleshooting is essential.

*Answers A, C, and D are correct because your administrative troubleshooting responsibilities will include diagnosing problems using your Windows NT architectural knowledge, troubleshooting the Windows NT boot process, and researching Microsoft Windows NT documentation. **Answer B** is incorrect because creating user accounts is not a troubleshooting problem.*

607   MICROSOFT TROUBLESHOOTING METHODOLOGY

Q: *What is the Microsoft acronym for its troubleshooting methodology?*

Choose the best answer:

    A.   SAMPLE

    B.   DETECT

    C.   SAVE

    D.   FIND

As you learned in the previous Tip, successfully troubleshooting a network (whether a single-domain model LAN or a multiple-platform WAN) is a crucial skill for Windows NT administrators. Successfully troubleshooting a network does not take any extraordinary skills. The best troubleshooters are administrators who possess a reasonable amount of deductive skills and a basic understanding of how the network works. If you have a basic understanding of what system components the network requires for which system functions, you can usually determine relatively easily and quickly why a system is not responding properly. As you may have guessed, the more you work on a particular system, the better you will get at diagnosing system problems. Although having prior experience with a system is not essential, you will be faster at troubleshooting systems with which you do have experience. Microsoft conducted a poll of administrators to determine why they felt they were successful at troubleshooting. The administrators attributed the majority of their success to knowledge and prior experience, but the polled group also felt that their innate problem solving abilities, research, and luck were crucial in their success. Most professionals find that using a methodology—a pre-set series of steps—to troubleshoot makes their efforts more successful. Microsoft has coined the acronym *DETECT* to define a troubleshooting methodology. Table 607 explains the components of Microsoft's DETECT acronym.

Acronym Letter	Troubleshooting Directive
D	Discover the problem—determine what is causing the breakdown.
E	Explore the boundaries—find what segments of the network the problem effects.
T	Track possible approaches—consider the possible alternatives that you execute to resolve the problem.
E	Execute the approach—after you decide which alternative will best address the problem, apply the solution to the network.
C	Check for success—make sure that the approach you select does not cause additional problems or, worse yet, not solve the original problem.
T	Tie up loose ends—secure hardware cases, collect tools, and return the network or the computer to its original state, ready for the end-user.

Table 607 Using the DETECT acronym to troubleshoot system problems.

Answer B is correct because DETECT is the Microsoft acronym for its troubleshooting methodology. DETECT means Discover the problem, Explore the boundaries, Track possible approaches, Execute the approach, Check for success, and Tie up loose ends. Answers A, C, and D are incorrect because none of the answers accurately state the Microsoft acronym for troubleshooting methodology.

608	UNDERSTANDING THE IMPORTANCE OF THE MICROSOFT WINDOWS NT SERVER RESOURCE KIT

Q: Which of the following statements best describe the importance of the Microsoft Windows NT Resource Kit?

Choose the best answer:

   A.   The Microsoft Windows NT Resource Kit is good to have, but not essential to your network administration.

   B.   The Microsoft Windows NT Resource Kit is essential to your Windows NT administration.

   C.   The Microsoft Windows NT Resource Kit is completely unnecessary to your Windows NT administration.

   D.   The Microsoft Windows NT Resource Kit is only necessary if you have more than one-hundred users in your network.

When you purchase Microsoft Windows NT server or workstation, the documentation for the product is on the CD-ROM. Although you will find the on-line documentation useful in administering and troubleshooting your Windows NT system, the best source of reference materials for Windows NT is the *Microsoft Windows NT Resource Kit*. Essential to administering your Windows NT network, the *Microsoft Windows NT Resource Kit* contains information and utilities you will not find anywhere else.

The *Microsoft Windows NT Resource Kit* is a set of books and utilities that provide an extensive reference library for the Windows NT administrator. You will find examples of information and utilities from the *Windows NT Resource Kit* throughout this book.

Answer B is correct because the Microsoft Windows NT Resource Kit is essential to the administration of your Windows NT network because it contains information and utilities you will not find anywhere else. Answers A, C, and D are incorrect because you will need the Microsoft Windows NT Resource Kit to properly administer your Windows NT network.

609	UNDERSTANDING HOW TO USE THE MICROSOFT WEB SITE FOR TROUBLESHOOTING

Q: Which of the following Web site addresses is the one you will use for Microsoft technical support?

Choose the best answer:

   A.   www.microsoft.com/techsupp

   B.   www.microsoft.com/help

   C.   www.microsoft.com/technet

   D.   www.microsoft.com/support

As you have learned, to properly administer your Windows NT network, you will need more documentation than you get with Windows NT itself. In Tip 608, you learned how the *Microsoft Windows NT Resource Kit* is essential to administering your Windows NT network. In addition to the *Microsoft Windows NT Resource Kit*, you may also elect to use the Microsoft Web site to help you troubleshoot your Windows NT network. The *Microsoft Windows NT Resource Kit* has all the information on how Windows NT works, and the components that makeup the system. On the other hand, the Microsoft Web site contains information from network professionals who have had problems with Windows NT systems.

The Microsoft Web site has documentation on known system problems with Windows NT and how other networking professionals fixed those problems. The address for the Microsoft Web site technical support page is *http:// www.microsoft.com/support*. When you get to the Microsoft technical support home page, simply select which product you want to get help with, and then follow the on-screen instructions. Figure 609 shows the home page for the Microsoft technical support Web site at *http://www.microsoft.com/support*.

Figure 609 *The Microsoft technical support Web site home page at* **http://www.microsoft.com/support**.

Answer D is correct because **http://www.microsoft.com/support** *is the Web site address you will use to help support your Microsoft Windows NT network. Answers A, B, and C are incorrect because none of the answers point to a Microsoft Web site.*

610	INTRODUCTION TO WINDOWS NT COMMAND LINE DIAGNOSTICS

Q: *The Windows NT Command Line Diagnostics program is a non-graphical version of WinMSD.*

True or False?

As you learned in Tip 180, Microsoft Windows NT workstation and server both come with the Windows NT Diagnostics (*WinMSD*) program, which lets you view important system configuration information. The *Microsoft Windows NT Resource Kit* comes with a non-graphical version of the Windows NT Diagnostics: the Windows NT Command Line Diagnostics program. The main advantage to the Windows NT Command Line Diagnostics is you can run it from a command prompt and automate a printed report. The standard Windows NT Diagnostics, because you have to perform steps within the program to generate the report, requires you to manually print a report. For more information on the Command Line Windows NT Diagnostics, you can refer to the *Windows NT Resource Kit*.

*The answer is **True** because the Windows NT Command Line Diagnostics is a non-graphical version of the regular Windows NT Diagnostics (WinMSD).*

611 **INTRODUCTION TO THE DRIVERS.EXE PROGRAM**

Q: *You can only use the Driver.exe program if you have installed the Windows NT Resource Kit.*

True or False?

In several Tips, you have learned about Windows NT services. Windows NT has lots of services, including all the Microsoft *BackOffice* products, which means you must have a Windows NT server to run them. Each Windows NT service will have one or more drivers that Windows NT must load before the service will run. If a service does not start, you will want to examine the drivers that Windows NT has loaded to ensure the drivers for the service that did not start have loaded properly.

The *Microsoft Windows NT Resource Kit* comes with a utility to examine drivers that Windows NT has loaded. The *Drivers.exe* program will display a command-line screen that will show you which drivers Windows NT initialized, and when it linked the drivers to the system. The *Drivers.exe* program will display the driver data in a table with severaln columns. Table 611 lists the columns and describes what each column means.

Column	Description
ModuleName	The name of the driver.
Code	The non-paged code in the image.
Data	The initialized static data in the image.
Bss	The data in the image that Windows NT has not initialized.
Paged	The amount of data that Windows NT has paged.
Init	The data Windows NT will not need after initialization.

Table 611 *The columns the **Drivers.exe** program uses to display the driver data.*

*The answer is **True** because the Drivers.exe program is in the Microsoft Windows NT Resource Kit.*

612 **EXAMINING STOP SCREENS**

Q: *Which of the following pieces of information could you gather from a Windows NT Stop screen?*

Choose all answers that apply:

A.   *The address that generated the error*

B.   *The drivers that Windows NT has loaded*

C.   *The kernel's build number*

D.   *The name of the application that generated the error*

When a Windows NT computer encounters a fatal system error, the system will generate a blue screen, called a *Stop screen* (also called "the blue screen of death"), with debugging information. If you have configured your Windows NT system to do so, the system will write the contents of physical memory to a file for future examination. You will learn more about system recovery in Tip 617.

A Stop screen contains five sections, each with its own unique purpose. The Stop screen's first section contains the *debug port status indicators*, which will appear if you have connected a null-modem cable to the system (to obtain debugging information about the system) and you have set the debug parameter in the *boot.ini* file.

The next section is the *bugcheck information* section, which contains the error code after the word *Stop*. An application developer can specify up to four parameters in the bugcheck information section to help an administrator debug the Windows NT system. The third section is the *driver information* section, which contains a three-column list of drivers that Windows NT loaded. The fourth section is the *kernel build number and stack dump* section.

In the fourth section, the kernel build number is the build number of Windows NT and the stack dump is the range of memory addresses that may pertain to the driver that failed. However, a full stack trace would require a kernel debugger. The last section is the *debug port information* section, which provides information on the port parameters that the debugger is using. The Stop screen, as you can see, provides significant, useful information to the administrator in the event of a system failure.

Answers A, B, and C are correct because, from the Stop screen, you can determine the memory address that generated the error, the drivers that Windows NT has loaded, and the kernel's build number. Answer D is incorrect because a Windows NT Stop screen will not display the application name that generated the error.

613   **UNDERSTANDING DEBUGGING TERMINOLOGY**

Q: *Which of the following are examples of debugging terminology?*

Choose all answers that apply:

     A.   *Symbol file*

     B.   *Memory dump*

     C.   *Stack trace*

     D.   *Structured exception handling*

Microsoft will not require you to become proficient at debugging Windows NT code to become a Microsoft Certified Systems Engineer (MCSE). However, Microsoft does require you to know some of the basics. One task Microsoft may ask you to do, as a network administrator, is to configure a Windows NT system so a remote technician can debug it.

Before you can assist anyone in debugging your system, you must understand basic Microsoft debugging terminology. Table 613 contains the most common terms that Microsoft uses in debugging Microsoft systems.

Answers A, C, and D are correct because symbol files, stack traces, and structured exception handling are all debugging terms. Answer B is incorrect because a memory dump is a Windows NT term for how Windows NT will manage a critical system error, but it is not a Microsoft debugging term.

Term	Meaning
Stack trace	A stack trace is a history of events in the stack. The *stack* is an area of memory that Windows NT uses to store data that the system was using when the error occurred.
Exception	An exception is an unexpected event within an application or from system hardware that the system cannot handle.
Structured exception handling	The structured exception handling information is code a developer writes to handle exceptions. In Windows NT structured exception handling is active, which means Windows NT will try to trap an exception, so structure exception handling code can then try to deal with the exception without terminating the application.
Host computer	A host computer, in debugging, is the computer on which you run the debugging software. A host computer should be at least the version of Windows NT that you are running on the computer you want to debug.
Target computer	A target computer, in debugging, is a computer that you are having problems with and want to debug.

Table 613 Common Microsoft debugging terms that you will encounter.

---

614 **DEBUGGING UTILITIES FOR WINDOWS NT**

Q: *Which of the following are Microsoft debugging utilities?*

Choose all answers that apply:

A. *NT Symbolic Debugger (NTSD)*

B. *Code Debugger (CDB)*

C. *Kernel Debugger (KD)*

D. *Windows Debugger (WinDBG)*

When you have an application or system process that cannot execute properly, that code is said to have a bug. As you learned in Tip 278, processes can run in Windows NT in one of two modes, user or kernel. Because software code runs in two different modes, you must have two debuggers. Microsoft provides several debugging utilities for debugging your Windows NT systems, which Table 614 lists.

Debugger	Description
CDB	The Windows NT code debugger is a user-mode debugger that you run from a separate computer. Output from the debugger travels through the kernel debugger port.
NTSD	The *NT Symbolic Debugger* is the same as CDB, except it adds a command window that will let you input debugging commands.
KD	The *Kernel Debugger* is a kernel-mode debugging utility with built-in modem control. The *Kernel Debugger* runs from the command prompt.
WinDBG	The Windows Debugger *WinDBG* debugger is a kernel-mode and user-mode debugger. You can get the *WinDBG* utility from the *Microsoft Windows NT Software Developer's Kit (WINNTSDK)*.

Table 614 The Windows NT system debugging utilities that Microsoft provides.

Answers A, B, C, and D are all correct because Microsoft provides the NTSD, CDB, KD, and WinDBG utilities to help you debug your Windows NT system.

615   **USING THE KERNEL DEBUGGER UTILITY**

Q: *The Kernel Debugger (KD) utility will help you determine if all the proper system drivers are loading on your Windows NT system.*

True or False?

You can debug your Windows NT system in many ways. One way to debug your Windows NT system is to use a kernel debugger to perform live debugging. The *Kernel Debugger (KD)* utility is a kernel-mode debugger that comes with Windows NT, which will let you examine files that Windows NT is loading during the system boot and load sequences. When you run the *Kernel Debugger*, it will display the drivers and services that Windows NT loads during system initialization. You must know what drivers and services should be running in order to use the *Kernel Debugger* to determine if one of the drivers or services your Windows NT system should have running is not present. Microsoft recommends running the *Kernel Debugger* on your system when it is functioning normally to determine what drivers and services your system is loading.

The answer is **True** *because the Kernel Debugger utility will let you verify drivers that Windows NT is loading.*

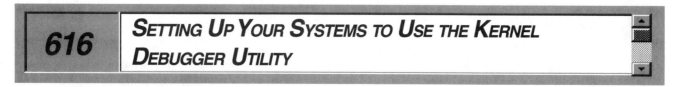

616   **SETTING UP YOUR SYSTEMS TO USE THE KERNEL DEBUGGER UTILITY**

Q: *Which of the following does Windows NT require for you to use the Kernel Debugger utility?*

Choose all answers that apply:

     A.   *A null-modem cable*

     B.   *Two Windows NT-based computers*

     C.   *An edited autoexec.bat file*

     D.   *The appropriate symbol files*

To use the *Kernel Debugger* utility, you must have two computers, one to run the debugging software (host computer), and one which is the system you want to debug (target computer). Microsoft recommends using the same version of Windows NT on both computers. When you use the *Kernel Debugger* utility, you must configure both systems, which means you must link the two computers together. The best way to link the two computers for debugging is to use a null-modem cable to connect the computers' serial ports.

After you have connected a null-modem cable to both computers, you must prepare the target computer. As you have learned, the target computer is the computer you want to debug. At the target computer, you must edit the *boot.ini* file and add the */debug* command to the end of the line for the operating system that you will load. You will then have configured your target computer. For example, the line might appear as follows:

`NTSERV40.EXE /debug`

Next, you must configure the host computer. The host computer is the Windows NT computer on which you will run the debugging software. To configure the host computer, you must copy the Windows NT *symbol files* off the Windows NT CD-ROM. The symbol files are Windows NT code files that contain the debugging code that Microsoft removed from the retail version of Windows NT.

You can locate the symbol files on the Windows NT CD-ROM with the following pathname: *\Support\Debug\platform* (for example *\Support\Debug\i386*). You can copy the entire folder from the CD-ROM to your host computer. In addition to the symbol files, you must set certain environment variables on the host computer for debugging to proceed properly, during which process you will configure the port settings for your debug session. Table 616 shows the environment variables and their descriptions.

Environment Variables	Description
_NT_DEBUG_PORT	The serial communications (COM) port you are using on the host for debugging.
_NT_DEBUG_BAUD_RATE	The maximum baud rate for the debug port. On x86-based computers, the maximum baud rate is 9600 or 19200 bps for modems.
_NT_SYMBOL_PATH	The variable you will use to specify the path to the symbols directory.
_NT_LOG_FILE_OPEN	An optional variable. You would use the _NT_LOG_FILE_OPEN variable to specify the filename to which you want to write a log of the debug session.

*Table 616 The environment variables you can use with the **Kernel Debugger** utility.*

To learn more about how to configure your Windows NT systems to use the *Kernel Debugger* utility, see the *Microsoft Windows NT Resource Kit*.

Answers A, B, and D are correct because to use the Kernel Debugger utility you must have a null-modem cable, both computers must be Windows NT-based systems (preferably the same version), and you will require the appropriate symbol files. Answer C is incorrect because you must edit the boot.ini file, not the autoexec.bat file.

617 CONFIGURING YOUR SYSTEM FOR CRASHDUMP

Q: *You are the administrator of a Windows NT network. You have configured your Windows NT server so that the partition that contains your Windows NT directory does not have a pagefile. Every time you restart the Windows NT server computer, Windows NT creates a new pagefile. Why is this happening?*

Choose the best answer:

A. *Windows NT automatically creates a pagefile on the system partition at every system start.*

B. *You have CrashDump turned on. CrashDump requires a pagefile on the boot partition.*

C. *Windows NT automatically creates a pagefile on the boot partition at every system start.*

D. *In Disk Administrator, you have the Create System Pagefile at Startup option turned on.*

As the administrator of your Windows NT system, you can configure the system to write the contents of physical memory to a file if the system encounters a critical error. You can then send the file, called a *CrashDump* file, to Microsoft, where specially-trained Windows NT technicians will interpret the *CrashDump* file's contents to help you determine the cause of the system crash.

If you configure your Windows NT system to automatically create the *CrashDump* file when the system encounters a critical error, you must have a pagefile (virtual memory file) on your Windows NT computer's boot partition. If you do not have a pagefile on the system's boot partition, Windows NT will automatically create one at the next system start. To configure your system to create the *CrashDump* file on a critical system error, perform the following steps:

1. From the Windows NT Desktop, right-click your mouse on the My Computer icon. Windows NT will display a pop-up menu.

2. Within the pop-up menu, click your mouse on the Properties option. Windows NT will display the System Properties dialog box.

3. Within the System Properties dialog box, click your mouse on the Startup/Shutdown tab. The System Properties dialog box will display the Startup/Shutdown sheet.

4. Within the Startup/Shutdown tab, click your mouse on the *Write Debugging Information To* checkbox. Then, click your mouse on the OK button. Windows NT will configure the CrashDump option and close the System Properties dialog box.

Answer B is correct because Windows NT requires a pagefile to be on the boot partition on the system if you are using CrashDump. Answers A and C are incorrect because Windows NT will not create a pagefile automatically, unless you have turned on the CrashDump option or the system has no other pagefile. Answer D is incorrect because Disk Administrator does not have an option for Windows NT to automatically create pagefiles.

---

618   INTRODUCTION TO DUMP ANALYSIS UTILITIES

Q: *Which of the following are utilities that Microsoft provides for CrashDump file analysis?*

Choose all answers that apply:

     A.   *Dumpchk*

     B.   *Dumpflop*

     C.   *Dumpexam*

     D.   *Crashexm*

As you learned in Tip 617, if the network administrator has configured the system to do so, Windows NT will dump (write) the contents of physical memory to a *CrashDump* file, should the system encounter a critical error. To assist you in troubleshooting the cause of the error, Microsoft provides utilities you can use to verify the *CrashDump* file before you send it to Microsoft. To start, the *Dumpchk* utility checks the validity of the *CrashDump* file. You will invoke the *Dumpchk* utility from the command-line, as shown here:

```
C:\> Dumpchk [options] <CrashDumpFileName>    <ENTER>
```

CrashDumpFileName corresponds to the name of the *CrashDump* file. Table 618.1 lists the *Dumpchk* syntax and options.

Options	Description
-?	Displays a Help message that lists the options
-p	Instructs the utility to print the *CrashDump* file's header only and to not validate the file
-q	Instructs the utility to perform a quick test on the *CrashDump* file
-v	Instructs the utility to use verbose mode—which displays more information

*Table 618.1 The **Dumpchk** utility options that Microsoft provides.*

In addition to the *Dumpchk* utility, Microsoft also provides the *Dumpexam* utility that lets you view the *CrashDump* file's contents. You will invoke the *Dumpexam* utility from the command-line, as shown here:

```
C:\> Dumpexam [options] <CrashDumpFileName>  <ENTER>
```

Table 618.2 lists the *Dumpexam* utility options.

Options	Description
-?	Displays a message that lists the options
-v	Instructs the utility to use verbose mode—which displays more information
-p	Instructs the utility to print the *CrashDump* file's header only; do not validate file
-f filename	Specifies the output filename
-y pathname	Sets the symbol search pathname

*Table 618.2 Options for the **Dumpexam** utility that Microsoft provides.*

Note: *If the **CrashDump** filename is empty, Windows NT uses the default name that the Registry specifies. If the symbol search path is empty, Windows NT uses the computer's first CD-ROM drive for the symbol path.*

Finally, the *Dumpflop* utility lets you write the *CrashDump* file information to a set of floppy disks. You will invoke the *Dumpflop* utility from the command-line as shown here:

```
C:\> DUMPFLOP [opts] <CrashDumpFile> [<Drive>:]    <ENTER>
```

The first command stores the *CrashDump* file onto floppies. The second command reassembles the *CrashDump* file from floppies. Table 618.3 lists the *Dumpflop* command-line options.

Options	Description
-?	Displays a Help message that lists command-line options
-p	Prints the *CrashDump* header only on an assemble operation (that is, when you reassemble the file from floppies)
-q	Formats a floppy disk (if the floppy is not previously formatted) during a store operation (when you save the *CrashDump* file to disk) and overwrites an existing *CrashDump* file during an assemble operation
-v	Shows compression statistics

*Table 618.3 The **Dumpflop** utility options that Microsoft provides.*

Answers A, B, and *C are correct because Microsoft provides the Dumpchk, Dumpexam, and Dumpflop utilities to help you examine your CrashDump file's contents before you send the file out to a technician.* **Answer D** *is incorrect because the Crashexm utility does not exist.*

619   **INTRODUCTION TO DR. WATSON**

Q: *Dr. Watson is a simple run-time debugger utility.*

      True or False?

Windows NT has many built-in features that help it handle applications when the applications encounter or create errors. One utility you can use to help determine what caused an application error is *Dr. Watson*. When an application crashes in Windows NT, you can use *Dr. Watson*, a simple run-time debugger utility, that you can optionally instruct to perform a crash dump and to maintain a log of application errors. *Dr. Watson* is not much immediate help in the event of a crash. However, if you find an application is crashing repeatedly, having the logs *Dr. Watson* generates available may help you diagnose the problem or at least give you valuable information that you can give to the application's vendor. You can learn more about *Dr. Watson* in the *Microsoft Windows NT Resource Kit*. Figure 619 shows the *Dr. Watson* utility's main screen.

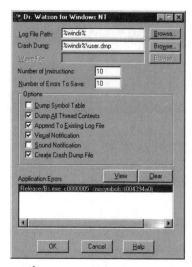

Figure 619 *The main window for the Dr. Watson utility.*

The answer is **True** *because Dr. Watson is a simple run-time debugger utility.*

621   **INTRODUCTION TO EXAM #70-58: NETWORKING ESSENTIALS**

Q: *To get the Microsoft Certified Systems Engineer (MCSE) certification, you must pass four core exams and two electives. Of the four core exams, three test your knowledge on a specific operating system, while one exam tests your general knowledge of networks. Which of the following exams test general network knowledge that Microsoft requires as a core exam for the MCSE certification?*

Choose the best answer:

    A.   Networking Essentials

    B.   Networks and You

    C.   Data transfer and communication standards

    D.   Basic networking

Of the exams you will take to acquire the MCSE certification, Exam #70-58: Networking Essentials is arguably the most diversified, because it requires you to draw from a broad base of information and experience. Because the Networking Essentials exam deals with general networking knowledge, the topics vary from the configuration of a Network Interface Card (NIC) to detailed knowledge of minimum and maximum lengths of cable types to the range of wireless networking. Microsoft requires Exam #70-58: Networking Essentials as a core exam and you must pass it to get the MCSE certification.

Answer A is correct because Exam #70-58: Networking Essentials tests general networking knowledge and Microsoft requires it as a core exam for the MCSE certification. Answers B, C, and D are incorrect because the answers list exam names that do not exist.

| 622 | **UNDERSTANDING THE FOUR SECTIONS OF THE EXAM #70-58: NETWORKING ESSENTIALS** |

Q: *Which of the following are sections of the Exam #70-58: Networking Essentials?*

Choose the best answer:

    A.   Planning

    B.   Implementation

    C.   Troubleshooting

    D.   Standards and Terminology

As with all the Microsoft Certified Systems Engineer (MCSE) exams, Microsoft broke Exam #70-58: Networking Essentials into different sections. Each section specifically tests you on knowledge that is necessary to support networks. The following lists describe the topics Exam #70-58: Networking Essentials tests, in accordance with the *Microsoft Exam Preparation Guide*.

The Standards and Terminology section tests your network standards, the terms you must use to describe them, and communications protocols. Specific topics the section covers include the following:

- Define common networking terms for LANs and WANs

- Compare a file-and-print server with an application server

- Compare user-level security with access permission assigned to a shared directory on a server

- Compare a client/server network with a peer-to-peer network

- Compare the implications of using connection-oriented communications with connectionless communications

- Distinguish whether SLIP or PPP is used as the communications protocol for various situations

- Define the communication devices that communicate at each level of the OSI model

- Describe the characteristics and purpose of the media used in IEEE 802.3 and IEEE 802.5 standards

- Explain the purpose of NDIS and Novell ODI network standards

The Planning section tests you on your ability to select the appropriate media for various situations. The section includes questions about media choices, situational elements, protocol choices, connectivity devices, and WAN specific questions. Specific topics the section covers include the following:

- Selecting between the four common media types, Twisted-pair cable, Coaxial cable, Fiber-optic cable, and Wireless connections

- Analyzing situational elements, including Cost, Distance limitations, and Number of nodes on the network

- Select the appropriate topology for various token-ring and Ethernet networks

- Select the appropriate network and transport protocol or protocols for various token-ring and Ethernet networks

- Understanding the common network and transport protocols, including DLC, AppleTalk, IPX, TCP/IP, NFS, and SMB

- Select the appropriate connectivity devices for various token-ring and Ethernet networks

- Understand the common connectivity devices and their uses, including Repeaters, Bridges, Routers, Brouters, and Gateways

- List the characteristics, requirements, and appropriate situations for WAN connection services

- Understand the common WAN connection services and the benefits and drawbacks, including X.25, ISDN, Frame relay, and ATM

The Implementation section tests you on your ability to analyze any situation and suggest and implement the correct network for the situation. Specific topics the section covers include the following:

- Choose an administrative plan to meet specified needs, including performance management, account management, and security

- Choose a disaster recovery plan for various situations

- Given the manufacturer's documentation for the network adapter, install, configure, and resolve hardware conflicts for multiple network adapters in a token-ring or Ethernet network

- Implement a NetBIOS naming scheme for all computers on a given network

- Select the appropriate hardware and software tools to monitor trends in the network

The Troubleshooting section tests you on your ability to identify and resolve common network issues. Specific topics the section covers include the following:

- Identify common errors associated with components required for communications

- Diagnose and resolve common connectivity problems with cards, cables, and related hardware

- Resolve broadcast storms

- Identify and resolve network performance problems.

Answers A, B, C, and D are all correct because the sections of Exam #70-58: Networking Essentials are Planning, Implementation, Troubleshooting, and Standards and Terminology.

623   **EXAM PREPARATION FOR NETWORKING ESSENTIALS**

Q: *Unlike other exams in the MCSE certification process, Exam #70-58: Networking Essentials, is an open book exam and you should bring your Networking Essentials study materials with you to the exam.*

True or False?

When you take an exam for the Microsoft Certified Systems Engineer (MCSE) certification, you must go to an authorized Prometric testing center (as you learned in early Tips within this book), which will require two valid forms of identification. You must schedule your test in advance and Prometric will require you to pay for the exam, unless you cancel within 24 hours prior to the exam. MCSE exams are knowledge-based and you may not take anything with you into the exams. The Prometric center will provide a pencil or pen and scratch paper if you ask for them.

Note: *The Microsoft Web MCSE Web site at **http://www.microsoft.com/aatp/** has practice exams you can download and take to help you prepare for the exam.*

*The answer is **False** because Exam #70-58: Networking Essentials is a knowledge-based exam and you cannot bring any written material with you to the exam.*

624   **INTRODUCTION TO COMPUTER NETWORK CONCEPTS**

Q: *A network is two or more computers connected together so they may share resources.*

True or False?

A *computer network* in its simplest form is two computers connected together so they may share resources. *Networking* is really just the act of connecting two or more computers together with some form of communication. Networking lets you share a variety of resources so all connected users can benefit from a single resource, such as a printer. Additionally, networks let you easily implement e-mail systems and client–server applications. Most of today's networks start out as local-area networks (LANs), which are networks in which the design of the network connects all computers on the network through the same cable system.

As networks grow, they sometimes become larger than a single building or cable system. When a network becomes so large, administrators often combine two LANs through a modem or other communication device to make a wide-area network (WAN). When you visualize a WAN, keep in mind that WANs can range from two small LANs connected with a modem to multi-national networks with advanced communication methods.

*The answer is **True** because the term network generally describes two or more computers connected together so they may share resources.*

625 INTRODUCTION TO CENTRALIZED COMPUTING

Q: *You are the administrator of a small network that consists of a single Windows NT server and 15 Windows 95 client computers. Each of the Windows 95 computers log onto the Windows NT server and the server authenticates them. This network is an excellent example of centralized computing.*

True or False?

Centralized computing refers to implementations of mainframe-like systems. In centralized computing, users use multiple terminals located throughout the cable system of the network to access a single computer that does all the processing. Early implementations of business computers used the centralized computing model to let many users access the company computer. The terminals used in centralized computing are sometimes called *dumb terminals* because they cannot perform any function without being connected to the central computer and are not, at least in the way most users think of a computer, computers themselves. Dumb terminals lack an operating system, storage media, their own RAM, and other important characteristics of personal computers.

*The answer is **False** because centralized computing describes a single computer with multiple access terminals connected through a cabling system that cannot perform any functions without the central computer.*

626 INTRODUCING LOCAL-AREA NETWORKS (LANs)

Q: *Which of the following best describes a local-area network?*

Choose the best answer:

    A.   *Two or more computers located in the same office.*

    B.   *Two or more computers the same physical cable system connects.*

    C.   *Five or more computers the same physical cable system connects.*

    D.   *Twenty-five or more computers the same physical cable system connects.*

As you have learned, administrators can connect computers to form a network. The most common network system, a *local-area network (LAN)*, consists of two or more computers in a single building or in several buildings that use the same physical cable system. To find out if a network is a LAN, simply follow the cable system to find out if a modem or other communication device connects the network. It is important to note that a LAN refers solely to the hardware (cabling) that connects the computers—not the protocols that the computers use to communicate.

*Answer **B** is correct because a local-area network (LAN) uses the same physical cable system to connect two or more computers. **Answer A** is incorrect because a computer's location in a local-area network is not limited to the same office. **Answers C** and **D** are incorrect because a local-area network must have at least two computers.*

627 UNDERSTANDING BASIC LOCAL-AREA NETWORK (LAN) TERMINOLOGY

Q: *Which of the following answers best describe the term "client" as it relates to local-area networks?*

Choose the best answer:

> A.   *A computer that asks to use another computer's resource.*
>
> B.   *A computer that grants access to another computer's resource.*
>
> C.   *A user who is connecting to a computer through the network.*
>
> D.   *A customer of the organization whose data the network contains.*

The term *client* can refer to either a computer on the network that must log onto the server for authentication (that is, the operating system and computer itself), or to a client–server application's front-end (that is, part of a program that communicates with another program on a server). As a network administrator, you must understand the context in which you are using the term client. However, similar to the word "client," many other aspects of network terminology may take different meanings in different contexts. Table 627 describes a few simple terms associated with local-area networks as well as wide-area networks, which you will learn about in later Tips.

Term	Definition
client	A computer that requests access to another computer's resource.
server	A computer that grants another computer access to its resource.
NIC	A network-interface card, which every computer on the network must use to connect to the network's physical cabling.
workgroup	Two or more computers in a network that do not have a central administration point. Also called a peer-to-peer network, workgroups can be complex to manage and understand because every computer in the workgroup can be both client and server, depending on the current activity a user is performing.
domain	A network design that describes the network and its authentication method (that is, how it verifies user access to the network). Domains always have at least one authenticating server. To learn more about domains, refer to this book's section on Windows NT Server.
share	A resource that a server makes available to users over the network. Shares may include printers, files, folders, CD-ROM drives, and other resources.
LAN	Local-area network.
WAN	Wide-area network. You will learn more about WANs in later Tips.

Table 627 LAN terminology.

Answer A is correct because the term client as it relates to a local area network (LAN) is a computer that requests the use of another computer's resource. Answer B is incorrect because the server in a LAN is the computer that grants access to a resource for another computer (the client). Answers C and D are incorrect because the term client, as it relates to a local-area network (LAN), describes a computer, not a user or customer.

628   UNDERSTANDING A NETWORK ADMINISTRATOR'S ROLE

Q: *Which of the following is a network administrator's concern?*

Choose the best answer:

     A.   *Network Security*

     B.   *Network Functionality*

     C.   *Data Security*

     D.   *All of the above*

A network administrator's role varies from organization to organization and is often difficult to pinpoint. Generally speaking, the network administrator must manage, support, and document the network. Depending on the organization's size and the number of administrators, duties may range from instructing users to merely doing a daily backup or managing other simple tasks as part of a team of administrators.

To manage the network, an administrator must (in many cases) first determine a budget and plan the structure on which the network will operate—although, in many cases, upper-level management may set the network budget, in which situation it becomes the network administrator's responsibility to ensure that he or she selects hardware and software for the network consistent with the budget.

After the administrator determines how much to spend on the network (and, therefore, the hardware and software that compose the network), the administrator must install and maintain the network's machinery and software, implement and plan the data security and backup strategy, plan and grant appropriate rights to resources, and restrict resources, when necessary.

To support the network, the administrator may have to repair computers and solve software problems, provide solutions to new network problems, and instruct users on proper network computer use. In smaller environments, the administrator may only have to perform minimal support of clients on the network.

To document the network, administrators must sometimes repair or upgrade the hardware and software on which the system operates. For example, many network administrators will upgrade the client computers' operating system as the operating system vendor releases new versions of the operating system. Documenting the network may additionally include the documentation of repairs, new machinery, backups, events, problems, violations of policy, and unauthorized accesses that the security system detects. Documenting the network is one of the most crucial responsibilities of the network administrator, and is also often the most neglected. Maintaining a document trail, whether for training manuals, or for documenting unauthorized system access for possible prosecution, is an important task that you should never ignore.

As you can see, the network administrator has a great many duties which provide network functionality, security, data security and much more. As you have also learned, the organization's requirements and the specific network requirements will determine your role as an administrator.

*Answer **D** is correct because network security, network functionality, and data security are all concerns the network administrator must address. Although **Answers A, B,** and **C** are correct, the best answer is **D** because a network administrator must address all these concerns.*

629   UNDERSTANDING WHY PASSWORDS ARE IMPORTANT

Q: *Local-area networks use passwords to verify user access. Which of the following are valid examples of local-area network password use?*

Choose all answers that apply:

    A.   *A password can validate the user at logon.*

    B.   *A password can validate access to a resource.*

    C.   *A password can determine the level of access to a resource.*

    D.   *A password can validate access to the network from a remote user a modem connects.*

Although administrators can use many methods to implement network security, the most popular method is the password. You can implement passwords in many ways to secure different parts of the network. For example, users may place passwords on individual files to prevent other users from accessing that file. An administrator may also apply passwords to shared resources (such as files, folders, printers, and so on) to authorize access to some users and deny access to others. In addition, you can use password and username combinations to grant initial access to the network— whether the user's computer is directly connected to the network or dialing in remotely.

Although passwords can prevent unauthorized access, it is important to choose passwords that other users will not be able to guess—much as banks warn you that you should not choose your birthday for your ATM pin number. Many users try to choose easy-to-remember passwords, such as names or items with personal meaning. However, such passwords can be too easy for other users to figure out and therefore could lead to an unauthorized user accessing a confidential or other sensitive file. When you issue passwords for use on a Windows NT network, the operating system will let you place certain restrictions on passwords (for example, a minimum length for passwords). You learned about password restrictions earlier in this book. In addition, administrators can establish a password creation policy users must follow to ensure that all users choose secure passwords.

Answers A, B, C, and D are all correct because, depending on the network's configuration, a password might validate the user at logon, might validate access to resources, and might determines a user's access level to those resources. In addition, a network might use passwords to validate a remote computer's access to the network.

630   PROTECTING YOUR NETWORK AGAINST DATA THIEVES

Q: *Networks do not require protection from unauthorized access if there is no modem attached to the network.*

    True or False?

As you have learned, most networks will use one or more passwords to protect the network against unauthorized attacks. When network administrators first begin to consider security issues, they most commonly focus on protecting their network from external attack. In fact, many organizations initially feel that *internal security* (that is, security against theft or attack from an employee or other individual that the company grants access to the network) is not an issue for them. Assuming that internal security is not an issue within any organization is not only a generally false assumption, it is potentially dangerous for your organization. For example, a sales organization (or business center) that assumes it is not necessary for it to have internal security because it stores no "top secret" data on the network may later regret a lack of security when other companies use a contact database that an unscrupulous employee had stolen.

Internal security is a concern for many organizations even if the organization's decision makers do not know it. Part of the network administrator's or consultant's responsibility is to bring security concerns to the attention of an organization's decision makers—either during the network's design phase or during regular administration of the network. In addition, the administrator must give the decision makers complete information as to the nature of security concerns, offer them appropriate choices for their organization, and so on. If an organization's decision makers feel that a particularly high threat exists, the network administrator or consultant must use every available security measure to protect the network from unauthorized access and data theft—both from internal dangers and from external dangers.

*The answer is **False** because many organizations must protect their networks from unauthorized access, even from their own employees and on the physical network backbone.*

631   UNDERSTANDING DISTRIBUTED PROCESSING AND NETWORKS

Q: Which of the following terms is interchangeable with the term "distributed processing"?

Choose the best answer:

> *A.   Multi-user*
>
> *B.   Client–Server*
>
> *C.   Multi-processing*
>
> *D.   Centralized Computing*

As you have learned, distributed processing is an application strategy in which the application distributes processing tasks it must perform among multiple computers. Client–server applications, such as Microsoft *SQL Server* and Microsoft *Exchange Server,* are excellent examples of distributed processing-style applications, because the user runs a front-end component on the client, which performs some processing, and the server runs a back-end component, which also performs processing of its own. One component that all client–server applications have in common is the network, which establishes communication between the participating computers. Communication is essential for a distributed application to function. For example, when you use Microsoft *Exchange Server* to implement an e-mail system, the client (that is, the component that the user's computer executes), which is running on the user's computer, can perform several services for the user. However, the client must communicate with the server (that is, the component that one or more network server computers executes) so that it can send and receive e-mail.

*Answer B is correct because the term "client–server" refers to the distribution of processing tasks to different computers on the network and is interchangeable with the term "distributed processing." **Answer A** is incorrect because the term "multi-user" means that multiple users may access the resource simultaneously and is not interchangeable with the term "distributed processing." **Answer C** is incorrect because the term "multi-processing" refers to the use of multiple processors within the same computer and is not interchangeable with the term "distributed processing." **Answer D** is incorrect because the term "centralized computing" refers to mainframe-type systems where all processing takes place on a central computer and is not interchangeable with the term "distributed processing."*

632   UNDERSTANDING NETWORK COMMUNICATION BASICS

Q: *Communication speeds in a local-area network are much faster than the inter-computer communication speed using a modem.*

True or False?

As previous Tips discuss in detail, networks are a method of communication between computers, similar to communications over a phone line. However, network communication provides a more consistent, often end-to-end connection between multiple computers, and is typically capable of faster communications speeds than are telephone transmissions. Network communication is a complex process that involves many components of the computer (such as the Network Interface Card) and the computer's software (such as the operating system, the network protocols, and so on). However, in basic terms, a series of interpreters establish communication between computers, and then change the data's structure into a format that the network's hardware can understand and transmit.

Communication on a local-area network (LAN) is similar to the communication between two computers a phone line and two modems connect, but at (generally) much higher speeds. An application that requires access to a remote resource will notify the operating system of its requirement. The operating system will then pass the request on to specialized software (often called network software or protocol software), which converts the request into a format the modem or network card can understand. Next, the operating system will transmit the request to the remote computer over the phone lines or network cable. The modem or network card on the other end will receive the request and pass it to the operating system. Finally, the operating system reconstructs the request into a format the resource can understand. After the resource performs its processing, the receiving computer performs the same steps as the transmitting computer (except in reverse) to send information back to the transmitting computer.

*The answer is **True** because network communication is much faster than communication using a modem.*

633   INTRODUCTION TO NETWORK RESOURCES

Q: *The general goal of a local-area network (LAN) is to make limited resources available to multiple users. Which of the following answers are valid examples of resources that a LAN can share?*

Choose all answers that apply:

    A.   *Printers*

    B.   *Files*

    C.   *Folders*

    D.   *Modems*

As you learned in previous Tips, one of the primary reasons for businesses to implement a network is so that many users can access a limited resource or set of resources. A *limited* resource is any resource that you cannot duplicate for every computer on the network—whether physical limitations, such as the cost of printers and the space they require, govern that duplication, or whether control limitations, such as centralized databases (which store corporate information a single, manageable location), govern the duplication. Resources can take many forms on a network, including modems, printers, plotters (specialized printers for drawing), files, folders, centralized databases, and so on.

Network administrators define a *network resource* as a component on the network that one or more network users may access remotely. In most networks, administrators also consider as a network resource any component on the network that the administrator can secure from remote access (through changing user's access permissions and so on).

Answers A, B, C, and D are all correct because they all list valid resources that computers on a local-area network (LAN) can share.

634   **UNDERSTANDING SERVERS**

Q: Which of the following answers best describe a server?

Choose the best answer:

     A.   A computer that is always running.

     B.   A computer that requests access to a shared resource from another computer.

     C.   A computer that grants access to a shared resource for another computer.

     D.   The computer from which the network administrator performs network backups.

In Tip 627, you learned that the phrase "client" can refer to several different characteristics of a computer or application on a network. You also learned that properly understanding the different roles computers may play in a network is vital to your ability to support all networks. In broad terms, a computer on the network can take the role of a client, a server, or a standalone computer (which may or may not have a physical connection to the network cable). Client computers are basically those on which users perform their day-to-day work.

Standalone computers are the same as client computers except they do not have access to the network—that is, the users have no access to the network's functions or resources, and may or may not actually have a physical connection to the network itself. For example, many network administrators use a standalone computer to scan disks for viruses before they let a user insert the disk into a networked computer. Server computers generally perform specific functions for the client computers and have different roles based on what service they perform. You will learn more about the different Server types in Tip 644.

You can generally think of a Server as a computer that performs a service for another computer. For example, a computer on the network that handles only printing requests from network users is a *dedicated print server*. Another example of a server is if you (as a client computer) share a folder, which means that your computer grants access rights to other users on the network. In such a case, your computer is acting as a *non-dedicated file server*. As a direct response to a client computer that asks to use a resource from another computer, the server will grant access to a shared resource to the requesting computer.

Answer C is correct because a server grants access to a resource for a client computer. Answer A is incorrect because a computer that is always running may be a client, a server, or a standalone system. Answer B is incorrect because a computer that requests access to a shared resource from another computer is a client computer. Answer D is incorrect because the computer from which the network administrator performs a network backup does not have to be a server.

635 UNDERSTANDING CLIENTS

Q: A networked computer can be both a client and a server at the same time.

True or False?

As you learned in the previous Tip, client computers are the computers at which users perform their day-to-day work. More specifically, client computers are computers that do not perform a service to other computers on the network. Understanding a "true" client computer can sometimes be difficult because most present-day operating systems create an environment in which the average computer can take the role of both a client and a server at the same time. For example, a Windows 95 computer at which a user performs day to-day-work is typically a client computer. However, if that computer also has a printer attached to it and shares the printer with another user who has no printer, the Windows 95 computer also takes the role of a print server.

The software components that let a computer request resources on a network are also known as *clients*. An example of a client component is the installable *Client for Microsoft Networks* protocol, which lets a Windows 95 computer connect and request resources on a Microsoft network.

The answer is **True** *because a computer at which a user normally performs day-to-day work and also shares resources to the network can be both a client and server at the same time.*

636 INTRODUCTION TO CLIENT FRONT-ENDS FOR APPLICATIONS

Q: You are the administrator of a Windows NT network. You have a large-scale Microsoft SQL Server database a Windows NT Server maintains that a Microsoft Access application on a client computer can access. The application operates on several Windows 95 computers on a local-area network. Which component in this example would you consider the Front-end?

Choose the best answer:

> A.   *The Microsoft SQL Server database*
>
> B.   *The Windows NT Server computer*
>
> C.   *The Microsoft Access Application*
>
> D.   *The Windows 95 computers*

As you have learned, the term "client' can mean different things depending on the context in which you use it. Therefore, you must ensure that your context is clear, whether you are writing or talking about clients. For example, if you were discussing the Microsoft *Exchange Server* program with another administrator and wanted to reference the component the user interacts with, you would commonly refer to that component as the client. Because the user-level computer in a basic network is also a client, you should take care to qualify the term "client" with a secondary description, such as *client computer* or *client application* (or, in this particular case, *Exchange* client).

In a client–server application, the component with which the user interacts is the *client application*. The component that performs central storage or transfers is the *server application*. The application that the user sees on his or her screen is always the client application, which administrators also commonly refer to as the *front-end application*. Likewise, administrators often refer to the server application as the *back-end application*.

Answer C is correct because the Microsoft Access application is the component that performs user-level operations such as data entry, and is the front-end component. Answer A is incorrect because although the Microsoft SQL Server database performs server-level operations, such as data storage or large-scale indexing, the user does not directly interact with it; therefore, it is the back-end component. Answers B and D are incorrect because the computers and operating systems do not determine the client–server relationship's front or back end.

637 **UNDERSTANDING DEDICATED AND NON-DEDICATED SERVERS**

Q: You are the administrator of a small network that consists of eleven Windows 95 computers. You have used Windows 95's built-in tools to implement e-mail, and have stored the Post-Office back-end on a user's computer because that user does not do all of his or her work on the computer, and the computer is the least-used computer the network. You can therefore describe this user's computer as a non-dedicated server.

True or False?

As you learned in Tip 635, a computer in a modern network can act as both a client and a server at the same time. Because computers can perform both functions, the term *dedicated server* has become an industry-standard term to describe a computer that performs services only for other computers on the network. Similarly, *non-dedicated server* is the industry-standard term for a computer that acts as both a client and a server. Understanding dedicated and non-dedicated servers is an important part of network design and troubleshooting. For example, non-dedicated servers may prove to be inadequate in some networks (because they slow network performance too greatly) while dedicated servers may be unnecessary and not cost-effective in others (because the network does not require a single computer to only perform services). In most enterprise networks (that is, networks which deal with multiple departments within an organization), you will generally find a combination of dedicated and non-dedicated servers.

The answer is **True** *because the user's computer in this case is both a standard client and the e-mail server and is therefore a non-dedicated server.*

638 **INTRODUCTION TO PEER-TO-PEER NETWORKS**

Q: The Peer-to-Peer configuration is ideal for networks that consist of haw many users?

Choose the best answer:

    A.   Less than ten

    B.   Less than twenty

    C.   Less than fifty

    D.   Less than one hundred

Most enterprise networks consist of networks that contain both dedicated and non-dedicated servers. However, occasionally it may be most useful or cost-effective to create a network that contains no dedicated servers. Network administrators use terms such as "peer-to-peer" and "workgroup" to describe a network that contains no dedicated servers. Because each network's configuration has its strengths and weaknesses, you must know the configuration before you can accurately troubleshoot some problems. In earlier Tips, you have learned about the domain model—a network configuration in which one or more servers control access to the network and all the network's resources.

In a Peer-to-Peer network, all the computers are equals—that is, every computer is a client, and every computer is also a server. No one computer performs service or authentication for the network. You can describe a Peer-to-Peer network as a configuration that has no dedicated server. In addition, you can use the term workgroup interchangeably with Peer-to-Peer to describe a network configuration with no dedicated server.

Peer-to-Peer networks tend to be small and simple, because of the lack of a centralized set of resources and authentication. Because it has no dedicated server, a Peer-to-Peer network usually costs less than a domain model-based network (that is, a network with one or more dedicated servers that handle resources and authentication). An excellent example of a Peer-to-Peer network would be ten Windows 95 computers connected to a simple network backbone (for example, through an active hub). Each computer in the network can act as both a client and a server, and each user can act as his or her computer's administrator. Peer-to-Peer networks are ideal for businesses that have ten or fewer users who are all located in the same general area, and where security is not an issue (that is, there are no specific resources that the organization wishes to protect). You should implement Peer-to-Peer networks only in such situations, and only when you expect little or no network growth.

Answer A is correct because the Peer-to-Peer configuration is ideal for networks that consist of less than ten users. Answers B, C, and D are incorrect because in networks that have more than ten users, the Peer-to-Peer configuration becomes less effective (because of the lack of security, speed, and so on).

639   **INTRODUCTION TO PASSWORD-LEVEL SECURITY**

Q: *Which of the following answers are available options when you use password-level security to configure a shared resource?*

Choose all answers that apply:

    A.   *Determine which users may or may not access the resource.*

    B.   *Specify a password for full access to the resource.*

    C.   *Specify a password for read-only access.*

    D.   *Specify which groups may or may not access a resource.*

As several previous Tips indicate, determining an organization's security needs is important for determining what network type to design. In fact, one of the most popular terms that network administrators use, and one of the most important considerations in any network design, is *security*. You can use the term security to describe a wide variety of networking issues—from validating network users to protecting the physical network machinery (such as computers and network cable) from theft.

Network administrators frequently use the term security to describe the process that protects network resources from unauthorized access. For example, assume that you have a folder on your Windows 95 computer that you want to make available to another user on the network. However, the folder contains sensitive files and you want to ensure that only that user can access the files in this folder. You can configure Windows 95 to provide secure access to the files in two different ways, depending on the network's configuration. *Password-level security* is the method that Windows 95 automatically implements for file and print sharing (that is, the user must enter a password to access the file or print share). *User-level security* is available only if you have a server on the network that provides authentication; therefore, you must manually configure user-level security (you must integrate it with the authenticating server). You will learn more about user-level security in Tips 641 and 646.

Password-level security is the most commonly implemented security level in workgroups and is the default security setting for Windows 95. You will implement password-level security (sometimes called *share-level security*) at the shared resource (such as the file or printer to share). Password-level security does not require a server on the network. Windows 95 limits the options available for password-level security to *No password* (meaning anyone can access the resource), *Read-only password* (meaning that the password lets the user read, but not modify, the share's contents), and *Full-access password* (which means the user can read, modify, and delete the share's contents).

Answers B and C are correct because password-level security lets you configure a password for read-only or full access with no access being granted for an incorrect password. Answers A and D are incorrect because password-level security does not let you specify a user or group who may or may not have access to a shared resource.

640   **UNDERSTANDING SECURITY ISSUES IN A PEER-TO-PEER NETWORK**

Q: *In a peer-to-peer network, each user acts as the network administrator for his or her computer.*

       True or False?

As you learned in the previous Tip, you can implement password-level security in a workgroup or peer-to-peer network without using a server to validate network or share access. In fact, password-level security is the only network security you can implement on a peer-to-peer network because the network has no central server to validate its users. Because each user has control over his or her computer's security, administering a workgroup network can be difficult. Security issues may increase because users configure their own computers differently from other computers in the workgroup— or, in some cases, fail to configure security at all. Although advanced Windows 95 configuration lets you restrict users from performing certain functions, the process is time-consuming and a user can easily disable or avoid the restrictions if a user has sufficient knowledge of the operating system. Because of the lack of a coherent security model, and many other security limitations of the Peer-to-Peer network model, if security is an issue on your network, a domain configuration (which does not have such limitations) is a better choice.

*The answer is **True** because in a peer-to-peer network, each user acts as the network administrator for his or her computer.*

641   **BETTER UNDERSTANDING USER-LEVEL ACCESS**

Q: *You are the administrator of a Windows NT domain that consists of one Windows NT Server and 33 Windows 95 Client computers that log on to the server. You want to enable user-level security on shared resources throughout the domain. Where in Windows 95 can you configure the security level for shared resources?*

Choose the best answer:

     A.   *Within the Control Panel's Accessibility Options dialog box*

     B.   *Within the Control Panel's System dialog box*

     C.   *Within the Control Panel's Network dialog box*

     D.   *Within the Control Panel's Passwords dialog box*

As you learned in Tip 639, user-level security requires a machine on the network to authenticate users and provide security (a *security provider*). In most networks, including Windows NT networks, the security provider is usually a server on the network. An external Server must manage security because user-level security relies on a different computer to verify a user's access to a resource.

When a user tries to access a resource that the resource's manager has used user-level security to share to the network, the operating system queries the security provider to determine whether the administrator has authorized the user to access the resource. Verifying user access in such a manner is known as *pass-through authentication* because the network passes the request for access through the computer that hosts the resource to the server which, in turn, validates the request. Then, the server will either grant or deny access to the resource.

Answer C is correct because you can configure security levels for shared resources in Windows 95 from the Control Panel in the Network option. Answer A is incorrect because the Accessibility Option in the Windows 95 Control Panel controls options such as sticky keys and advanced options for enhancing user-input functionality, but cannot configure the security level for shared resources. Answer B is incorrect because the System option in the Windows 95 Control Panel can configure many hardware and device driver settings, but cannot configure the security level for shared resources. Answer D is incorrect because the Password option in the Windows 95 Control Panel controls passwords that Windows stores, as well as User profiles and remote administration information, but cannot control security level for shared resources.

642   BETTER UNDERSTANDING SHARE-LEVEL ACCESS

Q: *The two different levels of resource security that you can implement are Share-level and User-level. You can implement Share-level security on a resource on a given computer without that computer belonging to a server-based network.*

True or False?

As you have learned, Password-level security (sometimes called Share-level security) means that you can choose to apply a password to a shared resource that a user must enter before the operating system grants the user access to the resource. The Windows 95 options for Password-level security include No password, Read-only password, and Full-access password. You can use the Windows 95 options to share a resource so that anyone can access it without a password, or you can share the resource with a password that grants either Read-only access or Full access. One advantage to Password-level security is that anyone in a workgroup can implement the security. Another advantage is that you can simply tell a user the appropriate password that will grant him or her access to a resource. A disadvantage to Password-level security is that anyone who knows or figures out the password has access to the resource. In addition, you can use different passwords to provide varying security levels for different shared resources. As Tip 638 indicates, you should use Password-level security and workgroups only in small, unsecure network environments. You can configure Windows 95 Share-level security options in a shareable resource's Sharing tab within the Properties dialog box.

*The answer is **True** because you apply Share-level security at the share level and it does not require a server to function.*

643 | **INTRODUCTION TO SERVER-BASED NETWORKS**

Q: *Networks that have a Windows NT Server are always Server-based networks.*

True or False?

As previous Tips explain, there are two general types of networks—Server-based networks and peer-to-peer networks. To quickly identify a network as a Server-based network, you can check to see if it has a security-providing server, which most or all the client computers must log onto so they can access network resources. A Windows NT Server installed as a domain controller is an example of a security-providing server. However, a dedicated server on the network does not automatically make it server-based.

For example, peer-to-peer networks may have a dedicated print or file server, but still rely on each user to implement security for the resources on the user's computer. To gain access to network resources on a Server-based network, users must enter a name and a password that identifies them as authorized network users. The security provider then verifies the password and determines which resources a specific user can access.

*The answer is **False** because you can install a Windows NT Server as a standalone server, and you can connect the Server to the network so that it does not perform security validation. In other words, although you have installed and connected a Windows NT Server to your network, if you do not install it as a domain controller and if the network has no other security provider, your network is still a peer-to-peer network.*

644 | **INTRODUCTION TO SERVER TYPES**

Q: *Which of the following answers describe specific roles of a network server?*

Choose all answers that apply:

A.   *File and Print Server*

B.   *Mail Server*

C.   *Application Server*

D.   *Protocol Server*

As you learned in Tip 634, network servers are those computers that perform one or more services for other computers. Servers perform a variety of services and administrators commonly give them qualifying names (for example, *PrintServer1)* based on the service they perform for the network. For example, an administrator would often call a computer that contains the central storage and routing control for a network's E-mail system the *MailServer.* Table 643 describes some server types and their functions.

***Answers A, B,** and **C** are correct because File, Print, Mail, and Application are all valid server roles in a network environment. **Answer D** is incorrect because a protocol sets the communication rules on a network, and both the client and the server must implement those rules.*

Server Type	Function
File servers	Central storage locations for data files. Users access File servers to access files and to save new files so that other users can access them.
Print servers	Computers that manage the printers connected to the network. Print servers add functionality to the network by dedicating themselves to printing requests. Dedicated print servers, in turn, let the client computers finish the print job faster and return to other tasks.
Mail Servers	Computers that act as a central host for e-mail systems. A Windows NT Server that an administrator has dedicated to running Microsoft *Exchange Server* is an excellent example of a Mail server.
Application servers	Computers that perform application processing as a service to less powerful computers. Application servers let organizations install an application centrally and manage it from a single location, and simultaneously let users access and run the application from multiple client computers.

Table 644 Different network servers and their roles on the network.

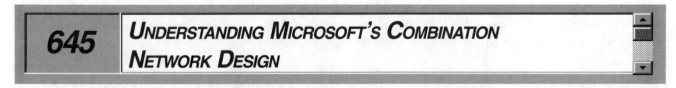

645   *UNDERSTANDING MICROSOFT'S COMBINATION NETWORK DESIGN*

Q: *You are the administrator of a small network that consists of 15 Windows 95 computers and two Windows for Workgroups computers. The network also includes a simple cable system that connects five printers to the network. Users who perform normal work use each Windows 95 computer daily. One of the Windows for Workgroups computers contains the central post office for the Microsoft Mail e-mail system and the other Windows for Workgroups computer controls the five network printers and manages the print jobs users send to it. This network is a server-based network*

True or False?

As you have learned, a network can have dedicated servers and still be a peer-to-peer configuration. Additionally, server-based networks may have standalone computers that do not participate in the network authentication process (that is, the verification of each network user's identity). In both home-based training guides and reference material, Microsoft calls a network with dedicated servers that still has a peer-to-peer configuration a *combination network* configuration.

A Windows NT domain that has a single Windows 95 computer connected to the network but does not log on to the domain is another excellent example of a combination network configuration (because the dedicated server does not force the computer into the domain security model).

The answer is **False** *because server-based networks receive authentication from a server-level security provider, such as a Windows NT server functioning as a domain controller. Although the Windows for Workgroups computers are acting as dedicated Print and Mail servers, the example uses a peer-to-peer configuration and is not a server-based network.*

646   *INTRODUCTION TO USER-LEVEL SECURITY*

Q: *You are a user in a medium-sized Windows NT domain. Your computer is a Windows 95 computer that an administrator has configured to implement User-level security for access to shared resources. You want to share a folder to the network so that people in your department can access files for a current project. What options must you include in the share's configuration before users will be able to access your files?*

Choose the best answer:

A.   *You must specify the passwords for Read-only and Full access to the share.*

B.   *You must type in the users' names who will have access to the share.*

C.   *You must choose users or groups who will have access to the share from a list the domain controllers provide.*

D.   *You must first type in the users' names who will have access and then enter a Read-only password or a Full-access password.*

As you have learned in previous Tips, User-level security is a process in which the network uses a security provider to secure network resources. In other words, an authentication server, such as a Windows NT Domain controller, provides a list of users and groups from which the administrator can choose when he or she grants access to a shared resource. Additionally, the authentication server verifies all requests for access to a shared resource for the computer that is hosting the shared resource. You will configure User-level security differently, depending on the operating system. Windows NT, for example, uses User-level security automatically, but you must configure Windows 95 to do so. To configure User-level security on a Windows 95 computer, perform the following steps.

1. Within Windows 95, click your mouse on the Start menu and select the Settings submenu Control Panel option. Windows 95 will open the Control Panel.

2. Within the Control Panel, double-click your mouse on the Network option. Windows 95 will open the Network dialog box.

3. Within the Network dialog box, click your mouse on the Access Control tab. Windows 95 will display the Access Control sheet.

4. Within the Access Control sheet, click your mouse on the *User-level access control* option button. Windows 95 will insert a dot in the User-level access control checkbox to indicate your selection.

5. Type the security provider's name in the *Obtain a list of users and groups from* field. Windows 95 will insert the text you type into the field.

6. Within the Network dialog box, click your mouse on the OK button. Windows 95 will verify that it can use the security provider you specify and prompt you to restart your computer to save the changes. If Windows 95 cannot use the security provider you specify, it will alert you and prompt you for another provider.

7. Click your mouse on the Yes button to restart your computer.

Note: *The operating system will destroy all existing resource shares. You must then use the new security model (that is, the domain model) to re-create the resource shares.*

After you configure the operating system for User-level security, the Sharing tab for a shareable resource looks different (it provides you more specific options) and you must configure the users or groups that will have access to a resource and their access levels.

Answer C *is correct because you must choose the users or groups who will have access to the share from a list the domain controllers provide.* **Answer A** *is incorrect because User-level security will not let you configure passwords for shares.* **Answer B** *is incorrect because user names must be chosen from the list of users provided by the domain controllers.* **Answer D** *is incorrect because you cannot configure passwords for shares when using user-level security.*

647   INTRODUCTION TO NETWORK TOPOLOGIES

Q: Which of the following answers best describe the term network topology?

Choose the best answer:

> *A.   The network software and protocols the administrator has implemented.*
>
> *B.   The domain model the administrator has chosen for the network.*
>
> *C.   The physical arrangement of the network's computers, cables, and other equipment.*
>
> *D.   All of the above.*

As you learned in Tip 627, network administrators use many different terms to describe networking concepts. Some of these terms (such as network topology) are not self-descriptive and are difficult to understand without a definition that conveys the administrator's meaning.

The term *network topology* describes the physical layout of computers, cables, printers, and other network-related equipment (such as routers, bridges, and so on). Topology usually has a qualifying word, such as *Star*, before it to create a descriptive phrase. In most cases, network administrators use the word "topology" to describe the a network's cable structure. For example, an administrator may use the phrase *Star Topology* (which you will learn about in Tip 648) to describe a network's design to a new administrator or to a colleague. You will learn more about specific topologies in the following Tips.

Answer C is correct because network topology is the physical arrangement of the network's computers, cables, and other equipment. Answers A and B are incorrect because network topology describes neither the software and protocols, nor the domain model. Answer D is incorrect because it includes the incorrect Answers A and B.

648   UNDERSTANDING THE STAR TOPOLOGY

Q: Which of the following answers best describe the Star topology?

Choose the best answer:

> *A.   A single run of cable with terminators on each end.*
>
> *B.   A loop of cable with no terminators and no ends.*
>
> *C.   Individual lengths of cable that run from each computer to a central hub.*
>
> *D.   A combination of a single length of cable with a central hub on each end and individual lengths of cable between each computer and a hub.*

As you learned in the previous Tip, network topology is a phrase that administrators will often use to explain a network's design. Topologies get their names from the shapes they resemble when they appear in a two-dimensional drawing or sketch. The Star topology has a center (the server or *hub*) and points (client computers, generally five or more), and resembles a star, as shown in Figure 648.

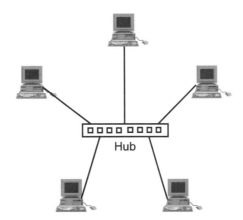

Figure 648 *The Star topology.*

Star topologies require a *hub*, which is a central piece of equipment that connects separate computers or network segments together. In a basic Star topology, each computer has its own cable length that connects to the central hub. The client computer also electrically terminates the network cable on its own end (either internally to the NIC or with a small metal attached called a *terminator*, depending on the network cable).

Answer C is correct because the Star topology requires a central hub with an individual cable length that runs from each computer to the hub. Answer A is incorrect because a single cable length with terminators on each end describes a Bus topology. Answer B is incorrect because a loop of cable with no terminators and no ends describes a Ring topology. Answer D is incorrect because a combination of a cable with a central hub on each end and individual cable lengths that run from each computer to a hub is an example of a Star-Bus topology.

649   **UNDERSTANDING THE RING TOPOLOGY**

Q: *Which of the following answers best describes the Ring topology?*

Choose the best answer:

     A.   *Individual lengths of cable that run from each computer to a central hub.*

     B.   *A loop of cable with no terminators and no ends.*

     C.   *A single run of cable with terminators on each end.*

     D.   *A combination of a single length of cable with a central hub on each end and individual lengths of cable between each computer and a hub.*

As you have learned, network topologies get their names from the shapes they resemble in a two-dimensional drawing. Just as the Star topology resembles a star, the Ring topology is similar to a ring or circle, as shown in Figure 649. In Ring topologies, network cable runs from one network interface card (NIC) to the other with no free ends (that is, the network cable makes a complete, closed circle).

Ring topologies were common until the early 1990s, when advances in network technology (such as the creation of new cable types) let network administrators create more complex networks that did not require the creation of a ring (which creates certain design issues).

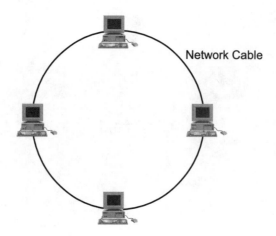

Network Cable

Figure 649 *The Ring topology.*

*Answer B is correct because the Ring topology is best described as a loop of cable with no terminators and no ends. **Answer** A is incorrect because individual lengths of cable that run from each computer to a central hub describe a Star topology. **Answer C** is incorrect because a single run of cable with terminators on each end describes a Bus topology. **Answer D** is incorrect because a combination of a single cable length with a central hub on each end and individual lengths of cable between each computer and a hub describes a Star-Bus topology.*

650   **UNDERSTANDING THE BUS TOPOLOGY**

Q: *Which of the following answers best describe the Bus topology?*

Choose the best answer:

> *A.*   *A single run of cable with terminators on each end.*
>
> *B.*   *Individual lengths of cable that run from each computer to a central hub.*
>
> *C.*   *A loop of cable with no terminators and no ends.*
>
> *D.*   *None, there is no such network topology as a Bus topology.*

In previous Tips, you have learned about the Star topology and the Ring topology, two very common network topologies. The *Bus topology* is the simplest topology and requires the least amount of cable to implement. To create a Bus topology network, simply run a single cable length and connect computers to it with T-shaped connectors (connectors that have three ends: two for network cable lengths, and one for the NIC). The administrator uses a *terminator*, which stops network transmissions, at each outside end of the network cable, to cap each end of the cable to prevent signal bounce. Without a terminator, the cable will continue to bounce network signals (which are, at their most basic level, electrical pulses) back and forth along the cable and prevent computers from sending new signals. In addition , signal bounce can corrupt other signals. Figure 650 shows a basic Bus topology

*Answer A is correct because a single run of cable with terminators on each end best describes the Bus topology. **Answer B** is incorrect because individual lengths of cable that run from each computer to a central hub describes a Star topology. **Answer C** is incorrect because a loop of cable with no terminators and no ends describes a Ring topology. **Answer D** is incorrect because there is a Bus topology..*

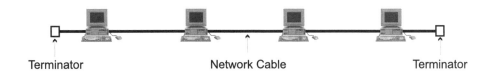

Figure 650 *The Bus topology.*

| 651 | UNDERSTANDING THE STAR–BUS TOPOLOGY |

Q: *Which of the following answers best describe the Star–Bus topology?*

Choose the best answer:

> *A.* *Individual lengths of cable running from each computer to a central hub.*
>
> *B.* *A combination of a single length of cable with a central hub on each end and individual lengths of cable between each computer and a hub.*
>
> *C.* *A single run of cable with terminators on each end.*
>
> *D.* *A combination of several separate loops of cable that also connect to a central hub.*

As networks grow, topologies that administrators originally implemented as simple, basic topologies may become more complex topology combinations. For example, while you might originally implement a small LAN using a ring topology, as you add more users to the LAN, or if you bring another department onto the LAN, you may start using a star topology for the additions, while keeping the original ring topology in the initial installation location. In general, you should use the topology which is most efficient for each installation.

The *Star–Bus topology*, for example, is a combination of the Star and Bus topologies. At its simplest, the Star-Bus Topology takes the shape of two Star topologies connected together with a Bus, as Figure 651 shows.

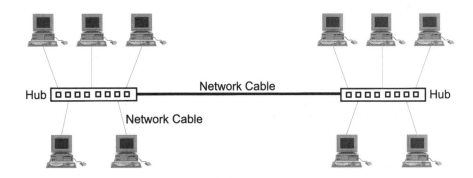

Figure 651 *A simple Star–Bus topology combination design.*

There are many situations in which you might encounter a combination Star-Bus topology, or one of its variations. As you learned in previous paragraphs, the most common occurrence of combination topologies is when you (or a previous administrator) design a certain portion of a network, and later add additional sections to the network. In the Star–Bus topology example, you might design a network with a single-domain model (the first star), then later add a second domain (the second star) to the first and convert the network to a master-domain model. The original star, then, would likely become the master domain.

Answer B is correct because the Star–Bus topology is a combination of a single length of cable with a central hub on each end and individual lengths of cable between each computer and a hub. Answer A is incorrect because individual lengths of cable running from each computer to a central hub describes a Star topology. Answer C is incorrect because a single run of cable with terminators on each end describes a Bus topology. Answer D is incorrect because a combination of several separate loops of cable that also connect to a central hub describes a Star–Ring topology.

652	INTRODUCTION TO THE STAR–RING TOPOLOGY

Q: Which of the following answers best describe the Star–Ring topology?

Choose the best answer:

A.   *A single run of cable with terminators on each end.*

B.   *A combination of several separate loops of cable that also connect to a central hub.*

C.   *A combination of a single length of cable with a central hub on each end and individual lengths of cable between each computer and a hub.*

D.   *A loop of cable with no terminators and no ends.*

Another combination of basic topologies that administrators will commonly develop, either because of network growth or to satisfy a specific implementation requirement, is the *Star–Ring topology*. Administrators create Star–Ring topologies from separate Ring topologies that are connected to a central Ring or hub by a length of cable—resulting in a star configuration, with rings at that end of the star, rather than single computers, as Figure 652 shows.

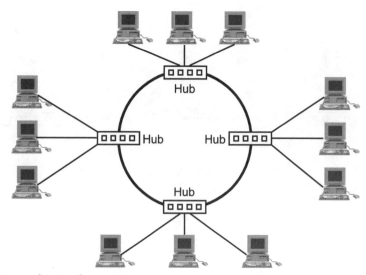

Figure 652 A simple Star–Ring topology implementation.

*Answer B is correct because the Star–Ring topology is a combination of several separate loops of cable that also connect to a central hub. **Answer A** is incorrect because a single run of cable with terminators on each end describes a Bus topology. **Answer C** is incorrect because a combination of a single length of cable with a central hub on each end, and individual lengths of cable between each computer and a hub, describes a Star–Bus topology. **Answer D** is incorrect because a loop of cable with no terminators and no ends describes a Ring topology.*

653   **INTRODUCTION TO HUBS**

Q: *You are the administrator of a small network you have configured as a Star topology. Each of the computers has a length of cable that runs to a central piece of equipment. What is the name of the central piece of equipment?*

Choose the best answer:

     A.   Centerpoint

     B.   Heart

     C.   Hub

     D.   Server

As you have learned, some network topologies require a central piece of equipment that connects computers or network segments together. Administrators call this central piece of connecting equipment a *hub*. A hub is a device that provides an electrical connection between different cable lengths (that is, a hub closes the electrical circuit). When hubs first became common, they were known as *passive hubs*, and they simply passed electrical signals through the hub onto all wires on the hub. Over time, hubs have become more powerful, and today you may find hubs from the simplest passive hub to *active hubs* that manage hundreds of cable connections and direct electrical transmissions. You will learn how to differentiate between hubs in the following Tips.

*Answer C is correct because the central piece of equipment in a Star topology is a hub. **Answers A** and **B** are incorrect because they do not describe networking components. **Answer D** is incorrect because a server is a computer that performs service for other computers on the network and is not the central component in a Star topology.*

654   **INTRODUCTION TO PASSIVE HUBS**

Q: *You can best describe a passive hub as a hub that does not amplify or enhance signals.*

     True or False?

As Tip 653 explains, a hub is an electronic device on the network that provides connections between network cables and lets the network transmissions (which are electrical pulses) pass from one cable on the network to another. A *passive hub* is one that simply provides a connection between different cables on the network and cannot perform any enhancements to network signals. In other words, a passive hub simply provides a connection between cables—it does not, for example, amplify signals that pass from one cable to another. One common example of a passive hub is a *network patch* panel, where administrators bring together and join within a single panel cables for the network that run throughout the building. In the past, administrators most commonly used passive hubs (because they are relatively inexpensive), but now they are becoming less popular because newer, active hubs can add functionality to the network. For example, newer hubs can increase a network's effective transmission distance, manage network traffic and, in some cases, direct network transmissions only down certain parts of the network.

*The answer is **True** because a passive hub does not amplify, regenerate, or enhance signals as it passes them between network segments.*

655   ## INTRODUCTION TO ACTIVE AND HYBRID HUBS

Q: *You are the administrator of a medium-sized network that consists of many different operating system types and two different cable systems. You want to connect the two different cable systems, so you purchase a hub that can accommodate both cable types and that boosts the signals as they pass through it. Which of the following statements about your new hub are true?*

Choose all answers that apply:

    A.   *The hub is active.*

    B.   *The hub is passive.*

    C.   *The hub is a hybrid.*

    D.   *The hub is a repeater.*

As you learned in Tip 654, passive hubs connect different lengths of cable together to create a single network. Passive hubs simply provide a connection that electrical signals can traverse to go from network cable to network cable. *Active hubs*, on the other hand, are hubs that can both connect cables and amplify or enhance the network signals as they pass through the hub to increase the network's effective transmission distance. Networks with greater distances between computers use active hubs to reduce data loss and increase network functionality.

Hybrid hubs, on the other hand, are hubs that can connect two or more kinds of cable together on the same network. A hybrid hub is always an active hub, because the hub must act on the electrical signals from one cable type before the hub can transmit the signals along the second cable type. This interconnection lets growing networks that originally implemented one cable structure use a more effective cable structure in newer areas of the network without having to replace the old cable structure. In turn, active hybrid hubs can significantly reduce the cost of network growth by combining cable types and extending a network's transmission distances.

*Answers **A**, **C**, and **D** are correct because the hub in the example is an active, hybrid, and repeater hub. It is an active hub, and also a repeater, because it boosts or amplifies signals as they pass through it. It is a hybrid hub because it can connect two different cable types. **Answer B** is incorrect because the hub amplifies signals and is therefore not passive.*

656   ## INTRODUCTION TO INTELLIGENT HUBS

Q: *Network administrators use hubs to connect computers to the network or to connect segments of a network together. Hubs are connection devices and cannot perform tasks more difficult than passing or amplifying signals.*

True or False?

In addition to passive and active hubs, another hub type is the *intelligent* (or *smart*) hub. An intelligent hub is an active hub that can provide an additional service to the network by ensuring that the hub sends signals when it should and holds back signals when the network is busy. As a network grows, it will become more common that a given computer will frequently try to send a signal at the same time another computer tries to send a signal. When two or more computers attempt to send signals simultaneously, problems can develop in the network because when signals collide, all computers stop transmitting for a period of time and then begin again. Frequent signal collisions will cause the network to become slower and slower as the collision rate increases.

In turn, network collision can increase tremendously at the point where *network segments* connect (such as two Star topology segments connecting at a bus). For example, if you have two separate network segments consisting of 20 computers each, collisions may not be a problem for signals within each segment. However, if you connect the segments together with a hub, you create a network with a total of 40 computers, and you might now have a problem with signal collisions. Intelligent hubs prevent problematic signal collisions by monitoring the network segments and passing signals through the hub only when no other computer is sending signals. Intelligent hubs are so named because they actively monitor the network and make decisions about when to send signals through.

The answer is **False** *because intelligent (smart) hubs can prevent problems on the network by sensing the network's current transmission state and determining the best time to send a signal.*

657   **CHOOSING YOUR NETWORK TOPOLOGY**

Q: *You are an MCSE hired to install a network for a small office. One of the organization's primary concerns is cost. Which of the following network topologies make the most economical use of cable?*

Choose the best answer:

    A.   *Ring*

    B.   *Bus*

    C.   *Star*

    D.   *Star–Bus*

Choosing a topology for a network can be difficult. You must carefully consider the requirements the organization will have for the network initially and in the foreseeable future. Therefore, you must know the advantages and disadvantages of each topology in order to make a good decision.

The Ring topology creates an environment where all computers on the network are "equal," which means that no one computer has a higher priority than another and that network performance will be the same for all computers in the network. However, the Ring topology is a *continuous network*, which means that a problem with a single computer can impact the entire network. Therefore, problems on the network will be difficult to isolate because the entire network will fail. Additionally, adding or removing computers to or from the network will disrupt the network while you do so.

The Bus topology is the simplest to implement and the most economical in terms of cabling because it requires the least amount of cable. However, the Bus topology has slower network performance when network traffic is high, and, like the Ring topology, problems with one computer or the cable can halt the entire network. Finally, problems may be difficult to isolate because the entire network will fail—rather than just a given segment, meaning you must manually inspect every computer and all the cable on the bus.

The Star topology offers a central management point, is easy to modify because adding and removing computers does not disrupt the entire network, and is easy to troubleshoot because problems with one computer will not halt the entire network. However, the Star topology has a higher initial installation cost and if a problem occurs with the hub, the network will fail completely.

Answer B is correct because the Bus topology requires the least amount of cable to implement and is therefore the most cost-effective topology, based on cable alone.

658   **INTRODUCTION TO NETWORK INTERFACE CARDS (NIC)**

Q: *Network interface cards must have a network address that is unique on the network. Where can you configure the network address for a network interface card?*

Choose the best answer:

     A.   *From the Network option in the Control Panel*

     B.   *From the System option in the Control Panel*

     C.   *With special software the network interface card manufacturer provides*

     D.   *You cannot configure the network address on a network interface card*

As you have learned, network interface cards (NIC) provide the physical connection between a computer and a network. A network interface card's primary functions are to prepare data for transmission, establish communication with another network interface card, send information across the network, and verify that the receiving computer received the data correctly. Network interface cards are communication devices, so they require computer resources such as the Interrupt-Request (IRQ) address the card should use, the base Input/Output (I/O) address the card should use, and the base memory address the card should use. You can configure these resources on most network interface cards either by changing dip-switches on the actual network interface card or by using software programs the network interface card's manufacturer provides.

However, one aspect of a network interface card is its *network address*, which must be unique on the network. Every network interface card manufacturer is issued a range of network addresses. The manufacturer then chooses a network address from this range and programs the address into the chips on a card before it sends the card out for sale. Because the memory address is programmed into the card's chipset, users cannot configure network addresses. Therefore, network address numbers cannot be changed by users because the numbers must be unique on the network in order for the network to function. Very rarely, you may somehow put two cards with the same address into your networked computers. In such situations, simply replace the second card with a different card.

Answer D is correct because you cannot configure a network interface card's network address, which the manufacturer hard-wires into the card. Answers A, B, and C are incorrect because you cannot configure a network interface card's network address.

---

659 | **UNDERSTANDING NETWORK INTERFACE CARD (NIC) DRIVERS**

Q: *Network interface cards all use a standard device driver that is included with the operating system.*

True or False?

Network interface cards (NIC) require special *device drivers*—software components that let the operating system communicate with a piece of hardware—to function within a specific operating system. Although many operating systems come prepackaged with a variety of device drivers, network interface card manufacturers may also provide the device drivers for your cards, depending on the card and the manufacturer. Therefore, when you install the NIC into your computer, you might have to load the drivers from a floppy disk that comes with the network interface card, obtain the correct drivers for your operating system from the manufacturer and load them, or simply use the drivers that the operating system includes.

Windows-based operating systems require only one set of device drivers for a network interface card because applications do not communicate directly with the hardware. Instead, applications installed on a Windows-based computer communicate with the operating system which, in turn communicates with the hardware through the device drivers.

*The answer is **False** because each network interface card has a unique device driver. Although many operating systems come prepackaged with a variety of common device drivers, you must install the correct driver for a network interface card to function.*

---

660 | **UNDERSTANDING DATA TRANSFER FROM YOUR COMPUTER TO YOUR NETWORK INTERFACE CARD (NIC)**

Q: *One of a network interface card's primary functions is to convert the data transfer method into a format computers can transmit over a cable. Which of the following statements accurately describe the way the computer communicates data to the network?*

Choose the best answer:

A.   *The computer sends information to the network interface card in parallel format.*

B.   *The network interface card sends data over the network in serial format.*

C.   *The network interface card receives data in serial format and passes it to the computer in parallel format.*

D.   *All of the above.*

Computers transfer information internally along pathways (collections of wires) called *buses*, which are internal, electrical paths that run throughout the computer parallel to each other (side-by-side). Data moves in bits along the bus from component to component (for example, from the microprocessor to the system RAM). Computer buses have changed over time to accommodate faster communication between components inside the computer. The original IBM personal computer used an 8-bit bus, which meant that data could travel through the computer along a bus that could transport 8 bits side-by-side through the computer. The modern-day Pentium computer, by comparison, uses a 32-bit bus, which means that data can travel through the computer along a bus that can transport 32 bits side-by-side through the computer. The term for transporting data in individual bits traveling side-by-side along a bus is *parallel communication*. However, the data bits that comprise network communications, such as e-mail, must travel in a single line. The term for single-line transmission (as opposed to side-by-side transmission) is *serial communication*. Therefore, a computer's network interface card must be able to accept parallel communication and translate it into serial communication before the card can send data over the network. Likewise, the network interface card must be able to accept serial communication from the network and translate it into parallel communication for the computer.

Answer D is correct because it includes all the correct answers. Answers A, B, and C are also correct but each does not include the other correct answers, which you must have to answer the question accurately.

661   ## UNDERSTANDING NETWORK INTERFACE CARD (NIC) NEGOTIATION

Q: *Network interface cards communicate directly with each other before sending and receiving data for their host computers.*

True or False?

Because networks may have a wide variety of network interface cards (NIC) and the cards may have different capabilities, the network interface cards involved in data transfer will first communicate with each other to establish the rules for a data transfer session. The network interface cards do not save or reuse the rules, and the communication between cards takes place before every data transfer session. The communication that takes place between network interface cards before they actually send and receive network data is called *network interface card negotiation* (commonly called *card negotiation*). During card negotiation, the network interface cards agree on the items shown in the following list:

- The transmission speed
- The amount of data to be sent before confirmation
- The amount of time to wait before confirmation is sent
- The amount of time to wait before sending data chunks
- The overflow limit each card has for data storage
- The maximum size of data to be sent in each chunk

*The answer is **True** because network interface cards first communicate directly with each other to establish the rules for a data transfer session.*

662   ## UNDERSTANDING NETWORK INTERFACE CARD (NIC) BUS TYPES

Q: *Which of the following answers are valid bus types for network interface cards?*

Choose all answers that apply:

A.   ISA

B.   EISA

C.   Micro channel

D.   PCI

As you have learned, personal computers transfer information from component to component internally along path-ways called busses. Over time, personal computer manufacturers have developed a variety of *bus types* to enhance computers' internal communication and increase communication speed and efficiency. Computer professionals some-times refer to a computer's bus type as its *architecture*. For example, the original IBM PC, XT, and AT computers implemented the *Industry Standard Architecture (ISA)* bus type, which was originally an 8-bit bus and could transfer information internally eight bits at a time with parallel communication. Designers have since extended ISA to a 16-bit bus to improve transmission times. Today, the term ISA describes both the 8-bit and 16-bit bus type.

The *Extended Industry Standard Architecture (EISA)*, which was introduced in 1988, describes a bus type that can support 32-bit transfer while maintaining ISA compatibility. In other words, a computer can continue to transmit to an EISA card just as it did to an ISA card, only more quickly. Designers created the EISA architecture to keep pace with the increasing speed of other computer transmissions, such as those along the motherboard.

Also, in 1988, computer designers introduced the *Micro channel* architecture, which can support 16- or 32-bit bus types. Micro channel architecture is also known as *bus mastering* because several independent processors devoted to internal communication can control it. IBM designed the Micro Channel bus to support their line of PS/2-compatible computers. All card designs for the Micro Channel bus must meet the physical and design guidelines outlined in the *Micro Channel Interface Specification* published by the Micro Channel Developers Association.

The most common bus type in use today is the *Peripheral Component Interconnect (PCI)* standard architecture, which is a 32-bit bus type. The PCI architecture, because of its speed, upgrade capability, and setup simplicity (almost all PCI cards are "plus-and-play"), has rapidly become the most common bus type on IBM-compatible computers. While most PCI busses in use today are 32-bit busses, the upgrade to 64-bits of the PCI bus is built into the PCI structure.

Manufacturers have produced network interface cards for each of these bus types, so you can purchase a card for whichever bus type your computer has. Refer to your computer's documentation to find out which bus type it has. Most computers will support both EISA and PCI busses.

Answers A, B, C, and D are all correct. You can obtain network interface cards for ISA, EISA, Micro channel, and PCI bus types.

663   CONFIGURING NETWORK INTERFACE CARD IRQS

Q: *Network Interface Cards require an interrupt request (IRQ) so that they may interrupt the processor and begin communication. How many IRQs are present in a personal computer?*

Choose the best answer:

A.   10

B.   15

C.   16

D.   20

Devices (such as network interface cards, disk drives, printer ports, and so on) use interrupt requests (IRQs) to request processor time from the computer. Intel-based PCs have 16 IRQ addresses that devices can use to interrupt the processor. The computer will process interrupt requests based on the request's priority. The lower an IRQ's number (a simple means to reference its address) is, the higher the request's priority is. In other words, the central processing unit will process requests that come into IRQ 0 before requests that come into IRQ 15.

Moreover, the central processing unit will process *every* request that comes into a lower IRQ address before it processes the requests at a higher level. Manufacturers typically set network interface cards to IRQ 3 or 5 by default (which gives network information a relatively high priority), but if another device is already using IRQ 3 or 5, in most cases you can configure the network interface card to use another IRQ: How you configure the IRQ of a network interface card depends on the card itself. That is, you can configure some network interface cards by changing physical settings on the card, but you will configure others with a program the manufacturer provides.

Answer C is correct because there are 16 IRQ addresses in a personal computer.

664   **CONFIGURING NETWORK INTERFACE CARD (NIC) I/O BASES**

Q: *Which of the following I/O base ranges for personal computers do administrators typically assign to network interface cards?*

Choose the best answer:

     A.   *200 to 20F*

     B.   *300 to 30F*

     C.   *2F0 to 2FF*

     D.   *3B0 to 3BF*

As you learned in Tip 663, personal computers use IRQs to let devices (such as network interface cards) signal the processor that they require processor time. The system BIOS strictly reserves the IRQ for signaling the processor (in other words, the IRQ can hold only a flag), which means that other information that must travel between the processor and the device must follow a different channel than the IRQ address.

The channel along which a device will transfer information to the processor is the *base I/O address*. Even though the channel is a port through which information passes, the processor interprets it as an address that it will use for input and output.

Administrators will typically assign network interface cards a base I/O address between hexadecimal memory addresses 300 and 30F or between 310 and 32F. If another device is already using these ranges, you can set the card to a different address. As with the IRQ, how you configure the base I/O address for a network interface card depends on the card itself.

Note: Diagnostic programs such as Microsoft Diagnostic (MSD) will display available addresses for you.

Answer B is correct because network administrators typically assign network interface cards a base I/O address between 300 and 30F or between 310 and 32F. Answers A, C, and D are incorrect because they specify ranges of I/O addresses network administrators do not typically assign to network interface cards.

665 UNDERSTANDING NETWORK INTERFACE CARD (NIC) PERFORMANCE ISSUES

Q: *Which of the following answers are common methods of speeding up network interface card performance?*

Choose all answers that apply:

   A.   *Direct Memory Addressing (DMA)*

   B.   *Shared system memory*

   C.   *Shared adapter memory*

   D.   *None; you cannot speed up network interface card performance*

As you have learned, network interface cards (NIC) are an important part of the hardware design of your network. Although all network interface cards comply with a certain level of functionality (that is, they convert parallel data to serial data and back again), some offer features that can enhance their performance and make the cards more useful within your network. Typically, the features offer enhanced memory management of data going to and coming from the card—and therefore, more speed. When determining what network cards to buy for your networks, you may wish to consider using cards with enhanced features if you find that network performance is slow for certain users. Table 665 describes various features that can enhance network interface card performance.

Feature	Description
Shared system memory	A network interface card that will reserve a section of the computer's physical memory and use it to process data.
Shared adapter memory	A network interface card that has its own physical memory that the computer will identify as if it were system memory. The network interface card will use this memory to process data.
Direct Memory Access (DMA)	A network interface card that can transfer data directly into a computer's physical memory without using the processor.

Table 665 *Features that enhance network interface card performance.*

Answers A, B, *and* **C** *are correct because Direct Memory Addressing (DMA), shared system memory, and shared adapter memory are all common methods of speeding up network interface card performance.* **Answer D** *is incorrect because you can enhance network adapter card performance.*

666 INTRODUCTION TO SPECIAL NETWORK INTERFACE CARDS (NICs)

Q: *Which of the following network interface cards would be classified as special?*

Choose the best answer:

   A.   *Cards with special connectors*

   B.   *Wireless Network Adapter Cards*

C.   *Remote-boot PROMs*

D.   *None of the above; network interface cards all share the same classification*

Most network interface cards (NIC) simply connect the computer to and provide communication with the network. However, some network interface cards, called *special network interface cards*, can perform additional features or connect a computer to the network in a unique way. To be a special network interface card, a card must perform a function beyond connecting a computer to the physical cable system on the network. Examples of special network interface cards include *remote-boot Programmable Read Only Memory (PROM) network interface cards* and *wireless network interface cards*.

First, remote-boot PROMs are network cards that have additional programmable Read Only memory chips you can program to automatically connect to the network and load an operating system from a server. Administrators most commonly implement remote-boot PROMs in high-security installations where hard drives or floppy disks are considered security risks because a user could copy or remove data from the computer. In such situations, administrators may decide to use *diskless workstations* (computers without any hard or floppy drives) as network clients. If a client has no permanent storage space (that is, no disk drives), it must obtain its operating system from somewhere else. The remote-boot PROM obtains the operating system for the client and loads it into the client's RAM.

Second, *wireless network interface cards* are network connection devices that can transmit network communications without using cable systems. Wireless systems require two basic components: one that connects to the computer (a card or other peripheral) and one that connects to the network (generally, a reception device of some type). Wireless connections use radio signals to let users stay connected to the network while they move lightweight, portable computers around as they work. Wireless connections also let you add a computer to a network where no cable exists. Because wireless connections generally cost more than normal network interface cards and cables, administrators usually install workstations with wireless connections only when there is no way to run a cable or when running the cable would be particularly expensive. A second, less common, type of wireless network interface card is an *infrared network interface card*. Infrared network interface cards transmit an infrared beam of light to a receiving device, which receives data down the infrared beam. Infrared cards are typically used to cover short distances, and most commonly with laptop computers, where multiple users may sit down at a given location, upload and download data from the network, and move on.

Answers B and C are correct because wireless and remote-boot PROM network interface cards are special because they perform functions that normal network interface cards cannot. Answer A is incorrect because a normal network interface card might have any number of special connectors attached to it, but will not perform any function that other cards cannot. Answer D is incorrect because some network interface cards are classified as special.

667	## Understanding How Modems Are Used in LANs

Q: *Network administrators most commonly implement modems to extend the reach of a network beyond a physical cable system.*

True or False?

Computers communicate with each other using digital (electronic) signals while standard telephone lines can only transmit analog (sound) signals. Therefore, in order for computers on a network to communicate over a telephone line with a remote computer, both the network and the remote computer must include a means to translate the communication signals from digital to analog and back again. A *modem* is a device that can translate digital signals into analog signals and translate analog signals into digital ones. The term modem is actually an acronym that stands for *Modulator Demodulator*. Network administrators use modems to extend a network's communication distance beyond the physical cable system. As an example, a given network might include workstations too far away to be joined with normal cable systems, or a remote client, such as a laptop or home computer user, that might need network access. In such a case, a user who works from home and who requires network access can use a modem to connect to the network.

*The answer is **True** because network administrators most commonly implement modems to extend the reach of their networks beyond the physical cable system.*

| 668 | **INTRODUCTION TO MODEM STANDARDS** |

Q: *The standard method for rating the speed of modems is the Baud rate, which is equivalent to the modem's bits per second (bps) transfer capabilities.*

True or False?

In order to understand modem standards, you must know some information about the modem's history. In the early 1980s, Hayes Microcomputer Products, Inc., developed a new modem that could dial a number while the telephone handset was still hung up. Up until that time, modems actually held the phone handset inside a rubber sleeve called an *acoustic coupler*, and you had to dial the phone and then place it into the coupler. The new *Hayes Smartmodem* quickly became the modem to which people compared all other modems. Therefore, the term *Hayes-compatible* soon became an industry standard phrase for describing a modem's capability. The speed at which a modem can send and receive data is measured in *bits per second (bps)*. The first Hayes *Smartmodems* could transmit and receive data at a rate of 300 bps. Similarly, the unit of measurement for data transmission over a telephone line is the *Baud rate* (from a French signal corps officer whose last name was Baudot). The Baud rate is a measurement that describes the properties of a specific sound wave on which a bit of data can travel over a telephone line. Initially, 300 Baud was equal to the Hayes *Smartmodem's* transfer speed of 300 bps, so many people became confused and thought that the Baud rate and bps were the same measurement.

As the computer industry became more proficient at transmitting data, techniques for compressing and encoding data made it possible for sound waves to carry more than one bit of data. Therefore, modems today can transmit data in bps at a much higher level than a modem's Baud rate. For example, a 28,800 Baud modem can transmit data in excess of 115,000 bps, and new compression standards allow for even higher transmission rates. Today, the *International Telecommunications Union (ITU)* determines the specifications for standard modem speeds (including how the compression applies to the data within the sound table). Table 668 illustrates some of the different versions of these standards (which the ITU, imaginatively, refers to as the V series, for version). As you can see, some of the standards have the word *bis* after the standard number. *Bis*, the French word for second, refers to a revision of an existing standard.

Standard	BPS
V.22	2400
V.32	9600
V.32bis	14,400
V.34	28,800
V.42	57,600

Table 668 Modem standards and their speeds.

Note: *Table 668 describes modem speed and does not include compression standards. You can use any compression standard with any speed modem. However, the compression standards will vary based on the modem speed—that faster the modem is, the more compressed the data is.*

The answer is **False** *because although the Baud rate and a modem's bps rate were initially the same, modern modems can transmit a higher bps rate than the Baud rate can.*

669   INTRODUCTION TO NETWORK CABLING

Q: Network cables fall into three major groups. Which of the following answers name a group of commonly implemented network cable types?

Choose the best answer:

    A.   Coaxial

    B.   Untwisted pair

    C.   Twisted pair

    D.   Fiber optic

The foundation of any network is the cable that carries the data. Network cable comes in many forms but are generally divided into three major groupings: *twisted pair*, *coaxial*, and *fiber optic*. Twisted-pair cable uses copper wiring, and uses multiple wires to transmit data. Coaxial cable uses a single cable to transmit data, and requires the use of T-connectors and terminators. Fiber-optic cable, the most expensive and fastest cable standard, uses a light beam (rather than electrical pules, which both twisted pair and coaxial cable use) to transmit data along the network. The following Tips will discuss each of the different cable type's properties, strengths, and weaknesses.

Answers **A, C,** *and* **D** *are correct because the three major groupings of network cable are coaxial, twisted pair, and fiber optic.* **Answer B** *is incorrect because there is no cable group named untwisted pair.*

670   UNDERSTANDING SIGNAL ATTENUATION

Q: Which of the following networking components can help solve an attenuation problem on a network?

Choose the best answer:

    A.   A BNC connector

    B.   A terminator

    C.   A repeater

    D.   None of the above; attenuation occurs on most networks and cannot be solved

As you have learned, as a network administrator, you will encounter various problems that you must solve to restore normal network function or to make the network function as efficiently as possible. One network communication problem you may encounter on a network is *signal attenuation*, which is the deterioration of a signal as it travels farther away from its point of origin. Signal attenuation is often difficult to solve, as its deteriorated signals may be readable by the receiving computer at one point, but not at another, depending on the signal's contents. Figure 670 illustrates the signal attenuation concept.

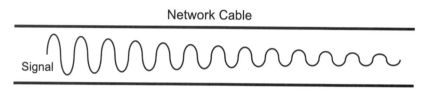

Figure 670 Understanding signal attenuation.

As you can see from Figure 670, signal attenuation is the result of networks using electrical pulses to transmit information. An electrical pulse is, essentially, a wave—and the internal resistance of the cable will cause the wave to grow smaller and weaker, until the signal is unreadable. You can solve signal attenuation by installing *repeaters*, which are devices that can clean up and amplify a signal before passing it on in the network. The repeater, basically, re-amplifies the signal and makes it more powerful, then passes it along the network. In addition to simple repeaters, active hubs (also known as multi-port repeaters), will perform signal enhancement during the routing of the electrical signals.

Answer C is correct because a repeater will clean up and amplify a weak signal before passing it along the network. Answer A is incorrect because a BNC connector is merely a form of cable connector and cannot solve signal attenuation. Answer B is incorrect because a terminator stops a signal and does not solve signal attenuation. Answer D is incorrect because only networks with long cable runs suffer from signal attenuation, which you can solve with repeaters.

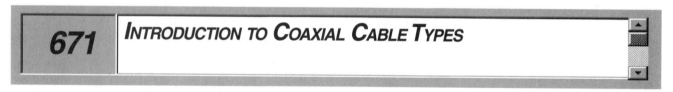

671 INTRODUCTION TO COAXIAL CABLE TYPES

Q: *Coaxial cable is more resistant to electrical interference and signal attenuation than twisted-pair cables.*

True or False?

As you have learned, network cable falls into three general categories: coaxial, twisted pair, and fiber optic. *Coaxial* cable has been very popular with networking professionals for a long time because it is easy to work with. It is more resistant to noise interference than twisted pair cable because the cable surrounds the actual communication wire with a woven or stranded metal shield, outside a protective plastic (or other non-communicative substance) wrap, that absorbs stray electronic signals. Absorbing outside signals (commonly called *noise*) is an important concern, particularly in today's offices, where many users have power cables, network cables, monitor cables, and so on, all crammed into a very small space.

The types of coaxial cable that networks use are divided into two categories: *Thicknet* and *Thinnet*. Thicknet cable is about ½ inch in diameter, and Thinnet cable is about ¼ inch in diameter. Networking professionals most commonly use Thicknet cable as the backbone for medium to large networks because it can transmit signals farther than Thinnet. However, Thicknet is less flexible and more costly than Thinnet. Network administrators most commonly use Thinnet cable in network segments of a medium to large network or as the only cable in small networks. Although Thinnet is more flexible and easier to work with than Thicknet, it cannot transmit data as far, and is more sensitive to external noise factors.

*The answer is **True** because the stranded protective sleeve that surrounds coaxial cable can absorb interference and helps reduce signal attenuation. Coaxial cable is more resistant to interference and attenuation than twisted pair.*

672   UNDERSTANDING COAXIAL CABLE CONSTRUCTION

Q: *Coaxial cable is constructed of a core cable and several layers of protective material, including at least one layer called shielding. What material is most commonly used in shielding?*

Choose the best answer:

> *A.*   *Plastic or Teflon®*
>
> *B.*   *Glass*
>
> *C.*   *Woven or stranded metal*
>
> *D.*   *Paper*

As you learned in Tip 671, coaxial cable consists of several layers. Each cable has a *core* that is made of either stranded or solid wire that carries the electronic signals over the cable. A layer of *insulation* made of Teflon®, plastic, or some other non-conductive material, surrounds the core. The insulation is surrounded by one or more layers of *shielding*, which is usually made of woven or stranded metal and protects the cable from outside interference by absorbing stray electronic signals. Finally, a layer of material called the *outer shield* surrounds the entire cable. The outer shield is made of plastic or rubber and protects the cable from outside elements (such as sharp corners on desks). Figure 672 illustrates the construction of a coaxial cable.

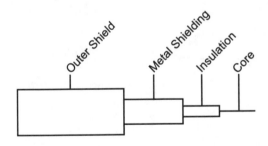

Figure 672 *Coaxial cable's construction is in layers.*

Answer C *is correct because the shielding layer of coaxial cable is designed to absorb stray electronic signals and is most commonly made of woven or stranded metal.* **Answers A, B,** *and* **D** *are incorrect because plastic, Teflon, glass, and paper are materials that would be ineffective at absorbing electronic signals.*

673   INTRODUCTION TO BNC COAXIAL CABLE CONNECTORS

Q: *Which of the following answers describe the definition of the acronym BNC?*

Choose the best answer:

A.   *Basic Network Cable*

B.   *Basic Network Connector*

C.   *British Naval Connector*

D.   *Basic Non-specific Connector*

Networks using coaxial cable systems use *British Naval Connector (BNC)* connectors to attach the cables to network interface cards and other network devices. In fact, you are probably familiar with the BNC connector because you use it with the coaxial cable most cable television systems use (in a cable television hookup, the connector is the BNC cable connector—a round connector that exposes the cable in its center). BNC connectors come in a variety of forms to accommodate different connection requirements. You will commonly find in an average computer network the BNC connectors Table 673 describes.

Connector	Purpose
BNC cable connector	Attaches to the end of a coaxial cable for connections
BNC T connector	Connects two cables together while allowing for a third input, such as a network interface card
BNC barrel connector	Joins two cable ends together
BNC terminator	Resides on the end of a Bus topology network to prevent signal bounce

Table 673 Common British Naval Connector (BNC) connectors.

Answer C *is correct because the acronym BNC stands for British Naval Connector.* **Answers A, B and D** *are incorrect because they do not accurately represent the definition for the acronym BNC.*

674   REVISITING TERMINATORS

Q: *Some network topologies require the presence of terminators. Which of the following answers describe a problem that a terminator can solve?*

Choose the best answer:

A.   *Signal attenuation*

B.   *Cross talk*

C.   *Signal bounce*

D.   *Network noise*

As you have learned, in a ring, bus, or simple star network (in other words, any network without a device to stop or manage transmissions), electronic signals (network communications) travel along the entire network. As you learned in Tip 650, a signal will not stop automatically when it reaches the end of a network (which may be either the end of the bus in a bus network or any of the points in a star network). To ensure the signal stops correctly, you must install a terminator, which is a device to stop the signal after it reaches the computer the packet is addressed to. If you have not installed a terminator at the network's ends, the signal will bounce back and forth along the network and prevent computers from introducing new signals. The bouncing back and forth of electronic signals is called *signal bounce*.

Terminators come in a variety of shapes, sizes, and ratings so that administrators can use them on different networks (for example, terminators come in both Thinnet and Thicknet sizes). In turn, terminators are rated in *ohms*, which are a measure of electronic *resistance* (the opposition offered by a body or substance to the passage through it of a steady electric current). A terminator's resistance must match the network's resistance or the network could fail.

Answer C is correct because signal bounce is the effect of an electronic signal bouncing back and forth along a length of cable; you solve signal bounce with terminators. Answer A is incorrect because attenuation is the degradation of signal strength as it travels farther from its point of origin; you cannot solve attenuation with a terminator. Answer B is incorrect because cross talk is electronic interference adjacent cables generate; you cannot solve cross talk with a terminator. Answer D is incorrect because network noise is electronic interference any number of electronic devices surrounding the cable generate; you cannot solve network noise with a terminator.

---

675   INTRODUCTION TO VAMPIRE-TAP CONNECTORS

Q: Which of the following answers is another acceptable industry-standard term for vampire-tap connector?

Choose the best answer:

     A.   Piggy-back connector

     B.   Cable-draining connector

     C.   Piercing-tap connector

     D.   Plug-in connector

As you have learned, Thinnet-cable networks will typically use different British Naval Connector (BNC) connectors to connect the network to computers, hubs and other devices, and to terminate the network. Thicknet cable networks, however, do not typically use BNC connectors to connect to the various points on the network. As Tip 671 explains, Thicknet cable is larger than other cable types, so administrators must use connection methods other than the standard BNCs to connect Thicknet cable to network devices.

The most common connector type for Thicknet cable is a combination of a *vampire-tap* connector and a *transceiver*. A vampire tap is a connecting device with sharp teeth-like protrusions on its edges that clamp to the cable. When you attach the vampire tap to the outside of a cable, the sharp protrusions pierce the cable and make contact with the core. Because the vampire-tap connector actually pierces the cable itself, the term *piercing-tap connector* is actually the original industry-standard term for this connector type. However, network administrators use the term vampire-tap connector so frequently that it has become an accepted industry-standard term.

The vampire tap (which actually penetrates the network cable) is, in turn, connected to a transceiver. The transceiver acts as a network interface card (that is, it translates serial communications to parallel communications) and provides communication to the computer through a 15-pin connector called the *DB-15 connector*—a parallel connection which, in turn, connects to a bus inside the computer.

Answer C is correct because network administrators use both the standard industry terms Vampire-tap and Piercing-tap connector. Answers A, B, and C are incorrect because they do not list standard industry terms that describe the Vampire-tap connector.

676   **INTRODUCTION TO ATTACHMENT UNIT INTERFACES (AUIs)**

Q: *Network administrators use other standard industry terms to describe the Attachment Unit Interface (AUI) connector. Which of the following answers list standard industry terms that are equivalent to the Attachment Unit Interface connector?*

Choose the best answer:

     A.   *Vampire-tap connector*

     B.   *DIX connector*

     C.   *DB-15 connector*

     D.   *BNC connector*

As you learned in Tip 675, vampire-tap connectors connect directly to transceivers (which convert the serial pulses to parallel pules), which then connect to computers or other network devices through a 15-pin connector called the DB-15 connector. The component in the computer or network device that can accept a connection from a DB-15 connector is an *Attachment Unit Interface (AUI)*.

Digital Equipment, Intel, and Xerox cooperatively developed the Attachment Unit Interface. Thus, another standard industry term for the DB-15 connector combines the first initial of each company into DIX (Digital, Intel, Xerox), resulting in the term DIX connector. In other words, you can call the connector that attaches a vampire-tap to the computer or other network device a DIX connector, a DB-15 connector, or an Attachment Unit Interface.

Answers B and C are correct because network administrators also know the Attachment Unit Interface connector as the DIX connector and the DB-15 connector. Answer A is incorrect because the Vampire-tap connector connects directly to a cable and does not describe the Attachment Unit Interface connector. Answer D is incorrect because the British Naval Connector (BNC) connects directly to a cable and does not describe the Attachment Unit Interface connector.

677   **INTRODUCTION TO TWISTED-PAIR CABLE TYPES**

Q: *Engineers and system administrators list twisted-pair cable by category to describe its capabilities. Which of the following is the category of twisted-pair cable that can only support up to 10mbps (megabits per second) of data transmission?*

Choose the best answer:

     A.   *Category one*

     B.   *Category three*

     C.   *Category four*

     D.   *Category five*

As you have learned, one of the most important decisions you can make when you design a network is the type of underlying cable that you use within the network. The most popular cable type network administrators use today is *twisted-pair cable* because it is easy to work with, flexible, and inexpensive. Twisted-pair cable also has proved its reliability through extensive use as telephone cable. Twisted-pair cable comes in two basic forms, *unshielded twisted-pair* and *shielded twisted-pair*. Shielded twisted-pair cable is much more expensive than unshielded twisted-pair and, therefore, network administrators implement it much less frequently than unshielded twisted-pair cable.

Manufacturers construct unshielded twisted-pair cable by twisting the core cables around each other as the cable moves through the protective outer cover. The more twists that occur for each foot of cable, the greater resistance the cable has to interference from outside electrical noise. Manufacturers construct shielded twisted-pair cable by grouping each of the twisted-pairs of core cables and surrounding each with a shielding material that reduces interference significantly. Shielded twisted-pair combines the convenience of twisted-pair cable with the interference shielding of coaxial cable. Figure 677 illustrates the construction of twisted-pair cable.

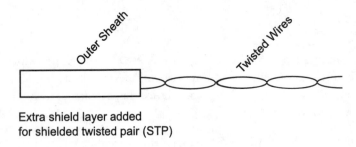

Extra shield layer added
for shielded twisted pair (STP)

Figure 677 A simple cross-section of twisted-pair cable's construction.

Engineers break unshielded twisted-pair (UTP) cable into five categories that rate the cable's capabilities. Table 677 describes each category of UTP cable.

Category	Description
Category one	Certified to carry voice, but unable to carry data. Category one cable corresponds to standard telephone cable.
Category two	Certified for data transmission of up to 4mbps.
Category three	Certified for data transmission of up to 10mbps.
Category four	Certified for data transmission of up to 16mbps.
Category five	Certified for data transmission of up to 100mbps.

Table 677 The unshielded twisted-pair cable categories.

Note: Most telephone cable installed today is a minimum of category 2 cable.

Answer B is correct because category three cable can support up to 10mbps of data transmission. Answer A is incorrect because category one cable cannot carry data. Answer C is incorrect because category four cable can support up to 16mbps of data transmission. Answer D is incorrect because category five cable can support up to 100mbps of data transmission.

678 DEFINING CROSSTALK

Q: What causes crosstalk?

Choose the best answer:

> A.   *A direct short between cables.*
>
> B.   *A high voltage device directly adjacent to a cable.*
>
> C.   *Cables running close to each other.*
>
> D.   *Using the wrong connectors.*

As you have learned, all communications across a normal, cable-based network are electrical pulses that the computers connected to the network interpret as data transmissions. When too many cables are near each other or when the administrator installs cables that do not have sufficient shielding for the cable's closeness, the electrical signals running down the cables may interfere with each other. *Crosstalk* is the term network administrators use to refer to electronic interference that other cables lying nearby generate. Crosstalk most commonly occurs in unshielded cables. Figure 678 illustrates crosstalk interference.

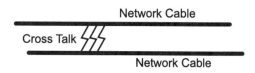

Figure 678 Crosstalk between two or more cables interferes with a data transmission.

*Answer **C** is correct because crosstalk is the electronic interference adjacent cables generate. Answers **A**, **B**, and **D** are incorrect because, although each answer could produce a problem on the network, none of the problems would be crosstalk.*

679   INTRODUCTION TO THE **RJ-45** CONNECTOR

Q: You must be careful when you choose connectors for your network because the RJ-45 connector is the same size and houses the same number of wires as the RJ-11 connector.

True or False?

In Tip 673, you learned about the BNC connectors you must use to connect coaxial cable. However, manufacturers construct twisted-pair cable differently from coaxial cable. Twisted-pair cable also requires a different connector. The *registered jack* (RJ) series connectors are the connectors you will use with twisted-pair cable. RJ connectors come in a variety of sizes, but the two most common connectors are the RJ-45 and the RJ-11 connectors. The RJ-45 connector is comparable in shape to the RJ-11 connector, but it is not the same size; it houses eight wires and it will not fit into a receptacle designed for an RJ-11 connector. RJ-45 connectors are the most common connectors for network cables. While you can use RJ-11 connectors with network administration, most administrators stick with the RJ-45 connector because it does not fit into an RJ-11 jack, making it harder for users or technicians to inadvertently put the wrong jack in the wrong hole. Additionally, the RJ-45 jack can handle more wires than the RJ-11 jack, making it more trustworthy for data communication (and faster).

*The answer is **False** because the RJ-45 connector is comparable in shape to the RJ-11 connector, but the RJ-45 connector is not the same size and it houses twice as many wires.*

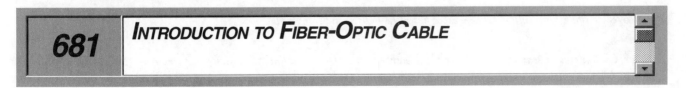

680   INTRODUCTION TO THE *RJ-11* CONNECTOR

Q: *The RJ-11 cable connector will fit into a receptacle designed for an RJ-45 connector.*

True or False?

As you learned in Tip 679, although they are similar in shape and only slightly different in size, the RJ-11 and RJ-45 connectors (because they accept different numbers of wires) are actually quite different, and have different uses. Commonly, telephone systems use the RJ-11 connector, while networks use the RJ-45. The RJ-11 connector houses four wires and is smaller than the RJ-45 connector. You must be careful when you choose prefabricated cables with connectors already attached because, even though the RJ-11 connector is smaller than the RJ-45, it will still fit into a receptacle designed for an RJ-45 connector. However, the RJ-11 connector will not fit the receptacle correctly, and the cable will not pass communications along the network.

The answer is **True** *because the RJ-11 connector will fit into a receptacle designed for an RJ-45 connector. RJ-45 connectors, however, will not fit into receptacles designed for an RJ-11 connector.*

681   INTRODUCTION TO FIBER-OPTIC CABLE

Q: *Which of the following network cable systems is the most expensive to install?*

Choose the best answer:

    A.   *Coaxial*

    B.   *Twisted-pair*

    C.   *Fiber-optic*

    D.   *Ethernet*

As you have learned, most networks use either coaxial cable or twisted-pair cable. In recent years, as high-speed data access has continued to become more important, some network administrators have begun to use fiber-optic cable as their network foundation. Fiber-optic cable is costly in terms of the cable itself and the expertise required to install it. Therefore, network administrators do not frequently choose fiber-optic cable as the cable system for a local-area network (LAN). Network administrators mostly install fiber-optic cable in medium to large networks (whether a LAN or WAN), because it can carry data over long distances at high rates of speed, and it is not subject to attenuation (that is, you do not need repeaters to maintain signal strength). Fiber-optic cable systems are the most expensive to install, but fiber-optics can carry data further and faster than other cable types. Because it uses light pulses to transmit data, fiber-optic cable is also more secure than electronic transmission cable because it is much more difficult for unauthorized users to tap into the cable and listen to data transmissions.

Answer **C** *is correct because fiber-optic cable systems are the most expensive to install both in terms of cable cost and the cost of labor due to fiber-optic installations requiring a higher level of expertise. Answers* **A** *and* **B** *are incorrect because coaxial and twisted-pair cable systems are less expensive to install than fiber-optic cable systems. Answer* **D** *is incorrect because Ethernet is a communication standard, not a cable system.*

682 UNDERSTANDING FIBER-OPTIC CABLE CONSTRUCTION

Q: Manufacturers can make the cladding of a fiber-optic cable from plastic or glass.

True or False?

As you learned in Tip 681, fiber-optic cable is the most expensive cable system to install both because working with fiber optics requires a high level of expertise and the cable itself is costly. Manufacturers construct fiber-optic cable similarly to coaxial cable, but with different materials. A single cable consists of a core made from glass surrounded by a layer of glass or plastic called the *cladding*. Then, a protective outer sheath made of plastic or rubber encases the cladding. The light pulses go through the core where the cladding keeps the pulses clear and amplifies them, which extends the distance a normal pulse of light could travel. You must be careful when you choose your cable because, although cable with a plastic cladding is less expensive, it also has a much lower maximum distance over which it can carry data. In fact, in some cases, depending on the plastic's quality, the maximum distance may be as little as half the maximum distance with glass cladding.

*The answer is **True** because, although plastic cladding cable cannot transmit light pulses as far as glass cladding cable, fiber-optic cable is sometimes made with a plastic cladding.*

683 UNDERSTANDING FIBER-OPTIC CONSIDERATIONS

Q: Which of the following answers are true statements about fiber-optic cable systems?

Choose all answers that apply:

    A.   Fiber-optic cable systems are easier to install than other cable systems.

    B.   Fiber-optic cable systems can carry network transmissions further than other cable systems.

    C.   Fiber-optic cable systems are more expensive than other cable systems.

    D.   Fiber-optic cable systems transmit data at very high speeds.

As you have learned, choosing a cable system requires careful consideration of issues, such as the distance data must travel, the budget available for cable and installation, and security. The following list contains true statements about fiber-optic cable, which may help you determine if fiber-optic cable is the right choice:

- Fiber-optic cable can transmit data over long distances, sometimes many miles. However, each turn or bend in the cable reduces the maximum distance.

- Fiber-optic cables can carry data at very high speeds, which can be well over 100mbps.

- Fiber-optic cable is extremely difficult to tap into and, therefore, is very secure.

- Fiber-optic cable is the most expensive cable type to install, both in terms of cable cost and installation expertise.

*Answers B, C, and D are correct because fiber-optic cable systems can carry network transmissions over much longer distances at higher speeds than other cable systems, but tend to be more expensive to install. **Answer A** is incorrect because fiber-optic cable systems require higher levels of expertise and are more difficult to install than other cable systems.*

684 | INTRODUCTION TO IBM's CABLING SYSTEM

Q: What is the major difference in the IBM-designed cable system?

Choose the best answer:

    A.   IBM constructs the cables from different materials.

    B.   IBM constructs the cables in a different way.

    C.   IBM constructs the connector in a different way.

    D.   None of the above; the IBM cable system is no different from other cable systems.

In previous Tips, you have learned about common cabling standards that network administrators use when they design networks. The IBM corporation has its own set of cabling standards, which are similar in many respects to the non-IBM standards. You can match most IBM cable directly to a non-IBM standard cable type. The major difference in the IBM cable system is the connector because IBM cable types do not use the British Naval Connector (BNC). The IBM corporation designed its IBM cable connector differently and did not separate it into male and female components. Therefore, you can connect all IBM connectors to all other connectors of the same size. Generally, you would only use the IBM cabling system if you had a contract with IBM to install the system. You are most likely to encounter the IBM cabling system on legacy networks that have been in place for an extended period of time.

In addition, IBM has its own classification system for rating cables, which is similar to the categories that classify twisted-pair cables. IBM calls its categories *types* and each type has various properties that describe the cable. (Tip 685 describes IBM's cable types in more detail.) To rate cables, IBM first ranks them by what IBM designed them to do. Next, IBM rates the cables by their thickness in accordance with the American Wire Gauge (AWG) standard.

*Answer C is correct because, although the IBM cables are basically the same as other cable systems, manufacturers do construct the connector differently. **Answers A and B** are incorrect because, although IBM rates the IBM cables differently, they are virtually identical in construction and materials as other cable systems. **Answer D** is incorrect because manufacturers do construct the IBM cable system's connector differently from other cable systems.*

685 | UNDERSTANDING IBM's CABLE TYPES

Q: Which of the following IBM cable types did IBM design for use in false ceilings?

Choose the best answer:

    A.   Type one

    B.   Type nine

C.   *Type seven*

D.   *Type eight*

As you learned in Tip 684, IBM has its own cable design and identification system which refers to cables as types. The IBM Corporation designed each type of IBM cable for a different purpose and each type has different capabilities. Table 685 describes the different IBM cable types.

IBM Type	Description
Type one	Shielded twisted-pair cable.
Type two	Voice and data grade cable. Consists of six twisted-pair cables, two cables for data and four cables for voice communication.
Type three	Voice grade cable. Consists of four twisted-pair cables for voice communication.
Type four	IBM has not defined this cable type in order to reserve it for future cable type developments.
Type five	Fiber-optic cable.
Type six	Data-patch cable. A shielded twisted-pair cable designed for short connections.
Type seven	IBM has not defined this cable type in order to reserve it for future cable type developments.
Type eight	Carpet grade cable. A twisted-pair cable with a flat, protective outer shield designed for use under carpeting.
Type nine	Plenum grade cable. A twisted-pair cable that IBM lists as *fire safe* and specifically designed for use in false ceilings.

Table 685 The IBM cable types that IBM rates.

Answer B is correct because IBM type nine cable is Plenum cable, which IBM designed for use in false ceilings and other areas that require fire-safe cable. Answer A is incorrect because IBM type one cable is standard twisted-pair cable, which IBM did not specifically design for use in false ceilings or other areas that require fire-safe cable. Answer C is incorrect because IBM type seven cable is an undefined type for which no real cable exists. Answer D is incorrect because IBM type eight cable is carpet grade cable, which IBM did not specifically design for use in false ceilings or other areas that require fire-safe cable.

686   *UNDERSTANDING MAXIMUM CABLE LENGTHS*

Q: *Network administrators frequently choose 10BaseT twisted-pair cable over 10Base2 coaxial cable because it can carry network transmissions for a greater distance.*

True or False?

Each kind of network cable has different characteristics, which includes a maximum cable length beyond which network transmissions are likely to deteriorate. Although the maximum length for each cable type increases as technology improves, each cable has a generally accepted maximum functional length that network administrators use as a guideline for choosing cables. Table 686 lists each cable type and its maximum cable length.

Cable Type	Maximum Functional Length
Thinnet (10Base2 coaxial)	607 feet
Thicknet (10Base5 coaxial)	1640 feet
Twisted-pair (10BaseT)	328 feet
Fiber-optic	6562 feet

Table 686 The maximum cable lengths for each cable type.

*The answer is **False** because 10Base2 coaxial cable can carry network transmissions for a maximum distance of 607 feet, but 10BaseT twisted-pair cable can carry network transmissions for a maximum distance of 328 feet.*

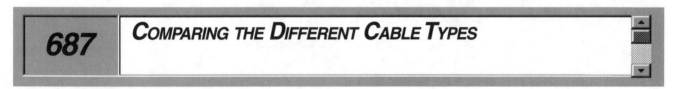

687   **COMPARING THE DIFFERENT CABLE TYPES**

Q: *Network administrators frequently choose 10BaseT twisted-pair cable over 10Base2 coaxial cable because it is less expensive.*

True or False?

As you have learned, each cable type has different properties and capabilities, and network administrators must choose the appropriate cable for a specific network. When considering your network's design, you will consider such issues as cost of cabling, ease of installation, maximum transmission speed, maximum cable length, and how upgradable the cable is as your network traffic needs increase. To help you determine which cable type would be best for your network, Table 687 describes some features about each cable type.

Cable Type	Features
10Base2 coaxial (Thinnet)	Thinnet cable costs more than twisted-pair cabling, but less than Thicknet cable. Thinnet cable is flexible, easy to install, and is fairly resistant to interference because it has shielding. Thinnet cable can support data transmissions at about 10mbps.
10Base5 coaxial (Thicknet)	Thicknet cable costs more and is less flexible than Thinnet cable, but Thicknet cable can carry data much further and is still easy to install. Thicknet cable can support data transmissions at about 10mbps.
10BaseT twisted-pair	Twisted-pair cable is the least expensive cable type. Also, twisted-pair cable is the most flexible cable type and is very easy to install. Depending on the grade of cable you buy, twisted-pair cables can support data transmissions at speeds between four and 100mbps.
Fiber-optic	Fiber-optic cable is the most expensive cable type. In addition, fiber-optic cable is not flexible, which makes installation difficult and requires high levels of expertise. Fiber-optic cable is not susceptible to electronic interference, is very secure, and can support data transmissions above 100mbps.

Table 687 Understanding each cable type's features.

*The answer is **True** because 10BaseT twisted-pair cable is the least expensive cable type.*

SELECTING THE PROPER CABLE TYPE

688

Q: *You are an independent network consultant a company has hired to design a network. Which of the following answers are issues you must consider when you choose a cable system?*

Choose all answers that apply:

A.   *The probable level of network traffic.*

B.   *The specific security requirements of the proposed network.*

C.   *The cost of the cable compared to the available budget.*

D.   *The maximum distances over which the network must carry data.*

With all the differences between cable types, you may find choosing a cable difficult. As a Microsoft Certified System Engineer, you must consider many issues when you choose a cable type. For example, if you chose twisted-pair cable for a medium-to-large network just because it was cheaper, you may find that the company is initially pleased with the lower cost. However, the company may not like that the network performs slowly or has problems due to an inadequate ability to carry data the required length. To help you avoid network problems, the following bulleted list describes some of the issues you must consider when you choose a cable type:

- The cost of the cable compared to the available budget

- Security issues for the network and its users

- The probable level of network traffic

- Maximum distances each length of cable must cover

- The total distance of the network between the client computers furthest from each other

- The location of the cable as it relates to electrical equipment or other cables

- Other possible sources of electronic interference

Answers A, B, C, and D are all correct because you must consider each of the issues the answers list when you choose a cable system for a proposed network.

INTRODUCTION TO BASEBAND TRANSMISSION

689

Q: *Baseband transmission is a standard industry classification for systems that transmit signals in which of the following formats?*

Choose the best answer:

A.   *Analog*

B.   *Digital*

C.   Low range radio frequencies

D.   High range radio frequencies

The *baseband* transmission system is a classification for systems which use digital signals to transmit data. Digital signaling uses the entire available bandwidth of the cable as it travels and only a single frequency. *Bandwidth* is defined as the difference between the highest and lowest frequencies a cable can carry. Also, digital signaling transmits data bi-directionally, which means you can transmit data in both directions along the cable. Digital signals have a value of only on or off. A *waveform* (a graphic representation of the shape of the digital signal wave that indicates the wave's characteristics, frequency, and amplitude), which is block-like in appearance, represents the digital signals during transmission.

Answer B is correct because baseband transmission is a standard industry classification for systems that transmit data in digital format. Answer A is incorrect because systems that transmit data in analog format are broadband transmission systems. Answers C and D are incorrect because the standard industry term baseband transmission does not describe a system that transmits data over high or low range radio frequencies.

690   INTRODUCTION TO BROADBAND TRANSMISSION

Q: While baseband transmission systems transmit data in both directions on a cable, broadband transmission systems transmit data in only a single direction on each cable.

True or False?

The *broadband* transmission system is a classification for systems which use analog signals to transmit data. Analog signals are more complex than digital ones because they can be any specific frequency within the cable and you can transmit multiple frequencies at the same time. Sound waves are excellent examples of analog signals (because the frequency and amplitude of the wave are important—otherwise, all sound traveling across a cable would sound the same on the receiving end). Analog signaling systems transmit data in a unidirectional path, which means data transmissions flow only one way along the cable.

*The answer is **True** because broadband transmission systems use analog signals, which communicate in only a single direction.*

691   INTRODUCTION TO WIRELESS NETWORKS

Q: Which of the following answers list the maximum transmission distance for wireless networks?

Choose the best answer:

A.   50 meters

B.   150 meters

C.   500 meters

D.   None. Some wireless networks can transmit data an unlimited distance

Wireless networking is a fairly new data transmission method for computer networks, having become common only within the past several years. Manufacturers are rapidly developing highly effective methods of transmitting data signals through the air (until recently, they could only effectively transmit analog signals through the air). Wireless networks take a variety of forms. In fact, wireless network components range from very low speed networking components with limited range, to components that can transmit data to different corners of the world at high speeds without a direct connection to any network or cable. You can achieve wireless networking with different methods. The next seven Tips will discuss each of the common methods that network administrators are currently implementing.

Answer D is correct because some wireless communication methods can transmit data an unlimited distance. Answers A, B, and C are incorrect because the distance limitations in these answers may apply to some wireless networking systems, but not to all wireless networking systems.

692   **INTRODUCTION TO INFRARED NETWORK TRANSMISSION**

Q:	*Other light sources can interrupt infrared wireless transmission systems.*

True or False?

As you have learned, there are various types of wireless transmissions. *Infrared* wireless transmission systems all operate by transmitting data over a beam of infrared light. Infrared network communication systems are available in several different varieties. However, there are two systems that are most common. One infrared system uses a line-of-sight method wherein all transmission devices must have a clear and direct path to the other devices. Another wireless system uses a bounce method that lets you bounce the infrared beam off walls and ceilings to reach other devices. Regardless of which method the wireless network uses, it must have devices capable of translating the electronic signals the computers in the network send into infrared beams and back again. Such devices typically are small boxes with an infrared transmitter and receiver that either plug into the computer's parallel port, network interface card (NIC), or other location from which the computer can receive data input.

Infrared networks can transmit data at speeds up to about 10mbps. However, most infrared communications devices have an effective maximum distance of only 100 to 150 feet. In addition, other light sources, such as common office lighting or sunlight, can interrupt infrared signals. Most infrared devices, therefore, generate a powerful light beam to offset the effects of outside lighting sources. The most commonly-used infrared devices provide print sharing services and network connections for computers which are difficult or impossible to connect directly to network cable.

*The answer is **True** because other light sources can interrupt weak transmissions from infrared wireless transmission systems, which means infrared systems must generate powerful signals.*

693   **INTRODUCTION TO LASER-BASED NETWORK TRANSMISSION**

Q:	*Network administrators do not frequently choose laser-based wireless transmission systems because they are costly and require a direct line-of-sight between components.*

True or False?

In Tip 692, you learned how infrared wireless systems use an infrared beam of light to transmit data between devices on the network. *Laser-based* wireless networking systems are similar in function to infrared systems. Laser-based systems transmit data over a beam of light and must have a line-of-sight between components. Proper placement of light emitting and receiving components (that is, the two ends of the wireless communication) is important because people walking through the office could disrupt the network if you place the components poorly. Any break in the line-of-sight will disrupt a laser-based network—because the light-emitting component will continue transmitting data, but the receiving component will not receive the data. Such disruptions may crash the network, result in corrupted transmissions, or simply slow communications.

Although they are less susceptible to interruption from other light sources (because the laser's light beam is significantly stronger than any infrared light beam), laser-based networks are less popular than infrared networks. Laser-based networks do not provide greater enhancement in data transfer speed and generally cost more than other systems. Worse, the line-of-sight consideration with a laser-based network makes it a less viable alternative for most offices.

The answer is **True** *because network administrators do not frequently choose laser-based wireless transmission systems because they require a direct line-of-sight between components and can be more expensive than other wireless networking systems.*

694	INTRODUCTION TO SPREAD-SPECTRUM RADIO TRANSMISSION

Q: Which of the following answers contain true statements about spread-spectrum wireless radio transmission systems?

Choose the best answer:

A.   *Spread-spectrum wireless transmission systems carry data at speeds above 20mbps.*

B.   *Spread-spectrum wireless transmission systems use codes to prevent unauthorized users from listening to data transmissions.*

C.   *Spread-spectrum wireless transmission systems are easy to install.*

D.   *Spread-spectrum wireless transmission systems use multiple channels and jump from channel to channel while transmitting data.*

In the previous two Tips, you learned about infrared and laser-based wireless systems—both of which use light beams to transmit data. More commonly, however, wireless communications use radio signals or other wave-based transmissions to send and receive data. Another wireless communication system is the *spread-spectrum radio* transmission network. Networks can use the spread-spectrum radio method over a range of radio frequencies, which are divided into *channels* (sometimes called *hops*). You must attach all participating computers and other network components to a device that you synchronize with the rest of the devices on the network. As data transmits across the network, the devices which interpret the radio messages will move from channel to channel in a preset sequence. Because all the devices on the network know which channel to move to and when, channel switching (hopping) does not interrupt network communication. Spread-spectrum wireless transmission devices also contain codes that validate them on the network. Therefore, between channel switching and the built-in code system, unauthorized users listening in on data transmissions is virtually impossible. The main reason that network administrators do not widely use spread-spectrum radio transmission wireless networks is the networks transmit data at a very slow rate when you compare them to other network systems. Spread-spectrum radio transmission wireless networks usually can transfer data at between ½ and two megabits per second.

Answers B, C, and D are correct because spread-spectrum wireless radio transmission systems are easy to install, use multiple channels, jump from channel to channel while transmitting data, and use codes to prevent unauthorized users from listening to data transmissions. Answer A is incorrect because spread-spectrum wireless radio transmission systems transmit data at very slow rates, usually around two megabits per second.

695   INTRODUCTION TO NARROW-BAND WIRELESS TRANSMISSION

Q: *What is the average transmission speed of a narrow-band wireless transmission system?*

Choose the best answer:

     A.   4 to 6mps

     B.   10 to 15mbps

     C.   10 to 20mbps

     D.   25 to 50mbps

In Tip 694, you learned about the spread-spectrum radio transmission wireless network, a highly secure wireless network which, unfortunately, is also very slow. A second radio-frequency-based transmission system is the *narrow-band* transmission system, which basically transmits data the way a radio station transmits music. Like a radio, you can tune in devices on the network to both transmit and receive data at a specific frequency.

Unfortunately, even without hopping across a spectrum, narrow-band transmission systems are still fairly slow, transferring data at speeds between four to six megabytes per second. In addition, narrow-band transmission systems use a high frequency, which prevents them from passing through heavy walls or structures made from iron and steel. However, as with spread-spectrum and laser-based networks, the main reason network administrators seldom use narrowband systems is the slow speed of data transmission.

Answer A is correct because narrow-band wireless transmission systems average a communication speed of four to six megabits per second. Answers B, C, and D are incorrect because each of the answers list a communication speed that exceeds the speed of the average narrow-band wireless transmission system.

696   INTRODUCTION TO SATELLITE NETWORK TRANSMISSION

Q: *Satellite networking systems are the most common wireless networks that network administrators use for long distance transmissions.*

     True or False?

You have learned about several different types of wireless transmissions systems, none of which seems to be a particularly useful alternative to standard, cable-based network. However, the most common wireless transmission system for communicating over large distances is the *satellite* transmission system, which is also known as the *microwave* transmission system. Microwave transmission systems are very common for medium-to-large networks that have multiple buildings in the same city or area. Microwave transmissions are relatively inexpensive, depending on whether the network uses its own directional antenna or whether the network communicates using access time on a satellite. Microwave transmissions tend to be fast (moving at the speed of light), though they are slowed by the "bounce time" which accrues during the initial transmission to the satellite and back. Microwave transmission is also popular because it is a tried-and-true technology—first tested for communications in 1933 (although satellites were not integrated with the transmissions until much later). To create a connection, microwave systems use directional antennas pointed at each other that require line-of-sight to operate. Less commonly seen, but also in use, are large microwave communication devices installed in satellites, which then broadcast signals to directional antennas or "dishes" that point to the satellite. As small, hand-held computers with wireless connections continue to become more common, satellite access for remote networking is also becoming a more common solution.

The answer is **True** *because satellite networking systems are the most common wireless networks that network administrators use for long distance transmissions.*

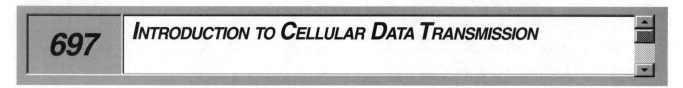

697   INTRODUCTION TO CELLULAR DATA TRANSMISSION

Q: *Which of the following statements accurately describe a property of cellular data transmission systems?*

Choose the best answer:

    A.   *Cellular data transmission systems suffer from long delays in data transfer.*

    B.   *Cellular data transmission systems require specialized equipment and you cannot use them with normal cellular telephones.*

    C.   *Cellular data transmission systems work only over digital cellular systems.*

    D.   *None of the above.*

Cellular networking is becoming more and more popular because you can often create a link to a network from anywhere within range of the cell sites (a geographical mapping that determines a cellular phone's "home area"). Mobile users with laptop computers and cellular telephones can now dial into a network from just about anywhere—and access the network as if they were physically connected to it, just as they would from their desk. Additionally, some small computers (such as hand-held computers) have built-in cellular capabilities.

Cellular digital packet data (CDPD) transmission operates with the same cell sites that cellular telephones use. The cellular tower will transfer the data within the packets it receives when the network is not busy with normal telephone users (making cellular communications notoriously slow). Cellular networks have transmission delays that typically last less than a second, which creates networks easily capable of transmitting data at an acceptable speed. The remaining factor which governs the network connection is modem speed—which, as you have learned, is significantly less than cable speed, but still fast enough for most remote activities.

Answer D is correct because none of the statements accurately describe a property of cellular data transmission systems. Answers A, B and C are incorrect because the statements do not accurately describe a property of cellular data transmission systems.

698   INTRODUCTION TO BRIDGES

Q: *Network administrators use bridges to separate and connect various segments of a large network. What is the part of a bridge that lets it segment a network?*

Choose the best answer:

> A.   The network locator service.
>
> B.   The routing table.
>
> C.   The port identification chip.
>
> D.   None of the above; bridges are unable to segment a network.

Frequently, as organizations grow, the network will begin to slow down as you add more and more users to it—because the increased traffic will result in more collisions. Network administrators often use bridges to separate a network's transmission loop into segments and then connect those segments. Such segmentation enhances network performance because it reduces collisions across the network as a whole. *Bridges* are devices which connect segments of a network together. A common misconception is that a bridge, like a hub or multi-port repeater, simply connects the network segments, and passes all network traffic on to all other segments. However, bridges are actually intelligent devices that can make decisions about which segment will receive a specific transmission.

To make segment decisions, a bridge uses a *routing table* (a reference of addresses on the network) that the bridge either builds over time automatically or that you can program directly. The routing table in a bridge contains the network addresses of computers and network devices, and their locations on segments of the network. When a network transmission enters the bridge, the bridge reads the network address and determines on which segment it can find the intended recipient. The bridge then passes the network transmission to that segment only, which reduces total network traffic.

Network administrators also use bridges when they begin to design medium or large networks, so they can go ahead and separate the network segments. In addition, using bridges from the start of a network lets network administrators connect different cable types, such as coaxial and twisted-pair cables, on the same network. Simply put, a bridge reduces network traffic on the network as a whole by confining it to local segments of the network, simplifies the connection of different network types, and is a valuable ally in your effort to control network traffic safely and efficiently.

Answer B is correct because the routing table lets a bridge segment a network. Answers A and C are incorrect because a bridge does not have a network locator service or a port identification chip. Answer D is incorrect because bridges can segment a network.

699	INTRODUCTION TO REMOTE BRIDGES

Q: *Wireless bridges can be examples of spread-spectrum wireless transmission systems.*

True or False?

As you learned in Tip 698, network administrators use bridges to connect a network's segments. One commonly-used type of bridge is the *remote bridge*. Network administrators use remote bridges to integrate two separate networks (that is, networks in different geographical locations) into one network. For example, if you have a small organization with two offices and each office has its own local-area network (LAN), you may want to combine the LANs so that all users can easily connect to each other.

You could use a remote bridge at each location to connect the two networks together over standard telephone lines, other data-grade communication lines, or even use a wireless bridge. Wireless bridges are typically spread-spectrum communication-based. Because of the amount of traffic that passes through the bridges, and because administrators commonly use them to communicate between distant networks (leaving them more open to signal interception), the pre-programmed hop sequence provides the wireless bridge with much-needed security.

The answer is True because wireless bridges can use spread-spectrum wireless transmission systems.

700 INTRODUCTION TO ROUTERS

Q: *Which of the following network protocols can a router not route?*

Choose the best answer:

 A. *TCP/IP*

 B. *NetBEUI*

 C. *NWLINK*

 D. *AppleTalk*

As you have learned, bridges can add functionality to a network and reduce network traffic by separating network segments and controlling transmissions between segments. An enhancement to the bridge is the *router* because a router cannot only separate a network's segments, it can also connect separate networks and determine the best path for a data transmission across the multiple networks.

Routers function by maintaining a list of network properties, such as the addresses of resources on the network, how to connect to other networks, the possible paths to other routers, and the costs in performance to use each path. When a network transmission intended for another network comes into the router, it will use the list of network properties to determine the location of, and best path to, the intended network. However, a router cannot route all network protocols. There are several reasons for this, but the most common is because the protocol's designers simply did not allow for routing of transmissions when they designed the protocol. The following bulleted list indicates some of the protocols that you can use a router to route:

- TCP/IP
- AppleTalk
- NWLINK (IPX)
- DECnet

Answer B is correct because a router cannot route the NetBEUI protocol. Answers A, C, and D are incorrect because TCP/IP, NWLINK, and AppleTalk are protocols a router can route.

701 INTRODUCTION TO STATIC ROUTING

Q: *The administrator must configure static routers' internal routing tables.*

True or False?

In Tip 700, you learned that you can use routers to connect separate networks and to determine the most appropriate path data should travel over the network to reach the intended computer. When you consider which routers to install onto your network, you can categorize routers into two basic types: *static routers* and *dynamic routers*.

An administrator must configure static routers' internal routing tables. In other words, static routers require that the person setting up the router has knowledge about the various networks the router will connect and how to appropriately determine data paths between the networks. Because the administrator predetermines and sets the data path, all transmissions will follow the same path, which will result in a higher security level than a dynamic router will provide.

In contrast, dynamic routers will transmit data along different data paths—even packets which are directly subsequent to each other may follow a different path, which makes it more difficult to ensure the data is not passing through a "hostile" computer. You will learn more about dynamic routers in the following Tip. Figure 701 shows how a static router routes data along a consistent path.

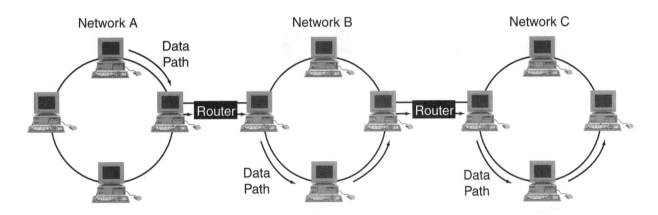

Figure 701 A static router routes data along a consistent path.

Although using a static router will provide a more secure data-path transmission, the fact that the static routing table instructs data transmissions to always follow the predetermined route can severely impact network performance, particularly when the data path is not the shortest or least resource-intensive path.

*The answer is **True** because an administrator must configure static routers' internal routing tables.*

702   **INTRODUCTION TO DYNAMIC ROUTING**

Q.   *Which of the following answers contain reasons why network administrators frequently choose static routers over dynamic routers?*

Choose all answers that apply:

     A.   *Dynamic routers are more expensive.*

     B.   *Static routers are easier to set up and configure.*

     C.   *Static routers provide more security.*

     D.   *Static routers can send packets over different routes.*

As you learned in Tip 701, routers are divided into two basic groups: static routers and dynamic routers. Dynamic routers build their internal routing tables automatically, using information the routers gather from the network. In other words, dynamic routers are easier to set up and configure than static routers because the administrator must configure only the initial network—the router itself senses everything else it must know to transmit packets effectively. Because a dynamic router can choose any path along the network to transmit data, a dynamic router can transmit sequential packets across a network along different paths, depending on the network's current traffic. Figure 702 shows how a dynamic router will transmit sequential packets across a network along different paths.

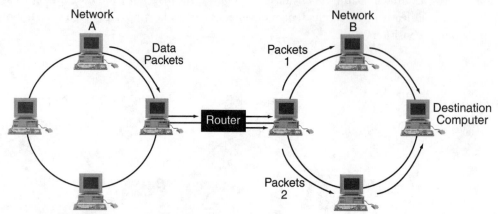

Figure 702 A dynamic router transmits data along different paths.

However, because dynamic routers are more sophisticated than static routers, they are typically more expensive. Therefore, network administrators frequently choose static routers over dynamic routers in smaller networks because the static router is less expensive or because the dynamic router is less secure—a direct result of data having an undetermined network route. On the other hand, administrators might choose dynamic routers instead of static routers because dynamic routers are easier to set up. However, dynamic routers can send data transmission packets over different routes because they evaluate the network before transmitting each packet and can choose a path for each that might be less resource-expensive than the path the previous packet used—a significant benefit in larger networks or high-traffic networks.

Answers A and C are correct because dynamic routers are more expensive than static routers and are less secure. Answer B is incorrect because dynamic routers are easier to set up and configure than static routers. Answer D is incorrect because static routers cannot split up packets over different routes.

703	**INTRODUCTION TO GATEWAYS**

Q.   Network administrators use gateways to perform what function?

Choose the best answer:

> *A.   Separate network segments.*
>
> *B.   Connect two or more separate networks together.*
>
> *C.   Provide communication between two or more different network architectures.*
>
> *D.   Provide access to the network for remote clients using the same network architecture.*

As you have learned, you can use routers when you design a network to connect different sections of a network. A router, however, generally presumes that both sections of a network have similar networking architectures or protocols.

To connect two network sections that use different architectures or protocols, you must use a different networking device, known as a *gateway*.

A gateway is a networking device that can connect dissimilar networking architectures or protocols. In other words, a network that transmits and receives data using only TCP/IP can transmit data to the gateway. The gateway, in turn, will translate the data into IPX-protocol communications for a network that transmits and receives data using only IPX. Another example would be devices that translate information for personal computers on a Local-area network (LAN) into a format that a mainframe computer originally designed to only understand communication from dumb terminals can recognize. Because the communication methods the mainframe and the LAN use are different, administrators must use a gateway for personal computers to access the mainframe. Figure 703 shows how a gateway receives, translates, and transmits information across two networks.

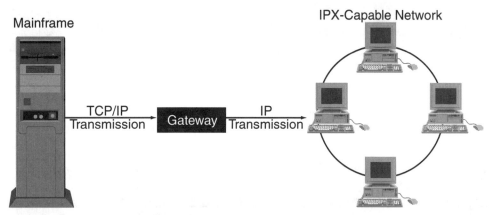

Figure 703 *The gateway bridges different network protocols.*

Note: Administrators can implement gateways as software components on normal LAN-based servers.

Answer C is correct because network administrators use gateways to provide communication between two or more dissimilar network architectures. Answer A is incorrect because different network segments are connected with a bridge or router. Answer B is incorrect because you can connect two or more separate networks with a router. Answer D is incorrect because remote access to a network is granted through a modem or other communication device.

704 **INTRODUCTION TO REPEATERS**

Q.   Network administrators frequently use repeaters to reduce network traffic by separating network segments.

True or False?

As you have learned, you can use various devices along a network to ensure that different sections of a network can communicate with each other. As your networks become more complex, it is possible that your network will become large enough to exceed normal allowable transmission distances for your network's cable or other transmission medium. In such cases, you should use a repeater to ensure the network's performance. As you learned in Tip 670, a repeater is a device that amplifies or enhances network transmissions so they can travel greater distances than would usually be possible. Network administrators frequently use repeaters to extend the maximum length of cable that can normally exist between network hosts such as computers, servers, or network printers. Some hub types (such as active hubs) can amplify or enhance a network's signals, and are commonly called multi-port repeaters—because they can receive and transmit along many different lengths of cable, and they amplify and enhance all transmissions that they process.

Repeaters do not have the ability to differentiate between network segments, so you cannot use them in place of bridges or routers. Instead, repeaters will amplify a signal and then pass it on to all segments of a network. Figure 704 shows how you might place a repeater on a network to amplify a signal.

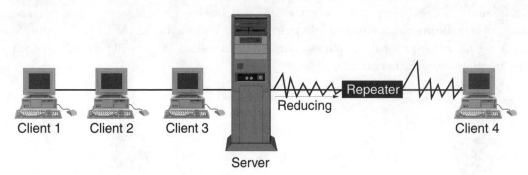

Figure 704 A repeater receives a network transmission, amplifies it, and retransmits it along the network cable.

Note: *Some bridges and routers can perform signal amplification as well as segment a network.*

The answer is **False** *because repeaters cannot filter data, but instead send all data they receive to all segments of the network.*

| 705 | UNDERSTANDING THE IMPORTANCE OF TRAFFIC CONTROL |

Q.   *What happens to data transmission packets when they collide with each other on the network?*

Choose the best answer:

    A.   *The packets move around each other and continue moving until they reach the destination computer.*

    B.   *The packets are destroyed.*

    C.   *The packets return to the computer of origin and begin again.*

    D.   *Packets cannot collide on a network.*

Imagine what it would be like if there were no street lights, signs, or police to manage the streets you drive your car on. Now think what it would be like if all roads were so narrow that only one car at a time could fit onto a street. It is easy to see how collisions would occur in such circumstances. This example corresponds to a computer network, with the network cable acting as the narrow street and the data transmission packets (groups of electrical pulses) taking the role of the cars. Without some form of traffic control, collisions will occur—and, just as in real life, even with traffic control, collisions still sometimes occur.

When data transmission packets collide with each other, both packets are destroyed. If packets from all the computers on the network were permitted to travel the network at the same time, collisions would be so common that nothing would ever get to its destination. Therefore, to communicate, computers and other devices on the network must take turns transmitting data on the network. There are several different and complicated methods of controlling network traffic, each of which the following Tips will detail. All networks that you work with will use at least one method of controlling network traffic, and some networks will use several or all the different methods across different network segments.

Answer B is correct because if data transmission packets collide on a network, the packets are destroyed. Answers A and C are incorrect because packets are destroyed when they collide. Answer D is incorrect because data transmission packets can collide in some networking systems.

706 | **INTRODUCTION TO TOKEN PASSING**

Q.   *Token-passing networks do not suffer from collision and contention problems.*

True or False?

As you learned Tip 705, different network architectures will use various traffic control measures to ensure that the number of data-packet collisions on the network remains at a minimum. One of the most common types of traffic control is known as *token passing networks*, which are based on a simple principle of token possession to enable transmission. In other words, in order for a computer to transmit data on the network, the computer must first possess a special packet of data called a *token*.

The token travels the network checking in with each computer to see if it is waiting to transmit data. If the computer is waiting to transmit data, the computer will transmit the data only when it receives the token. When the computer is finished transmitting data, it will generate a new token and pass it to the network.

Because only one token exists on the network, token passing networks do not suffer from *packet collision* or *network contention* (contention occurs when two or more computers try to send data onto the network at exactly the same time), which is the result of two or more computers requesting or attempting to transmit data at the same time. Figure 706 shows how a token passes from computer to computer along a token-passing network.

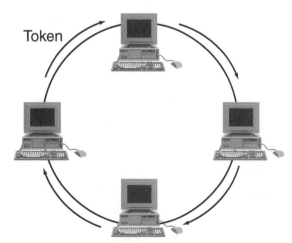

Figure 706 Each computer receives a token, transmits its data, and passes a token to the next computer.

Token-passing networks most often use the Ring or Star–Ring topology because the token must visit each computer and then move on to the next. The token moves in only one direction on the network cable, which prevents a computer from never receiving the token.

*The answer is **True** because only one computer on the network can possess a token at any time, so token-passing networks do not suffer from collision or contention.*

707   INTRODUCTION TO DEMAND PRIORITY

Q.   *Which of the following will occur if contention occurs in a demand priority-based network?*

Choose the best answer:

     A.   *All computers will stop for a period of time and begin transmitting again.*

     B.   *The data transmission packets will collide and be destroyed.*

     C.   *The network will transmit the data request with the highest priority first.*

     D.   *None of the above. Demand Priority-based networks do not suffer from contention problems.*

In Tip 706, you learned about token-passing networks, which control network traffic by ensuring that only a single computer at a time can transmit data. Token-passing networks have two significant limitations: First, after every transmission, each computer must pass the token. Second, if a single computer has a large number of transmissions to make, transmission time can be very slow because the token must pass around the network after each transmission. In large token-passing networks, such requirements can slow network performance significantly. However, as networks become larger, engineers design newer communication types to address such issues. One of the new communication types is known as *demand priority* network communication. Demand priority is a relatively new method of traffic control that uses the star or star–bus topology and works with 100Mbps Ethernet (a specific transmission protocol that you will learn more about in later Tips) networks. Demand priority uses intelligent hubs that network administrators can configure to assign priority levels to certain forms of data. (As you learned in Tip 656, intelligent hubs monitor the network and send signals based on how busy the network is.) Because each computer is connected directly to the hub, and the hub controls which computer can or cannot transmit on the network, packet collision does not occur. Contention on a demand priority network takes place when two or more computers request use of the network at the same time. How the hub handles the contention depends on what priority level the request has. For example, if two computers request use of the network at exactly the same time, the hub will grant use of the network to whichever data request has the highest priority. Figure 707 shows how an intelligent hub accepts requests and resolves contention.

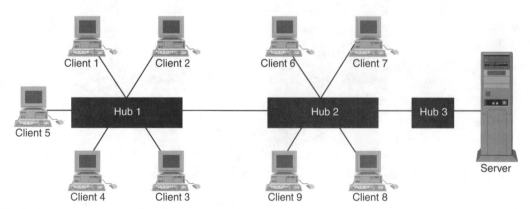

Figure 707 *The hub accepts, requests, and resolves contention issues.*

Answer C *is correct because the network will transmit the data request with the highest priority first.* **Answer A** *is incorrect because every computer assigns a data request priority in demand priority-based networks and the network will process the data with the highest priority first.* **Answer B** *is incorrect because the hub will determine priorities, the higher priority data request will transmit first, and collision will not occur.* **Answer D** *is incorrect because contention can take place on a demand priority-based network.*

708 UNDERSTANDING THE FEATURES OF DEMAND PRIORITY

Q.   Which of the following answers describe what will occur if two data requests with the same priority cause network contention?

Choose the best answer:

A.   The hub will randomly choose one data request and process it first.

B.   The intelligent hub will process data requests at the same time, alternating between packets.

C.   The intelligent hub will deny both data requests and force the requesting computers to start again.

D.   The hub will decide priority based on the originating computers' location.

As you learned in Tip 707, demand priority-based networks use intelligent hubs that can make decisions about which data request to process, based on the data request's priority. Demand priority-based networking systems can also alternate network use in much the same way a processor's time is divided in a multitasking operating system. For example, if two computers request network use at the same time and their data requests have the same priority level, the hub will process both requests at the same time by alternating packet transmissions so that each packet request receives a turn on the network.

Demand priority-based networks use a special cable scheme that uses four pairs of wires so that a computer to transmit and receive data at the same time. Features of demand priority networks include a lack of collisions, the fact that transmissions are not broadcast to the entire network, the capability for more than one computer can transmit data at the same time, and the ability of computers to transmit and receive data at the same time.

Answer B is correct because the intelligent hub will process both data requests at the same time and will alternate transmission at the packet level. Answer A is incorrect because the hub cannot randomly choose a data request. Answer C is incorrect because the intelligent hub will not deny data requests but will process them simultaneously. Answer D is incorrect because the hub cannot assign priority based on anything other than its configured priority table.

709 DEFINING NETWORK CONTENTION

Q.   Which of the following answers best describe the concept of network contention?

Choose the best answer:

A.   The data transmission packets collide with each other.

B.   Two or more computers attempt use of the network at exactly the same time.

C.   Too much data is on the network at one time.

D.   Electronic interference is corrupting data transmission.

As you have learned in previous Tips, network contention occurs when two or more computers try to use the network or request the network's use at the same time. In addition, you have learned that collision occurs when two data transmission packets collide with each other on the network and are destroyed. Although some network hubs detect contention because of collisions, the two terms do not mean the same thing. Some networks—such as those that use a demand priority traffic control method—can have contention, but, by their nature, will not allow collisions. Contention is a fundamentally different situation than collision—because, while some networks (such as token-ring networks) will never have packet collisions, there will always be contention so long as you connect multiple computers to the network.

Answer B is correct because network contention occurs when two or more computers request use of the network at the exact same time. Answer A is incorrect because when data transmission packets collide, they create collision, not contention. Answer C is incorrect because too much data on the network is called saturation, not contention. Answer D is incorrect because electronic interference does not produce contention.

710	**INTRODUCTION TO CARRIER SENSE MULTIPLE ACCESS WITH COLLISION DETECTION (CSMA/CD)**

Q.   *In networks that use a Carrier Sense Multiple Access with Collision Detection traffic control method, each computer listens to the network for collisions that might make it wait.*

True or False?

As you learned in previous Tips, some networks use both token-passing and demand priority for data transmission and collision reduction. However, most smaller Ethernet networks will use a third network type, *the Carrier Sense Multiple Access with Collision Detection (CSMA/CD)* network. In CSMA/CD-based systems, networking components, such as the network interface cards (NIC) and hubs, are always listening to the traffic on the network and detecting collisions and transmissions on the network. Such cards and hubs use *carrier sense* to listen on the network. When collisions occur, all cards on the network stop for a period of time and then begin transmitting again. Because each network interface card will wait a different amount of time, one computer will begin transmitting before others. Computers on the network that sense transmission taking place will wait until the transmission stops before beginning to transmit information themselves. The reason CSMS/ CD systems are popular in smaller networks, and not in larger ones, is because as network traffic grows, the chance of collision increases. When the number of computers on the network grows too large, collisions will occur so frequently that the network will become unacceptably slow or not function at all.

The answer is True because in CSMA/CD-based networks, each computer listens or senses the network for collisions that might make the computer wait.

711	**INTRODUCTION TO THE OPEN SYSTEMS INTERCONNECTION (OSI) NETWORK MODEL**

Q.   *Which of the following answers best describe the OSI model?*

Choose the best answer:

A.   *A three-dimensional drawing that details a personal computer's internal workings.*

B.   *An internationally accepted model that describes how hardware and software should function together to produce network communication.*

C.   *The blueprints for the first network.*

D.   *A set of networking specifications that describes valid variables in network hardware, such as network interface cards.*

In 1984, the *International Standards Organization (ISO)* created the Open Systems Interconnection (OSI) model. The OSI model defines a series of layers that each describe a part of the process that takes data from an application and transmits it over a network. Table 711 describes the seven OSI model layers.

Layer	Description
Application	The application layer contains details about network-wide applications.
Presentation	The presentation consolidates common functions that networks must repeatedly use during network communications.
Session	The session layer negotiates connections between processes or applications on different host computers.
Transport	The transport layer delivers (or transports) data within the host computer.
Network	The network layer determines the route or path that data follows to reach its destination on the network. It is responsible for handling network traffic, congestion, and transfer rates across the network's transmission lines.
Data Link	The data-link layer transfers data between the physical layer and the network layer. The network interface card (NIC) is typically the data-link layer, though in Thicknet networks the vampire-tap connector and the transceiver compose the data-link layer.
Physical	The physical layer transmits data through the network. This layer typically contains cable, routers, and so on.

Table 711 The seven layers in the Open Systems Interconnection (OSI) model.

As you have learned, your computer must transform information to pass it along the network—from parallel bits to serial bits. However, at a more global level, the computer and the network must transform information from the format that an application understands into a format that a network can understand and successfully transmit. Each OSI model layer describes what happens to a piece of information as it passes from layer to layer. (The following Tips describe each layer's details.) Figure 711 shows how you can best visualize the layers in the OSI model.

	Layer	Data Type
7	Application Layer	Messages
6	Presentation Layer	Messages
5	Session Layer	Messages
4	Transport Layer	Messages
3	Network Layer	Packets
2	Data-Link Layer	Frames
1	Physical Layer	Bits

Figure 711 Understanding the layers in the OSI model.

Answer B is correct because the OSI model is an internationally accepted model that describes how hardware and software should function together to produce network communication. *Answers A, C, and D* are incorrect because they do not describe the OSI model.

712	### UNDERSTANDING THE *OSI* MODEL'S APPLICATION LAYER

Q.   Which of the following OSI model layers is responsible for handling general network access, flow control, and error recovery?

Choose the best answer:

   A.   Presentation

   B.   Application

   C.   Data Link

   D.   Session

As you learned in Tip 711, the uppermost layer of the OSI model is the Application layer. As its name implies, the Application layer handles the services that directly support applications. The Application layer performs functions such as providing access to the network or creating a logical drive letter that an older application can use for access, passing information out at an acceptable pace, and passing information over the network again if one of the lower levels in the model detected an error. Overall, the Application layer is responsible for general network access, flow control, and error recovery.

Answer B is correct because the OSI model's Application layer handles general network access, flow control, and error recovery. Answer A is incorrect because the OSI model's Presentation layer is responsible for translating application data into a format the network sub-components that operate in the lower levels of the OSI model can recognize. Answer C is incorrect because the OSI model's Data-link layer is responsible for the creation and transmission of data frames through the Physical layer. Answer D is incorrect because the OSI model's Session layer is responsible for establishing a link between the participating computers and monitoring the transmission so that if a network failure occurs, the host computer will only retransmit the data that the target computer did not successfully receive.

713	### UNDERSTANDING THE *OSI* MODEL'S PRESENTATION LAYER

Q.   Which of the following OSI model layers is responsible for translating data from an application into a format that the networking sub-components that prepare data for transmission can recognize?

Choose the best answer:

   A.   Application

   B.   Presentation

   C.   Session

   D.   Network

The OSI model's Presentation layer is responsible for translating data from applications into a format that the networking sub-components that operate at lower levels of the OSI model can recognize. The Presentation layer is also responsible for translating data from lower levels into a format that applications can recognize. The Presentation layer converts protocols, manages data compression and encryption, and converts character sets. Network components such as the redirector (which intercepts local application requests and transmits them across the network to a remote machine) operate in the Presentation layer.

On the sending side of a transmission, data destined for a remote location on the network passes from the Application layer to the Presentation layer which, together with the lower levels of the OSI model, prepares and eventually transmits the data across the network. On the receiving side of a transmission, data that lower levels of the OSI model reconstructed passes to the Presentation layer, which then converts the data back into a format that the intended application will understand.

Answer B is correct because the OSI model's Presentation layer is responsible for translating data from applications into a format the network sub-components can recognize. Answer A is incorrect because the OSI model's Application layer is responsible for general network access, flow control, and error recovery. Answer C is incorrect because the OSI model's Session layer is responsible for establishing a connection between participating computers and monitoring transmission so that the host computer does not have to retransmit data the target computer already received. Answer D is incorrect because the OSI model's Network layer is responsible for addressing data transmissions and determining the best route over the network.

714   UNDERSTANDING THE **OSI** MODEL'S SESSION LAYER

Q.   *Which of the following OSI model layers is responsible for establishing a connection between the participating computers and monitoring transmission so that host computer does not have to retransmit data the target computer already received?*

Choose the best answer:

     A.   Presentation

     B.   Application

     C.   Session

     D.   Network

As you learned in Tip 713, the OSI model's Presentation layer translates data from the Application layer and passes it down into the OSI protocol stack (the *protocol stack* refers to all the layers in the OSI model). After the Presentation layer has translated that data into a commonly recognized format, the Presentation layer passes the data to the Session layer which, in turn, resolves network names into physical network addresses and then establishes a link with the data's intended recipient. The Session layer also monitors the transmission by placing special checkpoints into the data at regular intervals so that the host computer does not have to retransmit data the target computer already received if the network fails. At this point, the participating processes on each computer agree on transmission specifications, such as the length of transmission, when each side will transmit, and when each side will receive.

Answer C is correct because the OSI model's Session layer is responsible for establishing a connection between participating computers and monitoring transmissions so that the host computer does not have to retransmit data the target computer already received. Answer A is incorrect because the OSI model's Presentation layer is responsible for translating data from applications into a format that the network sub-components that operate at lower levels of the OSI model can recognize. Answer B is incorrect because the OSI model's Application layer is responsible for general network access, flow control, and error recovery. Answer D is incorrect because the OSI model's Network layer is responsible for addressing data transmissions and determining the best route over the network.

715 UNDERSTANDING THE *OSI* MODEL'S TRANSPORT LAYER

Q.   *Which of the following layers of the OSI model ensures that the network delivers data transmission packets in the correct sequence, with no errors, losses, or duplications?*

Choose the best answer:

   A.   *Network*

   B.   *Presentation*

   C.   *Application*

   D.   *Physical*

As you have learned, when the participating computers have established a communication session and agreed upon the transmission terms set in the Session layer, the data passes to the Transport layer which, in turn adds additional specifications to the connection between computers. The Transport layer converts the data from frames (large blocks of data internal to the computer) into packets (generally smaller blocks of data that the network can transmit). In other words, larger portions of information are broken up while portions that are too small are combined into data transmission packets that are about the same size, which facilitates efficient communication. The Transport layer checks each packet to ensure that the network delivers the data without errors, losses, or duplications.

Answer A is correct because the OSI model's Transport layer ensures that the network delivers data transmission packets in the correct sequence, with no errors, losses, or duplications. Answer B is incorrect because the OSI model's Presentation layer is responsible for translating data from applications into a format that the network sub-components that operate in lower levels of the OSI model can recognize. Answer C is incorrect because the OSI model's Application layer is responsible for general network access, flow control, and error recovery. Answer D is incorrect because the OSI model's Physical layer is responsible for the actual transmission of data over hardware.

716 UNDERSTANDING THE *OSI* MODEL'S NETWORK LAYER

Q.   *Which of the following OSI model layers are responsible for addressing data transmissions and determining the best route over the network?*

Choose the best answer:

   A.   *Presentation*

   B.   *Application*

   C.   *Network*

   D.   *Physical*

As you learned in Tip 715, the Transport layer divides information into packets in preparation for the data's transmission across the network. Conversely, the Transport layer on the receiving computer recombines the packets into data the receiving application can understand. After the Transport layer divides the information into packets, it passes the packets to the Network layer. The OSI model's Network layer is responsible for addressing packets and determining the best route over the network to the destination computer. Then, the data transmission packet is given the instructions it requires to navigate the network and find the destination computer. On the receiving computer, the Network layer is responsible for removing the addresses and passing the packet up into the Transport layer. Figure 716 shows how the Network layer adds addressing to a packet before transmission.

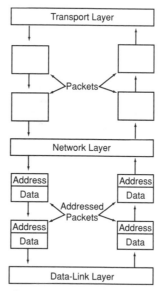

Figure 716 The Network layer adds the addressing information to the packet.

Answer C is correct because the OSI model's Network layer is responsible for addressing data transmissions and determining the best route over the network. Answer A is incorrect because the OSI model's Presentation layer is responsible for translating data from applications into a format that networking sub-components that operate at lower layers of the OSI model recognize. Answer B is incorrect because the OSI model's Application layer is responsible for general network access, flow control, and error recovery. Answer D is incorrect because the OSI model's Physical layer is responsible for actual transmission of data over network hardware.

717 UNDERSTANDING THE OSI MODEL'S DATA-LINK LAYER

Q.   *Which of the following OSI model layers is responsible for constructing data frames?*

Choose the best answer:

A.   *Physical*

B.   *Application*

C.   *Presentation*

D.   *Data-Link*

As you have learned, the OSI model's lower layers actually divide the data to transmit into smaller sections, address the sections, and prepare the information for transmission. The model's next-to-lowest layer, the Data-link layer, is perhaps the most interesting because this layer converts the packet data the Network layer constructs into electrical frames, or a series of pulses, that the physical network layer can transmit. The Data-link layer constructs the frames and transmits them through the Physical layer to the destination computer. The Data-link layer on the receiving computer sends a response indicating that it received the frame with no errors. If the sending computer does not receive a response or receives a response that indicates an error, the Data-link layer will retransmit that frame. You can associate the data-link layer with your network interface card. Figure 717 shows how the Data-link layer formats frames and passes them to the Physical layer for actual transmission.

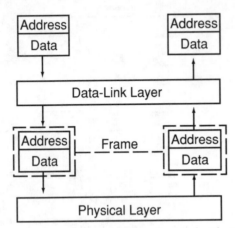

Figure 717 The Data-link layer formats frames for transmission and passes them to the Physical layer.

Answer D is correct because the OSI model's Data-link layer is responsible for constructing data frames and transmitting them through the Physical layer. Answer A is incorrect because the OSI model's Physical layer is responsible for actual transmission over networking hardware. Answer B is incorrect because the OSI model's Application layer is responsible for general network access, flow control, and error recovery. Answer C is incorrect because the OSI model's Presentation layer is responsible for translating data from applications into a format that the networking sub-components that operate at lower layers of the OSI model recognize.

718	UNDERSTANDING THE OSI MODEL'S PHYSICAL LAYER

Q.   Which of the following OSI model layers is responsible for the actual transmission of data over networking hardware?

Choose the best answer:

A.   Data Link

B.   Network

C.   Physical

D.   Application

As you have learned, the OSI model has seven layers. The first six layers perform data-conversion, addressing, monitoring, transmitting, and other higher-level functions in the network communications process. The last (bottom) layer is the Physical layer, which is responsible for the actual transmission and reception of data. The Physical layer is responsible for controlling the network interface cards (NIC) and media attachments, such as a cable. Unlike the other layers in the OSI model, the Physical layer does not perform processing, or analyze the data that passes through it. Instead, the Physical layer simply corresponds to the physical media that actually transports the data from one computer to another on the network.

Answer C is correct because the OSI model's Physical layer is responsible for actual transmission of data over network hardware. Answer A is incorrect because the OSI model's Data-link layer is responsible for constructing data frames and transmitting them through the Physical layer. Answer B is incorrect because the OSI model's Network layer is responsible for addressing data transmissions and determining the best route over the network. Answer D is incorrect because the OSI model's Application layer is responsible for general network access, flow control, and error recovery.

719   UNDERSTANDING THE RELATIONSHIP BETWEEN OSI LAYERS

Q.   *Each OSI layer works independently and is unaware of other layers.*

True or False?

The OSI model's layers are designed to function as if they were actually communicating with their equivalent layers on the destination computer. This communication, however, is *virtual*—that is, the layers on the two computers do not actually communicate directly with each other, as every communication goes down the protocol stack on the sending computer and comes back up the protocol stack on the receiving computer. While virtual communication exists between each layer in the protocol stack and the corresponding layer on the remote machine, only the Physical layer actually sends and receives data from other computers on the network. In other words, each layer in the stack places certain information into the data that the Physical layer transmits which its corresponding layer on the receiving computer will process when it receives the data. Figure 719 illustrates the path that data follows as it passes between applications on separate computers and the virtual communications between layers.

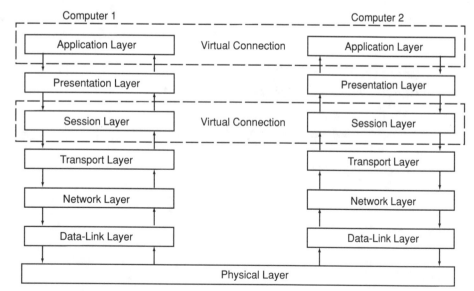

Figure 719 Data transmission in the OSI model.

The answer is **False** because the OSI model layers work together to create network transmissions. Each layer depends on others to perform its function. Although the layers are designed as if they communicated directly with the same layer on another computer, the actual process involves layers communicating with each other and the Physical layer actually transmitting and receiving data.

720   **UNDERSTANDING PACKET CONSTRUCTION**

Q. Which of the following answers are components of a data transmission packet?

Choose all answers that apply:

    A. Header

    B. Footer

    C. Trailer

    D. Data

As previous Tips have indicated, a packet is a piece of data that transmits over the network. Each layer in the OSI model adds additional information to the packet to ensure that the correct computer receives the information in the packet, and that the packet contains no errors.

Packets have three sections: *Header*, *Data*, and *Trailer*. The Header contains information such as the destination and source computers' addresses and the time the packet is transmitting, which information the receiving computer can use to ensure that it reconstructs the data in the proper order. The Data section contains the actual data the packet is transmitting. The Trailer section contains the *Cyclic Redundancy Check (CRC)* value, which is error-checking information that operates using mathematical calculations to verify the data's integrity after transmission.

Answers A, C, and D are correct because data transmission packets are made up of the Header, Data, and Trailer. **Answer B** *is incorrect because there is no component in a packet called the Footer.*

721   **INTRODUCTION TO THE 802 PROJECT**

Q. When was the 802 project started?

Choose the best answer:

    A. February 1980

    B. January 1980

    C. February 1982

    D. March 1982

In February 1980, the Institute of Electrical and Electronics Engineers (IEEE) began a project intended to define network communications and design standards. Named for the year (1980) and month (February) that it began,

Project 802 eventually became 12 categories that define various network standards. These standards, although split into different categories, all relate to the physical connection of network hardware, such as network interface cards (NIC), hubs, and repeaters for a specific network type, as well as the software the network uses. Because development of Project 802 and the OSI model occurred at roughly the same time, and because both committees shared information during development, many standards in Project 802 directly correspond to or enhance OSI model layers.

Answer A is correct because the 802 project is named for the second month of 1980 (February 1980), which is the year the project began. Answers B, C, and D are incorrect because they list incorrect starting months or years.

722   INTRODUCTION TO THE *802* CATEGORIES

Q.   *Which of the following 802 categories defines the standards for CSMA/CD?*

Choose the best answer:

     A.   *802.1*

     B.   *802.2*

     C.   *802.3*

     D.   *802.4*

As you learned in Tip 721, Project 802 defines 12 categories of network standards. Each of the Project 802 categories describe important, network-relevant information that describes the network's physical composition, collision and contention detection, and resolution standards. Table 722 describes each category.

Category	What Project 802 defines
802.1	Internetworking
802.2	Logical Link Control (LLC) sub-layer
802.3	Carrier Sense Multiple Access with Collision Detection (CSMA/CD)
802.4	Token Bus Local-area networking (LAN)
802.5	Token Ring Local-area networking (LAN)
802.6	Metropolitan Area Networking (MAN)
802.7	Broadband Technical Advisory Group
802.8	Fiber Optic Technical Advisory Group
802.9	Integrated Voice and Data Networking
802.10	Network Security
802.11	Wireless Networking
802.12	Demand Priority Networking

Table 722 The twelve Project 802 categories.

Answer C is correct because the IEEE category 802.3 defines the Carrier Sense Multiple Access with Collision Detection (CSMA/CD) Ethernet LAN standards. Answer A is incorrect because 802.1 defines the internetworking standards. Answer B is incorrect because 802.2 defines the Logical Link Control (LLC) standards. Answer D is incorrect because 802.4 defines the Token Bus LAN standards.

723   COMPARING PROJECT 802 AND THE OSI MODEL

Q.   *To which layer of the OSI model does Project 802 standards give more detail?*

Choose the best answer:

    A.   *Application*

    B.   *Network*

    C.   *Data-Link*

    D.   *Physical*

Because Project 802 deals specifically with the connection of network devices to computers and transport media, Project 802 affects the OSI model's Data-Link and Physical layers. As the IEEE committee worked with the OSI model's Data-Link layer, they found that the original, single-layer definition was not sufficient to describe the actions the layer performs. Therefore, the IEEE committee subdivided the Data-Link layer into two sub-layers—the Logical Link Control (LLC) layer and the Media Access Control (MAC) layer. Figure 723 illustrates the OSI model's LLC and MAC sub-layers.

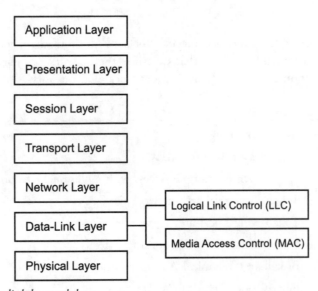

Figure 723 *The OSI model's Data-link layer sub-layers.*

Answer C is correct because the Project 802 standards subdivided the Data-link layer into the Logical Link Control layer and the Media Access Control layer. Answers A, B, and D are incorrect because they list layers that Project 802 standards did not enhance.

724   UNDERSTANDING THE LOGICAL LINK CONTROL SUB-LAYER

Q.   Which category of the Project 802 standards defines the Logical Link Control sub-layer?

Choose all answers that apply:

    A.   *802.1*

    B.   *802.2*

    C.   *802.12*

    D.   *802.11*

As you learned in Tip 723, the Logical Link Control (LLC) layer is a sub-layer of the Data-link layer. The LLC sub-layer defines the use of *Service Access Points (SAP)* that the Data-link layer uses to transfer information to the OSI model's upper layers. Service Access Points are software-interface points that let applications, services, and drivers communicate. Category 802.2 of the Project 802 standards defines the standards for Service Access Points. Category 802.1 of the Project 802 standards defines the LLC portion that concerns network management.

Answers A and B are correct because categories 802.1 and 802.2 of the Project 802 standards define the Logical Link Control sub-layer. Answers C and D are incorrect because the categories listed do not define the Logical Link Control sub-layer.

---

725   UNDERSTANDING THE MEDIA ACCESS CONTROL SUB-LAYER

Q.   Which of the following Project 802 categories help define the Media Access Control sub-layer?

Choose all answers that apply:

    A.   *802.3*

    B.   *802.4*

    C.   *802.12*

    D.   *802.5*

As you learned in Tip 723, the Media Access Control (MAC) is a sub-layer of the Data-Link layer. The MAC sub-layer defines the standards for communicating with a network interface card, as well as how network interface cards communicate on specific cable types. Various categories of the Project 802 standards define different network types. For example, category 802.3 defines Carrier Sense Multiple Access with Collision Detection (CSMA/CD) networks, and category 802.4 defines Token Bus networks. In turn, category 802.5 defines Token Ring networks, and category 802.12 defines Demand Priority networks.

Answers A, B, C, and D are all correct because each of the listed categories defines the Media Access Control sub-layer in a different type of network. 802.3 defines Carrier Sense Multiple Access with Collision Detection (CSMA/CD), 802.4 Defines Token Bus, 802.5 defines Token Ring, and 802.12 defines Demand Priority.

---

726   UNDERSTANDING THE NECESSITY OF PACKETS

Q.   *What standard industry term can you use interchangeably with the term packet?*

Choose the best answer:

    A.   *Data*

    B.   *Chunk*

    C.   *Piece*

    D.   *Frame*

You can think of packets as small, combined groups of information (data) transmitting over the network. The information packets that users work with every day and often send across a network are usually very large. However, users cannot send large amounts of data over the network all at once for several reasons. If you were to dump a large file onto the network all at one time, no other computer would be able to use the network until the receiving computer got the entire file. The receiving computer, in addition, would be unable to respond until the file transfer was complete. Even worse, if there were an error in a file transmission, you would have to retransmit the entire file (rather than just a small section of the file, as you do with packets), which action would halt the network yet again.

To avoid such problems, the network protocols divide all information into packets prior to transmission. Network administrators frequently use the term *frames* to describe packets, and they use the two terms interchangeably—even though, as you have learned, the network model allows for two different frame types: page frames within the computer, and electrical frames across the network. However, when working with data that transmits across the network, you can use either packets or frames to describe the data groupings, and most network administrators will understand what you are referring to.

***Answer D** is correct because you can use the standard industry terms frame and packet interchangeably. **Answers A, B, and C** are incorrect because the terms data, chunk, and piece are not standard industry terms and you cannot use them interchangeably with the term packet.*

727   **UNDERSTANDING PACKET CREATION**

Q.   *At what layer in the OSI model do packets begin to form?*

Choose the best answer:

    A.   *Application*

    B.   *Network*

    C.   *Data Link*

    D.   *Transport*

As you learned in Tip 720, packets are essentially pieces of data for transmission across the network that the network protocol stack separates out of the main data source. Each packet, in addition to the information from the original data source that it contains, includes information that lets the packet find the destination computer and check itself to ensure the transmission resulted in no errors. Because a packet begins as data, packet creation begins in the Application layer where the data originates and passes down through the other layers. As the packet passes through the Presentation, Session, Transport, and Network layers, each layer in the protocol processes the data and adds header information for each piece to the Packet Header. At the Data-link layer, the network protocol creates the Trailer with the Cyclic Redundancy Check (CRC) that lets a packet check itself for content when it arrives at the destination computer. When the packet finally arrives at the Physical layer, it contains information from each of the other layers in the OSI model. The Physical layer actually transmits the packet and all its contents to the receiving computer. On the receiving computer, the layers work in the opposite direction, reading and stripping away the additional information the packet contains until the application receives only the original data.

Answer A is correct because packets begin to form from data at the Application layer of the OSI model. Answers B, C, and D are incorrect because packets have already begun to form when they reach the remaining layers of the OSI model.

728 UNDERSTANDING PACKET ADDRESSING

Q. What portion of a packet contains the addresses of the destination and source computers?

Choose the best answer:

　　A.　Data

　　B.　Header

　　C.　Trailer

　　D.　Route

As you have learned in previous Tips, in order for a network to function properly, computer communication must take one of two forms. Either one computer must be able to send data to only one other computer and no others (which is very uncommon), or each computer must be able to send data to all computers on the network. In most network environments, communication takes place between only two computers or between one computer and another device, such as a printer or router.

Because most networking systems transmit data from one computer to all computers, on most networks all the network interface cards (NIC) on a segment of the network will see all packets moving on that segment. Each NIC must read the address on the packet that specifies the destination computer. When a NIC reads an address that matches its own, it will pass the packet up through the layers of the OSI model—otherwise, the NIC will simply ignore the packet.

Sometimes the computers on the network or other network devices must police the network to ensure that packets reach the intended destination and that packets do not travel to segments of the network where they should not be. Network devices use two methods to control the passage of packets: *packet forwarding* and *packet filtering*.

In packet forwarding, a network device can send a packet on to the next segment based on the packet's destination address. Packet filtering uses pre-specified criteria to determine whether the filtering device should or should not pass a packet to the next segment of the network. If packet filtering finds criteria that matches the restrictions (in other words, it finds that the packet does not need to transit to the next segment), it does not pass the packet on to the next segment.

Answer B is correct because a packet's Header portion contains the addresses of the destination and source computers. Answer A is incorrect because a packet's Data portion contains data. Answer C is incorrect because a packet's Trailer portion contains the Cyclic Redundancy Check (CRC). Answer D is incorrect because Route is not a portion of a Packet.

| 729 | **UNDERSTANDING PROTOCOLS' ROLES IN NETWORK COMMUNICATION** |

Q.   *Protocols only carry data across networks.*

True or False?

As you have learned, protocols establish rules for communication. Protocols actually come in a variety of forms and perform different jobs on networks and computers. Although network administrators frequently use the terms Network protocol and Transport protocol interchangeably, these are actually different kinds of protocols that perform different functions. You can divide protocols into three major categories: *Application* protocols, *Transport* protocols, and *Network* protocols. When you work with protocols, you will generally combine them into groupings known as *protocol stacks* or *protocol suites*—two terms that refer to the same grouping of individual protocols. It is the protocol stack, then, that a network administrator often refers to when he or she says Transport or Network protocol. For example, when you install the TCP/IP protocol (a common way to describe installation), you are actually installing a *stack* of protocols that work together to produce communication.

Protocols let different software components communicate within the computer prior to transportation over a network, let the software components communicate with the hardware, establish the rules for transportation, and establish the required data formatting so that it can transmit without error.

*The answer is **False** because protocols provide a wide variety of services to data prior to transmission.*

| 730 | **UNDERSTANDING HOW PROTOCOLS WORK** |

Q.   *Protocols define the steps software will perform to break apart data, transmit it over a network, and reconstruct it.*

True or False?

As you have learned, when you install network support, you actually install software that implements a protocol stack onto a computer. After you install a protocol stack onto a computer or other network device, the operating system or hard-burned BIOS binds the protocol stack to the computer's network interface card (NIC). In addition to letting the computer use the protocol to perform network operations, the binding process determines the order in which the computer will use protocols to establish communication. For example, assume you have both the NetBEUI and TCP/IP protocols installed on your computer and you have bound them so that NetBEUI is the first protocol. When you try to send or receive data to or from a remote computer, your system will try to establish communication first using the NetBEUI protocol. If you cannot achieve communication with NetBEUI, your computer will then try to establish communication with the TCP/IP protocol. After protocols are bound, they perform almost all the work involved in transforming data into a format that can transmit over a network. Each layer within a protocol stack may perform operations on data to prepare it for transmission. On the receiving computer, the protocol layers are responsible for reading and reconstructing the packets into a format that the application the data is intended for can recognize.

*The answer is **True** because protocols define how software performs various network operations.*

| 731 | UNDERSTANDING THE RELATIONSHIP BETWEEN PROTOCOLS AND THE OSI MODEL |

Q. Which of the following statements about protocols are true?

Choose the best answer:

A. Protocols work only in the upper layers of the OSI model

B. Protocols work only in the lower layers of the OSI model

C. Protocols work in all layers of the OSI model

D. Protocols work only in the Transport layer of the OSI model

As you have learned, protocols perform a variety of tasks both inside the computer prior to network communication and on the actual networking hardware that transmits the data. You can understand what a protocol's function is and where it operates in the OSI model from the description given to the protocol. For example, Application protocols work in the first three layers of the OSI model, but Network protocols operate in the last three layers. Figure 731 illustrates where protocols function in the OSI model.

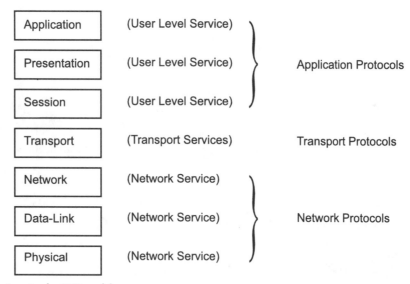

Figure 731 *Protocol locations in the OSI model.*

Answer C *is correct because protocols can work in all layers of the OSI model.* **Answers A, B, and D** *are incorrect statements.*

| 732 | COMPARING ROUTABLE AND NON-ROUTABLE PROTOCOLS |

Q. Which of the following are examples of routable protocols?

Choose all answers that apply:

    A.   IP

    B.   NetBEUI

    C.   AppleTalk

    D.   IPX

In general network terms, a *network* is defined as a series of computers that can directly communicate with each other. Therefore, two computers physically located on opposite sides of the world can be a network if they can communicate with each other directly. Conversely, you can have two networks on the same physical cable backbone if the protocols' configuration for the two networks makes it impossible for computers in one network to communicate directly with the computers on the other one (although the amount of traffic would probably make both networks very slow).

Different networks sometimes must communicate with each other. Therefore, design engineers specifically constructed some protocols so that, if a computer that does not exist within their immediate network addresses, the network can pass the transmission to the network on which the destination computer does exist. These protocols are *routable protocols* because data that computers transmit using one of the protocols can move, or transfer, from one network to another.

Not all protocols or protocol stacks are routable. For example, networks cannot route the NetBEUI protocol. The primary reason that NetBEUI does not support routing is that Microsoft moved much of its network structure to the TCP/IP protocol (which is routable) in recent years, and simply did not feel as if they needed to make NetBEUI routable. Therefore, if you have a wide-area network (WAN) or even a local-area network (LAN) that has more than one network defined within it and your computers must sometimes communicate with computers on other networks, you must be careful to choose a routable protocol. The following list includes some routable protocols:

- TCP/IP

- AppleTalk

- NWLINK (IPX/SPX)

- DECnet

*Answers A, C, and D are correct because IP, AppleTalk, and IPX are routable protocols. **Answer B** is incorrect because NetBEUI is not a routable protocol.*

| **733** | **UNDERSTANDING APPLICATION PROTOCOLS** |

Q.   Which of the following are examples of Application protocols?

Choose all answers that apply:

    A.   SMTP

    B.   TCP

    C.   FTP

    D.   NetBEUI

Application protocols operate in the upper levels of the OSI model and provide services such as application-to-application communication and data exchange. Commonly, application protocols manage distributed network services such as mail services, directory services, file transfer services, and so on. The following list provides examples of Application protocols:

- Simple Mail Transfer Protocol (SMTP)
- Lightweight Directory-Access Protocol (LDAP)
- File Transfer Protocol (FTP)
- Simple Network Management Protocol (SNMP)
- X.400
- X.500

Answers A and C are correct because Simple Mail Transfer Protocol (SMTP) and File Transfer Protocol (FTP) are examples of Application protocols. Answers B and D are incorrect because the Transmission Control Protocol (TCP) and the NetBIOS Extended User Interface (NetBEUI) are examples of Transport protocols.

734 UNDERSTANDING TRANSPORT PROTOCOLS

Q.   Which of the following are examples of Transport protocols?

Choose all answers that apply:

    A.   *TCP*

    B.   *SPX*

    C.   *IPX*

    D.   *DDP*

Transport protocols operate in the OSI model's Transport layer and provide services such as establishing the communication between computers and preparing data for error-free transmission. By far, the most commonly used protocol is the Transmission Control Protocol (TCP) (which all computers on the Internet use). However, both Microsoft and Novell have their own, custom protocols to manage transport across their networks. Sequential Packet Exchange (SPX), for example, is the original transport protocol for Novell networks. Today, most Novell networks use some combination of SPX and TCP to handle network transmissions. The following list contains some examples of Transport protocols:

- Transmission Control Protocol (TCP)
- NWLINK (the Microsoft-designed IPX/SPX-compatible protocol)
- Sequential Packet Exchange (SPX)
- NetBIOS Extended User Interface (NetBEUI)

Note: *NetBEUI is an example of a self-contained protocol that is both a Transport and Network protocol.*

Answers A and B are correct because the Transmission Control Protocol (TCP) and the Sequential Packet Exchange (SPX) protocols are examples of Transport protocols. Answers C and D are incorrect because the Internetwork Packet Exchange (IPX) and the Datagram Delivery Protocol (DDP) are examples of Network protocols.

---

735   UNDERSTANDING NETWORK PROTOCOLS

Q.   Which of the following are examples of Network protocols?

Choose all answers that apply:

A.   TCP

B.   IP

C.   IPX

D.   DDP

Network protocols function in the lower layers of the OSI model and provide functions such as error checking, packet addressing, and communicating with specific network hardware or media. As you have learned, network protocols work hand-in-hand with transport protocols to manage network transmissions. For example, whenever you refer to the Transmissions Control Protocol (TCP), you will also refer to the Internet Protocol (IP), combining the two protocols into a stack or suite (as TCP/IP). The same is true for IPX/SPX. However, as Tip 734 indicates, NetBEUI is a *self-contained protocol*—meaning that a single protocol includes both the network and transport protocols. Examples of Network protocols include those in the following list:

- Internet Protocol (IP)
- NWLINK (the Microsoft-designed IPX/SPX-compatible protocol)
- Internetwork Packet Exchange (IPX)
- NetBIOS Extended User Interface (NetBEUI)
- Datagram Delivery Protocol (DDP)

Answers B, C, and D are correct because the Internet Protocol (IP), Internetwork Packet Exchange (IPX), and Datagram Delivery Protocol (DDP) protocols are all examples of Network Protocols. Answer A is incorrect because the Transmission Control Protocol (TCP) is an example of a Transport protocol.

---

736   INTRODUCTION TO STANDARD PROTOCOL STACKS

Q.   Which of the following protocols is limited to Microsoft-based networks?

Choose the best answer:

     A.   TCP/IP

     B.   IPX/SPX

     C.   NetBEUI

     D.   AppleTalk

As you have learned, different networks support and implement different protocol stacks—depending on the network operating system (NOS), the network's use and, in many cases, the network's age. The computer network industry uses some protocol stacks more frequently than others. In turn, network administrators frequently refer to these protocol stacks as being standard because people use the terms so often. Table 736 describes some of the most frequently used protocol stacks.

Protocol Stack	Description
TCP/IP	The Transmission Control Protocol/Internet Protocol is the protocol stack network administrators most frequently use in internetwork environments and is the standard for Internet access. TCP/IP is a routable protocol and is supported by almost all networking implementations. Although the size of the TCP/IP protocol stack caused some problems on earlier MS-DOS-based networks, current operating systems do not suffer because of its size.
NetBEUI	The Network Basic Input Output System (NetBIOS) Extended User Interface (NetBEUI) is a self-contained, self-configuring protocol supported by Microsoft operating systems. NetBEUI is easy to install and requires no configuration. Disadvantages include the facts that NetBEUI is non-routable and is restricted to Microsoft-based networks.
AppleTalk	AppleTalk is the proprietary protocol stack designed to let Apple Macintosh computers share files and printers.
IPX/SPX	The Internetwork Packet Exchange/Sequential Packet Exchange protocol stack is the default protocol for Novel networks. IPX/SPX is routable and about the same speed as TCP/IP. NWLINK is the IPX/SPX-compatible Microsoft-designed protocol included with Microsoft operating systems.

Table 736 Standard protocol stacks.

Answer C is correct because the NetBEUI protocol is limited to Microsoft-based networks. Answers A, B, and D are incorrect because you can implement TCP/IP, IPX, and AppleTalk on operating systems other than those Microsoft makes.

737   INTRODUCTION TO THE APPLETALK PROTOCOL

Q.   *Most computers Apple Macintosh makes have a built-in ability to be networked. Which of the following protocols do Apple Macintosh computers automatically support for this built-in networking?*

Choose the best answer:

      A.   *TCP/IP*

      B.   *IPX*

      C.   *AppleTalk*

      D.   *NetBEUI*

The *AppleTalk* protocol is a proprietary protocol that Apple engineers designed to let Apple Macintosh computers share files and printers over built-in networking components called *LocalTalk* that come with all Apple Macintosh computers. Windows NT supports the AppleTalk protocol to let Apple Macintosh computers access or store files on printers Windows NT computers control. Apple Macintosh computers automatically support AppleTalk—you do not have to install it.

Answer C is correct because the built-in networking Apple Macintosh computer components (LocalTalk) automatically support AppleTalk. Answers A, B, and D are incorrect because LocalTalk does not automatically support TCP/IP, IPX, or NetBEUI.

738   INTRODUCTION TO THE *DEC*NET PROTOCOL

Q.   *The DECnet protocol is routable.*

True or False?

The *DECnet* protocol stack is a proprietary protocol stack designed to support the Digital Equipment Corporation's *Digital Network Architecture (DNA)*. DECnet is fully routable and can support other protocol stacks, such as TCP/IP. DECnet is available in several revisions, or *phases*. You will generally only encounter the DECnet protocol stack on legacy Digital Equipment installations. Most modern-day Digital servers use Windows NT, NetBEUI, and TCP/IP, rather than the DECnet protocol stack.

The answer is **True** *because the DECnet protocol is routable.*

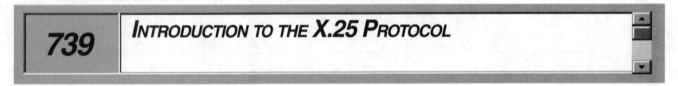

739   INTRODUCTION TO THE *X.25* PROTOCOL

Q.   *The X.25 protocol breaks data into packets, attaches source and destination addresses and routing information, and then transmits the data over a specific route to the destination computer.*

True or False?

The *X.25* protocol defines a packet-switched wide-area networking protocol that lets users create connections to remote networks by using a public network similar to the Internet concept. X.25 networks are medium-speed public networks that support speeds up to 56,000 bits per second (bps). The X.25 protocol is popular for organizations with multiple sites because X.25 connections are available worldwide.

The X.25 protocol breaks data into packets and attaches a source and destination address. Packets move across internal network switches without regard to sequencing or routing, and rely on the remote networks to route the packets themselves. When the packets arrive at the destination address, the protocol is responsible for reassembling them into the proper format.

The answer is **False** *because the X.25 protocol transmits data indiscriminately, relying on the remote networks to route themselves.*

740   INTRODUCTION TO NETWORK ARCHITECTURE

Q.   *What does a network architecture consist of?*

Choose all answers that apply:

    A.   *Standards*

    B.   *Topologies*

    C.   *Protocols*

    D.   *Cables*

In general network terminology, *network architecture* refers to the combination of communication standards, media standards, topologies, and protocols that comprise a network. Therefore, almost every aspect of a network is combined with some other aspect of the network and so is under the "umbrella" reference of network architecture. However, network administrators will frequently use the term network architecture to refer only to the carrier standard for the network, such as Ethernet or ArcNet.

Each network architecture has its own history, strengths, weaknesses, and restrictions, and the following Tips will discuss each individually.

***Answers A, B, C, and D** are all correct. Although network administrators frequently use the term network architecture to describe the base structure of the network and its standards, such as Ethernet or Token Ring, network architectures actually are combinations of standards, topologies, protocols, and specific cable types.*

741   **INTRODUCTION TO THE ARCNET NETWORK ARCHITECTURE**

Q.   *Which of the following categories of Project 802 describe the functionality of ArcNet-based networks?*

Choose the best answer:

    A.   *802.2*

    B.   *802.3*

    C.   *802.5*

    D.   *None. ArcNet predates Project 802 and is not described in any of the categories.*

In 1977, the Datapoint Corporation developed the *Attached Resource Computer Network (ArcNet)*. Therefore, ArcNet predates the IEEE Project 802 and is not defined in any of Project 802's categories. The Project 802 category 802.4, however, defines the standard for Token Bus networking, which is similar enough to the ArcNet standard that you can use it as a reference. ArcNet, which became quite popular in the mid-1980s, is a simple networking model designed for small networks. Its popularity has, for the most part, been supplanted by Ethernet. You will learn more about Ethernet in later Tips. ArcNet is a token-passing network that can use the bus or star–bus topologies. Originally transmitting data at about 2.5Mbps (2.5 megabits per second), newer ArcNet versions, *ArcNet Plus*, can transmit at rates of 20Mbps.

***Answer D** is correct because the ArcNet architecture predates Project 802 and, although it is very similar to the 802.4 category, none of the Project 802 categories actually describe it. **Answers A, B, and C** are incorrect because none of the Project 802 categories describe ArcNet.*

742   UNDERSTANDING HOW ARCNET WORKS

Q.   *ArcNet-based networks use which of the following traffic control methods?*

Choose the best answer:

     A.   *CSMA/CD*

     B.   *Token passing*

     C.   *Demand Priority*

     D.   *CSMA/CA*

As you have learned, the ArcNet protocol defines a token-passing network. As you learned in Tip 706, a token-passing network forces a computer to possess a special packet, called a token, before it can transmit data on the network. The protocol passes the token from computer to computer in numeric (addressed) order, regardless of where a computer may physically be located on the network.

Therefore, the token will pass from computer 1 to computer 2, even if computer 2 is on the opposite side of the network. *Numeric passing* ensures that each computer on the network will get a chance to transmit data no matter where the computer may be physically located. Figure 742 illustrates the token path on a Bus topology. Note how the sequential addresses are on opposite sides of the network.

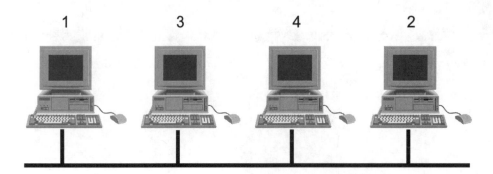

Figure 742 Token passing order on a Bus topology.

ArcNet can support both the bus and star–bus topologies and, depending on the chosen topology, you might connect computers on an ArcNet Network to a hub (if it is a star-bus topology). Standard cable for an ArcNet network is coaxial cable, although ArcNet can also support twisted-pair or fiber-optic cable.

The maximum transmission distance ArcNet can support depends on what type of cable you use, with coaxial cable typically having a maximum transmission distance of 2,000 feet and twisted-pair having a maximum transmission distance of 1,000 feet.

Answer B is correct because ArcNet-based networks are token-passing networks. Answers A, C, and D are incorrect because ArcNet does not use Carrier Sense Multiple Access with Collision Detection or Avoidance (CSMA/CD-CA) or Demand Priority traffic control methods.

743 INTRODUCTION TO THE APPLETALK NETWORK ARCHITECTURE

Q.   *The phrase AppleTalk only refers to a network communications protocol.*

True or False?

As you have learned, the operating system on Apple Macintosh computers automatically supports network communication. This feature has been in place since 1983, when the Apple Computer corporation released *AppleTalk*. AppleTalk is both the proprietary protocol designed for Apple Macintosh computers and the network architecture that the Apple Macintosh computers automatically support. There is also an enhanced version of the network architecture called *AppleTalk Phase 2*.

If you connect an Apple Macintosh computer to an AppleTalk network, the new computer will first choose an address from a list of allowable addresses and then broadcast it to the network to see if another device is using the address. If the address is in use, the computer will choose another address from the list and the process will repeat until the computer finds an available address on the network, which the computer will store for future use.

The AppleTalk architecture includes support for the AppleTalk protocol and describes installations using the built-in hardware and software for LocalTalk. The architecture also includes the additional hardware and software you can install to support the *EtherTalk* and *TokenTalk* protocols, which let Apple Macintosh computers connect to networks using the Ethernet and Token Ring protocols.

The answer is **False** *because AppleTalk is both a protocol and the network architecture for Apple Macintosh computers.*

744 INTRODUCTION TO LOCALTALK

Q.   *What is the maximum number of computers that an AppleTalk network can support on a single LocalTalk zone?*

Choose the best answer:

      A.   12

      B.   32

      C.   64

      D.   128

As you have learned, Macintosh computers use the AppleTalk protocol by default. LocalTalk is the standard network architecture normally associated with AppleTalk networks. LocalTalk uses a Carrier Sense Multiple Access with Collision Avoidance (CSMA/CA) traffic control method over a Bus topology. LocalTalk is also a description for the specialized cables and connectors that the built-in networking components of Apple Macintosh computers use. LocalTalk is limited to a maximum of 32 computers in a single *zone*. A zone is a logical separation of network segments that lets you expand a network beyond a 32-computer limitation and subdivide the network using friendly names to make network use easy on users.

Answer B is correct because a single LocalTalk zone can support up to 32 computers. Answers A, C, and D are incorrect because they list numbers of computers that are either higher or lower than the actual maximum number of computers a single LocalTalk zone can support.

745 | **INTRODUCTION TO APPLESHARE**

Q.   *Apple Macintosh computers include both client and server software.*

   True or False?

An *AppleShare* is basically the file server that an AppleTalk network uses. Although Apple Macintosh computers include the client software you require for network access, you must buy the server-level software separately, or purchase one or more Macintosh computers specifically designed as servers which include the software. As in Windows NT, you should ensure that your networks contain one or more file servers (AppleShares) for the network to be most useful.

*The answer is **False** because Apple Macintosh computers include client software and automatic support for the AppleTalk protocol.*

746 | **UNDERSTANDING THE ETHERNET ARCHITECTURE'S ORIGINS**

Q.   *What traffic control method does the Ethernet network architecture use?*

Choose the best answer:

   A.   *Carrier Sense Multiple Access with Collision Detection (CSMA/CD)*

   B.   *Carrier Sense Multiple Access with Collision Avoidance (CSMA/CA)*

   C.   *Demand Priority*

   D.   *Token Passing*

The network architecture that is now called *Ethernet* originated in Hawaii in the 1960s. The University of Hawaii designed a wide-area network (WAN) to connect computers throughout a campus that was spread over a large area. The University called this network ALOHA. One of the ALOHA network's greatest contributions to network design was the implementation of the Carrier Sense Multiple Access with Collision Detection (CSMA/CD) traffic control method (commonly called an *access method*), which is the access method that Ethernet uses even today.

In 1975, the Xerox Corporation introduced the original Ethernet version, which was designed to carry data between 100 computers over a 1 Kilometer cable at a speed of almost 3 Megabits per second (Mbps)—a stunningly high transmission rate at the time. Xerox later joined together with the Intel and Digital Equipment Corporations to design an Ethernet standard that could support up to 10 Mbps. The 10 Mbps standard provided the basis for the IEEE Project 802's 802.3 (CSMA/CD) specification.

Answer A is correct because Ethernet uses a CSMA/CD traffic control method. Answers B, C and D are incorrect because Ethernet does not use CSMA/CA, demand priority, or token-passing methods.

| 747 | INTRODUCTION TO THE ETHERNET NETWORK ARCHITECTURE | |

Q.   What transmission speeds is Ethernet capable of?

Choose all answers that apply:

> A.   10Mbps
>
> B.   100Mbps
>
> C.   1024Mbps
>
> D.   2000Mbps

Ethernet is by far the most popular network architecture in use today because it is fast and reliable, works on various topologies, and is easy to install and maintain. Ethernet supports most popular cable types and transmission speeds of 10Mbps or 100Mbps, depending on network hardware. The Project 802 category 802.3 (CSMA/CD) defines Ethernet, which uses a baseband transmission signal structure.

Ethernet cabling is passive, meaning that the network interface cards power the cable, which itself requires no power source to function. Ethernet cable will not fail unless a physical problem, such as the cable being severed, occurs. However, network problems such as signal bounce may result if you have not properly terminated the cables that comprise the network (you learned about terminating network cables in earlier Tips). Ethernet uses a CSMA/CD access method and may suffer performance loss as the number of connected devices increases. In most larger networks, administrators will use one or more active hubs, and generally multiple network segments, to reduce the amount of traffic (and therefore collisions) across their Ethernet networks. In fact, as Ethernet networks grow, using active hubs, routers, bridges, and other network segment connection devices is a crucial part of network management.

Answers A and B are correct because Ethernet can support either 10 Megabits per second (Mbps) or 100Mbps. Answers C and D are incorrect because Ethernet cannot support 1024 or 2000Mbps.

| 748 | UNDERSTANDING THE ETHERNET FRAME FORMAT | |

Q.   Ethernet breaks data down into a format that is different from other network architectures.

True or False?

One major difference between Ethernet and other network architectures is the format data is broken into for transmission. Ethernet breaks data into frames instead of the packets most other network architectures use. Although many networking professionals use the terms frame and packet interchangeably, there actually are differences between frames and packets. Specifically, aside from how protocols construct frames and packets differently, the essential difference is that frames are based on a connected protocol (that is, the transmitting computer will not send additional frames until it confirms reception of the first frame) while packet transmissions are built around a connectionless protocol (the transmitting computer will continue to send packets without necessarily receiving confirmation of the reception of the first packet).

An Ethernet frame can be between 64 and 1,518 bytes long and can carry quantities of data between 46 and 1,500 bytes because the frame itself uses 18 bytes. Each frame contains information that controls its transmission, reception, and verification on the network. For example, the Ethernet 2 frame always consists of the sections Table 748 describes.

Section	Description
Preamble	A piece of data that marks the beginning of the frame so that receiving computers know where to start interpreting data.
Destination	The intended destination computer or device's network address.
Source	The source computer or device's network address.
Type	Identifies the network layer protocol.
Data	The actual data that the frame contains.
CRC	The Cyclic Redundancy Check, a value that represents a mathematical calculation of the data's contents. The receiving computer compares the CRC value that it computes against the CRC value within the frame to verify the data's integrity.

Table 748 Sections of an Ethernet 2 frame.

The answer is **True** *because Ethernet breaks data into frames. Although networking professionals frequently use the terms frame and packet interchangeably, there actually are differences between the terms.*

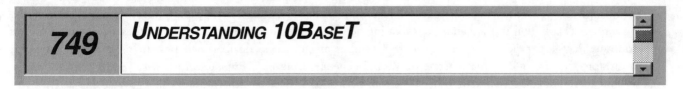

749   UNDERSTANDING 10BASET

Q.   *What is the maximum length of a 10BaseT segment?*

Choose the best answer:

    A.   *100 feet*

    B.   *328 feet*

    C.   *500 feet*

    D.   *1,024 feet*

As you learned in Tip 721, Project 802 defines 12 categories of standards for networking. Category 802.3 (CSMA/CD) defines the use of Ethernet over a variety of cable types, including twisted-pair, Thinnet (coaxial), Thicknet (coaxial), and fiber-optic cable. As earlier Tips in this section explain, *10BaseT* describes the specification for using Ethernet with twisted-pair cable. 10BaseT stands for *10Mbps, baseband, twisted-pair cable.* Networks using 10BaseT typically use a bus, star, or star–bus topology, can support up to 1,024 computers or other network devices, and are capable of transmitting data 100 meters (328 feet) without a repeater.

Note: *Maximum transmission distances may be reduced if lower-grade cables are used. For the best results, you should always use Category 5 Unshielded Twisted-Pair (UTP) or Shielded Twisted-Pair (STP) cable.*

Answer **B** *is correct because a 10BaseT segment can support a maximum length of 328 feet for a single segment. Answers A, C, and D are incorrect because they list lengths that are either higher or lower than the actual maximum length of a single 10BaseT segment.*

| 750 | **UNDERSTANDING 10BASE2** |

Q.   What is the maximum possible length of a single 10Base2 segment?

Choose the best answer:

> *A.   500 feet*
>
> *B.   804 feet*
>
> *C.   607 feet*
>
> *D.   953 feet*

10Base2 is the 802.3 (CSMA/CD) specification that describes the use of Ethernet with Thinnet (1/4 inch coaxial cable). 10Base2 stands for *10Mbps baseband transmission up to a maximum of about 200* meters (the actual limitation is 185 meters or 607 feet). Thinnet networks generally use a bus topology that connects computers directly to the cable using a BNC T connector. Thinnet networks are inexpensive, easy to install, and can support up to 30 computers on each segment. As you learned earlier in this section, Thinnet networks are very common in smaller network installations. Because of the wrapping and shielding of 10Base2 cable, it provides more protection against electrical interference than 10BaseT. However, it is also more expensive than 10BaseT, harder to administer (because of the bus topology), and administrators today generally do not use Thinnet as a network backbone, except for the smallest networks.

***Answer C** is correct because the maximum possible length of a single 10Base2 segment is 607 feet. **Answers A, B,** and **D** are incorrect because they list lengths that are higher or lower than the actual maximum length a single segment of 10Base2 cabling can support.*

| 751 | **UNDERSTANDING 10BASE5** |

Q.   What is the maximum possible distance for a single 10Base5 cable segment?

Choose the best answer:

> *A.   1640 feet*
>
> *B.   640 feet*
>
> *C.   500 feet*
>
> *D.   5000 feet*

As you learned in previous Tips, 10BaseT is the 802.3 specification that defines the use of Ethernet with twisted-pair network cable. *10Base5* is the 802.3 specification that defines the use of Ethernet with Thicknet (1/2 inch coaxial cable). The term *10Base5* stands for *10Mbps baseband transmission and 500 meter segments,* which means a single segment of 10Base5 cable can carry data a maximum of 500 meters or 1,640 feet. A 10Base5 cable is thicker and less flexible than 10Base2 or 10BaseT cable, and network administrators typically install it as the foundation for a network. A 10Base5 cable can support up to 100 computers or network devices on each segment.

As you have learned, Thicknet cable uses vampire-tap connectors to attach the transceiver to the computer or other network device. The vampire-tap connector to transceiver connection costs more than other cable types that have the transceiver built into the network interface card (NIC).

Answer A is correct because a single 10Base5 cable segment has a maximum possible distance of 500 meters or 1,640 feet. Answers B, C, and D are incorrect because the answers list distances that are either higher or lower than the actual maximum distance for a 10Base5 cable segment.

752   UNDERSTANDING 10BASEFL

Q.   What is the maximum possible distance for a single cable segment of 10BaseFL?

Choose the best answer:

    A.   5,000 feet

    B.   5,250 feet

    C.   6,560 feet

    D.   6,800 feet

As previous Tips indicate, 10Base specifications explain the use of Ethernet networks over specific cable types. Similarly, 10BaseFL is the 802.3 specification for using Ethernet with fiber-optic cable. As previous Tips indicate, fiber-optic cable is the most expensive cable type and the hardest to install, in part because its lack of flexibility requires a high level of expertise. Network administrators typically implement fiber-optic cables as foundations or as connections between extraordinarily long cable runs between repeaters. The maximum possible distance for a segment of 10BaseFL cable is 2,000 meters or 6,560 feet.

Answer C is correct because a single 10BaseFL cable segment can carry data over a maximum possible distance of 2,000 meters or 6,560 feet. Answers A, B, and D are incorrect because the answers list distances that are higher or lower than the actual maximum possible distance for a single 10BaseFL cable segment.

753   SUMMARIZING ETHERNET FEATURES

Q.   Which of the following cable structures support the most computers on a single cable for each segment?

Choose the best answer:

    A.   10BaseT

    B.   10Base2

    C.   10Base5

    D.   Cable structure does not determine the maximum number of computers on a single cable for each segment.

Over the last several Tips, you have learned about Ethernet and the different specifications for using Ethernet with a variety of cable types. Although Ethernet can use many cable types, the three most common types are 10BaseT, 10Base2, and 10Base5. Choosing which cable type is right for your network depends on cost, distances, the number of computers or other network devices, and the level of difficulty involved to install a cable type. All Ethernet implementations use the Carrier Sense Multiple Access with Collision Detection (CSMA/CD) access method, so if you choose Ethernet, using CSMA/CD is not a consideration. The following considerations apply when you consider using 10BaseT cable within your network:

- 10Base T is the least expensive cable type

- 10Base T is very flexible and easy to install

- 10Base T requires a hub and uses a Star or Star–Bus topology

- 10Base T supports a maximum distance of 100 meters (328 feet) for each segment

- Supports a maximum of one computer or other network device attached to a single cable (each cable runs from a device to the hub)

The following considerations apply when you consider using 10Base2 cable within your network:

- 10Base2 costs more than 10BaseT, but is less expensive than 10Base5

- 10Base2 is flexible and easy to install

- 10Base2 uses a Bus topology

- 10Base2 supports a maximum distance of 185 meters (607 feet) for each segment

- 10Base2 supports a maximum of 30 computers or other network devices for each segment

The following considerations apply when you consider using 10Base5 cable within your network:

- 10Base5 costs more than 10Base2

- 10Base5 is less flexible and more difficult to install

- 10Base5 supports a maximum distance of 500 meters (1640 feet) for each segment

- 10Base5 supports up to 100 computers or other network devices for each segment

Answer C is correct because 10Base5 cable segments can support up to 100 computers or network devices. Answers A and B are incorrect because a 10Base2 cable supports up to only 30 computers on a single segment, and a 10BaseT cable can support only one computer because you must connect each computer to the hub with its own cable. Answer D is incorrect because cable structure does determine the maximum number of computers or network devices on a single cable for each segment.

754 INTRODUCTION TO THE *100MBPS IEEE* STANDARD

Q.   *Which of the following Project 802 categories define networks supporting transmission speeds of up to 100Mbps?*

Choose all answers that apply:

A.   *802.3*

B.   *802.5*

C.   802.12

D.   802.10

The Institute of Electrical and Electronic Engineers (IEEE) has developed new standards for Ethernet transmission. The new standards support transmission speeds of 100 Megabits per second (Mbps) over 10BaseT cable. The new Ethernet standards have given networks the ability to transmit large amounts of data at previously impossible speeds. Newer applications, such as applications that support video transmission, can perform at real-time speeds using the new standards.

The two 100Mbps standards IEEE set are the *100VG-AnyLAN* and *100BaseX* standards, which IEEE defines in two categories. The 802.5 category for Token Ring standards defines the 100VG-AnyLAN standard, and the 802.12 for demand priority network communications standards defines the 100BaseX standard. Because the new standards can use existing 10BaseT cable structures, you can easily and inexpensively upgrade some legacy networks from a 10Mpbs transmission speed to a 100Mbps speed.

Answers B and C are correct because Project 802's 802.5 category defines 100Mbps transmissions with Token Ring network architecture and the 802.12 category defines 100Mbps Ethernet transmissions with twisted-pair cable. Answer A is incorrect because the 802.3 category defines 10Mbps Ethernet transmissions. Answer D is incorrect because category 802.10 defines network security.

755   INTRODUCTION TO THE *100VG-ANYLAN* STANDARD

Q.   *Which of the following access methods does the 100VG-AnyLAN standard use?*

Choose all answers that apply:

A.   *CSMA/CD*

B.   *CSMA/CA*

C.   *Demand priority network communications*

D.   *Token Passing*

One of the two standards that the Institute of Electrical and Electronic Engineers (IEEE) developed for 100Mbps transmission speeds is the 100VG-AnyLAN standard, which means 100Mbps Voice Grade-Any Local Area Network. IEEE specifically calls the 100VG-AnyLAN standard AnyLAN because IEEE designed it to function using either Ethernet or Token Ring network architectures. Network administrators will frequently use a variety of names for the 100VG-AnyLAN standard, including 100VG-AnyLAN, 100BaseVG, AnyLAN, and VG.

The 100VG-AnyLAN standard uses a Token Passing or demand priority access method (capable of supporting low and high priority levels). In addition, 100VG-AnyLAN can use category three, four, or five twisted-pair cable and supports both Ethernet frames and Token Ring Packets. The AnyLAN architecture generally uses a Star topology with all the hubs connected to each other and all computers or other network devices connected directly to a hub. A central hub (the Parent hub) is the star's center and all other hubs (the Child hubs) branch out from the Parent, as Figure 755 shows.

Answers C and D are correct because IEEE designed the 100VG-AnyLAN standard specifically to function on either Ethernet or Token Ring network architectures. Answers A and B are incorrect because 100VG-AnyLAN does not use Carrier Sense Multiple Access (CSMA) methods.

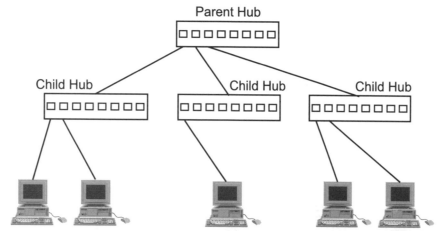

Figure 755 The 100VG-AnyLAN standard's Star topology.

Note: *100VG-AnyLAN is the only Ethernet-compatible standard that does not use* **Carrier Sense Multiple Access (CSMA).**

Answers C and D *are correct because IEEE designed the 100VG-AnyLAN standard specifically to function on either Ethernet or Token Ring network architectures.* **Answers A and B** *are incorrect because 100VG-AnyLAN does not use Carrier Sense Multiple Access (CSMA) methods.*

756	INTRODUCTION TO THE *100BASEX* STANDARD

Q.   Which of the following access methods does 100BaseX use?

Choose the best answer:

>   A.   CSMA/CD
>
>   B.   CSMA/CA
>
>   C.   Demand Priority
>
>   D.   Token Passing

As you learned in Tip 755, one new 100Mbps standard IEEE developed is the 100VG-AnyLAN standard. The other standard IEEE developed is 100BaseX. Network administrators sometimes call the 100BaseX standard *Fast Ethernet* because 100BaseX is so much faster than the standard 10Mbps Ethernet, but it still uses an Ethernet frame. Because the 100BaseX standard is still Ethernet, it uses a Carrier Sense Multiple Access with Collision Detection (CSMA/CD) access method.

The 100BaseX standard got its name because it has three different standard cable types. The 100 in the name stands for 100Mbps, and the Base stands for baseband transmission. However, the X is a variable that represents three standards, which are T4, TX, and FX. Table 756 describes the difference between the T4, TX, and FX standards.

Answer A *is correct because the 100BaseX network architectures use the Carrier Sense Multiple Access with Collision Detection (CSMA/CD) access method.* **Answers B, C, and D** *are incorrect because the 100BaseX network architectures do not use the Carrier Sense Multiple Access with Collision Avoidance (CSMA/CA), Demand Priority, or Token Passing access methods.*

Standard	Specification
100BaseT4	100Mbps, baseband transmission, with twisted-pair cable consisting of four telephone-grade pairs (pairs of wires).
100BaseTX	100Mbps, baseband transmission, with twisted-pair cable consisting of two data-grade pairs.
100BaseFX	100Mpbs, baseband transmission, over fiber-optic cable consisting of two strands.

Table 756 The100BaseX standard variations.

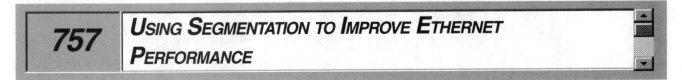

757 **USING SEGMENTATION TO IMPROVE ETHERNET PERFORMANCE**

Q.   *Segmentation is a method of improving network performance by dividing the total network into branches.*

True or False?

As you have learned, networks built around the Ethernet network architecture will suffer degradation of network performance as the number of computers or other devices on the network increases, due to network contention. In addition, you have also learned network contention refers to the number of collisions that occur when two or more computers try to use the network at the same time. As the number of computers or other network devices increases, the chance for collision also increases and the network's performance decreases.

You can solve network contention on an Ethernet network only by segmenting it. *Segmentation* is a method of dividing the network into branches that bridges, routers, and other segmentation devices govern. Segmentation improves the network's performance because the bridges and routers prevent signals from entering network branches to which the signals do not need access. Because network signals do not travel on all segments, the chance for collision and, therefore, network contention, decreases.

The answer is **True** *because segmentation is a method you can use to expand a network and improve performance by dividing the total network into branches.*

758 **INTRODUCTION TO THE TOKEN RING NETWORK ARCHITECTURE**

Q.   *Which of the following Project 802 categories define the standards for the Token Ring network architecture?*

Choose the best answer:

A.   *802.3*

B.   *802.4*

C.   *802.5*

D.   *802.6*

The most popular network architecture that uses a Token Passing access method is the version of Token Ring that IBM developed in 1984. Token Ring networks use twisted-pair cable and a Ring or Star–Ring topology. The basis for the Token Ring network is a simple ring of cable that runs into and out of each computer's network interface card (NIC). To expand on the original Ring topology, newer networks now use a Star–Ring topology that lets you connect each computer to a hub. The ring is not readily apparent in the Star–Ring topology because it is actually inside the hub. Figure 758 illustrates the Star-Ring topology with its internal ring.

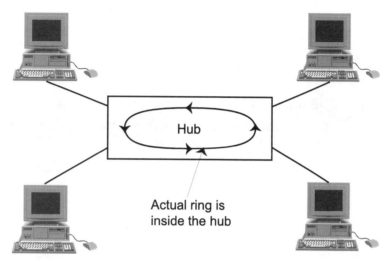

Figure 758 The Star-Ring topology showing the ring internal to the hub.

Answer C is correct because Project 802's category 802.5 defines the standards for the Token Ring network architecture. Answer A is incorrect because category 802.3 defines the standards for the Ethernet network architecture. Answer B is incorrect because category 802.4 defines the standards for the Token Bus network architecture. Answer D is incorrect because category 802.6 defines the standards for the Metropolitan Area Network (MAN) network architecture.

759	UNDERSTANDING THE TOKEN RING FRAME FORMAT

Q. *What section of the Token Ring data frame indicates the frame's priority level?*

Choose the best answer:

> *A.* *Start Delimiter*
>
> *B.* *Frame Control*
>
> *C.* *Access Control*
>
> *D.* *End Delimiter*

The Token Ring network architecture provides an excellent example of how standard industry terms can be confusing. The data transmission unit's structure is called the frame format, but Token Ring networks actually use packets to transmit data. Ethernet is the only network architecture that uses a frame. (Remember, the difference between frames and packets is minor and you can use the two terms interchangeably.) IBM divided the Token Ring frame format into nine sections, which Table 759 describes.

Section	Description
Start Delimiter	Indicates the frame's beginning.
Access Control	Indicates the frame's priority level. (This section also identifies whether the frame contains a Token or data passing along the network.)
Destination Address	Contains the intended receiving computer's network address.
Frame Check	Contains the Cyclic Redundancy Check (CRC) value.
Frame Control	Carries Media Access Control (MAC) information.
Frame Status	Identifies the frame status. (For example, if the frame is a copy of an original frame which did not transmit correctly, or if the frame is a data the network returned to the sending computer because the network could not locate the destination address.)
Source Address	Contains the sending computer's network address.
Data	Identifies the actual data the frame contains—which may be either token information or data passing along the network.
End Delimiter	Indicates the frame's end.

Table 759 The Token Ring data frame's sections.

Answer C is correct because the Token Ring data frame's Access Control section indicates the frame's priority level. **Answer A** is incorrect because the Start Delimiter section indicates the frame's beginning. **Answer B** is incorrect because the Frame Control section contains Media Access Control information. **Answer D** is incorrect because the End Delimiter section indicates the frame's end.

760   INTRODUCTION TO THE HARDWARE IN TOKEN RING ENVIRONMENTS

Q.   Which of the following standard industry terms describe the hub that Token Ring networks use?

Choose all answers that apply:

     A.   Multi-station Access Unit (MAU)

     B.   Multi Station Access Unit (MSAU)

     C.   Smart Multi-station Access Unit (SMAU)

     D.   None of the above; the term for the hub in Token Ring networks is simply the hub.

The Token Ring network architecture uses networking hardware found in other networks, such as hubs, repeaters, cables, and network interface cards (NICs). Although the networking hardware components perform the same functions in Token Ring networks that they do in other network architectures, the components must function differently because of the Token Ring access method. For example, the network interface card accepts, reads, and then regenerates each Packet as it moves through the network, which means Token Ring networks do not frequently require repeaters because each network interface card on the network acts as a repeater.

One important hardware component that Token Ring networks use is the Token Ring hub, which maintains the internal ring structure and passes the Token from port to port. Each computer or other network device connects to a port on the hub and accesses the network through the hub. Network administrators frequently use a few standard industry terms to describe the Token Ring hub, which the following bulleted list describes:

- Multi-station Access Unit (MAU)

- Multi Station Access Unit (MSAU)

- Smart Multi-station Access Unit (SMAU)

You can connect Multi-station Access Units (MAUs) together to form larger rings through special ports. In addition to the regular ports through which individual computers or devices connect to the hub, each Multi-station Access Unit has two special ports that you can use to connect additional MAUs to the MAU, called Ring-In and Ring-Out. To connect two or more Multi-station Access Units together, you simply use twisted-pair cable to connect the special ports together. The main detail to remember is you must connect the Multi-station Access Units so they form a single ring.

Answers A, B, and C are all correct because each listed term is a standard industry term that describes the hubs Token Ring networks use. Answer D is incorrect because the terms in Answers A, B, and C do describe the Token Ring network hub. Although you can call a Token Ring hub a hub, typically, network administrators do not because the Token Ring hubs function differently from the hubs other network architectures use.

761	UNDERSTANDING NETWORK INTERFACE CARDS IN TOKEN RING ENVIRONMENTS

Q.   At what speeds can Token Ring network interface cards operate?

Choose all answers that apply:

     A.   10Mbps

     B.   4Mbps

     C.   16Mbps

     D.   1,000Mpbs

As you have learned, Token Ring network interface cards (NICs) are unique because they perform the same function as repeaters by regenerating each Packet prior to passing it to the rest of the network. You can purchase Token Ring network interface cards capable of either 4Mbps or 16Mbps. The 16Mbps cards can scale back to function at 4Mbs for backwards compatibility, but the 4Mbps network interface cards cannot operate at 16Mbps.

Note: New network interface cards capable of 100Mbps using the 100VG-AnyLAN standard are now available.

Answers B and C are correct because Token Ring network interface cards can operate at either four Megabits per second or 16Mbps. Answers A and D are incorrect because Token Ring network interface cards cannot operate at speeds of 10Mbps or 1,000Mbps.

762	REPEATERS IN TOKEN RING NETWORKS

Q.   Token Ring networks can use repeaters to increase the length of cable between Multi-station Access Units (MAUs).

True or False?

As you have learned, Token Ring network interface cards (NICs) regenerate packets as they function, which reduces the need for repeaters (devices that amplify and enhance network signals) in Token Ring networks. Typically, Token Ring networks use repeaters to amplify or enhance signals between Multi-station Access Units (the special hubs that Token Ring networks use). If you have significant distance along a single cable between two Multi-station Access Units, you can use repeaters to increase the maximum possible distance a cable can carry a signal.

*The answer is **True** because Token Ring networks can use repeaters to increase the maximum possible cable length between Multi-station Access Units (MAUs).*

763   REVISITING THE FEATURES OF TOKEN RING NETWORKS

Q.   *What is the maximum number of segments possible on a Token Ring network?*

Choose the best answer:

> A.   *11*
>
> B.   *33*
>
> C.   *42*
>
> D.   *103*

In previous Tips, you have learned about the Token Ring network architecture's different characteristics. Token Ring networks use twisted-pair cable (shielded or unshielded) and the networks can support up to 260 computers, depending on the cable type. In addition, Token Ring networks can support up to 33 Multi-station Access Units (MAUs) on a single network. Each Multi-station Access Unit can support one segment, which means a Token Ring network can have only 33 segments (with the MAU's number of ports determining the number of computers per segment). Token Ring networks can support a maximum length from between 160 to 650 feet for a single length of cable.

Answer B is correct because a Token Ring network can support up to 33 Multi-station Access Units, which means the total number of segments on a single Token Ring network is also 33. Answers A, C, and D are incorrect because the answers list numbers that are higher or lower than the maximum number of possible segments on a Token Ring network.

764   COMPARING TOKEN RING AND ETHERNET

Q.   *The Token Ring network architecture does not suffer from collisions.*

True or False?

The Token Ring network architecture is one of the most popular network architectures in use today. Although it is usually more expensive to install than an Ethernet network, Token Ring offers some advantages that are very appealing to many network administrators. Because of the Token Passing access method, Token Ring networks do not suffer from collisions (network contention) which is a problem that Ethernet networks will increasingly experience as computers or other network devices increase in number. Additionally, the Token Ring Packet can carry more data than an Ethernet frame. Ethernet frames have a maximum size of 1½Kb (about 1,500 bytes), while Token Ring packets have a maximum size of 17Kb (about 17,000 bytes). Therefore, to transfer a piece of data with Ethernet Frames takes about ten times as many frames as it would with Token Ring Packets.

*The answer is **True** because the Token Ring network architecture uses the Token Passing access method and does not suffer from collisions.*

765   INTRODUCTION TO NETWORK APPLICATIONS

Q.   *Which of the following application types do network administrators consider to be network applications?*

Choose all answers that apply:

    A.   *E-mail*

    B.   *Word Processors*

    C.   *Spreadsheet programs*

    D.   *GroupWare*

The computer industry has always taken advantage of new technologies very quickly. As the use of personal computers became popular in organizations, the computer industry was quick to develop word processing applications and spreadsheet programs to increase productivity. As the use of networking in organizations became popular, the computer industry quickly developed network-dependent applications, such as e-mail systems and *GroupWare* (which lets you create, track, and manage a project involving many users), to increase user productivity. Over the next several Tips, you will learn more about applications software companies specifically designed for network use that depend on the network to function properly. Applications that depend on the network to function are *network applications*.

While the line between network and standalone applications remained relatively clear for many years, recent advances in network technology and the integration of the Internet and corporate intranets into the network is blurring the line. GroupWare application (such as Lotus *Notes*) are still a specific category of software, but word processors and spreadsheets are becoming more GroupWare-like. For example, Microsoft *Word's* integration of the Internet-model now lets users create links within their own documents to other files—graphics, documents, spreadsheets, and so on—on other computers on the network. While word processors and spreadsheets will always remain standalone capable, it seems likely that their integration into the network will continue to become more and more common.

*Answers **A** and **D** are correct because software companies designed e-mail and GroupWare applications to use networks and depend on networks to function properly, which means you can consider them network applications. **Answers B** and **C** are incorrect because word processor and spreadsheet applications can function without a network, which means you cannot consider them network applications.*

766   INTRODUCTION TO E-MAIL

Q.   *In order to communicate with another user through e-mail, what information must you have?*

Choose the best answer:

A.   The user's network address.

B.   Routing information required to locate the user's network.

C.   The user's e-mail address.

D.   The same e-mail program as the other user.

E-mail systems are probably the most common network applications in use today. E-mail systems provide a powerful communication tool to users, a tool that lets them send virtually anything they can create on a computer to other users, either on their local-area network (LAN) or on the other side of the world. In addition, e-mail systems are very user-friendly because they are easy to use and require little or no networking or advanced computing knowledge. To send a message or file to a user, you must know only the user's e-mail address (which you can frequently choose from a list), and generally understand the e-mail program you are using.

Another tremendous advantage of e-mail systems is the user receiving the message does not have to be at his or her computer at the time you send it. After you send the message, it will wait until the receiving user's computer is on, and the e-mail program has checked to see if new messages are waiting. If the receiving user's e-mail program determines messages are waiting, the program will deliver them to a storage area where the messages will again wait for the user to actually read them.

However, not all e-mail systems are equal—either in features or in transmission capability. Some systems can send messages over the Internet, while others can send messages back and forth only on the local-area network. Additionally, some e-mail systems can send and receive only text messages. If you cannot send files in their original format or pictures, you are using an e-mail service that does not support *attachments*, which are items (other than plain text) you place inside an e-mail. For example, you can place many items other than a letter, into an envelope and send them through the mail. Likewise, on many systems you can place items you created in your computer inside an e-mail and send the items through the e-mail system. If you are using an e-mail system that does not support attachments, you can only type and send text.

Answer C is correct because you must have the user's e-mail address to communicate with the user. Answer A is incorrect because you do not require the user's network address to communicate with the user. Answer B is incorrect because you do not require the routing information to the user's network. The e-mail server will determine the routing information. Answer D is incorrect because many e-mail systems can communicate with each other, even if users use different e-mail programs.

767 INTRODUCTION TO E-MAIL STANDARDS

Q.   How do e-mail systems that use different e-mail standards communicate with each other?

Choose the best answer:

A.   Through a router

B.   Through a repeater

C.   Through a gateway

D.   E-mail systems using different e-mail standards cannot communicate with each other

As networks grew beyond the local-area network (LAN) and Internet-working became a worldwide reality, the nature of applications on the network began to change. The computer industry realized, with the stunning growth of the

Internet, that like networking itself, e-mail systems required standards that would ensure a high level of compatibility between e-mail systems and encourage electronic communication. Today, several standards apply to e-mail systems, including the standards in the following bulleted list:

- X.400

- X.500

- Simple Mail Transfer Protocol (SMTP)

- Message Handling Service (MHS)

Because not all e-mail systems use the same standard and not all standards can communicate directly with each other, the computer industry began to develop programs and devices called *gateways* that could translate messages from one standard to another. Gateways also let an organization that uses one e-mail standard receive messages from and send messages to an organization or organizational department that uses a different e-mail standard.

Answer C is correct because e-mail systems using different e-mail standards can communicate with each other through a gateway. Answer A is incorrect because a router finds the best path between networks and cannot translate e-mail standards. Answer B is incorrect because a repeater enhances network signaling and extends the maximum possible cable distances. A repeater cannot translate e-mail standards. Answer D is incorrect because e-mail systems using different e-mail standards can communicate with each other using a gateway.

768   **INTRODUCTION TO THE X.400 STANDARDS**

Q.   *The X.400 standard is a single standard that describes the structure of electronic messaging.*

True or False?

One early standard the computer industry established for e-mail systems was the X.400 standard. However, the X.400 standard is actually a group of standards that range from the original X.400 to X.460, but network administrators generally refer to the standards collectively as the X.400 standard. Many e-mail systems in use today are X.400 compliant.

The X.400 standards define a structure for transferring messages using public networks, such as the Internet or an X.25 network. In addition, the X.400 standards are a set of rules that describe a client program's optimal structure, the format messages must adhere to for a receiving or transfer program to understand them, and the transfer programs or devices themselves. Designed to be both software and hardware independent, the computer industry wrote the X.400 standards in the form of recommendations. Tip 769 discusses the X.400 recommendations in detail.

*The answer is **False** because the X.400 standards are actually a set of standards ranging from the original X.400 to X.460.*

769   **UNDERSTANDING THE X.400 RECOMMENDATIONS**

Q.   *What do the X.400 recommendations specify?*

Choose all answers that apply:

A.   User-level applications for e-mail messaging.

B.   The structure of message transfer agents.

C.   Communication and addressing between e-mail applications.

D.   Communication between message transfer agents.

As you learned Tip 768, the computer industry wrote the X.400 standards in the form of recommendations. The X.400 recommendations specify many rules for creating user-level applications that will perform messaging, including the actual message structure and the structure of message transfer agents. In addition, the X.400 recommendations specify the communication and addressing required for messages, the transfer of messages between applications, and more. The major components the X.400 standards describe include the *user agent (UA)*, the *message transfer agent (MTA)*, and the *message transfer system (MTS)*. The user agent is the user-level application the user will use to perform messaging activities. The message transfer agent accepts messages from a user agent, performs any necessary formatting, and forwards the messages to another user agent or message transfer agent, depending on the message's destination. (Many message transfer agents typically make up the e-mail interface that the user sees.) The message transfer system is the service or software component responsible for transferring all messages to a user agent.

Note: The Telecommunication Standardization sector of the International Telecommunications Union (ITU TS) "Red Book" series details the X.400 standards. The International Telecommunications Union was formerly the Consultative Committee on International Telephone and Telegraphy (CCITT). If you wish to obtain further information about the X.400 standard, contact the ITU-TS.

Answers A, B, C, and D are all correct because the X.400 recommendations define the structure of, and the communication between, users, user-level applications, message transfer agents, and messages themselves.

770   INTRODUCTION TO P1, P2, AND P3 IN X.400

Q.   Which of the following X.400 protocols define communication between message transfer agents (MTAs)?

Choose the best answer:

A.   P1

B.   P2

C.   P3

D.   None of the above; message transfer agents do not communicate directly with each other.

As you learned in Tip 769, the X.400 standards include recommendations for transferring e-mail messages and describe the major messaging components. In addition, the X.400 standards describe three protocols required for communication between user agents (UAs) and message transfer agents (MTAs). Table 770 describes the three X.400 protocols.

Protocol	Description
P1	Defines standards for communication between message transfer agents.
P2	Defines standards for communication between user agents.
P3	Defines standards for communication between a user agent and a message transfer agent.

Table 770 The X.400 protocol standards.

Answer A *is correct because the X.400 P1 protocol defines the communication standard between message transfer agents.* **Answer B** *is incorrect because the X.400 P2 protocol defines communication between user agents.* **Answer C** *is incorrect because the X.400 P3 protocol defines communication between a user agent and a message transfer agent.* **Answer D** *is incorrect because message transfer agents do communicate directly with each other in the P1 protocol.*

771 INTRODUCTION TO THE **X.500** STANDARD

Q.   *The International Telecommunications Union's Telecommunication Standardization sector (ITU TS) developed the X.500 standard to make locating addresses in large networks easier.*

True or False?

As Internet-working became popular, messaging between users, either individually or on large networks, became difficult due to the large number of users. In short, the sheer volume of users that servers had to reconcile addresses for made messaging very slow. To help alleviate messaging problems, the International Telecommunications Union's Telecommunication Standardization sector (ITU TS) developed the X.500 standard.

The X.500 standard is an add-on to the X.400 standards that provides a set of directory services which makes locating e-mail addresses on large or public networks easier. The X.500 standard uses a variety of services to determine the network name and address for messages. Also, the X.500 standard provides a directory that lets users browse a list of friendly names (as opposed to IP addresses) for sending messages. (The directory service will then match the name to a network address.)

The answer is **True** *because the X.500 standard defines directory services that make locating addresses in large networks easier.*

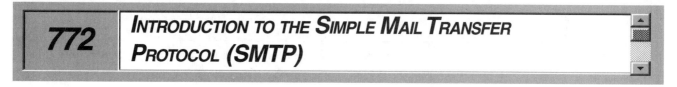

772 INTRODUCTION TO THE SIMPLE MAIL TRANSFER PROTOCOL (SMTP)

Q.   *Of what standard protocol stack is the Simple Mail Transfer Protocol (SMTP) a component?*

Choose the best answer:

A.   *IPX/SPX*

B.   *TCP/IP*

C.   *NetBEUI*

D.   *NWLINK*

In addition to the X.400 and X.500 standards, another popular e-mail standard is the Simple Mail Transfer Protocol (SMTP), which the computer industry designed to be a simple language that can carry messages over local-area networks (LANs) or over public networks, such as the Internet. The Simple Mail Transfer Protocol is a protocol that works with user applications designed for e-mail to provide both a client and a server component, which lets remote computers communicate with each other. Included as a component of the TCP/IP protocol stack (within the application layer), the Simple Mail Transfer Protocol is the Internet's e-mail standard.

Answer B is correct because the Simple Mail Transfer Protocol is a component of the TCP/IP protocol stack. Answers A, C, and D are incorrect because IPX/SPX, NetBEUI, and NWLINK do not contain the Simple Mail Transfer Protocol.

773 UNDERSTANDING SIMPLE MAIL TRANSFER PROTOCOL (SMTP) COMMANDS

Q.   Which of the following Simple Mail Transfer Protocol (SMTP) commands indicates the sending SMTP computer's identification on the network?

Choose the best answer:

    A.   <Send>

    B.   <Mail>

    C.   <Data>

    D.   <Hello>

As you have learned, the Simple Mail Transfer Protocol (SMTP) is a simple e-mail protocol that lets two remote computers communicate with each other when you combine them with an e-mail application. Network administrators consider the commands the Simple Mail Transfer Protocol uses to be user-friendly and simple, which explains the name Simple Mail Transfer Protocol.

In addition, the Simple Mail Transfer Protocol commands are not case sensitive, which means that a mistake in case will not cause the message to fail. For example, a Simple Mail Transfer Protocol component will read the words *HELLO*, *Hello*, *HeLLo*, and *hello* as all the same. Table 773 describes some examples of commands the Simple Mail Transfer Protocol uses (for more information on SMTP commands, see the Internet documents Request For Comment (RFC)-821 and RFC822, as well as RFC1123).

Command	Description
<Hello>	Indicates the sending SMTP host computer's identification (including network address).
<Mail>	Initiates a mail transaction between SMTP hosts and identifies the terminal to which the receiving SMTP host should deliver the message.
<Send>	Initiates a mail transaction between SMTP hosts and identifies the mailbox to which the receiving SMTP host should deliver the message (similar to the <Mail> command, but specifies a storage area instead of a terminal).
<Data>	Indicates to the receiving SMTP host that the text which follows the <Data> command is the actual message.
<Rcpt>	Specifies the recipient to which the SMTP host should deliver the message.

Table 773 Some Simple Mail Transfer Protocol commands.

Answer D is correct because the <Hello> command indicates the sending Simple Mail Transfer Protocol (SMTP) host's identification. Answers A, B, and C are incorrect because the <Send>, <Mail>, and <Data> commands do not indicate the sending SMTP host's identification.

774 INTRODUCTION TO GROUPWARE

Q.   Which of the following answers best describe the term GroupWare?

Choose the best answer:

     A.   A network-based program that lets you manage groups of users.

     B.   A network-based program that lets you effectively create, maintain, and manage a project involving multiple users.

     C.   A network-based program that lets you effectively create, maintain, and manage multiple users.

     D.   A network-based program that lets many users access a single data source at the same time.

One of the most recently developed network application types is GroupWare. Software companies designed GroupWare products to increase the productivity of a group of users by providing a way to create, track, manage, and maintain a specific project that involves many users. You can add documents of all types to storage areas and store notes with documents or files, in addition to storing and updating communication sessions between users in the group. Also, in most GroupWare products, shared scheduling features (that is, schedules available to other users on the network) let users check another user's availability, and you can manage and monitor an entire project from your computer without having to meet with all users in the group in one place.

Answer B is correct because the best description for the term GroupWare is a network-based program that lets you create, maintain, and manage a project involving multiple users. Answers A and C are incorrect because network administrators do not define GroupWare programs as programs that let you create, maintain, or manage users. Answer D is incorrect because a network-based program that lets many users access a single data source at the same time is a shared data source or a client server application, and does not describe the term GroupWare.

775 INTRODUCTION TO LOTUS NOTES®

Q.   Lotus Notes® is an example of GroupWare.

True or False?

Lotus Notes® is an excellent example of a powerful GroupWare product that incorporates messaging, security, directory services, connectivity, add-on applications, and management into a single application that focuses on multiple-user projects. The Lotus Corporation (a division of IBM) has released several versions of *Lotus Notes* and it is currently one of the most popular GroupWare products in use. You can get *Lotus Notes* for almost every major operating system and easily integrate it with existing applications and networking utilities. In the Windows NT environment, *Lotus Notes* is only partially Backoffice™ compatible, which means *Lotus Notes* databases will integrate with the Windows NT security system to a certain extent, but not completely.

*The answer is **True** because Lotus Notes is one of the leading GroupWare products available today.*

776 INTRODUCTION TO MICROSOFT EXCHANGE

Q.   Which of the following features does Microsoft Exchange Server include?

Choose all answers that apply:

    A.   Group Scheduling

    B.   Forms

    C.   Application Design

    D.   Remote control of client computers

As you learned in Tip 775, one of the most important advances that new, faster networks and high-bandwidth transmissions have resulted in is a new category of applications known as GroupWare. The best known example of GroupWare is *Lotus Notes®*, a program which companies can use to promote greater interaction between members of a group—in many cases, realizing important goals which the group may otherwise have taken much longer to achieve or perhaps never have achieved at all. In addition to *Lotus Notes*, there are several other popular and powerful GroupWare applications.

One of the other, commonly used (and powerful) GroupWare applications available today, is Microsoft *Exchange Server*, which combines a powerful e-mail system with additional features, such as group scheduling capabilities, the use of e-mail-enabled forms (simple forms that users can easily e-mail to other users), the ability to design or alter applications without programming (aside from drag-and-drop placement and simple scripting), and more. *Exchange Server*'s features let users perform all the tasks that GroupWare professionals typically associate with group processing.

Microsoft's *BackOffice* suite of server-based tools, which runs only on the Windows NT Server, includes *Exchange Server*. One of the most powerful features of *Exchange Server*, which sets it apart from *Notes* and other GroupWare productions, is the program's close integration with the Windows NT security model. In other words, you can use Users and Groups that you create rights for within the operating system within *Exchange Server* without creation of new Users or Groups.

Answers A, B, and C are correct because Microsoft Exchange Server includes Group Scheduling, Forms, and Application Design features. Answer D is incorrect because Microsoft Exchange Server does not include remote control of client computers.

777 UNDERSTANDING NETWORK MANAGEMENT AND CONTROL

Q.   *The network administrator should always be the person who knows the most about the organization's networking and computers.*

True or False?

As you have learned in previous Tips, installing and configuring a network is a complex and detailed process. Planning and careful implementation during installation and configuration of the network is crucial for the network to work properly. Unfortunately, installing and configuring a network does not ensure that it will continue to function correctly over the network's lifetime. Networks will have problems, the organization must regularly back up data on the network, user and group rights will change, and such tasks must be managed correctly and documented for the network to maintain its usability. The network administrator is the person who is responsible for the network's upkeep.

The network administrator is not necessarily the person who knows the most about computers and networking. Rather, in most enterprises, the network administrator should be a person with a general understanding of computers and networking, and who has a demonstrated history of performing his or her duties. Network administration is more a managerial task than a technical one. Therefore, the administrator should also have good management skills—from working with people to ensure that they use the network correctly, to ensuring that his or her staff completes all daily tasks, as necessary.

Larger networks may have numerous administrators, with one person who manages all the other network administrators to ensure that the various administrators accomplish all network-related work. Both network operating system (NOS) companies and third-party vendors have developed many tools and programs to help network administrators identify problems and obtain the data they require to maintain accurate and useful network documentation. These tools will help administrators perform nearly every task they may require, from common tasks, such as checking password validity and aging, to complex tasks, such as analyzing the network's entire directory structure. The following Tips will introduce you to some of these tools and how a good network administrator will most commonly use the tools to best administer the network.

*The answer is **False** because the network administrator should be a responsible person with good management skills and a demonstrated history of accomplishing tasks.*

778	**INTRODUCTION TO THE SIMPLE NETWORK MANAGEMENT PROTOCOL (SNMP)**

Q.   Which of the following answers best describe the Simple Network Management Protocol (SNMP)?

Choose the best answer:

> *A.   A piece of software that provides communication between network managers.*
>
> *B.   A standard for network management software.*
>
> *C.   A special packet that carries information about network management.*
>
> *D.   A set of guidelines you can use to manage your network.*

As you have learned, networking has been an important part of computing ever since the first mainframes were brought on-line in the 1960s. However, as networking increased in popularity with smaller organizations, and more network types became available to address the varying needs of such organizations, the computer industry began to create programs and software packages to help administrators manage networks. Such software and related tools are generally known as network management software.

Network management software originally came in a wide variety of implementations—many of which were extremely proprietary (that is, you could only buy the network management tools from the company that developed the network operating system). Today, most network management software follows some standard that lets products operate cooperatively to help the network administrator as much as possible. The most commonly used standard within the computer industry is the Simple Network Management Protocol (SNMP). Most networks in the enterprise today, including Novell Netware and Windows NT, support SNMP to some extent. You will learn more about characteristics of SNMP is the next several Tips.

Answer B is correct because the Simple Network Management Protocol (SNMP) is a standard for network management software. Answers A, C, and D are incorrect because they do not describe the Simple Network Management Protocol (SNMP).

779   UNDERSTANDING **SNMP** AGENTS

Q.   *The SNMP agent collects statistical information from the network and devices on the network, including computers, printers, and so on.*

True or False?

As you learned in the previous Tip, the Simple Network Management Protocol (SNMP) defines a series of rules for network management software operations. SNMP uses *agents*, which are special programs that run on each computer in the network and monitor the computer's and the network's status, as well as the connection between the two. Agents gather various kinds of information and store the information in a special file. Central software components then analyze the data to prepare reports for the network's administrator. The administrator can set the central software component, in turn, to alert the administrator if pre-specified conditions (such as excessive traffic or collisions) exist on the network.

Depending on your network management goals, and the network's construction, you will use different agents and different types of agents to gather information. For example, while the agents that you will use to gather information about computers on the network will be similar, they will be different in construction if you have both Windows and Macintosh machines on your network. Similarly, you must use a different type of agent to obtain management information about network devices (such as hubs, routers, and bridges) than you will use to retrieve information from computers on the network.

Note: *Not all network components can use SNMP agents. You are likely to find that hubs, routers, and bridges that can respond to SNMP agents are typically more expensive than those that cannot.*

*The answer is **True** because SNMP agents collect statistical information from the network and the devices which attach to the network.*

780   INTRODUCTION TO THE MICROSOFT SYSTEMS MANAGEMENT SERVER **(SMS)**

Q.   *Which of the following features does the Microsoft Systems Management Server include?*

Choose all answers that apply:

    A.   *Application Sharing*

    B.   *Hardware and software inventory collection*

    C.   *Remote control of client computers*

    D.   *Troubleshooting tools*

One of the widely-used examples of network management software is the Microsoft *Systems Management Server (SMS)* for Windows NT networks. SMS uses the Simple Network Management Protocol (SNMP) standard to collect data about hardware and software (such as transmissions speeds, collisions, contention rates, and so on) from sources all over the network. *Systems Management Server* can then use the data it collects to produce detailed reports of network status, alert administrators to potential problems (such as transmission bottlenecks), and provide the administrator with insight into network performance that may indicate to the experienced administrator a need to upgrade components on the network. *Systems Management Server* provides many features, such as application sharing to remote network clients, hardware and software inventory, remote control capabilities that lets an administrator solve problems, help users, and even install new software without leaving his or her desk.

Answers A, B, C, and D are all correct because Systems Management Server includes all the features each answer lists.

781 UNDERSTANDING PROTOCOL ANALYZERS

Q.   *Network analyzers can look inside packets.*

True or False?

As you have learned, network administrators use various specialized tools (such as SNMP agents) to detect and repair problems on the network. In addition to the software tools that you have learned about, administrators generally also require manual tools (such as wire cutters, voltmeters, and so on) to effectively administer networks. Some of the administrator's tools are general electronic repair tools, while others are designed specifically for use on networks.

The *protocol analyzer* (also sometimes referred to as a *network analyzer)* is a device that you can physically attach to the network. After you attach the analyzer to the network, it will then gather information about the network and provide that information to you to help you determine the cause of network problems. Protocol analyzers can capture and look inside network packets (network data transmissions) and read the information the packets contain which, in turn, lets you identify problems, that may otherwise be difficult to isolate, such as a single computer that is generating bad packets on the network. Additionally, network analyzers can identify cabling problems such as short circuits, network cross-talk, and other interference problems (either resulting from bad terminators, electrical interference, or from other sources).

The answer is True because protocol analyzers (also called network analyzers) can look inside packets and read the information the packets contain.

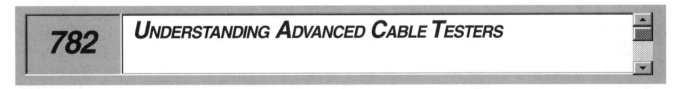

782 UNDERSTANDING ADVANCED CABLE TESTERS

Q.   *Advanced cable testers can detect problems such as collisions.*

True or False?

As you have learned, networks most often carry data over some form of cable. While you can perform most administrative activities from a computer on the network, from time to time you may require direct access to the electrical pulses on the network cable. As Tip 781 explains, you can use a protocol analyzer to perform direct analysis of the network cable's transmissions. However, there are also other devices that you can use to check the physical cable. These cable testers range from simple units that merely check for cable shorts, to advanced units that can detect problems with transmission, such as packet collisions or packet losses.

Although a network analyzer can detect network transmission problems as well as, and frequently more efficiently than, an advanced cable tester, network administrators often select an advanced cable tester as their primary tool because they are less expensive and more portable than network analyzers—making them easier to move from segment to segment of larger networks..

The answer is **True** *because, in addition to testing the physical cable, advanced cable testers can detect collisions and other network problems that do not necessarily result from a problem with the cable.*

783 — UNDERSTANDING DIGITAL VOLT METERS

Q. *How can you ensure that you have properly adjusted a digital volt meter to read resistance?*

Choose the best answer:

> *A.* *Check a store-bought cable's resistance.*
>
> *B.* *Send the meter to a calibration laboratory before each use.*
>
> *C.* *Touch the lead wires together.*
>
> *D.* *Digital volt meters are always correct.*

As a network administrator, you will often use physical tools in addition to your software management tools to ensure the network is working properly or to troubleshoot problems when the network is not working properly. A *digital volt meter* is one of the simplest and most common tools that a network administrator uses to identify network problems. Digital volt meters are non-specific electronic test units that can check network cable properties, such as voltage along the cable or the cable's electrical resistance.

The ability to test resistance is particularly important in network management because network cables rely on proper resistance to carry their data correctly over the network. For example, the resistance of 10BaseT cable will differ from the resistance of 10Base2 cable—and if the resistance on your cables is wrong, the network performance will likely diminish. A cable's resistance is a specific measurement (of how resistant the cable is to electrical transmissions) and you must be sure that your meter is properly calibrated (adjusted) before you test a cable. The simplest way to ensure that you have correctly calibrated your digital volt meter is to touch the lead wires on the volt meter together and check the amount of resistance between them.

Note: *Consult your digital volt meter's documentation for specific instructions on checking calibration and what the correct return values should be when you touch the lead wires together.*

Answer C is correct because you touch the volt meter's lead wires together to check a digital volt meter's resistance accuracy. Answer A is incorrect because a store-bought cable could nevertheless have the wrong resistance level. Answer B is incorrect because, although you can send the volt meter to a calibration laboratory before each use, it is time-consuming and not cost-effective. Answer D is incorrect because a digital volt meter is not always correct.

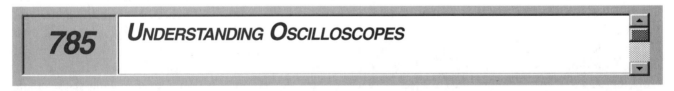

784   UNDERSTANDING TIME-DOMAIN REFLECTOMETERS (TDRs)

Q.   *Which of the following detection methods perform operations that are similar to the operations a Time-Domain Reflectometer performs on the network?*

Choose the best answer:

     A.   *Motion sensors*

     B.   *Radar*

     C.   *Sonar*

     D.   *Video cameras*

As you have learned, many network architectures rely on the transmission of electronic signals over a cable to communicate. At times, a crimp or a break in the physical cable can interrupt communication. Most network analyzers contain a *Time-Domain Reflectometer (TDR)*, which is a popular device that can detect crimps or breaks in cables. TDRs perform operations that are similar to sonar (a detection method that sends sound pulses into an area and reads the pulses that bounce back from that area).

Like sonar, TDRs send signals in the form of pulses—except TDRs use electrical pulses, and transmit them only down a network cable. The TDR then uses the pulses and their reflections to locate crimps or breaks in the network cable. Such crimps or breaks are impossible for network signals to pass over, and using a TDR lets you identify them more quickly—which can significantly simplify troubleshooting in larger networks.

Answer C is correct because Time-Domain Reflectometers perform operations that are similar to a sonar's operations. Answers A, B, and D are incorrect because the devices in these answers do not perform operations that are similar to a Time-Domain Reflectometer's operations.

785   UNDERSTANDING OSCILLOSCOPES

Q.   *Which of the following network problems can an Oscilloscope display?*

Choose all answers that apply:

     A.   *Cable short circuits*

     B.   *Broken cables*

     C.   *Bent or crimped cables*

     D.   *Attenuation*

In previous Tips, you have learned about devices that you can use to perform direct testing on a network's cables to help detect where breaks in the cable and similar problems occur. Another general electronic testing device that you can use when you test a network for possible problems is an *oscilloscope*, a device that displays electronic signals (the transmit network packets along the network) on a display monitor. The network administrator can then read the way the oscilloscope displays the signals to reveal details about the signals and the media (network cable, fiber-optic cable, or other physical backbone) that carries the signals (such as signal amplitude, network resistance, and so on). Network administrators frequently combine a Time-Domain Reflectometer (TDR) and an oscilloscope to identify network problems. Network analyzers usually include both TDRs and oscilloscopes in a single unit.

Answers A, B, C, and D are all correct because an oscilloscope can display each network problem the answers list.

786 — UNDERSTANDING VIRUS PROTECTION IN THE LAN ENVIRONMENT

Q.   *Because most viruses do not affect Windows NT, it is not necessary for you to check for viruses when you use a Windows NT Server.*

True or False?

While network problems that result from physical breakdown in the network are common during installation, and occur from time to time during the normal course of the network's operation, they do not pose as common and consistent threat to the network's viability as other network problems might. Most network problems that significantly threaten the network's usefulness, security, and stability are the result of software.

While there are many types of damaging software, there are very few things that a network administrator fears more than a *computer virus*. For example, a simple computer virus (the so-called Morris Worm) that took only a few hours to create brought the entire Internet to its knees in 1988. Specifically designed to damage computer files or hardware, computer viruses are very persistent and spread quickly. Frequently, viruses self-multiply (that is, they copy themselves throughout other files and operating systems they can access) as it functions—a process referred to as *infecting* other files.

The computer industry, in general, has produced and designed many programs (called anti-virus programs) to check for, prevent, and repair damage computer viruses cause. Unfortunately, these programs cannot find or prevent all viruses (because statistics indicate that about 10 new viruses per day appear on the Internet). The network administrator, therefore, must take every step possible to prevent a virus from infecting the entire network (such as blocking users' ability to download files from the Internet, making sure that every computer on the network has the most recently-updated anti-virus software, and so on). Although some network operating systems, such as Windows NT, are inherently resistant to some computer viruses' effects (because of how the operating system's designers built the operating system programs), network infection is still threatening because the operating system will not remove viruses from infected files—it was not designed to do so. Infected files may then wait in an inactivated state until users copy an infected file to a different operating system, where the virus the file contains can activate and begin to do damage (such as destroying the computer's operating system).

Although scanning and prevention programs (which every network design should include) help prevent network infection, they are not enough by themselves. Properly educating network users about the threat computer viruses may pose (such as lost work, a downed network, and even their termination, depending on the corporate security policy) and most common computer virus sources (such as the Internet and floppy disks that users bring in from home) is just as important and often more effective than scanning files with a virus protection program.

*The answer is **False** because although most viruses do not affect Windows NT, you should still regularly check all files for viruses.*

787 — **UNDERSTANDING WIDE-AREA NETWORK (WANs)**

Q.   Which of the following answers best describe the term "wide-area network" (WAN)?

Choose the best answer:

   A.   A series of computers that are connected together for communication.

   B.   One or more computers spread over a wide geographical area that communicate with each other.

   C.   Two or more local-area network segments a that a router connects.

   D.   Two or more local-area network segments that a bridge connects.

Throughout the last 185 Tips, you have learned about designing and implementing networks, as well as the protocols and architectures that most networks use. However, much of what you have learned is about local-area networks (LANs). As networking became more popular and spread throughout larger organizations, those organizations decided that they wanted to connect their disparate local-area networks (LANs) together. In some cases, large distances (miles, even continents) separated LANs and it became necessary for engineers to create ways to help these spread-out networks communicate.

A *wide-area network (WAN)* is two or more computers spread over a wide geographical area that communicate with each other. In the next several Tips, you will learn more about the various communication methods that connect computers together over large distances to form a WAN.

Answer B is correct because a network is two or more computers that communicate with each other, and doing so over a wide geographical area makes the network a wide-area network (WAN). Answer A is incorrect because a series of computers connected together for communication could be simply a local-area network (LAN). Answers C and D are incorrect because a bridge or a route's presence does not automatically define a network as a WAN.

788 — **INTRODUCTION TO DIGITAL WIDE-AREA NETWORK (WAN) LINKS**

Q.   What percentage of data that networks use digital communication methods to transmit is error-free?

Choose all answers that apply:

   A.   50%

   B.   75%

   C.   99%

   D.   100%

As you have learned, you can use a wide-area network (WAN) to connect computers that a large geographic distance separate. The earliest WAN communication methods used normal telephone lines to communicate and transmit data in the form of sound (analog communications). Because communication methods that use sound translate high-volumes of data into sound bursts, such methods tend to have high error levels in data transmission. Because analog transmissions so commonly have errors, the protocols that defined the transmissions also included extensive error-checking procedures to ensure that the receiving computer received the data correctly.

Needless to say, analog transmission was slow, both because of the limits of sending digital data in an analog format and because the network required such extensive error-checking procedures. As digital media became more widely installed, network communication stopped using analog communication and instead moved to digital transmission methods that have a much lower error level. Digital communication methods typically experience less than a one percent error rate (the data is 99 percent error-free), which means that information can be carried over a digital line much faster because the transmission protocols have to do less error-checking on the data.

Organizations may choose to implement their own digital transmission systems in their wide-area networks (WANs), but because of the costs involved (which are prohibitively expensive), usually depend on public networks to transmit data. Digital transmission methods that public networks offer are grouped into a Digital Data Services (DDS) category and are available in many formats, including T-1, T-3, T-4, and switched 56. The DDS T-1, T-3, and T-4 methods are called *leased lines* because an organization who wants to use T-line transmission services leases the service (and, in many cases, the actual physical cable to construct the line) from a provider (such as a telephone company) base. The organization can lease either a T-1, T-3, or T-4 line, depending on the transmission speed the organization requires. Table 788 lists the various speeds over which a leased line can carry data.

Line type	Transmission speed
T-1	1.5 megabits per second
T-3	44 megabits per second
T-4	274 megabits per second

Table 788 Leased line transmission speeds.

Switched 56 lines are digital communication lines that are capable of transmission speeds up to 56 kilobytes per second. Organizations frequently choose Switched 56 lines as a communication method because providers bill Switched 56 lines based on how long the line is actually transmitting data, instead of a constant, monthly fee that providers will assess for a leased line independent of the actual transmissions over the line.

Answer C is correct because digital communication methods transfer data 99 percent error-free. Answers A, B, and D are incorrect because these answers list percentages that are higher or lower than the actual data percentage that digital communication methods transfer error-free.

789   INTRODUCTION TO PACKET-SWITCHING NETWORKS

Q.   *Packet-switching networks are fast because the network transmits each data packet over the fastest path instead of all packets traveling the same path, even if that path becomes slower.*

True or False?

As you have learned, communications over larger networks create speed and quality issues when the network uses analog communications. Digital communications provide faster, more reliable communications across networks of all sizes. Digital communication methods have evolved over the years and today, there are several public network types that use digital communications to manage network transmissions. One of the most common public network types uses a form of transmission called *packet switching*. Packet-switching networks are fast because the network contains many intelligent devices that read the entire network and identify the quickest transmission path between two locations. These devices check the network status before they transmit each packet, which means that when a transmission is sent, some data will follow one route and other data will take a different route, but both will reach the same destination. Additionally, packet-switching networks use very small packets to transmit data (rather than larger frames or entire data files). The packet-switching network's use of small packets means that if an error occurs with a sent packet, the transmitting computer will only have to re-send a small amount of information to the receiving computer. Packet-switching networks use *intelligent hubs*, *demand priority networking*, and *dynamic routers* (all of which you have learned about in previous Tips) to manage the traffic of packets across the network.

*The answer is **True** because packet-switching networks transmit every packet along the fastest path available. The network devices evaluate the path for each packet before the packet's transmission and ensures the fastest data transmission possible.*

790   **UNDERSTANDING SWITCHED VIRTUAL CIRCUITS (SVCS)**

Q.   *Which of the following standard industry terms can you use interchangeably with "switched virtual circuit?"*

Choose the best answer:

    A.   *Switched circuit transmission*

    B.   *Virtual link transmission*

    C.   *Point-to-many-point transmission*

    D.   *Cooperative signaling*

As Tip 789 explains, packet switching networks are common digital networks. Some packet switching networks use *virtual circuit networking*, which is a variation on the original implementation of packet switching networks. *Virtual circuits* establish a series of software-based connections (meaning that the application layer in the protocol stack creates the connections) between the sending and receiving computers. The computers may establish the connection using any point in the physical media (cable, routers, hubs, other computers, and so on) that separates the computers. Software both creates and maintains the virtual circuit—meaning it has no specific physical construction in its creation—and the software also checks for errors in the communications and establishes communication rules for the circuit (such as speed, protocols, and so on).

One example of virtual circuit networking is the *Switched Virtual Circuits (SVC)* method of establishing a specific route across the network. Programmers also refer to SVCs as *point-to-many-point* connections. All transmitted data will follow this route during transmission and the route will be maintained until the connection is terminated. Each time the connection is established, the network will choose a new route that is based on the quickest path, but all packets use the same route as long as the connection exists. SVCs speed network transmissions because the network does not need to analyze the network and determine a path for each packet, and they also provide greater security for individual transmissions than a standard packet-switched network does. Such common protocols as the Point-to-Point Tunneling Protocol (PPTP), a Microsoft protocol for remote access to a wide-area network, use the basic principles of switched virtual circuits, with the two ends of the connection agreeing on a transmission path when the remote computer connects to the network.

Answer C is correct because the standard industry term point-to-many-point transmission is interchangeable with switched virtual circuit. Answers A, B, and D are incorrect because they list terms that are not interchangeable with switched virtual circuit.

791 UNDERSTANDING PERMANENT VIRTUAL CIRCUITS (PVCs)

Q.   Organizations frequently use permanent virtual circuits (PVCs) instead of leased lines because PVCs are less expensive.

True or False?

Tip 790 detailed switched virtual circuits (SVCs), a virtual circuit that exists between two computers or other network devices only so long as the connection between the two devices remains in use. On the other hand, *permanent virtual circuits (PVCs)* are similar to leased lines because the connection (and the virtual circuit path) is permanent and the data transmissions are very fast. The difference between PVCs and leased lines is that the customer pays only for the time the network actually transmits data. PVCs are examples of virtual networking because a physical connection between computers does not exist and networking software maintains the connection logically—that is, there is only a "virtual" connection between the devices.

The answer is **True** *because although leased lines and permanent virtual circuits (PVCs) function almost identically, PVCs are significantly less expensive.*

792 INTRODUCTION TO X.25 NETWORKS

Q.   Which of the following answers best describes the X.25 PAD?

Choose the best answer:

    A.   A terminal similar to a typewriter that can communicate over an X.25 network.

    B.   A device that translates networking protocols into X.25 format.

    C.   A device that acts as a router for X.25 networks.

    D.   A device that receives asynchronous characters and assembles them into X.25 packets.

As you have learned, many wide-area networks (WANs) use packet-switching technology to improve network speed and simplify communications. However, one of the first WANs that was widely used in business was the X.25 network, which originally used normal telephone lines (and, therefore, analog communications) to connect local-area networks (LANs) together. X.25 networks are still very common in larger, multi-national organizations, because most countries support X.25 connections (while they may not support other connection types). X.25 networks were slow because they used analog connections to communicate and modems to establish connections. In addition, they required higher error-checking levels than digital communications—because, as you have learned, analog transmissions suffer from a much higher error level than digital transmissions.

Today, the X.25 network's structure is the same, but it uses faster transmission methods—both digital communications and certain "tricks" to speed communications. For example, many X.25 networks use a *Public Data Network (PDN)* and a *Packet Assembler/Disassembler (PAD),* which receives asynchronous characters (data transmissions) from the transmitting computer or terminal and, in turn, packages them into packets that the PDN transfers to the receiving computer or network's PDN. Sending the information in packets lets the computers more easily manage transmissions and error corrections. At the receiving computer or network, the PDN sends the packets to the receiving PAD, which then disassembles the packets into the original asynchronous characters (data transmissions) and sends the characters to the receiving computer or terminal.

Answer D is correct because the X.25 Packet Assembler/Disassembler (PAD) receives asynchronous characters and assembles them into packets, and, when receiving, disassembles the packets into asynchronous characters. Answers A, B, and C are incorrect because they do not describe the X.25 PAD.

793   **INTRODUCTION TO FRAME RELAY NETWORKS**

Q.   *Frame relay networks are examples of Permanent Virtual Circuit (PVC) networking.*

True or False?

As you learned, X.25 systems were the earliest systems and were popular because of their wide accessibility and low cost. However, as more data transits public networks, speed is becoming a more and more significant issue for most companies. Today, *frame relay transmission systems* are becoming one of the most popular packet-switching network systems because frame-relay communications are both fast and cost effective. Frame relay systems are similar to X.25 systems but were designed for digital transmission and do not require or have the extensive error checking functions the X.25 has—making frame-relay communications faster not only during transit, but also when the receiving computer accepts the data.

Frame relay systems use permanent virtual circuit (PVC) networking to establish a logical connection across which the system transmits data, and the customer only pays for the length of time that the network is actually transmitting data. The systems are called *frame-relay systems* because they transmit data in data frames (which, as you have learned, are packets of data that travel across the networks), and because each frame transits one or more specific relay points along the PVC when it travels between the computers or networks.

*The answer is **True** because frame relay transmission uses permanent virtual circuit (PVC) networking to establish wide-area network connections.*

794   **INTRODUCTION TO ASYNCHRONOUS TRANSFER MODE (ATM) NETWORKS**

Q.   *What is an ATM network's currently possible maximum transmission speed?*

Choose the best answer:

    A.   *1.2Gbs per second*

    B.   *622Mbs per second*

    C.   *1.2Mbs per second*

    D.   *622Gbs per second*

As you have learned, there are several different types of packet-switching networks. The *Asynchronous Transfer Mode (ATM)* transmission standard is a packet-switching technology that is capable of high transmission speeds that developers designed for use on fiber-optic cable systems.

ATM *switches* (the ATM equivalent of intelligent hubs) break up data, structure the data into the appropriate format, add addressing and error-checking information to the data, and then place the data into a wrapper that is always the same size (53 bytes). Packet-switching networks can carry packets that are the same size much faster than they can carry packets that vary in length because the networking hardware requires less processing—determining the fastest network path is easier when packets are a constant size.

In theory, ATM networks can transmit data at 1.2Gbs. However, the maximum speeds currently possible in fiber-optic transmission limit the ATM network's speed. Currently, an ATM network's maximum possible speed is 622Mbs

Answer B is correct because an ATM network's current maximum possible speed use is 622Mbs. Answer A is incorrect because, although in theory, an ATM network's structure could transmit data at 1.2Gbs, fiber-optic cable transmission systems' maximum transmission speed (622Mbs) limits the ATM's actual maximum speed. Answers C and D are incorrect because they list speeds that are either higher or lower than an ATM network's currently possible maximum transmission speed.

---

795   UNDERSTANDING ATM HARDWARE

Q.   *Which of the following answers best describe an ATM switch?*

Choose the best answer:

A.   *A multi-port device that chooses an appropriate path for data.*

B.   *A multi-port device that serves only as a hub on ATM networks.*

C.   *A multi-port device that serves only as a router on an ATM network.*

D.   *A multi-port device that serves as either a hub or a router on an ATM network.*

As you have learned, Asynchronous Transfer Mode (ATM) networks use network switches to break network transmissions into fixed-size packets. ATM networks use networking hardware similar to the hardware other networks use, such as hubs, routers, and special network interface cards (NICs) to connect computers to the network.

However, only an ATM network has an *ATM switch*, which is an intelligent multi-port device (similar to a multi-port hub) that can act as a hub to connect many computers to the network. In addition, the ATM switch can act as a router to determine the best path between segments on an ATM network.

Answer D is correct because the ATM switch is a multi-port device that serves as either a hub or a router, or both, on an ATM network. Answer A is incorrect because ATM networks use a predefined path and do not require a device that determines an appropriate path. Answers B and C are incorrect because an ATM switch can act as either a hub or a router on an ATM network.

---

796   INTRODUCTION TO INTEGRATED SERVICES DIGITAL NETWORK (ISDN) NETWORKS

Q.   How many B channels are available in a Primary Rate Interface (PRI)?

Choose the best answer:

> A.   2
>
> B.   23
>
> C.   32
>
> D.   64

As you have learned, most wide-area networks (WAN) use digital communications today rather than analog communications. One of the more popular digital connection methods you can use to connect small networks or individual computers together is the *Integrated Services Digital Networking (ISDN)* standard, which comes two basic forms: *Primary Rate Interface (PRI)* and *Basic Rate Interface (BRI)*.

ISDN line providers typically bill ISDN lines as dial-up (on demand) connections in which the customer pays only for the time the network actually transmits data. Primary Rate Interface (PRI) ISDN provides 23 digital-transmission lines with speeds of 56Kbs to 64Kbs, or *B channels*, that carry data for the network or users. In addition, the Primary Rate Interface ISDN provides a single 16Kbps transmission line, a *D channel*, that carries special link-management data. Primary Rate Interface ISDN uses special devices that can divide the channels and maintain links to multiple sources—meaning that multiple computers and networks can use a single ISDN line for communications. Because ISDN supports multiple concurrent transmissions down a single cable, a Primary Rate Interface ISDN link is an excellent choice for an organization with multiple branches that require a connection to a central office. Moreover, a single computer can perform parallel transmissions down multiple B-channels simultaneously—yielding very high-speed transmissions.

Note: When all a Primary Rate Interface's B channels are combined, transmission speeds equal those of a T-1 leased line.

Basic Rate Interface ISDN provides users with two B channels (56 to 65 Kbps) and one D channel (16 Kbps). A Basic Rate Interface's advantage is that the user can combine the communication channels into a single link that has a 128 to 146 Kbps maximum transmission speed. Basic Rate Interface ISDN is an excellent choice for branch offices that require a connection to a central office that uses a Primary Rate Interface, or for fast dial-up Internet access.

Answer B is correct because a Primary Rate Interface (PRI) has 23 B channels. Answers A, C, and D are incorrect because they list quantities that are either higher or lower than the actual number of B channels a Primary Rate Interface (PRI) includes.

797   INTRODUCTION TO FIBER DISTRIBUTED DATA INTERFACE (FDDI) NETWORKS

Q.   What access method does the FDDI network architecture use?

Choose the best answer:

> A.   Carrier Sense Multiple Access with Collision Detection (CSMA/CD)
>
> B.   Token Passing
>
> C.   Demand Priority
>
> D.   Carrier Sense Multiple Access with Collision Avoidance (CSMA/CA)

As previous Tips indicate, there are many different constructions of wide-area network specifications. Most specifications use a combination of network cables. The *Fiber Distributed Data Interface (FDDI)* is a networking specification designed for organizations that require transmission speeds greater than those the original Ethernet and Token ring network architectures provided.

Released in 1986, FDDI is a network architecture that uses fiber-optic cabling and can transmit data at faster than 100Mbps. Organizations that require exceptionally high transmission speed, such as those that consistently transmit video or very large graphic files across the network frequently, use FDDI as a network architecture because of its speed. Larger organizations are also moving to FDDI as their network backbone because of the increased transmission distances of fiber-optic cable over other cable types.

FDDI networks use a token-passing access method over a Dual-Ring topology and can support up to 500 computers or other network devices (such as printers) while it carries data up to 62 miles (depending on cable restrictions). You will learn more about the special Dual-Ring topology that FDDI uses in Tip 799.

Answer B is correct because the Fiber Distributed Data Interface (FDDI) network architecture uses a token-passing access method. Answers A, C, and D are incorrect because FDDI uses a token-passing access method.

798	UNDERSTANDING *FDDI* ADVANTAGES OVER STANDARD TOKEN-PASSING

Q.   *The Fiber Distributed Data Interface network architecture uses a token-passing access method that is identical to the method the Token Ring network architecture uses.*

True or False?

As you have learned, the Fiber Distributed Data Interface (FDDI) network architecture uses a token-passing access method. However, the method FDDI uses is different from the token-passing method the Token Ring network architecture uses. As you learned in earlier Tips, Token Ring passes the token along the network only after the computer that currently possesses the token finishes transmitting and the receiving computer confirms its reception of the transmission.

The token-passing method that FDDI uses lets a computer transmit as many packets as it can produce in a specified time frame and then immediately releases the token and passes it to the next computer on the network. The computer that receives the token can then transmit its data immediately. In other words, transmissions from more than one computer can travel the FDDI network at the same time.

The FDDI network's unique sharing of transmissions (multiple simultaneous transmissions from multiple computers) gives FDDI networks a high level of functionality (because of the sheer volume of transmissions that can potentially transit the cable at one time) and speed that other network architectures are unable to compete with.

FDDI network architectures are less common than other architectures because they are expensive to install and maintain (because of the difficulties of working with fiber-optic cable), and require a high level of expertise to manage (because of the multiple concurrent transmissions on the network).

The answer is **False** *because although FDDI uses a token-passing access method, the implementation is different from the one that the Token Ring network architecture uses.*

799   Introduction to *FDDI's* Dual-Ring Topology

Q.   *What is the main purpose of the Dual-Ring topology that FDDI uses?*

Choose the best answer:

     A.   *Redundancy*

     B.   *Faster transmission speed*

     C.   *FDDI network interface cards transmit on one ring and receive on the other*

     D.   *The Dual-Ring topology lets you connect more computers to the network*

As you learned in Tip 797, the Fiber Distributed Data Interface (FDDI) network architecture uses a special Dual-Ring topology that other network architectures do not have. The Dual-Ring design consists of two fiber-optic cable rings that transmit data in opposite directions around the network, as shown in Figure 799.

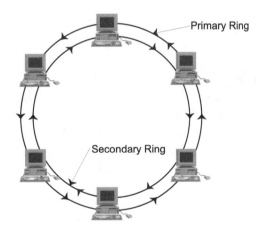

Figure 799 *FDDI's Dual-Ring topology.*

As you can see, the primary ring in Figure 799 carries data clockwise around the network, while the secondary ring carries data counter-clockwise around the network. The primary purpose of the Dual-Ring topology is to provide redundancy. Usually, the network carries data only on the *primary ring*.

If a network problem occurs or the primary ring fails, the network will automatically reconfigure itself to transmit data on the *secondary ring*. Some installations, however, use both rings at the same time to increase *throughput*—as you learned in Tip 798.

When the installation uses the dual rings to increase throughput, the first ring will transmit the first computer's data, while the second ring transmits the second computer's data. As soon as either ring becomes available, the token will pass to a third computer. In such cases, some computers may not be connected to both rings and how the computer reacts to a network failure will depend on its location on the network.

Computers that you connect to both the primary ring and the secondary ring are *Class A* computers.

Likewise, computers that you connect only to a single ring are *Class B* computers. If a network failure should occur, Class A computers can reconfigure themselves to use the secondary ring, but Class B computers will stop functioning because they have no redundant ring to use.

In the event of a network failure, networks which administrators configure for increased throughput (using both rings) will fall back on the single-ring as well.

Answer A is correct because the main purpose of the Dual-Ring topology that FDDI uses is for redundancy. Data typically flows only on the primary ring; the network can use the second ring if a problem develops with the primary ring. Answers B, C, and D are incorrect because they do not describe the purpose of the Dual-Ring topology that FDDI uses.

800	UNDERSTANDING THE ROUTING INFORMATION PROTOCOL (RIP)

Q: To connection to a TCP/IP network from a remote PC, you use the RIP (remote IP) protocol.

True or False?

Within a network that uses dynamic routers, the routers require a way to exchange routing-table information. One such protocol is RIP, the Routing Information Protocol. Using RIP, routers exchange 512-byte messages that contain network IDs and a metric that indicates the network's distance (which network administers sometimes refer to as a hop count). RIP restricts a network's hop count to 15 (a network that requires 16 or more hops is considered unreachable). By adjusting a network's hop count, network administrators can compensate for slower networks (by assigning a slow network a higher hop count which would make the network less desirable for use).

Within a network, RIP routers advertise their routing tables every 30 seconds, by broadcasting messages to all attached networks. If a router does not hear from another router for a period of three minutes, the first router assumes that the silent router has crashed.

Because the RIP protocol uses 512-byte messages, routers must often send their routing-table information within multiple messages. Depending on the networksize, a routing table can easily contain several hundred or possibly several thousand entries.

Only dynamic routers exchange routing-table information using RIP. Static routers do not exchange routing information. Likewise, some routers, which network administrators refer to as silent routers, receive RIP messages, but do not send any messages in return.

The answer is False because the RIP protocol is not used for remote PC access, but rather, to exchange routing table information between network routers.

801 INTRODUCTION TO EXAM 70-40: IMPLEMENTING AND SUPPORTING MICROSOFT WINDOWS 95

Q: You must pass Exam 70-40: Implementing and Supporting Microsoft Windows 95 for certification as an MCSE.

True or False?

Exam 70-40: Implementing and Supporting Microsoft Windows 95 is acceptable as a core exam for Microsoft Certified Systems Engineer (MSCE) certification. Of the client-level operating system exams you can take to become certified, the Windows 95 exam is one of the more difficult exams because it covers a wide subject area and requires detailed knowledge of various other operating systems and networking topics.

Although Exam 70-40 the will satisfy one of the core exam requirements for MCSE certification, you are not required to take it in order to certify because other client-level operating systems, such as Windows NT Workstation, have their own exams that also satisfy the client-level operating system requirement.

*The answer is **False** because Exam 70-40: Implementing and Supporting Microsoft Windows 95 is acceptable as a client-level operating system exam, but is not the only choice.*

802 UNDERSTANDING THE WINDOWS 95 EXAM SECTIONS

Q: Exam 70-40: Implementing and Supporting Microsoft Windows 95 is one of the easier exams you can take that will satisfy one of the core exams required for certification as an MCSE.

True or False?

Following their standard exam format, Microsoft breaks the Windows 95 exam into sections. Each section specifically tests you on knowledge that is necessary to support Windows 95 client computers. The following lists describe the topics Exam 70-40: Implementing and Supporting Microsoft Windows 95 tests, in accordance with the *Microsoft Exam Preparation Guide.*

The Planning section tests you on your ability to develop an appropriate implementation model to meet specific requirements. Specific topics the section covers include the following:

- Choose between a workgroup configuration or a domain model

- Develop a security strategy

- Implement security using system policies, user profiles, and file and printer sharing

The Installation and Configuration section tests you on your ability to install and configure a Windows 95 workstation. Specific topics the section covers include the following:

- How to install Windows 95 given different network configurations

- How to perform the various Windows 95 installation types, including automated Windows setup, a new Windows 95 installation, a Windows 95 upgrade installation, a Windows 95 uninstall, and a dual-boot combination with Microsoft Windows NT

- How to install and configure the network components of a client computer and server.

- Demonstrate and explain how to install and configure the different network protocols that Windows 95 supports, including NetBEUI, the IPX/SPX-compatible protocol, Transport Control Protocol/ Internet Protocol (TCP/IP), Microsoft DLC, and Point-to-Point Tunneling Protocol/Virtual Private Networks (PPTP/VPN)

- Demonstrate and explain how to install and configure modems and printers within Windows 95

- How to configure system services, including the *Internet Explorer*® Web browser.

- Demonstrate how to install and configure tape drive and the Windows 95 *Backup* application.

The Configuring and Managing Resource Access section tests you on your ability to use the Windows 95 operating system to manage resources. Specific topics the section covers include the following:

- How to assign access permissions for shared folders, using passwords, user permissions, and group permissions

- Demonstrate and explain how to create, share, and monitor resources.

- Explain how to manage and access remote resources, including network printers, shared fax modems, and Unimodem/V.

- Show how to set up user environments by using user profiles and system policies.

- Demonstrate knowledge of or ability to backup data and restore data, manage hard disks, perform disk compression, partition disks, and establish application environments for Microsoft MS-DOS® applications.

The Integration and Interoperability section tests you on your ability to integrate Windows 95 with network products and operating systems. Specific topics the section covers include the following:

- How to configure a Windows 95 computer as a client computer in a Windows NT network

- How to configure a Windows 95 computer as a client computer in a NetWare network

- How to configure a Windows 95 computer to access the Internet

- How to configure a client computer to use Dial-Up Networking for remote access

The Monitoring and Optimization section tests you on your ability to monitor the performance of the operating system after installation, as well as your ability to optimize installations for speed, efficiency, and manageability. Specific topics the section covers include the following:

- How to monitor system performance using *Net Watcher* and *System Monitor*

- Tune and optimize the system using Disk *Defragmenter*, *ScanDisk*, and *DriveSpace*

The Troubleshooting section tests you on your ability to resolve post-installation issues that may cause computers with the Windows 95 operating system to act incorrectly. Specific topics the section covers include the following:

- How to diagnose and resolve installation failures

- How to diagnose and resolve boot process failures

- How to diagnose and resolve connectivity problems using *WINIPCFG, Net Watcher*, and the troubleshooting wizards

- How to diagnose and resolve printing problems

- How to diagnose and resolve file system problems

- How to diagnose and resolve resource access problems

- How to diagnose and resolve hardware device and device driver problems using *MSD* and the Add/Remove Hardware Wizard

- How to perform direct modification of the Registry, when appropriate, using the *Registry Editor* (*regedit.exe*)

The answer is **False** *because Exam 70-40: Implementing and Supporting Microsoft Windows 95 is one of the more difficult exams that will satisfy one of the required core exams for MCSE certification. To take Exam 70-40, you must have extensive knowledge of Windows 95, general networking, Windows NT domain structure, and other network operating systems' features.*

803   P*REPARING FOR THE* W*INDOWS* **95** E*XAM*

Q: *Most people pass Exam 70-40: Implementing and Supporting Microsoft Windows 95 the first time.*

True or False?

As you have learned, you must take an exam for the MCSE certification at an authorized Prometric testing center. The center will require two valid forms of identification. You must schedule the test in advance (at least 24 hours) and you will be required to pay for the exam if you cancel within less than 24 hours. You can help prepare yourself for Exam 70-40 by taking practice exams, and by applying the knowledge you will learn within this section. The Microsoft Web site has practice exams you can download and take as part of your exam preparation.

Do not be discouraged if you do not pass the exam the first time—many people fail an exam more than once before they do pass it. The Windows 95 exam, especially, tends to be surprisingly difficult for most exam takers—because the material the exam covers is often material that exam takers have not encountered in their own network installations. Remember that if you fail an exam, the best thing to do is study the weak areas immediately while the questions are still fresh in your mind and then take the exam again in a short period of time. If you wait too long to retake an exam, you might second-guess answers that you correctly answered the first time. As with all the MCSE exams, the most important step is to ensure that you study the material the exams covers carefully, and that you be prepared to answer questions of any form about the material—whether the questions be true/false, multiple choice, or multiple choice/ multiple answer.

The answer is **False** *because many people fail Exam 70-40 more than once before they pass it.*

804   I*NTRODUCTION TO THE* W*INDOWS* **95** F*EATURES*

Q: *Which of the following are Windows 95 features?*

Choose all answers that apply:

      A.   *A graphical user interface*

      B.   *Built-in networking support*

      C.   *Support for applications designed for the Windows 3.x operating systems*

      D.   *Support for the NTFS file system*

The Windows 95 operating system, which is designed for both home and work use, is the successor to the Windows *3.x* operating systems. Windows 95 is a major enhancement to Windows 3.x because it supports 32-bit applications and utilities, has built-in networking support, and provides backward compatibility for MS-DOS-based and Windows *3.x*-based applications. In addition, Windows 95 is the first product Microsoft released with the *Graphical User Interface (GUI)* that replaces the Program Manager in Windows 3.x and Windows NT 3.x.

Since the first Windows 95 version release, Microsoft has made various changes to the system, in the form of patches, service packs, and newer Original Equipment Manufacturer (OEM) Service Releases 2 of the operating system. Many people refer to the newer OEM release as Windows 95 *Revision B* or simply *Rev. B*. One of the major changes to Windows 95 that is available in the OEM Service Release is support for the new File Access Table 32-bit (FAT32) file system, which is a new, enhanced File Access Table (FAT) file system version that can support hard drives of up to two terabytes in size (FAT cannot support drives larger than 2Gb). FAT32 is a source of confusion for many people because the FAT implementation within Windows NT 4.0 also provides enhancements to the original FAT implementation—however, the Windows NT FAT implementation does not include all the enhancements of FAT32. In fact, the two file systems are actually very different and, just as only Windows NT can use the NTFS file system, only Windows 95 OEM Service Release 2 can use FAT32.

Answers A, B, *and C are correct because all versions of Windows 95 include a graphical user interface, built-in networking support, and support for applications designed for Windows 3.x operating systems.* *Answer D is incorrect because no version of Windows 95 can support the NTFS file system.*

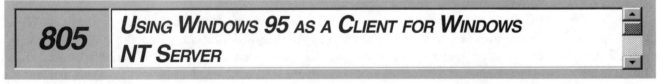

805	USING WINDOWS 95 AS A CLIENT FOR WINDOWS NT SERVER

Q: *What additional software must you add to enable Windows 95 to act as a client for Windows NT server?*

Choose the best answer:

      A.   *The Windows NT client software in the client's folder on the Windows NT server CD-ROM*

      B.   *Special network software third-party vendors provide*

      C.   *Nothing. Windows 95 includes the ability to act as a client for Windows NT server*

      D.   *Nothing. Windows 95 cannot act as a client for Windows NT server*

As you have learned, Windows 95 has built-in support for networking. This support enables Windows 95 to create a simple network between other Windows 95 computers or to act as a client to powerful server-based networks, such as Microsoft Windows NT or Novell NetWare. The Windows 95 source files include client software for both Microsoft Networks and Novell Networks and it is through these clients that you establish networks. For example, to use Windows 95 as a client for a Windows NT domain, you must install the *Client for Microsoft Networks* protocol and configure it to log on to a Windows NT domain by entering in the domain's name within the space the operating system provides.

Answer C is correct because no additional software is required to enable Windows 95 to act as a client for Windows NT server. All the required client software is included on the Windows 95 CD-ROM or floppies. Answers A, B, and D are incorrect because Windows 95 can, with no additional software, act as a client for Windows NT server.

806   INTRODUCTION TO THE WINDOWS 95 INTERFACE

Q: *Which of the following industry standard terms describe the main working area of the Windows 95 user interface?*

Choose the best answer:

     A.   *Workshop*

     B.   *Shortcut screen*

     C.   *Desktop*

     D.   *Tabletop*

As you learned in Tip 803, Windows 95 is the first operating system that Microsoft released with the new Graphical User Interface (GUI) and that replaces the Program Manager in Windows 3.x and Windows NT 3.x operating systems.

The new GUI is quite different than the interface previous Microsoft operating systems used. The idea behind the new interface is to provide the user with an area of space called the Desktop, upon which users place objects that control the operating system. The Desktop is the main working area of Windows 95 and is the first thing you see when you start Windows 95. You use *objects* located on top of the Desktop to perform tasks such as launching applications (the Start menu) and configuring software components or hardware devices inside the computer (the My Computer icon). Examples of Desktop objects include the My Computer and Network Neighborhood icons and the Windows 95 Taskbar.

Answer C is correct because the main working area of the Windows 95 user interface is the Desktop. Answers A, B, and D are incorrect because they are not standard industry terms to describe the main working area of the Windows 95 user interface.

807   USING THE WINDOWS 95 NETWORK NEIGHBORHOOD

Q: *The Desktop always contains a Network Neighborhood icon.*

True or False?

In Tip 806, you learned that you control Windows 95 through objects such as the My Computer and Network Neighborhood icons, which are located on the Desktop. Although you will almost always have a My Computer icon, you will not have a Network Neighborhood icon unless you configure your computer for connection to a network.

Network Neighborhood is the icon that lets you see network resources. For example, if you are operating Windows 95 on a small network and you want to use a resource located on the network, you will access Network Neighborhood to both view and access the resource. In addition, you can use the right-mouse button to open the Network Neighborhood's Network Properties dialog box. Within the Network Properties dialog box, you can configure networking components and software, including protocols, sharing rules, and so on.

*The answer is **False** because the Network Neighborhood icon appears on the Desktop only if you have configured network functions.*

808   ## USING THE WINDOWS 95 TASKBAR

Q: Which of the following tasks can you perform using the Windows 95 Taskbar?

Choose all answers that apply:

    A.   Quickly switch between open applications

    B.   Quickly start applications

    C.   Format a disk drive

    D.   Change the color scheme for Windows 95

The Windows 95 *Taskbar* is probably the object you will access most frequently while using Windows 95. The Taskbar contains the Start menu, which is the primary tool for accessing configuration options and launching applications in Windows 95. The Start menu also indicates all open windows and lets you quickly switch between applications. The Windows 95 Taskbar automatically resides at the bottom of the screen when you install Windows 95, but you can move it to the top or either side of the screen, depending on what you prefer. Figure 808 shows the Windows 95 Taskbar.

Figure 808 *The Windows 95 Taskbar.*

***Answers A and B** are correct because you can quickly start and switch between applications using the Windows 95 Taskbar. **Answers C and D** are incorrect because you cannot format a disk drive or change the Windows 95 color scheme using the Windows 95 Taskbar.*

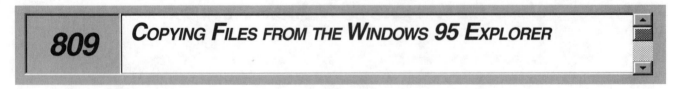

809   ## COPYING FILES FROM THE WINDOWS 95 EXPLORER

Q: The Windows 95 Explorer takes the place of what program in Windows 3.x operating systems?

Choose the best answer:

    A.   Print Manager

    B.   File Manager

C.   *Program Manager*

D.   *Control Panel*

The Windows 95 *Explorer* is the program that replaces the old Windows 3.x File Manager and is the primary tool in Windows 95 for file and folder management. The *Explorer* provides a dual-window view of the computer and network (if applicable) so that users can select a drive or directory in the left window and view its contents in the right window. Figure 809 shows the *Explorer*.

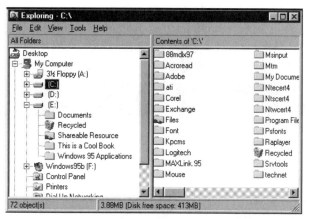

Figure 809 *The Windows 95 Explorer.*

The Explorer displays drives and folders with a plus (+) or minus (-) symbol if they contain subfolders. These symbols let you quickly determine if a drive or folder has subdirectories. In turn, you can expand or collapse a drive or folder's directory tree by clicking your mouse on the plus symbol to expand the drive or folder and the minus symbol to collapse the drive or folder.

As a Windows 95 user, you will perform file copying, file moving, folder creation, and other file-related tasks from within the *Explorer*. File copying is much easier to do in the Explorer than it was in older file management utilities because you can see both the original location of a file or folder and its intended destination at the same time.

For example, if you wanted to copy a file from the Windows folder on the *C:* drive to a folder on the *D:* drive, you would simply expand both drive letters by clicking your mouse on the plus symbols. You would then click your mouse on the Windows folder to select it. In turn, the Windows folder's contents would be displayed in the right window, where you could easily view them.

To copy a file, find the file you want to copy in the right window and use your mouse to drag it to the destination folder in the left window (while you hold down your keyboard's CTRL key—which forces the Explorer to copy, as opposed to move, the files). Additionally, the *Explorer* provides a pop-up menu that you will invoke with the right mouse button that you can use to perform many tasks, including copying files and folders, creating new folders, and so on.

Answer B is correct because the Windows 95 Explorer is a replacement for the File Manager program in Windows 3.x operating systems. Answers A, C, and D are incorrect because the Windows 95 Explorer does not replace the Print Manager, Program Manager, or Control Panel.

---

810   USING THE SHIFT KEY TO MOVE FILES TO YOUR WINDOWS 95 DESKTOP

Q: *You are dragging a file named Text.doc from a folder on the D:\ drive to the Windows 95 Desktop. Throughout the entire operation, you hold down the SHIFT key. What will Windows 95 do when you release the mouse button?*

Choose the best answer:

    A.   *Create a shortcut to Text.doc on the Desktop.*

    B.   *Create a copy of Text.doc on the Desktop.*

    C.   *Move Text.doc to the Desktop.*

    D.   *Nothing. Holding down the SHIFT key disables the drag-and-drop function in Windows 95.*

As you have learned, you can copy and move files in the Windows 95 *Explorer* just by dragging them with your mouse. You can also copy or move files from the *Explorer* to other locations, such as your Desktop, in the same way. For example, if you want to move a file from a folder on the *C:* drive to your Desktop, you can use your mouse to drag the file from the Explorer window to the Desktop. The *Explorer* will move a file from a folder on one drive to any other location on the same drive when you drag the file. If you drag a file from one fixed drive to another, the Explorer will copy the file instead of moving the file. You can force the Explorer to move files from one drive to another by holding down the SHIFT key while you drag your mouse. For example, if you want to move a file from the *D:* drive to your *C:* drive, hold down the SHIFT key and then drag the file from its current location onto the *C:* drive icon in the *Explorer* window's left pane.

Note: *When you use the SHIFT key to force a move during a drag-and-drop procedure, you must release the mouse button before you release the SHIFT key; otherwise, the file or folder will only copy, not move, to its new location.*

Answer C is correct because holding down the SHIFT key while dragging Text.doc from one disk drive or partition to another will result in Text.doc moving when you release the mouse button. **Answer A** is incorrect because if you simply drag Text.doc from one disk drive or partition to another, Windows 95 will create a shortcut, but if you hold down the SHIFT key while dragging, you force Windows 95 to move Text.doc instead of creating a shortcut. **Answer B** is incorrect because holding down the SHIFT key while dragging Text.doc from one disk drive to another forces Windows 95 to move Text.doc and does not copy it. **Answer D** is incorrect because holding down the SHIFT key does not disable the Windows 95 drag-and-drop function.

---

811   USING THE CTRL KEY TO DRAG FILES TO YOUR WINDOWS 95 DESKTOP

Q: *You are dragging a file named Text.doc from a folder on the C:\ drive to the Windows 95 Desktop. Throughout the entire process, you hold down the CTRL key. What will Windows 95 do when you release the mouse button?*

Choose the best answer:

    A.   *You will create a copy of Text.doc on the Desktop.*

    B.   *You will create a shortcut to Text.doc on the Desktop.*

    C.   *You will move Text.doc to the Desktop.*

    D.   *Nothing, holding down the CTRL key disables the Windows 95drag-and-drop function.*

As you learned in Tip 810, you can hold down the SHIFT key to force the Windows 95 *Explorer* to move files between drives. You can also use the CTRL key to force the *Explorer* to copy between drives or directories. For example, if you want to copy a file from the *D:* drive to your Desktop, hold down the CTRL key and then drag the file from the *Explorer* to the Desktop.

Note: When you use the CTRL key to copy files during a drag-and-drop procedure, you should release the mouse button before you release the CTRL key.

Answer A is correct because you can hold down the CTRL key while dragging Text.doc from one location to another on the same disk drive or on any other disk drive to create a copy of the file you are dragging. Answer B is incorrect because dragging Text.doc from one location to another on the same disk drive will not create a shortcut unless you use the right (not left) mouse button. Answer C is incorrect because while dragging a file from one location to another on the same disk drive will normally move the file, holding down the CTRL key while dragging the mouse will force Windows 95 to create a copy. Answer D is incorrect because holding down the CTRL key does not disable the Windows 95 drag-and-drop functions.

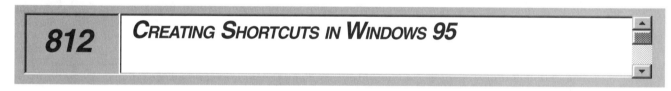

| 812 | CREATING SHORTCUTS IN WINDOWS 95 |

Q: *Which of the following answers list valid methods of creating a shortcut in Windows 95?*

Choose all answers that apply:

> *A.* *Drag a file from one location to another on the same disk drive or partition.*
>
> *B.* *Drag a file from one disk drive or partition to a location on another disk drive or partition.*
>
> *C.* *Use the right mouse button to drag a file from one location to another and choose the Create Shortcut(s) Here option from the menu that appears when you release the mouse button.*
>
> *D.* *Use the Create Shortcut Wizard included with Windows 95.*

As you have learned, Windows 95 is the successor to, and an improvement on, the Windows 3.x operating systems. One of the powerful new features that Windows 95 supports are special objects called *shortcuts* that point to other objects stored on your computer. Shortcuts let you create graphical reference points to applications, files, and folders that you use frequently. A Shortcut is simply an icon in a convenient location that contains an internal reference to the file's actual location. Using shortcuts, you can place references to your most commonly-used programs and files within convenient locations without actually moving the files themselves to those locations. The most common place to put a shortcut is on your Windows 95 Desktop.

Although there are various ways to create shortcuts (just as there are multiple ways to copy or move a file), the easiest method is the *New Shortcut Wizard*. To use the New Shortcut Wizard, perform the following steps:

1. Right-click your mouse on the Desktop. Windows 95 will display a pop-up menu.
2. From the pop-up menu, choose New and then Shortcut. Windows 95 will open the New Shortcut Wizard.
3. Click your mouse on the Browse button. Windows 95 will open the Browse Dialog box.
4. Navigate through the Browse dialog box to locate the file or application for which you are creating the Shortcut and click the Open button. Windows 95 will insert the complete pathname into the *Command Line* field.

5. Click your mouse on the Next button. The Create Shortcut Wizard will display the Select a Title for the Program dialog box.

6. Within the Select a Title for the Program dialog box, type a name for the shortcut and click your mouse on the Finish button. Windows 95 will close the dialog box and create a shortcut with the name you typed.

Answers B, C, and D are correct because each of the options listed will create a new shortcut. Answer A is incorrect because dragging a file from one location to another on the same disk drive or partition will not create a shortcut.

813   ARRANGING WINDOWS IN WINDOWS 95

Q: In addition to the Minimize All Windows option, what options are available for arranging windows when you right-click your mouse on the Windows 95 Taskbar?

Choose all answers that apply:

A. Maximize All Windows

B. Cascade

C. Tile Horizontally

D. Tile Vertically

Because windows tend to cover each other as they open, it can sometimes be difficult to work with more than one application because you cannot see all the windows that are open at the same time. To make it easier for you to work with multiple applications, Windows 95 provides you with several choices for arranging windows.

From the Windows 95 Taskbar, you can arrange windows in a *tiled* display, which means the windows are side by side on the Desktop, much as you would arrange floor tiles. You can also arrange windows in a *cascaded* display, which means the windows are layered at an angle, from the Desktop's top left corner to its bottom left corner. Although cascaded files always look the same, you have the option of tiling windows either vertically or horizontally.

To arrange windows on the Desktop, right-click your mouse on the Windows 95 Taskbar and choose an option from the pop-up menu that appears. Figure 813 shows the Desktop after you select Cascade Windows from the Taskbar's pop-up menu.

Figure 813 *Cascading windows on the desktop.*

Answers B, C, and D are correct because, in addition to the Minimize All Windows option, the Cascade, Tile Horizontally, and Tile Vertically options are available when you right-click your mouse on the Windows 95 Taskbar. Answer A is incorrect because Maximize All Windows is not an available option on the Taskbar pop-up menu.

814 — USING THE SHIFT KEY TO CLOSE MULTIPLE WINDOWS

Q: *What will happen if you hold down the* SHIFT *key and click the left mouse button on the Close Window button at the top-right of an open window?*

Choose the best answer:

A.   *Only that window will close*

B.   *Nothing*

C.   *That window and all windows you opened in sequence to reach that window will close*

D.   *All open windows will close*

As the previous Tip explains, working with multiple applications or windows can be difficult, although Windows 95 provides you with tools (such as cascading and tiling windows) to simplify your work with multiple windows. However, if you have opened too many unnecessary windows in sequence to reach a specific file, network resource, or application, you may want to close some or all of those windows after you access the file or network resource. In particular, you will commonly open multiple windows in sequence when you use My Computer or Network Neighborhood. However, to fix the problem of having too many open applications, you can use a quick but often overlooked method of closing all the windows you opened in sequence with a single mouse click. For example, if you opened seven windows in sequence to reach a specific destination and you now want to close them all, hold down the SHIFT key and click your mouse on the Close Window button of the last window you opened. In turn, Windows 95 will close all seven windows.

Note: *You can only use the* SHIFT+*Close Window method to close windows that you open either from within My Computer or Network Neighborhood or that you open using the pop-up menu's Open option in* **Explorer**—*in other words, you can only close folders and drives with* SHIFT+*Close Window.*

Answer C *is correct because holding down the* SHIFT *key and clicking the left mouse button on the Close Window button at the top-right of a window will close that window and all windows you opened in sequence to reach it.* **Answers A, B, and D** *are incorrect because they do not accurately describe what will happen if you hold down the* SHIFT *key while clicking the left mouse button on the Close Window button at the top-right of a window.*

815 — SWITCHING BETWEEN OPEN APPLICATIONS IN WINDOWS 95

Q: *You must learn to use the Windows 95 Taskbar to switch between applications in Windows 95 because the Windows 3.x* ALT+TAB *function does not work in Windows 95.*

True or False?

One of the most elementary requirements for a multi-tasking operating system is the ability to switch between applications. In Windows 3.x operating systems, you could switch between applications by pressing the ALT and TAB keys simultaneously. To make the transition between operating systems easier for users, Windows 95 also supports the ALT+TAB keyboard combination to switch between applications or windows. As an alternative, you can use the Windows 95 Taskbar to switch between applications by clicking on the application's Taskbar representation. Figure 815 shows the Windows 95 Taskbar with representations of open, minimized windows.

Figure 815 *Representations of open, minimized windows on the Windows 95 Taskbar.*

The answer is **False** *because although the Windows 95 Taskbar is an effective method for switching between applications, the ALT+TAB function that performed application switching in Windows 3.x operating systems will still switch between applications in Windows 95.*

816 CHANGING AN ICON'S APPEARANCE IN WINDOWS 95

Q: *You can change the appearance of an icon only for MS-DOS-based application shortcuts.*

True or False?

Windows 95 gives you a superior control over the way your interface appears. You can change your Desktop wallpaper (background) and your screen savers, and you can even change the icons that represent your computer's various files and applications. You can also change the appearance of any shortcut and even some actual program files, although it is generally a good idea to work with shortcuts and not change actual executable files.

To change a shortcut's appearance, perform the following steps:

1.   Right-click your mouse on the icon that represents the shortcut. Windows 95 will display a pop-up menu.
2.   Within the pop-up menu, select the Properties option. Windows 95 will display the shortcut's Properties dialog box.
3.   Within the Properties dialog box, select the Shortcut tab. Windows 95, in turn, will display the Shortcut sheet. Within the Shortcut sheet, click your mouse on the Change Icon button. Windows 95 will display a list of icons to choose from.
5.   Within the list, click your mouse on an icon to select it. Next, click your mouse on the OK button. Windows 95 will return to the shortcut's Properties dialog box.
6.   Click your mouse on the OK button. Windows 95 will change the icon for the shortcut.

The answer is **False** *because you can change the appearance of almost any Windows 95 icon.*

817 ADDING OR REMOVING PROGRAMS FROM STARTUP

Q: *Which of the following answers describe valid methods of adding shortcuts to the Startup group?*

Choose the best answer:

> A.   *Right-click your mouse on the Windows 95 Taskbar and use the Start menu Programs tab.*
>
> B.   *Copy a shortcut into the C:\Windows\Start Menu\Programs\Startup folder.*
>
> C.   *Use the Add/Remove Programs option in the Windows 95 Control Panel.*
>
> D.   *You cannot add shortcuts to the Windows 95 Startup group.*

Windows 95 can start programs automatically when the system initializes. To configure Windows 95 to start a specific application automatically, you must place a shortcut to the application in the Start menu's Startup group. Windows 95 provides a tool you access from the Taskbar's Properties dialog box that lets you add or remove shortcuts to the Start menu and its submenus. Alternatively, you can copy a shortcut into the Startup folder (*C:\Windows\Start Menu \Programs\Startup*). Figure 817 displays the Taskbar Properties dialog box's Start Menu Programs tab.

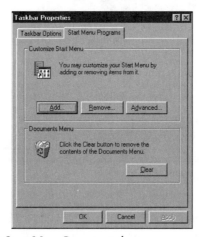

Figure 817 *The Taskbar Properties dialog box's Start Menu Programs tab.*

Answers A and **B** *are correct because either right-clicking on the Taskbar and using the Start Menu Programs tab or copying shortcuts to the C:\Windows\Start Menu\Programs\Startup folder will let you add shortcuts to the Startup group.* **Answer C** *is incorrect because the Add/Remove Programs option in the Windows 95 Control Panel will not let you add shortcuts to the Startup group.* **Answer D** *is incorrect because you can add shortcuts to the Windows 95 Startup group.*

818   ADDING OR REMOVING HARDWARE IN WINDOWS 95

Q: *Windows 95 supports only plug-and-play hardware.*

True or False?

As an MCSE, you will, at some point, install new hardware components into a computer running Windows 95. In turn, the procedure you must follow will depend on the hardware itself. Windows 95 includes support for both plug-and-play and legacy hardware devices.

Plug-and-play devices include information within the device itself (usually in the device's read-only memory) which lets the operating system recognize the hardware automatically. Legacy devices (that is, devices that do not support plug-and-play) do not contain such information, and, therefore, you must configure them manually.

In some cases (with plug-and-play hardware), merely installing the hardware is enough and Windows 95 will recognize the hardware when it initializes. Other times (with legacy hardware), Windows 95 will not automatically detect the hardware so you must use the Add New Hardware Wizard, which you can find in the Windows 95 Control Panel. Finally, occasionally you must configure the legacy device using command line instructions in the *config.sys* and *autoexec.bat* files.

When Windows 95 automatically detects hardware, you typically must answer a few questions about the hardware so that Windows 95 can set it up properly. The Add New Hardware Wizard gives you the option of letting Windows 95 search for a device or only identifying it and loading the appropriate device drivers. You should always let Windows 95 try to identify the hardware first, and configure hardware yourself, only if Windows 95 is unable to identify it. Figure 817 shows the Add New Hardware Wizard that you will generally use to manually configure hardware.

Figure 817 The Add New Hardware Wizard dialog box.

*The answer is **False** because Windows 95 supports both plug-and-play and legacy hardware devices.*

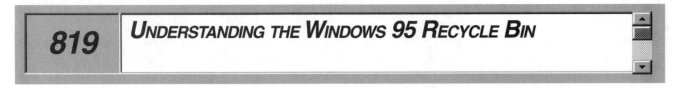

819 — UNDERSTANDING THE WINDOWS 95 RECYCLE BIN

Q: *Unless you change its configuration, the Windows 95 Recycle Bin will hold every file you ever delete forever.*

True or False?

The Windows 95 Recycle Bin provides protection to prevent a user from losing mistakenly deleted files and folders. The Recycle bin stores deleted files and folders until a user undeletes them, deletes them permanently, or replaces them with other deleted files. Windows 95 configures the Recycle Bin during installation to take a maximum of 10 percent of the hard drive, but the user can configure it to take more or less room or even not store files at all.

Whenever the operating system reaches the largest possible size for the Recycle Bin, it will begin to delete files within the Recycle Bin automatically, starting with the file that has been in the Recycle Bin the longest. Figure 819 shows the Windows 95 Recycle Bin Properties dialog box where a user can perform configuration.

*The answer is **False** because the Windows 95 Recycle Bin has a limited amount of space and, when full, will begin to delete files permanently, beginning with the files that have been in the Recycle Bin the longest.*

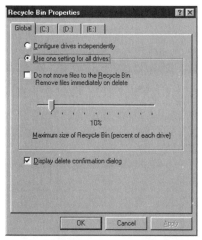

Figure 819 *The Windows 95 Recycle Bin Properties dialog box.*

820	**USING THE WINDOWS 95 BRIEFCASE**

Q: *Which of the following answers best describes the purpose of the Windows 95 Briefcase?*

Choose the best answer:

    A.   *A program designed to merge the changes of three or more users*

    B.   *A program designed to merge the changes of two or more users*

    C.   *A program designed to merge changes made on two computers by the same user*

    D.   *An icon shaped like a briefcase which holds presentations.*

Because users often have portable computers or more than one computer where they perform work, Windows 95 includes a method of synchronizing changes users make to files on various systems. The Windows 95 *Briefcase* is a program that manages a special folder in which users can place files and then take them home or to a different location to work on. After the users return to the original computer, they can synchronize changes they made to files with a few mouse clicks. For example, if you copied a file into the Briefcase and then copied the Briefcase onto a floppy disk, you would be able to take the files home and work on them at a different computer. After you returned to the original computer, you would simply insert the floppy disk into the computer and then right-click your mouse on the Briefcase icon on the Desktop. Windows 95 would display a pop-up menu that would let you simultaneously synchronize all files in the Briefcase folder with the original files located on the computer's hard drive. Figure 820 shows the pop-up menu you will see after you right-click your mouse on the Briefcase icon.

Figure 820 *The Windows 95 Briefcase pop-up menu.*

Answer C is correct because the Windows 95 Briefcase is best described as a program designed to merge changes one user made on two computers user. Answers A, B, and D are incorrect because they do not accurately describe the Windows 95 Briefcase's purpose.

821 USING THE WINDOWS 95 FIND FEATURE

Q: Which of the following operations can you perform using the Windows 95 Find Feature?

Choose the best answer:

> *A.   Find a file by its name.*
>
> *B.   Find a file by the date it was last changed.*
>
> *C.   Find a file by text it contains.*
>
> *D.   Find a computer name on the network.*

As you have learned, Windows 95 provides several file management features. In addition to moving and copying files, users can also find misplaced files and forgotten filenames. Windows 95 provides the Find utility to help users who have forgotten where a file is on the system or even what the file's name is. Windows 95 *Find* is a powerful tool that can locate files by name, by the date last changed, or by text the file contains. *Find* can even locate computer names on a network. To start the *Find* utility, select the Find option from the Start menu. Figure 821 shows the Find: All Files dialog box.

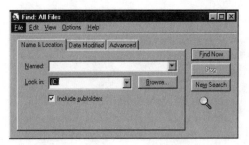

Figure 821 The Find utility's Find: All Files dialog box.

Answers A, B, C, and D are all correct because the Windows 95 Find utility can locate a file based on name, date last changed, or text the file contains. The Find feature can also find computer names on the network.

822 ADDING SUBMENUS TO THE START MENU IN WINDOWS 95

Q: The Windows 95 Start menu and its submenus are actually just folders on the hard drive.

True or False?

As you learned in Tip 817, you can add shortcuts to the Startup group in the Windows 95 Start menu to easily access programs or folders you frequently use. You also learned that the Start menu replaces the Windows 3.x Program

Manager and its program groups. The Windows 95 Start menu is really a series of folders on the hard drive that the system implements as menus and submenus. That is, you can create submenus simply by creating new folders inside an existing folder. In turn, all folders that are subfolders of *C:\Windows\Start Menu* will create a submenu on the Windows 95 Start menu (and folders that are subfolders of the *Start Menu\Programs* folder will appear as program groups within the Programs submenu. However, instead of manually creating folders, you can add items to the Start menu (and its submenus) within the Taskbar Properties dialog box. To access the Taskbar Properties dialog box, perform the following steps:

1. Right-click your mouse on the Windows 95 Taskbar. Windows 95 will display a pop-up menu.

2. Choose Properties from the pop-up menu. Windows 95 will display the Taskbar Properties dialog box.

3. Click your mouse on the Start menu tab at the top of the dialog box. Windows 95 will change your view to the Start Menu sheet.

4. To add shortcuts directly to the menu, click your mouse on the Start Menu sheet Add button. Windows 95 will display the Create Shortcut dialog box, from which you can create a shortcut as you learned in Tip 812. Alternatively, to create new groups or multiple shortcuts, click your mouse on the Advanced button. Windows 95 will open the Windows 95 *Explorer*. The *Explorer*, in turn, will display the Start Menu folder's contents.

The answer is **True** *because the Windows 95 Start menu and its submenus are really folders on the hard drive.*

823   *USING THE WINDOWS 95 HELP UTILITY*

Q: *You are the administrator of a small network. You have a new user who is taking over a computer another user previously operated. You want to enable the Welcome screen again until the user knows enough to turn it off. After you have disabled it, how can you re-enable the Windows 95 Welcome screen?*

Choose the best answer:

    A.   *You cannot re-enable the Windows 95 Welcome screen.*

    B.   *You must edit the Registry and change the value within the Welcome key in the Registry to On.*

    C.   *You must re-install Windows 95 over the top of the old installation.*

    D.   *You must use the Windows 95 Help utility.*

As a new Windows 95 user, you will find that an important support tool, built into the operating system, is the *Help* utility. Windows 95 *Help* is a program that contains descriptions of various operating system features, step-by-step instructions on configuration procedures, and troubleshooting Wizards that help you identify problems. The first section of the *Help* utility that most users see is the Welcome screen that appears when you first install Windows 95. Users frequently disable the Welcome screen from automatically starting (either intentionally or inadvertently), but later those users or an administrator will want to re-enable the Welcome screen. Administrators will perform this process from within the *Help* utility.

To open the Windows 95 *Help* utility, select the Start menu Help option. Windows 95 will display the *Help* utility dialog box. The Windows 95 *Help* utility is divided into three tabs: Contents, Index, and Find. Each of the tabs provides users with a different way to use *Help*. The Contents tab displays topics grouped into categories represented by book icons. You can double-click on a book icon to display its help descriptions and subcategories. Figure 823.1 shows the Windows 95 *Help* utility's Contents tab.

Figure 823.1 The Contents tab of the Windows 95 Help utility.

The Index tab lets users scroll through topics, type in an entire word, or type in the first letters of a word, which action will automatically advance the topic list to words beginning with the letters. For example, if you type in *rep*, the list will scroll down to *repaginating documents*, followed by a list of other words beginning with *rep*. You can then choose which word you want from the list. From within the Index tab, if you select the *Welcome screen, viewing* item, the Help utility will re-display the welcome screen. Figure 823.2 shows the Windows 95 *Help* utility's Index tab with the *Welcome screen, viewing* item selected.

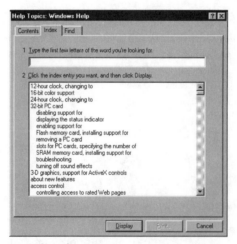

Figure 823.2 The Index tab of the Windows 95 Help utility.

Finally, the Find tab lets users type in a word or phrase and search through the text in *Help* to locate a description or Wizard. The first time you try to type in a word or phrase, the *Help* utility will build a help database, which it will then search for close matches to the word or phrase. Figure 823.3 shows the Windows 95 *Help* utility's Find tab.

Answer D is correct because the Windows 95 Help utility can display the Welcome screen. Answer A is incorrect because you can re-enable the Windows 95 Welcome screen. Answer B is incorrect because there is no Welcome key in the Windows 95 Registry and editing the Registry should always be a last resort. Answer C is incorrect because you are not required to re-install Windows 95 to re-enable the Welcome screen.

*Figure 823.3 The Find tab of the Windows 95 **Help** utility.*

824 **USING CTRL+ALT+DELETE IN WINDOWS 95**

Q: *What will happen if you press the CTRL, ALT, and DELETE keys simultaneously in Windows 95?*

Choose the best answer:

   A.   *The computer will restart*

   B.   *A log-on dialog box will appear*

   C.   *The Close Program dialog box will appear*

   D.   *Nothing*

Computer users who have worked with older operating systems, such as MS-DOS and Windows *3.x,* are familiar with the CTRL+ALT+DELETE keyboard combination as a method of restarting the operating system without turning power to the computer off and then on again. Windows 95 has reassigned this keyboard combination to provide users with a greater level of control over the operating system.

When users press CTRL+ALT+DELETE simultaneously in Windows 95, the Close Program dialog box will appear. The Close Program dialog box lets users view all the programs currently running within Windows 95. Additionally, users can choose to shut down the computer (Shut Down) or close any single program (End Task) in the list. Figure 824 shows the Close Program dialog box.

Note: *As in older operating systems, you can still make the system restart by using the CTRL+ALT+DELETE keyboard combination—you must simply use it twice in succession within Windows 95.*

Answer C *is correct because in Windows 95, the CTRL+ALT+DELETE keyboard combination will display the Close Program dialog box. **Answers A, B,** and **D** are incorrect because they do not describe what will happen if you use the CTRL+ALT+DELETE keyboard combination.*

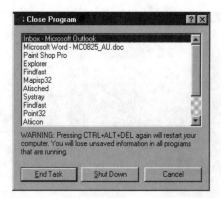

Figure 824 *The Close Program dialog box.*

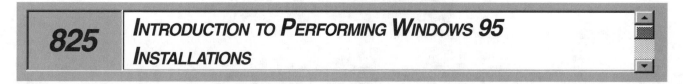

825 INTRODUCTION TO PERFORMING WINDOWS 95 INSTALLATIONS

Q: *You can install Windows 95 to run from a server for a computer that has no physical disks.*

True or False?

Installing Windows 95 is usually a very simple process. If you purchase a computer that had the Windows 95 operating system included with it, the installation is automatic and mostly complete when you buy the system. When you initialize the system for the first time, Windows 95 will ask a few questions about customization options and ask you to verify the license agreement before you begin using the system.

If you are installing Windows 95 to a non-manufacturer-installed computer for the first time, you can customize the Windows 95 installation with a high level of control. For example, you can install Windows 95 with a varied amount of files—you might exclude built-in graphics files, multimedia presentations, and so on, depending on your requirements. You can even install Windows 95 to run from a server so that computers that have no physical disks (diskless workstations) can run Windows 95. In the following Tips, you will learn about each installation type you can perform and the various installation stages.

The answer is **True** *because you can install Windows 95 to run from a server for diskless workstations.*

826 HARDWARE REQUIREMENTS FOR WINDOWS 95 INSTALLATIONS

Q: *What is the minimum amount of Random Access Memory (RAM) required to install and run Windows 95?*

Choose the best answer:

A.   *4Mb*

B.   *8Mb*

C.   *16Mb*

D.   *32Mb*

In previous Tips, you learned about the different methods that you can use to install Windows 95 onto a computer. However, before you set up Windows 95, you must ensure that your computer meets the minimum hardware requirements. Your computer must have at least a 386DX 20Mhz or higher processor, 4Mb of Random Access Memory (RAM), a VGA display adapter, and a pointing device, such as a mouse. Depending on the type of installation you perform, your computer may not require hard drive space.

As you have learned, server-based installations let you install Windows 95 on computers that have no physical disk drives. It is important to recognize that the figures in this Tip are absolute minimum requirements, and that Microsoft does not necessarily suggest that you *should* have computers that only meet the minimum requirements. In fact, most network professionals agree that Windows 95 runs best on at least a Pentium® computer with 16Mb of RAM.

Note: *The minimum amount of RAM increases to eight megabytes if you are using the Microsoft* **Exchange** *Client or the Microsoft* **Network** *(MSN).*

*Answer A is correct because the minimum amount of RAM required to install and run Windows 95 is 4Mb. **Answers B, C, and D** are incorrect because the answers list values that are higher than the minimum amount of RAM required to install and run Windows 95.*

827 INTRODUCTION TO THE *WINDOWS 95* HARDWARE COM-PATIBILITY LIST (HCL)

Q: *Windows 95 will not run on hardware the Windows 95 Hardware Compatibility List (HCL) does not list.*

True or False?

When you are determining whether your computer and network are Windows 95-capable and compatible, it is important to consider hardware (both the computer and devices you may attach to the computer). Microsoft produces a list of hardware called the *Hardware Compatibility List (HCL)* that has proven to be compatible with Windows 95. The HCL list describes computers and peripheral devices that have undergone testing procedures that ensure they will function properly with Windows 95. You can get a copy of the Windows 95 HCL from Microsoft by either accessing the Microsoft Web site or using the Microsoft Fax service, which will fax a copy to you directly.

If you use hardware that is not on the Windows 95 HCL, such omission does not mean that the hardware will not function properly with Windows 95. In fact, Windows 95 will function with many hardware components that are not on the HCL. Instead, using hardware the HCL does list simply means that you are using hardware Microsoft has previously tested with the operating system. Aside from a physical problem with the hardware (such as the hardware having a pin-connector that is incompatible with an Intel-based PC's standard ports), using hardware that is not on the list means you take the chance it will not function or that it may produce unpredictable results.

*The answer is **False** because, although you may experience unpredictable results, Windows 95 will run on many hardware components the HCL does not list.*

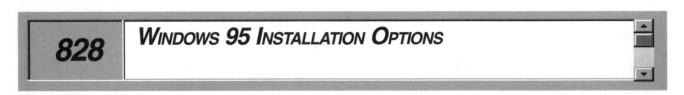

828 *WINDOWS 95* INSTALLATION OPTIONS

Q: *You must install Windows 95 from a CD-ROM.*

True or False?

After you determine that your hardware can support Windows 95, and that Windows 95 can, in turn, support your hardware, you can begin to install Windows 95. You can install Windows 95 in a variety of ways, with a variety of options, and from a variety of sources. For example, you can install Windows 95 from a CD-ROM, from a floppy disk, or from a network server to which you have copied or installed source files. In addition, you have choices about the type of installation you can perform based on your computer's specific requirements—such as whether or not the computer contains a hard drive or a compact disk drive. The following Tips discuss each installation type in detail.

The answer is **False** *because you can install Windows 95 from a CD-ROM, a floppy disk, over a network, or from source files copied directly to the computer's hard drive.*

829   INTRODUCTION TO SERVER-BASED WINDOWS 95 INSTALLATIONS

Q: *Which of the following server types can serve as a Windows 95 installation source?*

Choose the best answer:

    A.   *Windows NT server installed as a Domain controller*

    B.   *Novell NetWare server*

    C.   *Windows NT server installed as a standalone server*

    D.   *Windows NT workstation*

As Tip 828 indicates, you have several different installation options to choose from when you install Windows 95. One of the installation options is to install Windows 95 from a network server (known as *server-based installation*). You can install Windows 95 on a network server in order to run client computers directly from the server. The *netsetup.exe* utility program will prepare a server so you can run the *Setup.exe* Windows 95 setup program from client computers to create installations that run from the server (rather than from the client computer's own hard drive).

Running multiple installations of Windows 95 from a server can be very demanding on the server and the network. Therefore, using a powerful computer (one with a high-speed processor, lots of RAM, and large hard drives) as the server is generally a good idea—because the client computers will not wait as long for the operating system to respond. It is also important to have a fast network—a 2Mbps network will generally not perform well for server-based installations. However, any computer on the network can perform as the server if it has enough hard-drive space for the installations.

Note: *You must have at least one computer on the network already running Windows 95 because the* **netsetup.exe** *utility will run only from Windows 95.*

Answers A, B, C, and D are all correct because the answers all describe computers on the network that can both store and share the source files that can act as a Windows 95 installation source.

---

830   INTRODUCTION TO CUSTOMIZED INSTALLATIONS FOR WINDOWS 95

Q: *Which of the following installation types will let you install applications at the same time you install Windows 95?*

Choose the best answer:

     A.   *Typical*

     B.   *Custom*

     C.   *Portable*

     D.   *None of the above. Special installations that install applications are not part of the standard installation types.*

Network administrators and consultants who are installing large numbers of clients and still want to exercise control over the installation can create special scripting (that is, files which perform tasks in a sequence the administrator pre-defines) files that alter the way they install Windows 95. Combined with other files, the customized scripting files let you install Windows 95 with little input from the user. In addition, the scripting files configure Windows 95 to comply with the administrator's design during the installation process.

In other words, an administrator can simply execute a single command line to perform the installation, until the Windows 95 setup process is complete. Also, the computer will not require additional configuration because the special script and other files the administrator instructed the installation to use provided all the configuration during the setup process. The administrator can even install additional applications during *Setup.exe*'s execution, which is an option not available in any of the standard Windows 95 installation types.

Answer D is correct because only a special installation script will let you install applications at the same time you install Windows 95. Answers A, B, and C are incorrect because the answers list installation types that install a predefined list of components and do not let you install additional applications.

---

831   UNDERSTANDING THE FILES WINDOWS 95 REQUIRES FOR A CUSTOMIZED INSTALLATION

Q: *Which of the following files does Windows 95 require only if you are customizing an installation that includes the NetWare Terminate and Stay Resident (TSR) programs?*

Choose the best answer:

     A.   *msbatch.inf*

     B.   *apps.inf*

     C.   *wrkgrp.ini*

     D.   *netdet.ini*

As you learned in Tip 830, you can customize the installation procedure for Windows 95 to create an installation that performs every configuration during the install. To customize an installation, you need several files that contain the information the operating system requires to configure various aspects of Windows 95. Table 831 describes the files required to customize a Windows 95 installation.

File	Description
msbatch.inf	The main scripting file that contains setup information.
netdet.ini	The initialization file for the *NetWare Terminate* and *Stay Resident* programs.
apps.inf	The file that specifies additional application settings for the installation.
wrkgrp.ini	The file that controls workgroup membership.
grpconv.exe	The file that converts program groups during an upgrade or restores default Start menu settings.

Table 831 The files Windows 95 requires for you to customize a Windows 95 installation.

Answer D is correct because the netdet.ini file contains configuration information specific to NetWare Terminate and Stay Resident programs. Answer A is incorrect because the msbatch.ini file contains standard script information Windows 95 requires for all Windows 95 customized installations. Answer B is incorrect because the apps.inf file contains information for setting up applications during a Windows 95 installation. Answer C is incorrect because the wrkgrp.ini file contains information that controls group membership during a Windows 95 installation.

832   COMPARING THE WINDOWS 95 UPGRADE AND OEM VERSIONS

Q: *The Windows 95 Original Equipment Manufacturer (OEM) version contains advanced network and communication tools you cannot find in the Windows95 Upgrade version.*

True or False?

Although you may occasionally run across a customized version, Windows 95 basically has only two versions. Microsoft distributes the Original Equipment Manufacturer (OEM) version of Windows 95 only to computer manufacturers, meaning you can get it only with a new computer. The other version of Windows 95 is the Retail version, which is also known as the Upgrade version, because Microsoft typically sells it as an upgrade to an existing version of Windows *3.x*.

Microsoft has not fundamentally changed the Windows 95 Upgrade version from the time the company first released it, so it contains no new components or functions that Microsoft has added to the Windows 95 operating system since its release. Instead, new hardware support and function changes are available as service packs, which you can usually get from Microsoft for free. To obtain service packs for Windows 95, go to the Microsoft Web site at *http://www.microsoft.com*.

The Windows 95 OEM version is currently available in Service Release 2. Microsoft has changed the OEM version to support newer hardware components and function changes so new computer users do not have to install service packs. In addition, a major difference between Windows 95 OEM and Upgrade versions is you cannot install the OEM version over an existing operating system and have the operating system include no means for you to remove the Windows 95 installation (for example, to change the operating system to Windows *3.x*).

*The answer is **False** because the Windows 95 Upgrade and OEM versions contain the same network and communications component, although the OEM release may include support for newer hardware, and you cannot install an OEM version over another operating system.*

833   PLANNING YOUR WINDOWS 95 INSTALLATION

Q: *You are the administrator of a small network. You are upgrading the computers in the network from a Windows 3.x operating system to Windows 95. What choices do you have for network configuration when you install Windows 95?*

Choose the best answer:

     A.   *Form a workgroup*

     B.   *Join a Domain*

     C.   *Form a Domain*

     D.   *Designate a preferred server for NetWare*

Planning the installation of Windows 95 is vital to an administrator who is distributing a new operating system to a large number of computers. The impact to productivity the users could suffer due to a mistake in planning the implementation or functional problems from software incompatibilities might be very high. Considerations such as configuring the networking components to form a workgroup, joining a Microsoft domain (requires a Windows NT server), or designating a preferred NetWare server are minor issues when you deal with a single computer. However, the same considerations can be catastrophic when you install hundreds, or even thousands, of computers. Additionally, administrators must decide between standard or customized installations, fully functional clients or server-based installations, the kinds of restrictions they will apply to general users, and more.

Note: Administrators planning a shift to the Windows 95 operating system should get planning and implementation guides, such as the Windows 95 Resource Kit, before they start the shift.

Answers A, B, *and* **D** *are correct because you can form a workgroup, join a domain, or designate a preferred server in a NetWare environment.* **Answer C** *is incorrect because you can only form a domain using the Windows NT server.*

834   DUAL-BOOTING WINDOWS 95 AND WINDOWS NT

Q: *When you install Windows 95 and Windows NT to dual-boot on a single computer, you must install Windows 95 first.*

     True or False?

As you have learned, Windows 95 and Windows NT are fundamentally different operating systems. However, you can install Windows 95 and Windows NT to alternately run on the same computer. Network administrators commonly call this type of an installation *dual-booting* because you must restart the computer to choose which operating system you want to run at that time. Dual-booting a computer is an economical way to test two operating systems on the same computer or to test two operating systems with a network (because you do not have to use multiple computers for the testing and you do not have to entirely reinstall the operating system when you want to switch between the two).

To install a dual-boot with both Windows 95 and Windows NT, you must install Windows 95 first and then install Windows NT into a different directory. Because the Windows 95 File Access Table (FAT) file management component is so very different from the Windows NT NT File System (NTFS) file management component, installing Windows NT first will either prohibit you from installing Windows 95 or cause serious problems. Commonly reported problems with NT-first installations include Windows 95's ability to start, file corruption, increased program failures, and so on.

*The answer is **True** because, although you could accomplish a dual-boot installation if you installed Windows NT first, most network administrators (and Microsoft) agree that Windows 95 must be the first operating system installed when you install both Windows 95 and Windows NT to dual-boot on a single computer.*

835 **PARTITION REQUIREMENTS FOR A WINDOWS 95 INSTALLATION**

Q: Which of the following statements about installing Windows 95 are true?

Choose all answers that apply:

    A.   You can install Windows 95 only to a primary partition that is active.

    B.   You can install Windows 95 on an extended partition if you install Windows NT to dual-boot with Windows 95 on the computer.

    C.   You can install Windows 95 to a primary partition even if it is not the active partition.

    D.   You can install Windows 95 on a Windows NT volume set.

As you learned in earlier Tips, you can install Windows NT to either an NT File System (NTFS) partition or a File Access Table (FAT) partition. Unlike Windows NT, you can install Windows 95 only on FAT partitions. The partition must be a primary partition and must also be the active partition, or Windows 95 will not boot (because the computer's BIOS will not know where to look for Windows 95). You can install Windows 95 onto partitions that you compress with most compression utilities (if, for example, your primary, active partition is very small) using one of the command-line switches available with the Windows 95 *Setup* program.

*Answer A is correct because you can install Windows 95 only to a primary partition that is also active. **Answers B** and **C** are incorrect because you can install Windows 95 only on a primary partition and that partition must be active. **Answer D** is incorrect because you cannot install Windows 95 on a Windows NT volume set.*

836 **INTRODUCTION TO THE WINDOWS 95 INSTALLATION TYPES**

Q: Which of the following installation types will install the least amount of files to a computer's hard drive?

Choose the best answer:

    A.   Typical

    B.   Portable

    C.   Compact

    D.   Tiny

As you have learned, you have several installation choices when you install Windows 95 (including both standard and network installations). You will most frequently use the standard installation. A standard installation of Windows 95 gives you four choices for configuring the operating system. Microsoft designed each installation type to provide maximum functionality for the specific requirements of different computer configurations. Table 836 describes the different installation types.

Installation Type	Description
Typical	The default installation type Microsoft recommends for most installations. Microsoft requires you to verify the installation directory, provide identification for the user and computer, and specify whether to create a Windows 95 Startup disk.
Portable	The installation type Microsoft specifically designed to install the required files and programs for users with portable computers, including the *Briefcase* and *Direct Cable Connection* utilities for transferring files between computers.
Compact	The installation type that copies the least amount of files to the local hard drive and that Microsoft designed for users with limited free space on their hard drive.
Custom	The installation type Microsoft designed for advanced users and system administrators. The Custom type gives you the most control over the installation.

Table 836 The standard Windows 95 installation types you can use to configure an operating system.

Answer C is correct because the Compact installation type installs the least amount of files to a computer's hard drive. Answers A and B are incorrect because the answers list installation types that install more files to the hard drive than the Compact installation type. Answer D is incorrect because Tiny is not an installation type.

837 UNDERSTANDING A WINDOWS 95 TYPICAL INSTALLATION

Q: *Which of the following choices are available to you when you perform a Typical installation of Windows 95?*

Choose the best answer:

> A. *Confirm the installation folder*
>
> B. *Provide computer and user identification*
>
> C. *Create or do not create a Startup disk*
>
> D. *Choose custom application settings*

As you have learned, Microsoft designed the Typical installation type for most computers and recommends it as the installation type for most users. When you perform a Typical installation, Microsoft will require you to verify the installation directory, provide user and computer identification, and specify whether to create a Windows 95 Startup disk.

A Typical installation with operating system's Upgrade version requires 44.2Mb of free space and occupies 30Mb of disk space after it completes the installation. When you install Windows 95 on a blank hard drive, Setup requires 52.6Mb of free space and occupies 44.2Mb of disk space when it completes the installation. Table 837 lists the Windows 95 components a Typical installation installs.

Typical Installation Components

Accessibility Options	*Calculator*	Disk Defragmenter	Document Templates
Flying Windows screen saver	Hyper Terminal	Media Player	Object Packager
Paint	Phone Dialer	Quick View	ScanDisk
Standard Windows 95 files	Video Compression	Windows 95 Tour	*Winpopup*
WordPad			

Table 837 The Windows 95 components the Typical installation will install.

Answers A, B, and C are correct because you can only confirm the installation folder, provide computer and user identification, and tell Setup whether to create a Startup disk when you use the Typical installation type for Windows 95 installations. Answer D is incorrect because custom application settings are available only in the Custom installation type.

838 UNDERSTANDING A WINDOWS 95 PORTABLE INSTALLATION

Q: Which of the following installation types automatically install the Direct Cable Connection software utility that Windows 95 requires to transfer files through a serial connection?

Choose the best answer:

    A.   Custom

    B.   Typical

    C.   Portable

    D.   Compact

As you learned in Tip 836, Microsoft designed the Portable installation type for users who have portable computers. The Portable installation type includes software components, such as the *Direct Cable Connection* utility and the *Briefcase* utility, for transferring files between computers. An Upgrade Portable installation type requires 43.3Mb of free disk space to install and occupies 29 megabytes of disk space when it completes the installation. When you install Windows 95 onto a blank hard drive, the Portable installation type requires 52.5Mb of free disk space and occupies 43.9Mb of disk space when it completes the installation. Table 838 lists the Windows 95 components the Portable installation type installs.

Portable Installation Components

Briefcase	Dial-up Networking	Direct Cable Connection
Disk Defragmenter	Hyper Terminal	Media Player
Object Packager	Phone Dialer	*ScanDisk*
Standard Windows 95 files	Video Compression	*Winpopup*
WordPad		

Table 838 The Windows 95 components the Portable installation type will install.

Answer C is correct because the Portable installation type automatically installs the Direct Cable Connection software Microsoft requires for transferring files through a serial connection. Answers A, B, and D are incorrect because the answers list installation types that do not automatically install the Direct Cable Connection software.

839 UNDERSTANDING A WINDOWS 95 COMPACT INSTALLATION

Q: For what purpose did Microsoft intend network administrators to use the Compact installation type?

Choose the best answer:

> A.   *To install Windows 95 to a laptop computer.*
>
> B.   *To install Windows 95 to a computer with limited disk space.*
>
> C.   *To install a base version of Windows 95 for testing or troubleshooting.*
>
> D.   *Windows 95 does not have a Compact installation type.*

In Tip 836, you learned the Compact installation type copies the least amount of files to a local hard drive and Microsoft designed it for computers with limited disk space. The Upgrade Compact installation type requires 40 megabytes of free space to install and occupies 27Mb of disk space when it completes installation. When you install Windows 95 to a blank hard drive, the Compact installation type requires 50.1Mb of free space and occupies 40.8Mb of disk space when it completes installation. Table 839 lists the Windows 95 components the Compact installation type installs.

Compact Installation Components		
Disk Defragmenter	Object Packager	ScanDisk
Standard Windows 95 required files	Winpopup	

Table 839 The Windows 95 components the Compact installation type will install.

Answer B *is correct because Microsoft designed the Compact installation type to install a minimal version of Windows 95 to a computer with limited disk space.* **Answers A and C** *are incorrect because the answers do not accurately describe for what purpose Microsoft intended the Compact installation type.* **Answer D** *is incorrect because Windows 95 does have a Compact installation type.*

840 UNDERSTANDING A WINDOWS 95 CUSTOM INSTALLATION

Q: Which of the following installation types let you specify custom application settings?

Choose answers that apply:

> A.   *Typical*
>
> B.   *Custom*
>
> C.   *Portable*
>
> D.   *Compact*

As you have learned, there are several different types of common installations. Microsoft designed the first three types, Typical, Custom, and Portable, for easy use to satisfy particular installation requirements (such as installation on a laptop computer). Microsoft designed the Custom installation type for advanced users and system administrators. Default settings for the Custom installation type are identical to a Typical installation, but the administrator or user can then modify them (adding additional components, such as disabled-user support, and removing other components, such as Hyper Terminal and Phone Dialer). The amount of disk space the Custom installation type will require depends on the modifications and custom application settings the administrator or user makes.

Answer B is correct because only the Custom installation type lets you specify custom application settings when you perform the Windows 95 installation. Answers A, C, and D are incorrect because the answers list installation types that do not let you specify custom application settings during the installation of Windows 95.

841 UNDERSTANDING THE WINDOWS 95 SETUP COMMAND-LINE SWITCHES

Q: Which of the following command-line switches lets you install Windows 95 without checking for disk space?

Choose the best answer:

   A.   /IM

   B.   /ID

   C.   /IS

   D.   /IQ

When you run the Windows 95 *Setup* program from the command prompt, you have several execution opions. You can use the *Setup* command either alone or with additional instructions that take the form of command-line switches that initiate the installation process. Command-line switches are commands that you add at the end of an executable file's invocation and implement by adding a backslash (/) and following it with a letter, letters, or numbers. Table 841 describes the various command-line switches and their functions.

Switch	Description
/?	Provides a description of command-line switches.
/C	Tells the *Setup* command not to use the *SmartDrive* disk cache.
/D	Forces the *Setup* command to load its own Windows files during setup, even when an existing version is available on the computer's hard drive.
/ID	Forces the *Setup* command to skip the disk space check.
/IH	Lets you see the results of the *SCANDISK* sequence. (You will use the /IH switch to troubleshoot if the *Setup* program initially fails during the *SCANDISK* sequence.)
/IL	Forces the *Setup* program to load the *Logitech* mouse driver.
/IM	Forces the *Setup* program to install Windows 95 without checking the system's total memory.
/IQ	Forces the *Setup* program to skip the *SCANDISK* sequence when you start the program from the MS-DOS prompt.

*Table 841 The command line switches for the Windows 95 **Setup** program. (continued on the following page)*

Switch	Description
/IS	Forces the *Setup* program to skip the *SCANDISK* sequence when you start the program from Windows.
/NOSTART	Copies a minimum set of Windows Dynamic-Link Library (DLL) files to the hard drive, and then exits to MS-DOS.
(name of scripting file)	Designates a scripting file that Setup should use (typically *msbatch.inf*).
/t:(name of temp folder)	Specifies a temporary directory where the *Setup* program can copy files. (The directory must already exist.) The *Setup* program will delete the files you copy into a temporary directory when the program completes its execution.

*Table 841 The command line switches for the Windows 95 **Setup** program. (continued from the previous page)*

Answer B *is correct because the command-line switch /ID, when you use it with the Setup command, lets you install Windows 95 without checking for disk space.* **Answer A** *is incorrect because the /IM switch lets you install Windows 95 without checking for system memory.* **Answer C** *is incorrect because the /IS switch lets you install Windows 95 without running the standard system check.* **Answer D** *is incorrect because the /IQ switch lets you install Windows 95 without checking for cross-linked files.*

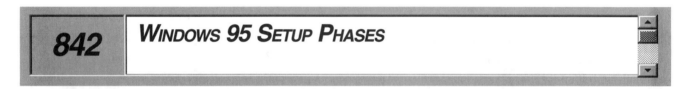

842   WINDOWS 95 SETUP PHASES

Q: How many sections does the Windows 95 installation have?

Choose the best answer:

    A.   *Two*

    B.   *Three*

    C.   *Five*

    D.   *Seven*

As you have learned, the Windows 95 Setup process lets you exercise considerable control over how you install Windows 95 on your computer. After you make your determinations, the program will begin the actual Setup process itself. The actual Windows 95 Setup process has three sections and each section performs a series of tasks. Microsoft designed the Setup process so if an installation failure occurs, the user or administrator performing the installation can quickly identify the problem based on where in the installation process the failure occurred. The sections of the installation process are Gathering System Information, Copying Windows 95 Files, and Final Installation, which takes place when Windows 95 starts for the first time.

In the Gathering System Information section, you will verify the installation directory (where Setup will install Windows 95), provide user and computer identification (such as names and serial numbers), determine whether to create a Windows 95 Startup disk, make selections for optional components (such as Hyper Terminal), and configure networking components. The Setup process, in turn, will conduct system checks and perform hardware detection.

In the Copying Windows 95 Files section, the Setup process will create the Startup disk and copy the appropriate Windows 95 files to the hard drive. The files that Setup copies will depend on the selections that you made in the Gathering System Information section of the Setup process. However, Setup will always copy certain required files

(Windows 95 system files), no matter what configuration you select. Upon completion of the Copying Windows 95 Files section, Setup will prompt you to reboot your computer. The Final Installation section takes place after your system reboots. In the Final Installation section, Windows 95 lets you address the final configuration options for the operating system on your computer. Final configuration options include your selection of the appropriate Time Zone for your area and acceptance of the Windows 95 License agreement.

Answer B is correct because the Windows 95 installation has three sections, Gathering System Information, Copying Windows 95 Files, and Final Installation. Answers A, C, and D are incorrect because the answers list values that are either higher or lower than the actual number of sections in the Windows 95 installation.

843   **UNDERSTANDING WINDOWS 95 CAB FILES**

Q: *Windows 95 Cabinet (CAB) files are very similar to ZIP files in structure.*

     True or False?

The installation files the Windows 95 Setup process uses to store most files are known as *Cabinet (CAB)* files, which are similar to ZIP files because they are compressed files that store other files. The Setup process extracts the files it requires from the CAB files during installation.

You can extract files from the Windows 95 CAB files, if necessary, using either the Windows 95 Power Tool called *Cabview*, which you can download from the Microsoft Web site, or using Windows 95's built-in *Extract* utility. After you install it, the *Cabview* utility lets you look inside CAB files and drag individual files from within the CAB to another location. The *Extract* command invokes a command-line utility that can extract individual files from a CAB file, but it requires you to know which CAB file contains the system file you want and the system file's name within the CAB file. For the *Extract* utility's complete syntax, type *Extract /?* at the MS-DOS command prompt.

*The answer is **True** because CAB files are single files that have had many files compressed and stored in them. Therefore, ZIP files are very similar in structure.*

844   **UPGRADING WINDOWS 95 FROM WINDOWS 3.x**

Q: *You are the administrator of a small network. You are upgrading a Windows 3.x computer with Windows 95, and you want the applications you have already installed on the computer to function with Windows 95. What must you do to ensure the Windows 3.x applications still function after you install Windows 95?*

Choose the best answer:

     A.   *You must reinstall the applications to Windows 95.*

     B.   *You must install Windows 95 to the Windows 3.x system directory.*

     C.   *You must install Windows 95 to a different directory from the Windows 3.x system directory.*

     D.   *Windows 3.x applications will not function in Windows 95.*

As you have learned, you can install a Retail (Upgrade) version of Windows 95 over an installation of a Windows *3.x* operating system as an upgrade. Upgrading is a desirable option for many users because Microsoft retains the Windows *3.x* applications and custom settings in Windows 95. To upgrade, you must install Windows 95 into the same directory in which you installed the Windows *3.x* operating system. When you upgrade, Windows 95 gives you the option of saving the previous operating system settings so you may remove the Windows 95 installation, if necessary (for example, if your other programs are not Windows 95-compatible). Although you will not be able to run the Windows *3.x* operating system without removing Windows 95, you will be able to boot into the previous version of MS-DOS using a boot menu.

Note: You cannot upgrade or remove an installation with an OEM version of Windows 95.

Answer B is correct because installing Windows 95 into the Windows 3.x system directory will ensure that the previously installed applications function with Windows 95. Answer A is incorrect because you do not have to reinstall the applications if you install Windows 95 to the Windows 3.x system directory. Answer C is incorrect because installing Windows 95 to a directory other than the Windows 3.x system directory will result in the previously installed applications not functioning. Answer D is incorrect because Windows 3.x applications will function with Windows 95.

845 UNDERSTANDING DISK SPACE REQUIREMENTS FOR WINDOWS 95

Q: *You are the administrator of a small network. You are upgrading a computer from Windows 3.1 to Windows 95 using a Typical installation type. Approximately how much free disk space will the installation require for the upgrade?*

Choose the best answer:

    A.   *10Mb*

    B.   *20Mb*

    C.   *30Mb*

    D.   *40Mb*

In previous Tips, you have learned the various disk space requirements each type of Windows 95 installation imposes. If you are trying to determine the requirements for multiple computers, and you are using a variety of installation types, determining the disk space requirements can become quite confusing. For quick reference, Table 845.1 describes each installation type's hard drive requirements for Windows 95 upgrade installations.

Installation Type	Hard Drive Requirements for an Upgrade
Typical	Requires 44.2Mb to install and occupies 30Mb when it completes the installation.
Portable	Requires 43.3Mb to install and occupies 29Mb when it completes the installation.
Compact	Requires 40Mb to install and occupies 27Mb when it completes the installation.
Custom	Installation and normal execution requirements depend on the components you install.

Table 845.1 Each installation type's disk space requirements for Windows 95 upgrade installations.

As you learned, however, the installation requirements for a Windows 95 original installation are different than those for an Upgrade installation. Table 845.2 describes each installation type's hard drive requirements for Windows 95 original installations.

Installation Type	Hard Drive Requirements for a Blank Hard Drive
Typical	Requires 52.6Mb to install and occupies 44.2Mb when it completes the installation.
Portable	Requires 52.5Mb to install and occupies 43.9Mb when it completes the installation.
Compact	Requires 50.1Mb to install and occupies 40.8Mb when it completes the installation.
Custom	Installation and normal execution requirements depend on the components you install.

Table 845.2 Each installation type's disk space requirements for Windows 95 original installations.

Note: All space requirements are additional requirements to space the hard drive is already using.

Answer C is correct because when you use the Typical installation type for an upgrade from Windows 3.1 to Windows 95, it requires approximately 30Mb of free disk space. Answers A, B, and D are incorrect because the answers list values that are either higher or lower than the actual amount of free disk space the upgrade requires.

846   *RUNNING A SERVER-BASED WINDOWS 95 SETUP*

Q: *You can run the Windows 95 Server-based Setup program (netsetup.exe) only from a computer running Windows NT server.*

True or False?

As you have learned, you can install Windows 95 to run from a network server to create shared installations for remote client computers. Shared installations include computers that start from a local hard drive, and then connect to the server for most of the Windows 95 operating system. However, the computers can also boot from a floppy disk, and then connect to the server for the Windows 95 operating system. Additionally, you can create shared installations for remote client computers with computers that boot from a special network card and connect to the server for the Windows 95 operating system.

Shared installations all begin with preparing the server to host the installations—that is, placing the information the server must have to perform the installations onto the server. You can prepare the server with a program called *netsetup.exe* that Microsoft includes with the Windows 95 CD-ROM. You must have at least one computer on the network running Windows 95 to prepare a server because the *netsetup.exe* program will operate only from within Windows 95. Because setting up a shared installation of Windows 95 is more difficult and involves more steps than a normal installation, the following Tips will discuss each step in detail.

*The answer is **False** because you can run Windows 95 Server-based Setup (netsetup.exe) only from a computer running Windows 95.*

847 CREATING MACHINE DIRECTORIES FOR SHARED WINDOWS 95 INSTALLATIONS

Q: *You are the administrator of a small network. You are installing Windows 95 as a shared installation from which all client computers will run Windows 95. Each client computer will start from a boot image on its local hard drive, and then connect to the server to actually run Windows 95. How can you determine the correct number of machine directories Windows 95 will require?*

Choose the best answer:

   A.   *One machine directory for each user.*

   B.   *One machine directory for each computer.*

   C.   *One machine directory for each computer type.*

   D.   *Windows 95 does not require any machine directories; machine directories are optional for computers booting from a local hard drive.*

As you have learned, you can use a server to perform shared installations of Windows 95. Some types of shared installations require special directories, called *machine directories,* on the server that store configuration information for each type of client computer to which you are installing Windows 95. Machine directories contain items necessary for the operating system to execute correctly, such as the *win.com* file and the Windows 95 Registry.

In addition, machine directories contain configuration files, such as *system.ini,* a default *user.dat* file, the Windows swap file and temp directory, files that define Start menu settings, and spool files for printing. In general, the machine directories contain all the computer-specific information for Windows 95 to execute correctly on the corresponding computer.

You must create a machine directory for each computer you are installing as a component of the shared Windows 95 installation (not each user—as the same computer may support multiple users). You can create machine directories using the *netsetup.exe* program. In the *netsetup.exe* program, you have the option of setting up one machine or setting up multiple machines.

When you set up one machine, you simply type in the pathname you want for the machine directory and the computer's name. When you set up multiple machines simultaneously, you must create a text file that contains the computer names and machine directory pathname variables. For specific instructions about structuring a multiple installation file, you can refer to Chapter 4 of the *Microsoft Windows 95 Resource Kit.*

Answer D *is correct because computers booting from a local hard drive to a shared installation of Windows 95 do not require machine directories.* **Answers A, B,** *and* **C** *are incorrect because Windows 95 does not require machine directories for this type of shared installation.*

848 CREATING A DEFAULT SETUP SCRIPT FOR WINDOWS 95

Q: *If you choose to create a default setup script during a Windows 95 Server-based Setup, what will the Server-based Setup automatically name the script on the server?*

Choose the best answer:

>   A.   *setup.inf*
>
>   B.   *mssetup.inf*
>
>   C.   *batch.inf*
>
>   D.   *msbatch.inf*

As previous Tips explained, customizing an installation of Windows 95 requires a text file (typically called *msbatch.inf*) that contains installation information from which the *Setup* program will read information to determine how to install certain files and what configuration options to perform. Previously, administrators had to learn the scripting language the *msbatch.inf* file used and manually create the file before using it. Today, administrators can use a script file creation tool called the *Batch Script Editor*, which Microsoft includes with the Windows 95 Resource Kit, to create the *msbatch.inf* file quickly and with little knowledge of scripting. Figure 848 shows the Batch Script Editor's Setup Information window.

Figure 848 The Batch Script Editor displaying the Setup Information window.

Answer D is correct because the Server-based Setup process will automatically name the default setup script msbatch.inf. Answers A, B, and C are incorrect because, although you may name additional setup scripts any name you choose, the Server-based Setup process will automatically name the default setup script msbatch.inf.

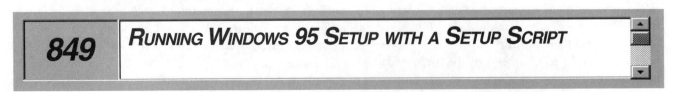

849	RUNNING WINDOWS 95 SETUP WITH A SETUP SCRIPT

Q: *You are the administrator of a small network. You are installing Windows 95 on client computers and want to use a setup script named scriptname.inf that you created previously. Which of the following commands lets you run Windows 95 Setup with the setup script scriptname.inf?*

Choose the best answer:

>   A.   *setup /B scriptname.inf*
>
>   B.   *setup scriptname.inf*
>
>   C.   *setup /batch scriptname.inf*
>
>   D.   *setup /s scriptname.inf*

Depending on how many different computer configurations you have on your network and what applications or rights you want to apply to different users, you may have multiple script files that you use when you install Windows 95 across the network. Merely installing the shared files on the server is not sufficient to create a shared installation of Windows 95. You must still run the *Setup* program for each computer configuration present on the network and, for computers that boot from a local hard drive, the installation must take place at the client computer. Whatever installation you are performing, if you have created a custom script to provide installation details to the *Setup* program, you must specify your custom script when you start the Setup process. You can specify a scripting file by typing the scripting file's name after the word Setup at the command line. For example, if you are using the default name *msbatch.inf* for your scripting file and want to begin an installation, you would type *setup msbatch.inf* at the command prompt.

Answer B is correct because the Windows 95 Setup program will let you use a Setup Script simply by typing Setup, a space, and then the setup script's name. Answers A, C, and D are incorrect because the answers list examples that will not let you use a setup script to install Windows 95.

| 850 | EXAMINING THE BATCH SCRIPT EDITOR'S CONFIGURATION OPTIONS |

Q: How many configuration windows does the Batch Script Editor have?

Choose the best answer:

    A.   Four

    B.   Three

    C.   Seven

    D.   Nine

As you learned in Tip 848, you can use a tool called the Batch Script Editor to create scripting files for customized installations of Windows 95. The Batch Script Editor is a series of four configuration windows that list various configuration options. To create the scripting file, the administrator simply fills in the appropriate areas on the configuration windows to specify the scripting options that the administrator wants, and saves the file. Figure 850.1 shows the Main Configuration window.

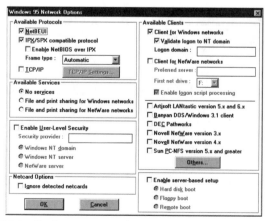

Figure 850.1 *The Batch Script Editor's Main Configuration Window.*

In addition to the Main Configuration window, administrators can use three other windows to configure the script file: Network Options, Installation Options, and Optional Components. The Network Options window contains fields that customize Windows 95's network components. Figure 850.2 shows the Network Options configuration window.

Figure 850.2 *The Batch Script Editor's Network Options configuration window.*

The Installation Options window lets you configure the rules the Windows 95 *Setup* program will follow during installation. Figure 850.3 shows the Installation Options configuration window.

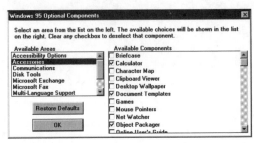

Figure 850.3 *The Batch Script Editor's Installation Options configuration window.*

The Optional Components configuration window applies only to custom installation types and lets you specify which Windows 95 components to install.

Answer A is correct, because in addition to the Main Configuration window, the Batch Script Editor has three additional configuration windows, which makes the total number of configuration windows four. Answers B, C, and D are incorrect because the answers list numbers that are either higher or lower than the actual number of configuration windows the Batch Script Editor contains.

851   USING THE BATCH PROGRAM TO CREATE SETUP SCRIPTS

Q: *Where can you get batch.exe?*

Choose the best answer:

     A.   *Windows 95 automatically installs batch.exe in the system folder of Windows 95 computers.*

     B.   *You can find batch.exe on the Windows 95 compact disk and you must install it separately.*

     C.   *You can only access batch.exe through Windows 95 Server-based Setup.*

     D.   *No program called batch.exe exists.*

As you have learned, administrators will often create scripts to assist in the installation of Windows 95 to a large number of computers. The *batch.exe* utility is a program administrators trying to script installations frequently overlook. Microsoft includes the *batch.exe* program with the Windows 95 CD-ROM, and it provides the same functionality as the Batch Script Editor that Microsoft provides with the Microsoft Windows 95 Resource Kit (that is, you can use it to create scripts just as you would the Batch Script Editor).

Although you must install the *batch.exe* utility separately from the Windows 95 installation itself, it provides a graphical interface that is almost identical to the Batch Script Editor. The four configuration windows you use to create scripting files with *batch.exe* are the same as those in the Batch Script Editor. The *batch.exe* program is a 32-bit program that runs on Windows 95, Windows NT 3.51, or later. Figure 851 shows the *batch.exe* program's main configuration window.

*Figure 851 The **batch.exe** interface.*

Answer B is correct because Microsoft includes batch.exe with the Windows 95 CD-ROM, but you must install it separately. Answer A is incorrect because Windows 95 does not automatically install batch.exe on Windows 95 computers. Answer C is incorrect because you can install batch.exe separately from the Windows 95 CD-ROM without running the Server-based Setup process. Answer D is incorrect because Microsoft does include a program called batch.exe with the Windows 95 CD-ROM.

852 UNDERSTANDING THE MSBATCH.INF FILE'S COMPONENTS

Q: *You may edit a setup script file, such as msbatch.inf, with any text editor.*

True or False?

As you have learned, you can use a scripting file to install Windows 95 with little or no input from the user. Scripting lets administrators control an installation and provide configuration options for multiple computers during the installation. When administrators use scripting, they do not have to configure each computer with utilities from the Windows 95 or Microsoft Windows 95 Resource Kit CD-ROMs.

Regardless of which utility the administrator uses to create a script (*batch.exe* or the Batch Script Editor), there may be times when you must edit a script file directly. You can use any text editor to edit a script file. In addition, many times the information you need is available in other files and you can simply copy and paste it into the script file. For example, if you are creating a script file for a series of computers that will contain identical Windows 95 installations, you can create a single script for all the installations. If you have a computer that has an identical Windows 95 installation to the computers in the series, you can copy much of the *System* and *Optional Component* sections from the configured computer's *setup.exe* file directly into the script. You must make sure to use a text editor, such as *Notepad*, and not a word processor, such as *Wordpad* or Microsoft *Word*, because word processors include non-printing characters that will cause errors in an installation script.

The operating system looks at script files in sections. The operating system will perform different functions during setup based on the corresponding section's contents. When you edit a script file, you must put configuration options into the correct section or the script will fail during installation. Table 852 describes some sections of a Windows 95 installation script file (you can use the *Windows 95 Resource Kit* to learn more about installation script file sections).

Section	Description
Install	Sets parameters for copying additional files as part of a Windows 95 installation.
InstallLocationsMRU	Specifies the pathnames to add to the list of directories the user can choose from when the Windows 95 *Setup* program prompts the user for a pathname. For example, the *[InstallLocationsMRU]* section could specify local and network file locations.
MSTCP	Sets parameters for Microsoft Transport Control Protocol/Internet Protocol (TCP/IP).
NameAndOrg	Defines the name and organization for the Windows 95 Setup process and specifies whether Windows 95 will show the user the Name and Organization dialog box.
Netcard_ID	Sets parameters for a specific network adapter, as the *[netcard_NDI]* sections of the network device *inf* files that Microsoft provides and Windows 95 defines. The actual name for the *[netcard_ID]* section is the identifier for the network adapter, as the related *inf* file defines.
Network	Specifies the parameters and options for installing network components.
NWLink	Specifies the parameters of the settings for the IPX/SPX-compatible protocol and the parameters are valid only if you also specify the *protocols=nwlink* switch in the Setup Script.
NWRedir	Determines NetWare client configuration options.
NWServer	Controls the properties specific to NetWare clients.
OptionalComponents	Contains the descriptions that appear in the Optional Components dialog box in Windows 95 Setup.
Printers	Installs one or more printers during the Setup process. To install printers, specify a user-defined name for identifying the printer, the model name, and the printer port. Each printer you install must have a separate entry in the *[Printers]* section.
Setup	Sets parameters for control of the Setup process—such as the command-line switches you learned about in previous Tips.
System	Sets parameters for modifying the system settings.
VRedir	Determines Microsoft client configuration options.
VServer	Controls the properties specific to Microsoft clients.

Table 852 Some of the Windows 95 installation script file sections.

The answer is **True** *because you may use any text editor to edit a Setup Script.*

853 INSTALLING SOFTWARE IN WINDOWS 95 USING CUSTOM SCRIPTS

Q: Windows 95 Server-based Setup can install additional applications to Windows 95.

True or False?

Although it is possible to create custom scripts that you can call from a Windows 95 installation script, Server-based Setup cannot configure a Setup Script to install additional software. To install additional software, you must create additional script files that control the software's installation, and make changes to the installation script's *Install* section.

The Microsoft *Windows 95 Resource Kit* includes a utility called the *INF Installer* that you can use to customize a setup script and copy all files the script requires to a server-based installation directory for any application that uses *inf* files for installation. You must install applications that do not use *inf* files for installation either manually (at each computer) or using network management software, such as Microsoft *Systems Management Server (SMS)*.

To use the INF Installer, you already must have used *netsetup.exe* to prepare a server for shared installations. After you prepare the server for shared installations, you can use the INF Installer to copy installation files for additional software and modify the installation script simultaneously. Figure 853 shows the INF Installer dialog box.

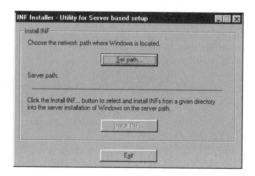

Figure 853 *The INF Installer dialog box.*

The answer is **False** *because Windows 95 Server-based Setup cannot install additional applications.*

854 UNDERSTANDING WINDOWS 95 PUSH INSTALLATIONS

Q: You can perform push installations only from a Windows NT server.

True or False?

Administrators of large networks who want to install a large number of client computers frequently choose a *push installation* method (so-called because it "pushes" data from the server to the client) because it lets them install client computers without having to travel to each client's physical location. Push installations are completely automated (that is, after you design them, they will run without interaction from the user or yourself) and use server-based source files and customized installation scripts. You can perform push installations from any network location, such as a Windows NT server, a NetWare server, or even a Windows 95 computer that shares the files to the network.

Some push installations are shared installations in which the client computer runs the operating system or application directly from the server. Other push installations are simply automated installations that copy all the required files over the network to the client computer. You can push an installation by configuring all the installation files and scripts or using network management software, such as Microsoft *Systems Management Server (SMS)*.

The answer is **False** *because you can perform push installations using Windows NT server, Novell NetWare, or third-party network management software, and you can store source files on any shared network location.*

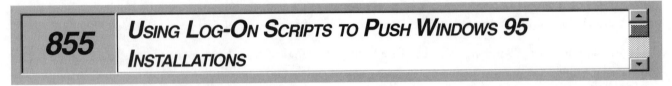

| 855 | USING LOG-ON SCRIPTS TO PUSH WINDOWS 95 INSTALLATIONS |

Q: Which of the following statements are true about using log-on scripts to perform a push installation?

Choose the best answer:

A. You should put the installation commands in the log-on script of the network users.

B. You should use a special user account devoted to performing installations.

C. You can use log-on scripts only to perform push installations on Windows-based operating systems.

D. You can use the Novell NetWare NETX client to perform a push installation with a log-on script, but you cannot use the Novell NetWare VLM client to do so.

As you have learned, push installations let administrators install software on client computers without having to go to each client's physical location. Some types of network management software let administrators begin push installations by issuing commands from a server-based application. Other types of push installations require administrators to initiate the installation process from the client computer.

To initialize an installation, you can put the installation commands in the log-on script of a user account that you dedicate to software installation and create specifically for such purpose. Although you could put the installation commands into every user's log-on script, doing so is usually not a good idea because users may begin the installation process over and over again as they try to log on. Using a special user account lets you specify an installation command in a log-on script that will install the software from a server location. When you are ready to distribute the software to client computers, you simply instruct the users to log on using the special account the first time, and then to log on normally when the installation is complete.

You can initialize push installations through any Microsoft client's log-on scripts, including MS-DOS, LAN Manager, and Windows for Workgroups *3.11* network components that log on to a Windows NT server. Additionally, NetWare VLM and NETX clients can initialize a push installation from a NetWare log-on script.

Answer **B** *is correct because you should use a special user account to perform push installations.* **Answer A** *is incorrect because putting installation commands in the log-on scripts of network users may result in users repeating the installation process unnecessarily.* **Answer C** *is incorrect because MS-DOS or Windows 3.x operating systems can use log-on scripts to perform push installations.* **Answer D** *is incorrect because both the Novell NetWare NETX and VLM clients can use log-on scripts to perform push installations.*

856 | SETTING UP A WINDOWS *NT* SERVER FOR A WINDOWS 95 PUSH INSTALLATION

Q: *If you are using a Windows NT server to perform a push installation of Windows 95, you must store the Windows 95 source files and the msbatch.inf file on the Primary Domain Controller (PDC).*

True or False?

As you learned in Tip 855, you can use a log-on script to initialize the installation of software in a networked environment that implements an authentication server (that is, a server that authenticates users). Although you could use any shared network location as a source directory for installation files, network administrators most commonly use the authentication server itself. For example, if you want to use a push installation to install Windows 95 as a shared installation in a Windows NT domain, you must prepare the server for the installation. To prepare the server, perform the following steps:

1. Run Server-based Setup and install the Windows 95 source files into a shared directory on the authentication server.

2. After you create the Server-based Setup, use one of the Windows 95 Setup script creation utilities to create and modify an *msbatch.inf* scripting file. After you create the scripting file, use the Windows *Explorer* to copy the script into the shared directory where the Windows 95 shared installation resides.

3. Within Windows NT's User Manager for Domains, create a user account named *Upgrade* (any name will work) and specify the password as *Upgrade* (any password will work). Ensure you have set the User Cannot Change Password and Password Never Expires options in the account.

4. Use *Notepad* or another text editor to create the custom log-on script that contains the installation commands. After you create the script, save it into the *NetLogon* service's folder (*winntroot\system32\repl\export\scripts*).

5. Within User Manager for Domains, assign the log-on script you create to the Upgrade user account.

Note: You must prepare the server for installation—including creating the Upgrade account and the custom logon script—for each domain to which users may log on.

When you are ready to begin push installations, give users the installation user's account name and password. Next, instruct users to log on to the installation user account one time, and then to log on normally when the installation is complete.

*The answer is **False** because you can store the Windows 95 source files and the msbatch.inf file on any shared location on the network. However, you must store the log-on script you use to initialize a push installation in a domain controller's NetLogon directory,*

857 | SETTING UP A NETWARE SERVER FOR A WINDOWS 95 PUSH INSTALLATION

Q: *When you perform a push installation from a NetWare server, what must the password for the Upgrade user be?*

Choose the best answer:

    A.   *User1*

    B.   *Upgrade1*

    C.   *Password*

    D.   *Any password you choose*

In Tip 855, you learned that NetWare's NETX and VLM clients can use a command in the log-on script to initialize a push installation of software over the network. The Windows 95 Client for NetWare Networks can also use a command in the logon script to initialize a Push Installation of software over the network. In NetWare environments, you must prepare the NetWare server to execute the push installation. To prepare a NetWare server for a push installation, perform the following steps:

1. Run Server-based Setup and install the Windows 95 source files to a shared directory on the NetWare server.

2. After you create the Server-based Setup, use one of the Windows 95 setup script creation utilities to create and modify a *msbatch.inf* scripting file. After you create the scripting file, use the Windows *Explorer* to copy the script into the shared directory where the Windows 95 shared installation resides.

3. On the NetWare server, use the *Syscon* utility to create a user account named Upgrade (any name will work) and specify the password as Upgrade (any password will work). Ensure you have set the Allow User To Change Password and Force Periodic Password Changes options to No.

4. With the *Syscon* utility, assign the User account to the preferred server that users will access.

5. Create the special log-on script that contains the installation commands and assign it to the Upgrade user account. Put the log-on script in the appropriate log-on directory for that server.

When you are ready to begin push installations, give users the installation user account's name and password. Next, instruct users to log on to the installation user account one time, and then to log on normally when the installation is complete.

Answer D *is correct because you can use any name for both the user account and the password to perform a push installation using a log-on script.* **Answers A, B, and C** *are incorrect because you do not have to use any specific password for the user account when you perform a push installation using a log-on script.*

858   CREATING THE WINDOWS 95 STARTUP DISK

Q: *How can you create a Windows 95 Startup disk from within Windows 95?*

Choose the best answer:

    A.   *You can use the Disk Administrator option in the Administrative Tools group.*

    B.   *You can use the System Recovery tool in the Control Panel.*

    C.   *You must copy the files that Windows 95 requires for startup to a floppy disk.*

    D.   *You can use the Add/Remove Programs option in the Control Panel.*

One feature of Windows 95 is the Windows 95 Startup disk, a floppy disk that can boot your computer and perform various diagnostic functions. In most installations, Windows 95 will ask if you want to create a Windows 95 Startup disk during installation. If you choose to create the Windows 95 Startup disk during installation, the Windows 95 Setup program creates the disk prior to copying any files to the hard drive. If you choose not to create the Startup disk during installation, and later decide you want one, you can still create a Startup disk from the Add/Remove Programs dialog box that you open from the Windows 95 Control Panel. To create a Windows 95 Startup disk after installation is complete, perform the following steps:

1. Click your mouse on the Start menu and select the Settings group Control Panel option. Windows 95 will open the Windows 95 Control Panel.

2. Within the Control Panel, double-click your mouse on the Add/Remove Programs icon. Windows 95 will open the Add/Remove programs dialog box.

3. Within the Add/Remove Programs dialog box, click your mouse on the Startup Disk tab at the top of the dialog box. Windows 95 will change your view to the Startup Disk sheet.

4. Within the Startup Disk sheet, click your mouse on the Create Startup Disk button. Windows 95 will prompt you to insert a floppy disk into your computer, and will specify the drive letter of the drive into which you should insert the disk. Insert the floppy disk into the drive.

5. Within the Insert Startup Disk prompt, click your mouse on the OK button. Windows 95 will create a Windows 95 Startup disk.

During the Startup disk creation process, Windows 95 will copy the files Table 858 lists to the disk and make the disk bootable.

Windows 95 Startup Disk Files

attrib.exe	*chkdsk.exe*	*command.com*	*config.sys*
debug.exe	*drvspace.bin*	*ebd.sys*	*edit.com*
fdisk.exe	*format.com*	*himem.sys*	*io.sys*
msdos.sys	*regedit.exe*	*scandisk.exe*	
scandisk.ini	*sys.com*	*uninstal.exe*	

Table 858 The files Windows 95 will copy to the Startup disk.

Note: *The Startup disk creation utility relies on a file that users can possibly edit; and therefore, some computers may copy more or less files.*

Answer D *is correct because the Add/Remove Programs icon in Windows 95 Control Panel opens a dialog box that lets you create a Windows 95 Startup disk.* **Answer A** *is incorrect because Windows 95 has no Administrative Tools group and no Disk Administrator option.* **Answer B** *is incorrect because Windows 95 has no System Recovery tool in the Control Panel.* **Answer C** *is incorrect because, although you could format a disk with system files and then copy other necessary files to create a Startup disk, it is not necessary to do so because Windows 95 provides you with a tool to create the Startup disk.*

Q: *You can uninstall any version of Windows 95.*

True or False?

Because upgrading a computer's operating system can produce unpredictable and sometimes undesirable results, Windows 95 Upgrade versions have the ability for you to uninstall them. Network administrators prefer uninstalling as the way to remove Windows 95 from a computer they have upgraded because it restores the computer to the condition it was in prior to the Windows 95 installation.

To successfully uninstall Windows 95, you must have a Startup disk and you must have specifically instructed Windows 95 to save the old operating system's configuration files during setup. Although you can create a Startup disk at any time, only during installation does Windows 95 give you the option of saving the files the old operating system requires. If you have the Startup disk and you have instructed Windows 95 to save the old files, you can uninstall Windows 95 by simply booting the computer with the Windows 95 Startup disk and typing *uninstal* at the command prompt.

Note: *As you learned in previous Tips, Original Equipment Manufacturer (OEM) versions of Windows 95 cannot upgrade an existing operating system and you cannot uninstall OEM versions.*

*The answer is **False** because you cannot uninstall OEM versions of Windows 95.*

860 TROUBLESHOOTING A WINDOWS 95 INSTALLATION

Q: *Which of the following files does Windows 95 create during Windows 95 Setup that contains information with which you can troubleshoot a failed Windows 95 installation?*

Choose all answers that apply:

    A.   *setuplog.txt*

    B.   *detlog.txt*

    C.   *detlog.log*

    D.   *detcrash.log*

As a Microsoft Certified Systems Engineer (MCSE), it is likely that you will experience problems with a Windows 95 installation. During installation, Windows 95 creates several files that contain information you can use to identify a problem and determine if you can successfully install Windows 95 on a specific computer. Table 860 describes the files created during a Windows 95 installation.

File	Description
detlog.txt	Maintains a record of all devices identified during the *Hardware Detection* phase of the Setup process.
detcrash.log	Records information during the *Hardware Detection* phase to ensure the Windows 95 Setup process will not crash or hang up on the same detection procedure more than one time.
setuplog.txt	Records the *Hardware Detection* phase's events, both the successes and failures.

Table 860 *The files Windows 95 Setup creates during installation.*

Answers A, B, *and* **D** *are correct because the answers list files created during Windows 95 Setup that contain information with which you can troubleshoot a failed Windows 95 installation.* **Answer C** *is incorrect because Windows 95 Setup does not create a file named detlog.log.*

861 — UNDERSTANDING FAILURE DETECTION AND SAFE RECOVERY

Q: What should you do if Windows 95 Setup hangs up during the Hardware Detection phase?

Choose the best answer:

> A.   Turn off the power, restart the computer, format the hard drive, and begin again.
>
> B.   Turn off the power, restart the computer, and begin Setup again.
>
> C.   Turn off the power, restart the computer, and start Setup again using the /IS command switch.
>
> D.   Turn off the power, restart the computer, and use Server-based Setup.

As you have learned, Windows 95 creates files during installation that maintain records of the installation process. The Windows 95 Setup program can use one file, *detcrash.log*, to detect failures and ensure that a computer will not crash or hang up while it performs the same hardware detection sequence which caused the initial crash. If Windows 95 Setup did not use the *detcrash.log* file, it is entirely possible that you could never complete a specific Windows 95 installation because the Setup program would always crash at the same point.

When Windows 95 Setup enters the *Hardware Detection* phase, Setup will create the *detcrash.log* file, insert a reference to a specific hardware detection sequence, and mark the sequence as Failed. Setup will run the hardware detection sequence only after it marks the sequence as Failed. If the sequence is successful, Setup will then change the log information within the *detcrash.log* file to indicate a successful hardware-detection sequence. If the sequence halts the computer or hangs up, the administrator will restart the computer, restart the installation, and choose the Safe Recovery option when Setup displays a prompt. When Windows 95 Setup reaches the detection sequence it marked Failed, Setup will pass over and not perform that sequence. Setup marks each detection sequence in the same way so that Windows 95 Setup will never crash or hang up on the same sequence. Theoretically, Setup could hang up or crash multiple times during installation and you could still successfully install Windows 95.

Answer B is correct because if Windows 95 Setup hangs up during the Hardware Detection phase, you should turn off the power, restart the computer, and begin Setup again. When hardware detection results in a hang up, Setup will not repeat it in subsequent installations. Answers A, C, and D are incorrect because the answers do not describe what you should do if Windows 95 Setup hangs up during the Hardware Detection phase.

862 — INTRODUCTION TO THE CONTROL PANEL IN WINDOWS 95

Q: Which of the following icons in the Windows 95 Control Panel lets you configure Sticky keys?

Choose the best answer:

> A.   Fonts
>
> B.   Keyboard
>
> C.   Accessibility Options
>
> D.   System

After you install Windows 95, you will often have to configure the operating system further for specific reasons. Most of the configuration for Windows 95 takes place in the Control Panel, which contains various icons that let you run small utilities within which you can configure different Windows 95 options. Table 862 describes some of the different icons in the Windows 95 Control Panel and the utilities they open when you double-click the mouse on them.

Icon/Utility	Description
Accessibility Options	Configures the way you interact with the system and includes configuration settings for Keyboard, Sound, Display, Mouse, and General. You can configure options, such as Sticky keys (which lets you use the CTRL, ALT, and SHIFT keys in combinations without holding the keys down), in this option.
Add New Hardware	Installs new hardware devices.
Add/Remove Programs	Manages optional components for Windows 95, installs or removes additional applications, and creates a Startup disk.
Date/Time	Manages the Time, Date, and Time Zone settings for Windows 95.
Display	Controls video devices, background settings, and how Windows 95 objects and menus appear.
Fonts	Adds, removes, and manages Fonts.
Internet	Contains configuration settings for Microsoft *Internet Explorer*.
Keyboards	Controls Keyboard type, speed, special key functions, and language.
Mail and Fax	Controls settings for the Exchange client, Fax service, and other messaging programs.
Microsoft Mail Postoffice	Creates and manages a Microsoft Workgroup Postoffice (not included with OEM Service Release 2).
Modems	Installs, removes, and manages modems.
Mouse	Controls the buttons, icons, animation, and mouse type.
Multimedia	Controls multimedia functions, such as audio, image compression, video codecs (video players and drivers), MIDI settings, and the mixer.
Network	Configures all aspects of Windows 95 networking.
Passwords	Changes passwords, enables remote administration, and determines user profile usage.
PC Card (PCMCIA)	Configures, manages, and starts or stops PCMCIA (PC Card) devices.
Printers	Installs, removes, views, and manages Printers.
Regional Settings	Specifies special settings, such as language format, currency format, number format, and Time and Date formats.
Sounds	Changes the assignment of sounds to system events.
System	Controls system settings such as memory parameters, CD-ROM settings, and other devices. Also, the System option lets you view system configuration.

Table 862 Some common options for the Windows 95 Control Panel.

Answer C is correct because Accessibility Options in Windows 95 Control Panel let you configure Sticky keys. Answer A is incorrect because the Fonts option lets you add, remove, or manage fonts installed in Windows 95, but does not let you configure Sticky keys. Answer B is incorrect because the Keyboard option lets you manage various aspects of your keyboard, but does not let you configure Sticky keys. Answer D is incorrect because the System option lets you manage various general configuration options relating to the system, but does not let you configure Sticky keys.

863   INTRODUCTION TO THE NETWORK PROPERTIES DIALOG BOX

Q: *Which of the following options found in Windows 95 Control Panel lets you add and remove transport protocols?*

Choose the best answer:

     A.   *System*

     B.   *Network*

     C.   *Protocols*

     D.   *Add/Remove Programs*

As you have learned, Windows 95 includes built-in support for networks. You will perform all configuration settings for Windows 95 networks (with the exception of older MS-DOS-based configurations) in the Network Properties dialog box. The Network Properties dialog box lets you add and remove network interface cards (NICs), network protocols, network services, network clients, and more, while letting you manage the settings for all these components.

Answer B is correct because the Network option in Windows 95 Control Panel lets you add and remove transport protocols. Answer A is incorrect because the System option lets you manage various configuration options relating to the system, but does not let you add and remove transport protocols. Answer C is incorrect because Windows 95 Control Panel does not have a Protocols option. Answer D is incorrect because the Add/Remove Programs option lets you add and remove applications, but does not let you add or remove transport protocols.

864   INTRODUCTION TO INTERPROCESS COMMUNICATION MECHANISMS (IPCS) IN WINDOWS 95

Q: *Which of the following Interprocess Communication Mechanisms (IPCs) does Windows 95 support?*

Choose all answers that apply:

     A.   *Named Pipes*

     B.   *Remote Procedure Calls (RPCs)*

     C.   *Windows Sockets*

     D.   *NetBIOS*

Client–server applications, and some Windows 95 operating system functions (such as Dial-Up Networking), require a component that can establish direct communication between the client and server applications. The components which establish connections between the client and server are *Interprocess Communication Mechanisms (IPCs)*. Windows 95 includes the following Interprocess Communication Mechanisms:

- Mailslots
- Named Pipes

- NetBIOS

- Remote Procedure Calls (RPCs)

- Windows Sockets

In general, the IPCs are invisible to both the administrator and the user—that is, programs written for Windows 95 use the IPCs directly, but you must only know that they exist. However, the Remote Procedure Calls (RPCs) protocol is a critical protocol for Windows 95, and, therefore, you will learn more about it in the next Tip.

Answers A, B, C, and D are all correct because Windows 95 supports Windows Sockets, Remote Procedure Calls (RPC), NetBIOS, Named Pipes, and Mailslots as Interprocess Communication Mechanisms (IPCs).

865   **UNDERSTANDING REMOTE PROCEDURE CALLS IN WINDOWS 95**

Q: *Which of the following Interprocess Communication Mechanisms (IPCs) can Remote Procedure Calls (RPCs) use in Windows 95?*

Choose answers that apply:

     A.   *NetBIOS*

     B.   *Named Pipes*

     C.   *Windows Sockets*

     D.   *Mailslots*

As you learned in Tip 864, Windows 95 supports Remote Procedure Calls (RPCs) as Interprocess Communication Mechanisms (IPCs). Remote Procedure Calls are a unique communication method because they use other Interprocess Communication Mechanisms to communicate between the client and server components across a network. Windows 95's support of Remote Procedure Calls (which can differ from the support for Remote Procedure Calls that other operating systems provide) lets Remote Procedure Calls communicate using the following Interprocess Communication Mechanisms:

- NetBIOS

- Named Pipes

- Windows Sockets

Answers A, B, and C are correct because Windows 95 supports Remote Procedure Calls (RPCs) using NetBIOS, Named Pipes, and Windows Sockets. Answer D is incorrect because Windows 95 does not support Remote Procedure Calls (RPCs) with Mailslots.

866   **UNDERSTANDING THE NETWORKS THAT WINDOWS 95 SUPPORTS**

Q: *For which of the following types of network environments does Windows 95 include built-in support?*

Choose all answers that apply:

   A.   *Novell NetWare*

   B.   *Microsoft Windows NT*

   C.   *IBM 3270 Mainframes*

   D.   *AppleTalk*

Microsoft designed Windows 95 with built-in support for a variety of network environments. In general, Microsoft designed Windows 95 to work with most commonly-available local-area network (LAN) environments. Specifically, Microsoft designed Windows 95 to work with the following environments:

* Artisoft Lantastic version *5.0* and greater

* Banyan VINES version *5.52* and greater

* DEC PATHWORKS (Protocol only)

* Microsoft Networking including LAN Manager, Windows for Workgroups *3.x*, and Windows NT

* Novell NetWare version *3.11* and greater

* SunSoft PC-NFS version *5.0* and greater

You can install some network clients at any time, while other client support must exist on the computer prior to the installation of Windows 95 to function correctly. Specifically, both the DEC protocol and the SunSoft NFS protocol must exist on the computer prior to your Windows 95 installation. Additionally, some network clients can provide support for network environments other than those environments that meet the description. For example, the Client for Microsoft Networks protocol (that you use to connect to Windows for Workgroups, Windows 95, and Windows NT networks) can also provide connection to IBM 3270 Mainframes for character-based applications.

Answers A, B, and C are correct because Windows 95 inherently supports networks in environments Novell NetWare, Microsoft Windows NT, and IBM 3270 Mainframes (through the Client for Microsoft Networks) define. Answer D is incorrect because Windows 95 does not inherently support networks in an environment AppleTalk defines.

867   **UNDERSTANDING NETWORK CONFIGURATION IN WINDOWS 95**

Q: *You can form a network using only network hardware, computers, and the Windows 95 operating system.*

   True or False?

As you learned in Tip 866, Windows 95 includes support for a variety of established network environments. Windows 95 can also form a Peer-to-Peer (workgroup) network using just the network hardware and a client, such as the Client for Microsoft Networks. To configure a Peer-to-Peer network in Windows 95, you must verify you have installed and configured correctly the network hardware, such as the network interface cards (NICs). Also, you must add a client, such as the Client for Microsoft Networks, and choose a protocol that is common for all computers. Additionally, you must decide which computers will share files and printers, and add the File and Print sharing service to those computers. You do all the configuration for Windows 95 networks in the Network Properties dialog box. To access the Network Properties dialog box, perform the following steps:

1. Click your mouse on the Start menu and select the Settings group Control Panel option. Windows 95 will open the Control Panel.

2. Within the Control Panel, double-click your mouse on the Network icon. Windows 95 will open the Network Properties dialog box.

After you open the Network Properties dialog box, you can use it to add protocols, set up file and print sharing, and so on for the Windows 95 computer. After most changes, Windows 95 will prompt you to restart the computer.

The answer is **True** *because you can form a network using only network hardware, computers, and the Windows 95 operating system.*

| 868 | INTRODUCTION TO THE WINDOWS 95 SUPPORTED NETWORK PROTOCOLS |

Q: Which of the following protocols does Windows 95 support?

Choose the best answer:

   A.   *TCP/IP*

   B.   *NetBEUI*

   C.   *IPX/SPX*

   D.   *DLC*

Throughout this book, you have learned that networks require protocols to communicate over a network. Just as different networks may use different protocols to communicate internally to the network and externally to the network (such as over the Internet), Windows 95 will also use different protocols for communications—which may differ for internal network connections and external network connections. Windows 95 must also use protocols to establish network communication and includes support for the following protocol suites:

• Transmission Control Protocol/Internet Protocol (TCP/IP)

• NetBEUI

• IPX/SPX

• Data-Link Connection (DLC) or Frame Relay

Answers A, B, C, and D are all correct because Windows 95 supports TCP/IP, NetBEUI, IPX/SPX, and DLC as protocol suites.

| 869 | CONFIGURING *TCP/IP* IN WINDOWS 95 |

Q: *What information must you enter to create a valid minimum Transmission Control Protocol/ Internet Protocol (TCP/IP) configuration?*

Choose all answers that apply:

   A.   *The IP address*

   B.   *The Subnet Mask*

   C.   *The Default Gateway*

   D.   *The DNS configuration*

As you have learned, Windows 95 supports several different network protocols, including the Transmission Control Protocol/Internet Protocol (TCP/IP) protocol suite. Because of its addressing scheme, the TCP/IP protocol suite frequently requires more configuration than other protocols. The TCP/IP protocol's addressing scheme consists of three sets of numbers that establish its address and communication path for other networks. A basic configuration for TCP/IP consists of the Internet Protocol (IP) address, the Subnet Mask, and the Default Gateway address.

Advanced implementations of TCP/IP that use a Dynamic Host Configuration Protocol (DHCP) server to provide addresses can make the configuration of clients easier. However, advanced implementations also require more knowledge of the TCP/IP protocol and the server operating system that supplies addresses when you design the server. To configure a client to use DHCP, simply add the TCP/IP protocol stack to the computer's network protocols and ensure you have selected the Use DHCP checkbox in the TCP/IP Properties dialog box.

Answers A, B, and C are correct because a minimum TCP/IP configuration consists of the IP address, Subnet Mask, and the Default Gateway. Answer D is incorrect because Microsoft requires the DNS configuration only for advanced Internetworking and not for a minimum TCP/IP configuration.

870   **USING THE TRACERT.EXE PROGRAM IN WINDOWS 95**

Q: *Which of the following switches let you specify not to resolve hostnames when you use the Tracert utility?*

Choose the best answer:

   A.   *-D*

   B.   *-H*

   C.   *-J*

   D.   *-W*

There may be times when using a Transmission Control Protocol/Internet Protocol (TCP/IP) network or the Internet is confusing or difficult to negotiate. As a result, you may be unable to reach the intended address of a remote computer that exists on a different network. The *Tracert* utility lets you identify the route the TCP/IP packets and protocol suite must take to reach a remote computer.

The *Tracert* utility is a command-line executable that runs from the MS-DOS prompt in Windows 95. You can use command-line switches to control how *Tracert* performs its functions. Table 870 describes some command-line switches that you can use with the *Tracert* utility.

Command-line Switch	Description
-D	Instructs *Tracert* not to resolve hostnames.
-H	Specifies the maximum number of hops (that is, server addresses away from the computer's server) *Tracert* will search for an address.
-J	Used with a file that contains a list of hosts and routers (speeds up *Tracert's* performance).
-W	Specifies the amount of time *Tracert* will wait for a reply.

*Table 870 Some command-line switches for the **Tracert** utility.*

Note: You can learn more about the **Tracert** utility within the Windows 95 Resource Kit.

*Answer A is correct because the -D switch lets you specify not to resolve hostnames when you use TRACERT. **Answer B** is incorrect because the -H switch lets you specify the maximum hops TRACERT will search for an address. **Answer C** is incorrect because the -J lets you specify a hostname list for TRACERT to use. **Answer D** is incorrect because the -W switch lets you specify an amount of time TRACERT will wait for a reply from a host.*

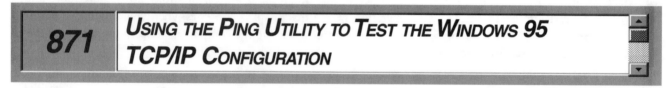

871 — USING THE PING UTILITY TO TEST THE WINDOWS 95 TCP/IP CONFIGURATION

Q: You can use the Ping utility to test the configuration of TCP/IP on your network.

True or False?

If you experience communication problems in the network while using Transmission Control Protocol/Internet Protocol (TCP/IP), your first step in troubleshooting is to verify you can reach other computers. You can verify TCP/IP communication using the *PING* utility, a command-line executable that runs from the MS-DOS prompt in Windows 95. You can use command-line switches to control how *PING* performs its functions. Table 871 describes some command-line switches you can use with the *PING* utility in Windows 95.

Command-line Switch	Description
-A	Resolve addresses to hostnames.
-F	Sets a "Do not fragment" flag in the ping packet.
-I	Specifies the time to live for pings (how long a ping can exist before destroying itself).
-J	Specifies a hostname list to use while pinging.
-K	Specifies a strict hostname list to use while pinging.
-L	Instructs *Ping* to send the buffer size.
-N	Specifies the number of echo requests (pings) to send.
-R	Instructs *Ping* to count the hops in the route it takes when pinging.
-S	Instructs *PING* to time stamp each hop in the route it takes when pinging.
-T	Will continue to ping until interrupted.
-V	Specifies the type of service.
-W	Specifies the time to wait for each reply.

*Table 871 Some command-line switches for the **Ping** utility in Windows 95.*

Note: You can learn more about the **Ping** utility within the Windows 95 Resource Kit.

The answer is **True** because you can use the Ping utility to test the configuration of TCP/IP on your network.

Q: What is the default frame type for the IPX/SPX compatible protocol?

Choose the best answer:

A. 802.2

B. 802.3

C. Auto

D. Ethernet 2

Although TCP/IP is the protocol that requires the most configuration, other protocols, such as the Internetwork Packet Exchange/Sequential Packet Exchange (IPX/SPX), also require configuration. Usually, the IPX/SPX protocol (the default communications protocol for Novell networks) will function properly when you install it.

However, some situations do require you to configure the protocol. For example, in a network that uses two frame types, such as 802.2 and 802.3, Windows 95 may choose the wrong frame type for the network to which you want the client to connect.

Windows 95 may choose the wrong frame type because the default frame type for IPX/SPX in Windows 95 is Auto, which means that the protocol will try to determine the frame type on the network. If more than one frame type is present, the protocol may choose the wrong frame type for your network design. Table 872 describes the configurable options for the IPX/SPX protocol.

Option	Description
Force even-length packets	Specifies even-length packets. Windows 95 enables the Force even-length packets option only for Ethernet 802.3 on monolithic implementations that cannot handle odd-length packet sizes.
Frame Type	Specifies the frame type, such as Auto, 802.2, 802.3, Ethernet 2, and Token Ring.
Maximum Connections	Specifies the maximum number of connections that IPX will allow.
Maximum Sockets	Specifies the maximum number of IPX sockets.
Network Address	Specifies the IPX network address in four byte value.
Source Routing	Specifies the cache size to use with source routing (Token Ring only).

Table 872 Configurable options for the IPX/SPX protocol in Windows 95.

Answer C is correct because the default frame type for the IPX/SPX compatible protocol is Auto. **Answers A, B,** and **D** are incorrect because, although the answers are all valid IPX/SPX frame types, only Auto is the default frame type.

873   SETTING A COMPUTER'S NETBIOS NAME IN WINDOWS 95

Q: *Which of the following rules must you adhere to when you assign a NetBIOS name to your computer?*

Choose all answers that apply:

> A.   *The NetBIOS name must contain numbers.*
>
> B.   *The NetBIOS name must contain text.*
>
> C.   *The NetBIOS name must be unique.*
>
> D.   *The NetBIOS name must be 15 characters or less.*

When you open the Network Neighborhood, if there are other computers on the network that you connect to, you will frequently see a list of computers that contain shared resources you may be able to access (depending on your security permissions). The names that appear in the list are NetBIOS names that identify computers on NetBIOS networks. In Windows 95, you specify the NetBIOS name for a computer in the Network Properties dialog box. NetBIOS names must be unique on the network or the network operating system will generate an error. Additionally, a NetBIOS name cannot exceed 15 characters in length.

Answers C and D are correct because a NetBIOS name must be unique on the network and can be no greater than 15 characters in length. Answers A and B are incorrect because a NetBIOS name can contain numbers or text, which is at the administrator's discretion.

874   USING LMHOST AND HOSTS FILES IN WINDOWS 95

Q: *You must always have an LMHOST file to use TCP/IP in Windows 95.*

True or False?

Almost all Transmission Control Protocol/Internet Protocol (TCP/IP) environments use hostnames that identify computers in a user-friendly way. For example, when you surf the Internet, you connect to the Jamsa Press Web site at *http://www.jamsa.com*—not the twelve-digit IP address for the Web site's host computer. You can configure TCP/IP in Windows 95 to search a special file called a *HOSTS* file to map hostnames to Internet Protocol (IP) addresses. Windows 95 creates an example of the *HOSTS* file when you install TCP/IP, and you can reference the example to create a custom file.

Although the *HOSTS* file can map hostnames to IP addresses on a local-area network (LAN), it cannot extend into a larger network environment through a gateway or over a router. To create a file that maps hostnames to remote addresses and provides routing at the same time, you must use an *LMHOST* file. As with the *HOSTS* file, Windows 95 creates an example of the *LMHOST* file when you install TCP/IP, and you can use the example as a reference to create a custom file.

*The answer is **False** because you require an **LMHOST** file only if the network requires access to undiscovered routes.*

875   Configuring the Client for Microsoft Networks for Domain Log on in Windows 95

Q: Where can you specify the information Windows 95 requires for a computer to join a Windows NT domain?

Choose all answers that apply:

A.   *In the Network Neighborhood Properties dialog box*

B.   *In the My Computer Properties dialog box*

C.   *In the System dialog box that you open from the Control Panel*

D.   *In the Network Properties dialog box that you open from the Control Panel*

If you want to use Windows 95 as a client computer in a Windows NT domain, you must configure the Client for Microsoft Networks to log on to a domain. To configure the Client for Microsoft Networks for domain log on, perform the following steps:

1. Click your mouse on the Start menu and select the Settings group Control Panel option. Windows 95 will open the Control Panel.

2. Within the Control Panel, double-click your mouse on the Network icon. Windows 95 will open the Network Properties Dialog Box.

3. Within the Network Properties dialog box, click your mouse on the *Client for Microsoft Networks* item. Windows 95 will indicate your selection by highlighting the *Client for Microsoft Networks* item.

4. Within the Network Properties dialog box, click your mouse on the Properties button. Windows 95 will open the Client for Microsoft Networks Properties dialog box.

5. Within the Client for Microsoft Networks Properties dialog box, click your mouse on the Log on to Windows NT Domain checkbox. Windows 95 will indicate your selection by displaying a check mark in the checkbox.

6. Within the Client for Microsoft Networks Properties dialog box, type your domain's name in the *Windows NT Domain* field. Windows 95 will insert the text you type into the *Windows NT Domain* field.

7. Within the Client for Microsoft Networks Properties dialog box, choose between the Quick logon and the Log on and Restore Network Connections option buttons, based on your network design and your computer's speed. Windows 95 will indicate your choice by displaying a dot in the option button you choose.

8. Within the Client for Microsoft Networks Properties dialog box, click your mouse on the OK button. Windows 95 will return you to the Network Properties dialog box.

9. Within the Network Properties dialog box, click your mouse on the OK button. Windows 95 will prompt you to restart your computer.

10. Within the dialog box that prompts you to restart your computer, click your mouse on the OK button. Windows 95 will restart your computer and display a Domain Logon dialog box when Windows 95 restarts.

Note: *You can also reach the Network Properties dialog box by right-clicking your mouse on the Network Neighborhood icon and choosing the Properties option from the pop-up menu that Windows 95 displays.*

Answers A and D are correct because you can specify the required information to cause Windows 95 to join a Windows NT domain on the Network Properties dialog box. You can reach the Network Properties dialog box through the Network option in Control Panel or the Properties of Network Neighborhood. Answers B and C are incorrect because you cannot reach the Network Properties dialog box through the Systems option in Control Panel or the Properties of My Computer. You can reach the System Properties dialog box through the System option in Control Panel or the Properties of My Computer.

---

876 CONFIGURING THE PRIMARY WINDOWS 95 CLIENT FOR NETWORK LOGON

Q: *The Primary Network Client in Windows 95 is the client that runs a log-on script.*

True or False?

As you have learned in previous Tips, Windows 95 will let you set up multiple network clients on a single computer. Although you can load multiple network clients into Windows 95 at the same time, you must designate one client you load as the *Primary Network Logon*. The Primary Network Logon is the client that loads first and looks for and loads a System Policy if a Policy is present on either the computer or the network. For example, if you want to use system policies that the administrator has previously stored on a Windows NT Server, you must designate the Client for Microsoft Networks as the Primary Network Logon.

Additionally, Windows 95 will compare the log-on credentials the Primary Network Logon supplies against other client log-on credentials, and provide a single log-on dialog box if all the client protocols' usernames and passwords match. For example, if your computer has the Client for Microsoft Networks and the Client for NetWare Networks installed, and the username and password for both the Windows NT domain and the NetWare server are the same, Windows 95 will produce a log-on dialog box only for the Primary Network Logon. If the user supplies proper credentials for the first Client, Windows 95 will assume the credentials for the second Client will also be accurate and automatically insert the username and password into the secondary client, and process any log-on scripts that result.

Windows 95's Network log-on can be confusing to watch because Windows 95 might display a Client for Microsoft Networks log-on dialog box, and then process a NetWare log-on script. Windows 95 may display a log-on box for one network type and process a log-on script for another network type, all without user intervention, because any client protocol Windows 95 loads can run a log-on script even if it is not the Primary Network Logon. To designate a Network Client as the Primary Network Logon, perform the following steps.

1. Within Windows 95, click your mouse on the Start menu and select the Settings group Control Panel option. Windows 95 will open the Control Panel.

2. Within the Control Panel, double-click your mouse on the Network option. Windows 95 will open the Network Properties dialog box.

3. Within the Network Properties dialog box, click your mouse on the Primary Network Logon drop-down list box. Windows 95 will display the choices in the drop-down list.

4. Within the drop-down list, choose the logon method you want to be Primary. Windows 95 will insert your choice in the *Primary Network Logon* field.

5. Click your mouse on the OK button. Windows 95 will close the Network Properties dialog box and prompt you to restart your computer.

6. Click your mouse on the OK button to restart your computer. Windows 95 will restart.

*The answer is **False** because each client you load in the Network Properties dialog box can run a log-on script. The Primary Network Client is the client that loads first.*

877 UNDERSTANDING WINDOWS 95 IN A WORKGROUP ENVIRONMENT

Q: *How can you configure the Client for Microsoft Networks to log onto a Workgroup?*

Choose the best answer:

> A.   *Type the Workgroup's name in the Windows NT Domain field on the Client for Microsoft Networks dialog box.*
>
> B.   *Type the Workgroup's name in the Identification sheet's Workgroup field on the Network Properties dialog box.*
>
> C.   *Place a check mark in the Logon to Workgroup checkbox in the Client for Microsoft Networks Properties dialog box.*
>
> D.   *Install the Windows 95 Workgroup Client.*

As you have learned, Windows 95 can create a networking environment without an authentication server, such as Windows NT server or a Novell NetWare server. You can refer to a network that does not require an authentication server as either a Workgroup network or peer-to-peer network. The term peer-to-peer, however, is the most descriptive for a network with no authenticating server because it describes each network computer's role on the network. In a peer-to-peer network, each computer on the network can be both a client and a server at the same time).

New users and network administrators alike often use the term "workgroup" to describe a Peer to Peer network, which is technically incorrect because workgroups can exist in domains and networks that use other authentication schemes (such as the Windows NT domain model). A workgroup is a group of computers a network administrator groups together under a single NetBIOS name for easy browsing. Misuse of "workgroup" is common, and you should be aware of the correct meaning of workgroup and where its meaning is correct.

Peer-to-peer networking has no authentication server. Instead, each computer is both a server and a client and each user is his or her computer's administrator. In Windows 95, you can install the Client for Microsoft Networks, a protocol suite (such as NetBEUI), and networking hardware (in other words, cards, cable, and other network devices) to create a peer-to-peer network. The Client for Microsoft Networks will automatically assume it is in a peer-to-peer environment unless you configure it to log onto a domain.

On the other hand, a Workgroup is a group of multiple computers that share a single NetBIOS name. To form a Workgroup in Windows 95, type your Workgroup's name in the *Workgroup* field in the Network Properties dialog box's Identification tab on each computer you want to include in the Workgroup.

Answer B is correct because when you type your workgroup's name in the Workgroup field on the Network Properties dialog box, it identifies the computer as being a Windows 95 workgroup member. Answer A is incorrect because when you type the workgroup's name in the Client for Microsoft Networks dialog box's Domain field Windows 95 will search for a Windows NT Domain that has same name. Answer C is incorrect because the Client for Microsoft Networks Properties dialog box has no Workgroup checkbox. Answer D is incorrect because there is no such thing as a Windows 95 Workgroup Client.

878 CUSTOMIZING THE WINDOWS 95 FILE SYSTEM TO SUPPORT SERVER OPERATIONS

Q: *How can you configure the Windows 95 file system to better support server operations?*

Choose the best answer:

A.   *During installation, you must choose Network Server as the installation type.*

B.   *Change the Typical Role of this Machine drop-down list in the File System Properties dialog box.*

C.   *Change the Typical Role of this Machine drop-down list in the Network Properties dialog box.*

D.   *You cannot configure Windows 95 to act as a Network Server.*

As you reviewed in Tip 877, a Peer-to-Peer network does not include an authentication server and, typically, computers on the network can be both server and client. However, in a peer-to-peer environment, you may decide at some point to dedicate a computer to such networking functions as a Print Server, a Mail Server, or a File Server. When a Windows 95 computer assumes a dedicated server's duties, you can optimize the file system to better perform server functions. To optimize the Windows 95 file system to better support server operations, perform the following steps:

1. Within Windows 95, click your mouse on the Start menu and select the Settings group Control Panel option. Windows 95 will open the Control Panel.

2. Within the Control Panel, double-click your mouse on the System option. Windows 95 will open the System Properties dialog box.

3. Within the System Properties dialog box, click your mouse on the Performance tab at the top of the System Properties dialog box. Windows 95 will display the Performance sheet.

4. Within the Performance sheet, click your mouse on the File System button. Windows 95 will open the File System Properties dialog box.

5. Within the File System Properties dialog box, click your mouse on the Typical Role of this Machine drop-down list. Windows 95 will display the choices in the Typical Role of this Machine drop-down list.

6. Within the Typical Role of this Machine drop-down list, choose Network Server from the list of choices. Windows 95 will insert Network Server into the *Typical Role of this Machine* field.

7. Click your mouse on the OK button. Windows 95 will close the System Properties dialog box and prompt you to restart your computer.

8. Click your mouse on the OK button to restart your computer. Windows 95 will restart.

*Answer B is correct because you can change the Typical Role of this Machine field to Network Server in the File System Properties dialog box. **Answer A** is incorrect because there is no Network Server installation type. **Answer C** is incorrect because the Network Properties dialog box does not have a Typical Role of this Machine field. **Answer D** is incorrect because you can configure Windows 95 to act as a network server.*

---

879   UNDERSTANDING WINDOWS 95 WITH WINDOWS NT CLIENT ACCESS LICENSE ISSUES

Q: *Windows 95 includes a client access license for Windows NT.*

True or False?

In many businesses and other enterprise environments, administrators will use Windows NT for the network server and Windows 95 for the operating system on the client computer. One of the most common misconceptions about Windows 95 is that the operating system includes a client access license for Windows NT or Novell NetWare, which is not true. Windows 95 includes a license only for Windows 95.

Unless the computer or software package that you purchase includes verifiable documentation for other licenses, you should assume that you must purchase licenses separately for that product. For example, suppose you have a network that includes ten Windows 95 computers (all licensed) and a single Windows NT Server that includes five client access licenses. In such a case, you must purchase an additional five client access licenses so that all the client computers on your network can legally log onto the Windows NT server.

*The answer is **False** because you must purchase Windows NT client access licenses separately.*

880   **INTRODUCTION TO THE MICROSOFT NETWARE CLIENT FOR WINDOWS 95**

Q: *The Microsoft Client for NetWare Networks cannot log onto a NetWare 4.0 server*

True or False?

As you have learned, Windows 95 provides built-in client protocols that you can use to connect to various network types, such as Windows NT networks and Novell NetWare networks. To provide connectivity to Novell networks, Windows 95 includes a Novell NetWare network client that can log onto and use any Novell NetWare Server's (version 2.15 and higher) file and print sharing services. The Microsoft Client for NetWare Networks can provide authentication and network management through the *SYSCON* utility. However, it cannot use all the network management tools available with newer NetWare versions. Novell also makes a Windows 95 client that it specifically designed to support these new network management applications—such as the Light Directory Access Protocol (LDAP).

If you want to connect a Windows 95 computer to a Novell NetWare Server, but you do not have the Novell-provided client, perform the following steps:

1. Within Windows 95, click your mouse on the Start menu and select the Settings group Control Panel option. Windows 95 will open the Control Panel.

2. Within the Control Panel, double-click your mouse on the Network option. Windows 95 will open the Network Properties dialog box.

3. Within the Network Properties dialog box, click your mouse on the Add button. Windows 95 will open the Select Network Component Type dialog box.

4. Within the Select Network Component Type dialog box, click your mouse on the Client option in the Network Component list. Windows 95 will highlight the Client option to indicate your selection.

5. Within the Select Network Component Type dialog box, click your mouse on the Add button. Windows 95 will search through a built-in database of client protocol entries and display the Add Network Client dialog box.

6. Within the Add Network Client dialog box's Manufacturers list, click your mouse on Microsoft. Windows 95 will highlight Microsoft and display the Microsoft choices in the Network Clients list to indicate your selection.

7. Within the Network Clients list, click your mouse on the Client for NetWare Networks option. Windows 95 will highlight the Client for NetWare Networks option to indicate your selection.

8. Within the Add Network Client dialog box, click your mouse on the OK button. Windows 95 will add the Client for NetWare Networks to the list of installed components in the Network Properties dialog box.

*The answer is **False** because although some NetWare management tools will not function when you use the Microsoft Client for NetWare Networks, the client can still log onto a NetWare 4.0 server.*

881 **UNDERSTANDING NOVELL-SUPPLIED NETWARE CLIENTS FOR WINDOWS 95**

Q: Which of the following answers describe reasons to install the NetWare Client for Windows 95?

Choose the best answer:

A.   *Windows 95 does not include a client for NetWare networks.*

B.   *The Windows 95 Client for NetWare Networks cannot log onto some NetWare servers.*

C.   *The Windows 95 Client for NetWare Networks does not support some network management tools NetWare provides.*

D.   *The Novell Corporation legally requires you to use the NetWare client.*

As you learned in Tip 880, Windows 95 includes a Microsoft-designed Client for NetWare Networks that provides the following for Novell NetWare Servers: connection, authentication, file and print sharing services, and simple network management functions (such as password changes). Novell produces a network client for Windows 95 because the Microsoft-designed client cannot support some of the new network management applications available with newer NetWare. Novell specifically designed its network client to support the newer applications available with newer NetWare versions that the Microsoft Client for NetWare Networks does not support. If you have a NetWare Server version 4.0 or higher, and want to use some or all the advanced network management utilities it includes, you must install the Novell-designed network client.

Note: *Some applications and their associated tools also require the Novell-designed network client for Windows 95.*

***Answer C** is correct because the Windows 95 Client for NetWare Networks does not support some network management tools NetWare provides. **Answer A** is incorrect because Windows 95 does include a client for NetWare networks. **Answer B** is incorrect because the Windows 95 Client for NetWare Networks can log onto all types of NetWare servers. **Answer D** is incorrect because the Novell Corporation legally requires you to have licenses to access their servers, but does not require you to use the NetWare client.*

882 **CONFIGURING NETWARE SERVERS TO SUPPORT LONG FILE NAMES WITH WINDOWS 95 CLIENTS**

Q: NetWare Servers automatically support long file names

True or False?

As you have learned, you must use a network client (either Microsoft or Novell) to connect your Windows 95 computer to a Novell NetWare computer. If you use Windows 95 to connect to a NetWare Server and store files on the server, you may experience problems with the long filenames that you can create in Windows 95—specifically, NetWare may tell you that you cannot save the files, or NetWare may truncate the filenames to a length it accepts. To solve such problems, you must specifically configure NetWare to natively support long filenames.

NetWare servers that the administrator has configured to use the OS2 Name Space can support filenames up to 254 characters long. However, they will truncate file names to support file browsing for 8.3-restricted applications, which can read only MS-DOS-compatible file names. NetWare servers use a different algorithm to create MS-DOS-compatible filenames than Windows 95 does. If two filenames on a NetWare server are similar and a user is trying to use an 8.3-restricted application to browse files, they will appear as follows:

```
thisisalongfilename.txt      will become      thisisa1.txt.
thisisalongerfilename.txt    will become      thisisa0.txt.
```

In Windows 95, however, the operating system would truncate the files differently, making the files appear as follows when you display them within a MS-DOS window:

```
thisisalongfilename.txt      will become      thisis~1.txt.
thisisalongerfilename.txt    will become      thisis~2.txt.
```

*The answer is **False** because you must configure NetWare servers to support long file names.*

883	**RUNNING NETWARE UTILITIES ON A WINDOWS 95 CLIENT COMPUTER**

Q: Which of the following NetWare utilities can you run when you use the Windows 95 Client for NetWare Networks?

Choose all answers that apply:

   A.   *SYSCON*

   B.   *NWADMIN*

   C.   *NETADMIN*

   D.   *NWUSER*

As you have learned, the Client for NetWare Networks that Windows 95 includes cannot support all the new applications services available with newer NetWare versions. For example, the Microsoft-designed client for NetWare Networks can support the NetWare *SYSCON* utility that most NetWare versions include (which you use to manage users and groups, network access, and so on). However, it cannot support the *NWADMIN* or *NETADMIN* utilities that NetWare version 4.0, and higher, includes because they require Novell Directory Services (NDS) to operate correctly. Neither the Microsoft-designed Client for NetWare Networks nor the *NWUSER* utility support NDS. Additionally, the Microsoft Client for NetWare Networks does not support the *NWUSER* utility, which is a NetWare *2.x* Virtual Loadable Module (VLM) utility.

Although it is always best to employ or temporarily hire a networking professional who is proficient with NetWare, cost restrictions may prevent you from doing so. If you must support a NetWare server, you should carefully review all documentation both Microsoft and Novell provide to see if the Microsoft Client for NetWare Networks does not support any utilities you want to use. If the Microsoft Client for NetWare Networks does not support your utilities, you must obtain and load the Novell-designed network client for Windows 95.

Answer A is correct because SYSCON is an example of a NetWare 3.x utility that the Windows 95 Client for NetWare Networks supports. Answers B and C are incorrect because NWADMIN and NETADMIN are examples of NetWare 4.x utilities that require NDS and the Windows 95 Client for NetWare Networks does not support them. Answer D is incorrect because NWUSER is a NetWare 2.x VLM utility that the Windows 95 Client for NetWare Networks does not support.

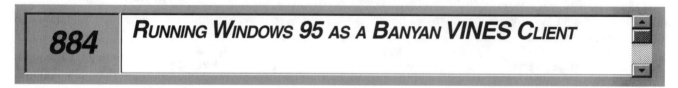

884 ― RUNNING WINDOWS 95 AS A BANYAN *VINES* CLIENT

Q: Windows 95 includes a 32-bit client to connect to Banyan VINES as a primary network.

True or False?

As you have learned, Windows 95 supports several different network clients, including network clients for Microsoft networks and NetWare networks. It also includes support for other network clients. Some network clients Windows 95 includes require special considerations when you load them. For example, if you want to use a Banyan VINES network client as the primary network logon, the Client for Microsoft Networks, and the Client for NetWare Networks, you must get a 32-bit client from Banyan. Windows 95 includes a 16-bit Banyan VINES client for MS-DOS and Windows 3.x that you cannot combine with 32-bit clients, such as the Client for Microsoft Networks or the Client for NetWare Networks. In other words, if you implement the Windows 95 default Banyan VINES client as a primary network logon, you cannot use the Microsoft and NetWare clients in the same Network Neighborhood. There may be times when you must install an MS-DOS-based client before you install Windows 95 so that Windows 95 will recognize and properly connect to the network. You must ensure that if you install Windows 95 into a networking environment that is neither Microsoft- nor NetWare- based, you are familiar with that particular networking environment's client issues—such as the 16-bit client issue with the Banyan VINES client. Windows 95 includes only two 32-bit network clients, the Client for Microsoft Networks and the Client for NetWare Networks. All other clients Windows 95 includes are 16-bit clients that might require additional software from the manufacturer or special loading procedures to function properly.

*The answer is **False** because Banyan provides a Windows 95 32-bit client to connect to Banyan VINES as a primary network, but Windows 95 does not include the client.*

885 ― RUNNING WINDOWS 95 AS A DEC PATHWORKS CLIENT

Q: Which of the following DEC PATHWORKS versions does Windows 95 automatically support?
Choose the best answer:

     A.   *Version 4.x*

     B.   *Version 5.x*

     C.   *Versions 5.x and 4.x*

     D.   *None. Windows 95 does not support DEC PATHWORKS.*

As you learned in Tip 884, not all network clients Windows 95 includes are 32-bit and may require additional software or special installation procedures to function properly. Additionally, you can support some networking environments within Windows 95 without a dedicated network client. An excellent example of network support without a dedicated network client is connecting a Windows 95 computer to Digital Equipment Corporation's (DEC) PATHWORKS networks.

To successfully operate Windows 95 in a DEC PATHWORKS environment, you must load both the Client for Microsoft Networks and the DEC PATHWORKS protocol. (Windows 95 does not include a DEC PATHWORKS client.) After you have installed the Windows 95 *autexec.bat* file, you must edit it to contain the *startnet.bat* command (which will load the DEC PATHWORKS client). In addition, a *startnet.bat* file, which starts DEC PATHWORKS, must be present on the computer and in the command path. Using the nested batch files to load the PATHWORKS client will let you support DEC PATHWORKS version *5.x.* Windows 95 can support older DEC PATHWORKS versions, but you must have additional software and follow special installation procedures. For example, to support DEC PATHWORKS version *4.1,* you must install appropriate support (that is, the network client) into Windows for Workgroups 3.11 and then upgrade Windows for Workgroups with Windows 95.

Answer B is correct because Windows 95 automatically supports DEC PATHWORKS version 5.x. Answers A and C are incorrect because although Windows 95 can support DEC PATHWORKS version 4.x, you must install the support before you install Windows 95. Answer D is incorrect because Windows 95 does support DEC PATHWORKS.

886   **INTRODUCTION TO WINDOWS 95 BROWSING**

Q: *How can you ensure that a Windows 95 computer will not become a master browser on the network?*

Choose the best answer:

> A.   *Disable the Browse-Master option in the Client for Microsoft Networks Properties dialog box.*
>
> B.   *Disable the Browse-Master option in the File and Print Sharing Properties dialog box.*
>
> C.   *You must edit the Windows 95 Registry.*
>
> D.   *Windows 95 computers cannot become master browsers.*

As you learned earlier in this section, Windows 95 uses NetBIOS names to produce the list of computers it displays within the Network Neighborhood window. You also learned that in Windows 95, you enter a computer's NetBIOS name into the Network Properties dialog box on the Identification tab. To produce a list of NetBIOS names for you to choose from, the network must perform a behind-the-scenes browsing action that gets the names from each computer and keeps them in a list. Because network speeds would slow significantly if every computer on the network performed such browsing to obtain NetBIOS names, Microsoft networks use a scheme in which certain computers browse and others do not. In Tips 373 through 374, you learned about the different roles that a computer can take in the browse process and how browsing functions on a NetBIOS network.

In some networking environments you may want to instruct a Windows 95 computer to either browse or not browse. In Windows 95, you configure the browse options in the File and Print Sharing Properties dialog box. To open the File and Print Sharing dialog box, perform the following steps:

> 1. Within Windows 95, click your mouse on the Start menu Sand select the settings group Control Panel option. Windows 95 will open the Control Panel.

2. Within the Control Panel, double-click your mouse on the Network option. Windows 95 will open the Network Properties dialog box.

3. Within the Network Properties dialog box, click your mouse on the File and Print Sharing option in the list of installed network components. Windows 95 will highlight File and Print Sharing to indicate your selection.

4. Within the Network Properties dialog box, click your mouse on the Properties button. Windows 95 will open the File and Print Sharing Properties dialog box.

5. Within the Property list, click your mouse on the Browse Master option. Windows 95 will highlight Browse Master to indicate your selection.

6. Within the File and Print Sharing Properties dialog box, click your mouse on the Value drop-down list. Windows 95 will display the options in the Value drop-down list.

7. Within the Value drop-down list, choose between Enabled, Disabled, or Automatic based on your requirement. Windows 95 will insert your choice in the *Value* field.

8. Within the File and Print Sharing Properties dialog box, click your mouse on the OK button. Windows 95 will return you to the Network Properties dialog box.

9. Within the Network Properties dialog box, click your mouse on the OK button. Windows 95 will close the Network Properties dialog box and prompt you to restart your computer.

10. In the Restart dialog box, click your mouse on the OK button to restart your computer. Windows 95 will restart.

Answer B is correct because if you disable the Browse-Master option in the File and Print Sharing Properties dialog box, a Windows 95 computer will not become a Master Browser on the network. Answer A is incorrect because the Client for Microsoft Networks Properties dialog box does not have a Browse-Master option. Answer C is incorrect because Windows 95 does not require you to edit its Registry to prevent a Windows 95 computer from becoming a Master Browser on the network. Answer D is incorrect because a Windows 95 Computer can become a Master Browser on the network.

887   **CONNECTING TO SHARED NETWORK RESOURCES WITH WINDOWS 95**

Q: Which of the following answers best describe the term "shared network resource"?

Choose the best answer:

    A.   *A special device that lets you connect more than one computer to a single power outlet.*

    B.   *A folder or printer that the administrator has made available to network users.*

    C.   *The Internet.*

    D.   *The network hub that connects all computers when using a Star topology for the network architecture.*

As previous Tips detail, Windows 95 provides a set of network clients that you can use to easily connect your Windows 95 computer to a network. Additionally, the built-in networking support in Windows 95 lets you easily connect to *shared network resources* with a few mouse clicks. A shared network resource is a folder or printer that the network administrator has made available to network users. Most of the time you will connect to shared network resources through the Network Neighborhood. To activate the Network Neighborhood, double-click your mouse on the Network Neighborhood icon on your Desktop.

After you open the Network Neighborhood, it will display a list of computers, workgroups, and domains. The computers that appear in the initial list are part of your workgroup. To reach other computers, you must expand the workgroups and domains and view the computers in the expanded list. When you have identified the computer that hosts the shared resource you want, double-click your mouse on that computer. Windows 95 will open another window that displays the shared resources that computer hosts.

*Answer B is correct because a shared network resource is best described as a file, folder, or printer that the network administrator has made available to network users. **Answers A, C, and D** are incorrect because they do not describe the term shared network resource.*

888   ***Understanding Mapped Drives***

Q: *Where in Windows 95 can you "map" a drive letter to a shared network resource?*

Choose all answers that apply:

     A.   *My Computer*

     B.   *Windows 95 Explorer*

     C.   *Network Neighborhood*

     D.   *You cannot "map" drive letters to shared network resources in Windows 95*

In Tip 887, you learned how use the Network Neighborhood to connect to a shared resource on the network. Another way to connect to a shared resource is through *"mapped" drive*s, which are semi-permanent logical connections to shared network resources that are given a drive letter, similar to your hard drive's letter. Mapped drives are important because many applications cannot use Universal Naming Convention (UNC) paths to reach a shared resource and must have a drive letter.

To map a drive letter to a shared network resource, locate the resource in the Network Neighborhood and right-click your mouse on it. Windows 95 will produce a pop-up menu that includes the option "Map Drive." When you use the Map Drive option, you can choose a drive letter for the resource to which you want to map a drive. Additionally, network administrators or advanced users can type in the UNC path from within My Computer, Network Neighborhood, or Windows Explorer to map drives.

*Answers A, B, and C are correct because you can map drives in My Computer, Windows 95 Explorer, and Network Neighborhood. **Answer D** is incorrect because you can map drives in Windows 95.*

889   ***Sharing Network Resources with Windows 95***

Q: *Where can you configure sharing for a resource on a Windows 95 computer?*

Choose the best answer:

A. *You cannot; only resources on a Windows NT Server can be shared.*

B. *In the Properties dialog box for Networking.*

C. *In the Properties dialog box for the resource.*

D. *In the Properties dialog box for the System.*

In Tip 888, you learned how to connect to a shared network resource. Just as someone shared that other network resource because they felt it was important for you to have access to it, you may also want to create shared network resources on your computer for other users to access. For example, suppose you have a printer that you want other computers in the network to be able to print to, or you have files you want to share with other users.

You can "share" your resources on the network so other users may attach to or access the printer or files, and you must do so from the resource's Properties dialog box. In other words, if you have a folder named Files and you want to share it on the network, you must access the Files folder's Properties dialog box. To access a resource's Properties dialog box, perform the following steps:

1. Within Windows 95, right-click your mouse on the resource you want to share. Windows 95 will display a pop-up menu.

2. Within the pop-up menu, choose the Sharing option. Windows 95 will open the resource's Properties dialog box and display the Sharing sheet.

Note: *You must install File Sharing support on the Windows 95 computer to enable the Sharing tab (and the sharing option on the pop-up menu).*

The steps you follow to share your resources depend on the security method you have chosen. For Password-level sharing, you can either share the resource with one password for Read-only and another password for Full-access, or you can share the resource with no password. For User-level sharing, you must add users or groups with whom you are sharing the resource, as well as their access levels. Refer to Tip 646 for more information about User-level security in Windows 95, and Tip 639 for more information about Password-level security in Windows 95.

Answer C is correct because you can configure sharing for a resource in its Properties dialog box. Answer A is incorrect because you can share resources on a Windows 95 computer. Answers B and D are incorrect because you cannot configure sharing for a resource in either the Networking Properties or the System Properties dialog boxes.

| 890 | ADDING FILE AND PRINT SHARING FOR WINDOWS 95 AFTER INSTALLATION |

Q: *You can click your mouse on the File and Print Sharing button in the Network Properties dialog box to install the special software components that file and print sharing require.*

True or False?

In Tip 889, you learned how to share a resource to the network, and that you must install File and Print Sharing support on the Windows 95 computer to share that resource. Although you typically install File and Print Sharing components during Windows 95 Setup, you can still do so after Setup.

File and Print Sharing components are specific to the network client on which you want to share files. Additionally, you can have only one File and Print Sharing components set installed at a time. For example, if you have both the Client for Microsoft Networks and the Client for NetWare Networks installed on the same Windows 95 computer, you can install a File and Print Sharing components set for only one client network program, which can then share files and printers to the other network. To install File and Print Sharing components, perform the following steps:

1. Within Windows 95, click your mouse on the Start menu and select the Settings group Control Panel option. Windows 95 will open the Control Panel.

2. Within the Control Panel, double-click your mouse on the Network option. Windows 95 will open the Network Properties dialog box.

3. Within the Network Properties dialog box, click your mouse on the Add button. Windows 95 will open the Select Network Component Type dialog box.

4. Within the Select Network Component Type dialog box, click your mouse on Services in the list of network components you can install. Windows 95 will highlight Services to indicate your selection.

5. Within the Select Network Component Type dialog box, click your mouse on the Add button. Windows 95 will open the Select Network Service dialog box.

6. Within the Select Network Service dialog box, click your mouse on Microsoft in the list of Manufacturers. Windows 95 will highlight Microsoft and display the Microsoft Services in the Network Service list to indicate your selection.

7. Within the Select Network Service dialog box, click your mouse on the File and Print Sharing for (Microsoft or NetWare) Networks option. Windows 95 will highlight your selection.

8. Within the Select Network Service dialog box, click your mouse on the OK button. Windows 95 will return you to the Network Properties dialog box.

9. Within the Network Properties dialog box, click your mouse on the OK button. Windows 95 will close the Network Properties dialog box and prompt you to restart your computer.

10. Within the Restart prompt, click your mouse on the OK button to restart your computer. Windows 95 will restart

*The answer is **True** because you can click your mouse on the File and Print Sharing button in the Network Properties Dialog box to install the software components that file and print sharing require.*

891 CONFIGURING NETWORK BINDINGS FOR WINDOWS 95

Q: Which of the following configuration options can you perform on protocol bindings in Windows 95?

Choose all answers that apply:

    A.   Bound

    B.   Unbound

    C.   Primary Protocol

    D.   You cannot configure protocol bindings in Windows 95

In Tips 354 and 355, you learned about network protocol bindings and how to configure them in Windows NT. Although the control level is not as high in Windows 95 as it is in Windows NT, you can also configure the network protocol bindings in Windows 95.

You must configure the network protocol bindings in Windows 95 in each protocol's Properties dialog box. Configurable options include Bound, Unbound, and Primary Protocol. In other words, you can turn a protocol's binding on or off and specify one protocol as the primary (or first) protocol the operating system will search. To set a protocol as the Primary Protocol, perform the following steps:

1. Within Windows 95, click your mouse on the Start menu and select the Settings group Control Panel option. Windows 95 will open the Control Panel.

2. Within the Control Panel, double click your mouse on the Network option. Windows 95 will open the Network Properties dialog box.

3. Within the Network Properties dialog box, click your mouse on a protocol. Windows 95 will highlight the protocol to indicate your selection.

4. Within the Network Properties dialog box, click your mouse on the Properties button. Windows 95 will open the Properties dialog box for the protocol you selected.

5. Within the Properties dialog box, click your mouse on the Advanced tab. Windows 95 will display the Advanced sheet.

6. Within the Properties dialog box's Advanced sheet, click your mouse on the Set This Protocol to be the Default Protocol checkbox. Windows 95 will place a check mark in the checkbox to indicate your selection.

7. Within the Properties dialog box, click your mouse on the OK button. Windows 95 will return you to the Network Properties dialog box.

8. Within the Network Properties dialog box, click your mouse on the OK button. Windows 95 will close the Network Properties dialog box and prompt you to restart your computer.

9. Within the Restart prompt, click your mouse on the OK button to restart your computer. Windows 95 will restart.

Answers A, B, and *C are correct because you can configure a protocol as either bound to a specific device or unbound to a specific device, and you can set a protocol as the computer's primary protocol. Answer D is incorrect because you can configure protocol bindings in Windows 95.*

---

892   UNDERSTANDING NETBIOS OVER IPX/SPX

Q: *How can you configure Windows 95 to send application requests that normally use NetBIOS over the IPX/SPX protocol?*

Choose the best answer:

     A.   *Install NetBIOS and the IPX/SPX compatible protocol and unbind NetBIOS.*

     B.   *Place a check mark in the Enable NetBIOS over IPX/SPX checkbox in the IPX/SPX Properties dialog box.*

     C.   *Place a check mark in the Enable NetBIOS over IPX/SPX checkbox in the File and Print Sharing Properties dialog box.*

     D.   *You cannot configure Windows 95 to send application requests that normally use NetBIOS over the IPX/SPX protocol.*

As you have learned, Microsoft networks use the NetBIOS protocol and Novell NetWare networks use the IPX/SPX protocol. Because so many applications use NetBIOS to function, but many networks do not use NetBIOS or a

NetBIOS-based protocol, Windows 95 must provide a means for applications to communicate on non-NetBIOS networks. The Windows 95 IPX/SPX compatible protocol has an option that lets you instruct applications that normally use NetBIOS to instead use the IPX/SPX protocol. You can configure the IPX/SPX protocol substitution option from the IPX/SPX Properties dialog box.

Answer B is correct because when you place a check mark in the Enable NetBIOS over IPX/SPX in the IPX/SPX Properties dialog box, Windows 95 will send application requests that normally use NetBIOS over the IPX/SPX-compatible protocol. Answers A and C are incorrect because they do not describe how to configure Windows 95 to send application requests that normally use NetBIOS over the IPX/SPX compatible protocol. Answer D is incorrect because you can configure Windows 95 to send application requests that normally use NetBIOS over the IPX/SPX compatible protocol.

893 TROUBLESHOOTING WINDOWS 95 PROTOCOL PROBLEMS

Q: *The NET DIAG tool can tell you if a computer is communicating on the network but requires that you run it on two computers to function properly.*

True or False?

After you install and configure the protocols that Windows 95 requires to connect to a network, you may occasionally find that the computer still will not communicate on the network. Troubleshooting network problems can be difficult and frustrating (because there are so many potential problems), whether you are a small network administrator with a simple Peer-to-Peer network or a networking professional with ten different network protocols within different domains.

Problems that prevent a computer's connection to the server can occur in the networking hardware, the cable system, the protocol, the network services, or from a user error. Many of the tools and techniques you have learned in this book will help you to troubleshoot networking problems. One tool that is specific to Windows 95, and that network administrators frequently overlook, is the *NET DIAG* command.

NET DIAG is a utility program that requires two computers to perform its full functions, but can provide insight into some problems (such as the operating system not loading the correct protocols) on a single computer. To initiate the program, type *NET DIAG* at the command prompt. *NET DIAG* will produce a list of loaded protocols to use for the network communications test.

If you know a protocol has previously been loaded onto the computer but it is not present, you have a problem with the protocol and should remove and reinstall it. Next, choose a protocol with which *NET DIAG* should perform the network communications test. *NET DIAG* will try to locate a *NET DIAG* server. If it does not find one, it will give you the option to act as the *NET DIAG* server.

After a computer is acting as a *NET DIAG* server, initiate the program again on another computer and choose the same protocol for the network communications test. If *NET DIAG* returns positive test results, you have verified the network card, cable, and protocol presence on the network of both computers.

Note: NET DIAG does not test across and will not recognize the TCP/IP protocol.

*The answer is **True** because the NET DIAG command can easily tell you if a computer is communicating on the network but requires two computers to function.*

| 894 | CONFIGURING WINDOWS 95 CLIENTS TO USE WINPOPUP | |

Q: *Windows 95 will automatically install the winpopup.exe program with either the Client for Microsoft Networks or Client for NetWare Networks that Windows includes.*

True or False?

A program that many network users find helpful and that most Windows 95 installation types automatically install is the *winpopup.exe* program, a network communication utility that lets users send instant messages to each other. In addition, you can configure *winpopup.exe* to receive administrative alerts. To start the *winpopup.exe* program, type *winpopup* at the Run command or at an MS-DOS command prompt. You can also place a shortcut to *winpopup.exe* in the Windows 95 Start menu's Startup group to configure Windows 95 to always start *winpopup.exe* at system start.

The answer is **True** *because Windows 95 automatically installs winpopup.exe with both the Client for Microsoft Networks and Client for NetWare Networks.*

| 895 | SETTING UP SECURITY FOR WIN95 SHARED RESOURCES | |

Q: *What is required for Windows 95 to use User-level security on shared resources?*

Choose the best answer:

    A.   *An authentication server (Windows NT Domain Controller or NetWare Server).*

    B.   *A list of users on the network.*

    C.   *Exchange must be installed.*

    D.   *Nothing. Windows 95 can always use User-level security.*

As you have learned, Windows 95 can use either Password-level or User-level security to share resources. Although User-level security requires an authentication server, such as Windows NT Server or Novell NetWare, you can implement Password-level security in a workgroup using only Windows 95. You must manually configure Windows 95 to take advantage of User-level security because the operating system does not automatically activate Windows 95 when an authentication server is present. You perform the User-level security configuration in the Network Properties dialog box on the Access Control tab. To configure User-level security, perform the following steps:

1.   Within Windows 95, click your mouse on the Start menu and select the Settings group Control Panel option. Windows 95 will open the Control Panel.

2.   Within the Control Panel, double-click your mouse on the Network option. Windows 95 will open the Network Properties dialog box.

3.   Within the Network Properties dialog box, click your mouse on the Access Control tab at the top of the dialog box. Windows 95 will display the Access Control sheet.

4. Within the Access Control sheet, click your mouse on the User-level Access Control check box. Windows 95 will place a dot in the User-level Access Control checkbox and enable the *Obtain list of users and groups from* field.

5. Within the *Obtain list of users and groups from* field, type your authentication server's name. Windows 95 will insert the text you type into the field.

6. Within the Access Control sheet, click your mouse on the OK button. Windows 95 will search the network for the authentication server, verify its presence, and then prompt you to restart your computer.

7. Within the Restart prompt, click your mouse on the OK button to restart your computer. Windows 95 will restart.

Answer A is correct because Windows 95 requires an authentication server, such as a Windows NT Domain Controller or a NetWare Server. Answers B, C, and D are incorrect because without an authentication server, Windows 95 cannot use User-level security.

896	INTRODUCTION TO THE MICROSOFT EXCHANGE CLIENT THAT WINDOWS 95 INCLUDES

Q: *What is the minimum amount of physical memory Windows 95 requires to run the Microsoft Exchange Client?*

Choose the best answer:

    A.   *4Mb*

    B.   *8Mb*

    C.   *16Mb*

    D.   *32Mb*

Along with the *winpopup.exe* program and other network-based applications, Windows 95 includes the Microsoft *Exchange Client* program, which is a general messaging tool that can serve as a center for on-line faxing, an Internet e-mail client, or a client to Microsoft Mail or Exchange Server for internal network messaging.

The *Exchange Client* is extremely memory-consumptive and doubles the minimum amount of physical memory Windows 95 requires to run from 4Mb to 8Mb.

You can use the Microsoft *Exchange Client* and the Microsoft Workgroup Mail tools Windows 95 includes to create an internal e-mail system on a peer-to-peer network. Each user can use the *Exchange Client* to send and receive e-mail to and from other users on the network.

Note: Windows 95 OEM Service Release 2 does not include the tools to create a Workgroup post office.

Answer B is correct because although the minimum amount of physical memory Windows 95 requires to run is four megabytes, it requires an additional four megabytes to run the Microsoft Exchange Client, which results in a minimum of eight megabytes. Answers A, C, and D are incorrect because they list values that are higher or lower than the actual amount of physical memory Windows 95 requires to run with the Microsoft Exchange Client.

897 — INTRODUCTION TO MICROSOFT FAX IN WINDOWS 95

Q: *Which of the following components does Microsoft Fax require to operate?*

Choose all answers that apply:

    A.   *A modem*

    B.   *Dial-up Networking*

    C.   *Microsoft Exchange*

    D.   *Third-party faxing software*

As you learned in Tip 896, Windows 95 includes the Microsoft *Exchange Client* messaging program. Another messaging program Windows 95 includes is the Microsoft *Fax* service, which is a program that lets you send and receive faxes from applications that have been specifically designed to send faxes to a fax service, such as Microsoft *Word* or the Microsoft *Exchange Client*. Microsoft *Fax* has built-in security features and supports binary file transfer (BFT), which lets you attach a document to an e-mail message. In addition, Microsoft *Fax* is compatible with most popular fax modems. When you install Microsoft *Fax*, you are actually installing a series of special device drivers and software components. The device drivers and software components include the fax viewer that lets you quickly read and browse faxes, as well as document examples, such as fax cover sheets. To install Microsoft *Fax*, perform the following steps:

1. Within Windows 95, click your mouse on the Start menu and select the Settings group Control Panel option. Windows 95 will open the Control Panel.

2. Within the Control Panel, double-click your mouse on the Add/Remove programs option. Windows 95 will open the Add/Remove programs dialog box.

3. Within the Add/Remove programs dialog box, click your mouse on the Windows Setup tab. Windows 95 will display the Windows Setup sheet.

4. Within the Windows Setup tab, choose Microsoft *Fax* from the list of optional components and click your mouse on the OK button. Windows 95 will install Microsoft *Fax*.

Answer A is correct because Microsoft Fax requires a modem to operate. Answers B, C, and D are incorrect because you can install and use Microsoft Fax without Dial-up Networking, Microsoft Exchange, or third-party faxing software.

898 — INTRODUCTION TO DIAL-UP NETWORKING IN WINDOWS 95

Q: *Which of the following network protocols must you manually install for Dial-up Networking to function?*

Choose the best answer:

    A.   *TCP/IP*

    B.   *IPX/SPX*

    C.   *NetBEUI*

    D.   *None; Windows 95 automatically installs some protocols when you install Dial-up Networking.*

In the Windows NT sections of this book, you learned about Windows NT's Remote Access Service (RAS), which lets remote users access the network over a phone line or an Internet connection as is they were physically connected to the network. Windows 95 includes Dial-up Networking, which is an optional component that lets you use a normal telephone line to connect to remote networks or the Internet. You can use Dial-up Networking with any Windows 95 computer that has a modem. Windows 95 Dial-up Networking can dial into such remote access servers as a Windows 95 dial-up server, a Windows NT Remote Access Service (RAS), Shiva servers, NetModem, LanRover, and Novell NetWare Connect. To connect two computers over a normal telephone line requires that the computers both use a series of protocols that can both establish communications and carry data between the computers.

The first set of protocols that remote access requires are Connection Protocols, which define the communication rules over Wide-Area Networks (WANs). Windows 95 Dial-up Networking supports the following Connection Protocols:

- Point-to-Point Protocol (PPP)
- Novell NetWare Connect
- Windows NT 3.1 Remote Access Service (RAS)
- Serial Line Internet Protocol (SLIP)

Remote access communication (which begins only after the connection completes) also requires a network protocol that can define the standards for data exchange. When you install Dial-up Networking, Windows 95 will automatically bind any network protocol you have already installed on the computer to the device drivers for Dial-up Networking. Additionally, Windows 95 will automatically install the IPX/SPX and NetBEUI protocols if they are not present. Windows 95 Dial-up Networking supports the following Network Protocols:

- IPX/SPX
- NetBEUI
- TCP/IP

Dial-up Networking will use a Connection Protocol to establish a connection to a remote computer The Connection Protocol then acts as a logical tunnel through which a Network Protocol can carry data. Not all Connection Protocols can support all Network Protocols. For example, the SLIP Connection Protocol can support only the TCP/IP Network Protocol. Table 898 shows you which Connection Protocols can support which Network Protocols.

Connection Protocol	Network Protocols supported
Point to Point Protocol(PPP)	TCP/IP, IPX/SPX, NetBEUI
Novell NetWare Connect	IPX/SPX
Windows NT 3.1 RAS	NetBEUI
Serial Line Internet Protocol(SLIP)	TCP/IP

Table 898 Connection Protocols and the Network Protocols they support.

Answer D is correct because Windows 95 automatically installs some network protocols (NetBEUI and IPX/SPX) when you install Dial-up Networking. Answers A, B, and C are incorrect because Windows 95 does not require you to manually install any protocols for Dial-up Networking to function.

899 **USING WINDOWS 95 AS A DIAL-UP SERVER**

Q: How many remote clients can simultaneously access a network through a Windows 95 Dial-up Networking Server?

Choose the best answer:

>   *A.   1*
>
>   *B.   10*
>
>   *C.   20*
>
>   *D.   0 (Windows 95 Dial-up Networking Servers cannot grant access to the network.)*

In Tip 898, you learned that Windows 95 Dial-up Networking lets you connect to remote servers, such as a Windows NT Remote Access Service (RAS) Server or a Windows 95 Dial-up Server, over normal telephone lines. Windows 95, however, does not include the ability to become a Dial-up Server (that is, it cannot receive an incoming Dial-up Networking connection). You must purchase and install the Microsoft Plus Pack for Windows 95 to configure Windows 95 as a Dial-up Server. The Windows 95 Dial-up Server software the Microsoft Plus Pack includes can act as a gateway to a network for remote Dial-up clients and can route TCP/IP through the network to the remote client. The Dial-up Server supports one connection at a time and cannot support more, even if you install more than one modem. The Windows 95 Dial-up Networking Server can support the following clients:

- Windows 95 Dial-up Networking Client

- Windows for Workgroups

- Windows 3.1 RAS

- Any PPP client

Answer A is correct because one remote client at a time can access a network through a Windows 95 Dial-up Networking Server. Answers B and C are incorrect because they list values that are higher than the actual maximum number of remote clients that can simultaneously access a network through a Windows 95 Dial-up Networking Server. Answer D is incorrect because Windows 95 Dial-up Networking Servers can grant access to the network.

900   **UNDERSTANDING DIAL-UP SERVER SECURITY**

Q: You cannot use User-level security when you connect to the network over a Windows 95 Dial-up Networking Server.

True or False?

As you have learned, you can use the Dial-up Networking Server that the Microsoft Plus Pack includes to configure Windows 95 to act as a gateway to a network. You have also learned in previous Tips about the Password-level and User-level security that can secure the access to shared network resources in Windows 95. When Windows 95 uses Dial-up Networking to connect to a remote network, many times the user or administrator will want to use User-level security to protect shared resources on the remote client—just as if the user were directly using the network.

When you configure Windows 95 to use User-level security over Dial-up Networking, the user must log onto the authentication server when he or she connects. For example, if you have a Windows 95 computer at home and you connect to a Windows NT domain over Dial-up Networking, and you have configured the Windows 95 computer to use User-level security, the following will be true.

- When you turn on your computer at home, you will not receive a log-on dialog box for the domain.

- When you connect to the network, Windows 95 will display a domain log-on dialog box.

- Only users you have chosen from a list may access resources on the Windows 95 computer that you have marked as shared.

- The Windows NT authentication server will validate users who are trying to access your resources.

In addition to using User-level security on Windows NT servers, you can also use User-level security on Windows 95 Dial-up Servers. In other words, a Windows 95 computer you have configured as a Dial-up Networking Server can grant access only to certain users based on their network logon instead of only a password. User-level security in a Dial-up Server increases control over network access because an unauthorized user must know the dial-up phone number, a valid user name, and the associated password. Users and administrators are also more likely to change their network logon password more frequently than they would on a Password-level Dial-up connection—because that password controls access to the entire network, not just a single resource.

*The **Answer** is **False** because you can use User-level security when you attach to a network through a Windows 95 Dial-up Networking Server.*

901 INTRODUCTION TO THE MICROSOFT NETWORK (MSN)

Q: MSN is which of the following?

Choose the best answer:

> *A.   A network of computer professionals who can assist you in troubleshooting your Microsoft systems.*
>
> *B.   An on-line service that will provide you with Internet access and other related services.*
>
> *C.   A description of local-area networks (LANs) that use Microsoft products.*
>
> *D.   A popular news channel.*

The *Microsoft Network (MSN)* is one of the more popular on-line services to which you can connect with your computer and modem. MSN provides you with Internet access and additional services, such as virtual chat rooms, newsgroups, and Internet e-mail. MSN has changed since its original implementation (a dial-in service with a proprietary front-end) and is now primarily a series of secure Web sites that you connect to with *Internet Explorer*, and only if you are an MSN member. MSN is a billable service and, although the software is free and you can obtain it from Microsoft, you must pay for the time that you are using the service, usually on a monthly flat-rate basis.

Windows 95 includes a program that will help you install MSN as long as you have a modem. However, depending on the Windows 95 version you have, you may have to download or otherwise install the new software MSN requires. If the software your Windows 95 version includes does not install the new MSN, you can download or order a copy of the new software from Microsoft.

***Answer B** is correct because the Microsoft Network (MSN) is an on-line service that will provide you with Internet access as well as other on-line services. **Answers A, C,** and **D** are incorrect because they do not describe MSN.*

902   SETTING UP A MODEM IN WINDOWS 95

Q: *Which of the following are methods of installing a modem in Windows 95?*

Choose all answers that apply:

     A.   *Use the Microsoft Windows 95 Modem Installer application.*

     B.   *Plug in the modem and let Windows 95 automatically detect your modem at system startup.*

     C.   *Use the Control Panel Modem dialog box.*

     D.   *Use the Device Manager's Install button in the System Properties dialog box.*

As you have learned, to use Dial-up Networking or the Microsoft Network, your computer must have a modem. Many new computers come with a modem already installed that you will configure during the Windows 95 Setup process. You can, however, install a modem after Setup either by letting Windows 95 detect the modem after you have installed it, or by using the Modems option in Windows 95 Control Panel. To install a modem that Windows 95 did not automatically detect, perform the following steps:

1. Click your mouse on the Start menu and select the Settings group Control Panel option. Windows 95 will open the Control Panel.

2. Click your mouse on the Modems Option. Windows 95 will open the Install New Modem Wizard, which will give you a choice to automatically detect the modem or to install it. You should always let the Wizard attempt to detect your modem first, and you should install it only if the Wizard is unable to find the modem.

3. To install the modem, click your mouse on the *Do not detect my modem I will select it from a list* checkbox. Windows 95 will indicate your selection by placing a check mark in the checkbox.

4. Click your mouse on Next. Windows 95 will display the Install New Modem dialog box.

5. Within the Install New Modem dialog box, choose your modem's manufacturer and model from the appropriate lists within the dialog box and click your mouse on the Next button. Windows 95 will display the next Install New Modem dialog box in the Wizard.

6. Within the Install New Modem dialog box, choose the communication port your modem is installed on and click your mouse on the Next button. Windows 95 will install your modem.

Answers B and C are correct because you can install a modem either by using the Control Panel Modem dialog box or by letting Windows 95 automatically detect your modem. Answer A is incorrect because there is no Microsoft Modem Installer program in Windows 95. Answer D is incorrect because you can view modem information or refresh an automatic detection only from the Device Manager dialog box, which has no Install button.

903   UNDERSTANDING THE MODEM REGISTRY KEY IN WINDOWS 95

Q: *To find the modems attached to your Windows 95 computer in the Registry, you would have to go to HKEY_LOCAL_ MACHINE\System\CurrentControlSet\Services\Class\Modem.*

True or False?

As you have learned, in general, you should not edit the Windows 95 Registry unless you have no other option. However, there may be times when you must directly edit the Registry to accomplish your goal—for example, to set specific modem properties. You can edit the Windows 95 Registry with the *Registry Editor* (*regedit.exe*) program that Windows 95 includes.

You will learn more about the Windows 95 *Registry Editor* program in Tip 919. Although the Windows 95 Exam 70–40: Implementing and Supporting Windows 95 does not test you on specific configuration settings in the Registry, it may ask you the location of modem settings. To answer such questions, you must know the Registry key for modem settings, *HKEY_LOCAL_MACHINE\System\CurrentControlSet\Services\Class\Modem*.

The answer is **True** *because modem configuration information is stored in the Windows 95 Registry under HKEY_LOCAL_ MACHINE\System\CurrentControlSet\Services\Class\Modem.*

904   **USING HYPERTERMINAL IN WINDOWS 95**

Q: *Which of the following are tasks you can perform using the HyperTerminal program?*

Choose all answers that apply:

    A.   *Connect to a remote server to access your e-mail.*

    B.   *Establish a remote NetBIOS node session to a Windows NT server.*

    C.   *Connect to a Bulletin Board System (BBS).*

    D.   *Fax documents.*

Another program Windows 95 includes that uses a modem to function is *HyperTerminal*, which you can use with a modem to connect to a remote computer. Generally, you will use *HyperTerminal* to connect to certain dial-in computers that require a terminal emulator. You can also use *HyperTerminal* to send and receive files or to connect to computer *Bulletin Board Services (BBS)* and other information programs. In addition, *HyperTerminal* can connect to another computer using a serial cable and can communicate with non-Windows computers.

Windows 95 automatically installs *HyperTerminal* on your computer when you use the Portable installation type. Other installations do not install *HyperTerminal* unless you specify (such as within a Custom installation). To install *HyperTerminal* after you install Windows 95, perform the following steps:

1. Click your mouse on the Start menu and select the Settings group Control Panel option. Windows 95 will open the Control Panel.

2. Within the Control Panel, click your mouse on the Add/Remove Programs icon. Windows 95 will open the Add/Remove Programs dialog box.

3. Within the Add/Remove Programs dialog box, click your mouse on the Windows Setup tab. Windows 95 will change your view to the Windows Setup tab.

4. Within the Windows Setup tab, double-click your mouse on the Communication option. Windows 95 will open the Communications dialog box.

5. Within the Communications dialog box, click your mouse on the HyperTerminal option. Windows 95 will indicate selection by placing a check mark in the checkbox next to the HyperTerminal option.

6. Click your mouse on the OK button. Windows 95 will return you to the Add/Remove Programs dialog box.

7. Within the Add/Remove Programs dialog box, click your mouse on the OK button. Windows 95 will install *HyperTerminal* and close the Add/Remove Programs dialog box.

After you have installed *HyperTerminal*, it will add a folder that contains a series of pre-configured icons with the communication settings for specific connections to your Accessories group on the Start menu. Additionally, you can choose a generic icon and configure it to connect to any type of computer's terminal-based interface.

Answers A and C are correct because you can use HyperTerminal to connect to BBS or remote servers for e-mail. Answer B is incorrect because you cannot use HyperTerminal to establish NetBIOS sessions. Answer D is incorrect because you cannot use HyperTerminal to fax documents.

905   *UNDERSTANDING USER PERMISSIONS IN WINDOWS 95*

Q: *What permission levels can you apply to a shared resource in Windows 95 when you use User-level security?*

Choose the best answers:

    A.   *Read Only*

    B.   *Full Access*

    C.   *Custom*

    D.   *No Access*

As you have learned, Windows 95 can use two forms of security: Password-level and User-level security. (In Tips 639 and 646, you learned the details of these security models and the network requirements to implement them on individual computers.) As you learned, in Windows 95 you can implement User-level security only if the Windows 95 computer is logging onto an authentication server, such as a Windows NT server or a NetWare server. When you share a resource using User-level security, you must add the users and groups who will have access to the resource. Where you add the users or groups determines the level of access the user or group will have to that resource. The Sharing tab of the Properties dialog box that you use to share a resource with User-level security will display the users who currently have access and their permission levels. The Sharing tab also lets you share or not share the resource and add new users to the access list. If you choose to share the resource, you must give it a share name.

When you click your mouse on the Add button within the Sharing dialog box, the Add Users dialog box appears. The Add Users dialog box lets you add users or groups to one of the list areas that determine the user or group's access level. You can add users or groups to the Read-Only, Full Access, or Custom list areas. If you add users or groups to the Read-Only or Full Access list areas, Windows 95 will not require any additional input to share the resource. However, if you add users or groups to the Custom list area, when you click your mouse on the OK button, a Change Access Rights dialog box will appear. The Change Access Rights dialog box lets you specify access rights to users and groups using the options in the following list:

- Read Files

- Write to Files

- Create Files and Folders

- Delete Files

- Change File Attributes

- List Files

- Change Access Control

The terms for Custom access rights can be misleading. However, you must choose the access rights depending on the operation you want the user to be able to perform. Table 905 describes the rights that users will require before they can perform various operations.

Operation	Required Rights
Read a file	Read Files
See a file's name	List Files
Search a folder for files	List Files
Write to a file	Write, Create, Delete, Change file attributes
Run a program	Read, List Files
Create a file	Create Files
Copy files from the resource	Read, List Files
Copy files into the resource	Write, Create, List Files
Create a folder	Create Files
Delete a file	Delete Files
Delete a folder	Delete Files
Change file attributes	Change File Attributes
Rename a file	Change File Attributes
Change access rights to the resource	Change Access Control

Table 905 A list of rights you must grant users to perform specific operations on a shared resource.

Answers A, B, C, and D are correct because each correspond to permission levels you can assign when you use User-level security.

906   CHANGING YOUR USER PASSWORD IN WINDOWS 95

Q: *Where in Windows 95 would you change your password?*

Choose the best answer:

     A.   *From within the System Properties dialog box, on the Passwords tab*

     B.   *From within the Windows 95 Control Panel, in the Password Properties dialog box*

     C.   *From the command prompt, using the setpass command*

     D.   *From the Network Logon dialog box*

As you have learned, when you connect your Windows 95 to a computer, the user will have to enter a password to access the network. However, Windows 95 also uses passwords for your Windows 95 User account whether or not your system is connected to a network. In turn, there may be times when you want to change your Windows 95 User account password (for example, if you use dial-up networking to access a remote network and your network password changes). You can change the Windows 95 User account password in the Passwords option within the Windows 95 Control Panel. To change your User Account password, perform the following steps:

1. Click your mouse on the Start menu and select the Settings group Control Panel option. Windows 95 will open the Control Panel.

2. Within the Control Panel, double-click your mouse on the Passwords option. Windows 95 will open the Password Properties dialog box.

3. Within the Password Properties dialog box, click your mouse on the Change Windows Password Button. Windows 95 will open a Change Windows Password dialog box that will ask you if you want to change other passwords at the same time. If you want to change the password for any of the listed options, click your mouse in the checkbox next to the option. Then click your mouse on the OK button. Windows 95 will open the Change Windows Password dialog box that lets you change passwords.

4. Within the Change Windows password dialog box, type your old password in the *Old Password* field. Then, type your new password into the *New Password* and *Confirm New Password* fields and click your mouse on the OK button. Windows 95 will insert asterisks into the fields as you type and will change your password when you click your mouse on the OK button.

Answer B is correct because you will change your password in Windows 95 from the Control Panel, in the Password Properties dialog box. Answers A and D are incorrect because you cannot change your password from the System Properties dialog box or the Network Logon dialog box. Answer C is incorrect because the setpass command is not a Microsoft command.

907   **INTRODUCTION TO WINDOWS 95 USER PROFILES**

Q: *A user profile contains which of the following?*

Choose all answers that apply:

     A.   *Your background screen image*

     B.   *Your color scheme*

     C.   *Your screen saver*

     D.   *Mapped network drives*

Windows 95 lets you use *user profiles* to configure the same computer for different users. User profiles store configurable information, such as the Windows 95 color scheme, the background image, the screen saver, and what drives are mapped to which network resources. User profiles are actually a part of the Windows 95 Registry and reside in a file named *User.Dat.*

When you enable user profiles, Windows 95 will create multiple copies of the *User.Dat* file and store them in a special user folder, *C:\Windows\Profiles\User.* Windows 95 will load the *User.Dat* file from the user's special folder, depending on which user logs onto the computer or network. In addition, you can store the *User.Dat* file on a network server for Windows 95 computers that participate in a network that uses an authentication server.

Answers A, B, C, and D are all correct because Windows 95 will store your background image, color scheme, screen saver, and all your mapped network devices.

908   ENABLING USER PROFILES

Q: *Where in Windows 95 will you enable user profiles?*

Choose the best answer:

     A.   *From the Control Panel, in the Profiles dialog box*

     B.   *From the Control Panel, in the Users dialog box*

     C.   *From the Control Panel, in the Passwords Properties dialog box*

     D.   *From the Control Panel, in the System Properties dialog box*

As you learned in Tip 907, Windows 95 can store and use different settings for multiple users with user profiles. You can enable user profiles for any Windows 95 computer, provided you have sufficient disk space to store the various *User.Dat* files for each user on that computer. To enable user profiles, perform the following steps:

1. Click your mouse on the Start menu and select the Settings group Control Panel option. Windows 95 will open the Control Panel.

2. Within the Control Panel, double-click your mouse on the Passwords option. Windows 95 will open the Password Properties dialog box.

3. Within the Passwords Properties dialog box, click your mouse on the User Profiles tab. Windows 95 will change your view to the User Profiles tab.

4. Within the User Profiles tab, click your mouse on the *Users can customize their preferences and desktop settings* option button. Windows 95 will indicate your selection by placing a dot in the option button and enabling the additional checkboxes at the bottom of the dialog box.

5. Within the User Profiles settings area, click your mouse on any options you want. Windows 95 will place a check mark in any checkbox you click.

6. Click your mouse on the OK button. Windows 95 will close the Password Properties dialog box and prompt you to restart your computer.

7. Click your mouse on the OK button to restart your computer. Windows 95 will restart.

Answer C is correct because you will enable user profiles from the Control Panel in the Password Properties dialog box. Answer A is incorrect because the Profiles dialog box does not exist. Answers B and D are incorrect because you cannot enable user profiles from either the Users dialog box or the System Properties dialog box.

909   MAINTAINING ROVING USER PROFILES

Q: *Which of the following steps must you complete to enable Windows 95 users to use roving user profiles?*

Choose all answers that apply:

A.   For each Windows 95 computer, make sure that user profiles are enabled.

B.   Within the Network option in the Control Panel, make sure you selected Client for Microsoft Networks as the Primary Network Logon client.

C.   You must create a log-on script for each Windows 95 user.

D.   On the Windows NT server, ensure each user is properly set up and has an assigned home directory on a Windows NT network server.

As you have learned, user profiles let you store user-specific information for multiple users on a single Windows 95 computer. Additionally, network users can store profiles on a network server in an authenticated environment to create a *roving user profile*.

Roving users are users who work at more than one computer in the network. Roving users can use stored user profiles to produce their custom Desktop on whichever computer they are using on the network, without having to configure each computer or change their settings multiple times.

To configure a roving user's profile, you must be running Windows 95 on a network that implements an authentication server, such as a Windows NT server or a NetWare server. To maintain the roving profile, each participating Windows 95 computer must have user profiles enabled, the *User.Dat* file must be stored in a folder on the server that is always available to that user, and you must set an appropriate client as the Primary Network Client. For example, if you want to enable user profiles on a Windows NT server-based network, you must enable user profiles on all participating Windows 95 client computers, the Client for Microsoft Networks must be the Primary Network Client, and you must store the user's *User.Dat* file in the user's assigned home directory.

Answers A, B, and D are correct because to enable roving user profiles for each Windows 95 user, you must enable profiles on each Windows 95 computer, configure the Microsoft network client to be the primary logon, and have a user home directory for each user. Answer C is incorrect because you will not have to create a log-on script for your Windows 95 clients.

910	CONFIGURING A NETWARE SERVER TO USE MANDATORY USER PROFILES FOR WINDOWS 95 CLIENTS

Q: Where must you place a mandatory profile (config.pol) on a NetWare server?

Choose the best answer:

A.   In the user's Home directory

B.   In the user's Mail directory

C.   In the server's Netlogon directory

D.   You cannot use mandatory profiles with NetWare servers

In the Tip 909, you learned that user profiles will let roving users use their custom Windows 95 settings on any computer in an authenticated network. Setting up roving users on a NetWare server can be confusing for many users and administrators because NetWare does not implement home directories. NetWare does, however, have a *Mail directory*, which is always available to a specific user. NetWare network clients for Windows 95 are designed to search the *Mail* directory for a user profile when the administrator has enabled user profiles on a Windows 95 computer. To set up roving users on a NetWare server, all participating Windows 95 client computers must have user profiles enabled, the Client for NetWare Networks must be the Primary Network Client, and the users' *User.Dat* files must be stored in the users' assigned *Mail* directory.

Answer B is correct because you must place profile files (User.Dat) in the user's Mail directory on a NetWare server. Answer A is incorrect because users may not have a Home directory on a NetWare server. Answer C is incorrect because you do not place a profile file in a NetWare server's Netlogon directory. Answer D is incorrect because you can use mandatory profiles with NetWare servers.

911 — **INTRODUCTION TO WINDOWS 95 SYSTEM POLICIES**

Q: *You will use Windows 95 system policies to restrict user access to specific Windows 95 functions.*

True or False?

Many network administrators choose to restrict the configuration options users have for their computers because users tend to make changes to their computers that can sometimes cause problems on the computer or network, which a network administrator must fix (such as changing their computer's TCP/IP address). In Windows 95, one of the primary tools for restricting the configuration options available to a user is the *System Policy Editor* program.

As you learned in Tip 239, you can use system policies to implement local restrictions for computers and users on Windows NT and Windows 95 systems. Windows 95 names system policy files *config.pol* and you must store them in a log-on directory on the authenticating server that the Windows 95 client will automatically search. The directory that contains the system policy is different for each server type. For example, the *config.pol* file would be in the Windows NT server's *Netlogon* directory, but would be in a NetWare server's *Public* directory.

*The answer is **True** because you will use Windows 95 system policies to restrict user access to certain Windows 95 functions.*

912 — **INSTALLING THE WINDOWS 95 SYSTEM POLICY EDITOR**

Q: *The Windows 95 Setup process automatically installs the Windows 95 System Policy Editor.*

True or False?

As you have learned, you will create system policies with the *System Policy Editor*, which Windows 95 includes but which you must install separately because no Windows 95 installation type will automatically install it. To install the *System Policy Editor* on a Windows 95 computer, perform the following steps:

1. Click your mouse on the Start menu and select the Settings group Control Panel option. Windows 95 will open the Control Panel.

2. Within the Control Panel, double-click your mouse on the Add/Remove Programs icon. Windows 95 will open the Add/Remove Programs dialog box.

3. Within the Add/Remove Programs dialog box, click your mouse on the Windows Setup tab. Windows 95 will display the Windows Setup sheet.

4. Within the Windows Setup sheet, click your mouse on the Have Disk button. Windows 95 will open the Install From Disk dialog box.

5. Within the Install From Disk dialog box's *Copy Manufacturer's Files From* field, type in or browse to your CD-ROM drive and on the Windows 95 CD-ROM, locate the *Admin\Apptools \Poledit* folder and click your mouse on the OK button. Windows 95 will open the Have Disk dialog box with the installable options for the designated folder listed in the Components list.

6. Within the Add/Remove Programs dialog box, click your mouse on the Group Policies and System Policy Editor options. Windows 95 will indicate your selection by placing a check mark in the checkbox next to each option.

7. Within the Add/Remove Programs dialog box, click your mouse on the Install button. Windows 95 will install the *System Policy Editor* and the sample group policies.

8. Click your mouse on the OK button to close the Add/Remove Programs dialog box. Windows 95 will close the Add/Remove Programs dialog box.

Figure 912 shows the Have Disk dialog box with the *System Policy Editor* and the group policies options.

Figure 912 *The Have Disk dialog box.*

The answer is **False** because you must install the Windows 95 System Policy Editor.

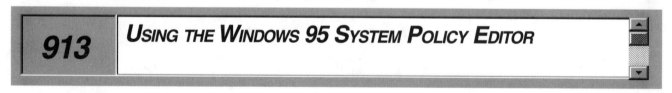

913   USING THE WINDOWS 95 SYSTEM POLICY EDITOR

Q: *You can use the Windows 95 System Policy Editor in one of two modes. Of the following, which are Windows 95 System Policy Editor modes?*

Choose all correct answers:

     A.   *Registry mode*

     B.   *Safe mode*

     C.   *Policy mode*

     D.   *Admin mode*

As an administrator, you can create a system policy quite easily. Actually, creating a system policy is simply a matter of clicking your mouse in the correct areas. A Windows 95 system policy can always place machine restrictions on a Windows 95 computer, but to enforce user restrictions with a system policy you must have enabled user profiles on the Windows 95 computer. To create a system policy, perform the following steps:

1. Click your mouse on the Start menu and select the Program menu. Within the Program menu, select the Accessories submenu System Tools group System Policy Editor option. Windows 95 will open the *System Policy Editor*.

2. After you open the *System Policy Editor*, you can either open an existing file or create a new one. To create a new file, click your mouse on the File menu and select the New File option. Windows 95 will then create a new file with two icons—Default User and Default Computer. Figure 913.1 shows the *System Policy Editor* with a new file loaded.

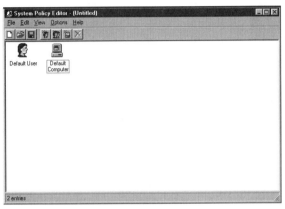

Figure 913.1 The System Policy Editor after you load the new policy file.

To add a restriction to the policy, you must open one of the policy's icons. All policies have the Default User and Default Computer icons, but you can add additional icons for a specific user, group, or computer from the Edit menu. A good policy is one in which the Default User and Default Computer icons represent the most restrictive accounts and an Administrator icon represents the least restrictive account.

To place a restriction, you must double-click your mouse on one of the icons. Windows 95 will display a dialog box with the restrictions list. You must expand the list of restriction groupings, and click your mouse on a specific restriction. After you select the restriction, Windows 95 will add the restriction to that group. Figure 913.2 shows the *System Policy Editor* with the Default Computer icon's restrictions list expanded.

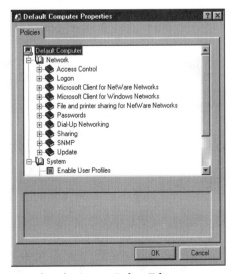

Figure 913.2 Applying system policy restrictions within the System Policy Editor.

Note: *While adding restrictions to a policy is simple, creating a sound set of system policies for all the computers on a network is a lengthy and detailed process. For detailed information, see Chapter 15 of the* **Microsoft Windows 95 Resource Kit,** *by Microsoft Press.*

Answers A *and* **C** *are correct because the Windows 95 System Policy Editor's two modes are Registry and Policy.* **Answers B** *and* **D** *are incorrect because neither answer is a Windows 95 System Policy Editor mode.*

914	CREATING POLICIES FOR USERS AND COMPUTERS FOR WINDOWS 95

Q: *You can create Windows 95 system policies so that the policy applies to any user on a specific computer.*

True or False?

In Tip 913, you learned that you can use the *System Policy Editor* to create system policies and that good system policies provide the most restrictions to the Default User and Default Computer groups. To create a good system policy, you must add specific users, groups, or computers that have few restrictions and place the most restrictions on the Default User and Default Computer options, which all system policies have.

To add a specific user, group, or computer, you simply add an icon from the Edit menu and name it with the user's log-on name, the group name, or the computer's NetBIOS name. For example, to add a setting for the Administrator account, perform the following steps:

1. Within the *System Policy Editor*, click your mouse on the Edit menu and select the Add User option. Windows 95 will open the Add User dialog box.
2. Within the Add User dialog box, type in the word *Administrator* in the *Dialog Box* field or click your mouse on the Browse button to locate the Administrator account.
3. Click your mouse on the OK button. Windows 95 will add a user icon for the Administrator account.

Figure 914 shows the *System Policy Editor* after you have added an Administrator group icon.

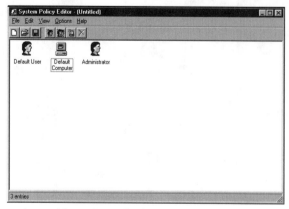

Figure 914 The System Policy Editor with an additional icon for the Administrator account.

The answer is **True** *because you can create a system policy that will apply to any user on a certain computer.*

915   CREATING POLICIES FOR GROUPS IN WINDOWS 95

Q: *You can configure a system policy to apply only to groups you have created on the local Windows 95 computer.*

True or False?

As you have learned, you can create a system policy that will apply to only one user on a certain computer. You can also apply user-level restrictions to entire groups of users with a system policy, as long as the administrator has already defined the group in the authentication server. Windows 95 will enforce restrictions you add to a group option on all users who are a part of that group and who also work at a Windows 95 computer for which you enabled user profiles. To add a group option to a system policy, perform the following steps:

1. Within the *System Policy Editor*, click your mouse on the Edit menu and select the Add Group option. Windows 95 will open the Add Group dialog box.

2. Within the Add Group dialog box, type in or browse to locate the name of the group you want to add (for example, *Sales*). Click your mouse on the OK button. Windows 95 will add the group to the policy.

Figure 915 shows the *System Policy Editor* after you have added a Sales group option.

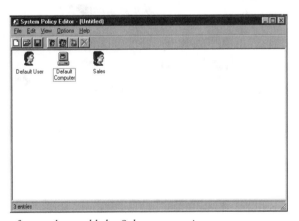

Figure 915 *The System Policy Editor after you have added a Sales group option.*

*The answer is **False** because you will use groups from the Windows NT domain for system policies.*

916   CREATING A MANDATORY USER PROFILE IN WINDOWS 95

Q: *How would you create a mandatory user profile?*

Choose the best answer:

A.   Within Windows NT and the User Manager for Domains program, click your mouse on the Profile tab in the User Properties dialog box of the user to whom you want to give a mandatory user profile and select the Mandatory checkbox.

B.   Within Windows NT and the User Manager for Domains program, go to the User Properties dialog box of the user to whom you want to give a mandatory user profile and rename the user's profile to include a .man extension.

C.   Rename the User.Dat file for the user to user.man. You now have a mandatory user profile.

D.   Set the user's User.Dat file attribute to Read-Only. You now have a mandatory user profile.

As you have learned, you can use user profiles within Windows 95 to restrict a user's access to resources on the network. In addition to using user policies to restrict users' access, you can also restrict users' actions in Windows 95 by creating *mandatory profiles*, which have a higher priority in Windows 95 and will override any settings in a locally saved profile. In other words, if a mandatory profile is present on the server when a Windows 95 client logs on, Windows 95 will implement the mandatory profile over any other profile the Windows 95 client locally stores.

Additionally, Windows 95 will not save any changes the user made during a session to the mandatory profile stored in the user's *home* or *Mail* directory. Because profiles store user information—such as mapped drives, background patterns, and color schemes—and users cannot change the settings in a mandatory profile, you can use a mandatory profile to enforce pre-configured Desktop and Start menus. To make a mandatory profile, create a normal profile, save it to a user's *Home* or *Mail* directory, and use the Windows *Explorer* to change the file's name from *User.Dat* to *user.man*.

*Answer C is correct because you must only rename the user's User.Dat file to **user.man** in order to make the profile mandatory. Answers A and B are incorrect because you cannot make a user profile mandatory **from** User Manager for Domains. Answer D is incorrect because, although resetting the User.Dat file's attributes so the file is Read-Only will keep the user from making changes to the profile, doing so does not make the profile mandatory.*

917   CONFIGURING MANUAL DOWNLOAD OF SYSTEM POLICIES FOR WINDOWS 95

Q: *By default, all Windows 95 client computers will get their system policies only from the Windows NT Server Primary Domain Controller (PDC) or NetWare Preferred Server networks.*

True or False?

As you have learned, you can easily configure Windows 95 computers to download system policies from an authentication server on the network—either a standard user profile or a mandatory profile. Whenever a Windows 95 computers logs onto an authenticating server, the computer will automatically search the Primary Domain Controller for the user profile in a Windows NT network or the NetWare Preferred Server for the user profile in a NetWare network.

If you want the Windows 95 computer to download a policy from a different location than the default location, you must specifically instruct it to do so. You can instruct the computer where to download the policy from either within the system policy that you store on the Primary Domain Controller (or NetWare Preferred Server), if you are using a 32-bit protected mode client. If you are using a 16-bit real mode network client, you can instruct the computer where to download the policy within the system policy the Windows 95 computer stores locally.

You will use the Remote Update option to redirect a system policy to a non-default location. You can find the Remote Update option in the Any Computer option within a system policy. Figure 918 shows the Remote Update option.

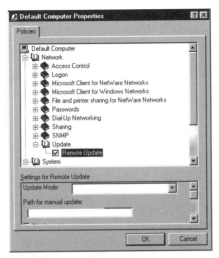

Figure 917 *The Remote Update option in a system policy.*

The answer is **True** *because, by default, all Windows 95 clients will get their system policies only from the Primary Domain Controller or NetWare Preferred Server. To configure a Windows 95 client to get its system policy from a system other than the Primary Domain Controller or NetWare Preferred Server, you must configure Remote Update within the policy.*

918 ACCESSING REMOTE WINDOWS 95 REGISTRIES WITH THE SYSTEM POLICY EDITOR

Q: *You can edit both Windows 95 and Windows NT system Registries from the System Policy Editor in Windows 95.*

True or False?

The *System Policy Editor* program is an extremely versatile tool and can provide a great deal of assistance to an administrator. In addition to creating and managing system policies, the *System Policy Editor* can directly edit the Windows 95 Registry, and if you have loaded the *Remote Registry* service, can open and edit remote Windows 95 computers' Registries over a network. However, the Windows 95 *System Policy Editor* cannot edit Windows NT computers' Registries. To open and edit a remote Windows 95 Registry, you must load the *Remote Registry* service on both Windows 95 computers. To load the *Remote Registry* service, perform the following steps:

1. Click your mouse on the Start menu and select the Settings group Control Panel option. Windows 95 will open the Control Panel.

2. Within the Control Panel, click your mouse on the Network option. Windows 95 will open the Network Properties dialog box.

3. Within the Network Properties dialog box, click your mouse on the Add button. Windows 95 will open the Select Network Component Type dialog box.

4. Within the Select Network Component Type dialog box, click your mouse on the Service option. Windows 95 will indicate your selection by highlighting the Service option.

5. Within the Select Network Component Type dialog box, click your mouse on the Add button. Windows 95 will open the Select Network Service dialog box.

6. Within the Select Network Service dialog box, click your mouse on the Have Disk button. Windows 95 will open the Install From Disk dialog box.

7. Within the Install From Disk dialog box, click your mouse on the Browse button. Windows 95 will open the Browse dialog box.

8. Within the Browse dialog box, find the *Admin\Nettools\Remotereg* folder on the Windows 95 CD-ROM. Windows 95 will insert the pathname into the *Path* field.

9. Click your mouse on the OK button. Windows 95 will return to the Install From Disk dialog box.

10. Within the Install From Disk dialog box, click your mouse on the OK button. Windows 95 will return to the Select Network Service dialog box and display the *Remote Registry* service in the list.

11. Within the Select Network Service dialog box, click your mouse on the OK button. Windows 95 will install the *Remote Registry* service and prompt you to restart your computer.

12. Click your mouse on the OK button to restart your computer. Windows 95 will restart.

After you have installed the *Remote Registry* service on both Windows 95 computers, you can connect to the remote computer by choosing Connect from the File menu in the *System Policy Editor*.

Note: As you have learned, you should be extremely careful when you edit any Windows 95 Registry.

The answer is **False** because the Windows 95 and Windows NT Registries are quite different. If you try to edit the Windows NT system Registry with any tool designed to edit the Windows 95 Registry, you could render the Windows NT system inoperable.

---

919 ACCESSING REMOTE WINDOWS 95 REGISTRIES WITH THE REGISTRY EDITOR

Q: You can edit both Windows 95 and Windows NT system Registries from the Windows 95 Registry Editor program.

True or False?

As you learned in Tip 918, you can open and edit a remote Windows 95 computer's Registry using the *System Policy Editor* program. You can also use another tool to open remote Registries—the *regedit.exe* program Windows 95 includes. In order to open and edit any remote Windows 95 computer's Registry, you must have the *Remote Registry* service installed on both computers. To open a remote Windows 95 computer's Registry from within *regedit.exe*, choose the Connect Network Registry option from the Registry menu and type the remote computer's NetBIOS name.

The answer is **False** because the Registry Editor program in Windows 95 is only for editing Windows 95 Registries. The Windows NT Registry is very different from the Registry in Windows 95. If you use the Windows 95 Registry Editor on a Windows NT system, you could damage the Windows NT Registry.

---

920 INTRODUCTION TO THE WINDOWS 95 REGISTRY

Q: Which of the following descriptions best fits the Windows 95 Registry?

Choose the best answer:

A. Schedules processes and threads

B. Is the section of Windows 95 code where the user registration information is stored

C. Is the licensing information about the local computer

D. Is a central repository for configuration information about the system and applications installed on the system

Windows *3.x* operating systems relied on real mode drivers and multiple initialization files to store configuration information. Windows 95 maintains many of these initialization files for backwards compatibility, but also uses a central repository of configuration information called the *Registry*. Microsoft's goal in using the *Registry* is to make it more difficult for end-users to directly manipulate information that is critical to the system.

Windows 95 stores one portion of the *Registry* in two files, *System.Dat* and *User.Dat*, while other Registry portions are built each time the computer starts. When Windows 95 starts, it combines information in the *System.Dat* and *User.Dat* files with information the system reads directly from the computer hardware to build the Windows 95 Registry. While Windows 95 runs, it stores the *Registry* in memory and you can edit it with a variety of programs to alter configurations that that you could not otherwise configure.

Answer D is correct because the Windows 95 Registry is a central repository of configuration information. **Answers A, B,** and **C** are incorrect because they do not accurately describe the Windows 95 Registry.

921 — UNDERSTANDING THE COMPONENTS THAT USE THE WINDOWS 95 REGISTRY

Q: Which of the following are part of the Windows 95 Registry?

Choose the best answer:

A. Device Drivers

B. Applications OLE information

C. System hardware configuration

D. User profiles

As you learned in Tip 921, the Windows 95 Registry is a central repository for configuration information. In other words, the Windows 95 Registry contains information about all aspects of the Windows 95 operating system, including references and special instructions for other files stored on the computer, such as device drivers and applications. Much of the information the Windows 95 Registry contains is stored in files on the computer. For example, the main hardware configuration information is stored in the *System.Dat* file and user information is stored in the *User.Dat* file. The Registry simply references other files, such as device drivers and applications, which the operating system must use. The Registry-referenced files are stored in files on the computer, either within application directories or in the *Windows* directory or its *System* subdirectory. Windows-based applications, such as *Word* for Windows or Microsoft *Excel*, use information the Registry contains to establish communication rules that the Object Linking and Embedding (OLE) entries define. OLE entries let the operating system reference and use other programs from within the currently-executing program. For example, when you embed a spreadsheet in a word processing document, you will use OLE to edit the spreadsheet from within the word processor.

Answers B, C, and **D** are correct because OLE information, hardware configuration, and user profiles are all aspects of the Windows 95 Registry. **Answer A** is incorrect because although the Registry contains references to device drivers, the drivers are actually other files stored on the computer.

---

922 EXAMINING THE HKEY_LOCAL_MACHINE SUBTREE IN WINDOWS 95

Q: *You will seldom, if ever, make any changes directly or indirectly to the HKEY_LOCAL_MACHINE subtree in the Windows 95 Registry.*

True or False?

Windows 95 divides information in the *Registry* into groups called *subtrees*. Each subtree in the *Registry* contains information about a different part of the Windows 95 operating system. For example, the *HKEY_LOCAL_MACHINE* subtree contains hardware configuration data that tells Windows 95 how to address the different hardware components installed in the computer, software settings that define how Windows 95 will interact with installed components and applications, and other information about the operating system in general. Windows 95 implements information the *HKEY_LOCAL_MACHINE* subtree contains the same way for every user. In turn, this subtree stores most configuration changes you make in Windows 95. Aside from the application- and operating-system-dependent information the *Registry* contains, the Windows 95 *Registry* is fundamentally identical to the Windows NT *Registry* that you learned about in earlier Tips, including Tip 223.

*The answer is **False** because you will make the most common system configuration changes to the HKEY_LOCAL_MACHINE subtree in the Windows 95 Registry.*

---

923 EXAMINING VARIOUS REGISTRY KEYS

Q: *Which of the following are keys under HKEY_LOCAL_MACHINE in the Windows 95 Registry?*

Choose all answers that apply:

A.   *Config*

B.   *Software*

C.   *Default*

D.   *User*

As you learned in Tip 922, the Windows 95 *Registry* stores most of the system configuration information for the computer in the *HKEY_LOCAL_MACHINE* subtree. Although you have learned that, in general, you should not edit the *Registry*, Exam 70-40: Implementing and Supporting Windows 95 might contains questions about the *HKEY_LOCAL_MACHINE* subtree. Windows 95 further divides the *Registry* subtrees (of which there are six) into other subtrees and then into objects called *keys*, which contain the Registry's actual configuration settings. The *HKEY_LOCAL_MACHINE* subtree contain the following other subtrees:

- *Config*

- *Enum*

- *Hardware*

- *Network*
- *Security*
- *Software*
- *System*

Answers A and B are correct because Config and Software are both HKEY_LOCAL_MACHINE keys in the Windows 95 Registry. Answer C is incorrect because Default is a key under HKEY_USERS, not HKEY_LOCAL_MACHINE. Answer D is incorrect because User is not a valid key in the Windows 95 Registry.

924   UNDERSTANDING THE WIN.INI FILE

Q: What information does the Win.Ini file contain?

Choose all answers that apply:

    A.   *Backgrounds*

    B.   *Font settings*

    C.   *Modem settings*

    D.   *Icon sets*

As you have learned, the Windows *3.x* operating systems store important operating-system information within a series of initialization files. Windows *3.x* systems store user information in the *Win.Ini* file, which contains information such as the background pattern, color scheme, font settings, icon sets, or personal group information. The *Win.Ini* file was not a required file for Windows *3.x* because it contained no hardware settings and the system would automatically re-create the file if it was missing when you started Windows 3.x. Windows 95 stores the same information that Windows *3.x* stored within the *Win.Ini* file within the file *User.Dat*, which it then incorporates into the Windows 95 *Registry*. Windows 95 still installs the *Win.Ini* file for backward compatibility, even if you install Windows 95 to a blank hard drive. If you install Windows 95 as an upgrade to Windows *3.x*, Windows 95 imports the *Win.Ini* settings into the Registry during the Setup process and stores the settings within the *User.Dat* file for future use.

Answers A, B, and D are correct because backgrounds, font settings, and icon sets are sections of the Win.Ini file. Answer C is incorrect because modem settings are not part of the Win.Ini file.

925   UNDERSTANDING WIN.INI SETTINGS IN THE REGISTRY

Q: Windows 95 parses the Win.Ini file and imports any configuration information into the Windows 95 Registry at system start.

True or False?

As you have learned, Windows 95 creates and maintains a *Win.Ini* file for backward compatibility with Windows 3.x applications, Furthermore, if you install Windows 95 as an upgrade to Windows 3.x, Windows 95 will import the settings in *Win.Ini* and store them within the Windows 95 *Registry*. After Windows 95 imports the necessary information, the system generally ignores the *Win.Ini* file because Windows 95 does not require settings that applications add. Windows 95 maintains the file to prevent older applications from having problems during installation.

Windows 95 does not need some of the information in the *Win.Ini* file and so does not import it. However, Windows 95 does parse and import specific information from the *Windows* section and the *WindowsMetrics* section of *Win.Ini*. Table 925 contains settings that the Windows 95 *Setup* process imports from the Windows 3.x *Win.Ini* file.

Windows Section Imported Setting	WindowsMetrics Section Imported Settings
Beep	BorderWidth
BorderWidth	CaptionHeight
CursorBlinkRate	CaptionWidth
DoubleClickSpeed	MenuHeight
KeyboardDelay	MenuWidth
KeyboardSpeed	MinArrange
MouseThreshold1	MinHorzGap
MouseThreshold2	MinVertGap
MouseSpeed	MinWidth
ScreenSaveActive	ScrollHeight
SceenSaveTimeOut	ScrollWidth
SwapMouseButtons	SmCaptionHeight
	SmCaptionWidth

*Table 925 Settings the Windows 95 Setup process imports from the Windows 3.x **Win.Ini** file during setup.*

*The answer is **False** because Windows 95 will parse the Win.Ini file when you install the system and then write any configuration information to the Windows 95 Registry. Windows 95 will never again parse the Win.Ini file.*

926   **UNDERSTANDING THE SYSTEM.INI FILE**

Q: *Windows uses the **System.Ini** file for global system configuration information.*

True or False?

In previous Tips, you have learned about some files (including the *Win.Ini* file) that Windows 95 imports and uses to create the Registry during the Windows 95 Setup process. Another Windows 3.x initialization file that Windows 95 Setup imports to Windows 95 during system setup is the *System.Ini* file. Windows 95 Setup also creates *System.Ini* if you are installing Windows 95 on a blank hard drive, so that Windows 95 will support backward compatibility with Windows 3.x applications.

In Windows 3.x, the *System.Ini* file stored global system configuration information, such as hardware configuration settings, pointers that identified the correct device drivers to use for hardware components installed on the computer, and operational specifications for application support and networking. In Windows 95, the Setup process stores the global system configuration information settings in the Registry and no longer requires the *System.Ini* file. Windows 95 migrates the changes applications or 16-bit installation programs make in the *System.Ini* file into the Registry.

*The answer is **True** because Windows uses the System.Ini file for global system configuration information.*

927   **UNDERSTANDING SYSTEM.INI SETTINGS IN THE REGISTRY**

Q: *When you install Windows 95, it will parse the System.Ini file and move the applicable settings to the Windows 95 Registry.*

True or False?

During a Windows 3.x to Windows 95 upgrade, Setup parses and imports almost every setting in the *System.Ini* file and makes changes to the entries within the *System.Ini* file to ensure that the drivers and other information the file contains references the correct files in the Windows 95 operating system The easiest way to consider the changes that the Setup process makes to the sections that comprise the *System.Ini* file's sections is to consider the affected sections in order. Setup adds the following entries to the *System.Ini* file's *Boot* section:

- *comm.drv=comm.drv*
- *dibeng.drv=dibeng.dll*
- *gdi.exe=gdi.exe*
- *sound.drv=sound.drv*
- user.exe=user.exe

Setup adds the following entries to the *System.Ini* file's *386Enh* section:

- *device=*vshare*
- *device=*vcd*
- *device=*int13*
- device=*dynapage

Setup deletes the following entries from the *System.Ini* file's *386Enh* section:

- *device=*vfd*
- *device=*configmg*
- *device=*serial.386*
- *device=*lpt.386*
- *device=*pagefile.386*
- *timercriticalsection=*
- *device=isapnp.386*

- *device=wshell.386*

- maxbps=

The answer is **True** *because, when you install Windows 95, it will search through the System.Ini and write configuration information in the Windows 95 Registry.*

928 SAVING AND RESTORING THE WINDOWS 95 REGISTRY

Q: *When you export Registry data to a file, what type of file extension does the export file have?*

Choose the best answer:

A.   *.log*

B.   *.txt*

C.   *.reg*

D.   *.exe*

As you have learned, the Windows 95 Registry is a central repository for configuration information that all aspects of the operating system require. In other words, almost nothing in Windows 95 can function without the Registry, and problems or incorrect settings in the Registry can cause system-wide malfunctions. You should regularly make a backup of your Windows 95 Registry to protect against file corruption that could affect the Registry. Additionally, you should always back up the Registry prior to editing Registry entries.

You can back up the Windows 95 Registry using the *Registry Editor* program's *(regedit.exe)* Registry menu Export Registry File option. When you export the Registry, *regedit.exe* will prompt you to enter a filename, and then add the *.reg* extension to the filename. For example, if you name your backup file *backup*, *regedit.exe* will create the file as *backup.reg*. To export a backup of the Windows 95 Registry, perform the following steps:

1. Click your mouse on the Start menu and select the Run option. Windows 95 will open the Run dialog box.

2. Within the Run dialog box, type *regedit* in the *Open* field. Windows 95 will insert the text you type into the *Open* field.

3. Within the Run dialog box, click your mouse on the OK button. Windows 95 will open the *Registry Editor* program.

4. Within the *Registry Editor*, select the Registry menu Export Registry File option. Windows 95 will open the Export Registry dialog box.

5. Within the Export Registry dialog box, choose a location to store your Registry. For example, if you want to export the Registry to the root folder of the C:\ drive, click your mouse on the Save in drop-down list at the top of the Export Registry dialog box and choose C:\ from the list that appears. Windows 95 will display the C:\ drive's files and folders in the Save in list.

6. Within the Export Registry dialog box, click your mouse in the *File name* field. Windows 95 will place the cursor in the *File name* field.

7. Within the *File name* field, type a name for your file. For example, type in the name *backup*. Windows 95 will insert the text you type in the *File name* field.

8.   Within the Export Registry dialog box, click your mouse on the Save button. Windows 95 will save the export file.

Note: *Registry export files can be several megabytes in size.*

Answer C *is correct because the Windows 95 Registry Editor saves the data you export as .reg files.* **Answer A** *is incorrect because the Registry Editor does not save files as* **.log** *files.* **Answer B** *is incorrect because a .txt file is a text file.* **Answer D** *is incorrect because an .exe file is an executable file.*

929   *RECOVERING REGISTRY DATA IN WINDOWS 95*

Q: *If your Windows 95 system's Registry becomes corrupt, what is the best way to restore the Registry?*

Choose the best answer:

A.   *Restore the Registry from a tape backup.*

B.   *Use the Windows 95 Registry Editor Import option.*

C.   *Windows 95 will automatically try to replace the System.Dat and User.Dat files with the System.da0 and User.da0 files.*

D.   *You cannot restore a corrupt Windows 95 Registry.*

In Tip 928, you learned you can export the Windows 95 Registry as a backup to help protect you from problems that result from file corruption. Windows 95 recognizes the threat of file corruption to Registry files and also backs them up. After a user logs on successfully and Windows 95 displays the Desktop, it creates backups of the *System.Dat* and *User.Dat* as *System.Da0* and *User.Da0* and stores the backups onto the hard drive. During system startup, if Windows 95 detects a corruption in the Registry, the startup process will halt and Windows 95 will display a message that tells you it has detected a corruption and it will try to restore the Registry from the backup files it prepared previously, and restart. When you click your mouse on the OK button, Windows 95 will replace *System.Dat* and *User.Dat* with *System.Da0* and *User.Da0*.

Note: *If file corruption damaged both the* **.dat** *and* **.da0** *files, Windows 95 will not be able to repair the Registry.*

Answer C *is correct because Windows 95 will automatically try to replace the System.Dat and User.Dat files with the System.Da0 and User.Da0 files.* **Answer A** *is incorrect because Windows 95 will automatically try to restore the Registry from backup files if the Registry is corrupt.* **Answer B** *is incorrect because, if your Windows 95 Registry is corrupt, you may not be able to boot Windows 95 to use the Import option in the Windows 95 Registry Editor.* **Answer D** *is incorrect because Windows 95 will automatically try to restore the Registry from backup files if the Registry is corrupt.*

930   *USING THE SECRET REGISTRY FILE (SYSTEM.1ST)*

Q: *Which of the following files does Windows 95 create during a Windows 95 installation, and then never updates again?*

Choose the best answer:

    A.   *System.Dat*

    B.   *User.Dat*

    C.   *System.Da0*

    D.   *System.1st*

In the previous Tip, you learned about the backup copies of the Registry that Windows 95 creates each time the user successfully logs onto the workstation. The Windows 95 Registry also has a "secret" file that stores a copy of the Registry's *System.Dat* file when you first install Windows 95. The "secret" file is *System.1st* and Windows 95 creates it during a Windows 95 installation and stores it in the boot partition's (*C:*) root directory as a hidden file.

The *System.1st* file's purpose is to provide the user or administrator with a method of restoring the Windows 95 Registry to the configuration that Windows 95 stored at installation. You can use the *System.1st* file to restore a corrupted Windows 95 Registry's *System.Dat* file. Because of the way Windows 95 implements application installations (by double-copying information to multiple files and rebuilding the Registry at boot-up), you will not lose any installed applications on your computer during the *System.1st* restoration process, nor will you lose most hardware configuration that you have done to the system since the original Windows 95 installation. Windows 95 sets the Read-Only and Hidden file attributes for the *System.1st* file, to minimize the risk of a user accidentally corrupting the file. To replace *System.Dat* with *System.1st*, you must remove the Read-Only and Hidden File attributes, rename *System.1st* as *System.Dat*, and copy the newly renamed file into the Windows\System folder. You can replace *System.Dat* with *System.1st* (and therefore rebuild a corrupted Registry) on a computer with a corrupted Registry by using the Windows 95 Startup disk.

Answer D *is correct because Windows 95 creates the System.1st file during a Windows 95 installation, and then never again updates or edits it.* **Answers A, B,** *and* **C** *are incorrect because, although Windows 95 creates each file during a Windows 95 installation, Windows 95 also constantly updates them.*

931   **UNDERSTANDING THE SETUP /P SWITCH AND SOME HISTORY OF GROUPS**

Q: *Windows 95 does not have group (.grp) files.*

True or False?

If you have worked with both Windows *3.x* operating systems and Windows 95 operating systems, you know that, in addition to the significant differences in processing between the two operating systems, there are also significant differences in the presentation the systems make to the user. One of the most easily recognizable examples of this difference is how Windows *3.x* and Windows 95 implement and display groups. Windows *3.x* operating systems divide control icons into groups and store the information about the groups in *group files*, which are basically text files with the *.grp* extension.

Windows *3.x* Setup installs several common groups that contain icons necessary to configure and control the operating system, and Windows *3.x* applications can create other groups when you install them. You can find instructions for creating groups and configuring the icons that Windows *3.x* stores in a group in installation files (*.inf*). For example, Windows *3.x* stores the configuration information for the standard Windows *3.x* groups in the *setup.inf* file that controls the installation of Windows *3.x* operating systems.

Recognizing that users may inadvertently delete groups that the operating system actually requires for configuration, Microsoft included a means for users to recreate the original groups and their associated icons by reading the *setup.inf* file. In Windows *3.x*, you can invoke the tool by adding a */P* to the end of the command *SETUP*. In Windows for Workgroups 3.11, you can add */P* to the end of the command *WINSETUP* to invoke the same function.

However, unlike the 16-bit Windows versions that preceded it, Windows 95 no longer requires group files because you can perform all configuration and program launching from the Start menu, and Windows 95 stores menus as folders on the hard drive. Windows 95 does, however, still create group files for backward compatibility and will import groups from Windows *3.x* during an upgrade installation. Additionally, Windows *3.x* applications may create group files. Windows 95 reads and imports these files to create menus for the applications.

The answer is **False** *because, although Windows 95 implements groups as categories on the Start menu and stores groups as folders, both Windows 95 and Windows 3.x applications can create group (.grp) files in the Windows folder. Then, Windows 95 will import and convert the group files into menu groups.*

932	USING THE GRPCONV.EXE UTILITY

Q: *Which of the following commands or utilities can recreate the original Windows 95 Start menu and its submenus?*

Choose the best answer:

    A.   *Setup /P*

    B.   *Winsetup /P*

    C.   *GrpConv.exe*

    D.   *None of the above; only by reinstalling Windows 95 can you recreate the original Start menu and its submenus.*

In Tip 931, you learned you can recreate the original groups in Windows 3.x operating systems using the *SETUP /P* command, and the same functionality exists for Windows for Workgroups 3.11. Because Windows 95 still has group files present and users may still inadvertently delete menus from the Start menu, Windows 95 also can recreate the original Start menu and its submenus. The Windows 95 command for recreating the Start menu is *grpconv.exe*.

The *grpconv.exe* utility is a multipurpose utility because, in addition to recreating original menus, it can convert existing group files (*.grp*) into menus. For example, Windows 95 Setup automatically runs *grpconv.exe* during installation to read information contained in *progman.ini* and to migrate existing Windows 3.x groups into the Windows 95 Registry. Windows 95 then maintains the Windows 3.x group entries, and any Windows 3.x applications that you install after you have installed Windows 95 will not make changes to the *progman.ini* file. If you try to make changes to the *progman.ini* file, Windows 95 will intercept your changes and add settings to the Registry instead. To run *grpconv.exe*, perform the following steps:

1. Click your mouse on the Start menu and select the Run option. Windows 95 will open the Run dialog box.

2. Within the Run dialog box, type in the program name *grpconv*. Windows 95 will insert the text you type in the *Open* field.

3. Within the Run dialog box, click your mouse on the OK button. Windows 95 will run the *grpconv.exe* utility.

*Answer C is correct because the GRPCONV.EXE command can recreate the original Start menu and its submenus. **Answer A** is incorrect because, although SETUP /P would recreate the original groups in Windows 3.x, it cannot recreate the Windows 95 Start menu and its submenus. **Answer B** is incorrect because, although WINSETUP /P could recreate the original groups in Windows for Workgroups 3.11, it cannot recreate the Windows 95 Start menu and its submenus. **Answer D** is incorrect because you can recreate the original Start menu and its submenus using the GRPCONV.EXE command.*

933   **INTRODUCTION TO THE CONFIGURATION MANAGER**

Q: *The Windows 95 Configuration Manager is a system component that coordinates system device configurations.*

True or False?

As you have learned, Windows 95 is a plug-and-play compliant operating system which supports both plug-and-play devices and non-plug-and-play devices. To help you manage both plug-and-play devices and non-plug-and-play devices, Windows 95 includes a software component called the Configuration Manager to govern hardware configuration. Configuration Manager maintains a list of all devices installed on the computer for the Windows 95 operating system.

In addition, Configuration Manager makes decisions about assigning resources to installed devices, such as Interrupt Request (IRQ) addresses, Input/Output (I/O) addresses, and memory addresses (DMA) to hardware devices that require them. For example, if you install a new plug-and-play device to Windows 95, which requires an Interrupt Request, Configuration Manager will determine if an Interrupt Request is available and assigns it. Configuration Manager also assigns priority to device types that require resources. For example, Legacy devices have a higher priority than plug-and-play devices in Windows 95 because Legacy devices cannot accept different configurations without input from the user. Configuration Manager always assigns resources to all Legacy devices before it assigns resources to plug-and-play devices.

*The answer is **True** because the Windows 95 Configuration Manager is a system component that manages system device configurations.*

934   **INTRODUCTION TO THE VIRTUAL MACHINE MANAGER**

Q: *The Windows 95 Virtual Machine Manager is a system component that manages the operating system's user interface.*

True or False?

In Tip 933, you learned that the Configuration Manager is the managing component that controls resource assignment to hardware devices. In the same way the Configuration Manager governs hardware devices, the *Virtual Machine Manager (VMM)* governs operating system software components and applications. The Virtual Machine Manager governs all virtual machines that run software in Windows 95, which includes the operating system, because Windows 95 itself runs in a virtual machine. The Virtual Machine Manager is responsible for the three major software services the operating system runs, as shown in the following list:

- Process Scheduling
- Memory Paging
- MS-DOS Mode Support

*The answer is **True** because the Windows 95 Virtual Machine Manager is a system component that manages the software resources the operating system or applications that may include the user interface require.*

---

935   UNDERSTANDING PREEMPTIVE MULTITASKING IN WINDOWS 95

Q: Which of the following best describe preemptive multitasking?

Choose the best answer:

> *A.   Preemptive multitasking means each application releases the system processor when the application wants to pass the processor's attention to another application.*
>
> *B.   Preemptive multitasking means the operating system manages each application's use of the system processor.*
>
> *C.   Preemptive multitasking means Windows 95 assigns a time value to each application. When the time value expires, the application will pass control of the processor to the next application that needs the processor.*
>
> *D.   Preemptive multitasking means each application can perform multiple tasks at the same time, such as an application copying files and making system configuration changes.*

As you have learned, the primary motive for most administrators in upgrading from Windows 3.x to Windows 95 was Windows 95's support for 32-bit processing. One of the most significant improvements "under the hood" in Windows 95 is its support for preemptive multitasking. Multitasking is a popular buzzword in the computer industry that describes an operating system's ability to share processor time between multiple applications. Windows 3.x operating systems support a process called *cooperative multitasking* in which the applications periodically release control of the processor so other applications can use it. The problem with cooperative multitasking is if an application hangs up while it has control of the processor, all other applications also hang up because they cannot access the processor to perform tasks. Engineers called the Windows 3.x multitasking support cooperative multitasking because applications must cooperate in order for the operating system to multitask. To share processor time between applications, Windows 95 uses *preemptive multitasking*—in which the operating system has control of the processor and applications make processor requests directly to the operating system. Engineers called the Windows 95 multitasking support preemptive multitasking because the operating system can preemptively interrupt an application and give the processor's use to a different application. You will learn more about how the preemptive multitasking process works in Tip 936.

*Answer **B** is correct because preemptive multitasking in Windows 95 means the operating system manages when each application can use the processor. **Answer A** is incorrect because the answer describes the cooperative multitasking that Windows 3.x uses. **Answers C and D** are incorrect because neither answer describes any type of Microsoft multitasking.*

---

936   UNDERSTANDING PROCESS SCHEDULING AND MULTITASKING

Q: *Which of the following are components of a process?*

Choose all correct answers:

     A.   *An executable program*

     B.   *A user interface*

     C.   *The program's memory address space*

     D.   *At least one thread*

As you have learned, Windows 95 supports preemptive multitasking, a multitasking type in which the operating system has control of the processor and determines which applications can access the processor and for how long. In Windows 95, applications that must use the processor must request processor access from the operating system. Because Windows 95 runs all applications in a virtual machine, the operating system even controls applications designed to access the processor directly, such as MS-DOS-based applications.

Each application, program, or system component running on Windows 95 is a *process* and a request for processor access is a *thread*. Each process can generate one or more threads depending on the process's design. For example, Windows 95 operates all Windows 3.x 16-bit (Win16) applications with a single range of memory addresses and a single thread. In other words, all Win16 applications must share a single thread. Windows 95 32-bit applications (Win32) each run with their own range of memory addresses and can each generate multiple threads. All threads have a base priority that determines their importance to the operating system.

The Windows 95 Virtual Machine Manager contains two components called the *Primary Scheduler* and the *Secondary Scheduler*. The Primary Scheduler determines the priority level of threads and grants access to the processor. The Primary Scheduler will grant processor access to the thread with the highest priority and make threads with lower priority wait. When two or more threads have the same priority level, the Primary Scheduler will evenly split the processor's time between the threads. The Secondary Scheduler periodically increases the priority of threads that have been waiting for the processor, so the Virtual Machine Manager eventually processes all threads.

Answers A, C, and D are correct because an executable program, the program's memory address space, and at least one thread, are all components of a single process. Answer B is incorrect because a user interface is not a component of a process.

937   UNDERSTANDING INSTALLABLE FILE SYSTEMS

Q: *Which of the following are installable file systems?*

Choose all correct answers:

     A.   *Virtual File Allocation Table (VFAT)*

     B.   *Compact Disk File System (CDFS)*

     C.   *Network Redirector*

     D.   *File Allocation Table (FAT)*

Windows 95 supports only the File Allocation Table (FAT) file system. Windows 95 OEM Service Release 2 (OSR2) provides additional support for the enhanced FAT32 file system. Other file systems and services (such as the file system

CD-ROMs use) you can implement as installable components that plug-in to the Windows 95 operating system are called *installable file systems*. Installable file systems provide special services (such as the ability to read the file structure on a CD-ROM) through the use of custom drivers that can provide instructions to Windows 95 to extend its functionality. Some components you can implement as installable file systems provide faster drive access, access to network file systems, and access to special file systems.

Answers A, B, and C are correct because VFAT, the Compact Disk File System, and the Network Redirector are all installable file systems. Answer D is incorrect because the File Allocation Table (FAT) is the Windows 95 file system and is always present.

938 INTRODUCTION TO THE INSTALLABLE FILE SYSTEM MANAGER (IFSMGR)

Q: *In Windows 95, the key to accessing disk and redirected devices is the Installable File System Manager (IFSMGR). The Installable File System Manager arbitrates access to file system devices and file system device components.*

True or False?

As you learned in Tip 937, installable file systems let Windows 95 access the FAT and FAT32 file systems faster, and provide access to network file systems and special file systems, such as the Compact Disk File System (CDFS). A Windows 95 component called the *Installable File System Manager (IFSMGR)* manages installable file systems. The Installable File System Manager receives requests for file access from the operating system and applications, and determines which installable file system should receive the request. The Installable File System Manager governs all 32-bit Network Redirectors, access to the base file system (FAT OR FAT32), and add-on file systems, such as the Compact Disk File System.

*The answer is **True** because the Windows 95 Installable File System Manager manages your system's access to local and remote devices, such as a network drive.*

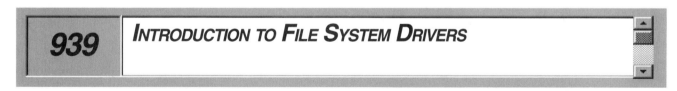

939 INTRODUCTION TO FILE SYSTEM DRIVERS

Q: *Which of the following are advantages of VFAT?*

Choose all correct answers:

    A. *Dramatically improved performance over real-mode disk caching software.*

    B. *VFAT does not require any conventional memory. (VFAT replaces real-mode SMARTDRIVE.)*

    C. *Better multitasking when your system is accessing information on disk.*

    D. *VFAT provides dynamic cache support.*

In Tip 938, you learned in Windows 95 the Installable File System Manager (IFSMGR) governs all file requests in the operating system, which includes access to the base file system (either FAT or FAT32. MS-DOS and Windows *3.x* systems using the *INT 21* function for file alteration. The MS-DOS and Windows *3.x* systems implemented Network Redirectors and Real mode device drivers that could intercept *INT 21* (a DOS interrupt address, similar in function to an IRQ) calls and determine if they should process the request or let the base file system handle it. The problem with such INT 21-based real-mode implementations is many drivers that third parties developed produced errors in file handling or simply did not function.

Windows 95 handles all file requests through installable file systems that it implements as 32-bit device drivers, and the Installable File System Manager controls. Windows 95 sends all *INT 21* functions directly to the Installable File System Manager, which evaluates them to determine which installable file system should handle the request. If the request is for a network resource, the Installable File System Manager will choose a Network Redirector. If the request is for CD-ROM access, the Installable File System Manager will choose the Compact Disk File System (CDFS). If the request is for a locally stored file or to create a new locally stored file, the Installable File System Manager will choose the Virtual File Allocation Table (VFAT).

The primary installable file system that is always present in Windows 95 is VFAT. Windows 95 implements VFAT as a 32-bit device driver for disk access and a 32-bit device driver for file access, although it does support 16-bit, real mode, file access device drivers if problems occur. The combination of 32-bit disk and file access improves the file Input Output (I/O). VFAT uses a 32-bit cache driver *(VCACHE)* that replaces the 16-bit read-ahead optimization the *SMARTDRIVE* disk caching driver software (which MS-DOS and Windows 3.x operating systems include) provides. *VCACHE* is more versatile than *SMARTDRIVE* because it can cache information from FAT, FAT32, CDFS, and Network Redirectors. Additionally, *VCACHE* allocates memory based on availability, and does not require you to set aside an area of memory as *SMARTDIVE* does. In other words, *VCACHE* will dynamically adjust the amount of memory it uses for caching as the user or the operating system starts or stops applications.

Answers A, B, C, and D are all correct because each answer is a benefit of using VFAT.

940   **UNDERSTANDING THE CORE SYSTEM COMPONENTS**

Q: *Which of the following are Windows 95 core system components?*

Choose all correct answers:

     A.   *User*

     B.   *Kernel*

     C.   *Memory Manager*

     D.   *The Graphics Device Interface (GDI)*

In Tip 934, you learned the Virtual Machine Manager (VMM) manages Windows 95 software-based resources. The primary software-based resources in Windows 95 are the file handles that control the various aspects of an application, such as the window structure, button bars, menus, and fonts. Grouped together, the Windows 95 software-based resources are known as *system resources*.

System resources are components that manage a variety of tasks, and Windows 95 implements them as 32-bit Dynamic Link Library (DLL) files. Although most Dynamic Link Library files have a *.dll* extension, Windows 95 stores the core system components (without which the operating system will not run) as executable files *(.exe)*. The three files that make up the Windows 95 core are *user32.exe, gdi32.exe,* and *kernel32.exe.* Table 940 describes each file's function.

File	Description
user32.exe	Manages input from devices, such as the keyboard and mouse, but is also responsible for other input devices (such as a light pointer) and the output of such devices to the display. The *user32.exe* file also interacts with the system timer and communication ports.
gdi32.exe	Manages the Windows 95 interface. Everything you see on your monitor *gdi32.exe*, in part, controls. Additionally, *gdi32.exe* manages graphical support for printing and drawing applications.
kernel32.exe	Is the operation system code that specifies the operations that Windows 95 performs and provides links to the system's Registry. You perform all Windows 95 system operations using code contained in *kernel32.exe*.

Table 940 The Windows 95 core components.

Each core component has a 16-bit counterpart responsible for providing 16-bit code that Windows 95 may require for backward compatibility from time-to-time. These files perform 16-bit operations that some applications (such as legacy DOS or Windows 3.1 applications) will require. Each filename is similar to its 32-bit counterpart, differing only in name, as the following bulleted list shows:

- *user16.exe*
- *gdi16.exe*
- kernel16.exe

Windows 95 will perform as many operations as it can using 32-bit code. In some cases, Windows 95 translates 16-bit code into 32-bit code for 32-bit processing and then translates the results back into 16-bit code. The translation between 32- and 16-bit code is a process called *thunking,* and the *user32.exe* and *user16.exe* files handle the thunking. In other cases, 16-bit code can actually run faster than 32-bit code because it requires less attention and verification for processing. When 16-bit code will run faster, Windows 95 processes the code entirely in 16-bit format, which the 16-bit core components handle.

Answers A, B, and D are correct because the three sets of executable files, the user, kernel, and gdi files make up the Windows 95 core system. Each component is actually two executables, one 16-bit and one 32-bit. Answer C is incorrect because the Windows 95 Memory Manager is not a Windows 95 core system component.

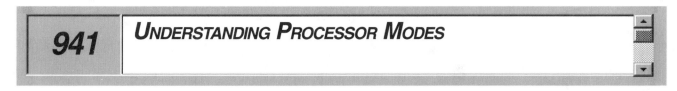

941   **UNDERSTANDING PROCESSOR MODES**

Q: *In which two modes can an Intel processor run?*

Choose all correct answers

     A.   *Real mode*

     B.   *User mode*

     C.   *Protected mode*

     D.   *Kernel mode*

In order to better understand many of the device drivers a 32-bit operating system, such as Windows 95, implements, you must understand the different processor modes in which an Intel processor can run. Intel processors can run in two modes, *Real mode* and *Protected mode*. Although extra processor modes are available for compatibility with other architectures, all Microsoft operating systems running on Intel processors use only the two modes. In Real mode, the processor is emulating the original 8088 Intel processor and can address only 1Mb of physical memory. The most drastic limitation Real-mode processing imposes is that the application must fit into the first 640Kb of physical memory, which network administrators generally call *conventional memory*—no minor feat, when you consider that an application such as Microsoft Word is over 5Mb in size—nearly 10 times the size of conventional memory.

MS-DOS programs have always required that you run them in the first 640Kb of physical memory. To maintain compatibility with older programs, MS-DOS kept the 640Kb limitation. You could use any memory over 640Kb only for data storage, not for executing programs. Over time, the computer industry invented add-on boards that could add memory to computers. However, the add-on boards required special drivers that could switch information between the add-on board and the area of physical memory MS-DOS could address. Later still, the computer industry developed a method of adding more physical memory to the main computer board. Unfortunately, the method still required special drivers to "switch" information back and forth between the extra memory and the area MS-DOS could address (using either Extended Memory drivers or Expanded Memory drivers).

Although the Intel processor has long been able to address more memory (since Intel's 80286 chip series), operating systems have maintained the limitation for compatibility reasons. Protected mode is really the processor mode that lets a computer address physical memory over one megabyte. Newer operating systems, such as Windows 95 and Windows NT, can use the Intel processor's Protected mode to address memory over 1Mb without a memory switching program. Addressing memory over one megabyte enables applications and device drivers that programmers have written using 32-bit code to access a computer's memory quickly and without translation.

Answers A and C are correct because the two modes in which an Intel processor can run are Real mode and Protected mode. Answers B and D are incorrect because neither answer correctly states an Intel processor's processor modes.

942   ## UNDERSTANDING PROTECTED MODE DRIVERS

Q: *How can you tell the difference between a Real mode device driver and a Protected mode device driver?*

Choose the best answer:

> *A.*   *Real mode device drivers always have an extension of .bin.*
>
> *B.*   *Real mode device drivers always have an extension of .vxd.*
>
> *C.*   *Real mode device drivers typically require an entry in the config.sys or autoexec.bat file.*
>
> *D.*   *You cannot tell the difference between Real mode and Protected mode device drivers.*

As you learned in Tip 941, Intel processors run in two modes, Real mode and Protected mode. Microsoft designed Windows 95 to be compatible with a wide range of hardware devices, device drivers, and applications. Therefore, you will find device drivers designed for either Real mode or Protected mode present on a Windows 95 computer at the same time. Windows 95 installs some of these drivers, while you may install other drivers during the installation of Legacy hardware devices or older applications. The major difference between Real mode and Protected mode device drivers is their designers created the device drivers to function in entirely different memory models. Real-mode device drivers operate in computers and operating systems that the original 8088 chip series, meaning the 1Mb memory address limitation restricts the program size and the device drivers are entirely in 16-bit code. Protected mode device drivers operate in computers and operating systems with a much higher range of memory addresses and programmers generally write them in 32-bit code.

Although some 32-bit device drivers have similar naming conventions to 16-bit Real mode drivers, you can generally recognize a 32-bit device driver by its extension. For example, device drivers that have an extension of *.vxd* are 32-bit Protected mode device drivers. One of the best ways to identify a 16-bit Real mode driver is that almost all Real mode drivers require an entry in the *config.sys* or *autoexec.bat* files, while 32-bit Protected mode drivers do not (the operating system may load some supporting Real mode drivers automatically, without their specific inclusion in the *config.sys* or *autoexec.bat* files).

Answer C *is correct because Real mode device drivers typically require an entry in the config.sys or autoexec.bat file.* **Answers A and B** *are incorrect because Real mode device drivers may have a variety of extensions.* **Answer D** *is incorrect because you can tell the difference between Real mode and Protected mode device drivers.*

943   INTRODUCTION TO THE *NET WATCHER* PROGRAM FOR *WINDOWS 95*

Q: *Windows 95 comes with a variety of system tools to help you administer your network. One tool that comes with Windows 95 is the Net Watcher program. Which of the following are functions of the Net Watcher program?*

Choose all correct answers:

> A.   *Net Watcher shows you which users are connected to your Windows 95 system.*
>
> B.   *Net Watcher lets you simultaneously monitor multiple Windows 95 computers.*
>
> C.   *Net Watcher lets you start and stop sharing directories on remote Windows 95 computers.*
>
> D.   *Net Watcher lets you capture network frames and analyze the contents.*

Windows 95 includes a utility program that lets you monitor network connections to shared network resources on your computer or other Windows 95 computers that are also providing shared network resources. The utility program is the *Net Watcher* program, an optional Windows 95 component that you can install from the Add/Remove Programs dialog box's Windows Setup tab. *Net Watcher* lets you monitor the following properties of a remote connection:

- User
- Computer
- Shares
- Open Files
- Connected Time
- Idle Time

Additionally, *Net Watcher* provides a window that displays which files are open and all the shared resources to which a user is connected. To install the *Net Watcher* program, perform the following steps:

1. Click your mouse on the Start menu and select the Settings group Control Panel option. Windows 95 will open the Control Panel.

2. Within the Control Panel, double-click your mouse on the Add/Remove Programs icon. Windows 95 will open the Add/Remove Programs dialog box.

3. Within the Add/Remove Programs dialog box, click your mouse on the Windows Setup tab at the dialog box's top. Windows 95 will change your view to the Windows Setup tab.

4. Within the Windows Setup tab, double-click your mouse on the Accessories option in the Components list. Windows 95 will open the Accessories dialog box.

5. Within the Accessories dialog box, click your mouse on the Net Watcher option. Windows 95 will display a check mark in the Net Watcher option checkbox to indicate your selection.

6. Within the Accessories dialog box, click your mouse on the OK button. Windows 95 will return you to the Add/Remove Programs dialog box.

7. Within the Add/Remove Programs dialog box, click your mouse on the OK button. Windows 95 will install the *Net Watcher* program.

Answers A, B, and C are correct because you can use Net Watcher to see which users are connected to your Windows 95 system, to monitor multiple Windows 95 computers simultaneously, and to start and stop sharing directories on remote Windows 95 computers. Answer D is incorrect because you cannot capture network frames using Net Watcher.

944 REMOTELY BACKING UP DATA ON A WINDOWS 95 COMPUTER

Q: *What are the two remote backup agents in Windows 95?*

Choose all correct answers:

    A.   *Microsoft backup agent*

    B.   *Arcada backup agent*

    C.   *Cheyenne ARCServe backup agent*

    D.   *Iomega backup agent*

Network administrators frequently want to back up client computers from across the network. To facilitate backing the client computers up for Windows 95 clients, Windows 95 includes two remote backup agents, the *Arcada backup agent* and the *Cheyenne ARCServe backup agent.*

To use either remote backup agent, you must have the corresponding software loaded on the server performing the back up. For example, if you had *Cheyenne ARCServe Backup* installed on a NetWare server on the network, you could install the Cheyenne ARCServe backup agent on Windows 95 client computers. Installing the Cheyenne ARCServe backup agent would let the backup software on the server access the client computer's hard drives directly, without having to share the drive as a network resource.

Answers B and C are correct because the two backup agents Microsoft includes with Windows 95 are the Arcada and Cheyenne ARCServe backup agents. Answers A and D are incorrect because Microsoft Windows 95 does not come with a backup agent for the Microsoft or the Iomega backup programs.

945   INSTALLING THE WINDOWS 95 NETWORK MONITOR AGENT

Q: From where in Windows 95 would you install the Network Monitor Agent?

Choose the best answer:

> A.   *Insert the Network Monitor agent disk into your disk drive. Run Setup.exe from the Network Monitor Agent disk.*
>
> B.   *In Windows 95 Control Panel, choose the Add/Remove Programs icon, and then point to the Network Monitor Agent software's pathname.*
>
> C.   *Windows 95 automatically installs the Network Monitor Agent with a normal system installation.*
>
> D.   *In the Network Properties dialog box, you will add the Network Monitor Agent as a service.*

Microsoft Systems Management Server (SMS) includes a utility called the *Network Monitor* that lets you gather information from all over the network that will assist you in locating potential problems or in optimizing your network. Windows 95 includes a network service called the *Network Monitor Agent* that Microsoft specifically designed to provide information from a Windows 95 client to the Systems Management Server. To install the *Network Monitor Agent* service, perform the following steps:

1. Click your mouse on the Start menu and select the Settings group Control Panel option. Windows 95 will open the Control Panel.

2. Within the Control Panel, double-click your mouse on the Network icon. Windows 95 will open the Network Properties dialog box.

3. Within the Network Properties dialog box, click your mouse on the Add button. Windows 95 will open the Select the Network Component Type dialog box.

4. Within the Select Network Component Type dialog box, click your mouse on the Service item within the list. Windows 95 will highlight the Service option to indicate your selection.

5. Within the Select Network Component dialog box, click your mouse on the Add button. Windows 95 will open the Install From Disk dialog box.

6. Within the Install From Disk dialog box, click your mouse on the Have Disk button. Insert the Windows 95 CD-ROM into your CD-ROM drive. Windows 95 will display the Open dialog box.

7. Within the Open dialog box, click your mouse on the Browse button and locate the *Admin\Nettools\Netmon* folder on the Windows 95 CD-ROM. Double-click your mouse on the folder. Windows 95 will display two entries in the File name list.

8. Within the Open dialog box, click your mouse on the OK button. Windows 95 will return you to the Install From Disk dialog box.

9. Within the Install From Disk dialog box, click your mouse on the OK button. Windows 95 will return you to the Select Network Service dialog box, but will display only the Microsoft Network Monitor Agent option.

10. Within the Install From Disk dialog box , click your mouse on the OK button. Windows 95 will install the *Network Monitor Agent* and prompt you to restart your computer.

11. Within the Install From Disk dialog box, click your mouse on the OK button to restart your computer. Windows 95 will restart your computer.

Answer D is correct because you would add the Network Monitor Agent as a new service from the Network Properties dialog box. Answer A is incorrect because the Network Monitor Agent software is on the Windows 95 CD-ROM and has no setup program. Answer B is incorrect because you will not add the Network Monitor Agent as a new application from the Add/ Remove Programs dialog box. Answer C is incorrect because Windows 95 does not automatically install the Network Monitor Agent.

946   **UNDERSTANDING WINDOWS 95 SYSTEM RESOURCES**

Q: *In Windows 95, systems resources refers to the amount of physical memory in the computer.*

     True or False?

In Tip 940, you learned system resources refers to the file system handles that the 16- and 32-bit versions of the core files *user, gdi,* and *kernel* manage. When Windows 95 loads the resource files to which system resources actually refer, it stores them within the computer's RAM in special memory areas called *heaps*. Each core system file produces at least one heap, and the *user* file produces two heaps. Each heap sets aside a non-configurable amount of memory that totals 6Kb in size. Windows 95 stores all file handles that control its various operations in one of six heaps that the core files create. Operations, such as business applications like as spreadsheets or word processors, require many different controls and will generally use space in more than one heap. Collectively, the heaps are also system resources. Windows 95 includes a utility program called the *System Resource Monitor* that can display a graph or percentage that tells you the remaining system resources left for your computer. The *System Resource Monitor's* percentage or graph always refers to the amount of space that is free in the heap that has the least amount of free space.

*Note: When you load it, the **System Resource Monitor** takes up heap space like any other application and does not provide you with any function other than a reading of remaining heap memory.*

*The answer is **False** because the Windows 95 system resources are a combination of 16-bit and 32-bit heaps (working memory).*

947   **INTRODUCTION TO VIRTUAL MEMORY IN WINDOWS 95**

Q: *Which of the following best describes virtual memory?*

Choose the best answer:

     A.   *The total amount of physical memory, plus the amount of system cache memory.*

     B.   *The total amount of system memory.*

     C.   *The amount of disk space that Windows 95 will use as physical memory.*

     D.   *The amount of physical memory the system requires to run a specific application.*

Virtual memory is really just a technical way of referring to the memory-management technique that Windows 95 creates to let users access more memory than is physically present within the computer. As you run programs, the

Windows 95 operating system uses a special, internal file (known as a *swap file*) to hold one or more programs that will not currently fit into memory. In general, the operating system treats the disk space within the swap file as if it were physical memory, which gives the Windows 95 operating system more memory with which to work. In fact, Windows 95 allocates a total of 2Gb of virtual memory to each process that runs on the computer (although most applications never approach that level of memory usage).

Virtual memory is slower that physical memory because reading and writing information to and from a disk is much slower than reading or writing information into your computer's fast electronic RAM. As you learned in the previous paragraph, Windows 95 uses virtual memory to store information that you load into memory, but you are not currently using. In other words, when Windows 95 requires physical memory for a process and no physical memory is available, it will store some information that you have previously loaded to the hard drive. Windows 95 will store information that is currently in memory, but that you have not accessed recently, on the hard drive to make room for additional processes. The file that Windows 95 uses to create virtual memory is known as a *Swap file* (so named, because Windows 95 swaps the information it contains back and forth between the hard drive and physical memory). The actual filename of the swap file is *win386.swp*.

The Windows 95 *Swap* file is not permanent unless the user specifies it to be permanent (permanent swap files can be faster than temporary swap files). In other words, the *win386.swp* file may not exist all the time on some Windows 95 computers—if the computer does not need the additional memory the swap file provides, it will either not create the swap file or delete the existing swap file.

Answer C is correct because virtual memory is the amount of disk space Windows 95 is using to emulate physical memory. Answers A, B, and D are incorrect because the answers do not describe virtual memory.

948 ADJUSTING THE WINDOWS 95 VIRTUAL-MEMORY SETTINGS

Q: *Where in Windows 95 will you adjust the virtual memory settings?*

Choose the best answer:

    A.   *From the Memory dialog box that you access through the Control Panel*

    B.   *From the System Properties dialog box that you access through the Control Panel*

    C.   *From the Performance dialog box that you access through the Control Panel*

    D.   *From the System Tuning dialog box that you access through the Control Panel*

In Tip 947, you learned about the Windows 95 *Swap* file and how it provides virtual memory for Windows 95. You can choose the settings for the *Swap* file in the Virtual Memory dialog box. To access the Virtual Memory dialog box, perform the following steps:

1. Click your mouse on the Start menu and select the Settings group Control Panel option. Windows 95 will open the Control Panel.

2. Within the Control Panel, double-click your mouse on the System option. Windows 95 will open the System Properties dialog box.

3. Within the System Properties dialog box, click your mouse on the Performance tab at the dialog box's top. Windows 95 will display the System Properties dialog box's Performance sheet.

4. Within the Performance sheet, click your mouse on the Virtual Memory button. Windows 95 will open the Virtual Memory dialog box.

Inside the Virtual Memory dialog box, you have the option of letting Windows manage your virtual memory settings or controlling them yourself. Letting Windows 95 control your virtual memory settings is the option Microsoft recommends—because the computer will automatically optimize the swap file access in most cases. If you must take control (for example, if you have significantly more space on another hard drive or partition than you do on the boot partition), you can specify the hard drive you will store the *Swap* file on, the minimum amount of drive space for the *Swap* file, and the maximum amount of drive space the operating system can use for the *Swap* file.

Answer B is correct because you will make configuration changes to virtual memory in Windows 95 from the System Properties dialog box in the Control Panel. Answers A, C, and D are incorrect because none of the Control Panel dialog boxes the answers list exist in Windows 95.

949 INTRODUCTION TO THE *WINDOWS 95* SYSTEM MONITOR UTILITY

Q: *The Windows 95 System Monitor is a graphical utility that will show you network traffic, file system performance, and other system statistics on remote computers.*

True or False?

As you have learned, Windows 95 includes a variety of utilities that assist you in determining your computer's status and configuring Windows 95 options. The primary utility included with Windows 95 for monitoring your computer is the *System Monitor*. As a graphical utility that lets you specify various system-level measurements, such as network traffic, file system performance, and processor usage, *System Monitor* will then monitor the system measurements you select. You can view these measurements as charts. Chart choices include numeric charts, bar charts, and line charts. Additionally, the *System Monitor* utility can connect to other Windows 95 computers, monitor statistical information about that system, and display it on your computer's screen.

The answer is **True** *because the Windows 95 System Monitor will show you a graphical view of system performance statistics on remote Windows 95 computers.*

950 INTRODUCTION TO *WINDOWS 95* DEVICE CLASSES

Q: *Which of the following are Windows 95 device classes?*

Choose all correct answers:

    A.   *Display*

    B.   *Modem*

    C.   *System Board*

    D.   *Monitor*

Over the next several Tips, you will learn how Windows 95 implements and supports plug-and-play for hardware devices. As you have learned, Windows 95 supports both plug-and-play and legacy (non plug-and-play) hardware devices and provides configuration methods for both kinds of devices.

For the purpose of managing the device drivers and specific settings that hardware devices and busses require, Windows 95 divides hardware devices and busses into groups called *device classes*. Remember that busses are the pathways inside a computer that information travels over from device to device, and different kinds of busses can exist in a computer. Some computers even implement more than one kind of bus in the same computer.

The Windows 95 Registry maintains a list of every device class installed on the computer and stores settings for configuring each device or locating the correct device driver for a device. Table 950 lists some examples of device classes (you can learn more about device classes within the Windows 95 Resource Kit).

Device Classes

Adapter	*CD-ROM*	*Display*	*EISA devices*	
FDC	*HDC*	*Keyboard*	*MCA devices*	
Media	*Modem*	*Monitor*	*Mouse*	
MTD	*Net*	*NetService*	*No driver*	
PCMCIA	*Ports*	*Printer*	*SCSI Adapter*	*System*

Table 950 Some of the device classes that Windows 95 maintains.

Answers A, B, and D are correct because Display, Modem, and Monitor are all Windows 95 device classes. Answer C is incorrect because System Board is not a device class.

951   INTRODUCTION TO WINDOWS 95 PLUG-AND-PLAY SUPPORT

Q: *Plug-and-play is a standard by which your Windows 95 computer will recognize and automatically set up new hardware.*

True or False?

Plug-and-play is a standard for hardware devices. Simply put, plug-and-play lets your computer automatically detect, set up, and initialize the hardware when you install the device. The plug-and-play standard is sometimes hard to understand because the phrase actually describes several standards.

For example, plug-and-play hardware for Apple–Macintosh computers describes hardware you can simply plug into the system and it immediately functions. Sometimes you can even install the hardware while the computer is running.

The plug-and-play standard for Windows 95 simply designates hardware devices that the operating system can configure dynamically, instead of requiring input from the user for configuration. Plug-and-play devices do not require entries in the *config.sys* or *autoexec.bat* files and the operating system accesses and operates the devices using 32-bit code.

The answer is True because Windows 95 will use plug-and-play to configure new hardware.

952   UNDERSTANDING BUS ENUMERATORS

Q: Bus enumerators are responsible for building (enumerating) the hardware tree on a plug-and-play system.

True or False?

As you have learned, the Windows 95 Registry is a central repository for configuration information. Additionally, you have learned that plug-and-play devices are devices the operating system can dynamically configure. For the operating system to configure a plug-and-play device, Windows 95 recognizes the device and gives it instructions that determine the computer resources. The operating system must then add the computer-resource information into the system's Registry so other components in the operating system know where the device is and how to access it. In Windows 95, a component called the *Configuration Manager* manages hardware devices and computer resources.

The Configuration Manager uses software components called *bus enumerators* to both receive information from and send information to hardware devices. A bus enumerator is a software component that enumerates a hardware tree (that is, it lists out each "branch" in the tree) in Windows 95. In other words, Windows 95 has a set of bus enumerators for each bus type installed in the computer. Bus enumerators travel their specific bus in search of hardware devices that identify themselves to the enumerators. The enumerators then carry information about the devices to the Configuration Manager, which, in turn, can assign computer resources to the devices. The same enumerators carry instructions back to the devices that specify which resources to use. After the operating system has configured the devices, the Configuration Manager updates the system's Registry with the information so other areas in the system can use them.

*The answer is **True** because, in Windows 95, bus enumerators build the hardware tree for the plug-and-play system.*

953   UNDERSTANDING HOW WINDOWS 95 PLUG AND PLAY WORKS

Q: The Windows 95 plug-and-play support will automatically configure any new piece of computer hardware.

True or False?

Because Windows 95 supports both legacy and plug-and-play devices, not all computers will respond in the same way to devices. You can achieve true plug-and-play functionality only if the computer's Basic Input Output System (BIOS), the devices attached to the computer, and the operating system are all plug-and-play compliant. If any of these components are not plug-and-play compliant, the computer will have restricted plug-and-play capabilities. For example, if a computer has legacy devices that you configured to use Interrupt Requests (IRQs) three, five, and seven, and you add a plug-and-play device that can function at Interrupt Request three, five, or seven, the plug-and-play device will not function because Windows 95 cannot reassign the Interrupt Requests of the legacy devices. If you change a legacy device's configuration to a different Interrupt Request, the next time you start the computer, Windows 95 will be able to configure and initialize the plug-and-play device.

Plug-and-play devices use components (plug-and-play drivers) that can identify themselves to Windows 95 and that the operating system can dynamically configure. Windows 95 can also automatically detect some other devices, but the operating system cannot dynamically configure them if they are not plug-and-play compliant (such as older network cards, CD-ROM drives, and so on).

*The answer is **False** because for Windows 95 plug-and-play support to recognize a piece of computer hardware, the hardware must be plug-and-play compatible.*

954   **INTRODUCTION TO PLUG-AND-PLAY DEVICE TYPES**

Q: *Which of the following are plug-and-play device types?*

Choose all answers that apply:

> *A.*   *Industry Standard Architecture (ISA)*
>
> *B.*   *Extended Industry Standard Architecture (EISA)*
>
> *C.*   *Modified Frequency Modulation (MFM)*
>
> *D.*   *Small Computer System Interface (SCSI)*

As you have learned, all computer devices must communicate with the computer. You have also learned that the pathways that carry information between devices and core computer components, such as the processor, are known as buses. Different computer configurations implement many types of buses, sometimes within the same computer. Plug-and-play devices must also use buses to send and receive information. Different manufacturers produce a variety of plug-and-play devices, which the manufacturers group into categories based on the type of buses they use. The following bulleted list names the plug-and-play device types:

- Industry Standard Architecture (ISA)
- Extended Industry Standard Architecture (EISA)
- Small Computer System Interface (SCSI)
- Personal Computer Memory Card International Association (PCMCIA)
- Peripheral Component Interface (PCI)

However, not all plug-and-play device types operate the same way. Some plug-and-play device types have restrictions that affect how and when they can actually operate in a plug-and-play environment. For example, many newer computers include a Peripheral Component Interface (PCI) bus as either a primary or secondary bus.

Plug-and-play devices designed for the PCI bus can use plug-and-play functionality only if the PCI bus is primary or if the primary bus is also plug-and-play. If the PCI bus is the secondary bus, and the primary bus is not plug-and-play compliant, PCI devices are unable to provide plug-and-play support, even if specifically designed for it.

***Answers A, B,** and **D** are correct because ISA, EISA, and SCSI are all plug-and-play device types. **Answer C** is incorrect because MFM is not a plug-and-play device type.*

955 | **INTRODUCTION TO THE WINDOWS 95 DEVICE MANAGER**

Q: How can you access the Windows 95 Device Manager?

Choose all answers that apply:

> *A.   From the Control Panel, double-click your mouse on the Device Manager icon.*
>
> *B.   Right-click your mouse on the My Computer icon on your Windows 95 Desktop and select the Properties option.*
>
> *C.   From the Control Panel, double-click your mouse on the System icon.*
>
> *D.   Click your mouse on the Start menu and select the Programs submenu Accessories group Device Manager option.*

In this book's Windows 95 section, you have seen several Tips that mention the *Device Manager* as the primary operating system utility that you will use when you configure or examine system hardware. The Windows 95 *Device Manager* is a graphical utility that lets you see all the system hardware in a device tree. Within the *Device Manager*, you can navigate through the device tree and configure your system's hardware. Windows 95 will also display hardware errors in the device tree, if any hardware is not functioning properly.

To access the *Device Manager,* you can use one of two methods. You can right-click on the My Computer icon on your Windows 95 Desktop, and then select the Properties option. Then, in the System Properties dialog box, select the Device Manager tab. The other way to access the *Device Manager* is to click your mouse on the Start menu and select the Settings submenu Control Panel option. Then, in the Windows 95 Control Panel, double-click your mouse on the System icon. In the System Properties dialog box, select the Device Manager tab. Figure 955 shows the Device Manager tab in the System Properties dialog box.

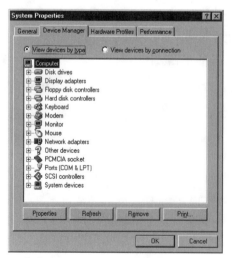

Figure 955 *The System Properties dialog box with the Device Manager tab selected.*

Answers B and C are correct because you can either right-click your mouse on My Computer on your Windows 95 Desktop and select the Properties option, or you can open the System dialog box from the System icon in the Control Panel. **Answers A and D** *are incorrect because neither answer describes how to access the Device Manager.*

956 INTRODUCTION TO HARDWARE PROFILES IN WINDOWS 95

Q: *You can use hardware profiles in Windows 95 only to turn the network support on and off.*

   True or False?

In previous Tips, you learned about user profiles, which let you control how a given user interacts with the computer and how the user's Desktop and other customizable configurations appear. *Hardware profiles* are configuration states for a specific computer, such as whether the computer is currently docked or undocked (with a portable computer). Hardware profiles enable Windows 95 to adjust system settings to match the hardware's current state. For example, when a notebook computer is undocked, Windows 95 removes the computer's print and network capabilities. You will learn more about the Windows 95 hardware profiles in Tip 957.

*The answer is **False** because you can use hardware profiles to set up your Windows 95 system in a variety of configurations.*

957 CONFIGURING HARDWARE PROFILES FOR WINDOWS 95

Q: *The best way to create a new hardware profile is to start with an existing profile and modify it.*

   True or False?

As you learned in Tip 956, hardware profiles let you create predefined configurations for your Windows 95 computer, and then you can select a configuration when the system starts. Creating predefined configurations with hardware profiles lets you have different configuration states for portable computers, such as notebook computers. To configure hardware profiles for your Windows 95 computer, perform the following steps:

1.   Right-click your mouse on the My Computer icon on your Windows 95 Desktop. Windows 95 will display a pop-up menu.

2.   Within the pop-up menu, select the Properties option. Windows 95 will display the System Properties dialog box.

3.   Within the System Properties dialog box, click your mouse on the Hardware Profiles tab. Windows 95 will display the Hardware Profiles sheet. Within the Hardware Profiles sheet, click you mouse on the Copy button. Windows 95 will display the Copy Profile dialog box.

4.   Within the Copy Profile dialog box, click your mouse in the *To:* field and type the name you want for the new profile (such as "undocked"). Then, click your mouse on the OK button. Windows 95 will close the Copy Profile dialog box and return you to the System Properties dialog box.

5.   Within the System Properties dialog box, click your mouse on the OK button. Windows 95 will close the System Properties dialog box and create your new profile.

Figure 957 shows the System Properties dialog box's Hardware Profiles tab.

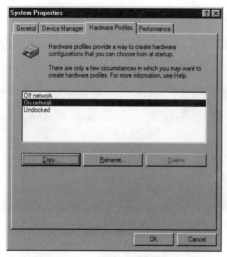

Figure 957 *The System Properties dialog box with the Hardware Profiles tab selected.*

*The answer is **True** because the best way to create a new profile is to modify an existing one the way you want, and then save it with a new name.*

958   CHANGING DISPLAY SETTINGS IN WINDOWS 95

Q: *Of the following methods, which can you use to get to the Display Properties dialog box?*

Choose all answers that apply:

     A.   *Click your mouse on the Start menu and select the Settings submenu Control Panel group.*

     B.   *Click your mouse on the Start menu and select the Programs submenu Administrative Tools group Display option.*

     C.   *Right-click your mouse on any blank area of the Desktop and select the Properties option from the pop-up menu.*

     D.   *Right-click your mouse on the My Computer icon on the Windows 95 Desktop and select Properties option.*

As with most other devices that you connect to a Windows 95 computer, Windows 95 lets you configure the display settings for your monitor. Windows 95 lets you configure your computer's display settings, such as the screen palette (the number of colors your system can display) and screen resolution (the number of dots that make up the images on your screen). The display settings control how sharp the images will appear on your screen. The sharper the image, the more system resources you must have. In older operating systems, if you wanted to change your screen resolution or color palette, you had to reboot your computer to implement them. However, Windows 95 lets you change your computer's display settings without rebooting the system (provided that the display card within the computer supports such on-the-fly changes, which some legacy cards may not). To change your display settings, perform the following steps:

1. Right-click your mouse on any blank area in the Desktop. Windows 95 will display a pop-up menu.

2. Within the pop-up menu, click your mouse on the Properties option. Windows 95 will display the Display Properties dialog box.

3. Within the Display Properties dialog box, click your mouse on the Settings tab. Windows 95 will display the Settings sheet.

4. Within the Settings sheet, click your mouse on the Color palette drop-down list or Desktop area slidebar to make configuration changes to your display settings. After you complete your changes, click your mouse on the OK button. Windows 95 will change your display settings and display a dialog box to prompt you to keep the new settings.

5. If you are satisfied with your display's new appearance, click your mouse on the Yes button. Windows 95 will return to the Display Properties dialog box. If you are not satisfied with your display's new appearance, click your mouse on No button. Windows 95, in turn, will revert the display settings to their original values.

6. After you finalize your display settings, click your mouse on the OK button within the Display Properties dialog box. Windows 95 will close the Display Properties dialog box and configure your settings.

Answer C is correct because, to access the Display Settings dialog box, you can right-click your mouse on any blank area of the Desktop and select the Properties option from the pop-up menu. Answers A, B, and D are incorrect because the answers do not describe how to access the Display Properties dialog box.

959   CHANGING MOUSE OPTIONS IN WINDOWS 95

Q: *In Windows 95, you can configure which of the following options for your mouse?*

Choose all answers that apply:

    A.   *Mouse length*

    B.   *Mouse speed*

    C.   *Mouse sensitivity*

    D.   *Double-click speed*

As you have learned, Windows 95 lets you customize your system to suit your individual needs. One item you can configure is your mouse, whose settings include the traveling speed, the double-click speed, and whether or not you want mouse trails. The mouse speed controls how quickly your mouse pointer will travel across the screen as you move your mouse across your desk. The mouse double-click speed controls how quickly you must double-click the mouse for Windows 95 to consider the action a double-click. Mouse trails are the graphical trails Windows 95 creates behind your mouse, wherever you move the mouse, to help your eye keep better track of the mouse's current position. To change your mouse's configuration, perform the following steps:

1. Click your mouse on the Start menu and select the Setting submenu Control Panel option. Windows 95 will display the Control Panel.

2. Within the Control Panel, double-click your mouse on the Mouse icon. Windows 95 will open the Mouse dialog box.

3. Within the Mouse dialog box, you can make your configuration changes. (The Mouse dialog box contains different options, depending on what type of mouse you have installed.) Then, click your mouse on the OK button. Windows 95 will close the Mouse dialog box and configure your settings.

Answers B and D are correct because you can control the mouse speed and the double-click speed. Answers A and C are incorrect because Windows 95 does not have mouse length or mouse sensitivity options.

960	CONFIGURING *COM* PORTS IN WINDOWS *95*

Q: To configure the existing COM ports on your system, which Windows 95 utility would you use?

Choose the best answer:

> A.   *The Device Manager utility in the System Properties dialog box*
>
> B.   *The Ports utility in the Control Panel*
>
> C.   *The Modems utility in the Control Panel*
>
> D.   *The Add New Hardware Wizard in the Control Panel*

Many different devices that you connect to your computer will use ports. For example, modems use communications (COM) ports, while most printers use parallel (LPT) ports. When you are using devices that require a port, sometimes you may have to configure the port (for example, you may have to set memory addressing information for the port). You can add new ports and configure existing ports in Windows 95, but not from the same dialog box. To add new ports, you must use the Add New Hardware Wizard in the Control Panel. To configure an existing port, you must use the Device Manager tab on the System Properties dialog box.

The configuration properties of a port include the port's Interrupt Request (IRQ) and the Input/Output base memory address (I/O base). If you do not set these addresses correctly (or let the Windows 95 plug-and-play drivers set the addresses), you may end up with device conflicts between the ports—and the ports will not work correctly. To configure a port, perform the following steps:

1. Right-click your mouse on the My Computer icon on your Windows 95 Desktop. Windows 95 will display a pop-up menu.

2. Within the pop-up menu, select the Properties option. Windows 95 will display the System Properties dialog box.

3. Within the System Properties dialog box, click your mouse on the Device Manager tab. Then, click your mouse on the Ports item within the device manager tree (each item represents a category of system hardware). The *Device Manager* will expand the Ports item.

4. Within the Ports type, click your mouse on the port you want to configure. Then, click your mouse on the Properties button. The *Device Manager* will display a Communication Port Properties dialog box.

5. Within the Communication Port Properties dialog box, make your configuration changes. (The Communication Port Properties dialog box contains various configuration sections.) Then, click your mouse on the OK button. Windows 95 will close the *Device Manager* (and the System Properties dialog box) and set your port configuration settings.

Answer A is correct because to configure an existing COM port, you will use the Device Manager tab in the System Properties dialog box. Answer B is incorrect because the Control Panel does not have a Ports dialog box. Answer C is incorrect because you cannot configure your COM ports from the Modems dialog box in the Control Panel. Answer D is incorrect because, although you can add new COM ports to your system from the Add New Hardware Wizard in the Control Panel, you cannot configure existing COM ports from it.

961 | USING A **PCMCIA** CARD IN WINDOWS **95**

Q: *You can configure your Windows 95 system's use of PCMCIA cards from which of the following?*

Choose the best answer:

> *A.* *You can configure PCMCIA cards from the Add New Hardware Wizard in the Control Panel.*
>
> *B.* *You can configure PCMCIA cards from the PC Card (PCMCIA) Properties dialog box in the Control Panel.*
>
> *C.* *You can configure PCMCIA cards from the PCMCIA dialog box in the Control Panel.*
>
> *D.* *You cannot configure PCMCIA cards in Windows 95; the operating system manages these devices automatically.*

Around 1990, computer manufacturers began making notebook computers with a new device type that let users interchange devices in their notebooks without having to make any system modifications. The new device type was the Personal Computer Memory Card International Association (PCMCIA). The PCMCIA cards are small interchangeable devices about the size of a credit card. You can get almost any type of device in a PCMCIA configuration. For example, you can purchase PCMCIA cards that contain modems, SCSI controllers, hard drives, and system memory.

Windows 95 automatically configures PCMCIA devices, so you will not have to configure them. In addition, Windows 95 supports *hot swapping* of PCMCIA cards, which means you can take out one PCMCIA card and insert another without rebooting your computer. However, to swap your PCMCIA device without damaging it, you must stop the *PC Card* service of the device you want to remove, and then insert the new device. To stop the Windows 95 *PC Card* service for a specific device, perform the following steps:

1. Click your mouse on the Start menu and select the Setting submenu Control Panel option. Windows 95 will open the Control Panel.

2. Within the Control Panel, double-click your mouse on the PC Card icon. Windows 95 will open the PC Card (PCMCIA) Properties dialog box.

3. Within the PC Card (PCMCIA) Properties dialog box Sockets sheet, click your mouse on the PCMCIA device you want to remove. Then, click your mouse on the Stop button. Windows 95 will stop the device and notify you that you may safely remove your PCMCIA device, as Figure 961 shows.

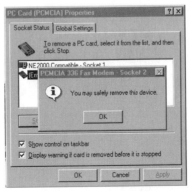

Figure 961 The PC Card (PCMCIA) Properties dialog box displaying a message box.

Answer B is correct because you can configure your PCMCIA cards from the PC Card (PCMCIA) Properties dialog box in the Control Panel. Answer A is incorrect because you cannot use the Add New Hardware Wizard to configure your PCMCIA cards. Answer C is incorrect because the Control Panel does not have a PCMCIA dialog box. Answer D is incorrect because you can use the PC Card Properties dialog box in the Control Panel to configure your PCMCIA cards.

962   INTRODUCTION TO **FAT32**

Q: The FAT32 file system extends the maximum partition size in Windows 95 to 4Gb.

True or False?

As you have learned in previous Tips, Windows 95 uses the File Allocation Table (FAT) file system to maintain files and directories on your computer's storage media (such as hard drives and floppy drives). The FAT file system divides the hard drive into *clusters,* which are essentially just groups of bytes, and then stores data in these clusters. When an application tries to retrieve a file, the file system finds the locations of all the clusters where it stored the data for the file and retrieves the file's data from these locations. Clusters let the file system optimize storage—that is, you can spread a 4Mb file over different sections of the hard drive, maximizing your use of the disk's available space.

The hard drive's size determines the cluster size; bigger drives use bigger clusters. For example, in FAT16, a 32Mb drive has a cluster size of 512 bytes and a 2Gb drive has a cluster size of 32 kilobytes. The drawback is a cluster can store data from only a single file. If the data does not fill the entire cluster, the cluster cannot use the rest of that disk space. For example, if a cluster is 16Kb, a 42Kb file would take up two full clusters, plus 10Kb of a third cluster. However, the six remaining kilobytes in the final cluster will remain unused.

The existing FAT system (FAT16) has two problems: it cannot address a hard drive larger than 2Gb without partitioning it, and the cluster sizes are too large. For example, on a 512Mb drive, a 277 byte Shortcut file stored on the Windows 95 Desktop requires16Kb of disk space. However, changes the FAT32 file system makes provide solutions to both issues. A FAT32 file system can address hard drives of up to two terabytes in size and uses smaller cluster sizes. For example, a 2Gb disk using FAT16 can implement a 32Kb cluster size, while the same disk using FAT32 implements a 4Kb cluster size.

Note: *Only Windows 95 OEM Service Release 2 (OSR2) can read the FAT32 file system.*

The answer is **False** *because the FAT32 file system extends the maximum partition size to two terabytes.*

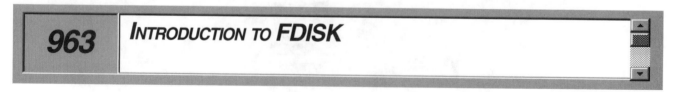

963   INTRODUCTION TO **FDISK**

Q: FDISK is a graphical utility for creating and managing hard drive partitions.

True or False?

As you learned in Tips 245 and 246, partitions are sections of disk space to which you can assign logical drive letters. To create partitions in Windows 95, you must use a non-graphical utility called *FDISK.* You can use *FDISK* to create primary and extended partitions, as well as logical drives within extended partitions, and to mark partitions as active. Microsoft has had the *FDISK* utility in its operating systems for years. In MS-DOS, you also had to use *FDISK* to create partitions. Figure 963 shows the *FDISK* utility's interface in a Command Prompt window.

Figure 963 *A Command Prompt window displaying the **FDISK** utility.*

*The answer is **False** because FDISK is a non-graphical utility for creating and managing hard drive partitions.*

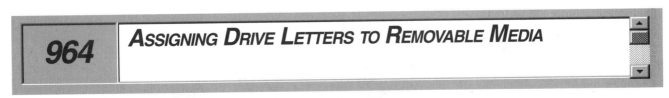

964 ASSIGNING DRIVE LETTERS TO REMOVABLE MEDIA

Q: Where in Windows 95 would you assign drive letters to removable media drives?

Choose the best answer:

> *A.   You would assign removable media drive letters from the System Properties dialog box's Device Manager tab in the Control Panel.*
>
> *B.   You would assign removable media drive letters from the Drives dialog box in the Control Panel.*
>
> *C.   You would assign removable media drive letters from the Add New Hardware Wizard in the Control Panel.*
>
> *D.   You cannot change drive letter assignments.*

As the computer industry evolves, computer users are requiring newer, better methods of data storage and transfer. The demand for large capacity, easily transferable storage has lead to the development of removable media disk drives. These drives come in a variety of sizes and types, such as optical and magnetic drives, which may support 100Mb, 125Mb, or even 1.2Gb of storage on a single disk. You can write to some removable media disk drives only one time, and to others you can write many times. Windows 95 will recognize most removable media drives and assign drive letters to them. However, if you want to, you can assign your own drive letter to a removable media drive. To assign a drive letter to a removable media drive, perform the following steps:

1. Right-click your mouse on the My Computer icon on your Windows 95 desktop. Windows 95 will display a pop-up menu.

2. Within the pop-up menu, select the Properties option. Windows 95 will display the System Properties dialog box.

3. Within the System Properties dialog box, click your mouse on the Device Manager tab. Windows 95, in turn, will display the Device Manager sheet. Within the Device Manager sheet,

click your mouse on the Disk Drives item. The *Device Manager* will display a list of all the drives on your Windows 95 computer.

4. Within the Device Manager tab, click your mouse on the removable media drive you want to change the drive letter on, and then click your mouse on the Properties button. The *Device Manager* will display the Drive Properties dialog box.

5. Within the Drive Properties dialog box, click your mouse on the Settings tab. Windows 95 will display the Settings sheet. Within the Settings sheet, click your mouse on the Start Drive Letter drop-down list and select the drive letter you want to assign to the removable media drive. Then, click your mouse on the OK button. The *Device Manager* will close the Drive Properties dialog box and return you to the System Properties dialog box.

6. Within the System Properties dialog box, click your mouse on the OK button. Windows 95 will prompt you to restart your computer.

7. Within the Restart dialog box, click your mouse on the OK button. Windows 95 will restart your computer.

Figure 964 shows the Drive Properties dialog box listing the settings for an IOMEGA ZIP 100 drive.

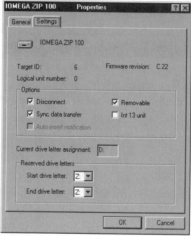

Figure 964 The Drive Properties dialog box displaying the drive settings for an IOMEGA ZIP 100 drive.

Answer A is correct because you can use the System Properties dialog box's Device Manager tab in the Control Panel to configure your drive letters. Answer B is incorrect because Windows 95 does not have a Drives dialog box. Answer C is incorrect because you cannot assign drive letter assignments from the Add New Hardware Wizard in the Control Panel. Answer D is incorrect because you can use the System Properties dialog box's Device Manager tab to change your removable media drive letter assignments.

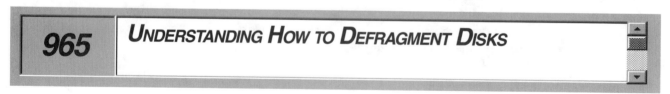

965 UNDERSTANDING HOW TO DEFRAGMENT DISKS

Q: *Windows 95 comes with a built-in disk defragmentation utility.*

True or False?

All personal computer systems sold today have built-in hard drives, which are mechanical devices for storing data. Hard drives have one or more disks (platters). As a hard drive reads and writes (with its *drive heads*, which are essentially small electro-magnets) information to a disk, the disk fills in a continuous pattern. When you save a file to the disk and then create a new file, as you make changes to the first file, it will become fragmented because the second file is blocking the continuous path. The hard drive will spread the first file out on the disk. The more files on your system become fragmented, the more your hard drive must work to gather the information to assemble a single file when you need it. Additionally, your system can become slow due to disk fragmentation.

To help resolve the problem of disk file fragmentation, Windows 95 comes with a built-in disk defragmentation utility called *Disk Defragmenter*. Windows 95 *Disk Defragmenter* is a graphical utility that takes information off areas of your disk and moves the information to a blank area on the disk. As *Disk Defragmenter* makes room at the beginning of the disk (by combining those clusters with the other clusters that contain the file), the utility will write the information from the end back to the front of the disk (The *Disk Defragmenter's* process is analogous with removing everything from a room to clean the room, and then moving everything back into the room—except in a different, more efficient structure. Figure 965 shows the *Disk Defragmenter* interface during a defragmentation process. The blue blocks represent defragmented clusters; the white blocks represent empty clusters.

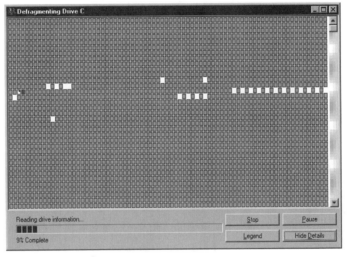

*Figure 965 The **Disk Defragmenter** utility's interface.*

*The answer is **True** because Windows 95 comes with a built-in disk defragmentation utility.*

966   Introduction to the *Windows 95* ScanDisk Utility

Q: *Which of the following Windows 95 utilities would you use to repair hard drive problems?*

Choose the best answer:

     A.   *DriveSpace*

     B.   *System Monitor*

     C.   *ScanDisk*

     D.   *Disk Defragmenter*

Windows 95 comes with most of the utilities you will need to manage your system. The tools at your disposal include disk compression, disk repair, and defragmentation utilities. The disk repair utility included with Windows 95 is *ScanDisk*. The MS-DOS version of *SCANDISK* runs automatically when you start the Windows 95 Setup process to check your drive for problems before you install Windows 95.

After you install Windows 95, you can use the Windows 95 *ScanDisk* utility on both uncompressed and compressed drives. *ScanDisk* checks compressed drives that you create with compression software from other vendors, but unlike *DoubleSpace* or *DriveSpace* drives, *ScanDisk* checks these drives as if they are uncompressed drives. *ScanDisk* can provide a detailed analysis of drives that you have compressed using the *DoubleSpace* or *DriveSpace* utilities. To run *ScanDisk* and check your system drives, perform the following steps:

1. Click your mouse on the Start menu and select the Programs submenu Accessories group System Tools subgroup *ScanDisk* program. Windows 95 will open the *ScanDisk* program.

2. Within the *ScanDisk* program, click your mouse on the drive you want to have *ScanDisk* examine. *ScanDisk* will highlight the drive. Then, click your mouse on the Start button. *ScanDisk*, will begin the examination of the drive you selected, as Figure 966.1 shows.

Figure 966.1 The ScanDisk program examining the C:\ drive.

3. After *ScanDisk* examines your drive, it will generate a disk error report in the ScanDisk Results window, as Figure 966.2 shows.

Figure 966.2 The ScanDisk program displaying a disk error report in the ScanDisk Results window.

4. Within the ScanDisk Results window, click your mouse on the Close button. *ScanDisk* will close the ScanDisk Results window and return you to the ScanDisk window.

5. Within the ScanDisk window, click your mouse on the Close button. Windows 95 will close *ScanDisk*.

*Answer C is correct because you would use ScanDisk to repair hard drive problems. **Answer A** is incorrect because you cannot repair a hard drive using the DriveSpace utility. **Answer B** is incorrect because you cannot use the System Monitor to perform any hard drive repairs. **Answer D** is incorrect because the Disk Defragmenter program will let you perform hard drive maintenance, but it will not let you perform any hard drive repairs.*

967 USING WINDOWS 95 DISK COMPRESSION

Q: *You can use Windows 95 disk compression to create more disk space on your system.*

True or False?

Even with today's very large disk drives, users often run short on disk space. To increase a disk's storage capacity, you can the Windows 95 disk compression program, *DriveSpace*. Using *DriveSpace*, you compress the files that reside on a disk, which, in turn, increases the disk's storage capacity. You can use *DriveSpace* to compress and uncompress data on floppy disks, removable media, or hard drives. The first time you use *DriveSpace* to compress data or space on a drive, the disk will have 50 to 100 percent more free space than it did before (depending on how much and what type of data is already on the disk). To compress a drive, perform the following steps:

1. Click your mouse on the Start menu and select the Programs submenu Accessories group System Tools subgroup *DriveSpace* program. Windows 95 will open the *DriveSpace* program, as Figure 967.1 shows.

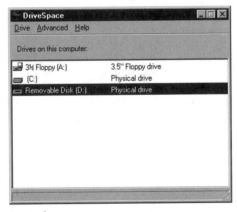

Figure 967.1 *The **DriveSpace** program's main window.*

2. Within the *DriveSpace* program, click your mouse on the drive you want to compress. *DriveSpace* will highlight the drive.

3. Next, click your mouse on the Drive menu and select the Compress option. *DriveSpace* will display the Compress a Drive dialog box.

4. Within the Compress a Drive dialog box, click your mouse on the Start button. *DriveSpace* will display the Are You Sure? dialog box.

5. Within the Are You Sure? dialog box, click your mouse on the Compress Now button. *DriveSpace* will begin compressing your drive. After *DriveSpace* completes the compression, it will display the Compress a Drive dialog box, which will show you the drive compression statistics.

6. Within the Compress a Drive dialog box, click your mouse on the Close button. Windows 95 will close the Compress a Drive dialog box and return you to the *DriveSpace* program window.

Note: Before you compress or uncompress a drive with the **DriveSpace** program or any other drive compression utility, you should first back up all contents of the drive, to protect against inadvertent loss of the data on the drive.

The answer is **True** because you can use the Windows 95 disk compression utility to create more disk space on your system.

Q: After you have compressed a drive in Windows 95, you cannot uncompress the drive unless you reformat it.

True or False?

As you learned in Tip 967, you can use the *DriveSpace* utility to compress the files on a disk drive. After you compress a drive, you can, later uncompress the drive at any time. Many users, for example, will uncompress a drive to improve their system performance. Although compressing a drive increases a disk's storage capacity, Windows 95 must decompress the file each time you use it and then later compress the file when you store its contents back to disk. The constant uncompressing and compressing of files requires many slow disk operations and also consumes processor time. To uncompress a drive in Windows 95, perform the following steps:

1. Click your mouse on the Start menu and select the Programs submenu Accessories group System Tools subgroup *DriveSpace* program. Windows 95 will open the *DriveSpace* program.
2. Within the *DriveSpace* program, click your mouse on the compressed drive you want to uncompress. *DriveSpace* will highlight the drive.
3. Next, click your mouse on the Drive menu and select the Uncompress option. *DriveSpace*, will uncompress your drive.
4. Within the *DriveSpace* program, click your mouse on the Drive menu and select the Exit option. Windows 95 will close the *DriveSpace* program.

Note: Before you compress or uncompress a drive with the **DriveSpace** program or any other drive compression utility, you should first back up all contents of the drive, to protect against inadvertent loss of the data on the drive.

The answer is **False** because you can uncompress any drive that you have compressed in Windows 95.

Q: What is Microsoft Windows 95 Plus!?

Choose the best answer:

    A.   *An enhanced version of Windows 95*

    B.   *A scaled down version of Windows 95 that Microsoft designed for small portable computer systems*

    C.   *A Microsoft add-on for Windows 95 that comes with system utilities and visual enhancements*

    D.   *A Microsoft Certification for Windows 95*

Microsoft Windows 95 Plus! is a companion (CD-ROM) product for Windows 95 that makes your PC look and run better than your basic version of Windows 95 does (whether Retail or Upgrade). Microsoft Windows 95 Plus! also adds graphical enhancements to your system, as well as system utilities. You can purchase Microsoft Windows Plus! at your local computer software retailer. The following bulleted list describes some of the Microsoft Windows 95 Plus! major features:

- *System Agent*—a background program scheduler that automatically schedules system maintenance tasks with utilities, such as *ScanDisk*, *Disk Defragmenter*, and *Compression Agent,* for times when you are not using your PC.

- *Internet Jumpstart Kit*—Microsoft's Internet Jumpstart Kit includes the *Internet Explorer*, which is Microsoft's World Wide Web browser for Windows 95. Internet Jumpstart Kit also includes a driver to allow the *Exchange* e-mail client in Windows 95 to receive Internet mail, and extensions to Windows 95 to let you create shortcuts to the Internet. You can also get the Internet Jumpstart Kit by downloading it from the Microsoft Network and other on-line services.

- *Advanced Disk Compression*—Microsoft Windows 95 Plus! disk compression includes *DriveSpace 3* with support for volumes up to two gigabytes in size and new compression algorithms that deliver much higher compression ratios than previous versions of *DriveSpace* (Windows 95 Retail and Upgrade versions come with *DriveSpace 2*). Additionally, the disk compression includes the *Compression Agent*, an intelligent, off-line compression utility that optimizes the compression of each file on the compressed drive—which results in maximum performance and minimum size.

- *Desktop Themes*—Microsoft Windows 95 Plus! includes 11 new user interface layouts for Windows 95 from the designers of the Windows 95 user interface. Each theme incorporates sounds, wallpaper, icons, new system fonts, color schemes, and more. The 11 themes included in Microsoft Windows 95 Plus! cover many subjects, from 1960s pop culture to the art of Leonardo da Vinci.

Answer C is correct because Microsoft Windows 95 Plus! is a Windows 95 add-on that installs system utilities and adds graphical enhancements to the system. **Answers A, B, and D** are incorrect because the answers do not describe Microsoft Windows 95 Plus!.

970   **USING COMPRESSION AGENT FOR WINDOWS 95**

Q: *The **Compression Agent** in Microsoft Windows 95 Plus! will let you configure how you want to compress files and folders on your Windows 95 system.*

True or False?

As you learned in Tip 969, Microsoft Windows 95 Plus! comes with advanced disk compression support, which includes *DriveSpace 3* with support for volumes up to 2Gb in size. Microsoft Plus! also includes new compression algorithms that deliver much higher compression ratios than previous ones, and the *Compression Agent*.

An intelligent off-line compression utility, the *Compression Agent* optimizes compression in each file for maximum performance and minimum size. You can use the *Compression Agent* to control which files Windows 95 will compress (you can use *exceptions* to instruct *Compression Agent* not to compress certain files) and what compression level each file will receive. To configure *Compression Agent* to use different compression methods for individual files or folders, or to leave individual files or folders uncompressed, perform the following steps:

1. Click your mouse on the Start menu and select the Programs submenu. Within the Programs submenu, select the Accessories group System Tools subgroup *Compression Agent* program. Windows 95 will open the *Compression Agent*.

2. Within the *Compression Agent* program, click your mouse on the Settings button. *Compression Agent* will open the Compression Agent Settings dialog box.

3. Within the Compression Agent Settings dialog box, click your mouse on the Exceptions button. Windows 95 will open the Exceptions dialog box.

4. Within the Exceptions dialog box, click your mouse on the Add button. *Compression Agent* will display the Add Exceptions dialog box.

5. Within the Add Exceptions dialog box, you must choose an exception to set. Depending on whether you want to set an exception on a file or a folder, click your mouse on either the File radio button (to set an exception for a file) or the Folder radio button (to set an exception on a folder). To set an exception for a particular file type, click your mouse on the All Files Of Specified Extension radio button. *Compression Agent* will display a dot on the button you select.

6. Within the Add Exceptions dialog box, type the name of the file, folder, or file type you want to set an exception for in the *Exception* field. If you are setting an exception for a file or folder, you can click your mouse on the Browse button to locate the file or folder instead of typing the item's name.

7. After you locate and select the file or folder, you must select a compression method. Click your mouse on the UltraPack, HiPack, or No Compression radio button to indicate the compression method that you want *Compression Agent* to use for the file, folder, or file type you specify. *Compression Agent* will display a dot on the button you select.

8. Within the Add Exceptions dialog box, click your mouse on the Add button. *Compression Agent* will close the Add Exceptions dialog box and return you to the Exceptions dialog box.

9. Within the Exceptions dialog box, click your mouse on the OK button. *Compression Agent* will close the Exceptions dialog box and return you to the Compression Agent Settings dialog box.

10. Within the Compression Agent Settings dialog box, click you mouse on the OK button. *Compression Agent* will close the Compression Agent Settings dialog box and return you to the *Compression Agent* program window.

11. Within the *Compression Agent* program window, click your mouse on the Exit button. Windows 95 will close the *Compression Agent* program.

The answer is **True** *because the Compression Agent in Microsoft Windows 95 Plus! will let you configure compression for your Windows 95 system.*

971 USING SYSTEM AGENT FOR WINDOWS 95

Q: *The Microsoft System Agent is a utility that manages network user connections to your Windows 95 computer.*

True or False?

Microsoft Windows 95 Plus! contains a scheduling utility called the *System Agent*. You can use the *System Agent* to schedule system maintenance tasks with utilities, such as *ScanDisk* and *Compression Agent*. The *System Agent* will usually run these system maintenance applications at night or when you are not using your Windows 95 system.

The *System Agent* utility has two sections, a scheduling engine *(sage.exe)* and a separate, user-viewable application *(sysagent.exe)* that displays and modifies the list of scheduled programs. The *System Agent* utility stores the list of scheduled programs in the *sage.dat* file, which Windows 95 places in the folder where you have Microsoft Windows 95 Plus! installed. Figure 971 shows the *System Agent* utility *(sysagent.exe)* displaying the program schedule.

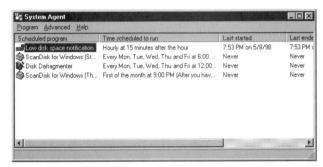

Figure 971 The System Agent utility showing a program schedule.

The answer is **False** *because System Agent is a utility that schedules system maintenance tasks with utilities, such as ScanDisk and Compression Agent.*

972   UNDERSTANDING THE HARD-CODED LIMITATION OF ENTRIES ON FAT PARTITIONS

Q: *You receive a call from a user complaining they have a FAT partition that should have 500Mb of free disk space on it. However, the user is getting an Out of Disk Space error message, even though the user has used only 200Mb of data on the partition. What could be causing this problem?*

Choose the best answer:

    A.   *The user's hard drive is faulty.*

    B.   *The user has a combination of 512 files or folders in the root of the partition.*

    C.   *The user is mistaken about how much data he or she has on the partition.*

    D.   *The files on the partition are compressed and Windows 95 is misrepresenting the free space.*

To ensure compatibility with MS-DOS, Windows 95 uses a standard File Allocation Table (FAT) file system. The FAT file system is a simple file system that Microsoft originally designed for small disks and simple directory structures. Microsoft has improved its design over the years (with the release of new operating systems) and now it can work more effectively with larger disks and more powerful personal computers.

Each file and folder on your Windows 95 system must have a FAT entry. However, the FAT file system has a hard-coded limitation of 512 entries in a partition's root. The 512 entry limitation means if you create 512 files or folders in a partition's root, you cannot add any more files or folders to the root. A FAT drive or partition's root directory has a fixed size and FAT stores it in a fixed location on the disk. All hard disk drives use 32 sectors of 512 bytes each to store the root directory, which limits the root directory on a hard disk drive to 16Kb (32 sectors x 512 bytes per sector = 16,384 bytes or 16Kb). MS-DOS uses one directory entry for each file and folder. Windows 95 uses additional directory entries to store long filenames and folder names, and the associated 8.3 aliases (MS-DOS filenames). Because Windows 95 uses additional entries, you can run out of directory entries with fewer than 512 files or folders in the root directory. If you encounter a user who complains of having a full hard drive or partition, but not enough information saved onto the drive or partition to fill it, you should examine the number of files and folders in the partition's root.

Answer B is correct because FAT partitions have a hard-coded limitation of 512 entries in a partition's root. If you exceed the 512 limitation, you will receive an Out of Disk Space error message. Answer A is incorrect because a faulty hard drive will not report incorrect free space. Answer C is incorrect because it is unlikely the user is mistaken about the amount of free space on the partition and how much data the user has already stored onto the partition. Answer D is incorrect because it is unlikely the system will misrepresent the free disk space.

973 **UNDERSTANDING ALIAS FILENAME CREATION IN WINDOWS 95**

Q: Each long filename in Windows 95 will get a short, operating system-generated filename.

True or False?

As you have learned, Microsoft Windows 95 supports long filenames. Until recently, when you used a PC, you could not create files with names longer than eight characters, with a three character extension to denote the file type. For example, *filename.txt* is a typical 8.3 filename (also known as an MS-DOS or Julian-style filename). However, Windows 95 supports filenames up to 255 characters in length and the new, long filenames can have multiple periods and spaces.

For every long filename you create, Windows 95 automatically generates an alias entry that complies with the 8.3 filename rules for backward compatibility. Windows 95 composes the short, auto-generated names with the filename's first six characters plus ~n (where n is a number) and the first three characters after the last period. Therefore, Windows 95 will create the Windows 95 alias file *1001MC~1.doc* to represent the filename *1001 MCSE Tips.doc*. If the alias name already exists within the same directory (that is, if there is already a *1001MC~1.doc*), the algorithm increments n, where n begins with two, until the system can find a unique filename.

*The answer is **True** because, for each long filename, Windows 95 will automatically generate a short 8.3 filename.*

974 **INTRODUCTION TO VFAT IN WINDOWS 95**

Q: You can disable VFAT in Windows 95.

True or False?

As you learned in Tip 939, the primary installable file system that is always present in Windows 95 is the Virtual File Allocation Table file system (VFAT). The Windows 95 operating system implements the VFAT file system as a 32-bit device driver for disk access and a 32-bit device driver for file access. However, VFAT also supports 16-bit, real-mode, file access device drivers if problems occur with the 32-bit device driver. The combination of 32-bit disk and file access improves the file Input Output (I/O) of Windows 95—both speed and reliability.

VFAT uses a 32-bit cache driver *(VCACHE)* that replaces the 16-bit read-ahead optimization the *SMARTDRIVE* disk caching software (which MS-DOS and Windows 3.x operating systems include) provides. *VCACHE* is more versatile than *SMARTDRIVE* because it can cache information from FAT, FAT32, Compact Disk File Systems (CDFS), and Network Redirectors (whereas *SMARTDRIVE* can only cache FAT file systems). Additionally, *VCACHE* allocates memory based on availability and does not require you to set aside an area of memory as *SMARTDRIVE* does. In other words, *VCACHE* will dynamically adjust the amount of memory it uses for caching as it starts or stops applications. Because VFAT is the primary installable file system, and Windows 95 uses VFAT to access the base file system (FAT), you cannot disable VFAT permanently. To do so would result in the operating system being unable to read from, or write to, hard drives or other disk drives. However, you can disable VCACHE for troubleshooting purposes.

*The answer is **False** because you cannot disable VFAT in Windows 95.*

975 INTRODUCTION TO THE WINDOWS 95 SYSTEM ARCHITECTURE

Q: Which of the following answers best describe the Windows 95 operating system architecture?

Choose the best answer:

  A.   *Windows 95 architecture is a linear design.*

  B.   *Windows 95 architecture is a circular design.*

  C.   *Windows 95 architecture is a modular design.*

  D.   *Windows 95 architecture is a closed design.*

The Microsoft *Windows 95 Resource Kit* describes the Windows 95 architecture as a modular design because Microsoft designed the components to interact with each other at specific levels, and yet function independently while performing specific tasks. As you have learned, Windows 95 is a versatile operating system that can support many types of hardware and software. Although completely discussing every aspect of the Windows 95 operating system is too much to cover in a single Tip, you can learn how the various managers and systems interact by understanding the relationships between the components Figure 975 depicts.

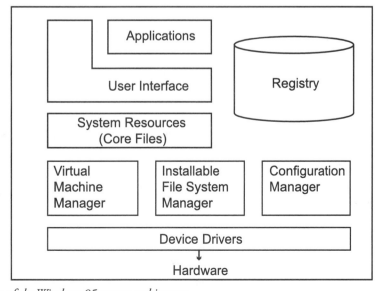

Figure 975 Some components of the Windows 95 system architecture.

Answer C is correct because Windows 95 architecture is a modular design. Answers A, B, and D are incorrect because the answers do not describe Windows 95 system architecture.

---

976 UNDERSTANDING THE RELATIONSHIP BETWEEN PROCESSES AND THREADS

Q: *A thread is a single request for processor use.*

True or False?

As you have learned, a *process* is any program, application, or operating system component that is running. Additionally, you have learned that a thread is a single line of executable code that is requesting to use the processor. Depending on its design, a process can use multiple threads. Windows 95, in turn, will processes each thread based on the thread's priority level. Each thread a process creates has a base priority that determines the thread's importance to the operating system. By assigning the CPU to threads based on each thread's priority, Windows 95 ensures can perform high-level functions first, without waiting for low-level application tasks.

Windows 95 places all threads in the system's thread queue (a line of threads that are waiting to use the processor). Windows 95 runs every program within its multitasking environment. Even applications that developers did not design for multitasking (such as MS-DOS-based applications) are multitasked when they run in Windows 95.

*The answer is **True** because a thread is a single request for processor use.*

---

977 RUNNING MS-DOS-BASED APPLICATIONS IN WINDOWS 95

Q: *If a Windows 95 computer is running two WIN32 applications, two WIN16 applications, and two MS-DOS applications, how many virtual machines are present in Windows 95?*

Choose the best answer:

    A.   Seven

    B.   Three

    C.   Five

    D.   One

As you have learned, Windows 95 is a preemptive multitasking operating system. To let the operating system control individual applications (and to let you halt an application when it has a problem), Windows 95 runs all applications in special environments, or *virtual machines*. The operating system treats each virtual machine as a standalone application container. The operating system itself and all Windows-based applications run in a single virtual machine, the *System Virtual Machine*. No matter how many Windows-based applications are running, the operating system uses only one virtual machine for all of the Windows-based applications.

On the other hand, each MS-DOS-based application receives its own virtual machine (which gives each MS-DOS program the illusion that it is running on its own system). Virtual machines are transparent to almost all MS-DOS-based applications, which means the MS-DOS application thinks it is running on a computer that is running MS-

DOS. Because each MS-DOS application receives its own virtual machine, you can multitask MS-DOS-based applications with other MS-DOS-based applications, as well as with Windows-based applications.

Answer B is correct because Windows 95 maintains a single virtual machine for the operating system and for all Windows-based applications, including Win16 and Win32, but will create a new virtual machine for each MS-DOS application (of which there are two in the question). Answers A, C, and D are incorrect because they list values that are higher or lower than the actual number of virtual machines Windows 95 requires to run the applications in the question.

---

978 RUNNING *WIN16* APPLICATIONS IN *WINDOWS 95*

Q: You are running three WIN16 applications in Windows 95. What is the maximum number of threads the WIN16 applications can generate?

Choose the best answer:

    A.   One

    B.   Three

    C.   Four

    D.   There is no maximum number of threads WIN16 applications can generate

As you have learned, all applications run inside a virtual machine that Windows 95 that emulates a computer and its resources. Windows 95 supports three basic application types: 32-bit Windows applications (*Win32*), 16-bit Windows applications (Win16), and MS-DOS-based applications. The Windows 95 operating system, *Win32* applications, and Win16 applications run in a single virtual machine, but the operating system gives each application (including itself) separate virtual-memory address ranges. The operating system divides memory ranges inside the System Virtual Machine as follows:

- The operating system receives 2Gb of memory addresses within which it stores its own programs and data and within which it allocates a section of memory that applications can share.

- Each WIN32 application receives its own 2Gb range of address in which to work.

The Windows 95 operating system consists primarily of Win32 processes that can generate multiple threads. Behind the scenes, each process will send its threads to the Virtual Machine Manager. The Virtual Machine Manager, in turn, will then preemptively multitask the application's threads with all other threads it is currently processing. A single Win32 application can generate multiple threads simultaneously, which the Virtual Machine Manager must process according to the thread's priority level. In Windows 95, all Win16 applications share a single thread. When a Win16 application takes control of that thread, it sets the Win16 MUTEX flag, which indicates to other Win16 applications that they must wait for the processor. When the application that has control of the thread voluntarily releases control, the operating system will release the Win16 MUTEX flag, and another Win16 application can then take control of the thread. Because each Win16 application cooperates with the other Win16 applications for processor use, they are generally considered *cooperatively multitasked* within their environment (in other words, Windows 95 emulates the Windows 3.x multi-tasking environment for those Win16 applications). The single thread that Win16 applications generate and share is sent by the Win16 virtual machine to the Virtual Machine Manager, which then preemptively multitasks it with all other threads.

Answer A is correct because all Win16 applications share the same memory address range and share a single thread to the processor in Windows 95. Answers B and C are incorrect because all Win16 applications share a single thread to the processor. Answer D is incorrect because the maximum number of threads that Win16 applications can generate is one.

979	USING THE WINDOWS 3.x PROGRAM MANAGER IN WINDOWS 95	

Q: The default interface in Windows 95 is the Program Manager.

True or False?

As you have learned, the initial screen that Windows 95 displays, on which you will display all other applications, is called the Windows 95 Desktop. The new Windows 95 Desktop interface was quite a change from what thousands of users were used to using because the previous Microsoft Windows interface (which was fundamentally different from the Windows 95 Desktop) had been around for years. Microsoft wanted to let previous Windows users, if they were uncomfortable with the new Windows 95 interface, revert to the old Windows 3.x interface, and therefore included the old Windows 3.x interface with Windows 95.

To use the Windows 3.x interface in Windows 95, click your mouse on the Start menu and select the Run command. Within the Run dialog box, type *Progman* and press ENTER. Windows 95 will open the Program Manager interface.

The answer is **False** *because Microsoft includes the Program Manager interface only for backward compatibility for users with Windows 3.x.*

980	CONFIGURING MS-DOS-BASED APPLICATION PROPERTIES IN WINDOWS 95	

Q: You are running an MS-DOS-based application in Windows 95 that is designed to perform a specific action when you press the ALT+TAB keyboard combination. When you press the ALT+TAB keyboard combination, Windows 95 switches between applications and does not perform the MS-DOS application's designated action. How can you disable the Windows 95 ALT+TAB keystroke for the MS-DOS application?

Choose the best answer:

   A.   Within the Keyboard option in Windows 95 Control Panel.

   B.   In the System Properties dialog box.

   C.   In any MS-DOS application's Properties dialog box.

   D.   You cannot disable the ALT+TAB keystroke.

As you have learned, Windows 95 runs each MS-DOS application in a separate virtual machine. Because Windows 95 creates a separate virtual machine for each MS-DOS application, you can configure each virtual machine so that it creates the optimum environment (such as letting you disable the ALT+TAB keyboard combination) for the application it runs. Special files that have the *.pif* extension store configuration settings for MS-DOS applications and their associated virtual machines. In Windows 95, the operating system automatically creates *pif* files for MS-DOS applications and, when the user runs the MS-DOS application, the operating system will actually execute the *pif* file first. The operating system stores the *pif* file's information within the application's shortcuts. You can configure virtual machines in the Properties dialog box for each application's Windows 95 shortcut.

Windows 95 divides the configuration options for MS-DOS applications into groups, which tabs separate on the Properties dialog box. The following list shows configuration groups for MS-DOS applications:

- Program

- Font

- Memory

- Screen

- Misc

The Properties dialog box for MS-DOS applications contains six tabs that let you control the options in the previous list, as well as the Shortcut's general file properties. Some of the settings inside the Properties dialog box apply specifically to the MS-DOS application and how it interacts with Windows 95. For example, if you have an application that uses a special keystroke to perform an action, and that keystroke is also a Windows 95 system keystroke, such as ALT+TAB, you can disable Windows 95's ability to use that keystroke while the MS-DOS application is running. The Misc tab in an MS-DOS-based application's Properties dialog box contains various settings (including screen saver support, Windows control key emulation, and so on) that let you control the way an application interacts with Windows 95.

Answer C is correct because you can disable the Windows 95 ALT+TAB keyboard combination in any MS-DOS application's Properties dialog box. Answers A and B are incorrect because neither the Keyboard option in the Windows 95 Control Panel nor the System Properties dialog box will let you disable the ALT+TAB keyboard combination in Windows 95. Answer D is incorrect because you can disable the ALT+TAB keyboard combination for MS-DOS applications in Windows 95.

981   CONFIGURING MEMORY SETTINGS FOR MS-DOS-BASED APPLICATIONS IN WINDOWS 95

Q: *Windows 95 can fool MS-DOS-based applications which were originally designed to use expanded memory into thinking expanded memory exists on the computer in the MS-DOS application's Properties dialog box.*

True or False?

As you have learned, because of backward compatibility issues (such as the 1 megabyte memory limitation) with earlier Intel chipsets, MS-DOS has maintained some of the memory limitations that the original Intel 8088 processor imposed on it. Because MS-DOS maintained these limitations, many applications written to run under MS-DOS were written to use the various methods that the computer industry developed to work around MS-DOS's memory limitations. Applications originally designed to use certain memory models require either the actual model or a way to emulate the model so that the application can run. In Windows 95, you can configure an MS-DOS Shortcut's properties to emulate memory models the application requires. The following list contains memory models and types for which you can configure specific settings:

- Conventional memory

- Expanded memory

- Extended memory

- MS-DOS protected-mode memory

Figure 981 shows an MS-DOS-based application's Memory sheet in the Properties dialog box that you can use to configure an MS-DOS program's memory requirements.

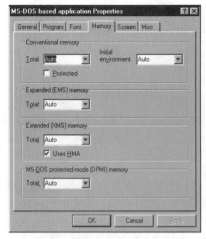

Figure 981 *An MS-DOS-based application's Memory tab in the Properties dialog box.*

Note: *Refer to the documentation for your specific application for its memory requirements.*

*The answer is **True** because an MS-DOS based application's Properties dialog box lets you specify memory settings, which include an expanded memory specification.*

982   CREATING UNIQUE CONFIG AND AUTOEXEC FILES FOR MS-DOS-BASED APPLICATIONS

Q: *You can configure MS-DOS-based applications that require unique config.sys and autoexec.bat entries to run in MS-DOS mode. Where must you store the unique config.sys and autoexec.bat files for such applications?*

Choose the best answer:

     A.   *In the boot partition's root directory.*

     B.   *In a special directory which the operating system sets aside for MS-DOS configuration files.*

     C.   *In the Properties dialog box of the MS-DOS Application's Windows 95 Shortcut.*

     D.   *You cannot specify unique config.sys and autoexec.bat files for any single application. You must start applications that require unique settings from a bootable disk.*

As you have learned, Windows 95 supports MS-DOS-based applications running in virtual machines; however, not all MS-DOS-based applications can run in a virtual machine. Certain types of MS-DOS-based applications (the most common example being full-screen games) do not function well in a virtual machine environment or require settings in *config.sys* and *autoexec.bat* that you do not want for other applications. To support such applications, Windows 95 lets you run MS-DOS-based applications in *MS-DOS mode*.

MS-DOS mode is a special set of instructions that causes Windows 95 to restart in a character-based environment, which is closer to MS-DOS. When you start an application whose *pif* you have set so that the application runs in MS-DOS mode, the computer will shut down and restart in the special character-based environment. When you close the application in MS-DOS mode, Windows 95 will restart the computer again and restore the normal Windows 95 interface and functionality. While the computer operates in MS-DOS mode, most of the Windows 95 operating system is not loaded and, therefore, the computer will not let you multitask different processes.

As part of the MS-DOS mode configuration, you can specify special settings (such as drivers) that would usually appear in a computer's *config.sys* or *autoexec.bat* files. Windows 95 will store the special settings as part of the Windows 95 shortcut and apply them in place of the real *config.sys* and *autoexec.bat* files when the MS-DOS mode application starts. You configure the MS-DOS mode in the Advanced dialog box. To access the Advanced dialog box, perform the following steps:

1. Within Windows 95, right-click your mouse on the Shortcut to the MS-DOS-based application. Windows 95 will display a pop-up menu.

2. Within the pop-up menu, click your mouse on the Properties option. Windows 95 will open the MS-DOS based application's Properties dialog box.

3. Within the Properties dialog box, click your mouse on the Program. Windows 95 will change your view to the Program tab.

4. Within the Program tab, click your mouse on the Advanced button. Windows 95 will open the Advanced Program Settings dialog box. Figure 982 shows the Advanced Program Settings dialog box.

Figure 982 *The Advanced Program Settings dialog box.*

Answer C *is correct because you can create special config.sys and autoexec.bat entries in the Properties dialog box of any MS-DOS-based application Shortcut.* **Answers A and B** *are incorrect because Windows 95 does not store special config.sys and autoexec.bat settings for a single application in files, but in the Properties dialog box of the MS-DOS Application's Windows 95 Shortcut.* **Answer D** *is incorrect because you can specify unique config.sys and autoexec.bat settings for MS-DOS-based applications running in MS-DOS mode.*

983 USING ALT+ENTER TO MAXIMIZE SCREEN SIZE

Q: Which of the following keyboard combinations will make a DOS window switch to full screen?

Choose the best answer:

     A.   C<small>TRL</small>+E<small>NTER</small>

     B.   C<small>TRL</small> +F1

     C.   A<small>LT</small>+ E<small>NTER</small>

     D.   S<small>HIFT</small>+ E<small>NTER</small>

As you have learned, Windows 95 lets you run MS-DOS applications within their own virtual machine. Microsoft Windows 95 will automatically open MS-DOS applications in a window, unless you specify to the operating system to run the application in MS-DOS mode. In other words, you must work with the MS-DOS application in a small window on your screen, as shown in Figure 983.1.

Figure 983.1 The MS-DOS application window.

At any time, you can make your MS-DOS applications run in a *full screen* view by pressing the ALT+ENTER keyboard combination. Full screen means that the application appears to be the only open window on your screen (in effect, you will have an MS-DOS screen), as shown in Figure 983.2.

Figure 983.2 An MS-DOS application in full screen view.

To toggle your MS-DOS applications between a window and full screen, press the ALT+ENTER keyboard combination.

Answer C is correct because the ALT+ENTER keyboard combination will maximize a DOS window to full screen. Answers A, B, and D are incorrect because none of the answers correctly state the keyboard combination you use to maximize a DOS window to the full screen view.

984   SETTING MS-DOS-BASED APPLICATION PROPERTIES TO MAXIMIZE THE SCREEN AT INITIALIZATION

Q: How can you specify the screen orientation (full screen or window) for an MS-DOS-based application at startup?

Choose all answers that apply:

A.   *The MS-DOS application's Shortcut will remember the condition that the application's screen orientation was in when a user last closed it and maintain that configuration.*

B.   *You can specify the screen orientation in each MS-DOS application's Properties dialog box.*

C.   *You can use the Console option in Windows 95 Control Panel to specify the screen orientation.*

D.   *You cannot specify the screen orientation for an MS-DOS application at startup. You must start all MS-DOS-based applications in a window and then use the ALT+ENTER keyboard combination to switch orientations.*

Over the last few Tips, you have learned some of the various configurations you can specify for MS-DOS-based applications and their virtual machines. Another configurable option for an MS-DOS-based application is the *Screen orientation*, which lets you specify whether the application should run full screen or in a window, the window's size, refresh properties, and the window's aspects that only Windows 95 includes.

Users commonly request MS-DOS-based applications to run full screen. You can configure an application to run with a full-screen display in two ways. First, you can specify that an application should start in a full-screen display in the MS-DOS-based application's Properties dialog box. Second, the application Shortcut will remember the display's condition when the user last closed the application and maintain that setting. For example, if you set an application for full screen and then close the application, the next time you start the application, it will start with a full screen display. Figure 984 shows an MS-DOS-based application's Screen tab in the Properties dialog box.

Figure 984 An MS-DOS-based application's Screen tab in the Properties dialog box.

Note: *Setting a MS-DOS application to display as a full-screen is not the same as telling the operating system to run the application in MS-DOS mode. The full-screen application will still run in its own virtual machine, and you will still have access to Windows 95 features during the application's execution.*

Answers A and B are correct because you can specify the startup screen orientation in each MS-DOS-based application's Properties dialog box and the MS-DOS applications' Windows 95 Shortcuts will remember the screen orientation that was in place when the user last closed the application and maintain that setting. Answer C is incorrect because the Windows 95 Control Panel has no Console option. Answer D is incorrect because you can specify MS-DOS applications' Startup orientation.

985   UNDERSTANDING *OLE* IN WINDOWS 95

Q: *Which of the following answers accurately describes the Windows-specific term OLE?*

Choose the best answer:

A.   *Objective Line Execution*

B.   *Object Linking and Embedding*

C.   *Overall Library of Executables*

D.   *Open Link Execution*

As you have learned, one of the biggest benefits of the Windows-based operating system is its ability to let applications communicate with each other. However, when Windows first became commonly available, the only way many applications could exchange data was via the Windows Clipboard. Microsoft first introduced the *Object Linking and Embedding (OLE)* model in Windows 3.x.

OLE is a lets users link together objects they create in one Windows-based program within a second document that they create using a second (possibly unrelated) program. For example, in the past, using the Clipboard, you could create a picture using the *Paint* utility and then copy and paste the image into a *Word* for Windows document.

Today, using OLE, the user could double-click their mouse on the image within the *Word* document and Windows 95 will start the *Paint* utility, loading the image for editing. When you place an object within a document using OLE, you have two choices. First, you can embed a copy of the object within document, which means the document has its own unique copy of the object. Second, you can link the object into the document. By linking the object to the document, should you ever later change the object, your change will appear within the document as well. That is because the document contains a link to the original object (that resides on disk) as opposed to a copy of the object.

Windows 95 supports a newer OLE standard than the one Microsoft implemented in Windows 3.x, but Windows 95 continues to support the original specification for backward compatibility. The Windows 95 dynamic-link library *storage.dll* manages OLE documents. OLE is an important concept for Microsoft, and for Windows 95 users, as it lets them interoperate more efficiently with other users and within their own applications. However, as a system administrator, it is sufficient for you to know that OLE exists.

Answer B is correct because the Windows-specific term OLE is an acronym that stands for Object Linking and Embedding. Answers A, C, and D are incorrect because they do not accurately describe the Windows-specific term OLE.

986	USING **WIN.COM** SWITCHES TO TROUBLESHOOT WINDOWS 95 BOOT PROBLEMS

Q: *Which of the following WIN.COM command-line switches let you start Windows 95 without 32-bit disk access enabled?*

Choose the best answer:

A.   */D:M*

B.   */D:N*

C.   */D:F*

D.   */B*

Troubleshooting the Windows 95 Startup process can be difficult and you may find that, in some cases, it requires less time to reinstall the operating system than it does to troubleshoot problems. If you decide to troubleshoot the Startup process, you should first use Safe mode and Safe mode with Network Support to try to start the operating system. Failing a successful startup in Safe mode or being unable to use the menu, you can start your system in MS-DOS mode and then type **WIN** at the command prompt to use the *WIN.COM* command file to start the operating system. To troubleshoot your system using *WIN.COM*, you must input additional information to troubleshoot problems. You can use the /D: command-line switch with the *WIN.COM* command to isolate possible problems. To use the /D: switch, type *WIN /D:* and follow the colon with a character that represents how you want to start Windows 95. Table 986 describes the additional characters that operate with the /D: command line switch.

Character	Description
F	Turns off 32-bit disk access.
M	Starts Windows 95 in Safe mode.
N	Starts Windows 95 in Safe mode with Network Support.
S	Instructs Windows 95 not to use ROM addresses between F000:0000 and FFFF:FFFF.
V	Instructs Windows 95 to use the ROM routine to handle disk controller interupts.
X	Instructs Windows 95 not to load adapters in physical memory areas between A000 and FFFF.

Table 986 Command line switches for Win.COM.

Answer C is correct because the /D:F command-line switch lets you start Windows 95 without 32-bit disk access enabled. Answer A is incorrect because /D:M lets you start Windows 95 in Safe mode. Answer B is incorrect because /D:N lets you start Windows 95 in Safe mode with network support. Answer D is incorrect because /B is not a valid command-line switch for WIN.COM.

987 **INTRODUCTION TO WINDOWS 95 PRINTING**

Q: *Which of the following answers best describes the term "device independence"?*

Choose all answers that apply:

A.   *Networking devices that can operate without a computer.*

B.   *An operating system that will run on all hardware.*

C.   *Hardware devices that do not require the Registry to work in Windows 95.*

D.   *A device that the operating system manages and, therefore, works with all applications.*

One of the biggest benefits of the Windows platform, and even more so with the Windows 95 platform, is that it hides (from the application programs) many low-level hardware specifics. For example, within the MS-DOS environment, the programmers who created applications (such as word processor) often had to program code to handle different video-card types, different networks, and even different printers. Today, the Windows platform hides many hardware settings from the user, making the programs device independent. In other words, an application does not care which specific devices your system uses—Windows 95, shields the program from the device—making the program, device independent.

Answer D is correct because the term "device independence" refers to a device the operating system manages and, therefore, works with all applications built for the operating system. Answers A, B, and C are incorrect because they do not accurately describe the term Device Independence.

INTRODUCTION TO PRINT DRIVERS IN WINDOWS 95

Q: *Mini-drivers written to function with the Windows 95 Universal Printer Driver also function with the Windows NT 3.5 Universal Printer Driver.*

True or False?

As you learned in the previous Tip, one of the most important features of the Windows 3.x operating system was its support for device independence. Windows 95 continues to support and provide device independence with enhancements to the print process (such as automatic queuing of print jobs) that lets Windows 95 print faster.

The Windows 95 printing subsystem uses a Universal Printer Driver (a single printer driver for all printers) that handles all software to hardware translations (that is, program output to actual printer output) for non-PostScript printers. When you add a specific printer to a Windows 95 computer, the operating system loads a mini driver that tells the Universal Printer Driver how to "talk to" the printer. Mini-drivers that have been specifically written to support the Windows 95 Universal Printer Driver also work with the Windows NT 3.5 Universal Printer Driver. PostScript printers must install a complete device driver for Windows 95 to support the printer.

*The answer is **True** because mini-drivers that hardware vendors write to function with the Windows 95 Universal Printer Driver also function with the Windows NT 3.5 Universal Printer Driver.*

989 **INSTALLING A PRINTER IN WINDOWS 95**

Q: *How can you access the Printers folder in Windows 95?*

Choose all answers that apply:

    A. *Click your mouse on the Start menu and select the Settings group Printers option.*

    B. *Double-click your mouse on the Printers option in Windows 95 Control Panel.*

    C. *Double-click your mouse on the Printers folder in My Computer.*

    D. *Type Printers at the command prompt.*

As you have learned, Windows 95 includes a Universal Printer Driver. When you install printers in Windows 95, you actually only install a mini-driver to help the Universal Printer Driver communicate with the actual printer. In Windows 95, you can install a printer from the Printers folder, which you can reach from the Start menu Settings option, from the Printers option in the Control Panel, or from My Computer.

Within the Printers folder, double-click your mouse on the Add Printer icon. Windows 95, in turn, will start the Add Printer Wizard which will walk you step by step through your printer installation. Figure 989 shows the Windows 95 Printers folder.

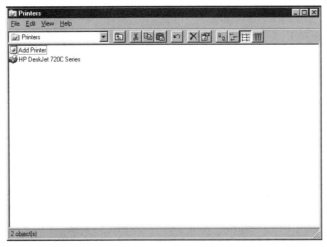

Figure 989 *The Windows 95 Printers folder.*

Answers A, B, *and C are correct because they all describe accurate methods you can use to access the Printers folder in Windows 95. Answer D is incorrect because typing Printers at the command prompt will not open the Printers folder.*

990	PRINTING A TEST PAGE IN WINDOWS 95

Q: *When you install a new printer in Windows 95, the operating system will require you to print a test page.*

True or False?

In Tip 989, you learned how to install a new printer in Windows 95, which tells the Universal Printer Driver what mini driver to use for that printer. After you install a new printer in Windows 95, you should test that printer to ensure that it is in good working order. Although you can use various methods to test the printer, the easiest way to check that the printer is working properly is to use the Print Test Page option, which is in the Printer Properties dialog box. Figure 990 shows the Printer Properties dialog box.

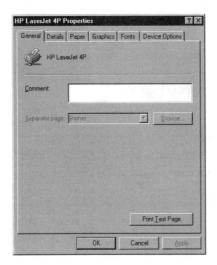

Figure 990 *The Printer Properties dialog box.*

To print a test page, perform the following steps:

1. Within Windows 95, click your mouse on the Start menu and select the Settings submenu Printers option. Windows 95 will open the Printers window.

2. Within the Printers window, right-click your mouse on the printer to which you want to print a test page. Windows 95 will display a pop-up menu.

3. Within the pop-up menu, click your mouse on the Properties option. Windows 95 will open the Properties dialog box for the printer you selected.

4. Within the Printer Properties dialog box, click your mouse on the Print Test Page button. Windows 95 will print a test page to the printer you specified.

The answer is **False** because you must specifically instruct the operating system to print a test page from the Printer Properties dialog box. The system will, however, provide you with the option to print a test page after a successful installation.

991   **USING POINT AND PRINT IN WINDOWS 95**

Q: *Which of the following answers best describe Point and Print functionality in Windows 95?*

Choose the best answer:

    A.   *Windows 95 computers can connect to a network print server and get information about the printer over the network.*

    B.   *Users can drag files directly onto a printer icon and the files will print.*

    C.   *Users can print to NetBIOS names on the network. If the NetBIOS name has a printer, it will accept the print job and process it.*

    D.   *Only Windows NT supports Point and Print, which is not available in Windows 95.*

As you have learned, you can install either local or network printers onto your Windows 95 computer. *Point and Print* is a process in which Windows 95 clients can connect to a network print server and get information about the printer over the network. In some cases, you can install the print drivers themselves over the network, using a remote printer becomes very easy. The information Windows 95 clients get over the network depends on both the print server type and the printer you install. Windows 95 print servers exist, to share printers with other client computers on the network. If you are using Windows 95 Point and Print to install a printer from a Windows 95 print server, the print server will transfer the printer's class, model, and name over the network to your computer. However, you must install the print drivers locally on your system.

Windows NT print servers can completely install and configure a printer on your computer, provided the printer's model name on the server matches a printer's model name in the Windows 95 *.inf* files. In such cases, the user requires no additional software and the printer is set up on the user's computer automatically.

Answer A is correct because Point and Print functionality in Windows 95 is the process in which Windows 95 computers can connect to a network print server and get information about the printer over the network. Answers B and C are incorrect because they do not accurately describe Point and Print functionality in Windows 95. Answer D is incorrect because Windows 95 does support Point and Print functionality.

992 | **USING MICROSOFT PRINT SERVICE FOR NETWARE**

Q: *Windows 95 includes a component that lets Windows 95 computers access some of a NetWare PSERVER's functionality. Which of the following files gives Windows 95 some of NetWare PSERVER's functionality?*

Choose all answers that apply:

> A. *pserver.exe*
>
> B. *unidriver.dll*
>
> C. *mspsrv.exe*
>
> D. *psvr.dll*

As you have learned, you can configure your Windows 95 client machine to print either locally or to a network printer. Windows 95 includes the *Microsoft Print Services for NetWare*, which is a Win32 utility that has a limited subset of the functionality NetWare PSERVER provides. In addition, Microsoft Print Services lets a NetWare server direct print jobs to Windows 95 computers which, in turn, print the job. The *mspsrv.exe* file provides this functionality and you can install it from the Windows 95 CD-ROM. To run the Microsoft Print Services for NetWare, you must install Microsoft Client for NetWare Networks on your computer and set it as the Primary Network Client.

The Microsoft Print Services for NetWare gives a network administrator a cost-saving option to enable PSERVER functionality on the network. The cost-saving option is worthwhile because the normal PSERVER functionality implementation uses MS-DOS-based dedicated print servers that cannot perform any other function on the network (that is, they cannot be file servers or other server types). The Microsoft Print Services for NetWare requires few system resources and will not interfere with other work users perform at the Windows 95 computer, which means the network requires fewer computers (because you do not have to dedicate any computers to print services).

Answer C *is correct because the mspsrv.exe file in Windows 95 provides the operating system with some of a NetWare PSERVER's functionality.* **Answers A, B,** *and* **D** *are incorrect because they do not list the file that provides some of NetWare PSERVER's functionality to Windows 95.*

993 | **USING DEC PRINTSERVER SOFTWARE FOR WINDOWS 95**

Q: *How do you install the software that lets Windows 95 Print to DEC PrintServers?*

Choose the best answer:

> A. *Install the software as a printer driver.*
>
> B. *Install the software as an installable port in Device Manager.*
>
> C. *Install the software as a Network Service.*
>
> D. *No additional software is required.*

As you have learned, Windows 95 provides specific support for network printing in different network environments. Part of the Digital Equipment Corporation's (DEC) networking support Windows 95 includes, is the ability for Windows 95 client computers to print directly to DEC PrintServers. You can install the optional component (the DEC PrintServer service) that provides the direct printing support as a network client from within the Network Properties dialog box. The DEC PrintServer service provides extensive bi-directional communication with the print server, which means that the server can send job and printer status back to the client computer. The DEC PrintServer service provides high levels of control over the print server. You can configure the PrintServer control levels to correspond to the different permission levels of user accounts on the network. In addition, the DEC PrintServer service lets you select such options as paper trays and single- or double -sided printing to control your print job.

Answer C is correct because you install the additional software that lets Windows 95 connect and print to a DEC PrintServer as a Network Service. Answers A, B, and D are incorrect because additional software is required for Windows 95 to print to a DEC PrintServer, but you must install the software as a Network Service.

994   USING HEWLETT-PACKARD'S JETADMIN UTILITY

Q: *The Hewlett-Packard JetAdmin utility lets Windows 95 computers manage printers that use a Hewlett-Packard JetDirect network printer interface card to connect directly to the network.*

True or False?

As you have learned, Windows 95 supports many different types of network print servers. However, Hewlett-Packard produces many products that let you connect printers directly to the network without first connecting the printer to a computer. Hewlett-Packard groups these devices into the general category of *JetDirect network printer interface cards.* Windows 95 includes the *JetAdmin* utility, which lets you manage Hewlett-Packard JetDirect cards from your Windows 95 client computer. You can use the *JetAdmin* utility to set up, configure, and delete printers you have connected to a JetDirect card. In addition, the *JetAdmin* utility will help you manage print jobs and modify settings on the printers. You will implement the Windows 95 *JetAdmin* utility as a Network Service and add it to the operating system from within the Network Properties dialog box.

*The answer is **True** because the Hewlett-Packard JetAdmin utility lets Windows 95 computers manage printers that use a Hewlett-Packard JetDirect network printer interface card to connect directly to the network /*

995   UNDERSTANDING FONTS IN WINDOWS 95

Q: *Which of the following font types does Windows 95 support without the installation of additional drivers?*

Choose all answers that apply:

     A.   Vector fonts

     B.   Raster fonts

     C.   TrueType fonts

     D.   PostScript Fonts

When you type at a computer, it uses special files, called *Fonts files,* to produce the characters you type. Fonts are more than simple type facing; they tell a computer how to form the characters, how to alter them (whether to bold or underline text), and how to display the characters on a computer screen. Windows 95 supports many font types which fall into the three general categories that Table 995 describes.

Font type	Description
Vector Font	Vector fonts are produced from mathematical calculations. Each character in a vector is defined by drawing lines from a series of predefined points. Vector fonts are very easy for computers to scale because the computer can expand the predefined points without losing the font's shape. Vector fonts are the only font type that a Plotter can use (because of their use of lines). Although you can install as many Vector fonts as you like, Windows 95 includes only one Vector font, which is *modern.fon.*
Raster Fonts	Raster fonts store font images within a series of font files. Each character is a bitmap and the computer or printer will produce the character as an array of dots. Raster fonts are most commonly associated with older dot-matrix printers and do not support scaling. You can typically recognize a Raster font in your application because the font will have only a few font size choices.
TrueType Fonts	TrueType Fonts (TTF) also store font and character definitions as mathematical models and a computer or printer can therefore scale the font to any size. TrueType Fonts are the most popular fonts and the easiest to work with because they appear on the screen the same way they appear on the printed page. The widespread use of TrueType Fonts let developers produce applications whose contents looked the same on the screen as they did when the user printed them. The similarity between the two outputs spawned the now industry-standard acronym WSIWYG, which stands for What You See Is What You Get. You can identify a TrueType Font from its extension, which is always *.ttf.*

Table 995 The font types Windows 95 supports.

Answers A, B, and C are all correct because each answer lists a font type that Windows 95 supports. Answer D is incorrect because you must install a type manager, such as Adobe Type Manager (ATM) for Windows 95 to support Postscript fonts.

996   INSTALLING ADDITIONAL FONTS IN WINDOWS 95

Q: *You can install TrueType fonts without the Fonts option in the Windows 95 Control Panel.*

True or False?

As you have learned, Windows 95 includes support and examples for three font types. You can install additional fonts and font types to enhance your word processing or to support specialized printing. For example, PostScript Printers require PostScript fonts, which you may have to install to use a PostScript printer. You install and manage fonts from the Fonts option in the Windows 95 Control Panel.

Note: *TrueType fonts install themselves to Windows 95 during the Windows 95 Setup process.*

*The answer is **True** because you can install TrueType fonts from a disk without using the Fonts option in the Windows 95 Control Panel.*

997	*TROUBLESHOOTING PRINTER PROBLEMS IN WINDOWS 95*

Q: *You are preparing a word processing document on a Windows 95 computer. When you have finished the file and try to print it, nothing happens. What is the first step you should take to troubleshoot the problem?*

Choose the best answer:

A. *Check the Windows 95 Registry to ensure that the printer description is accurate.*

B. *Print a test page.*

C. *Ensure that the printer is on.*

D. *Copy a file to the printer port from the command prompt.*

Throughout this book, you have learned how important it is to check for the simplest problem first when you troubleshoot any problem. Troubleshooting the printing process is no different. For example, if a printer does not respond to your print job request, the first thing to check for is whether the printer is on. Other troubleshooting steps may be valid, but if the printer is not on, you will have wasted valuable time for no reason. Many printer problems result from corrupted data in the *printer buffer*, which is physical memory that is installed on the printer. To solve such problems, the easiest thing to do is to clear the print buffer. Although many printers include a function that lets you electronically instruct the printer to clear its buffer, the simplest way to clear any printer's buffer is to turn off the power for five to ten seconds and then turn it back on. Other troubleshooting steps include the options in the following list:

- Print a test page

- At the command prompt, copy a file to the printer port (such as COPY CONFIG.SYS LPT1 <ENTER>)

- Check the printer cable

- Delete the printer from the Printers folder and the reinstall the printer

- Check the printer cable's length. Many computers experience problems with cables longer than ten feet

- Disable the EMF Metafile option in the Printer Properties dialog box. Some printers have problems with the EMF Metafile spooling method

All these options and more are valid steps you can take to troubleshoot printing problems. Although editing the Registry to ensure that the printer description is accurate should always be your final option, it is also a troubleshooting step you may take when the print process does not function correctly.

Answer C is correct because the first step you should take when you troubleshoot a print problem is to ensure that the printer is on and is on-line. Answers A, B, and D are incorrect because although each answer describes a valid troubleshooting process for Windows 95 printing, they should not be the first actions you take.

998	*DEFINING INTERNATIONAL SETTINGS IN WINDOWS 95*

Q: *Changing the international settings in Windows 95 will change the language in which Windows 95 displays messages.*

True or False?

When you install Windows 95, it will ask you for information during the Setup process about your geographical location, the language you prefer that Windows 95 display, and so on. Windows 95 includes an option in the Control Panel, *Regional Settings*, which lets you modify the international settings that govern the numbers and currency format and the Time and Date variables' structure in Windows 95. Portable computer users and users who have international associations (such as employees at large multinational corporations) may need to change the format and structure settings so that documents appear in the correct format.

A common misconception among users and administrators both is that when you change the regional settings, you also change the language in which Windows 95 displays text. Although there are international Windows 95 versions in other languages, you must install an international version, which will then only display the language for which Microsoft designed the version. When you change the international settings through the Regional Settings option in Control Panel, you will not change the language in which Windows 95 appears. Figure 998 shows the Regional Settings Properties dialog box.

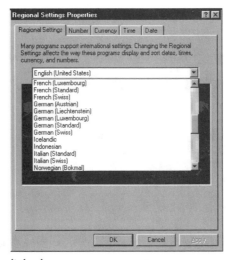

Figure 998 *The Regional Settings Properties dialog box.*

*The answer is **False** because changes to Windows 95's international settings affect only formatting and measurements, such as currency format and number format.*

999   **INTRODUCTION TO THE WINDOWS 95 SAFE MODE**

Q: *Windows 95's Safe Mode is a diagnostic mode with a minimal set of drivers installed.*

True or False?

When you start Windows 95, it will default to starting in its normal mode. However, there may be times when you start Windows 95 and it instead runs in Safe mode. Windows 95's *Safe* mode is a diagnostic mode, which is a Windows

95 Startup sequence that ignores all non-standard drivers, such as CD-ROMs, network services, and graphic drivers. When you start Windows 95 in Safe mode, the operating system bypasses the current normal-mode configuration and loads a minimal protected-mode configuration (without drivers and so on), disabling Windows 95 device drivers, and uses the standard Video Graphics Adapter (VGA) display adapter.

If you are having difficulty getting Windows 95 to boot properly, you may want to try to boot your system in Safe mode, which would help you diagnose if Windows 95 is loading device drivers that conflict. You can boot Windows 95 in Safe mode in three ways. First, you can press the F5 key when you see the Windows 95 logo appear at Startup. Second, you can press the F8 key when you see the *Starting Windows 95* message at Startup and select the Safe mode from the Startup menu. Third, you can press the F8 key when you see the *Starting Windows 95* message at Startup and select the Safe mode with Network Support from the Startup menu. You will learn more about the Safe mode in Tip 1000.

The answer is **True** *because the Windows 95 Safe Mode is a diagnostic mode which installs only a limited set of drivers.*

1000 INTRODUCTION TO WINDOWS 95 SAFE MODE WITH NETWORK SUPPORT

Q: *You are the administrator of a Windows 95 network. You are having problems with a Windows 95 computer that will not access the network. Every time you try to access network's resources, you are unsuccessful. Which of the following is the best option you can use to diagnose the problem?*

Choose the best answer:

A.   *Use the Net Watcher utility.*

B.   *Start Windows 95 in Safe mode.*

C.   *Start Windows 95 in Safe mode with Network Support.*

D.   *Reinstall Windows 95.*

As you learned in Tip 999, Windows 95 lets you start the system in a diagnostic mode to determine if Windows 95 is loading drivers that conflict with each other. Windows 95 also has a Safe mode that includes network support, which you can use to determine if you are having problems with your network configuration or drivers. You can use the Safe Mode With Network Support option in networking environments where users might require network connectivity to recover from a system problem (such as bad driver installation). If you can start an operating system in Safe mode, but not Safe mode with Network Support, you must examine that computer's network configuration, because it is likely the cause of the problem.

The following list contains examples from the *Windows 95 Resource Kit* of times you should use Safe mode with Network Support:

- When Startup stalls and Safe mode is unsuccessful

- If the computer stops responding when you are accessing a remote network

- If you cannot print to a network printer

- If the computer is running a shared Windows 95 installation

When you start Windows 95 in Safe mode with Network Support, the following drivers will load:

- *himem.sys* and *ifshlp.sys* (irrespective of the *config.sys* file's settings)

- *DoubleSpace* or *DriveSpace* drivers (if present)

- Windows 95

- Basic network drivers (such as the Client for Microsoft Networks)

Answer C is correct because you will want to start your Windows 95 system in Safe mode with Network Support, which will help you determine if your system's configuration is not working properly. Answer A is incorrect because you cannot use the Net Watcher utility to troubleshoot your Windows 95 network configuration problems. Answer B is incorrect because starting Windows 95 in Safe mode will not load any network drivers, so you will not be able to test your network configuration. Answer D is incorrect because reinstalling Windows 95 should never be your first troubleshooting approach.

1001 | **INTRODUCTION TO WINDOWS 95 STARTUP STEP-BY-STEP CONFIRMATION**

Q: *You would use the Step-by-Step confirmation Startup when you want to diagnose system boot problems.*

True or False?

As you have learned, you can use the Windows 95 Safe mode to try to troubleshoot problems with a Windows 95 computer. However, there may be times when you are having problems with a Windows 95 computer that will not boot properly, and you have tried the Safe mode approach but the computer still did not boot properly. In such cases, the next troubleshooting step is to step through each of the commands Windows 95 executes during the Safe mode boot sequence. As you step through the Startup process, try to determine if any devices fail to load. To step through the Safe mode boot sequence, restart your computer, press the F8 key when you see the *Starting Windows 95* message, and then choose Step-by-Step confirmation from the Startup menu. Windows 95 will prompt you to approve each driver that the system is loading so that you can determine if a particular driver is causing problems with your system.

The answer is True because you will use the Step-by-Step confirmation startup approach when you want to determine if a particular driver that your system is loading is causing a problem.

Index

Jamsa Press Runaway Bestsellers

Rescued by Upgrading Your PC, Second Edition

Every day thousands of users experience hardware problems. Worse yet, most users are afraid to open their systems. With the release of *Rescued by Upgrading Your PC, Second Edition*, users should fear no more. This book provides users with easy step-by-step instructions. Not only will users learn how to replace obsolete hardware, they will also learn how to locate system bottlenecks and how to fine-tune system settings.

$24.95 USA   ISBN: 1-884133-24-X
Available: Now!   272 full-color pages • 8 1/2 x 10 3/8"

By Kris Jamsa, Ph.D.

> *Rescued by Upgrading Your PC, Second Edition is a book for the PC users who want to keep their computers on the cutting edge without having to spend a lot of money.*
>
> —*Northwest View*

Rescued by Personal Computers

To complement our best-selling *Rescued by Upgrading Your PC*, Jamsa Press is pleased to announce *Rescued by Personal Computers*, an introduction to all aspects of computing. This book makes extensive use of full-color illustrations and an easy-to-read format that increases reader understanding and confidence while minimizing reader fears. Within the pages of *Rescued by Personal Computers* the reader will explore how to:

- Set up the personal computer

- Take the personal computer for a test drive

- Locate and run programs

- Use a word processor, spreadsheet, and database

- Create professional presentations

- Understand the Internet and Web

- Send and receive e-mail and faxes

- Experience multimedia on CD-ROMs and the Web

Rescued by Personal Computers is the ideal book for users who have just purchased a new PC or notebook computer, as well as for the employee whose new job requires computer literacy.

$24.95 USA   ISBN: 1-884133-54-1
Available: November '98   320 pages • 8 1/2 x 10 3/8"

By Kris Jamsa, Ph.D.

> *There's no better way to learn software on your own than to have Kris Jamsa at your side.*
>
> —Al Harrison, Member of Advisory Board, *PC World*

Jamsa's C/C++ Programmer's Bible

Jamsa's C/C++ Programmer's Bible, a follow-on to *Jamsa's 1001 C/C++ Tips*, is the most complete reference available about the C/C++ programming language. Along with the updated 1001 tips, this title also includes many additional tips that discuss Windows programming in detail. *Jamsa's C/C++ Programmer's Bible* was written by a programmer for programmers.

This book's companion CD-ROM contains a fully functional compiler and cut-and-paste source code for hundreds of ready-to-run programs.

$49.95 USA   ISBN: 1-884133-25-8
Available: December '97   704 pages • 8 1/2 x 10 3/8" • CD-ROM

By Kris Jamsa, Ph.D. and Lars Klander

> *The Jamsa manuals are well known for their excellent textbook-type computer manuals, written in very clear, easily comprehended text, yet very complete and informative.*
>
> —Herb Goldstein, *Sarasota PC Monitor*

Hacker Proof:
The Ultimate Guide to Network Security

Hacker Proof: The Ultimate Guide to Network Security provides a detailed examination of the security concepts network administrators, programmers, and Webmasters must know. Nonprogrammers will readily understand security threats and the steps they must perform to prevent them. Programmers will be thrilled with the detailed programming examples that demonstrate how hackers penetrate the most secure computer systems.

The book's companion CD-ROM includes software users can run to test their system's security.

$54.95 USA   ISBN: 1-884133-55-X
Available: Now!   688 pages • 7 3/8 x 9 1/4" • CD-ROM

By Lars Klander

1001 Visual Basic Programmer's Tips

According to Microsoft, over 3 million professional Visual Basic programmers use Visual Basic every day. *1001 Visual Basic Programmer's Tips* takes the programmer from "square one" with Visual Basic. The book teaches the "ins and outs" of the Visual Basic toolset and focuses on code, code, and more code.

Additionally, the CD-ROM contains all the supplemental files the user needs, including GIF files for image manipulation, audio files for ActiveX controls that play sound, and HTML files that provide the programs' Web interface.

$54.95 USA   ISBN: 1-884133-56-8
Available: Now!   708 pages • 8 1/2 x 10 3/8" • CD-ROM

By Lars Klander

> *A good way for folks who have been dabbling to understand more.*
> —*The Virginian Pilot*

Jamsa Press . . . Providing Solutions